Third Edition

FREEDOM AND CRISIS

AN AMERICAN HISTORY

Third Edition
FREEDOM

AND CRISIS

AN AMERICAN HISTORY

Allen Weinstein
Smith College

Frank Otto Gatell
University of California, Los Angeles

Random House New York

To Andrew and David, with love

Third Edition
98765432
Copyright © 1974, 1978, 1981 by Random House, Inc.

Grateful acknowledgment is extended to the following for permission to reprint previously published material.

Joan Daves: — From "I Have a Dream" by Martin Luther King, Jr.
  Copyright © 1963 by Martin Luther King, Jr.
Doubleday & Co., Inc.: — From *Six Crises* by Richard Nixon.
  Copyright © 1962 by Richard M. Nixon.
Alfred A. Knopf, Inc.: — From *In the Court of Public Opinion* by Alger Hiss.
  Copyright © 1957 by Alger Hiss.
Random House, Inc.: — From *Witness* by Whittaker Chambers.
  Copyright 1952 by Whittaker Chambers.
Charles Scribner's Sons: — From *The Spirit of St. Louis* by Charles A. Lindbergh.
  Copyright 1953 by Charles Scribner's Sons.

Library of Congress Cataloging in Publication Data

Weinstein, Allen
  Freedom and crisis.

  Includes bibliographies and index.
  1. United States — History. I. Gatell, Frank Otto,
joint author. II. Title.
E178.1.W395 1981b   973   80-39865
ISBN 0-394-32415-3

Cover Photograph: © John Veltri 1979/Photo Researchers, Inc.
Picture Research: Mary Jenkins
Photo Editor: R. Lynn Goldberg

Text design: Dana Kasarsky Design and Infield/D'Astolfo Associates
Cover Design: Dana Kasarsky Design

Project Researcher: Susan Sherer Osnos

Manufactured in the United States of America. Composed by Ruttle, Shaw & Wetherill, Inc., Philadelphia, Pa. Printed and bound by Von Hoffmann Press, St. Louis, Mo.

Contents

Pictorial Essays America As Seen By Foreign Observers

American Profiles

Maps and Charts

Author's Introduction

Freedom and Crisis is a book of discovery about the American past. The reader will quickly recognize, by glancing at the table of contents or by flipping through the pages, that this book is different from the ordinary "text." The difference is embodied in the way that *Freedom and Crisis* organizes the American experience.

Units are arranged in pairs of chapters. Every pair opens with a dramatic narrative of a significant episode in the American past. Each episode was chosen not only because it conveys an exciting story but also because it introduces many aspects of American life during the period under investigation. The chapter that follows then locates the episode within its appropriate historical context, interpreting the major forces that shaped the actions described in the episode.

This remains the book's basic format: a narrative chapter on a single episode, based on fresh documentary research, followed by an explanatory chapter linking historical fact and interpretation to the episode itself. The account of Jamestown in Chapter 3, for example, is followed by a chapter on seventeenth-century plantation colonies. Similarly, the Watergate drama serves as the basis for examining American politics and society during the 1970s in the accompanying chapter.

I have employed this novel approach to an introductory book on American history because my primary concern from the start has been to write a book that would hold the interest of today's students, perhaps the most inquisitive but skeptical generation of students ever. To do this, I felt that a book had to be readable and realistic. *Freedom and Crisis* is both. The book dramatizes critical moments in the American democratic experience and deals candidly with both the extension and the denial of liberty at those times.

Freedom and Crisis, then, is not a traditional book on United States history. Often such traditional books are written in the belief that there exists a certain body of data (election results, dates and outcomes of wars, treaties, major laws, and so forth) that comprises American history. I accept this idea only to the extent that most of the data of conventional texts can be found somewhere in this book. Sometimes, however, the information is located in maps, charts, and special features rather than in the text itself.

Frequently overlooked by students (and even by some teachers) is the point that this central body of data, the "facts," emerges only after a certain selection on the part of historians. There exists, after all, an almost infinite number of facts that could be chosen to represent the history of the human experience. In writing this book, I simply carried the usual selection process a step farther. Half the book is devoted to selected dramatic episodes. When linked to the accompanying chapters, the episodes form my bedrock of factual material. Using this foundation, students can then inquire into the fundamental questions of American history.

Most episodes can be read simply as absorbing stories. Thus readers will discover much about the country's past merely by studying such vivid incidents as the Boston massacre, the Lewis and Clark expedition, the Nat Turner revolt, the Custer massacre, the Triangle fire, the Philippines revolt, the attack on Pearl Harbor, and Watergate. But by using the interpretative chapter accompanying each episode, students will develop the ability to extract greater meaning from the facts in these dramas and, at the same time, acquire an understanding of related historical events.

Freedom and Crisis moves chronologically through the American experience, but certain themes recur and receive particular attention. The book devotes several episodes, for example, to patterns of race and ethnic relations, especially the treatment of blacks, Indians, immigrants, and other oppressed minorities. The struggle for political liberties and economic betterment, class conflicts, territorial expansion, technological change, and basic ideological and cultural disputes are also treated.

The constant interplay of factual drama and careful interpretation is the book's distinctive feature. Facts and concepts cross paths on each page, thereby avoiding the usual unhappy classroom extremes of concentrating either on what happened or on why it happened. *Freedom and Crisis* has no room for empty historical abstractions that leave students without a factual anchor. Nor does an uncontrolled flood of rampaging facts lacking solid conceptual boundaries spill endlessly off the printed pages. The paired-chapter format, I believe, avoids both these extremes.

The episode–explanatory chapter pairs present a concise but comprehensive introduction to the history of the United States. Yet although the book covers the American experience, I wrote with less urgent concern for coverage than for concreteness, drama, and interpretative depth. Almost every detail included in the narrative episodes has a larger meaning, so that students and instructors must work outward in this text from concrete detail to generalized understanding.

History as an act of inquiry involves putting great questions to small data, discovering general significance in particular events. *Freedom and Crisis* evolved from my belief that students are both willing and able to engage in the same process of inquiry as professional historians. In this manner each incident in the American odyssey, from the earliest European discoveries to our generation's exploration of the moon, can become a personal act of discovery for the reader, risky but rewarding.

The first two editions of *Freedom and Crisis* involved the joint efforts of myself and my collaborator, R. J. Wilson of Smith College, whose subtle intelligence contributed meaningfully to the book's success. This edition includes eighteen new chapters and thoroughly updates the others, so that it represents an entirely fresh attempt to make the paired-chapter format even more effective and useful to teachers and students. The popular short biographies of earlier editions have been supplemented with a series of "American profiles." Pictures and maps have also been revamped.

In the third and subsequent editions of *Freedom and Crisis*, Frank Otto Gatell joins me as co-author. Professor Gatell had contributed significantly, though without prior acknowledgment at his own request, to the book's first two editions.

The chapters that follow chart the authors' personal roadmap through American experience. This book will achieve its purpose only if it helps the reader begin his or her own private journey through the national past.

Allen Weinstein

Third Edition

FREEDOM AND CRISIS

AN AMERICAN HISTORY

The European conquest of the American continents was, like most momentous events in human history, a confused and complicated experience punctuated by a measure of greed, cruelty, and violence. The first pair of chapters in this unit of *Freedom and Crisis,* third edition, deals in general with the initial European discoveries, explorations, and attempts at colonization. For its specific example, it focuses in detail on the Spanish conquest of the elaborate and advanced Aztec civilization in Mexico.

From a modern perspective, the European triumph seems to have been an inevitable result of superior technology. But from the perspective of the sixteenth and seventeenth centuries, the European foothold in the New World appears to have been the precarious result of advantages won through daring exercises in ruthless desperation.

When the English managed to establish their first successful settlement in North America, they did not encounter Native American civilizations as advanced as those the Spanish found in Latin America. Nor did they find gold and silver. What they found was land—land that sometimes seemed impossible to conquer.

The early English settlements held on by a thread just as thinly stretched as the one that enabled Cortez and his men to survive in Mexico. They, too, encountered blood and suffering. Gradually, in the course of the seventeenth century, two successful centers of colonization developed, one in Virginia and the other in Massachusetts. Then, from these initial centers, English settlement fanned out into Maryland and the Carolinas, into Connecticut and Rhode Island, and into New York and Pennsylvania.

The two initial areas of English success—Virginia and Massachusetts—faced comparable problems of survival, although Virginia's were far more agonizing in the early years. Both colonies confronted the basic matters of feeding and sheltering their settlers, dealing with the native Americans they wished to displace, and ensuring an economic base with which to survive.

In the end, however, important economic and social differences developed between the plantation colonies of the South and the English settlements in New England and the "middle colonies." Differences in climate and soil reinforced settler preferences concerning the economic basis of colonization. By the century's end, Southern agriculture had become dependent upon slaves imported from Africa rather than upon the labor force of Europeans—free settlers or indentured servants—who dominated the remaining colonies. In Massachusetts and other New England colonies, moreover, variants of English Puritan society shaped colonial life for most of the century. Elsewhere in the Northern settlements, non-Puritan societies evolved displaying far greater religious and social tolerance.

This complex mosaic of English colonial existence emerges in the second and third pairs of chapters. Chapter 3 describes the Jamestown settlers' ordeal, while the accompanying chapter studies life in the Southern plantation colonies. Chapter 5 provides a vivid portrait of the Salem, Massachusetts, witchcraft trials, followed in Chapter 6 by a general discussion of seventeenth-century developments in Puritan New

COLONIAL AMERICA

UNIT ONE

England and the middle colonies. All three stories—the Aztec conquest, the founding of Jamestown, and the witchcraft trials—dramatize the lives of the men and women, European and native American, who helped to shape the first centuries of American settlement. They provide insight into the overall question of the European encounter, whether Spanish or English, with New World realities.

Cortez and Montezuma: I The Conquest of the Aztecs

For days Emperor Montezuma had eaten and slept badly. He feared for the safety of his kingdom. Strange ships had been sighted on the coast, and Montezuma anxiously awaited the return of messengers he had sent to greet the strangers, to present them with gifts of gold and precious jewels, and to urge them to leave Mexico at once. Montezuma believed the newcomers might be ancient Aztec gods, returning — as foretold in a prophecy — to claim his empire for their own. As a deeply religious man and a cautious ruler, the emperor wished neither to offend his gods nor to lose his throne.

Following Aztec religious practice at times of great crisis, the emperor ordered that upon the messengers' return, two Indian captives be brought to the city's largest temple and sacrificed to the supreme Aztec god, Huitzilopochtli. Montezuma's priests tore open the breasts of the captives, and the messengers were sprinkled with their blood. This was necessary because the messengers had completed a dangerous and difficult mission: their eyes had looked upon the gods' faces. They had even talked to the gods!

The messengers had sighted the white sails of gigantic ships on the coast of the Gulf of Mexico. Armed strangers had led them before a light-skinned but sunburned man, stocky and heavily bearded, who wore the armor of a warrior. This was the "god" himself, the returning Aztec deity Quetzalcoatl, god of learning and of the wind, whose sign was that of a serpent.

The messengers told the god that his vassal Montezuma, who ruled the kingdom for him, had sent them to pay homage. They dressed the god in Quetzalcoatl's vestments: a serpent's mask, armor, and other "divine adornments" heavy with jewels and gold. The other strangers — also light-skinned and bearded like the god himself, armor-clad and armed with swords — crowded around Montezuma's brown-skinned, clean-shaven envoys. Only when the messengers had completed their

Within the image:
apag. 2 22
RITR. DI MOTEZVMA
CAVATO DALL'ORIGINALE
VENVTO DAL MESSICO
AL SER.mo G.D. DI TOSCAna
Suor Isabella P. F.

A stylized portrait of Montezuma, emperor of the Aztecs, before his humiliation by Cortez and the first conquistadores. (Library of Congress)

ceremonial presentation did the god finally speak: "And is this all? Is this your gift of welcome? Is this how you greet people?"

The god ordered them chained by the neck and feet. The frightened messengers submitted without protest. They then watched several of the strangers walk toward a long iron cylinder tipped upward near the ship's edge. At the god's command, his men lit the cylinder with burning sticks, and the noise of the explosion that followed sent the messengers fainting onto the deck.

When they recovered, they were unchained, and once again the god spoke: "I have heard that you Mexicans are very great warriors, very brave and terrible. Supposedly one Mexican can pursue, overpower, conquer, and rout ten, even twenty, of his foes. I want to find out if you are truly that strong and brave."

The god next handed them swords, spears, and leather shields, ordering them to return at daybreak to fight his own men. The envoys protested strongly. If they fought with the strangers, Montezuma would surely put them to death. The god seemed amused by the frightened Aztecs. "No," he said, "it must take place. I want to see for myself." He dismissed the messengers and sent them back to their canoes. They paddled furiously away from the ship, some with oars and others with only their hands, fleeing from the god's command.

The messengers did not return. Instead, they hurried westward from the coast to report to Montezuma in the Aztec capital, Tenochtitlán (now Mexico City). From time to time they paused for food and water in villages or cities inhabited by Indians previously conquered by the Aztecs. Thus Montezuma's own messengers spread word among the conquered tribes about the arrival of strangers more powerful than the Aztecs themselves!

Once they had washed in the blood of the two sacrificed captives, the messengers told the emperor all about "Quetzalcoatl." Montezuma displayed evident fear when they mentioned the explosive weapon: "If the cannon is aimed against a mountain, the mountain splits and cracks open." But their description of the god and his followers was no less terrifying.

How fearsome, for example, did the god's companions dress!: Their trappings and arms are all made of iron. They dress in iron and wear iron cover-

An Indian view of Cortez on his march to Mexico City. The eagle perched on the cactus, at right, was the Aztec national symbol and today forms the Mexican coat of arms. (American Museum of Natural History)

ings on their head. Their swords are iron; their spears are iron. Their deer carry them on their backs wherever they wish to go.

And how strange their appearance!

Their skin is white, as if it were made of lime. They have yellow hair, although some of them have black. Their beards are long and yellow, and their moustaches are also yellow.

Montezuma hung on the messengers' every word. They confirmed all the earlier omens and signs, all the predictions of Aztec priests and magicians. His own messengers testified to the emperor's greatest fear: the return of Quetzalcoatl himself.

At once Montezuma began preparing himself for the arrival of Quetzalcoatl, much as one of his own fearful vassals would prepare himself for Montezuma's appearance. The sacred Aztec texts stated clearly that Quetzalcoatl's return meant the end of Montezuma's reign and the destruction of the Aztec Empire. It had taken several hundred years for Montezuma's ancestors to extend their control from their original home on the small island fortress of Tenochtitlán in the great interior Lake Texcoco, one of five interconnected lakes, until they ruled all of Mexico. Most of the other tribes feared them. The few villages or cities that continued to resist had to fight constant and generally losing battles against the Aztecs, battles aimed not at killing the enemy but at taking as many prisoners as possible: a constant supply of human sacrifices for the insatiable Aztec gods.

Now in their calendar year "13-Rabbit" (A.D. 1518), Aztec dominance over Mexico faced its major challenge. Montezuma brooded:

What will happen to us? Who will outlive it? Ah, in other times I was contented, but now I have death in my heart! Will our lord Quetzalcoatl come here?

At the same time, Montezuma began to search for means of determining whether or not the strangers were *truly* gods. "Strangers as powerful as gods"—but still human beings—might be dealt with more easily than Quetzalcoatl himself.

In the usual fashion of Aztec diplomacy, the emperor first sent magicians, along with his own personal wizards, to confront the strangers. He provided them with food for the visitors and with "captives to be sacrificed, because the strangers might wish to drink their blood." Traveling east, his magicians linked up with the gods moving westward from the coast. Immediately Montezuma's envoys began to sacrifice their captives, but as the strangers watched the Aztec ritual,

they were filled with disgust and loathing. They spat on the ground, or wiped away their tears, or closed their eyes and shook their heads in abhorrence. They refused to eat the food that was sprinkled with blood, because it reeked of it; it sickened them, as if the blood were rotted.

Montezuma's wizards had failed him: they had no magic powerful enough to turn the strangers back. And all along the route to Tenochtitlán, scores of Indians paid homage to the god and his few hundred com-

A sixteenth-century map presents a stylized view of Tenochtitlán. At the center stands the plaza with a great pyramid temple where important sacrifices took place. Causeways lead across Lake Texcoco to "suburbs"—here depicted as European fortresses. One Spaniard wrote on entering the city: "Gazing on such wonderful sights, we did not know what to say. Some of our soldiers even asked whether the things we saw were not a dream."

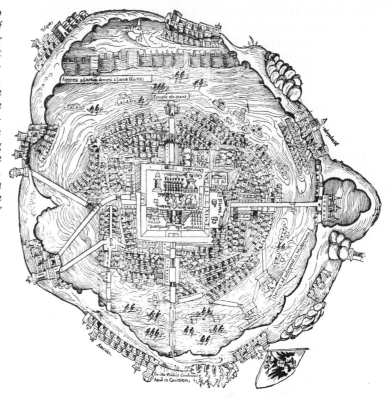

panions. Thousands joined the march, until it stretched out for miles along the royal road. Several times, the strangers fought against hostile tribes whom they encountered along the way. Each time, the god and his men triumphed.

One tribe in particular resisted ferociously. The Tlaxcalans, whose lands were to the east of those controlled by Montezuma and the Aztecs, had alternately fought with the Aztecs or lived in a state of uneasy alliance with them. Now, they battled the strangers three times before finally surrendering and pledging their friendship and alliance. After defeating the Tlaxcalans, the strangers marched on toward the Aztec capital, stopping at the town of Cholula. The Cholulans feigned friendship but planned to attack the strangers (acting at the direct orders of Montezuma). Through Doña Marina, his interpreter,[1] the god learned of this plan and launched an attack of his own. The Cholulans were defeated and, like the Tlaxcalans, joined the ranks of Indian tribes supporting the strangers' march toward Tenochtitlán.

---

[1] During his travels Cortez acquired several "interpreters." One such person was Jerónimo de Aquilar, a Spanish castaway who lived among the natives of Cozumel—an island off Mexico's Yucatan coast. The "god's" other chief interpreter was an Indian woman whom the Spaniards named Doña Marina. She was a "gift" from one of the first Indian tribes he and his men conquered. Doña Marina became Cortez's main interpreter with Indian messengers such as those from Montezuma.

One final time the emperor tried to appease the approaching strangers and to induce them to depart. He sent Aztec war chiefs rather than wizards this time, warriors who presented them with golden feathers and necklaces, at which point the gods began grinning.

> They picked up the gold and fingered it like monkeys; they seemed to be transported by joy. . . . For in truth they lusted for gold. Their bodies swelled with greed, and they hungered like pigs for that gold.

The strangers asked through their Indian interpreters whether the leading Aztec envoy was the emperor himself, to which that man replied, "I am your servant. I am Montezuma." The Indians who accompanied the strangers knew better. When they informed the gods of this lie, Quetzalcoatl himself shouted at the Aztec impersonator:

> You fool! Why try to deceive us? Who do you take us for? You can not fool, nor mock us, nor deceive us, nor flatter us, nor trick us, nor misguide us, nor turn us back, nor destroy us, nor dazzle us, nor throw dust in our eyes! You are not Montezuma, but he cannot hide from us either. Where can he go? . . . We are coming to see him, to meet him face to face.

As the god drew ever closer to the city, Montezuma abandoned all efforts to halt his progress. Many Indians were eager for the god's arrival, especially tribes like the Tlaxcalans, who had chafed under Aztec rule for two centuries. One such Indian was the prince of the city of Texcoco, who led his people not only in joining the strangers' army but in accepting their religion as well. Although the prince did not understand why Quetzalcoatl pretended to worship an even greater god, he listened as the god explained that "the emperor of the Christians had sent him here, so far away, in order that he might instruct them in the law of Christ." Upon hearing Quetzalcoatl describe the mysteries of this "Christ," the Texcocoan prince and most of his noblemen asked to be converted to the new religion. Thus the two strongest subject tribes of the Aztecs, the Texcocoans and the Tlaxcalans, had joined the strangers' small band on its inexorable march to Montezuma's city.

The strangers and their sprawling columns of Indian allies strode across one of the three causeways that led over the lake to the Aztec capital. This normally bustling, noisy thoroughfare was almost deserted. On most days, tens of thousands of tradesmen, nobles, priests, and commoners used the causeway. That day, however, "all lay quiet: the people did not go out or venture forth. . . . The people retired to their houses . . . and the common folk said: '. . . Now we shall die; we shall perish.'"

Across this deserted, water-borne highway strode a remarkable caravan: the pale-skinned strangers themselves — armed, iron-clad, many riding their strange "deerlike" animals, some carrying iron crossbows, still others pulling the dreaded cannon; the thousands of Indians who had joined the procession during its trip across Mexico; and the god himself, Quetzalcoatl, directing the entire operation from a position between his own companions and his Indian subjects.

When the god and his huge army entered Tenochtitlán, they were the first armed and possibly hostile force in centuries to walk unopposed through the elaborate and complex defenses that the Aztecs had constructed around their capital. "We entered Tenochtitlán," one of the soldiers later wrote,

> over a causeway wide enough for three or four or more horsemen to ride comfortably abreast. The causeway was built across the lake and had wooden bridges that could be raised or removed. The water was [so] full of canoes loaded with people who were watching us that it was frightening to see such multitudes.
>
> As we approached the city we could see great towers and churches of the kind they build, and large palaces and dwellings. There were over one hundred thousand houses in this city, each house built over the water on wooden piles, with nothing but a beam connecting one house to another, so that each one was a fortress in itself.

Montezuma, dressed in his imperial finery and attended by scores of Aztec princes, chieftains, and knights, awaited the god. The emperor himself presented gifts of flowers and precious ornaments to the visitors. Finally the god spoke: "Are you Montezuma? Are you the king?" The emperor replied that he was and then came forward, head bowed low, and made a welcoming speech:

> Our lord, you are weary. The journey has tired you, but now you . . . have come to your city, Mexico. No, it is not a dream. . . . I have seen you at last! I was in agony . . . [but] now you have come out of the clouds and mists to sit on your throne again.
>
> This was foretold by the kings who governed your city. . . . You have come back to us; you have come down from the sky. Rest now, and take possession of your royal houses. Welcome to your land, my lords!

The god ordered his Indian translator to respond to the emperor:

> Tell Montezuma that we are his friends. There is nothing to fear. We have wanted to see him for a long time, and now we have seen his face and heard his words.

Turning to Montezuma directly, Quetzalcoatl continued:

> We have come to your home in Mexico as friends. There is nothing to fear.

The strangers then took Montezuma by the hand and patted him on the back to demonstrate their affection. Dismounting from their horses, they entered the royal palace, accompanied by Montezuma and his chiefs. The god had arrived.

"Quetzalcoatl" was known to his troops as Hernando Cortez, no "god" but a Spanish soldier and adventurer who had sailed to the Mexican coast from Cuba with a small fleet. Cortez had been ordered by Cuba's Spanish governor, Velazquez, to explore for precious metal, which could then be divided among the king of Spain, the Cuban governor, Cortez, and his men.

Cortez learned from the coastal Indians that the many tribes of the Mexican peninsula had been formed into an empire by the Aztecs. The process resembled the recent Christian reconquest of Spain itself. But the Aztecs worshiped natural forces that the Spaniard and his men consid-

ered pagan deities. Cortez was particularly offended by the Aztec ritual of human sacrifice. From the moment he first learned of these Indian religious practices, Cortez determined not only to search for treasure, but to substitute Christian rituals for the Aztec forms of placating the gods.

Very early in the expedition, Cortez decided *not* to share any of the Aztec gold, silver, or precious stones with Governor Velazquez but, instead, to deal directly with the king of Spain. That way, Cortez would solicit his own royal honors while dividing up wealth and a new territory. Most of his men agreed. To keep those who remained loyal to the Cuban governor from returning to Havana and disclosing his treachery, Cortez resorted to a simple but drastic expedient. Once he and his men landed on the shores of Mexico, he burned his ships. From that moment on, he was legally a traitor to the Spanish king's representative, the governor of Cuba. Cortez realized that if he failed to stuff the king's coffers with Aztec gold, he would return to Spain in chains or be executed as a traitor in America.

Although his troops did not consider their captain a god, as Montezuma did, they rallied to Cortez's almost godlike self-confidence. The Spaniards fought few battles before reaching the halls of Montezuma. Yet they managed to force most of the Indian towns and villages they passed into submission. Upon their arrival in Tenochtitlán, they were welcomed as gods and escorted into the palace.

Although Montezuma soon realized that the strange warriors were not deities but mere men, the Aztec emperor continued to believe the ancient prophecies concerning the destruction of his kingdom. He became a prisoner in his own palace, and his power over the people of Mexico weakened at once. The Aztecs had offered no resistance to the white-skinned visitors, partly because of their own fears and partly because of Montezuma's commands. Their fears increased as they watched their own leaders either hiding from or bowing to "Quetzalcoatl." For several months the strangers ruled Mexico City by issuing their orders through Montezuma. Thus without shedding any Mexican blood, a mere three hundred heavily armed soldiers gained temporary control over an empire of millions.

When the Spaniards retired to their quarters on their first evening in the emperor's palace, they accidentally discovered the main Aztec treasure room, filled (as one Spaniard later wrote) with "a large quantity of idols, featherwork, jewels, precious stones, silver, and an astonishing amount of gold, as well as so many lovely things that I was amazed." For the moment Cortez decided to leave the treasure undisturbed. He ordered the secret room sealed. One of Montezuma's servants, who had watched the scene, reported to the emperor that "the Spaniards grinned like little beasts and patted each other in delight. When they entered the hall of treasures, it was if they had arrived in Paradise."

To placate his captor, Montezuma informed Cortez that he offered the contents of the room to the Spanish king, along with whatever else remained of his own personal treasure. Cortez and his men, "amazed at the great liberality of Montezuma," proceeded to divide the gold according to the custom of such expeditions: one-fifth for King Charles; one-fifth for Cortez, "captain general" of the band; a large portion to cover the expenses of mounting the expedition in Cuba and another substantial sum to pay for Governor Velazquez's destroyed ships; smaller shares for the various captains and officers who served under Cortez; and finally, shares for the ordinary troops, which were "so little that many of the soldiers did not want to take it and Cortez was left with it all."

At first, Cortez proved less successful in changing Aztec religious practice than he had been in obtaining Aztec gold. During his early days in Tenochtitlán, he urged Montezuma several times to forbid human sacrifice in the Aztec temples, but to no avail. Montezuma did grant Cortez's "request" for permission to erect a separate Christian place of worship, with a cross and a statue of Christ and the Virgin Mary, but he refused to abandon his own gods. Because the Spanish captain general hoped to dominate the Aztecs by using Montezuma as a figurehead emperor, he compromised for the moment. Cortez realized that an all-out fight within Tenochtitlán would find three hundred Spaniards and their Indian allies surrounded by three million Aztecs.

Once it became clear that Montezuma had been placed under "house arrest," his Aztec nobles began plotting to drive out the Spaniards. The emperor, however, observed his pledge of loyalty to Cortez and revealed their schemes. Montezuma even ordered the chief Aztec plotter, his nephew Cacama, seized and delivered to Cortez. Next Montezuma called a council of Aztec nobles, priests, and chief vassals, urging them all to submit to Cortez and to the Spanish king. Although they protested, the nobles obeyed, at least nominally, and pledged their loyalty.

Cortez was so confident of Montezuma's continued influence over his people by this time that he ordered the closing of Aztec religious shrines. For days thereafter, the Spaniards and their Indian converts to Christianity destroyed statues of Aztec gods, drove the native priests from their temples, cleansed the altars used for human sacrifices, and erected Christian shrines throughout Tenochtitlán.

Finally, the captain general decided to strengthen his authority over the Mexicans by completing the humiliation of Montezuma. First, Cortez displayed before the emperor two Aztec nobles who (according to Cortez) had confessed that Montezuma had ordered them to lead a revolt against the Spaniards. Then he ordered Montezuma placed in irons and forced the emperor to watch as the two Aztec prisoners were burned to death before his eyes.

If Cortez hoped to terrify the Aztecs and Montezuma by this action, he miscalculated badly. Even Montezuma now threw his support behind the secret plans of Aztec nobles and priests to organize armed resistance to the Spaniards. The emperor's uncertainty and fear of his captors disappeared; he began to recover his strength and resolve. At a private meeting, he warned the captain general to leave Mexico immediately because "the gods are very angry with me for entertaining you here." Montezuma indicated clearly to Cortez that he could no longer guarantee the Spaniards' safety against an Aztec attack.

Cortez stalled for time. For several weeks, Montezuma, reconfirmed in his authority, and Cortez, quietly encircled by hostile Aztecs, skirted each other uneasily. Both men waited for some decisive break in this contest of wills. The "break," like Cortez himself, came from the coast. A new expedition of nineteen ships arrived at Vera Cruz, a small settlement Cortez had founded. These ships brought soldiers from Cuba, sent by Governor Velazquez to destroy Cortez and his party. "Now you will not need to build ships," Montezuma told Cortez blandly. The emperor's agents had been in touch with the expedition's commander, Pánfilo de Narváez, and knew of its purpose.

Cortez left Tenochtitlán within days, taking most of his soldiers and Indian allies to confront Narváez. He left behind a small Spanish contingent under the command of one of his captains, Pedro de Alvarado. Montezuma remained a hostage, and most Aztecs seemed willing to wait, hoping that the soldiers of Cortez and Narváez would destroy one another. Then there would be time to deal with Alvarado's small rear guard.

But Alvarado proved restless as the appointed caretaker of Tenochtitlán, and shortly after Cortez departed, the pent-up conflict between Spaniard and Aztec, which seemed almost like a struggle between a bee and an elephant, broke into warfare. It was the bee that went on the attack.

The occasion for battle came when Aztec priests requested Montezuma's permission to celebrate the feast of their chief god, Huitzilopochtli. This major harvest festival in Aztec religious life included an elaborate, exhausting dance-and-song ceremony which Aztec warriors performed at night in the temple courtyard. Alvarado heard rumors that

This woodcut reconstruction of the great temple at Tenochtitlán and surrounding area suggests the extraordinary achievement of Aztec architecture, building design, and decorative arts. The great pyramid temple, site of Aztec human sacrifices, towers over the various subsidiary temples, government buildings, and fortress walls, suggesting the gigantic scale of Montezuma's capital city. (American Museum of Natural History)

the Aztecs planned to attack his troops once the dance ended. The hostility that Cortez's soldiers now encountered throughout Tenochtitlán, combined with the drum beatings, trumpet blarings, and frenzied dancing of the festival, struck fear in the Spaniards. Alvarado lacked Cortez's cool composure at such moments, and he mistakenly believed that the carnival-like ceremony foreshadowed a Mexican assault on his troops.

Alvarado ordered his men to block the temple's entrances. Then the Spaniards moved into the courtyard and massacred all those within. An Aztec narrative described the scene:

> They attacked all the celebrants, stabbing them, spearing them, striking them with their swords. They attacked some of them from behind, and these fell instantly to the ground with their entrails hanging out. Others they beheaded: they cut off their heads, or split their heads in pieces. . . . No matter how they tried to save themselves, they could find no escape.

When news of the slaughter spread through Tenochtitlán, the entire community exploded in anger and grief. Montezuma's captains assembled thousands of warriors within hours, and armed with only spears and javelins, they attacked. Alvarado and his men immediately took refuge in the palace. The first siege of Tenochtitlán had begun.

Alvarado ordered Montezuma shackled again, and his soldiers opened fire with cannon and muskets to defend themselves against a blizzard of Aztec spears. The Aztecs, enraged at the unprovoked slaughter of their temple dancers, scorned an emissary from Montezuma, who pleaded with them to return to their homes. "Who is Montezuma to give us orders?" they shouted at the envoy. "We are no longer his slaves!" Aztec captains and warriors denounced Montezuma himself for collaboration with their enemies. They put the emperor's servants to death, prevented food and supplies from entering the palace, and seized anyone attempting to enter. At the same time they watched closely the roads and causeways leading to the city, to guard against Cortez's return.

While Alvarado brought war to Tenochtitlán, Cortez managed to capture Narváez's expedition with a minimum of bloodshed. He first sent gifts of gold to Narváez's men and promised them more treasures if they joined him. Then he led his forces in a night attack on Narváez's camp. After some brief, half-hearted resistance, most of the eight hundred soldiers (Cortez had half that number) surrendered and swore loyalty to Cortez. Twelve days later, Cortez received a message from Alvarado describing his desperate situation. Cortez and his soldiers, now numbering perhaps a thousand, began a second march on the Aztec capital.

The Mexican siege had proved effective. By the time Cortez arrived in Tenochtitlán, Alvarado's men had almost exhausted their food and water. Cortez's column entered the city without resistance, since the Mexicans apparently hoped to trap *all* the Spaniards inside the royal palace. By this time, the Aztec nobles had deposed Montezuma as emperor in favor of his brother Cuitlahuac, a man long committed to total destruction of the white strangers. The Aztecs renewed their attack on the palace, opening a raging, four-day struggle.

During the battle, while still a Spanish captive, Montezuma died. The Spaniards later claimed that he had been fatally wounded by rocks thrown by his own people while pleading for peace from the palace roof. Aztecs insisted that he had been killed by the Spaniards.

The fierce bloodletting went badly for the Spaniards, and the royal palace, no longer a fortress, was fast becoming a death trap. Cortez decided to abandon Tenochtitlán and withdraw at night. By the time he fled the city, only four of the eight bridges on the causeway that led to safety were still in Spanish hands. Even these were under attack by Aztec warriors.

The captain general apparently hoped to surprise his opponents, but it proved impossible to hide from Aztec sentries the movement of a thousand Spaniards, several thousand "loyal" Indians, horses, cannon, and baggage. Cortez and his men also tried to cart away the *entire* Aztec treasure horde, most of it by then melted into ingot bars—a total of eight tons in gold. By the time this cumbersome procession reached the causeway's second bridge, the alarm had been sounded; thousands of Aztec warriors encircled the fleeing Spaniards. The lake was thick with canoes full of Indians, who swarmed over Cortez's retreating company. "The canal was soon choked with the bodies of men and horses," ran one Aztec account of the episode. "They filled the gap in the causeway with their own drowning bodies."

When the armies had finished hacking and slashing at one another in the dark, at least six hundred of Cortez's thousand men lay dead, while his Indian allies (chiefly the Tlaxcalans) numbered over two thousand fatalities. At least that many Aztecs also perished in the battle, an episode that Cortez's men referred to later as *la noche triste,* the night of sorrows.

Cortez's decimated army found itself harried mercilessly during the retreat that followed. Thousands of Aztec warriors remained behind in Tenochtitlán, many of them scouring the canals for gold and equipment abandoned by the Spaniards, but an even greater number marched north in pursuit of Cortez. They massed for a final attack, which occurred the following day (July 7, 1520) on a plain outside the village of Otumba. The battle ended indecisively, with the outnumbered Spanish and Tlaxcalan contingents still intact. The next day they reached the safety of the Tlaxcalans' own territory. The Aztecs pursued them but did not attack again, and for the moment "Quetzalcoatl" and his depleted company could rest.

"When the Spaniards left Tenochtitlán," wrote a Mexican chronicler, "the Aztecs thought they had departed for good and would never return. Therefore they repaired and decorated the temple of their god" and began again to hold traditional Aztec religious celebrations. Yet life in Tenochtitlán never returned to normal. Cortez proved a persistent and "mortal" enemy. He sent immediately to the Spanish coastal settlement at Vera Cruz for additional powder, weapons, and soldiers. Even more important, he managed to persuade his dispirited band of 400 survivors that they could reconquer the Aztecs and regain their gold.

The captain general and his men, several badly wounded (Cortez himself had lost two fingers on his left hand), marched after only three weeks' rest against the nearby Mexican town of Tepeaca. The defenders were easily overcome and most of them sold into slavery, a fate that Cortez decreed would await any Indian allies of the Spaniards who reneged on their promises of loyalty. The victory at Tepeaca had its desired effect. Indian tribes that had deserted the Spaniards after their flight from Tenochtitlán quickly rejoined their ranks, especially once they saw that Cortez was willing to allow his allies to continue their religious practice of ritual sacrifice.

Cortez prepared methodically for the assault on Tenochtitlán. He spent months gathering his Indian forces while constructing thirteen fortified sloops, known as brigantines, for use on Lake Texcoco during the coming battle.

Events in Tenochtitlán itself during this period worked to his advantage. Smallpox, a disease new to Mexico, spread quickly through the city, killing thousands (a fair return, one Spanish writer insisted, for the syphilis that the Indians had first transmitted to the Spaniards). Among those who died was the Aztec emperor, Cuitlahuac, who was replaced by one of Montezuma's sons-in-law, Cuauhtemoc. In the months from August 1520 to April 1521, the Spaniards and their Tlaxcalan allies raided a number of Mexican garrisons surrounding Lake Texcoco, seeking mainly gold and slaves while awaiting Cortez's order to begin the main assault.

By May 1521, Cortez's preparations were complete. He launched his brigantines on Lake Texcoco and sent messengers to his various Indian allies summoning them to battle. That month his entire force moved out, an impressive contrast to the scruffy band of stragglers that had taken refuge in Tlaxcala territory the previous year. Now, with new recruits from ships that had landed on the coast, Cortez had again managed to muster almost a thousand Spaniards, as well as eighty-six horses and plenty of powder for his cannon. Marching alongside the Spaniards were more than seventy-five thousand Indian soldiers.

Cortez directed the battles that followed from the deck of a brigantine, dividing the land forces into mixed Spanish-Indian units, each commanded by a Spanish captain. Soon after arriving at Lake Texcoco, his ships destroyed more than a thousand Aztec canoes. "We killed and drowned many of the enemy—the greatest sight to see in the world," Cortez later wrote to the Spanish king. More important, this early victory over the Aztecs assured the Spaniards control of the lake itself and thus helped seal the Aztecs inside Tenochtitlán, away from their allies and sources of supply across the lake.

The Aztecs, now encircled, were forced into an unfamiliar defensive role. The defenders of Tenochtitlán fought as bravely and ferociously to preserve their city as the Spaniards had fought the previous year to leave it. Several times Cortez himself nearly lost his life. He probably would have been killed if his Aztec pursuers had not been trying (unsuccessfully) to capture him alive for use as a sacrifice.

The Spaniards, while waging continuous battle against the warriors of Tenochtitlán, at the same time tried to starve out the city. Cortez's forces blockaded all the land and canal approaches to Tenochtitlán and seized relief supplies. For every Spaniard or Indian sacrificed to the Aztec gods, a thousand Mexicans perished through a longer, although not less painful, process, as the Aztec chronicles describe:

> The only food was lizards, swallows, corncobs, and the salt grasses of the lake. The people also ate water lilies and seeds, and chewed on deerhides and pieces of leather. . . . They ate the bitterest weeds and even dirt.

Several times the new Aztec emperor, Cuauhtemoc, and his chief nobles rejected Spanish demands for the city's surrender, while day by day Cortez and his army fought closer and closer toward the center of Tenochtitlán. At Cortez's orders, his Indian vassals systematically destroyed every building and structure they captured, choking off all possibility of Aztec ambush and escape. They leveled entire streets, turning the lake city of Tenochtitlán—only months before, the most majestic city in the Western Hemisphere—into a desolate island wilderness. In the last days of the battle, Cortez's forces slaughtered thousands of Mexico's army, now penned into less than one-eighth the city's area at its very center.

The battle ended on August 13, 1521, almost two years to the day after Cortez had begun his original march from the coast to Tenochtitlán. That day, over 15,000 Indians perished during a final assault by Cortez's troops. The remaining Aztec troops and nobles, including the emperor, fled by canoe into the city's maze of canals, but Cuauhtemoc was captured by a brigantine crew. With his surrender the independence and empire of the Aztecs ended.

> We found the houses full of corpses [wrote the Spaniard Bernal Diaz], and some poor Mexicans still in them who could not move away. Their excretions were the sort of filth that thin swine pass which have been fed on nothing but grass. The city looked as if it had been ploughed up. . . .

Of the 300,000 Aztec warriors who had begun the defense of Tenochtitlán, only 60,000 remained. Still the Spaniards' Indian allies continued killing indiscriminately, looting for gold, and taking Aztec captives, either as slaves or as victims for eventual sacrifice. Cortez himself acquired many Aztec nobles as his personal prisoners and ordered the entire city—which was strewn with unburied corpses—cleansed by fire.

Within days after his victory, Cortez and his Indian allies exchanged parting gifts. The bulk of their 200,000 troops marched homeward from Tenochtitlán, laden with gold and captives. The Spaniards, after celebrating a Thanksgiving Mass, began a systematic search for the Aztec gold lost during *la noche triste.* Despite the torture to which they subjected Aztec captives, however, only two of the original eight tons of gold were recovered. Much of that went to the coast for shipment to Spain as "the royal fifth," the share owed to King Charles.

Once the pillage and slaughter in Tenochtitlán ended, many of Cortez's men received not gold but Aztec slaves as compensation. Those who managed to survive the destruction of their nation faced a future as slaves, either to the Spaniards or to their own former Indian subjects. Cortez appointed himself Governor of Mexico. With Tenochtitlán destroyed and its population homeless, the last expression of Aztec culture came from poems written to mourn this monumental defeat:

> Broken spears lie in the roads,
> we have torn our hair in our grief.
> The houses are roofless now, and their walls
> are red with blood. . . .
>
> We have pounded our hands in despair
> against the adobe walls,
> for our inheritance, our city, is lost and dead.
> The shields of our warriors were its defense,
> but they could not save it. . . .
>
> Weep, my people; know that with these disasters
> we have lost the Mexican nation.
> The water has turned bitter, our food is bitter!
> These are the acts of the Giver of Life. . . .

Three ships left Vera Cruz for Spain in December 1522. Their cargo consisted of gold—"the royal fifth"—and of exquisite Aztec jewelry sent by the acting governor of Mexico, Hernando Cortez, to His Most Catholic Majesty, King Charles V. The ships never reached Spain. They were attacked and seized by a French privateer, who delivered their contents to his own sovereign, Francis I. But the real prize—the Aztec Empire and not the remnants of Montezuma's treasure house—would remain in Spanish hands for almost three centuries after Montezuma's messengers had first sighted the returning "Quetzalcoatl."

2 Exploring and Conquering the Americas

Cortez arrived in the New World more than twenty thousand years after the North American Indians. For hundreds of years, European scholars tried to demonstrate that the Indians were the survivors of the sunken continent of Atlantis or the ten lost tribes of Israel. But nothing so spectacular had happened. Instead, roving Mongolian hunters had slowly wandered through Siberia, across the prehistoric land bridge of the Bering Strait, and into Alaska.

It took several thousand years for them to spread throughout the entire Western Hemisphere—past the Mississippi and the Great Lakes, down along the Rockies and the Andes, and on to the islands of the Caribbean.

Only when they had settled at various points did these nomads begin acquiring traits linked with a sedentary life, such as agriculture and the domestication of animals. They then slowly developed complex civilizations varying in sophistication and size from the Aztecs to the Patagonians. None of them, however, could withstand the onslaught of the Europeans. Not all Indian states fell as quickly or as painfully as Montezuma's, and some would not have to contend with the whites for many years. But the Indians' control of the continents they had discovered had passed. Within two centuries of the first landing, the newcomers had divided up nearly fifteen million square miles among themselves.

DEVELOPMENT OF THE AZTEC EMPIRE

Since the Aztecs were perhaps as highly organized as any society the Europeans encoun-
tered, the building of their civilization deserves examination. The Aztecs borrowed freely from earlier cultures in the area. First came the people of Teotihuacán, who constructed a great city near the later site of Tenochtitlán. Teotihuacán flourished during the fourth and fifth centuries A.D. Here the Indians built pyramids, palaces, and temples.

A later people in the Valley of Mexico, the Toltecs, built another great city, Tula, just north of Teotihuacán. Under the leadership of a strong king named Quetzalcoatl, the Toltecs conquered a sizable territory, built beautiful palaces, and erected huge stone sculptures. Although Toltec rule collapsed, Indians in the Valley of Mexico retained Toltec cultural patterns. For example, they began worshiping Quetzalcoatl as a god. They believed that he had departed to the East, abandoning his people, but that one day he would return by ship from the other end of the world. This legend was the basis for Montezuma's initial fear that Cortez and his men were returning deities.

The Aztecs, initially bands of warriors, came into the Valley of Mexico from the north around 1215. Neighboring peoples helped to educate them in the fine arts and skills that had been handed down from the Toltecs. The Aztecs needed little training in the art of warfare, however. Within decades of their arrival in the valley, they had conquered every major city-state in the area.

The new overlords built upon the achievements not only of local peoples, but also of those in nearby regions, notably the Mayas. Mayan culture surpassed that of both the Aztecs and the Toltecs. Mayan civilization in Central America reached its height between A.D. 200 and 700. The people were not united under one government, but they lived clustered around such ceremonial cities as Tikal and Palenque.

THE INCAS

Because of their cultural achievements, the Mayas have sometimes been thought of as the Greeks of pre-Columbian America. Similarly, the Incas have been compared to the Romans because of their imperial political and administrative organization. The Inca Empire sprawled over the western part of South America. It covered large portions of modern Ecuador, Peru, Bolivia, and Chile—in other words, most of the land available for cultivation on the Andean Plateau. In the eleventh century, at roughly the same time the Toltecs were invading the Mayan region, the Incas began extending their control along the Pacific slope of the southern continent. At its peak in the sixteenth century, the Inca Empire stretched 1500 miles down the coast and 300 miles inland. It surpassed the Aztec state in communications and organization, as well as in size.

The Incas considered their emperor, known himself as "the Inca," to be divine. He ruled from the capital city of Cuzco, high in the Andes Mountains. An excellent system of roads and runners connected Cuzco to every part of the empire.

Superb Inca roads made it easy to move troops. "Not an insurrectionary movement could occur, not an invasion on the remotest frontier," wrote an American historian, "before the tidings were conveyed to the capital, and the imperial armies were on the march along the magnificent roads of the country to suppress it."

Although the Incas had a more efficient war machine than the Aztecs, they too were unsuccessful in resisting the Europeans. An adventurer named Francisco Pizarro had first heard of a rich inland kingdom while voyaging along the Pacific coast during the 1520s. In 1531 he led a group of Spaniards into the Inca domain. They found the empire in the throes of a civil war between two sons of the previous emperor. The more successful imperial contender, Atahualpa, had recently won control.

Because of this civil war, Inca forces were weakened and divided. They could not muster effective resistance when Pizarro attacked. The climax of Pizarro's campaign came in a scene resembling the episode in Tenochtitlán, when the Spaniards slaughtered the Aztecs at worship. Pizarro lured Atahualpa to a meeting, where he ordered Spanish troops to cut down thousands of poorly armed, unsuspecting Inca soldiers. Pizarro promised to release the Inca emperor after payment of a fantastic ransom in gold and silver worth an estimated ten million dollars. Once the Indians had delivered the ransom, Pizarro had Atahualpa executed, and the Incas (like the Aztecs) fell under Spanish rule.

NORTH AMERICAN CULTURES

The complex societies developed by the Aztecs, Mayas, and Incas contrasted with the simpler cultures of most North American Indians at the time of the European influx. On the one hand, the Indian population in Latin America was large; there were probably over fifteen million Indians south of the Rio Grande when the whites came. Societies were stable; people built cities and made a living by farming settled areas. Corn, the staple crop for almost all American Indians, was probably first cultivated in Mexico.

Probably no more than a million Indians, on the other hand, lived in what eventually became the United States and Canada. Instead of large civilizations like the Aztecs or the Incas, North American Indians formed small tribal groupings. Tribal societies in North America reflected the wide variety of climates and geographic features of the world's third largest continent. Alaska, Florida, the Great Plains, and the Rockies produced a striking diversity of lifestyles.

Remnants of some relatively advanced Indian cultures still exist in several regions of North America. One such culture flourished in southern Arizona, where an Indian-built complex of irrigation canals dating to the eighth century suggests highly sophisticated farming techniques. The Pueblos, the oldest inhabitants of the Southwest, lived in adobe villages built on high mesas. More warlike and nomadic tribes like the Navajos and the Apaches moved into the region later.

In the Mississippi Valley, early Indians known as Mound Builders heaped earth and rubble into pyramids and other structures used as temples

These Mayan buildings are among several at Chichen Itzá. At left is a temple to Kulkulcan, the Mayan counterpart of Quetzalcoatl. The round structure at right is an astronomical observatory, no longer standing. (George Halton/ Photo Researchers)

High in the Andes lies the Inca town of Macchu Picchu. Undiscovered by Spanish conquerors, it remained hidden in the mountains until an American explorer stumbled across it in 1911. (George Halton/ Photo Researchers)

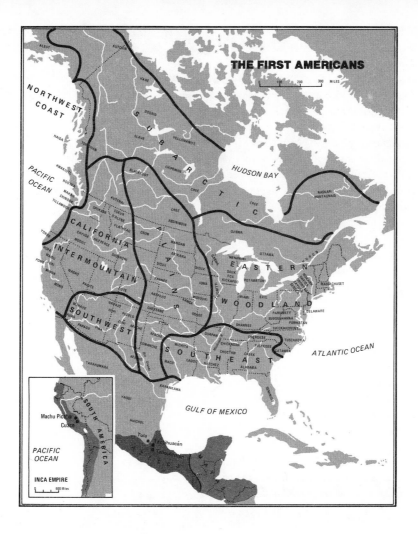

THE FIRST AMERICANS

or burial mounds; these have yielded many beautiful works of art.

In the large area to the north between the Rockies and the Mississippi River lived the Plains Indians: the Cheyenne, the Pawnee, and the Sioux. Although these tribes did some farming, hunting was the main source of their livelihood and the basis of their social organization. After the coming of the whites—and with them the horse—the Plains Indians happily gave up farming altogether and lived entirely by hunting the buffalo, which filled the plains in vast numbers.

Small tribes like the Shoshoni and the Ute roamed the bleak lands between the Rockies and the Pacific Ocean. They made a poor living gathering wild plants and eating small animals such as rabbits and snakes. In California—home of the Pomos, Hupas, and others—acorns were a staple food. Life was easier there, and people had time to make some of the finest basketwork in the world.

Tribes such as the Kwakiutl, Nootka, and Tlingit lived in what is now Oregon, Washington, and British Columbia. They based their economy on salmon and other fish available in the rivers, and on lumber from the great forests of cedars, using the wood to create handsome canoes and totem poles (many of which survive today).

Explorers landing on the East Coast encountered settled tribes living by a combination of fishing and hunting. Most of them dressed in deerskin and lived in bark-covered wigwams. The famous Iroquois confederacy occupied the New York State region. This league of five tribes consisted of the Mohawks, Oneidas, Onondagas, Cayugas, and Senecas. In the Southeast, Seminoles, Cherokees, and Creeks greeted the Spaniards coming up through Florida.

THE INDIAN WAY

Indian life clearly differed a great deal from group to group and place to place. But certain traits were common to almost all Indians and set them apart from other peoples—especially from the Europeans who settled in America. One of these characteristics was the Indian attitude toward land. Although a tribe might have hunting rights to a certain territory, its members no more owned this territory than the sky above it. Even among the complex farming societies of Latin America, land generally belonged to the community or perhaps to a god or spirit. Indians, in short, held a different concept of land ownership than did the Spanish invaders.

Indians also had different attitudes about warfare. For them battle was as much a ceremony as a conflict. Even in the Aztec Empire, where territory and tribute were important, the basic goal of war was to capture prisoners for religious sacrifice. To many North American tribes, war was almost a game. Plains fighters, for example, achieved as much glory for touching an enemy in battle as for killing him.

The first Europeans who came to America were accustomed to powerful monarchs, but even a ruler of Montezuma's importance did not possess *absolute* power. He was, in fact, elected to his post, and many of his duties were merely ceremonial. Few chiefs of North American tribes had the au-

Indians of a vanished era scratched these mysterious figures on a cliff wall in Wyoming. They may represent priests or perhaps gods held sacred by the tribe. (American Museum of Natural History)

thority to rule by themselves. When there was an issue to be decided, all the respected elders of a band would gather together and, after lengthy deliberations, try to reach a unanimous decision or, at least, a consensus.

Indian religious concepts differed greatly from those of Christianity. The idea of an afterlife was, at most, vague. They prayed not to one God but often to a multitude of gods or spirits. (The Aztecs worshiped more than 300 deities.) Indians were believed to have their own guardian spirits that helped them through life. Such spirits were also thought to inhabit trees, animals, rivers, and mountains. The Indians trusted in what we would call magic, but they soon found out that their magic could not make the white man disappear.

In America north of the Rio Grande, Indians created a number of distinctive styles. Typical of the Mound Builder culture is the kneeling stone figure at left, found in Tennessee. From New York State is the Cayuga Iroquois mask above, braided from corn husks. Masks like this were worn by members of the so-called False Face Societies—secret organizations whose members performed dances and other rituals to heal the sick. Below is a slate canoe sculpted by a Haida Indian of the Northwest. The figure in front is a shaman, or medicine man. He wears a crown of bear claws set in a rope of twisted cedar bark. The reclining figure at the back, with closed eyes. probably represents a dead person. (top left and bottom—Museum of Primitive Art; top right—American Museum of Natural History)

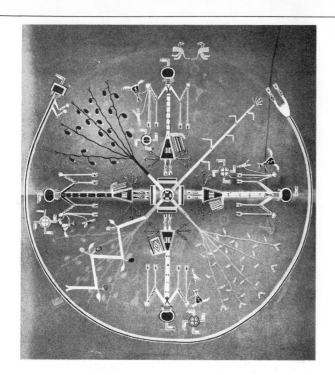

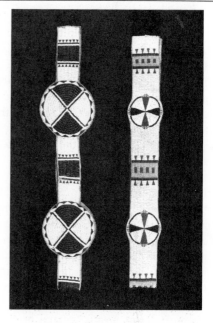

Navajo Indians of the Southwest are noted for their sand paintings, like the one above. Each one, combining sacred symbols and used as part of a healing ceremony, is formed by a priest in the morning and destroyed before nightfall. At right above are blanket bands woven by the Sioux Indians of the Great Plains. These were made after the white man came with beads for trade; in the early days, women fashioned similar designs using dyed porcupine quills or wampum (beads drilled from clam shells). The whale statuette at left was carved by a Chumash Indian of California. (top left—Bureau of Ethnology; top right—American Museum of Natural History; bottom—Museum of Primitive Art)

FIRST CONTACTS

Five hundred years before Cortez, in the far northeastern corner of the New World, Indians had in fact driven off the first European settlers. After raiding Ireland, France, and Italy, the red-bearded Vikings (or Norsemen) from Scandinavia also sailed far out into the North Atlantic. In the ninth century they established a settlement in Iceland. From this base of operations they conducted daring voyages of exploration farther westward.

Vikings led by Eric the Red discovered and settled Greenland during the tenth century. Around the year 1000, Eric's son Leif anchored his ship off the coast of what is now Newfoundland. He called the place Vineland the Good, and he and his men spent the winter there before returning to Greenland. A decade later, other Vikings sailed from Iceland to found a colony of farmers and tradesmen in Vineland. After spending two or three years fighting hostile Indians, however, they abandoned their settlement and returned to their Greenland base.

Cortez knew as little of his Scandinavian predecessors as Montezuma did. His knowledge that a New World existed came, of course, from much later visitors such as the Italian Christopher Columbus, who explored under the Spanish flag. In 1492 Columbus, with ninety men in three small ships, landed on a small island in the Caribbean, and promptly returned to Spain to announce that he had found China.

SPANISH AND PORTUGUESE EXPLORATION

Lacking the Vikings' pure thirst for adventure, the Spanish had a specific reason for sending out Columbus and the many Spanish explorers who followed him. For centuries, luxury products such as spices, jewels, and silk had come from Asia overland or across the Indian Ocean. In either case, the Italian middlemen transported the goods from the eastern end of the Mediterranean into western Europe. They had a monopoly on the trade, so they charged high prices. Nations on the Atlantic—Portugal and Spain, for example—decided to bypass the Mediterranean (and the Italians) and do their own trading with the East.

The Portuguese concentrated mainly on finding a route around Africa and then eastward to India and China. In the early fifteenth century, Prince Henry the Navigator sponsored a school of navigation on his country's southwestern coast. He devoted his life to sending out fleets of ships to explore the west coast of Africa. Year by year the Portuguese sailed farther south along the African coast. In 1488 Bartholomew Diaz voyaged as far as the Cape of Good Hope, at the tip of Africa. Vasco da Gama sailed around the cape and reached India in 1498, returning to Portugal with a rich cargo the following year. In 1500 Pedro Cabral, headed for India, was blown off course by trade winds and landed in what is now Brazil. This region of South America, claimed by Portugal, was the only area in the Western Hemisphere that the Portuguese exploited.

The Spanish, pursuing a different strategy, sent Columbus west to reach Asia. Although the admiral found only a scraggly village of naked Indians, he remained convinced that he had reached, if not China, certainly the outlying areas of Asia. On Columbus's three subsequent voyages, mainly to the Caribbean islands of Cuba and Hispaniola, the Spanish monarchs Ferdinand and Isabella sent along everybody needed to duplicate Spanish society in the New World. The ships carried missionaries, artisans, knights, soldiers, and field laborers. Unfortunately, even all this support could not establish a successful colony when the expected riches of the East failed to materialize. At one point the impatient Spanish rulers had Columbus brought back to Madrid in chains. Despite Columbus's lack of material success, he did set a pattern for future settlers.

The honor of having two continents named after him went not to Columbus but to a Florentine bank manager, Amerigo Vespucci. He claimed to have sailed to America several times. In widely read letters, he described his experiences in what he called the New World. In 1507 a geographer named Martin Waldseemüller suggested naming the new land "America, because Americus discovered it." (*Americus* is the Latin form of Vespucci's first name.)

In 1519 the Portuguese explorer Ferdinand Magellan, with Spanish backing, sailed around the southern tip of South America. He crossed the Pacific and thus found the westward route to the East. Magellan was killed by natives in the Philippine Islands. But his navigator, Sebastian del Cano, continued westward in the only ship that remained of the original five. He returned to Lisbon in 1522, having completed the first voyage around the world. The people of Europe then realized what many scholars had already known—namely, that the world is round. And they realized, too, that a whole "New World" lay to the west between Europe and Asia.

EARLY SPANISH EXPLORERS

In the fifty years after Columbus's first voyage, a host of Spanish explorers and conquerors performed incredibly daring and profitable feats all over America. Like Columbus, they dreamed of fame, of winning converts to the Christian faith, and of wealth; Spanish goals have been described as "glory, God, and gold."

For every Cortez or Pizarro who found the riches he had dreamed of, there were many who discovered only dusty, impoverished villages, bitter disappointment, and sometimes violent death. No Spaniard appears to have gotten rich exploring what is now the United States. Juan Ponce de León (who sailed to America on Columbus's second voyage) failed to find either gold or the legendary fountain of youth when he explored Florida in 1513. After trying unsuccessfully to found a settlement on the peninsula in 1521, he was wounded by Indians and died on his return voyage to Cuba. Searching for the legendary "Seven Cities of Cibola," said to be full of riches, Francisco Vasquez de Coronado explored much of the Southwest in 1540–42. When found, the "Seven Cities" turned out to be nothing more fabulous than the simple adobe villages of the Pueblo Indians. Hernando de Soto, leading a large military expedition from Cuba, wandered from Florida and the Carolinas to Texas and became the first white man to look upon the Mississippi. After finding only bloody battles with Indians, he died of disease and

disappointment in Louisiana. Not wanting the Indians to find a white body, his men wrapped and weighted his corpse and threw it into the river he had discovered.

CREATING AN EMPIRE

In spite of all these setbacks, the Spanish continued to come to the New World in tremendous numbers. They formed political units and appointed Spanish rulers. They built missions, military outposts, and towns, thereby creating an overseas empire.

By 1600, a quarter of a million Spaniards had settled in the Western Hemisphere. Here they introduced crops previously unknown in America—among them wheat, rye, oats, and barley. They found that bananas, peaches, and citrus fruits would grow well in America, too. Sugar cane became an especially important crop in tropical regions. The Spanish also brought draft animals—horses, mules, and oxen—and livestock, including cattle, hogs, and sheep. And the newcomers quickly learned to grow native American crops: corn, tomatoes, potatoes, beans, cacao, and tobacco.

Spanish civilization in the Americas prospered on gold and silver acquired from the Aztec and Inca empires. Fabulously rich silver mines were discovered in Mexico and Peru in 1545. Silver and to a lesser extent gold were for many decades Spain's chief exports from the New World.

SPANIARDS, INDIANS, AND AFRICANS

After the Spanish conquests of America, those Indians who survived war and epidemic diseases were virtually enslaved by their conquerors. Thousands labored in the mines digging and smelting silver and gold; others farmed and tended livestock.

Some Spanish friars and priests protested against mistreatment of the Indians. In time, the Spanish crown passed laws designed to limit the abuse of native labor. These efforts, however, were not notably successful in preventing cruelty and

Christopher Columbus

(Metropolitan Museum of Art—Gift of J. Pierpont Morgan, 1900)

We know more about the deeds of the adventurous, obstinate, and visionary mariner Christoper Columbus than about the man himself, especially his earliest years. Born the eldest son of an Italian wool weaver in 1451, possibly a weaver himself for a time, Christoper Columbus (the English version of a name which began as "Cristoforo Colombo" in Genoa and became "Cristobal Colon" during later years in Spain) left his native Genoa to become a sailor in about 1472.

The popular literature on Columbus, written after he became famous, described the young sailor as engaged in numerous adventures. It was said that when his ship caught fire in battle off the Portuguese coast, Columbus swam to safety. We know that he lived in Portugal—when not on voyages—for most of the period between 1476 and 1486. He married there, and studied navigation and geography among the circle of interested scholars and seamen who seemed almost too numerous in that maritime kingdom. Columbus knew about the Portuguese discoveries elsewhere in the world and he absorbed an idea, familiar to the more expert sailors of his day, that it might prove possible to reach the Far East by sailing westward across the uncharted ocean. Columbus was fascinated by the accounts which the Italian traveler Marco Polo wrote in the thirteenth century of his visit to Kublai Khan, the Mongol ruler of China ("Cathay"), and to other Far Eastern kingdoms. Columbus began dreaming of an ocean voyage westward to the Far East and, in the mid-1480s, set out in search of royal support and money to finance the voyage.

After being rebuffed by King Joao of Portugal from 1483–84, Columbus turned his attention to the devout Catholic rulers of Spain, Ferdinand and Isabella, then busily engaged in military campaigns to drive the remaining Moors from the Iberian peninsula and reunite their kingdom under Christian overlordship. Columbus emigrated to Spain and followed Ferdinand and Isabella from town to town, petitioning them to sponsor his expedition. Although impressed by the Italian's evident religious faith and dynamic personality, the king and queen of Spain persistently rejected his proposals over the next six years while waging war against the Moors. Finally in 1492, just as Columbus was preparing to leave Spain to try his luck with the king of France, Isabella summoned him and agreed to finance the voyage.

The forty-one-year-old Columbus set sail westward from Palos for "the Indies" on August 3, 1492, with three ships and less than a hundred men. After stopping at the Canary Islands in September, the ships proceeded across the ocean. On October 12, only two days after a near-mutinous crew had debated throwing "Admiral" Columbus overboard, the Spaniards sighted land, a small island in the Bahamas which Columbus named San Salvador (Spanish for "Holy Savior"). Convinced that he had arrived in the East Indies, he named the island's inhabitants "Indians." Columbus continued sailing through the West Indies, however, mistakenly naming islands he came to after places in Marco Polo's chronicle: Cuba became "Cathay" and Hispaniola, later Santo Domingo, "Cipango" (Polo's Japan). When Columbus set sail for Spain, he persisted in believing he had reached his original goal and left behind a small settlement of sailors on Hispaniola to wait for his return.

All of Europe rejoiced with the news that Columbus had discovered the "Indies" (albeit the

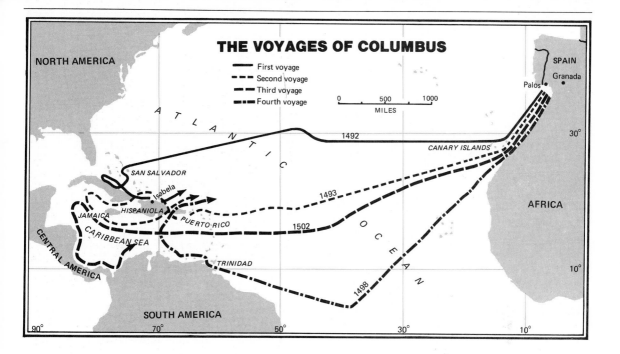

THE VOYAGES OF COLUMBUS

— First voyage
--- Second voyage
-·- Third voyage
-··- Fourth voyage

0   500   1000
MILES

NORTH AMERICA

SPAIN
Granada
Palos

ATLANTIC

1492

CANARY ISLANDS

30°

SAN SALVADOR
Isabela
HISPANIOLA
JAMAICA
PUERTO RICO
CARIBBEAN SEA

1493

1502

AFRICA

OCEAN

CENTRAL AMERICA

TRINIDAD

1498

10°

SOUTH AMERICA

90°   70°   50°   30°   10°

wrong ones, West and not East, though he never admitted that fact). His *second* voyage took place in 1493 with seventeen ships and 1500 men intent upon gaining quick profits for Ferdinand and Isabella from discoveries of gold, jewels, and other treasures. Missionaries intent upon converting the Indians to Christianity accompanied the adventurers, and the ships contained a social microcosm of Imperial Spain: knights, artisans, courtiers, and field laborers. By the time they reached Hispaniola —where they established the framework of a Spanish town—no trace of the garrison left behind remained. Columbus discovered Puerto Rico, Jamaica, and other New World islands on this voyage, but his more ambitious plans never materialized. His men found neither precious metals (except in small supply) nor the great Asian cities that Columbus believed were just over the horizon. Cruel treatment of the Indian tribes led to a rebellion in which, after three years of sporadic warfare, the Spaniards wiped out two-thirds of the native population and enslaved the rest.

Columbus returned to Spain in 1496 without substantial treasure but persuaded Ferdinand and Isabella to sponsor a third voyage in 1498. This time, he discovered Trinidad and the coast of

South America. Because of a revolt against Columbus's rule in Hispaniola, the Spanish rulers dispatched an investigator who ordered Columbus returned to Spain in chains. After convincing the king and queen of his innocence, Columbus obtained his release and made a fourth and last voyage to America from 1502 to 1504, on which he sailed along the eastern coast of Central America before returning home.

The "Admiral of the Ocean Seas," as he was called in his agreement with the Spanish rulers, found little tangible wealth for Spain on his voyages. The slave trade became the only consistent source of revenue during the decade he ruled Hispaniola, and Columbus shipped hundreds of Indians to Spain. Few Spaniards appeared grateful for his labors, and once when his two children walked through the streets of Granada, mobs of townspeople reportedly pursued them shouting, "There go the sons of the Admiral of the Mosquitoes, who has found lands of vanity and delusion, the grave and misery of Castilian gentlemen!" Still persuaded that he had discovered some fringe territories of Asia, not a new and unsuspected world to the west, Christopher Columbus died in 1506 at Valladolid. His death went virtually unnoticed.

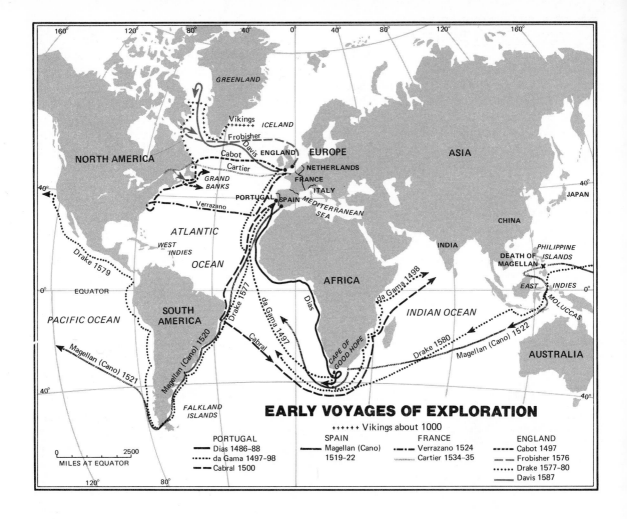

EARLY VOYAGES OF EXPLORATION

++++ Vikings about 1000

PORTUGAL	SPAIN	FRANCE	ENGLAND
—— Dias 1486–88	—— Magellan (Cano)	— ▪ — Verrazano 1524	----- Cabot 1497
········ da Gama 1497–98	1519–22	········ Cartier 1534–35	— — Frobisher 1576
— — Cabral 1500			········ Drake 1577–80
			—— Davis 1587

0 — 2500
MILES AT EQUATOR

exploitation. Cortez, Pizarro, de Soto, and other Europeans of that time regarded Indians as barely human. After a century of Spanish rule, the Indian population of Mexico, through maltreatment and white men's diseases, had been reduced from five million to one million. The Mexican experience was not unique. Elsewhere in the New World—in Peru and on the Caribbean islands, for example—the Indian population decreased at comparable rates and for similar reasons.

Since many Indians died or fled from Spanish settlements, another steady source of cheap labor was necessary, for raising crops like sugar cane required a large labor force. So the Spanish began importing black slaves from Africa. The first slaves came as early as 1510. Later, Europeans kid-napped and bought hundreds of thousands of Africans to ship to the New World.

Packed tightly into cramped cargo spaces, on ships called "floating coffins," some blacks preferred to jump overboard rather than accept slavery. Many more died of disease on board. Only a fraction of the slaves survived the journey, but enough reached America to make the trade profitable, and their numbers increased. They were more resistant to the diseases of the whites than the Indians were, since they had already been exposed to them in Africa. Due to their previous experience with agriculture, the blacks also proved to be better at it than the Indians, many of whom—especially those in the Caribbean and in North America—had done relatively little farming.

THE SPANISH EMPIRE:
THEORY AND REALITY

Spain dominated sixteenth-century European politics, diplomacy, warfare, and economic life as gold and silver flowed in from its American possessions. This vast influx of precious metals had serious consequences for the Spanish economy. It caused an enormous rise in prices and a decline in the real value of money—that is, inflation. Prices rose about 400 percent in Spain during the sixteenth century—a tremendously high rate of inflation for those times. The Spanish government often found it impossible to collect enough tax revenue to pay its debts.

Furthermore, inflation made it difficult for Spanish farm or manufactured goods to compete with cheaper foreign imports. Thus the same harvest of gold and silver that gave Spain temporary dominance in Europe also helped cripple her long-range chances as a food-producing, manufacturing nation.

Spain's overwhelming desire for precious metals grew out of a certain view of economic life

held by most European governments. According to this view, the true measure of any nation's economic prosperity and power was the amount of gold and silver it controlled. Later economic writers gave the name *mercantilism* to this set of ideas, which had generally governed the economic behavior of European nations since the fifteenth century. Spain's New World possessions, and the gold and silver found there, allowed Madrid to put such ideas into practice.

Spain alone had the mines from which to acquire gold and silver directly. Every other European power turned to foreign commerce to increase its stock of precious metals. The goal was to maximize exports and minimize imports from other countries; this was known as a favorable *balance of trade.* Mercantilists believed that gold and silver could best be kept within a country by achieving such a favorable balance of trade. To this end, the ships of Portugal, Holland, England, France, and other European nations crossed and recrossed the oceans in search of new opportunities for trade. Spain, by contrast, never developed a strong commerce, partly because of her smug certainty that

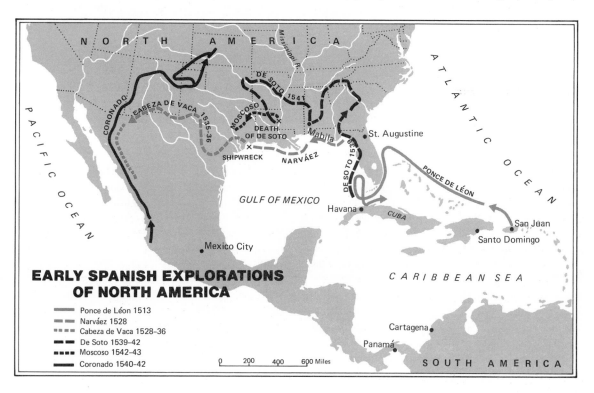

**EARLY SPANISH EXPLORATIONS
OF NORTH AMERICA**

- Ponce de Léon 1513
- Narváez 1528
- Cabeza de Vaca 1528-36
- De Soto 1539-42
- Moscoso 1542-43
- Coronado 1540-42

0   200   400   600 Miles

New World mines would eternally provide all the gold and silver she needed.

Unfortunately for Spain, those sources ran dry in the seventeenth century. Her great period of national prosperity soon waned, as did her political and military influence in Europe. What endured from decades of Spanish conquest and exploitation was not the treasure itself. Instead, there remained a vast imperial domain studded with great plantations, ranches, and orchards. Through it ran an equally impressive network of Catholic missions and churches, strung like rosary beads along the Spanish-American countryside. And over all lay the veneer of Spanish language and culture.

FRANCE IN THE NEW WORLD

King Ferdinand of Spain, the patron of Columbus, called himself "His Most Catholic Majesty." Therefore, when he wished to have his claims to the new discoveries made legitimate, he knew exactly whom to consult. In 1494, Pope Alexander VI, strongly influenced by the Spanish and Austrian ruling family of Hapsburg, drew a line down the Atlantic from north to south, cutting along the western border of Brazil, with all of North America to the west of it. He proclaimed that all new lands east of the line belonged to Portugal; west of it, to His Most Catholic Majesty of Spain.

Predictably, other European nations did not accept this division as happily as Spain and Portugal did. Francis I, who became king of France in 1515, reacted strongly. "Show me the will of Adam," he demanded, "dividing the world between Spain and Portugal." In challenging Spain's claim to the New World, Francis was only opening a new front in his European war with the Hapsburgs. From 1521 to 1559, France fought a perpetual battle with Charles V and his heirs. In hopes of bringing in some badly needed revenue, Francis sent Giovanni de Verrazano, a Florentine navigator, across the ocean in 1523. He told Verrazano to find a water route through North America to China. This idea of a "northwest passage" would fascinate explorers for the next century.

Unlike the first Spanish explorers, Verrazano had a fairly good idea of what he would find.

For twenty years, French fishermen had sailed to Newfoundland to gather codfish. Verrazano navigated along the eastern coast of the continent from the Carolinas to Newfoundland, establishing a French claim to North America, but he found no route to China.

Distracted by civil war, France did not attempt to develop her claim for sixty-five years; then Henry IV sent out his friend Samuel de Champlain. Champlain founded Quebec and reached the Great Lakes, but he failed to establish anything comparable to Spanish colonization in Mexico or Peru. Instead, French exploration continued at a leisurely pace. It was not until almost the end of the seventeenth century that René Robert Cavelier, sieur de La Salle, reached the foot of Lake Michigan and then journeyed down the length of the Mississippi to New Orleans. After one hundred and fifty years of fitful efforts, with long periods of neglect, France could claim an enormous North American empire — half of modern Canada plus the valley of the Mississippi.

The society of New France differed greatly from that of New Spain. The Spanish took the Aztecs' gold and land, destroying the Indians in the process. The French never found gold, and very few Frenchmen wanted to come to Canada to take the Indians' land. Thirty years after Champlain had founded Quebec, only two French farmers had immigrated. The only economic value Canada had for the French was the fur trade, which required amicable relations with the Indians.

THE PROTESTANT POWERS IN AMERICA

After the Protestant Reformation had swept across Europe in the first half of the sixteenth century, Spain and France, the western European superpowers, remained Catholic. But others nations that had adopted various types of Protestantism now had new reason to challenge the Spanish domination of the New World. As would often happen in the future, European conflicts extended overseas.

After a long and hard-fought war of rebellion, the Netherlands by 1600 had won their in-

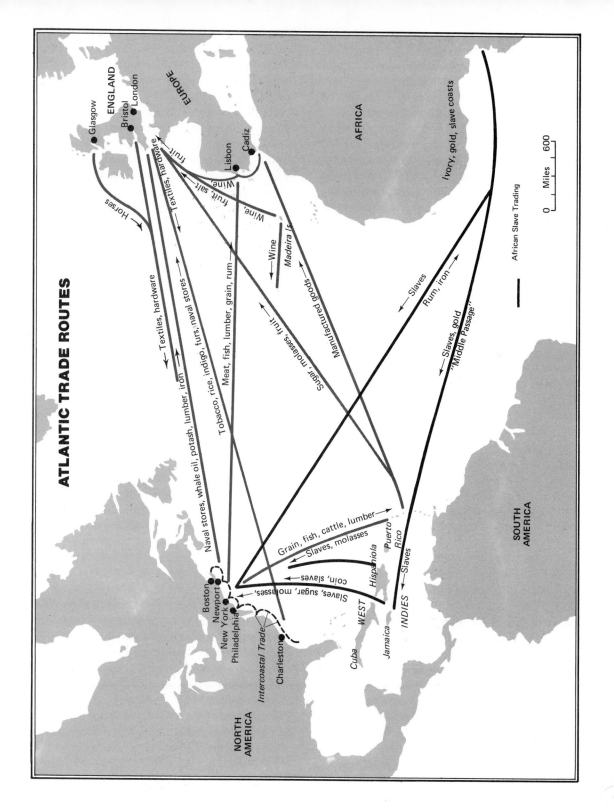

ATLANTIC TRADE ROUTES

ENGLAND
Glasgow
Bristol
London

EUROPE

Lisbon
Cadiz

AFRICA

Ivory, gold, slave coasts

0   Miles   600

African Slave Trading

fruit
Textiles, hardware
Wine, salt, fruit
Wine
Madeira Is.
Wine
Horses
Textiles, hardware
Tobacco, rice, indigo, furs, naval stores
Naval stores, whale oil, potash, lumber, iron
Meat, fish, lumber, grain, rum
Sugar, molasses, fruit
Manufactured goods
Slaves
Rum, iron
Slaves, gold
"Middle Passage"

NORTH
AMERICA

Boston
Newport
New York
Philadelphia
Intercoastal Trade
Charleston

Grain, fish, cattle, lumber
Slaves, molasses
coin, slaves
Slaves, sugar, molasses
Puerto
Rico
Hispaniola
WEST
Cuba
Jamaica
INDIES
Slaves

SOUTH
AMERICA

Exploring and Conquering the Americas 33

dependence from Spain. During the struggle, the Spanish had attempted to destroy the Dutch Reformed Church. The Dutch, who had won largely by virtue of their superior seamanship, preyed profitably upon Spanish shipping before actually attempting their own overseas colonization.

In 1609 the Dutch sent an Englishman named Henry Hudson to try to reach Asia around the top of Europe. Turned back by ice, Hudson instead sailed to America, up the New York river that now bears his name. His sailors brought the story of a rich land back to the Netherlands. A dozen years later, the Dutch founded the Dutch West India Company, largely as a weapon against the Spanish. While concentrating on the plunder of the Spanish and Portuguese colonies, the company established a small colony on Manhattan Island, as well as some nearby forts.

But Dutch farmers proved no more eager to cross the Atlantic than French farmers. New Amsterdam rapidly became a polyglot colony with residents from all nations, especially after the Dutch annexed a small Swedish colony on Delaware Bay. The company lost interest, and the colonists exhausted themselves in a long war with the Algonquin Indians. Forty years after its founding, New Amsterdam was itself annexed by the greatest Protestant power, England. (See Chapter 6, p. 118.)

BACKGROUND OF ENGLISH COLONIZATION

As early as 1497, the English crown had sent an exploratory expedition to the New World. Henry VII sent John Cabot, a Genoese born Giovanni Caboto, to discover an English northwest passage to Asia. Like Columbus, Cabot had kept company with a wide circle of Italian geographers and believed that Asia could be reached by sailing west across the Atlantic. By sailing over the old Norse westward routes (Cabot believed the Vikings had reached the Asian coast centuries earlier), Cabot expected to establish the precise locations of Japan and China. Instead his voyage took him to a landing somewhere in the rich fishing grounds of what is now Newfoundland or Canada's Maritime

Provinces. Convinced he had reached the Asian mainland, Cabot coasted for several hundred miles along the shoreline before returning to the English port of Bristol, whose merchants had helped finance the trip.

On a second voyage from Bristol in May 1498, Cabot had five ships, the merchants of both Bristol and London having competed in assembling cargo for him to trade with the "Asians." A number of English adventurers joined Cabot, hoping to share in the expected wealth. One ship put in at Ireland for repairs. History does not record the fate of Cabot or of four of his ships, however. Presumably if Cabot reached "New Found Land" (as he called it), he confirmed the plentiful presence of fish and the disappointing absence of Chinese. We shall never know. But given the failure of Cabot's second expedition, Henry VII, a tight man with a shilling in the best of times, refused to finance future voyages.

His son, Henry VIII, was too busy getting married and unmarried, and forming a new Protestant Church of England, to support colonial ventures. Eventually the English Reformation would serve to populate Massachusetts, but under Henry it prevented any colonization at all. Henry's elder daughter, Queen Mary, was a Catholic who had married King Philip II of Spain and had no interest in encroaching upon her husband's domains. She channeled English adventuring around the top of Europe, and chartered the Muscovy Company to trade with Russia in 1555. Although English merchants and sailors profited from such dealings, they hungered for the richer (and warmer) trade with America.

Their opportunity came with the succession to the throne of Henry's younger daughter, Elizabeth I, one of the most remarkable women of history. The red-haired Virgin Queen was as strong a Protestant as her sister had been a Catholic, and had little respect for Spanish claims or property. She also cared little for the Pope's division of the New World, especially when the papacy had declared her an illegitimate and illegal occupant of the English throne. Soon after she became queen in 1558, English ships again turned west and once more began to make voyages across the Atlantic.

In some ways England seemed an unlikely candidate to challenge Spain's power in the New World. A relatively small country on the fringes of Europe, England did not even control the entire island of Great Britain (Scotland remained independent until 1603). England had about as many people as the Netherlands, half as many as Spain, and one-quarter as many as France. Finally, parliamentary control of the purse strings greatly limited the moneys available to Elizabeth, preventing the kind of explorations that kings of Spain had financed personally. From Cabot's initial voyage, therefore, to the subsequent centuries of New World settlement, English efforts in America depended to a considerable extent upon the financial investments of its merchant class, and consequently upon the uneasy collaboration of the British monarchy, adventurous aristocrats, and ambitious middle-class entrepreneurs.

Hundreds of thousands of black-faced sheep grazing quietly in the English countryside lay behind the largest European migration to America. For centuries English merchants had carried on a large and lucrative trade in wool across the Channel. Consequently, private citizens, when gathered together in joint stock companies (the forerunners of modern corporations), possessed enough capital to underwrite settlements in Massachusetts and Virginia.

The sheep had also helped produce settlers for the new land. For several decades, landowners had been involved in the process of *enclosure*—fencing in what had been common farmland—in order to raise more sheep, a more profitable endeavor than simple crop growing. The process forced many farm laborers off the land, resulting in an extremely high rate of unemployment in sixteenth-century England. In some places, as much as one-third of the population lived on poor relief.

Finally, England's long history of shipping wool to Europe involved the development of a large fleet of ships and men who knew how to sail them. In what would essentially be a naval contest with Spain in the Atlantic, England's skilled and experienced—if somewhat informal—navy might prevail even over Spain's greater resources in gold and population.

EARLY ELIZABETHAN EXPLORATION

The idea of a northwest passage to the Orient fascinated Elizabeth as much as it had her grandfather Henry VII. Starting in 1576, she dispatched Martin Frobisher on three voyages over the top of Canada. Frobisher explored Labrador and became the first European to encounter the Eskimos, but found no shortcut to China.

Some English sailors set their goals beyond the ice floes of Hudson's Bay. Although England had not officially declared war against Spain, the rich Spanish treasure fleets were tempting targets. English captains also kidnapped slaves from Africa and smuggled them into Spanish America, which tried to limit the number of slaves brought in. Elizabeth's sailors believed strongly in an aggressive Protestantism, which allowed them to rationalize dealing in slaves not only for quick profits but also as a means of Christianizing blacks, and permitted them to justify anything done against Catholic Spain.

Queen Elizabeth supported and encouraged this slave dealing and semiofficial piracy. She hoped to add funds to her royal coffers while reducing Spanish power. From 1562 to 1568, Sir John Hawkins made three voyages, smuggling slaves from Sierra Leone and returning to England with ginger, sugar, and pearls. In 1570 Elizabeth commissioned Hawkins's cousin, Sir Francis Drake, as a *privateer*—essentially a pirate who split his booty with the crown. The following year Drake led a group of seventy sailors in an ambush of a Spanish mule train lumbering across the Isthmus of Panama with a cargo of silver from Peru. After pillaging a Spanish town on the Panama coast in mid-1573, Drake returned safely to England with his prizes.

DRAKE SAILS AROUND THE WORLD

In 1577 Drake set out with five ships and 164 officers and men to break Spain's monopoly in the Pacific. His squadron sailed near the Cape

Drake's campaign of the 1580s was his first act of open warfare against the Spanish. He commanded a fleet of twenty-nine ships. One successful episode was the sack of Santo Domingo, above. While the fleet lay at anchor, foot soldiers—their ranks bristling with spears—attacked the walled city from the left. Drake was a daring man who much enjoyed what the English of his day called "singeing the king of Spain's beard." (NYPL/Rare Book Collection)

Verde Islands, where he captured Spanish and Portuguese ships. Proceeding southward along the east coast of South America, Drake beat back an attempted mutiny, losing ships and men along the way. He rounded Cape Horn and reached the Pacific in September 1578 with only one remaining vessel, the *Pelican,* which was later renamed the *Golden Hind.*

Drake then turned north, seizing treasure and provisions from Spanish ships and towns along the way. To escape enemy attack he kept heading north—sailing, he wrote, "on the backside of America." Along the coast of California he stopped at a "fair and good bay"—what may be the San Francisco Bay of today. Finding no northwest passage to take him back to England, he crossed the

Pacific (taking on a valuable cargo of pepper in what is now Indonesia), rounded the Cape of Good Hope, and sailed up the west coast of Africa to reach Plymouth in September 1580.

Drake reached England uncertain of his reception. Spain was demanding the return of Drake's booty and his execution as a pirate, and hinted at war if Elizabeth refused. After a time of uncertainty, the queen, influenced by Drake's new status as a popular hero (and the estimated twenty-five-million-dollar value of his prizes), knighted Drake and allowed him to continue his raids on Spanish America.

ENGLISH VENTURES

The voyages of her "sea dogs" made the New World appear so attractive to Elizabeth that she took yet another step. In the 1580s she began to authorize other English adventurers—not pirates this time, but enterprising businessmen among the nobility—to explore and to found settlements.

Sir Humphrey Gilbert, attracted by the profits and glory of dealing with the New World, now persuaded Elizabeth to give him a charter to discover and settle such lands. Gilbert made two attempts at colonization. In 1578 he was either forced back by bad weather or diverted by the more attractive possibilities of piracy (historical accounts differ on this point). He tried again in 1583 with a larger expedition. This time he reached Newfoundland and took possession of a surprised international colony of summer fishermen. Soon afterward, however, he perished in a storm.

The dream of an English colony in America was carried further by Gilbert's half brother, Sir Walter Raleigh. He took over Gilbert's charter in 1584 on even more favorable terms than those granted his relative. Raleigh sent out an advance party that year to search for a suitable place. After Gilbert's misadventures in the chilly climate of Newfoundland, Raleigh decided to look farther south. His scouting party found a promising site, which it called Roanoke Island, along the Atlantic coast south of Chesapeake Bay. Raleigh named the entire coastal region Virginia, in honor of Elizabeth, England's Virgin Queen.

THE INVINCIBLE ARMADA

Spain, the most powerful nation in Europe, would not tolerate activities like Raleigh's—or like Drake's—forever. In 1588 King Philip II of Spain, hoping to ensure Spanish control of the Americas and the Atlantic, and to reclaim England for the Catholic Church, sent a large fleet against his sister-in-law Elizabeth. Hundreds of ships departed from the same port Columbus had used, carrying soldiers for invasion and priests for reconversion.

The sailors who had ravaged Spain on the oceans now rallied to the defense of their homeland. Drake, Hawkins, Frobisher, and other veteran captains moved their ships into the Channel, bringing a new idea of naval warfare. According to the traditional stategy, as used by the Spanish, ships were mainly transportation for soldiers, who would capture enemy ships by hand-to-hand fighting. Accordingly, the Spanish galleys were large and cumbersome, and were propelled largely by oarsmen. Expertly sailing their smaller ships in and out of the Armada, Drake and the English destroyed many of the invading ships. Others, heading northward, went down in a series of furious storms off the Scottish and Irish coasts.

Although the Armada came to grief thousands of miles from America, the battle proved crucial for future English settlement. England now controlled the Atlantic and could establish and supply projected colonies without fear of Spanish blockades.

Soon after the defeat of the Armada, England established its first permanent colonies in the New World. "He who rules the sea," proclaimed Raleigh jubilantly, "rules the commerce of the world, and to him that rules the commerce of the world belongs the treasure of the world and indeed the world itself." If England did not yet rule the world, it would soon rule a large part of North America.

THE ROANOKE SETTLEMENT

Raleigh's enthusiasm for English commercial expansion had taken tangible shape even before the Armada's destruction. In 1585 he dispatched an expedition of settlers to the recently

The mysterious end of the Roanoke or "lost" colony reached the awareness of other British explorers only in 1591, when they returned to the settlement to find all of its inhabitants missing without having left any indication of their whereabouts except for the word "CROATOAN" (the name given to a nearby island) carved on a doorpost. This later sketch shifts the location to a tree. (NYPL/Picture Collection)

explored Roanoke Island. The members of the group devoted most of their energy to roaming the countryside in search of gold. They also explored nearby rivers seeking the Pacific Ocean. They failed at both, of course, and since they had no interest in colonizing the area, most of the participants returned the following year.

In 1587 Raleigh sponsored yet a third expedition, this time commanded by an artist, John White, a veteran of the previous expedition. This group contained the first women and children to come to America, further evidence that the expedition anticipated a more permanent settlement in the Chesapeake Bay area than earlier expeditions. Although their English sponsors expected them to establish a "Citie of Ralegh in Virginia" elsewhere in the region, White's band disembarked at Roanoke Island. They searched vainly for fifteen men who had remained behind after the 1585 expedition and, finding their houses "standing unhurt," remained on the island. White helped the 118 settlers organize their colony, but a month later, in August 1587, he returned to England for supplies.

The Armada's assault and disorders within England prevented his immediate return, but White finally sailed back to America in 1590. When he reached Roanoke, he found the settlement in ruins. The entire colony had vanished without a trace, except for the single word CROATOAN — the name of a nearby island and site of an Indian village — carved on a doorpost. White's own daughter and his granddaughter, the first English child born in America, were among the missing. A storm forced White to abandon the search, return to his ships, and leave Roanoke without solving the mystery of its "Lost Colony." A subsequent expedition by Raleigh in 1602 shed no further light on the settlers' fate. It was not until 1607 that the English attempted another settlement in the area, this time along a river named (along with the town itself) for England's new monarch, Elizabeth's successor, James I. While exploring the James River, one of the colony's first settlers described his encounter with "a Savage Boy about the age of ten yeeres, which had a head of haire of a perfect yellow and a reasonable white skinne, which is a Miracle amongst all Savages." Was the "Miracle Savage Boy" the belated child of an ill-fated Roanoke settler? None of the subsequent English colonists, either at Jamestown or elsewhere on the North American coastal mainland, could ever resolve that mystery.

Suggested Readings
Chapters 1-2

Cortez and Montezuma

Charles Gibson, *The Aztecs Under Spanish Rule* (1964); Hammond Innes, *The Conquistadors*; Miguel Leon-Portilla, *Broken Spears: The Aztec Account of the Conquest of Mexico* (1962).

Discoveries and Explorations

John B. Brebner, *The Explorers of North America*; Samuel Eliot Morison, *Admiral of the Ocean Sea* (1942), *The European Discovery of America: The Northern Voyages, A.D. 500-1600* (1971), and *The European Discovery of America: The Southern Voyages: A.D. 1492-1616* (1974); John H. Parry, *The Age of Reconnaissance* (1963).

Indian Cultures

Woodrow Borah, and Sherburne F. Cook, *The Aboriginal Population of Central Mexico on the Eve of the Spanish Conquest* (1963); H. E. Driver, *Indians of North America* (2nd ed., 1970); J. A. Hester, Jr., and Kenneth MacGawan, *Early Man in the New World*; Alvin M. Josephy, Jr., *The Indian Heritage of America* (1969); G. R. Nash, *Red, White and Black: The Peoples of Early America* (1974); Carl O. Sauer, *Sixteenth-Century North America: The Land and People As Seen by Europeans* (1971); George C. Vaillant, *Aztecs of Mexico*; W. E. Washburn, *The Indian in America* (1975).

Spanish America

C. R. Boxer, *The Portuguese Seaborne Empire* (1969); A. W. Crosby, Jr., *The Columbian Exchange: Biological and Cultural Consequences of 1492* (1972); Charles Gibson, *Spain in America* (1966); Lewis Hanke, *The Struggle for Justice in the Conquest of America* (1949); Clarence H. Haring, *The Spanish Empire in America* (1947); James Lang, *Conquest and Commerce: Spain and England in the Americas* (1975); James Lockhart, *Spanish Peru, 1532-1560* (1968); John H. Parry, *The Spanish Seaborne Empire* (1966).

England and the New World

Wallace Notestein, *The English People on the Eve of Colonization, 1603-1630* (1954); David B. Quinn, *England and the Discovery of America, 1481-1620* (1974) and *Roanoke Voyages, 1584-1590* (1955); A. L. Rowse, *The Elizabethans and America* (1959) and *The Expansion of Elizabethan England* (1955); J. A. Williamson, *Voyages of the Cabots and the English Discovery of North America Under Henry 7th and Henry 8th* (1929).

3 Death and Survival: The Founding of Jamestown

The Indian king refused to kneel and receive the cheap copper "crown" brought to his village by the band of armed and unwelcome Englishmen. The visitors in turn kept careful watch on Powhatan's hundreds of warriors, who crowded in to watch the coronation. Finally, several of the English shoved Powhatan's shoulders down slightly to allow one of them to place the crown upon the unwilling Indian's head. Not to be outdone, Powhatan presented his cloak and moccasins to a surprised "guest." The ceremony was over.

Led by Captains John Smith and Christopher Newport, the Englishmen had come from the nearby settlement of Jamestown, which had been founded a year before, in 1607. The survival of Jamestown remained in doubt when Smith and Newport brought their men, bearing gifts, through the forest to Powhatan's village of Werowocomoco, home of the Pamunkey Indians. Powhatan, undisputed leader of the area's Indians, had refused Smith's invitation to come to Jamestown. He suspected that the English would lay a trap for him: "If your king has sent me presents," Powhatan had told Smith, "I also am a king and this is my land."

The gifts came not from James I of England, in fact, but from the London Company, the settlement's sponsor in England. Newport had recently arrived from there with fresh supplies for Jamestown and a curious assortment of presents designed to please Powhatan's fancy and thereby reduce the threat of Indian attack on the colony's outnumbered whites.

But what could Powhatan do with a wooden bed, several pieces of furniture, cutlery, and fashionable European clothing? Did the English expect Powhatan to move to Jamestown and imitate their ways?

The Indian leader remained unappeased and distrustful, although he accepted the gifts and admired the bravery (and resourcefulness) of John Smith, who had even taken pains to learn the Indian language. When asked after the coronation ceremony to allow Newport to explore the sur-

POWHATAN
Held this state & fashion when Capt. Smith was deliuered to him prisoner 1607

Appamatuck

rounding countryside, Powhatan refused. He did give his guests some corn, a most welcome present, since Jamestown residents rarely had enough food. In the end, Smith and Newport left Werowocomoco with their followers, uncertain whether their actions had made Powhatan into a friend or had placed Jamestown's future in even greater jeopardy.

The Founding of Jamestown **41**

The first voyage to Jamestown had taken more than four months. Three ships sailed from England in mid-December 1606, reaching the entrance to Chesapeake Bay by late April 1607. The London Company had placed Newport in command of the vessels, a 100-ton flagship, *Susan Constant*, and two smaller escort vessels, the *Godspeed* and *Discovery*. Surprisingly, the long winter ocean passage proved fatal to only one of the more than one hundred men who shipped out. They achieved this in part by making long island stopovers, first at the Canaries and then in the Caribbean, where they took on fresh food and water.

About a third of those who sailed with Newport were considered "gentlemen," according to prevailing English standards, enjoying some measure of either wealth, influence, or position through birth into a leading family or through personal achievement. Such gentlemen often saw their role in the new settlement as *supervisors* rather than *followers*, overseers and not workers. This ambitious crowd of "captains," minor noblemen, and lesser gentry found it easier to give orders than to take them. Unfortunately, this left an extremely large number of potential "leaders" for the work of colonization which lay ahead. The London Company further complicated the problem by keeping secret the names of those who would form Jamestown's governing council. These were listed in a sealed envelope given to Newport with instructions to open the envelope only *after* the ships had reached America.

Fortunately the *Susan Constant* and her two escort ships also carried a number of craftsmen: blacksmiths, carpenters, bricklayers, masons, laborers, and even a surgeon. These would prove far more valuable in building a *permanent* English colony in North America, the company's goal, than would many of the gentlemen, who schemed to dominate the settlement even before the ships left port.

Why did these people come? Reasons varied with each person. Most of them probably shared hopes, nurtured by the London Company, of wealth and glory in America, just as similar goals had driven the first Spanish *conquistadores* more than a century earlier. Surely the land contained exploitable minerals, possibly even gold. Many of the adventurers, John Smith included, had often sailed against the Spaniards in voyages and sea battles in the Caribbean and South America that aided their own fortunes while bolstering English power in the New World.

Smith, a short muscular man, lived an adventurous life even before leaving for America. While still in his teens, he fought for Austria against the Turks. A fearless self-promoter, Smith later wrote vivid accounts of his experiences, claiming that once he actually chopped off a Turkish commander's head. But the Turks captured and enslaved Smith. Eventually he escaped and wandered across Europe, Asia, and North Africa before returning to England in 1603. After this sort of warrior's life on three continents, Smith, at the age of twenty-six, cast his fortunes with Newport and the others, sailing to Virginia in December 1606 to become one of its "first planters."

On reaching Chesapeake Bay in April 1607, Newport began exploring the countryside for a site on which to build the colony, while trying to

John Smith seizes the Indian chief Openchancanough during a struggle between the English and the Indians in the first years of Jamestown's settlement. The illustration comes from one of Smith's own books on his Virginia adventures. (The Granger Collection)

C.Smith taketh the King of Pamavnkee prisoner 1608

make contact with Indians. The land proved more agreeable than the Indians, who attacked a landing party. The incident reminded Newport and the others that the London Company had instructed them to build a fort and town at some *inland* point, not on the coast. A new colony hugging the shoreline might attract Spanish warships only too eager to emulate the raids of people like Walter Raleigh, who had attacked *Spanish* outposts in the New World.

After sailing thirty miles up the largest of the rivers emptying into Chesapeake Bay, the vessels reached a peninsula. Though marshy and low-lying, the site afforded good visibility of both the river and the countryside. They named both the river and the town they began building after England's King James I.

Who would run Jamestown? The London Company's charter virtually guaranteed an initial period of disorder in the colony, since a company council, which remained in England, supposedly governed Jamestown. In Virginia, actual authority fell to a *local* council appointed by the parent body in England. Most Jamestown settlers, therefore, had no voice in choosing their leaders, for seven men had already been selected by the company. Newport and Smith were named to the council.

The settlers faced grave problems. They had to build up the town's defenses, stockpile enough food to last through the winter, and explore the countryside to find "exports" which Newport could take back to England. But council members bickered endlessly, neglecting the work

A contemporary mural depicts Jamestown in the early years. In the foreground is the James River. Farmers beyond the town would take refuge inside the palisade in case of attack. (Photo by Thomas L. Williams, mural by Sidney King—Jamestown Foundation)

that had to be done. The situation got so bad that one of the councillors was executed as a mutineer. Newport finally sailed for England in June. While uneasily awaiting his return and continuing their struggle for personal power, the remaining leaders managed somehow to mobilize the settlement against Indian attack.

The Paspahegh Indians living near Jamestown attacked only a few days after the English colonies built their first shelters. They were led by a *werowance* (an Indian captain) named Wowinchopunk, who owed no loyalty to Powhatan. Wowinchopunk was understandably angered over a white man's settlement on the Paspaheghs' traditional hunting grounds. Three days after the ships unloaded, Wowinchopunk and a hundred armed warriors appeared outside Jamestown. The Indians proposed that the whites drop *their* weapons and join in a feast, but Wowinchopunk's band fled hurriedly after one Englishman killed a warrior who tried to take a hatchet.

Soon many more Indian soldiers surrounded Jamestown. They waited until Smith, Newport, and several dozen heavily armed whites boarded one of the ships to explore land farther upriver. Then, in late May, the Indians attacked in force, taking the remaining colonists completely by surprise. As unsuspecting Englishmen worked in the field outside the town's primitive palisades, the Indians, as Smith later described the scene, "came up almost into the fort, shot [arrows] through the tents, [and] appeared in this skirmish, which lasted hot for about an hour, a very valiant people."

At first it seemed as if the attackers would overrun the settlement. Suddenly a blast of cannon shot came from the two remaining ships, and the tide of battle turned. Wowinchopunk and his warriors knew nothing of the wonders and terrors of artillery. The Indians collected their dead and wounded, and faded into the forests. Two settlers had been killed and ten more wounded, but for the moment, Jamestown had avoided extinction, the fate of Raleigh's earlier Roanoke colony.

Jamestown's troubles had only begun. The Indians who surrounded the settlement attacked sporadically, though now without the element of surprise. Newport's exploring party returned after the big battle, and the settlers fought off the Indians for the next three weeks while steadily reinforcing the town's fortifications. When Wowinchopunk's raids stopped, the English continued to scan nearby forests. The colony remained on alert for weeks expecting new attacks.

Newport, having sailed back to England in late June 1607, had supervised the loading of *Susan Constant* and *Godspeed* with whatever could be sold in England. He hoped to demonstrate Jamestown's economic potential and carried clapboard, ore samples for testing (since gold and other precious metals remained an obsession of Jamestown's founders), and sassafras roots. Englishmen of that day believed sassafras would heal and cure venereal disease.

Within weeks of Newport's departure, most of the hundred men still at Jamestown had to contend with a malaria and yellow fever epidemic, for the low and marshy ground, a virtual swampland, encouraged the diseases. The settlers' relentless work schedule left them exhausted, and they were unnerved by the strain of anticipated Indian attacks.

That first summer, only a half dozen or fewer men were normally available to patrol the palisades or perform other essential work. One of them, Captain George Percy, later wrote of those agonizing months:

> There were never Englishmen left in a foreign country in such miserie as we were in this new discouvered Virginia. Wee watched every three nights, lying on the bare-ground, what weather soever came; . . . which brought our men to bee most feeble wretches . . . [We heard] the pitifull murmurings and outcries of our sick men without reliefe, every night and day for the space of six weeks; in the morning their bodies being trailed out of their cabines like Dogges, to be buried.

Half of the original one hundred settlers in April were dead by September. By the time Newport returned in January 1608, the company had been further reduced to thirty-eight survivors.

One of these was John Smith. Although ill that first summer, Smith managed to recover and bring some order to the colony's desperate search for food. Shortly after the Paspaheghs' attack, friendlier Indians from other villages came near the fort to trade beans and corn. By then,

Newport had returned to England again seeking fresh supplies, and Smith became the settlement's chief trade negotiator. Not content to await the arrival of Indian goods, Smith led expeditions up the James River and its tributaries seeking out Indians willing to barter food for English-made items such as hatchets, household utensils, and copperware. Smith refused to supply the Indians, however, with guns and ammunition. That fall he returned from several boat trips into the country of the Chickahominy Indians bearing bargeloads of corn and beans, obviously increasing his influence in Jamestown.

During one expedition, Smith's luck ran out. He had journeyed into the territory of normally friendly Chickahominy Indians. Smith left seven of his nine white followers guarding the barge, while he, two Indian guides, and two companions went upstream by canoe. An Indian ambush wiped out all seven members of Smith's rearguard, while a second surprise assault by Powhatan's Pamunkey warriors cut down one of the whites in Smith's canoe. Smith's guide, whom he had been using as a shield, cried out to the surrounding Pamunkey Indians that Smith was a *werowance* of the whites. The Indians let him live, although Smith had already shot down two of the attackers. Smith's captors brought him to Powhatan. Ever resourceful, Smith had managed to persuade the leader of his captors, Powhatan's brother Opechancanough, that unless news of his capture was delivered to Jamestown, Englishmen (whose numbers Smith exaggerated) would seek revenge on the Pamunkeys. Opechancanough agreed to have his men carry the news.

Ever the survivor, Smith managed to keep his captors entertained by performing tricks with an ivory pocket compass and with his endless supply of adventure stories (and tall tales) translated by the Indian guide (at this point, Smith had not yet mastered Indian speech). After passing through a series of Indian villages, Smith carefully observing customs and ceremonies, the prisoner and the Pamunkeys finally reached Powhatan's village, Werowocomoco. A year after the encounter, Smith wrote that he had first seen Powhatan

> proudly lying upon a bedstead a foot high, upon ten or twelve mats, richly hung with many chains of great pearls about his neck, and with a great covering of [raccoon skins]. At his head sat one woman, at his feet another. On each side, sitting upon a mat upon the ground, were ranged his chief men on each side of the fire, ten in a rank, and behind them as many young women, each with a great chain of white beads over their shoulders, their heads painted in Red.

Surprised to discover such regal bearing "in a naked savage," Smith described his host as "grave and majestic."

Although he probably did not expect to leave Powhatan's camp alive, Smith tried to reassure the great chief that Jamestown people were friendly, denying that the London Company intended to establish permanent settlements on Powhatan's land. When the Indian chief asked him "the cause of our comming," Smith replied that the English "being in fight with the Spaniards our enemie, being over powred, [sic] neare put to retreat," came ashore. Then, because their ships had supposedly leaked,

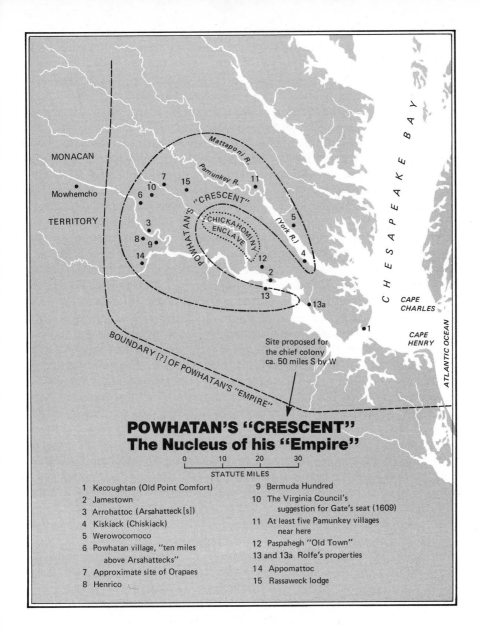

POWHATAN'S "CRESCENT"
The Nucleus of his "Empire"

```
0        10       20       30
         STATUTE MILES
```

1 Kecoughtan (Old Point Comfort)
2 Jamestown
3 Arrohattoc (Arsahatteck [s])
4 Kiskiack (Chiskiack)
5 Werowocomoco
6 Powhatan village, "ten miles
     above Arsahattecks"
7 Approximate site of Orapaes
8 Henrico

9 Bermuda Hundred
10 The Virginia Council's
     suggestion for Gate's seat (1609)
11 At least five Pamunkey villages
     near here
12 Paspahegh "Old Town"
13 and 13a Rolfe's properties
14 Appomattoc
15 Rassaweck lodge

"wee were inforced to stay to mend her, till Captaine Newport my father came to conduct us away."

Why, then, asked Powhatan, had Smith and his friends continued to explore so close to Indian villages? Again, John Smith answered deceitfully. The English, he explained, were searching for a great sea on the other side of the mountains (a clear reference to the continuing European pursuit of a westward passage to China). Despite the fact that Powhatan probably did not believe much of Smith's explanation, in the end, he welcomed Smith as a friend, "appointed" him the *werowance* of a nearby village, and agreed to provide guides who would deliver him safely back to Jamestown.

Powhatan exerted great power throughout the region, although Smith could not have known how much. As the chief of thirty Indian tribes spread along the coast of Virginia, Powhatan ruled a loosely knit kingdom, which would be dubbed a "confederacy" by Thomas Jefferson a century and a half later. But his authority, like Montezuma's in Mexico, was roughly equivalent to that of European monarchs such as James I. The Indian tribes spoke a common language, Algonkian, and shared common cultural beliefs and practices as well as Powhatan's leadership. In the years before Jamestown's settlement, Powhatan had expanded and consolidated control over many Virginia tribes. Thus, although he came to respect the military power commanded by the gun-carrying white newcomers, Powhatan displayed no apparent sense of inferiority. He welcomed John Smith as a potential ally against his remaining Indian enemies, especially the tribes that had escaped his domination by remaining in the mountainous Piedmont region beyond the coast. Powhatan evidently liked the notion of trading food (his tribes had plenty) for European weapons and military support.

When, seventeen years later, Smith wrote of his captivity at Powhatan's village, he mentioned for the first time an episode involving the Indian's favorite daughter, twelve-year-old Pocahontas. While eating a meal prepared by guards, according to Smith's 1624 account, he was abruptly bound and tied to boulders, presumably as the prelude to execution. Suddenly, although the Indians were "ready with the clubs, to beate out his braines, *Pocahontas* the King's dearest daughter . . . got his head in her armes, and laid her owne upon his to save him from death: whereat the Emperour was contented he should live. . . ." The tale of Pocahontas's rescue of Smith, whether or not it happened, has survived in myth and memory.

Several days after his alleged brush with death, Smith and Indian guides bearing gifts of food returned to Jamestown. He showed the Indians the fort and demonstrated the power of its cannons by firing a load of stones at nearby icicle-laden trees, terrifying them much as Cortez's demonstrations had struck fear in Montezuma's envoys.

But things were not well at Jamestown. Having survived probable death at the hands of Indians, Smith now faced the wrath of his English peers. His opponents held Smith responsible for the deaths of those on the exploratory trip. They tried and convicted Smith, and prepared for a hanging. Only Newport's arrival from London on January 2, 1608, saved Smith's life. Newport backed him against his enemies on the council.

The squabble over Smith's behavior receded days later, on January 7, when the attention of all settlers turned to putting out a major fire in the town, which destroyed buildings and supplies. Food and equipment were now even scarcer, at a time when the fresh recruits Newport had brought from England increased the colony's ranks to over a hundred mouths to feed. But Smith's "friendship" with Powhatan came in handy.

Twice in the days after the fire, gifts of food and raccoon skins arrived from the Indian monarch. Powhatan evidently sought a truce, although not an alliance, with the English intruders.

During the next few years, relations between the region's Indian tribes and the English remained tense and uncertain. Smith and his fellow settlers continued to explore the Chesapeake Bay region, striving always to forge friendly ties with Indians, especially those who opposed Powhatan's dominance. Smith traded beads and other European-made goods for food wherever he could, and he searched unsuccessfully for precious metals.

The Jamestown settlers, however, never dropped their guard against the Indians. Powhatan, for his part, appeared content to postpone a full-fledged assault on the English, possibly because of a fear of their superior weaponry, but he remained just as cautious in dealing with Jamestown as the English were with him. In 1609, for example, Powhatan moved his headquarters from Werowocomoco, only fifteen miles from Jamestown, to a more distant village. Nevertheless, in the early years of white settlement, Powhatan carefully avoided breaking off relations with Smith, even sending occasional delegations with gifts of food to Jamestown. These delegations sometimes included Pocahontas, Powhatan's impressionable daughter, who openly expressed her delight with life at the English settlement.

Pocahontas's preference for "city life" aside, the rhythm of relations between the two groups often became discordant. When Indians came upon whites exploring tribal lands, the intruders were often attacked. Such incidents inevitably led to English reprisals. When the Indians proved unwilling to "trade" food for the cheap goods bartered by the English, their towns and possessions were burned. In daily practice, both sides behaved as harshly toward one another as circumstances allowed, despite the London Company's instructions that the American settlers should be fair and friendly toward the natives (even this happened a few times, as when young Indians were brought to Jamestown to study white customs). It galled the colonists that, despite their superior arms and farming methods, even despite their *moral* status as Christians and cultural virtues as Englishmen, they depended upon the Indians for food with which to survive. If the Indians were indeed "savages," as many at Jamestown believed, how did they manage to keep the colony at bay so easily? Irritation at this inability to dominate and master the Indians turned easily to anger and, from there, to bloody killings and torture by the whites on many occasions. One thing, however, is certain: without the continuing supply of native corn and beans and other food over the years, the colony would have perished.

Having failed to hang John Smith, council members elected him their president. In September 1608, Smith clearly embodied the colony's best hope for surviving the coming winter. He ordered storehouses built to hold food supplies; he conducted military drills; and he ordered greater vigilance to prevent surprise attacks, all previously neglected measures.

To the unruly colonists, Smith offered a simple choice: cooperate or suffer the punishment. No work, in short, no food.

Newport's ship had finally arrived bringing much needed supplies as well as additional settlers: fourteen artisans, fourteen laborers, two women, and a less helpful resupply of twenty-eight gentlemen recruits. Several Polish and German craftsmen came to develop a glass factory and other manufacturing projects. These schemes had no realistic place in the desperate condition of Jamestown that winter, where food remained scarce and workmen had to stay inside the fort because of possible Indian attacks.

Newport had received still another series of unhelpful orders from the company's council, directives even more foolish than the notion that tiny Jamestown could become a manufacturing center overnight. The London Company wanted the search for gold stepped up and thus gave Newport a gold refiner—just in case. The captain was also to resume the impossible search for a westward passage to Asia, using a monstrously unwieldy five-section barge, which was to be carried across the mountains and reassembled on some westward-flowing river for the journey to the "South Seas." Finally, the search for the lost Roanoke colony was to be continued. Later that fall, Newport led 120 men up the James River. He found neither gold nor a South Sea passage, and other exploratory parties failed to turn up the Roanoke settlers.

Once Newport had returned empty-handed, Smith and the other council members set about, more practically, loading Newport's vessel for its return to England with *something—anything—*available near Jamestown that might please their English sponsors. They hoped that additional timber, loads of clapboard, and samples of glass (also pitch and tar) might suggest to the London Company that such goods—if produced in large quantity—would repay their investments in Virginia.

As winter approached, Smith also tried to increase trade with nearby tribes. But the Indians now proved more reluctant to part with corn and beans in exchange for English tradegoods, possibly (Smith suspected) following Powhatan's orders. John Smith then used an iron fist, menacing Indian villages until they agreed to "trade" their food supplies. Newport sailed for England in December, leaving behind a hungry community of two hundred people, half of them sick or disabled even before the start of winter.

Smith ruled Jamestown dictatorially for the next several months, imposing stern discipline despite his frequent absences while he foraged for food. He divided the colony into work details of ten to fifteen men and maintained constant patrols at the palisades. He staged weekly drills and frequent musket firings to impress watchful Indians, who lurked on the outskirts of Jamestown.

In January 1609, Smith traveled to Powhatan's village, at the Indian monarch's request, to build him an "English-style" wooden house (possibly to hold the earlier gifts, although Powhatan may have hoped to lure Smith into an ambush). Eventually, Smith cajoled and pressured Powhatan into agreeing to load his boat with corn. After that, Smith and

7. their Danceing.

(8) the manner of Praying to their Idol.

9. the Town of Pomeiooc

his men left abruptly because Pocahontas supposedly provided another timely warning that her father's warriors planned to kill him.

Smith sailed off with his corn. At Opechancanough's village Smith, never at a loss for adversaries, challenged the *werowance* to hand-to-hand combat, the winner to rule the other's troops. When Opechancanough hesitated, Smith grabbed his hair, stuck a pistol against his chest, and shoved him out in front of all his warriors. The Englishman then threatened the Indian captain and his people with bloody reprisals unless they supplied more corn. The shaken Indians delivered their supplies, and Smith left hastily for yet another "trade."

Thanks largely to Smith's stern rules within the fort and to his effective, if unusual, methods of strong-arming bargeloads of corn from the Indians, almost none of the settlers perished because of starvation or disease during the winter. When spring came, Indians again began arriving at the fort to trade corn, beans, and newly killed game. Smith had intimidated them, and now the Indians even delivered over to him those tribal members accused of stealing goods from Jamestown, usually weapons. Smith punished them sternly.

Governing partly through clever bluffs and partly through an extremely harsh but effective system of personal justice, Smith proved a master at dealing both with the Indians and with his own people. He ruled Jamestown arbitrarily but well until the end of his one-year term as president of the council. Despite obvious achievements, Smith received no second term. Complaints about his harsh dealings with the Indians had reached London when Newport arrived there early in 1609. By that time, the company had already decided to revise its plans for Jamestown. The struggling settlement on Chesapeake Bay received a new charter in 1609, a new president, a new local council, and most important of all, a new supply of a most vital resource — manpower.

The new charter came first, handed down by King James to the

London Company, assigning more powers to the company's leading figures and promising less royal interference. In exchange, the charter abolished the Jamestown council and appointed, instead, a governor to be advised by a *new* council and by other appointed officials, all of whom would be under the governor's absolute authority. The company named an able figure as Jamestown's first governor, Lord Thomas de la Warr, with Sir Thomas Gates as his lieutenant governor. De la Warr could not leave immediately, so Gates—who had sailed to America with Sir Francis Drake in 1585—went instead to assume command.

With the new charter and the new frame of government, enthusiasm for Jamestown's future soared in England. Excitement over the future prospects for developing America led more than 650 individuals and 56 city companies to subscribe stock in the reorganized London Company. This outpouring of support for England's experiment in American colonization was most amazing because Smith, Newport, and the other settlers had failed either to discover valuable metals or to find a new passage to Asia.

Six hundred new settlers joined the nine-ship fleet that sailed from England to Jamestown in June 1609. But it was not simply the larger numbers that distinguished the fleet. This "supply" expedition also differed from the earlier ones in qualitative ways. It included more than a hundred women, children, and servants, indicating clearly that the company had decided on a permanent venture in America. Jamestown as a virtually all-male preserve of "adventurers," gentlemen, and skilled craftsmen was dead.

Most of the vessels arrived at Jamestown in August, but the crossing was perilous. Gates's ship was wrecked in Bermuda, so that the new governor did not reach Jamestown for ten more months. The newcomers informed Smith and the old settlers of the revised London Company charter and its altered frame of government. Still Smith declined to quit as president until he had met with Gates. Once it became known that Smith's rule would soon end, however, the factionalism that had been firmly checked for the past year quickly reappeared.

Old enemies and long-standing grievances surfaced. The bickering Jamestown settlers, now tripled in number with the new arrivals, neglected the vital tasks of food collecting and town building, which Smith had directed so smoothly though harshly. At one point, Smith claimed that his enemies on the council, some of whom had returned with the new settlers, tried to murder him. Enough was enough. He decided to leave for England in October. Although John Smith kept in touch with events in Virginia, and although he later wrote several short books on his experiences, he never returned to America.

Winter was coming. Smith had sailed for England, and Governor Gates remained stranded in Bermuda. The Jamestown settlers lacked legitimate, effective leadership. An English nobleman named George Percy took over temporarily, but Smith's departure increased Indian confidence. Powhatan promptly resumed attacks on the white intruders. Thus when Captain John Martin, an original settler, left with seventeen men to trade for food, the entire party disappeared without a trace. Elsewhere, the bodies of several recently slaughtered whites were found. Percy sent Captain John Ratcliffe to negotiate with Powhatan for food. Ratcliffe went up the James River with fifty armed men and two Indians ("Powhatan's son and daughter," according to one account) as hostages. After reaching the Indian village, Ratcliffe succumbed to the type of false welcome from Powhatan that had never fooled John Smith. When Ratcliffe released the hostages, Powhatan's soldiers killed two-thirds of the Englishmen before the rest escaped.

Powhatan saved a special fate for Ratcliffe. According to George Percy, the luckless and trusting captain was

> bound unto a tree, naked, with a fire before [him]. And by women his flesh was scraped from his bones with mussel shells, and before his face thrown into the fire. And so for want of circumspection [he] miserably perished.

Discipline among the desperately hungry settlers quickly deteriorated. Percy had sent a few colonists to an outpost given the hopeful name Point Comfort. There, thirty miles from the fort, they eked out a tolerable existence that winter eating shellfish and boar meat. But the Point Comfort settlers never provided supplies for their starving brethren in Jamestown. On another occasion, Percy ordered Captain Francis West and three dozen men to trade for food with the Potomac tribe. West did well for himself, stocking the boat with corn, after handling the Indians savagely, even cutting off the heads of two Potomac warriors. West and his men then brazenly set sail for England, to the amazement and horror of Percy and his hungry colonists.

"A world of miseries ensued," Percy wrote after that agonizing winter, ". . . in so much that some to satisfy their hunger have robbed the store, for the which I caused them to be executed. Then, having fed upon horses and other beasts as long as they lasted, we were glad to make shift with [such] vermin as dogs, cats, rats, and mice."

Life in Jamestown during the winter of 1609–10 later came to be called "the starving time," a period of almost unbearable misery for those who endured it. John Smith, though himself far from the scene, collected accounts of the period from survivors, and described those grisly months when suffering and hunger could be alleviated at times only by munching upon "roots, herbes, acornes, walnuts, berries, now and then a fish . . . yea, even the very skinnes of our horses":

> Nay, so great was our famine, that a Salvage [an Indian] we slew and buried, the poorer sort took him up again and eat him; and so did divers one another boyled and stewed with roots and herbs. And one amongst the rest did kill his wife, powdered [i.e., salted] her, and had eaten part of her before it was knowne, for which he was executed, as he well deserved: now whether she was better roasted, boyled, or carbonado'd [i.e., grilled], I know not, but of such a dish as powdered wife I never heard of.

Such cases of cannibalism were not unique, not if George Percy is to be believed. He later recalled "things which seem incredible, as to dig up corpses out of graves and to eat them—and some have licked up the blood which hath fallen from their weak fellows." As for the man who murdered his wife for food, Percy had him tortured to obtain a confession before executing him by the slow and agonizing method of burning him alive, a clear enough warning to other settlers.

Some colonists simply ran off into the woods, apparently hoping to find friendly Indians willing to share their food, with unknown but probably fatal results. Others were killed by Indian attacks while wandering through the forests and riverbeds searching for food. A number of settlers died inside the fort, not only from starvation but also from the many diseases that had plagued Jamestown since its earliest days. Others relapsed into numbness, seemingly incapable of working or searching for food, although not actually sick. John Smith's iron discipline had been effective the previous winter at snapping the lethargic settlers out of such stupors. But many in the winter of 1609–10 wandered through their days at Jamestown in a deathlike trance, unable to function.

When Thomas Gates, Christopher Newport, and the others who had spent a relatively comfortable winter shipwrecked in Bermuda finally reached Jamestown in May 1610, they found the settlement close to total starvation. Gates and his 150 settlers had not brought much food with them, expecting to encounter a prosperous colony. What they saw left them stunned. The previous fall's six hundred colonists had been reduced to fewer than sixty survivors; most of the remainder had died, although some had fled to England with West, and others kept their distance at Point Comfort. As for Jamestown, it appeared (in John Smith's words) "rather as the ruins of some ancient fortification, then that any people living might now inhabit it."

It seemed evident to Gates that the colony could not be maintained as it stood. Food remained scarce, and with 150 additional people to feed, Gates decided to abandon Jamestown in favor of an English outpost far to the north, Newfoundland. Available grain would be rationed, and from Newfoundland, the party hoped to make its way back to England.

More than two hundred people boarded the four fragile boats on June 7, 1610, for yet another long journey. Many wanted to burn Jamestown to the ground, a fitting end to so much misery. Gates refused. Even without a fiery finale, it seemed evident that this ambitious English experiment in America had ended as miserably, though not so tragically, as Roanoke.

But the Jamestown refugees never reached open seas, thanks to what their more devout members considered Divine intervention and even the less reverent considered a miracle in timing. The colony's governor, Lord de la Warr, had succeeded in wrapping up his affairs in England and had sailed for Virginia in April 1610 with three ships, several hundred immigrants, and plenty of food and other supplies. De la Warr reached Point Comfort first, and he learned of Gates's plans to leave Virginia for Newfoundland. Lord de la Warr immediately dispatched a ship up the James River to alert Gates and scotch the project. Gates promptly and happily complied. Once again, the recently abandoned town throbbed with excitement and anticipation, preparing for the arrival of de la Warr's new recruits—and his food.

The new governor quickly asserted his authority and set the colonists to rebuilding Jamestown. Sounding remarkably like John Smith in earlier days, de la Warr addressed the community, denouncing their previous "idleness" and promising to restore both internal discipline and a strict work schedule. Every able-bodied person in Jamestown, including the gentlemen, would spend at least six hours a day at hard labor in repairing fortifications, planting crops, and constructing new buildings. Twice daily, the entire colony paused for communal prayers. The new governor also brought with him a new set of tough laws to deal with every breach of behavior and decorum. Killing an animal without permission, for example, was punishable by death; washing filthy items near the village well—chief source of the colony's fresh water supply—punished by whipping; cursing or fighting by being "tied head and feete together" every night for a month. Although de la Warr did not enforce the new code rigidly, the lawful threat of such extreme punishment helped to maintain peace at Jamestown, much as John Smith had done earlier.

But even under the sternest administration, Jamestown retained its nasty climate. Another muggy and unhealthy summer season arrived, undermining de la Warr's plans for recovery. At least 150 people died during that "sickly season" of 1610 from diseases such as dysentery, malaria, and scurvy. The Bermuda newcomers proved especially vulnerable to the spread of sickness and to that lethargic weakening of the will to live (and to work) that had always bedeviled the colony.

The most prominent casualty was de la Warr himself. Soon after arriving at Jamestown, the governor later wrote, he was "welcomed by a hot and violent Ague which . . . disease had not long left mee, till . . . I began to be distempered with other greevous sickness, which successfully & severally assailed me. . . ." After suffering bouts of what he described as "the Flux," "the Gout," more "Ague," and finally scurvy, de la Warr fled Virginia to escape sure death, leaving Jamestown in the far less competent hands of George Percy. Another "supply" arrived from England in March 1611, commanded by Sir Thomas Dale and carrying three hundred more settlers, and Dale soon replaced Percy as deputy governor.

Under Dale's leadership, de la Warr's earlier efforts to strengthen the colony continued. Work parties scurried around the settlement, planting crops and repairing buildings while organizing for winter. Sensitive to the decimation continually wrought at Jamestown, Dale directed a search for a new and healthier site for colonizing. Eventually, he supervised the development of a site fifty miles upstream, which Dale called Henrico (after Henry, the Prince of Wales), near the point at which the

Sir Thomas Dale was a successor to Lord de La Warr as governor of Virginia. He continued de La Warr's system of rigid control and strict discipline. Under his leadership, the colony expanded up and down the James River and into the surrounding area. (Virginia State Library)

James and Appomattox rivers meet. Henrico became Virginia's most important community for a time, better fortified and in a healthier location than Jamestown itself.

But Dale became known chiefly for his attempt to enforce a legal code even more stringent than earlier ones, a code that became known as the "Laws Divine, Moral and Martial." Dale's laws seemed designed to coerce a colony that consisted largely of rebellious or lethargic settlers into behaving responsibly; in short, the laws were savage and probably appropriate to Jamestown.

Trial by jury and other rights that the Jamestown settlers had known back in England were denied under Dale. Persons convicted of crimes were dealt with in an extraordinarily brutal manner—some burned at the stake, others hanged or shot, still others lashed to wheels to be broken into pieces. When the Virginia assembly (which did not exist in the time of Smith and Dale) issued a description in 1624 of the bad old days under Dale's rule, the details defied belief. Many settlers fled to the Indians in order to escape being punished for minor infractions of the "Laws Divine, Moral and Martial." If recaptured, they were normally put to death or subjected to punishments such as these: "one for steeling . . . 2 or 3 pints of oatmeal had a bodkin [dagger] thrust through his tongue and was tyed with a chain to a tree untill he starved. . . . Many through these extremities, being weary of life, digged holes in the earth and there hid themselves till they famished." When Thomas Gates replaced Dale in August 1611, the change did not noticeably lighten the burdens of ordinary Virginians.

Throughout the years of stern leadership under Dale, de la Warr, and Gates, the threat of English–Indian hostilities never abated. Both sides raided back and forth. Neither side displayed much pity toward the other. On one campaign, George Percy's men raided a Paspahegh village, cutting off the heads of several Indians and later throwing captured children overboard from their ship, shooting out their brains in the water. Rarely did the English take prisoners. Powhatan encouraged his warriors and subject tribes to attack, especially small, relatively defenseless groups of Englishmen caught outside the fortifications of Jamestown or Henrico. These forays, in turn, interrupted tobacco and corn cultivation. Both Dale and Gates had successfully encouraged the latter for winter food supplies. Tobacco, which King James I (an ardent opponent of smoking) called that "noxious weed," had rapidly become Virginia's leading hope for economic stability.

A kidnapping, and the semi-dynastic marriage that followed, brought Jamestown eight years of relative peace with most of the Chesapeake Bay Indian tribes. In the spring of 1613, when Powhatan refused to surrender eight white prisoners and some captured English weapons, the English took his daughter Pocahontas hostage. Pocahontas, now practically a woman, had always been friendly toward the Jamestown settlers. Early in 1613, Captain Samuel Argall was sailing along the Rappahannock River, seeking corn supplies, when he came upon Pocahontas visiting the king of the Potomac Indians, a tribe that wanted to be friendly with the English. Argall demanded and got Pocahontas, who then became a pawn in negotiations between Powhatan and the Virginians.

Shortly afterward, Dale and Argall took her up the James River, well-guarded. The English demanded that Powhatan either fight or return his cache of captured supplies, and they set a ransom for Pocahontas: five hundred bushels of corn. When Powhatan refused both demands, the English returned to Jamestown with their prisoner, warning the Indian king to comply by harvest time or else.

Events soon passed out of Dale's control, however, when a gentleman of Jamestown, a widower named John Rolfe, asked the leaders of the colony for permission to marry Pocahontas. The government approved the request after the Indian princess agreed to become a Christian. She

and Rolfe were married in April 1614. Powhatan refused to attend, but one of Pocahontas's uncles represented him, bringing her father's reluctant approval for the wedding.

In the eight years that followed, until Powhatan's death, the Virginia settlements enjoyed peace largely because of Pocahontas's marriage and Powhatan's subsequent pledge to avoid further conflict. Old by then, tiring of the constant struggle against the English, and deeply disappointed in his daughter's decision to join the company of his enemies, Powhatan had no heart for further battle. His decision encouraged tribes hostile to Powhatan's confederacy to make separate peace with the English, lest the full force of Jamestown's weaponry be turned against them. A number of treaties with tribes such as the Chickahominy turned most of the neighboring Indians into English vassals, who agreed to furnish regular tributes of corn and—when required—even warriors to fight for the English.

Pocahontas did not live to watch the years of peace descend upon the Chesapeake Bay region. She and John Rolfe toured England in 1616 before admiring crowds. She was received by the king in court, became celebrated by London society, and made several sentimental visits to her old friend, John Smith. Shortly after boarding a ship to return to Virginia with her husband in March 1617, "Rebecca Rolfe," born Pocahontas, died after a brief illness. She left as her legacy a grieving husband, a two-year-old child, and a moment of amity between Virginia's whites and Indians, which lasted for another five years.

When Powhatan died the following year, 1618, and his brother, Opechancanough, succeeded him as head of the confederation, Jamestown had yet another governor, Captain George Yeardley. Barely half a decade from the time Gates prepared to abandon the settlement, Jamestown had grown rapidly. Hundreds of new recruits came each year from

England; and despite a fearfully high death toll from disease, the population continued to increase. Newer tracts in the countryside came under corn and tobacco cultivation. Fear of Indian attack had receded after 1613, more a bad memory than a present reality. Tobacco, meanwhile, ensured the colony's growth and future.

The English had purchased most of their tobacco from Spanish colonies before the settlement of Virginia. By importing seeds of tobacco varieties planted in Spanish America, John Rolfe experimented to improve the unpopularly strong tobacco grown by Indians near Jamestown. Rolfe's mixture soon captured the English market with some help from King James, who craved additional revenue more than he despised tobacco. Thus, in 1612, the king granted the London Company a seven-year exemption from customs duties on its imports from America.

A tobacco boom was under way, especially after settlers began acquiring land privately in 1614 to grow crops. Governor Dale found himself forced to *order* all planters to grow at least two acres of *corn* to ensure an adequate food supply. If they did not, they risked having their tobacco crop forfeited. Still, tobacco production soared. In 1615, Virginians shipped only 2000 pounds of tobacco back to England, but by 1620, exports exceeded 40,000 pounds, and by 1622, 60,000. Only four years later, in 1626, the amount reached 500,000 pounds, and by 1629, a record 1.5 million pounds! Despite periodic declines in the English market in the decades ahead, either because supply outpaced demand or times were hard, the emergence of tobacco as its major export crop guaranteed the future of Virginia.

The newer immigrants from England spread out across the territory, surrounding Jamestown and other recently fortified towns. But despite the tobacco prosperity, the incidence of disease remained high. It proved as difficult for most new immigrants to adjust to unhealthy Virginian conditions as it had a decade earlier. Thus, although over 1000 settlers flocked to the colony each year from 1619 to 1622 (the population in 1618 had been about 700), the London Company complained that massive migration to Virginia had become little more than a "regulated kind of killing of men." The company estimated that over 3000 people died in Virginia between 1618 and 1622. Almost none of the fatalities could be blamed on Indians. The culprits remained disease in its usual varieties, hunger, malnutrition, and that extreme passivity that often afflicted otherwise healthy persons at Jamestown.

Powhatan's successor, Opechancanough, finally broke the peace in 1622 in a last desperate effort to force the whites from Indian lands before they themselves were completely driven off. The slaughter of English settlers that followed, although significant, involved only a tenth of the number that had perished from supposedly "natural" causes over the preceding three years.

The attack came suddenly, without warning. On March 22, some Indians paid their usual visits to English plantations and homes throughout the area to trade. Occasionally the Indians completed their exchanges, sat down for meals with their white hosts—and only then began the bloodletting, "not sparing either age or sex, man, woman, or childe." The killing assumed a special horror, even by Virginian standards, because often the whites and Indians involved had known one another well and lived peacefully alongside one another for almost a decade. Bodies were butchered, heads chopped off, and extremities defaced. That single day's carnage cost 347 white settlers their lives. Most of the atrocities occurred on farms spread out at a good distance from the fortified towns. Jamestown, warned of the impending attack by friendly Indians, mobilized its forces. Other communities, less fortunate and unsuspecting, suffered costly surprise assaults.

The reprisals taken by white settlers over the next several years proved even more terrible than the events of March 22. The English abandoned all efforts at friendship with the Indians. The colony's governor declared at Jamestown that there existed an "irreconcilable" conflict between the two cultures: "All trade with them must be forbidden, and without doubt either we must cleere them or they us out of the Country." Several expeditions, led by the colony's leaders, left from Jamestown to wipe out all tribes in the region.

Although Opechancanough himself escaped capture, the English exacted fearful retribution against the Indians whom they managed to track down: burning villages, slaughtering their inhabitants indiscriminately, and setting the torch to nearby cornfields after confiscating whatever food could be found. Throughout the region, white Virginians set up a series of fortifications to protect the outlying plantations. Bloody warfare between Indians and whites in the Chesapeake Bay area persisted for decades, with the English forcing out the remaining tribes and enlarging their territories bit by bit each year.

The Massacre of 1622 had another immediate effect, this one in England. It helped to stir opposition by many influential persons to the way in which the London Company had managed its American settlement under *both* old and new charters. Company critics complained about the shockingly high death rates (especially among new immigrants), the company's failure to diversify its economic base (where was the *gold* so confidently predicted by the "first settlers"?), and the obvious mismanagement by most of the colony's presidents and governors from the start. Finally, in May 1624, responding to a crescendo of complaints about the company, a royal court annulled and recalled its charter. Virginia fell under direct supervision of the crown.

By then, however, the defunct company's most important contribution to the growth of Virginia was already half a decade old. Governor Yeardley had been instructed in 1619 to summon a "general assembly," which would then meet annually, so that settlers "might have a hand in the governing of themselves." Although the governor and his advisory council would attend the assembly's meetings, two representatives (to be called "burgesses") would be elected from each plantation "freely . . . by the inhabitants thereof; this assembly to have power to make and ordain whatsoever lawes and orders should by them be thought good and proffittable for our subsistence."

Yeardley's instructions also abolished Dale's "cruel laws by which we had so long been governed," substituting instead "those free laws which his Majesty's subjects live under in Englande. . . ." Apparently most adult males in the colony, except for indentured servants, could meet the qualifications and vote for burgesses.

The first general assembly met in the Jamestown church on July 20, 1619, convened after June elections had chosen twenty-two burgesses.

The assembly sat in session for almost a week debating many problems. It devised a new and milder criminal code to replace Dale's draconian sentences. Acting as the colony's supreme court, it also sentenced quite leniently a number of lawbreakers. The burgesses petitioned members of the London Company to resolve a series of land disputes within Virginia. Most important, the assembly showed from the start that it intended to assert the *exclusive* power to pass tax measures in Virginia. Although the governor could veto its actions, and although the London Company could also disallow its existence, the general assembly proved surprisingly aggressive even at its initial meeting in 1619.

Despite more than a decade of starvation and warfare, Jamestown colony managed to survive. By the time the first assembly met in 1619, tobacco planting had guaranteed the Virginians a steady source of income. The Indian tribes that had once dominated the region had been pushed back. The general assembly brought representative government to the New World for the first time in a form that would serve as a model for other English colonies.. The fragile roots set down at Jamestown had taken hold in spite of mismanagement from England and inept actions by leaders in Virginia itself.

When the general assembly adjourned on August 4, 1619, it noted "the intemperature of the Weather, and the falling sick of diverse of the Burgesses." That same month, Pocahontas's again-widowed husband, John Rolfe, wrote a letter, published later by John Smith in his *Generall Historie of Virginia,* which mentioned in passing the following news item: "About the last of August came in a dutch man of warre that sold us twenty Negars. . . ." Those "twenty Negars," the first Africans to reach the English colonies, arrived almost at the very moment that representative government began. Both came upon the scene at Jamestown during the worst disease-ridden weeks of midsummer. So preoccupied were Virginians with the problems of death and survival that the coincidence passed without comment. Although unnoticed then, the origins of both slavery and freedom converged in Virginia during the summer of 1619, inextricably bound together in time and place. Thus began the ordeal that would harness them together for the next 250 years.

4 American Origins: The Plantation Colonies

he English investors in the London Company's venture at Jamestown had hoped for a quick and substantial profit. A ship had been sent back to England with its hold full of New World soil. Yet there were no minerals or precious metals to be found in all that dirt, no gold or silver as the Spaniards had found in Mexico and Peru. If there were profits to be made, they would have to come from more prosaic sources, and a government that would encourage and protect new sources of wealth would have to be created.

Tobacco did not make the Virginia company's investors immediately wealthy, but it eventually gave rise to a class of wealthy planters in Virginia itself. Some of the idle Englishmen who had so resentfully performed the manual labor needed to grow food after the first ships landed in Jamestown now began enthusiastically to cultivate the profitable crop of tobacco to meet the increased European demand. Tobacco leaves would even serve as currency in early Virginia.

The success and expansion of the tobacco crop helped heighten a problem already present in Jamestown—internal divisions within the settlement. Virginia had been regarded as a land where English gentlemen might make fortunes for themselves and, also, as a place where the poor and unemployed could be sent to ease the economic stress caused by the depression in England's textile industry. Would there be enough land to make both gentleman and laborer wealthy tobacco planters? If not, how would government and society react to the formation of distinct economic and social classes in England's first successful mainland settlement? The answers were defined over the next half-century of settlement and dramatized in a revolt against the colonial governor in 1676.

TOBACCO AND EXPANSION

The Virginia colonists had sent their first exports of tobacco back to England in 1615; by 1626 they were shipping over 500,000 pounds, and three years later, the figure had reached 1.5 million pounds. King James had granted huge areas of land to the Virginians' English sponsors. Those Englishmen who wanted land were willing to work as sharecropping tenants on the land of wealthier planters for several years if, at the end of their service, they could obtain land of their own. As the price of tobacco rose in the 1620s, the colonists continued to grow more and more of the crop, but they still would not grow enough corn to feed themselves. By 1624, in the midst of an economic boom, white Virginians were still dependent on Indian corn to stay alive.

New immigrants with their eyes on land often did not survive even with sufficient corn to eat. Ship captains would overload their Virginia-bound vessels, causing food shortages and deaths during the voyage. Those who survived the journey frequently died of scurvy shortly after reaching port. Although from 1625 to 1640, a period of significant migration from England, the population increased from 1300 to 8100, thousands (especially the newcomers) died of malaria, typhoid fever, and other diseases. One man observed that 1800 people perished in 1635 alone. In 1638, when the king proposed that tobacco production be limited, the House of Burgesses questioned the proposal because the burgesses could not estimate precisely what the population's current or future size might be.

Widespread disease helped create a feeling that everything was temporary. One was not quite certain what the next year, or even the next

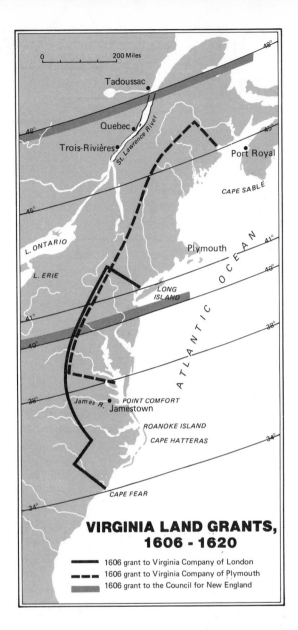

VIRGINIA LAND GRANTS, 1606 - 1620

——— 1606 grant to Virginia Company of London

– – – 1606 grant to Virginia Company of Plymouth

▬▬▬ 1606 grant to the Council for New England

change location soon. Masters purchasing servants, who were usually white and agreed to be "indentured," that is, to work for a period of years in exchange for their passage and the hope of land, often found that the servants did not survive long enough for a profit to be made from their labor. Since land was so abundant and cheap, and servants' life spans so uncertain, few planters were able to acquire huge fortunes during those early decades.

Yet, despite heavy death rates and declining tobacco prices in the 1630s, white servants remained cheap enough for planters to continue to purchase them. During the 1640s and 1650s, a combination of elements worked to make many master planters rich. For one thing, large planters adopted better methods of tobacco cultivation. Also, diseases that had killed so many newcomers began to decline in intensity, and Virginia's population increased sharply beginning in 1644. For Virginia's first half-century of settlement, the vast majority of indentured servants were whites, the major source of labor in the colony during those decades. Since servants now normally lived to fulfill their obligations, planters enjoyed additional profits that could help them purchase still more servants and plant still more tobacco. The cycle continued yearly. The growth of a class of wealthy planters, once it occurred, would have a profound impact upon Virginia society and the government that reflected the society.

BURGESSES AND PLANTERS

The London Company had paved the way for representative government by revising its charter in 1618. It instructed the new governor sent from England to call an assembly each year, and the House of Burgesses had met for the first time in 1619. The governor and the council which he appointed, however, clearly exercised greater power during the colony's early years. They often appropriated the labor of men the company sent to Virginia for themselves, thus furthering their own private fortunes. After hearing rumors regarding the exploitation of newcomers, King James I appointed an investigating committee that con-

month, might bring. Small planters often spent their tobacco profits on liquor, expensive clothing, or other luxuries. In many recorded cases, rather than invest their return from tobacco in building a substantial house, men continued to live in the shacks they had thrown up in the belief they might want to abandon them should the soil become exhausted or simply because they might want to

firmed the rumors. In 1624 he abolished the company's control and declared the settlement a royal colony under his officials' supervision. Although the king did not provide for the House of Burgesses to continue its meetings, the assembly was revived in 1629.

Some of the very first acts of the House of Burgesses were designed to secure the rights of planters to "own" servants. The members established a registration of all servants in the colony, noting the date of the expiration of their terms of service. The governor's council was composed of men with many servants. Even after the king had dissolved the London Company, its of-

ficials continued to hold many of the privileged positions that allowed them to control the labor of others. Since laws had been designed to protect the masters' property in servants, the poorer newcomers had few, if any, rights. Planters holding the transportation contracts of servants sold, hired out, lent, and even gambled away their human chattels. Servants could be shuffled from one master to another without their consent. The government refused to restrict the right of a master to punish a servant, and severe beatings of Englishmen by other Englishmen were seemingly condoned.

As the privileges of planters in the House of Burgesses grew, so did the power of this represen-

The 1622 Indian attack on Virginians, as imagined by an artist. Gory pictures of Indian atrocities appealed to Europeans, who held contradictory views of native Americans as either violent brutes or noble savages untouched by the vices of civilization. (Bry, America, Part XIII— NYPL/Rare Book Collection/Astor, Lenox, and Tilden Foundations)

tative assembly within the colonial government. Even before the London Company's abolition, the governor's council and the House of Burgesses had declared that the governor, appointed by the king, would have no power to levy taxes without the consent of the assembly. After 1629, a new governor, John Harvey, made peace with the Indians, questioned the illegal bargains of council members, and tried to persuade Virginians to raise crops other than tobacco. For his efforts, he was unceremoniously (although temporarily) shipped back to England in 1635. When the colonists defied an English law prohibiting trade with the Dutch, Parliament sent an armed force to Virginia in 1652. The governor, William Berkeley, persuaded the English authorities that the colonists required a certain amount of free trade to ensure their prosperity. Meanwhile the members of the Burgesses drew large salaries paid by their constituents, making them more powerful than ever.

PRELUDE TO DISASTER

With most indentured servants living out their terms of obligation, which usually ran up to seven years, it seemed that the dreams of poorer English immigrants might eventually be fulfilled. By 1660, however, developments that had created a wealthy class of planters were also restricting the hopes of the poor. The increase in population had enlarged the labor force and, thus, the output of tobacco. With the increase in tobacco production and the passage, in 1660, of the Navigation Act, which outlawed direct sales to the Dutch, the price of the crop fell, requiring the planting of additional acres. Land now became still more expensive, making it increasingly difficult for a newly freed servant to become a tobacco planter on his own.

Wealthy planters saw the profits to be made by speculating on the best remaining lands in the colony and quickly began to buy them up. The largest of these planters also became merchants, loaning goods to smaller farmers and exercising their role as creditors to increase their privileged standing in society. Many of them became tax collectors, keeping a handsome share of the government's revenue for themselves. Governor Berke-

ley compiled an impressive private fortune, for example, receiving 200 pounds of tobacco for every marriage license issued and 350 pounds annually from taverns that held a liquor license.

The new freeman, the former servant, found it increasingly difficult to prosper. He normally had to pay between 100 and 200 pounds of tobacco in taxes each year. If he could not afford to buy his own land and remained a tenant, the landlord still might require him to pay the tobacco tax. Since the wealthy were buying up the best lands, the smaller farmer often had to pay expensive transportation costs to market his crop. It was often easier and less expensive to sell his crop to a wealthy neighbor, who would then market it. If the recently freed farmer could not afford or find new land, he sometimes had to sell his labor again to another farmer and return to servitude. The decline of social mobility in those years is illustrated by the fact that no servant who arrived in Virginia after 1640 ever became a member of the House of Burgesses.

Wealthy planters in the Burgesses enacted laws making it even more unlikely that servants would ever rise too high. If former servants were allowed to acquire land and grow tobacco, they would be competing with their former masters and add to the excessive volume of tobacco production, further lowering the market price. Thus large planters passed laws increasing the length of indenture for servants, often by as much as three years beyond the original indenture agreement.

Sir William Berkeley— shown here before the time of Bacon's Rebellion—was not always a harsh ruler. But after his bloody revenge on the insurgents, King Charles II remarked, "The old fool has killed more people in that naked country than I have done for the murder of my father." (Berkeley Castle— Courtesy, Virginia Historical Society)

They also provided for longer terms as punishments for servants who ran away, stole, or violated the society's strict moral codes.

Freed servants with no land, and small farmers who could not maintain their freehold, were anything but happy over this situation. These young men increasingly joined the wandering poor who traveled from county to county, avoiding the tax collector while hunting and stealing to stay alive. Discontent grew in the plantation counties among the large number of new freemen, but their unrest was not directed solely against the government in Jamestown. The counties with the largest numbers of ex-servants also contained the highest number of Indians. Like the poorer whites, Indians had been pushed inland by the wealthy planters, who had come to dominate the better lands near the shoreline, the Tidewater. By the 1670s, the wandering whites had grown desperate. Some action needed to be taken, but would they strike against the colony's ruling elite and Jamestown— or against their more immediate competitors for land, the Indians?

BACON'S REBELLION

Governor William Berkeley of Virginia was well aware that these angry white men posed a threat to the colony's existing social order. When the Dutch attacked along the James River in 1673, Berkeley and many large planters refused to arm servants and even feared to leave them behind when the Virginia militia went into battle. The militia itself contained a large percentage of landless freemen whom Berkeley distrusted as potential rebels.

After the king made large land grants to two of his friends the next year, 1674, outraged Virginia land speculators sent a representative to England to protest, taxing every planter in the colony 100 pounds of tobacco to pay for the mission. There was no question that an entrenched elite was running Virginia. The last election for the House of Burgesses had been held in 1661; thus the same men had held office nearly fifteen years.

The tension between Indians and the encroaching poor whites led to violence in 1675. A group of Doeg Indians took some hogs from a white planter, claiming that he had not paid them for goods purchased earlier. The planter then gathered some men who recovered the hogs after some fighting with the Indians. When the Doegs struck back in a raid on nearby settlements, the county militia killed fourteen Susquehannah Indians whom they had mistaken for Doegs. Eventually settlers began to believe that all Indian tribes had banded together to destroy the whites, and hysteria swept through Tidewater and backcountry Virginia alike.

The reaction or, more appropriately, the inaction of Governor Berkeley and the assembly angered settlers. Just as Berkeley was ready to dispatch a large force against the Indians, he suddenly recalled them, deciding instead on defensive measures. Berkeley ordered whites to withdraw from areas near Indian land and locate behind a line of forts at the falls of the rivers. The governor offered good pay to farmers to enroll as soldiers, probably more than a small tobacco farmer could make in a year, and decided to build frontier forts. But security came with a high price tag: imposing a large tax for the construction of these forts. Moreover, wealthy members of the assembly intended to build the forts on *their* land, helping to increase its worth.

These decisions from Jamestown disgusted Nathaniel Bacon, a twenty-eight-year-old planter of aristocratic background who had come from England several years earlier. Governor Berkeley, his cousin by marriage, had given Bacon a seat on the council. He had also received a land grant of a thousand acres up the James River in the frontier interior. Here, Bacon could see the discontent of the wandering poor embittered with Virginia's self-absorbed ruling oligarchy. As an official, Bacon saw the advantages of leading these men against Indians as a way of satisfying their craving for land of their own.

Berkeley continued to maintain his defensive strategy, perceiving his young cousin as merely a troublemaker and a possible threat to his authority. When Bacon applied for a commission to lead a force against the Indians, the governor turned him down. Bacon intended to carry out his plan in any case, although he wrote a conciliatory

Nathaniel Bacon demanded permission from Governor Berkeley to make wholesale war on the Indians of the region. When denied this, he led unsanctioned settler warfare against both the Indians and the governor, throwing the entire Virginia colony into turmoil. (Culver Pictures)

letter to the governor explaining the need for independent action. In May 1676, Berkeley denounced Bacon and expelled him from the council. Then, for the first time in fifteen years, the governor called for a new election of burgesses. The new representatives, he explained, could air their grievances to him in a proper legal manner.

But Bacon's forces were already on the march. They no longer discriminated between tribes that had been friendly toward the colonists and those that had been hostile. After friendly Oceaneechees captured a number of Susquehannahs for them, Bacon's men turned on the friendly Indians and promptly massacred them. When Bacon returned to Jamestown, Berkeley urged him to repent his actions and offered to allow him to sail to England if he wished to ask for a king's pardon. Bacon refused to apologize, however, renewing his request for a commission. Berkeley finally denounced Bacon and all of his followers as rebels, calling for a militia to be raised to suppress the entire group.

In a situation where the discontent of land-less colonists had become widespread, Berkeley's action proved unwise. Now, many humble Virginians focused their anger not only upon the Indians along the frontier, but upon the Jamestown government as well. Even the new elections brought a majority of representatives sympathetic to Bacon. Elected himself, Bacon arrived in Jamestown to take his seat in the Burgesses, surrounded by fifty armed men. Berkeley managed to capture him, however, and to extract a confession. Surprisingly, then, the governor decided to placate the group of wealthy Virginians who thought Indian fighting a perfectly appropriate activity for discontented poor whites such as many of Bacon's followers. Berkeley pardoned Bacon, restored his seat on the council, and promised him a commission. He warned cousin Nathaniel, however, to stay out of New Kent County, center of the discontented poor.

Meanwhile the new representatives passed badly needed reforms designed to reduce the level of discontent. The right to vote in Virginia was granted to landless freemen. Members of the council were no longer exempt from taxes, and tax collectors, sheriffs, and other officials were now forbidden to take a percentage of the government revenues they received. The burgesses dropped the proposal to build frontier forts for defense, voting to raise a thousand troops instead. They offered attractive pay for soldiers and guaranteed them the plunder of all Indian goods they could carry, including the right to enslave captive Indians.

Bacon, who had disobeyed Berkeley's orders to stay away from New Kent, now appeared in Jamestown with 500 frontiersmen demanding his promised commission. At gunpoint, Bacon obtained the commission and the authority to raise as many volunteers as he wanted to lead. When eight whites were killed by Indians in New Kent, Bacon's men responded by entering prosperous Gloucester County and taking whatever horses and supplies they could find to avenge the deaths. Berkeley's supporters, meanwhile, were able to draw up a petition, signed by Gloucester landholders, protesting Bacon's high-handed action and requesting protection from the man. Berkeley then declared that Bacon's commission was void and marched to the county himself. He found that al-though the inhabitants were willing to fight Indians under his command, they were hesitant to attack their fellow Virginians led by Bacon. When the latter learned that Berkeley was gathering a force to use against him, he marched after the governor, forcing him to retreat by ship.

The young Bacon was now ready to challenge Berkeley for leadership in Virginia. In a "Declaration of the People," he condemned the levying of taxes for public projects that would create fortunes for certain officeholders. As an English aristocrat, Bacon was also convinced that many of the men who had accumulated these fortunes were upstarts socially inferior to true gentlemen like himself. He saw himself now as a person determined to curb the oligarchy's power and influence, as a kind of Robin Hood who would redistribute their wealth. Bacon's forces thus began to pillage large estates and to attack Indians in the back-country. His cause was first dealt a blow when his top two assistants, sent out to capture Berkeley, were themselves caught by the governor's men. Berkeley now issued an appeal for support, promising Virginians the plunder of the estates of Bacon's supporters. To prevent landholders from supporting Bacon, he even promised freedom to the servants of those who had signed an oath of support for Bacon.

Bacon and his followers were now at the height of their power. After more Indian fighting in New Kent, they had captured both Indians and their possessions. As a show of strength, Bacon marched his prisoners through Jamestown. Servants and slaves of those loyal to Berkeley now joined the rebellion, greatly adding to Bacon's forces. With the governor and his following in retreat aboard ships, Nathaniel Bacon's troops burned Jamestown to the ground. The rebels spent the next weeks looting their wealthy opponents' homes.

But the rebellion lacked any positive program of reform or revolutionary goals, as was soon evident following Bacon's sudden death from the "bloody flux" (probably dysentery). With no real direction, men gradually began to switch sides or lay down their arms. Significantly, the last of the rebel forces to surrender were slaves and twenty English servants. Governor Berkeley hanged the remaining leaders, even though the king had sent a pardon for all those who had engaged in the rebellion.

Had the uprising decided anything? Servants continued to arrive, live out their terms of indenture, and seek land, which would provide a better life, in the New World. Large planters, eager to maintain their privileged status, still required a labor force to produce massive quantities of tobacco. The labor problem, present in Jamestown when the first English ships reached North America, remained a dilemma in 1676. Bacon's Rebellion, however, had taught the ruling planter class that some changes were necessary to avert another violent conflict. That next outburst might not only disrupt their political and social standing in the colony, as Bacon had managed to do, but cost them their lives as well.

SLAVERY AND PLANTATIONS

By the time of Bacon's Rebellion, the idea of enslaving Africans to create a steady supply of forced labor was hardly new. Spanish and Portuguese slave traders had begun bringing African slaves to Latin America in the early sixteenth century. The Dutch, and then the English, had been drawn into the trade. In 1671, black slaves made up less than 5 percent of Virginia's population, while there were three times as many white indentured servants. But in the English colony of Barbados in the Caribbean, where a sugar-producing settlement required back-breaking work that discouraged the immigration of English indentured servants, many thousands of African slaves toiled and died under the tropical sun. Slavery had also been introduced into England's other colonies along the Atlantic coast but on a smaller scale.

When Negroes first arrived in Virginia, it was not assumed that they would all become

Slaves gather for festivities on a Carolina plantation. According to one expert, both the drum and the dance depicted are of Yoruba origin. (Many American slaves were descended from the Yoruba people, whose home is near the coast of West Africa.)

slaves. From the time when a Dutch ship arrived with twenty black captives, in 1619, to the middle of the century, all Africans *arrived* without fixed legal or social status. In the early decades, they achieved different destinies: some became slaves; some became servants for a term of years; and others became free. Some slaves were allowed to buy their freedom, and black servants and freemen were often treated comparably to their white indentured counterparts. Black and white servants worked and lived together, although firm evidence of racial practices in early Virginia remains incomplete. Early Virginia society *seemed* to make little distinction between those of different color, though we may never be certain of this point.

Economic trends, however, soon led wealthy white planters to favor black slaves over white indentured servants. Initially, because of the heavy death rate in the colony, it had not been advantageous to spend the extra money to purchase more expensive black slaves for life instead of buying the labor of white servants for a period of years. As life expectancy began to increase, however, the lower mortality rate of white servants gave planters more money and more confidence in buying the labor of a Negro for life. There is evidence, also, that blacks proved healthier than whites in the Southern climate and more immune to diseases such as malaria and yellow fever because of their African experiences. Also, an improving English economy induced fewer laborers to emigrate to the colonies. Bacon's Rebellion, moreover, helped induce the planter class to stop relying primarily upon a white indentured labor force. A black labor force, which could be kept *permanently* enslaved, seemed both safer and more reliable. Now such investors arrived in the New World, bought slaves, and settled on immense plantations. By 1700 half of Virginia's labor force was enslaved.

Just as they had passed laws before to lower the status and mobility of white servants, Virginia aristocrats now enacted legislation that discriminated between whites and blacks, demeaning Negroes and leading to a policy of permanent enslavement. Actions of the assembly that lowered the status of Negroes helped to reinforce feelings of racism, which apparently characterized large and small white planters alike. In 1662, the assem-

This leaflet advertising an upcoming slave auction illustrates the concern of potential owners for the health of their investments. (Library of Congress)

bly decided that even with Christian baptism, a slave remained a slave, and that all offspring of slave mothers automatically became slaves. All blacks were declared slaves in 1682, just six years following Bacon's Rebellion. In 1691 the assembly set strict penalties for miscegenation (interracial sexual relations). The same phrases that wealthy Englishmen had used to describe the supposed "natural" inferiority of the white poorer classes were now ascribed to African slaves.

The development of racist feelings was strongly aided by the rising opportunities for small white farmers. Bacon's battles with the Indians and subsequent campaigns greatly weakened the power of coastal tribes, and whites drove the natives farther and farther into the interior. This, along with the decline of immigration, allowed poorer whites to move into new areas and become landowners. In 1705, the Virginia assembly, now fearing that the greater threat came from black slaves rather than from poor whites, voted to provide freed indentured servants with money, clothes, and firearms. Small farmers also enjoyed a reduction of the poll

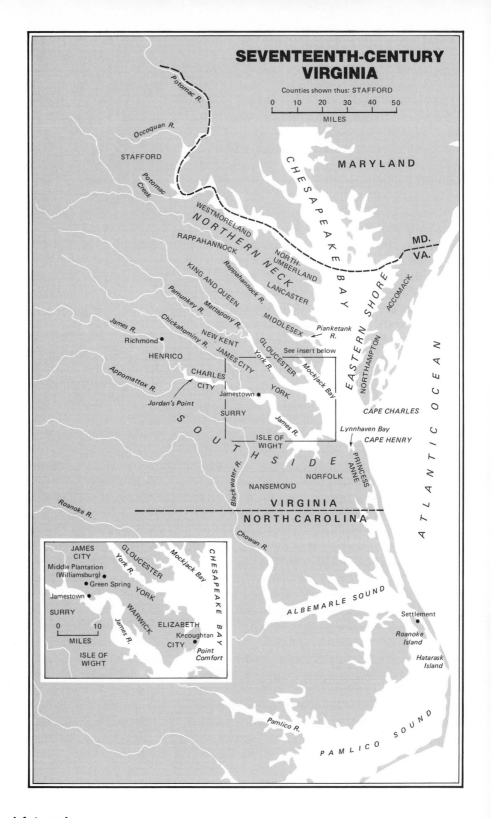

SEVENTEENTH-CENTURY VIRGINIA

Counties shown thus: STAFFORD

0 10 20 30 40 50
MILES

tax and, by the eighteenth century, had begun prospering with growth in the international tobacco market. Small white farmers no longer represented the bottom rung of Virginia's social ladder now that black enslavement had become institutionalized. Large and small planters both used the same racist rationalizations to justify the exploitation of the African peoples who now provided the bulk of plantation society's steady but unwilling labor supply.

PLANTATIONS AND SOCIETY

Despite the oppression inherent in racial slavery, black slaves in colonial Virginia fared better than those in other areas of the New World. Unlike the British West Indies, where staggering profits in sugar growing led planters to work slaves to death in order to increase their yields, the relatively less strenuous task of raising tobacco, and the prudence with which Virginia planters viewed their human "investment," created conditions under which black slaves could survive, procreate, and to an extent, experience stable family life. Beginning with the second generation of slaves, black women began to have more children, and more survived to adulthood. Nowhere else in the Western Hemisphere did the black slave population reproduce more than in the British colonies along the Atlantic coast. Still sexual exploitation of slave women by their white masters, and forced separation of women from their husbands and children, placed enormous stresses on the black family. Oppression, however, may also have driven black people into closer personal ties; when planters refused to provide enough food for slaves, they supplemented their meager rations by growing food near the cabin, involving all family members in the process.

The introduction of African slaves on a large scale, more than a half-century after Jamestown's founding, made the existence of huge, almost self-sufficient plantations possible. Wealthy planters often bought up the crops of smaller farmers, selling them retail goods, repairs, home manufactures, and slaves. Some powerful slaveholders built up their own individual "kingdoms." They were able to offer services from their flour mills, textile-weaving centers, blacksmith shops, and even iron foundries. White indentured servants, and increasingly black slaves, were taught the skills of tailor, carpenter, or blacksmith. The relative ease with which white farmers obtained land created opportunities for slaves to fill these roles as artisans, and the situation meant that they, along with the house servants, had close associations with the planter or his assistants. This closer proximity often earned slaves privileges, inside information, and perhaps an opportunity to become literate. It might also intensify the frustrations of enslavement and leave those slaves feeling deeply alienated from the larger number of blacks who labored more routinely and rigorously as field hands.

Most plantations did not contain mills or clothing manufactures but existed almost solely for the production of tobacco and, sometimes, other crops. The planter's large house usually faced a river, with the slave cabins in the distance. The Westmoreland County mansion that had thirty-three buildings around it, including a brewery and a spinning center, was indeed an exception. Few plantations contained more than a thousand acres or more than one hundred slaves.

Yet leadership in Virginia society remained dominated by a small elite group of large planters. Aristocratic families such as the Carters, Lees, Byrds, and Randolphs maintained their power through close association and intermarriage. By the eighteenth century the grandeur of their Georgian-style mansions overshadowed the humbler dwellings of their predecessors. The most stylish and expensive European furniture was imported to fill their huge stately rooms. If the appropriate articles could not be found, artisans could be employed to create worthy imitations. The atmosphere of wealth and a life of ease led this ruling class to pursue pleasures of the present, although (superficially, at least) in a more dignified manner than had its predecessors when tobacco had first brought easy riches. By the eighteenth century, the Virginia elite's days were filled with horse racing, fox hunting, and partying. Even after the founding of the College of William and Mary in Williamsburg in 1693, few planters' sons ever gave more thought to serious studies than had their fathers.

Although they might live on self-sufficient plantations, needing only to sell tobacco to England in return for the much-demanded luxury items, the planters' association with one another and their elevated social position above other farmers required that they assume active leadership in directing the colony. The interest of large planters in buying the crops of smaller farmers, selling them goods in turn and lending their less prosperous neighbors money, moved the tobacco elite toward directing politics within Virginia, both through the local county courts and as members of the House of Burgesses. These few great families also held themselves responsible for managing the religious life of the colony, usually through the appointment of Anglican ministers. The supreme irony of the Virginia planters' world occurred in the mid-eighteenth century when, out of this social context of elitism and slavery, there emerged the greatest champions of freedom and liberty in the American Revolution: men such as George Washington, Thomas Jefferson, James Madison, James Monroe, and Patrick Henry. But earlier in the eighteenth century, these "gentlemen freeholders" and their families held no particular thoughts of rebellion from the comforts of provincial society and benign English rule.

THE LATER SOUTHERN COLONIES

Maryland

Unlike Virginia, the colony of Maryland was founded when King Charles I gave a grant of land to a *single* proprietor and not a company. Initially the grant was made to Sir George Calvert, the first Lord Baltimore, who had been a stockholder of the London Company and had made an unsuccessful earlier effort to establish his own colony in Newfoundland. He had then emigrated to Virginia, but was ordered out for maintaining his Roman Catholic faith. Baltimore died before the Maryland charter received final approval in 1632, but his son, Leonard,[1] led the first group of Catholic settlers to

---

[1] Leonard's older brother, Cecelius, the second Lord Baltimore and first proprietor of Maryland, remained in England to defend his charter against Protestant attacks.

St. Mary's at the mouth of the Potomac River in 1634. They did not suffer through any period of starvation as their southern neighbors had at Jamestown; the Virginia settlement was near, and the newcomers maintained friendly relations with the coastal Indian tribes (unlike Virginia's more brutal experiences).

Despite its Catholic origins, the colony eventually allowed Protestants to settle there as well. Maryland provided a haven for English and Irish Catholics who faced oppression at home, but once Protestants began settling, the Baltimore proprietors urged that they be treated civilly. During the English Civil War in the 1640s, Virginia's loyalty to the crown helped spur anti-Puritan feelings in that colony, but Maryland allowed hundreds of Puritan immigrants to seek refuge there. This influx of Protestants led Baltimore to introduce his Toleration Act in 1649 to protect what had become, by then, a Catholic *minority* in the colony. Although the act required belief in Christianity, the document set a standard of religious tolerance for the Southern colonies of North America by endorsing the coexistence of different Christian sects —no small achievement in that age of religious warfare in England itself. Only Rhode Island further north practiced comparable religious tolerance toward dissenters.

After Oliver Cromwell and the Puritans triumphed in England in 1650, Puritans eventually came into power in Maryland, repealing the Toleration Act and helping to precipitate a small-scale religious war. Baltimore had summoned an assembly, since the royal charter guaranteed that all freemen should have a role in the making of laws. But the proprietor allowed the assembly little power, while awarding most of the important offices to relatives and Catholic friends. The outbreak of hostilities in Maryland in 1654 reflected the antagonism between Protestant small farmers and Catholic larger planters and lords. By 1657, Baltimore had recovered control of the colony, which again served as the tolerant home of Catholics and Protestants alike. At the same time, Maryland became prosperous, growing tobacco in the same soil and climate that Virginians had for decades—and growing wealthy like their neighbors across Chesapeake Bay.

William Byrd

I n the beginning, all America was Virginia." The author of those words, William Byrd of Westover (1674–1744), was an archetypal member of Virginia's plantation aristocracy: farmer, writer, colonial official, businessman, surveyor, and bibliophile (among his many interests). Byrd's life spanned the transforming decades in provincial American society—from Bacon's Rebellion to the mid-eighteenth century. As a leading member of the colonial elite, Byrd lived within the orbit of an Anglo-Virginian cultural world that would produce, one generation later, many of the leaders of the American Revolution. In his own time, however, politics lacked any focus beyond Virginia's borders. Gentlemen such as Byrd consumed their energies in a wide variety of economic, literary, and personal pursuits.

Raised on a plantation in frontier territory, son of a wealthy planter also named William Byrd, he was shipped off to relatives in England for education while still a boy. Eventually he studied law at the Middle Temple in London while also cultivating a taste for the literary life. Byrd became friendly with famous playwrights such as Congreve and Wycherley before returning to Virginia in 1692. Already a widely-known figure in the colony because of his father's economic position and his own large circle of influential friends, Byrd was elected to the House of Burgesses the year he returned from England. He became active in the colony's political life and, in 1697, again traveled to England where, the following year, he became Virginia's agent. (Byrd served two periods as colonial agent in England, 1697–1705 and 1715–26.) When the elder Byrd died in 1705, his son returned to the family estate at Westover and married within his class the following year.

Byrd resumed his political career and became a member of the Virginia Council of State in 1709. Over the next decade, Byrd and other members of the plantation gentry battled with the Lieutenant-Governor, Alexander Spotswood, who unsuccessfully attempted to assert royal prerogative against the interests of the leading planters. In 1718, Spotswood failed in an attempt to have Byrd removed from the Council and, in 1720, himself lost his post.

Turning increasingly to economic interests, Byrd pursued a relentless policy of land accumulation and speculation, increasing his acreage from 26,000 to 180,000 before his death. Like other Virginia planters, he was, at the same time, sometimes forced to sell slaves and land to pay his debts. He was a commissioner or surveyor of boundary lands between colonies, owned much land in frontier regions, and was committed to Virginia's expansion westward both for strategic reasons (to deny the French access to the territory) and economic ones. Byrd's *History of the Dividing Line* (between North Carolina and Virginia), a book first published in 1841, several other manuscripts, and voluminous private correspondence revealed Byrd's urbane and lively imagination. A Fellow and corresponding member of the Royal Society of London, Byrd owned what was probably the largest private collection of books (over 4,000 volumes on all subjects) in the American colonies at the time.

Byrd pursued his energetic and varied interests virtually to the time of his death in August 1744. Only with the posthumous publication of his manuscripts and letters, however, has the full measure of William Byrd of Westover—Virginia patrician—finally emerged. "A library, a garden, a grove, and a purling stream are the innocent scenes that divert our leisure," Byrd wrote of his Westover, Virginia, mansion. He might as easily have added his *outdoor* pursuits to the list: planter, councillor, speculator, surveyor, entrepreneur, and unofficial one-man cultural ambassador between the American and English Enlightenments.

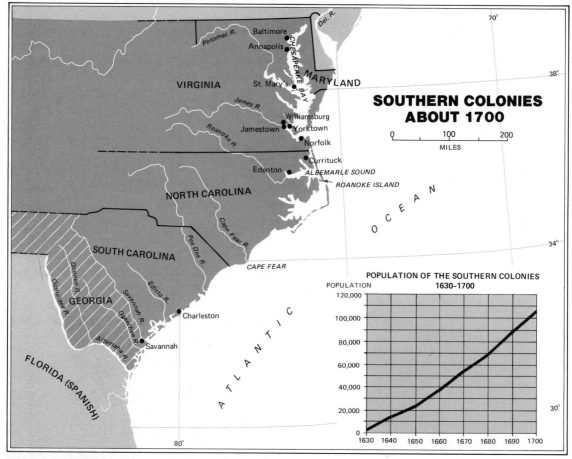

SOUTHERN COLONIES ABOUT 1700

POPULATION OF THE SOUTHERN COLONIES
1630-1700

Permanent English settlement in the Southern colonies began after the Virginia grant of 1606. From then on, English kings carved big chunks of land out of Virginia to form the four other Southern colonies.

Land north of the Potomac River was given in proprietorship to Lord Baltimore in 1634. Land south was given to eight noblemen as proprietors by King Charles II in two separate grants in 1663 and 1665. The king hoped that this new colony, Carolina, would serve as a buffer state, protecting Virginia from Indian and Spanish attack. The first settlers to Carolina came in 1653 from Virginia. They settled in the northeast, along Albemarle Sound. Carolina was treated as one colony until 1712, when it became known as North Carolina and South Carolina.

The last mainland colony to be claimed was the land southwest of Carolina, between the Savannah and Altamaha rivers. Georgia was founded not as a proprietory nor as a corporate colony, but rather under the trusteeship of a group of Englishmen. The most famous of these trustees was James Oglethorpe. Oglethorpe's goal was to create a refuge for worthy Englishmen imprisoned for debt. The founding of this new colony delighted South Carolinians, who saw Georgia as a bulwark against the Spanish in Florida. By 1700 the population of the Southern colonies (excluding Georgia) was 104,588. Virginia was the most populous.

The Carolinas

After the death of Oliver Cromwell and the restoration of royal authority in England in 1660, interest in New World settlement revived. Just as his father before him had done with Lord Baltimore, Charles II made a large grant of land to eight of his noble friends in 1663. All of the eight had been extremely helpful in assisting Charles to recover the throne, and their reward was "Carolina," an enormous grant that included the area between Virginia and Spanish Florida, extending theoretically to the Pacific Ocean.[2] Some of these men had made fortunes in sugar plantations on the Caribbean colony of Barbados, and they now needed more land to expand their American ventures. Early Carolina, therefore, has been aptly described as the colony of a colony.

Even before Barbadians established the first permanent settlements along the Atlantic coast, the northern area of the colony, in the region of Albemarle Sound, had already been partially settled (without any land tenure rights) by poor Virginia farmers, criminals, and runaway slaves. They grew some tobacco but mainly dealt in subsistence farming. The new Carolina proprietors gave them a separate governor in 1664, and a popularly elected assembly sat for the first time in 1665. The region contained only about four or five thousand small farmers by 1700, but in 1729, King George II took control from the proprietors. The area became the royal colony of North Carolina.

The first expedition sponsored by the eight proprietors was undertaken in 1670 when English colonists from the Barbados as well as from the mother country established themselves at Charles Town (later Charleston) near the confluence of the Ashley and Cooper rivers on the Atlantic coast. There, the new settlers engaged in a thiving trade with local Indian tribes, acquiring furs and hides, as well as Indians captured from other tribes, which they sold as slaves to the Caribbean. By the early eighteenth century, there were over a thousand Indian slaves in the Carolina colony.

In Barbados, wealthy planters had created a society in which the vast majority of the population were Negro slaves, and by the early 1700s, blacks outnumbered whites in Carolina as well. In that colony, neither Barbados sugar nor Chesapeake tobacco became the colony's staple and primary source of wealth; that place was reserved for rice plantations. As in Virginia, high initial costs had kept down the number of slaves in the beginning, but Carolina's close ties with Barbados reinforced the idea of slave ownership as a source of social prestige. With the length of the white indentured servants' terms declining by the 1680s, black slaves became increasingly involved in all facets of the colony's economy: guiding ships through the river marshes, herding cattle, trading with the Indians, and serving as blacksmiths. African slaves helped to teach the English colonists how to plant, tend, and harvest rice—the key to Carolina's survival.

The ruling whites of South Carolina faced challenges from both red and black, Indians and Africans, as they expanded their economy during the first half of the eighteenth century. Whites insisted that the Yamasees, a tribe with whom they frequently traded, had fallen into debt to them, and therefore began seizing Indian women and children to be sold as slaves as partial repayment. The Yamasees were then able to forge alliances with other tribes and mount an impressive attack in 1715 against the whites, who survived, first, because they had taken the risk of arming their black slaves against the Indians and second, because they persuaded the Cherokees to fight with them against the Yamasees and the latter's allies, the Creeks (ancient enemies of the Cherokees).

By the 1730s, the colony's elite took steps to encourage the immigration of more whites, while passing laws that took skilled jobs away from blacks and assigned them to more menial duties. Fear of a black uprising remained when expansion of rice cultivation required the importation of large numbers of West African slaves. In 1739, a rebellion near Charleston of newly arrived blacks brought death to twenty-five whites in a region where rice cultivation was intensive and the black population highly concentrated. As a result, white South Carolinians passed a Comprehensive Negro Act reducing slave importations and outlawing private manumissions (freeing) of slaves. As in Virginia, the labor force needed to be secure and reliable for South Carolina's white planters, whatever the human cost to African slaves and local Indians.

Georgia

In 1732 George II made a grant of land that became the last colony founded on the North American mainland under English royal auspices.

---

[2] Carolina was named for King Charles, whose name in Latin is "Carolus." The Carolina proprietors included Sir William Berkeley, Governor of Virginia during Bacon's Rebellion.

Charles Calvert (child), the third Lord Baltimore, was governor of Maryland during a period of traumatic upheaval both in England and in the colony. His Catholic co-religionists had become Maryland's minority by then. Despite Calvert's efforts, his family's charter was abandoned after the Glorious Revolution in England in 1689. (Courtesy, Enoch Pratt Free Library)

He gave the unsettled southernmost part of Carolina to James Oglethorpe, who hoped to use the new settlement to create a home for thousands of the English poor and imprisoned. (Many of Georgia's earliest settlers came directly from English prisons.) Oglethorpe and the first hundred colonists arrived in 1733 and founded the city of Savannah near the South Carolina border. The founders of Georgia hoped that the new colony would also serve as protection against Spanish incursions, from Florida outposts, into England's more northerly provinces, while producing badly needed silk to export to the mother country.

The trustees of Georgia, led by Oglethorpe, hoped to reach their humanitarian goals by creating a society of small, hardworking farmers not unlike those in the New England colonies and in Pennsylvania. Capital for this project came from Parliament and from private donations by the trustees themselves. With the Spanish close by and always threatening, settlements in Georgia were kept small and compact. Land sales were prohibited to avoid speculation and expansion. Slavery was outlawed at first, landholdings limited to 500 acres, and the settlers forced to grow silk which was less profitable than tobacco or rice. Alcohol was also prohibited to encourage both greater productivity and an elevated moral level in the colony. The controls exercised by the trustees discouraged migration and private investment.

Pressure from newcomers and South Carolinians soon forced the abandonment of Oglethorpe's noble experiment, however. Farmers within Georgia were discontented with their compulsory military service, restrictions upon expanding their land holdings, and the paternalistic bureaucratic controls exercised by the Georgia proprietors. By 1742, the ban on rum had been removed, and by 1750, slavery was permitted. This led, in turn, to an increase in the number of rice plantations and in the size of estates. When Georgia finally became a royal colony in 1752, it had already acquired the social structure common to neighboring provinces, including slavery and a racist caste structure, which would separate its interests and those of the other Southern colonies from the patterns that characterized English settlements farther to the north. Nor must it be forgotten that the whole process of English settlement in the Southern colonies stretched out over more than a century, with Georgia being established a century-and-a-quarter after Jamestown. The arc of settlement in the South from Jamestown to Georgia had its Northern counterpart in the more than half-century of colonization running from Pilgrim Plymouth to Quaker Philadelphia.

Suggested Readings
Chapters 3-4

Jamestown

Philip L. Barbour, *Pocahontas and Her World* (1969) and *The Three Worlds of Captain John Smith* (1964); Carl Bridenbaugh, *Jamestown, 1544-1699* (1980); E. H. Campbell, *Jamestown: The Beginning* (1974); Frances Mossiker, *Pocahontas: The Life and the Legend* (1976); Bernard Sheehan, *Savagism and Civility: Indians and Englishmen in Colonial Virginia* (1980); Alden T. Vaughan, *American Genesis: Captain John Smith and the Founding of Virginia* (1975).

Colonial Virginia and English Backgrounds

C. M. Andrews, *The Colonial Period in American History*, (Vols I-III, 1934-1937); Carl Bridenbaugh, *Vexed and Troubled Englishmen, 1590-1642* (1968); Verner Crane, *The Southern Frontier, 1670-1732* (1977); W. F. Craven, *The Southern Colonies in the Seventeenth Century, 1607-1689* (1949); Hugh Honour, *The New Golden Land* (1975); Edmund S. Morgan, *American Slavery, American Freedom* (1975); Richard L. Morton, *Colonial Virginia* (2 vols., 1960); J. E. Pomfret and F. M. Shumway, *Founding the American Colonies* (1970); David B. Quinn, *England and the Discovery of America, 1481-1620* (1974); A. L. Rowse, *Elizabethans and America* (1959); James M. Smith, ed., *Seventeenth Century America* (1959); Clarence L. Ver Steeg, *The Formative Years, 1607-1763* (1964); Wilcomb E. Washburn, *The Governor and the Rebel* (1957); G. F. Willison, *Behold Virginia* (1951); Louis B. Wright, *The Cultural Life of the American Colonies, 1607-1763* (1964).

Southern Colonies

Carl Bridenbaugh, *Myths and Realities: Societies of the Colonial South* (1963); L. C. Gray, *History of Agriculture in the Southern United States to 1860* (2 vols., 1933); Marcus W. Jernegan, *Laboring and Dependent Classes in Colonial America, 1607-1783* (1931); Hugh T. Lefler and Albert R. Newsome, *North Carolina* (1954); T. R. Reese, *Colonial Georgia* (1963); M. Eugene Sirmans, *Colonial South Carolina* (1966); A. E. Smith, *Colonists in Bondage* (1974).

Indians, Blacks, and the Problem of Slavery

Philip D. Curtin, *The Atlantic Slave Trade* (1970); David Brion Davis, *The Problem of Slavery in Western Culture* (1966); Carl Degler, *Neither Black Nor White* (1971); H. R. Driver, *Indians of North America* (2nd ed., 1970); John Hope Franklin, *From Slavery to Freedom* (1980 ed.); Eugene D. Genovese, *The World the Slaveholders Made* (1970); Wilbur R. Jacobs, *Dispossessing the American Indian* (1972); Winthrop D. Jordan, *White Over Black: American Attitudes Toward the Negro, 1550-1812* (1968); A. L. Kroeber, *Cultural and Natural Areas of Native North America* (1939 and later eds.); Edmund S. Morgan, *American Slavery, American Freedom* (1975); Gary Nash, *Red, White, and Black: The Peoples of Early America* (1974); Wilcomb E. Washburn, *The Indian in America* (1975); Peter Wood, *Black Majority* (1974).

5 The Witches of Salem

The charge: witchcraft. Dragged from her sickbed to be questioned at the Salem Village meeting house on March 23, 1692, seventy-three-year-old Rebecca Nurse calmly awaited her accusers. Ailing and nearly deaf, she could barely hear herself charged with "suspicion of having committed . . . acts of witchcraft and thereby having done much hurt and injury to the bodies of Ann Putnam, the wife of Thomas Putnam of Salem Village, and Ann Putnam, the daughter of said Thomas Putnam, and Abigail Williams, etc."

Twelve-year-old Abigail Williams had been the first to name Goodwife Nurse[1] as a witch four days earlier when, at the Putnam home, Abigail suddenly broke into what one observer described as a "grievous fit":

> sometimes makeing as if she would fly, stretching up her arms as high as she could and crying "Whish, Whish, Whish" several times; Presently after she said there was Goodw. N [Nurse] and said "Do you not see her? Why, there she stands!" And then said Goodw. N offered her The Book, and she was resolved she would not take it, saying Often, "I won't, I won't, I won't take it. I do not know what Book it is; I am sure it is none of God's Book, it is the Devil's Book, for ought I know." After that she run to the Fire, and begun to throw Fire Brands about the house. . . .

Another twelve-year-old, Ann Putnam, supported Abigail's charges two days later at the examination of Martha Cory, another Salem woman accused of witchcraft. "She thought Goodw. N. Praying . . . to the Devil," Ann told a meeting house "thronged with spectators." Although "she was not sure it was Goodw. N., she thought it was."

By the time Rebecca Nurse appeared before Magistrates John Hathorne and Jonathan Corwin on March 24, the lists of her accusers had grown. Ann Putnam's mother, also named Ann, had gone into a fit the previous day, which she blamed on a visit from Rebecca Nurse's "apparition." When Deodat Lawson, a former minister of Salem Village, saw

---

[1] "Goodwife" was the favored term of respect for married women in Puritan New England.

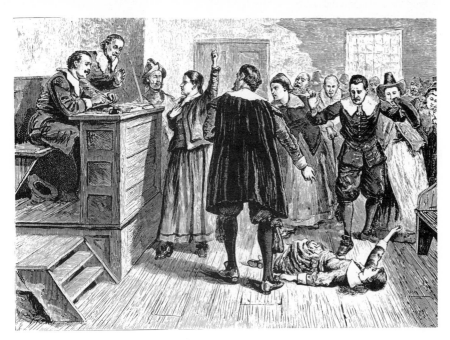

Goodwife Putnam that day, she "was so stiff, she could not be bended . . . [then] quickly began to strive violently with her Arms and Legs . . . and as it were to Converse personally with Goodw. N., saying, 'Goodw. N. Be gone! Be gone! Be gone! Are you not ashamed . . . to afflict a poor Creature so?'" During her examination by the magistrates, a pair of seventeen-year-olds, Mary Walcott and Elizabeth Hubbard, chimed in accusing Rebecca's apparition of having hurt them "most grievously."

But to her large family and her many friends in the village, Rebecca Nurse seemed a most unlikely witch. She and her husband Francis Nurse were among Salem's most respected figures, tilling a prosperous three-hundred-acre farm alongside their four sons and four daughters. A deeply religious woman, Rebecca differed from most of the unsavory or unpopular women in Salem Village who had recently been charged with witchcraft (for Rebecca was not the first person to be so accused). Thus, when the magistrates questioned Rebecca on March 24 to decide whether she should stand trial, even they seemed uncertain. "If you have confessed and give Glory to God," commented one a bit confusingly, "I pray God clear you, if you are innocent. And if you be guilty, discover you."

The examination proved a bedlam. Shrieks from Rebecca's "afflicted" accusers frequently punctuated the questions that Salem Village's minister, the Reverend Samuel Parris, dutifully recorded:

MR. HATHORNE: What do you say (speaking to one afflicted), have you seen this woman hurt you?

Yes, she beat me this morning.

Abigail, have you been hurt by this woman?

Yes.

Ann Putnam, in a grievous fit, cried out that she hurt her.

[HATHORNE]: Goody Nurse, here are two—Ann Putnam the child and Abigail Williams—complain of your hurting them. What do you say to it?

N. [NURSE]: I can say before my Eternal Father, I am innocent, and God will clear my innocency . . . I never afflicted no child, never in my life.

[H.]: You see these accuse you. Is it true?

[N.]: No

[H.]: Are you an innocent person, relating to this witchcraft?
Here Tho. Putnam's wife (Ann) cried out: Did you not bring the Black man with you? Did you not bid me tempt God and die? How oft have you eat and drunk your own damnation? What do you say to them?

Suddenly the "afflicted" girls and woman began howling as if stirred by Ann Putnam Senior's shouted question, screaming out that Rebecca Nurse's apparition was pursuing them. Hathorne complained to the witness: "It is very awful for all to see these agonies, and you, an old professor, this charged with contracting with the devil by the effects of it, and yet to see you stand with dry eyes when there are so many wet."

Rebecca snapped back: "You do not know my heart . . . I am as clear as the child unborn." She denied having caused her accusers any pain. Yet, at virtually every movement of Rebecca's hands or body, "the afflicted persons were seized with violent fits of torture." Rebecca agreed with Hathorne that the afflicted females appeared "bewitched," but she could not explain the cause of their suffering: "I cannot help it," she finally conceded; "the Devil may appear in my shape."

Exhausted by the questioning, Rebecca hung her head down to one side. Immediately, Elizabeth Hubbard's neck drooped to the same position, while Abigail Williams screamed: "Set up Goody Nurse's head, [or] the maid's neck will be broke." Those closest to Rebecca raised her neck to an unright position, after which Elizabeth Hubbard's neck also straightened out at once.

With such strong evidence, the magistrates ordered Rebecca Nurse imprisoned to await trial. Their indictment charged her with having committed against Ann Putnam Junior, Mary Walcott, Elizabeth Hubbard, and Abigail Williams "certain detestable arts called Witchcraft and Sorceries." According to the charges, Rebecca had allegedly "hurt, tortured, afflicted, consumed, pined, wasted, and tormented" all of the accusing girls. Her apparition had appeared before them a number of times, moreover, pummeling and otherwise injuring them by "Biting, Pinching, Bruising, Tormenting, at their Breasts, by her Leaning, and when, bended Back, as if their Backs were Broken." The afflicted girls also claimed that Rebecca had confessed to them a variety of murders (with six children among the alleged victims). Most of the accusers also mentioned the presence of a black man hovering near Rebecca and occasionally whisper-

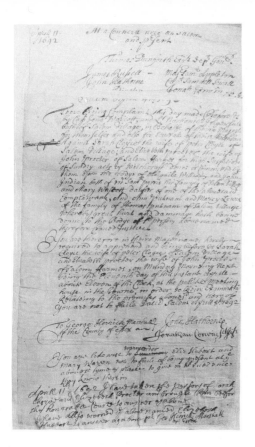

A fragment of the "Examination of Rebecca Nurse" at Salem Village in the handwriting of Rev. Mr. Parris. (Courtesy, Essex Institute, Salem, Mass.)

ing instructions to her, presumably a reference to the Devil images associated with "blackness" in that era among Englishmen and other Europeans.

When Rebecca's trial took place on June 30, her accusers repeated their earlier statements: Goody Nurse's apparition had tormented them. Again, Rebecca protested her innocence. Other witnesses linked Rebecca to various deaths in the Salem community. A neighbor's widow even claimed that Rebecca had caused her husband's sudden death after an argument they had had because his pigs had accidentally strayed into the Nurses's fields.

Possibly the strangest (yet in a sense the most *tangible*) "evidence" presented for Rebecca Nurse's alleged witchery came from a local physician, one "J. Barton, Surgeon," who had inspected five women then being tried for witchcraft—including Rebecca Nurse—assisted by several other women of Salem. According to their deposition, the group found on Nurse and two others "a preternatural excrescence of flesh between the pudendum and anus, much like to teats, and not usual in women"—in short, "witches' tit" markings considered "proof" of devilish connection. More startling still, according to this account, when inspected three or four hours later, Rebecca's skin was "dry," free, and clear of any "preter-

Judge William Stoughton was the overbearing deputy governor of Massachusetts colony, who presided at most of the witchcraft trials. (Culver Pictures)

natural excrescence." The evidence of "J. Barton, Surgeon" suggested some supernatural tampering with Rebecca's body, but the accused woman protested the conclusion. Any marks upon her ancient flesh, Rebecca avowed, came from a simple and *natural* cause—aging.

The jury brought back an unexpected verdict of *"not guilty"* for Rebecca, a tribute to her reputation within Salem considering the array of witnesses against her. Unfortunately, the nearly deaf woman failed to hear the verdict. Nor, though she watched the scene, could she hear the commotion which followed when her small group of accusers reacted to it:

> Immediately all the accusers in the Court, and suddenly all the afflicted out of Court, made a hideous out-cry, to the amazement, not only of the Spectators, but the Court also seemed strangely surprised; one of the Judges expressed himself not satisfied, another of them as he was going off the Bench, said they would have her Indicted anew.

Through all this, Rebecca stood patiently awaiting the court's instructions. But the accusers' shrieks and Rebecca's own flawed hearing now doomed her.

Massachusetts Bay's newly arrived governor, Sir William Phips, had assigned Chief Justice William Stoughton, the colony's lieutenant governor, to try the witchcraft cases. Stoughton asked whether jury members had "considered one Expression of the Prisoner's, when she was upon Tryal, viz. That one Hobbs, who had confessed her self to be a Witch, was brought into court to testify against her, the Prisoner turning her head to her, said 'What, do you bring her? she is one of us,' or to that effect."

The jury withdrew to reconsider its verdict, stirred by Stoughton's question and by the "Clamours of the Accused." They came to no agreement, returned to court, and repeated the allegedly offensive words to Rebecca Nurse for an explanation. By "one of us," had she meant another witch? Had this been an inadvertent confession of guilt? But Rebecca failed to hear the jury's question and, therefore, failed to reply. Again the jury left the court, this time returning with a verdict of "guilty." (Later, when the matter was finally explained to her, Rebecca Nurse insisted that she had referred to Deliverance Hobbs only as another *defendant* — "one of us" — but by then the damage was done.)

Several days later, the ailing woman was carried in a chair from prison to the meeting house to "hear" both her death sentence and her excommunication from the Salem church. Forty Salem residents petitioned Govenor Phips on Rebecca's behalf, and at first, Phips granted a reprieve of her death sentence. But upon learning of this, "the Accusers renewed their dismal outcries against her," and the governor withdrew his reprieve. Rebecca Nurse and four other women convicted of witchcraft were hanged on Salem's Gallows Hill on July 19. The five bodies were cut down from the gallows and thrown into a barely covered grave on the spot.

Rebecca appears to have gone to her death as quietly and uncomplainingly as she had lived with her ordeal from the beginning. Not so for another of her companions that day. When the Reverend Nicholas Noyes asked Sarah Good one last time to confess and save her soul by admitting her witchcraft, Sarah shouted, back: "You're a liar. I am no more a witch than you are a wizard! If you take my life away, God will give you blood to drink."

Why did Nurse, Good, and the others have to die? How had witchcraft first become an issue in the apparently peaceful Massachusetts Bay colony community of Salem? The trouble started two months before Rebecca Nurse was accused, in January 1692, in the home of Salem Village's minister, Samuel Parris, with the strange illness of his nine-year-old daughter Betty. The child would suddenly lapse into uncontrollable fits of weeping or, on other occasions, would wander distractedly through the house without any thought of those around her. Sometimes Betty sat quietly for hours oblivious to the world, as if in a trance, and when shaken out of the mood, she would scream frantically. The minister and his wife prayed intently for their daughter. But Parris tried to keep Betty's bizarre behavior secret until her cousin, Abigail Williams (age twelve), began displaying similar and even more alarming signs of affliction.

By then it was February, and the sickness, however caused, had spread to other young women in Salem: Elizabeth Hubbard (age seventeen), Mary Walcott (age sixteen), Mercy Lewis (age nineteen), Ann Putnam, Junior (age twelve), and Mary Warren (age twenty). Their behavior began to terrify the entire Salem community. The girls appeared prey to hysterical and abrupt convulsions. "Their arms, necks, and backs," wrote the Reverend John Hale, who had been summoned to witness and pray for the afflicted, "were turned this way and that way, and returned back again, so it was impossible for them to do of themselves, and beyond the power of any epileptic fits, or natural disease to effect."

All of the young women hallucinated regularly and complained about apparitions which bit and pinched them. Sometimes the victims displayed physical evidence of bites and punctures on their bodies. Often the girls could be found, according to one description, "getting into Holes, and creeping under Chairs and Stools, and [using other] Odd Postures and Antick Gestures, uttering foolish, ridiculous Speeches, which neither they themselves nor any others could make sense of."

To New England Puritans of the 1690s, the signs seemed unmistakable. But the Reverend Parris, possibly because his own daughter and niece were involved, tried to avoid thinking about them at first. "When these calamities first began," Parris later wrote, "which was in my own family, the affliction was several weeks before such hellish operations as witchcraft were suspected."

Ministers from nearby Massachusetts Bay towns rode into Salem, summoned for their opinions. On March 11, Parris invited several of his godly colleagues from neighboring parishes to join him for a day of public prayer and fasting. The spectacle must have unnerved the ministers. During the prayer sessions, the afflicted girls kept silent. Between prayers, however, "they would Act and Speak strangely and Ridiculously." Abigail Williams would lapse into occasional convulsions, "her Limbs being twisted several ways, and very stiff" before her fits ended. Even before that day, one Salem doctor, William Griggs, had pronounced to Parris his personal judgment: Griggs "was afraid they were Bewitched." Sometime later that month, Samuel Parris sent his daughter Betty out of Salem Village to stay in nearby Salem Town, and the child never figured in the terrible events that followed.

Like most Europeans in the seventeenth century, Protestant or Catholic, the New England Puritans believed devoutly in the existence of evil supernatural forces, which often affected daily life, either directly or through malevolent "apparitions." These forces could change the behavior or warp the minds of *apparently* good and innocent Christians. The *reality of* witches and wizards (their male counterparts) seemed as obvious to those in the deeply religious towns of Massachusetts Bay as the existence of the Devil himself. They believed also that the Devil and his helpers often worked their "black magic" through the youngest and most innocent members of a community, a useful conviction since it served to bolster their belief that young people had to be severely controlled.

A crude English drawing of 1655 shows the hanging of witches. A hangman climbs up to check the bodies. Below stand three condemned women and various officers of the law. (R. Gardiner, England's Grievance Discovered, 1655)

Nor had Salem escaped the problem in earlier days. Massachusetts Bay's great early governor John Winthrop had written of one Dorothy Talbie, a Salem woman hanged in 1638 for murdering her three-year-old daughter, Difficult Talbie. The mother, according to Winthrop, "was so possessed with Satan, that he persuaded her (by his delusions, which she listened to as revelations from God), to break the neck of her own child...." But New England's history of punishing suspected witches had been remarkably mild when compared with Europe's. Thousands of accused persons were burned at the stake or hanged as convicted witches in seventeenth-century Europe, and in "old" England at the time, numerous "witches" lost their lives. But in the New England Puritan colonies, excepting Salem in 1692, fewer than twenty persons died on the gallows as witches during the entire century, while many more than this number were acquitted of witchcraft at their trials.

Yet the *scent* of witches may have first reached Salem from the larger and more influential neighboring city of Boston, where, in 1688, a

A very influential minister in Boston during the Salem trials, Cotton Mather was also the author of numerous books, among them a "study" of witchcraft. (NYPL/Picture Collection)

Gaelic-speaking old Irish woman, Goodwife Glover, was executed after confessing to having "afflicted" four young girls. The distinguished minister Cotton Mather had followed the case closely and even taken one of the girls into his home afterward in order to "cure" her affliction. Mather wrote extensively on the episode in a 1689 book, *Memorable Providences*, restating the accepted Puritan belief in an "invisible world" of witchcraft. Later, in 1692, Mather would be drawn to Salem, fascinated by its unfolding drama of that world. *If* the afflicted girls were telling the truth, it seemed evident almost from the start of the troubles that Salem Village harbored a massive "coven" (or group) of witches.

First to be named, according to most accounts, was a West Indian slave, Tituba. The Reverend Parris had brought her to Salem from the British island of Barbados, where he had lived as a merchant prior to becoming a minister. Parris had also brought Tituba's husband, another Caribbean native whom Salem residents called John Indian, and the couple both served the Parris household. Tituba later admitted to the magistrates that she had entertained young people with tales of the occult and with magical experiments recalled from her Caribbean youth, both undoubtedly influenced strongly by African cultural survivals in the West Indies. Tituba's first "circle" of listeners included Betty Parris and her cousin, Abigail Williams, but the group's size grew as word of Tituba's wondrous tales spread.

Late in February, at the request of Mary Siblet, "afflicted" Mary Walcott's aunt, Tituba and John Indian prepared a "witch's cake," a popular test at the time in England for exposing the presence of devilish behavior. They mixed rye meal with the afflicted children's urine, baked the "cake," and fed it to the Parrises' dog, which, considering Betty's initial involvement, had been considered a prime suspect as a possible "familiar" (an agent of the Devil who worked closely with the responsible witch). Apparently the dog survived and thus proved its innocence.

Although Samuel Parris complained bitterly, when he learned about the "witch's cake" test, that it smacked of "going to the Devil for help against the Devil," the problem was now clearly viewed by Parris and other village leaders as a virtual epidemic of witchcraft in their community, affecting by then almost a dozen of Salem's young women. After sharp and relentless questioning, the afflicted girls finally had named as the witches responsible for their suffering three people, all women of poor reputation in Salem: Tituba, the West Indian slave; a sharp-tongued young mother named Sarah Good; and Sarah Osborne, an old woman well-known for lying and a poor record of church attendance.

The afflicted girls had chosen well, since almost no one in Salem Village could be expected to step forward to defend the innocence of any in this trio of suspected witches. All of these unfortunate women were arrested on March 1.

To examine the three women, two members of the Massachusetts Bay legislature who lived in nearby Salem Town (five miles from Salem Village), John Hathorne and Jonathan Corwin, came for what would be the first of many pretrial questioning sessions. Hathorne, who handled most of the examination, usually assumed the accused guilty, and acted like a prosecutor seeking confessions:[2]

HATHORNE: Sarah Good, what evil spirit have you familiarity with?

GOOD: None.

HATHORNE: Have you made no contract with the devil?

GOOD: No.

HATHORNE: Why do you hurt these children?

GOOD: I do not hurt them. I scorn it.

. . . HATHORNE: What creature do you employ then?

GOOD: No creature. But I am falsely accused.

At that point, Hathorne ordered Good's accusers to look at her directly and confirm that Sarah had been the one who hurt them: "and so they all did look upon her and said this was one of the persons that did torment them. Presently they were all tormented." The shrieking and apparently agonized behavior of the afflicted girls while confronting the accused became one of the major proofs of a witch's guilt.

But Sarah Good persisted in her denials. When asked who was responsible, then, she replied, "It was Osborne." But naming Sarah Osborne only confirmed the magistrates' belief that Good herself was a witch. How else would she *know* another one? Nor did the testimony of William Good, Sarah's husband, help her case. Of his wife, a petulant woman whom Magistrate Hathorne said had answered his questions "in a very wicked, spiteful manner . . . with base and abusive words," William noted only that she "either was a witch or would be one very quickly." Although William denied having seen Sarah behave in a supernatural manner (an admission that would have led the trial directly to him), he described Sarah's "bad carriage to him" and, apparently with no pun intended, ended by observing: "I may say with tears that she is an enemy to all good." Even Sarah's four-year-old daughter Dorcas gave evidence against her mother, claiming that Sarah had used as familiars three birds that "hurt the children and afflicted persons." Dorcas, herself, though only four, was arrested on suspicion of witchcraft later in March and held chained in a dungeon for eight months before being released!

Of the three women originally arrested, only Tituba confessed her guilt. She tried in her testimony to divert the magistrates' and the girls' attention from her husband, John Indian, who might easily have faced arrest as the likeliest local candidate for the role of mysterious "black man" whom the possessed young women often mentioned in their narratives. Not only did Tituba implicate Sarah Good as her accomplice in evil (indeed, Tituba's testimony left no doubt that Good was the groups' ringleader), but more importantly, she confirmed for the magistrates what

---

[2] John Hathorne's great-great-grandson, Nathaniel, would change the spelling of the family name to "Hawthorne." Nathaniel wrote brilliantly of the Puritan mentality in his novel *The Scarlet Letter.*

Tituba was a slave in the house of Samuel Parris where the first two "afflicted" girls lived. She had come from the West Indies, and her exotic stories and "magic" tricks contributed to the emotional tension that underlay the girls' early seizures. (Library of Congress)

they evidently most wanted to hear: that the pain and suffering of the afflicted girls was *real* and caused by the presence of witches and at least one wizard.

"The devil came to me and bid me serve him," Tituba swore, adding that she had seen "four women sometimes hurt the children" along with a single man. The man was white-haired and clothed in black, a "tall man from Boston"—in short, a white stranger and *not* Salem's own John Indian! The man sometimes brought two other female witches with him from Boston, hence the *four* women. Always, the group forced Tituba to join their devilish work *against her will.* The "tall man from Boston" was evidently Tituba's description of the Devil, who also appeared on occasion in the shape of an animal: "a thing all over hairy, all the face hairy, and a long nose." He had brought the obligatory "Devil's book" with him, in which the names of witches such as Sarah Good were written and Good's mark signed (a symbol used as a signature by those unable to read and write).

Tituba described the Devil's procedures vividly. She included sketches of familiars used by Sarah Good, such as a yellow bird and a cat. The Caribbean slave also recalled riding on "a stick or pole and Good and Osborne behind me . . . taking hold of one another. . . ." And again, Tituba: "Sarah Good appeared like a wolf to [Elizabeth] Hubbard. . . . Good caused her to pinch the children. . . ."

Tituba's examination had sent the afflicted girls into convulsions inside the meeting house. When Hathorne demanded to know the tormenter's name, Tituba once more volunteered the news that she had seen Sarah Good's apparition at work. The young women agreed, and soon Tituba herself began convulsing: "I am blind now. I cannot see." The magistrates were persuaded. All three women were held for later trial, though only Sarah Good ever faced one. (Osborne died in jail, and Tituba was eventually sold by her jailer when the Reverend Parris refused to pay the jailer his fees.)

Without Tituba's startling testimony, the pursuit of witchcraft at Salem Village might have ended as inconclusively as had most earlier alleged outbreaks of the "invisible world" in New England. Even without her confession, the affair might have been blamed only on the three women—Tituba, Good, and Osborne—whose reputations set them apart from more respectable citizens. But the girls continued to experience fits and hysterical outbursts of even greater intensity. When Samuel Parris held his day of prayer and fasting on March 11, for example, they punctuated every pause in the proceedings with shrieks. At some level, conscious or otherwise, the afflicted youngsters—joined by some older women who also professed to be tormented—had begun to recognize that they enjoyed an extremely powerful hold upon the adults in their fear-ridden community. Naming someone as a witch or wizard could taint that person forever in the eyes of other Salem residents, even if the person managed to "prove" her or his innocence. And the girls' behavior was not only tolerated but encouraged by the examining magistrates and attending ministers (by the colony's traditional sources of authority, in short), supported also by the Parris and Putnam families, which (between them) accounted for a majority of the afflicted persons.

The hysterical girls soon found additional targets for their deadly accusations. The first three women named had been outcasts of questionable reputation. Many in Salem Village now wondered whether the charge of witchcraft could be sustained against more prominent churchgoing people.

The answer came on March 20. At Sunday prayer meeting, the afflicted girls found a new target, an articulate and respected woman named Martha Corey. The girls began their usual fits that day without first naming any tormenter, until Abigail Williams shouted out: "Look where Goodwife Corey sits on the Beam suckling her Yellow bird betwixt her fingers." Ann Putnam and others took up the cry about a yellow bird (Tituba had described such a bird as one of *Sarah Good*'s familiars), and the following day, Martha Corey found herself being examined at the crowded meeting house as a suspected witch.

When Martha entered the room, the afflicted girls began their full performance, screaming out that Martha was torturing them with bites and pinches. One Salem woman (claiming that Corey was "tearing out" her bowels) threw her muff and shoe at the accused witch, scoring a direct hit on Corey's head. When Goodwife Corey told the magistrates at the start that she wished to pray (and not *immediately* answer the allegations), the several hundred assembled townspeople murmured at her insolence.

Corey denied having afflicted the girls and protested that she was a God-fearing "Gospel woman," at which her accusers shouted back: "Ah! She was a Gospel witch." The girls followed each movement of Corey's with a physical display of pain, producing marks on their bodies which they alleged Corey was inflicting upon them even at that very moment. One witness, Deodat Lawson, later provided this description of the way in which the magistrates often allowed afflicted girls to direct the examination (Corey persisted in denying all charges):

> They affirmed, she [Corey] had a Yellow-Bird, that used to suck betwixt her Fingers, and being asked about it, if she had any Familiar Spirit, that attended her, she said, She had no Familiarity with any such thing . . . The afflicted persons asked her why she did not go to the company of Witches which were before the Meeting house mustering? Did she not hear the Drum beat? They accused her of having Familiarity with the Devil, in the time of Examination, in the shape of a Black man whispering in her ear . . . They told her, she had Covenanted with the Devil for ten years, six of them were gone, and four more to come.

The most startling piece of news to those at Martha Corey's hearing was the "company of Witches" supposedly mustering directly outside the meeting house while beating on drums. That drum beat, more than any previous accusations by the afflicted, signaled the escalation of the girls' assault upon respectable members of the church and village with accusations of complicity in witchcraft. It was also at Martha Corey's interrogation that Ann Putnam first raised Rebecca Nurse's name as another witch. After Corey was held for trial, Rebecca was summoned from her sickbed to begin her long ordeal to the gallows.

Thus even the most prominent, wealthy, and respected figures in Salem Village were no longer safe from the screams of the afflicted girls. The matter had become a colony-wide concern, in fact, and the examinations that followed Nurse's, on April 11, were moved to Salem Town's larger meeting house. Those hearings were not only attended by Magistrates Hathorne and Corwin but were also observed by Deputy Governor Thomas Danforth (who would be replaced by William Stoughton later that year), half a dozen additional magistrates, and a number of concerned ministers.

The "company of witches" grew with each feverish outburst by the afflicted girls. Thus Abigail Williams found on March 31 that "she saw a great number of Persons in the Village at the Administration of a Mock Sacrament, where they had Bread as red as raw Flesh, and red Drink"—a kind of black mass linked to witchcraft ceremonies. No longer was it even safe to be related to an accused person, as Sarah Cloyce, Rebecca Nurse's sister, discovered on April 3, when she suddenly stood up and walked out of The Reverend Parris's "Sacrament Day" sermon after Parris named his Text: "6. John, 70. *Have I not chosen you Twelve, and one of you is a Devil.*" When the wind shut the meeting house door with a long bang behind Sarah, suspicions spread immediately: "she was soon after complain'd of, examin'd and Committed" to arrest on witchcraft charges.

Those courageous enough to challenge the genuineness of the afflicted girls' torments found themselves immediately suspect. John Proctor, a prosperous Salem Village farmer, discovered this when he came

to take home his servant, Mary Warren, one of the accusers, the day after Rebecca Nurse's examination. Proctor did not bother hiding his contempt for the witch hunt or for what he considered the shameful gullibility of the magistrates who believed the young women: "If they were let alone, we should all be devils and witches quickly," Proctor stated according to one account. "They should rather be had to the whipping post. But he would fetch his jade [that is, Mary Warren] home and thrash the Devil out of her." Within days of this incident, John Proctor's *wife* Elizabeth had been denounced as a witch and arrested.

One of Elizabeth Proctor's chief accusers (he also denounced Sarah Cloyce as a witch) was Tituba's husband, John Indian, who had joined the girls as a prime witness for the examining magistrates. Stories of witches' conclaves at Salem had become even more elaborate by this time. Mary Walcott and Abigail Williams, for example, now identified those attending one such gathering as Rebecca Nurse, Martha Corey, Sarah Good, and Sarah Cloyce. The combinations seemed ever more expandable as "old" witches and newly accused ones shared the spotlight in the revised tales of the invisible world.

When Elizabeth Proctor's turn came to deny the accusations on April 11, the girls went through their usual repertoire of convulsions and fits timed to coincide with Elizabeth's movements, John Indian joining in the ranks of tormented ones this time. Elizabeth, who was then pregnant, denied their charges: "I take God in heaven to be my witness that I know nothing of it, no more than the child unborn."

Not content to denounce Goodwife Proctor alone, Abigail Williams and Ann Putnam Junior suddenly cried out that *John* Proctor's apparition floated above them on a high beam in the meeting house along with his wife's, which meant that Proctor was a wizard. Proctor's arrest and jailing provoked the first recantation among the afflicted girls. His "jade," the impressionable Mary Warren, evidently infatuated with Proctor, began retracting her own earlier testimony. Mary now insisted that she and the other young women had been making false charges from the beginning. Even their fits, she asserted to a stunned meeting house audience, had been false and contrived. After this, Mary Warren confronted the magistrates next on April 19, not as one of the afflicted but—given the twisted logic of the examining magistrates—herself accused of witchcraft.

Hathorne asked the inevitable question: "You were a little while ago an afflicted person. Now you are an afflicter. How comes this to pass?" Mary Warren: "I look up to God and take it to be a great mercy of God." Hathorne: "What! Do you take it to be a great mercy to afflict others?" When the remaining group of afflicted girls greeted Mary's testimony with the inevitable convulsions and hysteria, Mary lost her nerve. Apparently confused beyond words about what to say or believe, she began to babble: "I will speak. . . . Oh! I am sorry for it, I am sorry for it . . . Oh Lord help me! Oh good Lord save me!" Shaking with seizures herself by this time, which alternated with minutes of stony silence, Mary Warren finally blurted out "I will tell, I will tell," only to "tell" nothing. Then she indicated the latest direction of her mind by screaming, "I will tell! They did! They did! They did! . . . I will tell! They brought me to it!"

Days later, Mary Warren returned quietly to the ranks of the afflicted, not only confirming for the magistrates that John and Elizabeth Proctor were guilty but also denouncing several others as witches within Salem. As for the Proctors, once they went to prison, the sheriff of Essex County (of which Salem Village formed a part) followed the letter of the law, which allowed confiscation of property in such cases. He

> came to Proctor's house and seized all the Goods, Provisions, and Cattle that he could come at, and sold some of the Cattle at half price, and killed others, and put them up for the West-Indies; threw the Beer out of a Barrel, and carried away the Barrel; emptied a Pot of Broath, and took away the Pot, and left nothing in the House for the support of the Children: No part of the said Goods are known to be returned. . . .

Over two dozen people at Salem Village *confessed* to some complicity in witchcraft during 1692, either as "afflicted" persons or as accused witches and wizards. Many of them suffered from the same psychological pressures that had turned young persons like Mary Warren into fearful hysterics. Many of the "confessions," therefore, must be considered (for whatever reason) voluntary ones *up to a point*. Others came only through coercion. Magistrates such as Hathorne browbeat terrified witnesses into bargaining for their lives by making false and extravagant statements about their lives as witches or wizards (and about the complicity of others in the community). Those who confessed a role in the in-

Giles Corey was the husband of Martha Corey, an accused witch who was later executed. Giles was tortured for refusing to give testimony at his own trial. The stones placed on his chest were meant to persuade him to speak, but he insisted on his innocence to the end. (Library of Congress)

visible world usually lived to survive those terrible months, while accused persons who claimed to be innocent and challenged the afflicted girls' reliability often paid with their lives.

Some confessions were coerced by barbaric means. Thus John Proctor wrote from Salem prison in July 1692 to a group of Boston ministers (who had expressed concern over the events at Salem Village) about five of his fellow prisoners whose confessions "we know to be Lies":

> Two of the 5 are [Martha] Carrier's [Sons], Young-men, who would not confess any thing till they tyed them Neck and Heels till the Blood was ready to come out of their Noses. . . . My son William Proctor, when he was examin'd, because he would not confess that he was Guilty, when he was Innocent, they tyed him Neck and Heels till the Blood gushed out at his Nose. . . .

One stubborn victim of the witchcraft craze, Martha Corey's husband Giles, "stood mute" and refused to stand formal trial. Huge boulders were placed on Gile's chest as punishment in an effort to force him to testify against Martha or himself. But Corey, "pressed" to death, went to his grave unrepentant, his last words of contempt reportedly: "More weight!"

Despite the many accusations, inquisitors remained unpersuaded that the young women had identified the *leader* of this local "company of witches." Then, on April 20, Ann Putnam Junior "discovered" him. The news could not have been worse.

As her father and others watched Ann lapse into one of her seizures, she suddenly shouted out: "Oh, dreadful, dreadful! Here is a minister come. What, are ministers witches too? . . . Oh dreadful, tell me your name that I may know who you are." By this time, according to Ann, "Dreadful" had begun choking and hurting her in the usual fashion of witches and wizards. Surprisingly, the apparition proceeded to identify himself to Ann Putnam and to catalog his iniquities.

It took only a few days for Ann's intimate cohorts — among them Abigail Williams, Mary Walcott, Mary Warren, Mercy Lewis, and the confessed witches Abigail and Deliverance Hobbs — to confirm the devilish presence of this ministerial apparition. Ann Putnam Junior later described her initial encounter with "Dreadful":

> . . . he told me that his name was George Burroughs, and that he had had three wives, and that he had bewitched the first two of them to death, and that he killed Mistress Lawson because she was so unwilling to go from the village [with him], and also killed Mr. Lawson's child . . . and that he had bewitched a great many soldiers to death . . . and that he had made Abigail Hobbs a witch, and several witches more. And he has continued ever since, by times tempting me to write in his [Devil's] book and grievously torturing me by beating, pinching, and almost choking me several times a day. And he also told me that he was above a witch, he was a conjurer.

The Reverend George Burroughs seemed to many at Salem a likely candidate for the role of "conjurer" or even chief wizard. Burroughs had served as Salem Village's minister from 1680 to 1683 before leaving for a frontier congregation in the Maine wilderness. Reports of his cruelty toward his first two wives, and of somewhat mysterious personal habits while at Salem, fueled the hostility toward him. From the start, the magistrates were willing to believe the accusations made by Putnam and the others against Burroughs. On April 30 they ordered the minister arrested and returned to Salem for questioning. When examined on May 9, Burroughs denied the charges. Throughout the hearing, Ann Putnam Junior and the other girls performed their fits at appropriate moments. Burroughs's testimony that he had not received the sacrament of the Lord's Supper for "so long . . . he could not tell" weighed heavily against him. The magistrates sent him off to prison to join the four dozen other accused witches and wizards of Salem, who now crowded the dungeons of Boston's jail awaiting trial.

The delay in bringing this accused "company of witches" to trial stemmed from the fact that Massachusetts Bay lacked a legal government or governor for much of the period. James II, the last Stuart king of England, had revoked the old Puritan charter in 1684, declared Massachusetts a *royal* colony, and appointed Sir Edmund Andros as governor. Andros ruled despite the opposition of most Puritan ministers and political figures until overthrown peacefully early in 1689 following England's Glorious Revolution, which deposed James II and placed William and Mary of Orange on the throne.

Although the Puritans behaved briefly as if the old charter had been restored, few people in Massachusetts were surprised when the new governor, Sir William Phips, reached Boston in mid-May 1692, confirm-

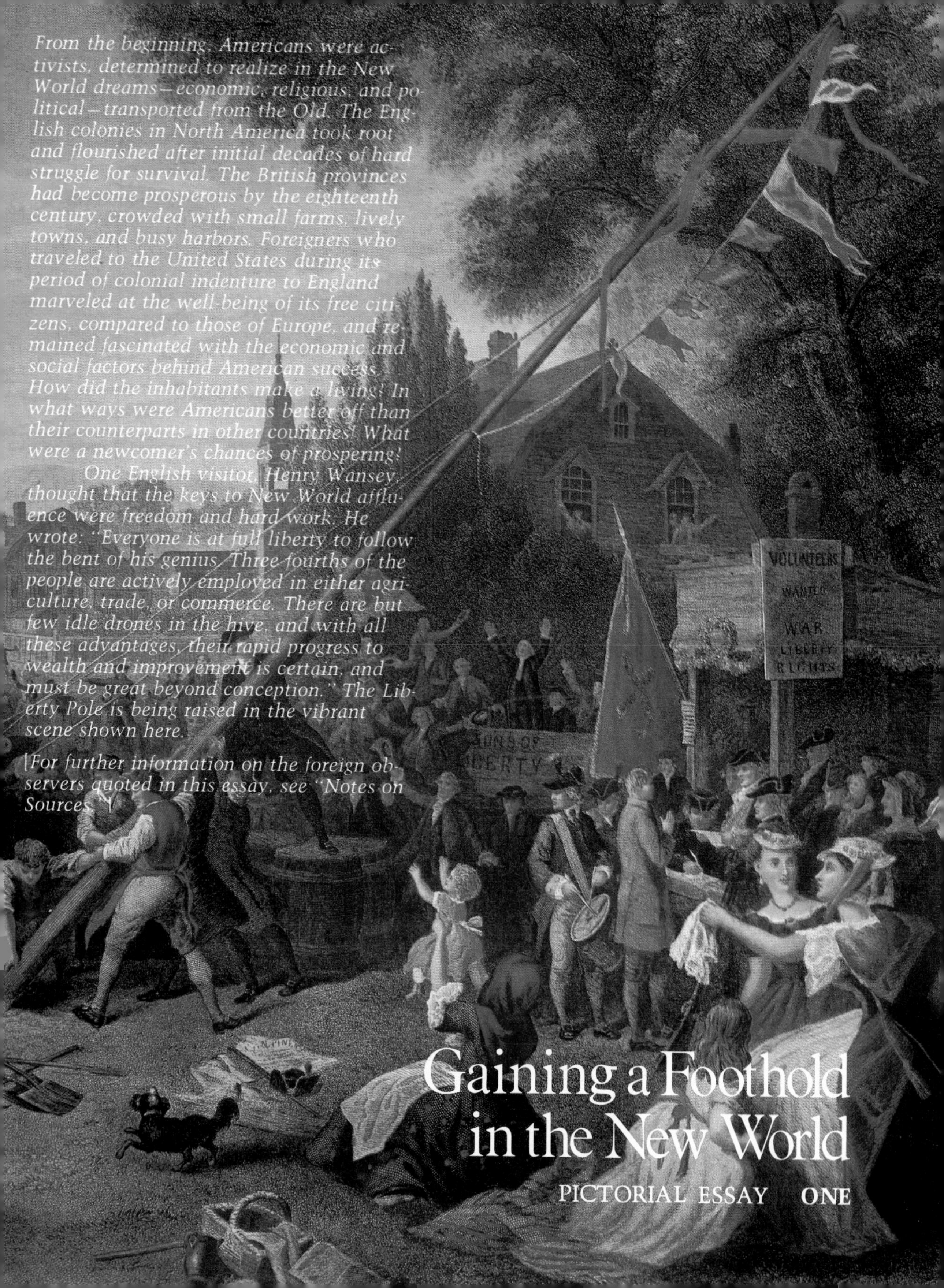

From the beginning, Americans were activists, determined to realize in the New World dreams—economic, religious, and political—transported from the Old. The English colonies in North America took root and flourished after initial decades of hard struggle for survival. The British provinces had become prosperous by the eighteenth century, crowded with small farms, lively towns, and busy harbors. Foreigners who traveled to the United States during its period of colonial indenture to England marveled at the well-being of its free citizens, compared to those of Europe, and remained fascinated with the economic and social factors behind American success. How did the inhabitants make a living? In what ways were Americans better off than their counterparts in other countries? What were a newcomer's chances of prospering?

One English visitor, Henry Wansey, thought that the keys to New World affluence were freedom and hard work. He wrote: "Everyone is at full liberty to follow the bent of his genius. Three fourths of the people are actively employed in either agriculture, trade, or commerce. There are but few idle drones in the hive, and with all these advantages, their rapid progress to wealth and improvement is certain, and must be great beyond conception." The Liberty Pole is being raised in the vibrant scene shown here.

[For further information on the foreign observers quoted in this essay, see "Notes on Sources."]

Gaining a Foothold in the New World

PICTORIAL ESSAY   ONE

All of Maryland that we have seen is high land, with few or no meadows, but possessing such a rich and fertile soil, as persons living there assured me, that they had raised tobacco off the same piece of land for thirty consecutive years. The inhabitants, who are generally English, are mostly engaged in this production. It is their chief staple, and the means with which they must purchase everything they require.

[JASPAR DANCKAERTS, 1679]

A view of early Baltimore, with tobacco growing on the hill at right

The Blue Mountains, [the Catskills] which reared their towering summits above all the other mountains, were now seen before us towards the north, but at a great distance. The farms became very numerous, and we had a view of many grain fields between the hills.

[PETER KALM, 1748]

Sawmill operated by water power

A New York farm, with the Catskills in the background

New England produces very good timber. The firs are of an extraordinary growth, for masts, yards, and planks. The sumac is much used by the tanners and dyers. The cedar produces sweet gums, besides being extremely useful in making shingles for coverings for their dwellings, as being the most durable and least injured by the weather. But the treasure and glory of the woods are the monarch oak, the spruce, and fir trees, which are in such abundance that the navy of England might be supplied with all sorts of naval stores at a cheaper rate than from the Baltic.

[THOMAS ANBUREY, 1778]

Swedes trading with the Indians

In dealing with the Indians, you must be positive and keep to your word, for if they persuade you to lower your price, they will spend time in higgling for further reductions, and seldom conclude any bargain. Sometimes, you may with brandy or strong liquor dispose them to give you ten times the value of your commodity. At other times they are so stubborn that they will not offer half the market price, especially if they are aware that you plan to influence them with drink, or that they think you have a desire for their goods, which you must appear to slight and disparage.

[JOHN LEDERER, 1669]

Unloading and drying fish at Newfoundland

The fishermen take yearly upon the coasts many tons of cod, hake, haddock, and pollack, which they split, salt, and dry at their stages, making three voyages in a year. When they share their fish at the end of every voyage, they separate the best from the worst. The first they call merchantable fish. These they sell to the Massachusetts merchants, who send them to Lisbon, Bilbao, Bordeaux, Marseilles, and other cities of France. The refuse fish they sell to the Caribbean islanders of Barbados, Jamaica, and so on, who feed their Negroes with it.

To every shallop belong four fishermen — a master or steersman, a midshipman, a foremastman, and a shore man who washes the fish, dries it, and tends their cookery. These often get in one voyage £8 or £9 a man for their shares, but it does some of them little good. For the merchant at the end comes in with a traveling tavern — a boat laden with the legitimate blood of the rich grape, and with brandy, rum, and tobacco. Coming ashore, he gives them a taste or two, which so charms them that for no persuasions that their employers can use will they go out to sea for two or three days, nay sometimes a whole week, till they are wearied with drinking. If a man of quality chance to come where they are roistering, he must be sociable and rolypoly with them or else be gone. For when wine in their guts is at full tide, they quarrel, fight, and do one another mischief.

[JOHN JOSSELYN, 1674]

Trade card of a manufacturer of spermaceti (whale oil) candles

In Rhode Island and particularly in the small town of Nantucket, famed for its fisheries, spermaceti candles are made, which in whiteness rival those of wax, but they do not give so pure and equal a light.

[FELIX DE BEAUJOUR, 1810]

The principal branch of American manufacture is the building of vessels. The Americans excel in naval architecture, and in this particular point certainly rival the most industrious people of Europe. The annual tonnage of vessels built in the different yards is estimated at about 100,000 tons.

[FELIX DE BEAUJOUR, 1810]

Launching the ship *Fame* at Salem, Massachusetts, 1802

In the heart of New York City's commercial district, 1797

Wasteland, unhealthy climate, poor people, ragged clothing — such is approximately the general idea of this continent in Europe. But oh how far from the truth is this! The land requires too little work to remain uncultivated. The robustness of the men and the fine color of the women attest to the healthiness of the climate. Not only the abundance, but also the luxury in which people live belies their reputed poverty. And the pleasure which everyone who is introduced to their society experiences is incontestable evidence of their gracious manner of living. The [American] peasant does not know what misery is; he eats meat four times a day and drinks tea twice a day. If money is scarce, everything is cheap. At present such is the competition here among ships from Europe (where perhaps they imagined that the Americans were all naked) that they are obliged to sell their merchandise at a loss. The quantity of all kinds of lumber, fish, oil, blubber, material for soap, flour, and salt meat will, before long, bring to this continent enough money to enable it to be recognized as a wealthy country.

[FRANCESCO DAL VERME, 1783]

Elijah Boardman, a wealthy Connecticut merchant

Merchants' counting house in Philadelphia

Philadelphia, if we consider that not eighty years ago the place where it now stands was a wild and uncultivated desert, inhabited by nothing but ravenous beasts and a savage people, must certainly be the object of everyone's wonder and admiration. It contains about 3,000 houses, and 18 or 20,000 inhabitants.

The Pennsylvanians, as to character, are a frugal and industrious people: not remarkably courteous and hospitable to strangers, unless particularly recommended to them; but rather, like the inhabitants of most commercial cities, the reverse. They are by far the most enterprising people upon the continent. As they consist of several nations, and talk several languages, they are aliens in some respect to Great Britain: nor can it be expected that they should have the same filial attachment to her which her own immediate offspring have. However, they are quiet, and concern themselves but little, except about getting money.

[ANDREW BURNABY, 1760]

Table for converting currency

*Forges are established in New Jersey,
Pennsylvania, Maryland, and Virginia.
In several states, particularly the northern ones, utensils of iron the most necessary for agriculture and buildings are
manufactured.*

[FELIX DE BEAUJOUR, 1810]

Air furnace for casting iron, from an early advertisement

Early American flask,
decorated with an eagle

*Went with a party to see Dickson's cotton manufactory. There are two large
buildings four stories high and eighty feet long. Twelve or fourteen workers from
Manchester. All the machinery in wood, steel, and brass was made on the spot
from models brought from England and Scotland. They are training up women
and children to the business, of whom I saw twenty or thirty at work. They give
the women two dollars a week, as well as board and lodging. The children are
bound apprentice till twenty-one years of age, with an engagement to board,
clothe, and educate them.*

[HENRY WANSEY, 1794]

Carding machine constructed
by English immigrant
Samuel Slater in 1790

ing a previously announced new charter that maintained *royal* supremacy in the colony. The thirty-nine-year-old Phips was a New Englander himself, born to a humble family, who rose to wealth and prominence after a romantic career fighting Spaniards as a Caribbean "sea dog." Phips then married a rich English noblewoman.

When Phips arrived in Boston, the witchcraft controversy at Salem topped his agenda of unresolved problems. The new governor decided to skirt direct involvement, but, before leaving to organize a military campaign against the French in Canada, he appointed the lieutenant governor, William Stoughton, as chief justice of a special seven-man "Court of Oyer and Terminer" to dispose of the backlog of trials involving accused witches. Stoughton began the trials at Salem Town on June 2.

First to be judged was Bridget Bishop, a woman reputed to have a "smooth and flattering manner" with Salem's more flirtatious men and notorious for her extravagant habits of dress. Bridget had been suspected of witchcraft much earlier, in 1679 at the time of her second marriage, but had gained release after trial without punishment. Now, even her current spouse, tavern owner Edward Bishop, denounced her as a witch when the afflicted girls renewed their accusations. Also, several reputable men of Salem testified that they had seen Bridget employ spells and charms in making advances toward them, claiming that their loved ones had been injured after they rebuffed her proposals. Bridget's movements in the courtroom provoked the usual round of shrieks and complaints from the afflicted, who were joined now by a confessed witch, Deliverance Hobbs, in denouncing Bridget's devilish activities.

Evidently Magistrates Hathorne and Corwin selected Bishop to lead off the trials in order to make the strongest possible case at the start. The *new* judges had to be convinced concerning the validity of their earlier examinations. Thus not only were statements that had been made by accusers and accused prior to trial admitted in evidence (in this and all subsequent trials), but a "medical" examination of Bridget turned up the obligatory testimony concerning a witch's tit that subsequently disappeared. Also, a search of her house produced rag dolls in the cellar allegedly stuck with pins. "There was little occasion to prove the witchcraft, this being evident and notorious to all beholders," the Reverend Cotton Mather observed of Bridget's trial. Mather's comments probably reflected the views of most orthodox Puritan ministers in Massachusetts Bay.

Although the jury found Bridget guilty and the judges sentenced her to hang, they paused before carrying out the sentence until the Massachusetts General Court (the colony's legislature) on June 8 restored an earlier law that made witchcraft punishable by death. Bridget then became the first convicted witch of Salem Village to walk to her doom on Gallows Hill (which Salem residents began calling "Witches Hill") on June 10.

Despite pressures to begin new trials quickly, Stoughton delayed matters for over two weeks. All the judges were important figures in the colony, but only one came from Salem, and a majority of the others were

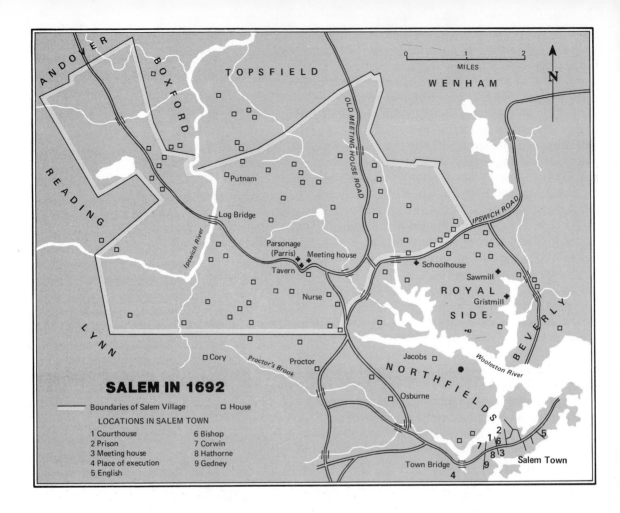

SALEM IN 1692

— Boundaries of Salem Village □ House

LOCATIONS IN SALEM TOWN

1 Courthouse
2 Prison
3 Meeting house
4 Place of execution
5 English
6 Bishop
7 Corwin
8 Hathorne
9 Gedney

from Boston. They believed in the reality of witches and their invisible world, to be sure, but as shrewd and practical men, they also recognized the problem of dealing with testimony that might be tainted by Salem's family feuds and town quarrels.

The judges were particularly concerned with evaluating "spectral evidence," in other words, the afflicted girls' testimony that they had witnessed apparitions of witches commiting dreadful acts or apparent indications of "spectral" influence on the girls' behavior in court. Without such spectral evidence, one member of the court pointed out, it would not have been possible to convict even as mischievous a woman as Bridget Bishop. But by allowing admission of such evidence, the court had already weighted the scales heavily against *all* accused persons. Stoughton and his colleagues also accepted as fact the pretrial depositions of the afflicted, and they promised not to punish witches who confessed, thereby possibly encouraging false admissions even from the innocent.

Should such spectral evidence have been allowed? To resolve the question before starting trials, the court relied on a conference of twelve leading Bay colony ministers summoned in Boston on June 15 and presided over by Cotton Mather. The document produced there apparently cautioned against accepting spectral evidence of witchcraft from afflicted persons, at least against accepting it *uncritically* and without additional proof, especially when the accused "have been persons formerly of unblemished reputations." By such restraint, the ministers seem to have thought that a number of those awaiting trials could be cleared. Mather and his colleagues urged "a very critical and exquisite caution [in using spectral evidence] lest by too much credulity of things received only upon the devil's authority there be a door opened for a long train of miserable consequences." The ministers thus evidently agreed with a point made earlier by the doomed Rebecca Nurse, namely that the "demon may assume the shape of the innocent."

Despite these reservations, the ministers' statement praised the previous efforts by Parris, Hathorne, Corwin, Stoughton, and the others involved in pretrial examinations and trial of accused witches. Yet these men had relied heavily, often exclusively, and most certainly "uncritically" upon the spectral testimony of afflicted girls like Ann Putnam Junior and Abigail Williams, or on similar evidence by confessed witches like Tituba and Deliverance Hobbs. Moreover, Mather and his colleagues went on to "humbly recommend the speedy and vigorous prosecution of those as have rendered themselves obnoxious."

Thus the ministers straddled the issue of spectral evidence, leaving its admissibility in the hands of Stoughton and his fellow judges. Since the ministerial recommendations remained secret at the time in any event, accused witches could not even refer to the explicit warnings against careless use of such evidence. In the trials that followed, therefore, when the afflicted girls cried out against their tormenters' apparitions, such spectral presences remained *hard proof* of witchcraft for the judges. One of them, Nathaniel Saltonstall, resigned from the court because he refused to believe such evidence, but he was promptly replaced by Magistrate Jonathan Corwin, who had no doubts on the matter. (As might be expected, after Saltonstall's resignation, some of the afflicted began complaining that *his* apparition had been pursuing them.)

When the court resumed on June 29, it tried five cases in a single day, among them that of Rebecca Nurse. The jury found all five guilty, although only Stoughton's intervention caused its change of decision on Nurse. All five were hanged on July 19. The Reverend George Burroughs came up for trial on August 5, along with John and Elizabeth Proctor and three others. One of them, John Willard, the former Salem Village constable, had been accused only after expressing doubts about the charges raised by the afflicted girls. Another, a lame old man named George Jacobs, who swung about the courtroom aided by two canes, ridiculed the proceedings. He called one of his accusers, Sarah Churchill, his house servant and a new recruit to the ranks of the afflicted, a "witch bitch." Jacobs complained that his granddaughter, Margaret, who had been ar-

Witchcraft victims on their way to the gallows. (Painting by F. C. Yohn. Courtesy, Essex Institute, Salem, Mass.)

rested and thrown into prison, had been tricked into testifying against him. (Margaret later recanted her confession in court.) And Jacobs told the judges: "You tax me for a wizard; you might as well tax me for a buzzard!"

All six were convicted and sentenced to hang, although Elizabeth Proctor, pregnant at the time, had her sentence stayed until after she gave birth. The others went to their deaths on Gallows Hill on August 19. Most of the crowd's attention that day went to George Burroughs, the "chief wizard," who spoke briefly and again declared his innocence before climbing the ladder to the scaffold. Burroughs apparently shook the confidence in his guilt of many of those present. A number of them wept as Burroughs concluded his oration with a flawless recital of the Lord's Prayer, something that no agent of the Devil supposedly could accomplish. There even seemed a possibility that the crowd would try to stop the execution, when Cotton Mather, who had been mounted on a horse as he watched the event, suddenly called for everyone's attention. He declared that Burroughs was not even an ordained minister, that "the Devil has often been transformed into an Angel of Light," and that Burroughs was surely guilty. The mood of uncertainty dissolved, and without further interruption, George Burroughs and the four others were dispatched, after which their bodies were thrown into a two-foot-deep hole between the nearby rocks.

The trials continued. Within the next several weeks, fifteen more accused witches were convicted. Eight of these were hanged on September 22. Of the remainder, five had confessed and therefore escaped execution; the sixth had her sentence delayed because of pregnancy; and the final one, Mary Bradbury, escaped from prison with the help of friends.

Strife within the Salem Village community increased after each execution. Despite the hysteria, twenty-one of John Proctor's Salem neighbors had signed a petition affirming their belief in his religious piety. Ninety-three of Mary Bradbury's Salem friends and associates had petitioned on her behalf. Thus even in Salem and the surrounding towns, not everyone trusted the spectral revelations made by afflicted young women as devoutly as did William Stoughton and his fellow judges. The hangings themselves—and especially the sight of Giles Corey's body crushed to death on September 19—also helped persuade many that the *real* afflicters were the girls who had leveled charges of witchcraft upon so many innocent persons.

The eight hanged on September 19 included Giles Corey's wife, Martha; another sister of Rebecca Nurse's, Mary Easty; and a man named Samuel Wardwell, who had confessed but recanted at his trial. Wardwell's previous confession, supported by spectral evidence from the afflicted girls, doomed him. While making a final speech from the scaffold protesting his innocence, Wardwell began choking on the tobacco smoke from the Executioner's pipe, which had been blown into his face. The afflicted girls then cried delightedly that "the Devil hindred him with smoak." As all eight bodies dangled from the gibbet, the Reverend Nicholas Noyes, an early supporter of the hunt for witches, intoned to all who would listen: "What a sad thing it is to see Eight Firebrands of Hell hanging there." Although neither Noyes nor anyone else in the crowd knew this at the time, there would be no further executions.

Witchcraft had ceased to be a local problem by then. It affected virtually every town in Essex County and other communities in the Massachusetts Bay colony. The jails of Boston alone held over one hundred accused witches and wizards in September 1692, all awaiting trial, while other suspects were being examined each day. At first, the afflicted young women had made their charges only against those who lived in or near Salem Village. But after the initial dozen accusations, the net broadened to involve others outside the vicinity of the village. Joined by accusations from "afflicted" persons elsewhere in Essex County, they soon spread to towns over a wide area, and of those awaiting trial in September for witchcraft, barely a dozen came from Salem itself.

As the spring and summer of 1692 wore on, each fresh burst of accusations were aimed at more highly placed figures in the colony. Prominent persons in Massachusetts Bay affairs were now cried out against and joined the ranks of accused witches and wizards, although most of these people managed to avoid arrest or imprisonment.

One who did not was Captain John Alden of Boston, the son of neighboring Plymouth's best known couple, John and Priscilla Alden. Ordered to appear for questioning by Deputy Governor Stoughton himself, Alden confronted the afflicted girls—whom he called the "Salem wenches"—in that town on May 28. The girls had identified Alden as another plausible candidate for the role of chief wizard. They had described him in seizures as a "tall man from Boston" following Tituba's initial statement. Unfortunately for Alden, George Burroughs, also high up the Devil's ladder in the girls' eyes, was a short, stubby man from back-country Maine.

Alden arrived in Salem furious at having been dragged into the whole affair, and he quarreled intemperately with both the girls and the judges. The magistrates, still uncertain about the identification of Alden, ordered the accusers to form a ring around him and identify the accused, at which point one of the girls cried out: "There stands Alden, a bold fellow with his Hat on before the Judges, he sells Powder and Shot to the Indians and French, and lies with the Indian Squaws, and has Indian Papooses." Alden was arrested on the spot and brought to the meeting house to be examined. He denied the girls' charges that he had tormented them. He also bickered with one of the judges, Bartholemew Gedney, an old friend who now seemed to accept his accusers' account. Taken back to Boston under arrest, Alden was confined for the next fifteen weeks to his house (and not in Boston prison, where less influential "wizards" were kept) until he finally escaped, fleeing the colony for safety in New York, where he remained for the next year.

Other important personages in Massachusetts Bay found themselves and their loved ones under threat of similar imprisonment and death. One wealthy Salem man, Philip England, and his wife Mary, friends of Governor and Lady Phips, were also placed under house arrest in Boston and fled to New York as Alden had done. Nathanial Cary, a rich shipowner from Charlestown, arranged the escape of his wife from prison. Both went first to Rhode Island and then to New York.

No one, no matter how powerful, appeared to be safe from the afflicted girls' accusations. George Burroughs paid with his life, and another minister, John Hale, who had originally championed Abigail Williams and her cohorts, found his own wife accused of witchcraft. Wealthy members of Boston's mercantile and political "first families" found their names dragged into the "Devil's mud." There seemed no end to it. After Nathaniel Saltonstall withdrew as a judge in disbelief at spectral evidence, the girls cried out against him. One of them went to the top, implicating Cotton Mather. Several named Lady Mary Phips, the governor's wife! But by now — nine months, nineteen hangings, and one crushed body later — the afflicted young women of Salem had finally overreached themselves.

Again the ministers took the lead, this time in bringing the witchcraft trials to a halt. As early as mid-August, Cotton Mather had written John Foster, a member of the governor's council, repeating even more strongly his earlier assertion that spectral evidence alone from afflicted persons "is not enough to convict . . . of witchcraft" and that "devilish presences" sometimes could enter innocent bodies — even his own. The point was made with still greater authority by Mather's father, Increase Mather, the colony's most respected minister. In a sermon preached to a conclave of ministers at Cambridge on October 3, Increase Mather denounced categorically the use of spectral evidence. In that sermon, soon published as *Cases of Conscience Concerning Evil Spirits Per-*

sonating Men, he also criticized as inadequate most other types of "evidence" used in the Salem witchcraft trials and argued: "It were better that ten suspected witches should escape, than that one innocent person should be condemned."

Most of Mather's ministerial audience evidently agreed with him. They shared by then a widespread consensus among Massachusetts Bay's civil and religious authorities that matters at Salem had gotten out of hand. Nine days after Mather's sermon, Governor Phips issued instructions banning any further arrests or trials for witchcraft. Later that month, the Massachusetts legislature passed a bill calling for a ministerial meeting to advise civil authorities on the best way to handle cases involving the accused witches who remained in jail. A short time later, Phips abolished the special Court of Oyer and Terminer which had been appointed to try the cases and freed on bond many of those in prison awaiting trial.

Another special court met at Salem early in 1693 to deal with the imprisoned persons. Stoughton was again its chief judge, but this time Governor Phips instructed the judges that no accused witch could be convicted *solely* on spectral evidence. Only three of the fifty-two cases tried ended in conviction, and in all three cases, the "witch" had confessed. The remaining forty-nine accused witches were acquitted. Stoughton sentenced all three found guilty to hang along with five others, including Elizabeth Proctor, who had been convicted earlier but spared because of her pregnancy. Governor Phips promptly reprieved all eight, giving obvious vent to his displeasure with Stoughton's attempt to salvage one final act of bloody retribution from the Salem tragedy. The lieutenant governor could hardly contain his outrage at Phips's action: "We were in a way to have cleared the land of the witches!" he complained. "Who is it that obstructs the course of justice I know not. The Lord be merciful to the country!"

Stoughton knew perfectly well who had "obstructed" the "justice" of spectral evidence. When his court resumed hearing witchcraft cases in Boston that April, others accused of the crime were also cleared, including one mentally ill woman who had confessed. Meanwhile, Governor Phips proclaimed John Alden innocent of the charges against him and, in May 1693, decisively ended the episode by freeing those who remained in jail on witchcraft charges.

Phips also proclaimed a general pardon for the fortunate people who had fled the colony when accused. The governor had written to the earl of Nottingham in February 1693 defending his belated decisiveness in terminating the witch hunt as necessary in order to dissipate "the black cloud that threatened this Province with destruction" and to relieve the threats against innocent victims of the afflicted girls, including "some of the principal persons here." Even Phips's pardon did not free some of those in jail, since payment of prison fees was then a prisoner's responsibility and not the state's. Only when the jailer had been reimbursed for expenses could the accused buy their way out of jail, a costly procedure that kept a number of them in jail long after their pardons.

Slowly Salem Village regained its earlier peaceable state. But supporters and opponents of the Reverend Samuel Parris, in whose house the affair had germinated, continued to bicker for several years. The afflicted young women returned to their homes, subdued finally by fear of the governor's displeasure. Pro-Parris and anti-Parris factions in the Village fought so fiercely within the church that, in April 1695, a special conference of neighboring clergymen met at Salem to mediate. Their conclusions gave Parris little comfort, since the ministers agreed (in a model of understatement) that Parris had taken "unwarranted and uncomfortable steps" against those of his parishioners accused of witchcraft. Still, the visiting ministers pleaded with survivors of the ordeal to display "compassion" toward Parris and toward his followers, presumably including the afflicted girls. Parris eventually agreed to resign as minister and leave the community, *if* he received his unpaid back salary (approximately £79 or $4000 by today's standard). Raising the money proved easy, so badly did even those who had supported Parris yearn to close the wounds that he had opened in Salem Village.

Samuel Parris resigned in July 1696 and left the village forever in the following year to become a schoolmaster and merchant in another town. By then, Parris had come to recognize the enormity of his responsibility for the events that had taken place. So had others involved in stirring up the witchcraft craze (including the "afflicted" Ann Putnam Junior, who later begged forgiveness for her actions). "To see a dear friend torn, wounded, and the blood streaming down his face and body, will much affect the heart," Parris had preached in an August 1693 sermon. "But much more when those wounds we see, and that streaming blood we behold, accuseth *us* as the vile actors . . . much more when our consciences tell us that we, our cruel hands, have made those wounds, and the bloody instruments by which our dearest friend was gored, were of our own forging."

When he left Salem, Samuel Parris took with him his daughter Betty, whose strange sickness had begun the events of 1692 in the village, and his younger son Noyes, born during those hysterical months and named after the Reverend Nicholas Noyes, a prime supporter of the Salem witchcraft trials. No record tells us whether Betty Parris ever recovered from her afflictions. As for Noyes Parris, he grew to adulthood only to become insane and to die in that unfortunate condition.

6 Puritan New England and the Middle Colonies

The *Speedwell* leaked so badly that it could not be trusted to cross the Atlantic. The ship had made two unsuccessful starts from Plymouth, England. The twice-disappointed passengers, thirty-five Pilgrims, as they later called themselves, were members of a small sect of religious dissenters who had sailed to Plymouth on the *Speedwell* from the Dutch city of Leyden. Several hundred Pilgrims had taken refuge at Leyden years earlier. Now the thirty-five joined dozens of other passengers, Pilgrims and non-Pilgrims alike, aboard a larger vessel, the *Mayflower*, which sailed for the Virginia colony on September 16, 1620. The 102 passengers had accepted an offer made by London merchants to settle in Virginia and exchange their hard work in return for the chance to build new lives in the wilderness.

The uncomfortable trans-Atlantic voyage lasted nine weeks. Men, women, children, chickens, pigs, and goats all jostled for room on the overcrowded *Mayflower*. Although illnesses struck passengers and crew, all but one person survived the crossing, and two babies were born during the voyage. Somehow the ship managed to drift hundreds of miles northward and off course, far to the north of Virginia, anchoring first near the tip of Cape Cod on November 11. Although they lacked legal title to the land, the group determined to sail no farther. They would build their community somewhere in the vicinity, but less exposed to storms than at the ocean's edge on Cape Cod.

Even before the Pilgrims found a town site, and in the absence of either a royal charter or authority from their merchant sponsors, those aboard ship committed themselves to organizing a government. Forty-one of the forty-four men on the *Mayflower* signed a document, the Mayflower Compact, in which they agreed to form a colony and to obey its laws and its officials. There were no other English settlements in the region (such as those in Virginia, whose assembly had met for the first time the previous year) for the Pilgrims to associate with. The signers of the Mayflower Compact promised to "combine ourselves together into a civill body politick, for our better ordering and preservation and . . . to enacte, constitute, and frame such just and equall laws."

The *Mayflower* weighed anchor again and sailed up the coast, arriving on December 21 at another harbor, which the group named Plymouth. There they went ashore to build their colony, not knowing that only half the hundred or so settlers would survive that winter. The death toll mounted for reasons already familiar at Jamestown: disease, hunger, passivity, and the exhausting ocean voyage. In addition, the Pilgrims had not been prepared for the long and harshly cold New England winter. Those who survived gratefully accepted help from friendly local Indians as they learned to plant the local corn, trade for furs, and explore the surrounding forests and rivers of that unfamiliar countryside, soon to be called New England. In the fall of 1621, after harvest, the Pilgrims held a three-day festival of thanksgiving to which ninety Indians were invited.

The devout Pilgrims were simple and modest people who dealt fairly, both with the Indians and with their merchant sponsors back in England. Their colony—which existed independently until it was absorbed into the Massachusetts Bay colony in 1691—struggled for decades to repay debts owed in England, colonists working hard but without notable success to become solvent, and the colony expanded only slowly within the area. The population of Plymouth never increased, not

even in irregular spurts as it did at Jamestown; after a decade of settlement, there were still fewer than four hundred people. Nevertheless, William Bradford, the colony's first governor, wrote truly in his chronicle of the Pilgrim experiment, *Of Plymouth Plantation*: "as one small candle may light a thousand, so the light here kindled hath shone unto many . . ."

Portrayals of the Pilgrims praying together shortly before they disembarked at Plymouth (or earlier on Cape Cod) became a mythic part of America's colonial heritage during the nineteenth century, when this one was painted. (NYPL/Picture Collection)

William Bradford became governor of the Pilgrim's Plymouth colony in 1621 and was re-elected a number of times. His life was inseparable from that of the Pilgrim settlement, and he later became its most famous chronicler with Of Plymouth Plantation. *(Culver Pictures)*

THE PURITAN MIGRATION: ORIGINS OF THE "BIBLE COMMONWEALTH"

Beginning in the late 1620s another much larger group of English religious dissenters, the Puritans, migrated to New England to found another colony. They proved more aggressive, better organized, more expansionist, and wealthier than the Pilgrims. Leading Puritans (including John Winthrop, later first governor of the Massachusetts Bay colony) managed to gain a royal charter from Charles I in 1629. The charter provided for a governor and a number of "assistants" whom "freemen" or shareholders of the Massachusetts Bay Company would elect while meeting in a general assembly four times each year. These company officials were to manage the colony's affairs, make its laws, punish wrongdoers, assign lands, and otherwise run matters in Massachusetts Bay.

The company organized an advance expedition of "old planters" during the summer of 1629, five ships bearing several hundred colonists, cattle, supplies and Indian trade goods. They sailed to New England and took over a small settlement founded the previous year on the Naumkeag River, calling the new community "Salem" or "house of peace." It was at Salem, where witches would be pursued so avidly six decades later, that New England Puritan civilization first took root.

The following year, 1630, seventeen ships from England brought the Puritans' new governor, John Winthrop, and another thousand settlers. Because of religious persecution, Winthrop and his colleagues had decided to transfer the company's charter and government to the New World, safely out of the grasp of unfriendly royal officials.

Stopping first at Salem, where the older Puritan migrants struggled to survive in crude surroundings (many living in tents or Indian huts), the group's leaders judged the community a poor location for their chief settlement. Food and land capable of decent cultivation were in short supply, considering the many new settlers already on the way from England. Winthrop and his advisers decided to shift the center of Puritan control from Salem farther south, landing this time in Boston harbor where a new string of towns quickly developed in the surrounding bay area—foremost among them Boston itself. Within little more than a decade, over 20,000 additional settlers joined this Puritan "exodus" from Old England. This "Great Migration" gave New England by 1640 a population more than twice that of the Virginia colony, despite the latter's far longer history of settlement.

The Puritans came to create a society organized for God's purposes as they understood them. It would be a "covenanted community" in the American wilderness fit to serve as a model for Europeans to follow in completing the Protestant Reformation. Even before landing in America, John Winthrop had preached such a sermon aboard his

John Winthrop was a man of refinement and sensitivity. Though some questioned his arbitrary rulings (he had no faith in democracy), none doubted his integrity. (American Antiquarian Society)

ship, the Arbella. He defined the religious purposes for which Puritans had come to America. Their community would be "as a City set upon a hill, in the open view of all the earth; the eyes of the world are upon us . . ." Solving the problems of survival that had bedeviled the Jamestown colony became, if not easy, at least simpler than it had been for the Virginians because the Puritans had clearly stated goals. No massive search for gold or other treasures preoccupied Massachusetts Bay; nor did its settlers pursue imaginary inland routes to Asia, unrealistic manufacturing ventures, or unknown sites of "lost colonies"—all of which had been done at Jamestown.

The Puritans, like the Pilgrims before them, fished and farmed and sought after practical, easily developed sources of export trade (primarily lumber, furs, and fish). Nor did they suffer from a shortage of needed laborers or an excess of "gentlemen at leisure." Puritan immigrants, apart from hardworking farmers and cattle herders, included a variety of artisans, merchants, lawyers, ministers, and other groups which quickly gave each Puritan town a rich mixture of occupations. Nor was money or administrative talent in short supply, either in New England or among the English backers of the Puritan experiment. Thus the permanent settlements that spread out quickly along the coastline and inland sections of Massachusetts Bay never underwent the perilous *early* years of imminent disaster so familiar to the older settlers of Jamestown. Above all else, New England settlers of the 1630s shared common religious beliefs and values.

THE ENGLISH REFORMATION AND PURITAN BELIEFS

Most of those who settled the Virginia colony in its founding decades were members of the Church of England, itself a relatively recent creation of Henry VIII. Christians throughout Europe had lived for over a thousand years within the unifying orbit of Roman Catholicism, when, in 1517, a German Augustinian monk named Martin Luther began his world-shaking denunciations of papal rule, church corruption, and overly elaborate church ritual and hierarchy. Luther's Reformation received the backing of several German princes and, later, of rulers elsewhere in Europe, such as England's Henry VIII, who were anxious to staunch the flow of local wealth to Rome, to gain church lands for themselves, and to increase their authority over the populace—and their support within their countries—at the Papacy's expense. Henry's immediate concern was to ensure a legal divorce from

his then-wife, Catherine, who had failed to produce a male offspring as heir to the throne, so that he could remarry.

Protestantism, as the general movement for church reformation became known, gained powerful allies in the rising monarchs of nation-states such as England and among groups within society most affected by the social instability that religious upheaval both reflected and reinforced. Rising merchant classes, entrepreneurial landowners, professional classes, such as the new body of lawyers allied to monarchs in court or parliamentary roles—all of these "middle-class" elements within European society contributed meaningfully to the different Protestant sects.

Nothing distinguished the web of reformist doctrine more fully than conflicts between Protestant and Catholic views of "sin." Although all Christians believed (and believe) that mankind's "original sin" derived initially from the fall of Adam in the Garden of Eden, in practice Catholicism by the sixteenth century had come to view human decline with relative tolerance. So long as an individual relied regularly upon the authority of the church, his or her sins could be alleviated without extraordinary exertions.

But for Protestants, especially those who followed the stern teachings of the Swiss lawyer and theologian John Calvin, human beings were obliged to strive relentlessly against every manifestation of sin in their behavior and thoughts. Neither priests nor rituals could replace, in this view, the obligation of each person to pursue *actively* his or her own spiritual salvation. Like their Calvinist brethren on the Continent, English "Puritans"[1] believed that God had "predestined" some for eternal salvation and others for damnation. God's grace had determined the "elect" or "company of saints" from the beginning of time, not because of any intrinsic goodness on their part but of His own volition. Most human beings were to try and live devout lives, *as if* they had been chosen one of God's elect, while searching for signs of Gods grace (or the opposite). Nothing that occurred at Salem in 1692 during the witchcraft trials could have

---

[1] The term "Puritan" was used to describe individuals intent upon "purifying" the Church of England during the Protestant Reformation in that country.

surprised believing Puritans, at least with regard to the examining magistrates presenting "evidence" that persons considered moral pillars of the community were in reality agents of the Devil. For all true Puritans believed that only God knew with assurance which people *really* lived among the "invisible" company of the saved—or the damned.

Among Puritans, then, there existed an obligation to conduct at every moment a spiritual accounting. Only those who had undergone actual "conversion" experiences, those who had personally experienced God's grace, entered into the first ranks of Puritan society during the early seventeenth century. Since Puritans did not believe in the exoneration of sins by absolution, the pursuit of their own moral impurities offered constant activity for the Puritan conscience. The events at Salem in 1689, therefore, involving constant calibration of moral behavior and assessments of individual sinfulness that might have been deemed excessive in many *non*-Puritan communities at the time, seemed only the normal pattern of life within Puritan society.

Since, for the Puritans, individuals and not whole groups achieved salvation, freely given and predestined by God, the role of priests or churches underwent fundamental change. Puritan ministers devoted themselves to providing moral and theological guides by examining the Bible and sermonizing. Exact and comprehensive understanding of the Old and New Testaments replaced ritualized worship that Puritans thought extraneous to determining God's will and obeying it.

When Henry VIII broke with Catholicism, he hoped to minimize the changes in doctrines and rituals that his Church of England would follow, a policy continued by Henry's daughter, Queen Elizabeth. But Puritan attacks on the monarchy and on the Church of England intensified under James I (1603–25). The reformers demanded that all vestiges of Catholicism be abolished and that each congregation be considered self-governing (that is, Congregationalist).

Some dissenters dismissed the idea of reforming the Church of England. Among those "purifiers" who wanted *complete* separation were the Pilgrims or "Separatists." Others, non-separating Congregationalists, remained in England to battle

for church and political reform, among them the Puritans, though thousands of these "*non*-separating congregationalists" would later migrate to America. Thus the chief distinction between *Separatist* Pilgrims and *non-separatist* Puritans concerned a theological argument over whether to try and purify the Church of England from within or, as the Pilgrims believed, to abandon the effort entirely and *separate* from the "impure" English mother church to found an entirely separate sect.

James's son, Charles I, came to the throne in 1625. Charles attempted to extend royal authority by ruling and taxing without Parliament. His appointee as Archbishop of Canterbury, William Laud, began a full-scale campaign against the Puritans, demanding that all conform to the Church of England's practices. As the persecution continued, both on religious and political grounds, John Winthrop and the other leading Puritans of the Massachusetts Bay Company finally decided on a transfer of their colony's government and charter to New England, where distance alone would ensure less interference in religious and political practices by royal authority.

PURITAN SOCIETY IN NEW ENGLAND: THE PURSUIT OF PERFECTION

The transfer decision ensured that Puritanism in the New World would retain significant freedom from English restraints. Unlike Jamestown, where the Virginia Company had interfered continuously, Massachusetts Bay could devise its own laws and governing proceedings. This remarkable measure of independence allowed the Puritan communities of New England to evolve free from English restraints for more than a half-century.

Puritans based their government on a set of political ideas derived from religion. In this view, government represented a God-given mechanism for restraining man's innate sinfulness. *All* government derived from what Puritans considered a formal agreement—a "covenant"—between rulers and ruled under God. Those Puritans who made the Atlantic crossing to New England believed that their society had a *special* covenant with God to build their holy "City upon a Hill." All of Europe would turn to Massachusetts Bay as a model in time, or so they reasoned. Even aboard the *Arbella,* John Winthrop spoke for other Puritan leaders when he warned in a sermon that God "will expect a strict performance" from the new arrivals, since His covenant with Massachusetts Bay had "given us leave to draw our own Articles."

Political leadership in Puritan Massachusetts fell naturally into the hands of church members, those "visible saints" who could provide some evidence of genuine conversion experiences and of model Christian behavior. To consider oneself "converted" meant, for the Puritans, to have undergone a transforming personal religious experience which signaled—both to the individual in question and to other members of his church—apparently "visible" evidences of God's grace. Those who underwent such experiences continued testing themselves and their moral behavior most strenuously for continual confirmation of their position among the "saved."

Inevitably the Puritan ministers played a major role, not simply in church life but in the political lives of the towns as well (though not through holding elective office). Despite the close relations between church and state in Massachusetts Bay, never could the colony have been termed a genuine "theocracy," where ministers exercise political power by virtue of their *church* offices. Rather, the relation between ministers and the governing officials in Puritan New England, though intimate, clearly provided for distinct realms of authority. Moreover, many of the colony's leaders—from the 1630s to the witch trial period—from Winthrop to Phips—were vigorous and aggressive secular figures and not ministers: lawyers, landowners, merchants, and teachers among them.

When Winthrop and other members of the company gathered to organize their society, the structure of government emerged directly from the charter. It provided for the members or freemen of the company to meet four times yearly in a "General Court" which, once a year, would select a governor, deputy governor, and eighteen assistants. These officials would run the company—that is,

the colony—for a year until the next election by the company's full membership.

The General Court met for the first time in October 1630 in the newly founded community of Charlestown. At that time, "Company" formally became "Colony." In May 1631, most of the colony's church members—116 in all—became freemen, and the number expanded steadily in the years ahead. In order to keep control of the government in the hands of believing Puritans, church membership became a fixed condition for being made a freeman. Within the next few years, each town in Massachusetts Bay's commonwealth gained the right to elect representatives to the General Court, which had evolved into a representative colonial legislature comparable to Virginia's House of Burgesses.

But the Bay colony's affairs remained in the hands of a Puritan elite, despite constant pressure from freemen or those who wished to become freemen for a greater share of power. Thus John Winthrop served as governor for eleven years, although not continuously. His periodic ouster at election time by Puritan rivals showed that even the most respected leaders in the colony could not hope to rule continuously.

Puritans brought with them not simply a set of religious ideals but also English patterns and beliefs that often mixed uneasily in the new colony. Demands for a written legal code, for example, quickly arose among dissatisfied settlers, and the earliest Puritan efforts to create such a body of laws combined biblical injunctions, English common law, and statutes passed by the Massachusetts General Court. Finally, in 1648, a revised code known as the Laws and Liberties of Massachusetts—mixing all these elements—became the colony's fundamental legal code. Punishments were generally harsh by today's standards but not by those of the seventeenth century. In every town and county, a local court system had taken root, with the governor's council of assistants serving as Massachusetts's highest court of appeals. Special courts were also established for extraordinary occasions similar to the court that Governor Phips created to try accused witches.

Within each town, the Puritan church exercised remarkable influence and control. Both re-

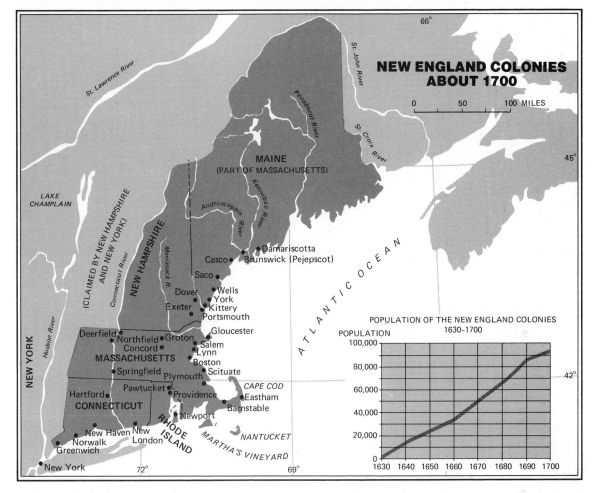

NEW ENGLAND COLONIES ABOUT 1700

POPULATION OF THE NEW ENGLAND COLONIES 1630-1700

By 1700, the New England colonies had a population of 92,763. Over three-fourths of this total lived in Massachusetts and Connecticut. Northern New England, as can be seen, had not yet taken on the form familiar to us today.

Maine's English beginnings went back to a grant to proprietors Sir Ferdinando Gorges and John Mason. In 1622 they received the land between the Merrimac and Kennebec rivers. They did little to build up a colony. Most early settlers came from Massachusetts, and the region remained part of that state until 1820.

In 1629 Gorges and Mason divided their lands. Mason received the region between the Piscataqua and Merrimac rivers, which he named New Hampshire. Like Maine, it had many ties to Massachusetts. The colony became a separate royal province in 1679. Both New Hampshire and New York claimed it, but there were no English settlements until the eighteenth century.

ligious worship and the monitoring of moral behavior were normal aspects of *daily* behavior for every churchgoer—not only church "members" but all residents—in Puritan New England. Although each congregation chose its own minister and particular pattern of worship without interference from other churches, every resident of a town had an obligation to attend services regularly, contribute money or goods toward a minister's support, and accept whatever scrutiny and criticism other church members might provide. Rarely have the members of a society watched one another as closely as in seventeenth-century Puritan New England. Rarely have members of a community

Harvard College was founded in 1636 in large measure to train ministers. The middle of the three halls pictured here was named for Judge William Stoughton of the Salem trials. (NYPL/Stokes Collection)

been bound by such intricate networks of religious, moral, and economic attitudes and regulations as those that affected the Puritan towns of New England.

Puritans placed high value on education. How else could a Christian know the Bible? Many Puritan leaders were university-educated, and Puritans determined to preserve this background in the American wilderness. Village schools were established in most towns, and parents were required by law to make certain that their children (and others in the household) learned to read. Secondary schools modeled after those in England also appeared, and Harvard College was established in 1636, using the same curriculum as that employed at the best English colleges. Massachusetts Bay had the first printing press in the English settlements; it published not only sermons but also almanacs, schoolbook primers, and psalms. The first book published in Massachusetts was the Bay Psalm Book in 1636.

New England Puritans led a communal existence compressed into towns sprinkled neatly across the landscape. From the early establishment of communities such as Salem and Boston along the seacoast to the development of town sites inland, the migrants to Massachusetts Bay often passed quickly through the older settlements only long enough to lay groundwork for newer towns of their own. All groups of freemen had the right to request from the Massachusetts General Court a grant of land upon which to establish a new town. Once settlers reached the site of their new community, they took pains to lay out a full plan for the town, complete with a central commons and a location for the church. By reserving a large portion of land as "common" land for grazing animals, they often achieved a combination of personal landholding and communal agriculture. The town pattern provided an effective compromise between the Puritan concern for a structure sufficiently closed to ensure supervision of religious and moral life and a structure sufficiently flexible to allow room for individual economic and social enterprise. Anyone dissatisfied with a specific town could always pack up and either move to another community or hope to find enough other malcontents to establish a town more to one's liking.

In later periods of communal stress, such as the one that preceded the Salem witchcraft trials, New England Puritans searched relentlessly for external, "visible" signs of God's disapproval to explain the *internal* turbulence. Indian wars, famines, plagues, foreign invasions, and political setbacks were usually seen as tokens of divine judgment. In the early decades, however, the ministers and governors of Massachusetts Bay had found more signs of divine *approval* than rejection.

A prosperous economic life seemed only the most notable of these signs. From the beginning of migration, New England Puritans practiced a mixture of economic pursuits that ensured self-sufficiency for most communities. Farming the rocky land adjacent to the New England coast proved less profitable than agriculture in the valleys farther inland in Massachusetts Bay and in the Connecticut Valley. Those who preferred not to farm often fished or traded with the Indians for furs, and an abundance of forest woods and plants served as additional staples of the export trade from earliest years. African and Indian slaves came to the colony by mid-century, but slavery itself never became as economically or socially important as in the Southern colonies. A number of merchants—men such as Salem's Philip England and Charlestown's Nathaniel Cary—grew wealthy, and such entrepreneurs became an increasingly significant element in the political and even religious life of Massachusetts Bay, not always to the satisfaction of the older ministerial class.

On the whole, however, the society that evolved under Puritan rule in New England held more freemen than servants, more craftsmen than merchants, and still more farmers and fishermen. There were far fewer gradations in rank and prosperity than in England or in the plantation colonies to the south. The bedrock of Puritan New England society seemed at all levels to be characterized by a remarkable measure of independence, self-sufficiency, and self-confidence. Only when all three had declined profoundly could an event as horrendous as the Salem witch trials have occurred. Had any such disorder threatened the colony's peace in their lifetime, the founders of New England would undoubtedly have moved swiftly to bring matters under stern control.

The Ben Franklin hand press. (Eliot Elisofon, Life Magazine © 1959 Time, Inc.)

NEW ENGLAND MIGRATIONS

Puritans seemed forever poised to move again. As wave after wave of migrants arrived in Massachusetts Bay from England during the 1630s, the "older" townships of the earliest settlers—Salem, Boston, Charlestown, Newton, Watertown, Dorchester, and Roxbury—often served mainly as departure points into newer communities. The movement went not only up the coast toward

Maine or south, impinging upon the Plymouth townships, but inland toward the forests and river-beds to the west. With the founding of each town, as the population spread out over the colony, the central authority of Massachusetts Bay's General Court became less binding. By the mid-1630s, Puritans had begun moving beyond the lands and authority of the commonwealth itself. Some had private visions of God's purpose in New England. Others wished greater authority both to enlarge their own lands and to practice variations of the doctrines that ruled in Massachusetts Bay.

The Founding of Connecticut

Expeditions by traders from Plymouth and Massachusetts Bay had reached the lush farming lands of the Connecticut Valley as early as 1632, and small groups of settlers began trickling into the valley by mid-decade. One of the Massachusetts Bay colony's leading ministers, Thomas Hooker, petitioned the General Court in 1635 to allow him to take his congregation there in order to found a new settlement, still nominally under the control of Massachusetts Bay. Political and religious disagreements figured in Hooker's unhappiness. He felt that ties between church and state were too close in Massachusetts and believed that participation in town affairs should not be limited to church members alone. During the next few years, other groups of migrants from Massachusetts joined Hooker's band and founded towns at Hartford, Wethersfield, Windsor, and additional points in the Connecticut Valley. Representatives from these towns issued in 1639 the "Fundamental Orders of Connecticut," a compact that served as a frame of government similar to that of Massachusetts Bay in many ways but different in one "fundamental": there was no religious test for town "freemenship," and all men acceptable to the majority of town householders would be "freemen" and voters. Unlike Massachusetts, then, the Puritan society of Connecticut would not be ruled by "visible saints," even in its earliest year. The colony finally obtained a charter from King Charles II in 1662 that confirmed its control over the Connecticut Valley towns.

Anne Hutchinson and Puritan Dissent

Two leading dissenters, Roger Williams (see p. 116) and Anne Hutchinson, migrated to the Narragansett Bay area. Anne Hutchinson, like Williams, had directly challenged the authority and beliefs of orthodox New England Puritans. Hutchinson showed, among other things, that a religiously trained and imaginative woman could effectively dispute theology with the major Puritan ministers of the period. The matter under contention went to the heart of Puritan concerns in the Bible Commonwealth. Hutchinson challenged the view that proper conduct, moral behavior, and Christian piety—visible evidence of what Puritans called "sanctification"—necessarily foreshadowed "justification" or the divine infusion of the Holy Spirit. Good "works," in short, did not determine divine "grace," according to Hutchinson. Puritans called this heresy (which had antecedents in the history of Christianity) "antinomianism." Anne Hutchinson had begun holding Tuesday meetings in her home where she and her friends would

Anne Hutchinson, who immigrated to Boston in 1634, soon became a figure of controversy within orthodox Puritan circles. Tried for blasphemy in 1637, she was exiled from the colony.

discuss orthodox theology and then her own views. Her arguments appeared to threaten the established order as too "individualistic," encouraging above all else personal communion with God and individual alertness to such divine "infusion." At a trial conducted by the General Court, Anne Hutchinson defended herself brilliantly but sealed her fate in the colony when she asserted an awareness of the deity through "immediate" personal revelation and not through the normal church practices. Hutchinson was ordered banished from Massachusetts Bay. She settled with her family and a number of followers on an island in Narragansett Bay (Aquidneck) in 1638. Five years later, having moved to what is now New York, she fell victim to a band of attacking Indians.

Both Roger Williams and Anne Hutchinson showed to orthodox Puritan leaders in Massachusetts Bay what effects *excessive* zeal could have on talented individuals. John Winthrop's "City upon a Hill" could handle the religiously lax more easily than it could absorb overenthusiastic believing spirits intent upon pursuing private religious truths. Such visions, Winthrop and his colleagues feared, might just as easily come from the Devil as from the Lord, which made first-generation Puritans extremely cautious, for example, when the occasional church member complained of "witches" or "evil presences" in their midst. Puritans guarded against such disruptions within the community during the earlier decades because they threatened to untangle the carefully maintained structure of religious and civil authority within Massachusetts Bay. For several generations, the colony's leaders proved confident and successful when handling such menacing signs. Communal pressures, jailings, banishments, and even executions could deal with those who chose direct communion with God in place of properly channeled church worship.

Catholic "New France"

From earliest settlement, the Puritans at Massachusetts Bay found themselves coming into contact with French traders and seamen from the North. At various times during the seventeenth century, the Puritans engaged in wary but amicable contacts with French officials in the area which came to be known as Canada, but the Puritans remained deeply suspicious of these occasional links to the Catholic foreigners so close to their borders.

The original European settlers in Canada were the French, who first came in the early seventeenth century. Like the English in Virginia, these colonists were sent by a trading company operating under royal charter. The stockholders were allowed to set up a fur trade, but they were also committed to establish colonies in Canada.

Once in Canada, however, men were lured from the stern task of hacking out pioneer farms by the free life of the forest and by dreams of a quick fortune made in the fur trade. They became hunters and trappers—often living with the Indians—rather than settling down to raise large broods of children. By 1660 there were only 2000 inhabitants in New France, compared with 75,000 in the thirteen English colonies. This scant population did not produce enough food to support itself, nor was it a match for hostile Indians. The French government took over the colony in 1663.

During the next hundred years the government made a systematic effort to people New France. Population did increase, but in 1760 the colony fell to the British in the French and Indian War. By 1763, the British controlled the four chief regions of Canada—Quebec, Nova Scotia, Newfoundland, and Rupert's Land. (See Chapter 8, p. 163.)

THE MIDDLE COLONIES: ORIGINS AND PATTERNS

From their earliest days of settlement, the Puritans considered themselves an embattled society. Not only did they suffer from *internal* strains but non-English colonial outposts hemmed them in on both the north and south. Thus, during the seventeenth century, Massachusetts Bay had at times to trade or negotiate with the authorities of Catholic "New France" along the St. Lawrence River. There was less contact with the Dutch Protestants of "New Netherland," although in some ways, this colony remained the most direct threat

Roger Williams

(Brown Brothers)

Salem symbolized not only the beginning but the end of Puritan control of the Massachusetts Bay colony. In 1692, the witchcraft trials and their aftermath signaled the death knell both of Puritan religious authority and of the colony's independence from royal control. More than a half-century earlier, however, the most explosive challenge to domination of Massachusetts Bay by its founding ministers and magistrates also began, appropriately, at Salem. Provoking the controversy with John Winthrop and the other Puritan leaders was a heretical minister and self-professed "Separatist" named Roger Williams.

Williams arrived in New England in 1631, age twenty-eight. He promptly stirred tempers in the colony by declining to fill temporarily the vacant post of minister in Boston. That church, he asserted, had not truly separated itself from the Church of England.

After a stint as a minister in Plymouth, marked as usual by controversies concerning religious "purity," Williams departed for Salem, where he was elected pastor in April 1635. By then, Roger Williams had managed to confront the authorities on other questions as well. He challenged the legitimacy of Massachusetts Bay's title to its lands, arguing that the English king had no right to grant lands owned by the Indians. Williams even suggested that the Puritans either return to Eng-

land or confirm their land title properly with the Indians. He opposed laws enforcing taxes to pay for church expenses and those that made church attendance mandatory.

Ironically, Roger Williams arrived at an acceptance of virtual religious *tolerance* precisely because of his uncompromising spiritual *intolerance.* Thus Williams believed in the complete *separation* of church and state because of the overriding importance he attached to *individual* pursuit of true faith. Spokesman for a vision of religious "purity" far more personal than the communal faith of Massachusetts Bay, Williams opposed strongly the oligarchical control exercised by the Puritan leaders. On virtually every fundamental issue, from church membership to political rights and from land titles to religious conscience, then, Williams disagreed. Small wonder that the colony's General Court tried him during the fall of 1635 and ordered him banished.

The dissenter fled Massachusetts Bay in midwinter and took refuge among the Narragansett Indians. In their midst, Williams and his few supporters established a new settlement, which he called Providence Plantation. Lacking a royal charter, Williams devised a "compact," which did not require church membership or any other religious test for voting in town affairs. It recognized no ecclesiastical role in civil matters whatsoever, demanding instead that laws be made simply "by the major consent of the present inhabitants." All sects were welcomed without prejudice to the community, and church and state were entirely separate, with the right to worship according to one's own creed guaranteed. Several other towns were founded in the Narrangansett Bay area by additional groups of Puritan dissenters and by other Protestants including Baptists and Quakers. In 1642, Williams traveled to England and obtained from Parliament in 1644 a charter for the "Incorporation of Providence Plantations." The four towns of Providence, Newport, Warwick, and Aquidneck (later Portsmouth) united formally under the charter in 1647, and the colony of Rhode Island, which evolved from this union, continued to reflect the representative and libertarian ideals of its founder, Roger Williams, who died in 1683.

to the cohesion of Puritan New England. Still, the relatively brief sea war between England and Holland (1652–54) did not greatly affect either Massachusetts Bay or New Netherland. England remained a land in turmoil for most of the decade preceding and the decade following the execution of Charles I in 1649. The English Civil War and Oliver Cromwell's Puritan Revolution affected life in New England more directly than any Dutch merchant colony on its borders.

The Puritan leaders in Massachusetts Bay found immigration drying up after the 1640s, and they also learned to their dismay that the City upon a Hill did not appeal to Cromwell, who regarded New Englanders' pretensions to a measure of political or religious leadership in *his* England as grotesque and absurd. By the end of Cromwell's Protectorate, the New Englanders' early notion of returning in triumph to a transformed England had been thoroughly shattered. New England Puritanism, as one historian wrote, had been "left alone with America." In some ways, therefore, the beginning of the end for New England Puritanism came *not* with the return of Charles II to England in 1660 but with the emergence of Oliver Cromwell's Protectorate two decades earlier. It was Cromwell's imposition of a degree of religious tolerance within England, not restoration of Anglican control two decades later, that dealt the first major blow to the values of Puritan New England, which treated its own dissenters less forgivingly.

New Netherland Becomes New York

The decision by a number of highly placed Massachusetts Bay residents accused of witchcraft during the Salem hysteria of 1692 to flee to New York for safety continued a pattern begun in the earliest years of Puritan rule. As early as the 1630s, Dutch New Netherland served as a refuge for religious dissenters. From its inception, the tolerance of the Dutch colony contrasted vividly with Puritan repressiveness. New Netherland allowed members of all Protestant sects to settle there, and even accepted Jews. At the beginning, however, the Dutch viewed their activites on the North American mainland as a part of more important trading concerns elsewhere. The Englishman Henry Hudson sailed up the large river that now bears his name as agent of the Netherland East Indies Company, seeking an American passage to Asia. Hudson had traded with the local Indians for furs, and more than a decade later, Dutch merchants founded the Netherland *West* India Company in order to develop American trade.

The company founded small trading posts from as far south as the Delaware Valley north to Long Island Sound on the Connecticut River. New Amsterdam on Manhattan Island's tip was established as a trading post in 1624, one of the Dutch outposts, which together came to be known as New Netherland. (In 1626, one of the early governors or "director generals," Peter Minuit, "bought" Manhattan Island from Indians for an amount estimated at from twenty-four to forty dollars in this century's money.)

New Netherland was ruled by its governor and council. There was no popular representation, a typical state of affairs given the status of the colony as a commercial joint stock company. The company's bylaws provided for worship in the Calvinist Dutch Reformed Church but explicitly allowed members of *all* Protestant groups to live in New Netherland without fear of persecution. A number of farmers emigrated along with merchants to New Amsterdam, the chief town within New Netherland, and more than a dozen languages were spoken in this cosmopolitan community. In 1629, the company further encouraged immigration by creating a Charter of Privileges for "Patroons" (great landowners), who were given huge tracts of land in return for bringing over fifty families of farm tenants. Within a few years, the Hudson Valley north of New Amsterdam had been divided into "patroonships" virtually under the feudal control of their owners. (When the English occupied New Netherland, they confirmed these land titles, thereby keeping the patroon system of estate ownership.)

The Dutch colony's most important governor was a soldier named Peter Stuyvesant, who came in 1647, and who extended the control of New Netherland over a Swedish settlement on the Delaware River ("New Sweden"). If religious life remained tolerant during these years, political

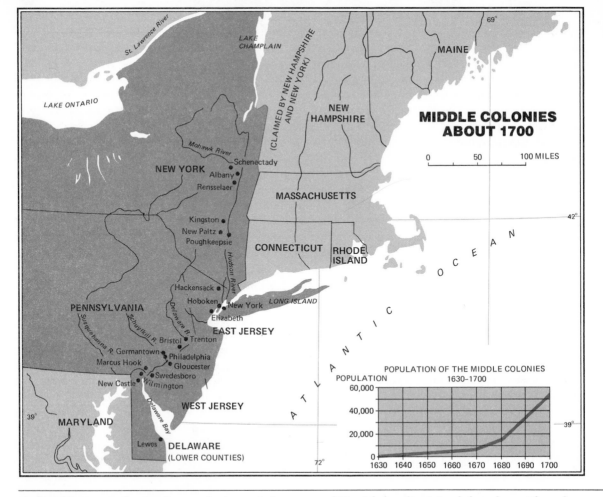

MIDDLE COLONIES ABOUT 1700

POPULATION OF THE MIDDLE COLONIES
1630–1700

The land between the Southern colonies and the New England colonies was known as the Middle Colonies. This region early attracted settlers from many different countries in Europe, and from other colonies.

The Dutch staked one of the first claims in the Middle Colonies on the basis of explorations by Henry Hudson in 1609. Dutch merchants established fur trading posts at Fort Orange (Albany), on the Connecticut River, and on the Delaware River. They called the land they claimed New Netherland. Dutch merchants negotiated a famous real estate deal with the Indians. They purchased Manhattan Island for twenty-four dollars' worth of goods, and changed its name to New Amsterdam.

The Dutch were also responsible for the settlement of Delaware. A Dutchman obtained a charter that organized a company headed by Swedes and Dutchmen. Fifty Swedes sailed up the Delaware River in 1638 and established Fort Christina, on the site of present-day Wilmington. Several Finnish families joined them later. The colony was called New Sweden.

In 1655 the Dutch strengthened their hold on this region by seizing Fort Christina. But New Sweden did not remain in Dutch hands long. King Charles II of England did not like having Dutch settlements wedged in between the English colonies. In 1664 he declared that all the territory between the Connecticut and Delaware rivers belonged to his brother James, the Duke of York. The Dutch, realizing they were in no position to fight, surrendered when an English fleet sailed into New Amsterdam. Thus ended Dutch colonial power in mainland America. The new proprietor, the Duke of York, promptly renamed the colony New York.

Included in James' grant was the region of New Jersey, which had been settled by Swedish and Dutch pioneers. James gave the land to two of his friends, Lord John Berkeley and Sir George Carteret. The province was soon divided into East Jersey and West Jersey. In 1702 England claimed all

life was arbitrary and economic affairs firmly in the hands of an oligarchy of merchants and patrons. Popular government never reached New Netherland. Tensions between Stuyvesant's regime and the English settlers to his north, including those Puritans who had migrated into various Long Island towns, remained serious. During the English Civil Wars of the 1640s and 1650s, however, it proved impossible to extend English control over New Amsterdam and the other Dutch possessions.

Once the monarchy was restored and Charles II took the throne in 1660, however, he began rewarding his favorite supporters with grants of titles and land. One of the largest went to the Duke of York, who received a grant in March 1664 of all the land between the Connecticut and Delaware rivers (including Long Island), most of which happened to belong to the Dutch at the time. The duke dispatched four ships and several hundred soldiers, many of them recruited at Puritan Boston, to New Amsterdam harbor, where they demanded the fort's surrender. Recognizing the futility of resisting the far superior English force, Governor Stuyvesant capitulated on September 8, 1664, and New Amsterdam became New York that same day. Shortly thereafter the British occupied the former Swedish settlements on the Delaware, and the Dutch ceased to be a factor in North America.

New Jersey as a royal colony. There is still a Board of Proprietors for East Jersey and one for West Jersey.

The most successful of the Middle Colonies was Pennsylvania. William Penn, a Quaker, received the land from Charles II in 1681. He envisioned his colony as a refuge for fellow Quakers. Arriving in Pennsylvania in 1682, he carefully studied his property before selecting the site of Philadelphia. Attracted by the prospect of good land, political liberty, and religious tolerance, people flocked to Pennsylvania. By 1700 Philadelphia had 10,000 people. It would eventually outstrip Boston as the largest city in colonial America.

In 1682 Penn convinced the Duke of York to grant him control of the southern portion of the Delaware River. This area, already inhabited by Swedes and Dutch, was known as "the lower counties." It became the colony of Delaware in 1704.

Puritan New England could not take heart from this transfer of power. If anything, it made the task of enforcing religious conformity more difficult, because the Duke of York's agents confirmed their intention to maintain the same standard of religious tolerance as the Dutch within the newly acquired domains. Now there w ere *two* English colonies on New England's borders — Rhode Island and New York — prepared to receive those who rejected the coercion of Puritan society. Another colony, New Jersey, would later emerge from a portion of the Duke of York's grant assigned to a pair of English proprietors, Sir George Carteret and Lord John Berkeley, although New Jersey became a *royal* province in 1702. But sales of land along the Delaware to various Quaker purchasers during the 1670s and 1680s, including a major purchase in 1682 by that sect's most well-connected and aristocratic young leader, William Penn, led to creation of *another* non-Puritan Northern colony, Pennsylvania. All of these circumstances confirmed both the growing importance of religiously "tolerant" provinces within English North America and the increasing isolation of that survivor from a more *intolerant* period in colonial affairs, Puritan New England.

Quakerism and Puritan Massachusetts

Although few Quakers tried to settle in Massachusetts Bay during the seventeenth century, the sect proved especially irritating to Puritan leaders. They reacted mercilessly to Quaker infiltration. The Quakers, also known as the Society of Friends, had emerged as a significant dissenting movement in England. Its leader, George Fox, advocated a form of spiritual individualism even greater than the variety that had caused Anne Hutchinson's banishment. Fox and the other Quakers challenged the notion that ministers stood apart from ordinary believers in any respect, thereby denying the hierarchy that even Puritan churches accepted as legitimate. The Quakers also denied the primacy of biblical authority, believing that Christ's "inner light" entered every human being. Elaborate church ceremonies and even formal preaching seemed without basic spiritual significance to the Quakers, who were also pacifists and egalitarian believers in universal brotherhood. Practically every basic tenet of Quakerism contradicted orthodox doctrine, whether Puritan or Anglican. Although thousands of Quakers were jailed in England, Quakerism became the most dynamic faith within English Protestantism in the second half of the seventeenth century.

Massachusetts Bay passed statutes banning Quakers, and when two Quaker women arrived there from Barbados in 1656, the authorities responded drastically. They had just hanged a local woman for witchcraft. Now the Quaker ladies were undressed and subjected to demeaning bodily examinations comparable to those given at Salem in 1692 in search of witches' tits and similar malign evidences. None were found, so the women were jailed and deported rather than hanged.

The laws governing Quaker intrusion at Massachusetts Bay were then made even more stern. One imprisoned Quaker was beaten unconscious for his beliefs. A Quaker couple failed to pay their fines and, as a consequence, witnessed their two children sold into slavery outside the colony. An old man who tried to help a pair of Quaker women starving in prison found himself banished to Rhode Island in midwinter. In 1658, the General Court approved the death penalty for Quakers who returned after banishment. The following year, two Quakers were hanged and a third, Mary Dyer, banished. When she returned to Boston in 1660, she too went to the gallows.

Quaker Pennsylvania

It was evident to Quakers in England that they needed more hospitable areas to settle in English America, and hundreds drifted into the colonies south of New England even before acquiring their own refuge. The person responsible for providing Quakers with a colony of their own, William Penn, was the son of Admiral Sir William Penn, a leading figure both in the Cromwellian era and during the Restoration period when Charles II "restored" the Stuart monarchy. Young William, born in 1644, converted to Quakerism in 1667 and became passionately devoted to the notion of beginning a colony in America that would receive all groups persecuted for political or religious reasons, not simply Quakers alone. Penn, although a Quaker, remained on good terms with prominent figures in the Stuart Restoration such as the Duke of York, whose troops had conquered New Netherland. With the duke's support, Penn managed to obtain a charter from Charles II (1681) for an area roughly the size of England itself around York's Delaware River territories. Penn and his heirs would hold the land in feudal tenure from the king (a situation that continued up to 1776) and would serve as sole proprietor and ruler, paying Charles only "two Beaver skins" and a fifth share of any precious metals found.

The arrangement was a colossal bargain for Penn and a boon to his fellow Quakers. The king ordered the territory named Pennsylvania, and its proprietor began immediately advertising both in England and on the European continent for farmers and artisans. Settlers were promised generous land grants for farms as well as complete freedom to worship and some political influence through a representative assembly.

Thousands of settlers quickly followed Penn to the new colony during the 1680s. Many came from other English colonies in the New World, while others migrated from Germany, Wales, Ireland, and Holland as well as from England. Penn-

---

Each colonial government had a governor and a legislature. All the legislatures except that of Pennsylvania had two houses. The upper house was usually called the council. The lower house was generally known as the assembly.

There were three main types of colonial governments—royal, proprietary, and self-governing. In a royal colony, the governor and council were appointed by the crown; the assembly was elected by freemen. In a proprietary colony, the proprietor (or his appointee) was appointed by the crown. He in turn named the council, while freemen elected the assembly. In a self-governing colony, freemen elected the governor, the council, and the assembly. In a self-governing corporate colony, directors of the corporation appointed the governor and council; freemen elected the assembly.

For additional information on the original thirteen colonies, see maps on pp. 76, 111, and 118.

Founding of the Thirteen English Colonies

Colony	Early Settlements	Year Founded	Type of Colonial Government
Connecticut	Windsor	1633	Self-governing corporate
	Wethersfield	1634	
	Hartford	1636	
	New Haven	1638	
Delaware	Zwaanedael (Lewes) (settled by Dutch)	1631	Proprietary to 1682/Part of Pennsylvania, 1682–1703/Self-governing corporate after 1703
	Fort Christina (Wilmington) (settled by Swedes)	1638	
Georgia	Darien	1721	Proprietary 1732–54/Royal after 1754
	Savannah	1733	
	Augusta	1735	
Maryland	St. Mary's	1634	Proprietary 1632–91/Royal 1691–1715/ Proprietary after 1715
	Annapolis	1648	
Massachusetts	Plymouth	1620	Self-governing corporate 1620–91/Royal after 1691
	Gloucester	1623	
	Salem	1626	
	Boston	1630	
New Hampshire	Rye	1623	Proprietary 1622–41/Part of Massachusetts, 1641–80/Royal after 1680
	Portsmouth	1624	
New Jersey	Glucester	1623	Proprietary 1664–1702 (divided into East Jersey and West Jersey 1676)/ Royal after 1702
	Hoboken	1630	
	Hackensack	1639	
	Swedesboro	1641	
	Elizabeth	1664	
New York	New Amsterdam (New York) (settled by Dutch)	1609	Colony of Dutch West India Company, 1624–64/Proprietary 1664–85/Royal after 1685
	Kingston (settled by Dutch)	1615	
	Fort Orange (Albany) (settled by Dutch)	1623	
North Carolina	Edenton	1658	Part of Carolina proprietary colony 1670–1712/Separate proprietary colony 1712–29/Royal after 1729
	Currituck	1672	
	Bath	1705	
	New Bern	1710	
Pennsylvania	Marcus Hook (settled by Swedes)	1640	Proprietary
	Bristol	1681	
	Philadelphia	1682	
	Germantown	1683	
Rhode Island	Providence	1636	Self-governing 1636–44/Self-governing corporate 1644–63/Royal after 1663
	Portsmouth	1638	
	Newport	1639	
	Warwick	1643	
South Carolina	Charleston	1670	Part of Carolina proprietary colony 1670–1712/Separate proprietary colony 1712–29/Royal after 1729
	Beaufort	1711	
Virginia	Jamestown	1607	Self-governing corporate 1607–24/Royal after 1624
	Hampton	1610	
	Newport News	1611	

William Penn was granted land on both sides of the Delaware River by Charles II in repayment for a debt owed Penn's father. The younger Penn established a Quaker society, guaranteeing an unusual amount of self-government and religious tolerance. In dealing with the Indians, he was consistently fair. (Colonial Williamsburg)

sylvania quickly became a cosmopolitan haven for dissenters from many countries. That suited the proprietor, who considered the venture his "Holy Experiment" in establishing religious freedom within a colony devoted to a belief in man's essential goodness.

Penn wrote a "Frame of Government" for the colony that provided for a governor (he served himself while in the colony from 1682 to 1684), an appointed council, and an elected assembly whose role remained largely advisory until 1701. Penn also supervised the work of engineers and architects who laid out the plan for his capital city of Philadelphia (the "City of Brotherly Love"), and he personally met with Indian chieftains to confirm through purchase from the Indians the land already granted him by the English king. (Roger Williams would have approved.)

Despite the goodness of man, quarrels broke out. Penn's representatives in the colony fought for power with assembly members demanding the right to *initiate* laws. Penn himself returned in 1699 to help devise "A New Charter of Privileges," which served as the colony's constitution until the revolution. Pennsylvania flourished economically from the start. Farmers spread out over the rich inland riverbed fields, while merchants traded for furs with the Indians and engaged in a variety of other commerce with England, the West Indies, and the other mainland colonies.

By the time he died, Penn recognized that his colonial experiment had become more prosperous than holy. A Quaker elite arose among Pennsylvania's merchants and large landholders and used the assembly as a base to contend for power with those representing the proprietor's interests. Still, Penn's efforts to guarantee religious liberty in his province served as a model for other mainland colonies, spreading the gospel of toleration that Roger Williams had preached without success when battling Puritan orthodoxy earlier in the century.

TOWARD THE WITCHCRAFT TRIALS: THE PARADOX OF PURITAN DECLINE

It is hard to imagine disillusioned Puritans, a scholar of Puritanism once wrote, if only because the group was conditioned to expect disappointment and suffering while obeying God. Nevertheless, from the mid-seventeenth century on, ministers preached constantly on the theme of "declension" or *decline* from the expectations of the founding generation. Even within their own churches, by the 1660s, the Puritans began watering down their stringent standards for membership. Rather than risk antagonizing a large body of believers, whose moral behavior was admirable but who had not undergone religious conversion, the churches of New England agreed in 1662 to a "halfway covenant" membership. Those who practiced high standards of personal behavior could now achieve a "halfway" status within the church, a status normally sufficient to allow freemanship and voting within the town as well as maintenance of their Puritan identity.

The founders had passed from the scene by that time. England had restored the monarchy under Charles II, and Puritanism was a declining faith in the mother country. Second- and third-generation New Englanders could not escape recognizing that their "errand into the wilderness" had been successful—but irrelevant as an example of a City upon a Hill. New England retreated even before the Restoration period into a defensiveness about its virtues, proudly independent from practically any English control and groping toward a new identity.

"I write the Wonders of the Christian Religion," Cotton Mather proclaimed in his *Magnalia Christi Americana*, "flying from the Depravations of Europe, to the American strand." Although Mather stressed the theme of declension—berating his own generation for failing to measure up to their revered fathers—the dilemma faced by late-seventeenth-century Puritans such as Mather reflected a problem of cultural transition. Committed to a set of beliefs that appeared increasingly archaic within their own environment, observing their religion even as faith gave way to economic activity or secular achievement, Puritan leaders like Mather and Stoughton in the 1680s and 1690s found no adequate way to reconcile their society's past and present.

Even the once humbled Indians of New England revived themselves for a final outburst that Puritans viewed as yet another evidence of declension and of God's disfavor. New England had not known a major Indian uprising since the Pequot War of 1636–37, which ended with the bloody suppression of the Pequots and the opening to settlement of the eastern Connecticut region. During the next four decades, white settlers—Puritans and non-Puritans—had driven New England's Indians from their lands, from Maine and New Hampshire south to the New York border. In 1661, Massasoit, king of the Wampanoag Indians who had befriended the Pilgrims, died and his son, Metacom, whom the whites called Philip, took charge. After years of trying to maintain friendly relations with English settlers only to be humiliated in return, Philip and his outnumbered subjects undertook a desperate final stand against the English. It began in June 1675 with an attack on the town of Swansea. Within months, frontier settlements in western Massachusetts had been attacked and destroyed. Philip's Wampanoags were joined by Maine's Abenaki Indians and by the normally peaceful Narragansett tribe from Rhode Island, so that the uprising spread throughout New England.

The Indians managed to wipe out entire settlements in Maine and Massachusetts over the next year, but the English gradually regained the initiative aided by thousands of loyal Indians. They began tracking down the rebellious warriors. Then

Philip's death in 1676 took the steam out of the war, which ended with the almost complete destruction of Indian culture in New England. By the time peace returned to the frontier, one out of every sixteen whites in the region had been killed along with a huge but uncounted number of Indians.

King Philip's war was only a temporary menace, but the English government's decision to revoke the Massachusetts Bay charter in 1684 proved a permanent disaster from which Puritan society never recovered. Massachusetts Bay authorities had alienated Charles II and his advisers almost from the moment he returned to the throne. First, the colony declined to enforce the Navigation Acts (see Chapter 8, p. 154), arguing that England could not regulate trade in its waters because Massachusetts Bay had no representatives in Parliament. Second, the Puritans would not allow other religious groups, including Anglicans, to practice their faith freely. In a number of other ways, the colony displayed its evident belief that it enjoyed freedom from English control in all but name. Massachusetts coined money without permission from the crown, and it refused to allow appeals to English courts. An official of the Lords of Trade, which supervised the colonies, Edward Randolph, toured New England in 1676, reporting back these and other offenses against English authority.

The following year, Massachusetts sent two agents to England to defend its rights, one of them being William Stoughton (later the magistrate at Salem's witch trials). The agents accomplished little, since the Puritan commonwealth could count on few defenders in England by then. Finally, after years of continued resistance by Massachusetts Bay to the Navigation Acts, the Lords of Trade persuaded the Court of Chancery to declare Massachusetts's charter forfeit in October 1684. By 1687, the charters of Connecticut and Rhode Island had also been annulled, thus clearing the ground for imposing direct royal control over New England.

The frustrations of Puritan leaders in Massachusetts Bay grew daily as they watched the old order crumble. Shortly after revocation of the charter in 1684, the first Anglican congregation began holding services in Boston. What would

Winthrop, John Cotton, and the other founders have thought had they witnessed the Anglican parson obtain permission to conduct services in the Puritan's historic Old South Church—while those who had come to attend regular Congregational services waited outside for the Anglicans to conclude their prayers? Adding to this *religious* humiliation came political subordination; that same year, 1686, brought a new royal governor to Massachusetts, Sir Edmund Andros. He ruled a "Dominion of New England"—Massachusetts Bay, Connecticut, Rhode Island, New York, and New Jersey—without a representative assembly. The dominion government also began enforcing the Navigation Acts, imposing taxes without assembly approval. Andros's council also challenged earlier New England land titles as part of the governor's campaign to break the power of the old Puritan oligarchy.

When Bostonians learned in the spring of 1689 that William and Mary of Orange had assumed the throne in England after the Glorious Revolution of 1688, ending the last Stuart king's rule, they promptly arrested Andros and shipped him back to England. There were revolts against Andros's rule in the other dominion colonies, and in New York, rebellious militia led by Jacob Leisler threw the province into a state of civil war for a time before a new royal governor arrived.

Puritan leaders promptly sent Increase Mather, whose ministerial authority would later help terminate the witchcraft agitation, to England on a desperate mission: gaining permission from William and Mary to restore the old Massachusetts Bay charter. Mather failed, and the new charter, which he brought back in 1691, left Massachusetts a crown colony, although with some aspects of limited self-rule. (The assembly, for example, and not the governor, would choose the members of the governor's council.)

By the time the first royal governor under the new regime, William Phips, reached Massachusetts in the midst of the witchcraft crisis in 1692, the end of the old Puritan order seemed complete. Because of Andros, Anglicans worshiped freely in the heart of Congregationalist Boston. Many of Massachusetts Bay's new *economic* elite, especially the merchant princes of Salem Town,

Boston, and other leading seaports, were either Anglicans or otherwise alienated from traditional Puritan dogma. The political disturbances of the Andros period had reduced the previously unchecked *local* authority of Puritan ministers and town officials throughout the commonwealth. Even before the first witchcraft outbreak at Salem, a general mood of uncertainty and foreboding prevailed in Massachusetts Bay. Teetering between the final collapse of *all* Puritan authority and the beginning of its new status under royal control, the leaders of Massachusetts in 1692 were ill-tempered and ill-prepared. They had difficulty in coping,

therefore, with that final assault upon *local* patterns of authority represented by the temporary triumph of the "afflicted" teenagers and their supporters at Salem. With the end of the the witchcraft trials, the Puritan ideal no longer dominated New England's political and social developments as had been the case up to then. The passing of the old Puritan order went unmourned by most New Englanders on the eve of the eighteenth century. They appeared more concerned with the processes of economic growth and social change than with any lingering allegations of spiritual "declension."

Suggested Readings
Chapters 5-6

The Salem Witch Trials

Paul Boyer and Stephen Nissenbaum, *Salem Possessed: The Social Origins of Witchcraft* (1974) and *Salem-Village Witchcraft: A Documentary History* (1972); Sanford J. Fox, *Science and Justice: The Massachusetts Witchcraft Trials* (1968); Chadwick Hansen, *Witchcraft in Salem* (1969); David Levin, *What Happened in Salem?* (1960); Marion L. Starkey, *The Devil in Massachusetts* (1949); C. W. Upham, *Salem Witchcraft* (reprinted, 1959).

Puritanism in New England

James Axtell, *The School Upon a Hill: Education and Society in Colonial New England* (1976); Bernard Bailyn, *The New England Merchants in the Seventeenth Century* (1955); Viola Barnes, *The Dominion of New England* (1923); Emery Battis, *Saints and Sectaries: Anne Hutchinson and the Antinomian Controversy* (1962); Sacvan Bercovitch, *The Puritan Origins of the American Self* (1975); Timothy H. Breen, *The Character of the Good Ruler* (1970); C. E. Clark, *The Eastern Frontier: The Settlement of Northern New England, 1610-1763* (1970); Lawrence A. Cremin, *American Education: The Colonial Experience* (1969); John Demos, *A Little Commonwealth* (1970); R. S. Dunn, *Puritans and Yankees: The Winthrop Dynasty of New England* (1962); Kai Erikson, *Wayward Puritans* (1966); D. H. Flaherty, *Privacy in Colonial New England* (1972); Charles Grant, *Democracy in the Connecticut Frontier Town of Kent* (1961); P. J. Greven, *Four Generations* (1969); David Hall, *The Faithful Shepherd* (1972); Michael Hall, *Edward Randolph and the American Colonies, 1676-1703* (1960); G. H. Haskins, *Law and Authority in Early Massachusetts* (1960); Sydney V. James, *Colonial Rhode Island* (1975); Mary J. A. Jones, *Congregational Commonwealth* (1968); George Langdon, *Pilgrim Colony: A History of New Plymouth, 1620-1691* (1966); Kenneth Lockridge, *A New England Town* (1970); Robert Middlekauff, *The Mathers* (1971); Perry Miller, *Errand Into the Wilderness* (1956), *The New England Mind: From Colony to Province* (1953), *The New England Mind: The Seventeenth Century* (1954), and *Orthodoxy in Massachusetts*

(1959); Edmund S. Morgan, *The Puritan Dilemma* (1958), *The Puritan Family* (1966), *Roger Williams: The Church and the State* (1967), and *Visible Saints* (1963); Samuel E. Morison, *Builders of the Bay Colony* (1930), *The Founding of Harvard College* (1935), and *Harvard in the Seventeenth Century* (2 vols., 1936); Sumner C. Powell, *Puritan Village* (1963); Darrett B. Rutman, *American Puritanism* (1970) and *Winthrop's Boston 1630-1649* (1965); Alan Simpson, *Puritanism in Old and New England* (1955); R. E. Wall, *Massachusetts Bay: The Crucial Decade, 1640-1650* (1972); Ola Winslow, *Master Roger Williams* (1957) and *Meetinghouse Hill* (1952); Larzer Ziff, *Puritanism in America* (1973).

Indians and Puritans

Francis Jennings, *The Invasion of America* (1975); Douglas Leach, *Flintlock and Tomahawk: New England in King Philip's War* (1958) and *The Northern Colonial Frontier, 1607-1763* (1966); Richard Slotnick, *Regeneration Through Violence* (1973); Alden T. Vaughan, *New England Frontier: Puritans and Indians, 1620-1675* (1965); Anthony F. C. Wallace, *The Death and Rebirth of the Seneca* (1970).

The Middle Colonies

Charles M. Andrews, *The Colonial Period of American History* (Vols. I and III, 1934-1937); Van Cleaf Bachman, *Peltries or Plantations* (1969); Daniel J. Boorstin, *The Americans: The Colonial Experience* (1958); Charles Boxer, *The Dutch Seaborne Empire, 1600-1800* (1965); Carl Bridenbaugh, *Cities in the Wilderness, 1625-1742* (1938); E. B. Bronner, *William Penn's "Holy Experiment": The Founding of Pennsylvania* (1962); Thomas J. Condon, *New York Beginnings* (1968); Wesley F. Craven, *The Colonies in Transition, 1660-1713* (1968) and *New Jersey and the English Colonization of North America* (1964); Mary M. Dunn, *William Penn: Politics and Conscience* (1967); M. B. Endy, *William Penn and Early Quakerism* (1973); Rufus Jones, *Quakers in the American Colonies* (1911); Michael Kammen, *Colonial New York* (1975); L. H. Leder,

Robert Livingston and the Politics of Colonial New York, 1654–1728 (1961); David S. Lovejoy, The Glorious Revolution in America (1972); Gary B. Nash, Quakers and Politics: Pennsylvania, 1681–1726 (1968); J. E. Pomfret, The Province of East New Jersey, 1609–1702 (1962) and The Province of West New Jersey, 1609–1702 (1956); Ellis L. Raesley, Portrait of New Netherland (1945); J. R. Reich, Leisler's Rebellion (1953); F. B. Tolles, Meeting House and Counting House: The Quaker Merchants of Colonial Philadelphia (1963) and Quakers and the Atlantic Culture (1960); Allen W. Trelease, Indian Affairs in Colonial New York: The Seventeenth Century (1960); Thomas J. Wertenbaker, The Founding of American Civilization: The Middle Colonies (1938); H. E. Wildes, William Penn (1974).

The British colonies in North America at the time of Bacon's Rebellion and the Salem trials had been little more than a series of isolated settlements scattered along the eastern coast. The planters of Virginia and the Puritans of Massachusetts, like other early colonists, were still basically Europeans. They continued to identify with the European concepts of home, family, culture, and government. Royal authority remained almost unchallenged, and when social crises occurred, more often than not, they were resolved by the exercise of British power. Thus Governor Berkeley in Virginia, backed by English soldiers, put an end to Bacon's rebels, and in similar fashion, Governor Phips in Massachusetts clamped a final lid on the Salem hysteria.

By the mid-eighteenth century, two generations after the fateful events described in the previous episodes, all this had changed. With remarkable speed, the British colonists and other settlers in English North America had created a distinctly new and American society. From Georgia to Maine, the settlement line was almost solid, as population expanded along with agriculture and commerce. Cities like Boston, Philadelphia, and New York became almost as large and as wealthy as many European urban centers.

Culturally, the new society remained mostly British, while it absorbed large clusters of German, Dutch, and Swedish immigrants (among others) who settled along the seaboard. But as it grew, British North America became increasingly conscious of its identity and style as distinctly American rather than English. The events that moved the thirteen colonies toward their fateful decision to break with England in the mid-1770s came at the end of two decades during which a multiplicity of actions had engraved American patterns of family life, religious and cultural values, economic behavior, and—most importantly—political autonomy upon the older British fabric of this society. The chapters that follow describe this process of "Americanization," the political strife that ensued from it, and the creation of a new nation from the turmoil of revolution.

Chapter 7 describes the background and drama of that March 5, 1770, event that occurred in Boston when a squad of British soldiers fired their weapons into a noisy and threatening crowd of Bostonians. One of a series of such conflicts that grew during the 1760s and 1770s between the American colonies and British authorities, the Boston Massacre symbolized the evolving separation of mother country and colonies. Chapter 8 details the chain of events leading to American independence.

But the winning of independence and the creation of a loosely connected confederation of thirteen distinct "nation-states" proved only the first part in a two-phase drama of nation building. To the surprise of many, including a number of their own leaders and citizens, the Americans managed to win the Revolutionary War. The hero of that war, General George Washington, retired to his Virginia plantation after directing American military efforts. Soon, he and many of his revolutionary associates came to believe that the new government they had brought into existence had not succeeded in consolidating the political society for which they had fought. After long and thoughtful deliberation, they concluded

REVOLUTIONARY AMERICA

UNIT TWO

that the Confederation had to be replaced. The culmination of the slow, painful process by which the revolutionary leaders reached this conclusion occurred at the Constitutional Convention held in 1787 at Philadelphia, the subject of Chapter 9. The new Constitution and frame of government for the United States of America is described in Chapter 10. Having entered the eighteenth century a small, weak, European, and divided people, Americans began their first century as an independent people in 1800 with a host of problems but also (with resources as a new country born of their three-decade-long struggle for survival) independence and nationhood.

7 The Boston Massacre

Some called the eleven-year-old boy Christopher Seider, others, Christian Snider. Whatever his real name, Christopher Seider (let us call him that) stood in a crowd outside Ebenezer Richardson's home in Boston's North End on the windy morning of February 22, 1770. Seider was one of several hundred Bostonians gathered there, many of them youngsters like himself. They had penned Richardson and his family inside, and now they pelted the house with eggs, fruit peelings, sticks, and stones. The crowd broke most of the house's glass windowpanes. One rock struck Richardson's wife. Others barely missed his two daughters. Richardson took an unloaded musket to the window and aimed it at the mob outside. The crowd broke down his front door, but continued to stand outside — probably because of its healthy respect for the gun — and bombard the house with stones.

Richardson loaded his musket with small birdshot pellets. He fired and hit several people in the crowd, some of whom were injured slightly. Christopher Seider less fortunate than others, fell to the ground with eleven pellets in his chest and abdomen. He died that evening.

The angry crowd surged into the house after the boy fell. It cornered Richardson, who surrendered without further resistance. The mob prepared to lynch the unfortunate man and doubtless would have except for the timely appearance of William Molineux, one of Boston's leading "radical" opponents of British authority. Molineux persuaded the angry crowd to turn Richardson over to the law officials. Within the hour Richardson appeared before four justices of the peace and a thousand onlookers in Faneuil Hall. Witnesses were heard at the open hearing, and Richardson was held in jail until the next session of the Massachusetts Superior Court, charged with "giving Christopher Seider a very dangerous wound." After Seider died, the charge became murder.

Before his death Seider had been unknown to most of Boston's 16,000 residents. On February 26, however, he received the "largest funeral perhaps ever known in America" up to that time. Several thousand Bostonians braved snow-clogged streets to pay tribute to his memory.

The funeral was organized by one of Boston's leading radicals, Samuel Adams, a lawyer and former town official with a reputation as an effective political agitator.

Seider's death provided Adams, and the cause of colonial resistance, with a perfect juvenile martyr to British tyranny. It was disclosed that Richardson had served in previous years as an informer for the British customs commissioners, who had been sent to Boston in 1767 to collect duties on colonial imports. These duties had been set by Parliament in the Townshend Acts.

A few days later, after Christopher Seider's death, Boston's townspeople poured into the streets again, this time not as a mob but as a funeral procession. The following opinion appeared in the *Gazette,* the unofficial newspaper of the Sons of Liberty: "Young as he was, [Seider] died in his Country's Cause, by the Hand of an execrable Villain, directed by others, who could not bear to see the enemies of America made the Ridicule of Boys."

Boston merchants, along with merchant groups throughout the North American colonies of Great Britain,[1] viewed the taxes imposed upon them by Parliament as both unfair and illegal. In an attempt to force Parliament to repeal the Townshend Acts, they organized a boycott of all British-manufactured goods, which was referred to as the nonimportation agreement. Those merchants and other colonists who protested against the taxes levied upon them by the king and Parliament came to be known as Whigs (a term used earlier for *English* opponents of royal tyranny) or Patriots; the more militant among them organized themselves into the Sons of Liberty. Their opponents, those colonists who believed Great Britain did have the right to tax them, were known as Loyalists or Tories.

After passage of the Townshend Acts, increasingly large and unruly crowds of Patriots began to roam the streets of Boston at night, intimidating Tories or crown officials with threats of violence—and with violence itself. British officials claimed that such mobs were directed by radical leaders like Samuel Adams and William Molineux, and some of them were. On occasion, a town meeting[2] could transform itself into a mob simply by moving from its usual meeting place in Faneuil Hall into the streets, where it had been summoned to help enforce the decisions of the town leaders, most of whom were Patriots. Crowds like these often included the city's most respectable merchants and politicians. Mobs also gathered spontaneously, their numbers swelled by the presence in that port city of sailors, itinerant workers and artisans, jobless teenagers, and local bullyboys. More often than not, the more spontaneous crowds were dominated by those with powerful lungs or muscles. The mob that

---

[1] In 1707 England was united with Scotland. After this date the governmental unit as a whole is usually referred to as Great Britain. Its overseas possessions together became known as the British Empire.

[2] Boston was governed by a town meeting consisting mostly of voters. It met whenever the need arose. It could bring as many as 3000 people together for several days running.

stormed Ebenezer Richardson's house had gathered in this fashion. They were reacting to Richardson's attempt, that same night, to keep another, more organized mob from interfering with a merchant who was reported to be violating the nonimportation agreement.

During the two years preceding this incident, the Patriots and the colony's royal government had struggled bitterly to control Boston's economic and political life. Patriots like Samuel Adams used the easily aroused mobs to exert pressure on even Tory merchants to endorse the nonimportation agreement. The royal governor of Massachusetts, Francis Bernard, troubled by the Patriots' effective economic boycott and their control of the city's streets, encouraged the British army commander in North America, Major General Thomas Gage, to send troops from the large garrison at Halifax, Nova Scotia, to help restore the authority of the crown in Boston. But Bernard himself could not directly request troops. He had first to secure the consent of the governor's council, the upper house of the Massachusetts legislature. This council, which was elected by the citizens, generally sided with the opponents of British taxation and control. Bernard outlined his dilemma, one shared in some measure by most royal governors in the American mainland colonies, in a letter written in July 1768 to an official in Great Britain:

> General Gage has now informed me that his orders to Halifax are that the Troops shall be collected & kept in readiness, but are not to move till I require them. I answer that then they will never move: for I shall not make such a requisition without the Advice of Council: & I never expect to obtain that: neither their popular Constitution nor the present intimidation

British soldiers disembark at Boston's Long Wharf in October 1768. According to engraver Revere's caption, the troops then marched up King Street "with insolent parade." (Henry Francis DuPont Winterthur Museum)

will permit it. . . . In short, my Lord, Troops are not wanted here to quell a Riot or a Tumult, but to rescue the Government out of the hands of a trained mob & to restore the activity of the Civil Power, which is now entirely obstructed. And if an open Defiance of the Authority of Great Britain: a persecution of all those who are supposed to be maintainers of that authority . . . are not sufficient to show the Expedience of quartering Troops at Boston, we must wait till it becomes more apparent.

But if Bernard could not order troops, the authorities in London could. In October 1768 Boston witnessed the arrival of the first redcoats from the two regiments to be stationed there—the Fourteenth and the Twenty-ninth. After a lengthy struggle with Boston's local officials to obtain adequate quarters for the soldiers (one regiment spent its first night in Faneuil Hall), the troops began regular patrols. Overnight, Boston became a garrisoned town; the center of colonial opposition to parliamentary and royal authority had been "occupied." But the presence of troops failed to check the townspeople's "mobbish disposition"; it succeeded only in helping to unify the various local factions that opposed British attempts to tax and govern. Before the soldiers came, these factions had few visible symbols of British authority to complain about. Neither the ineffective Governor Bernard, nor the talented but unpopular Lieutenant Governor Thomas Hutchinson—not even the customs commissioners—had managed to rally patriotic sentiment among the people as effectively as did the presence of the British troops, whose numbers ranged from 600 to 1000 men. In the months between the arrival of the troops and the death of Christopher Seider, tempers flared repeatedly on both sides.

During these months the troops controlled their sentry posts. The Patriots controlled the merchants and the town meeting. Crown officials controlled Boston by day. The mobs, when they appeared, controlled the streets at night. The royal governor controlled only his temper. He resigned in 1770 in favor of Thomas Hutchinson. As far as anyone could judge, however, none of the authorities controlled Boston itself with any certainty. Both royal officials and Patriot leaders freely predicted that any major incident could trigger an open rebellion against British authority in that edgy community.

Relations between Bostonians and the British troops were sometimes friendly, sometimes hostile. Two groups among the unwanted soldiers made them even less welcome to townspeople than they would otherwise have been. These were the many Irish Catholics, whose presence offended the town's Protestant citizens, and a number of black troops, an affront to those Bostonians who kept black slaves or servants.

Any occupying army, of course, must expect hostility from those whose territory it controls. The British army was no exception. From the moment the troops arrived, the town's Patriot newspapers filled their columns with accounts of friction involving townspeople. There were numerous fights (invariably begun by the soldiers, according to townspeople), many minor acts of harassment, and endless arguments as the red-

Thomas Hutchinson, a loyal servant to the crown, moved to England in 1774 and never returned to America. But he loved Boston and was homesick for it until he died in 1780. (Massachusetts Historical Society)

coats attempted to patrol the community. Soldiers who searched for quarters for their families in the town were overcharged shamelessly if they managed to obtain quarters at all, and few Boston merchants resisted the temptation to raise their normal prices for British customers. But what proved particularly galling to the troops and their officers was not the understandable bitterness of private citizens. It was the hostility of public officials, especially the magistrates of Boston's court system. Sentries who were instructed to challenge passersby at fixed guard posts throughout Boston, especially after dark, found that civilians could and often did swear out warrants against the sentries themselves for disturbing the peace! The civil magistrates generally fined harshly any soldiers on guard duty whom townspeople accused of rude behavior. "We are in a pleasing Situation," wrote one British officer, "who are ordered here to Aid & assist the Civil Magistrate in preserving the peace & protecting his Majesty's subjects, when those very magistrates are our Oppressers." Ordinary soldiers complained about unfair treatment at the hands of American justices of the peace with the same kind of outrage voiced by colonial merchants at their treatment by British customs commissioners. Each side believed that justice could rarely be gained in the other's courts. Both sides were usually correct.

By late 1769 it had become clear that both the Townshend Acts and the dispatch of troops to Boston had failed to enforce British taxation. The struggle to assert royal authority in Boston had ended in a political stalemate between crown officials and the city's Patriot leadership—neither the troops nor the mobs managed to control the streets unopposed. Bernard and Hutchinson were reluctant to risk a general uprising by trying to enforce the customs laws, which merchant signers of the nonimportation agreement continued to ignore. Samuel Adams and his fellow radical Patriots, for their part, proved equally reluctant to provoke outright rebellion against all British authority. British officials and most American Tories believed, however, that the Patriots wanted not only to abolish the onerous customs duties but to end British rule entirely. They viewed the Patriots, in General Gage's words, as "an illegal combination of people" conspiring to stir popular feeling against Britain as a first step along the road to revolution.

The Patriots did not consider themselves conspirators. But they did view the British authorities and Tories as schemers trying to deprive provincial America both of its traditional liberties and of its hard-earned income. "There was a cursed cabal [group of plotters], principally residing in this town," Samuel Adams wrote in 1769 of Boston's Loyalists, "who . . . were perpetually intriguing to bring about another parliamentary tax act; for no other purpose than that they might feast and fatten themselves upon the spoils and plunder of the people." Adams added:

> One man has as good reason to affirm that a few, in calling for a military force under pretense of supporting civil authority, secretly intended to introduce a general massacre, as another has to assert, that a number of loyal subjects, by calling upon one another to be provided with arms, according to law, intended to bring on an insurrection.

Although at times Adams argued the existence of this British–Tory "conspiracy," he also acknowledged his opponents' belief in a comparable Bostonian plot against British rule. That the 600 harassed British soldiers who occupied Boston in early 1770 "secretly intended to introduce a general massacre" against Boston's 16,000 residents seems improbable. But at the time many Bostonians believed it, and they acted accordingly. Tensions ran high in the early months of 1770. Each group feared an attack that it believed its opponents had plotted well in advance. More often than not, however, the violence that actually flared up was unplanned and disorganized.

The British troops recognized by 1770 that their role in Boston had little to commend it. The job was lonely. The soldiers were shunned by the town's Patriot majority, abused in the courts, challenged boldly on the streets, and threatened regularly by mobs—all this for extremely low wages. To supplement their pay, many soldiers braved local hostility and sought jobs during their off-duty hours. Unfortunately, there were few part-time jobs available in Boston; there had been a grave depression in local commerce because of the enforcement of the nonimportation agreement. Bostonians were worried about their own unemployed, whose numbers increased daily. Competition between off-duty soldiers and unemployed townsmen for the few available jobs provoked a number of noisy arguments and minor fights.

One such incident took place on March 2, 1770, only four days after Christopher Seider's funeral. With emotions still running high in the town, this minor flurry brought Bostonians and redcoats to the brink of major civil conflict. The trouble began at John Gray's "ropewalk,"[3] a large plant where a number of workers produced rope and cable. Temporary laborers' jobs were often available there. These attracted unemployed townspeople and British troops. On this particular day a British soldier named Thomas Walker of the Twenty-ninth Regiment entered the plant and asked for work. Ropemaker William Green, a Bostonian, asked him: "Soldier, do you want work?" "Yes, I do," replied Walker. Green responded with an amused smirk, "Well, then go and clean my outhouse." The other ropemakers roared with laughter, but Walker's face turned red with fury. "Empty it yourself!" he shouted at Green. The pair exchanged hard words for a moment longer. Then the fight began.

The ropemakers pounced on Walker and pummeled the unfortunate soldier badly before he managed to get away. He returned shortly with eight or nine other redcoats, and the slugfest resumed. Both sides fought mainly with wooden clubs, although the soldiers also slashed away at times with their swords. The Bostonians managed to chase Walker and his cohorts from the ropeworks. But the soldiers returned within minutes, bringing with them nearly thirty reinforcements. By then, the number of civilians had also grown. Soon Gray's ropewalk was jammed with troops and ropeworkers, cracking their clubs against all

---

[3] At this time rope was made in a long, low building. A ropemaker walked backward from one end to the other, paying out fiber from a bundle at his waist and braiding it as he walked.

comers. Both sides suffered casualties, some quite severe, until the soldiers were once more driven from the factory.

The following day, Saturday, March 3, a trio of redcoats returned to the ropewalk, where they renewed the battle against workers on the scene. This time, one of the soldiers suffered a fractured skull and arm before he and his friends withdrew. Sunday, March 4, seemed more peaceful, although a group of British officers visited the ropewalk searching for a missing British sergeant, whose comrades had reported him killed by the townspeople.

The sergeant's body was never found, but rumors spread among the troops that the Bostonians planned some larger dramatic gesture of revenge against the British soldiers. One private "remembered some ropemakers asking where the Twenty-ninth [Regiment] planned to bury its dead." A Bostonian later swore that he heard four soldiers from the regiment say that "there were a great many townspeople who would eat their dinners on Monday next [March 5], who would not eat any on Tuesday."

The day of Monday, March 5, passed without incident. A foot of snow covered the ground. Bostonians who braved the cold, windswept city walked cautiously over the ice sheets that covered most of the streets. Boston had no street lamps then. As darkness fell, people had only a first-quarter moon to light their way. Snow covered King Street, which housed both the Custom House and the Main Guard, British army headquarters.

No one in Boston knew then that in London, earlier in the day, the British Parliament had repealed most of the controversial Townshend Acts (all but the one on tea). This was a stunning victory for colonial protesters, but the news of repeal reached Boston only in late April. By that time Bostonians were preoccupied with the events that had occurred on King Street on the bitter cold evening of March 5. It was then that the fragile structure of civic peace in Boston finally collapsed.

The incident began as had similar ones in the past—with a nervous British soldier, a sharp-tongued young Bostonian, and a fight. The soldier, Private Hugh White of the Twenty-ninth Regiment, was on guard duty at a sentry box on the corner of King Street and Shrimton's Lane, down the street from both the Main Guard and the Custom House. Along came a young wigmaker's apprentice named Edward Garrick. Garrick spotted a British officer named Goldfinch, and shouted within earshot of Private White: "There goes the fellow that won't pay my master for dressing his hair." Joined by another apprentice, Garrick strolled through the King Street area, later returning to White's sentry post, where he resumed his criticism of Captain Goldfinch. At this point, Private White defended the officer as a gentleman who would pay all his debts. "There are no gentlemen in the Twenty-ninth Regiment," shouted Garrick, whereupon White left his post and joined Garrick in the street.

"Let me see your face," ordered White. Garrick obliged, and White immediately smashed his musket into the young wigmaker's head. Garrick cried out in pain, and his companion began exchanging curses with the angry sentry. Within minutes a crowd of some fifty townspeople had gathered in the street, surrounding the lone sentry, shouting at him to fight them. White loaded his musket, retreated down the block to the steps of the Custom House, fixed his bayonet, and faced the angry crowd.

The mob began throwing large chunks of ice at White, screaming as they flung their missiles: "Kill him, kill him, knock him down. Fire, damn you, fire, you dare not fire." The town watchman suddenly appeared on the scene and urged the sentry to restrain himself, pleading that most people in the mob were youths who would not hurt him. As the crowd continued nevertheless to pelt him with ice, White responded: "Damn them; if they molest me I will fire." Finally, he shouted for assistance from the nearby regimental headquarters: "Turn out, Main Guard!"

Meanwhile, similar mobs had appeared elsewhere in Boston. Just a few blocks from King Street, soldiers strolled along Brattle Street carrying clubs, bayonets, and other weapons, while a solitary Bostonian ran up and down the immediate area shouting the usual call for a mob to gather: "Town born, turn out! Town born, turn out!" A crowd collected quickly at a regimental encampment called Murray's Barracks near Brattle Street. Soon volleys of snowballs hurled at the soldiers accompanied the shouts of bystanders. Several British officers, including Captain Goldfinch, ordered the soldiers back into the barracks to forestall bloodshed. More than once, officers knocked their own troops to the ground to prevent them from shooting into the onrushing crowd.

Another throng gathered in Dock Square, only two blocks from Private White's sentry post on King Street. Several hundred townspeople poured into the empty stalls of Boston's town market. They ripped the legs off produce and butcher tables and shouted "Fire!" to attract additional recruits from the neighborhood.

The cry of "Fire!" sounded repeatedly through the dark Boston streets and attracted a number of sleepy townspeople. Boston depended on volunteer firefighting companies. So groups of such firefighters carrying buckets joined the three separate crowds of agitated Bostonians spoiling for a fight with the soldiers. At some point, church bells began tolling an additional call for firefighters.

Bostonians of all ages converged on King Street—some with buckets, others with sticks. Many ran from the Dock Square and Murray's Barracks fracases once those incidents had quieted down. The crowd in King Street varied in size from several dozen to several hundred over the next hour, as men and boys moved along the town's cramped lanes and alleys. "There is no fire," shouted one youth to a bystander. "It is the soldiers fighting." "Damn it, I am glad of it," came the response. "I will knock some of them on the head." A number of Bostonians left the sidewalks to join the unruly scene in the streets.

The mob that gathered in King Street surrounded White's sentry post but made no immediate attempt to overwhelm him. Meanwhile, the British officer of the guard that evening, Captain Thomas Preston, had

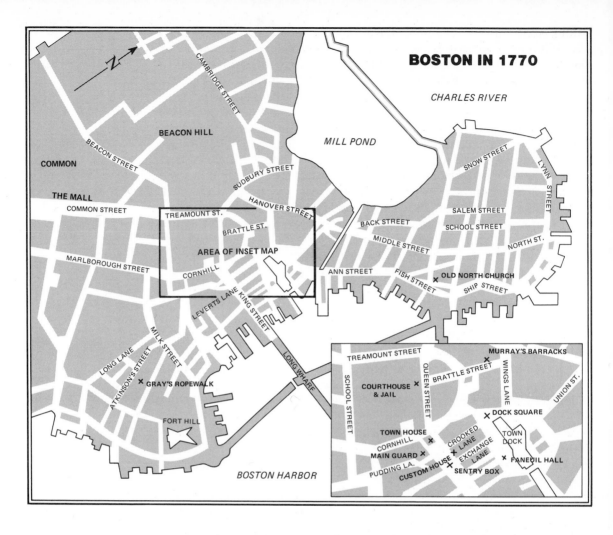

BOSTON IN 1770

CHARLES RIVER

MILL POND

BEACON HILL

COMMON

THE MALL

COMMON STREET

BEACON STREET

SUDBURY STREET

HANOVER STREET

TREAMOUNT ST.

BRATTLE ST.

AREA OF INSET MAP

MARLBOROUGH STREET

CORNHILL

CAMBRIDGE STREET

BACK STREET

MIDDLE STREET

ANN STREET

FISH STREET

LEVERTS LANE

KING STREET

LONG WHARF

LONG LANE

MILK STREET

ATKINSON'S STREET

× GRAY'S ROPEWALK

FORT HILL

BOSTON HARBOR

SNOW STREET

LYNN STREET

SALEM STREET

SCHOOL STREET

NORTH ST.

× OLD NORTH CHURCH

SHIP STREET

TREAMOUNT STREET

MURRAY'S BARRACKS

BRATTLE STREET

WINGS LANE

UNION ST.

SCHOOL STREET

COURTHOUSE & JAIL ×

QUEEN STREET

DOCK SQUARE

TOWN HOUSE

CORNHILL ×

CROOKED LANE

EXCHANGE LANE

TOWN DOCK

MAIN GUARD ×

PUDDING LA.

CUSTOM HOUSE ×

× SENTRY BOX

× FANEUIL HALL

been summoned from his dinner table by White's urgent request for reinforcements. He went to the Main Guard on King Street, and he surveyed the crowd. By now it had grown to at least several hundred (accurate estimates were difficult). After deciding to help the beleaguered White, Preston ordered up a relief party of sentries—six privates and a corporal. This group then marched toward the menacing crowd, their muskets empty and shouldered—but their bayonets fixed.

Preston's few soldiers managed to push through the crowd, loading their muskets after reaching White's empty sentry box. White still confronted the large throng from a position on the Custom House steps. At Preston's orders and without interference from the bystanders, he joined the other soldiers.

Preston had ordered the sentries out primarily to relieve White. Having done so, the captain tried to march his soldiers back toward the Main Guard. The surrounding mob either would not or could not allow the troops through, so great was the press of bodies. Some people in the throng began shouting at the redcoats: "Damn you, fire. You can't kill us all." Within moments Preston found himself and his men cut off from assistance. He ordered his soldiers to form a curved line with their backs to the Custom House. Although they tried to keep the crowd from encircling them, some Bostonians managed to slip behind the soldiers.

The crowd, obviously leaderless, shuffled angrily yet uneasily around the nervous redcoats, uncertain whether to attack or withdraw. To add to the confusion, the church bells kept tolling. Every few moments, more bucket-carrying Bostonians arrived at the scene. Many exchanged their buckets quickly for clubs or ice chunks when they understood the situation. Preston shouted for the crowd to disperse, but received in return only laughter, hooting, and a pelting with snowballs. The crowd taunted the soldiers to shoot, and the small company of British troops clenched their weapons tightly.

The only town official to brave the mob scene was one James Murray, a Tory justice of the peace, who arrived at King Street to read the Riot Act. By law, the statute forbidding riotous gatherings had to be read to a mob before it took effect. The crowd knew this. They knew, therefore, that Preston and his men would be on questionable legal ground if they fired without having first ordered the mob to disperse by a reading of the Riot Act.

The mob wanted to prevent the reading. A volley of snowballs and ice chunks soon sent Murray scurrying toward safety. The mob's anger increased when some of its members recognized at least two of the sentries, Privates Matthew Kilroy and William Warren, as participants in the battle at the ropewalk four days earlier. At the same time, Private White himself spotted a familiar face in the crowd, a young woman named Jane Whitehouse, whose home was near his own Boston living quarters. "Go home," he cried, taking her arm and pushing her toward the corner. "Go home, or you'll be killed."

The mob soon abandoned all restraint short of directly assaulting the soldiers. Individuals began pushing forcefully against Preston's troops, daring them to fire, denouncing them as cowards and scoundrels, challenging them to fistfights. "Why do you not fire? Damn you, you dare not fire. Fire and be damned," they continued to shout. There were small duels, as townsmen carrying clubs beat them against the guardsmen's musket barrels and bayonets. Preston continued to shout demands that the crowd disperse, at the same time restraining his frightened band of soldiers from opening fire. Several times the captain was approached by Patriot leaders in the crowd who asked whether he intended to fire. Each time he responded, "By no means, by no means."

A Tory dignitary urged the captain to disperse the unruly rioters with a warning volley of musket shot. At this, stressing his desire to prevent bloodshed, Preston placed himself directly in front of the muskets so that he would be the first victim of any shooting. The crowd cheered at Preston's predicament, which at the moment seemed an almost perfect reflection of the overall British situation in Boston—incapable either of maintaining public order or of withdrawing gracefully.

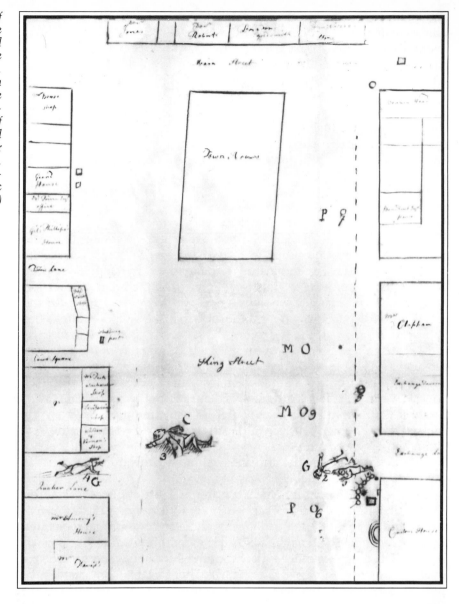

No more than a foot or two separated the line of soldiers from the nearest rioters. Suddenly a club went sailing from the midst of the crowd into the dimly lit street, hitting Private Hugh Montgomery. The private fell to the ground and dropped his musket on the ice. No one knows what triggered that particular act of violence, or what emotions Private Montgomery felt as he staggered to his feet and recovered his musket. But matters had reached the breaking point. Montgomery shouted, "Damn you, fire," and proceeded to pull his trigger. Within seconds, members of the crowd lunged at Preston and his troops, swinging their clubs wildly.

The soldiers managed to fight off these blows, but in an interval of from fifteen seconds to two minutes (the exact time remains unclear), the other troops also fired their weapons.

Preston neither ordered the shooting, nor did he—stunned at Montgomery's impulsive action—order it to stop. When the shooting finally ceased, the crowd continued to advance on the small group of soldiers, although few people got close enough to swing their clubs. The soldiers parried blows while reloading their muskets. They fired another round. Again the firing took place sporadically, with single shots being fired over a period of minutes. This time, several people in the crowd were wounded, and some fell to the ground. Finally, the crowd began to disperse, although it regrouped quickly once the firing had stopped, this time to recover the bodies of those who lay dead or wounded. The soldiers, fearing another attack, raised their muskets to fire a third round. By now, Preston had regained his composure and personally shoved down his soldiers' gun barrels before they could shoot, shouting, "Stop firing! Do not fire!"

The mob drew back for the moment, carrying the bodies of those hit by the troops. Preston's soldiers began to explain to their agitated captain that they had fired only after hearing what they believed to be *his* command. While emergency hospitals for the wounded were being set up in nearby homes, Preston marched his company back to the Main Guard. He then turned out the entire guard and placed it in formation on King Street between the Main Guard and Boston's Town House (the Old State House). The troops were drawn up in street-firing position, an eighteenth-century tactic for controlling urban riots in narrow streets. Rows of soldiers stood in single-file formation. The man at the head of the line would shoot, then move to the back of the line. There he reloaded and waited his turn to shoot once more.

In front of the Custom House, small groups of Bostonians passed grimly along King Street and stared at the bloodstains splattered on the icy thoroughfare. Word had spread quickly through town that, as a result of the shooting, five men lay dead or dying. Among the dead was one who would soon become the most famous martyr of the evening's bloodshed, Crispus Attucks. (Accounts differ as to whether he was a free black, a runaway slave, or an Indian of the Natick tribe.) Four others also died—an Irish Catholic immigrant named Patrick Carr; Samuel Gray, the son of the ropewalk owner; seventeen-year-old Samuel Maverick; and a young apprentice sailor named James Caldwell.

The withdrawal of Preston's men did not dispel the threat of further bloodshed that very night, as angry Bostonians filled the streets, hurling curses at the British troops and crying "To arms!" Every church bell in Boston began pealing. Even the town's official drums—which generally summoned the militia to combat—beat solemnly to announce the tragedy. Within an hour after the "massacre" itself, more than a thousand citizens crowded King Street. Rumors spread quickly among the townspeople that the soldiers planned a wholesale slaughter of the inhabitants. Local Tories were attacked and beaten in the streets. British officers and

Although only a mediocre artist, Paul Revere was a fine silversmith in addition to being an ardent Patriot. As a skilled craftsman, he cast cannon for the army, printed the first Continental money, and designed the state seal still used by Massachusetts. (Museum of Fine Arts, Boston— Gift of Joseph W., William B., and Edward H. R. Revere)

soldiers also found it dangerous to walk through Boston without armed escorts that night.

Moderate Patriot leaders pleaded with Lieutenant Governor Hutchinson, the leading civil official in town, to remove Preston's troops from King Street before their presence provoked further retaliation from the crowd. Hutchinson approached the troops and exchanged some harsh words with Preston. But he declined to order the soldiers back to quarters. Instead, he addressed the people from a balcony of the Town House. He urged them to retire peacefully, promising that he would do everything possible to ensure a full inquiry into the shooting. "The law shall have its course," he shouted. "I will live and die by the law." Apparently, this was also the view of the many Bostonians in the crowd who left quietly. The hundreds who remained demanded both immediate action against the British soldiers and removal of the troops from Boston's streets. Preston's superior officer, Lieutenant Colonel Maurice Carr, feared a renewed confrontation between the crowd and the troops. He ordered the soldiers on King Street to abandon street-firing formation and return to their barracks. As the troops marched off, the crowd—now silent and somber—dispersed.

At 2 A.M. on March 6 the town sheriff served a warrant on Captain Preston for his role in the episode. Preston surrendered an hour later. A few hours afterward, the eight redcoats in Preston's sentry party were also imprisoned. All nine were charged with murder.

After the arrest of Preston and his men, Boston drew back from the brink of civil disorder. Hutchinson and Carr were not the only ones who feared a bloodbath. Most responsible Patriot leaders shared their anxieties. They believed that the continued presence of troops among angry townspeople would only provoke violence on an uncontrollable scale. So they urged the removal of British troops from the town itself to Castle William, an island fort in Boston harbor.

Bostonians were still outraged over the massacre. At a town meeting on March 6, which was dominated by Samuel Adams and other Patriots, the people demanded removal of the British troops. Hutchinson tried to compromise between his loyalty to the crown and his recognition of the town's anger. He ordered only Preston's regiment, the Twenty-ninth, to Castle William.

The town meeting remained dissatisfied. On March 10 it sent a committee led by Samuel Adams to see Hutchinson. The group demanded that the remaining British regiment be ordered out of town. Hutchinson and his advisers had no choice but to submit. They ordered the Fourteenth Regiment, the last British troops in Boston, to depart the following day for Castle William. Boston now returned to the control of its own, Patriot-dominated town meeting. The remaining loyal dignitaries—Hutchinson, the customs commissioners, and lesser officials—could not direct the course of events without assistance from troops. The Patriots had no further need for nightly mobs to confront crown authority. Thus the immediate threat of civil disorder ended.

With the troops gone from Boston, the Patriots turned their attention to settling accounts with the imprisoned soldiers. On March 12 the *Gazette* employed the term "massacre" in connection with the events of March 5. This was the first public use of the term. A week later, on March 19, Boston's town meeting approved printing a version of the events that justified the behavior of the rioters and condemned the British soldiers. Entitled *A Short History of the Horrid Massacre at Boston*, the pamphlet was dispatched on fast ships to England to soften British anger at the Bostonians' conduct toward the troops. The Patriots decided not to distribute the pamphlet in Boston itself, lest it prejudice the soldiers' trials.

Also on March 19, the town meeting petitioned Hutchinson for an early trial of the prisoners. The lieutenant governor and other Loyalists resisted, considering the aroused state of emotions in Boston regarding Preston and his men. "I have assurances from the court," Preston wrote General Gage on April 1, "that they will continue [postpone] the trial . . . until the last week in May [although] great pain is being taken to intimidate the judges and compel them to bring it on sooner." Hutchinson's concern for a fair trial seemed even more understandable after the conclusion of Ebenezer Richardson's trial. On April 21 a Boston jury found Richardson guilty of the murder of Christopher Seider. They did so despite the judge's instruction from the bench that Richardson had clearly committed justifiable homicide in self-defense.

Soon after the "massacre," both Tories and Patriots began arguing that the incident had been part of a prearranged scheme of wholesale murder on the part of their opponents. Such assertions appeared in versions of the incident prepared by the British military authorities and in the town meeting's *Short History*. A town meeting on May 15 issued statements that referred to "a deep-laid and desperate plan of imperial despotism . . . for the extinction of all civil liberty" in the American colonies. On the other hand, Hutchinson viewed the behavior of Adams and the Patriots as simply the "designs of particular persons to bring about a revolution, and to attain to independency." In the aftermath of the massacre, belief in conspiratorial plots hardened into obsessions on both sides. Loyalists and Patriots seemed worlds apart, and Boston was split irrevocably into two camps. "They call me a brainless Tory," said one local gentleman. "But tell me . . . which is better—to be ruled by one tyrant three thousand miles away, or by three thousand tyrants not one mile away?" Aware of this tension, Hutchinson and other crown dignitaries employed various legal devices to delay proceedings against Preston and his soldiers. They were finally indicted in September.

Preston's trial began on October 24. Ironically, one of his prosecutors was a well-known Tory, Samuel Quincy. And his defense was undertaken by two of the colony's leading Patriot lawyers, John Adams (Samuel Adams's cousin) and Josiah Quincy (Samuel Quincy's brother). There is some evidence that Samuel Adams and other Patriot leaders encouraged John Adams and Josiah Quincy to act as defense counsel, not wishing the British to feel that Boston had failed to provide a fair trial.

John Adams was forty-one when this drawing was made, in 1776. His grandson later described him as "grave and imposing, but not unbending" and as one who "delighted in social conversation." (Massachusetts Historical Society)

Whatever their motives, Adams and Quincy performed brilliantly. Actually, Preston's chances for acquittal seemed good from the start, especially since five acknowledged Tories were among the jury. The failure or inability of Patriot leaders to pack the jury with hostile Bostonians suggests that the Patriots were less concerned with convicting Preston and his men than with exploiting the trial as propaganda.

A parade of prosecution and defense witnesses testified to the different British and Bostonian versions of the events on King Street. James Brewer's testimony for the prosecution summarized the claim that the soldiers had lacked sufficient provocation to fire into the crowd.

Q. Did you see anything thrown at the soldiers?

A. No.

Q. Did you hear anybody call them names?

A. No.

Q. Did you hear any threatening speeches?

A. No, except that the people cried "Fire! Fire!" The word "fire" was on everybody's mouth.

Q. Did you take that to be the cry of fire, or bidding the soldiers fire?

A. I cannot tell now what I thought then.

Q. Did you see anything extraordinary, to induce them to fire that gun?

A. Nothing, but a short stick was thrown, which seemed to go clear over all [the soldiers'] heads.

A typical statement for the defense came in the testimony of Newton Prince:

I ran to the door [of my house] and heard the cry of fire. I went out and asked where the fire was; somebody said it was something better than fire. I met some with clubs, some with buckets and bags, and some running before me with sticks in their hands . . . there were a number of people by the west door of the Townhouse; they said let's go and attack the main guard. . . . After a while they huzzaed and went down King Street; they went down to the Custom-house, and I went down . . . There were people all round the soldiers . . . I saw people with sticks striking on the guns.

Q. Did you hear at that time they were striking, the cry of fire, fire?

A. Yes, [the crowd] said fire, damn you, fire, fire you lobsters,[4] fire you dare not fire.

At several points during Captain Preston's trial—and later during the other soldiers' trial—John Adams threatened to resign as defense attorney because his co-counsel, Josiah Quincy, wished to introduce evidence that Bostonians had triggered the violence. Adams felt that the

---

[4] "Lobsters" was a slang term for British soldiers because of the red coats they wore.

British soldiers could be acquitted without putting Boston and the Patriot cause itself on trial.

From the manner in which they dealt with Boston itself, the closing arguments by prosecution and defense lawyers used at the soldiers' trial illustrated the basic issues of Preston's case as well. The chief prosecutor, Robert Treat Paine, tried to absolve the mob itself of blame for the shooting. He answered "yes" to his own questions: "Was it lawful for the inhabitants of Boston to walk the streets that evening with sticks? Was it lawful for them to run on the cry of 'fire!'?" And he responded "no" to this critical question: "Must they be answerable for the rude speech of every person that happens to be near them, when it does not appear they assented to them and joined in putting them in execution?" In other words, Paine thundered, Preston's company of sentries had no lawful right to fire into the crowd. They were, therefore, guilty of murder.

While Paine defended the radical mob's behavior, lawyer Josiah Quincy (defense lawyer for the sentries as well as for Preston) denied the importance, perhaps even the existence, of such a mob. He insisted that

> Boston and its inhabitants have no more to do with this cause than you or any other two members of the community. . . . The inhabitants of Boston, by no rules of law, justice, or common sense, can be supposed answerable for the unjustifiable conduct of a few individuals hastily assembled in the streets.

In other words, Quincy argued that the crowd's responsibility for provoking the incident was essentially different from the soldiers' guilt or innocence of the murder charge itself. Yet Quincy went on to defend the soldiers' innocence of murder, at the same time defending Boston against those who would criticize it.

Who, then, was to blame for the massacre? The prosecutor pointed to outside agitators who had provoked the violence, and he mentioned two such groups in his summation. One was "sailors and foreigners of the lower Class . . . who are fond of mingling with such Commotions and pushing on a disorder of which they feel not the Consequences." The other was the British army. The crowd's threatening words and hostile stirrings were only natural "among a free People Oppressed and galled with the ravagings of an ungoverned Soldiery [and were not] to be construed as Evidence of an Insurrection or a design to put in Execution the Supposed threats." John Adams picked up the outsider theme and made it the pivotal argument of his defense summation. Although the British did not come out unscathed, the soldiers' defender obviously directed his eloquence against the mob itself. But *what* mob? Composed of *whom*?

> The plain English is, gentlemen [that] most [of the mob] was probably a motley rabble of saucy boys, Negroes and mulattos, Irish teagues,[5] and outlandish jack tarrs [sailors]. . . . There was a mob in Boston on the 5th of

---

[5] "Teague," from the Irish name "Tadhg," was a nickname for an Irishman.

March that attacked a party of soldiers. . . . And indeed, from the nature of things, soldiers quartered in a populous town will always occasion two mobs where they prevent one. They are wretched conservators of the peace!

As for the role of Boston's citizens in the episode, Adams continued:

A Carr from Ireland, and an Attucks from Framingham, happening to be here, shall sally out upon their thoughtless enterprises, at the head of such a rabble . . . as they could collect together, and then there are not wanting, persons to ascribe all their doings to the good people of the town.

Judge Edmund Trowbridge, shrewdest of the three-judge panel that presided at both trials, told the jury that if they were satisfied "that the sentinel was insulted and that Captain Preston and his party went to assist him, it was doubtless excusable homicide, if not justifiable." Trowbridge went on to deny the conspiracy theories of the massacre. He stated that there had been "no concerted plan on either side," only the provocative actions of an angry crowd and the nervous reaction of frightened soldiers. In that situation "any little spark would kindle a great fire — and five lives were sacrificed to a squabble between the sentry [Private White] and Piemont's barber's boy [Edward Garrick]." The jury at Preston's trial agreed with the judge. On October 30 it found the officer not guilty.

The second trial began on November 27 and ended on December 5. Six of the eight soldiers were also found not guilty. The two others, Matthew Kilroy and Hugh Montgomery, were found guilty of manslaughter. Both soldiers later used a legal technicality to avoid imprisonment. Nine months from the day of the massacre itself, the eight men who had fired their weapons into the King Street crowd had all returned to their military posts. As for the massacre, its fame was only beginning.

Boston was peaceful for a brief period after repeal of the Townshend Acts. In colony after colony during 1770 merchants repudiated their nonimportation agreements. They swiftly resumed trade with Great Britain so that competitors from other provinces would not take over their business. In the rush to resume business as usual, only Boston held firm, demanding that England repeal the remaining duty on tea and renounce similar taxes in the future. Finally, even Boston had to accept the inevitable and abandon nonimportation.

By the end of 1770 the Patriot movement had lost momentum throughout British North America. The spark of rebellion that had flared momentarily at the time of the massacre now flickered low. Samuel Adams confessed in a letter of April 1771:

The Generality are necessarily engaged in Application to private Business for the Support of their own families, and when at a lucky Season the publick are awakened to a Sense of Danger [and] a manly resentment is enkindled, it is difficult, for so many separate Communities as there are in all the colonies, to agree in one consistent plan of Opposition.

Boston, as Samuel Adams recognized, was the symbol and center of colonial resistance. The game of rebellion would continue to be played first in that throbbing seaport town, where so many prominent political, economic, and intellectual leaders resided. As part of their campaign to rekindle colonial resistance to Great Britain, Boston's Patriots produced a number of posters, pamphlets, engravings, and poems. Many of them dealt with the massacre. The events of March 5 began filtering into the daily language of patriotic protest as American Patriots drew appropriate lessons from the massacre—namely, that the proper response to tyranny was resistance, and that true resistance usually meant the sacrifice of life as well as property. The following appeared in the Boston *Gazette:*

Let THESE Things be told to Posterity!

And handed down
From Generation to Generation
'Til time shall be no more!
Forever may AMERICA be preserved,

Crispus Attucks dies a martyr in the Boston Massacre. (The Bettmann Archive)

From weak and wicked monarchs,
Tyrannical Ministers,
Abandoned Governors,
Their Underlings and Hirelings!
And may the
Machinations of artful, designing wretches,
Who would ENSLAVE THIS People
Come to an end.

Every March 5, in the years that followed the King Street killings, Boston remembered. On that anniversary day a major speech was given to commemorate the five martyrs. The speeches were highly emotional in tone. They evoked the images of blood-stained streets and dying victims more than they asserted political and constitutional arguments for freedom. Leading Patriots delivered the orations. John Hancock spoke in 1774. The 1775 oration was given by Joseph Warren, whose heated remarks stirred a large audience in Faneuil Hall. When Warren cried out the words "Bloody Massacre" for the first time, an irreverent listener, presumably a Tory, shouted back, "Oh fie!" Many of those in the gallery, believing that the speaker had shouted "Fire!" began jumping out the windows. They collided on the ground with a passing regiment of parading British soldiers, whose fife and drum contingent blared so noisily that some of those inside the hall began to suspect another massacre. The incident amused bystanders and participants alike. But New England had no further humorous moments in connection with the annual observances of the massacre. On March 5 of the following year, Peter Thatcher addressed the gathering with a passionate plea for American independence. It concluded simply: "O God, let America be free!"

8 Eighteenth-Century America: From Provinces To Independence

The crisis of the 1770s in Massachusetts had actually been brewing for many decades throughout the British North American provinces. The troubles of Governors Bernard and Hutchinson had been experienced earlier by many other royal officials in other colonies. At least as far back as the days of Sir William Berkeley in Virginia, the relationship between American colonists and royal officials had been a troubled one. Powerful stresses and strains were built into the very structure of the British Empire. Many royal governors had complained about how the colonists tried to escape, bypass, or limit British control of colonial life and trade.

What had changed in the years since Berkeley had less to do with the type of quarrel between governors and colonists than with the context of their argument. Conflicts in Boston and elsewhere grew heated in the 1760s. They stemmed from rapidly changing views on both sides of the Atlantic as to the rights and obligations of American subjects under the British crown.

Before the 1760s, traditionally and in theory, colonists swore — and felt — loyalty to the British crown. But in practice they gave their own colony first allegiance. Politically, a colonial American's "country" was his province, and his public life centered in the towns, counties, and cities of that province. Intercolonial political contacts were rare before the 1760s. Within each province, colonists had always taken certain rights and privileges for granted. Among these were the common law, the protection of private property, the right to representative legislatures, and the privilege of trial by jury.

Colonial obligations to the mother country seemed equally clear. Many of these involved trade and its regulation.

A CENTURY OF "SALUTARY NEGLECT"

Mercantilism

In general, the British government followed a mercantilist policy in relation to its American colonies. The British believed that all their colonies existed mainly to bring benefits to the mother country. Mercantilism, in theory, represented a reasonable division of economic labor between colonies and mother country. The mother country would produce most of the manufactured goods needed by the empire. The colonies would produce raw materials. In some cases Britain even paid bounties (for example, on naval stores[1] and indigo) to encourage colonial production. With other products, such as tobacco, Englishmen living at home were forbidden to compete with colonial producers.

In carrying out its mercantilist policies, England passed a number of trade regulations known as the Navigation Acts. Their purpose was to ensure that American commerce would "terminate in the advantage of the Mother State, unto whom it owes its being and protection." Another purpose was to limit the amount of colonial produce car-

---

[1] Naval stores were certain products needed to operate British navy and merchant ships; they included hemp, tar, and resin.

ried to Europe in foreign ships, especially those of the Dutch.

The Navigation Act of 1660 was a major trade law affecting the American colonies. It declared that goods from the American colonies could be transported in English ships only. The English crown also wanted to limit profits made by colonial shippers from the sale of American produce. So the 1660 Navigation Act enumerated certain commodities such as tobacco, sugar, indigo, and cotton (most of English America's leading exports). These commodities could only be shipped to points outside the empire from England and not directly from American colonies. Later acts added to the enumerated list new sources of trade almost as fast as Americans developed them—molasses, naval stores, rice, and furs.

It was easier to pass such laws than to enforce them. Smuggling was common. It was not difficult for a colonial merchant to ship enumerated goods to French colonies in America or even to mainland Europe. Breaking the law was all the easier because British colonial administration during the seventeenth and eighteenth centuries was badly disorganized. Several different royal agencies in the British government helped to set early policies for the mainland colonies.[2] In 1696 an agency known as the Board of Trade was created to bring some degree of order to colonial administration. Throughout the eighteenth century the Board of Trade had primary responsibility for shaping royal policy in America. (It was the Board of Trade, for example, that approved the dispatch of troops to Boston in 1768.)

Administrative reorganization did not solve Britain's major colonial problems. For one thing, political conflicts, both internal and external, often preoccupied the mother country. Those responsible for colonial regulation were generally too busy with other concerns to worry about widespread smuggling in America. Even if British officials had wished to enforce the laws more rigorously, they had few customs officers and few ships for coastal patrol. Thus, from the viewpoint of British imperial control, the century after 1660 was accurately called a period of "salutary neglect."

---

[2] That is, British North American colonies other than those in the West Indies.

As far as the colonists were concerned, they had relatively few complaints about the imperial system during this period. It seemed to meet the needs of a largely undeveloped, labor-scarce group of provinces that specialized in producing raw materials. Colonial commerce and agriculture matured under mild royal supervision. Successive Board of Trade members rarely interfered when American merchants violated the Navigation Acts with regularity.

Colonial Government

From his distant London office, a British administrator may easily have winked at American violations of the law. It was much more difficult, however, for a royal governor stationed in one of the colonies to keep his good humor.

By 1760, eight of the thirteen colonies were under direct royal control. In these colonies, governors like Francis Bernard or Thomas Hutchinson received their appointments directly from the king. In every royal colony except Massachusetts (where the council was elective), the governor appointed a council, which usually included the wealthiest and most distinguished citizens in the colony.

On paper a royal governor looked unbeatable. His duties were numerous. He enforced royal legislation. He summoned and adjourned colonial assemblies—or dissolved them whenever their actions threatened royal authority. He vetoed colonial statutes if they conflicted with British law. He also commanded the provincial militia and appointed local judges. Despite these impressive powers, the governors often found themselves isolated among unfriendly colonists and lacking the means to enforce royal authority against colonial assemblies.

Few royal governors had an easy time in dealing with the colonial assemblies. For although the king appointed the colonial governors, the assemblies paid their salaries. And they did so irritably, ungenerously, and on a year-to-year basis. Each mainland British colony had an assembly that controlled the colony's purse strings. The assemblies had the right to initiate legislation, levy taxes, and appropriate money—including the governor's salary—on a yearly basis. Except for Pennsylvania, all the colonies had two-house (bicameral) assemblies. The elected lower house passed laws, assessed taxes, and dispensed funds. The upper house, appointed by the king in royal colonies, advised the governor.

By passing tax measures that had only limited duration, the colonial assembly ensured that it would be called into session regularly by any royal governor who needed more revenue quickly. By stating how money raised by specific taxes should be spent, an assembly limited the governor's freedom of action. In extreme cases of conflict with crown officials, the assembly resorted to the effective practice of withholding salaries. The assembly was powerful not only because it was elected by the people. Voters and nonvoters alike were kept aware of its actions by means of newspapers, political meetings, and even sermons.

Estimates differ concerning the number of colonists who met the requirements for voting in the mid-eighteenth century. Voters had to be Christians, though in a number of colonies not of any particular religious denomination. They were required to own a certain amount of property, but the amount of land or its monetary equivalent required was not unreasonably high. In almost every colony property qualifications for voting were met by a large majority of the *white, free, male* population. (These were, of course, important and massive restrictions, since they excluded free blacks, slaves, and women.) The exact proportion of voters probably ranged from 50 to 75 percent in most colonies. In Massachusetts, for example—a colony composed mainly of small, family-owned farms—more than 80 percent of the male population could have voted at the time of the Revolution.

Whatever royal governors or imperial legislation might have said on the matter, every colonial assembly already exercised the functions of local self-government by 1750. The assemblies had been generally successful in asserting their claims for colonial autonomy. Supporting the assemblies' actions were majorities of each colony's qualified voters. Even most leading Tories—men such as Thomas Hutchinson, for example—argued for a greater measure of internal self-government in the American provinces.

From their earliest days, the mainland English settlements had waged almost continuous warfare against the Indian tribes and European settlements along their borders. As the seventeenth century drew to a close, England's chief European rival for control of North America was France. Her trading posts and fortified settlements ringed the British colonies like a vise from the eastern tip of Canada to the mouth of the Mississippi River. Aiding the French were thousands of Indians—great tribes like the Algonquins and the Hurons—with whom they traded furs. The powerful tribes of the Iroquois Confederation, however, were allies of the British.

France and Britain fought a series of four wars between 1689 and 1763. At stake were territories in Europe and possessions throughout the overseas empires of the two nations. In America, British troops were aided by American militia and their Indian allies in their fight against combined French and Indian forces.

The first of these wars, known in America as King William's War (1689–97), ended inconclusively. In the next war, Queen Anne's War (1702–13), the British won most of the battles, both in Europe and America. As a result, Britain acquired Nova Scotia, Newfoundland, and the Hudson Bay region of Canada. The third conflict, called King George's War (1740–48) in America, ended as indecisively as King William's War. But the French and Indian War, the fourth and last round of fighting, proved decisive. It began in the spring of 1754.

The Albany Congress

At the start of war, the American colonies displayed in dramatic fashion their divided condition and mutual suspiciousness. What made the display even more striking was the fact that this first attempt to achieve intercolonial unity was organized by none other than the British Board of Trade.

The Board of Trade wanted the colonists to meet with Britain's Iroquois allies. The purpose of the meeting was to discuss defense measures to be taken against the French and their Indian allies.

Jonathan Edwards

Jonathan Edwards, the most influential religious teacher and writer in eighteenth-century America, spent most of his life concerned with the problem of spiritual decline and possible regeneration of the faith—and the faithful—in what was once Puritan New England. Edwards was America's most subtle and original student of religious psychology and modes of thought. Born in Windsor, Connecticut, in 1703, he was descended from influential Puritan ministers on both sides of his family, among whom his grandfather Solomon Stoddard of Northampton was probably the most famous.

He proved an intellectual prodigy, studying at home with his highly educated parents before entering Yale College when he was almost thirteen. Even before then, he had written brilliant essays on aspects of natural history. After graduating from Yale in 1720, Edwards studied theological

subjects for two years, briefly held a ministry in New York, and, in 1726, joined his grandfather, Solomon Stoddard, in the Northampton church. Although he later wrote of the deep religious feelings he had as a child, Edwards underwent a transforming conversion experience in 1721 which reinforced his pivotal belief in God's utter omnipotence and control over human affairs and persuaded him that he had been "saved" by an infusion of divine grace. Edwards associated this experience of salvation with an intuited moment of religious rapture quite distinct from any more pallid and rational "proofs" of salvation.

Solomon Stoddard did not share his grandson's fascination with the process of achieving personal redemption. In Stoddard's Northampton church, membership had been extended to all those interested in becoming church members, including any "morally sincere" persons who had not been converted. But Edwards had come to believe that *true* church members experienced an inner transformation prior to becoming saved through God's freely given grace, and he disapproved strongly of Stoddard's practice of admitting the entire congregation to the sacrament of the Lord's Supper as a method for converting the unregenerate. When Stoddard died in 1729, Edwards became Northampton's only pastor and almost immediately began tightening requirements for church membership.

Edwards stressed to his parishioners their inability to influence through personal efforts or moral behavior alone God's sovereign decisions over saving or damning individual human beings. Images of hell and divine punishment filled Edwards's sermons and terrified many of his audiences into a shocked awareness of their own helplessness before the deity. As for the unregenerate: "The

---

The British also wanted to encourage cooperation among the various colonial militias, which had been sadly lacking up to this time. The result was the Albany Congress, which met in June and July of 1754. Seven colonies sent delegates. Among

them were Thomas Hutchinson of Massachusetts and Benjamin Franklin of Pennsylvania.

Once the meeting began, Franklin went beyond the British agenda and proposed instead a general plan of intercolonial union. According to

devil is waiting for them, hell is gaping for them, the flames gather and flash about them, and would fain hold on them and swallow them up. . . . All that preserves them every moment is the mere arbitrary will and unconvenanted, unobliged forbearance of an incensed God."

Edwards's inspired preaching and fearsome admonitions led to the announced "conversions," in 1735, of dozens of his parishioners, especially young people, and a revival of religious enthusiasm which spread throughout the Connecticut Valley—the first such "revival" in American history—making Edwards famous on both sides of the Atlantic. His *Faithful Narrative* of the revival, published in 1737, was quickly translated into German and Dutch and served as a model for John Wesley, founder of the Methodist church. Edwards's activity in Northampton helped to prepare New England churches for the outburst of religious evangelism and spread of conversion experiences which attended George Whitfield's preaching in 1740–42. In the wake of Whitfield's tour of the colonies, evangelical ministers stirred up highly emotional conversion scenes throughout the American provinces. The infusion of divine grace often reached communicants in a profoundly dramatic manner. Screaming and writhing, fainting, and weeping accompanied many of the conversions during the "Great Awakening." And although Jonathan Edwards decried many of these emotional excesses for their possibly "devilish" origins, he welcomed the renewed stress on genuine spiritual transformations which the Awakening appeared to bring. His most significant analysis of the psychology of religion, *A Treatise Concerning Religious Affections,* was published in 1746. Among other points, Edwards defended the notion of man's necessary and total subordination to divine moral perfection, stressed the role played by emotions in apprehending God's holiness, but cautioned against excessive dependence on the intensity of emotions alone among truly devout persons.

Edwards's two decades as minister in Northampton had often seen stormy battles between pastor and parishioners. After one such dispute involving standards of church membership, the congregation dismissed him in 1750. The following year, Edwards settled with his wife and children in the frontier outposts of Stockbridge where he served both as pastor of the small church and as missionary to the Indians (the church itself included both white settlers and Indian parishioners). Although deeply in debt and virtually impoverished for the next seven years, Edwards remained in Stockbridge and wrote many of his most important religious treatises. The two most extraordinary works which further developed his uncompromising perspective on Godly control of human destiny appeared in 1754 (*A Careful and Strict Enquiry into the Modern Prevailing Notions of . . . . Freedom of* (the) *Will . . .*) and 1758 (*The Great Christian Doctrine of Original Sin Defended*). Edwards ended his Stockbridge isolation in January 1758, when he traveled to Princeton, New Jersey, to become president of the College of New Jersey. There he preached and taught theology for the next two months before dying of a fever on March 22, 1758, after receiving a smallpox inoculation.

Few subsequent theologians could match the rigor of Edwards's logic and theoretical rebuilding of Calvinist doctrine. His major legacy, however, remains a tradition of evangelical religious revivalism which Jonathan Edwards helped first to create and then to weave into the central tapestry of American Protestant belief.

Franklin's plan of union, the king would appoint a president-general, a kind of supergovernor, presumably with the usual lack of enforcement authority. The provincial assemblies would be represented in proportion to their tax payments in a grand council, a kind of superassembly somewhat like our present-day Congress. Taxes on each colony would support the grand council's control of intercolonial defense, Indian relations, and westward expansion. The central body would be allowed to raise an army and navy and build forts and settlements. The president-general, however (like the royal governors), could veto any laws in the king's name.

The Albany Congress approved the essential outlines of Franklin's plan and submitted it to the colonial assemblies. Three of these simply ignored the proposal. The other four rejected it, agreeing with the Boston town meeting that the Albany Plan endangered popular liberties. Throughout the French and Indian War, each colony preferred to protect itself. Whatever common defense did exist in British North America was led and staffed largely by regular units of the British army. None of the colonial assemblies was willing to surrender its taxing powers; nor, for that matter, did any assembly wish to allow any "grand council" to divide the unclaimed lands in the interior that some colonies hoped to acquire by driving out the French.

The French and Indian War

In the beginning, this conflict (also known as the Seven Years' War) went badly for the British. Colonial assemblies were reluctant to contribute men and money to the fight. The result was a series of British defeats along the frontier line with French Canada.[3] Not until William Pitt became prime minister in 1757 did the British war effort begin to take shape. For one thing, Pitt shifted the war's main emphasis from Europe (on which it had been centered during the earlier three Anglo-French conflicts) to the empire. Here Pitt assigned most of Britain's military strength. Pitt bankrupted the national treasury to pay for additional regiments of British troops to send to America.

In order to win over the colonial assemblies, Pitt directed British military officials to assume the cost of feeding and arming colonial militia. The British also promised to repay the assemblies for money they spent to supply additional volunteers. Such generosity swelled the ranks of colonial regi-

---

[3] One American who got his first taste of battle in this conflict was George Washington. As a young officer with British General Edward Braddock, he took part in an unsuccessful campaign against the French near what is now Pittsburgh.

ments that fought alongside British redcoats in subduing the French.

The British won a series of military victories under aggressive new commanders such as James Wolfe and Jeffrey Amherst. In 1759 they captured Quebec from the French, who were led by the Marquis de Montcalm. Within a year all of French Canada lay in British hands. In the Treaty of Paris in 1763, France surrendered all of her North American possessions east of the Mississippi from Canada to Florida. The exception was Louisiana, which France had earlier ceded to its ally Spain.

During the war all did not go smoothly between Britain and her colonies. For one thing, Pitt insisted on rigorously enforcing the Navigation Acts in America. British warships patrolled in force to choke off trade with the enemy.

Northern colonial merchants were also outraged by Britain's intensified hunt for smuggled goods through the use of so-called general writs of assistance. These were unlimited search warrants good for the entire period of a king's reign. They allowed customs officers to enter and search any building in daytime, without having prior knowledge of allegedly imported goods.

After the death of King George II in 1760, Boston merchants (many of whom later led the nonimportation campaign) retained James Otis, one of the colony's best lawyers, to argue the illegality of the writs in order to prevent their renewal under the new king, George III. Otis lost his case, and the writs were upheld. Often during the following decade, royal customs officials barged unannounced into Boston warehouses and homes searching for smuggled goods.

INCREASED BRITISH CONTROL

After the French and Indian War, it became clear that the British intended to regulate their American provinces much more closely and thoroughly in the future than they had in the past. One important decision involved the new trans-Appalachian territories recently acquired from the French. Even before 1754, settlers had begun moving into the rich Ohio Valley. Land companies were organized to take control of the region's fur trade and to explore other opportunities. Then the British government issued the Proclamation of 1763, banning, for an indefinite time, settlement and land grants beyond the crest of the Appalachian Mountains. Land speculators (among them George Washington) denounced British efforts to close off the West. Unofficially and in violation of British law, American settlement and land speculation continued.

Another problem was financial. Who would pick up the tab for Britain's costly victory over France? Pitt's war strategy had succeeded, but in the process England had spent £82 million, virtually bankrupting the treasury. Despite heavy wartime taxation, the British national debt had run up to £130 million by 1764. Every leading British minister during the 1760s and 1770s agreed that it was only fair for the American colonies to share in paying off the war debts. After all, they reasoned, the mainland provinces had achieved almost complete security on their borders at practically no cost to themselves.

Americans disagreed with the British argument that Parliament had the right to tax colonists along with other British subjects. This dispute over taxation, brought on by the British government's search for revenue, quickly became the major source of colonial unrest during the 1760s. Throughout the eighteenth century most Americans had accepted Parliament's right to legislate for the colonies. But they denied its right to tax them. Most Americans would probably have agreed with the Virginia legislature that, "Laws imposing taxes on the People ought not to be made without the Consent of Representatives chosen by themselves." Colonial assemblies believed that they had won the exclusive right to initiate taxes within their own provinces. Yet in April 1764, George Grenville, Britain's first lord of the treasury, steered through Parliament a law that challenged this right and, in the process, stirred up colonial resistance from New England to Georgia.

The Sugar Act

When George Grenville became British finance minister in 1763, he made an embarrassing discovery: the customs service in America cost the

George III, long thought to have become insane in later life, probably suffered from a rare inherited disease. (Colonial Williamsburg)

British government four times as much in salaries as it collected in revenues! Grenville's solution was a revenue-raising bill that came to be known as the Sugar Act.

Earlier in the century the British had taxed foreign molasses at the rate of sixpence a gallon in order to encourage colonials to purchase this product from the British West Indies. The regulation was largely ignored. American rum distillers found it much cheaper to bribe customs officials (at one penny or "pence" a gallon) so they could smuggle in cheaper molasses from the French West Indies. Grenville's Sugar Act of 1764 was designed to eliminate such colonial trading freedom.

The new statute lowered the molasses duty from six to three pence, thereby making payment of the duty more competitive with payment of the bribe—and much safer. The new duty applied to both British and foreign molasses entering the colonies. This provision transformed a trade-regulating device into a revenue-producing tax. The Sugar Act also placed new tax duties on such commodities as sugar, indigo, wine, and textiles.

More upsetting to the colonists than the taxes themselves was Parliament's obvious determination to enforce their collection. Colonial shipowners now had to file official papers for every vessel leaving and entering American harbors. Moreover, accused violators of the Sugar Act would be tried in admiralty (naval) courts distant from their hometowns or cities. Such courts operated without juries and under rules according to which a defendant was considered guilty until proved innocent. Provincial merchant-smugglers had come to depend on sympathetic local juries or judges (men like Boston's justice of the peace William Molineux, who had persuaded a mob to surrender Ebenezer Richardson). Local jurors and judges generally gave violators of British trade regulations what the defendants wished—freedom, not justice.

A storm of protest over the Sugar Act spread quickly through the colonies. It was sparked by commercial cities like Boston, which reminded their rural countrymen of the stake all Americans had in the new British policies. "If our Trade may be taxed, why not our Lands?" asked the Boston town meeting in a thumping denunciation of the Sugar Act. "Why not the produce of our Lands and every Thing we possess or make use of?" Similar complaints filled newspapers from Massachusetts to the Carolinas. Widespread smuggling continued. Yearly collections of revenue from the Sugar Act averaged a ridiculously small £20,000.

Grenville (and many other British officials) failed to realize that, to provincial Americans, their idea of freedom as British subjects included the right of their assemblies alone to levy taxes over them. Americans were as much concerned with the *precedent* set by the Sugar Act as with its actual enforcement. The rights of Englishmen, colonists argued, depended upon a person's right—as James Otis put it—to be "free from all taxes but what he consents to in person, or by his representative." Actually, although the colonists lacked representation in Parliament, by and large they did not want it. They recognized that this would lead to tighter and costlier English control of provincial affairs—taxation *with* representation.

Paying taxes to England became one of the most galling aspects of life for an American colonial in the 1770s. Often the tax man bore the brunt of communal anger, as portrayed in this 1774 British print, "The Bostonians Paying the Excise-Man, or Tarring & Feathering." (The Henry Francis DuPont Winterthur Museum)

Additional Regulations

Colonial protests over the Sugar Act did not lessen Grenville's interest in squeezing additional revenue out of North America. In March 1765 Parliament passed the Stamp Act. It required Americans to buy tax stamps for newspapers, legal documents, and other types of printed matter. Englishmen had paid such a tax for decades. Grenville made certain to mention that revenues raised from the new tax, which was to take effect in

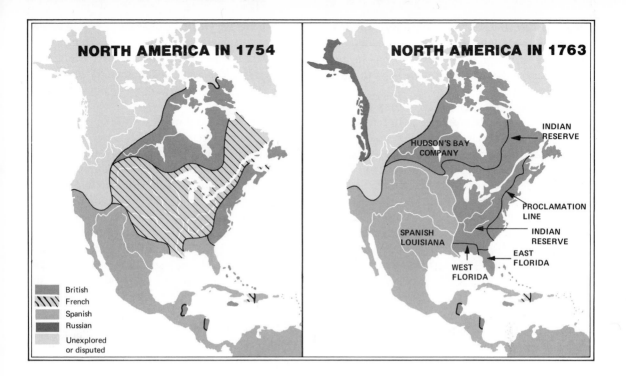

NORTH AMERICA IN 1754

British
French
Spanish
Russian
Unexplored or disputed

NORTH AMERICA IN 1763

HUDSON'S BAY COMPANY

INDIAN RESERVE

PROCLAMATION LINE

INDIAN RESERVE

SPANISH LOUISIANA

EAST FLORIDA

WEST FLORIDA

November 1765, would be applied entirely to "the Defense of the Colonies."

A related measure also sponsored by Grenville was the Quartering Act, passed by Parliament in March 1765. It obliged colonial assemblies to furnish British troops stationed in their colonies with adequate living quarters and provisions. Many colonists considered the timing strange. Britain had kept almost no royal troops garrisoned in America when the French, the Spanish, and the Indians menanced the western borders of almost every colony. Now, after this threat had been removed, she planned to station soldiers there. Americans realized that the troops were actually being sent to enforce royal authority—which they did with such mixed results in Boston three years later.

The Stamp Act and the Quartering Act fed a growing suspicion of England among knowledgeable Americans. Had the British government deliberately set out to deny them freedoms they had previously exercised? Some of these might be called *negative* freedoms—the absence of British taxation, the lack of a British army in their midst,

lax enforcement of the Navigation Acts. Others were more *positive*—trial by local juries, the liberty to expand westward.

None of the king's ministers would have denied that Britain meant to change its permissive ways in North America. They would have argued, though, that Parliament did not wish to deny *legitimate* colonial rights. It wanted only to remind the mainland colonies of their equally legitimate responsibilities toward the mother country. In practice, however, Britain's sudden effort to tighten the parental screws triggered an immediate protest from her fully grown New World children.

American Opposition

The Stamp Act generated the first successfully organized intercolonial opposition to British policy. It took the form of almost complete resistance to buying the required stamps. For a lawyer, merchant, newspaper editor, small businessman, or even a planter, the stamps represented both a costly expense and an illegal parliamentary attack on colonial liberties. As usual, resistance centered in the commercial cities and towns, to which Britain had sent most of the stamps and tax collectors. For the first (but hardly the last) time in the struggle, Boston became the center of both legal and violent protest.

The Massachusetts assembly took the lead in June 1765, when it proposed an intercolonial meeting to unify opposition to parliamentary taxation. Boston mobs—often organized by the same Sons of Liberty who would prove so effective later in the decade—ransacked the homes of several British officials, including the chief royal stamp collector. The mobs also burned Lieutenant Governor Thomas Hutchinson's elegant mansion to the ground, destroyed important government records, and forced several stamp distributors to resign their offices. Riotous Sons of Liberty played a similar role in New York City and elsewhere.

Meanwhile, peaceful forms of protest were having an even more unsettling effect on British policy. As early as May 1765, a young lawyer named Patrick Henry introduced a series of resolutions in the Virginia House of Burgesses. They asserted that this body alone had the right to tax Virginians. The House of Burgesses adopted the more moderate of Henry's resolutions, but it rejected his call for outright resistance to collection of stamp taxes. Most other colonial assemblies followed Virginia's lead and passed similar resolutions, all of which Parliament ignored.

But the British government could hardly overlook the resolutions passed by an intercolonial Stamp Act Congress, first proposed by Massachusetts. The assemblies of nine colonies were represented when this congress convened in October 1765 in New York City. Although the congress assured Parliament of "all due subordination," the phrase was negligible, since it went on to deny that Britain had the right either to tax the colonists or to try Americans in admiralty courts. Furthermore, the delegates demanded immediate repeal of both the Sugar Act and the Stamp Act.

In order to put teeth into these demands, more than a thousand colonial merchants from all the major trading cities quickly organized an effective boycott of British manufactured goods. This was the first of several times that colonial economic pressures through such nonimportation agreements were to force changes in British policy. The merchants played a crucial role in the struggle with Britain—so crucial that the strength of colonial resistance at any given moment depended to a large degree on the extent of merchant support, or lack of support.

The most important long-term result of the Stamp Act protests was that Americans of all classes and backgrounds began to learn the habit of resistance. Some Americans—including militants like Samuel Adams—even began to advocate independence and revolution. They argued that, both historically and legally, a people had the right to change or overthrow a government that systematically violated people's rights and exceeded its authority. Such opinions frightened members of Parliament. William Pitt urged repeal of the Stamp Act on the grounds that doing so would restore the loyalty to England of most *moderate* Americans and isolate the minority of *radicals:* "If we repeal the Act, we shall have all the sober part of America on our side, and we shall easily be able to chastize the few hot-headed republicans among them." Pitt might also have reminded his colleagues that the Stamp Act had proved a total failure. It earned no revenue, since no Americans could be found who were brave enough to collect the tax. American business continued as usual, while British manufacturers suffered from the boycott of their goods in America. Responding finally to economic and political pressures, Parliament repealed the Stamp Act in March 1766.

A DEEPENING CRISIS

Americans might have celebrated the repeal of the Stamp Act a bit more heartily had not Parliament coupled its repeal with passage of another measure. This was the Declaratory Act, which reaffirmed colonial subordination. It also asserted Parliament's right to pass any law it wished (presumably, therefore, any *tax* law), "to bind the colonies and people of America."

In 1767 a new British finance minister, Charles Townshend, exercised this dangerous option. He secured a new program of colonial duties, to be placed on imports of items such as paper, tea, lead, paint, and glass. Townshend believed somewhat naïvely that his move would produce much-needed revenue. Instead, he succeeded only in reopening the unsettled issues of the Stamp Act crisis.

Once more, Massachusetts led intercolonial resistance. This time its assembly sent a Circular Letter to the other colonial legislatures urging some form of united opposition similar to the Stamp Act Congress. The Circular Letter denied that Massachusetts advocated independence. Still, the British government considered the letter dangerous enough to demand that the assembly rescind it. When the assembly refused, Governor Bernard, on orders from London, prevented the legislators from meeting in 1768. Special town meetings summoned delegates to an extralegal convention to discuss the matter. It was at this point that two regiments of British troops were sent to occupy Boston in order to protect the unpopular customs commissioners.

The civic turmoil that ensued over the next two years would lead directly to the Boston Massacre. New York City was also the scene of protests and mob violence after Parliament dissolved the New York assembly for refusing to obey the Quartering Act.

As with the Stamp Act, however, the peaceful boycott of British goods by colonial merchants proved more effective with Parliament than threats or violence. Boston's nonimportation agreement was followed by other cities, among them Providence, Newport, and New York. In the Virginia assembly a set of resolutions sponsored by George Washington supported Massachusetts' Circular Letter. When the royal governor dissolved the assembly, its leaders regrouped informally and endorsed a nonimportation campaign. Throughout the colonies unrest died down only after Parliament had repealed all the Townshend duties except the tax on tea. The king's new prime minister, Lord North, had insisted that this tax remain in order to uphold the "supremacy of Parliament" in America.

Lacking a dramatic rallying point against Britain, many American Patriots lapsed back easily into provincial disunity. Even dogged fighters like Samuel Adams were hard-pressed to keep alive much bitterness toward royal authority during the few relatively quiet years that followed repeal of the Townshend Acts. Customs commissioners went about their business. British troops remained quartered in the colonies. And royal governors began to act more confidently.

To counteract this apathy, Samuel Adams and other Sons of Liberty in Boston created a Committee of Correspondence to publicize complaints against the British. The idea spread throughout the colonies and revived intercolonial cooperation. The committees found a convenient *cause célèbre* when Rhode Islanders burned a British customs patrol boat, the *Gaspée,* after it ran aground in Narragansett Bay in June 1772. This led to a royal investigation. To the Patriots' delight, the investigators could find no sign of the culprits. The incident also probably served as a model for another one, involving a shipload of tea, which took place in Boston harbor in December 1773.

The Boston Tea Party

Tea was the colonists' most popular beverage, and few Americans liked Lord North's decision in May 1773 to aid the financially ailing British East India Company by granting it a monopoly in America. Previously, the company had sold its tea to British wholesalers. They in turn sold to Americans wholesalers, who distributed the tea to local merchants. The British government now proposed to allow the East India Company to sell tea directly through its own agents in America. This step would eliminate both British and colonial middlemen.

The immediate effect was to *reduce* the retail price of tea considerably. But Americans grasped almost immediately the long-term effect of this action. In return for cheaper tea, they were being asked to accept a new royal interference in normal patterns of colonial commerce. If Parliament could so easily dispose of a profitable, long-standing colonial tea trade, then no portion of America's commerce would be safe from British interference.

Public protests against the Tea Act spread quickly throughout the colonies. They were fueled by passionate letters exchanged among the Com-

In December 1773, a group of Boston townspeople dressed as Indians dumped an entire cargo of tea into Boston harbor. The "Tea Party" was a reaction to the Tea Act, a British effort to by-pass colonial merchants in the highly profitable tea trade. The Tea Party stirred the imagination of those colonials intent upon resisting British authority at all costs. (The Bettmann Archive)

mittees of Correspondence and by the almost unanimous opposition of colonial newspapers. Once again the British government had unintentionally revived the colonial resistance movement. In New York and Philadelphia royal authorities, fearing violence, ordered the first East India Company tea ships back to Britain without attempting to unload them. In Charleston the tea was simply locked in a warehouse and not offered for sale.

Bostonians, as usual, thought of a more direct and effective way to rally patriotic sentiment and provoke royal anger. On December 16, 1773, a ship called the *Dartmouth* lay at dockside waiting for her captain to decide whether to try to unload her cargo of tea. That night, led by the Sons of Liberty, a band of townspeople disguised as Indians boarded the *Dartmouth*. A huge crowd of Bostonians cheered as the "Indians" dumped the cargo overboard.

Aftermath: The Intolerable Acts

Parliament responded to this "tea party" by passing a series of laws designed to punish Boston. These so-called Coercive Acts took away the city's

remaining liberties. One of them closed the port to all commerce until its residents had paid for the spoiled tea. Another authorized the transfer of cases involving British officials from Massachusetts to England in order to escape the hostility of local judges and juries. A third act revised the fundamental structure of Massachusetts' government to strengthen royal authority in the colony. The upper house (governor's council) would now be appointed by the king and no longer elected. Town meetings, in which the Sons of Liberty engaged in their most effective organizing, could be held only once a year. Once more British troops appeared in Boston. General Gage, commander-in-chief of all British troops in America, became military governor of Massachusetts. For Bostonians, British occupation and interference with normal political and economic life was far more sweeping than it had been during the controversy over the Townshend duties.

Another statute passed by Parliament at this time was the Quebec Act, which applied to the recently conquered French territory that Americans had already begun settling. The law recognized the practice of Roman Catholicism and

French civil law in that area—both unpopular with the largely Protestant and largely English colonists of the thirteen colonies. They dubbed the Coercive Acts and the Quebec Act the Intolerable Acts.

Supplies and pledges of support from all over the provinces flowed into Boston. The Intolerable Acts achieved something that had previously eluded Samuel Adams and the Sons of Liberty—the unification of colonial resistance to Britain.

OUTBREAK OF THE REVOLUTION

In June 1774 the Massachusetts assembly asked other colonies to send delegates to a congress where they could agree on common action against the Intolerable Acts. Fifty-five delegates from twelve colonies attended the First Continental Congress, which met at Philadelphia in September. (Georgia was unrepresented at this time, but later sent delegates.) The Congress rejected by one vote a compromise proposal for a new scheme of colonial government similar to Franklin's 1754 Albany Plan. The Congress then endorsed a set of resolutions proposed originally by a convention in Suffolk County, Massachusetts. These Suffolk Resolves demanded direct resistance to the Intolerable Acts. The Congress also adopted John Adams's Declaration of Rights and Resolves, a statement of the colonists' constitutional arguments.

The most practical step taken by the Continental Congress was to create an association to enforce a complete boycott against Britain. Delegates vowed not to import, export, or consume British goods until the crisis had been settled. Before adjourning in October 1774, the delegates also decided to meet again in May 1775.

King George and his ministers had erroneously believed that colonial resistance was confined largely to Massachusetts, and their reaction to the First Continental Congress reflected this mistaken judgment. They convinced themselves that stern measures in *that* colony would dampen unrest elsewhere. "The New England governments are in a state of Rebellion," George III remarked in November 1774. "Blows must decide whether they are to be subject to this country or independent."

General Gage, ordinarily as stubborn as George III himself about punishing colonial resistance, had been sobered by his new role as governor of Massachusetts. He tried to warn London of what lay ahead. The provincial militia was then gathering on the outskirts of Boston. To subdue it and reassert parliamentary authority in Massachusetts, Gage wrote Lord North, would require 20,000 additional troops. Until their arrival, Gage recommended that Britain suspend the Coercive Acts in order to reduce tensions in America. But his superiors responded by declaring Massachusetts to be in a state of rebellion. They sent Gage an additional 3500 men. They directed the general to suppress the rebellion and arrest "the principal actors in the provincial Congress." Gage attempted to obey this order on April 19, 1775, and, in the process, began the American Revolution.

Open Hostilities in Massachusetts

Not suprisingly, the conflict began in Boston. Massachusetts Patriots had been drilling for months, organized into extralegal militia companies sometimes called Minutemen. Gage had been informed that the Patriots were storing arms at Concord, west of Boston, and that Samuel Adams and John Hancock were also in the vicinity. The British general sent a force of some 700 regulars to confiscate the arms and arrest the Patriot leaders.

On April 19, arriving at Lexington on their way to Concord, the British found about seventy Minutemen assembled on the town common. The British commander ordered the Americans to disperse. Then someone—whether British or American remains unclear—fired a shot. Just as had happened six years earlier during the Boston Massacre, a single shot led to additional firing and a state of general confusion. When the smoke cleared, the Minutemen had fled, leaving eight dead and ten wounded. The British continued to Concord only to find that most of the colonial arms stored there had already been removed. The British destroyed what supplies they could find and fought several skirmishes with small groups of Minutemen.

Meanwhile, colonial militia had converged on Lexington and Concord throughout the day, the alarm having been spread the previous night by a

"Give Me Liberty, or Give Me Death!" This 1870
rendering of Patrick Henry's March 23, 1775,
oration to the Virginia assembly shows vividly
how later Americans viewed his famous "war
cry of the Revolution." (Culver Pictures)

few Boston Sons of Liberty, including Paul Revere.
Some 900 British reinforcements joined the first
detachment at Lexington for the march back to
Boston. But they found themselves outnumbered
and outvolleyed by more than 4000 colonial
marksmen, who fired from behind stone walls and
other cover. The colonists peppered the British
troops with musket fire along their 20-mile retreat.
Even the 1500 additional redcoats sent by Gage to
protect the retreat failed to prevent it from turning
into a chaotic stampede.

By the time the British straggled back to
safety in Boston, they had lost 73 men and suffered

149 wounded, compared to American casualties of
49 killed and 39 wounded. More ominously still,
the Minutemen did not return to their homes.
They began instead to surround Boston, and their
ranks grew. First they came from other Massachusetts towns. Then, within days, volunteers
began arriving from other colonies as well. Gage
and his undermanned British garrison now found
themselves under siege from all sides.

Two months later, reinforced by only 1100
troops, Gage attempted to break the colonial lines
ringing Boston. He fought colonial militia entrenched on two strategic high points, Breed's Hill

and Bunker Hill. After a furious day's fighting, on June 17, the British cleared both hills of American soldiers. The cost was high. The British suffered more than 1000 killed or wounded out of an attacking force of 2000 men. The Americans counted fewer than 450 men killed, wounded, or captured. As one of Gage's officers aptly remarked, "another such victory would have ruined us."

The Second Continental Congress

In May 1775, while 16,000 colonial militia penned the British garrison in its uncomfortable quarters among Boston's hostile townspeople, the Second Continental Congress met at Philadelphia. Its members now confronted not merely the older pattern of colonial grievances but also the new reality of armed revolt. After the British "victory" at Bunker Hill, George III had relieved Gage of his command and formally declared the colonies to be "in open rebellion." The Continental Congress endorsed the description and began the difficult job of trying to make the rebellion succeed.

One of the Congress's first acts was to appoint one of the delegates, George Washington of Virginia, as commander-in-chief of Continental forces. Delegates also prepared to requisition men and supplies for the new army.

Some of the men at Philadelphia still considered the revolt a *temporary* break with Britain. They believed that the grievances that had inspired it could be resolved by compromise. In deference to these moderates, the Continental Congress, in July 1775, adopted a conciliatory document that came to be known as the Olive Branch Petition. The delegates, "as faithful subjects," requested the repeal of all oppressive legislation and an end to tyranny.

The Second Continental Congress also passed a Declaration of the Causes and Necessities of Taking up Arms. This document was drafted by John Dickinson of Pennsylvania and a new delegate from Virgina, Thomas Jefferson. It defended colonial resistance as the only alternative to "unconditional submission to the tyranny of irritated ministers." It also denied that the American aim was complete independence and promised to lay down arms once Britain ceased its abusive behavior.

The declaration was a response to the so-called Conciliatory Act, passed by Parliament the previous February. The act had promised to exempt from British taxes those colonies that paid for royal expenses voluntarily. The declaration rejected this idea, however, and signaled the colonists' continued opposition to British policies.

Canada Remains Loyal

Renewed imperial controls, which followed the British victory of 1763, ran counter to a rising desire for independence in the thirteen colonies. Americans hoped that Nova Scotia and Quebec would sympathize with their grievances against Britain. (They did not consider Newfoundland or Rupert's Land, as they were too far away.)

Although part of the same empire, Nova Scotia and Quebec did not cast their lot with the thirteen colonies. Few of the American protests applied to Nova Scotia. The closing of the western lands did not affect the colony, which had many empty acres of its own. Nor was Nova Scotia a Massachusetts, ready to stand on its own feet in world trade.

In Quebec support for the colonies to the south was not forthcoming either. The Catholic Canadians had little love for the Protestant Americans, nor much interest in English traditions of government. In Quebec the French were a majority. But if Quebec combined with the other colonies, the French would be a minority. In addition, because of decades of warfare, the colonists of France and those of Britain still regarded each other more as enemies than as friends.

Despite Canadian neutrality, the American Revolution had a profound influence on Canada. She became a refuge for supporters of the crown—Tories to the Americans, United Empire Loyalists to the British. Over 40,000 moved north to Canada. Their descendants live there still.

SEVERING TIES WITH BRITAIN

All the actions taken to strengthen intercolonial resistance reinforced Lord North's belief, shared by George III, that the Americans wanted complete independence. Various proposals for compromise were defeated by Parliament. The British government's answer to the Olive Branch Petition was to send 25,000 additional troops to America. Britain also began to hire foreign mercenary soldiers. In August 1775 the king had declared the colonies to be in rebellion. In December Parliament outlawed trade with the colonies and declared American ships and cargoes subject to confiscation.

As far as Britain was concerned, she was at war with rebellious subjects in a conflict that permitted only one solution: the colonists' submission as dutiful subjects of the mother country and the king. As far as a growing number of Americans were concerned, the colonies had no choice left but to fight. This involved taking a more serious step toward independence: repudiating the basic symbol of British power—the British monarchy—and colonial allegiance to it.

Normal people do not surrender their customary loyalties easily or without overwhelming reasons. Many of the delegates at Philadelphia shrank from defying the king himself. To strike such a blow at the symbol of monarchy required someone who hated more bitterly than did most Americans, even in 1776, *both* the British crown and the ruler on whose head it now rested. The man who struck the blow was a recently arrived immigrant from England named Thomas Paine.

Thomas Paine had left England in 1774 for the colonies. He was a failure in marriage and a failure in business. More important, however, he was an ardent republican who believed in rule by the people rather than by a monarch. He made an enormous impact in America with his anonymously printed pamphlet, *Common Sense,* which first appeared in January 1776. Paine's pamphlet sold 150,000 copies in the critical months from January to July 1776.

Common Sense contained outspoken attacks on George III as "the royal brute of Britain." Paine assailed the idea of monarchy itself. He wrote: "Of more worth is one honest man to society and in the sight of God, than all the crowned ruffians that ever lived." Through Paine's influence enthusiasm for republican government spread quickly throughout the colonies.

In May 1776 the Continental Congress adopted John Adams's proposal urging all provincial assemblies to suppress any remaining vestiges of royal government, to establish constitutions, and to create new state governments based upon popular consent. Royal authority had already collapsed throughout the colonies by this time, as British officials fled to safety and American Tories retreated into silence. Colonial assemblies began functioning as independent, provisional state legislatures.

The Second Continental Congress had already begun acting as a provisional national government. It sought diplomatic and military assistance abroad. It authorized Americans to attack English shipping in retaliation for the British embargo on American trade. In addition, it opened American ports to foreign shipping, thus formally ending further pretense at recognizing England's right to regulate American trade.

The decisive step in the move toward independence came on May 15. Virginia's new revolutionary legislature instructed its delegates to the Congress to introduce a resolution proposing both independence *and* an intercolonial confederation. Many Virginians were already convinced that Britain was indifferent to colonial interests. This belief grew stronger after the efforts made by Virginia's last royal governor, Lord Dunmore, to recruit slaves into the British army by promising them freedom. Rumors of a British scheme to stir up a slave rebellion swept the South in 1776. Such rumors probably helped some fearful Southerners to overcome their reluctance and endorse a complete break with the mother country.

The Declaration of Independence

On June 7 Richard Henry Lee introduced Virginia's independence resolution into the Congress. A five-man committee was assigned the task of preparing an appropriate document defending colonial actions. The committee consisted of John Adams, Benjamin Franklin, Thomas Jefferson, Roger Sherman of Connecticut, and Robert Livingston of New York. The thirty-three-year-old Jefferson, the youngest man in the Congress, became chairman of the committee. Adams and Franklin made suggestions, but the draft was largely Jefferson's.

By late June more moderates had accepted the idea of a complete break. On July 2 Congress finally voted to approve Richard Henry Lee's earlier motion "that these united colonies are, and of right ought to be, free and independent states." Jefferson's Declaration of Independence was then submitted to the full membership of the Congress. Delegates altered some of the wording, but they made few substantial changes except to strike out a rather questionable passage blaming George III for the existence of slavery in America.

Most of Jefferson's draft had a familiar ring to the delegates. Perhaps most original was its attempt to attribute colonial oppression to *royal* rather than *parliamentary* tyranny. Much of the Declaration consisted of a list of the alleged "injuries and usurpations" by George III that had forced America to resort to rebellion. Some of the complaints were reasonable: the king's interference with representative assemblies, his abuse of civil rights, his use of an army of occupation without colonial consent, and his allowing Parliament to tax the colonies and restrain their trade. Other grievances had plainly been designed to arouse American fears, not to gain foreign support, especially charges that the king had incited slave and Indian insurrections, "plundered our seas, ravaged our coasts, burnt our towns, and destroyed the lives of our people."

Jefferson's preamble to the Declaration attempted to justify a people's right to rebel and to alter their form of government. He employed concepts that were thoroughly familiar to his associates in Congress and to his American readers. These included (1) the duty of a government to protect a people's unalienable "natural rights"—among which are "Life, Liberty, and the Pursuit of Happiness"; and (2) government's origin in the consent of those governed. The preamble also spoke of the obligation of a people to alter or abolish their government whenever their rights were persistently violated—in other words, it defended the right to revolution. (For the complete text of the Declaration of Independence, see the back of this volume.)

John Adams later said that there was "nothing new" in Jefferson's Declaration. Its author would have agreed. Most of these ideas had been included in earlier statements of colonial grievances against England. What *was* new about the Declaration, which Congress adopted on July 4, 1776, was its suggestion that Americans had become a single, separate people, and the "united colonies" a single, separate nation. The president of the Continental Congress, John Hancock, reportedly said as he signed the Declaration (the first to do so): "We must be unanimous; there must be no pulling different ways; we must all hang together." To which Benjamin Franklin supposedly replied: "Yes, we must indeed all hang together, or most assuredly we shall all hang separately." The exchange probably never occurred, but it suggests an important symbolic truth. During the previous decade, colonists had come to define their loyalties as *national* as well as provincial. They had begun to see themselves as Americans, not merely as Massachusetts people, New Yorkers, or Virginians.

From a sense of shared grievances and from efforts at common action, a broader definition of national loyalty had begun to evolve. This pattern of allegiance would be strengthened immeasurably in the revolutionary struggle that loomed ahead. Even for many of those who had hoped for a compromise settlement, there seemed to be no choice but to acknowledge their mutual peril as *Americans* in revolt.

THE WAR FOR INDEPENDENCE

War followed and continued throughout the next five years. Despite a number of defeats in battle and a variety of difficulties which plagued him and his officers, Washington managed to keep an army in the field—and thereby to keep the Revolution alive. The Continental Army he commanded rarely exceeded 5,000–10,000 men, although it was periodically reinforced by units of state militia, whose lack of discipline or zeal often exasperated the general. George Washington, a professional soldier by training and inclination, had served with valor and distinction during the Seven Years' War, and he had little fondness for the Minute Men and other citizen soldiers he now commanded.

Still he understood how effective such volunteers could be in battle, especially when fighting

An American cartoon satirizes the British retreat from Concord. British troops, portrayed with jackass heads, stop to burn and plunder in this distorted but lively drawing. (John Carter Brown Library)

on familiar ground against British troops unaccustomed to the terrain or the vastness of America's thirteen independent "nations." Thus, in May 1775, hardly a month after the initial clashes at Lexington and Concord, a force of patriotic Vermont irregulars known as "Green Mountain Boys," led by Ethan Allen, captured Fort Ticonderoga and Crown Point from the British. That fall, however, Americans led by Richard Montgomery and Benedict Arnold launched an unsuccessful assault against Canada in an effort to force Quebec to join the rebellion (See p. 163.)

By the time Washington took command of the Massachusetts militiamen who were confronting General Thomas Gage's troops near Boston, he had a clear notion of the difficulties that awaited him, especially the inequality in numbers and training between his own Continental Army and his British adversaries. Gage's replacement as British commander, General William Howe, decided

to evacuate the unfriendly city of Boston in March 1776 and shift the base of his military operations southward to New York. He sailed into its harbor that summer with a fleet carrying 30,000 troops, and for the next several years, Howe and other British generals pursued a logical—but eventually unsuccessful—strategy of attempting to sever and isolate New England from the other rebellious colonies. Although the British defeated Washington's army at the Battle of Long Island (August 1776) and later at the Battle of White Plains (October 1776), forcing him to abandon Manhattan Island and retreat southward with his bedraggled troops, Howe failed to obtain a single, decisive victory, as he had hoped, that would terminate the revolution by wiping out the American army. On December 26, 1776, Washington routed German mercenaries, employed by the British at Trenton, New Jersey (during the war, the British hired more than 30,000 such mercenaries), and eight days later, he defeated a force led by Charles, Lord Cornwallis, at Princeton.

Farther southward in 1776, patriots were victorious against a group of Loyalists at Moore's Creek Bridge, North Carolina, and Americans also repulsed a British naval attack on Charleston. (The British navy was then the largest in the world, and

This dramatic battle scene shows Washington's troops routing the British, obviously a popular theme during the Revolutionary War and subsequently. (The Historical Society of Pennsylvania)

at times, about half its ships participated in the effort to crush the American rebellion.) Howe's army proved more successful that year in pacifying insurgent areas of New Jersey and other Northern states, and thousands of Americans initially rushed to affirm their allegiance to the king, a process aborted in New Jersey only by Washington's victory at Princeton.

The two chief campaigns in 1777 took place in the North, involving British efforts to isolate New England. In June General John Burgoyne invaded upstate New York from Quebec, recapturing Fort Ticonderoga but allowing his supply lines and troops to become badly overextended in the process. Burgoyne was stopped at Bennington, Vermont, on August 16 by New Hampshire militiamen, and after savage fighting during September and October and subsequent defeats at Saratoga, he surrendered on October 19. Burgoyne's capitulation has often been called a turning point in the American struggle for independence, since it helped to persuade the French government to form an overt alliance with the revolutionaries. (Royalist France, England's traditional enemy, had been supplying the Americans with arms and other assistance even earlier.) Meanwhile, General Howe left New York by sea, intent upon capturing Phila-

delphia, seat of the Continental Congress. The British occupied Philadelphia, but their defeats of Washington at the nearby battles of Brandywine in September and Germantown in October came at the cost of any sustained effort to assist the unfortunate Burgoyne. Washington's army quartered at Valley Forge, Pennsylvania, where they spent an anguished and ill-supplied winter. Although the moment seemed desperate for the American cause, in retrospect, time had already begun to work against the British.

Early the following year, in February 1778, the French signed both military and commercial treaties with the Americans, shrewdly negotiated by Benjamin Franklin, our envoy in Paris. Franklin held over the heads of Louix XVI's ministers the threat that the "United States" might rejoin England under the terms offered by the so-called Carlisle Commission earlier that year. That body, appointed by the British government, conceded the

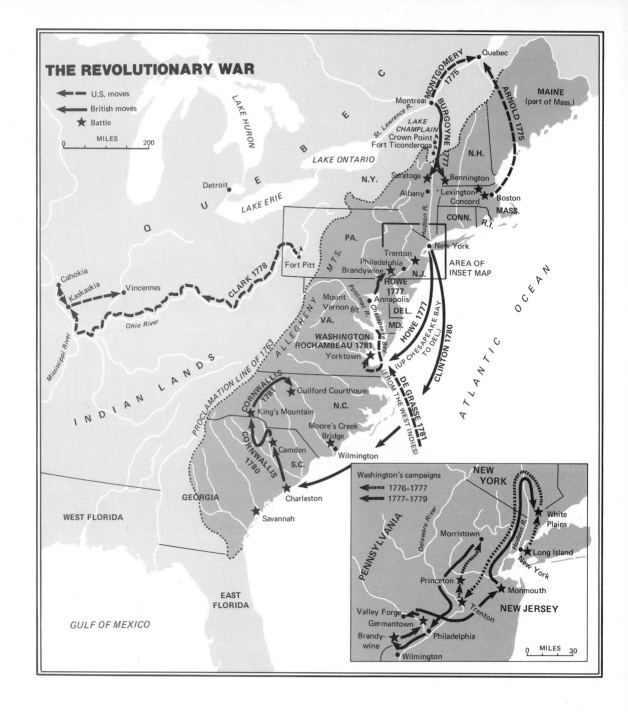

THE REVOLUTIONARY WAR

- →--- U.S. moves
- → British moves
- ★ Battle

MILES
0   200

LAKE HURON

LAKE ONTARIO

LAKE ERIE

Detroit

Quebec

MONTGOMERY 1775

Montreal

St. Lawrence R.

LAKE CHAMPLAIN
Crown Point
Fort Ticonderoga

BURGOYNE 1777

ARNOLD 1775

MAINE
(part of Mass.)

N.H.

N.Y.

Saratoga ★   Bennington ★

Albany

Lexington ★
Concord ★   Boston ★

MASS.

CONN.   R.I.

Hudson R.

New York

AREA OF
INSET MAP

Q   U   E   B   E   C

PA.

Fort Pitt

ALLEGHENY MTS.

Trenton ★
Philadelphia
Brandywine ★

HOWE 1777

N.J.

DEL.

Annapolis
Mount
Vernon

MD.

Potomac R.

Chesapeake Bay

HOWE 1777
(UP CHESAPEAKE BAY
TO DEL.)

CLINTON 1780

CLARK 1778

Cahokia
Kaskaskia   Vincennes

Ohio River

Mississippi River

INDIAN   LANDS

PROCLAMATION LINE OF 1763

VA.

WASHINGTON-
ROCHAMBEAU 1781

Yorktown

DE GRASSE 1781
(FROM THE WEST INDIES)

CORNWALLIS 1781

Guilford Courthouse ★

King's Mountain ★

N.C.

Moore's Creek
Bridge ★

CORNWALLIS 1780

Camden ★

S.C.

Wilmington

Charleston ★

GEORGIA

Savannah ★

WEST FLORIDA

EAST
FLORIDA

GULF OF MEXICO

ATLANTIC   OCEAN

INSET MAP

Washington's campaigns
- ◄···· 1776–1777
- ◄— 1777–1779

NEW YORK

PENNSYLVANIA

Delaware River

Morristown

Princeton ★

Valley Forge ★
Germantown ★
Brandy- ★
wine
Wilmington

Philadelphia

Trenton ★

Monmouth ★

NEW JERSEY

White
Plains ★

Hudson R.

Long Island ★

New York

MILES
0   30

rebellious colonies terms—a return to the pre-1763 status of noninterference by the mother country—that might have been acceptable as late as 1775 but had been overtaken by events since then. The following year, Spain joined with France in alliance against England, so that the Americans now had strong and reliable European patrons in their continuing struggle. The British, in turn, found themselves increasingly preoccupied with their disadvantageous position in the European struggle against France. Their tactics in America became increasingly defensive. Sir Henry Clinton, who replaced Howe in command of the British army, evacuated Philadelphia in 1778, and the British forces retired into strongholds in New York, Rhode Island, and the West Indies. Their only significant victory that year was Clinton's successful attack on Savannah beginning in December. But that summer, George Rogers Clark, a Kentucky militiaman under orders from Virginia, had pushed westward with 175 men and seized three British forts.

Neither side made significant gains in 1779, an indecisive period which ended the next year with a series of major British victories. After the surrender of 5500 American troops under General Benjamin Lincoln in May 1780, the British captured Charleston. Lord Cornwallis defeated another American force under General Gates at Camden, South Carolina, in mid-August, but an American victory at King's Mountain, North Carolina, in October kept Cornwallis from progressing farther in his avowed aim of pacifying the Southern states. American guerrilla bands under the famous "Swamp Fox," Francis Marion, also impeded British movements throughout the region.

The energetic Cornwallis went on the attack again the following spring, 1781, engaging a patriot army led by General Nathanael Greene in the Battle of Guilford Courthouse in March. Heavy losses forced Cornwallis's troops to retreat to Wilmington, North Carolina, while American units reoccupied most of the inland South that summer. Cornwallis withdrew his troops to Yorktown, Virginia, on the coast where he was trapped between the American and French army commanded by Washington and Comte de Rochambeau and a French fleet in the harbor commanded by the Comte de Grasse. Cornwallis surrendered his 8000 troops on October 19, 1781, in the last major engagement of the war. The military phase of the Revolution had ended.

It remained to conclude arrangements for peace. Negotiations for a treaty of peace began among commissioners of the three nations primarily involved in the war—the British, the French, and the Americans—in Paris in April 1782. Meanwhile, the British began evacuating their re-

Washington's army spent a freezing and hungry winter at Valley Forge in 1777. His ultimate triumph has inspired American patriots for more than two centuries. (NYPL/Prints Division)

maining garrisons in the coastal cities, although they remained in New York until November 1783, seven months after Congress (in April) ratified the terms of the peace treaty. Washington—the country's hero and easily its most popular choice for chief magistrate in any American government—gave up his command in December 1783, bidding farewell to his officers in an emotional scene at Fraunces' Tavern in New York on December 4. He traveled south toward his plantation home at Mt. Vernon, receiving tumultuous receptions from his grateful countrymen at Philadelphia and elsewhere. Finally, on December 23, he spoke to Congress, then meeting in Annapolis, and announced his retirement—however temporary—from "all public employments."

Washington's departure symbolized the shift in attention among Americans from the uppermost problem of survival during the Revolution's military phase to the political tasks of consolidating a system of government that would prove itself worthy of the hopes and ideals for which so many Americans had sacrificed.

Suggested Readings
Chapters 7-8

Boston Massacre

Richard B. Morris, *Government and Labor in Early America* (1946); Carl Bridenbaugh, *Cities in Revolt, 1743-1776* (1955) and *Mitre and Sceptre* (1962); Edmund S. Morgan and Helen M. Morgan, *The Stamp Act Crisis* (1953); Hiller B. Zobel, *Boston Massacre* (1976).

Economic Life

Lewis C. Gray, *History of Agriculture in the Southern United States to 1860* (2 vols., 1933); Arthur L. Jensen, *Maritime Commerce of Colonial Philadelphia* (1963); Richard Pares, *Yankees and Creoles* (1950).

Social and Cultural Life

J.T. Adams, *Provincial Society, 1690-1763* (1927); Bernard Bailyn, *Education in the Forming of American Society* (1960); Sacvan Berkovitch, *The Puritan Origins of the American Self* (1975); Daniel J. Boorstin, *The Americans: The Colonial Experience* (1958); Carl Bridenbaugh, *Cities in the Wilderness, 1625-1742* (1938) and *Myths and Realities: Societies of the Colonial South* (1952); Lawrence A. Cremin, *American Education: The Colonial Experience, 1607-1783* (1970), Alan Heimert, *Religion and the American Mind From the Great Awakening to the Revolution* (1966); James A. Henretta, *The Evolution of American Society, 1700-1815* (1973); Michael Kraus, *The Atlantic Civilization: Eighteenth Century Origins* (1949); Henry F. May, *The Enlightenment in America* (1976); Richard Slotkin, *Regeneration Through Violence* (1973); R. P. Stearns, *Science in the British Colonies of America* (1970); Louis B. Wright, *The Cultural Life of the American Colonies, 1607-1763* (1957); Michael Zuckerman, *Peaceable Kingdoms* (1970).

Politics and Government

Charles M. Andrews, *The Colonial Period in American History*, (vol. IV, 1938); Bernard Bailyn, *Origins of American Politics* (1968); Robert B. Brown, *Middle-Class Democracy and the Revolution in Massachusetts, 1691-1780* (1955); Robert B. Brown and B. Katherine Brown, *Virginia, 1705-1780: Aristocracy or Democracy?*

(1964); Lawrence H. Gipson, *The British Empire Before the American Revolution,* (15 vols., 1936-1970); Jack P. Green, *The Quest For Power* (1963); Michael Kammen, *Empire and Interest* (1969); Leonard W. Labaree, *Royal Government in America* (1930); Edmund S. Morgan, *The Birth of the Republic, 1763-1789* (rev. ed., 1977); Howard H. Peckham, *The Colonial Wars, 1689-1762* (1964).

Origins of the Revolution

John R. Alden, *The American Revolution, 1775-1783* (1969); Charles M. Andrews, *Colonial Background of the American Revolution* (1924, rev. ed., 1931); Bernard Bailyn, *Ideological Origins of the American Revolution* (1967) and *The Ordeal of Thomas Hutchinson* (1974); Thomas C. Barrow, *Trade and Empire: The British Customs Service in Colonial America, 1660-1775* (1967); John Brooke, *King George III* (1972); Robert M. Calhoon, *The Loyalists in Revolutionary America* (1973); Ian R. Christie and Benjamin W. Labaree, *Empire or Independence, 1760-1776* (1976); Oliver M. Dickerson, *The Navigation Acts and The American Revolution* (1951); Lawrence H. Gipson, *The Coming of the Revolution* (1954); Jack P. Greene, ed., *The Reinterpretation of the American Revolution, 1763-1789* (1968); George H. Guttridge, *English Whiggism and the American Revolution* (1972); Merrill Jensen, *Founding of a Nation* (1968); Pauline Maier, *From Resistance to Revolution* (1972); Jackson T. Main, *The Social Structure of Revolutionary America* (1965); Richard Merritt, *Symbols of American Community, 1735-1775* (1966); William H. Nelson, *The American Tory* (1961); R. R. Palmer, *The Age of the Democratic Revolution,* (2 vols., 1955-1964); J. R. Pole, *Political Representation in England and the Origins of the American Republic* (1966); John Shy, *A People Numerous and Armed* (1976) and *Toward Lexington* (1965); Willard Wallace, *Appeal to Arms* (1951); Chilton Williamson, *American Suffrage from Property to Democracy, 1760-1860* (1960); Garry Wills, *Inventing America: Jefferson's Declaration of Independence* (1978); Esmond Wright, ed., *Causes and Consequences of the American Revolution* (1966); Alfred Young, ed., *The American Revolutionary* (1976).

The
Constitutional 9
Convention

When General Washington arrived in Philadelphia on Sunday, May 13, 1787, he went immediately to call on Benjamin Franklin. With the convention that had brought him from Virginia scheduled to begin the next day, Washington had been greeted by chiming bells, an artillery salute, and a procession of soldiers. After that grand entrance into the city, Washington met with the eighty-one-year-old Dr. Franklin at his home off Market Street. Franklin had returned only two years before from Paris, where he had been negotiating for an alliance with the French. There he had impressed his Gallic hosts with his romantic, but contrived, "American" appearance: simple clothing, fur cap, unpowdered gray hair, and spectacles far down his nose. Acclaimed as a citizen of the world, Franklin had an international prestige that was perhaps unmatched by any man of his day.

His high standing, as well as his mostly honorary post as president of Pennsylvania and resident of Philadelphia, placed Franklin in the position of entertaining the delegates arriving for the convention. But Washington and others soon realized that it would be appropriate for Franklin to attend the convention himself, and shortly before it began, Franklin joined the roster of the Pennsylvania delegation by special act of the state legislature. It was perhaps the last great honor bestowed on the doctor. He had never been an effective public speaker (his pen had always done his best "talking"), and at age eighty-one, Franklin's analytic powers had begun to fade. As the great convention wore on, therefore, it became increasingly necessary for another delegate to be present at Franklin's lively dinners to sidetrack the conversation lest the old man inadvertantly reveal secrets of the convention to the guests.

What secrets had to be guarded? Nothing less than a new constitution. The presence of Franklin and Washington at the convention, originally called to correct the flaws in the government under the Articles of Confederation (the loose frame of government adopted for the thirteen sovereign states in 1777 by the Continental Congress), added stature and

James Madison has been called the "master builder of the Constitution." His journals are the main source for later knowledge of proceedings of the convention. (Thomas Gilcrease Institute)

legitimacy to proceedings that undertook the founding of a new government altogether. Delegates from the various states, including James Madison and Alexander Hamilton (Thomas Jefferson and John Adams were in Europe as diplomats representing the United States), drew upon their own experiences in colonial assemblies, town meetings, the Continental Congress, and the Confederation Congress. Many had also participated at conventions that drafted state constitutions and had been active in their state governments. Now these fifty-five men would ponder, debate, disagree, and try to compromise on a new plan for the American national government to safeguard their decade-old revolution.

But Washington and precious few other delegates managed to arrive on time. By May 14, scheduled to be opening day of the meeting, only the Pennsylvania and Virginia delegations were present. Rain had turned the new country's dirt roads into mud, making travel slow and uncertain. Two of Georgia's delegates had to travel over 800 miles under these adverse conditions to reach Philadelphia's State House, where the convention would be held. By the time they arrived, the Virginians had already decided upon fifteen resolves that would eventually stand as fundamental sections of the Constitution.

Proceedings were delayed until May 25, when enough delegates had come from seven states to form a quorum. Even then, only twenty-nine delegates had arrived, and for weeks to come, men straggled into the town of 43,000, then the largest city in the United States, to take part in the gathering. Finally twelve of the thirteen states were represented. Rhode Island alone among the thirteen states refused to send delegates. The state's earlier failure to ratify an amendment to the Articles of Confederation authorizing a 5 percent duty upon imports had contributed to the growing dissatisfaction with the present government. Under the Articles of Confederation, an impossible unanimity was often required before the government could take action. Thus, delegates at a trade convention in Annapolis, Maryland, in 1786 were led to call for

> the Appointment of Commissioners to meet at Philadelphia on the second Monday in May next, to take into Consideration the situation of the United States to devise such further Provisions as shall appear to them necessary to render the Constitution of the Federal Government adequate to the exigencies of the Union. . . .

As a small independent state, Rhode Island feared that a stronger national government would take away the sovereign powers it had exercised since the United States of America (the name took a *plural* form, recognizing state sovereignty) had become a nation. (Even three years after the Philadelphia meeting had concluded and the Constitution had been ratified and implemented, Rhode Island refused to ratify it. The state finally gave in when forced by practical necessity.)

Although Rhode Islanders sulked in their fiercely independent Narragansett Bay towns, the other twelve states sent as delegates a remarkable collection of men. Generally wealthy, influential, imaginative, and intelligent, many of them would later serve in the new national government they were helping to found: two as president, one as vice-president, and five on the U.S. Supreme Court, two of them as chief justice. Aside from the much-lauded George Washington, the Virginia delegates included tall, dignified Governor Edmund Randolph and the younger James Madison, short, slender, and scholar of politics. From Massachusetts came Elbridge Gerry, a signer of the Declaration of Independence who had prospered as a merchant and financier, and the handsome and eloquent Rufus King. Roger Sherman, the mayor of New Haven, Connecticut, excelled in his abilities as a politician, and John Langdon of New Hampshire had made a fortune in commerce and had served as president of his state under the Confederation government. From Pennsylvania came, along with Dr. Franklin, Scottish-born James Wilson, one of America's best and best-known lawyers, sharp-witted Gouverneur Morris, whose crippled arm and wooden leg did little to detract from his great speaking abilities, and English-born Robert Morris, who had served as superintendent of finance for the Confederation from 1781 to 1785 and was probably the richest man in America.

Overshadowing his older colleagues in the New York delegation was thirty-year-old Alexander Hamilton, the arrogant conservative intellectual who had served with Washington in the Revolution, later sitting in his state legislature and in the Continental Congress. The New Jersey delegation, which along with that of Virginia would prove profoundly influential at Philadelphia, included Irish-born William Paterson, long-time attorney general of his state and highly skilled in debate, and Governor William Livingston, a talented wit and writer.

Certainly the delegates had the advantage of a setting historically appropriate to their task. They sat in the east room of the State House,

Independence Hall (then called the Philadelphia State House) was the meeting place of the Continental Congress and the Constitutional Convention. This view, dating from about 1778, shows a cobbled street and the water pumps that served the neighborhood. (Historical Society of Pennsylvania)

site of the first meetings of the Continental Congress and the signing of the Declaration of Independence. The room now served as the meeting place for the Pennsylvania legislature, while the state supreme court met across the hall. The people of Philadelphia clearly had a keener interest in the activities of the legislature and the courts than they did in the curious convocation that now occupied the premises, though city officials tried to accommodate the proceedings. The city commissioner had even spread dirt along Chestnut Street to quiet the noise from passing horses and carriages. By noon the summer sun streamed through the side windows which occupied two walls of the room. New Englanders in woolen suits especially felt the heat and humidity. The windows were nearly always shut for the sake of secrecy, but even when air was let into the room, the delegates were pestered by annoying streams of flies, for the era of window screens had not yet arrived.

Finally the delegates began. After a quorum was achieved, those present went about the business of organizing the convention. The Pennsylvania delegation proposed that George Washington preside, and after the formality of balloting his uncontested nomination, the general was led to the high-backed speaker's chair to serve as president of the Federal

Convention. He modestly bemoaned his lack of experience for the office, but thereafter served with distinction and (all sides agreed) with as much impartiality as possible.

The vast majority of delegates now readily decided that convention proceedings should be kept secret. Such a rule would protect individual members from the pressures of public opinion in their own states and would suppress immediate public outcry over adoption of particularly controversial sections. Even the official secretary of the convention avoided recording any of the discussions and debates. But fortunately for posterity in general, and historians in particular, James Madison sat to the side of the room, faced all the delegates, and wrote down their speeches, debates, and other events of the convention. Others helped the young Madison with this record, which was published after his death in 1840, some fifty-three years later.

The delegates next decided that the Convention should be organized on the basis of state representation, with majority opinion within each delegation counting as one vote. Gouverneur Morris and other Pennsylvania men had argued that states with larger populations should receive greater representation. But Virginia delegates quickly intervened to stop the argument, realizing that it "might beget fatal altercations between the large and small states." It would be just such a conflict that would later bring the convention to its most serious impasse.

As representatives of the largest state both in size and population, the Virginia delegation, headed by Governor Edmund Randolph, now presented its proposals for the new government, drawn up before many of the delegates from other states had yet arrived. Called by some the Randolph Resolutions, the proposals actually seemed to reflect more the ideas of James Madison. They came to be collectively known as the Virginia Plan. Randolph began a long and detailed speech, which pinpointed the crucial weaknesses of the Confederation government. His loose, dark unpowdered hair brushed back from his forehead, Randolph presented not a *revision* of the Articles, which was what most of the delegates expected to hear, but rather fifteen resolves that would create an entirely new government. He "candidly confessed," it was said, "that they were not intended for a federal government — he meant a strong *consolidated* union."

The resolves contained many of the features of the Constitution that we recognize today. The government would be separated into three branches — the legislative, the executive, and the judicial. A legislative branch, which would make the national laws, would consist of two houses. The executive branch would carry out the laws, and national courts would help enforce them.

But the differences between these initial proposals and the final product shaped by many weeks of deliberations proved significant. Under the Virginia Plan the House of Representatives was elected by the people, but the Senate was to be elected — by the House! In both houses, the number of representatives from a state would depend not only on the state's population but also on the *wealth* of its citizenry, measured by the taxes paid. Congressmen would be ineligible for a second term and could be recalled from office by dissatisfied constituents at any time. Congress, in addition to having the power to act whenever the states alone would be incompetent (a vague declaration of power), was given the *absolute* right to veto *any* laws passed by individual states.

Under Randolph's proposals, the roles of executive and judiciary also differed from their modern function. The national executive would be chosen not by the people or the electoral college but by Congress. Instead of *one* president, whom Randolph feared might develop into a tyrannical monarch, the executive would consist of a council of three men, ineligible for a second term. The Supreme Court could join these three in a council of revision, vetoing acts of Congress before they were passed into laws. A veto by the Supreme Court, however, might be overruled by an overwhelming vote in Congress. Other provisions included the admission of new states by a less than unanimous vote, federal guarantee of a republican government to each state and territory, and the requirement that state officers take oaths promising to support the national government.

Randolph's lengthy speech concluded just before the time for that day's adjournment. Delegates decided that these far-reaching resolutions should be debated by all of their number at the next meeting rather than be consigned to committees.

The great debate on the fifteen Virginia Resolves began the next morning with Randolph again calling for a national government with supreme legislative, executive, and judicial branches. Representatives of small states, fearing that under a stronger central government they would lose their influence to the larger states, soon raised their voices in dissent. Pierce Butler of South Carolina and John Dickinson of Delaware argued that the states had no need for a stronger central government and that together they already composed one nation. Pennsylvania's Gouverneur Morris insisted that the states would only be forced to yield to the national government when their powers collided, a statement that only confused many delegates who could not imagine a government in which the state and central governments would share power. Morris's colleague, James Wilson, felt that individuals, not states, should be the focus of government.

One critical question was whether congressional representation should be based on the equality of states, on state populations, or on taxes paid by each states. This question dominated the first half of the convention. Roger Sherman of Connecticut insisted that the state legislatures, rather than people in certain districts, should elect the House of Representatives. This surely would uphold the interests of the states and would center people's interests on the affairs of their state rather than on the national government. The people, Sherman argued, "should have as little to do as may be about the [national] government. They want [i.e., lack] information and are constantly liable to be misled." Charles Pinckney of South Carolina supported Sherman, arguing that election by

state legislature rather than by the people would protect the interests of property from mass assault and thus be "a better guard against bad [i.e., popular] measures." Elbridge Gerry of Massachusetts, however, favored popular election but only because he feared the radicalism of the state legislatures more than that of the people. "The evils we experience," warned Gerry, "flow from the excess of democracy."

Gerry's sentiments, shared by most of the men present, stemmed from actions within the states under the Articles of Confederation. To protect the interests of their debtor farmer constituents, many state legislatures had issued bales of paper money. In some cases the dates for repayment of debts were postponed. In western Massachusetts, mobs of farmers temporarily prevented the collection of debts and protested political *under*representation in what came to be known as Shays's Rebellion.

It was no wonder that the wealthy and powerful delegates to the Federal Convention feared an "excess of democracy." To them the word "democracy" meant tyranny exercised by the uneducated, beastlike mob of common people, threatening their property with high taxes and reducing the debt due to wealthy creditors. Washington exclaimed, "Would to God that wise measures may be taken in time to avert the consequences we have but too much reason to apprehend." Hamilton asserted that "the people seldom judge or determine right." Few delegates to the convention agreed with the sentiments expressed by Thomas Jefferson in a letter from Revolutionary France: "God forbid we should every twenty years be without such a rebellion! What signify a few lives lost in a century or two? The tree of liberty must be refreshed from time to time with the blood of patriots and tyrants. It is its natural manure."

The first votes provided a victory for the Virginia Plan and for the larger states over the smaller ones, which had not yet mounted an organized and united front against the plan. Congress, all agreed, would consist of two Houses, and the people, not the state legislatures, would choose members of the House of Representatives. The authority of Congress over state laws was also approved. But realizing the small states' sensitivity over this issue, Virginia's Madison argued to postpone debate over the clause authorizing the use of federal troops against an offending state. His argument was thought reasonable, considering the widespread fear of executive tyranny among Americans, and the delegates retired to their lodgings by midafternoon on May 31, the initial day of balloting.

When they reassembled the following morning, they temporarily passed over the disputed question of congressional representation and debated, instead, the structure of the executive branch. When James Wilson of Pennsylvania rose to suggest that there be a single executive, silence fell upon the convention. The young nation had been free of royal control for only a few years, and the specter of a single, powerful president seemed (to many of the delegates, at least) to foreshadow creation of another monarch. With his steel-rimmed spectacles hooked on to his powdered wig, Wilson argued that the executive branch was best assigned to a single person to afford energy and speed of decision. This idea was immediately and bitterly opposed by Roger Sherman of Connecticut. Sherman viewed the new executive office as little more than a place from which to enforce the dominant will of Congress. Even Edmund Randolph, who had introduced the Virginia Plan, condemned the idea of a single executive as a fatal step toward monarchy. No doubt worried about the position of the South in a central government with its probable headquarters in Philadelphia or New York, Randolph believed that a single president would always come from the center of population, whereas *three* executives could be drawn from the different sections of the country.

Benjamin Franklin rose, with the slowness of age, to oppose the idea of a special "council of revision" that some had suggested, comprised of the chief executive and a section of the national judiciary, charged with administering the government. From what he had witnessed in Pennsylvania's colonial government, Franklin pointed out, the governor had often threatened to veto a measure unless he received special favors in the form of increased salary, bribes, or increased powers. But a *plural* executive rather than a single person, Franklin argued, serving without pay would guard against these natural tendencies toward ambition and avarice, to which most executives—whether kings, presidents, or governors—succumbed. In the end, however, the delegates voted for a single executive, although it was over two weeks before a decision was reached on the question of a presidential veto power over congressional legislation.

The delegates took up the question of a national judiciary on Tuesday, June 5, while also examining the Virginia Plan's remaining resolves. Should a set of inferior federal courts (beneath the Supreme Court) be created? James Wilson, a Pennsylvania delegate whose interests in western land speculation may account for part of the strength of his nationalist beliefs, argued for their creation with judges to be appointed by the president. But John Rutledge of South Carolina thought that if a single executive appointed the judges, that would too closely resemble a monarchy and that there would be no use for these inferior courts in any case. Roger Sherman—also intent upon limiting the powers of the new federal government—agreed that the existing state courts would serve the same purpose and save the expense of creating separate federal tribunals. Still the delegates voted in favor of the federal court system, although they postponed consideration of the methods of appointing judges. The very touchy issue of whether individual states should be allowed to ratify or reject the new constitution, which was being written without a specific mandate from the states of the Confederation government, was also postponed.

By 1787 Philadelphia had grown from a quaint Pennsylvania town into a thriving cosmopolitan city. The commercial interests of many delegates reflected a number of the concerns felt by influential men in this important market and port city. One Philadelphian had been working for a year on a new invention—the steam engine. Warehouses and vessels lined the waterfront of the Delaware River. Wandering through the city were such diverse people as German-American farmers from the countryside, Indians and frontiersman from the backcountry, and sailors who had come from many foreign nations. In the midst of this energetic urban setting, delegates, when not debating provisions of the new constitution, often enjoyed Philadelphia's convivial atmosphere; one evening, twelve delegates dining in a local tavern managed to consume no less than *sixty* bottles of Madeira port!

Yet there was hardly cause for celebration at that point. Having concluded their preliminary survey of the Virginia Resolves, the delegates now confronted the even more difficult issues presented in creating a new government. This time the small states took the offensive, arguing that the state legislatures and *not* the people should elect the members of the House of Representatives. Charles Pinckney of South Carolina observed that if state legislatures were excluded from participating in the new government or assigned a subordinate role, South Carolina might not ratify the Constitution. John Dickinson of Delaware feared both his small state's losing its independence and an uprising of the people, "the most dangerous influence of those multitudes without property and without principle with which our country, like all others, will soon abound." George Mason, along with Wilson and Madison, argued that at least *one* house should be democratically elected by the people: "The people will be represented; they ought therefore to choose the representatives. The requisites in actual representation are that the representatives should sympathize with their constituents, should think as they think and feel as they feel, and for these purposes should even be residents among them."

Delegates from both small and large states recognized the fundamental issue involved in this debate: how much *power* the new national government would possess. Thus when the subject turned to representation in the Senate, small-state delegates were again the first to respond. John Dickinson moved that senators be chosen by state legislatures, a motion seconded by Roger Sherman. Elbridge Gerry, who, as a Boston merchant, had been greatly frightened by Shays's Rebellion, also argued for election of senators by state legislatures because "the commercial and monied interest would be more secure than in the hands of the people at large."

Such belief in the need for an elitest Senate was widespread among the delegates. Thus James Madison asserted that the Senate should be composed of intelligent, thoughtful men. This idea reflected the sentiments of many delegates who wanted the Senate and the House to become American versions of the British House of Lords and House of Commons. James Wilson suggested that the Senate be elected by the people, but his suggestion was voted down. The delegates agreed that the upper house would *not* be elected by the people. But both sides of the argument had been concerned with the same problem—the need for a national government that would reflect the interests of property holders within the community, that would not permit the unregulated printing of paper money or otherwise threaten the security and stability of property.

Despite certain underlying assumptions such as these, seldom spoken but recognized by all the delegates, large- and small-state representatives continued to debate the proposed powers of the central government. On June 8 Wilson moved that the delegates consider the proposal that Congress have the power to veto *state* laws they judged improper. Gunning Bedford of Delaware worried that such a veto would be still another means by which massive entities such as Virginia and Pennsylvania (two states that contained one-third of the nation's population) could dominate small states such as Delaware (which held about one-ninetieth of the people). South Carolina's Pierce Butler saw the veto as denial of equal justice to states distant from the national capital. But Madison reminded the small states that they would be particularly hurt should the federal union dissolve completely, because of their virtual inability to defend their interests against larger neighbors and foreign countries. When it came to a vote, only the states containing the three largest populations—Virginia, Pennsylvania, and Massachusetts—had majorities in favor of the congressional veto. That idea was dead.

With their first taste of victory, the small states renewed the debate over proportional representation in Congress. David Brearley of New Jersey pondered the dilemma and called for eradicating existing state boundaries and redrawing state lines so that each area would have the same population, a utopian suggestion that died stillborn. His colleague, William Paterson, attacked the very nature of the discussion itself. The convention, Paterson reminded his colleagues, had been called only to consider the revision of the Articles of Confederation. As representatives of various states, he continued, the delegates had no authority to create a government that would annihilate state sovereignty. If the large states decided in favor of a stronger union, Paterson declared, let them go by themselves; they would have no cooperation from smaller states. Tension among the delegates had risen perceptibly as Paterson reached his dramatic conclusion: "I therefore declare that I will never consent to the present system, and I shall make all the interest against it in the state which I represent that I can. Myself or my state will never submit to tyranny or despotism."

Pennsylvania's Wilson jumped to his feet to reply, further accentuating the division. Were not Pennsylvanians equal to citizens of New Jersey? Wilson demanded to know. Why shouldn't his state, then, have a greater representation than New Jersey if it contained more citizens? Wilson threatened that "if the small states will not confederate on this plan, Pennsylvania, and I presume some other states, will not confederate on any other." Heated orations such as Paterson's and Wilson's threatened to tear the convention apart, and after the latter stepped down, the delegates wisely postponed the issue of proportional voting once more and adjourned the meeting.

But they returned on the morning of June 11 still divided on the crucial question. Connecticut's Roger Sherman rose from his chair to offer a compromise. Oddly shaped and awkward, Sherman was nevertheless a very shrewd and able politician. He called for proportional representation in the House and equal state representation in the Senate, thereby offering half a loaf to both large- and small-state delegates. Sherman's suggestion, however, went almost without comment. No other delegate seconded his plan, each side apparently unwilling to modify its stand.

Suddenly everyone began to introduce proposals for representation. John Rutledge and Pierce Butler argued that the vote in the House of Representatives should be according to "quotas of contribution," the original idea of the Virginia Plan. At once Elbridge Gerry of Massachusetts raised the question of slaves—would the Southerners insist that blacks be counted for purposes of representation? Pennsylvania's Wilson moved that a slave be counted as three-fifths of a person, a proposal that had already been made in the Confederation Congress of 1783. At this point, the convention agreed that congressmen should be paid out of the national treasury. More important, there was a majority at hand for the divisive proposal that the Senate as well as the House have representation proportional to a state's population. This final point shocked representatives of small states into concrete, unified action. On June 14 William Paterson of New Jersey demanded an immediate adjournment of the convention and a consideration of an entirely different plan, which he and his supporters wished to substitute for the Virginia Plan.

The next day the nine resolutions of the so-called New Jersey Plan were presented. Unlike the plan Virginia had proposed, the new plan did not create a *national* government but sought to amend the Articles of Confederation. Congress would remain one House with states having equal representation and members being elected by state legislatures. The first step toward reform was the authorization of additional congressional powers. Congress would be allowed to raise revenue through import duties, stamp taxes, and postal rates and to regulate trade and commerce. If more money was needed, Congress would have the power to collect revenue from the states in proportion to their population, counting three-fifths of the slaves. All acts of Congress and treaties entered into by the central government would be binding on all states, and the central Confederation government would be able to use force to require the states to submit in these cases.

The executive, under the New Jersey Plan, would be composed of several persons elected by Congress and would exercise no veto power. But the executive would appoint members of the one federal supreme court. It would handle impeachment cases and review state court decisions dealing with maritime subjects, foreigners, federal treaties, trade regulation, and collection of federal revenue. Had the New Jersey Plan's provisions been adopted by the Confederation government—or even proposed seriously—as late as the previous year, the Philadelphia Convention might never had met.

But now it had met and had gone a significant distance *beyond* simple amendment of the Confederation government toward creation of a new national structure. Paterson might continue to warn the delegates, before he sat down, that they had neither legal authority nor popular support for the creation of a stronger national government. But supporters of the more radical revision, such as Edmund Randolph, reminded their opponents of the perilous times that the United States confronted and for which the Confederation seemed (at least in their eyes) inadequate. Randolph rose to bemoan particularly the weak state of financial affairs that had beset the young nation: "France, to whom we are indebted in every motive of gratitude and honor, is left unpaid the large sums she has supplied us with in the day of our necessity [the Revolution]. Our officers and soldiers, who have successfully fought our battle, and the loaners of money to the public, look up to you for relief. . . ."

When the delegates assembled on Monday morning next, young Alexander Hamilton of New York spoke for six straight hours. But even before he opened his mouth, the delegates knew what to expect: an argument for a powerful national government with considerable safeguards *against* democracy. Hamilton had demonstrated his political skill at the Annapolis, Maryland, Convention the previous year. Designed to be a meeting at which problems of trade between various states would be ironed out, that convention had accomplished little, since only five states sent delegates. Hamilton saved the gathering from total failure by the adoption of his majority report, part of which called for a convention the following year to revise the Articles, a suggestion approved by the Confederation Congress.

Once the Philadelphia Convention opened, however, Hamilton had little use for mere amendment. He argued strongly for a new frame of government in which there would be a single president chosen for life by electors and with an absolute veto. Hamilton would agree to a lower house of Congress elected by the people, but he advocated senators elected for life to check democratic sentiments. The Virginia Plan had not been aristocratic enough for Hamilton's taste. He had only high praise for the House of Lords and the British government generally, which he called "the best in the world." Hamilton wanted a thoroughgoing nationalist regime with strong executive power. All state governors would be appointed by the central government, and each would exercise the power of absolute veto over state legislatures. The people, Hamilton argued, were starting to tire "of an excess of democracy." Even regarding the modified Virginia Plan, he argued: "What even is the Virginia plan, but pork still with a little change of the sauce?" But Hamilton seemed to be alone in his extremist nationalism, and there was no discussion of his proposals at the convention.

Worried that Hamilton's ultra-nationalism had driven many delegates into the small-state camp as advocates of merely amending the Articles of Confederation, Madison was on his feet as the meeting opened the next morning. The New Jersey Plan, he argued, would not prevent internal rebellions such as Shays's, nor would it do much to protect the union against foreign powers, either economically or militarily. Madison's eloquence strengthened majority opinion on the question, and the states attending then voted seven to three (with Maryland divided) in favor of the Virginia Plan. Only New Jersey, New York, and Delaware opposed. Had the New Jersey Plan been introduced at the beginning of the convention, it might have fared more successfully. But weeks of discussion of a stronger national government through the Virginia Plan, as well as Madison's pointed closing arguments, helped undercut the notion of simply revising the Articles of Confederation.

By this time, delegates' arguments over proposals often became angry and passionate. Embattled small-state interests now confronted the more nationalistic sections of the Virginia Resolves, including the crucially important issue of congressional representation. John Lansing of New York spoke against a congressional veto of laws passed by state legislatures: "Will the members of the general legislature be competent judges? Will a gentleman from Georgia be a judge of the expediency of a law which is to operate in New Hampshire?" Maryland's Luther Martin, whose sloppy, careless appearance and long-winded hostile speeches an-

Throughout the convention, Luther Martin of Maryland fought strongly for the rights of small states. Martin was a perennially disheveled figure at Philadelphia, noted mainly for his irritatingly long stem-winding speeches. (Culver Pictures)

noyed many at the convention, argued that there should be a single house in Congress to represent the state legislatures in the central government. (Martin and William Few of Georgia were the only delegates from a small-farmer background, the class which comprised the great majority of American whites at the time. Thus the many unfavorable comments about Martin's appearance—and the general hostility toward him displayed by other delegates—had a decided tinge of class snobbery about it.) Martin's and other comments revealed that the spirit of the New Jersey Plan remained very much alive, despite the nationalist onslaught.

Unable as yet to agree on the fundamentals of the new government, delegates wisely began to debate and settle lesser issues. Small states won two concessions: the convention did not insist upon paying members of Congress out of the federal treasury, and members of both houses continued to be eligible to hold office in their home states, although they could not hold another federal post simultaneously. Some had favored annual election of members to the lower house, as was done in elections for state legislatures, while others supported a provision in the Virginia Plan that set the term at three years. A compromise of two years was unanimously accepted, with six-year terms for senators. Delegates also voted that senators would be chosen by state legislatures and would have to be at least thirty years old. Clearly the delegates expected the upper house in the national legislature to check "popular" tendencies in the often-elected lower house.

As the heat and humidity of a Philadelphia summer set in upon the already wearied delegates, they sat with the worried expectation that the coming debate over representation and the powers of the national government might create enough anger and dissension to break up the convention. Another long speech by the exasperated and exasperating Luther Martin on June 28 only added to the frustration. Each delegate continued to present his own view, usually well-known by this point, with little or no progress. Madison insisted that the larger states would not conspire to further their particular interests in the national government. The three powerful and populous states of Virginia, Pennsylvania, and Massachusetts were concerned with tobacco, flour, and fish, respectively; what had they in common? Large states, Madison claimed, trying to assuage the fears of small-state delegates, were certainly more apt to become rivals than allies; Britain and France served as the clearest of examples. But Sherman of Connecticut and others continued to insist that bigger states should not have more votes than their smaller brethren.

Worried by the strong possibility of deadlock, Benjamin Franklin rose to urge delegates to display greater tolerance and patience. "The small progress we have made after four or five weeks," he said, "is methinks a melancholy proof of the imperfection of human understanding." Franklin proposed that a member of the Philadelphia clergy be brought in to lead daily prayers each morning. Hamilton and others opposed, believing that such a move might reveal to the public the extent of dissensions within the assemblage. Franklin then observed placidly that such a suspicion among the public might do more good than harm. Finally, Hugh Williamson of North Carolina stated the obvious—that the convention had no money with which to hire a chaplain!

Proceeding without the assistance of divine providence, Oliver Ellsworth reintroduced Connecticut's or Sherman's compromise plan that gave both large and small states an equal vote in the Senate. Madison angrily rejected the idea, charging that Connecticut had not even fully paid its federal requisition of funds during the American Revolution. Ellsworth then jumped to his feet shouting, "the muster rolls will show she had more troops in the field than Virginia!"

Such useless but emotional arguments later led Pennsylvania's Gouverneur Morris to observe that "the fate of America was suspended by a hair." Rufus King of Massachusetts proclaimed he would never listen to the argument that states should have equal representation in the Senate, but Gunning Bedford of Delaware retorted that self-interest blinded the big states: "I do not, gentlemen, trust you." Approval of the Virginia Plan, said Bedford, was not the sole alternative available to the smaller states: "The large states dare not dissolve the confederation. If they do, the small ones will find some foreign ally of more honor and good faith who will take them by the hand and do them justice." The thought had occurred to other small-state delegates at the convention.

The drastic threat of seeking a foreign patron, should the Confederation dissolve, was countered in kind by Gouverneur Morris: "This country must be united. If persuasion does not unite it, the sword will." Another vote on representation in the Senate took place. When Georgia, the final state to be called, divided its vote, the tally in states stood at five to five. All business had come to a standstill.

The deadlock which threatened to destroy the Convention troubled most of the delegates sufficiently to seek some novel means of resolving the apparently intractable disputes. After a few unheeded suggestions, a special committee was formed with one representative from each state to try to break the impasse. While the rest of the delegates adjourned to celebrate the Fourth of July, Franklin suggested that the committee consider a plan based on Sherman's neglected compromise measure. Under this scheme the House would contain one representative for every 40,000 (later reduced to 30,000) citizens, including three-fifths of the slaves. All money bills would originate in the House and could not be amended by the Senate. Each state would have an equal vote in the Senate. Gouverneur Morris strongly disapproved of the compromise, while most members from the small states generally favored the idea, although Paterson of New Jersey thought it conceded too much.

It remained for the delegates to agree on details. They determined that the first House should contain a total of sixty-five representatives distributed according to population. Also, a census should be taken every ten years in order to rearrange representation as needed. An amendment that would have counted black slaves equally with whites for representation was voted down eight states to two. Gouverneur Morris bitterly chided the small states, insisting that their plan would never bring efficient government. His comments so angered Robert Yates and John

Lansing (delegates from a large state, New York, but with localist attitudes on the issue) that they packed their bags and left Philadelphia as Alexander Hamilton had done previously (though in Hamilton's case, to attend to private business).

The slavery issue intruded again at this point. Southern states with much of their "property" tied to slavery insisted that enslaved Africans be counted as people for voting purposes. Paterson protested that New Jersey could "regard Negro slaves in no light but as property." Although Pierce Butler and Charles Pinckney of South Carolina moved that *all* slaves be counted for purposes of proportional representation, most Southern delegates asked only that three-fifths of the slaves be counted, a figure that had earlier been used by the Confederation Congress in its frustrating efforts to collect taxes. James Wilson of Philadelphia argued emphatically that this was a different situation, *not* an apportioning of taxes but representation for citizens: "Are the blacks admitted as citizens? . . . Then why are they not admitted on an equality with white citizens? Are they admitted as property? Then why is not other property admitted into the computation?"

Again a bitterly divisive issue threatened to disrupt the convention. The new quarrel over counting slaves had shifted the argument from large state–small state to North–South. William Davie of North Carolina threatened that his state and perhaps other Southern states would leave unless slaves were counted as three-fifths. Randolph, fearing that Northern states might someday gain control of Congress and choose to abolish slavery completely, insisted that the slave states needed the security of extra votes in Congress. Gouverneur Morris, objecting not to possible *Northern* influence but to the future role of the *West*, protested the taking of a regular census. Morris feared that population shifts to newly created Western states could threaten the power of the original thirteen. Most delegates, however, recognized the need to compromise on all these issues, and the entire compromise plan as formed in committee passed— though by a margin of only one state. Perhaps the cooler weather had helped cooler heads prevail.

Passage of what would come to be known as the Great Compromise seemed a victory for the small states. Their delegates no longer feared that the creation of a stronger central government would lead to oppression by the powerful states. The next discussion of the executive branch proceeded without the strong divisions that had plagued the convention earlier. Various proposals for selecting the executive came up: appointment by state executives, direct election by the people, and selection by a system of "electors" chosen by either the people, state legislatures, or Congress. Every possible length of term from four years to life was suggested, but many delegates came to favor the selection of a president by Congress for a single, seven-year term. Although a four-year term was not then adopted, the delegates voted to subject the president to possible impeachment.

The role of the judiciary also figured in debates. Disagreement continued as to whether the executive or the legislative branch should appoint judges. Most delegates agreed that the jurisdiction of national courts should extend "to all cases arising under the national laws and to such other questions as may involve the national peace and harmony."

On July 26, the convention appointed a Committee of Detail composed of Randolph of Virginia, Wilson of Pennsylvania, Nathaniel Gorham of Massachusetts, Ellsworth of Connecticut, and John Rutledge of South Carolina. Their purpose was to organize the various measures, amendments, and proposals the delegates had agreed on into a workable plan of government and to issue a report — in eleven days. The convention adjourned meanwhile, awaiting the plan and report, and delegates had good reason to frequent Philadelphia's taverns in a jovial mood. General Washington, the convention's quiet and stoic president, rode off into the country for some trout fishing with a few friends.

When the convention reassembled on August 6, the Committee of Detail presented an able draft for a plan of government. Wilson of Pennsylvania apparently took portions of a draft by Randolph and augmented it with ideas from the New Jersey Plan and a separate plan drawn up by Charles Pinckney of South Carolina. The influence of the Articles of Confederation and of the various state constitutions was also apparent in this preliminary document. After copies had been distributed, the convention adjourned to give delegates time for study and reflection. The committee's draft would be subjected to intense debate for five more weeks.

In many instances, the committee left questions unanswered for eventual action by the new government once it was in place; in other instances, the committee arrived at new solutions to conform to the governmental structure it was creating. Thus citizenship and residence requirements for membership in Congress were included, while property qualifications, if any, were omitted pending further debate. It was thought best to set suffrage requirements similar to those each state provided for electing the popular house in the state legislature. The more democratic House of Representatives would exercise the power of impeaching public officials, and all criminal prosecutions would be jury trials.

Some of the details worked out by the five members of the Committee of Detail went through without argument; others created prolonged discussion and debate. The delegates eventually voted against the committee's recommendation that members of Congress be paid by their state legislatures, providing instead for payment from the national treasury, a move that would make congressmen more independent from their states. The committee had defined treason, provided for the naturalization process, and granted powers for the levying of taxes and the regulation of commerce. It had also sought to foster greater interstate cooperation by providing for the extradition of criminals, imposing recognition by states of the laws of other states ("full faith and credit"), and granting the citizens of one state the privileges and immunities of citizens in the other states.

The degree to which the delegates at Philadelphia, despite their most heated disagreements, shared a common set of economic interests and political perceptions in forming the new government emerged clearly from the committee's draft. Some of the interests involved, though by no means all, were acutely personal. Many members had speculated in Western land, for example, and were especially concerned that when Western states were admitted to the union, the original states should retain power over them. Although such blatant control was voted down, the delegates did assign Congress the power "to dispose of and make all needful rules and regulations respecting the territory or other property belonging to the United States."

As members of America's economic and political elites, the self-interest of most Founding Fathers can also be traced to money matters. Many of them were creditors, holding bonds and securities that had been issued to fund the Continental Army and state militias during the Revolutionary War. Some delegates had argued that Congress should assume these state debts in order to ensure their repayment, but others realized that this tactic would mainly benefit those who had bought up the bonds from others when they were almost valueless, rather than those who more deservedly had earned compensation for their patriotism. By forbidding the states to print paper money or to alter contractual obligations, the men of the convention were protecting the property of creditors and guarding against the rising power of debtor farmers in state legislatures.

One of the chief defects in the Articles had been the inability of the Confederation Congress to regulate commerce among the several states and with foreign nations. A link between this issue of commerce and another problem soon appeared. Northerners would be greatly helped by the power of Congress to place tariffs on foreign goods and to regulate national trade, which Northern shipping interests dominated. None of this would be of much benefit to Southerners; their wealth lay largely in land and slaves. Pinckney of South Carolina asserted that "the power of regulating commerce is a pure concession on the part of the Southern states."

Southerners demanded some guarantees and safeguards in return. Tempers flared when the South asked that Congress be forbidden to stop the importation of slaves. Gouverneur Morris jumped up to condemn slavery as a "nefarious institution" and "the curse of heaven on the states where it prevails." John Rutledge of South Carolina denied that this was a moral issue, observing that the products of slavery served to enrich the Northern shipping interests. In the end most Northerners echoed the sentiments of Connecticut's Sherman, who said that it would be "better to let the Southern states import slaves than to part with them." The Northern states agreed that Congress could only pass a navigation law by a two-thirds margin in each house, that the import tax on slaves would not be over ten dollars per person, and that for purposes of both taxes and representation, a slave would be counted as three-fifths of a white citizen. In return the Southern states agreed that Congess could terminate all slave importations after 1808.

With the slavery compromise arranged, the hard business of the convention was nearly over. A Committee of Style and Arrangement now went to work on a final draft of the Constitution, an effort that took them only four days. The preamble—in contrast to the Articles of Confederation, which began with "We the undersigned delegates of the States . . ."—now, written by Pennsylvania's Morris, read "We the people of the United States . . ." George Mason of Virginia suggested logically that a national bill of rights should be inserted as a preface to the Constitution. Sherman argued that existing state bills of rights should be sufficient, since they would continue to operate under the new Constitution. The convention voted ten states to none against the adoption of a bill of rights. General Charles Cotesworth Pinckney of South Carolina observed during the debate that bills of rights "generally begin with declaring that all men are by nature born free. Now, we should make that declaration with a very bad grace, when a large part of our property consists in men who are actually born slaves." But the public later demanded that a bill of rights be inserted as one price for ratification of the Constitution.

As the day for signing the document arrived, forty of the fifty-five delegates who had attended at one time or another during the convention were present. Benjamin Franklin urged unanimous approval by the delegates and pleaded with them not to discuss their differences in public. Washington also urged the delegates to sign. By one ironic turn of events, Edmund Randolph's concern with local Virginia politics persuaded the man who had introduced the original Virginia Plan at the meeting's start *not* to sign the final draft. Randolph wished first to observe public reaction, which he believed would be largely negative. Elbridge Gerry of Mas-

The signing of the Constitution as rendered by a twentieth-century artist intent upon capturing an expressive realism for the occasion. (Library of Congress)

sachusetts feared that the Constitution created too strong a central government and might even help foment a civil war during the debate over ratification. He, too, would not sign. George Mason, still unhappy over the convention's refusal to adopt a bill of rights, returned to Virginia to oppose ratification. The remaining thirty-nine men from New Hampshire to Georgia wrote their names on the bottom of the parchment. After dining together at City Tavern, they packed up and returned to their states to renew the debate they had lived with over the past four months — this time with the people.

The signers of the Constitution, despite individual objections, were generally satisfied that they had created a stronger and more workable union of the states. The men who would come to be called Founding Fathers had authorized a new national government with specific powers to collect taxes, coin and borrow money, make treaties with foreign countries, and regulate commerce among the states and with other nations. The Constitution was "the law of the land" and therefore binding on all federal and state courts. The courts, in turn, were empowered to review laws to ensure their conformity with the new document, and the power of the executive and even the militia could enforce the laws made by Congress. Moreover, the new frame of government could not be changed hastily in the heat of public anger. The Constitution could be amended only if two-thirds of both houses of Congress and three-quarters of the state legislatures (or special conventions) agreed.

The delegates at Philadelphia, therefore, could presumably identify with the sentiments that James Madison's notes ascribe to Benjamin Franklin, who watched with evident pleasure as the last of the convention's members signed the new plan of government:

> Doctor Franklin looking toward the Presidents chair, at the back of which a rising sun happened to be painted, observed to a few members near him, that painters had found it difficult to distinguish in their art a rising from a setting sun. I have, he said, often in the course of the session, and the vicissitudes of my hopes and fears as to its issue, looked at that behind the President without being able to tell whether it was rising or setting. But now at length I have the happiness to know that it is a rising and not a setting sun.

10 The New Republic: Establishing a Workable Government

Returning to his home after the signing of the Constitution, Benjamin Franklin had good reason for optimism. He was born in 1706 in New England, some twenty-five years before the colony of Georgia was founded; his life spanned nearly the entire eighteenth century. He moved when young to Pennsylvania. From a small, strongly Quaker community, Franklin's Philadelphia had grown into the commercial and cultural center of the new nation. And Franklin had grown with the town. At the Albany Congress in 1754 (see Chapter 8, pp. 151–154) he had a plan that would have created an assembly with representatives from each colony in proportion to their tax payments, but it had been frustrated by individual colonies' fears of giving up powers and authority. Now that the colonies had become independent states, Franklin and others were not prepared in 1787 to allow a repetition of that disunity.

In the Continental Congress the states had provided the vehicle to raise funds and unite in the revolutionary struggle against Great Britain. By the time of the Declaration of Independence, the first loyalties of almost all the people were toward their particular states. In fact, the Declaration itself had proclaimed the colonies to be "Free and Independent States." When the First Continental Congress met in 1774, it did so in response to the colonial-wide crisis. Acting virtually on their own, without established procedures or obligations to constituents, the members raised an army, issued a continental currency, and conducted foreign relations. But the revolutionary leaders found it expedient to create a more permanent and legitimate government to be called The United States of America. Although in 1777 they drew up the Articles of Confederation, a plan for a loose union of the states, it was not until 1781 that every state approved the plan and the new government could go into operation.

Only six years later the Founding Fathers at Philadelphia's Constitutional Convention decided to replace their nation's first system of government. The convention had seen a heated battle between delegates from small states and those from larger and more powerful ones. The major question of which powers should be exercised by the central government—and which should be denied it—had been a point of contention from the Albany Congress to the Continental Congress, then during the debate over the Confederation government, later at the Annapolis Convention, and finally at the Constitutional Convention in 1787.

Leaders from many states were also worried, however, about growing democratic trends within the states, especially as these sentiments could be detected in the various legislatures. Yet the central government was so weak under the Articles that even a nationwide tariff could not be approved by the required unanimous votes of the states. Was formation of a new constitution and government needed to prevent the union of states from dissolving? Had government under the Articles of Confederation proved a failure? Most important, how did this debate reflect the manner in which Americans thought and acted during the years that followed independence?

COLONIES TO STATES

Even before the Declaration of Independence, the Continental Congress had advised the separate colonies to organize new governments "under the authority of the people." As states

191

sought immediately to create new constitutions, the Congress had begun to create its own successor in the central government: the Articles of Confederation. Resistance to British policies had centered in the colonial legislatures (directed against the royal governors and their councils), and it was the creation of new state governments that preoccupied the minds of most people in the new nation. Between May and December 1776, eight states drew up constitutions. The remainder quickly followed.

American revolutionary theory reflected prevailing ideas of constitutional law in the thirteen colonies at the time. Government derived its powers from the consent of the people. A written constitution drawn up by representatives of the people should embrace the concept of limited government, placing clear restraints upon the powers of executive, legislative, and judicial branches. Most of the new state constitutions also contained bills of rights barring the government from interfering with freedom of speech and conscience and —among other rights—assuring trial by jury and other legal guarantees. The English constitution had never been written down in a single codified document; it remained even in the eighteenth century a collection of laws and customs practiced within the institutions of the realm. But the constitutions of American states provided *written* guidelines. These written guidelines were distinguished from ordinary legislation by their fixed and fundamental nature.

Nonetheless the old, unwritten British constitution with its "balanced government" served as the model for Americans. Power in England, theoretically, was divided or balanced among the monarchy, the aristocracy (in the House of Lords), and the popular electorate (legislating in the House of Commons). In reality, the legislative branch (though growing in power) was probably the weakest of the three at the time of the American Revolution, with the aristocracy wielding significant power in the House of Commons.

The American states sought to correct this tendency by increasing legislative authority and decreasing the influence of state governors. In the colonial period, the greatest political struggles had been those fought between the colonial assemblies, elected by an increasingly higher percentage of the population, and the English royal governors. Now, however, the state legislatures and *not* the governors would have the power to declare war, create new courts, coin money, and raise armies. The Pennsylvania constitution, most radical of the state documents, even eliminated the office of governor entirely, resting the executive power in an elective council of twelve members chosen directly by the people. Since it also made provisions for a single-house legislature, doing away with the upper house, the entire concept challenged the basic idea of government balanced among its branches.

Most states, however, retained their upper houses — state senates whose members were often chosen by the vote of those who could meet higher property qualifications than those required to vote for the lower houses. The state senates had been an outgrowth in the United States of the royal governors' councils, and the new state constitutions generally provided that their power would not be greater than that assigned to the more popularly elected assemblies.

A stronger legislative branch, a weaker executive, and an independent judiciary were ways in which the new states implemented the lessons of the past and the principle of separation of powers, an idea popularized in the mid-eighteenth century by the French political philosopher Montesquieu. Frequent elections, a broad suffrage, and small electoral districts, where constituents could instruct their representatives on how to vote, were practices that gave rise to greater democracy through increased popular participation in government. Unlike the colonial practices of ignoring or underrepresenting new counties in the West, the new state constitutions quickly provided that the western areas be fairly represented in the legislature. Five states provided for periodic adjustments of representation to ensure an equal voice for all areas of the state according to population. Prohibition of plural office holding (occupying more than one political post at a time) would further ensure the separation of powers under the new constitutions, and moderate salaries for public officials to guard against corruption were also featured in many of the documents.

Although legislative power in the states was enlarged nearly to the point of primacy, the executive and judicial branches still exerted a substantial check on the lawmakers' powers. Governors received short and fixed terms. Their vetoes could be overridden, but their power to appoint some officials with legislative assent gave the governors considerable authority. A governor's prestige would also be enhanced by the fact that he entered office by the vote of the people of the entire state. Whereas individual legislators might have widely divergent and narrow interests reflecting the concerns of their constituents, the governor could claim to represent the aspirations of the people as a whole and to pursue the general interest of the state.

An independent judiciary would be nearly free from interference by a powerful legislature or popular governor. After their appointment, judges would serve for long terms or even for lifetime in the new states at salaries that could not be altered at the politicians' whim. Judges had not yet asserted the authoriy to determine the constitutionality of legislation; this power of judicial review would later develop from the need for a higher body, less involved in periodic political controversies, to enforce limits on the power to legislate. When this power evolved, the judiciary's power was further strengthened. These developments within the *state* constitutions—especially the manner in which the constitutions assured both separation of powers and checks and balances within a government—later strongly influenced the delegates to the Philadelphia Convention in their deliberations over creating a new constitution for the entire country.

DEVISING THE ARTICLES OF CONFEDERATION

The organization and structure of state governments, however, did not serve as the model for the new nation's *first* government. The Articles of Confederation were approved by the Continental Congress in 1777 but were not finally approved or ratified by the states until 1781 as the Revolution neared its end. Eight days after the signing of the Declaration of Independence, a committee had submitted the draft of a new government. But congressional approval had been held up by a sixteen-month debate over the apportionment of expenses and voting power under the Articles and over the equally thorny dilemma of Western land policy.

Under the Articles, the states actually surrendered very little of their independence or authority. They continued to enjoy the power to tax and to regulate commerce. In Article 9, Congress was authorized to pursue diplomatic relations, raise and administer military forces and the funds to support them, coin and borrow money, regulate Indian affairs, settle boundary disputes among states, and manage the public lands not yet brought under state control. A simple majority of states was required to decide minor matters, while nine states had to agree on more important questions such as declaring war, adopting treaties, and borrowing or coining money. There was no president or executive branch, although congressional committees were created from time to time in order to serve in an executive capacity. Any amendments to the Articles required the approval of every state.

The crucial powers of commercial regulation, taxation, and ultimate authority (sovereignty) remained within the state governments. The Confederation Congress could merely *request* money from the states; it had no powers of coercion or enforcement. Since the authority of Congress to conduct war and foreign affairs required revenues, the states even helped determine these policies in practice as well as through the payment—or withholding—of requested funds. The spirit of this loose confederation was best illustrated in Article 2, which declared that "each state retains its sovereignty, freedom and independence, and every power, jurisdiction, and right, which is not by this confederation expressly delegated to the United States. . . ."

The apportionment of representatives and taxes, questions that later threatened to break up the Constitutional Convention, became major stumbling blocks to ratification of the Articles. The smaller, less populous states refused to accept representation based upon population, so each state received one vote in the Confederation

Congress. An interesting sectional issue arose over apportioning state revenues to Congress. The New England states had relatively high land values and, therefore, argued that revenues should be raised in proportion to population—and *not* land values. Leaders in the Southern states, which had large populations (including thousands of slaves already counted as three-fifths for representation) but *lower* land values, pushed for taxation on the basis of property values. Supported by representatives from the middle states, Southerners got their way, and property values became the basis for revenue payments under the Articles.

Collecting these taxes from the states would prove far more difficult than agreeing upon the *formula* for collection!

The fact that some states claimed huge areas of Western lands also became a point of contention in approving the Articles. The colonial charters of Georgia, the Carolinas, Virginia, Connecticut, and

In 1787 the first covered wagon left Ipswich, Massachusetts, for new land near Marietta, Ohio. Settlement of the West was a continuing problem for the confederation. (NYPL/Picture Collection)

Massachusetts had claimed land stretching to the Pacific Ocean, while other provincial charters had no such provisions. Those without claims wanted Congress to restrict the western boundaries of the other states and to take control of the Western lands for the entire country. States *with* claims resisted any move to restrict their borders though they argued with one another over *conflicting* claims in the West. Before the Revolutionary War, despite complaints and opposition from Virginia's Ohio Company, speculators from Maryland, Pennsylvania, and New Jersey had purchased lands from Indians in the Ohio Valley. There they hoped to establish the new colony of Vandalia and, after the war, pressed Congress to recognize their project.

Virginia and other states with Western land claims, however, had been able to include a provision in the Articles of Confederation providing that no state would be required to relinquish such claims. Maryland refused to ratify the Confederation government's charter unless Congress took control of these lands, arguing that states with huge holdings in the West would be able to gain so much revenue through land sales that their citizens would pay almost no taxes. This, in turn, would cause many people to move to those states with Western lands and without taxes, leaving "landless" states sparsely populated. As the oldest state, Virginia had the largest land claims. Yet as the Philadelphia Convention would later show, sentiment in Virginia for a stronger central government overcame its more parochial interest in Western lands. When Thomas Jefferson led Virginia to offer Congress all of her land claims north of the Ohio River, Maryland ratified the Articles in the following month.

SOCIETY AND POLITICS IN THE 1780s

War, Social Disorder, and Democracy

The strains of the Revolutionary War had done much to upset the existing economic and social order. Many merchants who had traded under British mercantile patterns now found it hard to adjust to commercial conditions in an independent nation. Beginning in 1776, all govern-

mental power, held previously by British officials, passed to American control, while thousands of administrators and ordinary persons loyal to the crown fled the thirteen states. Over 100,000 of these Tories left for Canada, England, or the West Indies, while others who remained in the United States suffered the loss of wealth, status, and power to the revolutionaries. The new state governments required loyalty oaths and often punished wealthy Tories by confiscating their lands. Merchants, small farmers, and planters alike were forced to adjust to new situations in which their traditional markets and credit sources had been seriously altered. Southern planters lost their normal markets for tobacco, while many of their slaves had escaped to British lines, after receiving promises of liberation (largely broken) from British officials during the Revolution.

This economic disruption proved to have long-range benefits, however, both for upwardly mobile Americans and for the national economy as a whole. The loss of some tobacco markets only encouraged and accelerated the diversification of agriculture in the upper South and led to the establishment of new markets by agrarian entrepreneurs. In Massachusetts, newly prosperous merchant families moved quickly, in Boston and other port cities, to replace the fleeing or discredited Tories, helping to establish with remarkable rapidity a new commercial elite loyal to the Revolution. Operating without some of the British restrictions which had hindered them under the Navigation Acts and the restrictive legislation of the pre-Revolutionary decade and a half, American ships now traded with the West Indies, South America, and even China. The new commercial elite bought the confiscated property of loyalists at greatly reduced prices and speculated in depreciated Revolutionary paper currency. Merchants also used the state and central governments after 1776 to charter banks and other businesses as well as to develop resources for investment purposes. Although land speculators profited most from the outright confiscation of Tory property, the war also helped to eradicate the practice of quitrents, which many farmers had to pay annually to landlords. The Revolution also created a large market for the sale of surplus foodstuffs, which farmers could sell at inflated prices. Although exports remained an important feature of the American economy, interstate and interregional trade soon opened up significant new markets, pointing the direction toward eventual creation of a vast *national* market system within the United States in the century ahead.

The Revolution also intensified patterns of American social development that reached back into the early and mid-eighteenth century. With the British Proclamation of 1763 restricting Western land settlement no longer in effect, for example, and with the withdrawal of most British troops from the United States even before Yorktown, the westward movement of settlement was well under way by the 1780s. Natural increase was responsible for giving that decade the largest percentage growth of population in American history. Nor were the Appalachian Mountains, formidable though they were, proving to be insurmountable. By 1780, twenty thousand settlers occupied the Kentucky territory. The social effects of such movement emerged clearly. A mobile population helped partially to undermine traditional beliefs of social superiority and inferiority along well-defined class lines. The westward movement also brought in its wake "wars" between Indians and American migrants in Georgia, Tennessee, Kentucky, and elsewhere.

The Revolutionary War also encouraged independent religious feeling and weakened the remaining links between church and state within the various states. Denominations that tended to be more democratic and less rigid in their doctrines and rituals spread rapidly, while the older "high status" religious sects lost ground. States that had never known an "official" church during colonial days now wrote strong clauses in their constitutions separating church and state. Some states that had previously "established" the Anglican faith found the affiliation discredited, because of American Anglicanism's close ties to the Church of England, and dropped the official designation. Massachusetts, New Hampshire, and Connecticut retained their Congregationalist established churches into the next century. On the whole, however, people were now free from paying taxes for the church or from attending any designated "state" church, developments that furthered freedom of religion and thought, not only in public action but in the realm of private religious choice.

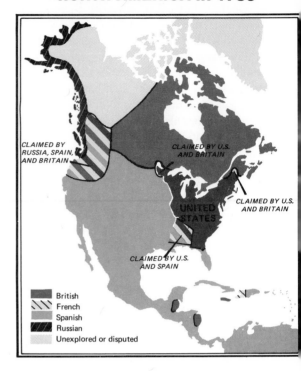

NORTH AMERICA IN 1783

CLAIMED BY RUSSIA, SPAIN, AND BRITAIN

CLAIMED BY U.S. AND BRITAIN

CLAIMED BY U.S. AND BRITAIN

UNITED STATES

CLAIMED BY U.S. AND SPAIN

British
French
Spanish
Russian
Unexplored or disputed

dom of religion and thought, not only in public action but in the realm of private religious choice.

Republican ideology, in addition to furthering developments already under way, also gave rise to growing democratic sentiments as a result of the Revolution. Upwardly mobile middle-class groups in the Northern states especially resented older concepts of deference to the aristocratic class. Membership in private clubs and the wearing of expensive foreign clothing, among other "snobbish" customs, drew criticism from the avidly democratic press. The most ambitious men of the time, however, aimed not at attacking the uneven distribution of income—an unevenness that the Revolution had actually accelerated—but sought instead to gain a higher place within the existing (and changing) economic structure. Social distinctions increasingly became founded more upon wealth and political position after the Revolution than upon association with powerful families from the pre-Revolutionary elite.

Egalitarian values that emerged from the ferment of the American Revolution also stimulated a serious antislavery movement in the new nation. Slavery now stood exposed as a glaring contradiction to the Declaration of Independence's proud assertion that "all men are created equal." As early as 1774, the Continental Congress had urged that the slave trade be abolished, and six state governments soon followed through. Shortly afterward, Philadelphia Quakers organized the world's first antislavery society in 1775, and other societies quickly emerged in both Northern and Southern states. During the war itself, the Continental Army and the militias of the Northern states (and Maryland) promised (and sometimes actually granted) freedom to blacks who enlisted to fight for the Revolutionary cause. Later, the Constitutional Convention would set an 1808 deadline for abolition of the foreign slave trade. In an even more fateful step, Pennsylvania became the first state, in 1780, to pass a statute granting slaves gradual emancipation. By the end of the eighteenth century, most Northern states had either taken similar action or were launched on the process of emancipation. Inevitably, the Southern states began to recognize the emerging distinctions between their social and economic patterns and those of their Northern brethren based upon the continuation—and expansion—of slavery below the Mason-Dixon line.[1]

Politics Within the States

The growth of greater popular participation in government stemmed partly from the extralegal activity of patriots during the Revolution. "Mobs" and groups protesting British actions or patrolling local streets had been a commonly accepted method for enforcing the will of a community upon town or city wrongdoers in colonial days. Al-though independence reduced the need for such vigilante behavior, many Americans continued to view all official institutions—even their own—with deep distrust. This suspicion was not confined to instructing representatives on how to vote in the state assemblies; citizens often organized committees and conventions appealing to the public as a whole for redress. Mobs helped enforce *economic* standards, for example, when Revolutionary state legislatures were unable to prevent prices from rising rapidly or to control war profiteering. By the mid-1780s, popular associations arose in several states to resist tax collections and judicial actions. State assemblies, by incorporating representatives from the newer Western sections, often included a greater number of small farmers and men of moderate wealth. Significant popular access to government was also achieved by moving several of the state capitals to towns in the interior, by opening assembly meetings to the public, and by reporting legislative debates in the daily and weekly press.

The state legislatures became increasingly the place to introduce laws benefiting local interests and the forum for debates between various interest groups. Older concepts of the public good based upon aristocratic or monarchical premises gave way to the idea of a complex, democratic separation of powers between the branches in which assembly, senate, and governor alike were all responsible—and accountable—to popular demands. Debtor farmers called for low taxes, court delays of debt payments, and printing of inflationary amounts of paper money. Artisan craftsmen wanted price regulation of farm produce, abolition of trade monopolies, and tariffs against competitive foreign imports. Merchant creditors asked for high taxes on land and protection of private contracts. Businessmen sought special legal and economic privileges. All the while, the powers of state legislatures continued to expand. They began to assume duties that belonged in colonial days to the executive or judicial branches by such practices as legislating to overrule judgments and decisions taken by the other branches. More important, however, through such actions as printing great quantities of paper money and delaying settlements against debtor farmers, the legislatures under the

[1] To settle a longstanding boundary dispute between Maryland and Pennsylvania, two British astronomers, Charles Mason and Jeremiah Dixon, surveyed the boundary between Pennsylvania and the colonies to the south —including Maryland—from 1763–67. The term "Mason-Dixon line" became a popular phrase in antebellum days for imaginatively dividing free Northern and slave Southern states.

Benjamin Franklin

Americans do not inquire concerning a stranger, *"What is he?"* but, *What can he do?"* So Benjamin Franklin commented on the opportunities available to anyone in colonial America. In America, he observed, any industrious young man could become "self-made," rising from poverty and obscurity to fame and wealth. One such individual was Franklin himself. On his deathbed in 1790, he could claim to have been a printer, author, scientist, inventor, philanthropist, and diplomat.

Franklin was born in Boston in 1706, the fifteenth child and youngest son of a family of seventeen children. He left school at the age of ten. First he was an apprentice to his father, a candle- and soapmaker, and then to his brother, a printer. At the age of seventeen he ran away to Philadelphia, with one Dutch dollar and a copper shilling in his pocket. He found employment in a print-shop, and soon demonstrated his ability. Through his brother-in-law, Robert Holmes, he met the eccentric Governor Keith, who sent Franklin off to London, where Franklin found work at Palmer's printing house. After two years in London, he returned to Philadelphia in 1726 and worked as a shop clerk, learning accounts and becoming an "expert in selling."

Within seven years Franklin had bought the weekly newspaper, the *Pennsylvania Gazette,* rescuing it from near bankruptcy. It ran profitably for the next thirty-six years. During these same years Franklin created the overwhelmingly popular *Poor Richard's Almanack,* published yearly from 1732 to 1757. It contained local information for all the colonies, and sayings on the virtues of thrift and hard work. It was "Poor Richard" who said that "A penny saved is a penny earned," "Time is money," and "Little strokes fell great oaks." The *Almanack* sold thousands of copies in America every year and was translated and reprinted in many European countries.

Franklin grew wealthy. He devoted much of his energy to making Philadelphia a better city. He initiated street lighting, police and fire protection, and a colonywide militia. He helped establish a circulating library — the first in the United States — the American Philosophical Society, and the University of Pennsylvania. His scientific and inventive genius, typically American in its practical outlook, produced bifocal eyeglasses, the Franklin stove, a stool that opened up into a ladder, and a rocking chair that fanned the sitter while rocking. By the age of forty Franklin was a distinctly successful man. But, he wrote his mother, he would rather have it said that "he lived usefully," than that "he died rich."

Unquestionably Philadelphia's most prominent citizen, Franklin was sent to London in 1767 to act as agent for Pennsylvania. He emerged as a spokesman for American independence. When he returned home, the Revolution had already broken out. He served in the Second Continental Congress and in 1775 went to France to negotiate for financial and military aid. Franklin charmed the French with his wit, wisdom, and kindness. His personal popularity added much to the success of his diplomatic mission.

When Franklin returned to his beloved Philadelphia, he received a hero's welcome. He was elected president (mayor) of the city. And at the age of eighty-one he became a delegate to the Constitutional Convention in 1787. His interest in the welfare of mankind prompted him to sign a petition to Congress calling for the abolition of slavery. Death claimed him three months later in April 1790. Philadelphia lost its most famous citizen, and the young nation lost a man who embodied its very spirit.

Articles of Confederation incurred the wrath of creditors, capitalists, and merchants—as well as many wealthy landholders—who debated appropriate actions to check what some considered an excess of democracy in the new republic.

THE ACHIEVEMENTS OF THE CONFEDERATION GOVERNMENT

Although the various weaknesses of the Confederation government, perceived or real, led in 1787 to the Philadelphia Convention's attempt to jettison the system, the loose Confederation could still show a respectable number of meaningful achievements. The new government had to face the enormous problems left by the economic and social dislocations created by the war. It also wrestled with the twin dilemmas of establishing viable, legitimate state governments and constructing a central government that could unite the nation while leaving most basic authority with the individual states. In the short time that it wielded power, the Confederation government managed to solve the problem of the Western lands, create an efficient government bureaucracy, and clear away many of the problems wrought by the financing of the war.

Perhaps the Confederation succeeded most impressively in a series of land ordinances culminating in the Northwest Ordinance of 1787. After Virginia relinquished claims to the Ohio country, speculators pressured Congress not to take over the area because they objected to the terms of the cession. When Congress finally gained control, it passed the land ordinances of 1784 and 1785. These ordinances provided for the territory to be surveyed into townships of six miles square along lines running east–west and north–south. Each township was divided into thirty-six lots one mile square. The Confederation government provided for land sales by auction at no less than a dollar an acre, the land to be sold in 640-acre plots (i.e., one square mile). This procedure gave large land companies and speculators a decided advantage over smaller farmers who neither needed 640 acres nor owned six hundred forty dollars. Congress retained four sections and set aside an-

other for the support of public education. The land sales at such a high price (at least for the 1780s) not only kept many low-income settlers from buying their own land but also paved the way for removal of squatter settlers and Indians.

If the terms of sale represented business sense, the terms of the Northwest Ordinance of 1787 were little short of enlightened. It provided for an initial period during which the governor, a secretary, and a three-court judge appointed by Congress would rule the Northwest area. Once the white population of the territory reached five thousand adult males, a representative legislature would be created. The area would be divided into three, four, or five territories, each to be admitted to the union as an equal state when its population reached 60,000. Slavery was forever forbidden. Political and religious freedom were guaranteed and public education encouraged. In creating the future states of Ohio, Indiana, Michigan, Illinois, and Wisconsin, the Confederation government had removed many of the questions regarding the status of new territories acquired by the United States, at least temporarily, thereby encouraging settlement of those and other Western lands. The procedures established in these ordinances also established important precedents for the admission of virtually all the remaining states of the Union.

Another major accomplishment of the Confederation government was the establishment of a federal bureaucracy. Elected by the Confederation Congress and responsible to it, civil servants worked in the departments of war, foreign affairs, finance, and the post office, whether or not Congress was in session. Several men who served in the Confederation's departments continued in their posts after ratification of the Constitution in 1789, notably one gentleman who served as the register of the treasury from 1779 to 1829! Most democratic revolutionaries distrusted such executive power, however, and insisted that congressmen themselves acting in committees should supervise the work of permanent employees.

The Board of Treasury was established to handle the numerous financial problems of the Confederation period. It supervised treasury officials who were settling accounts of military departments. Also, the board oversaw the continen-

United States map showing territorial claims and cessions:

NORTHWEST TERRITORY
Ceded 1784
Western Reserve Ceded 1800
Claimed by Massachusetts and Virginia Ceded 1784–85
Claimed by Conn. and Va. Ceded 1784-86

(VERMONT) Claimed by N.Y., N.H. and Mass.
(MAINE)
Claimed by N.Y. & Mass.
NEW HAMPSHIRE
NEW YORK
MASSACHUSETTS
RHODE ISLAND
CONNECTICUT
PENNSYLVANIA
NEW JERSEY
DELAWARE
MARYLAND
VIRGINIA

(KENTUCKY) Claimed by Virginia Admitted as state, 1792

Claimed by North Carolina Ceded 1790
NORTH CAROLINA

Ceded 1787
SOUTH CAROLINA

Claimed by Georgia Ceded 1802
GEORGIA

Claimed by Spain, United States & Georgia

FLORIDA (Spain)

ATLANTIC OCEAN

L. Superior
L. Michigan
L. Huron
L. Ontario
L. Erie
Missouri R.
Ohio R.
Mississippi R.
St. Lawrence R.

UNITED STATES AFTER 1783

0   100   200   300
MILES

tal loan officers within the several states as well as those commissioners settling accounts between the United States and various states or individuals. The board reviewed complaints about finance and disbursed payments to troops and civil employees of the government. One member of the board, Arthur Lee, worried over the wealthy speculators who had purchased so many of the Revolutionary War securities: "I am afraid, my dear friend," he wrote at one point, "that we will live to see the noble fabric we have labored so much to rear to liberty, honor, and independence, uprooted from its foundation from the rapacity for speculation which appears to me ascended from commissaries and quartermasters to legislators." Lee's fears would be realized during the first years of the new Confederation government.

PROBLEMS OF THE CONFEDERATION

The experience of many of the new nation's elite in the Continental Congress, Revolutionary War, and Confederation government—when combined with their personal and class perceptions of the situation—fostered a growing feeling of nationalism. The Confederation found itself confronted by tremendous inflation because of the large issues of paper money printed to finance the war, troubled by the states' refusal to pay their alloted requisitions to Congress, and frightened at the threats of mutiny that came from unpaid soldiers in the Continental Army. There occurred, moreover, a marked change in congressional leadership during the Confederation period. Now men as much inter-

A nineteenth-century American artist captures the mood and pedagogical style of a schoolroom in the newly independent United States. Revolutionary America placed great emphasis on the significance of primary and secondary school education. (Library of Congress)

ested in asserting public authority as popular liberty began reaching positions of influence. The Continental Army was intended partly to curb the power of local militias. Single appointees rather than congressional committees now ran the departments of war, foreign affairs, and finance, thereby strengthening the executive function.

By far the most powerful of these men was Robert Morris, a Philadelphia merchant and land speculator who would later argue for a strong nationalist position at the Constitutional Convention. As superintendent of finance, Morris wielded enormous power. In attempting to win support among creditors and merchants for a stronger central government, Morris convinced Congress to recommend to the states that they stop issuing paper money and require all taxes to be raised in

coin, or specie. This would help support the value of the new nation's currency, the paper money "continentals," forty dollars of which were worth only one dollar in gold or silver by 1780.

Finance

The key to the nationalist plan was adoption of an amendment to the Articles allowing the Confederation to set a 5 percent tax on imports. This would have given Congress regular funding independent of what the states might see fit to allocate. The Confederation government could then pay back its war debts, thus enhancing the standing of the United States government both domestically and with international creditors. That, in turn, would increase the value of any bonds and securities issued by the Confederation government. The amendment for this tariff passed every state except Rhode Island. But since the Articles required that amendments be ratified by unanimous consent of all the states, the proposal failed.

With the end of the Revolutionary War in 1783, the campaign for a stronger central government, promoted by mercantile and creditor interests among others, received even less support from state governments. A military *coup d'état* had been narrowly averted in 1783, when officers of Washington's army issued an address to Congress and plotted a takeover of the Confederation government. This crisis was prevented only by Washington's personal appearance and plea for restraint.

After the war, however, state autonomy and pride often led the different states to convert federal securities into state bonds, thereby completely subverting the intentions of nationalists like Morris and Alexander Hamilton, who hoped to link the interests of the monied elite closely with those of a stronger central government. Many wealthy individuals with property and interests to protect now looked instead toward their state governments for ultimate redress.

Foreign Relations

Despite the considerable skills of American representatives John Adams in London and Thomas Jefferson in Paris, no amount of diplomatic activity seemed to improve the new nation's standing with the European powers. England refused to surrender its forts in the western lands until Southern planters repaid the debts owed British creditors. The weak Confederation government could not force Southern states to enact the laws needed to comply with this debt repayment, so the British continued to reap the benefits of Western fur trade and retain the allegiance of Indian tribes, despite the pressures of American westward expansion.

In addition to the presence of British troops in the Northwest, the United States faced a Spanish threat in the Southwest. Americans in the Southern states had long eyed the abundant land and fertile soil existing between the Appalachian Mountains and the Mississippi River. Since the

John Jay—like Alexander Hamilton—distrusted the common people and believed that government should be controlled by men of means and education. (Yale University Art Gallery)

Spaniards insisted that no foreign powers could have the right of navigation or settlement on the lower part of the river or its environs, Southern agricultural interests were stymied.

Northern commercial interests met similar frustration at this time. The European governments and their mercantile communities proved reluctant to trade with thirteen virtually independent American states. Meanwhile, competing British goods flooded the American markets, while no American products were admitted—at least none legally—to either the West Indies or any other part of the British Empire. Influenced by Northern merchants, New Yorker John Jay negotiated a treaty with the Spanish minister opening Spain to American trade in return for recognizing Spain's right to refuse American access to the Mississippi. Although seven states voted in favor of ratifying this treaty, the angry South voted in a bloc against it, preventing the three-fourths majority needed to approve it. The incident demonstrated again that a weak Confederation could only advance the legitimate interests of one part of the union by sacrificing those of another, or so it appeared to the nationalists.

Even when American interests were *not* sectionally divided, the structure of the Articles prevented unified action in foreign affairs. Pirates in the Barbary states of North Africa, for example, had seized American ships and sold their crews into slavery for years. Even if Congress had agreed to pay the tribute demanded by the pirates for free navigation into the Mediterranean, there were not enough funds to do so. John Jay, a diplomat to Spain during the Revolution, and others hoped that these humiliating incidents would help mobilize public sentiment for strengthening the central government.

Congress as then set up was ill-equipped to handle any of these problems. It had neither courts nor executive authority with which to coerce states or individuals to obey its various resolutions and recommendations. It had no power to tax or to regulate commerce between the states or with foreign nations. It often took delegates several weeks after a session began to arrive, preventing the quorum needed to decide official business. Delegates were elected annually and prevented from serving more than three years in six. This rapid turnover in membership prevented continuity and experienced leadership from developing, while encouraging confusion and ineffectiveness. The Confederation Congress had met in Philadelphia, in fact, until 1783 when a mutiny in the army barracks there frightened the representatives into leaving the city. After that, Congress could not even decide upon a permanent meeting place, and the delegates wandered in embarrassment from sessions at Princeton to Annapolis to Trenton to New York.

Steps were already well under way by the mid-1780s to shore up the weaknesses of the Confederation. Mechants and land speculators, George Washington among them, helped to organize the Mount Vernon Conference of 1785. They hoped to open up the mouth of the Potomac River to trade with the hinterland. For this, the neighboring states of Maryland and Virginia would have to cooperate by enacting similar commercial legislation. During this period, some states had been tax-

ing the goods arriving from other states as "imports," and boundary disputes occasionally led to armed combat between states. In an attempt to relieve these problems, the Mount Vernon Conference decided to adjourn its meeting and summon a second conference on Confederation problems at Annapolis in 1786. Five states sent delegates to the Annapolis Convention which, though called for the specific purpose of strengthening national authority over commerce, quickly agreed on the necessity of a general revision of the Articles. Through the prodding of Alexander Hamilton and James Madison, *that* convention adjourned even before other states' delegations had arrived. The Confederation Congress, at the request of the Annapolis Convention's sponsors, then summoned yet another convention the following year, this time in Philadelphia, to make "the constitution of the Federal Government adequate to the exigencies of the Union."

Shays's Rebellion

Soon after the delegates had left Annapolis, they received news of a violent episode, which did much to strengthen their cause by persuading Americans of the urgency involved in revising the Articles. As had happened in the western sections of other states, Massachusetts's debtor farmers had taken the law into their own hands. Economic dislocation following the Revolutionary War had caused states to levy new taxes to repay the public debt, thus increasing the debt of already hard-pressed farmers. In western Massachusetts, a number of farmers organized local conventions to demand abolition of the "aristocratic" state senate (which took much of the blame for the high taxes), a lowering of taxes on land, and a reduction in fees charged by lawyers and county courts. Soon after the conventions had ended, mobs stopped the county courts from sitting to prevent mortgage foreclosures at least temporarily while depriving creditors of their rights to collect from debtors. Finally, during the winter of 1786–87, two thousand western Massachusetts farmers rose in armed rebellion. They were led by Daniel Shays, who had served as a captain during the Revolutionary War.

Captain Daniel Shays, a Revolutionary War soldier turned farmer, became the primary leader of "Shays's Rebellion" in western Massachusetts in 1786–87. The two thousand rebel farmers protesting tax and governmental abuses had an even greater impact in states other than Massachusetts, where the prospect of similar "rebellions" stirred support for a stronger central governing authority. (Culver Pictures)

Though Shays's Rebellion was easily put down by the Massachusetts militia, exaggerated reports of armed bands of rebels who conspired to confiscate all private property spread throughout the country. Wealthy merchants like Elbridge Gerry, as well as large landowners, speculators, and creditors throughout Massachusetts—and elsewhere—were horrified by rumors that Shays's men were marching to the federal arsenal at Springfield to seize enough arms to sack Boston and bring down the government of the state. The insurrection struck fear into the hearts of all highly propertied Americans. George Washington's reaction to the stories of spreading rebellion typified the concerns of wealthy slaveholding planters and land speculators everywhere: "I am mortified beyond expression when I view the clouds that have spread over the brightest morn that ever dawned upon any country. . . . Let us have a government by which our lives, liberties and properties will be secured; or let us know the worst at once."

The threat to creditors reached beyond the borders of Massachusetts, especially in Rhode Island where the legislature had made it illegal for anyone to refuse the state's worthless paper money as payment for a debt. Not surprisingly, Rhode Island was the only state that refused to send delegates to the Constitutional Convention, and it only joined the new government reluctantly after all other states had ratified. Perhaps more than any other single factor, Shays's Rebellion convinced the delegates preparing to attend the Philadelphia Convention of the need for overstepping their mandate and creating a new, more powerful central government. Simply revising and strengthening the Articles of Confederation, they reasoned, might not prove sufficiently effective against armed threats to "lives, liberties and properties" by rebellious debtors in other states as well.

RATIFYING THE CONSTITUTION

One of the last debates at the Philadelphia Convention had centered on the method for gaining public approval of the Constitution. In the final committee report, a blank had been left to designate the number of states sufficient for the new government to go into effect. The delegates knew that Rhode Island would not approve of the new document, yet the Articles of Confederation required that amendments receive the unanimous consent of the states.

To agree on less than unanimous consent would be to recognize that the Philadelphia Convention had thoroughly transformed the existing framework of government, which of course it had. James Wilson of Pennsylvania suggested that a simple majority of seven would be sufficient for purposes of ratification. Only the states that chose to approve the new Constitution, Wilson argued, would be bound to it. Pierce Butler of South Carolina sought to support this decision, as well as the delegates' other actions, by claiming the delegates were obedient to a higher law, which allowed for changing the government when the country was poorly governed. After extensive debate, three-quarters or nine states finally became the compromise number agreed upon for ratification.

The final question before the convention was whether the state legislatures or special conventions elected by the people would decide the fate of the new document. With visions of Shays's Rebellion fresh in his mind, Elbridge Gerry declared that the people had "the wildest ideas of government in the world." But many other delegates observed that members of state legislatures sworn to uphold the existing pattern of govern-

ment would be unlikely to support an entirely new government whose creation had never even been authorized. State legislators, moreover, would also feel inclined to vote against the Constitution on grounds of self-interest, perceiving it correctly as creating a new structure of government that undermined the currently dominant influence of the states. A minority of delegates continued to fret that the people should not be allowed to decide ratification through specially elected conventions. There was a "danger of commotions from a resort to the people," cautioned Maryland's Luther Martin, "and to first principles in which the government might be on one side and the people on the other." Nevertheless, in a decision as important as any previously taken, the convention voted nine to one for *popular* ratification through special conventions, and the campaign to win the confidence of the people in the new government began.

Supporters of the new Constitution had enormous advantages, tactically and doctrinally, over their opponents in the ratification controversy. Supporters declared themselves to be Federalists while labeling those opposed to the Constitution anti-Federalists. Since "federalism" describes a government in which both state and central authorities share power, it would have been more accurate, however, to describe those favoring ratification as "nationalists" and those who opposed it as believers in the existing "federalism." Still, the names stuck in the public mind, and the opposition was saddled with a major disadvantage in popular perception. Newspapers, moreover, reflecting the self-interests of urban printers and owners who relied on merchant readers and wealthy advertisers, overwhelmingly supported ratification.

The Federalist supporters of the Constitution worked closely across state lines during the ratification process. They comprised a group whose interests dictated such cohesion, and their frequent exchanges of correspondence dealing with strategy amd tactics during the ratification struggles in various states illustrated their superior organization. Nor did it help the anti-Federalists that the most prestigious Revolutionary leaders— Washington and Franklin among them—supported the Constitution. Such personal endorsements

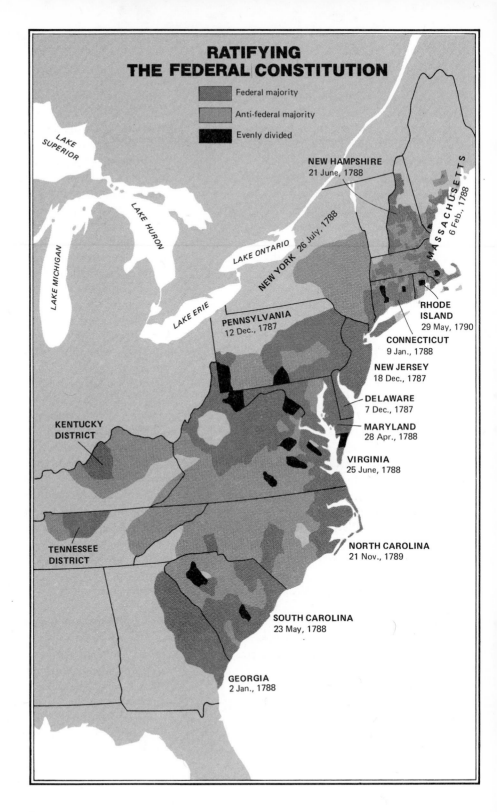

RATIFYING THE FEDERAL CONSTITUTION

- Federal majority
- Anti-federal majority
- Evenly divided

LAKE SUPERIOR

LAKE MICHIGAN

LAKE HURON

LAKE ONTARIO

LAKE ERIE

NEW HAMPSHIRE
21 June, 1788

MASSACHUSETTS
6 Feb., 1788

NEW YORK 26 July, 1788

RHODE ISLAND
29 May, 1790

PENNSYLVANIA
12 Dec., 1787

CONNECTICUT
9 Jan., 1788

NEW JERSEY
18 Dec., 1787

DELAWARE
7 Dec., 1787

KENTUCKY DISTRICT

MARYLAND
28 Apr., 1788

VIRGINIA
25 June, 1788

TENNESSEE DISTRICT

NORTH CAROLINA
21 Nov., 1789

SOUTH CAROLINA
23 May, 1788

GEORGIA
2 Jan., 1788

added great strength to Federalist arguments with the electorate. A collection of forceful pro-Constitution essays written by Hamilton, Madison, and John Jay were impressive both as political treatises and as political propaganda. Originally published in newspapers in New York City (and later in Virginia) to influence those states' ratification debates, the essays were later combined and printed as *The Federalist Papers*.

The promise of amendments later to be known as the Bill of Rights helped ease the hesitations of many who had been undecided. Finally, although they opposed the adoption of the Constitution, anti-Federalists disagreed among themselves over how the Articles should be revised. The absence of any genuine alternative or counter-

proposal to the new government also served to weaken their opposition.

Those who supported the Constitution often came from a broad sector of American opinion allied to commercial interests. Such people saw the new government's power to regulate commerce as leading to uniform procedures that would encourage stable trade routes, end the bickering between states, and create a climate more likely to stimulate foreign trade. This group included not only merchants but also skilled workers, master craftsmen or independent artisans with small shops. Coopers (barrel makers) and sailmakers, for example, were among those who depended directly upon the prosperity of the shipping industry. Some sold their products to mer-

This superb early-nineteenth-century lady's dressing table made in Baltimore—mahogany and mahogany inlaid with satinwood, with painted and gilt decoration—illustrates (as could many other pieces) the elegance and high quality of American crafts in the late-Revolutionary period. (Maryland Historical Society)

chants for export. Many hoped for a protective tariff from the new government to further shield their trade. Even large farmers who produced a sizable surplus crop for export, and ordinary agriculturalists with farms near rivers and streams that produced smaller but easily marketed surpluses, looked for an upsurge in commerce once the new government took power. Anti-Federalists usually had almost no commercial support. Instead, their ranks included many subsistence and debtor farmers in the western sections of states farthest from interstate or foreign markets. These men, like the ones who had marched with Daniel Shays, were more apt to remain suspicious of a new government that threatened to restrain the ability of states to inflate the currency or revise contractual obligations. To the anti-Federalists, such federal restraints smacked of a threat upon individual liberties comparable to the worst English abuses that had led to the Revolution. The anti-Federalists also feared a powerful central government located at some distant but as yet undetermined capital.

Despite Federalist advantages, the noncommercial and small farmer interests often provoked heated ratification battles in the states. Georgia, badly needing federal protection from the Indian tribes surrounding the state, was quick to approve. New Jersey and Connecticut bought goods imported in New York City, which placed a tax on the goods. Their approval reflected (among other things) a belief that though the tax helped to fund New York's debt, under the new Constitution, congressional import duties would use such taxes to fund the national debt as a whole.

The crucial battles were fought in the larger states of Virginia, Pennsylvania, Massachusetts, and New York. Many citizens of these important states were confident that they could continue prospering without a stronger central government. Influential public officials also proved unwilling to lose their power and status by agreeing to the changes incorporated in the Constitution. Despite several cliff-hangers during the ratification process in these states, eventually arguments that the Constitution's checks and balances would preserve states rights adequately—abetted by the shrewd political machinations of powerful Federalists—won by 1789 the votes of the nine states required.

North Carolina and Rhode Island held out briefly, but saw the inevitability of the situation and finally fell into line. The Philadelphia convention's handiwork became the law of the land.

THE BILL OF RIGHTS

In the process of ratifying the Constitution, six states had suggested that amendments be added limiting the power of the new government over popular rights and personal freedoms. James Madison had not considered this necessary during the convention itself, and other delegates shared his opinion. Madison believed at first that such guarantees were superfluous in a republic where the people made the laws on a regular basis and monitored their enforcement through the legislatures. Madison also felt that any declaration of rights in the new Constitution might prove too narrow and thus encourage the violation of rights other than those specified in the amendments. But many of the new government's first Congressional members arrived at the first capital of New York prepared to make good the promise of other Federalists, who had assured their supporters that such constitutional guarantees would be enacted once the new government began its work. Madison, himself, guided the amendments through Congress.

The first ten amendments to the Constitution, known collectively as the Bill of Rights, received ratification by the necessary three-fourths majority of states in 1791. The first nine amendments prohibited Congress from restricting freedom of speech, religion, press, the right to assemble, to petition the government, and to bear arms, while guaranteeing fair trials with due process of law. Also forbidden were general warrants, excessive bail, cruel and unusual punishments, and the quartering of troops in private houses. The Ninth Amendment relieved one of Madison's fears by providing that the simple listing of certain rights in the Constitution did not mean that the government could violate any others presently enjoyed by the people. The Tenth Amendment explicitly reserved to the states all power not delegated to the national government.

With the inauguration of George Washington as president and the establishment of a strengthened Congress equipped with powers to handle the problems confronting the country, the final page in America's book of revolution was closed. At the same time, the opening chapter of the history of a newly revitalized American nation began in that same year, 1789, with the newly empowered Federalists assuming the many unresolved tasks of protecting their young and fragile national identity.

Suggested Readings Chapters 9-10

The American Revolution

Thomas P. Abernethy, *Western Lands and the American Revolution* (1937); John R. Alden, *The American Revolution, 1775-1783* (1954); Samuel Flagg Bemis, *The Diplomacy of the American Revolution* (1935); Irving Brant, *James Madison: The Virginia Revolutionist* (1941); Wallace Brown, *The King's Friends* (1965); Robert M. Calhoun, *The Loyalists in Revolutionary America, 1760-1781* (1973); Marcus Cunliffe, *George Washington, Man and Monument* (1958); E. P. Douglass, *Rebels and Democrats* (1955); Robert A. East, *Business Enterprise in the American Revolutionary Era* (1938); J. T. Flexner, *George Washington in the American Revolution* (1968); Douglas S. Freeman, *George Washington* (7 vols., 1948-1959); James B. Hedges, *The Browns of Providence Plantation* (1952); Don Higginbotham, *The War of American Independence* (1971); J. Franklin Jameson, *The American Revolution Considered as a Social Movement* (1926); Lawrence S. Kaplan, *Colonies Into Nation: American Diplomacy, 1763-1801* (1972); Bernard Knollenberg, *Washington and the Revolution* (1940); Piers Mackesy, *The War for America* (1964); Jackson Turner Main, *The Sovereign States, 1775-1783* (1973); Dumas Malone, *Jefferson and His Time* (4 vols., 1948-1970); James K. Martin, *Men in Rebellion* (1973); John C. Miller, *Triumph of Freedom, 1775-1783* (1949); Edmund S. Morgan, *The Birth of the Republic, 1763-1789* (rev. ed., 1977) and *The Challenge of the American Revolution* (1976); Samuel Eliot Morison, *John Paul Jones: A Sailor's Biography* (1959); Richard B. Morris, *The Peacemakers: The Great Powers and American Independence* (1965); Mary Beth Norton, *The British-Americans: The Loyalist Exiles in England, 1774-1789* (1972); Howard Peckham, *The War for Independence* (1958); Benjamin Quarles, *The Negro in the American Revolution* (1961); Page Smith, *A New Age Now Begins* (1976); Clarence L. Ver Steeg, *Robert Morris, Revolutionary Financier* (1954); W. M. Wallace, *Appeal to Arms* (1951); Christopher Ward, *The War of the Revolution* (2 vols., 1952); Gordon S. Wood, *The Creation of the American Republic, 1776-1787* (1969); Esmond Wright, *Washington and the American Revolution* (1957); Alfred Young, ed., *The American Revolution: Explorations in the History of American Radicalism* (1976).

The Confederation Period: Government and Politics

H. J. Henderson, *Party Politics in the Continental Congress* (1974); Merrill Jensen, *The American Revolution Within America* (1974), *The Articles of Confederation* (1940), and *The New Nation: A History of the United States During the Confederation, 1781-1789* (1950); Jackson Turner Main, *Political Parties Before the Constitution* (1974) and *The Upper House in Revolutionary America, 1763-1788* (1967); Richard McCormick, *Experiment in Independence: New Jersey in the Critical Period, 1781-1789* (1950); Allan Nevins, *The American States During and After the Revolution* (1924); E. W. Spaulding, *New York in the Critical Period, 1781-1789* (1932); M. L. Starkey, *A Little Rebellion* (1955).

The Constitutional Convention and the American Constitution

Douglass Adair, *Fame and the Founding Fathers* (1974); Charles A. Beard, *An Economic Interpre-*

tation of the Constitution of the United States (1913); Irving Brant, *James Madison the Nationalist, 1780–1787* (1948); Robert Brown, *Charles Beard and the Constitution* (1956); J. E. Cooke, ed., *The Federalist* (1961); Jonathan Elliot, ed., *The Debates in the Several State Conventions on the Adoption of the Federal Constitution* (5 vols., 1876); Max Farrand, *The Framing of the Constitution of the United States* (1913) and *Records of the Federal Convention of 1787* (4 vols., 1911–1937); E. James Ferguson, *The Power of the Purse: A History of American Public Finance, 1776–1790* (1961); Merrill Jensen et al., *The Documentary History of the Ratification of the Constitution* (1976); Cecilia Kenyon, *The Antifederalists* (1966); Leonard Levy, *Essays on the Making of the Constitution* (1969); Staughton Lynd, *Slavery, Class Conflict, and the United States Constitution* (1967); Jackson Turner Main, *The Antifederalists: Critics of the Constitution, 1781–1787* (1961); Forrest McDonald, *E. Pluribus Unum: The Formation of the American Revolution* (1965) and *We the People: The Economic Origins of the Constitution* (1958); J. C. Miller, *Alexander Hamilton: Portrait in Paradox* (1959); Broadus Mitchell and Louise Mitchell, *A Biography of the Constitution of the United States* (1964); Clinton Rossiter, *Alexander Hamilton and the Constitution* (1964) and *1787: The Grand Convention* (1966); Robert A. Rutland, *The Birth of the Bill of Rights, 1776–1791* (1955) and *The Ordeal of the Constitution: The Antifederalists and the Ratification Struggle of 1787–1788* (1966); C. C. Tansill, ed., *Documents Illustrative of the Formation of the Union of the United States* (1927).

The first decades of the American nation proved to be a formidable testing time for the new republic. Although Americans took pride in their new government, and although they quickly accepted the Constitution's basic principles, the national government had to be established and protected. Its future, especially in the earliest years, was by no means assured. Many Americans—and our enemies abroad—asked themselves: Can the fledgling federal republic survive as a unique government in a world of monarchies, most of them autocratic and unfriendly?

The problem of reducing the danger of foreign intrusion into American affairs figured in Thomas Jefferson's bold decision, during his first term as president, to buy from Napoleonic France the massive expanse of western territory that became known as the Louisiana Purchase. Jefferson then directed his private secretary, an army officer named Meriwether Lewis, to explore the new American domain. The expedition led by Lewis and another young officer, William Clark, both advanced and dramatized the westward thrust of exploration and settlement in the new republic. Chapter 11 narrates the Lewis and Clark Expedition. Chapter 12, accompanying this account, examines the passionate political quarrels of the republic's founding decade, the 1790s, which pitted Federalists against Jeffersonian Republicans. After a decade of Federalist rule, which the chapter discusses, the Jeffersonians took power in 1801. The presidencies of Thomas Jefferson and James Madison were both characterized by troubled relations with the leading embattled European powers, England and France, conflicts that led eventually to another American war with Great Britain in 1812.

The United States managed to survive the fierce tangle of domestic and foreign problems that characterized the first generation of American nationhood. In the aftermath of the War of 1812, Americans began a period of relative political calm accompanied by extraordinary economic and geographic expansion. In the 1820s, after a so-called Era of Good Feelings, which followed the decline of Federalist–Jeffersonian arguments, a new brand of politics—and a new political party system—began to emerge. First in the states and then in the federal government, "the people" became supreme through universal white manhood suffrage and through a host of practical and symbolic changes. Symbolizing this process was the election of Andrew Jackson, a "common man" by birth and upbringing, as president in 1828. Chapter 13 describes Jackson's "Road to the White House"—his dramatic life from earliest days and military career to the presidency. Chapter 14 explores the nature of Jackson's political world. It examines the emergence of mass political parties, the growth of the presidency as an institution, and the key issues of this second party system.

The first half of the nineteenth century witnessed not only major political innovation in the United States but also massive economic, social, and cultural changes. The creation of a new factory system and an urban working class, expansion into farming areas (territories soon to become states) in the Southwest and Northwest, and the evolution of a

EXPANDING AMERICA

UNIT THREE

modern commercial capitalist economy were accompanied by a host of parallel developments outside the economic realm.

Prominent among these developments was the rise of an entire cohort of devoted social reformers, among them the small number who helped to found the women's rights movement. The first women's rights convention held at Seneca Falls, New York, in 1848 forms the subject of Chapter 15. Other major aspects of antebellum reformist sentiment included the temperance, peace, antislavery, and education movements. The religious developments in this era exercised a profound and complex impact upon the growth of reform concern. New religious groups spread throughout the country, often through revivalist methods, while older churches struggled to maintain their membership and influence. The newer sects ranged from sedate rationalistic Unitarians to more emotional groups like the Millerites holding millennial beliefs. Chapter 16 describes the range of reform and religious activities in American life during the first half of the nineteenth century.

213

Exploring a Wilderness:
II The Lewis and Clark Expedition

Not every junior officer in the American army received a letter from president-elect Thomas Jefferson that winter, especially not those who served in the distant Ohio territory. But the recently appointed regimental paymaster of American army outposts there, Captain Meriwether Lewis, learned through his commanding officer, General James Wilkinson, that such a letter had arrived for him. Captain Lewis's duties as paymaster took him away from headquarters at Pittsburgh and Detroit to other forts and outposts in the Ohio River Valley, so Jefferson had sent his message through Wilkinson. The February 23, 1801, letter held no ordinary change of assignment or rank for the young officer but offered, instead, a unique opportunity. Jefferson invited Lewis to serve as his private secretary at the recently constructed presidential mansion in Washington, a building not yet commonly known as the White House. Jefferson had special plans ahead for Captain Lewis's work as "private secretary."

Although Lewis rejoiced at the chance to join the president-elect, the opportunity did not come as a complete surprise. Jefferson had long known not only the twenty-six-year-old officer but most of the Lewis family well. Meriwether had been born in 1774 in Albemarle County, Virginia, where his family and the Jeffersons were neighbors. This small tight circle of the Piedmont elite included the Randolphs, Madisons, and other well-placed families, tied together often in kinship relations as well as by economic interests. Lewis's father, William, who died in 1779, had gained some fame and much acclaim by marching against Lord Dunmore, the colony's governor, after the British had seized Virginia's gunpowder supply at the outset of the American Revolution. Young Lewis, fascinated with natural history, settled down and managed his father's plantation for a time in the 1790s. His hard work there while still in his teens earned Jefferson's praise for being "an assiduous and attentive farmer, observing with minute attention all plants and insects he met with." Strong praise indeed from a man who valued both science and agriculture highly.

When the Whiskey Rebellion, a brief Pennsylvania tax revolt, broke out in 1794, Lewis did not hesitate to enroll in the Virginia militia. He never actually fought in the rebellion, but decided to remain with the small army of occupation stationed in Pittsburgh. In 1795 he was transferred to a company of sharpshooters commanded by William Clark (brother of the better-known George Rogers Clark), the man with whom Lewis's name would be linked in his own day and ours. Lewis received a second transfer in 1796, this one to the First U.S. Infantry Regiment, where he served with Indians on Cherokee Nation land, learning their language and culture. Other experiences helped qualify Lewis for his future role as Jefferson's "secretary." He became familiar, for example, with keelboats on the Ohio River while serving as paymaster for troops stationed in wilderness areas.

The president-elect evidently had a broader notion of Lewis's usefulness than merely wielding a secretarial quill pen and similar office duties. In his letter of appointment, Jefferson wrote, "Your knowledge of the Western Country, of the Army, and of all of its interests and relations has rendered it desirable for public as well as private purposes that you should be engaged in that office." Lewis quickly discovered after arriving in Washington what the new president meant by that vague job description.

The new secretary tackled his ordinary duties with customary energy, delivering Jefferson's first message to Congress and making himself totally available for the president's directives. But sometime in 1802 Jefferson and Lewis began to meet in the president's basement study to plan a Western expedition. As a scholar of natural history, and a former vice-president of the American Philosophical Society of Philadelphia, Jefferson had twice tried and twice failed to find a sponsor for an explorer who could catalog flora and fauna while seeking a good commercial overland route to the Pacific from the Eastern United States. American occupation of the upper Missouri country, where such a route lay (Jefferson felt), would achieve several things: it would snatch the North American fur trade away from British control, and it would provide a legacy of land for future generations of American farmers.

Their plans completed by 1803, Jefferson prepared to act. In a message to Congress on January 18, the president masked his true intentions. He argued that an expedition should be funded for the purpose of conferring with Indians from the Ohio country to the Pacific, in order to enlarge the activities of existing trading posts, and to allow purchase of additional Indian lands. Congress, so misadvised, appropriated the twenty-five hundred dollars that Jefferson requested. Lewis, meanwhile, began an intense study of natural science and available maps of the area. He also began recruiting for what now became known as the "Corps of Discovery." But Lewis asked for volunteers without disclosing the expedition's ultimate destination. During late April and May of 1803, the president's secretary went to Pennsylvania to purchase scientific equipment and medical supplies. At the Harpers Ferry landing in Virginia's western mountains, federal arsenal workers labored at constructing a collapsible

Although when the nineteenth century began, the U.S. Army was very small, it contained some men of great ability. Among them were Jefferson's young friend Meriwether Lewis (left) and William Clark (right). (Library of Congress)

iron-framed boat for Lewis's expedition, a vessel that weighed less than one hundred pounds and had been appropriately named the *Experiment.*

By June Lewis had decided on his former commanding officer, Lieutenant William Clark, as the second in command for *his* expedition. Clark proved both eager for the opportunity and delighted to join with a man of his own generation whom he respected from their earlier association. Lewis's letter to Clark about the proposal confided a state secret: that very favorable "expectations are at this time formed by our Govt. that the whole of that immense country watered by the Mississippi and its tributary streams, Missourie inclusive, will be the property of the U. States in less than twelve months from this date." Lewis provided no further word to Clark explaining the mysterious method by which this would happen.

Meriwether Lewis now journeyed to Pittsburgh, where wagons had brought all of the expedition's supplies. The young officer proved impatient with the boatbuilders, who took twelve days to get his oars and poles in place for the journey, describing them as "a set of most incorrigible drunkards" with whom he spent most of his time "alternately persuading and threatening." The equipment eventually loaded on board included astronomical instruments, various kinds of firearms and ammunition (including a new "airgun"), and camping supplies and clothing. The provisions also held many presents for the Indians who would be encountered on the trip, a motley assortment that contained (among other things) three pounds of beads, two dozen earrings, five hundred brooches, seventy-two rings, fifteen pewter looking mugs—and fifteen scalping knives! The total cost of provisions and gifts amounted to slightly over two thousand dollars.

Jefferson's final instructions to Lewis, dated June 20, 1803, took on a very specific and practical tone:

> The object of your mission is to explore the Missouri R. and such principal stream of it as, by its course and communication with the waters of the Pacific Ocean, whether the Columbia, Oregon, Colorado, or any other river, may offer the most direct and practicable water communication across this continent for the purpose of commerce. . . . Should you reach the Pac. Ocean, inform yourself of the circumstances which may decide whether the furs of those parts may not be collected as advantageously at the head of the Missouri . . . as at Nootka Sound, or any other point of that coast, and that trade be consequently conducted through the Missouri and U.S. more beneficially than by the circumnavigation now practiced.

The president also mentioned the importance of soil, plants, animals, and minerals. For Jefferson as head of the American government, rather than as Jefferson the naturalist, however, discovery of a Northwest passage to the Pacific and its commercial advantages had to receive priority.

Lewis's trip down the Ohio began on August 20 and on a frustrating note. The water level was so low that by the time the boat reached Wheeling, Virginia, the men had spent half the trip walking along the riverbed. On September 28, the crew rested at Cincinnati where Lewis gathered specimens of mammoth tusks to send back to Jefferson, only to find out later that they had been lost in a shipwreck. At Louisville, Kentucky, Lewis welcomed his partner, William Clark, aboard. Later that year, on December 8, Clark ran into the expedition's first trouble with America's foreign adversaries, when he presented his compliments to the Spanish governor of Upper Louisiana at St. Louis only to be denied permission to ascend the Missouri River.

The two men worked furiously with their men to prepare for the uncertain journey ahead. Lewis gathered information about the territorial population, number of settlements and social structure, as well as the trading patterns that existed between New Orleans merchants and both the United States and Canada. Clark, meanwhile, supervised the physical labor, keeping his volunteers busy cutting planks for the boats and hammering the craft together. News reached St. Louis at this time that ownership of Upper Louisiana had changed hands. On November 30 the Spanish had turned the keys of the city over to the French.

The following March 1804 Lewis witnessed the formal transfer of the territory from France to the United States, provided for by the Louisiana Purchase agreement negotiated the previous year. Jefferson's secretary took pride in signing the official record that day, and several days later, American soldiers of the First Infantry moved into St. Louis. With the international legal barriers now removed, the expedition was ready to depart.

One Private George Drouillard, who would prove valuable to the project's success, joined the expedition at this point. Drouillard's mother was a Shawnee Indian, and his French father had been a friend of George Rogers Clark. The private himself was a talented scout, Indian interpreter, and hunter. Two French-Canadian members of the expedition also knew various Indian dialects and languages.

The journey began. All the equipment was stowed in three boats: a twenty-two-oared keelboat, a seven-oared Frenchmen's pirogue, and a six-oared soldier's pirogue. The men were divided into three squads under the command of a sergeant, and each received a firearm, gunpowder, and one hundred balls. At 4 P.M. on May 14, 1804, a crowd gathered to give the explorers a send-off, after which Lewis and Clark got under way.

But the intrepid pair did not get very far at first. A rainstorm forced the explorers to stop and make camp only four miles upstream, and there were other problems. The boats had been badly loaded by Clark's soldiers. All the boats were stern-heavy, when they should have been heaviest in the bow so that if a boat hit a snag, it would not ride up on the snag and tear out its bottom.

While the soldiers reloaded the ships, Lewis had a narrow escape. Exploring Indian pictographs around a cave, he slipped and almost fell over a three-hundred-foot cliff. Fortunately, he fell onto a ledge twenty feet below, thereby avoiding certain death. When the journey continued, however, Lewis persisted in exploring the shore, making natural history and astronomical observations. Clark, the better boatsman and navigator, commanded the group of almost fifty men inching their way up the Missouri River.

Danger also lurked in the form of international sabotage. At the French settlement of La Charrette, they met Régis Loisel, a French trader with the Sioux who gave the two American officers much information concerning the country ahead of them. A few days later, Loisel was privately reporting to the Spaniards on the danger of American influence over the Indians and on American land claims to Spanish territory lying farther west. The Spanish governor of west Florida urged that Spanish troops be sent overland from Santa Fé or Chihuahua to capture the party or force it back. Agents actually stalked Lewis and Clark for some time before finally abandoning ideas of stopping them.

As the expedition approached the Platte River, the men began suffering from an outbreak of boils or intestinal upheavals. This forced a stop for several days to cement American friendship with the Oto and Missouri Indian tribes. The explorers told the warriors that they had been sent "by the great Chief of the Seventeen great nations of America" to tell them that their "old fathers the French and Spanish have gone beyond the great lake towards the rising Sun, from whence they never intend returning to visit their former red children in this quarter." The Indians must return French and Spanish flags and medals and receive those of the Americans instead.

In reply, the warriors promised not to injure white traders if the Americans would help them mediate their differences with the Omahas. The Lewis and Clark party then distributed medals, gunpowder, whiskey, and other presents. Soon after passing present-day Council Bluffs, Iowa,

This encounter with Indians in the Dakota country was typical of many such meetings experienced by Lewis and Clark. Most were friendly encounters, but when the situation was threatening, a show of force would normally be made. (The Bettmann Archive)

the explorers came to Pelican Island, covered with birds who had carpeted the surface of all the river with feathers and down. The men soon realized the significance of the sight and, casting out a net, caught over a thousand fish. Still exploring along the banks, Lewis found the remains of a forty-five-foot-long Cretaceous reptile which he ordered sent back to Jefferson.

Fifty or sixty miles above Bismarck, North Dakota, the expedition stopped at Fort Mandan to set up winter quarters. There, on the left bank of the Missouri, downstream from the Mandan villages where the white men could keep a sharp eye on both the Indians and the Canadian traders, the weary party started building a shelter against dampness and cold. Their stockade, completed by Christmas Eve, gave cause for celebration. The white men were amazed both by the aurora borealis, and by the Indians, who played lacrosse stark naked on the ice at 26°F. below zero. The Indians, in turn, were impressed with the skill of Lewis's blacksmith in making iron tools and weapons in the bellows. The Mandans gladly exchanged eight gallons of corn for each piece of metal, which they used to strengthen their weaponry. The Indians were also intrigued with York, Clark's black servant. After continuously trying to wipe the "warpaint" from the big boatsman's skin, they shifted attention to his hard curly hair which continued to fascinate them, a scene that would be repeated time and again with other Western Indians encountered by the expedition.

On November 11, 1804, a pregnant Indian woman, who looked as if she were hardly more than a child, walked into camp. Her name was Sacajawea, a Shoshone who had been captured by a rival tribe and finally

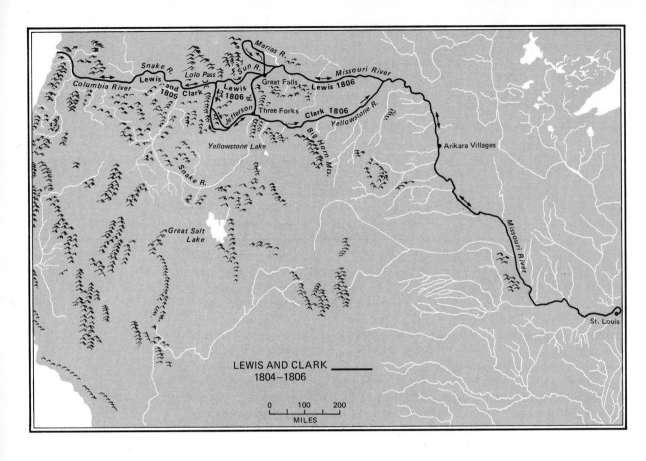

LEWIS AND CLARK
1804–1806

0   100   200
MILES

given to a French trader named Toussaint Charbonneau. The captains realized that Sacajawea and Charbonneau would be valuable when the expedition resumed in the spring. Charbonneau could interpret the languages of the river Indians, while Sacajawea, whose baby was born on February 11, knew the Shoshone tongue. These two would give Lewis and Clark their only chance to communicate with the Rocky Mountain Indians.

Throughout the winter, there was much work to be done. The travelers wove ropes, cured meat, and made battle axes which they exchanged for Indian corn. Lewis compiled Indian vocabularies and worked over his reports, while Clark busied himself with maps, updating his own topographical information by discussions with local Indians.

Most of the men on the expedition were less scientifically preoccupied. The two captains had great difficulty keeping their men away from the Indian villages. Clark noted: "Their womin verry fond of carressing our men &C." An Arikara chief inquired whether there were no women where the white men lived for "one might suppose they had never seen any before." By February 27, 1805, the men had put dalliance aside long enough to cut away the ice that trapped their boats, and about 5 P.M. on April 7, Lewis fired the swivel gun to announce officially their departure. The previous November, the Sioux had voted for a spring war against the whites and had moved to the banks of the Missouri that April but too late to trap the Americans. By then, Lewis and Clark had left.

The Americans had enough on their minds even without the distraction of an Indian war. As the boats continued up the Missouri, it became increasingly necessary for the men to wade in the water, towing the boats and holding up the canoes to escape dangerous waves. One huge wave threatened to scatter the expedition's journals, instruments, books, and medicines. But Sacajawea saved the day, calmly fishing important provisions out of the water. Even the highly skeptical Lewis admitted: "The Indian woman, to whom I ascribe equal fortitude and resolution with any person on board at the time of the accident, caught and preserved most of the light articles which were washed overboard." The men had become trail-hardened by then. Lewis's dog Scammon would catch animals, fish, even wild geese and bring them ashore to his exploring master, who wrote: "The flesh of the beaver is esteemed a delicacy among us. I think the tail a delicious morsel."

The party halted at Loma, Montana, where the river divides. Which stream ran nearest to the headwaters of the Columbia River? Lewis took a group sixty miles up the north fork, where he again barely avoided death, when, after slipping atop a ninety-foot precipice, he managed to grab a handhold. Realizing soon after this incident that he was following a tributary of the Missouri, Lewis named the stream Maria's River after his cousin and sweetheart. After journeying forty miles up the southern stream, Clark realized that he was on the right route. Once reunited, the leaders decided to bury their big red pirogue and much of the heavy baggage before continuing, interring them Indian style to be picked up on the return trip. Lewis had fallen victim to an intestinal illness, but he cured himself by making a concoction from choke cherry twigs that his mother used to administer. He had recovered by the time the party reached the Missouri Falls on June 13. Greatly impressed at the sight, which few, if any, whites had seen before him, Lewis recorded his observation that the spectacular waters "roll and swell into half-formed billows of great height which rise and again disappear in an instant."

The falls were beautiful but costly in time, forcing a detour to a more navigable part of the river. The expedition took a full month to cut a path and move the boats and supplies sixteen miles around the Missouri Falls. Much to Lewis's dismay, the tar substitute on the *Experiment* began to fall off and the collapsible iron ship had to be abandoned. Soon after the boats had been brought back to the water, the explorers came to three forks in the river. Ever conscious of Republican politics, Lewis named the rivers for Jefferson, Secretary of State Madison, and Secretary of the Treasury Albert Gallatin. As the party made its way up the Jefferson River, Sacajawea announced that they were nearing the land of the Shoshone, her own people. Lewis realized that the expedition could not find its way across the Rocky Mountains without someone who knew the trails and without horses to carry their baggage. September was approaching, and the party was not sure of the distance between the headwaters of the upper Missouri and the upper Columbia.

The Shoshone were hesitant about making contact with foreigners. They were a weak Rockies tribe, hemmed in by more powerful Indian nations on all sides, with little knowledge of the white men or access to trade. Their diet was necessarily meager, bordering on subsistence. Though the Americans were for the moment unaware of the Shoshone condition, they were all too familiar with their own. Lewis was suffering from dysentery, while Clark and others had severe attacks of boils. In addition, one of Clark's canoes had sunk in the rapids and another had turned partly over, ruining most of the remaining medical supplies.

The first contact proved helpful to both sides. Lewis spotted and caught up to an old Shoshone woman with a girl of about twelve. The women sat down and lowered their heads, waiting for this new warring tribe to murder them. When instead the explorer loaded them with beads, moccasins, and paint, they ran up to their chief displaying the gifts. The hungry Indians found they could get meat from Lewis's hunters, and they enthusiastically embraced the explorers. Sacajawea suddenly ran excitedly up to the Shoshone chief, discovering that he was her brother! She had also met with another Shoshone woman with whom she had been captured and sold away from the tribe.

The Shoshone realized that they could enjoy future benefits from trading with the whites, who might eventually shield them from their

The help Sacajawea gave to the Lewis and Clark expedition proved essential to its success. (Culver Pictures)

enemies while providing them with firearms to protect and feed themselves. Again, the explorers plied the Indians with gifts, in this case a medal with Jefferson's portrait and a military uniform coat. In return, Lewis seemed to eye the Shoshone horses enviously as when he recorded in an August 14, 1805, diary entry: "Drewyer who had had a good view of their horses estimated them at 400. Most of them are fine horses. Indeed many of them would make a figure on the South side of James River [in Virginia] or the land of fine horses. I saw several with Spanish brands on them, and some mules which they informed me that they had also obtained from the Spaniards." Lewis remained with the Shoshone long enough to rest his men, stock up on supplies, and bury what would be impossible to carry across the mountains. He could not, however, keep his men away from the Shoshone women.

Lewis acquired eleven horses and a mule, not enough for his purposes, but "the Indian women took the balance of the baggage." The expedition struggled down the Lemhi River. At the Bitterroot Mountains the party had to cut its way through with axes, battling also against sleet and snow, especially when crossing Lolo Pass. The men were lucky when they had wolfmeat and crayfish to eat. More often their dinner consisted of soup, snow water, bear grease, dried fish, and camass root flour. Moving down toward the valley known as Ross's Hole in the country of the Selish Indians, the party lost several horses that slipped down the slopes. They were also endangered by falling timber and attacking wasps.

Clark had found a branch of the Columbia River some fifteen or twenty miles ahead on September 22, where he had met with the friendly

Frederic Remington, the greatest artist of the American West, painted from his knowledge of history as well as from his own experience. This drawing shows Lewis and Clark conferring over one of the many decisions to be made (perhaps regarding plans for dividing the party). In the background are Sacajawea and Charbonneau; the men prepare the canoes. (Library of Congress)

Nez Percé tribe. While some sick men rested, others began felling trees for the first *downstream* part of the journey. A local chief and medicine man, Twisted Hair, made a map for the explorers, while the tribe agreed to take care of the animals obtained from the Shoshone. On October 7, four large canoes and one small one carried the party down the Columbia River. The boredom of the journey was spectacularly relieved by the rapids, which smashed two of the boats against the rocks. Bedding, shot pouches, and other important items were lost. During the next two weeks, they saw signs of Indian contact with Europeans: muskets, swords, brass armbands, shirts, and even overalls.

At the Short Narrows of the Columbia River, framed by high and jagged rock walls, many of the men disembarked, while French explorer Peter Cruzat shot the rapids. Afterward he played the violin, while Clark's servant York danced, delighting the local Indian spectators.

As they neared the ocean, the men grew ill from washing their dried fish in the increasingly salty water. Little game could be found. The increasing cold caused great hardship among the American explorers, who found their wet bedding and clothing rotting away from the salt water. Although from the expedition's actual location on November 7, 1805, Clark himself probably could not have seen what he recorded in his diary—the party had indeed almost reached its destination:

> Great joy in camp we are in *view* of the *Ocean,* this great Pacific Ocean which we been so long anxious to see. and the roreing or noise made by the waves brakeing on the rockey shores (as I suppose) may be heard distinctly.

How would the explorers return? If they found trading vessels at the mouth of the Columbia River, this problem would be solved, but if not, the tired men would face a second journey across the North American continent. Jefferson had not sent ships to wait for the party to appear on the river. He was afraid Spain, already disturbed over the French sale of Louisiana, would be angered further by a United States naval vessel so close to her California settlements.

Conditions remained miserable for the explorers. The men had little time and less cause for celebration. Waves were so high that the canoes were in constant danger of overturning, and many men became violently seasick. Camping in Gray's Bay on the north side of the Columbia on November 8, the group had to pile baggage on a tangle of poles to keep it above the tide. One canoe sank before it could be unloaded, and others filled and sank during the night. There was no level ground to lie upon and nothing to eat but dried fish. Indians took their rifles as they slept, although the rifles were later returned. The party moved three miles to the present site of Fort Columbia, opposite Astoria, near a Chinook village. Hunting improved and the Indians were willing to sell food. But they charged such high prices that the supply of trading goods was rapidly disappearing.

The expedition voted almost unanimously to cross the river and look for a winter site on its southern shore. With winter approaching, it

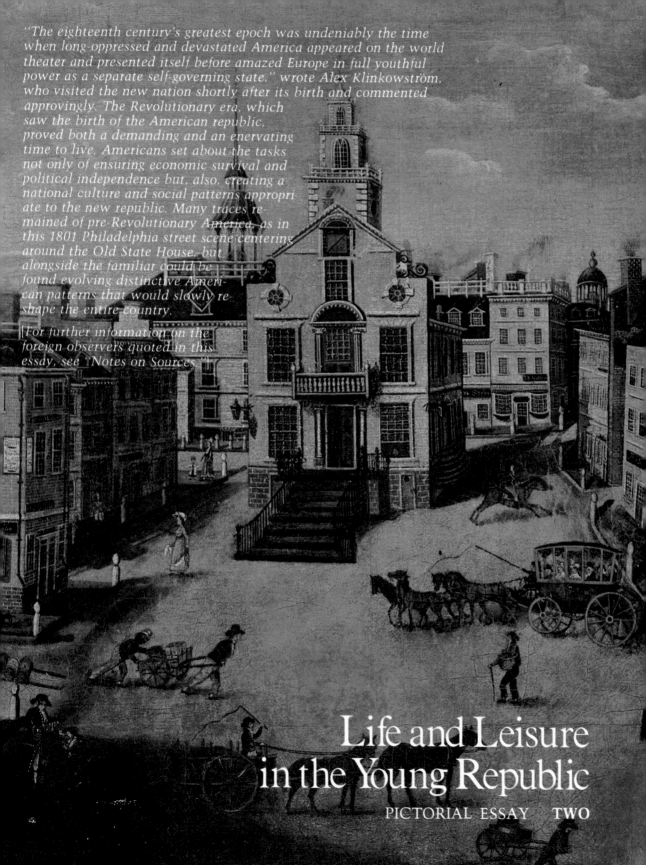

"The eighteenth century's greatest epoch was undeniably the time when long-oppressed and devastated America appeared on the world theater and presented itself before amazed Europe in full youthful power as a separate self-governing state," wrote Alex Klinkowström, who visited the new nation shortly after its birth and commented approvingly. The Revolutionary era, which saw the birth of the American republic, proved both a demanding and an enervating time to live. Americans set about the tasks not only of ensuring economic survival and political independence but, also, creating a national culture and social patterns appropriate to the new republic. Many traces remained of pre-Revolutionary America, as in this 1801 Philadelphia street scene centering around the Old State House, but alongside the familiar could be found evolving distinctive American patterns that would slowly reshape the entire country.

[For further information on the foreign observers quoted in this essay, see "Notes on Sources."]

Life and Leisure in the Young Republic

PICTORIAL ESSAY   TWO

The European instructors brought to teach in America have always admired the docility and modesty with which girls behave whenever they find themselves in a school with a regular discipline, at least if they are not spoiled to begin with. These qualities are united to a certain freeness and maturity of judgment rarely found elsewhere.

[GIOVANNI GRASSI, 1810–17]

Mary Lightfoot of Virginia, age seven

Pennsylvania Germans singing a birthday song

At Bethlehem, I went to the house of the "single men." I entered the manager's apartment, and found him busy copying music. He had in his room a piano, made in Germany. I talked music with him, and discovered that he was not only a performer but a composer as well. When we went into the chapel together, I asked him to play the organ. He played some improvisations, into which he introduced a great deal of harmony and chords in the bass.

[MARQUIS DE CHASTELLUX, 1782]

"The First, Second, and Last Scene of Mortality,"
needlework by Prudence Punderson of Connecticut

*In the United States on the seventh day of
every week, the trading and working life of
the nation seems suspended. All noises
cease. A deep tranquility, say rather the
solemn calm of meditation, succeeds the
turmoil of the week, and the soul resumes
possession and contemplation of itself.
Laying aside for a while the petty passions
which agitate life and the fleeting interests
which engross it, the American strays into
an ideal world, where all is great, eternal,
and pure.*

[ALEXIS DE TOCQUEVILLE, 1835]

*At about seven or eight o'clock of the eve-
nings when there are no formal dinners
they have tea. At tea the whole family is
reunited and friends, acquaintances, and
even strangers are invited. Tea in the evening is accompanied by a boring and dull
etiquette. The mistress of the house serves,
and passes the cups around. Until you turn
over the cup and put the spoon on top they
will keep bringing you fresh cups. There are
a thousand stories, true or false, of Frenchmen, ignorant of this customary signal,
who were drowned with that beverage.*

[M.-L.-E. MOREAU DE SAINT-MÉRY, 1794–98]

A Rhode Island family at tea

An English fashion plate of the late eighteenth century

Shopping at the furniture store of Duncan Phyfe, New York City

The taste in dress is chiefly English, extremely simple, neat, and elegant. The finest cloth and the finest linen are the greatest adornment. The women (as everywhere), seeking to please, allow themselves more variety of ornament than the men. Every year dressed dolls are brought from Europe, which, silent, give the law of the mode. However, distinction of rank among the feminine half is not striking as a result of any distinct costume. In the item of dress, each selects according to her taste, means, and circumstances.

[JOHANN DAVID SCHOEPF, 1783]

Blindfold an Englishman and convey him to New York, unbind his eyes, and he will think himself in an English city. The same sort of streets; shops precisely the same; the same beautiful and modest women crowding in and out of them; the same play-houses; the same men, same dress, same language. He will miss by day only the nobility and the beggars, and by night only the streetwalkers and pickpockets.

[WILLIAM COBBETT, 1817–19]

A dinner party in Boston

The dinner was served in the American, or, if you will, in the English, fashion. It consisted of two courses. One included the entrées, roast, and warm side dishes, the other, the sweet pastries and preserves. When the second course is removed, the cloth is taken off, and apples, walnuts, and chestnuts are served. It is then that healths are drunk; the coffee which comes afterwards serves as a signal to rise from table.

[MARQUIS DE CHASTELLUX, 1780]

Newspaper announcement
of a music teacher, 1785

The theater is on the southeast side of the park, and is a large, commodious building. The interior is handsomely decorated and fitted up in as good style as the London theaters, upon a scale suitable to the population of the city. The scenes are well painted and numerous. The machinery, dresses, and decorations are elegant and appropriate to the performances, which consist of all the new pieces that appear in London, and several of Shakespeare's best plays.

[JOHN LAMBERT, 1806]

Playgoers watching an English farce at the Park Theater, New York City

The crafts are greatly respected in this country. They have taken on a different character than in Europe. The rich merchant continues, in spite of his success and the public offices he may have held, to put his hands to his own work.

[AXEL KLINKOWSTRÖM, 1820]

A quilting bee in the South

Merrymaking at a Wayside Inn. by Paul Svinin

(Below left) Dancing, for the inhabitants of the United States, is less a matter of self-display than it is of true enjoyment. At the same dance you will see a grandfather, his son and his grandson, but more often still the grandmother, her daughter, and her granddaughter. If a Frenchman comments upon this with surprise, he is told that each one dances for his own amusement, and not because it's the thing to do.

[M.-L.-E. MOREAU DE SAINT-MÉRY, 1794-98]

Hunting in Virginia was a far different thing from its English original. The meaning of the latter is simple and explicit. A party of horsemen meet at an appointed spot and hour, to turn up or turn out a deer or a fox, and pursue him to a standstill. Here a local peculiarity — the abundance of game — upsets all system. The practice seemed to be for the company to enter the wood, beat up the quarters of anything from a stag to a snake, and take their chance for a chase. If the game went off well and it was possible to follow it through the thickets and morasses, ten to one that at every hundred yards up sprung so many rivals that horses and hunters were puzzled which to select. Every man, if he chose, could have a deer to himself — an arrangement, I was told, that proved generally satisfactory, since it enabled the worst rider, when all was over, to talk about as many difficulties surmounted as the best.

[JOHN BERNARD, 1799]

The End of the Hunt, artist unknown

The inhabitants of Marlborough [Massachusetts] are nearly all Congregationalists. The prayers of those Congregational ministers whom I have heard have been of a general and tolerant nature which embraces all sects and denominations of Christians, beseeching the safety and welfare of all men without respect of persons. Their sermons were generally zealous, but devoid of all absurd tenets, dogmas, and denunciations. Faith was earnestly recommended, but the necessity of good works was strenuously enforced.

[JOHN LAMBERT, 1808]

Tombstone of a minister, from a New England graveyard

Princeton is a college built by the state of Jersey some years before the war. I dismounted to visit this vast edifice for a moment. I was almost immediately joined by Mr. Witherspoon, the president. From him I learned that this college is a complete university and that it can contain two hundred students and more. There is only one class of the humanities. Two others are devoted to perfecting the young men in the study of Latin and Greek, a fourth to natural philosophy, mathematics, astronomy, etc., and a fifth to moral philosophy.

[MARQUIS DE CHASTELLUX, 1782]

Nassau Hall at the time of the Revolution

made no sense to return to the Rockies without adequate food and clothing. There was also the hope that a ship, any ship, might arrive before spring. Misery continued. Firewood was hard to come by, and there were no deer or elk for meat. The large officers' tent had practically worn out, while the other tent and sails were "so full of holes and rotten that they will not keep anything dry." Although plagued with dysentery, boils, and colds, the men worked in the constant rain to build cabins for winter.

The party rejoiced as best it could that Christmas, but in their exhausted condition, the merrymaking was understandably muted. The scarcity of wild game meant not only a shortage of food, but also a shortage of skins with which to make much-needed clothing. Somehow, through all this suffering, the Indians either deliberately deceived the Lewis and Clark party, or they had not been able to communicate properly the exciting news that the American trade ship *Lydia* lay just off the coast near their encampment! And it did not sail until August 12, 1806, long after the expedition had begun its long homeward trek—overland.

Lewis continued to work throughout the winter, recording each evergreen, shrub, fern, and grass he encountered. He also made observations regarding Indian costumes, canoe building, and domestic animals. There was the now familiar pattern of his men fraternizing with Indian women, and the resulting problem of venereal diseases. Lewis thought it best to ignore a situation he could neither end nor alleviate.

In preparing for the trip home, Lewis had to trade his fine laced uniform coat in order to buy another canoe. He was careful to leave behind, nailed on the fort, a document listing the names of many of his men and the purpose of the expedition. This notice later helped the United States stake out its claim to the Oregon Territory.

Clark, meanwhile, had been spending the winter completing a map from astronomical observations. The two leaders now realized they could save considerable time by traveling directly overland to the falls from the beginning of the Lolo Trail, avoiding the difficult canoe travel along the Missouri's upper waters. Since they now had horses, they could test this route on the way back.

Lewis and Clark knew that they must leave Fort Clatsop on the Pacific and reach the Rockies as soon as the mountain passes opened that spring. Otherwise the Nez Percé might take all their horses for buffalo hunting on the other side of the mountains, leaving the expedition stranded without a way to transport baggage over the Continental Divide. An early departure would also eliminate the need for passing another winter at Fort Mandan. They loaded the canoes, one of which they had stolen from the coastal Indians, and left for home on March 23, 1806. This time, they supplemented their dried salmon diet with game shot in the area.

Once the party reached the Nez Percé, they began scrounging for horses. Charbonneau literally traded the shirt off his back for an animal, not once but twice. One Indian traveler arrived with a number of horses, which he offered to sell or rent. While Clark and some of the men traded

for horses along the banks of the Columbia, Lewis commandeered the canoes upriver and kept the men busy making saddles and harnesses. Chief Twisted Hair was sorry to report that other chiefs, jealous of his previous meeting with the expedition, had taken the horses and part of the previously buried supplies. By the end of May, however, half of the lost saddles were found and almost all of the horses had been recovered. The whites, especially Clark, won great favor with the Nez Percé for medical services rendered to the tribe; when Clark opened an abscess on a woman's back, she slept so well that her grateful husband gave the Americans a horse. As a partial result of this medical diplomacy, the chiefs agreed to make peace with the impoverished Shoshones and to send emissaries with the party to make peace with the Blackfeet.

The expedition was now ready for a return assault on the Rockies. As the party stood at the foot of the great mountains on June 10, Lewis expressed some doubt: "I am still apprehensive that the snow and the want of food for our horses will prove a serious embarrassment to us, as at least four days' journey of our route in these mountains lies over heights and along a ledge of mountains never entirely destitute of snow." As they set out on the beginnings of the Lolo Trail on June 15, it soon became apparent that many landmarks pointing the way through the pass would be obscured by heavy snow. There was virtually no food for the men or the sixty-six horses, and a hard cold rain soaked everyone. One night many of the party ate the green fungi that grew in some places along the trail but which Lewis described as "truly an insippid taistless food."

After stopping for two hours to consider the crucial decision confronting him, Lewis decided that the situation called for retreat. Both men and horses might starve and freeze to death before the party found the precise paths that would lead them over the Continental Divide. Lewis and Clark would do all in their power to obtain an Indian guide whose knowledge of the terrain might shorten the journey.

Luckily they found such guides, and on June 24 the expedition began struggling up the slopes for a second attempt. In two days they located the equipment they had stored nine months before. The snowbanks were shrinking, and the three Nez Percé guides constantly led the explorers along the fastest route. By this time and at this pace, even bear oil and boiled roots made a tolerable meal. They came out of the snow on June 29 and descended down the northeast side of the mountains. Their Indian guides soon led them to a herd of deer and to a hot springs, where the weary Americans gratefully ate and bathed. Next night, they arrived at "Traveler's Rest" near Missoula, Montana—their old camp on their journey to the Pacific.

After a two-day rest, Lewis and Clark decided to separate and explore different routes to the Missouri River, where they would meet. The captains agreed that Lewis would probe the basin of Maria's River, traveling overland north to the Missouri. Clark, the better boatsman, would go south to the Yellowstone River and follow it down to the Missouri. The two groups split up on July 3. Nez Percé guides showed Lewis two routes to the falls, but after discovering signs of their enemy, the Prairie Minnetares, the Indian guides quickly asked for payment and returned back over the mountains to their own people.

Lewis's party made an easy trip to the falls. The fields were crowded with buffalo, who provided easy and abundant game for the party. Lewis wrote: "The bulls keep a tremendous roaring we could hear them for many miles and there are such numbers of them that there is one continued roar." Upon arriving at the falls on July 13, the men eagerly dug up their buried provisions. But the river had been so high the previous winter that, unfortunately, all of Lewis's bearskins, botanical specimens, and medical supplies had been destroyed. Luckily his damp papers could be dried out, and the chart of the Missouri was rescued unscathed. On July 17, Lewis took some men and headed for Maria's River, while those behind struggled with the job of carrying the expedition's supplies around the falls of the Missouri. This latter group was soon joined by some men from Clark's party, who came floating downriver in canoes, bringing supplies left the previous year at Jefferson's River, which had remained in usable condition.

Lewis and his handful of men found the going considerably rougher by this time. Hunting proved so poor at Maria's River that the group reverted to eating grease with mush made from roots, cooked over a buffalo dung fire in the absence of firewood. One afternoon Lewis scaled a high point. Through his spyglass, he observed a group of Indians looking down at a stream where Lewis's valuable scout and interpreter Drouillard had gone. Although he feared for his men's safety if they came out into the open, Lewis was more afraid of leaving Drouillard to the mercy of the hostile Minnetares. The men made their presence known to the Indians, and after many a wary glance, the Indians invited the Americans to spend the night at their camp.

Then came the most severe conflict with a native tribe during the entire expedition. Near dawn, after trying but failing to steal the whites' rifles, the Minnetares tried to make off with Lewis's horses. The explorers shot two of the Indians, while the others escaped. Fearing pursuit by a large group of Minnetares, Lewis and his men rode hard all day toward the bluffs of the Missouri, covering 120 miles in a little more than 24 hours. There they rejoiced to find the rest of their party and quickly scrambled on board the canoes to make their way downriver.

Meanwhile Clark's party suffered little more than minor mishaps, moving along the Bitterroot, then down Jefferson's River, to the Wisdom River and finally to the Yellowstone. This group found itself under attack, not by Indians, but by swarms of mosquitoes. Since Clark's party did not find Sacajawea's brother or his band of Shoshones, she traveled on with the explorer, who noted she was "of great service to me as a pilot through this country." On July 8, a few days after leaving Lewis, Clark's band found the buried canoes in their old camp. Starting down Jefferson's River on July 10, the expedition covered the same distance in three days downstream that had taken over a week to navigate upstream the year before.

Clark and his men continued to make their way east toward the Missouri, and Sacajawea guided them through Bozeman Pass into the Yellowstone Valley. Clark was alarmed over growing Indian thefts of his horses and directed Sergeant Nathaniel Pryor to take two men and drive the animals directly overland to the Mandan villages. From there Pryor was to head north, giving Canadian fur trader Hugh Heney a letter requesting him to persuade Sioux chiefs to travel to Washington, D.C., with Clark.

These plans were quickly dashed when, the second night out, Indians stole all of Pryor's horses. Pryor and his men then rushed to the Yellowstone River, only to find that Clark's canoes had already passed them. The stranded men began to shoot buffalo and use the skins to make tublike "bull-boats" on which they hoped to float down the Yellowstone to the Missouri. Clark's group reached the Missouri on August 3. Five days later, they were amazed to see the men they had sent on an *overland* mission come *floating* down the Missouri! The only major problem now was to find Captain Lewis and his men.

But the Lewis group was not far behind. The discovery of fresh meat on a pole and a campfire still burning meant to Lewis that Clark was close by. Lewis left the boats one afternoon to hunt for elk, accompanied by the French-Canadian Cruzat, known more for his virtuosity on the violin than his skill as a sharpshooter. The two men went their separate ways until a shot was fired, hitting Lewis "in the hinder part of my right thigh." Believing the shot to have come from the mistaken and nearsighted Cruzat, Lewis cried, "Damn you! You have shot me!" Cruzat was nowhere to be found, and Lewis hobbled toward the river and canoes, ordering his men to search the shore. At last the men found Cruzat, unhurt and apparently surprised at Lewis's misfortune. Although he would never admit the error, it was obvious that Cruzat had mistaken Lewis's leather-clad behind for an elk!

Soon the two groups were reunited. The Lewis party found a note from Clark and later met two white trappers who had just passed Clark's men. Finally, on August 12, the two parties met, and small arms and blunderbusses sounded a sharp salute. Lewis especially welcomed the presence of Clark at this time, since his injury had left him temporarily unable to exercise effective leadership:

> at 1 P.M. I overtook Capt. Clark and party and had the pleasure of finding them all well. as wrighting in my present situation is extreemly painfull to me I shall desist untill I recover and leave to my friend Capt. C. the continuation of our journal.

When they reached the Mandan villages, it was Clark who presided at a council of the Mandans and Minnetares. The Mandans welcomed the explorers warmly.

One of the men, John Colter, decided to travel to the Yellowstone with two passing trappers, where they would stay until they could "make a fortune." Lewis and Clark gave their reluctant consent only after the other men promised to return to St. Louis. After the Minnetare chiefs had refused to send a representative to Washington, Charbonneau announced his intention to stay with the Mandans along with Sacajawea and the baby. Despite their frequent complaints about his services on the journey, Lewis and Clark paid Charbonneau $500.33, while Sacajawea, considerably more valuable to the expedition, received nothing. The friendly Mandans now promised to make war only in self-defense, and one chief agreed to travel with the expedition to St. Louis and later to see the president in Washington.

By the time Lewis and Clark left the Mandans for St. Louis, most Americans had given them up for lost. Now they swept downstream at eighty miles a day. At the mouth of the Vermilion River, they met a fur trader who gave them "the news," including the information that former Vice-President Aaron Burr had killed Alexander Hamilton in a duel in 1804. On September 10, the men gratefully accepted a bottle of whiskey from a group of Frenchmen on their way to the Platte River. This party brought news that American Captain Zebulon Pike had begun an expedition up the Arkansas River, traveling up the Missouri just before the Corps of Discovery had come down. The Lewis and Clark group received cheers and salutes from five Missouri trading boats as they passed La Charrette. When the canoes landed at Fort Bellefontaine, Clark began writing to friends in Kentucky, and Lewis had already composed his report.

Next day, at noon on September 23, 1806, more than three years after the journey had begun, the expedition landed in the center of St. Louis. Clark reported that he allowed his men "to fire off their pieces as a Salute to the Town. We were met by all the village and received a harty welcome from its inhabitants &C."

The expedition had been a resounding success by every standard, accomplishing the goals set out in Jefferson's instructions plus others undreamed of by the president and his private secretary when they plotted the trip in the White House basement. Except for one death from an illness early in the journey, not a single man had perished, despite the many hardships undergone by the Corps of Discovery. While at St. Louis, the returning explorers enjoyed parties and a ball given in their honor. Meriwether Lewis greeted Jefferson in Washington again on December 30, with Clark following two weeks later. The two heroes found themselves feted continuously by Washingtonians during the months that followed.

Of far greater significance to America's destiny than the festivities celebrating the accomplishments of Meriwether Lewis and William Clark, however, was the report Lewis sent to Jefferson upon arriving in St. Louis the previous September. In this message, we can find the growing patriotic self-assurance and passionate optimism that would characterize the generation following Jefferson's. Lewis conveyed to the president his belief in an American manifest destiny to expand across the continent to the Pacific Ocean, stressing the significance of the fur trade and other commercial opportunities available to the United States. He advised the president to erect outposts on the upper Columbia River that could collect furs taken by neighboring trappers and traders while helping transfer goods arriving by ship from Asian ports. Lewis's vision of an American continental presence even included an explicit warning to Jefferson that the United States would have to check British competition in the Northwest if its own ambitions were to succeed, a prophetic warning that foretold British–American conflict over the Oregon Territory four decades later.

Of greatest importance about the lessons that Lewis and Clark drew from their journey, however, was the unswerving belief, held by both men, in the westward march of American society past even the new Louisiana Purchase, across the Rockies and beyond to the Pacific. Less than thirty years after the Declaration of Independence's signing, a president of the founding generation had placed his unique mark on the next century's pattern of development in America, all of which began in the nightly planning sessions between Jefferson and his capable secretary in the tiny basement study of an executive mansion not yet known as the White House.

12 The Embattled Republic: Federalist and Jeffersonian America

The explorations of Lewis and Clark had been a resounding success. President Jefferson was delighted at the diligence with which the two explorers had fulfilled his orders and recorded a great variety of information on the Western territories—natural, ethnological, and political—for use by the new national administration. Yet the Lewis and Clark venture also reflected complex, crucial issues that remained to be resolved. Jefferson, after all, had been forced deliberately to shade his intentions when asking Congress to finance the expedition, realizing that his controversial plan might arouse hostility from his political opponents.

But what sort of opposition, and operating under what guidelines? The Constitution made no mention of political parties. Indeed, most Founding Fathers had opposed the formation of "factions" as contrary to the healthy functioning of a republic. They had hoped, by constructing a government with adequate checks and balances, to minimize the impact of special interests and to encourage the formation of policies based solely on the national interest. The struggle over creation and ratification of the Constitution itself revealed sharply a diversity of interests based upon geography, class, and occupation.

As problems arose during the period from George Washington's Inaugural to Andrew Jackson's victory over the British in 1815—decades when the United States was a young and embattled republic—Americans disagreed profoundly on what constituted "the national interest." By the time of Jefferson's administration, the Lewis and Clark expedition could be seen almost as much as a *political* act, an assertion of Jeffersonian Republican principles, as a triumph of skill and daring.

American national development and domestic politics during this period, perhaps more than in any other, were closely linked to foreign affairs. Jefferson and Lewis had planned their project in secrecy, fearing the reactions of France, Spain, and Britain. A Spanish military detachment had even followed the explorers at the beginning of their journey. Americans argued over the continued European presence and interest in the North American continent and also disagreed over which side to support in the seemingly never ending European wars of that era.

There was also the question of the powers of the national government within the federal system. Did it have the power to create a national bank? Did the United States government have the authority to purchase territory without the direct consent of the existing states? Beyond that, how could the population of such a territory be prevented from creating a nation of its own? Would it even be possible to retain the existing states within one federal union? The extent to which powers had been delegated to the federal government and retained by the states under the Constitution created fundamental disagreements, and the new lands explored by Lewis and Clark intensified those disagreements.

WASHINGTON THE PRESIDENT

The stability of the new constitutional government was greatly enhanced when George Washington, the almost unanimous choice of his countrymen, agreed to serve as the first president of the United States. In leading the colonists to military victory and in his service as president of the Constitutional Convention, Washington had gained a well-deserved reputation for personal integrity. At the urging of Vice-President John Adams, the Senate voted that the president be called "His Highness the President of the United States of America and the Protector of the Rights of the Same." Fortunately, the House of Representatives failed to agree, and that bombastic subtitle was forever discarded. Citizens were confident that the general would not abuse his power to subvert the liberties of Americans. The passage of the Bill of Rights, guided through Congress by James Madison, further reassured people that the ship of state had been launched on a steady course.

Washington's selection of a cabinet also seemed to confirm his political neutrality. He appointed people from different states and different interests to fill federal offices. Alexander Hamilton of New York, who had been the general's personal aide during the Revolution, became secretary of the treasury. Secretary of State Thomas Jefferson and Attorney General Edmund Randolph were Virginia planters. Henry Knox of Massachusetts was chosen as secretary of war. Shortly after his inauguration on April 30, 1789, on a balcony overlooking Wall Street in New York City, the nation's first capital, Washington confided his anxieties in a letter to Knox. The new president believed he faced "an ocean of difficulties, without that competency of political skill, abilities, and inclination, which are necessary to manage the helm. . . . Integrity and firmness are all I can promise."

HAMILTON'S ECONOMIC PROGRAM

Washington brought prestige and stability to the new administration. Alexander Hamilton formulated financial policy in a brilliant and controversial manner, eventually stirring hostilities that would mar Washington's second term and force Hamilton from office. But first came the triumphs.

Born in the West Indies, Hamilton migrated to New York, where he attended King's College, now Columbia University, before becoming an ardent young participant in the Revolution. Hamilton gained status as a member of New York's elite,

despite his illegitimate birth, by marrying into one of the state's wealthiest families. Imaginative and ambitious, he saw his role in Washington's cabinet as tantamount to that of "prime minister." At the Constitutional Convention, Hamilton had fought for a powerful central government, a position he advocated forcefully after the convention as one of the authors of the Federalist Papers. Disappointed with the final result, Hamilton viewed the Constitution as transitory, once calling it a "frail and worthless fabric." Now, as secretary of the treasury, he was in a position to rectify what he considered its weaknesses by deliberately strengthening and enlarging the powers of the federal government. His methods were primarily economic: funding and assumption of the national debt, passage of a federal tariff, and creation of the Bank of the United States.

The first business of government was somehow to solve the problem of the nation's debt of fifty-four million dollars—no small sum in those days. In order to defray the costs of fighting the Revolution, the government certificates had been distributed by Congress to soldiers in the Continental army, promising future payment for their services. Since few Americans ever believed the government would pay back the entire debt, however, the certificates declined in value. Soon hard-pressed soldiers in need of ready cash sold their certificates to speculators, who bought them up at well below their face value. Foreigners purchased fully one-fifth of the debt.

Hamilton's twofold debt proposal was unexpected. First, he planned to fund and repay the *entire* debt at face value. Second, the federal government would take over or assume state debts. In this way, the creditors holding bonds would benefit greatly, and their interests would then be bound with those who favored a strong central government (or so Hamilton reasoned). Creditors would not even receive cash but, instead, would be given new government bonds, further cementing the alliance between business and government that Hamilton keenly desired. He also believed this policy would stimulate enterprise and assure the future revenue needs of the government. Although Madison argued in the House that the original bond holders should be compensated, Hamilton insisted

No man wielded more influence in the early days of the American Republic than did Alexander Hamilton. His nationalistic economic policies set the stage for the growth of effective national power. His antidemocratic political policies led to the rise to power of the Jeffersonian Republicans. (Culver Pictures)

that if the creditors were allowed to reap windfall profits by a complete funding of the debt, strong new confidence would be created in the young government. Congress agreed; the debt would be funded in full.

Federal assumption of state debts proved a more controversial plan. Many Northern capitalists had bought up discounted state securities in the South. Also, some Southern states had already taxed their citizens and repaid state debts on the certificates; they now opposed plans that required further taxation. Madison and the Virginia delegation led the opposition to assumption of state debts. Realizing that his plan was close to defeat and that the struggle might split the delicate bonds of union, Hamilton struck a bargain with Secretary of State Jefferson, who had been working closely with Madison on the issue. In exchange for their approval of assumption, Hamilton promised to support the future establishment of the national capital on the Potomac River in the South between

Maryland and Virginia, far from the commercial-minded North. Opposition then diminished and assumption passed in 1790.

Congress would now have to raise money to pay off these debts. The first tariff act of 1789 placed duties on imports to raise revenue. When this proved insufficient, Congress enacted an excise tax on distilled liquors in 1791. As confidence in the stability of the new nation increased, prosperity returned, giving rise to increased imports and greater tariff revenues. Merchants also enjoyed substantial gains by paying lower duties than those on goods brought in by foreign vessels.

Congress also acted in 1791 to satisfy another key element of Hamilton's program by creating the Bank of the United States (BUS). A major political controversy erupted within Congress and elsewhere in the government prior to passage of the bank legislation. Opponents viewed Hamilton's national bank as an unconstitutional extension of congressional authority. Supporters, in turn, argued that the Constitution gave Congress the right to create such an institution. This argument over "strict" versus "loose" construction of the Constitution would recur in every major debate over Hamilton's program.

Capitalized at far more than all of the other existing state banks combined, the new institution provided a stable circulating medium to make trading easier and stimulate economic development. The Bank of the United States was a semiprivate corporation, with the government owning one-fifth of the stock and naming one-fifth of the board of directors. Moveover, BUS stock could be purchased with government bonds, and recently enriched government creditors rushed to buy up shares in the new corporation. The bank's public character allowed the government to hold and disburse funds as it saw fit; yet its control by private individuals on the board gave them significant power in making loans and issuing notes to businessmen. The bank worked just as planned by the secretary of the treasury.

Hamilton continued to press for closer ties between government and business. He admired both British industrial development, then first getting under way, and the mixture of popular and hereditary features in the British government. In his

"Report on Manufactures" of 1791, Hamilton recommended subsidies and protective tariffs to encourage development of American industry, which would make the country less dependent on foreign products. The American economy had not yet reached the stage where such industrialization was feasible, but Hamilton believed it would eventually be possible through a strong government run by a shrewd elite class. The anti-Federalist agrarians and states rights defenders who had dreaded the creation of a new government based upon stronger central control now reacted angrily as they saw some of their worst fears enacted into law through Hamilton's program.

FOREIGN AFFAIRS UNDER WASHINGTON

From the days of the first settlements in Massachusetts, many Americans had felt that they were building a new and better form of society that would serve as an inspiration to the corrupt Old World, a "City upon a Hill," as Puritans had called their experiment. With political independence won, many Americans believed that the United States should set an example in amity for the entire world by trading freely with every country, while remaining independent and uninvolved in disputes between European powers. The policy also reflected practical considerations: the new nation could not hope to become militarily involved in any foreign conflict without suffering severe social and economic dislocation at home, if not outright military defeat. As events would show, however, neither could Americans hope to steer clear of conflicts that struck at the heart of the country's prosperity.

Within months after adoption of the Constitution and Washington's inauguration in 1789, the French Revolution began, sending tremors throughout the European monarchical world. Growing uneasiness with events in France helped persuade Great Britain to recognize and establish full diplomatic relations with the United States in 1791, if only to deflect any possible close links between the two "revolutionary societies" of America and France. By 1793, Britain and France (and many other European nations) were again at war, and this time the French Revolution lent the struggle a particular intensity.

American cabinet meetings soon reflected this passion. Secretary of State Jefferson had been U.S. minister to France in the 1780s and had even watched the beginnings of the French Revolution before returning home in 1789. He had developed a warm sympathy toward the French, and he increasingly supported the goals of their revolution, though he was shaken by the execution of Louis XVI and the ensuing Reign of Terror. Hamilton, on the other hand, saw the destruction of monarchy and aristocracy as the end of civilized society. Along with other American conservatives, he was further shocked when the revolutionists declared the "war of all peoples against all kings," a threat to Britain and Spain.

Attempting to use the crisis to terminate the U.S.–French alliance created under the Treaty of 1778, Hamilton argued that the fall of the French monarchy had nullified the agreement. The United States, he urged, should declare its neutrality and refuse to receive the new French minister, "Citizen" Edmund Genêt. Although agreeing that Americans should remain uninvolved, Jefferson viewed the treaties as still binding and urged that the government refrain from announcing its intentions to remain neutral.

On April 22, 1793, Washington issued a proclamation of neutrality addressed to American citizens, while formally recognizing Genêt and refusing to repudiate the treaties with France. This public announcement disappointed Jefferson, who had hoped that American intentions could be kept secret and used as a bargaining tool to negotiate the withdrawal of British troops, which still occupied parts of the American Northwest and controlled that areas's valuable fur trade. (That issue, the fur trade, would later concern Meriwether Lewis; upon his return from exploring the continent he warned Jefferson of Britain's continuing designs on the fur trade in the Pacific Northwest.) By 1793, Jefferson had seen how little his views counted and decided to quit the cabinet. This was the first major breach in Washington's national coalition government of leaders from the Revolutionary generation.

French Minister Genêt conducted himself foolishly, creating more opposition than support for his country's cause. Although only a foreign envoy, Genêt ignored the proclamation of neutrality and proceeded about his business as if directing a united Franco-American war effort. He commissioned privateers in American ports to fly the French flag and capture British vessels, set up courts to deal with the ships the privateers captured, and organized expeditions to march on Spanish and British territories in North America. Finally, even Jefferson grew disgusted with the French upstart, and Washington demanded Genêt's recall.

Still clinging to idealistic notions of foreign policy, Americans claimed a neutral's right to trade with nations at war. This idea, that "free ships make free goods," quickly ran aground in the summer of 1793, when the British navy began to seize American vessels trading with France and its West Indian possessions. Amid cries for war, Washington decided on calm. He sent John Jay, Chief Justice of the Supreme Court, to negotiate a settlement in London to protect the United States's neutral rights. Other issues, such as the continued presence of British military posts in the Northwest Territory, the British urging Canadian Indians to attack American settlements, and British failing to return American slaves seized during the Revolution, also needed attention.

Jay's mission, however, was marred from the beginning. Hamilton, anxious that peaceful relations be retained with Britain at all costs, had told the British secretly that Americans would do almost anything to avoid war. Bargaining from a weak position, undercut by Hamilton's intrigues, Jay returned with a treaty so one-sided that Washington only reluctantly submitted it to the Senate, which ratified it with equal reluctance. Britain promised to withdraw from posts in the Northwest but with certain conditions. The United States agreed to permit continued British fur trade with the Indians, and although the British agreed to compensate Americans for ships seized in the Caribbean, English creditors would now be allowed to collect pre-Revolutionary debts.

Great Britain clearly gained more than the United States from the Jay Treaty. She continued to refuse to compensate American slaveholders or to halt the seizure of American seamen who were then "impressed" into the Royal Navy. Although some commercial restrictions in England were liberalized, the United States did not gain significantly, since the British would not specifically agree to respect U.S. rights as a neutral. Ratification of the Jay Treaty created further political antagonisms among Americans. Denunciations in the press and popular meetings in Boston, Philadelphia, and New York soon illustrated that in a democratic republic citizens could combine patriotism and active opposition to their government's decisions. Although commonplace today, this idea was startling and revolutionary at the time.

THE DEVELOPMENT OF POLITICAL PARTIES

The division over Hamilton's economic program, the French Revolution, and the war between Britain and France all contributed to growing factionalism within the American government. Many Founding Fathers had feared such factionalism, but they had not been able to prevent it. Jefferson, Madison, and most other Southerners believed that Hamilton's financial measures would benefit bankers and capitalists in Northern seaports at the expense of Southern planters and small farmers in the North. As Jefferson unsuccessfully jockeyed with Hamilton for power in Washington's cabinet, Southerners charged that the secretary of the treasury was in league with Northeastern merchants and speculators in gaining an undue influence over Congress. Also embittered by the administration's pro-British sentiment and by the ratification of Jay's Treaty, Jefferson condemned Hamilton as "not only a monarchist, but for a monarchy bottomed on corruption."

By the 1790s, political differences had gone beyond factionalism to the creation of a pair of distinct political parties, the Republicans and the Federalists. Unlike factions, parties were organized on a more permanent basis for the purpose of seeking votes to elect candidates to office. In developing programs, they often drew different groups together to organize at local, state, and national

The Whiskey Rebellion (1794) was a revolt against the federal excise tax on whiskey. Western Pennsylvania farmers here manhandle the tax collector, burning his cabin and leaving him with a coat of tar and feathers. (Culver Pictures)

levels. They encompassed several issues and sought to be national, rather than sectional, in scope.

Such party organization eventually grew, specifically, from opposition to Hamilton's influence in the Washington administration, and generally, from conflicts over the scope and role of national power. While Jefferson attempted to transfer greater authority to the State Department and away from the Treasury, Madison rallied anti-Hamilton elements in the House. Madison's forces began referring to themselves as the "republican interest," and finally by 1792, as "the Republican party." In 1791, the first Republican newspaper devoted to national issues appeared, and local "Democratic Clubs" began to form in sympathetic imitation of the revolutionary Jacobin societies in France. Although Washington himself was not challenged in the election of 1792, an alliance between New York and Virginia Republicans led North Carolina, Virginia, and New York to cast their second vote for New Yorker George Clinton for vice-president rather than for John Adams.

Supporters of Hamilton and the British continued to refer to themselves as Federalists in order to link their opponents to the anti-Federalists of the preceding decade. This was no longer either accurate or effective, since most Americans realized that the Republican leaders had also supported the Constitution. Madison, after all, had even joined Hamilton in contributing to the Federalist Papers. The struggle over ratification had quickly become history, giving way during the 1790s to more immediate and pressing issues that divided Republicans and Federalists.

The Whiskey Rebellion

Soon Federalist policy received a more direct challenge far from the seat of national government. One of Hamilton's financial measures was to impose a federal excise tax on liquor. Because it was more difficult and more expensive to transport surplus grain over mountainous regions, western Pennsylvania farmers had distilled their corn crops into whiskey. The profit they made in Eastern markets was already small, and the excise tax would reduce it to practically nothing. Thus the tax was largely ignored, and when the United States marshal summoned violators to court, he met strong resistance from Pennsylvania farmers near Pittsburgh.

Their action openly defied national authority, and the Federalists expressed horror at this "rebellion," exaggerating the threat it posed to the government. In Federalist eyes, it was another Shays's Rebellion. Even though the governor of Pennsylvania believed that the courts could handle the situation, Hamilton persuaded Washington that military action was needed. The president himself then led 15,000 soldiers to the disaffected area in October 1794. No one fired a shot; Washington returned to Philadelphia (then the capital); and Hamilton arrested the leaders of the protest movement.

After his return, Washington gave a speech condemning all organized opposition to government policies. He implied that the Republicans and the Democratic Clubs had somehow been responsible for the disturbances. Ignoring the Constitutional right to assemble and to petition government, he urged that such organizations disband. His prestige still remained so great that most of them did dissolve, and Republican opposition suffered a major if temporary setback.

John Adams was our second president and the first of the Adams family to distinguish himself in politics. Adams was talented but unpopular, and his administration (1797–1801) witnessed the breakup and defeat of the Federalist party. (Culver Pictures)

The Election of 1796

Washington's impending retirement in 1796 set the stage for the United States's first contested election. Although Washington's farewell address warned of the dangers of political parties and foreign entanglements, political partisanship grew as arguments concerning the respective merits of British or French policies were hotly debated. The Federalists backed Vice-President John Adams, while Thomas Jefferson ran as the Republican candidate. The two parties also openly endorsed candidates for congressional seats.

The election was understandably bitter and surprisingly close. Federalists called the Republicans anarchists and accused them of trying to disrupt and bring down the government in the manner of the French Jacobins. The Republicans, in turn, denounced Federalist measures as elitist and designed to subvert American liberty as George III and the British Parliament had done. Passions ran remarkably high, inflamed by extreme

and inaccurate charges flung about by both parties. Adams won a close victory over Jefferson, receiving seventy-one electoral votes[1] to sixty-eight for the Virginian. Since he finished second in the electoral vote total, however, Jefferson became vice-president.

THE ADAMS PRESIDENCY

Despite his original intentions to dampen political strife when he took office, John Adams proved incapable of quieting the furious name-

---

[1] The Constitution provided *indirect* election of the president as a means of removing the office from direct popular control. Rather than vote for presidential candidates, voters would vote for "electors"—expected to be prominent men in their states—who would then meet and cast ballots for the president and vice-president. National political parties were not anticipated by the Founders, although they recognized the inevitability of political "factions."

He in a trice struck Lyon thrice Upon his head, enrag'd Sir, *Who seiz'd the tongs to ease his wrongs, And Griswold thus engag'd Sir.* *Congress Hall, in Philad.ª Feb. 15. 1798. S. E. Cor. 6.ᵗʰ & Chesnut.*

In 1798, Congress was the scene of a brawl between Republican Matthew Lyon, left, and Federalist Roger Griswold, right. In the Speaker's chair sits an amused Jonathan Dayton. (Library of Congress)

calling that had come to characterize both parties. He and Jefferson had been friends during the Revolution, and now the two resolved to reestablish their friendship. Adams again denied the Republican accusation that, because he favored a strong executive, he was a monarchist. He also denied that he felt only hostility toward France. Any moderating influence Adams's Federalist adminis-

tration might have achieved was soon undermined, however, by the composition of his cabinet. Weak and mediocre, the Adams cabinet remained under the influence of Hamilton, who sent them advice from New York, where he had returned to seeming semi-retirement. Hamilton himself considered Adams too moderate, and he had attempted to manipulate the electoral voting system in 1796 to elect Federalist Thomas Pinckney of South Carolina instead of Adams.

Under Adams, foreign events would continue to exercise a strong influence over American domestic policies. The French responded to the Jay Treaty by attacking American shipping and refusing to receive the American minister. The cabinet, manipulated by Hamilton, convinced President Adams to begin arming merchant ships and to establish an army. When an American three-man negotiating commission went to France to ease tense relations, French Foreign Minister Charles Talleyrand demanded a bribe of $250,000 through three go-betweens designated in official dispatches only as X, Y, and Z. They informed the Americans that the price of a treaty with France would run into millions of dollars.

Aided by French corruption and blackmail, Federalists saw another opportunity to further their own political fortunes. Hamilton believed that a standing army would not only protect the country against a French threat, but could also be used to suppress political opponents. Although he also sided with the British, Adams felt that it was more important to concentrate on building up a navy, since the nation would otherwise be helpless to oppose the British navy. But the Hamiltonians or "High Federalists" demanded a strong army too and a declaration of war against France. They believed that the war with France might eliminate Republican opposition by rallying patriotic feeling around the Federalist administration and, at the same time, permit creation of a strong anti-French alliance with Great Britain.

President Adams remained unwilling to go to war, however, and in 1799 he sent an American minister to Paris to negotiate differences between the two countries. These had led to an undeclared war between the French and American navies in the fall of 1798. Negotiations brought peace with France but split the Federalist party. An agreement in September 1800 finally released the United States from its defunct 1778 alliance with France and compensated Americans for lost ships and goods. Hamilton and his followers, frustrated by peace, again schemed to "dump" Adams, this time in favor of Charles C. Pinckney, the party's vice-presidential candidate.

Federalists of all sentiments had used the anti-French reaction to the XYZ Affair to pass the Alien and Sedition Acts in 1798, an attempt to discredit and eliminate Republican opposition. The Alien Act extended from five to fourteen years the length of the residence requirement for immigrants, who generally favored the Republicans,

before they could become voting citizens. The president was also given the temporary authority to deport any alien whom he believed to be dangerous.

The Sedition Act, one of the worst examples of political repression in American history, was also supposed to be temporary, expiring on the day the next president would be inaugurated. It called for fines and imprisonment for those who opposed "any measure or measures of the government of the United States" or anyone who spoke or printed any "false, scandalous and malicious writing against the government of the United States or either house of the Congress or the President." Twenty-five Republicans, including influential newspaper editors, were prosecuted under this law. Even a loiterer outside a New Jersey tavern was sentenced for wishing that the cannon shot fired in honor of Adams had struck the president's posterior!

Spurred by new taxes and by laws inhibiting free expression, Republican opposition grew, with Madison and Jefferson again leading the way. The two drafted the Virginia and Kentucky resolutions as a response by state legislatures to this latest Federalist threat. Both states declared the Alien and Sedition Acts unconstitutional and upheld the right of the states to judge the constitutionality of laws passed by Congress. Although no other states would join in the protest, this action strengthened Republican confidence while raising issues of federal and state authority that would be hotly debated among future generations.

THE ELECTION OF 1800

As the renewal of the contest between Federalist Adams and Republican Jefferson approached in the fall of 1800, bitter divisions within the electorate had developed. Neither Federalists nor Republicans accepted the legitimacy of a political opposition, and both parties considered their chief opponents enemies of constitutional government and the republican system, and bent upon destroying the new Administration.

One *older* elite group supplied much of the leadership, organization, and philosophy for the Republicans. Southern planters who had first felt alienated by Hamilton's pro-commercial economic policies now sought to challenge and obtain national power from New Englander Adams. In order to succeed, they drew support from rising Northern businessmen and from discontented artisans as well as from certain "non-established" ethnic and religious groups. New Englanders tended to favor the Federalists, while most Southern support went to Republicans. Many creditors and urban merchants found much to support in the Hamiltonian system, while many debtor farmers enthusiastically supported Jefferson.

The intensity of the campaign resulted both from increased Republican political organization and from the emotional nature of the issues involved. Jefferson's party had suffered losses in 1798 as a result of French conduct in the XYZ Affair, but a caucus of Republican congressmen set up state committees which supervised creation of powerful local political organizations in 1800. Candidates themselves remained aloof from campaigning by tradition, but newspapers, pamphlets, and public meetings echoed charges, real or imagined. Federalists accused Jefferson of atheism and French Jacobinism which would destroy both religion and property. Republicans called Adams a monarchist and British lackey, criticizing the taxes that Federalists had imposed to support the military buildup. Some Republican newspapermen were arrested and sentenced by Federalist judges, but most editors successfully defied the Sedition Act and lashed out against Federalist policies.

The Republicans won the majority of electoral votes, yet the election went into the House of Representatives. Since the Founding Fathers had not foreseen the formation of political parties, the Constitution had not provided for separate electoral ballots for the offices of president and vice-president. Thus presidential electors in 1800, "the electoral college," had cast seventy-three votes each for Jefferson and Burr, with sixty-five for Adams and sixty-four for Pinckney. So there was Aaron Burr, intended candidate for the vice-presidency, on the same footing with his party chief, Jefferson. When no presidential candidate receives a majority of the *electoral* ballots, then, according to the Constitution, the House of Representatives elects the president.

The Republicans had clearly intended Jefferson to be their presidential candidate, but the Federalists realized that they had been presented another opportunity to keep the "radical" Jefferson out of office by supporting Burr in the House. As usual, however, all Federalists could not agree. Hamilton in particular despised Burr, his political rival in New York City (Burr would later kill Hamilton in a duel in 1804). After thirty-nine House ballots, Hamilton persuaded three Federalist congressmen to submit blank ballots instead of voting for Burr, thereby electing Jefferson president. (The Twelfth Amendment, ratified in 1804, required separate ballots for president and vice-president, thereby eliminating this sort of constitutional problem.) Although the presidential election had been close, Republicans gained large majorities in both the House and the Senate. The elated Jefferson hailed the Republican victory as the "Revolution of 1800."

JEFFERSONIAN REPUBLICANISM

To what extent was the election of 1800 really a "revolution"? Republicans had charged that Adams was an aristocrat with monarchical tendencies, but Jefferson owned thousands of acres of land and several hundred slaves. Even though Jefferson was a member of the Virginia elite, his defense of democratic ideals, his attacks on Federalist "monarchism," his support for religious liberty, and his eloquence as a spokesman for human rights won widespread support. The slaveholding aristocrat brought a more democratic and modest style to the presidency than his predecessor, Adams, despite the latter's humbler personal background.

The election of Jefferson marked a change of emphasis, rather than a drastic change in the nature of American government and society. "We are all Federalists; we are all Republicans," Jefferson announced in his inaugural address. He did not believe in political parties any more than did the Federalist opposition. Still, Jefferson determined (as had Adams) to end political warfare by winning opponents over to his way of thinking rather than by attempting to use political repression (as in the

Jefferson's greatest personal attraction, according to one admirer, was "a countenance beaming with benevolence and intelligence." (White House Collection)

farmer who was economically independent would be the perfect citizen of a republic, since no one could wield economic or social power over him sufficient to control his voting or political opinions. Jefferson, moreover, believed that farmers, freed of the temptations and pitfalls of urban life, had a measure of genuine virtue sufficient to sustain a democratic society interested in advancing the common welfare: "Those who labor in the earth," he declared flatly and sincerely, "are the Chosen people of God."

Those whom Jefferson feared most, on the other hand, were those who had earned their fortunes through commercial and financial speculation in the growing cities and towns: the "perfect" citizens of Alexander Hamilton's ideal republic. These men had largely supported Hamilton's economic program and had benefited from it. Jefferson also saw dangers in industrialization. If American entrepreneurs built factories which attracted men, women, and even children from the surrounding countryside to work in them, then he feared the dreary conditions of industrial society that had already appeared in Europe would reach America, shattering his dream that the New World might someday teach corrupted Europe how to build the just (that is, agrarian) society. The growth of factories would make workers dependent upon their wages from owners, who would then (Jefferson believed) inevitably dictate the workers' voting behavior, a reasonable fear in a day before the existence of either labor unions or the secret ballot.

Jefferson was sworn in as president in the new capital of Washington, certainly a place where the Virginian had no cause to worry about urban decadence—not yet. Despite extravagant planning by a French engineer, Pierre L'Enfant, and despite the best engineering efforts of a black scientist, Benjamin Banneker, to lay out the streets, the new capital was not a city, not even a town. Washington was a clearing in the wilderness with wooden houses here and there. Only one wing of the Capitol building had been completed, and the rotunda had not yet been enclosed. Pennsylvania Avenue, leading from the Capitol to the White House, had been fairly well cleared, but stumps and bushes appeared occasionally in the road. Mosquitoes proved a constant nuisance and even brought malaria to

Alien and Sedition Acts) or outright violence. In this respect, Jefferson's election did constitute a revolution in American government: one group had replaced another at the head of a democratically elected republican government without civil war. A revolutionary movement had succeeded in institutionalizing the peaceful transfer of power from one party to another; few subsequent revolutions in world history could boast of any similar success in this endeavor.

The new administration would be influenced by Jefferson's personal philosophy. Although himself a wealthy planter, he professed to share the interests of small American farmers, who composed the vast majority of the United States population in 1800. Jefferson idealized the agrarian, believing that an ordinary American

The Jeffersonian White House. (Library of Congress)

some. Because much of the federal city remained swampy marshland, congressmen had little choice but to leave their wives at home and move into the crowded boarding houses where they lived for the few months Congress remained in session each year.

The primitive capital proved an appropriate setting for Jefferson to test his political philosophy. Jefferson lived simply, hosting state dinners only rarely. He abandoned the practice of reading his annual message in person because the practice reminded Jefferson too strongly of the British monarch reading a proclamation speech from the throne. Instead, Jefferson sent his secretary, Meriwether Lewis, to deliver it to a congressional clerk. Jefferson ordered that the White House doors be opened every morning and that visitors be accommodated according to the order of their arrival. Foreign dignitaries were often surprised to be greeted by the American president in a faded coat and slippers.

The New Economic Program

Jefferson's new financial policies, with the support of Secretary of the Treasury Albert Galla-tin, reflected his philosophy of limited government: the new president believed that the government that governed best governed least, especially at the national level. He determined to reduce the public debt, which, as it stood, he felt benefited the wealthy classes at the expense of all other Americans. Republicans had long urged debt reduction, and Jefferson and Gallatin reduced spending and economized wherever possible. The government reduced taxes, and Jefferson persuaded Congress to repeal the much-hated tax on whiskey, which had created great hardship for Western farmers. Increasing revenues from import duties helped Republicans reduce the debt, despite lower taxes, from eighty million to fifty-three million dollars in ten years.

Much of this decrease was made possible by a severe cut of military spending. The regular army was reduced from four thousand to twenty-five hundred men. Naval strength was also diminished, leaving only thirteen ships. The rest were sold to merchants. Jefferson believed that if state militia systems were improved and the U.S. Military Academy was established at West Point, such cutbacks would not seriously threaten national defense.

Republican Gains

Despite this new economic austerity, Jefferson also accepted the need to temper his idealism for purposes of political expediency. He was convinced that through argument and compromise, he could undermine the Federalists and end the two-party system, which he (like most Americans of the period, both Federalist and Jeffersonian) considered "unnatural." Republicans never sought to undo Hamilton's measures of funding and assumption, and they allowed the national bank to exist until its charter expired in 1811. Jefferson even appointed three New Englanders to his cabinet as a gesture toward reconciliation with that Federalist stronghold, and though he continued to believe in the fundamental importance of agriculture, he now admitted the need to make concessions to shipping interests in order to lure them away from the Federalist fold. Yet Jefferson drastically reversed one whole body of Federalist policies: he allowed the Alien Act to expire and quickly obtained the lowering of residence requirements for citizenship from Congress. After the expiration of the Sedition Act, Jefferson refunded all fines and pardoned all who had been imprisoned under the hateful law.

After the 1800 elections, Republicans also sought to undermine the last Federalist stronghold and power base within the national government—the judiciary. Following his defeat, President Adams obtained passage of the Judiciary Act of 1801 and appointed Federalists to sixteen new federal judgeships. These were known as "midnight appointments." Congressional Republicans promptly repealed the act as an unnecessary expenditure, but the political nature of the issue was undeniable. Jefferson had also begun slowly to remove Federalist officeholders from the executive branch and to replace them with Republicans, while trying to avoid an all-out patronage battle with angry Federalists. Meanwhile, Republicans in control of the House came close to impeaching Justice Samuel Chase of the U.S. Supreme Court, an important jurist who had often delivered Federalist harangues while passing judgment on Republican offenders.

Political battles in several states gave reality to the Republican creed by democratizing American life. As competition grew between political elites, it became increasingly necessary to appeal to different classes and groups which before had rarely participated in politics. Popular appeals through newspapers and rallies brought an end to "deference politics," where voters had yielded to the judgment of their better-educated local elite when choosing candidates for office. Political parties encouraged people instead to consider their own self-interest when voting. Parties also exploited existing local and state rivalries, as well as nationally binding symbols, while soliciting support from the different ethnic, economic, and religious groups. Although many Federalists still viewed the Republicans as dangerous revolutionaries, even after Jefferson's first term in office, a majority of Americans soon accepted the value of organized political parties. They especially delighted in the freedom of press arguments and open debate that accompanied enthusiastic partisan campaigning as legitimate means of political expression within a democratic society.

LOUISIANA AND THE WEST

The Louisiana Purchase

Years before Lewis and Clark made their trek across the continent to the Pacific, the American westward movement was well under way. By 1800, nearly a million people lived between the Appalachian Mountains and the Mississippi River. Four new states had entered the Union: Vermont in 1791, Kentucky in 1792, Tennessee in 1796, and Ohio in 1803. Soon American settlers began moving across the Mississippi into Spanish territory. In Pinckney's Treaty of 1795, Spain granted American flatboats the right of navigation on the river down to New Orleans, where they were allowed to leave their goods for shipment elsewhere.

In 1801 Jefferson was shocked to find that the previous year Spain had secretly transferred all of Louisiana to the powerful French government. When, in 1799, Napoleon declared himself dictator, Jeffersonian Republicans lost all sympathy for France. Now Napoleon attempted to re-create the French colonial empire in America that had been lost with the cession of Canada to Great Britain in 1763. Such an empire would serve as a geographic

John Marshall

This great American jurist, and Chief Justice of the United States Supreme Court from 1801 to 1835, came from a background remarkably like Thomas Jefferson's — the man who would become his chief adversary in public life. John Marshall was born in Virginia in 1755, the son of a planter, though not one of the colony's wealthiest. Although Marshall spent some time at William and Mary College, for the most part he educated himself in the law. As a young attorney at Richmond, Marshall won recognition as one of Virginia's best legal minds.

Marshall served in the Revolutionary forces, later observing that this experience had reinforced for him a belief in the importance of national unity. A supporter of the Constitution in 1787 and against strong anti-Federalist sentiment in Virginia, Marshall gravitated easily into the Federalist party during the 1790s. He rose in that decade to hold important diplomatic posts, serve in Congress, and finally, to gain appointment as John Adams's secretary of state in 1800. When Marshall was holding this office, at the close of the Federalist era, President Adams named him Chief Justice of the Supreme Court. Marshall had not been Adams's first choice, and many die-hard Federalists distrusted Marshall's nationalist avowals, apparently for no better reason than that he came from the Virginia of Jefferson and Madison.

Once on the Court, Marshall dispelled their unwarranted fears. He proceeded to make the Supreme Court an important factor in the American political process, and for most of the next thirty-four years, Marshall held tight reign over "his" Court. He seldom lost control of the majority, and he himself wrote nearly half of the 1,100 recorded opinions during the 1801–35 period.

Several of Marshall's decisions helped construct the basic fabric of American constitutional law. In *Marbury* v. *Madison,* an 1803 opinion, the Court established the principle of judicial review itself, declaring unconstitutional a 1798 congressional measure and thereby establishing the Court's authority to rule such statutes null and void when in violation of the Constitution. In the landmark *McCulloch* v. *Maryland* decision, Marshall disposed of an attempt by Maryland to tax the local branch of the Second Bank of the United States on the grounds that the attempt represented an unconstitutional state effort to tax a federal agency. Marshall not only asserted the principle of federal supremacy over state authority in this decision but also rebutted Maryland's argument that

limitation upon American expansion, a continuing interest of Jefferson's. Settlers in the Western lands, concerned, for their part, over selling their cash crops to foreign markets, were severely threatened when the French forbade Western farmers from sending their exports down the Mississippi to New Orleans. Alarmed, but wishing to solve the problem peacefully, Jefferson sent James Monroe to France to buy New Orleans and West Florida, authorizing up to ten million dollars for this purpose.

By the time Monroe reached Paris, Napoleon's interests had shifted away from America. In 1803 the emperor faced the threat of losing the

the Bank of the United States itself was unconstitutional, since the Constitution did not explicitly authorize creation of such a bank. "Let the end be legitimate," he wrote, "let it be within the scope of the Constitution, and all means which are appropriate, which are plainly adapted to that end, which are not prohibited, but [are] consist[ent] with the letter and spirit of the Constitution, are constitutional."

Nationalists cheered, while "strict constructionists" reeled as this and other decisions from the Marshall Court expanded federal and judicial powers in a variety of ways: protecting private property through application of the Constitution's contract clause, guaranteeing the right to appeal cases involving federal issues from state to federal courts, broadening "implied powers" under the Constitution, and interpreting federal authority broadly under the Constitution's interstate commerce clause. In the last area, the Court ruled in *Gibbons* v. *Ogden* (1824) that states could not create monopolies in areas under federal jurisdiction. The specific argument involved licenses to run steamboats in New York, but the general problem concerned monopolies on transportation arteries throughout the country. The decision effectively opened the waterways to competitive commerce (within a year after *Gibbons* v. *Ogden*, the number of steamboats sailing New York's inland waters had increased sevenfold).

John Marshall was the most prominent of President Adams's "midnight judges," the Federalists that he appointed to judicial posts with lifetime tenure at the last minute prior to his leaving office in 1801. Jeffersonians had attacked the appointments, but as time passed (and after Republicans had failed to remove Supreme Court justices

through congressional impeachment efforts), they grudgingly came to accept the Federalist judges, including Marshall. They reasoned that, in any event, Jefferson and other Republican presidents would have a chance to appoint their own loyalists to the federal bench and restore a balance. This hope proved to be in vain, since Marshall maintained his nationalist judicial ideas throughout the 1820s despite the presence of Jeffersonian-Republican colleagues. Sometimes, as in the case of Justice Joseph Story, a Jefferson appointee proved to be as nationalist as the Chief Justice.

The Marshall Court's principal contribution was to prevent state power from overwhelming the fragile national government's authority, that would have turned the United States into a loose confederation again despite the new Constitution. Marshall fought hard and regularly to keep the states at bay and to maintain — even expand, where possible — the grants of power to the federal government that he found in the Constitution. He was the supreme "loose constructionist," interpreting the Constitution in a manner that generally allowed the national government to function in any manner that it was not specifically prohibited from doing.

Marshall began to lose his grip on the Court by the end of the 1820s and during his closing years in the 1830s. Dissenters gained a majority more frequently, and the chief justice clashed with President Andrew Jackson regularly, especially over Indian policy. It proved yet another measure of Marshall's greatness and his impact upon the American constitutional system that when he died in 1835, his successor, a strong Jacksonian supporter named Roger B. Taney, modified but never abandoned his predecessor's vision of the Constitution and national power.

French colony of Santo Domingo (now Haiti) through an independence movement of slaves led by Toussaint L'Ouverture. He also feared that he could not obtain enough money to renew his war with Great Britain, and his vision of a restored "New France" in America had faded. When his foreign minister, Talleyrand, therefore, offered the

American negotiators not merely New Orleans but the entire province of Louisiana for fifteen million dollars, the American ministers did not hesitate to accept the offer. They did so despite their lack of any specific authority to make such a purchase, and despite the fact that the price was 50 percent more than their "budget." A bargain was a bargain.

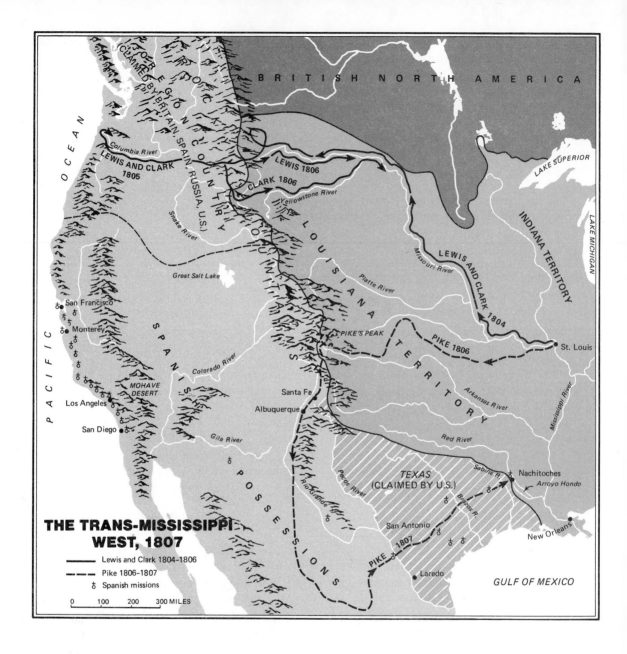

THE TRANS-MISSISSIPPI WEST, 1807

——— Lewis and Clark 1804–1806
– – – Pike 1806–1807
⚲ Spanish missions

0   100   200   300 MILES

Congressional debate over ratification of the purchase (which, parenthetically, did not stop the Lewis and Clark expedition from proceeding) centered around the question of constitutional authority. New England Federalists believed the new territory would become another Republican stronghold, further undermining the interests of the New England states and irrevocably damaging the Federalists in national politics. Federalists had always believed in a broad interpretation of the Constitution, that the national government had "implied powers" to act in furthering the country's welfare. Republicans adopted a strict construction view, arguing that the central government had only the specific powers delegated in the Constitution and little discretionary authority.

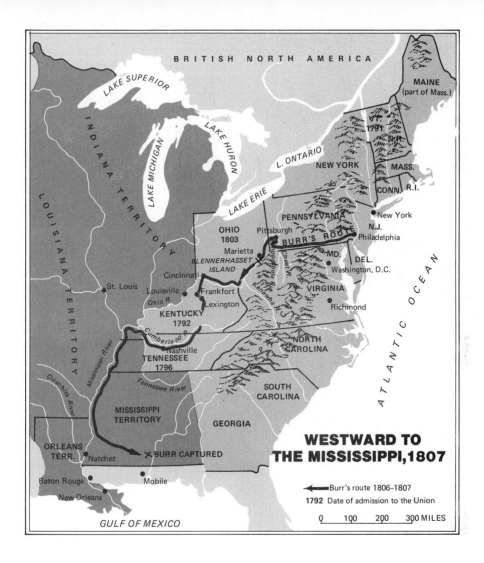

WESTWARD TO THE MISSISSIPPI, 1807

Burr's route 1806–1807
1792 Date of admission to the Union

0   100   200   300 MILES

The Louisiana Purchase "bargain" dented Republican principles. The Republicans now argued ironically that the federal government did have power to make the agreement, while many Federalists argued the opposite. Jefferson, though reluctant to assert that the government had implied powers that covered the transaction, realized that Napoleon might withdraw the offer if he waited for the long process of a constitutional amendment to ratify the purchase. He, therefore, supported congressional ratification of the treaty which, once achieved, confirmed the Louisiana Purchase.

Jefferson had compromised his constitutional ideals, but he remained consistent in championing the interests of farmers above all others. Within the Louisiana Territory, he believed, lay enough land for any number of farming generations to till, over eight hundred thousand square miles in all. Even before the Lewis and Clark Corps of Discovery had fully explored Louisiana, as early as 1804 in fact, the territory between the Appalachians and Mississippi began filling up with settlers who could purchase 160 acres of Western land from the government with a down payment of eighty dollars. Jefferson even approved of the con-

New Yorker Aaron Burr was a crafty politician, a Jeffersonian Republican who always looked out for Number 1 and almost slid into the White House in 1801. Unhappy as Vice-President, Burr plotted to set up an independent "empire" in the U.S. Southwest and Texas. In 1807, he was tried for treason—Chief Justice John Marshall presiding—and was acquitted. (Culver Pictures)

struction of a national road from Cumberland, Maryland, to Wheeling, Virginia, exercising still another power not explicitly mentioned in the Constitution. This road would cross the Appalachians, making it easier for farmers to transport surplus crops, and thus encourage Western settlement. By 1820, one out of ten Americans lived west of those mountains. After the Lewis and Clark exploring party returned successfully, the vision of westward settlement became fixed in the consciousness of an America fast becoming converted to the gospel of continental expansionism.

The Burr Conspiracy

One major politician of that era needed no encouragement to see the economic and political potential of the newly acquired Western lands. Aaron Burr, brilliant and ever-ambitious, had indicated an interest in promoting his own fortunes

at the expense of his country's in the Louisiana Territory even before stepping down from the vice-presidency in 1805. Burr had approached the British minister, Anthony Merry, asking a half-million-dollar "loan" to help arrange the secession of newly acquired Louisiana from the United States. Although Merry became intrigued with the proposal, his superiors in London dawdled in responding so that Burr turned to other schemes.

He sailed down the Mississippi River in 1806 on a well-equipped flatboat, stopping along the way to visit sympathizers (among them Andrew Jackson) and to propose various elaborate plans for gaining wealth and fortune in the West. Accounts of Burr's proposals differed but, at one point or another, he apparently entertained such disparate schemes as separating several of the Western states (Kentucky and Tennessee among them) from the Union, establishing a Western empire independent of the United States with himself as its president or king, and invading then-Spanish-ruled Mexico with an eye toward "liberating" it.

Burr's presumably treasonous intentions were betrayed to President Jefferson by one of Burr's closest co-conspirators: James Wilkinson, the highest ranking general in the American army and (on the side) a paid agent for the Spaniards. Jefferson ordered Burr's arrest, Burr fled the now-unfriendly Wilkinson's troops, and in February 1807, the former vice-president was finally captured near Mobile. Chief Justice John Marshall presided at Burr's lengthy trial for treason in Richmond, Virginia. After conducting a brilliant defense, much of it as his own attorney, Burr was acquitted. The government failed to produce sufficient evidence—or two witnesses—to show overt treasonous acts on Burr's part. After the not-guilty verdict on September 1, Burr escaped possible further harassment by Jefferson through exiling himself to France for the next four years. He returned to New York City in 1812 where he practiced law, dying there in 1836 at the age of eighty.

THE CRISIS IN AMERICAN SHIPPING

A truce between Great Britain and France, the treaty that Adams obtained with France in

1799, and Napoleon's dictatorship all combined to defuse the foreign issue for Americans, temporarily, and allowed Jefferson to focus attention on domestic policy during most of his first term. Yet as the previous decade had shown, the United States remained dependent on the international trading structure for exporting surplus grain and raw materials while importing manufactured goods. Any significant disturbance in that trade would bring economic dislocation and perhaps social turmoil. This situation would characterize Jefferson's second term in office.

There had already been some trouble early in his administration. Barbary pirates controlling the entrance to the Mediterranean from North Africa demanded periodic tribute from the American government to let our ships proceed. In 1801 Jefferson sent an expedition against one of the North African states, which stopped the pirates' interference and raised American morale and prestige. Yet pirates from other parts of North Africa continued to harass ships, and the American government was forced to pay bribes as late as 1816.

A more serious challenge to future prosperity came in 1803, when England and France went to war again. That war led directly to Napoleon's decision to sell Louisiana, and at first, as in the 1790s, American shipping took advantage of neutrality by importing goods from British and French colonies then reexporting them to the "mother countries" in Europe. The British had previously allowed Americans to deliver these goods to France as long as they first imported the merchandise into the United States. In 1805 an English court denied this right to Americans, and in the next year, Britain proclaimed a partial blockade of French-dominated western Europe. France promptly declared a blockade of England. Both countries began seizing American ships; between 1805 and 1807, the French seized about five hundred vessels, while the British confiscated over one thousand. American rights as a neutral, in short, had again come under sustained attack from both sides.

It quickly became evident that Britain posed the larger danger. Its superior navy had the power to enforce policy far more effectively than the French. The British seized or impressed sailors from American ships, whom they declared to be

The United States and Britain almost went to war in 1807 after the H.M.S. Leopard *(right) fired on the U.S.S.* Chesapeake *(left), then boarded the American warship in search of deserters. (Culver Pictures)*

deserters from the Royal Navy. As often as not, however, native-born Americans were taken mistakenly or purposely. Americans responded to this crisis much as they had during the Revolutionary period. Congress passed a Non-Importation Act in 1806 banning the consumption and importation of British goods. This proved to have a negligible effect, and the situation worsened when attempts to negotiate a solution failed in London. It was during this frustrating year that Lewis wrote Jefferson, warning him of British intentions to grab the Northwest trade.

One incident that represented a gross violation of the United States's neutral rights nearly pushed Americans into war. In June 1807 the British frigate *Leopard* fired on the American frigate *Chesapeake* in broad daylight as astonished Virginians looked on from the coast. The British captain had demanded to board the *Chesapeake* and search for deserters. The Americans replied that they did indeed have three deserters from the Royal Navy, but that all three were Americans who had escaped impressment! When the search was refused, the *Leopard* opened fire, killing three Americans and wounding eighteen.

The Embargo

After demanding compensation and an apology for the *Chesapeake* incident, Jefferson sought to punish the British in the Embargo Act of 1807. Congress prohibited all U.S. ships from sailing to foreign ports, outlawed all exports from the United States, and refused to import certain British manufactured goods. Jefferson believed that if Britain and France were deprived of their American trade, including goods from their colonies, they would be forced to relax shipping restrictions toward the United States and respect the United States's neutral rights.

The embargo failed miserably. Many American shipowners had no quarrel with British restriction and actually enjoyed higher profits because of the greater risk. Federalists and New England merchants objected, however, using the argument they had employed earlier in the debate over the Louisiana Purchase: that the government did not have the power to curtail trade. Many Republican farmers grew angry when their surplus crops could no longer be sold in the foreign market. Illegal trade with Canada and through Florida helped to subvert the goals of the embargo, leaving Jefferson increasingly frustrated and producing coercive enforcement laws.

But the real reason for its failure was that the embargo hurt Americans far more than it did the British or the French. Public pressure finally forced Congress to repeal the embargo, and Jefferson reluctantly signed this measure in 1809, just days before his good friend, James Madison, was to be sworn in as the next president. One effect of the embargo, curiously, proved more in line with Hamilton's vision of America than Jefferson's. By prohibiting certain British imports, the embargo helped stimulate American industry in ways that, one generation later, would turn Jefferson's vision of an agrarian society into an outdated fantasy.

Causes of the War

After decisively winning the presidential contest and enjoying a brief period of popularity with the embargo's repeal, Madison and the Republicans in Congress passed the Nonintercourse Act in 1809. The law reestablished trade with all countries except Britain and France. For a brief period, when the British minister to the United States violated his instructions in negotiating a treaty, it looked as if the crisis over neutral rights might be resolved. But the agreement was quickly invalidated upon the minister's return to London.

The United States then tried a different tactic. Congress lifted the ban on trade with the two countries in 1810, while authorizing the president to reimpose an embargo on one of the belligerents if the other should relax restrictions. When Napoleon falsely announced that restrictions on American shipping would be lifted, Madison immediately reestablished nonintercourse with Great Britain and severed diplomatic relations soon after. Surrounded by economic hardship and political strife, the British foreign secretary announced on June 23, 1812, that his country would suspend its restrictive maritime policy against American vessels. The move, however, came five days too late. Congress had already declared war on Great Britain.

Americans living in the South and West were the strongest proponents of the war. They had felt most strongly the foreign presence in Louisiana and Florida. They were the most affected by emotional appeals that the United States needed to reassert its independence and strength by successfully challenging Britain, putting an end to impressment and interference with neutral trade. It was also the agrarian South and West that were most keenly threatened by the closing of European markets to American foodstuffs.

Many land-hungry Westerners had also been disturbed by the belief that the British in Canada had been arming Indians to oppose American expansion. No one consulted Indian tribes when Napoleon decided to sell Louisiana to the Americans, and farmers often migrated to new areas before Indian land claims were settled. In the Ohio country, in fact, Thomas Jefferson—celebrator of the "noble savage"—even advised Governor Wil-

liam Henry Harrison on techniques for wheedling the tribes into making treaties that they did not understand! Two Shawnees, Tecumseh and his brother "the Prophet," organized various tribes against further white encroachment. In 1811 they mobilized a large force of warriors until defeated at the Battle of Tippecanoe. Here, thought many, was an example of what British deviousness could accomplish.

When it came, however, the War of 1812 proved one of the most unpopular and controversial conflicts in American history. Every Federalist in Congress voted against war. Even a minority of Republicans, remembering Hamilton's efforts to encourage federal spending for military needs, balked at the idea of taking on a major European power. Many blamed Madison personally for stumbling ineptly into war, and he barely won reelection in 1812 by a margin of one state's electors.

THE WAR OF 1812

The United States entered the war unprepared as well as divided. The government had

The British bombarded Fort McHenry, near Baltimore, throughout the night of September 13–14, 1814. The successful resistance of the Americans inspired a bystander, lawyer Francis Scott Key, to write the verses of "The Star Spangled Banner." (The New-York Historical Society)

waited too long to raise funds to build up the navy, and it depended upon volunteer enlistments for the general army and state militias which never came in the hoped-for numbers. Three attempts to conquer Canada ended dismally. The navy fared somewhat better, capturing several British ships on the Atlantic. The American navy also defeated a British fleet on Lake Erie, winning control of the Northwest in 1813. When the British turned the tide against France and defeated Napoleon in 1814, however, they were able to transfer resources and manpower to North America. They successfully blockaded the American coastline. In the gloomiest days of the war, in August 1814, a British fleet sailed up the Chesapeake, landing troops that captured Washington, burning the Capitol and the

The American plan called for attacks against the British from Detroit, Fort Niagara, and Plattsburg, New York. In **1812** William Hull marched from Detroit into Canada. Fearing trouble from Indians on his flank, however, he retreated and surrendered Detroit without a shot. In August the American garrison at Fort Dearborn was wiped out.

In **1813** Americans were more successful. In April Henry Dearborn sailed from Sackets Harbor, New York, across Lake Ontario and burned York (now Toronto). Oliver Hazard Perry's September victory on Lake Erie forced the British to abandon Detroit. William Henry Harrison, who had moved north from Cincinnati, pursued the retreating British into Canada and defeated them at the Battle of the Thames in October.

In **1814** the Creek Indians, allied with the British, attacked Americans along the frontier. Andrew Jackson, moving south through Mississippi Territory, dealt the Creeks a heavy defeat at the Battle of Horseshoe Bend. In September British troops under Robert Ross and Alexander Cochrane sailed up Chesapeake Bay. They burned Washington, D.C., but failed to take Baltimore. That same month a British force under George Prevost moved south from Montreal. Americans led by Thomas Macdonough went north to meet them and won an important victory at the Battle of Lake Champlain. Late in the year a large British fleet commanded by Edward Pakenham moved north from Jamaica. In **1815**, in the war's most spectacular battle, Jackson defeated them at New Orleans.

White House. Madison and his government fled ignominiously.

Fittingly, perhaps, the greatest American victory of the war occurred in the Southwest shortly after it had officially ended. On January 8, 1815, with both sides unaware that a peace treaty had already been signed, British Major General Sir Edward Pakenham led a direct frontal assault on New Orleans, keeping his troops in close column formation. His fifty-three hundred men faced an American force of thirty-five hundred composed of militiamen, two battalions of free black troops, disorganized frontiersmen, and pirates, including the notorious Jean Lafitte, all under the direction of General Andrew Jackson, a militia commander from Tennessee. Jackson won an astounding victory, killing two thousand British troops, including General Pakenham and the next two generals in command. Only thirteen Americans died in the action. The victory fired American nationalism, virtually silencing the war's critics, and it made Jackson—"The Hero of New Orleans"—a major overnight figure on the political stage. The war itself decided virtually nothing: on December 24, 1814, the Treaty of Ghent ended the war unconditionally; that is, each side dropped or postponed its demands. Each nation accepted—at least in theory—conditions as they had existed before the war.

Most people in New England continued to oppose the war as they had opposed Jefferson's embargo. Many commercial-minded Federalists viewed the war as one imposed by the South and West at New England's expense, suspecting Madison and the Republicans of trying to use the conflict for partisan political ends and sectional economic motives. It might be recalled that New Englanders had also opposed the Louisiana Purchase and would have opposed appropriations for Lewis and Clark's expedition had Jefferson fully revealed his intentions. Federalist governors opposed the use of state militiamen during the War of 1812, discouraging volunteer enlistments or increasing taxes.

In October 1814, representatives from most New England states gathered at Hartford, Connecticut, to draft a list of grievances and recommendations. Dismayed by their section's waning influence in the policy making of the national government, the Hartford delegates argued that the Constitution had failed to provide equal rights among the states. A few demanded secession from the United States, but the moderate majority proposed a series of constitutional amendments instead. They wanted abolition of the three-fifths compromise which gave greater representation to the Southern states plus a new requirement for a two-thirds vote in Congress either to declare war or to admit new states. With the war's end and Jackson's victory at New Orleans, however, the country was in no mood to listen to disaffected New Englanders. Federalists faced charges of treason from their more patriotic, belatedly pro-war countrymen, and the party never recovered from its opposition to the war. Nothing, other than the Battle of New Orleans, did more to enhance the war's popularity among Americans in all sections than the coming of peace.

Once the war had ended, its unifying effects became more apparent. Even the most remote frontiersman seemed eager to defend the country against foreign attack. Wartime curtailing of trade with Europe had encouraged greater interstate trade and cooperation as well as a growth of domestic industries. The doctrines of the Virginia and Kentucky resolutions (1799) and of the Hartford Convention (1814), one the work of Republicans, the other of Federalists, remained as warnings of what dissatisfied sections might do in the future. The rise of party politics had proved significant by providing, among other things, the means through which such sectional discontent could be channeled and compromised. If serious questions of principle could be resolved through party mechanisms and through the participation in politics of ever-expanding numbers of people, then both national unity and democratic sentiment might grow to an unprecedented degree. Whatever the future held, it seemed clear by 1815, at war's end, that the American republic had withstood successfully the major political and foreign challenges of its early embattled decades. Its energies began shifting toward economic and political expansion, much of it toward the West, thereby beginning to fulfill the promise of continental development foretold in the success of Lewis and Clark's trek through the American wilderness.

Suggested Readings
Chapters 11-12

The Lewis and Clark Expedition and the American Frontier

Thomas P. Abernethy, *The Burr Conspiracy* (1954); John Bakeless, *Lewis and Clark, Partners in Discovery* (1947); John D. Barnhart, *Valley of Democracy: The Frontier Versus the Plantation in the Ohio Valley, 1775–1818* (1953); Paul Russell Cutright, *A History of the Lewis and Clark Journals* (1976); Bernard De Voto, *The Course of Empire* (1952) and *The Journals of Lewis and Clark* (1953); Richard Dillon, *Meriwether Lewis: A Biography* (1965); William H. Goetzmann, *Army Exploration in the American West 1803–1863* (1959); David Freeman Hawke, *Those Tremendous Mountains: The Story of the Lewis and Clark Expedition* (1980); E. Wilson Lyon, *Louisiana in French Diplomacy 1759–1804* (1954); Arthur K. Moore, *The Frontier Mind: A Cultural Analysis of the Kentucky Frontiersman* (1957); Francis Paul Prucha, *American Indian Policy in the Formative Years* (1962); Bernard W. Sheehan, *Seeds of Extinction: Jeffersonian Philanthropy and the American Indian* (1973); Henry Nash Smith, *Virgin Land: The American West as Symbol and Myth* (1950).

The Federalist Era

James M. Banner, Jr., *To the Hartford Convention: The Federalists and the Origin of Party Politics in Massachusetts, 1789–1815* (1969); Morton Borden, *Parties and Politics in the Early Republic, 1789–1815* (1967); Irving Brant, *The Bill of Rights* (1965); James H. Broussard, *The Southern Federalists 1800–1816* (1978); Richard Buel, Jr., *Securing the Revolution: Ideology in American Politics 1789–1815* (1972); William N. Chambers, *Political Parties in a New Nation* (1970); Joseph Charles, *The Origins of the American Party System* (1956); Marcus Cunliffe, *The Nation Takes Shape 1789–1837* (1960); Alexander DeConde, *Entangling Alliance: Politics and Diplomacy Under George Washington* (1958); M. J. Heale, *The Making of American Politics* (1977); Linda K. Kerber, *Federalists in Dissent* (1970); Stephen G. Kurtz, *The Presidency of John Adams* (1957); John C. Miller, *The Federalist Era 1789–1801* (1960); Curtis P. Nettels, *The Emergence of a National Economy 1775–1815* (1962); Robert V. Remini, *Andrew Jackson and the Course of American Empire 1767–1821* (1977); James M. Smith, *Freedom's Fetters: The Alien and Sedition Laws* (1956); Paul A. Varg, *Foreign Policies of the Founding Fathers* (1963); Leonard D. White, *The Federalists: A Study in Administrative History* (1948).

The Jeffersonians

Thomas P. Abernethy, *The South in the New Nation, 1789–1819* (1961); Henry Adams, *A History of the United States During the Administrations of Jefferson and Madison* (9 vols., 1889–1891); Irving Brant, *The Fourth President: A Life of James Madison* (1970); Roger H. Brown, *The Republic in Peril, 1812* (1964); Harry L. Coles, *The War of 1812* (1965); Noble E. Cunningham, *The Jeffersonian Republicans 1789–1801* (1958) and *The Jeffersonian Republicans in Power* (1963); Richard Ellis, *The Jeffersonian Crisis: Courts and Politics in the New Republic* (1971); David H. Fischer, *The Revolution in American Conservatism* (1965); Reginald Horsman, *Causes of the War of 1812* (1962), *Expansion and American Indian Policy 1783–1812* (1967), *Jefferson and Civil Liberties* (1963), *The Jeffersonian Image in the American Mind* (1960), and *The War of 1812* (1969); L. S. Kaplan, *Jefferson and France* (1967); Ralph Ketcham, *James Madison* (1971); Leonard Levy, *Legacy of Suppression: Freedom of Speech and Press in Early American History* (1960); Dumas Malone, *Jefferson and His Times* (four vols to date, 1948–1969); Bradford Perkins, *Prologue to War: England and the United States 1805–1812* (1961); Merrill D. Peterson, *Thomas Jefferson and the New Nation* (1970); Julius W. Pratt, *The Expansionists of 1812* (1925); Norman K. Risjord, *The Old Republicans: Southern Conservatism in the Age of Jefferson* (1965); Marshall Smelser, *The Democratic Republic 1801–1815* (1968); Burton Spivak, *Jefferson's English Crisis: Commerce, Embargo and the Republican Revolution* (1979); Leonard D. White, *The Jeffersonians 1801–1829* (1951); Charles M. Wiltse, *The Jeffersonian Tradition in American Democracy* (1935); James S. Young, *The Washington Community 1800–1828* (1966).

Andrew Jackson: The Road to the White House

13

The Seminole Indian chiefs stood on the shore and watched the soldiers hang the old man. Almost alone among white men, Alexander Arbuthnot had cared about the Seminoles and had tried to help them. For his pains, the Scottish trader's body now dangled limply from the yardarm of his own schooner under the hot Florida sun in the spring of 1818.

Arbuthnot had been caught up in a war between the United States and the Seminoles, an offshoot of the Creek Indian confederacy who lived mostly in Spanish Florida and occasionally crossed the border to raid American settlements in Georgia and Alabama. The U.S. government, eager to stop the raids and anxious to acquire Florida, sent Major General Andrew Jackson and several thousand men into Spanish Florida. Jackson's forces found few Indians willing to fight, but after several skirmishes he did capture two Seminole leaders, whom he promptly hanged in April 1818. He also ran across two Britons. "My love," the general wrote to his wife Rachel, "I entered the Town of St. Marks on yesterday. I found in St. Marks the noted Scotch villain Arbuthnot . . . I hold him for trial." Farther to the east, American forces encountered Lieutenant Robert C. Armbrister, formerly of His Britannic Majesty's Royal Marines. Both Britons were jailed as allies of the Seminoles.

The War of 1812 had ended only three years earlier, and Americans still believed that the British stirred up the Creeks and Seminoles to raid into the United States. Jackson, acting as commanding general, ordered a court martial for Arbuthnot and Armbrister. His legal basis for trying two British subjects on Spanish soil in an American military court was shaky at best. But when Andrew Jackson felt he was right, technicalities rarely impressed or stopped him.

The case against Arbuthnot, a tall, white-haired, carefully dressed man in his seventies, consisted of one letter, a bill of sale, and two witnesses. Arbuthnot had written the letter to his friend, the Seminole leader Bolecks ("Bowlegs" the American dubbed him), warning him to avoid battle with Jackson's powerful army. Jackson insisted, however, that the letter contained military information and provided advice to the

Indian enemy. The bill of sale listed ten kegs of powder Arbuthnot had sold to the Indians. The witnesses, both personal enemies of the Scotsman, testified to having seen a letter he had written to the Seminoles urging them to attack the Americans. The letter itself was not produced.

Arbuthnot defended himself in a simple but eloquent speech to the court. He denied advising the Seminoles to go to war, since he wished to avoid bloodshed. The sale of a few powder barrels to be used in hunting was, he pointed out, a normal part of a trader's business. How long, after all, would ten kegs have lasted in a war? Arbuthnot pointed to the flimsy nature of the documentary evidence and the hearsay nature of the oral testimony. He swore that he was no agent of the British government.

The case against Armbrister *appeared* to be more serious, though it showed him as pathetic rather than malevolent. The young Royal Marine had been removed from his regiment for dueling with another British officer and had gone to stay with his uncle, the British governor of the Bahama Islands. Armbrister came to Florida on a holiday. To impress the Indians, he said that he was a British agent and that his uncle would be sending them arms and other supplies to use against the Americans. Armbrister was all talk—but the talk was to cost him his life. The very manner of his capture revealed how unthreatening he was. Wandering through the night with an attendant and two slaves, he simply stumbled across the American army!

Armbrister confidently threw himself on the mercy of the court. "I should have no fears, as I am in the hands of Christians," he told his captors. "I know they will not murder me." The tribunal, headed by Jackson's second-in-command, Major General Edmund Gaines, consisted of fourteen American officers. They decided the case rapidly. Alexander Arbuthnot would be hanged as a spy; Lieutenant Robert Armbrister would be shot as a spy. But the court then reconsidered and commuted the young, bumbling Armbrister's sentence to fifty lashes and a year at hard labor.

A courier brought news of the sentences to Jackson for approval. The general, who was with his troops in the field, quickly signed Arbuthnot's death warrant—but he rejected the court's clemency for Armbrister. Instead, he scribbled out an order restoring the original sentence. The ex-marine would be shot.

Jackson, as major general of the United States Army of the South, had bigger things to do than watch the execution of two spies. He marched his army off toward Pensacola, the capital of Spanish Florida. Jackson's aim was to seize the principal Spanish forts and to ship the colonial governor off to Havana, Cuba. He believed (and so, he thought, did President Monroe) that the Seminole threat could never be ended while Spain kept Florida.

Armbrister still could not believe that he was to die. Frantically, he demanded to know whether Jackson had left a pardon before marching away. He had not. Still, it took the dread music of fife and drum summoning the firing squad to convince the ebullient Armbrister of his doom. "I have heard that sound in every corner of the globe," he reflected quietly, "and now I hear it for the last time." The shots rang out a few minutes later; Armbrister collapsed in the dirt; and several soldiers rowed Arbuthnot out to his ship. As the rope went around his neck, the Scotsman swore that Great Britain would avenge his death. The Americans let his body hang for about twenty minutes before cutting it down.

Arbuthnot's threat almost came true. London exploded with anger at the news of the executions. In the streets and in newspaper columns, Jackson and other Americans were damned as murderers. War would have been declared, admitted the foreign secretary, "if the Ministry had but held up a finger." But the British then had more than enough problems in Europe to keep them occupied, and a third war with America was out of the question.

Jackson had more to fear from his own government. When word of the executions, and of his occupation of Spanish Florida, reached Washington, President James Monroe and all but one cabinet member favored relieving Jackson of his command immediately. Fortunately for the general, the lone dissenter, Secretary of State John Quincy Adams, persuaded the others not to admit American fault. Adams, a leading authority on international law (among other things), promised his colleagues that he could justify Jackson's activities and defend the United States position.

"It is an established principle of the laws of nations," Jackson had argued in ordering the executions, "that any individual of a nation making war against the citizens of another nation, they being at peace, forfeits his allegiance, and becomes an outlaw and a pirate." Unfortunately, nobody but Jackson had heard of any such "principle." So Adams's defense had to be a masterpiece of legal distortions and diversions. Rather than defend the lawfulness of Jackson's actions themselves, Adams (like Jackson) went on the attack. He denounced Arbuthnot as a "pretended trader" and argued that anyone who aided "savages" to fight civilized nations could not claim protection under the rules of war. Furthermore, while agreeing *in principle* that all occupied territory in Florida should be returned to Spain (Adams was then negotiating for American purchase of the territory), the secretary refused to admit that Jackson had been wrong to seize the Spanish forts. On the essential points, in short, Adams argued for Jackson's correctness.

After defeating the Seminoles and the Spaniards in Florida, Jackson had returned to the Hermitage, his plantation manor house outside Nashville, Tennessee. There he learned that opponents of the Monroe administration, led by the ambitious Speaker of the House of Representatives, Kentucky's Henry Clay, planned a thorough investigation. Jackson decided to make the long ride to Washington to defend his actions. He had no intention of answering to Congress for his behavior or of letting rival politicians in the capital bandy his name about. If Congress insisted on stirring up the issue, Jackson would make them answer directly to him. This was hardly an idle boast, considering his character, his ambitions, and—especially—his past.

In 1788, Andrew Jackson had crossed the Appalachian Mountains into Tennessee (then part of North Carolina) with a horse, a slave girl he had bought for two hundred dollars, and a commission as traveling prosecutor. The twenty-one-year-old lawyer was accompanying a friend to a new town called Nashville. The friend had been lucky enough to obtain appointment as a judge in the new community, and Jackson tagged along, hoping to secure a good position there also.

His legal training and knowledge were decidedly limited. Jackson had experienced one personal tragedy after another from his earliest days (his father had died shortly before his birth in 1767; his two brothers and his mother had all died of war wounds or epidemic diseases during the Revolution), and he had attended school only irregularly. To the end of his long life—he died in 1845—Jackson might spell a word two or three different ways in the same document or letter. The best that any well-disposed friend could claim for him was that at least he spelled better than either Washington or Napoleon. Jackson had gathered his scant store of legal knowledge by reading law in an attorney's office in western North Carolina for two years. But a good deal of that time had been spent not at study but in taverns and at racetracks; and very early in his young manhood, Jackson had fought the first of his several duels.

Still, to impose the law upon a frontier territory such as Tennessee, determination and physical courage were often more important than legal acumen. Jackson and his fellow lawyers traveled the state with knife and rifle close at hand. And if, at times, he had to *catch* a suspected criminal before he could prosecute, Jackson could handle that as well.

His tall, lanky figure, topped with a shock of red hair and blazing blue eyes, became well known throughout the new state. Men feared his temper but, at the same time, respected his courage and honesty. When Tennessee entered the Union in 1796, Jackson, then a twenty-nine-year-old prosecutor (and protégé of the state's first governor, William Blount), served as delegate to the convention that wrote the Tennessee constitution. He soon became the state's first member of the House of Representatives, a passionate supporter of Jefferson's Democratic-Republican party.

Philadelphia, then the nation's capital, failed to charm the new congressman, and, in turn, even a leader of his own party found him an "uncouth-looking personage, with manners of a rough backwoodsman." An extreme anti-Federalist, Jackson opposed a resolution praising the previous administration and wishing ex-President Washington a pleasant retirement. Jackson also refused to wear a powdered wig, then the fashion, and instead wrapped his long hair in an eel skin. Nor did he care much for all the talk and paperwork of Congress. He soon resigned his House seat, but political duty then dictated that he accept a promotion to the United States Senate. Blount, his benefactor, had been expelled from that body in 1797, so Jackson went back to serve during one Senate session. Again, he resigned as soon as Congress adjourned.

By that time Jackson's personal affairs, both financial and domestic, required his full attention. Although he had rapidly grown wealthy in

Rachel Donelson Robards Jackson, born in Virginia in 1767, migrated with her family to a frontier Kentucky farm and later to Tennessee. After her turbulent early marriage to Lewis Robards, and her two weddings to Andrew Jackson (both before and after her divorce), she managed the Hermitage, from which Jackson was frequently absent, and raised a dozen foster children, mainly the sons of relatives. She died shortly after Jackson's election in 1828. (Library of Congress)

land speculation, a panic in 1795 had wiped away most of his gains and left Jackson with an abiding suspicion of banks and paper money. It would take him nearly nineteen years to climb out of debt.

Jackson had also acquired a wife, in 1791. Rachel Donelson Robards, recalled one contemporary, was "irresistible to men." They admired her figure and her dark eyes, and even forgave her addiction to smoking a corncob pipe. At first meeting, Jackson found her enchanting. He also found her married, although she and her husband, Lewis Robards, already lived apart. Jackson clearly played an important role in making the couple's separation permanent. On hearing that Rachel's husband was approaching Nashville in an unpleasant frame of mind, Jackson escorted Rachel out of danger and down to the Mississippi River port town of Natchez. Frontier social mores were reasonably permissive for their day, but Jackson's three-hundred-mile, unchaperoned trip with another man's wife raised eyebrows and caused gossip. Upon reaching Natchez, the couple heard that Robards had obtained a divorce. Andrew and Rachel were promptly and happily married.

Too promptly, as it turned out. For Rachel's first husband had not yet obtained a final divorce decree; he had only started proceedings for one. For two years before the true situation was uncovered, the Jacksons unwittingly lived in adultery and bigamy. When they discovered the confusion, and after Rachel's divorce from Robards had finally taken effect, Andrew and Rachel went through another marriage ceremony. But even

In a duel fought in 1806, Charles Dickinson meets his match and his fate at the hands of Andrew Jackson. (Granger Collection)

this did not prevent the tangled episode from plaguing the Jacksons for the rest of their lives.

Tennesseans, however, rarely discussed Jackson's marital affairs in public, since the duel still settled many personal disputes in that day. Even the most amusing bit of gossip at Andrew Jackson's expense seemed too costly if it meant a challenge from the hot-tempered Jackson to meet over pistols. Nashville's lack of interest was even more pronounced after Charles Dickinson's experience in 1806.

Jackson's quarrel with Dickinson began over a horse race. But it assumed an uglier dimension when the latter made disparaging allusions to Rachel Jackson. Jackson's second son called on Dickinson and arranged a meeting over pistols at dawn across the border in Kentucky. According to the rules of the dueling code, combatants faced each other twenty-four paces apart and fired once upon command. The seconds then reloaded pistols for another exchange — if necessary.

Charles Dickinson was an accomplished marksman; his seconds rarely had to reload. Dickinson had a reputation as a sure shot and boasted that he would kill Jackson with his first bullet. Jackson, not a quick shooter, decided to let Dickinson fire first. Even if hit, he reasoned, his willpower would sustain him until he had killed the man who had maligned his wife.

The opponents stood and awaited the signal. On the cry of "Fire!" Dickinson's arm flashed out and a gunshot pierced the early morning silence. But Jackson did not fall. He did not even move. His second saw only a puff of dust arise from his jacket.

"Oh God!" cried the horrified Dickinson, stumbling backward. "Can I have missed him?" For answer, he heard only Jackson's second say sharply, "Back to the mark, sir!" Dickinson returned to his position. Jackson carefully sighted along the barrel of his gun and shot his enemy down. The bullet split an artery and Dickinson died that evening.

Only after Dickinson had been carried off to bleed to death did a servant boy notice that Jackson's right boot was full of blood. The victor now opened his coat, and his second saw for the first time where Dickinson's bullet had lodged. It had missed Jackson's heart by inches, breaking two ribs. But Jackson had refused to give his opponent the satisfaction of knowing that he had been hit. "I would have killed him," Jackson swore later, "even if he had shot me through the brain."

Charles Dickinson had many friends and influential allies, so Jackson's revenge proved costly at first to his political ambitions. For the next six years he lived quietly on his cotton plantation. When Congress declared war on Britain in 1812, however, Jackson soon regained his old rank (acquired years earlier) as major general of the Tennessee militia. Although as untrained in war as he had been when starting out as a lawyer, Jackson led three expeditions during the war.

The first campaign, though aborted, helped build his public reputation. Residents of Tennessee and Georgia liked the idea of acquiring Florida from Spain—by force if necessary—and Jackson shared their goal. He assured the secretary of war that his men, unlike certain militia units from Northern states who had refused to cross into Canada, had "no constitutional scruples, and, if the Government orders, will rejoice at the opportunity of placing the American eagle on the ramparts" of Spain's Florida forts.

Thus, by early 1813, Jackson had marched with several thousand volunteer soldiers to Natchez and stood poised to invade eastern Florida. President Madison and Congress decided otherwise. The military authorities in Washington ordered Jackson to dismiss his troops and thank them but said nothing about pay, provisions, or transport for their return home. Jackson was furious and reassured his men that, if necessary, he would march them back "on my own means and responsibility." Although the general's worth as a military strategist was still untested, the combination of devotion to his men with stern enforcement of discipline among them had earned Jackson the affectionate yet appropriate nickname "Old Hickory" (a wood noted for its toughness).

In his second campaign, the quarrelsome major general fought Indians and not American bureaucrats, building a personal legend. Jackson was recovering from wounds received in a brawl with Thomas Hart Benton (later a senator from Missouri) and his brother Jesse. One of the Bentons had put a bullet in Jackson's shoulder, where it remained when Jackson set out in 1813 to fight the Creeks, the only major group of Southern Indians actively hostile to the United States during the War of 1812. On the way into Creek territory (in what is Alabama today) Jackson had to threaten personally to shoot those militiamen whose one-year enlistment period had expired and who wished to return to Tennessee. In March 1814 his troops won a decisive victory over the Creeks at Horseshoe Bend on the Tallapoosa River. Ten times as many Indians as whites died in the battle, and the surviving Creeks fled into Spanish territory.

Jackson's third campaign of the war, against the British at New Orleans, assured him lasting fame. When Andrew Jackson arrived in New

Andrew Jackson's victory over the Creeks at Horseshoe Bend, when he was 46, not only established his national reputation as an Indian fighter, but resulted in his promotion from a Tennessee militia general to commander of the southern division of the regular army. In this climactic battle of the long Creek War, 800 out of 1000 Creek warriors were killed, the greatest number in any Indian battle, although there were few casualties among Jackson's troops and Indian allies.

Orleans in December 1814 with only two thousand troops, chances for additional victories appeared remote. Despite his victory over the Creeks and his commission as a major general in the regular army, many felt that he did not fit the part of a great general. Certainly he did not look it. An aristocratic Creole lady caught one glimpse of Jackson and winced; he resembled a "Kaintuck flatboatman." Worried residents of New Orleans had further cause for complaint: Jackson had divided his forces. The latest messages from Washington had warned the general of a possible British attack at either Mobile or New Orleans. Jackson accepted that estimate until very late in 1814 and, therefore, divided his men between a force at Mobile, and one upriver at Baton Rouge, where they could move toward New Orleans *or* Mobile, depending upon where the British attacked.

Meanwhile, a thousand miles to the southeast, the British had assembled their assault fleet off the West Indian island of Jamaica. Ten thousand sailors manned the ships that would carry almost eleven thousand fighting men, veteran soldiers and marines, many of whom had taken part either in the Napoleonic Wars or in the capture and burning of Washington that spring. Jackson's uncertainty over the scene of battle was realistic, since the British did not decide on New Orleans until late November, a decision made by the admiral of the fleet, not the commanding general, who had not yet arrived. (In matters of mismanagement, disorganization, and upset timetables, the professional British military proved every bit as adept as the amateur Americans.)

The enemy's army commander, Major General Sir Edward Pakenham, had served ably against the French forces in Spain. When he caught up with his armada, he agreed that New Orleans, near the mouth of the Mississippi, represented a far more valuable prize than Mobile. The British also hoped that the French residents of Louisiana, who had been Americans for only a dozen years—that is, since the Louisiana Purchase —would refuse to fight for the Stars and Stripes (the same mistake made by Americans invading Canada in 1812, who had convinced themselves that French Canadians would turn on the British and help the invaders). Pakenham carried with him a royal commission as governor of Louisiana. Once he had pushed out the Americans, he would rule, in trust for Spain, all the territory "fraudulently conveyed by [Napoleon] Bonaparte to the United States."

The British hoped to improve their chances still more by enlisting the help of the pirates of Barataria Bay for the invasion. From this inlet one hundred miles south of New Orleans, Jean Lafitte, himself a landloving businessman (although many called him a "pirate"), directed a very profitable operation against all sorts of shipping. Louisiana's Creole leaders regarded the Baratarians tolerantly, and Lafitte was willing to dicker with all sides. Britain offered him cash (something he always needed), plus amnesty and a Royal Navy commission (neither of which he needed), if he would fight against the Americans.

To make the most of a tangled situation, Lafitte now wrote to the governor of Louisiana. The governor had recently put a $500 price on Lafitte's head—the pirate had responded by offering a $30,000 reward for the governor's. But such acrimony was now behind him. Calling himself "a lost sheep who desires to return to the fold," Lafitte promised, if not to reform, at least to fight the British. When Jackson heard this, he ignored his previous description of the Baratarians as "hellish banditti" in the pay of the British and graciously accepted the pirates as allies. Soon afterward, Lafitte's brother managed somehow to escape from jail.

The general's quick and positive response to Lafitte showed his awareness of his side's weakness. Even with his Tennesseans, the Baratarians, Creole businessmen of the city militia, the Kentucky sharpshooters, and a group of friendly Choctaw Indians, Jackson needed more troops. He agreed to use two battalions of New Orleans free blacks, already organized, as well as a third battalion which was quickly shaped up, to form a regiment. Jackson appointed white officers for the unit, but let the soldiers select their own noncommissioned officers. To an army paymaster reluctant to disburse wages to the new regiment, Jackson sent a curt note: "Be pleased to keep to yourself your opinions upon the policy of making payments to particular corps."

Earlier, Jackson had been undecided about which city the British would attack. Now he faltered briefly in guarding against their invasion route. Although all approaches to New Orleans had been ordered blocked, the Tennessean had not ensured that the job was actually done. Nor had he acquired sufficient supplies for his troops. Two days before Christmas, he first learned that the enemy was encamped nine miles from the city. They had moved two thousand men up through an unguarded bayou. A prudent (and less effective) general might have immediately concentrated on his fortifications. "Gentlemen, the British are below," Jackson announced to his officers. "We will fight them tonight." The ensuing battle, a night attack by the Americans, was a standoff, with about equal casualties on both sides — but it saved New Orleans. Reasoning that Jackson must command overpowering force (fifteen thousand men at least) to come out and attack in that risky fashion, the British commander decided to advance no farther. That gave Jackson two vital weeks to organize his forces.

Preparations for battle continued on both sides over the Christmas holidays. Pakenham brought seventeen heavy cannon from his ships. But he never established superiority in artillery, a mistake that would cost him dearly. On January 4, 1815, a large Kentucky militia contingent marched into the American camp, but few of the men even had rifles. "I don't believe it," Jackson supposedly complained. "I have never seen a Kentuckian without a gun and a pack of cards and a bottle of whiskey in my life." As Jackson rode off to the front line, a New Orleans resident asked him if the women should leave the city. "Say to the ladies not to be uneasy," answered the general. "No British soldier shall enter this city unless over my dead body." The remark seemed, at that moment, as much a prediction of things to come as a promise of safety.

At six o'clock on the morning of January 8, the Americans saw two red rockets streak up from the British lines. This, they knew, signaled an attack. The band of Battalion d'Orleans struck up "Yankee Doodle," as the Americans waited. Except for the artillery, Jackson's troops would hold their fire until the British came within two hundred yards. In the heavy fog and early-morning semidarkness, the defenders, four deep behind their mud and timber wall, could hear the bagpipes of the Ninety-third Highlanders before they could see anything. When the breeze cleared patches in the fog, they began to distinguish the many lines of British troops still off in the distance but approaching at a measured pace. The red-coated British infantry had pushed the French out of North America, twice driven back American invasions of Canada, and just defeated Napoleon. Awaiting the nine thousand advancing Britishers were half as many backwoods farmers, New Orleans businessmen, newly organized free blacks, pirates, Indians, and a very few American army regulars.

Only when Jackson was sure that the redcoats were within range of his men's muskets did he give the command to fire. The American artillery, already very effective, had stopped to let some of the smoke clear from the field. Hundreds of rifles barked out as one, and as the front rank dropped behind to reload, the second came forward to fire. By ranging his troops in four lines, Jackson could maintain a constant wall of flame in the face of the invaders. The Baratarians, the only nonregulars on the American side who could handle cannon, helped blow great holes in the enemy lines.

Soon the advancing British had to step over the bodies of dead and wounded comrades. Their red lines first buckled and then broke under a "leaden torrent no man on earth could face," in the words of one British officer who watched the carnage. There was no lack of valor on the attackers' part, officers or enlisted men. But Jackson held a superb defensive position, with the river on one flank and a swamp on the other. When a

British flanking maneuver on the Mississippi's west bank produced no real results, the frontal attack then under way became suicidal. Pakenham, trying desperately to rally his men, caught two bullets and died on the field, as did the handful of attackers who reached the American parapet. As the troops retreated, some in panic, others more slowly, the commander of the British reserve units saw no point in continuing the slaughter, and he ordered the attack ended.

It all took less than half an hour. Two thousand British soldiers lay on the battlefield, dead or dying. The defending Americans had seven killed and six wounded. Four of the casualties were black soldiers, so eager for battle that they had left their lines to chase the retreating British. Shattered in spirit, the British invaders sailed away eleven days later, after burying their dead. They had time to dig only shallow graves, and that summer the stench of death hovered over New Orleans. The body of Pakenham, who had expected to become His Britannic Majesty's Royal Governor of Louisiana, was returned to London preserved in a barrel of rum.

In mid-February, Jackson, still governing New Orleans under martial law, finally received news from Washington. The British and American governments had signed a peace treaty at Ghent, Belgium, on December 24. The Battle of New Orleans, in short, had been fought fifteen days after the war's end.

But the two-month lag in communications was to prove of enormous benefit to the United States. By January 1815, the Americans were still mired in the war's bad news. The British burning of Washington only confirmed their military dominance in the conflict. True, a few naval victories had interrupted the parade of American defeats, but New England was demanding an end to the war at almost any cost, and talk of secession ran through Massachusetts and Connecticut. When Northerners heard nothing from New Orleans, newspapers accused President Madison of concealing the city's loss. "If an attack has been made on Orleans," despondently reasoned the New York *Post,* "the city has fallen."

Word of Jackson's victory burst upon this gloomy atmosphere, and the country went wild. "GLORIOUS!!! UNPARALLELED VICTORY!" screamed the headlines. Jackson immediately became the nation's hero and made a triumphant return from New Orleans to Nashville. Every state legislature passed a resolution of gratitude. New York's tribute, written by a young state senator named Martin Van Buren, called Jackson's triumph "an event surpassing the most heroic and wonderful achievements which adorn the annals of mankind."

The Battle of New Orleans, by removing the sting from a stalemated, often humiliating war, caught the popular imagination. Volunteers, mainly farmer soldiers, had routed England's professional troops, a fact that seemed to confirm everything Americans liked to believe about republics and democracy. (The country quickly forgot the many times during the War of 1812 when royal forces had smashed republican militiamen.) In the popular mind, Jackson's victory had proved American freemen invincible and, therefore, had demonstrated our national superi-

ority. "The Hunters of Kentucky," a minstrel show ballad about the battle, swept the country, becoming the nation's most popular song.

That a nonprofessional soldier had led the army helped swell the legend considerably. All Americans soon knew the story of Andrew Jackson, a poor orphan who had achieved wealth and influence through his own efforts. It helped considerably that Jackson was a product of the frontier, where American society seemed to be functioning in its most classless and democratic form. That Jackson had come to own a large plantation with many slaves indicated to his many enthusiasts only the extent of opportunity in America.

Jackson's friends in Tennessee watched with great interest the national wave of adulation. The country had once made a military hero president; might it not be persuaded to do so again? Their thoughts ran not to 1816, when Secretary of State James Monroe would probably run for the White House, but to 1824, by which time Monroe would have completed two terms and Jackson would still be only fifty-seven. In 1815, Jackson responded publicly to the proposal with appropriate modesty: "No sir, I know what I am fit for. I can command a body of men in a rough

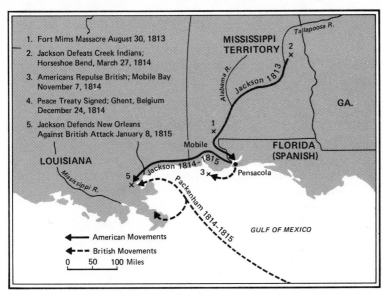

JACKSON'S MILITARY CAMPAIGNS

1. Fort Mims Massacre August 30, 1813
2. Jackson Defeats Creek Indians; Horseshoe Bend, March 27, 1814
3. Americans Repulse British; Mobile Bay November 7, 1814
4. Peace Treaty Signed; Ghent, Belgium December 24, 1814
5. Jackson Defends New Orleans Against British Attack January 8, 1815

way, but I am not fit to be President." But while Jackson, with decreasing sincerity, told this to visitors, two of his close friends published a popular biography of the hero. The Jackson legend grew still further with his conquest of Spanish Florida three years later.

Thus, the angry Jackson who approached Washington in 1819 to face official censure for his high-handed conduct in Florida bore the strengths of a popular idol and the potential of a long-shot presidential candidate. The capital was full of other hopefuls who wanted to see Jackson eliminated. Two of them, Secretary of the Treasury William Crawford and Secretary of War John C. Calhoun, had just voted in the cabinet to recall Jackson in disgrace from Florida. A third, Speaker of the House Henry Clay, would now have his turn.

The House Military Committee, which Clay controlled, had voted without dissent to recommend censure of Jackson, both for hanging Arbuthnot and shooting Armbrister and for seizing Spanish Florida. The House had then begun a twenty-seven-day debate of the censure move. During its deliberations, Jackson arrived in Washington.

The general refused to appear in public at first, remaining in his hotel until the House had voted. Jackson boiled with rage at his accusers, feeling that he had not only done nothing wrong but had carried out the accepted policy of the Monroe administration. Secretary of State Adams tried to calm Jackson, assuring the general that his conduct could be justified by the great theoreticians of international law, Grotius, Vattel, and Puffendorf. "Damn Grotius! Damn Vattel! Damn Puffendorf!" exploded Jackson. "This is a matter between Jim Monroe and myself."

Clay led off the House debate with a long warning of the danger military heroes posed to democracies. He later denied implying that he meant to indict Jackson as a threat to the government, but if Clay's speech did not mean that, it meant nothing. Jackson believed deeply in the Constitution and in democratic civil government. No accusation could have infuriated him more, and from that day Jackson, an unrelenting hater, hated Henry Clay.

But Jackson also had brilliant defenders in the House, led by the Tennessee delegation. The representatives of the Southwest believed, as Jackson did, that only firm action could deal with the Indian menace to settlements on the frontier. On the final vote, the House not only refused, by a vote of 90 to 54, to condemn Jackson for the executions, but, by a 91-to-65 tally, it endorsed his seizure of Florida.

Vindicated, the hero of New Orleans now emerged from his hotel in triumph and journeyed to celebrations in his honor held at Philadelphia and New York. On these occasions, only once did anyone have the temerity to raise the subject of Arbuthnot and Armbrister. "They were spies," answered Jackson coldly. "They ought to have been executed. And I tell you, sir, that I would do the same thing again."

Jackson returned to Washington to find that the Senate had launched its own investigation of his conduct in Florida. But the Senate soon lost interest, and when the United States finally bought Florida from Spain two years later, Monroe sent Jackson there as territorial governor. Jackson accepted the job for a short time—as a symbol of vindication rather than because of any real interest in the post. He returned to Tennessee within a year.

A very different Andrew Jackson appeared in Washington in December 1823 as United States senator and candidate for president. Since spring, he and his friends had been writing amiable, fence-mending letters to political figures in all parts of the country, and Jackson now even spoke and wrote an occasional kind word or two about his old enemies. "General Jackson's manners," admitted an opponent, "are now more presidential than those of any of the candidates." But such niceties were soon forgotten when Jackson suddenly indulged himself in one of those outbursts of temper for which he was famous. The cause this time was political.

Four rivals for the White House, all more experienced in politics than he, now confronted the new senator from Tennessee. William Crawford claimed the support of the old Republicans, including Jefferson himself. John Quincy Adams, son of the only Northern president, counted on the united vote of New England. John C. Calhoun, younger than the rest, would become a major candidate if, as he expected, Pennsylvania lined up with the South on his behalf. Clay of Kentucky represented the young West and a program of high tariffs and government aid to economic development. None of the four professional politicians considered Jackson, although a national hero, to be a major threat. Adams indirectly offered him the vice-presidency, which, Adams suggested, "would offer an easy and dignified retirement to his old age." (The considerate Adams was exactly 118 days younger than Jackson.)

Two events swiftly altered the situation. Crawford, considered to be the front-runner, suffered a stroke. Although his supporters gamely predicted recovery, they found it difficult to press the claims of a man who could neither move nor speak. Then, several months later, a Calhoun meeting in Pennsylvania overruled its chairman and endorsed Jackson. The secretary of war now shelved his dreams of the presidency and announced himself as a vice-presidential candidate under Jackson.

Thus, the hero of New Orleans, without having taken a public stand on any major issue, became almost overnight the leading candidate for the White House. Professional politicians could not understand his popular appeal. But many ordinary Americans saw Jackson as a simple and able person who had already served his country well and now asked only for the chance to serve again—a man of action, not words, who scorned the tangled political world of party machines, caucuses, and Eastern business interests. When skeptics asked where Jackson stood on the issues of the day, his followers replied with rapturous descriptions of the Battle of New Orleans.

In 1824, the states of the Union chose presidential electors on different days and by various methods. But long before the last returns reached Washington from Louisiana (by this time a state), it became clear that no candidate had won a majority. Adams's strength was concentrated in the Northeast; Crawford's in three Southern states; and Clay's in the West. Only Jackson could point to national support, having won eleven states from New Jersey to Illinois and southward to Calhoun's South Carolina. But even with his ninety-nine electoral votes, Jackson had still finished thirty-two short of victory. The House of Representatives would choose the new president.

This should have worked to the advantage of Clay, Speaker and virtual ruler of the House. But the Constitution states that the House can choose only among the top three contenders, and Clay had finished fourth, a few votes behind Crawford. The other candidates quickly recognized that Clay, although he could not himself attain the presidency, would probably determine who among them would gain the office. Emissaries of Adams, Jackson, and Crawford soon besieged the Speaker. Clay enjoyed the attention, but he had vowed that, having missed the presidency this time, he would negotiate primarily with a view to improving his chances for the future.

Every political reason led him to support Adams. Both Clay and Jackson came from the Southwest, but Clay would be more likely to succeed a New Englander like Adams. Even were Jackson, if acclaimed president, to name Clay secretary of state, Calhoun, who had been elected vice-president, would surely press his prior claim to be Jackson's heir. Also, although this probably did not greatly influence the Speaker, his political stance corresponded closely with Adams's beliefs. Finally, Clay did not think that Jackson would make a good president. "I cannot believe," he wrote a friend, "that killing two thousand five hundred Englishmen at

New Orleans qualifies a man for the various difficult and complicated duties of the Chief Magistracy."

Clay met with Adams on January 9, 1825. Communications between cities were slow at the time, but news traveled fast through Washington—then, as it does today. Within hours, the capital knew that Speaker Clay had joined with Secretary of State Adams. Jacksonians fumed indignantly, still hoping that Adams could be stopped. Each state would cast one vote in the House, and Adams needed thirteen for victory. New York, still in doubt, could provide the thirteenth vote. For a month, pro- and anti-Jackson forces worked to gain the New York vote. It boiled down to the decision of a vacillating and aged New York Dutch aristocrat, Steven Van Rensselaer. First Clay and Daniel Webster, then Jackson's supporter Martin Van Buren, extracted promises of support from the eighty-one-year-old congressman. On election day, February 9, Van Rensselaer, confused and undecided, tottered onto the House floor. As tellers passed the ballot box around, he looked upward for heavenly guidance. Receiving none, he hung his head and saw an Adams ballot at his feet. Convinced that the Almighty works in mysterious ways, Van Rensselaer picked up the slip and put it in the box. John Quincy Adams would be president of the United States.

For the second time, the House of Representatives—as in 1801—had chosen the president. The process, though constitutionally correct, produced a national uproar. Jackson and his followers felt deprived, if not defrauded outright. When Adams named Clay his secretary of state, they unleashed a storm of protest. "The Judas of the West has closed the contract," raged Jackson, "and will receive the thirty pieces of silver." Jackson, offended but hardly Christlike, was playing sarcastically upon one of Henry Clay's nicknames, "Harry of the West." In the Senate, Jackson and fourteen others voted unsuccessfully to block Clay's confirmation.

Soon after Adams's inauguration, Jackson resigned from the Senate. The Tennessee legislature had again nominated him for president. Jacksonians in all parts of the country, convinced that their man had been cheated out of the White House, now impatiently awaited the 1828 rematch. While they still boasted of New Orleans, they now also denounced the Adams–Clay "corrupt bargain," in which the presidency had been bought and sold. "Why is Adams on shaky ground?" ran a popular riddle spread by Jackson's friends. The answer: "Because he stands on slippery Clay." Administration members tried vainly to deny the charges —and their denials only gave more currency to the accusation. Politically the issue ruined Clay for years.

Jacksonians received additional assistance from Adams's policy proposals. The president sent to Congress an ambitious national economic program, one calling for a higher tariff, government sponsorship of road and canal construction, and even a national university. Adams also recommended that the federal government operate a chain of observatories, or what he called "lighthouses of the skies." Old-line Jeffersonians, who still believed in limiting the powers and activities of the federal government, reacted in horror. The younger Adams seemed to them as much a Federalist as his father, perhaps more of one, and in 1828 many of the Old Republicans took shelter in Jackson's camp.

The Jackson forces organized efficiently for the next presidential election. They established hard-hitting, sometimes slanderous, newspapers across the country. By denouncing Adams and Clay at countless rallies and ridiculing the president's call for astronomical "lighthouses," they gave a decided anti-intellectual tone to the Democratic campaign. In Congress, led by Martin Van Buren of New York, Jackson men obstructed most administration moves. Many federal officeholders, from the postmaster general on down, worked openly for Jackson, and Adams refused to stop them. The upright New Englander did not believe in firing government officials for political reasons.

But, as the election approached, Clay rallied the administration (National Republican) forces into a semblance of a counterattack. They circulated thousands of copies of the "Coffin Handbill"—a campaign document charging Jackson with the unjust and merciless hanging of six militiamen in 1815. They raked up the story of his duels with Charles Dickinson and others and invented many more incidents of Jackson's mayhem. Worst of all, at least in the candidate's mind, they reopened the subject of Jackson's marriage. "Ought a convicted adulteress," inquired one editor unctuously, "and her paramour husband to be placed in the highest office of this free and Christian land?"

On this subject, Jackson did not have control over his rage. He considered Clay responsible for the attacks and called the secretary of state "the basest, meanest scoundrel that ever disgraced the image of his God." Jackson's advisers kept him, with difficulty, from challenging Clay to a duel, and they lived in fear that Jackson would do something to ruin their carefully planned campaign. "For Heaven's sake, for your country's sake," warned one friend, "do remember that but one man can write you down—and his name is Andrew Jackson."

Politicians who thought they had seen everything watched the campaign of 1828 in shock. Torchlight parades and libelous attacks on opponents would apparently decide the next president. From a thousand stumps and platforms, the Jacksonians denounced the "corrupt bargain" and the "lighthouses of the skies." The old general, they cried, was a man of the people; Adams was a Boston aristocrat who had installed a billiard table in the White House! The supporters of Adams dismissed Jackson as an illiterate and an adulterer, a military chieftain who endangered the liberties of all Americans. Supporters of Jackson retaliated by suggesting that Adams, a former Harvard College professor and professional diplomat, had acted as a pimp for the czar of Russia while serving as minister to St. Petersburg! Both sides resorted time and again to such absurd charges. No slander was too vile or unjust to be rejected by the supporters of either candidate.

Except perhaps for the size of Jackson's majority, the election result surprised few people. The military hero and uncertain speller had swept the West and the South, while also taking Pennsylvania. Adams won only New England, New Jersey, and half of the New York vote. And, in a statistic then calculated for the first time—the popular vote—Jackson led Adams by 150,000. Four times as many men voted in 1828 as had voted four years before, slightly more than half of all those eligible.

At the peak of Jackson's triumph, Rachel Jackson died. Her husband refused to accept that fact and spent an entire night sitting beside her lifeless body. For the rest of his life, Jackson believed that campaign slander had killed his beloved wife. As he had done in 1819 and again in 1823, Jackson began the long trip by horse and flatboat from Nashville to Washington. But the president-elect now journeyed in sorrow. "May God forgive her traducers," he told a friend. "I know that I never shall."

Meanwhile, Washington nervously awaited the coming of its new leader. The capital had known its past presidents well—they had lived there, holding high political offices before moving into the White House. But, except for his brief service in House and Senate, Jackson had not. Washingtonians knew of him mainly by rumors, most of which they hoped were untrue. As one uneasy resident wrote: "General Jackson will be here [about] 15. of Feb—Nobody knows what he will do. My opinion is that when he comes he will bring a breeze with him. Which way it will blow I cannot tell."

14 The Jacksonian Era

Jackson brought more than a breeze with him; within weeks his political enemies were calling it a hurricane. In the eight years before Old Hickory returned to his home at the Hermitage, he permanently remodeled and strengthened the office of the presidency. Moreover, he helped to create a new political party system and to recast the electorate's ideas of what is expected from government.

Before the 1820s, politics in the United States had worked in a relatively genteel fashion. Most states had limited the right to vote to male property owners, and in both the North and the South, wealthy merchants or large landowners had dominated public affairs. Many states had come to be so thoroughly under the control of one party—the Federalist or the Jeffersonian Republican party—that competition hardly existed. Presidential elections in those times were very different from the bitter Jackson–Adams contest of 1828.

This genteel state of affairs had begun to change long before Jackson entered the White House, but the country's first frontier president clearly helped to speed up the process.

THE ERA OF GOOD FEELINGS

At the time that Jackson threw back the British at New Orleans, American politics had already begun to change. The declining Federalists were further weakened by charges of wartime disloyalty because of the Hartford Convention, and by 1820 they had all but disappeared. For nearly ten years a so-called Era of Good Feelings characterized the political scene, with political competitions occurring mainly among groups within the all-powerful Republican party.

This all-inclusive Republican party was not the same one that Jefferson had fashioned. When the war ended, Republicans adopted some of the same measures that they had condemned in the past. This proved especially true with regard to the national bank and the tariff.

The Second Bank of the United States, a corporation with both private and public directors, chartered in 1816, had branches in the major cities and provided most of what little regulation existed of the American financial system. As Jackson rose steadily to power in the 1820s, so did the bank, on a collision course that would provoke the most spectacular political confrontation of the 1830s.

The same war that had made a hero of Jackson had caused the creation of his eventual adversary. The federal government had gone deeply into debt during the war, and it needed more revenue. Dozens of new banks had sprung up after the expiration of the charter of Hamilton's Bank of the United States in 1811. The state banks had operated poorly during the war, and the country now clearly needed a better financial system. The government had to pay off its debts. Moreover, there was growing pressure on it to take a more active role in promoting economic growth. Many Americans wanted federal money to be spent on building a network of roads and canals—internal improvement, as it was then called—especially west of the Appalachian Mountains.

Swallowing pride and party principles, Republicans responded to these pressures by chartering a second national bank. President Madison overcame his previous objections to such a bank. A young South Carolina representative of the Southern planter interest, John C. Calhoun, introduced the bank recharter bill. It passed in 1816, providing for a bank to run until 1836.

Andrew Jackson, seventh president of the United States, and the first president to be born in a log cabin. (Library of Congress)

Next came the tariff. Like the bank issue, debate on the tariff in 1816 began with patriotic statements and a nationwide agreement, but it ended before long in fierce political squabbling. American manufacturers, located mainly in New England, were just then getting started. They wanted higher tariff duties so that Americans would buy fewer foreign goods and more of their own products. They wanted not just a revenue tariff, to bring in funds, but a protective tariff—one set high enough to protect American producers from foreign competition.

In 1816, Calhoun and many other Southerners voted in favor of a higher, protective tariff. They did so not to enrich the New England manufacturers but to bring in the additional revenue then needed by the federal government. National security was one of their primary concerns at the time. Southerners—like Americans in all sections—feared the outbreak of yet another war with Britain, since the War of 1812 had been a standoff. The United States must be better prepared, militarily and financially, argued Southerners, than it had been in 1812.

There was less agreement on internal improvements. The country needed a better transportation system, and Congress passed a bill authorizing national funds. But here, Madison's constitutional conservatism stood in the way. Despite his lapses from Jeffersonianism on the tariff and the bank, Madison could not convince himself that the federal government had the right to spend money in this way. The president vetoed the bill, and for the next two generations each state had to build its own roads and canals.

The Federalists offered little opposition to the candidacy of Secretary of State James Monroe to be Madison's successor. And again, four years later, Monroe received every electoral vote but one for reelection. Throughout his administration, Monroe issued soothing calls for an end to all party divisions. The composition of his cabinet—with the ex-Federalist Adams in the State Department, the Old Jeffersonian Crawford of Georgia in the Treasury, and the Southern nationalist Calhoun as secretary of war—showed that all elements of the political spectrum now coexisted within the Republican party. Harmony had indeed been established in national politics—for a brief moment.

The Panic of 1819

But trouble was already brewing. The first sign was a financial panic. Since the War of 1812, people had been speculating heavily in foreign trade and Western lands. They bought on credit, hoping to reap a large profit before having to pay off their debts. Then, in 1819, the Second Bank—under new management—began calling in loans. As a result, many state banks stopped paying hard money for their notes or closed, and numerous investors went bankrupt.

The Panic of 1819—the first of a series of economic downturns that would continue to occur in the United States at approximately twenty-year intervals until 1929—affected the whole nation, although Western states were the hardest hit.

The national bank, then just three years old, was widely blamed for the hard times. Many Americans attacked the bank as a corrupting agent of aristocracy and privilege, and several state legislatures tried to tax its branches out of existence. The Supreme Court ruled such laws unconstitutional. But the strong antibank feelings that had surfaced never really disappeared. Politicians would capitalize on them throughout the 1820s, and Jackson would find in such feelings a reservoir of political support during the 1830s.

Americans had distrusted banks even during the colonial period—often with good reason, given the high rate of bank failures. In the 1820s, Kentucky and Tennessee witnessed "relief wars," during which debtors organized against creditors. Everywhere, private banking interests were on the defensive. These struggles were a prelude to the Jacksonian battles of the 1830s. They also provided a training ground for several important politicians who would later join Jackson's antibank crusade.

The Missouri Compromise

Another sign that the short-lived Era of Good Feelings (1816–24) had its own tensions came when the always troublesome problem of slavery surfaced again. In the same year as the panic, the issue of statehood for Missouri came to a head. The Missouri Territory was part of the original Louisiana Purchase. Its residents had applied for admission to the Union in 1817. But, at the time, a congressman from New York had demanded that slavery be prohibited in the state as the price of admission. The uneasy sectional truce on the question of slavery quickly evaporated. Congress was deadlocked on the issue for over a year. Southerners had equal voting strength in the Senate, since the nation then had the same number of slave states and free states. Northerners controlled the House of Representatives, however, because the North had acquired a larger population since 1789. Antislavery representatives argued that Congress could and should make prohibition of slavery a condition for admitting new states. Southerners retorted that all states, old or new, were sovereign and could decide the matter of slavery for themselves.

The very mention of the slavery question in Congress terrorized Southerners. As the struggle went on in Congress, Richmond, Virginia, was said to be as "agitated as if affected by all the Volcanic Eruptions of Vesuvius." Southerners, who always suspected that the North wanted to destroy their "peculiar institution" of slavery, now felt their suspicions confirmed. They readied themselves for a long fight on what they considered a life-or-death issue. "To compromise is to acknowledge the right of Congress to interfere and to legislate on the subject," wrote one prominent Southern politician; "this would be acknowledging too much."

Yet compromise they did, when Maine, then a district of Massachusetts, petitioned Congress to become a separate state. Southerners would not admit Maine as a free state unless Missouri joined the Union with the right to permit slavery. Henry Clay, Speaker of the House and a Kentucky slaveholder more identified with the West than with the South, now piloted a three-part compromise through Congress, with a different coalition backing each part. Maine would be admitted as a free state, Missouri as a slave state, and slavery would be banned in the remaining areas of the Louisiana Purchase and in future acquisitions above 36°30' latitude.

The Missouri crisis frightened Americans in the North and West as well as in the South and with good reason. They knew that truly national politics and parties could not exist if slavery became an active issue bitterly dividing the sections of the country. This "momentous question, like a fire-bell in the night, awakened and filled me with terror," wrote Jefferson, in retirement at Monticello. "I considered it once as the knell of the Union . . . this is a reprieve only, not a final sentence." Many other anxious politicians agreed with this analysis, although few were willing to admit it publicly.

The South in particular regarded the compromise uneasily, especially its limitation on the future expansion of slavery. "Instead of joy," one Southern editor mourned, "we scarcely ever recollect to have tasted of a bitterer cup." All three Southerners in Monroe's cabinet advised him that the restriction of slavery was unconstitutional. Sixty percent of the Southern congressmen who voted for the compromise were not returned to the next Congress.

Both Southerners and Northerners now hoped that the slavery issue could be kept quietly localized. The Missouri debates had exposed the deep division between supporters and opponents of slavery. These sectional issues and attitudes had the power to rip the Union apart. Throughout the Age of Jackson, however, politicians would strive to keep the slavery genie bottled up.

In President James Monroe's annual message to Congress on December 2, 1823, he included the principles of foreign policy later known as the Monroe Doctrine. Monroe and his Secretary of State, John Quincy Adams, wanted to clarify the American position in two specific problem areas. They succeeded in a wider sense, as one historian states, by planting their principles "firmly in the national consciousness."

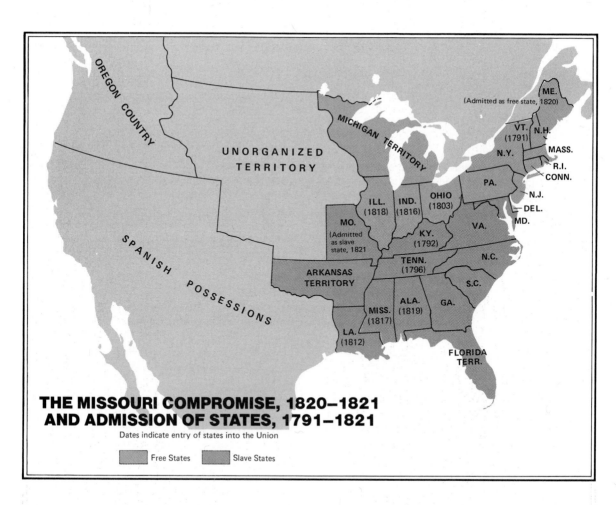

THE MISSOURI COMPROMISE, 1820–1821 AND ADMISSION OF STATES, 1791–1821

Dates indicate entry of states into the Union

Free States Slave States

The first problem area was the Northwest. Since 1821 Russia had been encroaching on the Oregon country, claimed jointly by Britain and the United States. In October 1823, Adams stated bluntly that "the American continents are no longer subjects for any new European establishments." This principle was repeated in Monroe's speech.

South America was the second problem area. Eight new republics had declared their independence from Spain, but their existence was precarious. Despotic regimes in Europe were successfully crushing revolutions on the Continent, and it was evident that Spain was eager to regain her lost colonies. In August 1823 the English foreign secretary proposed a joint British–American manifesto to warn Europe against intervention. British merchants wanted to retain their profitable new markets in South America, now open to them after the breakup of the Spanish monopoly. And Britain could back up a threat with naval power.

Adams, however, did not want the United States to be "a cockboat in the wake of the British man-of-war." He suspected that the British might restrict American expansion in some way as a price for their support. Also, Britain had not officially recognized the new republics, as the United States was doing. So Adams suggested an independent course of action. Monroe agreed and decided to include a warning in his message to Congress.

Monroe declared that intervention by European monarchies in the democracies of the New World would be judged as "the manifestation of an unfriendly disposition toward the United States." He pledged the United States not to interfere with any existing European colonies in the New World and to keep out of the "internal concerns" of Europe.

The speech was acclaimed at home but viewed abroad as "arrogant." Yet the European powers took no action. Why? Two months earlier, unknown to Adams and Monroe, the English had pressured France to agree not to assist Spain in any invasion of her ex-colonies. Thus the issue had already been defused. Russia, unable to gain support for intervention, withdrew its claims to the Pacific Northwest early in 1824. The South American republics seemed indifferent to the speech. They

President James Monroe, last of the Revolutionary era executives, has gone down in history as the co-author of the Monroe Doctrine and as the man who presided over the demise of the first American political party system. Monroe's years in office were less an "era of good feelings," however, than an era of no national parties and much factional infighting.

were more impressed with "the oaken fleets of Britain" than with "the paper shield of Monroe."

So the significance of Monroe's declaration was widely discounted at first. In years to come, however, its principles were invoked with great reverence by American nationalists, often to rationalize U.S. intervention in Latin American affairs.

A RETURN TO PARTY POLITICS

The election of 1824, as we have seen, emphatically closed out the Era of Good Feelings. It also destroyed the method that Americans had first used to select presidential candidates, the congressional caucus or party meeting. The caucus had often been denounced as aristocratic and undemocratic. After Crawford, who was nominated by this means in 1824, lost the election, nobody suggested holding another caucus in the future. Politicians had to find a new process, one that at least *seemed* more democratic.

They found the answer during the next few years in a new nominating device, the convention. Conventions were supposed to be more representative of a party's membership and thus more democratic than the caucus. Only members of the national or state legislature could attend a legislative party caucus. But, in theory, any party member could become a convention delegate. Grass-roots political elements could be represented at a convention, as could groups or factions that had not been able to elect their leaders to Congress.

This change reflected the general movement toward increasing popular participation in the governmental process. Throughout the 1820s, state constitutional conventions revised the old Revolutionary constitutions, lowering or abolishing the property qualifications for voting. More offices were now filled by direct vote of the people; in some states even presidential electors were now chosen by direct vote.

At first, old-line politicians resisted the changeover to conventions. Yet they had little to worry about. Party bosses found that it was not difficult to manipulate convention delegates. On the other hand, conventions gave the *appearance* of equality in an age when political operations were becoming more and more democratized.

For the presidential election that followed the Adams-Clay victory in the House of Representatives, Americans required neither caucus nor convention to indicate the candidates. Jacksonians hungered for their next electoral bout with John Quincy Adams. Only with a brilliantly successful administration could the president hope to fend off their challenge, and for that, Adams was the wrong man at the wrong time.

Like his father, John Adams—another crusty, stubborn, and inflexible man—John Quincy Adams believed in government by the most able and talented. Also like his father, John Quincy Adams learned quickly that such a belief did not make him popular with the majority of his fellow Americans. Adams had been preparing for the presidency all his life, but once in the White House, he found that his hands were tied. He became a minority president, without any real control over Congress. He also lacked the ability to make either himself or his programs popular with the public. Adams was bound to fail, and fail he did.

For four distressing years this very capable individual fussed and floundered. The job called for

talents Adams did not possess and could not acquire. He was reserved—a "cold fish" to most people who met him. He was short-tempered with any person he considered a fool, and he claimed to have met many—especially in politics. Most importantly, he was totally unwilling to compromise.

President Adams's expansive first message to Congress, calling for "lighthouses of the skies," ended whatever survival chances his administration might have had. It especially shocked Martin Van Buren, opposition Senate leader, political boss of New York's Albany Regency, and a confirmed Jeffersonian. Van Buren now traveled to Virginia to confer with leaders of the so-called Richmond Junto, the clique that dominated the politics of the state. Van Buren proposed a North–South Republican alliance that would not only oust Adams but prevent Adams's ideas from becoming dominant in the future.

Jackson, Van Buren argued, could accomplish the first end and would be a reasonable president. He was already very popular. He did not support the extreme states' rights position, but neither did he favor a strong national government. Furthermore, Van Buren promised that his Northerners would see that slavery was kept out of national politics. The Southern states would thus be free from antislavery attacks during Jackson's presidency, and presumably afterward as well. In short, after Jackson's victory in 1828, Van Buren wanted to revive the coalition originally formed by Burr of New York and Jefferson and Madison of Virginia. Both the original Jeffersonian group and the new Jacksonian alliance were known as Democratic-Republicans. But the Jeffersonians were more generally referred to as Republicans, while the Jacksonians called themselves Democrats. Anti-Jackson Republicans were first known as National Republicans, later as Whigs.

JACKSON AS PRESIDENT

Few people knew what would happen when Jackson took office. He had been deliberately vague about issues while campaigning, and the Jacksonian Democrats were then more of a faction gathered about a leader than a party with a plat-

form. His inaugural address revealed little except a call for "reform." This word was political shorthand, an indication that Jackson intended to reward his friends and punish his enemies. During the previous generation of one-party, Republican rule, turnover among public officeholders had not been great. The last large-scale shift in government employees had occurred when Jefferson had become president and removed a good many Federalists from office. Since that time a Republican elite, many of them anti-Jackson, had settled cozily into federal jobs, some for a quarter century. Jacksonians understandably demanded that the new president replace these older officials with loyal Jackson supporters.

Although, in fact, Jackson went only about as far as Jefferson had, he and his supporters made more noise about it. He removed about 10 percent of the federal officeholders during his first year as president and a total of about 20 percent in eight years. It was not the clean sweep hoped for by the

Voting day in Philadelphia, as elsewhere in the Jacksonian era, occasioned much rowdy excitement. During this period the number of voters increased, not only because suffrage requirements were eased but also because people took more interest in politics. (Historical Society of Pennsylvania)

Democratic politicos. But the Jacksonians did radically change the nature of federal patronage, in the sense that Jackson openly defended the principle of rotation in office—what came to be known as the spoils system. He agreed with Senator William L. Marcy of New York—an associate of Van Buren— that "to the victor belong the spoils." Jackson acted on the theory (if not always the practice) that, in a democracy, persons of normal intelligence could capably fill most public offices. To Jackson's political opponents this view seemed dangerous. Yet rotation in office, at all levels of

American government, became the standard practice after Jackson and lasted for decades.

Strengthening the Office

Jackson's opponents saw him as a tyrant, an uncouth military man from the West. Obviously, this opinion did not conform to Jackson's vision of himself as an "Old Republican," a true Jeffersonian. But Republicanism had changed significantly since Jefferson's presidency. Jackson hoped to revive what he called the "Republican principles of [17]98." He did not want national power to increase at the expense of the states. Yet his role as a strong president and his ability to dramatize political issues for ordinary people in every section stimulated the growth of national power. Just as Jefferson had strained his principles to purchase Louisiana, Jackson would sometimes find his ideas fairly elastic when put to the test.

Old Hickory's "Old Republicanism" took several forms. In his first annual message, the president criticized the national bank. He also rejected the idea of a high, protective tariff. (Unlike some Southerners, however, he did not deny the tariff's constitutionality.) On the issue of internal improvements, Jackson held views like those of the Republican presidents prior to John Quincy Adams. In 1830 he vetoed the Maysville Road Bill, which would have involved the federal government in a road-building project in the state of Kentucky. He argued that such matters should be left in local hands. He believed, though, that the national government could contribute to interstate projects. This is why he favored national support for the Cumberland Road, an east–west improvement that passed through several states. Jackson received firm support on this question from Martin Van Buren, who was his secretary of state from 1829 to 1831. Van Buren's state, New York, had completed the Erie Canal in 1825 without federal money, and further major internal improvements in the state were unlikely.

Jackson did much to strengthen the American presidency. He was by far the strongest chief executive up to his time and one of the most forceful in American history. Since Jefferson's first term, power had been steadily slipping out of presi-

dential hands and into those of the Congress. Jackson, however, reversed the process.

During his eight years as president, Jackson restored the White House as the focal point of national politics. Where Congress had largely dictated to the last three presidents, Jackson now set out to manage Congress. Working closely with loyal Jacksonians like House Speaker Andrew Stevenson and Senator Thomas Hart Benton—whose bullet the President still carried in his shoulder—he tried to get Congress to support his policies and to defeat bills he did not like. Anti-administration congressmen soon found it difficult to get presidential patronage for constituents hungry for jobs. When his policies failed with Congress, Jackson had no hesitation about vetoing bills. Twelve times he refused his assent to a bill passed by both houses of Congress—three times more than his five predecessors combined. A favorite device of his was the pocket veto—delay in signing a bill until Congress adjourned. Perhaps most important, Jackson vetoed some bills just because he thought them unwise, not necessarily because he regarded them as unconstitutional.

Jackson introduced another innovation into his conduct of the office. Previously, presidents had relied for advice mainly on their cabinets, often consisting of politicians as interested in their own careers as in the nation's problems. Jackson now assembled around him his own personal advisers—a so-called kitchen cabinet that included Van Buren and two newspapermen, Francis Prescott Blair and Amos Kendall. Blair edited the administration newspaper, the Washington *Globe,* and Kendall held a minor job in the Treasury Department, but both were available to advise Jackson on strategy, to consult with party leaders, or to draft Jackson's messages to Congress.

Finally, Jackson was the undisputed head of his party, as well as leader of the government. His power in each role strengthened him in the other, and his extraordinary personal popularity helped him in both. Democrats all over the country followed the administration line as it appeared in the *Globe,* or they soon ceased to be Democrats.

Jackson brought a new concept of the presidency to the White House. Some previous occupants, as well as his political opponents, saw the president's duty as only to administer the government, while Congress, representing the people, made the laws. But Jackson saw himself as the direct representative of the American people, elected by the entire nation, with an obligation to lead the country forcefully.

The "Eaton Affair"

Dramatizing Jackson's concept of the presidency was an intensely personal issue that frayed relations between himself and his vice-president, John C. Calhoun, whose support had helped gain Jackson victory in 1828. Embittered by Jackson's evident preference in assigning cabinet posts for Van Buren and his political allies, Calhoun lost most of his remaining influence in the administration as a result of an episode that came to be known as the "Peggy Eaton affair."

Jackson enjoyed the social company of Peggy O'Neill Eaton, wife of his friend, Tennessee Senator John H. Eaton, whom the president appointed secretary of war. Mrs. Eaton was the daughter of a tavern keeper and a widow at the time she married Eaton, and other Washington wives gossiped incessantly about her morals while spreading rumors that she had engaged in a love affair with John Eaton while her former husband still lived. Once Eaton joined the cabinet, Mrs. Calhoun and other wives of leading Jackson administration officials refused all social contact with the Eatons while continuing their slander mongering.

Nothing could have guaranteed Jackson's anger toward the gossips more easily than what he treated as an obvious comparison to his political enemies' earlier slanders about his beloved dead wife Rachel. The president turned this social flap into a test of political loyalty and insisted that cabinet members deal respectfully with Mrs. Eaton. Caught between their wives and their president, most—including Calhoun—stood ground and continued to question Peggy Eaton's virtue (and virtues). Martin Van Buren, however, a widower, found it easier—and politically useful—to cultivate the Eatons' friendship, something that did not pass unnoticed by Jackson. After many months of battling within the administration over the "Eaton affair," Jackson (with the approval of Van Buren) finally forced the resignation of his entire cabinet in 1831 as a means of reorganizing it with friendlier—and more compliant—figures. Van Buren went to England as American minister where he remained until the Senate voted against his confirmation by a single vote—Calhoun's, casting a tie-breaking ballot as vice-president. The entire episode strengthened Van Buren's claims on Jackson while rupturing the president's personal links to Calhoun.

Nullification

In the crisis over nullification, Jackson most strongly demonstrated his forcefulness and his claim to represent all the American people. Trouble had been brewing over the federal tariff law for many years. In 1828 the South Carolina legislature published an *Exposition and Protest*. It branded protective tariffs as unjust and unconstitutional and termed the 1828 version, supported by Jackson, the Tariff of Abominations. Changes must come, the *Exposition* warned, or South Carolina would act.

Improbably, the man behind the *Exposition* was the vice-president of the United States, John C. Calhoun. Brilliant, ambitious, and totally humorless, Calhoun had begun his political career as a strong nationalist, favoring both a national bank and a protective tariff. But the shifting political sands of South Carolina could no longer support such a stand, and Calhoun now attempted to devise means of protecting his and other states from the national government. Like the rest of the South, he had been profoundly impressed by the Missouri crisis and felt the slave states required strong defenses against a potentially hostile national government. Explained Calhoun, "I consider the Tariff but as the occasion, rather than the real cause of the present state of things."

Calhoun thought he had found a solution in the Virginia and Kentucky resolutions, written by Madison and Jefferson in the late 1790s. He now interpreted them to mean that a state could nullify (refuse to enforce) an act of Congress that it considered unconstitutional. Obviously, the South would find Calhoun's solution extremely useful against any antislavery laws passed by Congress. The aging

Madison denied that the resolutions carried Calhoun's interpretation, but South Carolina accepted that view.

As Southern complaints about the tariff continued, Jackson tried to arrange for a compromise bill to lower import duties. But he never lost sight of the fundamental issue, state defiance of federal law. Jackson rejected nullification totally, vowing to preserve the Union by any means necessary. He applied all the power of the presidency and all the force of his personality to block nullification and denounce John Calhoun.

Nevertheless, South Carolinians went ahead and declared the 1828 tariff "null and void" in their state. What would Jackson do? Though he might compromise on tariff rates, he would not compromise federal authority. "I consider . . . the power to annul a law of the United States, assumed by one state, incompatible with the existence of the Union," he proclaimed in December 1832. South Carolina should not think that it could nullify the Constitution peacefully, and, he warned: "Disunion by armed force is treason." Jackson got Congress to pass a Force Bill reaffirming the president's right to use troops to put down rebellion and enforce the laws. In fifteen days, he wrote a South Carolina Unionist, he could send forty thousand armed troops to South Carolina to put down rebellion; in forty days, two hundred thousand. The Hero of New Orleans would not look far for a general to command them. "I repeat to the Union men, fear not, *the union will* be preserved."

Meanwhile, South Carolina had received no substantial support from other Southern states. The state's isolation left it no real hope of defending itself or nullification. Early in 1833, Clay and Calhoun worked out a compromise bill reducing tariff rates over the next ten years to an acceptable level. The nullification issue collapsed, though to save face, South Carolina declared the Force Bill unconstitutional. An armed clash had been avoided. The Union stood firm. Jackson emerged from the struggle with more strength and greater prestige than before. The president had shown character, political skill, and moral courage—all of which he would need in his next major campaign, the war against the Second Bank of the United States.

The Bank War—and After

Why did Jackson oppose the Second Bank of the United States and come to hate its president, Nicholas Biddle? As an investor, Jackson had lost money in a panic in the 1790s, and he had distrusted banks ever since. As a Jeffersonian, he regarded the bank as a dangerous institution. He thought it was too large and too national in scope. To him, it represented a concentration of economic power, created by the federal government, that endangered states' rights and the rights of the people. The Supreme Court declared the Second Bank of the United States constitutional, but Jackson felt that the president had as much right as the Court to interpret the constitution.

The existence of the bank became the primary issue in the election of 1832. Although the bank's twenty-year charter did not lapse until 1836, Biddle took the advice of Henry Clay and asked for a twenty-year recharter four years early. Clay, running for president as the National Republican candidate, needed an issue on which to challenge Jackson. Clay identified himself totally with the bank and even took on one of its attorneys as his running mate.

Jackson never refused a challenge. After Congress had passed the bank recharter bill, the president vetoed it in a stinging message drafted by Amos Kendall. The powers of the bank, he charged, were "unauthorized by the Constitution, subversive of the rights of the states, and dangerous to the liberties of the people." He called the bank an instrument used by wealthy merchants to oppress the workers and farmers. "It is to be regretted," he warned, with at least one eye on the fall elections, "that the rich and powerful too often bend the acts of government for their own purposes."

The election of 1832 transformed the *Jacksonian* party of 1828 into the *Democratic* party, a coalition with issues and a party constituency. The cementing issue was the Bank of the United States, which symbolized Democratic objections to many other kinds of concentrated government power, such as a high protective tariff and internal improvements.

The Democratic constituency largely reflected the Van Buren–Ritchie agreement of the

Peter Cooper

(The Cooper Union)

As an old man looking back, Peter Cooper said that his life had fallen into three parts — thirty years to get started, thirty years to gain a fortune, and thirty years to distribute it wisely. As inventor, manufacturer, and philanthropist, Cooper became a legendary figure. One historian called him "as distinctly an American type as Benjamin Franklin, and as quickly taken to the American heart."

Born in 1791 in New York City, the young Cooper revealed a restless nature and a talent for tinkering. As a boy, he made shoes and hats and even a simple washing machine. For his first child he devised a mechanically rocked cradle attached to a musical instrument, patented as a "Pendulous and Musical Cradle." Some of his ambitious projects, such as propelling ferryboats by compressed air, were grotesque failures. Others, such as an endless chain to haul canal boats, went unrecognized. "I was always fussing and contriving," he wrote, "and was never satisfied unless I was doing something difficult — something that had never been done before, if possible."

He came to a turning point in 1821, when he bought a glue factory in New York. It became the foundation of his fortune. In a few years he had a monopoly in the field and was able to pursue other interests. Cooper invested in real estate and railroads. In 1830, for the Baltimore and Ohio Railroad, he built and piloted the first steam locomotive in the United States, nicknamed "Tom Thumb." With a good sense of the demand for iron in an increasingly industrialized economy, he bought iron mines and ironworks, producing the first structural iron for fireproof buildings. As president of the giant North American Telegraph Company, he supported Cyrus Field in his project for laying the Atlantic cable.

In 1856 Peter Cooper calculated that he was a millionaire. So he turned to the realization of his long-held dream: a workingman's institute in New York City for "the advancement of science and art." He was painfully aware of his own lack of formal education, and yet he was distrustful of much "book learning." Thus he wanted to develop a school "so that the boys and girls of this city who had no better opportunity than I had to enjoy means of information would be enabled to better their condition." Cooper Union opened in 1859, offering free courses in science, technology, art, and design, as well as a library and a museum.

Cooper's public career included reform politics. Some of his ideas were far in advance of his time — controlled currencies, unemployment relief works programs, and government regulation of railroads. In his last years, according to one writer, he became "an unwearied figure for social justice."

Cooper's personal qualities explain the esteem in which the public held him. He had the self-confidence and optimism of the master craftsman. Though hardworking, he was never ruthless. At his funeral in 1883, this tribute was paid: "Here lies a man who never owned a dollar he could not take up to the Great White Throne."

Bank War, Stage I, 1832. President Jackson takes on Biddle's Monster, wielding his bank recharter bill veto sword. (Smithsonian Institution)

previous decade, including most of the South and most urban workers in the North. The latter Democratic constituency was steadily increasing: between 1820 and 1860, three million Irish and two million Germans streamed into the United States, most of them into the ranks of the Democratic party. The Democrats could also count on the support of many backwoods farmers of the West, who supported Jackson and disliked the Eastern bank.

In 1832, workers and farmers both saw the bank as a tool of the rich; they wanted to be paid for their labor and their crops in gold and silver, rather than in banknotes. But Jackson's supporters also included many ambitious entrepreneurs who disliked the bank for exactly the opposite reason. They felt it was restricting the flow of paper money too tightly, keeping other banks from issuing their own banknotes freely enough to encourage economic growth. But they joined with the other Jacksonians in alleging that the bank only helped to make the rich richer.

Jackson's opposition had an issue and a leader—but not much else. Henry Clay, with only the limited and ineffectual organization of the National Republican party, counted on the bank issue to provide the rest of his votes. For Clay and the National Republicans, the bank stood for many other issues. It was part of Clay's "American system," a plan of positive government action to encourage manufacturing and tie the country together. The system consisted of the bank, a high protective tariff, and extensive internal improvements. For the system, swore Clay, he "would defy the South, the President and the Devil."

The South and the president, at least, defeated Clay roundly in 1832. Whether the bank issue helped or hurt Jackson's campaign is difficult to judge. Although he improved his showing in the electoral college, he was less popular with the voters than when he had run as a fresh and untried candidate in 1828, and his percentage of the popular vote declined. Some Southerners reacted unfavorably to his anti-nullification stand, and a new party in the North called the Anti-Masons siphoned off additional votes. In fighting the bank, Jackson had seemingly raised the threat of class war. Many of his opponents, including wealthy businessmen in New York City and elsewhere, thought that he was trying to set the poor against the rich. All this was more than offset, however, by the incredibly bungled campaign waged by Clay and the National Republicans.

Having gained another four years in the White House, Jackson was convinced that the American people wished him to crush the bank forever. He was also sure that anyone who attacked the bank was for him, and anyone who supported it was against him. Those who wanted to remain Jacksonian Democrats in good standing had to join the antibank crusade. Those who felt they could not support Jackson on this issue switched over completely to the opposition. But Jackson was not a man to let such defections bother him. He would now begin the second battle of the Bank War.

Bank War, Stage II, 1833. Jackson sends the pro-Bank political and economic forces scurrying for safety. He has pulled down the Bank's foundations by ordering removal of U.S. government deposits. (Courtesy, The New-York Historical Society)

Distrusting Biddle, Jackson now wished to remove all government deposits from the bank, to weaken it, and perhaps kill it. By law, only the secretary of the treasury could order the removal of deposits. Jackson found it necessary to replace two men before he found a secretary who would remove the deposits—future Supreme Court Chief Justice Roger B. Taney. The government would now put its money into selected state banks, many of them controlled by Democrats eager to obtain interest-free government deposits. These favored institutions soon acquired the nickname "pet banks."

Biddle now counterattacked. The Philadelphia banker, a man of considerable talent and arrogance, liked to boast that he wielded, as president of the bank, more power than the president of the United States. He would not see that power destroyed without a struggle. He stopped issuing new loans and called in many that the bank had previously granted. The nation immediately plunged into a serious recession. Biddle watched the situation with satisfaction, hoping that he might yet get his recharter. "Nothing but the evidence of suffering," he explained coolly, "will produce any effect on Congress."

Many people felt that Jackson had gone too far and that both the party and the economy had been permanently damaged. Petitions poured into Congress asking for recharter of the bank. Among the thousands of signatures were the names of prominent Democratic merchants, including a sizable number from Northern cities. Some merchants, perhaps a bit braver than the rest, actually went to see Jackson to plead their case. "What do you come to me for?" asked the president, enjoying himself greatly. "Go to Nicholas Biddle. We have no money here, gentlemen. Biddle has all the money."

As calmly as he had once taken physical aim at Charles Dickinson, Jackson had taken political aim at Nicholas Biddle. Any plan aimed at breaking Jackson's will was doomed to failure. Before he would recharter the bank, the president told Van Buren, "I would cut off my right hand from my body."

But would the issue be decided over Jackson's head? Both sides recognized that the congressional elections of 1834 would have an important influence on the outcome of the Bank War. To fight those contests, Jackson's opponents now created a new party, the Whigs. They took their name from the British party that usually opposed the king. After all, they explained, they opposed "King Andrew I." The party consisted mostly of the National Republicans, plus Democrats who had left the party over the bank issue. Apparently, however, not enough had defected. Despite the economic hardships of the winter and spring, Jackson's candidates did well at the polls that year. They even made slight gains in the fall elections for Congress.

Jackson had won the Bank War. The Second Bank of the United States was dead. Biddle later obtained a charter for his bank from the Pennsylvania legislature. But the institution was no longer a national bank, thus it was no longer as powerful as it had been. In 1839 Biddle resigned. In 1841 his bank went bankrupt. He died soon afterward.

Since the mid-1820s the nation had once more prospered, and in the early 1830s the economy began to boom. The government was taking in far more money than it spent. In fact, the national debt completely disappeared during Jackson's tenure—one of the few times in American history that it did so. Speculation in Western lands had become almost a mania. American capitalists were heavily involved, as were European investors. Since the United States was still an underdeveloped, credit-hungry nation, there was a demand for additional capital. Many new banks were chartered. Their promissory notes (written promises to pay a specified sum of money, either on demand or at a certain time) circulated as unofficial paper money.

The speculative boom worried Jackson. In 1836 he issued the Specie Circular, an executive order directing government land agents to accept only gold and silver specie (hard money) as payment. The Deposit Act of that same year included the first federal regulation of the pet banks. But the Whigs added a rider providing that the federal government's surplus revenues should be distributed among the states. This money, in state hands, caused more inflation. Thus it worked against Jackson's Specie Circular.

JACKSON AND THE SUPREME COURT

After the Bank War, Jackson enjoyed one more triumph before leaving the White House. Since 1801, Jeffersonians and Jacksonians had unhappily regarded the Supreme Court under Chief Justice Marshall constantly upholding the power of the federal government and the sanctity of contract. Attempts by anti-Marshall presidents to outnumber Chief Justice Marshall with their own appointments had failed to affect the decisions of the Court.

Jackson had had one serious run-in with Marshall, over a subject to which the president was highly sensitive—Indian policy. The Cherokee Indians in Georgia had developed a modern farming society, with their own written language and their own elected government, based on an 1827 constitution in which the tribe declared itself an independent Cherokee Nation. Georgia officials, anxious to open Cherokee lands to white settlers, in turn declared state authority over the Indians and ordered the seizure of Cherokee land. White Georgians planned to ship the Cherokees across the Mississippi, as they had done earlier in the case of the Creeks, a course of action approved by Jackson. The Cherokee Nation brought suit, claiming that their treaty with the United States government allowed them to remain unhindered where they were. Marshall spoke for a majority of the Supreme Court in upholding the Cherokees in two cases—*Cherokee Nation* v. *Georgia* (1831) and *Worcester* v. *Georgia* (1832)—directing Georgia state officials to allow the Cherokees to continue running their own affairs and on their own territory. According to Marshall, Georgia's laws did not apply to the Cherokees and white settlers. Even state officials could not enter the Indians' lands without permission from the Cherokees. Georgia ignored the order and proceeded to seize Cherokee lands, while Jackson, for his part, did nothing to

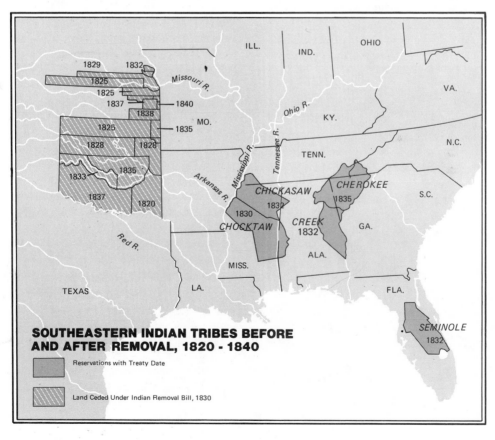

SOUTHEASTERN INDIAN TRIBES BEFORE AND AFTER REMOVAL, 1820 - 1840

Reservations with Treaty Date

Land Ceded Under Indian Removal Bill, 1830

compel state obedience to federal law. "John Marshall has made his decision," he is reputed to have said; "now let him enforce it."

Several years after a small handful of renegade Cherokees signed an 1835 treaty ceding its Georgia lands in exchange for an Indian Territory (later Oklahoma) reservation and a five-million-dollar settlement, Jackson sent an army led by General Winfield Scott to direct the removal of sixteen thousand Cherokees from Georgia. Unwilling to leave their homes, the Cherokees, along with remnants of other tribes, were forced, at rifle and bayonet point, on the arduous trek west during the winter of 1838. Bitter frosts, starvation, and disease took the lives of several thousand Indians before they arrived at the dry wasteland of "Indian Terri-

This later painting of the "trail of tears" portrays the forced removal of the Cherokee Nation in the winter of 1838 from Georgia to Western "Indian Territory," guarded by United States soldiers as the caravan moved along. (Courtesy, Woolaroc Museum, Bartlesville, OK.)

tory." The march became known afterward among American Indians as "the trail of tears." While Jackson's Indian policy led to the removal of most Cherokees, Creeks, Seminoles, Chocktaws, and Chickasaws from the South, similar efforts in the new northwestern states had decimated—and expelled—tribes like the Fox and Sac Indians who stood in the way of white settlement in Illinois and Wisconsin. By the 1840s, most Indian tribes east of the Mississippi River had completely lost control of tribal lands and lapsed into the status of federal (or state) wards, where they had not been physically removed to desolate and unpopulated areas west of the Mississippi.

Several tribes resisted removal forcibly, the most notable instance being the Seminoles led by Chief Osceola in Florida. Pressured to leave for western "Indian Territory" in compliance with an 1833 treaty, the Seminoles revolted, supported by a number of runaway black slaves who had joined the tribe in preceding years. Fighting, for a time, a successful guerrilla-style war against federal troops

The steady westward movement of the American people has been one of the most important elements in the national experience. Americans traveled through tangled forests, down rivers, and along newly built wagon roads, carting their families and their belongings to new homes in what were, until recently, wilderness areas. As white settlement pushed westward, the Indian tribes of the old Northwest and Southwest found themselves moved, often forcibly, into the sparsely populated plains and prairie states, where the buffalo hunt portrayed in this painting occurred. Throughout the antebellum decades, Americans overcame obstacles to national expansion with amazing energy. During this period, they not only moved relentlessly across a continent but, in the process, created whole new cities, among them Cincinnati, Louisville, Chicago, St. Paul, and San Francisco.

Alexis de Tocqueville praised the fearlessness of the pioneers: "Millions of people are marching at once toward the same horizon. Their languages, their religion, their manners differ; their object is the same. Fortune has been promised to them somewhere in the West, and to the West they go to find it."

[For further information on the foreign observers quoted in this essay, see "Notes on Sources."]

An Expanding Frontier

PICTORIAL ESSAY   **THREE**

On our way to Pittsburgh we met with various specimens of the backwoodsman, and I must say that, when clad in their green hunting shirts, with deerskin caps and leggings, their muscular attitude fully displayed in the free handling of their long rifles, they presented the most picturesque appearance I had ever seen. They had a way of leaning on their guns and surveying a stranger which struck me as singularly intelligent. It implied conviction, not inquiry. It was a look that said, not "Who are you?" but "I know you."

[JOHN BERNARD, 1800]

Engraving of Daniel Boone, said to be the earliest print made west of the Mississippi

A squatter is a person who, without any title to the land, or leave asked or granted, squats himself down and declares himself the lord and master of the soil for the time being. There is nobody to question his right. These hardy fellows are sometimes called the pioneers of the wilderness — and justly so — for they go ahead of the more orderly and civilized population and clear away the grounds in the line of march.

[BASIL HALL, 1828]

The Squatters, by George Caleb Bingham

Setting Traps for Beaver, by Alfred Jacob Miller

From camp all the trappers — some on foot, some on horseback, according to the distance they have to go — start every morning in small parties in all directions ranging the distance of some twenty miles around. There is much anxiety and danger in going through the ordinary routine of a trapper's duty. For as the enemy is generally lurking about among the rocks and hiding places, watching an opportunity, the hunter has to keep a constant lookout, and the gun is often in one hand while the trap is in the other.

[ALEXANDER ROSS, 1810–25]

The driver stopped and came to tell us ladies that he was sorry to trouble us to get out, but that an emigrant's wagon had blocked up the ford of a creek which we had to cross. It must not be supposed a common circumstance that an emigrant's wagon was left in a creek. The "camping out" is usually done in a sheltered, dry spot in the woods, not far from some little stream, where the kettle may be filled and where the dusty children may be washed.

[HARRIET MARTINEAU, 1835]

Emigrating westward, a family camps beside a stream

Methodist missionary on his way west

At one lone dwelling we found a neat, respectable-looking female, spinning under the little piazza at one side of the cabin, which shaded her from the sun. Her husband was absent on business. She had no family, and no companion but her husband's faithful dog, which usually attended him in his bear hunting in the winter. She was quite overcome with "lone," she said, and hoped we would tie our horses in the wood and sit awhile with her during the heat of the day. We did so, and she rewarded us with a basin of coffee. Her husband was kind and good to her, and never left her without necessity, but a true lover of bear hunting — which he pursued alone, taking only his dog with him, though it is common for hunters to go in parties to attack this dangerous animal.

[MORRIS BIRKBECK, 1818]

Indiana housewife outside her log cabin

At intervals a log cabin, with its little space of cleared land about it, nestles under a rising ground and sends its thread of blue smoke curling up into the sky. Sometimes the ground is only just now cleared, the felled trees lying yet upon the soil and the log house only this morning begun. As we pass this clearing, the settler leans upon his axe or hammer and looks wistfully at the people from the world.

[CHARLES DICKENS, 1842]

Pioneers cutting trees in a clearing

A lively scene from Davy Crockett's Almanac

PE THREE/4

Inside a backwoodsman's home

A squatter came splashing through the mud to the spot where I was and begged me to take a paddle with him in his canoe, hollowed out, as he told me, by his own hands from the trunk of a cypress. I went along with him and found his wife seated in a very nice, clean, roomy cottage made of logs, with a large fireplace lined with mud on one side, the whole white-washed and very neat. An air of comfort pervaded the whole establishment, which I had not expected. The squatter was really quite active in his hospitality.

[BASIL HALL, 1828]

These lonely settlers are poorly off. Their corn for bread must be ground thirty miles off, requiring three days to carry to the mill and bring back the small load of three bushels. Articles of family manufacture are very scanty, and what they purchase is of the meanest quality and excessively dear. Yet the people are friendly and willing to share their simple fare.

[MORRIS BIRKBECK, 1818]

Pushed by the European population toward the northwest of North America, the Indians come, by a strange destiny, to die on the very shores where they landed in unknown centuries to take possession of America. In the Iroquois language, the Indians call themselves the "men of forever"—Ongoue-onoue. These "men of forever" have gone, and foreigners will soon leave to the heirs of a whole world only the earth of their tombs.

[FRANCOIS-RENÉ DE CHATEAUBRIAND, 1791]

The Mill Boy, by George Caleb Bingham

Chippewa chieftain with a white trader

Every boy, as soon as he can lift a rifle, is constantly practicing with it, and thus becomes an astonishingly expert marksman. When I was in Kentucky, a hunter offered to fire twenty times at a dollar at a distance of 100 yards, on condition that I should give him a dollar every time he struck it and that he would give me one every time he missed it. But I had seen such specimens of their rifle-shooting that I did not choose to accept his offer.

[WILLIAM BLANE, 1822–23]

Shooting for the Beef, by George Caleb Bingham. (The cow at left goes to the winner.)

When several families settle at the same time and place, the colonists do not become brutalized as easily as the solitary settler. When he is surrounded by gloomy woods and closed horizons, cut off from associations with his fellows, he soon loses those civilized habits that a community develops.

[AXEL KLINKOWSTRÖM, 1820]

Frontier neighbors at a community scutching (beating flax to separate the fibers)

It is a peculiarly happy feature of the Constitution of the United States that every state has itself an independent government. The western states of America are each a nursery of freedom. Every new settlement is already a republic in embryo. They extend political life in every direction. Every new state, therefore, is a fresh guarantee for the continuance of the American Constitution and directs the attention of the people to new sources of happiness and wealth. It increases the interest of all in upholding the general government and makes individual success dependent on national prosperity.

[FRANCIS J. GRUND, 1837]

Stump Speaking, by George Caleb Bingham

The next moment
St. Paul was before us,
standing upon a high
bluff on the eastern
bank of the Mississippi.
The town is one of the
youngest infants of the
Great West, scarcely
eighteen months old,
and yet it has in this
short time increased to
a population of two
thousand persons. In a
very few years it will
certainly be possessed
of twenty-two thousand,
for its situation is as
remarkable for beauty
and healthiness as it is
advantageous for trade.

[FREDRIKA BREMER,
1850]

Whatever may be the talents of the persons who meet together in society, the
very shape, form, and arrangement of the meeting is sufficient to paralyze
conversation. The women invariably herd together at one part of the room,
and the men at the other. In justice to Cincinnati, I must acknowledge that
this arrangement is by no means peculiar to that city, or to the western side of
the Alleghenies. The gentlemen spit, talk of elections and the price of produce,
and spit again. The ladies look at each other's dresses till they know every pin
by heart, and talk of Parson Somebody's last sermon on the day of judgment
or Dr. T'otherbody's new pills for dyspepsia. When the "tea" is announced,
they all console themselves together for whatever they may have suffered in
keeping awake.

[FRANCES TROLLOPE, 1828]

St. Paul, Minnesota, in 1856

sent by Jackson, the Seminoles and blacks held out in the Everglade jungles for several years before their eventual defeat (their leader, Osceola, had been seized deceptively under a flag of truce and shipped off to prison where he died). Whether through actual battle, as in the Seminole War, or through his contemptuous dismissal of Marshall's Supreme Court decisions, Jackson displayed a marked contempt for the rights of Indian Nations. But Jackson was not unique in this view. Rather, he held the attitude toward Indians—that they could not coexist with an expanding white settler civilization—which characterized most of his contemporaries and guided the actions of most nineteenth-century presidents.

In 1835, Marshall died, just in time for Jackson to name his successor. Jackson chose Roger B. Taney, the secretary of the treasury who had finally removed the deposits. Jackson soon saw a difference in the Court's rulings. In the *Charles River Bridge* case (1837), Taney ruled that a state charter, in this case for a bridge, did not constitute an unbreakable monopoly if a second bridge was required by traffic. Property rights were important; but the public, too, had rights. The states must use their powers, ruled Taney, "to promote the happiness and prosperity of the community."

VAN BUREN'S UNHAPPY REIGN

Jackson had been a towering figure as president. But his stature appeared even greater in comparison with the president who preceded him and the one who followed him—both of whom had unfortunate administrations. John Quincy Adams, returning to national politics in the 1830s and 1840s as an antislavery congressman from Massachusetts, must have felt some satisfaction over the difficulties faced by Martin Van Buren, or the Little Magician, as he was called.

The Panic of 1837

Martin Van Buren was Jackson's handpicked choice for the Democratic nomination in the 1836 presidential election. The Whigs could not muster a single strong candidate, and Van

Buren won easily over several regional candidates. But even during the campaign, it became clear that economic problems would soon loom large. No sooner had Van Buren been inaugurated in the spring of 1837 than he faced an economic panic, the worst the country had ever known. There were several causes. One was the Specie Circular, which had made much paper money worthless. Another was the fact that British banks raised interest rates and called in loans. In May 1837, New York banks suspended specie payments; that is, they refused to pay out hard cash in exchange for paper money. Other banks soon followed.

All parts of the American business system suffered in the Panic of 1837 and the depression that followed. The price of cotton, America's chief export item, tumbled. Land sales fell from 20 million to 3½ million acres in a year. Merchants found that they could not sell their goods. When sales dropped, factory owners laid off workers. Debtors could not make payments and went bankrupt.

Van Buren responded to the panic by asking Congress to create an independent Treasury system. Like many other Democrats, he had, by then, come to associate the economic crisis with banking itself, whether in the form of a national bank or the pet banks. Van Buren proposed that the United States should simply deposit its funds in "subtreasuries," owned and managed by the government itself. Thus public funds would be separated completely from the private banking structure. Despite three years of successful resistance by Whigs and conservative Democrats, Congress finally enacted the subtreasury plan in 1840. But it did not seriously affect the nation's economic growth, either favorably or otherwise.

The Locofocos

Jacksonian Democrats had attacked the Second Bank of the United States as an undemocratic institution. These attacks went too far for Whig businessmen and politicians, who saw a threat to their economic and political freedom. But they did not go far enough for a small group of radical Democrats called Locofocos, who hated the bank in particular and the wealthy in general.

Most of the Locofocos were artisans, workers, and small businessmen in the urban East.

Many had lost their jobs in the Panic of 1837, displaced by new manufacturing techniques that were part of the growing factory system. They had previously organized themselves into early trade union and local workingmen's parties, many of which achieved some success in winning reforms from state legislatures. Ardently supporting political and economic equality, they hoped to turn the Democratic party into an even more strongly antibank and pro-workingman party than it was under Jackson and Van Buren. Van Buren's own antibank policies had already led many Whigs to brand the entire Democratic party as Locofoco.

Specifically, the Locofocos wanted to prevent private banks from issuing too much paper money and engaging in speculation. Such activities, they felt, had led to the financial panics of 1819 and 1837. Many Jacksonians—workers, farmers, and middle-class Americans—were still reeling from the effects of the recent economic crisis. They hoped to restore a currency system based almost entirely on gold and silver. Some of them even wanted to eliminate paper money altogether.

A HIGH POINT FOR WHIGS

As Van Buren's first term drew to a close, the Whigs marshaled their forces to unseat the Democrats. They had the support of most wealthy Americans, and had recently received a new influx of Democrats who had swallowed Jackson's bank policy but could not endorse Van Buren's. The Whigs also held some appeal for voters among the middle class and working people. Some working people voted Whig out of fear and hatred of the (largely Democratic) immigrants. The Whigs found support in the South among the wealthiest planters, those who had heavy dealings with Eastern businessmen and thus identified with their financial interests. The Whigs also had a hard core of support in the West, among recent settlers from New England, the party's stronghold.

In addition, the Whigs attracted business interests concerned with economic and social expansion. Rejecting Jacksonian fears about panics and paper money, these Whigs argued that the country needed *more* economic development. They wanted more roads, canals, and railroads, and more credit for investors. Government, including the federal government, should play a more active role in spurring development for the benefit of all.

The Whigs smelled victory in the presidential election of 1840. Their factions seemed united at last. Besides, Van Buren, as the president in office, shouldered responsibility for the depression. He had warned that "all communities are apt to look to government for too much." This negative attitude toward federal power did not help in his search for votes.

Van Buren had other problems as the election approached. The "Little Magician" could not make the slavery issue disappear. By trying to keep slavery out of national politics, he was losing votes on both sides. Many Southerners attacked him for refusing to annex Texas after American settlers there had set up an independent republic (see Chapter 20). Many Northerners regarded him as "soft" on slavery and attacked him for refusing to support abolition in the District of Columbia. People like Calhoun and Adams were beginning to destroy the North–South gentleman's agreement, which Van Buren had been instrumental in devising.

Taking advantage of the anti–Van Buren feeling, Whigs decided to mute their own differences. Party managers turned their backs on the Whigs' leading politicians and chose, instead, a candidate with a popular Jacksonian image. He was a military hero and a Westerner, General William Henry Harrison of Ohio.

When a Democratic editor unwisely tried to discredit Harrison as a man content to sit in front of a log cabin drinking hard cider, Whigs turned the slur into a boast. They decorated their floats with log cabins and dispensed hard cider at rallies. They rarely mentioned that Harrison was born in a Virginia mansion belonging to his father, a signer of the Declaration of Independence. Campaigning for Harrison, Daniel Webster actually apologized: "Gentlemen, it did not happen to me to be born in a log cabin; but my elder brothers and sisters were born in a log cabin. Its remains still exist. I make to it an annual visit. I weep."

At the same time, Whigs depicted Van Buren, the son of a small-town tavern keeper, as an

A Harrison campaign poster features a trumpeting angel and includes as well a cheering crowd and the inevitable log cabin and cider barrel. (Benjamin Harrison Home)

Americans—almost 80 percent of those eligible to vote—participated in this national election.

The Whig party had finally arrived, but for how long? When Harrison took over in March 1841, it appeared that the Whigs would remain in power for many years, and that a real two-party system had been established. Even the Whig leaders bypassed as presidential candidates had cause for satisfaction. Daniel Webster became secretary of state. Clay intended to run the administration from the Senate, where he was the most influential Whig, especially since Harrison's inaugural address promised that Congress, not the White House, would lead the way in national affairs. Harrison regarded the veto—so often used by Jackson to browbeat Congress—as a last resort, to be used sparingly, if at all.

But Whiggery's triumph lasted exactly twenty-nine days. Harrison caught cold during his inaugural and died. John Tyler of Virginia became the first vice-president to succeed to the presi-

This early photographic portrait of Daniel Webster, the great Whig senator from Massachusetts, suggests the commanding presence and penetrating gaze which allowed Webster to become one of the most impressive orators of his age. (Library of Congress)

overdressed, would-be aristocrat. They said he lived in luxury, perhaps on dishonestly acquired money. The charges were nonsense, for Van Buren was too smart to be dishonest. Yet, the president's earlier reputation as Jackson's political wirepuller and party chieftain did him no good.

In 1840, the Whigs came of age as a popular party. The National Republicans had previously presented a faintly aristocratic image that was politically damaging. But the new Whig coalition of 1840, which now included hard-fighting political pros from both the Democratic and Anti-Masonic parties, changed all that. The party launched a typically Democratic campaign, with the issues drowned out by songs, rallies, and torchlight parades. One Democratic politician remarked bleakly, "We have taught them to beat us."

The Whigs had learned the lesson well and piled up a Whig landslide. Many states went Whig for the first (and last) time. A record number of

dency. Tyler won a crucial point at the outset. He quickly rejected the suggestion that decisions be made by majority vote of the cabinet. This change — one that Harrison apparently had been considering favorably — would have permanently crippled presidential power. Though not elected to the presidency (his opponents called him His Accidency), Tyler made a vital contribution to maintaining the prestige and power of the office. He established the precedent that a vice-president would inherit the full power of the office, rejecting all attempts to call him *"Acting* president."

Tyler scored lower as a party leader and as a direct representative of the people. A states' rights Southerner, he had been put on the ticket to broaden its appeal. He now demonstrated the dangers of such a policy, infuriating Whig leaders (and damaging the party permanently) by his vetoes of legislation that would have carried out their program. Two national bank bills met with vetoes at Tyler's hands. All of the cabinet except Webster resigned, and the president was officially read out of the Whig party. For a while Tyler hoped

he might be vindicated by winning the election of 1844. He tried to build his own organization by offering jobs to cooperative politicians. Except for fellow Virginians and a few hungry office seekers, however, Tyler did not win over many regular Whig party members.

Instead, Tyler devoted much of his "accidental" presidency to foreign affairs. Webster negotiated a treaty with Britain over the boundary between Canada and the northeastern United States. Tyler himself became obsessed with annexing Texas. He ignored warnings that such a move would shatter the fragile sectional truce on slavery. In 1844 he appointed the Democrat John C. Calhoun as secretary of state and ordered the negotiation of a Texas annexation treaty. The Senate rejected the treaty, partly because the South Carolinian had urged it as necessary for the defense of slavery. Calhoun's undiplomatic statement underlined what everyone knew. Slavery, by then, had replaced the Second Bank and related financial concerns as the single most important issue in American political life.

Suggested Readings
Chapters 13-14

Andrew Jackson: The Road to the White House

James C. Curtis, *Andrew Jackson and the Search for Vindication* (1976); Marquis James, *Andrew Jackson: The Border Captain* (2 vols., 1977); Robert V. Remini, *Andrew Jackson and the Bank War* (1967) and *The Election of Andrew Jackson* (1963).

A Return to Party Politics

James S. Chase, *The Rise of the Presidential Nominating Convention* (1973); Robert G. Gunderson, *The Log-Cabin Campaign* (1957).

Jackson as President

Lee Benson, *The Concept of Jacksonian Democracy: New York As a Test Case* (1961); George Dangerfield, *The Awakening of American Nationalism, 1815–1828* (1965); Michael Feldberg, *The Turbulent Era: Riot and Disorder in Jacksonian America* (1980); William W. Freehling, *Prelude to Civil War: The Nullification Controversy in South Carolina, 1816–1836* (1966); Thomas P. Govan, *Nicholas Biddle* (1959); Bray Hammond, *Banks and Politics in America from the Revolution to the Civil War* (1957); Richard B. Latner, *The Presidency of Andrew Jackson: White House Politics, 1829–1837* (1979); Richard M. McCormick, *The Second American Party System* (1966); Marvin Myers, *The Jacksonian Persuasion* (1957); Sydney Nathans, *Daniel Webster and American Democracy* (1973); Edward Pessen, *Jacksonian America* (1969); Leonard L. Richards, *The Advent of American Democracy, 1815–1848* (1977); Ronald N. Satz, *American Indian Policy in the Jacksonian Era* (1975); Arthur M. Schlesinger, Jr., *The Age of Jackson* (1945); Glyndon G. Van Deusen, *The Jacksonian Era* (1959); John W. Ward, *Andrew Jackson: Symbol for an Age* (1955); Leonard D. White, *Jacksonians: A Study in Administrative History, 1829–1861* (1954).

Jackson and the Supreme Court

Stanley I. Kutler, *Privilege and Creative Destruction: The Charles River Bridge Case* (1971); Michael Paul Rogin, *Fathers and Children: Andrew Jackson and the Subjugation of the American Indian* (1975); Malcolm Rohrbaugh, *The Land Office Business* (1968); Ronald N. Satz, *American Indian Policy in the Jacksonian Era* (1975).

15 Women in Revolt: The Seneca Falls Convention

Tea time on a midsummer Sunday in the upstate New York village of Watertown was normally a quiet occasion, even in 1848 when revolutions seized Europe and antislavery insurgency had begun to spread across America. But this Sunday proved different, at least in Jane Hunt's parlor. Five women sat around an antique mahogany center table that humid July afternoon sipping tea and discussing not only their families but also "things." Confessions seemed in order. Each of the five told of her personal struggle to achieve respect and dignity as an educated woman in the United States. The most impassioned remarks came from Elizabeth Cady Stanton, who had come to Watertown that day for a long-awaited reunion with her friend Lucretia Mott, another guest in the Hunt parlor. Both women were married and had children: Stanton lived in nearby Seneca Falls and Mott in Philadelphia. "I poured out, that day," Stanton later wrote of the July 13 gathering, "the torrent of my long accumulating discontent, with such vehemence and indignation that I stirred myself, as well as the rest of the party to do and dare anything."

Impulsively and without any prior arrangement, the five women decided on the spot to "do and dare" something that had never been done in this country. They decided to organize a women's rights convention, the first ever held in the United States. Nor did they spend much time in preparation. They decided to hold the meeting that week in Stanton's hometown, Seneca Falls. Sitting around the tea table, they wrote a "call" for the occasion to be inserted the following day in the local weekly, the *Seneca County Courier*, and on July 14 New Yorkers throughout the region—many of them doubtless startled by the news—read the following *unsigned* announcement in that paper:

SENECA FALLS CONVENTION

WOMAN'S RIGHTS CONVENTION—A Convention to discuss the social, civil, and religious condition and rights of woman, will be held in the Wesleyan Chapel, at Seneca Falls, N.Y., on Wednesday and Thursday, the 19th and 20th of July, current; commencing at 10 o'clock A.M. During the first day the meeting will be exclusively for women, who are earnestly

294

invited to attend. The public generally are invited to be present on the second day, when Lucretia Mott of Philadelphia, and other ladies and gentlemen, will address the convention.

Lucretia Mott had been one of the five women who prepared the call for the convention. Mrs. Mott's participation in other reform activities, notably abolitionism, had already given her a considerable reputation in the North. In addition to Mrs. Mott and her friend, Elizabeth Cady Stanton (reunited with Mrs. Mott after years of separation), the others at Watertown that day included Mrs. Mott's sister, Martha C. Wright, Mary Ann McClintock, and their hostess, Mrs. Jane Hunt.

No calculated plan, only a casual network of family ties and friendship had brought the women to Watertown that day. Of the five, only Mrs. Mott and Mrs. Stanton had any background in reform activity —though some of the others had also worked in Quaker affairs. Mrs. Mott, in fact, had come to the area originally both to visit her sister, Mrs. Wright, and to attend the Society of Friends' annual meeting in western New York. Western New York had already proved sympathetic to a variety of new religious and social reform movements. Would this prove to be the case with women's rights? None of the five knew if their advertisement would draw a single additional person to the hastily called meeting. Would anyone other than its organizers attend the Seneca Falls Convention on July 19?

For Lucretia Mott and Elizabeth Cady Stanton, the daring notion of that first American women's rights meeting had come eight summers earlier in London, where both women and their husbands attended the World Anti-Slavery Convention. Opponents of slavery demanding immediate "abolition" of the institution had gathered in London that year, 1840, from all parts of Europe and the United States. One of the American delegates, Henry Brewster Stanton, later a prominent lawyer and journalist as well as reformer, had brought his bride, Elizabeth, with him. The Stantons had married in May 1840 at a ceremony in which the word "obey" had been omitted from the traditional vows at Elizabeth's insistence. In London, they met the merchant and Quaker leader James Mott and his wife, Lucretia Coffin Mott, both already well-known in abolitionist circles.

Despite protests by William Lloyd Garrison and other leading American antislavery advocates, the London convention refused to allow women to be seated as official delegates. The ladies were relegated to silence in the spectators' galleries behind a curtained grill. A majority of the convention delegates refused to allow the abolitionist women to participate entirely on grounds of their sex, a circumstance that outraged both Lucretia Mott and Elizabeth Stanton.

Denied access to the proceedings, the two women spent a great deal of time walking through London discussing not only the injustices suffered by slaves but those inflicted upon women. So fierce did Mrs. Mott's opposition become to the convention's exclusion of women that male delegates took to calling her the meeting's "lioness." As the older of

Susan B. Anthony, shown here in an early portrait, was possibly the leading women's rights advocate in nineteenth-century America. She began her lifelong activism on behalf of the movement in the years following Seneca Falls and continued steadily until her death in 1906. Her daring and tactical brilliance led some to call her "the Napoleon of the women's rights movement." (Meserve Collection)

the two women, forty-seven-year-old Lucretia Mott dominated her conversations with Elizabeth Stanton (then twenty-five), and educated her young friend in the problems women encountered when pursuing equal treatment in a male-dominated society.

Lucretia Mott had been raised in the sturdily independent environment of Nantucket, the New England fishing community, and had become first a teacher and then an "acknowledged minister" of the Society of Friends. Long before coming to London, Mrs. Mott had preached on a variety of reform concerns: antislavery, temperance, peace, and women's rights. She had helped to organize the American Anti-Slavery Society and served as president of Philadelphia's separate *female* antislavery society (which she had worked to bring into existence). At the time of the London convention, Mrs. Mott was probably the best-known woman in the American abolitionist movement. Her services as a speaker were prized by reform groups and Quaker meetings alike. Thus Lucretia Mott was the obvious person for the other four organizers to list as the featured speaker in the July 14, 1848, call for a women's rights convention at Seneca Falls.

Elizabeth Cady Stanton had been raised in a Johnstown, New York, household that was far more educated and worldly than the Nantucket

When Elizabeth Cady Stanton was ten, she wanted to take a scissors and cut out of her father Judge Cady's books "all the laws that make women cry." When she grew up, she did everything she could to abolish these laws. She died in 1902, hours after writing to President Theodore Roosevelt urging him to support woman's suffrage. (Brown Brothers)

family in which Lucretia Mott grew to adulthood. Elizabeth's father was a judge and her mother a member of the prominent New York Livingston family. The atmosphere at home was both highly religious and scholarly. Under the tutelage of a Presbyterian minister, Elizabeth studied at the Johnstown Academy, learning Greek, Latin, and mathematics. She then attended Emma Willard's "femle seminary" at Troy, New York, graduating in 1832. In later life, Elizabeth credited her earliest detailed knowledge of women's grievances to the hours spent as a child in her father's law office eavesdropping upon women while they unburdened to Judge Cady the many threads of abuse and discrimination in which they were tangled. Elizabeth also became close to a cousin interested in such matters, Gerrit Smith of Peterboro, New York, later a leading New York merchant and antislavery advocate, before meeting and marrying the reformer Henry Stanton.

As the two committed reformers, Mrs. Mott and Mrs. Stanton, reviewed their exclusion in London from the 1840 conference, they vowed that upon their return to the United States they would organize a women's rights convention. But the project became sidetracked as both women returned to their own communities and resumed their respective lives. At the time, the Stantons lived in Boston, while James and Lucretia

Mott were Philadelphians. Elizabeth began pursuing a career as a reformer, working for both temperance and antislavery groups while also laboring for several years along with other women's rights advocates in New York State to obtain enactment of a statute protecting married women's property rights which was finally passed by the legislature in 1848.

The turning point in Elizabeth Stanton's life came in 1846 when she and her husband moved to the isolated New York village of Seneca Falls, where she was deprived of the lively companionship and social amenities of Boston. Elizabeth, the judge's daughter with a classical education who had married intent upon somehow living in non-coercive domesticity, now found herself overwhelmed in upstate New York by personal isolation and household responsibilities as wife and mother. She watched herself grow daily more embittered by what she later described as a "general discontent" felt with "woman's portion as wife, mother, housekeeper, physician, and spiritual guide . . . [requiring] constant supervision . . . ." For the first time, the dilemmas she confronted as a member of the small educated minority of American women had merged with those of the ordinary, overworked female majority. It was at this point, Elizabeth Cady Stanton recalled, that she identified strongly with these women for the first time.

The sudden appearance in Watertown of her old friend and adviser,

This antifeminist 1851 lithograph, "Two of the Fe'he Males," ridiculed the comfortable, innovative mode of dress—jackets draped over loosely fitted "Turkish" trousers—which was advocated by Amelia Bloomer and other women's rights leaders. (Culver Pictures)

Lucretia Mott, triggered thoughts and feelings that Elizabeth Stanton had kept closely veiled until that unexpected tea time conclave. "My experiences at the World Anti-Slavery Convention, all I had read of the legal status of women, and the oppression I saw everywhere, together swept across my soul, intensified now by many personal experiences," Stanton would later write. "It seemed as if all the elements had conspired to impel me to some onward step. I could not see what to do or where to begin — my only thought was a public meeting for protest and discussion." Now that they had taken the initial step, however, Elizabeth and her four associates realized that they had yet to formulate a clear notion of what they hoped to achieve at the convention — assuming that anyone but their immediate circle actually showed up.

The women met again on Sunday morning, the 16th of July, this time in Mary Ann McClintock's parlor (without Jane Hunt) to draft proposals and resolutions for Wednesday's meeting. Recognizing that they lacked explicit models for organizing women's rights demands, they scanned reports and pamphlets issued by other reform groups — among them the proceedings of antislavery, peace, and temperance conventions — searching for usable examples upon which to pattern a description of the present condition and future aspirations of American women like themselves. In the end, none of the current examples seemed more suitable than the Declaration of Independence, which they then paraphrased skillfully into a "Declaration of Sentiments." The four women labored the entire day on their "Declaration" (see pp. 299–300).

Drafting a series of resolutions which embodied their call for complete equality of the sexes, resolutions that included a demand for women's right to vote, the four organizers concluded their preparations. The Motts planned a brief trip to Philadelphia before the meeting. Elizabeth Stanton and the other two local women returned to their homes, while the *Seneca County Courier* — and word-of-mouth — spread news of the impending convention throughout western New York. Three days remained until the opening session.

Plans for the meeting were suddenly threatened by domestic discord and unexpected illness. When Henry Stanton learned that Elizabeth intended to present the convention with an explicit demand that women receive the right to vote, and not simply with a general set of women's grievances, her normally sympathetic husband balked. Henry Stanton's convictions as a reformer did not extend to the "radical" doctrine of female suffrage, and he threatened to disavow the meeting and leave Seneca Falls for its duration if Elizabeth persisted in demanding the suffrage. When his wife refused to give ground, Stanton followed through on his threat, fleeing the town and returning to his family only after the convention.

When the Motts returned to Philadelphia, meanwhile, James was suddenly taken ill. Lucretia wrote her cohorts in New York explaining that because of this misfortune she and her husband might not be able to

Declaration of Sentiments

When, in the course of human events, it becomes necessary for one portion of the family of man to assume among the people of the earth a position different from that which they have hitherto occupied, but one to which the laws of nature and nature's God entitle them, a decent respect for the opinions of mankind requires that they should declare the causes that impel them to such a course.

We hold these truths to be self-evident: that all men and women are created equal; that they are endowed by their Creator with certain inalienable rights; that among these are life, liberty, and the pursuit of happiness . . .

The history of mankind is a history of repeated injuries and usurpations on the part of man toward woman, having in direct object the establishment of an absolute tyranny over her. To prove this, let facts be submitted to a candid world.

He has never permitted her to exercise her inalienable right to the elective franchise.

He has compelled her to submit to laws, in the formation of which she had no voice.

He has withheld from her rights which are given to the most ignorant and degraded men — both natives and foreigners.

. . . he has oppressed her on all sides.

He has made her, if married, in the eye of the law, civilly dead.

He has taken from her all right in property, even to the wages she earns.

He has made her, morally, an irresponsible being, as she can commit many crimes with impunity, provided they can be done in the presence of her husband.

In the covenant of marriage, she is compelled to promise obedience to her husband, he becoming, to all intents and purposes, her master . . . . He has monopolized nearly all the profitable employments, and . . . closes against her all the avenues to wealth and distinction which he considers most honorable to himself . . . .

He has denied her the facilities for obtaining a thorough education, all colleges being closed against her.

He allows her in Church, as well as State, but a subordinate position . . . .

He has created a false public sentiment by giving to the world a different code of morals for men and women, by which moral delinquencies which exclude women from society, are not only tolerated, but deemed of little account in man.

He has endeavoured, in every way that he could, to destroy her confidence in her own powers, to lessen her self-respect, and to make her willing to lead a dependent and abject life.

Now, in view of this entire disfranchisement of one-half the people of this country, their social and religious degradation — in view of the unjust laws above mentioned, and because women do feel themselves aggrieved, oppressed, and fraudulently deprived of their most sacred rights, we insist that they have immediate admission to all the rights and privileges which belong to them as citizens of the United States.

In entering upon the great work before us, we anticipate no small amount of misconception, misrepresentation, and ridicule; but we shall use every instrumentality within our power to effect our object. We shall employ agents, circulate tracts, petition the state and National legislatures, and endeavour to enlist the pulpit and press in our behalf. We hope this Convention will be followed by a series of Conventions embracing every part of the country.

attend the meeting. Without Mrs. Mott as the featured speaker, the organizers at Seneca Falls lacked a prominent attraction for their conclave. Besides, the women had hoped to use James Mott as chairman of the gathering, both because of his previous experience in such roles and because of their anxiety lest public reaction be overly hostile to a woman as chairman. As it turned out, James recovered in time, and the Motts showed up in Seneca Falls on the eve of the great day. Somewhat to Elizabeth's surprise, Lucretia Mott showed no more enthusiasm for raising the suffrage issue at the meeting than did Henry Stanton. In Mrs. Mott's case, however, the reason was tactical. She urged Mrs. Stanton to tread cautiously, lest the controversial issue of women voting distract public attention from more urgent women's rights problems demanding attention and action. Lucretia stated her complaint to Elizabeth in pithy terms: "Lizzie, thee will make us ridiculous. We must go slowly."

A crowd scene greeted the five delighted organizers at the Wesleyan Chapel on the first day of the convention. Dozens of carriages surrounded the church on the morning of July 19, and many more people, who had walked to attend the proceedings, stood waiting patiently for admission. They had come from every part of western New York. Among those who stood waiting for the meeting to open were a few of the most prominent figures in the reform community, men such as the black abolitionist Frederick Douglass, who published an antislavery newspaper called *The North Star* in the nearby city of Rochester. More than 250 women and at least forty men, the latter drawn to Seneca Falls by sympathy or curiosity, clustered around the chapel. Several of those present later recalled that they had expected to be among the few people daring enough—or foolhardy enough—to risk community disapproval and attend the convention, only to find to their astonishment that the single newspaper "call" had drawn a packed house.

To everyone's surprise, the chapel door proved to be locked, an act that turned out to be one of neglect and not hostility. A nephew of Mrs. Stanton's was hastily called into service, and he climbed through a window to unlock the entry door. The crowd pushed into the church, filling every seat, forcing the Seneca Falls organizers to change their planned format on the spot. They abandoned their earlier plan to bar men from the opening day's proceedings, which "proceeded" with an integrated audience: white and black, male and female. Without further ceremony, the speeches began.

James Mott chaired the meeting wearing his ordinary Quaker garb, his wife and other organizers having agreed (in Mrs. Stanton's words) that "this was an occasion when men might make themselves pre-eminently useful." One of the women, Mary McClintock, was appointed secretary after which Lucretia Mott rose to deliver the keynote oration. Mrs. Mott ranged eloquently on the far-reaching subject of women's "degraded condition . . . the world over," urging that a movement be started to "educate and elevate" women. But the most effective speaker that day proved to be Elizabeth Cady Stanton, despite her inexperience as a platform orator. "I

Y^E MAY SESSION OF Y^E WOMAN'S RIGHTS CONVENTION—Y^E ORATOR OF Y^E DAY DENOUNCING Y^E LORDS OF CREATION.

should feel exceedingly diffident to appear before you at this time, having never before spoken in public," she began, "were I not nerved by a sense of right and duty, did I not feel that the time had come for the question of woman's wrongs to be laid before the public, did I not believe that woman herself must do this work; for woman alone can understand the height, the depth, the length and the breadth of her degradation." (According to one local woman who attended, Mrs. Stanton could hardly be heard at first, so softly did she speak before gaining in confidence—and volume— as her talk continued. So recalled Amelia Bloomer, who then managed the Seneca Falls post office with her husband but who would shortly make her own career as a feminist.)

Mrs. Stanton read the Declaration of Sentiments previously prepared by the organizers plus an accompanying series of resolutions which the five women hoped the convention would adopt. Following her to the pulpit were other speakers who described the property bill for married women that the New York legislature had passed and reviewed the discussion of women's rights at a recently held state constitutional convention. A young law student, Samuel Tillman, "read a series of the most exasperating statutes for women, from English and American jurists, all reflecting the *tender mercies* of men toward their wives, in taking care of their property and protecting them in their civil rights." The audience responded enthusiastically to all the speakers.

This nineteenth-century print satirizes the proceedings at the Seneca Falls convention. (Library of Congress)

The hundreds who jammed into Wesleyan Chapel seemed to agree on every issue but one. When the Declaration of Sentiments was read, the assemblage adopted it with only minor changes in wording. The convention than adopted all but *one* of the resolutions without protest. It went on record urging women's equality in all spheres of society, revision of laws that discriminated against women, opportunities for education and vocational advancement for women, and acceptance of female equality in "capabilities and responsibilities." The Seneca Falls gathering also demanded in those same resolutions that women gain the right to enter the universities, enjoy complete equality within marriage, have control over their property, and equal status in the courts among other rights.

Only Resolution Nine stirred passionate debate during the meeting: *"Resolved,* That it is the duty of the women of this country to secure for themselves their sacred right to the elective franchise." Opponents of the resolution feared that an immediate demand for women's suffrage would provoke public ridicule and stir animosity toward *all* feminist demands, including those that lay within reach more easily. The resolution's main supporters included Mrs. Stanton and Frederick Douglass, whose outspoken speech urging its passage probably swayed a number of those present to favor the resolution. Douglass believed that obtaining the vote would prove decisive in forcing gains on every other women's rights demand. After an extended round of angry debate, Resolution Nine passed by a small majority. At the meeting's conclusion, only one hundred people (sixty-eight women and thirty-two men), one-third of those attending, signed the Seneca Falls Declaration of Principles which incorporated (among other resolutions) the controversial suffrage proposal. Even some of these would later remove their names and disassociate themselves from the declaration, once opponents of women's rights gathered force. Elizabeth Cady Stanton's own father rushed to Seneca Falls after reading about the convention and pleaded with his daughter to disavow her own handiwork. She refused, firmly and absolutely.

Although the two days of discussion and debate at Seneca Falls had continued well into the evenings, the convention adjourned on July 20 without having completed all items on its agenda. The delegates voted to reconvene two weeks later in Frederick Douglass's home city of Rochester. Once the Seneca Falls proceedings were published and distributed, a firestorm of complaints against the actions there filled editorial and letter columns in newspapers throughout the East. In almost every Seneca Falls church as well as in pulpits throughout the state, clergymen denounced the women—and their male supporters—who had arranged the convention. The complaints centered on the efforts by women's rights reformers, in the eyes of their opponents, to "unsex" American females and to destroy the sanctity of traditional women's roles and obligations. Unfortunately for the antifeminists, however, even as they denounced the Seneca Falls convention, they could not help publicizing the work done there—including its now notorious Declaration of Sentiments and the accompanying resolutions. The Declaration of Sentiments was "a most amusing document," explained the New York *Herald.* "The amusing part is the preamble where they asserted their equality." Many women learned for the first time of the new reform movement through journalists' and clergymen's bitter attacks upon its handiwork.

When the convention reassembled at Rochester on August 2, the Unitarian Church which served as its headquarters was as crowded as the Wesleyan Chapel had been at Seneca Falls. At the start, three of the initial contingent of organizers—Mary McClintock, Lucretia Mott, and Elizabeth Stanton—found themselves locked in bitter disagreement with an even bolder and more "radical" stroke taken by a majority of those who arranged the Rochester meeting. The Rochester contingent insisted upon electing a *woman* to chair the convention and an exclusive slate of women to serve in all other official roles at the meeting. Neither Mrs. Mott nor Mrs. Stanton, however, felt persuaded that a woman could prove effective in presiding over such a large, lively, and possibly unruly gathering. "To our great surprise," deadpanned the official "Report" of the Rochester convention, "two or three . . . women, glorious reformers, well deserving the name, coming from a distance to attend the meeting, at first refused to take their seats upon the platform, or otherwise co-operate with the Convention" if Abigail Bush—the person selected as "president" to preside over the meeting—served in that capacity. Lucretia Mott and Elizabeth Cady Stanton actually threatened to leave the convention, a step that would have left the fledgling movement in disarray, but the two women eventually backed down and remained. Before doing so, they listened to some opening remarks by the person whom the Report would describe as "our gentle but heroic President" Bush.

The meeting began with a prayer. The Report continues: "The minutes of the preliminary meeting [at Seneca Falls] were then read by SARAH L. HALLOWELL, at which time much anxiety was manifested concerning the low voices of the women, and whenever reading or speaking was attempted, without giving time for adapting the voice to the size of the house, cries of 'louder,' 'louder,' 'louder,' nearly drowned every other sound." Unlike the Seneca Falls experience, there were clearly some hecklers in the crowd in Rochester, possibly bent upon disrupting the convention.

At that point, although untested in her ability to maintain control over an orderly meeting, President Abigail Bush rose to quell the complainers: "Friends," she began, "we present ourselves here before you, as an oppressed class, with trembling frames and faltering tongues, and we do not expect to be able to speak so as to be heard by all at first, but we trust we shall have the sympathy of the audience, and that you will bear with our weakness, now in the infancy of the movement. Our trust in the omnipotency of right is our only faith that we shall succeed."

Whether Abigail Bush's eloquent opening words stilled the complaints or whether the succeeding speakers managed to pitch their voices louder remains unclear. The remainder of the Rochester meeting proceeded without serious incident, however, though not without an occasional heckler. By now, the speeches must have seemed familiar to veterans of the Seneca Falls meeting. Lucretia Mott rose to defend men against

The photo portrays vividly several generations of women's rights leaders. In the front row are Susan B. Anthony (second from left) and Elizabeth Cady Stanton (fourth from left). (Culver Pictures)

the accusation raised by some women's advocates that they were innately malevolent and oppressive: man, she avowed, "was not a tyrant by nature, but had been made tyrannical by the power which had, by general consent, been conferred upon him." A letter from Elizabeth Stanton's cousin, the abolitionist Gerrit Smith, commending the gathering became part of the official record. Elizabeth read once more the Declaration of Sentiments adopted at Seneca Falls which the Rochester meeting proceeded to adopt as its own. At that point, "a Mr. COLTON, of Connecticut," though miles from his own home, rose to express the hope that woman would remain in *her* home—"her empire and her throne"—rather than try to occupy the pulpit: "He loved the ladies as well as they loved themselves, but he would not have woman exceed her proper sphere . . . engaging in the strife and contention of the political world." Lucretia Mott rose to reply, noting that Colton thought too much of the clergy's pulpit and not enough of the Bible which, she asserted, "had none of the prohibitions in regard to women" as religious teachers. Several speakers complained about allowing women to vote, but Frederick Douglass again delivered an impassioned defense both of women's suffrage and of the feminist struggle for full equality.

Douglass had hardly returned to his seat when a recently married woman named Rebecca M. Sandford stepped forward to the altar and asked whether she might not say a few words. The audience listened attentively as the young bride, who had never before participated in any reform activity, described how she had been on her way west with her husband when she learned of the Rochester convention. The couple had arranged later train transportation so that they could attend the gathering (as she spoke, her husband stood near her and listened with evident approval).

With unstudied eloquence, Rebecca pleaded for both the abolition of slavery and the achievement of women's rights, linking the two "emancipations" as they had been tied in the minds of many American and British reformers. Mrs. Sandford's primary theme was *women's emancipation*:

> Give her the privilege to cooperate in making the laws she submits to, and there will be harmony without severity, and justice without oppression. Make her, if married, a *living being* in the eye of the law—she will not assume beyond duty; give her right of property, and you may justly tax her patrimony as the result of her wages. Open to her your colleges—your legislative, your municipal, your domestic laws may be purified and ennobled. *Forbid her not,* and she will use moderation.

When Mrs. Sandford stepped down, the audience had been stirred as no professional speaker could have done on that occasion. "It was a scene never to be forgotten," Elizabeth Stanton recalled, and it suggested the way in which the cause of women's rights had begun to influence ordinary women normally outside the circles and concerns of avid reformers.

The speeches continued as did the bristling rejoinders by antifeminists who had come to harass. That evening a Mr. Sulley, for example, demanded to know who would decide matters when husband and wife disagreed, if each family had *two* heads. Did not St. Paul, he demanded to know, "strictly enjoin obedience to husbands, and that man shall be head of the woman?" Mrs. Mott appeared to have been waiting for the inevitable question about St. Paul's instructions, and she plunged into the argument. Among Quakers, Lucretia Mott pointed out, the absence of a promise of *obedience* in the marriage ceremony had never raised difficulties as long as "an appeal to reason" was possible. As for the Apostle Paul, she argued, "many of the opposers of Woman's Rights, who bid us to obey the bachelor, St. Paul, themselves reject his counsel—he advised us not to marry."

But who should hold the property in a family, one Mr. Pickard queried, "and whose name should be retained" after marriage. Elizabeth Stanton responded to Pickard, arguing that the Bible, if "rightly understood, pointed to a oneness of equality, not subordination, and . . . property should be jointly held." She also questioned the appropriateness under all circumstances of taking one's husband's name upon marriage, attacking the custom as a "main reason for woman's inferior status." Fortunately, the exuberant Mrs. Stanton did not attempt to include that argument in any of the convention's resolutions. At the time, it might have provoked debate as heated as a suffrage resolution. Before adjourning, the Rochester gathering endorsed a set of resolves comparable to those adopted at Seneca Falls—again including one that urged the vote for women.

Other women's rights conventions followed in the next few years, spreading from New York State to Massachusetts in 1850, Indiana in 1851, Pennsylvania in 1852, and elsewhere throughout the North. As the

Susan B. Anthony (standing) and Elizabeth Cady Stanton, friends and associates in the women's rights movement, photographed during the early 1890s, after more than four decades of struggle on behalf of their cause. (Library of Congress)

movement spread and gained adherents, so did the anti-feminist opposition become more fervent. When the Massachusetts Women's Rights Convention met at Worcester in 1850—jeeringly attacked in the press by opponents as the "Hen Convention"—one minister warned his parishioners that he would expel anyone caught attending the meeting. Those who came listened to a number of speakers, among them the militant black abolitionist Sojourner Truth, who demanded direct action to gain equality: "If women want any rights more'n they've got," she exclaimed, "why don't they just take 'em and not be talking about it."

During the 1850s, Sojourner Truth, Susan B. Anthony, Lucy Stone, Elizabeth Cady Stanton, Lucretia Mott, and a growing number of activists spread the gospel of women's rights across the nation through meetings and rallies, mixing their advocacy of equality for women with demands for other reforms, especially the abolition of slavery. None proved so adept, yet direct, in stirring audiences for *both* pivots of American reform —*both* "emancipations"—as Sojourner Truth, as when she stared down into an Akron, Ohio, women's rights gathering in 1851, raised her bare hand in the air, and exclaimed:

> Look at my arm! I have ploughed and planted and gathered into barns, and no man could head me—and ain't I a woman? I could work as much and eat as much as a man—when I could get it—and bear the lash as well! And

Abolitionist orator Sojourner Truth, born a slave named Isabella in 1797 in upstate New York, traveled widely as a speaker for antislavery. An itinerant preacher, mystic, and former domestic, she drew great crowds with her statuesque bearing, resonant voice, and fervent denunciation of slavery. (Brown Brothers)

ain't I a woman? I have borne thirteen children, and seen most of 'em sold into slavery, and when I cried out with my mother's grief, none but Jesus heard me—and ain't I a woman?

None of the organizers of that first women's rights convention at Seneca Falls lived to witness the triumph of their disputed Resolution Nine on women's suffrage. Attending that meeting, however, unnoticed by the more prominent persons in the audience, was a nineteen-year-old farm girl named Charlotte Woodward. Attracted by the convention's announcement in the *Seneca County Courier*, Charlotte rode off to the meeting in a farm wagon along with some friends and watched the entire two days' proceedings quietly from a back-row seat. Charlotte never spoke but, at the convention's end, strode forward to sign the Declaration of Sentiments and its accompanying resolutions. Pressures from hostile family members, ministers, and newspaper editorialists in the days that followed the Wesleyan Chapel convention led a number of signers to withdraw their names from the declaration. Not Charlotte. She stood firm and remained committed to women's rights for the remainder of her life. At the close of that life, in 1920, after the Nineteenth Amendment guaranteeing woman's suffrage had been ratified, ninety-one-year-old Charlotte Woodward—the sole survivor of Seneca Falls—finally voted for a president.

16 Religion and Reform in Antebellum America

Religion and the various reform causes were inseparably linked during the decades prior to the Civil War. Often religious motivation explained those individuals who chose to devote themselves to one or another reform activity, as when Lucretia and James Mott expressed their Quaker antislavery convictions through participation in the abolitionist movement. Devout Protestants from all denominations joined the ranks of antislavery, women's rights, temperance, peace, and other reform movements. Reformers regularly cited biblical texts and arguments as justifications for the various social changes they sought—this occurred throughout the Seneca Falls and Rochester conventions—and such arguments were crucial, considering the strong religious orientation of most Americans who fought in the antebellum era for major reforms within their country.

Nor could it be otherwise, at a time when for the great majority of persons, the Bible remained the ultimate and most meaningful moral guide. During the first half of the nineteenth century, Americans paid more serious attention to religion than at any other time in their history except, possibly, in seventeenth-century Puritan New England. Between the Revolution and the Civil War, while American nationality was shaped and institutionalized, Americans (which at the time meant primarily Protestants) grappled with problems of God and country. For many, those problems were inseparable.

As the eighteenth century ended, American religiosity seemed on the wane. Many of the nation's leaders (Jefferson and Franklin, among others), had embraced the religion of Reason. Deism represented an attempt to bypass orthodox forms of religion. It substituted, instead, belief in an imprecise God who had created a very precise universe. To orthodox Christians—whether Congregationalists in New England or Episcopalians in the South—deism meant little more than atheism sugar-coated with spirituality. During the election of 1800, Jefferson's religion (or lack of it) became a campaign issue, though not enough of a negative factor to cost him the presidency.

THE SECOND GREAT AWAKENING

Americans in that era were experiencing a remarkable and wide-ranging religious experience called the Great Revival (or the Second Great Awakening). Beginning in the late 1790s, a wave of religious enthusiasm swept most of the country. Revival meetings, especially those in the frontier states west of the Appalachian Mountains, converted thousands and attracted much attention. In the West, as open a society as then existed in the United States, older, more established religious customs and doctrines gave way to an exuberant religiosity. Preachers stressed a gospel of salvation, and thousands responded with conversions and commitments that, although sometimes short-lived, were nonetheless sincere.

The Great Revival fundamentally altered American Protestantism. Sixty years earlier, during the First Great Awakening, itinerant preachers in countryside and city had been able to rekindle some of the fire of Calvinism, with its doctrine of election and predestination. But by the time of the Great Revival, American Calvinists (found mainly in the Congregationalist and Presbyterian churches by this time) saw doctrinal purity replaced for many of their number by the happier promise of eternal life. Denominations such as the

This highly emotional revival meeting resembled thousands of such meetings that took place throughout the United States during the antebellum era. Many were marked by numerous conversion experiences that increased the membership of newer, evangelical Protestant sects. The great revivals of the early-nineteenth century decreased the influence of older, more established religious groups. (Courtesy, The New York Historical Society)

Baptists and Methodists offered salvation. No longer need one live with the terrible uncertainties of Calvinist damnation hanging over one's head. A positive commitment to God could bring, if not the certainty, then at least the probability of salvation. Men and women could become active instruments of their own salvation. Works, not faith alone, counted for something in the great scoreboard in the sky.

Even more startling, preachers began telling Americans that God *wanted* them to be saved, that God meant love. Hellfire and damnation preaching did not become outdated, as evidenced by the conduct of some evangelical preachers who warned of terrible things in store for those resisting God's message. Yet if hell still existed and eternal damnation still threatened, believers also knew that God was in heaven, gladly awaiting the arrival of the saints.

Unitarianism

The replacement of the Puritan God of wrath by a gentler God of love also helped create several new sects. Though hardly a mass movement, Unitarianism was one of the most important. It began late in the 1700s, in Boston and in outlying Congregationalist churches, and won many followers among well-educated middle-class New Englanders early in the nineteenth century.

In 1803 a Unitarian gained appointment to the professorship of divinity at Harvard College. The struggle for the post clearly revealed the split between religious reformers and the more orthodox Calvinists in New England. Unitarianism included several beliefs that more orthodox Protestants could not accept. First, as their name indicates, Unitarians rejected the Trinity, believing Jesus to be a great religious teacher but not the son of God. Unitarians denied original sin, insisting on mankind's innate goodness and stressing the human capacity for moral improvement. Their most prominent leader, William Ellery Channing of Boston, preached the Unitarian message with a clarity and benevolence that made him a national figure. He was also involved in a variety of reform activities, as were many of the leading Unitarian preachers.

Transcendentalism

The best known of these preachers, Ralph Waldo Emerson, went beyond Unitarianism to expound ideas that made him *the* popular philosopher of nineteenth-century America. Unitarians fostered a belief in the potentially divine character of human life. Beginning with this conviction, Emerson and a number of intellectuals in the Boston area developed the philosophy called transcendentalism, forming a Transcendental Club that remained small in numbers but culturally influential. During the early 1840s Ralph Waldo Emerson, Margaret Fuller, Henry David Thoreau, and other transcendalists published a journal of literature and the arts, The *Dial*, that offered an effective sounding board for these religious and philosophical rebels.

Transcendentalists believed in mankind's natural goodness and perfectibility, and in the active presence of a divine spirit within each human being. God lived within each individual. This meant that everyone remained open to direct moral guidance. In effect, each person became his or her own church. There was no need for actual churches or ministers to mediate in the search for God. "Why should not we enjoy an original relation to the universe?" Emerson wrote in his book *Nature*, published in 1836. "There are new lands, new men, new thoughts. Let us demand our own

works and laws and worship." According to transcendentalist doctrines, each person possessed an "oversoul," an inner soul or spirit, which, when correctly instructed by divine insight, would point the way to perfection and salvation.

Yet, Unitarianism was too geographically restricted and transcendentalism too highbrow to affect the lives of most Americans. Emerson became a successful lecturer and a nationally known personality, but probably no more than a handful of his listeners understood his explanations of the oversoul. A far more numerous group of Americans responded to what today would be called "old-time religion"—a blend of evangelical fervor and strenuous piety, of joyous commitment combined with intolerance toward sin and sinners.

Revivalism

These religious currents converged with spectacular results in New York State's "burned-over district." There, in central and western New York, site of the Seneca Falls convention and many others, evangelical American Protestantism flowered as never before. Starting in the early years of the nineteenth century, when the region was still sparsely settled, revivalism steadily gathered strength. By the 1830s it had peaked in new cities of the area, such as Rochester and Buffalo. The religious ferment of the burned-over district involved a diluting, almost a breaking down, of older organizational forms. In "the district," Presbyterians and Congregationalists joined together in a short-lived merger, and the denominational label of a revivalist preacher counted for less than the force of his message (sometimes *her* message—since a few women were able to break through the sex barrier and do some of the preaching). A Baptist might exhort in a Presbyterian church, and vice versa. Although conservative clergymen were less than happy when the revivalists came to their areas, there was no way to contain the enthusiasm of their congregations.

Among the revivalist preachers were those who believed that Christ was preparing momentarily for his second coming. Ministers who followed this biblical interpretation, sometimes known as Adventism, crisscrossed the northeast-

Charles Grandison Finney was among the best-known and most influential evangelical preachers of the Second Great Awakening. He toured central and western New York in the 1820s, then turned his attention to the cities in the 1830s. (Brown Brothers)

the greatest revival preacher of his day, a man named Charles G. Finney. Finney was originally a skeptic. He had decided to study law. But a pious fiancée and a gnawing belief that "lawyering" was not an *honest* profession turned him toward the ministry. He began preaching in the small towns of central and northern New York, riding circuit, just as lawyers did. Finney attracted larger and larger audiences and won many converts. Finney became pastor of the Second Free Presbyterian Church of New York City in 1832 and ran it successfully—gaining many converts—until he withdrew in 1836. The following year, he helped establish a theological department at the antislavery college newly founded at Oberlin, Ohio, where he remained for more than three decades. His was not a fire-and-brimstone approach; it was a hopeful message, though not a simple-minded one. Finney, like many other clerics of his day, tried to retain the pious intensity of Calvinism while discarding some of its more rigid theological doctrines. The attempt was doomed, but the effort shaped the contours of much of modern American Protestantism.

Finney, along with many other evangelical ministers of the nineteenth century, stressed the importance, for churches and their members, of good works and constant involvement in practical morality. Finney himself, like the more decorous Bostonian Reverend Channing, ended his days as a strong antislavery reformer. One of Finney's many converts, Theodore Weld, became a leading abolitionist.

Mormonism

Charles Finney was thoroughly conventional when compared with Joseph Smith, founder of the Mormon church—another product of the burned-over district. Young Smith, born in 1805, became a part-time gold digger, one who could supposedly divine the location of buried gold. Soon, Smith struck it rich beyond his wildest dream. According to Smith, an angel appeared to reveal the location of a book written on gold pages and in a strange script. In the late 1820s Smith translated the text, he said, while fellow believers transcribed what he dictated.

ern United States, attracting between 50,000 and 100,000 Americans—possibly even more—to their vision of the Last Judgment's imminence. Although *most* Adventist ministers avoided assigning a precise date to the event, one controversial group had no uncertainty on this score. They were known as the Millerites, organized by a New York farmer and self-taught preacher named William Miller, assisted by the Reverend Joshua V. Himes. The Millerites became a major force throughout New England and upstate New York during the early 1840s, attracting thousands of followers. But the sect lost most of its adherents after two judgment days that it had predicted—one in 1843 and another the next year—failed to terminate the world. The Adventist movement, however, has remained one of American Protestantism's most vigorous components from that period to the present.

New York's burned-over district produced

Born in Vermont and raised in New York, Joseph Smith underwent a revelation and founded the Church of Jesus Christ of the Latter Day Saints (Mormon). Persecuted at every turn, Mormons moved west to Ohio, Michigan, Missouri, and Illinois, where Smith was murdered by an anti-Mormon mob in 1844.

The result, the Book of Mormon, is today the sacred text for the Church of Jesus Christ of the Latter-Day Saints, founded in 1830 in Seneca County, New York. Mormons had to withstand the scorn of unbelievers, but in the case of Smith and his followers, opposition was much more extreme. The Mormons left New York in 1831 and, like many thousands of others, went west, first to Ohio, then to Missouri, and, in 1839, established the Mormon town of Nauvoo in Illinois. But there would be no peace even there. With economic rivalry as an underlying cause, and opposition to Smith's next major revelation (polygamy) as the

stated objection, an Illinois mob set upon and murdered Smith in 1844. The Mormons, now led by Brigham Young, then pushed still farther westward and settled in Utah near the Great Salt Lake.

Anti-Catholic Nativism

Mormons were not the only religious minority to fall victim to violence at the hands of rejuvenated, militant Protestant Americans. Although the United States legally proclaimed religious freedom, and although church and state had been separated, toleration did not imply acceptance. At times, even toleration was lacking. The status of Catholics had remained an uneasy one, for example, since colonial times. As more and more Catholic immigrants arrived in the early nineteenth century, Protestants (who, often as not, fought the good fight against one another) could unite temporarily in opposition to Catholics. The idea of a vast Papist conspiracy against Protestant America, which had strong roots in the colonial

Brigham Young took over leadership of the Mormon Church after Smith's death. He led the arduous, but successful, move to the new Mormon Zion near Utah's Great Salt Lake. (The Bettmann Archive)

era's anti-Catholicism, began to spread. During the 1830s, small but insistent "nativist" movements sprang up in Eastern cities. The groups denounced Catholicism as un-American, criticized unrestricted immigration from Catholic countries, and were particularly angered by the ease with which immigrant Americans could gain the vote. Samuel F. B. Morse, better known as the inventor of the telegraph than as a nativist, led one such group in New York City.

For the most part, anti-Catholicism during the 1830s remained nonviolent, with one notable exception: in 1834, the good citizens of the Boston area burned down a Catholic convent in Charlestown. No lives were lost, but the crowd's murderous fury demonstrated once again that religious passion can sometimes lose all restraint. The Charlestown outrage foreshadowed the much more vigorous nativist movement that afflicted America in the 1850s, following the massive Irish and German Catholic immigration of 1847–56. A relatively minor Catholic population in the United States of slightly over 300,000 in 1830 had grown to more than 3 million by 1860, most of the newcomers impoverished and uneducated Irish and Germans who settled in the cities.

Conflicts between the largely working-class Catholic population of the urban North during the 1830–60 period and the Protestant native-born majority focused often on the question of public school education. In state after state, Protestant nativists fought successfully to deny public funding to Catholic denominational schools. These victories had the effect of leaving the public schools nominally nonsectarian but, in fact, strongly Protestant (often evangelical) in moral orientation. Such practices as regular study of and readings from the King James Bible, for example, were common in the nominally "secular" public schools. Catholics proved less successful in gaining a share of tax revenues for schools in which their doctrines would be taught with public funds. Instead, a number of states during the 1840s embarked on a program of developing a privately financed system of parochial school education (based on tuition payments and the contributions of the faithful). This program would provide religious training along with secular teaching—but within schools run by the Catholic church, so that American-born Catholic youths could be shielded in their formative years from the educational influences of the predominately Protestant culture.

SOCIAL CRUSADES OF ANTEBELLUM AMERICA

Background and Motivation of Reformers

What brought the "delegates," men and women alike, to Seneca Falls? What led people to try to change so many of their society's customs and institutions? One important factor was the widespread belief in progress. Many Americans during the antebellum decades came to feel that progress was apparent in all areas of national life. They believed that rapid economic growth could be matched by steady improvement in society and values.

The belief in a divine mission for America had been understood in religious terms by the seventeenth-century Puritans. Eighteenth-century American leaders had thought of it largely in political terms. Now it was seen in social terms by nineteenth-century antebellum reformers. They wanted to liberate Americans by correcting personal defects and eliminating social wrongs. They aimed at achieving *worldly* perfection within the nation itself (not the celestial perfection of evangelical Protestants) and in their own lifetimes. Most reformers believed that, in the struggle to perfect American life, they would also achieve their own moral perfection.

This utopian dream was certainly not confined to the United States at this time. American reformers borrowed ideas from (and corresponded regularly with) their counterparts in Europe. For example, American abolitionists learned much from the British movement to abolish slavery. Many American reformers, especially the Utopians, were influenced by French socialist-communitarian thinkers. Generally, though, the American reformers resembled religious crusaders more than their European counterparts did. American reform was closely connected to the evangelical

Ralph Waldo Emerson

In the history of American writing, the Jacksonian period was a very special moment. In the life span of a single generation, a dazzling new literature burst suddenly into view. The novels of James Fenimore Cooper, Nathaniel Hawthorne, and Herman Melville constituted as fine a body of fiction as was being produced in any nation in the world. Henry David Thoreau's *Walden* and Walt Whitman's *Leaves of Grass* took their places among the most imposing works of art in the English language. Indeed, what Noah Webster and other intellectuals had yearned for so much at the beginning of the century—a new, authentic, and distinctive American culture—was, by mid-century, a flourishing reality.

At the center of this exciting phenomenon stood a quiet, even shy, former Unitarian minister, Ralph Waldo Emerson. He was not as popular a writer as was Cooper. He produced no single work of art as lastingly important as *Leaves of Grass*. But Emerson had a special significance. In his lectures, his essays, and his poems, he brought together all the principal themes and questions that preoccupied the major intellectuals of the period. And because of this, some of his essays became a bible of sorts for young Americans who decided to pursue careers as writers, poets, reformers, or philosophers. Emerson's life—first as a Boston minister, then as a free-lance writer and lecturer living in Concord—was extremely quiet. But he carried on an intense internal struggle—a struggle of ideas and symbols. From this struggle, and from the famous *Journals* where he recorded it, came radical positions on the primary issues of the century— radical positions which themselves soon became a new orthodoxy among writers and artists.

Emerson's radicalism, which he announced in controversial lectures and essays in the 1830s and 1840s, was primarily a radicalism of celebration. He celebrated "Nature" as against "civilization." He was the philosopher and the poet of the "self-reliant" individual. And against the legitimate needs of such an individual, Emerson counted the requirements of society very little. He praised instinct, intuition, experiment, and freedom. He condemned dry logic, routine, and law. He wrote excitedly about whatever was new and young, and he talked constantly of escape from the "sepulchres of the fathers" and the "dry bones of the past." And these commitments led directly and obviously to a celebration of what was "American," and to the repudiation of much of what was "European."

From all this, Emerson's readers could draw a clear and somewhat radical picture of an ideal "American scholar"—as Emerson called the writer. He should plant himself firmly on his own private instincts. He should have no reverence for established customs, and no patience with law. He should be young, and if he could not be young, he should side with the young in almost everything. He should ruthlessly question every rule and institution to see whether they were in tune with "Nature." He should be innovative and daring, always ready to risk public criticism and rejection. And the scholar should do all these things in an acute and continuing consciousness of his identity as an American.

As Emerson put it in his most popular lecture, "Trust thyself: every heart vibrates to that iron string. Whoso would be a man, must be a nonconformist. A foolish consistency is the hobgoblin of little minds, adored by little statesmen and philosophers and divines."

Protestant movements of the day. Nevertheless, although religion and reform were indeed linked, antebellum reform had a distinctly *this*-worldly tone in its concentration on altering existing human institutions or creating new and improved models.

Many Americans lent part-time support to one or another reform activity, but a small number of people devoted their entire lives to the task of achieving social perfection. The dedicated reformer emerged during the 1830s and 1840s as a distinct social type in the United States. Men and women pursued reform as a vocation, especially in New England (no longer Puritan but still puritanical) and to a lesser extent in the Middle Atlantic and Middle Western states. The novelist Nathaniel Hawthorne was once such a reformer. He wrote:

> We were of all creeds and opinions, and generally tolerant of all, on every imaginable subject. Our bond, it seems to me, was not affirmative, but negative. We had individually found one thing or another to quarrel with in our past life, and were pretty well agreed on the futility of lumbering along with the old system any further. As for what should be substituted, there was much less agreement.

Hawthorne raised a question that many have asked about American reformers: Why did some people try to change society while a majority of their countrymen remained content to tolerate existing conditions? What were the reformers' motives? The answers have been as varied as the reform activities themselves. Unfriendly observers and skeptical historians have identified antebellum reform with the personal frustrations or unfulfilled ambitions of the reformers, with psychological or emotional disturbance, even with derangement. Enthusiasts have responded that intense commitment, even fanaticism, is a praiseworthy reaction in the face of evil or in response to obvious social problems.

Although the motivation of each individual reformer can be judged only on its own merits, it is helpful to remember that the antebellum American reform movements occurred during an unsettled period. The economy was undergoing rapid change. A new transportation network of roads, canals, and, later, railroads was opening up the American West to mass settlement. This meant that Western farmers could have access to Eastern or even overseas markets—markets that offered tremendous opportunities for both economic growth and crises, as when the economy plummeted downward in the panics of 1837 and 1857. At the same time industry grew. That growth, in turn, created demands for cheap, reliable labor in the new factories.

At first, Americans naively thought that industrialism could be fostered in a happy, benign atmosphere, free from the horrors of the Industrial Revolution in Britain: the New World would, in this regard as in all others, instruct the Old. The capitalists who owned the textile mills in Lowell, Massachusetts, thought (like Voltaire's Dr. Pangloss) that theirs could be the "best of all possible worlds," with happy young female workers making cotton cloth and happy factory owners making money. It worked for a while, from the 1820s to about the mid-1830s. But economic downturn, wage cuts, strikes, and the replacement of Yankee mill hands with more easily bossed Irish immigrants put an end to the Lowell dream—though not to the growth of industry or profit making.

Antebellum America was a society in motion. Thousands of people were moving westward. Many hundreds of thousands were moving into the fast-growing cities, where social problems, being more concentrated, were also becoming more visible. Boatloads of immigrants, expectant and exploitable, arrived daily during the 1840s and 1850s. Whatever the personal factors involved, whatever the motivation—philanthropy or arrogance—no reforming spirit could remain unaffected by at least some of these developments.

The Cold Water Army

On the night of April 2, 1840, six friends met at a Baltimore tavern, as was their custom, and prepared for a night of hard drinking. Nearby, at a local church, a temperance advocate prepared to deliver a sermon on the evils of alcohol. As a lark, the six decided to attend the lecture—and these sinners who came to scoff remained to pray. Afterward, they organized the Washington Temperance Society, the parent organization of a loose-knit network of prohibition societies that spread to

From a sip to a shot. The inevitable progress of the drinker, as pictured by the temperance advocates. (Fruitlands Museum, Harvard, Massachusetts)

most parts of the country and challenged the legitimacy of "demon rum" eighty years before the prohibition era of the Roaring Twenties.

The fervor of the Protestant crusade of 1800–60, and its potential both as a reforming factor and as a method of social control, is amply illustrated in the crusade for temperance. At first, "temperance" did not necessarily mean prohibition. For one thing, Americans of the colonial and early national periods were a hard-drinking lot. Wheat and rye were plentiful and cheap. So was corn. Rather than let those crops rot once their normal markets had been exhausted, American farmers generally turned them into liquor. The home "still" was as much a part of a well-run American

DEVELOPMENTS IN TECHNOLOGY, 1750-1860
(DATES REFER TO PATENT OR FIRST SUCCESSFUL USE)

YEAR		CONTRIBUTION	IMPORTANCE/DESCRIPTION
1750	Benjamin Franklin	LIGHTNING ROD	Protected buildings against damage from electrical storms.
1775	David Bushnell	SUBMARINE	First American submarine; submerged by taking water into tanks and surfaced when water was pumped out.
1787	John Fitch	STEAMBOAT	First successful American steamboat.
1793	Eli Whitney	COTTON GIN	Simplified process of separating fiber from seeds; helped make cotton a profitable staple of Southern agriculture.
1798	Eli Whitney	JIG FOR GUIDING TOOLS	Facilitated manufacture of interchangeable parts.
1802	Oliver Evans	STEAM ENGINE	First American steam engine; led to manufacture of high-pressure engines used throughout eastern United States.
1813	Richard B. Chenaworth	CAST-IRON PLOW	First iron plow to be made in three separate pieces, thus making possible replacement of parts.
1830	Peter Cooper	RAILROAD LOCOMOTIVE	First steam locomotive built in America.
1831	Cyrus McCormick	REAPER	Mechanized harvesting; early model could cut six acres of grain a day.
1836	Samuel Colt	REVOLVER	First successful repeating pistol.
1837	John Deere	STEEL PLOW	Steel surface kept soil from sticking; farming thus made easier on rich prairies of Middle West.
1839	Charles Goodyear	VULCANIZATION OF RUBBER	Made rubber much more useful by preventing it from sticking and melting in hot weather.
1842	Crawford W. Long	FIRST ADMINISTERED ETHER IN SURGERY	Reduced pain and risk of shock during operations.
1844	Samuel F. B. Morse	TELEGRAPH	Made long-distance communication almost instantaneous.
1846	Elias Howe	SEWING MACHINE	First practical machine for automatic sewing.
1846	Norbert Rillieux	VACUUM EVAPORATOR	Improved method of removing water from sugar cane; revolutionized sugar industry and was later applied to many other products.
1847	Richard M. Hoe	ROTARY PRINTING PRESS	Printed an entire sheet in one motion, vastly speeded up printing process.
1851	William Kelly	"AIR-BOILING PROCESS"	Improved method of converting iron into steel (usually known as Bessemer process because English inventor had more advantageous patent and financial arrangements).
1853	Elisha G. Otis	PASSENGER ELEVATOR	Improved movement in buildings; when later electrified, stimulated development of skyscrapers.
1859	Edwin L. Drake	FIRST AMERICAN OIL WELL	Initiated oil industry in the United States.
1859	George M. Pullman	PULLMAN CAR	First sleeping-car suitable for long-distance travel.

farm as the grist mill. Anyone seeking to control or limit the production and consumption of alcoholic beverages in America obviously would have a difficult task.

Early temperance advocates hoped to rely on persuasion, and they made limited demands. Hard liquor became the prime culprit, with beer and wine apparently exempt from the temperance injunction. Neither high taxes nor horror stories on the evil effects of drink seemed to work, however,

so the temperance forces shifted their line of appeal. The citizens of a godly republic, they argued, must be prepared to discharge their civic and religious duties. But how could a drunken sot vote intelligently for political representatives or pay due homage to God? Obviously, he or she could not.

The American Society for the Promotion of Temperance (founded in 1826) and allied groups, working especially through the churches, urged people to sign a pledge of total abstinence. Many thousands did, and often signing the pledge formed part of a religious conversion. By the mid-1830s the society could claim over a million persons on the temperance (total abstinence) wagon. Still the evils of drink would not go away. Those who refused to give up alcohol, and who thereby polluted society, might have to be coerced into godly behavior.

After the start of the Washington movement in 1840, demands for legal action through state prohibition laws — forbidding the sale of alcoholic beverages — became the hallmark of the antiliquor campaign. But laws must to some extent reflect public opinion; to influence the public, to educate it to the need for prohibition laws, temperance men and women mounted a tremendous publicity campaign — one that resembled in many ways the organized enthusiasm of Harrison's concurrent Whig presidential campaign in 1840.

Rallies, parades, picnics, mass meetings — all marked the efforts of the so-called cold water army. Writers and poets poured (to overfilling) their talents into the crusade. Miss C. B. Porter's *The Silver Cup of Sparkling Drops* included the lines:

> I gazed upon his pallid cheek
>   And asked him how his cares begun —
> He sighed, and thus essayed to speak,
>   "The cause of all my grief is *rum.*"

Timothy Shay Arthur, a writer who specialized in rum demonology, produced a best seller, *Ten Nights in a Bar Room.* But the heaviest guns of the cold water army were the preachers who inveighed against drink as strenuously and as sincerely as they fought against the devil.

Temperance became a political force to be reckoned with, especially in the Northeast. But its advocates may have overreached themselves and become overconfident on the basis of a few legislative victories. In 1838, Massachusetts had passed a "fifteen gallon" law, stipulating that sales of liquor had to be in amounts of fifteen gallons or more. This obvious discrimination against the poor had one unexpected but understandable effect: a Democrat was elected governor of Massachusetts for the first time. The law was then repealed. Nearby, the state of Maine made legislative history in 1846 by becoming the first state to ban alcoholic bever-

In 1837, Horace Mann dropped a promising career as lawyer and state legislator to become the first State Superintendent of Education in Massachusetts. During his twelve-year tenure, the state's public schools were impressively reformed: teaching standards were raised, the school year was lengthened, state appropriations were doubled, and "Normal Schools" were established to train teachers. (Brown Brothers)

ages altogether. Other states, including some in the West, followed suit; when New York (which had adopted local option in 1845) went for prohibition in 1854, the victory of the temperance advocates seemed an accomplished fact.

It was not. First, the rest of the nation did not rush to emulate Maine's example. Much of the South pretended to be blissfully unaware of the crusade, and the Middle Atlantic states remained ambivalent. Second, some of the prohibition laws had been badly drafted, opening them up to lawsuits. Pre–Civil War temperance suffered perhaps its most severe setback in 1856, when the New York courts ruled that state's prohibition law unconstitutional because it deprived citizens of vested rights in property (their liquir) without due process of law.

Education

Although the movements urging the spread of educational facilities—especially tax-supported primary schooling for all—were not so directly a part of the Protestant crusade as was the temperance movement, the religious factor was present nevertheless. The free primary school—what came to be called "the little red schoolhouse"—was, at first, very definitely a Protestant schoolhouse. Catholics objected that, when public school instruction included Bible readings using the Protestant, King James version of the Bible, then public institutions were being used to serve sectarian purposes. (This was long before anyone in authority paid much attention to the few who objected to having any Bible readings in the public schools at all.)

Diffusion of schooling, it was felt, would wipe out illiteracy, a scourge as bad as alcoholism; at the same time the school system would instill in pupils proper moral attitudes and values. In short, along with its altruistic and humanitarian purposes, advocates of the public school argued that it would provide a superb agency for social control in a society that was becoming increasingly individualistic, unruly, and downright "licentious."

Whatever their definition of "progress," most reformers agreed that the surest road to progress in the United States was through education. They worked to reduce illiteracy. (Although literacy in America was relatively high in compari-son to other societies of that time, it is probable that before the Civil War a majority of Americans could not read or write.) The reformers also tried to improve educational opportunities in a variety of ways. Outside of the South, belief in state-supported primary education for every child became widespread. Public school systems were established throughout the North. In the South, a more limited number of children—mainly from the wealthier classes—continued to attend private academies or to receive instruction from tutors.

The leader of the Northern public school movement was Horace Mann of Massachusetts, ably seconded by Henry Barnard in neighboring Connecticut. The New England common school system, established in colonial times and calling for state aid to towns that established primary schools, had fallen into decay. Many economy-minded small towns had no schools at all; others had ramshackle schoolhouses with poorly paid teachers (mostly males at that time). During the 1830s and 1840s, Horace Mann worked to reorganize his state's school system, raise teacher salaries,

Oberlin College, in Ohio, became a center of controversy because it was coeducational and interracial. Its school of theology was very liberal and heavily supported by prominent Eastern reformers and abolitionists. (Brown Brothers)

and upgrade teacher training. Massachusetts, which doubled its educational budget under Mann's prodding, established the first teacher training institution in 1839. Formal education at the secondary school level also grew in importance. A number of progressive schools—primary and secondary—opened in New England. But it should be stressed that, in the pre–Civil War period, secondary education remained far out of reach of the vast majority of young people, and even primary education was by no means universally available.

Horace Mann, as state secretary of education in Massachusetts, stated his case for education in well-publicized annual reports. Appropriations time brought this warning from Mann:

> In a republic, ignorance is crime. . . . If we do not prepare our children to become good citizens, if we do not develop their capacities, if we do not enrich their minds with knowledge, imbue their hearts with the love of truth and duty, and a reverence for all things sacred and holy, then our republic must go down to destruction.

Mann's well-publicized twelve annual reports (1837–48) as secretary of the state board of education in Massachusetts brought to the attention of reformers and officials throughout the country not only the specific problems of Massachusetts schools but the more general concerns and issues of public education. In 1838, he began editing a magazine called the *Common School Journal* devoted to spreading the gospel—and highlighting the problems—of public school education. Under Mann's leadership in Massachusetts, the salaries of teachers improved significantly, and the number of children enrolled in public schools increased yearly. Elementary school curriculums were modernized, and new methods of teaching reading to the young and the illiterate received his special attention. Mann resigned as secretary in 1848 after being elected to Congress as an antislavery Whig, although not an abolitionist. He became the first president of the newly founded Antioch College at Yellow Springs, Ohio, in 1852, where he taught and administered until his retirement in 1859. Only weeks after retiring, Mann died, still the most influential leader of public education in his generation.

Higher education expanded, too. State universities were established in several Southern and Midwestern states. New private colleges and universities also sprang up. Oberlin College in Ohio, founded in 1833, was the first coeducational college in the country. It was also one of the few schools to admit blacks, and it became a center of antislavery agitation. Antioch College was another antislavery and coeducational institution.

Mount Holyoke in Massachusetts, founded in 1837 as Mary Lyon's Female Seminary, was the first to offer women advanced education. During the period, such opportunities for women increased but at a pitifully slow pace. Women were different, mentally as well as physically, argued the men who dominated American society and who had as little sympathy for the idea of formal education for women as they did for the notion of allowing women to vote. Although men like Horace Mann and Henry Barnard also faced difficulties, the *women* who fought for educational reform—Emma Willard, who started a "female seminary" in Troy, New York (which Elizabeth Cady attended); Mary Lyon, who did likewise in Massachusetts; and Elizabeth Blackwell, who earned and insisted on receiving the first medical degree awarded an American woman—were the ones who fought the hardest fight against prevailing sex prejudice.

Mass education of a more informal kind also flourished in the antebellum period. Breakthroughs in machine technology had resulted in a "printing revolution" that permitted the low-cost production of reading material by steam-powered rotary presses. Hundreds of mass circulation newspapers and magazines, catering to almost every segment of public taste, made their appearance. The famous "penny press" dated from 1833. In that year, the New York *Sun* demonstrated the possibility of profitably increasing readership by cutting its price to one cent. Weekly editions of such leading papers as Horace Greeley's New York *Tribune* (founded in the early 1840s) became the equivalent of the first national magazines for a mass audience. Periodicals such as *Harper's Weekly* and *Godey's Lady's Book* were only two of many serving the apparently insatiable reading appetite of an increasingly literate America.

Schoolteacher Mary Lyon raised the funds to establish Mount Holyoke College by soliciting contributions, door-to-door, from other Massachusetts women. Although the "Seminary" for girls that she founded in South Hadley, Massachusetts, in 1837 was not chartered as a college until 1886, after her death, the level of instruction and entrance requirements from the outset were on a par with those at men's colleges. The pious Miss Lyon also insisted upon a religious atmosphere and, since she believed in the virtue of manual labor, required all students to assist with the housework. (Culver Pictures)

Educator Emma Hart Willard, who was determined to improve women's education—and to prove that women could master as difficult subjects as men—campaigned in New York (unsuccessfully) for the state funding of girls' schools. In 1821, she established the Troy Female Seminary, with financial support from the town, and introduced an advanced curriculum that included math, history, geography, and a wide range of sciences—rather than the hodge-podge of handicrafts usually offered at girls' schools. Mrs. Willard was particularly devoted to teacher preparation and trained two hundred of her graduates to enter the teaching profession. (Culver Pictures)

The most influential form of adult education in this period—again outside the South—was the lyceum movement. It originated in New England in 1826. Lyceums were established by the hundreds throughout the North and Middle West. They were basically lecture halls with small libraries and facilities for discussion and study groups. Lyceums drew a steady stream of well-paid lecturers on regional and even national tours. No better device existed for mass education in a country that still lacked universal literacy but which valued the arts of public speaking and debating.

Almost any cause could gain an attentive audience (and perhaps some converts) easily by sending a speaker to tour the lyceums. Hundreds of reformers—ranging from such rarified philosophers as Emerson to more down-to-earth men and women advocating a variety of nostrums guaranteed to elevate mankind—all followed the lyceum circuit hoping to arouse America to the need for change.

There proved to be no shortage of causes to expound. In addition to temperance and education through formal schooling, reformers called for the end of capital punishment; some demanded changes in the prison system through the establishment of penitentiaries that would rehabilitate and not merely punish; others lectured on spiritualism or the principles of phrenology (character analysis by measuring the contours of the head); still others urged the total renunciation of

war; some wanted the few Jews then living in America converted to Christianity; many demanded equal rights for women; still more demanded the abolition of slavery. Lyceum lectures were not exclusively reform platforms, but the lecture-study circuit never lacked for reformers—those who saw and fretted about the imperfections of a society that they thought should be constantly striving to improve itself. In this connection, note the relative ease with which the women of Seneca Falls quickly organized their convention—and attracted a large audience.

Treatment of the Handicapped

One cause that received a great deal of attention for the first time during the antebellum decades was the manner in which Americans treated

Three writers of the American renaissance 1830–60. (Above) Nathaniel Hawthorne (1804–64), the literary voice of New England's nineteenth-century romantic neo-Puritanism; (below left) Edgar Allan Poe (1809–49), Philadelphia journalist and author, a brilliant and mordant maverick, his

fiery fantasies were at first more admired in Europe than in America; (below right) William Cullen Bryant (1794–1878), poet, editor, and abolitionist, for over half a century New York City's first citizen. (All photos are from The Bettmann Archive)

the mentally ill. Foremost among those responsible for changing public attitudes on this controversial question was Dorothea Dix, a Boston schoolteacher, who spent years studying conditions in the country's insane asylums. Dix found most inmates "confined in cages, closets, cellars, stalls, and pens, where they were chained, naked, beaten with rods, and lashed into obedience." When she exposed these inhuman conditions, all of which she had seen personally, some critics denounced her agitating; but with the help of people like Horace Mann and the young politician Charles Sumner, Dix persisted. Her detailed reports to state legislatures on the hideous conditions, and her long campaign for public recognition of the problem in and outside of Massachusetts, led to many improvements in state-supported mental hospitals.

Among those who helped Dorothea Dix in her campaign to ease the sufferings of mental patients was Dr. Samuel Gridley Howe. A romantic figure, who had fought in the Greek war for independence, Howe was also a very practical reformer. He had concentrated on the education of the deaf and the blind and had succeeded in educating a young woman named Laura Bridgman, a blind deaf-mute. His "feat" in so doing, which attracted a great deal of curiosity and attention, greatly aided Howe in raising money for his Perkins Institute for the Blind. Before he opened his school for the blind, Howe spent several days blindfolded so that he might gain a better understanding of the problems faced by his future pupils.

Other reformers, forerunners of the modern social worker, helped the "neglected poor," the unemployed, the newly arrived immigrant. The work of such individuals as Joseph Tuckerman of Boston and Charles Loring Brace of New York called attention to poverty amid the plenty of the nation's developing cities.

Pacifism

The peace movement gained many followers in the early nineteenth century. A Maine merchant named William Ladd founded the American Peace Society in 1828. It was weakened after a few years, however, when it split into warring factions over the question of whether nations might use force to defend themselves. Some pacifists condemned the use of force under any circumstances, arguing that there was no such thing as a "just" war. Among their leaders was abolitionist William Lloyd Garrison. He led those who believed in absolute pacifism into a much smaller society, the New England Non-Resistance Society, which condemned violence even in self-defense.

Pacifism gradually lost followers as the slavery controversy heated up during the 1840s, and the Mexican War of 1846–48 created a second convulsion within the American Peace Society. A group of dissidents, led by Elihu Burritt, wanted the war condemned. Failing in that, they founded the League of Universal Brotherhood. But the "war" that did the most to undermine organized pacifism was the "war against the slave power." Many of the leading pacifists like Garrison and Burritt were also abolitionists. When faced with the choice of fighting or giving in to slavery, such men renounced pacifism. Thus Garrison ended by praising John Brown's raid on Harpers Ferry and supporting the Civil War.

Woman's Rights

Women were active in almost every progressive cause in antebellum America. In the process of trying to improve conditions for others, they came to recognize the degree to which they themselves were deprived of equal citizenship. The treatment of Elizabeth Stanton, Lucretia Mott, and other women at the World Anti-Slavery Conference in London in 1840 dramatized this fact. They had no political rights, and upon marriage, they lost some of their civil rights, in particular, control over whatever property they had owned. Most of all, women suffered from limited professional and social opportunities. They were refused admission to most secondary schools and universities. Practically all careers but marriage were considered "unfeminine."

Yet women were expected to work. On the nation's farms and in the small towns, where a majority of Americans then lived, women did their share of the work—perhaps more than their share, since they also did most of the work involved in child rearing. But male society threw up powerful barriers against women working outside the home, rural or urban, or participating in public activity.

The woman's rights movement, which began in an organized manner at the Seneca Falls Convention in 1848, next to abolitionism,[1] was the most controversial of antebellum reform crusades. Some male reformers, notably Garrison, Wendell Phillips, Gerrit Smith, and Samuel Gridley Howe, actively supported the feminists. Others, especially clergymen worried about conventional morality, and journalists, looking for a good story, attacked or ridiculed the movement. On one point both clergy and press were united: that the "Bloomer-style" of dress temporarily adopted by leading feminists was shocking. Actually, it was only different, since it consisted of a knee-length jacket over a pair of "Turkish" trousers that were not form fitting. The costume as a whole was no more revealing or provocative than conventional dress. But Bloomerism proved such a handicap to feminism, it evoked so much criticism, that feminists reluctantly returned to less comfortable petticoats and gowns.

Nevertheless, American women made some progress during the pre–Civil War years. Women were allowed to become elementary and then high school teachers. State legislatures began to award married women control over their own property: Mississippi was the first, in 1839; New York followed in 1848 after extensive work by Elizabeth Cady Stanton and other feminists. Girls began attending secondary schools in small numbers, and a few colleges offered higher education to women.

Probably the most important breakthroughs were stubbornly personal. Distinguished careers pursued by individual reformers and intellectuals — such as Blackwell, Dix, Mott, and Stanton — dented the dominant image of woman's mental and emotional unfitness for serious vocations outside the home. In educational institutions like Willard's Female Seminary, which taught mathematics, history, and philosophy, a small percentage of American women began to find themselves intellectually. These reforms came at a time when women were thought incapable of learning much

besides singing and embroidery and when most women seemed permanently imprisoned by their "circumstance." Susan B. Anthony, an ardent feminist (and abolitionist) who worked to gain the vote for women, once declared that she "would ignore all law to help the slave, and ignore it all to protect an enslaved woman."

Utopian Communities

The idealism and social unrest of the period were perhaps best symbolized by the Utopian communities that sprang up in the antebellum era. From the 1820s through the 1840s more than a hundred colonies were set up. Most were inspired by one or another religious belief, although some were secular, established as proving grounds for new economic or social theories.

The purpose of New Harmony, Indiana, according to its founder, was "to introduce an entire new system of society." He was a successful Scottish industrialist named Robert Owen, who believed that capitalism represented selfishness and that only socialism (communitarian socialism) could bring harmony to society. In 1825 Owen purchased a ready-made colony of 30,000 acres from a German religious group. Within six weeks he had brought together eight hundred colonists. But New Harmony also attracted its share of crackpots and loafers. Quarrels broke out over major and minor issues. And Owen's frequent absences left the group without strong guidance. Within two years, New Harmony was disbanded.

Brook Farm, a few miles west of Boston, operated on a smaller scale but with a more distinguished group of adherents. It began in 1841 as a progressive prep school and cooperative farm, with all pupils and group members sharing daily chores. Its leader, George Ripley, former Unitarian minister and sometime member of the Transcendental Club, believed in "plain living and high thinking." He thought that people could develop more fully when freed from competition. Many intellectuals were associated with Brook Farm. Emerson considered it a nice place to visit, but he did not want to live there. Nathaniel Hawthorne was a group member. (He later satirized the experiment in his novel *The Blithedale Romance*.) When a highly

---

[1] For a full account of abolitionism, see Chapter 22.

structured, more impersonal working and living system was introduced in 1845 (in other words, when it became more regimented), the farm lost its appeal for many supporters. A fire in 1846 destroyed the main building and brought the experiment to an end. Brook Farm, according to Transcendentalist Orestes Brownson, had been "half a charming adventure, half a solemn experiment."

Less intellectual, and unconcerned with charm, was the Oneida Community in upstate New York, started by John Humphrey Noyes in 1848. Noyes believed that small industry provided a better economic base for a colony than did agriculture. So the community produced and marketed animal traps, furniture, and other consumer goods. Property was owned jointly and distributed equally. Conventional marriage was replaced by "complex marriage," a system in which all group members were considered married to each other. Noyes and his followers believed that no manmade laws could separate them and that they belonged to one another. These doctrines were criticized severely by the outside world. The Oneida Community, like the Mormons, paid the price for their sexual unorthodoxy and financial success. The group finally abolished complex marriage in 1879. Soon afterward, the community itself was dissolved, becoming a joint stock company that specialized in manufacturing silverware.

Most American Utopian communities were unable to become truly self-sufficient or to maintain their cherished isolation from the outside world. Many floundered when it came to putting their high ideals into practice. Yet a few made noteworthy contributions. New Harmony sponsored some important educational innovations—the kin-

The Oneida Community's sexual practices created much controversy. Here, the Oneidans vote on whether to allow the union of two members under their highly regulated scheme of "complex marriage." (Culver Pictures)

dergarten and the trade school. Brook Farm's combination of work and culture was highly praised, and its school was much admired. As for Oneida, its members pioneered in eugenics and in what, today, would be called encounter sessions.

Most Americans knew about the Utopian communities; but few approved of them, and even fewer actually participated in these early American experiments in communitarianism. Utopian withdrawal offered no solution to a mass society, innovative though some communities might be. To outsiders they appeared, at best, as exotic retreats. Most Americans still believed that piecemeal reform — working to correct gradually the abuses in society as a whole, rather than creating new minisocieties — offered greater hope. Some approached the task of reform with the sour anxiety of a Lyman Beecher, orthodox Congregationalist from Connecticut; others were blessed with the cheerful and optimistic spirit of a William Ellery Channing, the Boston Unitarian. Yet both were clergymen imbued with the belief that mankind could and should better its lot on earth, and approach closer to moral perfection. Such attitudes made the starburst of American reform in the antebellum years a reality and offered a more certain prospect for the future than did the Adventist hopes of William Miller and his followers or the *secular* Utopias.

Origins of the Abolition Movement

Of all the reforms influenced by religion, the one with the closest connections was abolitionism. Certain religious groups had been particularly active in the antislavery movement from its beginning in the eighteenth century. These included the Methodists, Episcopalians, and, particularly, the Quakers, whose opposition continued into the nineteenth century, as evidenced by the activities — among others — of James and Lucretia Mott. Ethical opposition to slavery inspired many leading figures of the Revolutionary period to free their slaves. It also influenced Northern states to abolish slavery gradually by the 1820s.

A leading antislavery organization of the early nineteenth century was the American Colonization Society, founded in 1817. It worked to obtain gradual, compensated emancipation of slaves. After being freed, slaves were to be transported immediately elsewhere, preferably to Africa. The society actually colonized very few blacks. But it did help found Liberia in 1822 as a refuge for ex-slaves. Many Southerners joined the American Colonization Society in an effort to resolve their moral doubts over slavery, but the society lost most of its support in the South after a slave insurrection in 1831 that helped shape attitudes for the next three decades — the Nat Turner Revolt.

Suggested Readings
Chapters 15-16

The Seneca Falls Convention and Early Women's Rights Movement

Lois W. Banner, *Elizabeth Cady Stanton* (1980); Barbara J. Berg, *The Remembered Gate: Origins of American Feminism 1800–1860* (1978); Otelia Cromwell, *Lucretia Mott* (1958); Carl N. Degler, *At Odds: Women and the Family in America, 1776 to the Present* (1980); Ellen DuBois, *Feminism and Suffrage: The Emergence of an Independent Women's Movement in America, 1848–1869* (1978); Eleanor Flexner, *Century of Struggle: The Women's Rights Movement in the United States* (1959); Elinor Rice Hays, *Morning Star: A Biography of Lucie Stone* (1978); Blanche Glassman Hersh, *The Slavery of Sex: Feminist-Abolitionists in America* (1978); Alma Lutz, *Created Equal: A Biography of Elizabeth Cady Stanton* (1940) and *Susan B. Anthony: Rebel, Crusader, Humanitarian* (1959); Keith Melder, *Beginnings of Sisterhood: The American Woman's Rights Movement, 1800–1850* (1977); Judith Nies, *Seven Women: Portraits from the American Radical Tradition* (1977); Elizabeth Cady Stanton, *Eighty Years or More: Reminiscences, 1815–1897* (1898); Elizabeth Cady Stanton, Susan B. Anthony, and Matilda Jocelyn Gage, eds., *History of Woman Suffrage* (Vols. 1–3, 1881–1886).

Religious Reforms

Sydney E. Ahlstrom, *A Religious History of the American People* (1972); Ray A. Billington, *The Protestant Crusade, 1800–1860* (1938); Carl Bode, *The American Lyceum* (1956); Fawn M. Brodie, *No Man Knows My History: The Life of Joseph Smith* (1971); Whitney R. Cross, *The Burned-Over District: Enthusiastic Religion in Western New York, 1800–1850* (1950); Mark Holloway, *Heavens on Earth* (1951); Daniel W. Howe, *The Unitarian Conscience: Harvard Moral Philosophy, 1805–1861* (1970); Ralph L. Lusk, *The Life of Ralph Waldo Emerson* (1949); Perry Miller, ed., *Transcendentalists: An Anthology* (1950); Thomas F. O'Dea, *The Mormons* (1964); Timothy L. Smith, *Revivalism and Social Reform in Mid-Nineteenth Century America* (1965); Bernard A. Weisberger, *They Gathered at the River: The Story of the Great Revivalists and Their Impact Upon Religion in America* (1958).

Social Crusades

Arthur E. Bestor, Jr., *Backwoods Utopias: The Sectarian Origins and the Owenite Phase of Communitarian Socialism in America: 1623–1829* (1950); Peter Brock, *Pacifism in the United States: From the Colonial Era to the First World War* (1968); Michael Fellman, *The Unbounded Frame: Freedom and Community in Nineteenth Century American Utopianism* (1973); Gerald N. Grob, *Mental Institutions in America: Social Policy to 1875* (1973); Michael Katz, *The Irony of Early School Reform: Educational Innovation in Mid-Nineteenth Century Massachusetts* (1968); John A. Krout, *The Origins of Prohibition* (1925); W. David Lewis, *From Newgate to Dannemora: The Rise of the Penitentiary in New York, 1796–1848* (1965); William G. McLoughlin, *The Meaning of Henry Ward Beecher* (1970); Jonathan Messerli, *Horace Mann* (1971); David S. Rothman, *The Discovery of the Asylum* (1971); Harold Schwartz, *Samuel Gridley Howe, Social Reformer* (1956); Ronald G. Walters, *American Reformers, 1815–1860* (1978); Rush Welter, *Popular Education and Democratic Thought* (1962).

Change in American Thought

Rowland Berthoff, *An Unsettled People: Social Order and Disorder in American History* (1971); Daniel Boorstin, *The Americans: The National Experience* (1965); Clifford S. Griffin, *The Ferment of Reform, 1830–1860* (1967); Neil Harris, *The Artist in American Society: The Formative Years, 1790–1860* (1966); Oliver W. Larkin, *Art and Life in America* (1949); F. O. Mathiessen, *American Renaissance: Art and Expression in the Age of Emerson and Whitman* (1941); Perry Miller, *The Life of the Mind in America* (1965); Ernest L. Tuveson, *Redeemer Nation: The Idea of America's Millennial Role* (1968); Alice Felt Tyler, *Freedom's Ferment: Phases of American Social History from the Revolution to the Outbreak of the Civil War* (1964).

Shortly after the Missouri Compromise of 1820, Thomas Jefferson and John Adams, aging patriots, exchanged letters on the one remaining major problem that seemed to threaten the nation's stability. "The real question, as seen in the states afflicted with this unfortunate population," wrote Jefferson in 1821, "is, Are our slaves to be presented with freedom and therefore a dagger? Are we then to see again Athenian and Spartan confederacies? To wage another Peloponnesian War to settle the ascendancy between them?" Adams was equally skeptical. "Slavery in this country," he responded, "I have seen hanging over it like a black cloud for half a century." The "black cloud" was still there when the two Founding Fathers died, in an awesome coincidence, on the same day — July 4, 1826, the fiftieth anniversary of American independence.

During the 1820s and 1830s economic issues such as the Bank War and land policy deflected popular attention from the "black cloud." Only in the 1840s did the landscape once more become overcast with the problem, as Americans grappled with the question of slavery's expansion. Even then, slavery did not completely preoccupy the American people. The nation doubled its population between 1830 and 1850. An industrial factory system began to develop in the North and Middle West. Millions of European immigrants landed on American shores. The country fought a war with Mexico and gained huge new territories in the West. Yet all these events occurred within a society torn by a fundamental and unresolved social problem — the place of blacks and slavery in American life.

The four pairs of chapters that follow examine various phases of the American experience from the 1830s to the 1870s, with special emphasis on changing reactions to the problems of slavery and race. Chapter 17 tells the story of the most important slave revolt in United States history, led by Nat Turner. It serves as a focal point for the discussion of slavery in Chapter 18 which portrays the patterns of Southern society as they affected both slaves and their masters. Chapter 19 deals with the drama of congressional efforts to achieve a compromise over the issue of slavery in the Western territories. The resultant Compromise of 1850 and surrounding events provide a vehicle for exploring, in Chapter 20, three dominant themes of the 1840s and 1850s: Northern economic growth, westward expansion, and the politics of sectional conflict.

John Brown's raid, the subject of Chapter 21, triggered extreme sectional hysteria in both South and North. It can also be understood in relation to a general climate of reform, described in Chapter 22, which characterized the antebellum period. Sectional differences in the United States culminated in civil war and continued in the bitter Reconstruction era that followed. The meaning of the Civil War in human terms is dramatized in Chapter 23 through an account of Sherman's devastating march through Georgia. Chapter 24 describes the major events of the Civil War and Reconstruction — the climactic struggles of a tragic period in our national past.

DIVIDED AMERICA

UNIT FOUR

17 Slaves in Revolt: The Nat Turner Uprising

Six poorly clad black men huddled around their campfire in the woods drinking brandy and barbecuing a pig. They had arrived at this meeting place about noon, started the fire, and waited in silence. Toward mid-afternoon another black man suddenly emerged from the surrounding trees. The six turned to greet him. They had been waiting for this short and stocky figure. His name was Nat Turner. A later description of him reads:

> Five feet 6 or 8 inches high, weighs between 150 and 160 pounds, rather bright complexion, but not a mulatto. Broad shoulders, large flat nose, large eyes. Broad flat feet, rather knockkneed, walks brisk and active. Hair on the top of the head very thin, no beard, except on the upper lip and the top of the chin. A scar on one of his temples, also one on the back of his neck. A large knot on one of the bones of his right arm, near his wrist, produced [by] a blow.

Turner greeted the other blacks and joined them around the campfire. We know his companions only by their first names—Sam, Nelson, Hark, Will, Henry, and Jack.

Turner sat down, stared directly at Will, and demanded to know something he already knew quite well. Why had Will come to his rendez-vous? According to Turner's later account, Will replied that "his life was worth no more than others and his liberty was as dear to him." Turner continued the questioning: "I asked him if he thought to obtain his freedom. He said he would, or lose his life."

The seven men spoke further about their plans until some time after sunset. Then, at a command from Turner, they trudged back out of the woods and through ripe tobacco fields to a clearing. Here stood a large, handsome frame house. It belonging to a white man named Joseph Travis, who happened to own Nat Turner. An eighth black, Austin, joined them at the Travis home. Then, as Turner later recounted, "they all went to the cider press and drank, except myself."

About midnight the group gathered in front of the house. Turner climbed through a window, opened the doors to his men, and gave them

guns that had been stored inside. His men now insisted that he "spill the first blood." Armed with a hatchet and accompanied by Will, Turner entered Travis's bedroom and swung wildly at the sleeping man. The blow merely grazed Travis's skull, and he jumped out of bed screaming for his wife. A second later, Will bashed his head in with an ax. Within moments, wielding his ax, Will also killed Mrs. Travis, their three oldest children, and an apprentice, none of whom ever awoke.

The band of black men then searched the house for arms, collecting a half-dozen rifles and several pounds of gunpowder. They left soon afterward and started walking down a road that led to the town of Jerusalem (now Courtland), some fifteen miles away. They had gone only a short distance when someone remembered that the Travises had another child, a baby who slept in a cradle near its parents' bed. "Henry and Will returned and killed it," Nat Turner later observed. He formed the others "in a line as soldiers" and marched his seven-man "army" down the road. With the murder of this one family began the greatest slave revolt in the history of the United States. It started on Sunday, August 21, 1831, in the sleepy Virginia county known as Southampton.

Southampton County, in southeastern Virginia, was an important agricultural area. It had several large farms that employed slave labor and might have been called plantations. Such was the Travis homestead. More common were small farms tilled by poor whites who owned no slaves. The federal census in 1830 showed that Southampton was second among Virginia counties in growing rice and potatoes. A decade later, it led the state in cotton production.

Southampton County's planters might have felt an occasional twinge of concern over their safety. Blacks in the area (most of them slaves) outnumbered whites by almost two to one. Among the 9501 Southampton blacks counted by the 1830 census takers was a thirty-year-old, Bible-reading, visionary slave preacher named Nat Turner.

Turner was born in Southampton County on October 2, 1800. At the time, members of his family were slaves of a man named Benjamin Turner. (It was common for slaves to be given the last name of their master.) When Nat was only three or four years old, he already felt that he had been singled out by God to achieve some great work. As he said later, he thought he "surely would be a prophet." Young Nat certainly seemed a prodigy to his elders. His upbringing was unusual for a slave child, in several ways. At an early age he was taught to read and write by his parents. As a youth, he spent much time at prayer. Also, he was apparently spared much physical labor. Instead, he had free time when he could study schoolbooks belonging to his master's children or simply be alone with his thoughts. He remembered other slaves turning to him for help because of his "superior judgment."

At a very early age, Turner decided to pursue a lonely, almost friendless, life while awaiting the great works for which he believed God had prepared him. "Having soon discovered myself to be great, I must appear so, and therefore studiously avoided mixing in society, and wrapped myself in mystery, devoting my time to fasting and prayer."

Several times as a young man in his twenties, Turner claimed to have divine visions. His reputation as a preacher spread among whites as well as blacks in Southampton County. Yet he appeared aloof and puzzling to most of his fellow slaves. One time he escaped. But, instead of trying to reach shelter in the Great Dismal Swamp—some twenty-five miles away—he stayed in the woods for thirty days. Then he casually returned to his owner. "The Negroes found fault, and murmured against me," Nat later remarked, "saying that if they had my sense they would not serve any master in the world." By this time, however, Nat Turner believed himself destined for a greater role than that of an escaped slave, skulking in swamplands to avoid recapture. "I now withdrew myself as much as my situation would permit, from the intercourse of my fellow slaves, for the avowed purpose of serving the Spirit more fully."

Turner's vision of a divinely inspired slave revolt came to him in 1828, according to his account. "The Spirit instantly appeared to me," he said, and told him of the task ahead: "I should arise and prepare myself, and slay my enemies with their own weapons." A heavenly sign would instruct him when to begin. The signal that triggered his actual plan to revolt was an eclipse of the sun in February 1831. That month, Turner outlined his general scheme to Henry, Hark, Nelson, and Sam, who later brought in Will and Jack. Turner's men began to call him the Prophet because of his mystical statements. The small band of plotters could gather easily at church meetings or barbecues to plan the rebellion, since few whites in the Jerusalem area had the slightest suspicion of an impending uprising.

Nat Turner's master in 1831, Joseph Travis, had acquired him in 1830 after marrying the widow of his former owner. Turner remembered Travis as "a kind master, [who] placed the greatest confidence in me; in fact, I had no cause to complain of his treatment to me." But Travis was a slaveholder. As such, he was marked by "the Prophet" for destruction.

To the very moment of revolt Nat Turner spoke more easily with the God whose commands he believed he was obeying than with his own black followers. After agreeing to meet his six companions in the woods at noon on the fateful Sunday, he joined them instead hours later, for "the same reason that had caused me not to mix with them for years before." However, once the Travis family had been chopped to pieces and the revolt was under way, Turner's aloofness no longer affected them. The killing began in earnest.

Some distance from the Travis house lived Salathiel Francis. His home was the rebels' next stop as they obeyed Turner's command to "carry terror and devastation" along the road to Jerusalem. Their work was aided by the fact that the rebellious slaves knew most of the families in the neighborhood. When they arrived at the Francis house, Sam knocked at the door and shouted that he had a letter to deliver. It was after midnight. Yet the unsuspecting planter opened the door immediately, only to be dragged outside and beaten to death. No one else was home, so Turner and his men marched on to the home of a Mrs. Reese, whose door they found unlocked. They murdered Mrs. Reese in her bed.

By sunrise on Monday other slaves had joined the group. They now numbered fifteen, with nine mounted on horses. Monday morning they arrived at the house of Elizabeth Turner, whom Will killed, along with Sarah Newsome. No woman was raped either then or at any point during Nat Turner's march of destruction. At each stop along the way, however, the rebels destroyed whatever valuable property they found, and they seized money, guns, and ammunition.

From the Turner residence the blacks on horseback rode on to the home of Richard Whitehead, while the others detoured to kill a slave-holding family named Bryant. As the nine armed blacks rode onto his property, Richard Whitehead stared unbelievingly from a nearby cotton patch. The blacks called him, and as he walked toward them, Will's ax dropped him in his tracks. Dismounting, the slaves tore through the house, putting to death the entire family. Here occurred the only murder Nat Turner acknowledged having committed personally during the entire uprising—that of Whitehead's daughter Margaret. Margaret "had concealed herself in the corner. On my approach she fled, but was soon overtaken, and after repeated blows with a sword, I killed her by a blow on the head, with a fence rail."

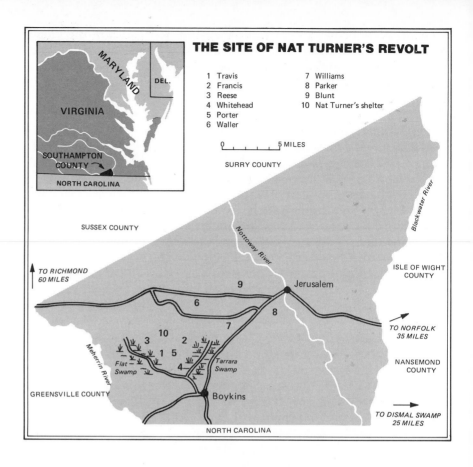

THE SITE OF NAT TURNER'S REVOLT

1 Travis
2 Francis
3 Reese
4 Whitehead
5 Porter
6 Waller
7 Williams
8 Parker
9 Blunt
10 Nat Turner's shelter

By then the six blacks who had detoured to the Bryant home returned, having "done the work of death assigned them." The entire party moved on toward Jerusalem. The mutinous slaves again broke into small bands, since several scattered slaveholding families lay in their path. The main group, led by Turner himself, rode on to Richard Porter's home, only to discover that Porter had escaped with his family. "I understood there," Nat later acknowledged, "that the alarm had already spread, and I immediately returned to bring up those sent to other plantations."

Richard Porter's family was not alone in escaping from Nat Turner's wrath. By dawn on Monday, August 22—less than twelve hours after the revolt began—small numbers of whites began straggling into Jerusalem from the direction of the killings, rousing the town to the threatened black invasion. Within hours, a rider left Jerusalem and headed north for the state capital at Richmond, about seventy miles away. He carried an urgent letter appealing for military help.

Wild rumors spread quickly across the state. In the absence of more accurate information from Southampton, the rumors threw white Virginians into a panic. Thousands of angry slaves, it was said, had banded together to take over the state. According to reports, the rebels were well armed and commanded by soldiers from Haiti.[1] Rumor had it that Northern abolitionists had helped incite the insurrection.

Whole companies of the state militia were hastily called up, and they headed for Jerusalem. By the time the first outside help had arrived, however, the uprising had already been crushed by Southampton County's own militia groups and armed white farmers. They had begun riding out after the small band of black rebels shortly after Richard Porter and others first sounded the alarm.

When he found Porter's family missing, Nat Turner realized the importance of marching as quickly as possible to seize Jerusalem. He knew, too, that he should keep his band together at full strength in the event of an attack. At each house along the way the rebels slaughtered the white inhabitants and urged nearby slaves to join them. By the time Turner and his men reached the home of a Captain Harris, who had also fled with his family, their ranks numbered about forty. Most seemed untroubled by Harris's absence, as they jubilantly destroyed his valuables, drank his liquor, collected his rifles, and rode on.

By this time "General Nat"—as his men reportedly started calling him—had decided on his tactics. He ordered those on horseback to ride ahead, killing whomever they met along the way. This would frighten the remaining whites in the area so that they would flee from their homes, and even abandon Jerusalem to his men. Turner himself remained at the rear, directing his foot soldiers while coaxing the slaves he met to join the rebellion. When General Nat reached a house, its occupants had usually been killed, although he later commented: "I sometimes got in sight in time to see the work of death completed, viewed the mangled bodies as they lay, in silent satisfaction, and immediately started in quest of other victims." In this way, Mrs. Levi Waller and her ten children were killed, then William Williams and his two small boys. Mrs. Williams was caught running away and brought back to her dead husband's side. The rebels ordered her to lie down beside him and shot her. Several other families perished as well. By Monday afternoon the rebel band numbered between fifty and sixty, "all mounted and armed with guns, axes, swords, and clubs." They were only three miles from Jerusalem. Their leader urged them to press on into the town, but several of them insisted on stopping at the plantation of James Parker, where they had relatives. Most of Turner's men rode across the fields toward Parker's house to collect their kinfolk (the Parker family had already escaped), but Turner himself remained at the roadside with seven or eight of his soldiers. This delay proved fatal for the rebels.

A local militia captain, Alexander Peete, had ridden out from Jerusalem at the head of eighteen volunteers. He was probably as startled to find Nat Turner and his small band of blacks in front of the Parker

---

[1] In 1794 blacks in Haiti—led by Toussaint L'Ouverture—had overthrown French rule there. Although the French captured Toussaint, they failed to retake the colony. The success of the black revolt in Haiti frightened American slaveholders for decades afterward.

plantation as Turner was to see Peete. Turner coolly ordered his handful of followers to form ranks and prepare to fire. Shots rang out on both sides, and the white militiamen fled. The black insurgents pursued Peete's men until the retreating militiamen ran headlong into another party of armed whites who had left Jerusalem to hunt down the rebels. Turner's small band, now heavily outnumbered, scattered into the surrounding woods. Most of them were wounded. For the rest of Monday afternoon, General Nat backtracked across much of the area of his earlier march. He combed the woods for his men while evading the growing numbers of militiamen who searched for him. By evening he had collected almost forty men, including several new slave recruits. He placed guards around his camp and rested for the night. But the men on patrol panicked, believing the camp under attack. When order was restored, Turner's "army" had been reduced to about twenty.

"The Prophet" set out early on Tuesday morning to continue recruiting the slaves in the area. His group reached the home of Dr. Simon Blunt just before daybreak. Almost immediately, the rebels were fired on by a party of armed whites and by some of Blunt's slaves. Several of Turner's men were killed. The rest retreated to the home of Captain Harris, which earlier had been deserted. This time, another band of militia opened fire on the slaves from within the house. Most of the blacks fled into the woods, where they were quickly rounded up. Only two, Jacob and another slave named Nat, retreated to the woods with General Nat. They waited until evening, when Turner sent his last two followers in search of his original group. They never returned.

Sixty hours after the rebellion had begun, it was crushed. Nat Turner was left alone with the shattered wreckage of his mission. According to Turner's own account, God had not promised him success—only that he would perform the "great work" of "carrying terror and devastation wherever we went." This he had done. In less than three days his men had killed fifty-five whites from Southampton County slaveholding families: eleven men, fourteen women, and thirty children. At least as many blacks were also killed during and after the revolt by white militiamen. These militiamen seldom knew whether their victims had actually taken part in the revolt.

As for Nat Turner himself, he proved more skillful in defeat than in battle. He managed to remain free, eluding thousands of whites, for almost two months. During that period, throughout the country, the black "Prophet" of Southampton County became both famous and infamous.

Just as Virginians of the seventeenth century had studied the omens that foreshadowed Bacon's Rebellion, so did most white Southerners see a train of alarming events leading up to Nat Turner's Revolt. Had not an even more widespread plot among slaves and free blacks been discovered in Charleston, South Carolina, a decade earlier? This conspiracy was led by a free black named Denmark Vesey. It was exposed in 1822, and its leaders were executed. But rumors of such plots cropped up regularly in the years before the Southampton revolt. Had not a militant free black in Boston, David Walker, published a widely distributed *Appeal* in 1829 calling for slave uprisings throughout the South? And, in that same city, had not a journalist and printer named William Lloyd Garrison begun publishing a notorious abolitionist newspaper called *The Liberator*, which demanded immediate and total emancipation of all slaves?

Although Boston was 500 miles from Southampton County, many Southerners blamed the abolitionist writings of Walker and Garrison for stimulating a desire for rebellion in blacks such as Nat Turner. Some even suspected antislavery Northerners of actually plotting the Southampton revolt. Almost every white Virginian, for example, would have agreed with the sentiments of the state's leading newspaper, the Richmond *Enquirer*. Only a few days after the slave rebellion had been crushed, it printed this comment:

> When an appeal is actually made through the press to this unfortunate class of our community, calculated to mislead them, and while it involves us in serious trouble, leads those unhappy creatures to destruction, it is time for us to arouse from an indifference to a conduct which is daily augmenting and becoming worse and worse. To attempt to excite discontent and revolt, or publish writings having this tendency, obstinately and perversely, among us, is outrageous—it ought not to be passed over with indifference. Our own safety—the good and happiness of our slaves, requires it.

This criticism came from a newspaper whose editor, Thomas Ritchie, believed in the gradual emancipation of slaves. Obviously, the reaction of proslavery Southerners was much more hysterical. Thinking about the Nat Turner Revolt, supporters of the "peculiar institution"[2] may have remembered South Carolinian Edward D. Holland's warning at the time of the Vesey conspiracy:

> Let it never be forgotten, that "our NEGROES are truly the *Jacobins*[3] of the country; that they are the *anarchists* and the *domestic enemy,*" *the common enemy of civilized society,* and the barbarians who would, IF THEY COULD, become the DESTROYERS of our race.

Southerners were fearful that Turner's insurrection would inspire other slaves to rebel. They began acting on these fears, often in an incredibly barbaric manner. An antislavery Northern observer, E. A. Andrews, wrote:

> In every town and village, an active and vigilant patrol is abroad at such hours of the night as they judge most expedient, and no Negro dares, after the prescribed hour, to be found at a distance from his quarter. Great cruelty is often practiced by the patrols toward unoffending slaves. The principal object of such visits is to terrify the slaves, and thus secure their good behavior, and especially to prevent their wandering about at night.

---

[2] This term for slavery seems to have been used first by a South Carolina newspaper in the 1850s, which spoke of the dangers then threatening "the peculiar domestic institutions of the South."

[3] The Jacobins were a leftist political group of the French Revolution. Their name became synonymous with extreme and dangerous radicals.

Andrews went south prepared to find such cruelties, and he might therefore be expected to exaggerate. But many similar accounts filled the Southern press itself. The editor of the Richmond *Whig*, a militiaman himself, wrote the following typical account:

> A party of horsemen started from Richmond with the intention of killing every colored person they saw in Southampton County. They stopped opposite the cabin of a free colored man, who was hoeing in his little field. They called out, "Is this Southampton County?" He replied, "Yes, Sir, you have crossed the line by yonder tree." They shot him dead and rode on.

Nowhere was the punishment of innocent slaves for Nat Turner's brief uprising more ruthless than in Southampton County itself. Nathaniel Bacon's men over a century earlier had consoled themselves for failing to find any marauding Indians by slaughtering villages of peaceful ones. In the same manner, roving companies of militiamen and vigilante slave patrols—often drinking from the same stocks that had nourished Nat Turner's band during its brief lifetime—butchered many innocent slaves unlucky enough to fall into their hands. The situation became so offensive to the commander of military forces at Southampton, General Eppes, that he issued an order on September 6 threatening to shoot any of his own men caught mistreating local blacks. Eppes cautioned against further "acts of barbarity and cruelty" on the part of his own troops; but numerous slaves in the area paid with their lives before the carnage ended.

Throughout the South, state legislatures reacted to the acute fear of uprisings by further limiting the already restricted lives of slaves. The Virginia asembly endorsed the widely proclaimed "lesson" of Southampton County (to quote the Richmond *Enquirer*) that "no black man ought to be permitted to become a preacher" by passing a complete ban on "any assembly or meeting, for religious or other purposes" by either slaves or free blacks. Only whites could preach to black congregations, and slaves had to accompany their masters to church. Other new Virginia laws forbade free blacks to carry weapons, increased the penalties for blacks assaulting whites, prohibited the sale of liquor to slaves, and allowed whippings for blacks who expressed "seditious" thoughts.

In every other Southern state, within months after the Nat Turner Revolt, a flood of similar legislation tightened controls over both slaves and free blacks. These actions fulfilled the prediction made by Garrison's *Liberator* concerning the white Southerner's reaction to the Turner uprising. "In his fury against the revolters," wrote the abolitionist editor, "who will remember their wrongs?"

While Nat Turner remained free, the object of Southern fears and fury, forty-six other blacks were brought to trial in Jerusalem for taking part in the revolt. The militiamen had obviously cast their nets too wide, for five free blacks were included among the accused. Sixteen slaves and three freemen died on the gallows for their alleged role in the revolt. Seven more were sentenced to be deported to the harsher conditions of

The capture of Nat Turner. Turner had been hiding in a cave near the Francis farm for almost two months. (NYPL/Picture Collection)

Deep South[4] slavery. The others were acquitted, although several slaves in nearby counties were also convicted as accomplices in the uprising.

Meanwhile, Nat Turner lived a hand-to-mouth existence as a fugitive. After his last supporters had scattered on August 23, he returned to the Travis home and collected some food. In a nearby field he scratched out a shelter under a pile of fence rails. There he remained undetected for six weeks, just a short distance from his former slave cabin. Every evening the hunted rebel would leave briefly to drink water from a nearby stream. As the days wore on, he began to spend the entire night prowling through the neighborhood "gathering little or no intelligence, afraid of speaking to any human being, and returning every morning to my cave before the dawn of day."

One time when he returned, Turner saw a dog leaving his hiding place carrying a piece of meat. His days were now numbered. A few evenings later, two slaves, hunting with the same dog, passed his hideaway. The animal spotted Turner walking nearby and began barking. Turner later recalled:

> Thinking myself discovered, I spoke to the Negroes to beg concealment. On making myself known they fled from me. Knowing then they would betray me, I immediately left my hiding place, and was pursued almost incessantly until I was taken a fortnight afterwards by Mr. Benjamin Phipps, in a little hole I had dug out with my sword, for the purpose of conceal-

---

[4] The term "Deep South" refers to the southeastern states, especially Georgia, Alabama, Mississippi, and Louisiana. The older Southern states such as Virginia and Maryland are often known as the Upper South.

ment, under the top of a falled tree. On Mr. Phipps' discovering the place of my concealment, he cocked his gun and aimed at me. I requested him not to shoot and I would give up, upon which he demanded my sword. I delivered it to him, and he brought me to prison.

Turner was captured on October 30. Once locked in his Jerusalem cell, he was questioned by a white lawyer named Thomas R. Gray. The black insurgent apparently agreed to tell Gray his own story of the revolt. Turner's narrative, edited by Gray, appeared as a pamphlet, *The Confessions of Nat Turner*, early in 1832. At Turner's trial he pleaded not guilty, "saying to his counsel that he did not feel so." His narrative, however, was read to the court and served to convict him. After finding him guilty on November 5, Judge Jeremiah Cobb pronounced the inevitable death sentence, though with added fervor. He sentenced Turner to "be hung by the neck until you are dead! dead! dead!"

In talking to Gray, Nat Turner denied the existence of any widespread slave conspiracy. When he saw the lawyer's skeptical expression he said: "I see, sir, you doubt my word; but can you not think the same ideas might prompt others, as well as myself, to this undertaking?" The prisoner apparently impressed Gray considerably. Despite the attorney's proslavery beliefs, he defended Nat Turner against charges being made in the Southern press that he was an ignorant and cowardly black who had rebelled only to secure enough money to escape northward. "For natural intelligence and quickness of apprehension," Gray wrote, Turner "is surpassed by few men I have ever seen." Furthermore, Turner's Revolt could be understood, the lawyer argued, only as the action of "a complete fanatic warped and perverted by the influence of early impressions." Gray was probably referring to the childhood religious visions "the Prophet" claimed to have had. But elsewhere in the *Confessions,* Gray evoked this fearful image of Turner:

> The calm, deliberate composure with which he spoke of his late deeds and intentions, the expression of his fiend-like face when excited by enthusiasm, still bearing the stains of the blood of helpless innocence about him; clothed with rags and covered with chains; yet daring to raise his manacled hands to heaven, with a spirit soaring above the attributes of man; I looked on him and my blood curdled in my veins.

Most accounts at the time agree on the dignity with which Turner spoke to questioners such as Gray and confronted his final days. "Do you not find yourself mistaken now?" Gray once asked him shortly before his death. "The Prophet" quietly responded, "Was not Christ crucified?" Calmly and without recorded last words, Nat Turner went to his death at noon on November 11, 1831.

One man who was intensely concerned with the whole episode of the Nat Turner Revolt and its aftermath was the governor of Virginia, John Floyd. His diary provides an interesting account of what the insurrection meant to a moderate white Southerner.

Floyd, born in Kentucky, had trained as a surgeon before going into Virginia politics. He had served as a Democratic congressman from 1817 to 1829. Although originally a supporter of Andrew Jackson, he felt increasingly drawn to the views of Jackson's pro-Southern Vice-President, John C. Calhoun. Unlike Calhoun, however, he opposed slavery and advocated gradual emancipation.

Floyd had been governor for only a year when the Nat Turner Revolt occurred. He first heard of the rebellion on Tuesday, August 23, when the rider from Jerusalem reached Richmond. Floyd took immediate charge of preparations for quelling the uprising. Within hours he dispatched several companies of militia to Southampton County. By the end of the week the governor received definite news that the rebellion had been crushed. Yet, on August 29, his diary recorded a request from several other Virginia counties and from the town of Fredericksburg for militiamen to help quell other expected slave revolts. Virginians were obviously uneasy.

Governor Floyd insisted on being kept closely informed about the trials of those blacks accused of taking part in the rebellion. So completely did the Nat Turner Revolt obsess him that his diary in the following months mentions little else but the Jerusalem trials, rumors of other slave conspiracies, and reflections on their meaning. By mid-September, however, Floyd became suspicious of the many reports of black unrest that flowed into Richmond. None of them seemed to materialize once state militia were sent into the area. Of one such rumor he wrote: "I do not exactly believe the report. The slaves are quiet and evince no disposition to rebel."

On several occasions Floyd expressed concern over the fate of those blacks sentenced to be sent to the Deep South. The treatment of slaves was generally much harsher there. Floyd debated whether to commute the sentences rather than "endanger the lives of these Negroes." On other occasions he reprieved some slaves who had been sentenced to death in Jerusalem. Indeed, there is evidence that the governor reviewed personally almost every convicted rebel's trial record.

At the same time, Floyd could not contain his fury at those Northern abolitionists who, he believed, had encouraged the Nat Turner Revolt and similar conspiracies. On September 27 he wrote:

> I have received this day another number of the *Liberator,* a newspaper printed in Boston with the express intention of inciting the slaves and free Negroes in this and the other states to rebellion and to murder the men, women, and children of those states. Yet we are gravely told there is no law to punish such an offense. The amount of it then is this, a man in our states may plot treason in one state against another without fear of punishment, whilst the suffering state has no right to resist by the provisions of the federal Constitution. If this is not checked it must lead to a separation of these states.

When not complaining about the abolitionists, the governor's diary often denounced President Andrew Jackson. Floyd considered him dangerous to Southern interests, especially on such issues as a national tariff policy. After receiving South Carolinian guests returning from an antitariff meeting in Philadelphia, Floyd noted in his diary that the election of Calhoun would "turn out Jackson with all his unworthy officers, men not gentlemen, who lie and slander all men opposed to them to keep themselves in power."

The governor had little time for national politics, however. Requests for men and arms to combat expected slave revolts continued to pour into Richmond from every section of Virginia. Floyd's diary spoke constantly about the "Northern conspirators" who he believed were planning fiendish schemes. As late as October 20, Floyd recorded hearing of a plot by "Northern fanatics" in Philadelphia to stir up a general insurrection throughout Virginia and massacre its white population. Floyd treated the rumors coming from outside his state more seriously than he did those concerning slave conspiracies within Virginia itself, and his diary cautioned that, if the North refused to check the activities of abolitionists, "this Union is at an end as we [in the South] cannot consent to be tied up by the confederacy from doing ourselves justice, when the authorities of these states refuse to check the evil."

Turner's capture and execution only reinforced the determination of antislavery Virginians like John Floyd to prevent such future uprisings, not simply by supervising blacks in the state more closely but also by eliminating the source of discontent itself—that is, slavery. "There are still demands for arms in the lower counties," Floyd's diary commented on November 21. "I could not have believed there was half the fear amongst the people of the lower counties in respect to their slaves."

The problem never seemed to die down, as the governor's subsequent November entries indicate:

Twenty-third day. I have reprieved for sale and transportation southward several slaves.
Twenty-sixth day. I have received more applications for arms.
Twenty-eighth day. I am preparing a message to the General Assembly. It will be ultra states' rights.

By "ultra states' rights" Floyd meant that he would demand that Northern states begin controlling the activities of abolitionists; also he would denounce the federal government for raising tariff duties, in opposition to Southern desires for lower rates.

In his "message to the General Assembly" (the state legislature) the governor also planned to deal with the question of slavery itself. His diary notes: "Before I leave this government, I will have contrived to have a law passed gradually abolishing slavery in this state, or at all events to begin the work by prohibiting slavery on the west side of the Blue Ridge Mountains."

Floyd's plan may sound surprising to us today, but it had the support of many of his fellow Virginians. In large sections of the state slavery had never assumed great economic or social importance. Men like Floyd and Thomas Ritchie of the Richmond *Enquirer* spoke for many Virginians in supporting gradual freeing of the slaves. They favored compensated emancipation—that is, slaveholders would be paid for the slaves who were freed. Most of those who favored this type of emancipation also believed in colonization—resettling former slaves elsewhere. (Africa was the location most commonly thought of.)

Opposition to slavery was particularly strong in the hilly areas and lush valleys west of the Blue Ridge Mountains. There, blacks (whether slave or free) numbered less than 20 percent of the population. In the eastern sections of Virginia, plantation slavery was common and blacks numbered over 50 percent of the total population. Here, supporters of abolition were less numerous.

During the early decades of the nineteenth century, many antislavery voices such as John Floyd's were raised throughout the South. The leading organization devoted to gradual, compensated emancipation —the American Colonization Society—found many of its leaders, and followers, in the region.

When Floyd addressed the state legislature in December 1831, he urged its members to abolish slavery by gradual stages in Virginia. Debate began in January 1832. For three weeks Virginia's legislators wrestled with the problem of abolishing slavery. They engaged in the bluntest and most complete debate on this question ever to take place in the antebellum[5] South. Supporters and opponents of emancipation marshaled

Governor Floyd, though favoring gradual emancipation at the time of the 1831–32 debate in Virginia, soon afterward took a strong proslavery position. (Virginia State Library)

---

[5] "Antebellum" refers to the period prior to the Civil War. The term comes from Latin words meaning "before the war."

their arguments in long speeches detailing the benefits or dangers that would flow from such a policy. Even those who defended the institution did so mainly on the grounds that it was an unavoidable reality rather than a blessing.

A typical defense was that of a delegate named John T. Brown:

> And is there, then, no apology for slavery? Is it a sin of so deep a die that none dare vindicate it? For my own part, I am not the advocate of slavery in the abstract, and if the question were upon introducing it, I should be the very last to agree to it. But I am yet to be convinced that slavery as it exists in Virginia is either criminal or immoral. It was cast upon us by the act of others. It is our lot, our destiny, and whether, in truth, it be right or wrong—whether it be a blessing or a curse—the moment has never yet been when it was possible for us to free ourselves from it. This is enough to satisfy my conscience, and I contend that the happiness of the slave does not call for his emancipation. His condition is better than that of four-fifths of the human family. He enjoys far more of the comforts of life, than the peasantry of many of the nations in Europe. The greater part of mankind must, in the nature of things, be poor and ignorant, toiling anxiously for their daily bread. All cannot be raised to the top of the scale. The Negro, of all others, is the least susceptible of elevation.

The debate ranged over many issues. What might be the economic effects of emancipation? How should colonization be handled? (Both supporters and opponents of abolition were in agreement on the need for this step if blacks were freed.) What was the morality of slaveholding? The specter of Nat Turner hung plainly over the entire proceedings. Few speakers, whatever their views on emancipation, bothered to disguise their anxiety over the prospect of future slave revolts. A typical antislavery speaker, for example, pleaded with his colleagues for support by reversing a standard proslavery argument. James McDowell observed:

> It is true to the letter that there is no laboring peasantry in any other part of the world who, in all external respects, are better situated than our slaves—who suffer less from want—who suffer less from hardship—who struggle less under the toils of life or who have a fuller supply of the comforts which mere physical nature demands. In all these respects the slave shares in the equalizing and benign spirit of our institutions and age.
>
> But it is in this very circumstance, in this alleviated and improved condition, that we have a principal cause of apprehension from the slave. You raise his intelligence with his condition, and as he better understands his position in the world, he were not a man if it did not the more inflame his discontent. That it has this effect we all know. The truth is proverbial: that a slave is the more unhappy as he is the more indulged. He could not be otherwise; he follows the impulse of human nature in being so.

Petitions for and against emancipation reached the legislature from all over Virginia. Debate was halted on January 25. Finally, the legislature voted on a mild measure providing for gradual emancipation over a period of many years. It was defeated by a vote of 73 to 58. The representatives had divided along distinct regional lines. Delegates from west of the Blue Ridge Mountains (who held only 102 slaves among them) supported abolition, 49 to 6. Representatives from the eastern areas (men who together owned 1029 slaves) opposed emancipation by 67 to 9. The eastern counties were overrepresented in the legislature, as they had been since the time of Jamestown, and carried the day for slavery.

Antislavery Virginians such as Governor Floyd felt understandably disheartened. Floyd confided to his diary the thought that Virginia itself would split into states on the question:

> Both sides seem ready to separate the state if any one would propose it. I think that event from appearances highly probable.

Floyd was right, though the creation of a separate state—West Virginia—did not occur for another three decades.

As it turned out, the subject of abolition was never again debated anywhere in the antebellum South. Within months, antislavery Southerners like Governor Floyd shifted their attention to defending what they considered Southern rights over the question of tariff nullification. Yet the rebellion did force many white Southerners to confront their own deepest convictions about the relations between master and slave. Never again would this relationship seem as clear-cut as it had before the August rebellion in Southampton County.

The most lasting result of the Nat Turner Revolt turned out to be increasingly severe Southern control of both slaves and free blacks. Many whites in the region apparently shared the fears (if not the conclusions) of the antislavery Virginia legislator who asked in January 1831:

> Was it the fear of Nat Turner and his deluded and drunken handful of followers which produced or could produce such effects? Was it this that induced distant counties, where the very name of Southampton was strange, to arm and equip for a struggle? No, it was the suspicion eternally attached to the slave himself, the suspicion that a Nat Turner might be in every family, that the same bloody deed could be acted over at any time in any place, that the materials for it were spread through the land and always ready for a like explosion.

A remarkable story was told by a black preacher who was in Virginia during the Nat Turner Revolt. Shortly after the rebellion a Southampton County slaveholder went hunting in the woods with a trusted slave, who carried his master's gun. The black had been with the slaveholder's family for many years, and he had led his master and his family to safety during the uprising. In the forest the bondsman handed the gun to his master, saying that he could no longer live as a slave. He asked his owner either to give him his freedom or to kill him. The white man hesitated for a moment, then took the gun and shot the black man through the heart.

Although this episode might never have occurred, the choice it speaks of was given to white Virginians in the aftermath of the Nat Turner Revolt. Like the slaveholder in the story, they chose to kill the last promise of a peaceful emancipation.

18 Slavery in the Antebellum South

With the wisdom of hindsight, we can say that the issue of slavery was too complex to be resolved—even in one state—by a legislative debate such as that held in Virginia in 1832. The sons of these Virginians would go to war over the "peculiar institution." Their fathers and grandfathers had, after all, wrestled with the problem unsuccessfully since the time of the Revolution.

When news of the Declaration of Independence reached England, even British supporters of the colonial cause complained about one aspect of the American Revolution. The "assigned cause and ground of the rebellion," wrote one Englishman, "is that every man hath an unalienable right to liberty and here the words, as it happens, are not nonsense, but then they are not true; slaves are there in America, and where there are slaves, there liberty is alienated." The practice of slavery in "republican" America seemed a glaring contradiction not only to Englishmen but to the revolutionaries themselves—many of whom owned black slaves. The Declaration of Independence opened with lofty phrases about equality. But the Second Continental Congress cautiously decided to omit a passage in the original draft that denounced human bondage. Some American leaders from Southern colonies, such as Thomas Jefferson and George Washington, expressed concern over maintaining slavery within a democratic republic. But they did so privately.

The thirteen colonies contained about half a million slaves at the time of the Revolution. Every colony had some, but the great majority lived in the South. There were 200,000 in Virginia, 100,000 in South Carolina, and at least 70,000 each in Maryland and North Carolina. In some Southern colonies slaves comprised 50 percent of the population. There were also slaves in the North. New York had 25,000 and New Jersey had about 10,000. Pennsylvania and Connecticut each had about 6,000 slaves. There were about 5,000 in Massachusetts and 4,000 in Rhode Island.

Fear of slave uprisings was common in eighteenth-century colonial America, despite the fact that only a few insurrections actually took place. Boston's Patriots were outraged by the presence of black troops among the occupying British army before the Boston Massacre. They were also angered by rumors that the redcoats were stirring up the city's small black population. Virginians were just as outraged in 1776 when the departing royal governor urged slaves to revolt against their masters and join the British in exchange for their freedom.

Along with fear of blacks went an equal measure of contempt. Most ordinary "free" Americans of the Revolutionary era—even those who favored abolition—believed that blacks were innately inferior to whites. "Comparing them by their faculties of memory, reason and imagination," wrote Jefferson, "it appears to me that in memory they are equal to the whites, in reason much inferior, and in imagination dull and tasteless." Few people of Jefferson's time would have quarreled with his view (although some might have challenged that notion that a black person had a memory—or anything else—equal to a white's).

During the Confederation period, steps were taken to end slavery in large areas of the Republic. In the period between 1783 and 1786, Massachusetts, Connecticut, Rhode Island, New York, and New Jersey either abolished slavery outright or provided for its gradual disappearance. In Virginia the legislature passed an act in 1782 easing the

process by which owners could emancipate their bondsmen. At Jefferson's direction the Northwest Ordinance of 1787 prohibited slavery in the Northwest Territory. And even though the Constitution made no provision for slavery as an institution, it did provide that the foreign slave trade be abolished after 1808.

But what would happen to slaves who were freed? Since even *moderate* whites feared blacks or looked down on them, very few white Americans were prepared to accept a large free black population living among them. Most schemes for emancipation from the Revolutionary era up to the time of the Virginia legislative debate failed to resolve the underlying problem of freed slaves. Most supporters of gradual emancipation, from Thomas Jefferson to John Floyd, believed in the need for colonization—a policy that was easier to agree on in principle than to achieve in practice.

Slave auctions were regarded as a necessary evil by many slaveowners. After turning some of his "people" over to an auctioneer, one Southerner grieved: "I did not know until the time came what pain it would give me." (Culver Pictures)

The task of the North in emancipating its blacks after 1790 was relatively simple. The region contained only 40,000 slaves and 27,000 freed blacks; the white population totaled 1,900,000. Thus roughly 1 out of 28 people was a black. The situation was very different in the South, where there were 1,271,000 whites, 657,000 slaves, and 32,000 free blacks. In other words, over a third of the Southern population was black. By the time of the Nat Turner Revolt, through individual emancipation (a process known as manumission) and increases by birth, there were over 181,000 free blacks in the South.

Fears of an unstable free black population were obviously much greater among Southerners than among Northerners. Many white Southerners sincerely wanted to abolish slavery. But Southern leaders from the time of the Founding Fathers until the Virginia legislative debate of 1832—and beyond—were afraid of even *gradual* emancipation. They thought it would pose a threat to the safety, stability, and "racial purity" of white society. Besides, slavery was profitable.

THE ECONOMICS OF SLAVERY

The antebellum South comprised a million acres of territory. It stretched from Chesapeake Bay to western Texas and from the Ohio River south to the Gulf of Mexico. Although climate and terrain varied considerably in the South, most of the region had rainfall, temperature, and soil conditions adequate for producing a variety of staple cash crops.

During the colonial period, the major crops grown on Southern plantations were tobacco, rice, indigo, and (to a much lesser extent) cotton. In some areas more than one of these crops was important. In Southampton County, for example, farmers grew both rice and cotton on a large scale.

"King Cotton"

Tobacco had been the South's leading export before the Revolution. But after 1800 the Southern economy came to center on cotton. The most important single factor in this change was the cotton gin. ("Gin" is short for "engine.") It was invented in 1793 by a New Englander named Eli Whitney. Before this time, separating cotton fiber from the seeds was done by hand and took a long time. But with Whitney's machine one person could do the work of fifty. At the same time, improvements in technology enabled England's textile industry to process raw cotton into cloth much more efficiently. Thus, early in the nineteenth century, growing cotton became truly profitable in the United States.

Cotton cultivation spread throughout older states such as Georgia and South Carolina. Even more important cotton-growing areas were the sparsely settled regions that eventually became the states of Alabama, Mississippi, Louisiana, Texas, and Arkansas. The United States had exported only 3,000 bales of cotton in 1790. By the time of Nat Turner's Revolt this figure had grown to 805,000 bales. By 1859, on the eve of Civil War, the figure had skyrocketed to 4,500,000 bales. Cotton alone accounted for almost two-thirds of the total export trade of the United States. And the United States—or, more particularly, the American South—had become the world's leading cotton producer. Along with this phenomenal growth went a continuing demand for more slaves to raise the crop.

Tobacco growing remained important in nineteenth-century Virginia, Kentucky, and North Carolina. Rice cultivation prospered along the South Carolina and Georgia seacoasts. Sugarcane production dominated Louisiana agriculture. Elsewhere in the South the main crop was cotton.

Who Owned Slaves

The 1850 census showed that 1,815,000 slaves were employed in cotton production. Some 350,000 worked in the tobacco fields; 125,000 raised rice; 150,000 labored on sugar plantations; and 60,000 produced hemp. Smaller numbers worked as house servants and artisans on plantations. Several thousand labored as workers in the South's few mines and factories.

Throughout the nineteenth century, a constant flow of both white settlers and black slaves shifted millions of Southerners away from the older seaboard regions and into the newer regions of Alabama, Mississippi, Louisiana, Arkansas, and Texas. Older states such as Virginia and Maryland declined in economic importance in the South because they produced relatively little cotton (despite the output of scattered areas such as Southampton County). During the decades between Nat Turner's Revolt and the Civil War, more than 700,000 slaves were sold in the United States, mainly by owners in the Upper South to purchasers in the Deep South.

It would be incorrect to think of the Southern population as divided simply into two groups— white owners and black slaves. Most white South-

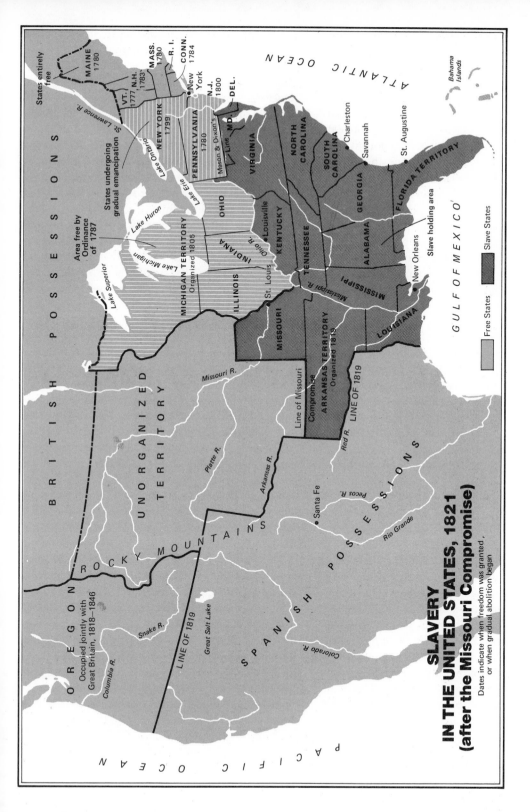

**SLAVERY
IN THE UNITED STATES, 1821
(after the Missouri Compromise)**

Dates indicate when freedom was granted,
or when gradual abolition began

States entirely free

States undergoing gradual emancipation

Area free by Ordinance of 1787

Slave holding area

Slave States

Free States

ATLANTIC OCEAN

Bahama Islands

GULF OF MEXICO

PACIFIC OCEAN

BRITISH POSSESSIONS

OREGON
Occupied jointly with Great Britain, 1818–1846

UNORGANIZED TERRITORY

ROCKY MOUNTAINS

SPANISH POSSESSIONS

LINE OF 1819

MAINE 1780

N.H. 1783

VT. 1777

MASS. 1780

R. I.

CONN. 1784

New York

NEW YORK 1799

N.J. 1800

PENNSYLVANIA 1780

DEL.

MD.

Mason & Dixon's Line

VIRGINIA

NORTH CAROLINA

SOUTH CAROLINA

GEORGIA

ALABAMA

MISSISSIPPI

FLORIDA TERRITORY

St. Augustine

Charleston

Savannah

New Orleans

LOUISIANA

ARKANSAS TERRITORY Organized 1819

MISSOURI

St. Louis

Louisville

KENTUCKY

TENNESSEE

ILLINOIS

INDIANA

OHIO

MICHIGAN TERRITORY Organized 1805

Line of Missouri Compromise

LINE OF 1819

St. Lawrence R.

Lake Ontario

Lake Erie

Lake Huron

Lake Michigan

Lake Superior

Ohio R.

Mississippi R.

Missouri R.

Red R.

Arkansas R.

Platte R.

Santa Fe

Pecos R.

Rio Grande

Colorado R.

Snake R.

Great Salt Lake

Columbia R.

Bahama Islands

erners owned no slaves at all. Most whites who owned slaves in Southampton County and other regions in the South worked alongside their own bondsmen in the fields.

The entire white population of the South in 1860 numbered approximately 7 million, with the total of white families estimated at 1,400,000. There were 383,635 slaveholders. This meant that almost three out of every four families owned no slaves. Only 2,292 landowners owned more than 100 slaves. Some 46,000 slaveholders owned between 20 and 100. The great majority of slaveholders—those owning fewer than twenty slaves—were not owners of large plantations but simply moderately successful independent farmers. Except in the richest cotton-producing areas, slaveholders generally formed a minority of local landowners.

Before the 1830s, some slaveowners freed their own slaves. Like Governor Floyd, they expected that the policy of a colonized, gradual emancipation would be generally adopted throughout the South. But new laws made the practice of manumission more difficult after the Nat Turner Revolt. In any case, most nineteenth-century slaveholders did not consider the possibility of emancipation very seriously.

SOUTHERN SOCIETY

The social structure of the antebellum South resembled a pyramid. The region's few thousand large planters stood at the top. Beneath them was the larger group of slaveholding whites, who owned enough slaves to staff a small or medium-size plantation. Further down the pyramid stood the majority of slaveholders, who owned fewer than twenty slaves. Below them was the great mass of landowning but nonslaveholding white farmers. Toward the base of the pyramid were the lowest white Southerners, the landless and luckless "poor whites," who generally farmed the region's less fertile hill-country areas. At the base of the pyramid were, of course, the slaves themselves, on whose labor rested the South's entire social and economic structure.

Several groups in the South stood outside the central structure of plantation power and influence. There were professionals and businessmen, people like the journalist Thomas Ritchie or the physician (and governor) John Floyd. Such people were often absorbed into the plantation aristocracy by marriage, political alliance, or slave purchases. There were also free blacks—roughly 228,000 in 1860. Most of them lived in the cities of the Upper South or in New Orleans. Though better off than slaves, they were distrusted and discriminated against by Southern whites.

The plantation gentry were the elite of the South. They and their supporters dominated Southern politics up to the Civil War. Their social events, held in the larger cities and towns, set the tone for Southern society. Their impressive mansions often became centers of social life for the surrounding communities.

Though they might be compared to foreign aristocrats, Southern planters differed from them in at least two ways. (1) They were a working aristocracy. The business records of countless plantations show that the men and women who ran them were constantly concerned with the many problems of cash-crop agriculture. (2) They lived on their lands much of the time, rather than being absentee owners. This direct involvement helps account for the fact that slaveholders in the American South worked out a systematic proslavery argument to justify their holdings (see pages 358–359). They were the only "master class" in the Western Hemisphere to do so.

Susan Dabney Smedes, a planter's wife, once observed that "managing a plantation was something like managing a kingdom." A planter often found himself playing many roles within a brief space of time. He was an absolute ruler of his slaves. He was an aristocrat among fellow planters. He was a democratic politician among white men of all classes. He was a fellow Christian when conducting plantation religious services (often for a mixed audience of family members and slaves). The strains of moving back and forth quickly among such different roles produced anguish among some planters, at least according to their own diary accounts.

Planter Society

The most typical of the South's few cities—as racially mixed and tolerant New Orleans was atypical—was Charleston, South Carolina, the cultural center of the Old South and a prosperous seaport since colonial times. The planters of the area, together with the town merchants, supported concerts, lectures, plays, and libraries when such refinements were unknown elsewhere in the colonies. Charlestonians could point to the following "firsts": public library (1698), theater (1736), symphony orchestra (1762), city college (1770), and museum (1773).

The ebb and flow of social life was governed by the customs of the planters. From May to November, when the rice fields were under irrigation, they lived in the city to avoid the dangers of malaria. The Christmas holidays were usually spent in the countryside. By the end of January, the planters were back in town for a round of races, dinners, balls, and other entertainments.

Fully half the population of the city—the slaves—did not share in these pleasures. They were subject to many restrictions because of their numbers and fears of a revolt. In colonial times, slave uprisings that had broken out in Charleston had been crushed with great severity. In 1822 came the Denmark Vesey plot. Vesey, a one-time West Indian slave who purchased his freedom, was charged with organizing a conspiracy among local slaves to revolt. Fifteen persons were executed and others imprisoned or deported after trials related to the alleged plot. Public gatherings of blacks were forbidden. Black sailors—free elsewhere—were jailed while their ships were in port. In 1815 Charleston had been the leading port for the export of cotton and rice. But, as cotton growing spread into the Deep South, the city gradually lost its importance.

Conditions Favoring Slavery

If only a minority of white Southerners actually owned slaves, why did the whole society support slavery so solidly from the Nat Turner Revolt to the South's secession in 1860? Probably a majority of the volunteer militiamen who had helped to quell Turner's uprising owned no slaves, yet they

This New Orleans poster of 1856 speaks for itself. (Courtesy, The New-York Historical Society)

seemed passionately committed to maintaining slavery. Why? At least one answer suggests itself immediately in light of the Southampton County experience. Fear of slave insurrections was intense and constant among antebellum white Southerners. As whites rode their nightly slave patrols in the years after the 1831 uprising, many of them must have remembered that Nat Turner's band slaughtered slaveholders and nonslaveholding whites alike. Thus concern for personal and family security helped bind together different economic classes in the South.

Southerners also favored slavery because of its psychological advantages. The existence of a slave class gave all whites—especially poor white landless farmers—some reassurance that they were superior. Black people like Nat Turner and his men had no status within Southern white society. Even the poorest, least educated white person meant more in the eyes of the law and in Southern society than a planter's brightest, most talented slave. Nat Turner acknowledged having received special treatment from his original owner. But Turner had few, if any, rights that any white person was bound to respect.

Belief in the inferiority of blacks was common among almost all Southern (and Northern) whites, whatever their class. This universal sense of white supremacy blurred the sharp contrast between the South's democratic political system and its rigid economic structure, controlled by a few. Planters and poor whites, if they shared nothing else, still felt a common concern for maintaining slavery and the white racial unity it represented.

Slavery influenced status in another way. Nonslaveholding white farmers could aspire to purchase slaves, and some managed to do so; a few even broke into the planter ranks. When this happened, it bolstered the prevailing belief among white Southerners that only an economy run by slave labor could ensure a broad range of economic opportunity.

In this way, anxiety, outright fear, and ambition combined to create a feeling among almost all Southerners that their "peculiar institution" should be retained and, if necessary, defended. One other factor reinforced the consensus. Southerners were subject to fewer outside influences and new ideas than other Americans. For one thing, most white Southerners were native-born and therefore familiar with the customs of their region. Only 4.4 percent of the Southern population in 1860 was foreign born, compared to 18.7 percent elsewhere in the country. Also, there were fewer big cities in the South than in other regions. Even places like Norfolk and Richmond were little more than overgrown country towns. The vibrant, unsettling qualities of urban life affected only a small minority. Most white Southerners lived on farms, on plantations, or in small towns such as Jerusalem. The bulk of the South's free blacks, however, lived in towns and cities—where they were closely watched and their movements rigidly supervised. Cities thus remained the most obvious breeding ground of discontent with the slave system. And free blacks were clearly the most dangerous element within the closed world of slave society.

The Treatment of Slaves

The conditions under which slaves lived varied considerably. They could be treated relatively mildly and with consideration. Nat Turner, for instance, said that he was well treated by both his original owner and his last one. But savagely harsh practices prevailed on rice and sugar plantations in the Deep South. Slaves from other regions of the South were sent there to be punished, as was the case after the Nat Turner Revolt.

Because slaves were valuable property, an owner seldom abused them so cruelly that they died. Short of this, however, a master could treat his slaves much as he pleased. In times of extreme social tension, whites subjected blacks to the most degrading punishment with little fear of legal action or social criticism. Most recent scholars agree, however, that, under ordinary circumstances, slaves in the United States were generally better fed, housed, and clothed than those in Latin America during the same period. The economic condition of many slaves probably compared favorably with that of many industrial workers in the North and elsewhere—as proslavery people argued. (Even black rebels such as Nat Turner did not complain primarily about their *economic* conditions.) Some slaves were allowed to grow crops on private patches and to keep animals, for their own use or for sale. Almost every plantation had a weekly day of rest and special holidays as well. Thus Nat Turner's companions were probably not missed by their owners as they spent that final Sunday eating roast pig, drinking brandy, and scheming rebellion.

Yet, no matter how kindly a master might treat his slaves, the slavery system was brutal, for it rested ultimately on force. "The whole commerce between master and slave," wrote Thomas Jefferson from his own experience, "is a perpetual exercise of the most boisterous passions. The most unremitting despotism on the one part, and degrading submission on the other." Slave codes, such as those strengthened throughout the South following the Nat Turner uprising, gave whites almost

Although some owners provided good housing for their slaves, much of it was poor, like this ramshackle cabin. Southern physicians often warned planters that they had to provide flooring, windows, and adequate space in order to prevent illness and disease. (Duke University Library)

unrestrained physical power over their slaves. A slave master had absolute authority to decide how long his slaves should work and under what conditions. The law permitted the whipping and beating of slaves. Southern newspapers and court records during the antebellum decades contained numerous accounts of how slaves had been mutilated, hanged, shot, starved to death, or even burned alive. (Indeed, the Southern press was the abolitionists' major source for reports on the mistreatment of blacks.)

The law seldom imposed more than minor penalties on whites found guilty of deliberately injuring or killing blacks. Most often, the offenders escaped punishment completely—as did the white militiamen who committed hundreds of atrocities against Southampton County blacks in 1831. Blacks, whether slaves or freemen, were not allowed to testify against whites in Southern courts of law.

It was often impossible for slaves to keep their families together as units. Slave marriages had no legal status. Slave families were separated, and the members were sold individually as a matter of course. How understandable, then, that the troops of "General Nat" broke ranks at the Parker plantation to collect their missing kinfolk!

ATTITUDES OF BLACKS

Acceptance vs. Resistance

In spite of massive oppression, many slaves appeared to be devoted to their masters, whether from affection, loyalty, or outright fear. This attitude emerges not only from the narratives of slave-holders themselves but from other sources. The slaves who belonged to Dr. Blunt defended their master by firing upon Nat Turner's retreating band. In the Vesey plot and in an 1800 conspiracy in Virginia—led by a slave artisan named Gabriel Prosser—fellow blacks were prominent among those who betrayed the plotters. There are at least two ways of looking at this situation. On the one hand, trusted and indulged slaves such as house servants and artisans had most to lose in any slave uprising—namely, their privileged status. There-fore, they might be expected to place loyalty to their white overlords above any feeling of kinship with rebel slaves. On the other hand, an effective slave rebellion was conceivable only among well-treated bondsmen such as Prosser or Turner. Such people could move easily among other blacks in their areas without arousing the white communi-ty's suspicion.

Often in history, those in an oppressed group who have privileged status, but most con-scious of their condition, are willing to risk all. So it was with the slave preachers, artisans, house ser-vants, and freed blacks who joined the Prosser, Vesey, and Turner conspiracies. It was easy for Nat Turner's original band of supporters—Will, Hark, Henry, Sam, Nelson, and Jack—to meet with their leader. They plotted rebellion for several months while attending church services and weekend gatherings, and on slave holidays, before finally deciding to strike. Their long period of preparation shows the confidence of slaveholders in the region concerning the loyalty of their most trusted bonds-men.

Slave revolts were relatively uncommon in the antebellum South. Yet blacks used a number of other ways to indicate how much they opposed the system. Many slaves tried to flee from bondage: al-most every plantation owner worried about run-aways. Some slaves reached freedom in the North, especially after abolitionists organized the "un-derground railroad" (see page 419). Others simply took off and hid in the woods for a while (as Nat Turner had done), often returning voluntarily as a sign of independence. The huge number of run-aways in the antebellum South showed that many slaves silently nursed a keen desire for freedom,

despite all the efforts by slaveholders to break the will of their blacks. Sabotage was also common. Blacks burned crops and stole supplies. They some-times pretended to be sick and found other, often ingenious, ways to express their hatred for the sys-tem.

The Role of Religion

In all the efforts by blacks to undermine slavery, the black church and its preachers played a significant role. Most slaves followed the religion of their masters, evangelical Protestantism.[1] It was hardly accidental that, after the Nat Turner Revolt, the Virginia legislature placed a ban on blacks like Turner wandering freely through the countryside preaching the Gospel. Most Southern states tried to restrict the activities of black church meetings from the 1830s on—and with good reason. For one thing, slaves bent on rebellion could plot in safety at such gatherings. For another, the Bible itself—especially the Old Testament—offered to blacks prepared to interpret it that way an ideology that justified resistance. Southern whites may have regarded as strange Nat Turner's claim that a heav-enly vision had instructed him to lead his people from bondage and to slaughter their oppressors. But most of his fellow slaves would have immedi-ately understood what he meant.

The spirituals sung by slaves in their churches and elsewhere expressed a great deal. They dwelt on the belief blacks held of themselves as a "chosen" people. "We are the people of God," said one. Another proclaimed: "I'm a child of God, with my soul set free." Such images probably helped keep many slaves from adopting their mas-ters' view of them as submissive children. The spirituals were "sorrow songs," telling of all the troubles and suffering that slaves experienced. They rarely spoke of black inferiority, inadequacy, or unworthiness.

In their religious lives, slaves found more than simply the strength to endure suffering, cer-

---

[1] In general, evangelical Protestants stress the teachings of the Bible rather than the authority of organized church doctrine. They also emphasize the importance of an indi-vidual's personal conversion.

John Randolph

John Randolph once said that asking a state to surrender part of its sovereignty was like asking a woman to surrender part of her virtue. This quip is typical of his wit. It also neatly summarizes his passionate belief in the sanctity of states' rights. To this proud, eccentric member of the Randolph family of Virginia, only Republican (anti-Federalist) principles could ensure personal liberty and freedom from the "tyranny" of strong central government. To the end of his life he espoused these principles, sacrificing political friendships and his own promising career for the often-reckless role of congressional gadfly.

In 1799, at the age of twenty-six, Randolph was elected to the House from Charlotte County. For the next thirty years, except for three two-year intervals (a single defeat, sickness, and service as a senator), he represented this district. His appearances on the floor of the House commanded attention. Usually a bit late, he would swagger in, whip in hand, booted and spurred, with one or two of his favorite hunting dogs. He would speak off the cuff in a rambling and theatrical fashion, scattering epigrams right and left. One historian described him as "one of the most brilliant figures that ever strutted and fretted his hour upon the American public stage."

Randolph's high point was his leadership in gaining congressional approval for the Louisiana Purchase in 1803. He did this although he felt that Jefferson was stretching his constitutional powers. Randolph himself believed in a strict interpretation of the Constitution in order to limit the scope of federal power.

His low point came in 1805, when he bungled the politically inspired impeachment trial of a Federalist judge and quarreled with Jefferson. In 1806 Randolph declared himself independent of his party, accusing Jefferson of "pulling Federalism forward." His opposition to the War of 1812, which swelled the power and popularity of the federal government, cost him his congressional seat.

Randolph returned to Congress in 1815 and opposed on principle the Bank of the United States, the tariff, and other nationalistic measures. His eccentric behavior remained unchecked, but he was

(The Bettmann Archive)

no longer a figure of influence. It was the Missouri Compromise of 1820 that brought him back to the limelight—as a spokesman for states' rights and for the Southern way of life. He first linked the ideas that John Calhoun later developed more fully. He also pitted himself against the architect of the compromise, Henry Clay. The two even fought a duel in 1826. According to Clay, Randolph's actions "came near shaking this Union to the center, and desolating this fair land."

Randolph's final position was not altogether congenial to him and to others of his generation who were uneasy about slavery. He regarded himself a friend to blacks. By the terms of his will he freed his four hundred slaves. When once asked whom he considered the greatest orator he had ever known, Randolph replied, "A slave, Sir. She was a mother, and her rostrum was the auction-block."

tain of a reward in heaven. Often, as in the case of Nat Turner, they also discovered the power to resist actively the efforts of those in authority to brutalize and degrade them. Spirituals, and the sermons of black preachers, were often prophetic. They promised a proud vision of betterment, justice, freedom, and personal worth. They taught that slaves could rise above slavery—not only in the next world, but in this one as well. Nat Turner and his fellow black ministers preached that their people could escape from bondage, through their own efforts and with the help of God. Countless deeds of slave resistance were inspired by this vision. It was embedded in the spiritual life of Southern blacks. Nat Turner's Revolt, the most extreme act of resistance by antebellum blacks, can be understood only as the product of such intense religious belief.

JUSTIFYING THE SYSTEM

While blacks found in the Bible a means of enduring slavery, white Southerners turned increasingly to it, and other writings, for evidence to help justify the system. Earlier proslavery advocates —such as those in the 1832 Virginia legislative debate—had apologized for slavery as a "necessary evil" inherited from the past. In the 1830s Southern political figures, led by Calhoun, began aggressively defending their peculiar institution. Southerners were disturbed for several reasons. They were shaken by such episodes as the Vesey and Turner revolts. The growth of abolitionism in the North frightened them. So did South Carolina's lonely championing of Southern interests in the nullification crises of 1832–33. In defense, they began arguing that their system of bondage was morally justified on all grounds. In 1837, Calhoun expressed this point of view: "Where two races of different origin, and distinguished by color and other physical differences, as well as intellectual, are brought together, the relation now existing in the slaveholding states between the two is, instead of an evil, a good—a positive good."

Slavery as a Positive Good

The "positive good" argument dominated the thinking of white Southerners between 1832 and the Civil War. The region's leading thinkers went to enormous lengths to devise a rationale for slavery. In doing so, they supported a set of beliefs that differed from the basically optimistic and democratic attitudes held by other Americans elsewhere in the country. These theorists argued that most men are naturally limited in their capacities. They said that human progress and achievement come only at the cost of enslaving peoples that are supposedly suited for such bondage. And they held that human society has always been characterized

An antislavery cartoon, published in 1840, mocks the idea, advanced by many Southerners, that blacks had to be treated like children. Depicting black people as competent and capable was part of the strategy of those who favored abolition. (Courtesy, The New-York Historical Society)

1840.] *Anti-Slavery Almanac.* 29

by class distinctions. Not even the extreme pro-slavery advocates during the 1831–32 Virginia legislative debates would have accepted such propositions. Yet, within a decade, they had become the orthodox Southern view of its "peculiar institution."

Governor James H. Hammond of South Carolina insisted that "in all social systems there must be a class to do the menial duties, to perform the drudgery of life." Without such a class, Hammond argued, "you would not have that other class which leads progress, civilization, and refinement." Slavery, then, "constitutes the very mudsill of society and of political government." George Fitzhugh, a brilliant proslavery spokesman, put it in a livelier way. He declared that "some are born with saddles on their backs, and others booted and spurred to ride them—and the riding does them good." These writers argued that whites could not be expected to perform the backbreaking tasks associated with cotton, rice, and tobacco cultivation. Slaves, therefore, became an economic necessity.

Proslavery people used a number of arguments in attempting to prove the virtues of slavery. They found citations in the Bible that justified enslavement, especially instructions that slaves obey their masters. They pointed to the glories of ancient Greece and Rome—both slave societies. They compared, unfavorably, the working conditions of Northern industrial laborers with those of Southern slaves. And, arguing from the false "scientific" theories of their day, they accepted the notion of the innate inferiority of black people.

Such proslavery advocates also glorified planters as an aristocracy of talent and grace. Southern gentlemen were pictured as chivalrous heroes, brave and quick to defend their honor. Southern ladies were portrayed as gentle noblewomen who devoted countless leisure-filled days to such "feminine" pastimes as needlework and music. These romantic images were highly unrealistic. Yet reality and myth agreed on at least one aspect of regional life. Even hostile accounts of the slave South usually acknowledged the longstanding planter traditions of hospitality and generosity toward friend and stranger alike.

Basic to the proslavery defense was a false image of black people. White Southerners insisted on describing blacks as submissive, contented happy-go-lucky children. "A merrier being does not exist on the face of the globe," wrote one Virginian, "than the Negro slave of the United States." This docile image fitted the hopes of Southern slaveholders better than it did the realities of slave life. But Southerners were concerned less with convincing outsiders than with persuading themselves that their proslavery arguments were true. So they harped on the supposed happiness and essential docility of their slaves, despite all evidence to the contrary.

UNCLE CLEM. " Say, Massa Jim, is I wan of them onfortunate Niggers as you was reading about?'
YOUNG GENTLEMAN. " Yes, Uncle Clem, you are one of them."
UNCLE CLEM. " Well, it's a great pity about me.—I'se berry badly off, I is."

Proslavery Americans undoubtedly enjoyed this pictorial jibe at the sometimes over-heated arguments of abolitionists. It appeared in Harper's Weekly *in 1861. (Library of Congress)*

Slavery in the Antebellum South **359**

SLAVE STATES, 1860
PROPORTION OF WHITE AND BLACK POPULATION
(Figures rounded off to the nearest whole percentage point.)

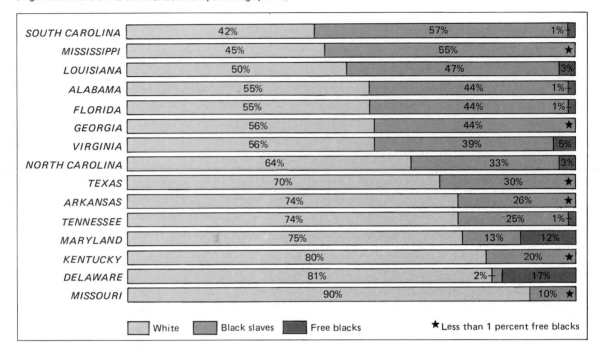

	White	Black slaves	Free blacks	
SOUTH CAROLINA	42%	57%	1%+	
MISSISSIPPI	45%	55%	★	
LOUISIANA	50%	47%	3%	
ALABAMA	55%	44%	1%+	
FLORIDA	55%	44%	1%+	
GEORGIA	56%	44%	★	
VIRGINIA	56%	39%	5%	
NORTH CAROLINA	64%	33%	3%	
TEXAS	70%	30%	★	
ARKANSAS	74%	26%	★	
TENNESSEE	74%	25%	1%+	
MARYLAND	75%	13%	12%	
KENTUCKY	80%	20%	★	
DELAWARE	81%	2%+	17%	
MISSOURI	90%	10%	★	

White · Black slaves · Free blacks · ★ Less than 1 percent free blacks

The End of Moderation

A frank and hard-hitting public debate in the South over the merits of slavery, like the one held in Virginia in 1832, would have been impossible a decade later. Even the idea of gradual emancipation, accompanied by colonization, could not be argued openly in the 1840s. By that time, no Southern state would have elected an emancipationist governor such as John Floyd. Opponents of slavery were driven from positions in Southern churches, universities, and newspapers. Freedom of speech and press on the slavery question no longer existed in the South during the decades before the Civil War. "Southern rights" were to be defended at all costs.

Even before this time, white fears and class tensions had made the South a notoriously violent region. The vengeance taken by militiamen against Southampton County blacks after the Nat Turner uprising did not appear excessive to most white Southerners. The antebellum South was noted for its expert brawlers, marksmen, and duelists. Most Southerners owned guns or at least bowie knives (also known as "Arkansas toothpicks").

Once the "positive good" argument took hold during the 1830s, the level of militancy rose among white Southerners. Planters and their overseers armed themselves, and slave patrols rode regularly through the hot Southern nights. Many plantations became tiny military fortresses, their owners obsessed with thoughts of runaways and rebellions. Southern life became "militarized," not only on the plantations but also in the cities, where militia and town guards watched free blacks closely. By the late 1840s most white Southerners had accepted a view that linked the defense of slavery to every other cherished virtue. The region's leading Presbyterian minister, the Reverend J. H. Thornwell, argued in 1850 that:

> the parties in this conflict are not merely abolitionists and slaveholders—they are atheists, so-

cialists, communists, red republicans, jacobins on one side, and the friends of order and regulated freedom on the other. In a word, the world is the battleground—Christianity and atheism the combatants; and the progress of humanity the stake.

Thornwell probably spoke for the great majority of white Southerners.

The uncharitable, suspicious, and militant South of Thornwell's day seems light years away from the more leisurely, less fearful world of John Floyd and his fellow Virginians. Antislavery Southerners, of either Jefferson's generation or Floyd's, would have found little worth praising in the positive good argument. Yet leaders like Floyd had helped prepare the way for the more aggressive Southerners who followed.

Floyd, after all, supported John C. Calhoun. Like Calhoun, he managed to combine a strong nationalist fervor with an equally passionate belief in Southern rights. He had endorsed South Carolina's attempt at nullification. He opposed slavery, but he had denounced abolitionists and roused public opinion against the "menace" of Northern "agitators." Floyd's generation found it possible to be-

lieve strongly in gradual emancipation while at the same time nursing a violent hatred for Northern advocates of immediate abolition.

But the next generation hardened its point of view. One Southerner who would have agreed with Thornwell was John Buchanan Floyd, son of the antislavery Virginia governor. John Buchanan Floyd believed wholeheartedly in slavery. Like his father, he went into politics. He served as secretary of war from 1857 to 1860 in the cabinet of President James Buchanan. While in this post, Floyd transferred an excessive number of arms from Northern to Southern arsenals. His aim was to stockpile military supplies for the sectional conflict everyone expected.

John Buchanan Floyd resigned from the Buchanan cabinet in December 1860, a convinced secessionist. After Virginia joined the Confederacy in May 1861, he volunteered his services to Virginia. Three decades earlier, his father had unsuccessfully urged the Virginia legislature to abolish slavery. Now John Buchanan Floyd accepted a commission from the same legislature. He would become a major general in an army dedicated to preserving the South's "peculiar institution."

Suggested Readings
Chapters 17-18

The Nat Turner Revolt

Herbert Aptheker, *American Negro Slave Revolts* (1943); John B. Duff and Peter M. Mitchell, eds., *The Nat Turner Rebellion: The Historical Event and the Modern Controversy* (1971); William Styron, *The Confessions of Nat Turner* (1967).

Slavery

John W. Blassingame, *The Slave Community* (1972); P. A. Davis, et al., *Reckoning with Slavery* (1976); Robert A. Fogel and Stanley L. Engerman, *Time on the Cross* (2 vols., 1974); John Hope Franklin, *From Slavery to Freedom* (1974); George M. Frederickson, *The Black Image in the White Mind: The Debate on Afro-American Character and Destiny, 1817–1914* (1971); Winthrop D. Jordan, *White Over Black* (1969); Kenneth M. Stampp, *The Peculiar Institution* (1956).

Slavery in America and Elsewhere

David B. Davis, *The Problem of Slavery in Western Culture* (1966); Carl Degler, *Neither Black Nor White: Slavery and Race Relations in Brazil and the United States* (1971); Stanley M. Elkins, *Slavery: A Problem in American Institutional and Intellectual Life* (1959); Lawrence J. Levine, *Black Culture and Black Consciousness: Patterns of Afro-American Folk Thought in the United States* (1976); William Stanton, *The Leopard's Spots: Scientific Attitudes Toward Race in America, 1815–1859* (1960); Allen Weinstein, Frank Otto Gatell, and David Sarasohn, eds., *American Negro Slavery: A Modern Reader* (3rd ed., 1978).

The Negro in the North

Leon Litwack, *North of Slavery: The Negro in the Free States, 1790–1860* (1961); George Rawick, *From Sundown to Sunup: The Making of the Black Community* (1973); Richard Wade, *Slavery in the Cities* (1964).

The Negro in the South

Clement Eaton, *A History of the Old South* (1975) and *The Growth of Southern Civilization, 1790–1860* (1961); Eugene D. Genovese, *Roll, Jordan, Roll* (1974); Herbert G. Gutman, *The Black Family in Slavery and Freedom, 1750–1925* (1976); William Scarborough, *The Overseer: Plantation Management in the Old South* (1966); Robert Starobin, *Industrial Slavery in the Old South* (1970); Charles S. Sydnor, *The Development of Southern Sectionalism, 1819–1848* (1948); William R. Taylor, *Cavalier and Yankee: The Old South and American National Character* (1961).

The Crisis and Compromise of 1850 19

Potomac River breezes chilled the air as legislators returned to Washington, D.C., in December 1849 for the opening of Congress. Senators and representatives tramped through muddy streets past the city's boarding houses, hotels, and half-finished public buildings. An incomplete stone tower jutted out like a bruised silo; when completed several decades later, it would be a monument to George Washington. The Capitol, still topped by a temporary dome, was being repaired and enlarged to make room for the growing number of congressmen who crowded into its corridors with the admission of each new state into the Union.

The mood in Washington when a new Congress convenes is normally charged with excitement. There was special reason, though, for intense feeling in December 1849. Politicians from the North and South feared that the issue of slavery would wreck the approaching Thirty-first Congress. Some brooded anxiously over the possible collapse of the Union itself.

American politicians had deliberately suppressed the slavery question in national politics since the days of the Founding Fathers. No other issue could arouse Americans to such emotion. No other issue had such power to overcome party loyalties. Southerners were particularly troubled. Fearful of abolitionist attacks since the Nat Turner uprising a generation earlier, they warned that Northern interference with slavery could lead to a breakdown of the national party system.

A struggle to elect a Speaker of the House of Representatives began almost from the moment Congress opened on December 3. The difficulty confirmed the fears about sectional political warfare. The Democratic party had dominated national politics since the days of Jackson. There were now 112 Democrats in the House and 109 Whigs. There were also nine members of the newly formed Free Soil party.

Normally the majority party in the House agrees on its candidate for Speaker and then elects him at the opening session. But these were not normal times. The third party representatives held the balance of power, preventing either major party from having a majority.

Bitterness over slavery and sectional issues strained party lines, threatening to break them beyond repair. The Whigs nominated Robert C. Winthrop of Massachusetts, a descendant of the Puritan governor. He opposed the extension of slavery into the Western territories, but he was not an abolitionist. Still, eight Southern Whigs stormed out of the party's caucus. When the Democrats chose Howell Cobb of Georgia, a supporter of slavery, a small but significant minority of Northern Democrats balked at the choice. These defections meant that neither party could exercise control.

Vote followed vote for three weeks. After sixty-two ballots, the House had still failed to select a Speaker. Even the withdrawal of Cobb's and Winthrop's names on various ballots could not break the stalemate. This frustrating inaction immobilized the entire government. Congress was paralyzed. The Senate could not function without the House. President Zachary Taylor could not deliver his annual message.

On December 22 both sides finally recognized the dangers, and they agreed to change the election system itself. House members resolved that, in order to be elected, a Speaker would in future need only a plurality of votes, not a majority. On the sixty-third ballot they finally chose Cobb. Several Northern Democrats who had opposed Cobb voted for him in the end. Some doubtless hoped to ease the tension. Others were simply tired. "Many members," observed Senator Daniel Webster of Massachusetts," wished to go home for the holidays."

The new Speaker was a moderate, genial man, popular with most members. He tried to heal some of the wounds by carefully allotting committee chairmanships to members from all sections of the country. But other quarrels in Congress showed that tensions remained high. Because the speaker was a Southerner, Northerners expected that someone from their section would be chosen clerk of the House, a position of some importance and profit for the holder. Two Northern Democrats in particular wanted the job. Several Democrats from the South broke party lines, however, to help elect a fellow Southerner (though a Whig) from Tennessee. One furious Northerner felt that this action taught a simple lesson. He wrote to his brother, stating angrily that if a Northerner:

> [does not] bow and humble and prostrate himself in the dust before their high mightinesses of the South, he must hope for nothing. My Yankee blood is fairly up in this matter, and I will see the South all d—to everlasting perdition before I will ever open my lips in its defense.

Even the president of the United States came under attack. Zachary Taylor, who owned several plantations and dozens of slaves, should have presented no problem to the South. His career had been devoted entirely to military service. He had never held public office, nor had he even voted. Taylor had never expressed a hostile opinion on slavery—or anything else. During the campaign of 1848 the South had

A cartoon of 1848 pokes fun at Taylor's unwillingness to commit himself on the issues of the day. The two disgruntled men at left have decided to turn to other candidates: John P. Hale, nominated by the Liberty party, and Van Buren ("Matty"), the Free Soil candidate. (Library of Congress)

QUESTIONING A CANDIDATE

clearly seemed more content with Taylor, a Whig, than with his two opponents. One was Lewis Cass of Michigan, a Democrat. He favored popular sovereignty—that is, allowing people in the territories to decide the slavery question for themselves. Ex-President Martin Van Buren ran on the Free Soil ticket, opposing the extension of slavery into any territory.

Taylor had encouraged Southern hopes by straddling most embarrassing issues or remaining silent. Attacks on him from antislavery spokesmen in the North clinched the matter. The South supported Taylor, and he won the election by a narrow margin.

As president, however, Taylor seemed less acceptable to Southerners. In good Whig fashion he promised to relax the use of the presidential veto. This position caused concern among Southern Whigs who feared that he might allow passage of the Wilmot Proviso.[1] In November 1849 a prominent Southern Whig visited the White House to learn what Taylor intended to do if Congress adopted the proviso. The president claimed to be neutral on the matter. But he added ominously that "if Congress sees fit to pass it, I will not veto it." He opposed the "coercion of the veto" as undesirable. Taylor had already stated publicly that "the people of the North need have no apprehension of the further extension of slavery." In reaction, a group of Southern Whigs vowed once more to leave the Union before they would accept the Wilmot Proviso.

Two presidential statements in 1849 did little to reassure Southerners. Taylor's message to Congress in December urged all sides to avoid agitating "exciting topics of a sectional character." But Taylor did just that. He advised that, since Californians had already decided against slavery, a free California should become a state at once, bypassing entirely the territorial stage. Southerners found this idea unacceptable. They regarded as even worse Taylor's observation, in a later speech, that the New Mexico Territory (present-day New Mexico, Arizona, and part of Colorado) would probably follow California's lead in framing a state constitution prohibiting slavery. "A good Whig document," said Webster of the message, "written in a plain and simple style." But to the South it was evident that Taylor was biased against introducing slavery into newly acquired territories.

On January 21, 1850, Taylor again pleaded for action on California. His special message advised, in effect, that the people in California and New Mexico should enter the Union immediately as states. Avoid complicating the issue, Taylor seemed to say, by extending the Missouri Compromise line all the way to the Pacific Ocean. Let the territorial problem solve itself.

Unfortunately for Taylor's program, the slavery problem in the territories would not go away. Slavery had already reentered national politics to stay. In the summer of 1848, during debates over the Oregon Terri-

---

[1] The Wilmot Proviso was first proposed in 1846. It stated that slavery should be prohibited in all of the lands acquired from Mexico. Congress did not adopt the provision in 1846, but many Northern politicians were committed to its passage (the proviso passed the House twice only to fail both times in the Senate).

tory, Thomas Hart Benton, a Democratic senator from Missouri, had likened the slavery issue to the biblical plague of frogs:

> You could not look upon the table but there were frogs, you could not sit down at the banquet table but there were frogs, you could not go to the bridal couch and lift the sheets but there were frogs! We can see nothing, touch nothing, have no measures proposed, without having this pestilence thrust before us.

Ill feeling over slavery did indeed seem to crop up with every issue. As Congress got under way in 1850, debate in the House seldom rose above the level of name-calling. "For two years," accused Ohio Free-Soiler Joshua Giddings, "the people of the North have been defrauded, deceived, and imposed upon." Georgia's Robert Toombs countered: "I do not hesitate to avow before this House and the country that if by your legislation you seek to drive us from the territories of California and New Mexico and to abolish slavery in this District of Columbia, I am for disunion."

The problem of fugitive slaves brought further trouble. Some Northern states and many Northern citizens had been ignoring or flouting the existing fugitive slave law of 1791. Early in January, Senator James M. Mason of Virginia presented a bill to make the return of captured runaway slaves easier and more certain. William H. Seward, an antislavery Whig from New York and a man close to Taylor, warned that he would try to nullify the effect of a new law by adding a guarantee of trial by local jury for an alleged runaway. The Senate then exploded into a predictable outpouring of sectional complaints and threats. Mississippi's Henry S. Foote branded Seward a fanatic who wished to punish the South. Mason himself, however, defended his proposed bill in reasonable language, and he even agreed to soften parts of it in a bid for Northern votes.

Within a few days two important Democratic senators, Daniel Dickinson of New York and Lewis Cass of Michigan, spoke in favor of milder language and sectional compromise. As tempers cooled, it became possible for someone to step forward and restore calm.

The man who took on this role was Henry Clay. He hoped to engineer the third major compromise of his long career. In 1820, while Speaker of the House, he had helped pass the Missouri Compromise. In 1833, together with John C. Calhoun, he had worked out a compromise tariff bill to lower import duties and thus ease the nullification crisis. The presidency had escaped him three times. But the seventy-three-year-old senator drew consolation from his reputation as a compromiser, and he gloried in the title of "the Great Pacificator" (peacemaker). Clay knew that the conflict of 1850 would be his last major political battle.

On January 29 Clay presented his program for compromise. It consisted of eight points, most of which would soon be joined in one comprehensive, or omnibus, bill. (1) Congress should accept California as a state with a free constitution. (2) In the New Mexico Territory — unfavorable ground for slavery, according to Clay and many others — there should be no congressional restriction or encouragement of slavery. (3) The slave trade should be abolished in Washington, D.C.

These were the pro-North points. Clay's additional proposals were designed to balance things sectionally. (4) The boundary between Texas and New Mexico should be established on a line favoring Texan claims. (5) The federal government should assume responsibility for the debts of Texas before it became a state. (6) Slavery itself was to be guaranteed in the District of Columbia. (7) Congress should pass a tougher fugitive slave law. (8) Congress should formally announce a policy of noninterference with the slave trade among the Southern states. (This eighth and final suggestion, an attempt to sweeten the pill for the South, was later dropped.)

The North stood to gain more from Clay's proposals than the South. Admitting California as a free state would destroy the sectional balance — parity between free and slave states — that still existed in the Senate. (The House already had a Northern majority because the North had more people.) Giving the North a majority in the Senate as well as the House seemed suicidal to proslavery forces.

As for leaving the New Mexico Territory question undecided, Southern extremists feared, with good reason, that free states would eventually emerge from it. Why did this matter to a slaveholder in South Carolina? Because when such states joined the Union, they would elect antislavery congressmen who might vote to abolish slavery. The proposals regarding the Texas boundary and debt would not alter the sectional power balance. And enforcing a new fugitive slave law would depend on Northern cooperation, risky and uncertain at best.

Yet Clay made his appeal primarily to the North, asking for generosity, since the more powerful section had more to give. Northerners, he warned, must be especially understanding about slavery. Although the institution did not figure in their economy or society, slavery was woven into the fabric of Southern society. To talk of abolition threatened the South's "habits, safety, property, life — everything."

Clay expected no help from extremists on the slavery question, and he got none. Northern antislavery advocates had never liked him much, but they bided their time and let Southern extremists voice the first criticisms of his proposals. Eight Southern senators tore into "the Great Pacificator." One angry "fire-eater" (Southern proslavery extremist) denied that Clay had proposed a compromise at all. It was, he said, "cowardly capitulation" to the North.

On February 5 Clay responded with his major speech defending the compromise. In an address which lasted two and a half hours, he ignored the extremists and appealed to Northerners.

> What do you want? What do you want — you who reside in the free states? Do you want that there shall be no slavery introduced into the territories acquired by the war with Mexico? Have you not your desire in California? And in all human probability you will have it in New Mexico also. What more do you want? You have got what is worth more than a thousand Wilmot Provisos.

In the manner of a true compromiser Clay pleaded for moderation.

Let me say to the North and to the South, what husband and wife say to each other. We have mutual faults; neither of us is perfect; nothing in the form of humanity is perfect; let us, then, be kind to each other — forbearing, forgiving each other's faults — and above all, let us live in happiness and peace together.

Henry Clay presents the compromise proposals to a crowded Senate. (The Bettmann Archive)

While Clay looked for votes and worked to generate "spontaneous" meetings, two leading Southerners, representing two generations of proslavery opinion, renewed the attack on his compromise proposals. Senator Jefferson Davis of Mississippi dismissed Clay's plan as misleading if not worthless. He pointed out what many congressmen perhaps chose to ignore in 1850 — that no fugitive slave bill, no matter what its provisions, would work if the North chose to sabotage it. Even the Missouri Compromise line, which Davis hinted might be extended to the Pacific Ocean (thus satisfying the South), could not legally bind the states involved.

In the early part of his career, Calhoun followed a nationalistic line, but by the 1830s, when he championed nullification, he had become the South's strongest voice. Abolition, he warned in 1836, "strikes directly and fatally not only at our prosperity, but our existence as a people." (Library of Congress)

According to Davis, Northern aggression had caused the crisis. "I see nothing short of conquest on the one side, or submission on the other." He claimed that the North sought to degrade Southerners, to make them "an inferior class, a degraded caste in the Union." Unless this stopped, warned Davis, Southerners would follow the example of the thirteenth-century English barons who rose up and forced King John to sign the Magna Charta.

The other Southerner who spoke at this time was John C. Calhoun. In contrast to Davis's emotional oration, Calhoun's logical address demanded specific concessions for the South. The South Carolinian had long demanded Southern unity. A year earlier Calhoun had drafted a Southern Address, a strong document of grievance and warning that was signed by forty-eight congressmen.

By 1850 Calhoun was old and sick. He knew that his career and life were almost over. He had already fainted in the Senate lobby several times. On one of these occasions he was carried into the vice-president's office to recuperate. Another South Carolinian, Robert B. Rhett, rushed over. "Ah, Mr. Rhett," Calhoun sighed, "my career is nearly done. The great battle must be fought by you younger men. . . . the South—the poor South!" On March 4 Calhoun presented his speech to the Senate. He did not actually speak, however, because of his feeble health. Senator Mason read his address for him.

Though broken in body, Calhoun remained as firm and uncompromising as ever. He argued that an exact political balance between North and South had to be maintained. No temporary, patchwork solution would do. Compromisers might chant the word "Union!" till doomsday, but it would have no more effect than intoning the word "Health!" over a dying person.

What could be done? As Calhoun saw it, the North had to give slaveholders a chance to settle the West. It had to return runaway slaves and discourage them from fleeing. It had to agree to a constitutional amendment creating a precise balance between Northern and Southern political power in the national government (despite the fact that Northern whites outnumbered Southern whites by more than 2 to 1). If the North could not accept the South on these terms, he concluded, "tell us so, and let the states we both represent agree to separate and part in peace. If you are unwilling we should part in peace, tell us so, and we shall know what to do when you reduce the question to submission or resistance."

Calhoun's defiant stand might represent the views of a minority, but still it demanded some direct response. The South Carolinian had attacked Clay's proposals and momentarily upset the majority's impulse to compromise. The man who accepted Calhoun's challenge was Daniel Webster of Massachusetts.

Webster was scheduled to speak in the Senate on March 7. In those days, a major congressional address was a great public occasion. Congressmen worked for days carefully preparing lengthy speeches. Their fellow legislators sat through the speeches and actually listened. Others, too, wanted to hear. Notice of an important speech on the congressional calendar set off a stampede for seats in the gallery. Spectators would line up for admission to the chamber, even if it meant crowding in the aisles, close-packed with other standees, for four or five hours. The Senate presented just such a picture when Webster gave his famous "Seventh of March" speech.

The portly senator rose, pulled his vest down over his paunch, raised his head, and struck a theatrical pose. "I wish to speak today," Webster began, "not as a Massachusetts man, not as a Northern man, but as an American. I speak today for the preservation of the Union. Hear me for my cause."

Webster traced the history of North–South differences. First, he emphasized the contrast between the North's easy abolition of slavery after the Revolution and the South's commitment to the institution after the invention of the cotton gin and the spread of cotton culture. He did not go so far as to claim that only lack of economic dependence had made slavery seem wrong to the North. But he did argue that his listeners had to bear in mind slavery's significance to the white South. Why then had sectional conflict grown? Because, Webster said, too many radicals in the North now contended that right could be distinguished from wrong "with the precision of an algebraic equation."

Then, Webster denounced both Northern abolitionists and Southern secessionists as dangerous extremists. Abolitionism was harmful, he asserted. The Wilmot Proviso was offensive and unnecessary; no one need "reaffirm an ordinance of nature nor reenact the will of God" by prohibiting slavery in territories "naturally" hostile to its existence. He dismissed the idea of sectional disunion. Secession and peace were mutually exclusive. Finally, Webster argued that, although sectional tensions obviously existed, they could be eased, and major political problems could be settled. Taking Clay's cue, Webster called on the North to keep its part of the basic sectional bargain. It must not harass the South over slavery, however repugnant the slave system. It must obey the law regarding slavery and even approve a new federal law to ensure that Southerners could recapture their fugitive slaves.

When he attacked the secessionists, Webster included Calhoun, the man "who, I deeply regret, is prevented by serious illness from being in his seat today." But Calhoun was there that day, having shuffled into the Senate shortly after Webster started. Calhoun shot back: "The Senator from South Carolina is in his seat." Webster continued with hardly a pause, saying that "peaceable secession is an utter impossibility." When he had finished, the galleries broke into sustained applause. Calhoun tried for the final word: "I cannot agree that this Union cannot be dissolved. Am I to understand that no degree of oppression, no outrage, no broken faith, can produce the destruction of this Union? The Union *can* be broken." These were Calhoun's last words in the Senate.

Webster had more to worry about from Northern reaction to his speech than he did from Calhoun. Webster had opposed slavery, though he was not an abolitionist. Now his call for justice to the South, especially his support for capturing and returning fugitive slaves, infuriated Northern antislavery advocates. They responded predictably and savagely. Horace Greeley, editor of the influential New York *Tribune*, wrote that the speech was "unequal to the occasion and unworthy of its author." William Cullen Bryant wrote a poem about the "fallen angel," the "Godlike Daniel." Theodore Parker, an abolitionist Boston preacher, claimed that he knew "of no deed in American history done by a son of New England to which I can compare this but the act of Benedict Arnold."

Other Americans, however, hailed Webster's speech for what it was—a significant and eloquent statement urging both sides to stop agitating the slavery question. Conservatives, North and South, read it with approval; 120,000 copies had been rushed into print. Even the Charleston *Mercury*, unfriendly to the North and its politics, noted that "with such a spirit as Mr. Webster has shown, it no longer seems impossible to bring this sectional contest to a close." Businessmen overwhelmingly supported the Clay-Webster position. They worried that all the squabbling about slavery would interfere with trade. William W. Corcoran, an important Washington banker, went further. He sent Webster a letter of congratulation with a check for $1000.

With Clay and Webster clearly speaking for an older generation, it remained for a different breed of politician to be heard from. While young Southern fire-eaters continued to regard Calhoun as their mentor (even after his death on March 31), a rising group of Northern politicians looked for new leadership. William H. Seward of New York, who had just arrived in the Senate, became their spokesman.

Seward, a little man of large ambition, had played the political game astutely since the middle 1820s, mainly in his home state. First an Anti-Mason, then a Whig, Seward's election as governor in 1838 broke the Democratic Albany Regency's domination of New York State politics. He knew the value of party organization and party discipline (even at the expense of party principles) far better than most older Whig leaders. He knew also that antislavery and anti-Southern feeling was rising in the North and would soon monopolize American politics.

The leader of the antislavery Whigs, William Seward spoke of a "higher law" than the Constitution. (Library of Congress)

Seward addressed the Senate on March 11. His speech was clearly a reaction to Webster's effort of four days earlier, although there was little similarity between the two in structure, delivery, or content. Seward read a prepared text in a monotone to a sparsely filled chamber. Still, leading senators (even Calhoun) attended because they realized the importance of Seward's views and those for whom he presumably spoke.

In essence, Seward rejected all plans for compromise. Since no real threat of disunion existed, he insisted, why compromise? Slavery, a barbarous relic of earlier and less enlightened times, would die a peaceful and natural death. Why encourage it? Congress could legislate for the territories, and it should prohibit slavery there. "I shall vote for the admission of California directly, without conditions, without qualifications, and without compromise."

Most of Seward's speech followed a Northern hard line on territorial questions, not far removed from President Taylor's stand. But the New Yorker added some statements that made his speech notorious. Did the Constitution protect slavery? "There is a higher law than the Constitution," answered Seward. Slavery must go. A moral question had been raised that transcended the "narrow creeds" of political parties. He dismissed slavery as "temporary, accidental, partial, and incongruous." Freedom, on the other hand, was "perpetual, organic, universal, and in harmony with the Constitution."

Southerners were outraged. Even many Northerners joined in attacking Seward's "higher law" doctrine as anarchy. President Taylor himself, previously close to Seward, ordered his administration newspaper to rap the New Yorker on the knuckles. These quick reactions revealed clearly that Seward, like Calhoun, spoke only for a congressional minority. But, just as clearly, his stand could not be ignored.

Stephen Douglas, Illinois's "Little Giant," was the ultimate mastermind of pro-compromise strategy. (Library of Congress)

The debate continued. On March 13 another Northerner, Stephen A. Douglas of Illinois, made an important speech. On the surface, Douglas was critical of Clay's proposals. Actually, however, he spent more time attacking Clay's enemies and upholding popular sovereignty, his preferred solution. Douglas regarded the will of local inhabitants in the territories as all-important. He felt that the Missouri Compromise restriction of 1820, which prohibited slavery in the Louisiana Territory north of 36° 30' latitude, was no restriction at all. Politicians in Washington, he believed, could neither establish nor forbid slavery in a territory. Local laws would prevail. They would inevitably reflect local environment and attitudes. Douglas also added his opinion that slavery could not expand west of the Mississippi beyond where it already existed — that is, Missouri, Arkansas, Louisiana, and Texas. His statement made many Southerners suspicious of Douglas and other so-called National Democrats.

At this point, a Senate fracas indicated how deep the impasse had become. It involved Thomas Hart Benton of Missouri and Henry S. Foote of Mississippi. Both were Democrats, and both wanted a compromise. Beyond this they parted ways. Benton was tall and burly, a polished and often bombastic orator. He had been in the Senate for thirty years, as long as Missouri had been a state. Although he represented a slave state, Benton did not believe in the extension of slavery. Let California join as a free state, he urged, and then solve other disputed sectional matters one by one.

In his last year as a senator, Thomas Hart Benton maintained his moderate views on slavery. (Library of Congress)

Foote was short, rotund, and animated. Other senators acknowledged his considerable talents yet regarded him as a bit eccentric. Previously, Foote had been close to the Southern extremists. But he now supported Clay's proposals for compromise and strongly urged combining them into an omnibus bill.

On April 17, Benton attacked Clay's omnibus approach as pandering to Southern hysteria. Foote labeled the charge a slander. Benton then rose and headed straight toward his adversary. No match for Benton at

Henry Foote's life seemed to embody inconsistency. A Mississippian, he opposed secession. Then he served in the Confederate congress. Still later, he quarreled with Jefferson Davis, resigned his seat, and left the South. (Library of Congress)

coining phrases, Foote decided on another equalizer. He pulled a gun. Other members of the world's greatest deliberative body—as the Senate likes to call itself—quickly moved to avoid catastrophe. As Foote was stopped by a friendly senator, Benton, who rarely let slip the opportunity to add drama to a situation, tore open his shirt front and shouted, "Let the assassin fire! I am not armed. I have no pistols. I disdain to carry arms. A pistol has been brought in to shoot me with—to assassinate me!"

"I brought it here to defend myself," Foote responded lamely, at the same time handing his gun to Senator Dickinson.

"Nothing of the kind, sir," Benton retorted. "It is a false imputation. I carry nothing of the kind, and no assassin has a right to draw a pistol on me."

Foote obviously did not want to shoot Benton; yet the outrageous incident could not be ignored altogether. A special Senate committee investigated. It reported two months later but declined to recommend any disciplinary action against Foote.[2]

Although congressional speechmaking played a more important role in 1850 than it does today, the real work of Congress—then as now—went on in committees. The day after the Benton–Foote confrontation, the Senate attended to more serious business. Foote moved that a select committee chaired by Clay work to resolve the sectional disputes. His resolution passed, 30 to 22. Thirteen senators world serve, seven Whigs and six Democrats. Seven were from slave states, and six were from free states. But only one senator from each section could be labeled an extremist.

For the next three weeks congressional activity creaked to a halt. Even the speechmakers were silent, waiting for Clay's committee to report. Its seven-point recommendation strongly resembled Clay's original plan. There was no minority report.

Few senators seemed satisfied with everything Clay's committee had proposed. When formal debate on the report began on May 13, almost every senator wanted to be heard, some several times.

The compromise faced another challenge—from outside Congress. The Mississippi legislature had called on representatives of the slave states to meet at Nashville, Tennessee, in June 1850 to adopt methods of "resistance to [Northern] aggressions." Calhoun had supported the Mississippi move enthusiastically. His spirit would certainly be present at Nashville. Daniel Webster predicted that if the Southern extremists actually convened at Nashville, Andrew Jackson's body would turn over in its nearby grave.

Nevertheless, the Nashville Convention did take place. But—like New England's Hartford Convention during the War of 1812—it proved a

---

[2] As usual, Benton had the last word. Foote later tried to patch up the quarrel, announcing his intention to write a small book in which Senator Benton would figure prominently. Benton countered with an announcement that he would write a large book that would not even mention Senator Foote. Both men kept their word.

bit of a dud. Only nine of the slave states sent delegates, and not all of them were leaders in their own states. There was a great deal of heated talk. The meeting's final report, drafted by South Carolina fire-eater Robert B. Rhett, honored Calhoun's memory and most of his principles. Yet the convention kept cool. Delegates did not abandon their desire to defend Southern rights. But most still waited for a decision in Congress.

Most Americans observed the Nashville Convention fiasco with satisfaction, and none more so than President Taylor. The general was the nation's most important opponent of Clay's compromise, and he was angry. Clay and other Whig leaders had slighted him. Some had even made fun of him as lacking intelligence. Clay went so far as to heap praise on another general and would-be president, Winfield Scott—Taylor's rival for military glory during the war with Mexico. The president's anger boiled over whenever he heard talk of secession. At one point, a group of worried Southerners had trooped into the White House to ask Taylor if he really meant to maintain the Union at all cost. Eyes blazing (possibly thinking of Andrew Jackson's sternness at such moments), the president swore that he would blockade every Southern port if secessionists took over federal facilities. He promised to head an army of Northern and Western troops to put down any rebellion.

The situation had not yet come to a head, though. In the spring and summer of 1850 the legislative process still seemed the best solution. Yet it looked as if no compromise could jump the hurdle of a presidential veto. Taylor opposed the omnibus bill. When his own newspaper began speaking kindly of Clay, Taylor had the editor replaced by someone who would follow the administration line. Clay argued that his proposals would heal at least some, if not all, of the country's wounds on the slavery question, whereas Taylor's would heal only one, the status of California. The White House responded tartly that the original congressional resolution concerned only California and the New Mexico Territory, with no mention of such inflammatory side issues as fugitive slaves or Texan debts.

Throughout June pro-compromise forces made no progress. Opponents were trying to mutilate the select committee report with amendment after amendment and delay it with parliamentary obstruction. "We shall have a warm summer," Webster predicted. "The political atmosphere will be hot, however the natural may be. I am for it and shall fight it out." Arguments of "no earthly consequence start up from time to time," admitted Clay glumly, "to discourage the stoutest heart." The omnibus was stalled, perhaps permanently.

There matters stood, until Washington heat, gluttony, and divine Providence intervened. On the Fourth of July, President Taylor attended ceremonies at the base of the unfinished Washington monument. Under a broiling sun he dutifully heard the ever-present Henry S. Foote (presumably unarmed this time) deliver the Independence Day oration. As the president got up to leave, aides asked him to stay and witness yet another ceremony. A handful of dust from the tomb of Thaddeus Kosciusko, the Polish hero of the American Revolution, was to be deposited in the monument. Taylor waited, standing exposed to the summer sun for an additional hour.

Back at the White House at last, Taylor refreshed himself with huge quantities of fruits, vegetables, and iced liquids. "Cucumbers and cherries with mush and milk," runs the most bizarre of the many accounts of what he consumed.

Taylor loved to eat—heartily and often. He ignored all danger warnings, verbal or internal, even one that appeared in his own official newspaper: "Do not unnecessarily heat yourselves, but, when heated, drink cold water in moderation. Ice water, in small quantities, is an excellent tonic; but some persons flood the stomach till internal chemistry can no longer overcome its effects." The president's internal chemistry broke down. He was overcome with nausea, stomach cramps, and fever. Taylor lingered on until July 9, when he died of acute gastroenteritis.

Into the White House came Vice-President Millard Fillmore. Like Seward, though always several rungs below him, Fillmore had climbed the ladder of New York Anti-Masonic and Whig politics. New Yorkers of all parties had a history of squabbling and splitting into factions. By 1850 Fillmore and Seward found themselves in warring camps. Taylor might have been on good terms with Seward, but Fillmore had no use for his fellow New Yorker. Where did Fillmore stand on the compromise? Most Southerners distrusted him, since he came from western New York, the most strongly antislavery part of the state. Fillmore's nomination and election to the vice-presidency in 1848 had caused an anxious stir in the slave states. But in that election the South had placed its faith and sectional interests in Taylor's hands.

As late as April 1850, Fillmore had indicated agreement with Taylor's policies. Sometime between April and early July, however, he became a supporter of Clay's compromise. He later claimed that, just before Taylor's death, he had told the president that if the Senate tied the vote on the compromise, he, as vice-president (and president of the Senate), would break the tie with a yes vote. Daniel Webster may have had something to do with Fillmore's conversion. As secretary of state, he emerged as the leading figure of the new administration. He exercised a strong influence over the conscientious but intellectually limited Fillmore. So did Clay, a semiofficial administration spokesman in Congress. Apparently all that remained was to push the omnibus bill through, have the new president sign it, and let peace reign. But this was not to be.

On July 31 the Senate was voting on a complicated series of amendments to the compromise. The omnibus was maneuvered by its opponents into a position where it could be killed. One by one, each of the bill's provisions was rejected by the Senate. The only part to be adopted was a bill granting territorial status to Utah. This passed easily, since the federal government wanted to reassert its authority over the Mormons (see pp. 313–14). Little else remained but disappointment for the pro-compromise forces and delight for Northern and Southern extremists. A reporter for a New York paper described the scene: "Jefferson

Davis's face grinned with smiles. Old Bullion's [Thomas Hart Benton] few hairs actually bristled with delight. *He* had routed *Clay*! *He* had smashed his omnibus to atoms! Seward was dancing about like a little top." The reporter went on to describe other gleeful senators—a Northern supporter of Seward whose "thick sides shook with sporadic spasms"; a Southerner who "looked solemn in solitary glory"; and an Ohio abolitionist shaking hands with a Louisiana fire-eater.

Clay walked out of the Senate chamber humiliated. He had fumbled his last great compromise effort. He soon left Washington for the resort town of Newport, Rhode Island—probably in a huff and surely very tired.

Clay's failure created Douglas's opportunity. Since the omnibus package had fallen to pieces, the energetic Douglas took the logical course of action. He worked on one bill at a time. There were five altogether in addition to the Utah bill.

First was the bill settling the Texan boundary and debt. It passed on August 9. Next came the question of California. Southerners wanted to divide the region into two states—one free and other undecided on slavery. Douglas, however, aimed to have the free-state California constitution adopted as it stood. Jeremiah Clemens of Alabama warned: "I do not know what Alabama may do, but if she determines to resist this bill by force, secession, by any means, I am at her service. If this be treason, I am a traitor—a traitor who glories in the name."

Despite talk of this kind, the Senate passed the California bill on August 13. Next to clear the Senate was the New Mexico territorial bill.

The measure strengthening the fugitive slave laws, which would soon become the weakest link in the compromise chain, passed on

In this bitter comment on the Fugitive Slave Act of 1850, Webster (center) helps a slave catcher chase a fleeing woman and child. In the accompanying caption, Webster is made to say: "Any man can perform an agreeable duty—it is not everyone that can perform a disagreeable duty." (Worcester Art Museum)

August 26. In view of later reactions Northerners were surprisingly calm on the measure, perhaps because several leading antislavery figures had left Washington for cooler parts by that time. Still, twenty-one senators (fifteen of them Northerners) failed to vote on the fugitive slave bill. Had they all responded to the roll call, the bill would probably have been defeated. Douglas had applied strong and effective pressures on his Democratic colleagues in the Senate. The final bill of the compromise was one outlawing the slave trade in Washington, D.C. Clay himself came back to Washington in time to shepherd it through Congress on September 16.

The House of Representatives played second fiddle to the Senate throughout the dramatic 1850 session. Once the bills were through the Senate, the House passed them with little trouble early in September.

The Compromise of 1850 had initially been a Whig venture—or so Clay and Webster saw it, despite their nonpartisan appeals. But it became a reality through a series of bills shepherded through Congress by Stephen A. Douglas, a Democrat who relied largely on the votes of Democratic congressmen. Of eleven senators who supported at least five of the six compromise measures, nine were Democrats. Votes in the House of Representatives revealed the same Democratic concern for compromise. The Democrats, the party of Jefferson and Jackson, had clearly committed themselves to a new version of their old policy—keeping the slavery issue out of national politics.

A Deepening Sectional Conflict 20

Passage of the Compromise of 1850 and its acceptance by most Americans, North and South, seemed to close a dangerous chapter in United States history. Americans felt that they had achieved peace. Or at least they hoped so —with a fervor that showed how afraid they had been. If slavery took root as a national issue, the country itself might split apart. The apparent escape from this danger led to a feeling of elation in 1850. Yet if the past decade was a true indicator of the future, the years ahead would be anything but placid.

Indeed, slavery was already a national issue, even though people might wish to think otherwise. It had become so through its relationship to newly acquired territories in the West—the very question that had led to the Compromise of 1850. Throughout much of American history, disruptive political crises have often been involved with issues of geographic expansion. The slavery controversy was no exception.

EXPANSION INTO THE FAR WEST

Americans have generally believed that they could move freely into unsettled territories wherever available. This belief was never more stoutly held than during the first half of the nineteenth century. In this period some Americans moved into land acquired through the Louisiana Purchase. Even more attractive, however, were Far West regions that did not belong to the United States. The most important of these were the Oregon Country, claimed by Great Britain, and the Mexican-held Southwest and California.

Americans had various reasons for wanting to expand westward. Merchants were attracted to trade possibilities. Oregon, for example, offered not only furs but also a possible base for commerce with Asia. Many Americans were looking for good farming or grazing land. Even those who stayed home in the East took pride in the idea of westward expansion.

Newspapermen and politicians wrote approvingly of national growth. The phrase that best expressed the current attitude was manifest destiny. The term was coined by John L. O'Sullivan, a Democratic editor from New York. He wrote in 1845 that it was the "manifest destiny [of the United States] to overspread and to possess the whole of the continent which Providence has given us for the development of the great experiment of liberty and federated self-government entrusted to us."[1]

In other words, it was manifest (obvious) that fate had destined the United States for an expansionist role. Americans had a God-given mission to establish the Protestant religion, a democratic political system, and a capitalist economy in all the lands from the Atlantic to the Pacific. Many Americans shared this imperial vision in some form.

The Oregon Country

Since the late eighteenth century, many nations had shown an interest in the Oregon Country—the region between the Rockies and the Pacific

---

[1] The term "manifest destiny" was first used in Congress by Robert C. Winthrop, the Whig nominee for Speaker of the House in 1849.

coast extending from what is now California northward to Alaska. At various times Spain, Russia, Britain, and the United States had laid claims to all or part of the area.

American merchants en route to the Far East sailed along the Oregon coast. So did traders in search of furs. In 1792 an American named Robert Gray explored and named the Columbia River. Lewis and Clark also explored the Oregon Country. In 1811 New York merchant John Jacob Astor founded a fur-trading post, Astoria, at the mouth of the Columbia River. When the War of 1812 broke out, however, he sold the post to a British company.

By 1825 both Spain and Russia had given up their claims to the Oregon Country. But British fur traders of the Hudson's Bay Company were quite active in the region. There was a spirited three-way rivalry between them, the American traders employed by the Rocky Mountain Fur Company, and Astor's American Fur Company. In 1818, Great Britain and the United States had agreed that the two countries would occupy Oregon jointly until 1827. When the agreement expired, it was extended for an indefinite period.

The settlement of American families in the Oregon Country was stimulated mainly by missionaries, who went to the area in the 1830s. Methodist minister Jason Lee opened a mission in the Willamette Valley near what is now Salem, Oregon. Marcus and Narcissa Whitman, backed by the Congregationalists and Presbyterians, established a mission on the Columbia River near present-day Walla Walla, Washington.

The missionaries' letters described in glowing terms Oregon's fertile soil, magnificent rivers, and excellent climate. Small groups of settlers moved westward in the early 1840s. The first major party of pioneers—a thousand strong—set out from Independence, Missouri, in 1843. The westward migration became so heavy in the late 1840s that it was known as "Oregon fever."

Pioneers made the trip to Oregon along the famous Oregon Trail. From Independence, the trail led northwest and then followed the Platte River, crossing the Rockies at South Pass. Travelers to Oregon proceeded northward through the valleys of the Snake and Columbia rivers.

In 1843, Americans in Oregon organized a provisional government and petitioned Congress for annexation. Settlers from the United States now far outnumbered those from Canada and Britain. The earlier arrangements for joint occupation of the region seemed unsatisfactory—at least to Americans.

Annexation of Oregon was one of the issues in the presidential campaign of 1844. The Whigs nominated Henry Clay, who tried to avoid the

U.S. GROWTH OF POPULATION, 1790-1860

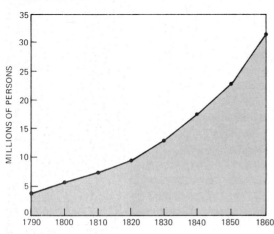

U.S. FOREIGN TRADE, 1790-1860

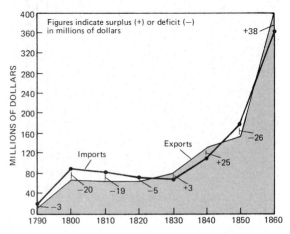

THE OREGON BOUNDARY DISPUTE

RUSSIAN TERRITORY

NORTHERN LIMIT OF U.S. CLAIM — 54° 40'

CANADA

ROCKY MOUNTAINS

VANCOUVER IS.

OREGON COUNTRY

LINE OF 1846 — 49°

PACIFIC OCEAN

CRUX OF DISPUTE 1846

Columbia R.

Astoria

Columbia R.

Ft. Walla Walla

Willamette R.

Ft. Vancouver

OREGON TRAIL

Snake R.

UNITED STATES

Ft. Hall

SPANISH AMERICAN BOUNDARY OF 1819 — 42°

MEXICAN TERRITORY

0 100 200 300
MILES

question of expansion. The Democrats chose James K. Polk, governor of Tennessee and former Speaker of the House of Representatives. Polk was an ardent expansionist, and the Democratic platform stressed "All of Oregon or none." In other words, said Polk, the United States should expand northward to the 54th parallel. The British insisted on the 49th parallel as a more reasonable dividing line, since it continued westward the already existing boundary that divided the rest of the United States from Canada.

After Polk's election, some expansionists demanded war if the British refused to yield to American demands. Their slogan was "54° 40' or Fight!" Other Americans took a calmer view, and in 1846, the Polk administration negotiated a set-tlement with Britain that established the 49th parallel as the boundary between the western United States and Canada.

An Independent Texas

While American settlement in Oregon led to tension with Britain, expansion into Texas brought on conflict with Mexico. Spain had ceded Florida to the United States in 1819. As part of the bargain, Americans had given up their claim to Texas—a claim they had asserted since the purchase of Louisiana. Americans, however, were already moving into the region. In fact, traders and military adventurers from the United States had helped the Mexicans win independence from Spain in 1821. In return the new Mexican government had confirmed a large land grant previously made by the Spanish to Moses Austin.

Austin, a Missourian, had planned to colonize the Brazos River area with Americans. He died in 1821. Stephen Austin, his son, carried out the plan. In 1822 he planted a colony of three hundred American families at Columbus, Texas. Most were Southerners, small slaveholders or nonslaveholding farmers. They were lured by the promise of practically free farmland for cotton cultivation.

During the next decade American settlers moved steadily into Texas. By 1830 there were at least twenty-five thousand whites and two thousand black slaves. Most of the newcomers remained Protestant despite the terms of the original Austin land grant, which committed American settlers to becoming Roman Catholics. Although Texas formed part of a state in the Mexican republic, the majority of its inhabitants were firmly committed to their American customs and beliefs.

The "invasion" of these American settlers frightened the Mexican government. Its leaders were afraid that the Texans would try to break away and join the United States. Mexico crushed one revolt in 1826. After this, Mexicans tried unsuccessfully to restrict further American immigration. They forbade the importation of slaves into Texas and placed heavy taxes on imported American goods. These efforts proved to be too little and too late. Americans in Texas were already encouraging their fellow countrymen to settle there. They were also agitating with the Mexicans for their own state government.

President Antonio López de Santa Anna decided to tighten Mexican control over Texas. Early in 1836 he led an army of 6000 into the region. On March 2 the Texans met at Washington, Texas, and declared their independence from Mexico. They adopted a constitution legalizing slavery and established a provisional government. As commander of the Texan army they named Samuel

In the last hours of the Alamo garrison Jim Bowie wields the knife named after him as the Texan defenders fight back Santa Anna's attacking Mexican army. (The Bettmann Archive)

Houston, former governor of Tennessee and a friend of Andrew Jackson.

Meanwhile, Santa Anna had begun his siege of the Alamo, a former mission at San Antonio. For twelve days a garrison of 187 Texans led by William B. Travis withstood an attack force of 3000. Finally, on March 6, the Alamo fell. Its defenders—including the famous frontiersman Davy Crockett—were massacred. Later in March 300 Texans were slaughtered in a similar fashion when they surrendered at Goliad. For several weeks Houston had to retreat before Santa Anna's army. Then, on April 21, he made a stand at San Jacinto. Shouting "Remember the Alamo!" and "Remember Goliad!" Houston's men defeated Santa Anna and took the Mexican general prisoner.

Santa Anna signed a treaty (which he later repudiated) recognizing the independence of Texas. In September 1836, Texas voters ratified their new constitution and elected Sam Houston president. At the same time, they indicated their desire for annexation to the United States.

Troubles Over Annexation

The annexation of Texas became a controversial issue. Northern antislavery forces did not want to add another slave state to the Union. President Jackson, who wished to avoid a sectional split, refused to endorse the proposal. So did his successor, Van Buren.

Texans then began to turn to Europe for recognition and aid, showing particular interest in Britain. Southern expansionists were alarmed by the prospect of a close alliance between cotton-hungry Britain and the cotton-producing Republic of Texas. They pressed for a treaty of annexation. So did President Tyler (who had come into office after Harrison's death in April 1841) and Secretary of State John C. Calhoun. A treaty that they negotiated in 1844, however, was rejected overwhelmingly by the Senate.

Texas, like Oregon, was an issue in the presidential campaign of 1844. One of Polk's slogans was a demand for "the reoccupation of Oregon and the reannexation of Texas." (The "re" in each case cleverly implied that the United States had always owned the disputed territories.)

After Polk won, but before he took office, President Tyler exploited the popular support for expansion. He pressed for a joint congressional resolution annexing Texas. Since it was not a treaty, the resolution did not require a two-thirds Senate vote, and thus it squeaked through. Texas ratified the resolution and joined the Union in December 1845.

The Mexican War

When Texas became a state, Mexico broke off diplomatic relations with the United States. This was not the only sore point between the two nations. The United States claimed that the Texan boundary extended to the Rio Grande, whereas Mexico set it at the Nueces River. Another Mexican grievance was the growing number of Americans in California.

Early in 1846 Polk ordered General Zachary Taylor, commanding a force of 1500, to take up a position along the Rio Grande. War fever grew among nationalists in both countries. The Mexicans refused to see John Slidell, an American diplomat sent to Mexico City to negotiate. A minor skirmish between Taylor's forces and the Mexican troops along the Rio Grande gave the eager American president an excuse for war. Polk blamed Mexico for shedding American blood; Congress declared war on May 11; and the House authorized the recruitment of an army of 50,000 volunteers.

The American troops, though fewer in number, were better supplied and better led than the Mexican forces. In fact, the Mexican War served as a training ground for many young officers who later commanded armies during the Civil War. Among them were Robert E. Lee, Ulysses S. Grant, J. E. B. Stuart, George B. McClellan, and "Stonewall" Jackson.

The United States won a series of victories on Mexican soil—at Monterrey, Buena Vista, and Veracruz. In September 1847, Americans took Mexico City itself. The United States also seized New Mexico and California with small military forces supported by American settlers. Mexico had to sue for peace.

The Treaty of Guadalupe Hidalgo ended the war. Mexico gave up California, New Mexico, and the disputed area east of the Rio Grande. In return

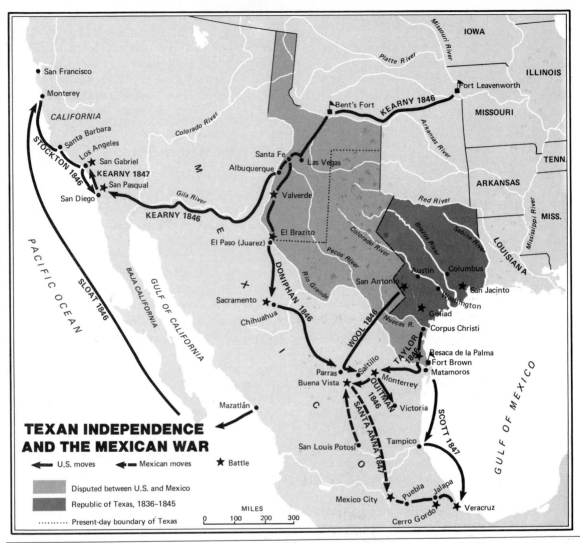

TEXAN INDEPENDENCE AND THE MEXICAN WAR

⬅— U.S. moves
⬅-- Mexican moves
★ Battle

▨ Disputed between U.S. and Mexico
▨ Republic of Texas, 1836–1845
········· Present-day boundary of Texas

MILES
0 100 200 300

In the spring of **1846,** before war was officially declared, Zachary Taylor engaged the Mexican army in two battles north of Fort Brown, Texas. After Palo Alto (May 8) and Resaca de la Palma (May 9), Taylor drove the Mexicans out of the disputed area between the Nueces River and the Rio Grande. He then crossed the lower Rio Grande and captured Matamoros (May 18) and Monterrey (Sept. 29). Before the end of the year Taylor, aided by John E. Wool, occupied Saltillo, and, along with General A. Quitman, then proceeded south to Victoria.

In the meantime Stephen W. Kearny led an expedition from Fort Leavenworth to Santa Fe (Aug. 15) and proclaimed New Mexico part of the United States. He left part of his army there, sent another detachment under Alexander W. Doni-

phan south to join Taylor, and proceeded to California. Doniphan, on his march from Sante Fe to Chihuahua, defeated the Mexicans at Valverde (Dec. 12) and El Brazito (Dec. 25). Meanwhile, Kearny had arrived in California, where John Sloat had already taken Monterey. After a temporary setback at San Pasqual (Dec. 6) Kearny joined Robert F. Stockton in San Diego.

In **1847** Kearny and Stockton were victorious at San Gabriel (Jan. 8-9). By February the Southwest was in American hands. Doniphan defeated the Mexicans at Sacramento (Feb. 28) and reached his goal, the provincial capital city of Chihuahua, on March 1. Taylor's army drove Mexican forces under Santa Anna out of a narrow mountain pass near the hacienda of Buena Vista (February 22-23).

This print of the American Army taking posses-sion of the Mexican capital in 1847 appeared in a history of the war written by George W. Kendall of the New Orleans Picayune. *Kendall was one of the first war correspondents ever to ac-company an army on its campaigns. (Library of Congress)*

In the winter of 1847 Winfield Scott led a force of about 10,000 with orders to take the for-tified city of Veracruz. His men landed on the beaches outside the city on March 9, launching the first large-scale amphibious operation in United States military history. On March 29 he captured the city, and began an advance toward the Mexican capital. Near Jalapa, he stormed a mountain pass at Cerro Gordo (April 17-18), routing Santa Anna's army. He reached Puebla in May. Scott badly de-feated Santa Anna at Contreras (Aug. 19) and Churubusco (Aug. 20), and captured the hilltop fortress of Chapultepec (Sept. 12). He smashed his way into Mexico City's last defenses on September 14, thus effectively ending the war.

it received $15 million and the Americans' prom-ise to assume their own citizens' outstanding claims against Mexico. The United States acquired an additional 529,000 square miles of territory at a cost of 13,000 American lives, most of them lost as a result of disease. Mexican casualties totaled ap-proximately 14,000 killed or missing in action.

Some rabid expansionists considered even these gains minor. They wanted the United States to pursue its supposed manifest destiny and seize all of Mexico. The Senate prudently disregarded these suggestions, however, and ratified the treaty of peace in March 1848.

Americans in California

Many Americans who moved west from In-dependence, Missouri, had destinations other than Oregon. At about the same time that Stephen Aus-tin led his settlers into Texas, merchants were opening up the Sante Fe Trail. Year after year their trade caravans left Independence and lumbered south, loaded with goods to be sold in New Mexico. Thousands of Americans started out on the Oregon Trail but turned off before reaching the Oregon Country. One group, the Mormons, went south into Utah (see pp. 313–315). Others pushed farther west on the California Trail; most of them went to either Sutter's Fort (Sacramento) or the Los Angeles area.

Like Texas, California originally belonged to Spain and, after 1821, to Mexico. In the early years of the nineteenth century it attracted relatively few Americans. There were only about seven hundred there in 1845.

Nevertheless, Polk had plans for California. Late in 1845 he wrote Thomas Larkin, the American consul at Monterey, asking him to stir up a revolt and encourage Americans in California to apply for annexation. Larkin received Polk's message in April 1846. At the same time, an explorer and military adventurer named John C. Frémont entered the picture. Moving south from Oregon, he helped lead a revolt of settlers in the Sacramento Valley. On June 14, 1846, at Sonoma, they declared California an independent republic.[2]

Meanwhile, Mexico and the United States had gone to war. American naval forces led by Commodore John Sloat took Monterey on July 7. San Francisco was captured two days later. In August, Commodore Robert Stockton (who replaced the ailing Sloat) declared California annexed to the United States—with himself as governor.

The situation in California was clearly getting out of hand. Polk himself sent in Colonel Stephen Kearny, who had recently taken Sante Fe. When Kearny arrived with a small force in November, he found Stockton and Frémont bickering over who should be in control. Early in 1847 Kearny succeeded in quelling remaining Mexican resistance in the region and in establishing his own authority as governor. California was ceded to the United States in the Treaty of Guadalupe Hidalgo, which ended the Mexican War.

Even before the treaty was ratified, an event occurred that would soon transform California.

---

[2] This event is known as the Bear Flag Revolt because the homemade flag raised by the rebels was adorned with a picture of a grizzly bear.

California goldminers pause for a photograph in 1852. In this type of sluice, water pushed gravel through, while heavier gold sank to the bottom of the trough.

This was the discovery of gold near Sutter's Mill in January 1848. When news reached the East, the Gold Rush was on, and in 1849, the "forty-niners" poured into California. By 1850 there were 100,000 people there, a figure that doubled in the next two years. Most of those who had joined the Gold Rush remained in California, although only a small proportion of them ever struck it rich.

NATIONAL POLITICAL TENSIONS

During the 1830s and 1840s the United States had extended its boundaries to the Pacific Ocean. But these territorial gains brought major political headaches. They were the unwanted and unexpected consequences of manifest destiny. Should Northern or Southern patterns dominate the new Western territories? Should the emerging new states be slave or free? And who would decide the slavery question, Congress or the territories themselves?

National party politics in the 1840s underwent many shifts and changes reflecting the uncertainties of a rapidly growing country. The system in existence at this time was the second American national party system. (The first, which took shape during the early 1800s, pitted the Federalists against the Jeffersonian Republicans.) The second system had arisen in the 1820s out of the struggle for national power between the Jacksonians and the National Republicans. It resulted in two major national parties, the Democrats and the Whigs.

The Democratic party had supporters in both the North and South, and it specifically pledged to keep slavery out of politics. The Whigs promised to do the same. In general Whigs kept this promise. Still, they usually fared better in Northern states, a fact that made them more antislavery in tone than the Democrats. Thus an antislavery politician was more likely to be a Whig than a Democrat.

Some antislavery politicians preferred to work outside the two-party system. Radical abolitionists shunned political parties altogether. Other Americans decided on organized political effort through a third party. In 1840 a small group of moderate abolitionists organized the new Liberty party. They nominated a "reformed" ex-slaveholder and former Alabaman, James G. Birney, for president. But they polled only seven thousand votes in the 1840 election, which helped to place Harrison in the White House. Four years later the Liberty party again ran poorly. But this time, by taking votes away from Whig candidates in several important states, it helped swing the election in favor of Democrat James K. Polk.

The Wilmot Proviso

Until the mid-1840s, party loyalties generally overcame American sectional differences. A Southern Whig, for example, considered himself a Whig first and a Southerner second, at least in matters in which party principle played a large role. But things changed, as the slavery issue emerged swiftly in national politics.

One man who helped bring about the change was an obscure Pennsylvania Democratic congressman named David Wilmot. In August 1846 he introduced a proviso (amendment) to an appropriation bill requested by President Polk to buy territory from Mexico. The Wilmot Proviso stated simply that slavery would be forbidden in any states formed out of territory acquired from Mexico.

Both of the major political parties tended to divide along sectional lines in the voting. Southerners—Whigs and Democrats alike—bitterly opposed the Wilmot Proviso. (The proslavery Whigs were sometimes known as "Cotton Whigs.") Some Northern Democrats also opposed the proviso. But many other Northerners—both Democrats and Whigs—favored it. (Northern antislavery Whigs called themselves "Conscience Whigs.")

One antislavery congressman from Illinois —a Whig named Abraham Lincoln—lost his reelection bid in 1848 partly because of his support for the Wilmot Proviso. The growing strength of antislavery feeling in the North can be seen from the fact that the proviso passed the House twice, only to be defeated both times in the Senate, where Southerners enjoyed equal voting strength.

Effects of the Mexican War

Another factor responsible for the growth of sectionalism was the Mexican War. The war was understandably popular in the South, because proslavery people wanted the new territories. Northern opponents of slavery denounced both the war and the prospect that the newly acquired territories might become slave states. Many Northerners saw the war as part of a conspiracy to extend the South's economic base and political power.

Even some thoughtful Southerners recognized the dangers. Calhoun supported the Mexican War, but he warned the Senate that "a deed has been done from which the country will not be able to recover for a long time, if ever. It has closed the first volume of our political history under the Constitution and opened the second."

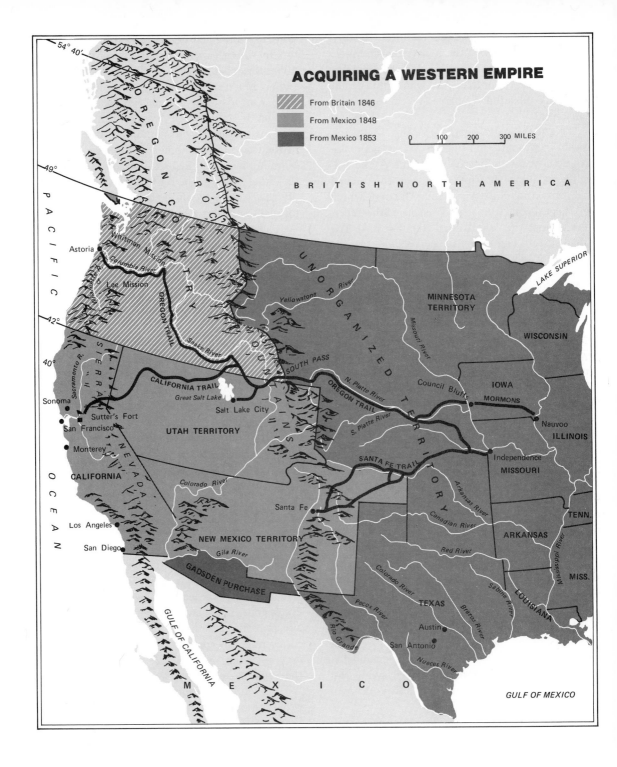

ACQUIRING A WESTERN EMPIRE

From Britain 1846
From Mexico 1848
From Mexico 1853

0   100   200   300 MILES

54° 40'

49°

42°

40°

PACIFIC

OREGON COUNTRY

OREGON ROCKY

BRITISH NORTH AMERICA

LAKE SUPERIOR

Astoria
Whitman Mission
Columbia River
Lee Mission

OREGON TRAIL

Yellowstone River

UNORGANIZED TERRITORY

MINNESOTA TERRITORY

WISCONSIN

Snake River

SOUTH PASS

N. Platte River

Missouri River

Council Bluffs

IOWA

Sonoma
San Francisco
Sutter's Fort
Monterey

SIERRA NEVADA

CALIFORNIA TRAIL

Great Salt Lake

Salt Lake City

UTAH TERRITORY

OREGON TRAIL

S. Platte River

MOUNTAINS

MORMONS

Nauvoo

ILLINOIS

Sacramento R.

CALIFORNIA

Colorado River

SANTA FE TRAIL

Independence

MISSOURI

Arkansas River

Los Angeles

San Diego

NEW MEXICO TERRITORY

Gila River

GADSDEN PURCHASE

Santa Fe

Canadian River

Red River

TENN.

ARKANSAS

MISS.

Colorado River

Pecos River

Rio Grande

TEXAS

Austin

San Antonio

Brazos River

Sabine River

Mississippi River

LOUISIANA

GULF OF CALIFORNIA

Nueces River

M E X I C O

GULF OF MEXICO

388   UNIT 4 Divided America

The Election of 1848

Throughout the North many politicians seemed increasingly willing to sever old party loyalties in order to commit themselves more fully to the antislavery cause. A number of Liberty party abolitionists, antislavery Democrats, and Conscience Whigs banded together in 1848 to form the Free Soil party. They nominated ex-President Martin Van Buren as their candidate for the presidency.

The Free Soil platform cleverly appealed to many different segments of the population. It contained the inevitable antislavery plank. But it also included Whig economic demands, such as support for federally sponsored roads and other internal improvements. In addition it advocated Democratic social values, as in its demand for a federal homestead act that would provide free farms on public lands in the West. "Free Soil, Free Speech, Free Labor, and Free Men" ran the party's motto.

Southerners were now also banding into a party of their own, though it had no name. In Congress, bloc voting on slavery issues created a Solid South that cut across earlier party lines. Thus from 1848 to 1860 Southern Whigs and Democrats usually voted as Southerners on regional questions, particularly slavery.

Despite growing sectionalism, the Whig party managed to elect its 1848 presidential candidate, Mexican war hero Zachary Taylor. Although it had been in existence for only three months, the Free Soil party did well. Its presidential candidate, Van Buren, received 290,000 votes, and the party elected nine congressmen and one senator.

Aftermath of the Compromise

The country soon found itself involved in the crisis over slavery in the new territories that led to the Compromise of 1850. When the sectional crises eased momentarily, tempers cooled. Public opinion in both North and South swung heavily behind such pro-compromise moderates as Stephen A. Douglas and the new president, Millard Fillmore.

Antislavery Northerners, however, continued to demand the exclusion of slavery from the new territories. Like Seward, they believed that "a higher law" had reserved the new lands for free labor. In 1851 Massachusetts sent Charles Sumner, a radical Conscience Whig, to the Senate. Everywhere in the North, abolitionists and their sympathizers denounced the new fugitive slave measure in the Compromise of 1850.

Southern fire-eaters found themselves badly undercut by the Compromise of 1850. Yet they did not give up. After passage of the compromise, a Georgia state convention warned that any further attempt by Congress to exclude slavery from the new territories or interfere with it elsewhere would lead to secession.

In 1852 the nation elected a Democratic president, Franklin Pierce of New Hampshire. Democrats also carried both houses of Congress. These victories were due partly to the fact that the Democrats, unlike the Whigs, had endorsed the Compromise of 1850. The Whig party lost in every section and never again ran a presidential candidate. Even the new Free Soil party suffered because of the general public support for compromise; it received only half as many votes as it had in 1848. In the South the Democrats took effective control of the region's political life. Except for the short-lived Reconstruction period, they were to maintain this monopoly for over a century.

DANGER SIGNALS

A majority of the nation wanted to bury the slavery question and exclude it from political debate. But factors still at work kept the issue alive.

Attempts to enforce the Fugitive Slave Act irritated and angered Northerners. The problem was more symbolic than real, though, since fewer than one in 5000 slaves escaped annually. In 1859 over 500 of the 803 runaways came from border states,[3] where owners displayed little interest in

---

[3] The border states—Delaware, Maryland, Kentucky, Tennessee, and Missouri—were slave states bordering the North that had more moderate views on controlling slaves (and, later, secession) than the rest of the South. West Virginia, which joined the Union in 1863, is usually considered a border state, too.

This daguerreotype of Harriet Beecher Stowe was taken shortly after the publication of Uncle Tom's Cabin. *(The Bettmann Archive)*

recovering their lost property. Only a handful came from the Deep South, which had demanded the tough new law, and where feelings ran highest.

Most of the runaway slaves actually recaptured were caught in the border states and received little attention. But the few slave catchers who roamed New England and the Middle West stirred up a hornets' nest. Abolitionists who stymied the efforts of "slave-nappers" became heroes to their neighbors. Few Northerners objected to the presence of runaway slaves despite their otherwise racist treatment of black people.

Moreover, even Northern moderates who despised abolitionists and endorsed the 1850 compromise reacted emotionally to antislavery appeals. Thousands wept over *Uncle Tom's Cabin*, Harriet Beecher Stowe's best-selling novel. Published in 1851, the book portrayed the sufferings of the fictional Uncle Tom and other slaves at the hands of their masters. Tom, the novel's black hero, was martyred at the end. He represented for Mrs. Stowe the ultimate triumph of the Christian in an evil society. *Uncle Tom's Cabin* probably won hundreds of thousands of sympathizers to the antislavery cause. Translated into twenty languages, the book sold 300,000 copies within a year. Dramatized versions appeared in Northern theaters throughout the 1850s.

President Pierce tried to keep the slavery issue out of politics by pursuing an expansionist foreign policy. During his administration, American ships under Commodore Matthew C. Perry opened Japan to Western trade. The $10 million Gadsden Purchase of land from Mexico rounded out American continental borders in the Southwest. Pierce also pressured China for commercial privileges and agitated for American expansion into Cuba and Central America. Pierce, Douglas, and other Northern Democrats hoped that by stressing the national interests of Americans abroad they could destroy the virus of sectionalism at home. For a time, at least, their policies seemed effective.

But sectional bitterness intruded even into the conduct of foreign affairs. Pierce had directed the American minister to Spain, a Louisianan named Pierre Soulé, to offer Spain $130 million for the island of Cuba, whose purchase many favored both on strategic and economic grounds. Soulé conferred on the matter with the American ambassadors to Great Britain and France (the former was James Buchanan, who himself became president in 1856). The three diplomats sent a confidential dispatch to the State Department after meeting at Ostend, Belgium, urging that—in the event Spain rejected America's offer—the United States should seize the island by force. After the "Ostend Manifesto" was leaked to Congress and the press, antislavery Northerners denounced this proposal as an outrageous bid by Southerners to extend slavery into yet another potential American territory. The controversy put an end to the possibility of acquiring Cuba peacefully.

The Kansas-Nebraska Act

Stephen A. Douglas himself, however, helped to stoke sectional bitterness over slavery and destroy the very compromise he had so skillfully pushed through Congress. In 1854 he introduced a Senate bill to organize the territories of Kansas and Nebraska, a sparsely settled region at that time. Douglas hoped to prevent further congressional furor over the morality of slavery expansion through popular sovereignty, allowing settlers to decide the issue for themselves. Once again, however, as in President Taylor's solution regarding California, it proved easier to devise a practical approach to the slavery issue than to enforce it.

Congress soon found itself embroiled in another quarrel between antislavery and proslavery members. Since Kansas and Nebraska lay within the area of the Louisiana Purchase, the status of slavery there should have been governed by the Missouri Compromise of 1820. This agreement kept slavery out of land that far north. Passage of the Kansas-Nebraska Bill would in effect repeal the Missouri Compromise. This prospect infuriated antislavery Northerners.

Douglas sponsored his bill in order to encourage settlement in the region. This would enable a transcontinental railroad to move across it to the Pacific. The bill's final version included several concessions to Southerners, whose votes Douglas needed. With the support of President Pierce the bill passed in May 1854 after months of furious debate.

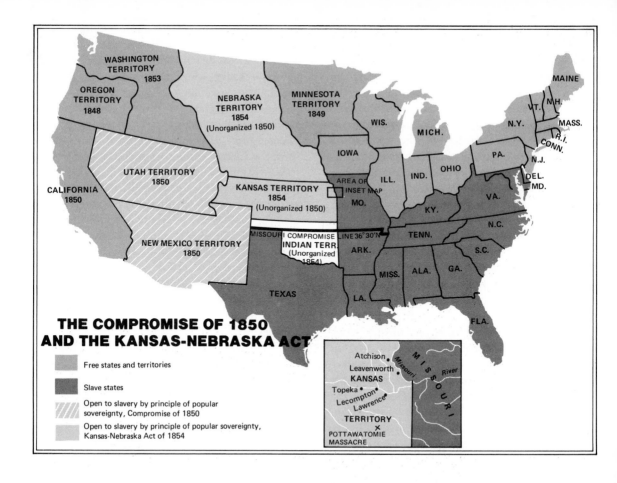

THE COMPROMISE OF 1850
AND THE KANSAS-NEBRASKA ACT

- Free states and territories
- Slave states
- Open to slavery by principle of popular sovereignty, Compromise of 1850
- Open to slavery by principle of popular sovereignty, Kansas-Nebraska Act of 1854

WASHINGTON TERRITORY 1853
OREGON TERRITORY 1848
NEBRASKA TERRITORY 1854 (Unorganized 1850)
MINNESOTA TERRITORY 1849
UTAH TERRITORY 1850
CALIFORNIA 1850
KANSAS TERRITORY 1854 (Unorganized 1850)
AREA OF INSET MAP
NEW MEXICO TERRITORY 1850
MISSOURI COMPROMISE LINE 36°30'N
INDIAN TERR. (Unorganized 1854)
TEXAS
WIS. MICH. N.Y. MAINE VT. N.H. MASS. R.I. CONN. N.J. PA. OHIO IND. ILL. IOWA MO. KY. VA. DEL. MD. N.C. TENN. ARK. S.C. MISS. ALA. GA. LA. FLA.

Inset map:
Atchison
Leavenworth
KANSAS
Topeka
Lecompton
Lawrence
TERRITORY
x POTTAWATOMIE MASSACRE
MISSOURI
Missouri River

Debate over the Kansas-Nebraska Act broke the uneasy truce that had more or less silenced discussions about slavery since 1850. It aroused Northern public opinion against slavery as no previous congressional measure—not even the Fugitive Slave Law of 1850—had ever done. Douglas's concessions to Southerners during the long debate over his measure—and some changes he made to please this camp—were one factor offending the antislavery forces. Another was the possibility, slim, but (in theory) conceivable under the bill's terms, that territories *north* of the 1820 Missouri Compromise line might somehow adopt slavery. Primarily, the measure became a rallying point for (and a symbol of) Northern fears of Southern intentions on the question of slavery's expansion into the Western territories.

Two New Parties

Northern outrage at passage of the Kansas-Nebraska Act took concrete form. Throughout the North in 1854 hundreds of thousands of people left the Democratic and Whig parties to join local anti-Nebraska political groups. In a few months these groups united to form the Republican party. It was a much broader coalition of Conscience Whigs, anti-Douglas Democrats, and abolitionists than the Free Soil party had been. The new party demanded complete exclusion of slavery from all remaining federal territories.

The Whig party was dying. Its members sought new political homes. While some became Republicans, others joined the recently formed American party. Members of the party were often

Sam Houston

When Sam Houston arrived in Washington, D.C., in 1846 as a senator from the new state of Texas, he was described as "a magnificent barbarian, somewhat tempered by civilization." He was a stately six-foot-three and had "a lion-like countenance capable of expressing fiercest passions." Flamboyant in speech and manner, he dressed in character. A favorite ensemble included a gold-headed cane, a panther-skin waistcoat, a large sombrero, and a Mexican blanket.

At age fifty-three, the freshman senator was a legend. A runaway youth on the Tennessee frontier, he lived for years with the Cherokees, who dubbed him "the Raven." He was a hero in the War of 1812. A long-time protégé of Andrew Jackson's, he became governor of Tennessee in his mid-thirties. His fame grew as the victorious commander in chief at the Battle of San Jacinto, which won independence for Texas. Twice president of the new republic, he was the prime mover in achieving annexation to the United States.

Texas was a slave state, and Sam Houston himself was a slaveholder. He was, as John F. Kennedy wrote, "a Southerner by birth, residence, loyalty, and philosophy." But he was also "one of the most independent, unique, popular, forceful, and dramatic individuals ever to enter the Senate chamber." He did not bind himself by sectional ties. As he said, "I know neither North nor South; I know only the Union." His was the only Southern vote for all five laws that made up the Compromise of 1850. He and a Tennessean were the only Southern senators to vote against the Kansas-Nebraska Bill.

Houston's staunch defense of the Union cost him his presidential ambitions in 1852 and again in 1856. He denounced "the mad fanaticism of the North" and the "mad ambition of the South," but he was caught between them. His vote against the Kansas-Nebraska Bill resulted in a formal censure by both the Texas legislature and the state Democrats. When he took his case to the people of Texas as an independent candidate for governor in 1857, he was defeated. But he served out his senatorial term and left the capital early in 1859. Still vigorous at age sixty-six, he was determined

(International Museum of Photography at George Eastman House)

to make a comeback. By autumn he had done so, running again for governor and winning handily.

Houston's term of office was cut short, however. The presidential election of 1860 brought on a secessionist crisis in Texas. Pitted against a hostile legislature, Houston delayed — but could not prevent — withdrawal from the Union.

When he refused in March 1861 to take the oath of allegiance to the Confederacy, he was deposed. Gallantly, with sorrow, he bid his farewell: "I have seen patriots and statesmen of my youth one by one gathered to their fathers, and the government which they have reared rent in twain. I stand the last almost of my race, stricken down because I will not yield those principles which I have fought for."

called "Know-Nothings." Their platform was secret, and when asked about it, a party member would answer "I know nothing."

The Know-Nothings were nativists—that is, they felt that immigrants presented a threat to "native Americans." (By "native Americans" the Know-Nothings were referring, not to Indians, but to families who had been in America for two or three generations.)

Know-Nothings were particularly opposed to Roman Catholics. Hundreds of thousands of such newcomers, mainly Irish, had migrated to America in the 1840s after a potato famine in Ireland. Nativists feared the newcomers' religion, and they felt that the Catholics would not fit into American society.

Anti-Catholic sentiment grew at a time when many Americans were fearful of subversive elements in their society, elements plotting in secret to undermine democratic freedoms. Know-Nothings feared a Catholic conspiracy. Slaveholders were afraid of an abolitionist plot. And abolitionists were convinced of a slaveholders' intrigue.

"Bleeding Kansas"

Many people moved to Kansas after passage of the Kansas-Nebraska Act. Most of them were farmers—from both the North and the South. Few seemed to care whether the state became slave or free. Unfortunately, this unconcern did not last.

Antislavery Northerners formed Emigrant Aid Societies, usually under the direction of abolitionists. These societies provided money, guns, and supplies for Northern settlers in Kansas—settlers who were determined that Kansas should be a free state. At the same time, a smaller group of proslavery settlers were backed by neighboring Missourians, who often crossed the border to vote and to fight.

Armed proslavery and antislavery forces clashed frequently and fiercely in what came to be called "Bleeding Kansas." Normal political processes broke down completely. Although a large majority of Kansas settlers voted for a free-state legislature, proslavery forces and Missourians elected their own assembly. Violence ruled the territory, and President Pierce could not maintain order.

The conflict reached Washington. In May 1856, Massachusetts Senator Charles Sumner delivered a fervent antislavery address, "the Crime against Kansas." His speech included an attack on Senator Andrew Butler of South Carolina. Butler's nephew was a hotheaded South Carolina congressman named Preston Brooks. Two days after Sumner's speech, Brooks—determined to avenge his family's honor—marched into the Senate chamber and beat the Massachusetts senator unconscious with a cane. Sumner was injured so severely that he did not reappear in Congress for three years.

As for "Bleeding Kansas," the fighting persisted between proslavery and antislavery irregulars for several more years. One of the antislavery militia leaders, the veteran abolitionist John Brown, would become involved in a dramatic incident in 1859—far from Kansas—that would prove even more significant than the caning of Charles Sumner.

Suggested Readings
Chapters 19-20

Crisis and Compromise in 1850

Holman Hamilton, *Prologue to Conflict: The Crisis and Compromise of 1850* (1964).

Expansion into the Far West

Ray A. Billington, *Westward Expansion* (1974) and *The Far Western Frontier, 1830–1860* (1956); Gene M. Brack, *Mexico Views Manifest Destiny* (1976); Frederick M. Merk, *Manifest Destiny and Mission in American History* (1963); John H. Schroeder, *Mr. Polk's War: American Opposition and Dissent, 1846–1848* (1973); Otis A. Singletary, *The Mexican War* (1960); George Rogers Taylor, *The Transportation Revolution, 1815–1860* (1951); Albert K. Weinberg, *Manifest Destiny* (1935).

National Political Tensions

Gerald M. Capers, *Stephen A. Douglas: Defender of the Union* (1959); Avery Craven, *The Growth of Southern Nationalism, 1848–1861* (1953) and *The Coming of the Civil War* (1963); Bernard DeVoto, *The Year of Decision, 1846* (1943); Don E. Fehrenbacher, *The Dred Scott Case: Its Significance in American Law and Politics* (1978). Eric Foner, *Free Soil, Free Labor, Free Men: The Ideology of the Republican Party Before the Civil War* (1970); Vincent C. Hopkins, *Dred Scott's Case* (1951); Robert W. Johannsen, *Stephen A. Douglas* (1973); Albert J. Kirwan, *John J. Crittenden* (1962); Philip S. Klein, *President James Buchanan* (1962); Allan Nevins, *The Emergence of Lincoln* (2 vols., 1950) and *Ordeal of the Union* (2 vols., 1947); Alice Nichols, *Bleeding Kansas* (1969); David M. Potter, *The Impending Crisis, 1848–1861* (1976); James A. Rawley, *Race and Politics: Bleeding Kansas and the Coming of the Civil War* (1969); Joseph G. Rayback, *Free Soil: The Election of 1848* (1970).

21 John Brown's Raid

The plot seemed so incredible that the secretary of war refused to believe it. John B. Floyd was relaxing at a Virginia resort late in August 1859 when he received an anonymous letter. It warned of a conspiracy to incite a slave uprising throughout the South. " 'Old John Brown,' late of Kansas," according to the writer, had stored a large quantity of arms in a Maryland hideaway. As the head of a "secret association," he planned to attack Virginia first, entering the state at Harpers Ferry, a northwestern border town.[1] The anonymous writer urged Floyd to send federal troops to the town.

The South had experienced no slave rebellion since the Nat Turner Revolt almost thirty years earlier. Floyd (the son of Virginia's governor at the time of the Turner uprising) was a fiery opponent of abolitionism. But he refused to believe that "a scheme of such wickedness and outrage could be entertained by any citizen of the United States." He took no action.

At this time John Brown was fifty-nine years old and a fugitive from justice. President Buchanan himself had authorized a $250 reward for his capture. Brown was wanted in connection with antislavery raids he had conducted in Kansas. It was partly because Brown's name was identified so closely with Kansas that Floyd did not take the Harpers Ferry plot seriously.

In Kansas, Brown had acquired notoriety but little else. In fact, his life was marked by almost total failure. He had struggled constantly to achieve financial security (an understandable goal for the father of twenty children). Brown failed first during the 1830s as an Ohio land speculator. Then, in 1842, he went bankrupt as a sheep rancher. A later career as a wool merchant also ended in failure. In 1855 Brown and his family migrated to the newly opened Kansas Territory. Here Brown soon gained a reputation as a ferocious opponent of slavery.

---

[1] Harpers Ferry and other West Virginia towns mentioned in this chapter were still a part of Virginia at this time; West Virginia did not become a separate state until 1863.

John Brown had always been an abolitionist. Before he moved west, his house had been a station on the underground railroad. In Kansas the situation was violent, with proslavery and antislavery forces struggling for control of the territorial government. Brown and five of his sons took an active role in what was practically a guerrilla war.

Brown was best known for an incident that took place at Pottawatomie, Kansas, in 1856. He led a small band that murdered and mutilated five proslavery settlers. This raid was apparently in retaliation for the burning of Lawrence, Kansas (a free-state town), by slave-state advocates. None of Brown's victims owned slaves. The common thread linking them was their association with a local court that soon would try a case in which Brown was the defendant.

In the fall of 1856 Brown went east with his sons. For the next three years he wandered across the North from Kansas to Massachusetts making speeches and holding private fund-raising meetings. Brown had long toyed with the notion of launching a direct assault on Southern slavery. He knew that this kind of action would frighten moderate abolitionists, so he usually described his aim as a simple raiding expedition southward to rescue a select handful of slaves. By early 1858, however, Brown began revealing his actual plan—"to overthrow slavery in a large part of the country."

Incredibly, Brown told about eighty Northern abolitionists of his scheme. Many had grave doubts about it. One such man was Frederick Douglass, the leading black abolitionist. Another dubious listener was an Iowa Quaker named David J. Gue. Gue had written the anonymous letter to Secretary of War Floyd. He hoped that, if Floyd ordered federal troops to Harpers Ferry, Brown would call off the raid before he and his men were all killed.

Brown could not have gotten as far as he did without the aid of six leading abolitionists, later known as the Secret Six. One was Gerrit Smith, a wealthy landowner in upstate New York. The other five were all from Massachusetts. Franklin B. Sanborn was a Boston schoolteacher. Thomas Wentworth Higginson and Theodore Parker were Unitarian ministers. George Luther Stearns was a prominent merchant and manufacturer of Boston. The sixth member of the group was a physician, Samuel Gridley Howe.

At first the Secret Six, like Brown's other abolitionist supporters, believed that their leader planned some new and dramatic strike against the proslavery forces in Kansas. But then Brown began to reveal his real intentions. Neither political action nor peaceful persuasion had settled the slavery question, he said. Only a slave uprising throughout the South would make slaveholders aware of their moral guilt. God had selected him, Brown continued, to organize and lead such an insurrection. The revolt would begin in Virginia. From there it would quickly spread like a raging brushfire across the entire South. Even if the plot failed, Brown believed that the hysteria that would then sweep the South would provoke a major sectional crisis, dividing a proslavery South and an antislavery North so that civil war might result.

John Brown was fifty-six when this photograph was taken, early in 1857. (Library of Congress)

Gerrit Smith. (Library of Congress)

Franklin B. Sanborn. NYPL/Picture Collection)

Thomas W. Higginson. (Boston Athenaeum)

Theodore Parker. (NYPL/Picture Collection)

George Luther Stearns. (Library of Congress)

Brown asked the Secret Six for financial help. He refused to discuss any tactical and strategic objections they might have. He offered them, as Sanborn later remarked, "only the alternatives of betrayal, desertion, or support." Brown claimed that he now wanted "men of action." What he really wanted—and had in the Secret Six—was a group of people who would raise funds and thus fulfill their private dreams of being something more than mere talkers.

Though some of the six wavered, in the end they all cast their doubts aside and supported Brown. Why should a slave revolt be condemned, they probably reasoned, when the "slave power" had inflicted so much violence on the free states during the previous decade? Hadn't there been undeclared warfare in Kansas? Wasn't there a massive effort by slave catchers to hunt down fugitive slaves? And what about the physical assaults on abolitionists, not to mention the savage beating of Charles Sumner on the floor of the Senate?

By the late 1850s many abolitionists—not only the Secret Six—had become convinced that there could be no peaceful solution to the slavery question. Gerrit Smith wrote the Republican governor of Vermont:

> Hitherto I have opposed the bloody abolition of slavery, but now, when it begins to march its conquering bands into the free states, I and ten thousand other peace [movement] men are not only ready to have it repulsed with violence, but pursued even unto death, with violence.

Samuel Gridley Howe. (Library of Congress)

John Brown represented, for Smith and the others among the Secret Six, the obvious instrument of what they believed to be justifiable violence. At the same time, Brown's supporters preferred being kept in the dark concerning his specific plans. They hoped to avoid being identified too closely with the scheme. "I have great faith in the wisdom, integrity, and bravery of Captain Brown," Gerrit Smith wrote Sanborn in July 1858. "Whenever he shall embark on another of his contests with the slave power, I shall again stand ready to help him." The limit on this support became clear only in the final sentences of Smith's note: "I do not wish to know Captain Brown's plans. I hope he will keep them to himself." Or, as

Samuel Gridley Howe put it to Brown himself, "Don't tell me what you are about or where you are going."

Brown's ultimate destination was Harpers Ferry, Virginia, but as a base of operations he chose a farm across the Potomac River in Maryland. Brown, posing as a New York cattle buyer named Isaac Smith, had rented the farm from the Kennedy family in July 1859. He arrived with two of his sons, Owen and Oliver. A third son, Watson, joined them later.

By late August there were fifteen recruits living on the Kennedy farm. Oliver's wife, Martha, and a granddaughter of Brown's, Annie, were brought to the farm to keep house and divert the suspicions of nosy neighbors. Most of the group were young. All but two of Brown's men were under thirty. The oldest, apart from the "commander in chief" himself, was a forty-eight-year-old free black named Dangerfield Newby. He had joined the company hoping to liberate his wife and seven children from a nearby Virginia plantation. As the group waited restlessly through the hot summer, hundreds of weapons reached the farm—200 revolvers, 198 rifles, and 950 iron-tipped pikes destined for use by insurgent slaves.

Several of the recruits still believed that they had come South to rescue a small group of slaves and escort them to safety in Canada. During the summer, though, Brown revealed his actual plan for a full-scale slave revolt that would spread quickly throughout the South.

Brown's men drilled, but their commander made few other preparations for the attack itself. He gathered almost no information about the slaves in the region. He did not even bother to scout the area's roads and hiding places. Nor did he develop a plan of escape in case the assault on Harpers Ferry failed.

The only preparation Brown made for possible failure was a curious effort to ensure that others besides himself would be blamed for the raid. Inside a trunk in the farmhouse, in plain view, Brown left letters that implicated his most prominent Northern supporters, among them the Secret Six.

A final handful of recruits drifted into the "Smith" farm in October. Brown decided to strike. He had already sent Martha and Annie back home and written last-minute notes to Northern relatives and friends.

There were now twenty-one "soldiers": five blacks and sixteen whites. On Sunday, October 16, Brown gathered them together for a final prayer service. He then explained his plan of attack to the newer recruits, three of whom had arrived only the previous day. First his men were to blockade the two bridges into Harpers Ferry. Then they would capture the armory buildings and a rifle factory. They would take hostages to use in the event of attack by federal troops or state militia. Once a sufficient number of blacks from the area had rallied to the invaders, the entire band would retreat toward the nearby mountains and regroup for their march southward.

At eight o'clock that moonless night Brown strode out of the farmhouse followed by eighteen of his men. He posted the remaining three as a rear guard. (One was to go to a nearby schoolhouse on Monday

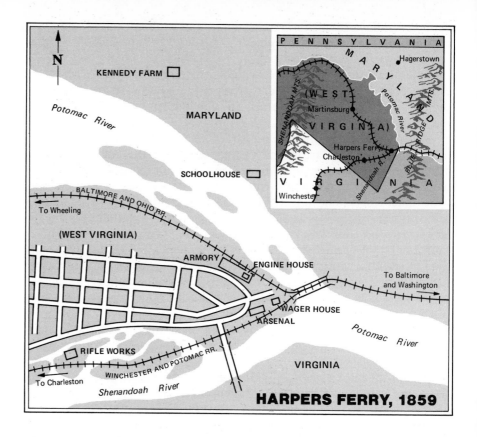

HARPERS FERRY, 1859

to await the escaping slaves who were expected to gather in the area.) Brown then climbed into a wagon filled with the weapons he had collected and rode toward a bridge that led into the silent, sleeping town across the Potomac.

Harpers Ferry was strategically located at the junction of the Potomac and Shenandoah rivers. Baltimore lay eighty miles east by rail and Washington fifty-seven miles by road. The town's main industry was arms manufacture. The federal government maintained a complex of buildings, including a fire-engine house, an armory, and an arsenal. There was also a private rifle works located on an island in the Shenandoah.

The town had a population of slightly more than 2500. Of this total 1251 were free blacks, and only 88 were slaves. Most of the white residents were Northerners employed as skilled craftsmen or government officials in the armory-rifle works complex.

Harpers Ferry was not a typical Southern town. There were no large plantations in the area. Neither cotton nor tobacco was grown there. The few slaveholders in the area owned small farms. Most of the local slaves were house servants. There was no large pool of plantation field hands to be rallied in the immediate area.

Several of Brown's recruits stationed themselves at the two bridges leading into Harpers Ferry. Another group overpowered the single watchman at the government-owned properties and seized control of the armory, the arsenal, and the engine house. They also took over the private rifle works. The invaders herded a small group of prisoners into the engine house as hostages. Now that he controlled millions in government munitions, Brown grew increasingly confident of success. He ordered the telegraph wires cut and dispatched a raiding party to secure more hostages from the nearby countryside. This band returned in the early morning hours of Monday, October 17, with ten freed slaves and three prisoners. Among the latter was the great-grandnephew of George Washington, a minor slaveholder named Lewis W. Washington. Brown had particularly wanted Lewis Washington as a prisoner "for the moral effect it would give our cause having one of your name."

A train whistle signaled the beginning of danger for John Brown's plans. Shortly after midnight an express passenger train from Wheeling reached Harpers Ferry en route to Baltimore. Trainmen found the railroad bridge barricaded and a wounded night watchman shouting warnings of armed night raiders. Brown's raiders began firing, forcing the engineer to back up the train until it was safely out of gunshot range. Just then the Harpers Ferry baggage master, a free black named Hayward Shepherd, wandered down the track. When he tried to run in spite of a raider's command to halt, he was shot down. Shepherd died soon afterward, the first fatality in John Brown's private war against slavery.

By dawn the alarm had sounded throughout the countryside. The residents of Harpers Ferry, except for the handful Brown had taken as hostages or prisoners, armed themselves and fled in panic to a hilltop behind the town. Many of the town's blacks—both slave and free—fled with them. Church bells throughout northwestern Virginia and Maryland tolled the warning signal for slave insurrections. Militia companies began collecting their forces throughout the Blue Ridge towns that bordered on Harpers Ferry, preparing to march on the town.

Up to this point most Virginians who knew of the incident believed that *blacks* had begun a slave uprising at Harpers Ferry much like the one three decades earlier at Jerusalem. Only later in the day would the truth filter out. Brown, amazingly enough, had allowed the Baltimore express train to continue on its way. Thus he ensured that news of his invasion would pass instantly across the telegraph lines from Baltimore to Washington, Richmond, and elsewhere. It is difficult to know whether he was too dazed to act decisively or whether he deliberately wanted to publicize what he had done. In any case, by Monday noon, he and his men had clearly lost the initiative in Harpers Ferry.

Not only did Brown allow the train to proceed. He actually dawdled away the morning. Instead of collecting his hostages and escaping to the nearby mountains, as several of his men urged him to do, he squandered time with his hostages at the engine house. He even ordered breakfast for all of them from a nearby hotel, the Wager House. He divided his

Harpers Ferry at the time of the 1859 raid was a small town in a dramatic setting. In this view, looking southeast, the Potomac curves down from the left and into the far distance; the Shenandoah flows past the church at the right. The government buildings are near the center, not far from the bridge over the Potomac. (Baltimore and Ohio Railroad)

already outnumbered forces, sending several raiders and a few freed slaves across the Potomac to join his rear guard at the schoolhouse.

In the morning, armed townspeople and men from nearby farms got the upper hand. Their rifle fire kept the raiders pinned down to their armory compound. Brown had obviously not expected his opponents to attack so quickly. Yet he remained in the town, either expecting slave reinforcements or perhaps simply making what he believed to be a divinely ordered last stand.

Brown's only means of escape, the two bridges, were retaken by militia late Monday morning. The militia dispersed the few raiders guarding the structures. One of them, the free black Dangerfield Newby, was the first of Brown's men to die in the assault. As he lay dead in the street, townspeople vented their fury at the raid on his body, beating it with sticks.

Brown finally began searching for a way to get out. Some of his men were still across the river in Maryland. Others were trapped in the rifle works. He and most of his raiders, guarding about thirty hostages by now, could not link up with either group. Brown decided to offer an exchange. He would release the hostages in return for a guarantee that he and his men could go free. Will Thompson, the first raider who carried these terms to the militia under a flag of truce, was seized by the crowd and taken away at gunpoint. Brown recognized his predicament at last. He took his remaining men, his few slave recruits, and eleven of his most prominent hostages. They barricaded themselves in the engine house. He then sent out three more people—his son Watson, another raider, and one of the prisoners. They approached the militia under another flag of truce.

The two raiders were shot down, although Watson managed to crawl back to the engine house.

The streets of Harpers Ferry were filled with drunken, hysterical townspeople and militiamen by late Monday afternoon. One group caught an escaping raider near the Potomac, killed him, and then spent hours puncturing his body with bullets. Brown's remaining three men in the rifle works received similar treatment when they were forced to flee toward the river. Two of them fell dead, riddled with bullets. The third, a black named John Anthony Copeland, was rescued from lynching by a local doctor, who protected him from a mob of captors until the arrival of slightly more sober militiamen.

Among the casualties on Monday afternoon was the mayor of Harpers Ferry, a gentle old man named Fontaine Beckham. (His will provided for the emancipation of a slave family owned by him.) He was shot by one of Brown's men. After Beckham's death the town went completely out of control. Residents and local farmers competed with frenzied militiamen in screaming at the raiders while senselessly firing their guns. A mob marched on the Wager House, where Will Thompson remained under guard. They dragged him down to the Potomac, as he shouted: "You may take my life, but eighty thousand will arise up to avenge me, and carry out my purpose of giving liberty to the slaves." The mob peppered his head with bullets before tossing the dead man into the shallow water.

The first word of the leader's identity came late Monday. He sent out yet another note from the engine house repeating his offer to exchange hostages for freedom. It was signed "John Brown." The offer was refused.

The night that followed must have been agonizing for Brown, as he struggled to retain some control over his future despite the obvious failure of his plan. Two of his sons, Oliver and Watson, lay dying. Brown and his four remaining able-bodied men took turns guarding their eleven hostages. Brown spent a good deal of time tending to his prisoners' comfort. Mainly, though, he strode quietly back and forth across the blood-spattered room, alone with his thoughts.

When Brown and his men peered out of their engine-house fortress at dawn on Tuesday, October 18, things had changed. They saw, not Monday's scruffy and jittery mob of local rabbit-shooting militia but a cool, well-dressed company of United States Marines. They were armed with rifles, bayonets, and sledge hammers for the siege that lay ahead. The marines were under the command of Colonel Robert E. Lee, accompanied by Lieutenant J. E. B. Stuart. Brown appeared neither shocked nor unhappy. One of his hostages, Lewis Washington, later observed:

> Brown was the coolest and firmest man I ever saw. With one son dead by his side, and another shot through, he felt the pulse of his dying son with one hand and held his rifle with the other, and commanded his men with the utmost composure, encouraging them to sell their lives as dearly as they could.

In this engine house Brown and his raiders took refuge on October 17. His small band pushed the fire engines up to the doors to impede entry, but Lee's troops broke in, using a heavy ladder as a battering ram. (Baltimore and Ohio Railroad)

Lieutenant Stuart approached the engine house under a flag of truce. He handed a note to Brown demanding unconditional surrender and promising him and his men protection from vigilante justice. Brown refused. He insisted that he would surrender only when he and his men were promised their freedom. Stuart repeated Lee's surrender terms and then, without warning, leaped away from the door waving his cap. While thousands of excited spectators cheered wildly, a party of soldiers began battering at the oak doors of the engine house. Brown's men responded with a volley of shots. Within moments one of the doors had been broken down, and armed marines began dashing into the engine house. The first two were shot. But others swarmed in, overpowering Brown and his four remaining raiders.

Two of the four raiders were quickly bayoneted and died soon afterward. The remaining two, a Quaker youth named Edwin Coppoc and a free black named Shields Green, were captured without being seriously wounded. Brown himself knelt on the floor, his rifle cocked while awaiting the assault. Lieutenant Israel Green, the officer leading the attack on the engine house, entered the building and struck Brown with a light sword before the weary man could fire. Green then tried to run him through with his sword, practically lifting Brown off the ground. Somehow the sword struck either a bone or a belt buckle and failed to inflict a fatal wound. Nevertheless, as Brown collapsed on the ground, Lieutenant

Green continued beating him over the head with his sword until his victim lost consciousness. Finally, the lieutenant regained his self-control. He ordered Brown and his men carried outside and placed on the grass, where their wounds were dressed.

Later that afternoon a detachment of militia confiscated boxes of revolvers and rifles from the Maryland schoolhouse where Brown's recruits had waited vainly for slaves to rally. Another patrol under J. E. B. Stuart occupied the Kennedy farm. By then the rest of Brown's rear guard had fled. They left behind not only hundreds of weapons but also the incriminating letters from the Secret Six and other abolitionists that Brown had abandoned so casually before the raid.

After his wounds had been dressed, Brown was taken to an office in the armory. He was guarded closely, since mobs in the streets of Harpers Ferry wanted to lynch him immediately.

On Tuesday afternoon Brown was visited by a group of politicians, military officers, and newspaper reporters who had just arrived in Harpers Ferry. Among them were Virginia Governor Henry A. Wise and Senator James M. Mason, also of Virginia. Brown did not shirk speaking to the visitors since, as he put it, he wanted "to make himself and his motives clearly understood." It was a new role for the militant man of action, who had often expressed his contempt for mere talkers. In Governor Wise's words, Brown spoke "freely, fluently, and cheerfully." Whether he spoke truthfully, however, is open to question.

Senator Mason asked the old man how he had financed the raid. "I furnished most [of the money] myself," he answered. "I cannot implicate others. It is by my own folly that I have been taken." Brown insisted throughout the interview on accepting completely responsibility for the raid: "No man sent me here; it was my own prompting and that of my Maker, or that of the devil, whichever you please to ascribe it to." (If Brown had sincerely wished to avoid implicating his Northern supporters, though, he might have done so more effectively by not leaving their correspondence in plain view at the Kennedy farm.)

Brown departed most strikingly from the truth when he discussed his motives in attacking Harpers Ferry. He denied any intention of leading a violent slave revolt. He claimed that his purpose had been simply to liberate a group of slaves and lead them to freedom: "We came to free the slaves," he insisted, "and only that."

"Do you consider yourself an instrument in the hands of Providence?" one bystander asked. "I do," Brown replied. "I pity the poor in bondage that have none to help them; that is why I am here; not to gratify any personal animosity, revenge, or vindictive spirit." Brown claimed that only fear for his hostages' safety had prevented his fleeing earlier. He said too that his decision to allow the Baltimore train to proceed stemmed from his concern for the lives of its passengers.

Brown was evidently trying to suggest to his interviewers a dramatic change in personality. His speech was free of the harsh and vindictive rhetoric that he had used formerly in talking of Southern slaveholders. There now emerged the image of a gentle and rather sorrowful agent of Providence. To Senator Mason, he said:

> I think, my friend, [that Southerners] are guilty of a great wrong against God and humanity—I say it without wishing to be offensive. . . . I wish to say, furthermore, that you had better—all of you people at the South—prepare yourselves for a settlement of that question that must come up for settlement sooner than you are prepared for it. . . . You may dispose of me very easily; I am nearly disposed of now; but this question is still to be settled—this negro question I mean—the end of that is not yet.

Brown was directing his words more toward the Northern audience that would read newspaper accounts of the interview than toward his Southern questioners. He was trying to convey to Northern readers the belief that had led him to Harpers Ferry—that slavery could no longer be fought by peaceful means but only by such methods as he had used in his unsuccessful raid.

By late Tuesday afternoon it was possible to tally the results of John Brown's invasion scheme. The slaves he had sent to the Maryland schoolhouse had deserted the previous night and returned to their masters. One unfortunate slave captured with Brown later died in a Charleston prison. Another of his reluctant slave recruits was later found drowned near Harpers Ferry.

Seventeen people were killed during the raid or died soon afterward: the two slaves, three townspeople, one slaveholder, and one marine; and ten of Brown's men, including two of his sons. Five raiders, including Brown, were captured, and the rest escaped into the Maryland mountains. Two others were caught in Pennsylvania a few days later, while five (including Brown's son Owen) fled to safety.

As a military effort, Brown's campaign had failed miserably. Yet, even at its moment of failure, it began to trigger exactly the kind of sectional crisis that Brown had predicted.

Moderates in the North tried to minimize the raid's importance. They dismissed John Brown as a solitary madman whose efforts did not have support among respectable Americans in any section. "It is now well understood," editorialized *Harpers Weekly* in late October 1859, "that the insurrection was merely the work of a half-crazed white." Republican party politicians were especially eager to disassociate their peaceful antislavery views from Brown's violent tactics. "John Brown was no Republican," insisted Abraham Lincoln, and not "a single Republican [has been implicated] in his Harpers Ferry enterprise."

On the other hand, Democrats in both the North and the South denounced the Brown plot as an extension of Republican antislavery agitation. In Virginia itself, a state legislative committee that later investigated the invasion probably spoke for most Southerners when it wrote:

> The whole argument against the *extension* of slavery is soon, by a very slight deflection, made to bear against the *existence* of slavery, and thus the anti-extension idea is merged in that of abolition. . . . The crimes of

John Brown were neither more nor less than practical illustrations of the doctrines of the republican party.

Senator Stephen A. Douglas, the leading Democratic spokesman of the North, called the scheme a "natural, logical, inevitable result of the doctrines and teachings of the Republican party."

More directly concerned, of course, were the Secret Six and Brown's other Northern abolitionist backers. They faced possible arrest and prison terms for their role in the episode. Newspapers throughout the country began reprinting the incriminating letters found at the Kennedy farm. Within a week after Brown's capture Sanborn, Howe, and Stearns had fled to Canada to escape prosecution. Frederick Douglass, after writing an editorial defending the Harpers Ferry raid, sailed to England. Edwin Morton, another of Brown's abolitionist backers, also went to England. (Parker, dying of tuberculosis, had already gone to Europe.)

Gerrit Smith broke down completely. In November friends took him to an asylum for the insane, where he remained until late December, by which time he had "recovered his reason."

Higginson was the only member of the Secret Six to stand his ground. He did not try to deny involvement in the raid. But he did insist that Brown's "acquittal or rescue would not do half as much good as being executed; so strong is the personal sympathy with him."

Higginson's view was shared by most abolitionists. They praised Brown for his actions—and they wanted the South to complete its work of immortalizing their hero. "Let no man pray that Brown be spared!" declared the Reverend Henry Ward Beecher. "Let Virginia make him a martyr!"

Virginia's Governor Wise seemed determined to oblige. Wise decided to charge Brown and his associates, under a Virginia statute, for treason against the state, rather than to hand over the men for trial in a federal court. The governor's position was legally questionable but politically shrewd. Brown's raid on the government arsenal and armory at Harpers Ferry had clearly broken federal laws. Nor did any of the raiders owe allegiance to Virginia. But Wise's action satisfied the general Southern clamor for swift (Southern) vengeance against the raiders. Virginia authorities, fearful that unruly mobs in Harpers Ferry might try to lynch Brown, shifted the trial and the prisoners to Charleston. On October 26 the grand jury indicted Brown and his four accomplices—two whites and two blacks—charging them with the murder of five people, conspiracy to provoke a slave revolt, and treason against the state of Virginia. All of the raiders pleaded not guilty. The judge agreed to separate trials, Brown's being the first.

The trial of John Brown began on October 27, with the defendant reclining on a cot confronting a packed courthouse. Brown's court-appointed lawyer, Virginian Lawson Botts, startled the courtroom audience by immediately producing a telegram from a man in Akron, Ohio. He asserted that Brown and others in his family (which had lived in the Akron area for a number of years) were insane.

Botts felt that the only way to save his client's life was to have the jury commit him to an insane asylum. But Brown was not interested in saving his life. He wanted to use his trial as a national forum for preaching the antislavery gospel. He did not wish to wither away in obscurity. Finally, because of Brown's objections, his attorneys abandoned the insanity defense.

The trial came rapidly to a conclusion. On October 31, after deliberating only forty-five minutes, the jury found Brown guilty on all charges. Two days later he was carried back into court for sentencing. Before the judge could pronounce his sentence, the prisoner was asked to speak. He talked for five minutes, addressing not the court so much as the country, which would read the text of his speech in newspapers the next day. He spoke slowly and eloquently, defending his actions at Harpers Ferry by distorting the facts and appealing directly—and in the most emotional way—for support from the antislavery North:

> In the first place, I deny everything but what I have all along admitted—the design on my part to free slaves. I intended to do as I did last winter, when I went into Missouri, and there took slaves without the snapping of a gun on either side, moved them through the country, and finally left them in Canada. I designed to have done the same thing again, on a larger scale. That was all I intended. I never did intend murder or treason, or the destruction of property, or to excite or incite slaves to rebellion, or to make insurrection. . . . I see a book kissed here, which I suppose to be the

A PREMATURE MOVEMENT.

John Brown. "Here! Take this, and follow me. My name's Brown."
Cuffee. "Please God! Mr. Brown, dat is onpossible. We ain't done seedin' yit at our house."

Trying to recruit a less than enthusiastic disciple to his cause, Brown is ridiculed in this pro-Southern view of the raid. (Library of Congress)

Bible, or at least the New Testament. That teaches me that all things whatsoever I would men should do to me, I should do even so to them. It teaches me further to "remember them that are in bonds, as bound with them." I endeavored to act up to that instruction.

Though Brown lied in his remarks about the plans for a slave revolt, he was truthful about his ultimate intention of liberating the slaves. This distinction was lost not only on many of Brown's Northern admirers but also on the judge, who sentenced him to die on the gallows on December 2. The four other captured raiders were also found guilty at their trials and, like Brown, were sentenced to hang.

In Brown's last month, he continued his efforts to replace his earlier public image as a vengeful border fighter with that of a forgiving yet sternly moral Christian, one who endured his final days as a prisoner with simple dignity. Brown's lawyers worked furiously to collect sworn statements from the condemned man's family and friends testifying to his insanity, in the hope of persuading Governor Wise to commit the condemned man to an asylum. They gathered a large number of such statements, many doubtless from people who were trying to save Brown's life but did not really believe him mad.

At the same time, many people wrote Wise pleading with him to spare Brown and not create an antislavery martyr, thereby increasing sectional tensions. The governor finally rejected the many appeals for clemency, declaring Brown perfectly sane — "cool, collected, and indomitable." "He is a fanatic," Wise wrote, "but firm, truthful and intelligent."

Brown could not have been more delighted at Wise's actions. He wrote: "I am worth inconceivably more to *hang* than for any other purpose."

Brown greeted a procession of visitors in his cell during his last month. Virginia officials also generously (perhaps foolishly) allowed their prisoner to receive and send a steady stream of letters to friends, family, and antislavery associates. These letters helped fix the view of Brown among Northerners as a Christian martyr for the abolitionist cause. The themes he dwelt on in his correspondence were constant: his "cheerful" resignation to death, comparisons of his own death with Christ's, his belief that his death would help achieve his aim of liberating the slaves, and his continued assertion that he served as a messenger of God. In only one month's time Brown made his execution a national event. Thousands now saw him only as a brave Christian going to his death with calm nobility.

On December 1, the afternoon before his execution, Brown received a last visitor, his wife, Mary. She had traveled south, having received Governor Wise's permission to return the bodies of her husband and two sons to their New York farm for burial. Brown and his wife shared supper and discussed family matters. Before going to bed, Brown wrote a final letter to his brother Jeremiah in which he described himself as "quite cheerful and composed."

A sentimental version of Brown on his way to his execution was painted by Thomas Hovenden in 1884. Just before, Brown had stopped by the cell of some of this fellow raiders and spoken to them, parting with the words: "God bless you, my men. May we all meet in Heaven." (MET, Gift of Mr. and Mrs. Carl Stoeckel, 1897)

Brown rose at dawn on December 2, read his Bible briefly, and wrote a final note to Mary. He enclosed his will and gave instructions for his tombstone inscription — simply "John Brown born May 9th 1800 was executed at Charleston, Va., December 2d 1859." Soon afterward his jailers came for him and escorted him down the corridor.

Brown walked briskly down the corridor. Pausing by the cell where the two blacks, Copeland and Green, were being held, he advised them: "Stand up like men, and do not betray your friends." At the cell shared by Cook and Coppoc, the two captured white raiders, Brown engaged in a brief argument with the pair over whether they had made false statements at their trial concerning his conduct. Finally, he shook hands with them both and walked on, shouting: "God bless you, my men. May we all meet in heaven."

Brown stepped out into a street jammed with armed men, observing wryly to his guards: "I had no idea that Governor Wise considered my execution so important." Climbing into a wagon that would take him to the gallows, Brown sat down on his own coffin. He handed one of the guards a last message (punctuated in his own unique style). It was obviously addressed to Americans in every section of the country and read as clearly as a battle order:

Charleston, Va, 2nd, December, 1859
I John Brown am now quite *certain* that the crimes of this *guilty, land: will* never be purged *away;* but with Blood. I had *as I now think: vainly* flattered myself that without *very much* bloodshed; it might be done.

At the gallows site 1500 federal troops and state militiamen waited, along with a huge crowd of onlookers. The day itself seemed much too pleasant for a hanging. Looking at the Blue Ridge Mountains in the distance and the cornfields that surrounded them, the doomed John Brown observed: "This *is* a beautiful country. I never had the pleasure of seeing it before."

The prisoner walked quickly up the steps of the scaffold with no hesitation. For ten minutes the officials in charge stumbled about trying to take their assigned positions. Brown himself seemed the most calm and least worried person on the platform. Finally, the preparations were completed, and a hush fell over the spectators as the officials walked off the scaffold, leaving Brown alone and "as motionless as a statue." Moments later, John Brown hung dangling before the huge crowd.

Some of the Southerners present felt, like Edmund Ruffin (a proslavery Virginian), that Brown had gone to his death with "complete fearlessness." Others, like a young actor named John Wilkes Booth, remained too bitter toward the dead man to admire his courage. Several Southern military leaders were present, including "Stonewall" Jackson, later to be a Civil War hero. But it was Colonel J. T. L. Preston's voice that first broke the stillness after Brown's death. "So perish all such enemies of Virginia," Preston exclaimed. "All such enemies of the Union! All such foes of the human race!"

Brown maintained his usual calm to the very moment of his death. A few days earlier he had written to his wife: "I have been whiped, but am sure I can recover all the lost capital occasioned by that disaster; by only hanging a few moments by the neck."

By the time Brown went to his death, he had become a symbol. In the North he had, of course, won the sympathies of convinced antislavery forces. But he had also captured the compassion of many who had previously been either indifferent or opposed to abolitionism. One such person was a prominent New York Democrat and conservative on the slavery issue named George Templeton Strong. A few days after the execution Strong wrote in his diary:

> Old Brown's demeanor has undoubtedly made a great impression—his simplicity and consistency, the absence of fuss, parade and bravado, the strength and clearness of his letters, all indicate a depth of conviction that one does not expect in an abolitionist (who is apt to be a mere talker). Slavery has received no such blow in my time as Brown's strangulation. The supporters of any institution are apt to be staggered and startled when they find that any one man, wise or foolish, is so convinced of its wrong and injustices as to acquiesce in being hanged by way of protest against it. One's faith in anything is terribly shaken by anybody who is ready to go to the gallows condemning and denouncing it.

When Brown died, in fact, few Republicans and Democrats in the North were willing to denounce openly the character and aims of a man whom, only a month earlier, many had attacked as an insane fanatic.

In the South the image of John Brown was naturally a different one. Here he was not the Christian martyr who was becoming increasingly popular in the North. He was, instead, a grim, avenging devil-figure who had tried to start a massive slave revolt. After November 1859, Northerners concentrated on the *words* that had come from John Brown's eloquent tongue and pen after his capture. But Southerners were more concerned with the *deeds* that he and his men had attempted at Harpers Ferry. After the raid several Southern towns had called militia units and vigilante companies into service, declared martial law, and began hunting down conspirators—real or imagined—in their midst. A wave of hysteria sent thousands of fearful whites, many of whom did not own slaves, patrolling their neighborhoods, searching for abolitionist invaders and unruly slaves.

The South mobilized much more quickly and effectively after John Brown's assault than it had after Nat Turner's insurrection three decades earlier. After all, Southerners had been predicting such an assault from the North for more than a generation.

Southerners regarded John Brown even more harshly after the election of Abraham Lincoln as president in November 1860. The impact of John Brown's raid was crucial in provoking what one historian has called a crisis of fear among Southerners concerning Northern-led efforts to stir up slave rebellions. It helped create the climate of intense sectional passion that led to secession and civil war.

Once the South had left the Union, John Brown provided a magnificent symbol for rallying a reluctant Northern public to war. "Fifty years hence," George Templeton Strong confided to his diary in February 1862, "John Brown will be recognized as the Hero or Representative Man of this struggle." He added that "a queer rude song about him seems to be growing popular." The song to which Strong refers was set to the music of another Northern tune, then also growing in popularity—"The Battle Hymn of the Republic"—whose eloquent verses were written by Samuel Gridley Howe's wife, Julia. But Brown would probably have enjoyed the "queer rude song," whose simplicity proved so appealing to the ordinary soldier:

> John Brown's body lies a-mouldering in the grave,
> John Brown's body lies a-mouldering in the grave,
> John Brown's body lies a-mouldering in the grave,
> But his soul goes marching on.

22 The Road to Civil War

ad John Brown launched his raid thirty years earlier, in 1829 instead of 1859, almost all of the North would have joined the South in shock and condemnation. Although Northern states had abolished slavery, and many Northerners viewed the slave system with hostility, few shared the overriding desire of John Brown and the Secret Six to interfere with slavery's operation in the South. Most residents of New England, the Middle Atlantic states, and the Upper Midwest supported the Missouri Compromise and accepted the existence of slavery in the South as a political necessity that cemented the Union of free and slave states.

But between the 1820s and the 1850s, Northern attitudes toward the South and slavery underwent a significant change. A small group of antislavery men and women—stubborn, committed, and intensely religious—could claim a good deal of the credit and assume much of the responsibility for bringing these changes about. At first, the agitators risked social ostracism and even physical injury. Several Southern states offered cash rewards for their arrest and extradition. But slowly these radical antislavery advocates, or abolitionists, gained a hearing for their belief that slavery was morally wrong and should not be subject to political compromise.

The great majority of Northerners never accepted this concept entirely. As late as the eve of the Civil War, the term "abolitionist" was used to smear political opponents. Yet, for various reasons, even the majority of "moderates" in the North began to believe that although slavery could not be snuffed out at once, the institution should not be allowed to extend farther into the new Western territories. Both abolitionists and slaveholders believed that such a policy of restriction would inevitably lead to the end of slavery in the South. So, when the new Republican party won a national victory in 1860 on a slavery restriction platform, Southerners and abolitionists were in agreement on another point: national political compromise on the slavery question had become impossible.

THE ABOLITION MOVEMENT

A leading antislavery (but not abolitionist) organization of the early nineteenth century was the American Colonization Society, founded in 1817. But the Colonization Society, after a promising start, did not prosper. Everybody seemed to have a different notion as to what it stood for and what it might accomplish. Free blacks feared the society as a trap for expatriating them forcibly, and some antislavery people agreed. Thus the society would not end slavery but merely siphon off free blacks. Southerners from the Deep South did not cotton to colonization and took the society's antislavery professions much too seriously. Politicians from such states as South Carolina and Georgia consistently and insistently fought against giving a federal subsidy to the society, an idea opposed by many Northerners too. The shock waves of fear that surged through all of the South in the aftermath of the Nat Turner Revolt in 1831 ended all realistic hopes for strong and widespread Southern support for colonization as a "solution" to the slavery question.

Garrison and His Followers

Abolitionism as an independent movement began in the 1830s. Without doubt its leading fig-

414

William Lloyd Garrison was stubborn, humorless, and courageous in his crusade for abolition. In 1854 he publicly burned a copy of the Constitution exclaiming, "So perish all compromises with tyranny!" (Courtesy, Dept. of Special Collections, Wichita State University)

ure was William Lloyd Garrison. Born in Massachusetts, he was influenced by a fanatically religious mother. For a time he edited the first temperance paper. Then he turned to the antislavery cause and founded an abolitionist journal, the *Liberator.* It was first published in Boston in 1831. Two years later Garrison organized the American Antislavery Society.

Much of Garrison's support came from free blacks in the North. But the movement quickly grew among white sympathizers as well. By 1837 the American Antislavery Society had 145 local chapters in Massachusetts, 274 chapters in New York, and 213 in Ohio (the Middle Western center of antislavery activity). By 1843 the society had over 200,000 members.

Other abolitionist leaders included Frederick Douglass and Wendell Phillips, Garrison's Boston lieutenant. Prominent figures in New York were Gerrit Smith and the Tappan brothers, Lewis and Arthur. Theodore Weld dominated the Middle West. Among the best-known speakers in the Northeast were Angelina Grimké and her sister, Sarah Grimké Weld.

Garrison and his followers broke deliberately with previous antislavery groups in several ways. First, they demanded the *immediate* rather than *gradual* abolition of slavery. Second, many of the abolitionists opposed the idea of colonization. They believed it was possible for black Americans to be absorbed into American society. Third, the "Garrisonians" abandoned the politeness of earlier antislavery groups. Instead they adopted a militant, aggressive style. Garrison set the tone himself in the first issue of the *Liberator:* "I *will* be as harsh as truth, and as uncompromising as justice. On this subject, I do not wish to think, or speak, or write with moderation. I am earnest—I will not equivocate—I will not excuse—I will not retreat a single inch—AND I WILL BE HEARD."

Changing Tactics

The abolitionists' religious beliefs helped determine their strategy. Most were devout Protestants. They believed that slavery was the country's greatest moral evil, a blot on the United States that had to be erased. Their main objection to slavery was moral. Therefore, they thought, it was essential to convince the mass of Americans, North *and* South, that slavery was immoral and unjust. Abolitionists believed that personal recognition of this fact would result in nationwide demands for an immediate end to slavery. This technique was called moral suasion.

During the 1830s Garrison and his associates made a strong effort to reach slaveholders by mailing hundreds of thousands of abolitionist newspapers and tracts to the South. After the Nat Turner Revolt, the postmaster general, a Southerner, allowed Southern postmasters to refuse to deliver abolitionist propaganda, violating both the law and the senders' civil liberties. Southerners burned antislavery material.

Although Turner's revolt dampened the prospects of colonization as a viable solution to slavery, American blacks continued to emigrate to Africa throughout the nineteenth century. The ship drawn here, a Dutch steamer, left Savannah, Georgia, in 1895 with two hundred blacks bound for Liberia. Founded to provide an African homeland for freed American slaves, Liberia broke away from the fading American Colonization Society in 1847 and established itself as an independent Republic. (Culver Pictures)

By the 1840s abolitionists recognized that moral suasion had failed to win over any significant number of slaveholders. They abandoned this tactic in the South, but they continued to use it in the North.

The abolitionists split into two separate wings—those who opposed Garrison and those who supported him. His opponents objected to him for several reasons. They resented his overbearing leadership. They also disapproved of his demand for equal status for women as abolitionist leaders, and for fusion of the woman's rights campaign with the antislavery movement. They disliked Garrison's constant attacks on the organized churches, many of whose leaders still opposed the drive for emancipation. And they wanted to involve the movement in practical political action. (Garrison wanted to focus on moral agitation.)

In 1840 the anti-Garrisonians withdrew from Garrison's organization and formed the American and Foreign Anti-Slavery Society. Both groups continued their propaganda campaigns to stir up Northern public opinion until the Civil War. But their major energies shifted during the 1840s into direct political agitation at the local, state, and national levels. Abolitionism was now the central concern of all American reformers, whatever their other interests.

From the beginning of settlement, Americans have been notoriously avid travelers. (One wag observed in the nineteenth century that the rocking chair was popular in the United States mainly because, although a person might be sitting down, he could at least keep moving.) A vast continental nation yielded first to the horses and covered wagons of the pioneers or to river steamboats, canal-floating barges, and sailing ships going round the tip of South America and back up to California and the Oregon Territory. Then, in the 1840s and 1850s, came the railroads.

"American railroads, the connecting ligaments of the great West," wrote historian Daniel J. Boorstin, "had appeared in a peculiar way. In England, for example, they were commonly built to connect one city with another, to carry an already heavy traffic for people who were already there. . . . Running often from 'Nowhere-in-Particular to Nowhere-at-All,' the American railroad was commonly built in the hope that it would call into being the population it would serve." In the Eastern states, of course, the people who rode the early railroads were already there, as in this scene from Edward Lamson Henry's painting, "The 9:45 Accommodation, Stratford, Connecticut."

[For further information on the foreign observers quoted in this essay, see "Notes on Sources."]

Travel in a Growing Nation
PICTORIAL ESSAY FOUR

I like traveling by the canal boats very much. Ours was not crowded, and the country through which we passed being delightful, the placid moderate gliding through it — at about four miles and a half an hour — seemed to me infinitely preferable to the noise of wheels, the rumble of a coach, and the jerking of bad roads. The only nuisances are the bridges over the canal, which are so very low that one is obliged to prostrate oneself on the deck of the boat to avoid being scraped off it. This humiliation occurs, upon an average, once every quarter of an hour.

[FANNY KEMBLE, 1838]

The Erie Canal near Little Falls, New York

The American has a perfect passion for railroads. It is not merely because his supreme happiness consists in that speed which annihilates time and space, but also because he perceives that this mode of communication is admirably adapted to the vast extent of his country, to its great maritime plain, and to the level surface of the Mississippi Valley. This is the reason why railroads are multiplied in such profusion, competing not only with each other but entering into a rivalry with the rivers and canals.

[MICHEL CHEVALIER, 1834–35]

An early railroad train meeting a steamboat at the dock

Stagecoach near Trenton, New Jersey

At Trenton we left our boat for the most detestable stagecoach that ever a Christian built to dislocate the joints of his fellow man. The change in our movement was not more remarkable than that which took place in the tempers and countenances of our fellow travelers. Gentlemen now looked more like victims than dandies armed for conquest. The pretty ladies too, with their expensive bonnets — how sad the change! As I looked into the altered eyes of my companions, I was tempted to ask, "Look I as cross as you?" Indeed, I believe that, if possible, I looked crosser still, for the roads and the vehicle together were quite too much for my calm.

[FRANCES TROLLOPE, 1830]

The steamboat was fitted for the twofold purpose of carrying as many bales of cotton as could be heaped upon it without sinking, and taking in as many passengers as could enjoy the luxuries which Southern manners and a hot climate require — especially spacious cabins, abundance of fresh air, and protection from the heat of the sun.

These steamers, notwithstanding their size, draw very little water. They cannot quite realize the boast of a Western captain that "he could sail wherever it was damp," but I was assured that some of them could float in two-foot water. The high-pressure steam escapes into the air by a succession of explosions alternately from the pipes of the two engines. It is a most unearthly sound, like that of some huge monster gasping for breath.

[SIR CHARLES LYELL, 1849]

A boatman on the Missouri River

Steamboat docked at New Orleans

Interior of a steamship

On the Great Lakes there is only one means of travel, and that is the steamship. The elegance of such a ship is quite remarkable. The vessel is equipped in every possible way for the convenience of the passengers. There is, for example, a barbershop. There is also a band. Its performance on brass instruments we found none too good, but in the evenings it won general approval by presenting comical Negro songs, accompanied by the guitar, and by playing dance music, to which the youthful Yankees executed their favorite cotillion, with many dainty skips and steps.

[OLE RAEDER, 1847]

Wooding Up on the Mississippi

In the evening we embarked on board the Philadelphia and started up the Mississippi. As the steamboats on this river burn nothing but wood, and as their engines are mostly high-pressure, the consumption of this bulky fuel is so considerable that they are obliged to call at least twice a day at the wooding stations on the banks of the stream. The Philadelphia used about one cord of wood an hour. When the supply on board began to run short, the pilot cast his eye round, and upon the first convenient opportunity, he steered the boat for one of the numerous piles of firewood which occurred every few miles along the way.

[BASIL HALL, 1828]

I was asleep when suddenly the coach stopped, which woke me up. I heard someone outside say, "Get out one at a time & throw up your hands." Then I knew in an instant that the coach was stopped by highwaymen. *The first thing I saw was a man with a double-barreled shotgun full cocked pointed at the driver and another behind the coach with 2 six-barreled pistols in his hands. When we were all out, the man with the pistols searched us. He began with me, he first took out my watch but he only looked at it & put it back & said he didn't want it. Then he searched the others. After they took our money, they handed round a bottle of whiskey for the passengers to drink. I took some just for the joke of it & because I was cold with standing out with my hands up.*

[SIDFORD HAMP, 1872]

A masked holdup man in the West

The trail is a very remarkable piece of work. To rise 3,000 feet vertically about 4 1/2 miles have to be traversed, and still the track is very steep. The ride up on our ponies was not absolutely free from danger, but, so long as the traveler does not lose nerve, the danger is slight. The ponies have the very sensible but slightly disquieting habit of walking to the very edge of the turns in order to make the inclined plane as easy as possible. But it was glorious! Every fresh turn, almost, introduced us to fresh views of this wonderful place. I affirm that, until I rode this trail and found myself looking down and around me from Glacier Point, I had no adequate idea of the beauty and grandeur of the Yosemite district.

[LORD RUSSELL OF KILLOWEN, 1883]   Yosemite Valley as seen from Glacier Point

I must take this occasion to say a word of the commodiousness and other advantages of the railroads in America, which I could well observe on my trip from Chicago westward. The possibility of covering long distances by rail in the United States under unfavorable climatic conditions depends on the use of materials and devices much superior to those that serve in Italy. The front of the locomotive is furnished with an apparatus capable of removing not only the little stones, but any objects that may obstruct the roadbed, especially animals and plants torn away from the sides. At the rear of the locomotive is a little glassed-in compartment designed to protect the engineer against the elements.

[GIOVANNI CAPELLINI, 1863]

Train stopped by buffalo on the plains

Railway traveling in America is not tiring; on the contrary, it is refreshing. A train on its way to San Francisco or to Mexico is a series of moving houses. The cars are divided into rooms, and are provided with all the necessaries of life. Spacious libraries, smoking rooms, and dining rooms open out of one another, and there are bathrooms and barbershops. In the anterooms are the servants, chiefly white-coated Negroes, who are there to carry out all orders.

[COUNT VAY DE VAYA UND LUSKOD, 1908]

I suppose the reader has some notion of an American railroad car, that long, narrow wooden box like a flat-roofed Noah's ark. Those destined for emigrants on the Union Pacific are remarkable only for their extreme plainness. The benches are too short for anything but a young child. Where there is scarce elbow room for two to sit, there will not be space enough for one to lie. In all other trains, a warning cry of "All aboard!" recalls the passengers to take their seats. But all the way to San Francisco, the train stole from the station without a note of warning, and you had to keep an eye upon it even while you ate.

[ROBERT LOUIS STEVENSON, 1879]

Coach car on a train

Railroad car carrying emigrants westward

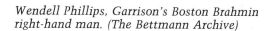

Wendell Phillips, Garrison's Boston Brahmin right-hand man. (The Bettmann Archive)

Reactions to the Abolitionists

The abolitionists aroused intense feelings that often led to violence. It was dangerous during the 1830s to advocate immediate emancipation, even in the North. Anti-abolitionist mobs, often including prominent community leaders, disrupted abolitionist meetings and destroyed antislavery printing presses. When a leading English abolitionist came to New England in 1835, Bostonians rioted. Garrison was led through the city's streets with a rope around his waist, until police took him into protective custody. (This incident helped convert Wendell Phillips to the abolitionist movement.) That same year in New York City a mob destroyed Lewis Tappan's home, and throughout that stormy decade dozens of anti-abolitionist riots and mobbings took place. Henry B. Stanton, another militant antislavery figure, claimed to have been attacked personally over two hundred times. The worst incident occurred in Alton, Illinois, in 1837. There, Elijah Lovejoy, an abolitionist editor, was shot dead by a mob while defending his home and his press.

Those outside the South who opposed abolitionism feared the reformers almost as much as Southerners feared the slave revolts. To conservative Northerners, the abolitionists seemed to threaten public order, national unity, and established institutions. In fact, race prejudice was as strong in the North as in the South. Certainly free blacks in the North suffered constant abuse and discrimination.

Even white abolitionists could not wholly shed their color prejudice. Only a few treated their black associates as complete equals. Garrison at one point urged the eloquent Frederick Douglass to use more "darky" mannerisms in his speeches. Such attitudes led Douglass to break with the Boston abolitionist.

Although Northerners did not lose their racial prejudices, they gradually became more sympathetic to the abolitionists. Federal interference with antislavery mail to the South won many converts to the abolitionist cause. Even those who did not share abolitionist beliefs disliked the practice of suppressing ideas. A number of Americans who began by defending the abolitionists' civil liberties ended by joining the movement itself.

Other Northerners became aroused by the "gag rule." This resolution, passed by the House of Representatives in 1836, provided that no antislavery petitions would even be considered. Every year a small group of congressmen, led by former President John Quincy Adams, tried to repeal the gag rule. They finally succeeded in ending this flagrant violation of the abolitionists' right of petition in 1844.

THE MOVE INTO POLITICS

The abolitionists' earliest efforts in politics were limited to questioning major party candidates regarding slavery and voting for the individual, if

The murder of editor Elijah Lovejoy made him the first martyr of the abolitionist cause. He aroused controversy by his antislavery principles, first in St. Louis, where his printing office was destroyed, and then across the Mississippi in Alton, Illinois. His murder by an anti-abolitionist mob sent a "shock wave as of an earthquake throughout this continent," according to John Quincy Adams. (Brown Brothers)

Frederick Douglass, born in Maryland, escaped from slavery in 1838. He broke with Garrison, believing in a more political approach to abolition. During the Civil War he organized two black regiments from Massachusetts. Later he served as minister to Haiti. (Nelson Library, Sophia Smith Collection, Smith College)

one could be found, whose answers were satisfactory—or the least unsatisfactory. Needless to say, this went on exclusively in the North. By this method, unpromising though it seemed, abolitionists hoped to hold the balance of power in some Northern districts and states. Only rarely did they succeed.

Many abolitionists yearned for bolder action. James G. Birney was an Alabama plantation owner and slaveholder who had become converted to abolitionism. Finding it unwise and unsafe to advocate abolition in the South, he left for Ohio to establish an antislavery newspaper. Birney had long differed with Garrison on the Boston editor's support for woman's rights and opposition to political action. In 1840, Birney ran for president as the candidate of the new Liberty party.

Both Harrison, the Whig candidate, and Van Buren, the Democrat, he argued, were totally unacceptable to abolitionists, and a new party had to be formed if abolitionists wished to cast a *moral* vote for president. But Garrisonians ridiculed the efforts of Birney and the Liberty party, and abolitionists found little more comfort in the slaveholding Harrison than in Andrew Jackson's hand-picked successor, Van Buren. Of 2.5 million votes cast in 1840, Birney got only seven thousand.

The abolition movement had now split. Garrison maintained headquarters in Boston; the Liberty-ites were headquartered in New York City (where they generated most of their financial support). Although disappointed at their showing in 1840, Liberty party people decided to stay in business. "The fewer we have now," wrote one after the election, displaying strong faith but shaky logic, "the more we have to gain before we carry our point." They continued to work in local and state elections in 1841 and 1842, and increased the party's vote slightly.

Garrison, meanwhile, expanded his antipolitical principles to new and broader dimensions. He had become a moral perfectionist, a pacifist, and a total nonresister, rejecting the use of force under any circumstances. In 1842, he proclaimed "it is morally and politically impossible for a just and equal union to be formed between Liberty and Slavery." By remaining in the Union, Northerners bore as much responsibility for slavery as the South. Only a breakup of the country could ease that guilt. Many who had remained loyal to Garrison up to then could not accept his new demand, or his perfectionism, or his commitment to various other reforms. Garrison for his part wanted no truck with such compromisers. He banished the doubters without a qualm, and forced the shrinking American Antislavery Society to accept his policy.

ABOLITIONIST ACTIVITIES

Antislavery Energies

Despite the bitterness of their split, abolitionists from both wings of the movement engaged in many of the same activities. Both the Garrison and the Liberty party groups maintained newspapers, produced pamphlets, and organized public meetings. They cited the same books and stories detailing atrocities committed against blacks on Southern plantations. And all abolitionists were regarded as equally detestable by slaveholders and conservative Northerners.

Probably no single aspect of the abolitionists' work did more to gain sympathy for them than their efforts to assist fugitive slaves. Black abolitionists made daring raids into the South to rescue some of those in bondage. Other blacks took to podiums to denounce slavery. Outstanding were a famous pair of black women, Harriet Tubman (see p. 421) and Sojourner Truth. A large network of Northern sympathizers, both white and black, maintained the Underground Railroad. In its "stations"—safe havens such as barns and cellars—escaped slaves could hide until "conductors" led them onward to freedom in the North and in Canada.

Many abolitionists actively interfered with slave catchers who came North to recapture runaways. To those who argued that the Constitution gave slaveholders the legal right to reclaim their slave property, people like James Birney replied firmly, "Whatever pledges of noninterference may be given they will be disregarded—at least so long as our body has any life or humanity in it, or any greater fear of God than of man." Even a conven-

The Underground Railroad was neither underground nor a railroad. But somehow it did work to gain freedom from slavery for several thousand blacks. (Library of Congress)

tional major party politician like William H. Seward, the New York Whig, during the Compromise of 1850 debates, warned of a "higher law" than the Constitution—the law of freedom.

The abolitionist attack on slavery also included criticism of the deplorable condition of free blacks in the North. Few Northern states allowed blacks to vote, and the little schooling offered them was substandard and on a rigidly segregated basis. Although white abolitionists found it easier to attack Southern slavery than to rid themselves of prevailing anti-Negro prejudices or to imagine blacks living in equality with whites, the movement still fought against the worst forms of Northern racial discrimination. "No proposition is more true," admitted one Liberty party speaker, "than that the wrongs which the North has done, and continues to do, to its colored people . . . furnish the most influential argument in favor of Southern oppression."

Abolition and Expansionism

By the time the Liberty party rallied for its second national campaign in 1844, the political abolitionists had acquired an issue with national appeal. The giant slaveholding republic of Texas, whose annexation to the United States (possibly as more than one state) the antislavery forces had steadily opposed, was about to be admitted by Congress. Once again, abolitionists organized meetings, printed anti-Texas petitions and newspapers, and tried to pressure Congress to refuse admission. This time, they began to gain support from other Northerners. Many of these did not care about slavery with the same moral intensity as the abolitionists, but they were leery of any action that

The most famous "conductor" on the Underground Railroad was a former slave, Harriet Tubman. In the years 1850 to 1861, from the passage of the Fugitive Slave Act to the outbreak of the Civil War, she made nineteen secret trips into the South rescuing some three hundred people. Offers of rewards for her capture eventually totaled $40,000. But she eluded her enemies successfully and was never caught. In later years she claimed that "on my Underground Railroad, I never ran my train off the track, and I never lost a passenger."

Born in 1820 or 21 on a plantation in Dorchester County, on Maryland's eastern shore, Tubman knew only cruelty as a child. She was one of ten or eleven children born to Benjamin Ross and Harriet Greene. (Her grandparents on both sides had come in chains from Africa.) She received no schooling and thus could not read or write. Because she was found to be too awkward and clumsy for housework, she was made to work as a field hand. When she was about thirteen years of age, an overseer struck her on the head with a two-pound weight and fractured her skull. This resulted in spells of somnolence that affected her for the rest of her life. In 1844, she married a free black named John Tubman, but the marriage did not succeed.

In 1849, Harriet Tubman's master died, and it was rumored that his slaves would be sold. The young woman decided that this was the time to make a break for freedom, which she did with the help of friendly Quakers. She reached Philadelphia and obtained employment in a hotel. There she met the black abolitonist, William Still, who recruited her for the Underground Railroad. He later said of her:

> Harriet was a woman of no pretensions, indeed, a more ordinary specimen of humanity could hardly be found among the most unfortunate-looking farm hands of the South. Yet, in point of courage, shrewdness, and disinterested exertions to rescue her fellowmen, by making personal visits into Maryland among the slaves, she was without her equal.

In December 1850, this single-minded, deeply religious woman began the first of her many trips back into the South to bring out slaves. First,

Harriet Tubman

(National Portrait Gallery, Smithsonian Institution)

she brought out her brother and his family and later that same year a family of eleven. On one of her most difficult trips, she returned, in 1857, to the eastern shore and brought back her aged parents in a hired wagon. Many tales are told of her tenacity and ingenuity. To inform prospective fugitives that she would be arriving shortly, she sent messages in the "double-talk" that blacks had learned to use in their communications and even in the texts of their songs (spirituals).

Harriet Tubman became well known among abolitionists and sometimes addressed their conventions. But she preferred to remain a woman of mystery whose whereabouts were generally unknown. It was in St. Catharines, Ontario, in April of 1858, however, that she counseled and encouraged John Brown in his plan to take action by force of arms. Only a flareup of her head injury kept her from joining him at Harpers Ferry.

When the Civil War broke out, "General Tubman" (as John Brown had called her) volunteered her services. For three years she worked for the "Union" forces securing information from black informants. She worked as a nurse and a cook, aiding freedmen who had joined the Union Army, supporting herself by selling chickens and eggs. After the war she returned to her farm in Auburn, taking in helpless old black people and black orphans as well. Her farm became the Harriet Tubman Home for Indigent Aged Negroes, which carried on even after her death in 1913.

would so greatly increase the South's size and national political power.

In the election of 1844, the Whigs' Henry Clay, making his last desperate stab at the presidential office he wanted so badly, tried to keep Texas out of the campaign. James K. Polk, the Democratic candidate, openly favored the annexation of Texas and westward expansion generally. Birney, running again on the Liberty party ticket, polled only sixty-five thousand votes, a disappointing total. But had his fifteen thousand votes in New York gone to Clay, Whigs would have carried the state and the election. For the first time, the abolitionists had flexed a small but significant bit of political muscle.

Texas joined the Union shortly after the election, and a year later Polk went to war with Mexico to gain New Mexico and California. Abolitionists opposed the war passionately, first because most of them were pacifists, and second, because they feared that the new territories would be added to the roster of slave states. A few went so far as Henry David Thoreau, who refused to pay his local taxes and spent a night in jail to symbolize his protest. They began to charge that the country was being taken over by an "aggressive slavocracy" (the Slave Power), which intended to crush all criticism of slavery in the North and West, just as it had stamped out dissent in the South. The slavocracy would then embroil the nation in foreign wars to increase its own slave territory and wealth.

Thousands of individuals all over the North, up to now unmoved by the plight of the slaves, rallied to this standard of opposition. "The Mexican War and Slavery," predicted Charles Sumner, a Massachusetts antislavery Whig, "will derange all party calculations." The Whigs of his own Bay State were soon split over the slavery extension issue into "Cotton" and "Conscience" factions. Northern Democrats, unhappy over their party's control by Southerners, now supported the Wilmot Proviso (see Chapter 20). Many Westerners supported it, too; they wanted the land west of the

In this pre-Civil War picture, the great abolitionist Harriet Tubman (far left) stands with a family of slaves, possibly one of the many groups Tubman bravely escorted from the slave South north to freedom. (The Sophia Smith Collection, Smith College)

Advertisements such as these proliferated after the passage of the Fugitive Slave Act of 1850. Despite the stronger law, slaves continued to seek freedom north of the Mason-Dixon line. (NYPL/Picture Collection)

Missouri River for small farms for white settlers, and wanted to keep both slavery and free blacks out of the area.

Although some Liberty men — and, of course, the Garrisonians — warned against accommodating these new allies, most of the party eagerly sought to construct antislavery coalitions. In 1846, New Hampshire Liberty-ites and independent Democrats elected John P. Hale to the U.S. Senate, and a growing number of congressmen openly declared themselves for slavery restriction. Whig Senator William Seward of New York was rapidly becoming the leader of a small group of national political figures committed to antislavery.

In August 1848, at a convention in Buffalo, the Free Soil party emerged — a coalition of Barnburners (antislavery New York Democrats), Conscience Whigs, independent Democrats from the Midwest, and Liberty party members. Both major parties had nominated unacceptable candidates: the Whigs named General Zachary Taylor, a Louisiana slaveholder; and the Democrats, Lewis Cass, widely considered a "doughface" — a Northern man with Southern principles. The new antislavery party adopted a platform opposing the admission of *any* new slave states or allowing slavery to exist in the territories. Yet its presidential nominee was none other than Martin Van Buren, the Jacksonian Democrat who had been so important two decades earlier in forging the "doughface" coalition of Northern and Southern Democrats.

Many abolitionists felt that too much had been conceded. The Free Soil platform said nothing about abolition, or about racial discrimination. Many recalled that only a decade before, Van Buren had been considered the worst of the doughfaces, a Northern president who would make no move to abolish slavery in the District of Columbia or speak out against the gag rule. Gerrit Smith, later of the Secret Six, led a small number of dissidents in forming the Liberty League to uphold the principles of the now disbanded Liberty party. Wendell Phillips, a close ally of Garrison, sneered at the "namby-pamby antislavery" of the Free Soilers.

THE GROWTH OF ANTISLAVERY SENTIMENT

The handful of antislavery men in the Senate, now including Seward, Hale, and a former Liberty-ite from Ohio, Salmon P. Chase, fought hard against the Compromise of 1850. Yet the Compromise, or rather one specific part of it, gave an enormous impetus to the antislavery movement.

The Fugitive Slave Law of 1850 granted almost unlimited power to the federal commissioners appointed to enforce it, and to private slave catchers seeking to profit by it. The latter roamed the Northern states during the 1850s, collecting bounties from Southern planters for capturing and returning blacks who had allegedly escaped from slavery. Some of the victims were indeed runaways; others were not. But commissioners could decide as they pleased — there was little due process and no right of appeal. Northern legislatures, responding to public disgust over the slave catchers, passed what came to be known as "personal liberty laws," to counteract the fugitive slave law. Under the personal liberty laws, state and local officials might delay or withhold help in the distasteful process of returning alleged runaways. Southerners understandably fumed over this Northern betrayal of the Compromise, this Northern version of nullification.

Abolitionists went a step further and actively assisted fugitive slaves. It has been estimated that Boston alone sheltered a minimum of six hundred runaway blacks at any given time. Abolitionists in that city even resorted to violence to keep Negroes out of the hands of slave catchers. Thomas Higginson, for example, led a Boston mob which prevented the return to slavery of a fugitive. Theodore Parker, who often hid runaways in his home, wrote sermons with a pistol within reach of his desk. But when the federal government decided to go into the slave-catching business seriously and with all its power, it usually had its way, as in the case of Anthony Burns of Boston, who was returned to slavery by a massive force of federal troops.

Still, the reaction to such activities showed how attitudes had changed. In the 1830s, Garrison had been led through the streets of Boston with a rope around his body (and placed under "protective custody") for opposing slavery. In the 1850s, when Anthony Burns was returned to the South through those same streets, thousands of protesters lined the streets, and church bells tolled the city's shame.

While persistently agitating the fugitive slave issue, Free Soilers sought to increase their political influence by forming coalitions with members of the major parties. The party might ally with Democrats in one Northern state, Whigs in another; and in yet a third state it might support a Democrat for one office and a Whig for another. Such tactics succeeded in some instances. In the early 1850s, when most Americans, North and South, wished to believe that the Compromise of 1850 had permanently settled the question of slavery, such "deals" may have been necessary to keep antislavery politics alive.

In 1852, both major parties endorsed the Compromise, and most of the Barnburners (Van Buren included) returned to the Democratic party, their natural home. One result of this was to make the Free Soil party decidedly more radical than it had been four years before. Its platform now declared "that slavery is a sin against God and a crime against man . . . and that Christianity, humanity, and patriotism alike demand its abolition." John P. Hale, New Hampshire's non-Compromise senator, became the party's presidential nominee. A natural result of *this* was a falling off in votes. Hale polled about half of Van Buren's total of 1848. Yet the election in 1852 revealed a hard core of 150,000 antislavery votes, a seed for growth should the right issue appear.

That issue was not long in coming. When Stephen A. Douglas introduced the Kansas-Nebraska bill in 1854, reopening the possibility of forming slave states from those and other territories, the North exploded. Free Soilers and other restrictionists formed the new Republican party. "Our position is now rather enviable," wrote one Free Soil congressman, "We lead the hosts of freedom." "Anti-Nebraska" Democrats, as they were known, fielded their own tickets in many states. The American (or Know-Nothing) party, anti-immigrant and anti-Nebraska, made a strong showing. (The two issues did relate to each other, since many immigrants were deeply anti-Negro and also strongly opposed abolitionism.) With the existence of so many parties, shifting coalitions, and candidates with unclear partisan allegiances, finding the winners in the congressional elections of 1854 proved difficult. Despite some doubt as to who had won, those who favored the *expansion* of slavery, under any formula or conditions, had very clearly been the losers.

EMERGENCE OF THE REPUBLICAN PARTY

The Republican party, like most newly formed political organizations, was a complex group. It enrolled virtually all of the Free Soilers, most Northern Whigs (whose party had recently fallen apart), and a significant minority of Northern Democrats for whom the Kansas-Nebraska Act had been too much to swallow. All of these groups united, with varying degrees of commitment, on a single issue: slavery should not expand into the territories. Beyond that, they differed widely. "There are Republicans who are Abolitionists," explained Horace Greeley's New York *Tribune,* "there are others who anxiously desire and labor for the good of the slave, but there are many more whose main impulse is a desire to secure the territories for Free White Labor, with little or no regard for the interests of negroes, free or slave."

Yet, from the start, the party felt the heavy influence of the first group, the "political aboli-

Fugitive Henry Box Brown attempted a most daring escape, after his master refused to purchase Brown's wife and prevent her sale to the South. In a specially constructed crate, 2 feet by 3 feet wide and 2½ feet high, complete with airholes, Brown had himself sent 350 miles by express to Philadelphia, where delighted abolitionists unpacked him. He had spent 27 hours in the box, much of the time upside down, awaiting his "resurrection from the grave of slavery." (Library of Congress)

tionists," who regarded the prevention of slavery's spread as only a first step to total elimination of America's "national sin." They succeeded in getting through a strong antislavery platform at the 1856 Republican convention. But the party's presidential nominee, a professional Western explorer and amateur politican named John C. Frémont, left much to be desired. Even Garrison, however, admitted grudgingly that "as between the three rival parties, the sympathy of every friend of freedom

Dred Scott, the central figure in the celebrated Supreme Court decision of 1857. (Missouri Historical Society)

must be with the Republican party, in spite of its lamentable shortcomings." Frederick Douglass led what little there was of the black vote in the new party, and Gerrit Smith, although running for president himself as the Abolition candidate, donated $500 to the "other" antislavery party.

After only two years of existence, the Republicans ran effectively in 1856. Receiving virtually no votes in the slave states, the new party swept New England and carried New York, Ohio, and several other Western states. The Democratic candidate, James Buchanan, another doughface, carried only five Northern states, some of them mainly because Know-Nothings had voted for their own candidate, ex-President Millard Fillmore. "We are beaten," conceded a leading Republican, "but we frightened the rascals awfully."

Another Weak President

By the time James Buchanan took office as president in March 1857, political parties could no longer appeal to voters on a nationwide basis. Republicans now dominated the North, but they had no following in the South. The Know-Nothing party was dead; so were the Whigs. Southern Democrats generally voted as a bloc. Only Northern Democrats were still trying to bridge the widening gap between the sections. And only an extraordinary, national-minded president, one skilled in the political arts of bullying and compromise, would have stood a chance of repairing all of this political damage. James Buchanan, an elderly, fussy bachelor, quick to please, slow to offend, soon proved the obvious—he was *not* that kind of president.

The Dred Scott Decision

Buchanan's first and only effort at sectional reconciliation produced immediate disaster. The Supreme Court, he stated blandly in his inaugural address, was about to decide the question of slaveholders' rights in the territories. The Court's decision, whatever it turned out to be, should be accepted by all sides, and the opinion should settle the dispute permanently. Dred Scott, a slave, had been taken from Missouri to Illinois and later to Wisconsin. Missouri was a slave state, Illinois a free state, and Wisconsin, at the time, a free territory according to the Missouri Compromise. In 1846, Scott sued for his liberty, claiming that residence in a free state and a free territory had put an end to his slave status. After passing through state courts and lower federal courts, the well-publicized case reached the U.S. Supreme Court.

Even before the decision, antislavery forces had rejected Buchanan's "offer." The Supreme Court of 1857 was controlled by slaveholders and doughfaces. Besides, slavery *did* enjoy protection from the Constitution and laws of the United States; Garrison and other radical abolitionists were right about that. In the twenty years before *Dred Scott* v. *Sandford*, the Supreme Court had upheld both the legality of the interstate slave trade and the rights of slaveowners to retrieve their property forcibly anywhere in the Union. In 1851, six years before *Dred Scott*, in *Strader* v. *Graham*, a case with very similar issues, the court had ruled that a slave going from Kentucky to Ohio remained a slave under the laws of Kentucky, rather than becoming free under the laws of Ohio. Such decisions led John Hale to denounce the Court as "the very citadel of American slavery," an exaggerated but not preposterous allegation.

Moreover, Buchanan's offer of March 1857 was not so generous and open as the president wished people to think. While reading the speech, he already knew (through confidential contacts with one of the justices) how the Court would decide. He had in fact helped persuade a justice from his own state, Pennsylvania, to join the five justices from slave states, so that the Court would not divide along totally sectional lines.

Chief Justice Roger Taney of Maryland, speaking for the majority, ruled against Scott, declaring that the plaintiff had no right to sue since a black could not be a citizen. Taney added gratuitously that white Americans had since colonial times considered blacks inferior human beings, possessing "no rights that a white man was bound to respect." Worst of all, from the North's point of view, Taney and the Court decided that slavery could not be excluded from *any* territory. Slaves, he explained, were property, and according to the Fifth Amendment, persons could not be deprived of property without due process of law.

Opponents of slavery reacted furiously, charging that their warnings about the aggressions of the Slave Power had been confirmed. Not only was the South demanding the possibility of opening all new territories for slavery but the logic of the Court decision could be taken even further. "Does the Constitution make slaves property?" an irate Republican wanted to know. "If so, slavery exists in Ohio today, for the Constitution extends over Ohio, doesn't it?" Northerners, who had considered Kansas-Nebraska too favorable to the South, now felt some of that rage which characterized Southern grievances over nonenforcement of the fugitive slave law. The Buchanan administration, only a week old, was already doomed.

The Emergence of Lincoln

Stephen A. Douglas had helped build the Compromise of 1850 — and he had helped to destroy it with the Kansas-Nebraska Act. In 1858 he ran for reelection to the Senate from Illinois. His Republican opponent was a popular former Whig congressman, Abraham Lincoln.

Born in Kentucky in 1809 to poor parents, Abraham Lincoln had moved with his family first to Indiana and then to Illinois. During his early years in these frontier areas the young man educated himself through extensive reading. He managed a general store at New Salem, Illinois, served as a captain of volunteers during a brief Indian war in northern Illinois, and worked as New Salem's postmaster while studying law. Lincoln was admitted to the Illinois bar in 1836. The next year he moved to Springfield and opened a law office.

Lincoln served as a state legislator from 1834 to 1842 while engaged in a private law prac-

The earliest known photograph of Lincoln was taken when he was a congressman—an obscure Whig and unpopular at home because of his opposition to the Mexican War. (Culver Pictures)

tice. He quickly acquired a reputation for his skill as a trial lawyer and his rough frontier humor. Elected in 1846 as a Whig, the young Illinois lawyer served one term in the House. He opposed the Mexican War but remained a member of the Whig party. Like many Northerners, Lincoln was pried loose from former party loyalties only by passage of the Kansas-Nebraska Act in 1854. He denounced the law and, in 1856, joined the newly formed Republican party.

Lincoln's views on slavery were typical of most Northern antislavery moderates. He believed that slavery was "a moral, social, and political wrong." But he denied having any intention of interfering with the institution in the Southern states. Like most Republicans, he felt that it would die out gradually as an unprofitable labor system. He did insist, however, that slavery should be totally excluded from the Western territories.

During a statewide series of public debates Lincoln kept Douglas on the defensive with questions about how, in view of the Dred Scott decision, settlers could legally exclude slavery from a territory under popular sovereignty. Douglas was reduced to arguing that a free-soil majority could simply refuse to enact a slave code, a weak counter to Lincoln's basic point.

In the short run the Lincoln-Douglas debates of 1858 helped to reelect Douglas. But in the long run they damaged him as a national leader. His view that a territory could effectively exclude slavery in spite of the Dred Scott decision gained him votes in Illinois, but it offended Southerners.

As for Lincoln, he emerged as a major national figure in the Republican party. He had dramatized in the debates the basic differences between Douglas Democrats and the Buchanan–Southern Democratic coalition.

Kansas and Collapse

President Buchanan scored no great successes. Perhaps his greatest failure was his Kansas policy, one inherited from fellow Democrat Franklin Pierce to deal with the miniature civil war which raged there. Pressured by Southerners in his cabinet, Buchanan submitted to Congress the "Lecompton Constitution," a document drafted by a proslavery minority in Kansas to serve as the basis for entry into the Union. The Lecompton Constitution legalized slavery, and prohibited agitation against the institution. Congress offered a huge land grant to Kansas if the state would ratify the document, but in 1858 free state settlers voted it down by a 9 to 1 margin. "Ever since the rendition [returning] of Anthony Burns," Thomas Higginson reported with pride, "I have been looking for *men*. I have found them in Kansas. . . . In Kansas, nobody talks of courage, for everyone is expected to exhibit it."

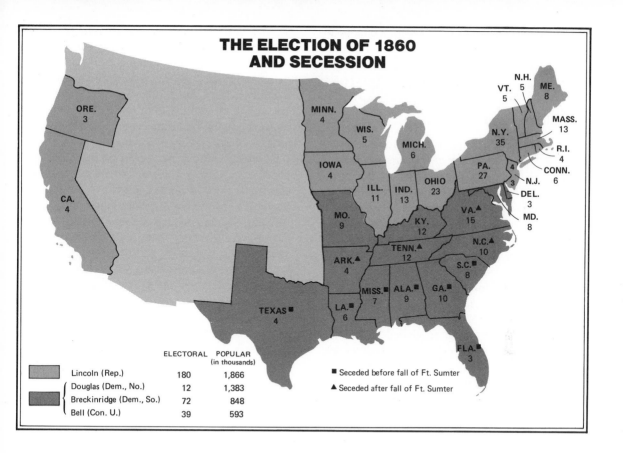

THE ELECTION OF 1860 AND SECESSION

	ELECTORAL	POPULAR (in thousands)
Lincoln (Rep.)	180	1,866
Douglas (Dem., No.)	12	1,383
Breckinridge (Dem., So.)	72	848
Bell (Con. U.)	39	593

■ Seceded before fall of Ft. Sumter

▲ Seceded after fall of Ft. Sumter

On the Lecompton issue, even Douglas, author of the Kansas-Nebraska Act, abandoned ship. Parly due to Lincoln's pressure in Illinois, partly due to obvious irregularities in the framing of the document, Douglas announced, "if this constitution is to be forced down our throats . . . I will resist it to the last." The Democratic party, the last national political institution, now broke in two: Southerners backed Buchanan; most Northerners supported Douglas.

THE FAILURE OF COMPROMISE

The reaction to John Brown's raid showed how fragile the political links between North and South had become. In the North even moderate antislavery advocates were outraged by the South's embittered defense of its "peculiar institution."

They regarded President Buchanan as a turncoat. Though Brown was in fact and by right a federal prisoner, Buchanan had simply handed him over to a Virginia court.

In the South, moderates had lost control of public opinion. People there had already begun preparing for possible secession, if not war. To most Southerners, Buchanan's pro-Southern attitudes no longer seemed adequate protection against "aggressions" (such as the Harpers Ferry raid) that the South believed Northern Republicans were planning. By 1860 armed defense against Northern attack seemed as reasonable to most Southerners as did violent assaults against the slave system to the antislavery North.

What was left to negotiate? How could either section compromise, when each one felt its most vital interests at stake? Brown's raid came at the end of a decade of bitter argument and violent conflict over slavery. It hastened the collapse of normal political life, since democratic politics requires moderation—which no longer had many spokesmen.

Election and Secession

The Democratic party split into sectional wings in 1860. Northern Democrats nominated Stephen A. Douglas for the presidency. The Southerners put forward their own candidate, John C. Breckinridge of Kentucky. He promised to sponsor federal laws that would protect slavery in the territories. The Republicans nominated Abraham Lincoln. A hodgepodge of former Whigs, Know-Nothings, and Democrats formed a new Constitutional Union party. They nominated a fourth candidate, John Bell, also of Kentucky. He pledged mainly to say and do nothing about the slavery question.

But a decade of agitation had eroded the basis for compromise solutions to the slavery question. It was no longer possible to avoid the issue by not talking about it. Douglas and Breckinridge split the Democratic vote. Bell carried three border states. Lincoln won the North. He became president with barely 40 percent of the popular vote, none at all from the Deep South.

Fear swept the South after Lincoln's election. "Secession fever" grew to epidemic proportions within days. South Carolina took the first step. Its legislature passed a secession ordinance on December 20, 1860, climaxing thirty years of leadership in defense of Southern nationalism. By February 1, 1861, six other states—Mississippi, Florida, Alabama, Georgia, Louisiana, and Texas—had adopted similar ordinances. Three days later, these seven states proclaimed the Confederate States of America in Montgomery, Alabama.

Four critical months separated the 1860 election and Lincoln's inauguration in March 1861. The "lame-duck" administration of James Buchanan did little to impede the course of secession. Buchanan condemned Southern actions and demanded obedience to federal laws. But neither he nor his government attempted to interfere as Southerners took control of federal forts, arsenals, and public property in their region.

There were various efforts to end the secession crisis by a political compromise in Congress, similar to the ones of 1820 and 1850. The most important of these was the Crittenden Compromise. It would have extended the Missouri Compromise line across the entire country, legalizing slavery south of it and prohibiting it to the north. By then, however, most Southerners were unprepared to accept any limitation, just as most Republicans opposed any extension, of the system. Lincoln proposed that the North agree to enforce the Fugitive Slave Act and protect Southern slavery by constitutional amendments if necessary. But his belated suggestions seemed inadequate to the secessionists.

Both the Confederate states and the new Republican administration waited in March 1861 to see whether states in the Upper South would also secede. Although fears about Republican intentions were widespread in states like Virginia and North Carolina, especially after John Brown's raid, there were also more Unionists there than in the Deep South.

Lincoln's Inauguration

Lincoln's inaugural address did little to calm the South. The new president promised not to invade the region or interfere with slavery where it already existed. But he made it clear that he believed the Union could not be dissolved at the whim of a state or group of states. He promised "to hold, occupy, and possess the property and places belonging to the federal government" throughout the country, including the South. And he pointed directly to the moral and political issue of slavery (and its extension) as the root of the conflict. "One section of our country," Lincoln said, "believes slavery is right, and ought to be extended, while the other believes it is wrong, and ought not to be extended. This is the only substantial dispute." Finally, he insisted that the question of war and peace was not in his hands but in those of his "dissatisfied fellow countrymen," the secessionists.

Lincoln's promise to maintain control of federal property in the South practically eliminated the possibility of a political compromise with the Confederate states. Lincoln was trapped be-

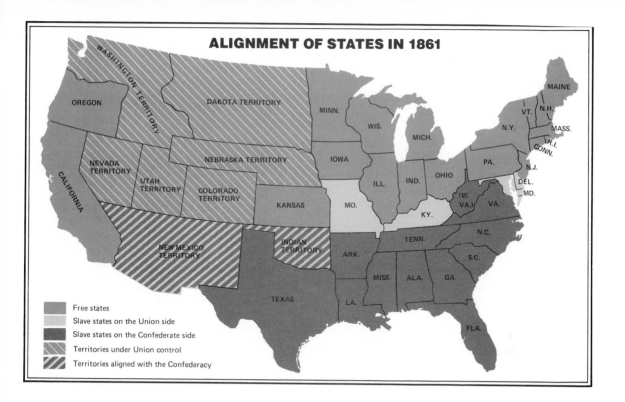

ALIGNMENT OF STATES IN 1861

Free states
Slave states on the Union side
Slave states on the Confederate side
Territories under Union control
Territories aligned with the Confederacy

tween a desire to mediate and a need to maintain national authority, lest it collapse throughout the Upper South as well.

For weeks Lincoln and his cabinet debated their course of action toward the Confederacy. They worried especially about whether to send relief supplies and troops to the few remaining federal posts in the region, such as Fort Sumter in Charleston harbor.

Finally, on April 4, Lincoln dispatched a relief expedition to Sumter. It carried only fresh supplies for the garrison, not reinforcements. Lincoln wanted to avoid the charge that he was making a hostile move toward the Confederacy. He even went so far as to inform the governor of South Carolina about his desire to supply Sumter peacefully. But the Confederate government demanded that the fort be entirely evacuated or, if necessary, destroyed. Charleston's harbor batteries opened fire at Sumter on April 12. Within two days Confederate forces had captured the fort. Virginia, Arkansas, and North Carolina all joined the Confederacy in the weeks that followed. So did Tennessee. Elsewhere in the border states—especially Maryland, Missouri, and Kentucky—Lincoln took firm measures to maintain Union control. "Both parties deprecated war," Lincoln later wrote, "but one of them would *make* war rather than let the nation survive; and the other would *accept* war rather than let it perish. And the war came."

Suggested Readings
Chapters 21-22

John Brown

R. O. Boyer, *The Legend of John Brown: A Biography and History* (1973); Stephen Oates, *To Purge This Land with Blood: A Biography of John Brown* (1970); J. Scott, *The Secret Six* (1979).

Abolitionism and the Antislavery Movement

Martin Duberman, ed., *The Antislavery Vanguard* (1969); Louis Filler, *The Crusade Against Slavery, 1830–1860* (1960); Larry Gara, *The Liberty Line: The Legend of the Underground Railroad* (1961); Aileen S. Kraditor, *Means and Ends in American Abolitionism . . . 1834–1860* (1967); Walter M. Merrill, *Against Wind and Tide: A Biography of William Lloyd Garrison* (1963); Russell B. Nye, *Fettered Freedom: Civil Liberties and the Slavery Controversy, 1830–1860* (rev. ed., 1963); Jane H. Pease and William H. Pease, *They Who Would Be Free: Blacks' Search for Freedom, 1830–1861* (1974); Gerald Sorin, *Abolitionism: A New Perspective* (1972); John L. Thomas, *The Liberator: William Lloyd Garrison* (1963).

Antislavery Politics

Eugene Berwanger, *The Frontier Against Slavery* (1967); F. J. Blue, *The Free Soilers: Third Party Politics, 1848–1854* (1973); S. W. Campbell, *The Slave Catchers* (1968); Avery O. Craven, *The Growth of Southern Nationalism, 1848–1861* (1953); David Donald, *Charles Sumner and the Coming of the Civil War* (1960); Don E. Fehrenbacher, *The Dred Scott Case: Its Significance in American Law and Politics* (1978) and *Prelude to Greatness: Lincoln in the 1850's* (1962); Eric Foner, *Free Soil, Free Labor, Free Men: The Ideology of the Republican Party Before the Civil War* (1970); Harry V. Jaffe, *Crisis of the House Divided: An Interpretation of the Issues of the Lincoln-Douglas Debates* (1959); Robert W. Johannsen, *Stephen A. Douglas* (1973); Roy F. Nichols, *The Disruption of the American Democracy* (1948); David M. Potter, *The Impending Crisis, 1848–1861* (1976); Richard H. Sewell, *Ballots for Freedom: AntiSlavery Politics in the United States, 1837–1860* (1976); Paul Sigelschiffer, *The American Conscience* (1973); Hans Trefousse, *The Radical Republicans* (1969).

The Secession Crisis

Steven A. Channing, *Crisis of Fear: Secession in South Carolina* (1970); David M. Potter, *Lincoln and His Party in the Secession Crisis* (1942); Kenneth M. Stampp, *And the War Came: The North and the Secession Crisis, 1860–1861* (1950).

Sherman's March to the Sea 23

Early on the morning of November 16, 1864, the Union columns headed out of Atlanta, Georgia, bound southeast for the coastal city of Savannah. Northern troops, over sixty thousand strong, with their horses, mules, and wagons, clogged the road. As they reached a hilltop, the soldiers turned to look back toward the town. Their commander, General William Tecumseh Sherman, recalled:

> Behind us lay Atlanta, smoldering and in ruins, the black smoke rising high in the air and hanging like a pall over the ruined city. Away off in the distance, on the McDonough road, was the rear of Howard's column, the gun-barrels glistening in the sun, the white-topped wagons stretching away to the south; and right before us the Fourteenth Corps, marching steadily and rapidly, with a cheery look and a swinging pace, that made light of the thousand miles that lay between us and Richmond. Some band, by accident, struck up the anthem of "John Brown's Body." The men caught up the strain, and never before have I heard the chorus of "Glory, glory, hallelujah!" done with more spirit, or in better harmony of time and place.

On that beautiful day of brilliant sunshine and clean, crisp air, the Civil War, already three and a half years old, seemed exhilarating, if not remote. Sherman later recalled experiencing a "feeling of something to come, vague and undefined, still full of venture and intense interest. Even the common soldiers caught the inspiration, and many a group called out to me—Uncle Billy, I guess Grant is waiting for us at Richmond!"

Although Richmond and victory for the Union were still five months away, Sherman had already made his mark in Georgia. The pall of smoke he and his troops saw above Atlanta came from the fires they had set in the town's railroad depot and machine shops. Flames soon swept into residential areas, destroying hundreds of dwellings. The general's reputation for toughness—"brutality" in the minds of most Southerners—took shape at Atlanta and on the subsequent campaign, his famous march to the sea. "We are not only fighting hostile armies," Sherman believed, "but a hostile people. We must make old and young, rich and poor, feel the hand of war."

Union invasion of the South devastated the Confederate terrain as well as its morale. Marching through Georgia in 1864, General Sherman's troops occupied Atlanta and demolished much of the city—ripping up railroad tracks, destroying the depot, burning down homes, and evacuating the remainder of the residents. The fire-swept shambles behind them, Sherman's men moved on to Savannah. (Culver Pictures)

Sherman, the tough-talking soldier, knew the South well. Born in Ohio in 1820, he attended West Point and, after graduation, spent most of his time on duty in military posts in the South. He resigned from the army in 1853. After working unsuccessfully as a bank manager in California and as a lawyer in Kansas, he tried to get back into the army. Rejected, he had to settle for the job of superintendent of a military academy in Louisiana. The school opened in 1859.

As the sectional crisis deepened, Sherman made it clear that, if Louisiana should secede from the Union, he would resign his post and do all he could to aid the national government. He kept his word when he heard of the Southern attack on Fort Sumter in April 1861. Secession, he thought, was "folly, madness, a crime against civilization." He immediately sought, and gained, reinstatement in the army. It was now more receptive to such applications, since so many regular officers had joined the Confederacy.

Sherman started as a colonel and rose rapidly in the Union high command. He served in the west as one of Grant's most trusted officers. By mid-1864, as a major general, he was assigned the mission of striking from Tennessee into Georgia and seizing Atlanta. The town, though relatively small, was an important railroad center. Confederate troops under General Joseph E. Johnston and, later, General John B. Hood fought hard to hold Sherman back. They were defeated in July at two crucial battles, those of Peachtree Creek and Atlanta. After a siege of several weeks, Atlanta fell.

Sherman's troops entered the city on September 2. Although Hood at first moved south toward safety, he later wheeled northwest toward Tennessee, hoping to harass Sherman's communications so badly that his forces would have to retreat. Inadvertently, Hood's actions may have influenced Sherman in his later decision to move to the sea without regard for communications or established supply lines.

For the time being, however, Sherman wanted to rest his troops and observe Hood's movements. He decided that Hood could be kept at bay by some detachments of his own army, plus Union troops in Tennessee.

Sherman meanwhile undertook some indirect negotiations with the governor of Georgia, Joseph E. Brown. His aim was to separate the state from the Confederacy. There was reason to hope that Georgia might pull out of the war. Brown had already withdrawn his state's militia from the rebel army. And, like many Southern politicians, he had come to detest Jefferson Davis, president of the Confederacy. Davis had stirred bitter reactions because of his insistent demands for troops and supplies from the hard-pressed Southern states. Nothing came of the negotiations, but they may have impressed on Sherman the need for bringing the hardships of war home to the Southern civilian population.

When the war started, Atlanta—not then the state capital—had only twelve thousand inhabitants. Many of them had fled as the Union troops approached. Others followed when Hood abandoned the town. When Sherman entered, he ordered the rest of the civilians to leave, since he did not want them clogging the town and interfering with his lines of communication. He and Hood agreed to a ten-day truce so that these civilians could move out.

By late October, Sherman had decided to march to the sea. On November 2 Grant wired: "I do not really see that you can withdraw from where you are to follow Hood without giving up all we have gained in territory. I say, then, go as you propose."

Sherman gained a reputation as a ruthless commander because of his march through the Confederacy. (Brady Collection, U.S. Signal Corps, National Archives)

Sherman's bold plan called for his army of sixty-two thousand men (five thousand of them cavalry) to move the three hundred miles to Savannah without supply lines and without communications until they reached the Atlantic coast. There the Union navy could provide cover and supplies. Sherman's troops carried enough provisions for twenty or thirty days, but those were considered emergency rations. Food on the march would be "provided" by the farms and plantations along the way—*not*, of course, on a voluntary basis—so Georgia would be made to "howl."

Sherman's Special Field Order #120 detailed the procedure he hoped to establish. Brigade commanders were responsible for organizing foraging parties. Every morning, these would move out from the four main columns under the direction of one or two "discreet officers." Foragers—or "bummers," as they soon came to be called (even by the Yankees themselves)—could seize available livestock and food supplies. They were not supposed to enter houses. Only corps commanders had the authority to order destruction of buildings, and then only in areas of resistance. Foragers for artillery units could take all the animals and wagons they needed.

If possible, foragers were to seize provisions from the rich planters rather than poor farmers. The wealthy were presumed to be more in favor

One of Sherman's "bummers" goes his way, so loaded with booty that he cannot hold the reins in his hands. (NYPL/Prints Division)

of the rebellion than their humbler fellow Southerners. (This assumption fitted Northern views of secession as a conspiracy of the elite. It did not square with the facts of Southern political life.)

Sherman's field order directed his men to "forage liberally." They obeyed with a will. Men would go out in the morning on foot, seize a wagon, and then load it with everything valuable and movable they could find. One of Sherman's aides, Major Henry Hitchcock, described a foraging expedition in his diary:

> Plenty of forage along road: corn, fodder, finest sweet potatoes, pigs, chickens, etc. Passed troops all day, some on march, some destroying railroad thoroughly. Two cotton gins on roadside burned, and pile of cotton with one, also burned. Houses in Conyers look comfortable for Georgia village, and sundry good ones along road. Soldiers foraging all along, but only for *forage* – no violence as far as I saw or heard. Laughable to see pigs in feed troughs behind wagons, chickens swinging in knapsacks. Saw some few men – Whites look sullen – darkies pleased.

Stories of Union brutality, supposedly encouraged by Sherman himself, began to circulate. (They continued to circulate for generations.) But his march to the sea, devastating as it was, did not degenerate into an orgy of murder, rape, and arson. Sherman later acknowledged "acts of pillage, robbery, and violence" undoubtedly committed by some of his men. But, he argued, "these acts were exceptional and incidental. I have never heard of any cases of murder or rape; and no army could have carried along sufficient food and forage for a march of three hundred miles; so that foraging in some shape was necessary."

To Sherman, the march became just what he had ordered – harsh but, in the main, well-disciplined. The destruction wrought by his "scorched-earth" policy centered on three main targets: railroads, the few factories on the route, and public buildings that could serve as temporary headquarters for military units.

Sherman marveled at the skill of his men in carrying out his order to "forage liberally." One fact among many proves how proficient they were: Sherman's army started the march driving five thousand head of cattle; they ended it with over ten thousand.

Where were the Confederate forces during these agonizing weeks? Some small cavalry units of the Confederate army did appear from time to time to raid foraging parties. But they had little overall effect. Hood's army had marched northwest to Tennessee and defeat. Since most Georgians of fighting age were serving with the Southern forces, the state militia had been reduced to several thousand old men and young boys. They tried to make a stand at the state capital, Milledgeville, but the Union forces swept them aside. After viewing the casualties, a Northern officer wrote: "I was never so affected at the sight of dead and wounded before. I hope we will never have to shoot at such men again. They know nothing at all about fighting and I think their officers know as little."

Milledgeville fell on November 23. Georgia state officials had fled a short time before. The invading Yankee officers decided to mock the "sovereign state of Georgia." They pretended to hold a session of the state legislature, complete with resolutions and fire-eating oratory. Then they decided to repeal the ordinance of secession. When Sherman heard about these antics, he laughed. Meanwhile, his Milledgeville "legislators" ordered the burning of public buildings in the town.

Sherman's soldiers sliced a path forty to sixty miles wide through central Georgia. Every white family along the way underwent its own particular ordeal and emerged with its own sorrowful story. Tales of the devastation became commonplace: houses broken into and sacked, food and valuables hidden only to be found by the recurrent searches of intruding "bummers," treasured family possessions tossed into the flames, cotton gins and public buildings put to the torch. "Everything had been swept as with a storm of fire," wrote one Macon newspaper. "The whole country around is one wide waste of destruction."

Contrary to Sherman's conception of his foraging troops as restrained and disciplined, most white Southerners in their path regarded them as greedy marauders. The experiences of two Georgia women, a mother and daughter, typified the ordeal. Mary Jones, the widow of a Presbyterian minister, owned three plantations in Liberty County, not far from Savannah. At the time of Sherman's march she and her daughter, Mary Jones Mallard, were living at the plantation known as Montevideo. Their letters and journals vividly portray the impact of war.

Mary Mallard's husband was captured on December 13 by Union cavalry near Montevideo. (Mrs. Mallard was then pregnant and expecting to give birth within days.) The first groups of "bummers" reached the Jones-Mallard household on December 15. They searched the house and made off with a number of family keepsakes. During the next two weeks,

Union raiding parties—sometimes large detachments, sometimes only a few stragglers—arrived almost daily at the home. Each group searched the premises, insulted the two women, and took what food, supplies, or family items remained to be carted away.

Mary Mallard confided unhappily to her journal on December 17.

> The Yankees made the Negroes bring up the oxen and carts, and took off all the chickens and turkeys they could find. They carried off all the syrup from the smokehouse. We had one small pig, which was all the meat we had left; they took the whole of it. Mother saw everything like food stripped from her premises, without the power of uttering one word. Finally they rolled out the carriage and took that to carry off a load of chickens. They took everything they possibly could.

"Everything" included seven of the Jones family's slaves, who— like hundreds of blacks elsewhere along the army's line of march—were pressed into service as porters, laborers, or mule drivers. "So they were all carried off," Mary Mallard grieved, "carriages, wagons, carts, horses and mules and servants, with food and provisions of every kind—and, so far as they were concerned, leaving us to starvation."

Occasionally an officer would apologize for the behavior of his men. One friendly Union soldier, a Missourian, offered to show Mrs. Jones where to hide her things. Mary Mallard noted: "He said he had enlisted to fight for the *Constitution;* but since then the war had been turned into another thing, and he did not approve of this abolitionism, for his wife's people all owned slaves." A few days later, a Virginian told Mrs. Jones that "there was great dissatisfaction in the army on account of the present object of the war, which now was to free the Negroes."

More often than not, however, the raiders stalked through the houses indifferent to its inhabitants. Never knowing whether soldiers coming to the door would behave politely or insolently, the two women lived in constant fear. Several times, "bummers" threatened to return and burn down their house. Yet on other occasions, Union commanders offered them protection and safe-conduct passes to Savannah, which was still in Confederate hands. The women declined to leave, partly because of Mary Mallard's pregnancy. On January 4, 1865, she gave birth to a daughter. Her mother noted in her journal:

> During these hours of agony the yard was filled with Yankees. They were all around the house; my poor child, calm and collected amid her agony of body, could hear their conversation and wild halloos and cursing beneath her windows. After a while they left, screaming and yelling in a most fiendish way as they rode from the house.

Mary Jones's journal makes it clear that Sherman had achieved his major purpose in marching through Georgia—to demoralize beyond repair what remained of the Deep South's fighting spirit. She wrote in January 1865:

> As I stand and look at the desolating changes wrought by the hand of an inhuman foe in a few days, I can enter into the feelings of Job. All our

pleasant things are laid low. We are prisoners in our own home. To obtain a mouthful of food we have been obliged to cook in what was formerly our drawing room; and I have to rise every morning by candlelight, before the dawn of day, that we may have it before the enemy arrives to take it from us. . . . For one month our homes and all we possess have been given up to lawless pillage. Officers and men have alike engaged in this work of degradation. I scarcely know how we have stood up under it. God alone has enabled us to "speak with the enemy in the gates," and calmly, without a tear, to see my house broken open, entered with false keys, threatened to be burned to ashes, refused food and ordered to be starved to death, told that I had no right even to wood or water, that I should be "humbled in the very dust I walked upon," a pistol and carbine presented to my breast, cursed and reviled as a rebel, a hypocrite, a devil.

Troubling Mrs. Jones almost as much as the behavior of Sherman's soldiers was the reaction of her slaves. During the first days of Union occupation, most of them stayed on the plantation, perhaps out of fear, perhaps out of loyalty. But when it became clear that the Northern army firmly controlled the area, a number of slaves left to join the Union columns marching on Savannah. "Many servants have proven faithful," Mrs. Jones wrote in January 1865, "others false and rebellious against all authority or restraint."

Sherman himself pursued an ambiguous policy toward the ex-slaves, who were considered "contraband." He did not want them as soldiers, despite the good record of black regiments in battle when they were

allowed to fight. He rejected the suggestion of General Ulysses S. Grant (by now in charge of all Union forces) that blacks be armed. He felt that his troops would object. And he had another reason. "My aim then," he later wrote, "was to whip the rebels, to humble their pride and make them fear and dread us. I did not want them to cast in our teeth that we had to call on *their* slaves to help us to subdue them."

Nevertheless, Sherman did order the formation of black "pioneer battalions"—construction units—for each army corps. "Negroes who are able-bodied and can be of service to the several columns may be taken along," Sherman instructed, "but each army commander will bear in mind that the question of supplies is a very important one, and that his first duty is to see to those who bear arms." In other words, the army was to keep blacks at a distance, using labor as needed but refraining from becoming a relief organization for ex-slaves who had left their plantations.

Sherman's prejudice against blacks was a crucial factor in his military policy. His brother John was an important antislavery Republican politician from Ohio, but William did not share his views. When still in Louisiana, he had assured Southerners that slavery was best for blacks.

"All the congresses on earth," he said, "can't make the Negro anything else than what he is"—namely a slave, or a second-class noncitizen. In a letter he stated:

> I would not if I could abolish or modify slavery. I don't know that I would materially change the actual political relation of master and slave. Negroes in the great numbers that exist here must of necessity be slaves. Theoretical notions of humanity and religion cannot shake the commercial fact that their labor is of great value and cannot be dispensed with.

Whatever Sherman's own attitudes, it was clear that, from the moment his troops left Atlanta, they sparked the imagination of Georgia's slaves. As Sherman rode through the town of Covington, a day's march from Atlanta, he found that "the Negroes were simply frantic with joy." He later recalled that "Whenever they heard my name, they clustered about my horse, shouted and prayed in their peculiar style, which had a natural eloquence that would have moved a stone."

During the following weeks, as Northern troops foraged their way across Georgia, Sherman witnessed "hundreds, if not thousands, of such scenes." He wrote later that he could still see "a poor girl, in the very ecstasy of the Methodist 'shout,' hugging the banner of one of the regiments."

Thousands of slaves did more than simply greet the liberating Northern army. They joined it, striding alongside or in back of the troop columns. Wrote Mary Jones: "Negroes in large numbers are flocking to them. Nearly all the house servants have left their homes; and from most of the plantations they have gone in a body." The ranks of contraband included strong young men and women in the prime of life, mothers carrying children, and the white-haired elderly.

More than thirty thousand blacks joined Sherman's army at one time or another during its four-week march. Yet only ten thousand remained with its ranks as it entered Savannah. Many had been actively discouraged from remaining by the soldiers. Neither Sherman nor most of his officers and men wished to add the task of foraging to feed a huge contraband population from the food collected each day.

Sherman later remembered personally telling an old black man at one plantation that:

> we wanted the slaves to remain where they were, and not to load us down with useless mouths. We could receive a few of their young, hearty men as pioneers. But if they followed us in swarms of old and young, feeble and helpless, it would simply load us down and cripple us in our great task. I believe that old man spread this message to the slaves, which was carried from mouth to mouth, to the very end of our journey, and that it in part saved us from the great danger we incurred of swelling our numbers so that famine would have attended our progress.

In any case, the thousands of slaves who remained with Sherman's forces did not all passively trudge along waiting to be fed and taken care of. Many played active roles. They carried supplies as porters and mule drivers. Some searched out food, animals, and equipment hidden by Con-

Freed Negroes joining Union lines in North Carolina. (Library of Congress)

federates along the way. Others built roads or repaired bridges so that Sherman's men, equipment, and supply wagons could keep to their ten-mile-a-day pace across the swampy stretches of central Georgia. Still others helped the soldiers to destroy railroads and other strategic targets. A favorite trick was to heat the heavy iron rails and twist them into "Sherman's neckties.")

Local blacks also served as reliable guides behind Confederate lines. One of Sherman's officers, General Oliver O. Howard, ordered one of his men to reach the Union fleet anchored off Savannah. After safely rowing a canoe past enemy posts along the Ogeechee River, the officer and his patrol:

> found some Negroes, who befriended him and his men and kept pretty well under cover until evening. Then they went ashore to get a Negro guide and some provisions [after which they passed through Confederate lines]. Soon after this they came to quite a sizable Negro house, went in, and were well treated and refreshed with provisions. When they were eating they were startled by hearing a party of Confederate cavalry riding toward the house. Of course they expected to be instantly captured, but the Negroes, coming quickly to their rescue, concealed them under the floor. The coolness and smartness of the Negroes surprised even Captain Duncan, though he had believed and trusted them. The cavalry stopped but remained only a short time, and the Negroes guided our men back to their boats.

Although few blacks aided the Union side quite so daringly during Sherman's march, the general himself acknowledged that the "large number employed as servants, teamsters and pioneers rendered admirable service."

Sherman's army marched into Savannah on December 21, along with ten thousand blacks marching behind the troops. The general sent a playful telegram to "His Excellency," President Lincoln: "I beg to present you as a Christmas gift the city of Savannah, with one hundred and fifty heavy guns and plenty of ammunition, also about twenty-five thousand bales of cotton."

The message was quickly published throughout the North. Northerners had considered Sherman's army "lost" when the general had broken communication after leaving Atlanta. Sherman and his men instantly became popular heroes. "Our joy was irrepressible," said one high Washington official, "not only because of their safety, but because it was an assurance that the days of the Confederacy were numbered." Even to many Southerners, Savannah's capture seemed to foreshadow final defeat. Given the suffering that Confederate soldiers and civilians had undergone by then, the prospect seemed almost welcome.

Sherman did not order the city's residents to leave, as he had done at Atlanta. With Union ships in the harbor and his troops in control of the surrounding countryside, he felt no useful military purpose would be served by evacuating or burning the city. In fact, Sherman decided to govern Savannah's twenty thousand inhabitants mildly—much to their amazement and that of other Georgians. He gave people the choice of remaining in Savannah or leaving for other cities that were still under Confederate control.

Sherman placed one of his generals in overall command of Savan-

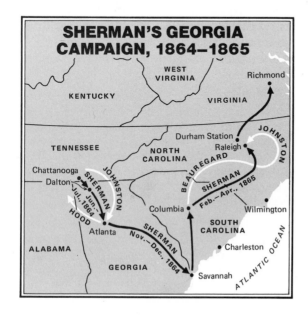

SHERMAN'S GEORGIA CAMPAIGN, 1864–1865

nah, but the Confederate mayor and city council handled most day-to-day matters. Relations between Northerners and Southerners were polite, almost cordial. Only a few hundred citizens left the city. Most people calmly went about their business. Relief ships organized by private citizens in the North arrived regularly in January 1865, bringing much-needed food and clothing. Supplies were distributed to freed blacks and indigent whites. Local markets selling meat, wood, and other necessities reopened under military supervision.

"No city was ever occupied with less disorder or more system than Savannah," Sherman wrote on December 31. "Though an army of sixty thousand men lay camped around it, women and children of an hostile people walk its streets with as much security as they do in Philadelphia." Confederate newspapers raged about the alleged "barbarities" of Sherman's forces on their march from Atlanta, exaggerating the amount of property burned, and the numbers murdered or raped. Meantime the "barbarians" occupied Savannah with little friction.

In Savannah, as on the march from Atlanta, Sherman became a hero to the liberated blacks. He wrote to his wife on Christmas Day: "They flock to me, young and old. They pray and shout and mix up my name with that of Moses and Simon and other scriptural ones as well as 'Abram Linkom'." Hundreds of blacks hurried to see the general, wrote an aide. "There was a constant stream of them, old and young, men, women and children, black, yellow, and cream-colored, uncouth and well-bred, bashful and talkative — but always respectful and behaved — all day long."

It would have come as a great shock to the blacks of Savannah to learn that their hero was at that very moment being attacked in the North for his policy toward ex-slaves. Late in December General Henry W. Halleck wrote Sherman to congratulate him on the march through Georgia and his capture of Savannah. He also warned him that powerful individuals close to the president spoke critically of him, alleging that he "manifested an almost *criminal* dislike" to the Negro. "They say," added Halleck,

> that you are not willing to carry out the wishes of the government in regard to him, but repulse him with contempt! They say you might have brought with you to Savannah more than fifty thousand, thus stripping Georgia of that number of laborers, and opening a road by which as many more could have escaped from their masters; but that, instead of this, you drove them from your ranks, prevented their following you by cutting the bridges in your rear, and thus caused the massacre of large numbers by Wheeler's cavalry.

Sherman defended his decision to discourage slave runaways from joining the march on the grounds that their presence would have overburdened his army and hindered its military success. In responding to Halleck, however, he acknowledged that his sympathy for freed blacks was limited:

Thank God I am not running for an office and am not concerned because the rising generation will believe that I burned 500 niggers[1] at one pop in Atlanta, or any such nonsense. The South deserves all she has got for her injustice to the Negro, but that is no reason why we should go to the other extreme.

It came as no surprise to Sherman, therefore, when Secretary of War Edwin M. Stanton arrived in Savannah on January 9, aboard the Union ship *Nevada.* Stanton was supposedly traveling on a vacation cruise and to supervise the disposition of captured Confederate cotton supplies. Actually he had come to check on Sherman's handling of matters involving blacks. Stanton strongly supported Sherman's military strategy in Georgia. But he disapproved of the general's rumored hostility toward the ex-slave population and of his refusal to use blacks as soldiers.

Sherman denied that any of his officers or troops had been hostile to slaves on their march from Atlanta. But Stanton wanted to hear about Sherman's behavior from the blacks themselves. At his request, therefore, Sherman invited "the most intelligent of the Negroes" in Savannah to come to his rooms to meet the secretary of war. Twenty black men attended the meeting with Sherman and Stanton on January 12, 1865.

Never before had any major American government official met with black leaders to ask what *they* wished for their people. Each man present began by introducing himself with a brief account of his life. The average age was fifty. Fifteen of the men were ministers—mainly Baptist and Methodist—and the other five were church officials of one kind or another. Five of the leaders had been born free. Of the others, three had bought their freedom; most of the rest had been liberated by Sherman's army.

Secretary of War Stanton sat at a table facing the black visitors, making extensive notes on their remarks. Sherman, restless and uneasy over the interview, stood with two of his aides apart from the seated group. He watched the proceedings warily, pacing across the room from time to time during the exchange. The blacks had selected as their spokesman sixty-seven-year-old Garrison Frazier, a Baptist minister. He responded firmly to each of Stanton's questions.

Stanton asked first whether the men were aware of Lincoln's Emancipation Proclamation. Frazier replied that they were.

STANTON: State what you understand by slavery, and the freedom that was to be given by the President's Proclamation.
FRAZIER: Slavery is receiving by irresistible power the work of another man, and not by his consent. The freedom, as I understand it, promised by the Proclamation, is taking us from under the yoke of bondage, and placing us where we could reap the fruit of our own labor, and take care of ourselves, and assist the Government in maintaining our freedom.

---

[1] This term was considered only mildly discourteous in the 1860s. It was commonly used, even by antislavery Northerners.

Stanton then asked how black people could best maintain their new freedom. Frazier suggested that young men should be able to enlist in the army, and that other blacks ought to receive land to farm: "We want to be placed on land until we are able to buy it, and make it our own."

The secretary of war then asked whether the men believed that freed blacks "would rather live scattered among the whites, or in colonies by yourselves?" Frazier answered: "I would prefer to live by ourselves, for there is a prejudice against us in the South that will take years to get over; but I do not know that I can answer for my brethren."

Frazier and his black associates may have considered Stanton's next question offensive. The secretary asked whether the ex-slaves of the South were intelligent enough to sustain their freedom while maintaining good relations with Southern whites. "I think there is sufficient intelligence among us to do so," Frazier replied simply.

The black minister was then asked what he believed were the causes and objectives of the Civil War, and whether blacks generally supported one or the other side. He responded shrewdly and at length. Frazier told Stanton that blacks wished only to help the Union subdue the rebellious Confederacy. He acknowledged that the North's first war aim involved bringing the South back into the Union and that Lincoln had issued the Emancipation Proclamation mainly as a means toward achieving this end. Only the South's refusal to emancipate its slaves "has now made the freedom of the slaves a part of the war." Frazier pointed out that the thousands of runaways who had followed the Union armies, "leaving their homes and undergoing suffering," spoke clearly for the pro-Union sentiments of blacks.

Stanton then indicated that he wanted to ask a question about Sherman. The general — silently furious — left the room. In Sherman's absence, Stanton inquired about "the feeling of the colored people in regard to General Sherman" and whether Negroes regarded "his sentiments and actions as friendly to their rights and interests." Frazier's answer probably surprised Stanton, considering the rumors current in Washington:

> We looked upon General Sherman, prior to his arrival, as a man in the providence of God, specially set apart to accomplish this work, and we unanimously felt inexpressible gratitude to him. Some of us called upon him immediately upon his arrival [in Savannah], and it is probable that he did not meet the Secretary with more courtesy than he met us. His conduct and deportment toward us characterized him as a friend and a gentleman. We have confidence in General Sherman, and think that what concerns us could not be under better hands.

The meeting soon ended, after Stanton had thanked his black visitors for their advice.

Stanton and Sherman spent the next three days discussing problems of policy toward the freedmen. They agreed that Sherman would issue a field order on January 16, the day after Stanton's departure from Savannah.

Special Field Order #15 set aside confiscated or abandoned land along rivers emptying into the Atlantic and on the Sea Islands — nearby islands that lie along the coast from Charleston, South Carolina, to Jacksonville, Florida. These lands were to be used exclusively for settlement by freed blacks. A freedman and his family taking up such land were to be given a "possessory title" to "not more than forty acres of tillable land" until Congress should regulate the title.

Sherman obviously viewed this scheme as a temporary one, needed in order to provide for freedmen and their families in the area during the rest of the war or until Congress acted. "Mr. Stanton has been here," he confidently wrote his wife on the day of Stanton's departure, "and is cured of that Negro nonsense." By now Sherman was impatient to begin his march northward. He appointed General Rufus Saxton as Inspector of Settlements and Plantations for the entire area covered by his field order. On January 21 Sherman's army left Savannah and marched into South Carolina, the symbol of Confederate resistance.

Saxton energetically arranged to transport homeless blacks in Savannah to coastal farms. He wrote urgent letters to Northern sympathizers asking for food and supplies to help sustain the new agricultural settlements. By midsummer of 1865 — with the war now over — Saxton and his aides had managed to settle more than forty thousand black people on lands covered in Sherman's order.

The people faced numerous hardships — neglected soil, old equipment (and little of it), poor seed, and shortage of supplies. But the hardworking freedmen, especially those on the Sea Islands of Georgia and South Carolina, successfully grew crops of cotton and various foodstuffs. They received support not only from Saxton and the military but also from Northern white teachers and missionaries, a number of whom traveled into the area to found schools.

Most of the planning and hard work, however, came from the freedmen themselves. Many started out with little more than the clothes on their backs. One party was led by Ulysses Houston, a minister who had been present at the interview with Stanton. Before leaving for Skidaway Island, he wrote a Northern reporter: "We shall build our cabins, and organize our town government for the maintenance of order and the settlement of all difficulties." The reporter later gave this account:

> He and his fellow-colonists selected their lots, laid out a village, numbered their lots, put the numbers in a hat, and drew them out. It was Plymouth colony repeating itself. They agreed if any others came to join them, they should have equal privileges. So blooms the Mayflower on the South Atlantic coast.

The impressive success of this resettlement led many Northerners to urge that Congress enact a general land distribution policy to help all freedmen. Landless ex-slaves also came to expect that, since forty thousand Deep South blacks had quickly and effectively settled new lands, others too would receive their forty acres in the near future. Such hopes were soon dashed.

Andrew Johnson became president after Lincoln was assassinated in April 1865. Many had believed that Johnson would favor a generous land distribution policy once in the White House, since he had been sympathetic to black rights earlier as governor of Tennessee. But a proclamation which he issued in May 1865 completely shattered this belief. Johnson pardoned all former Confederates except those whose taxable property exceeded $20,000 and those who had held high military or civil positions. (Even these groups could apply for special presidential pardon.)

For the great majority of white Southerners, Johnson's proclamation not only restored civil and political rights. It also restored their property—except for slaves—even if previously confiscated as a result of temporary wartime orders such as Sherman's. Not only did the new president omit mentioning the freedmen in his proclamation. He clearly intended them to resume their second-class economic status in the South, although no longer as slaves. Johnson made it plain that he wanted land-owning blacks such as those under Saxton's jurisdiction to surrender their newly acquired lands and return to their previous owners.

Saxton now administered the freedmen's new settlements in Georgia, South Carolina, and Florida as assistant director of the Freedmen's Bureau. This agency had been recently established by Congress to coordinate federal relief assistance to ex-slaves. Heading the bureau was Sherman's former subordinate, General Oliver O. Howard. He shared President Johnson's wish to conciliate the South. Unlike the president, though, he did not want to be generous at the expense of the freedmen.

Both Saxton and Howard tried to resist and delay the restoration of black-occupied lands to their former white owners. They were supported by Stanton, who attempted various maneuvers to stave off the move. But Johnson was determined. Sherman's field order was revoked in June 1865. Saxton even traveled to Washington to protest, but without success.

In September the former landholders of Edisto Island, then under Freedmen's Bureau control, petitioned Johnson for the return of their lands. The president directed Howard to visit the island and convince the freedmen to arrange a "mutually satisfactory solution." The president left little doubt that he wanted the blacks to pack up and leave.

Howard unhappily went to Edisto in late October. Trapped between his duty and his sympathies, he met with freed blacks in a local church. They crowded in, furious at the course of events. They refused to quiet down until a woman began the spiritual "Nobody Knows the Trouble I Seen."

The blacks then listened to Howard as he urged them to surrender their farms and return to work for the island's former white landholders. Angry shouts of "no, no" punctuated Howard's talk. One man in the gallery cried out: "Why, General Howard, why do you take away our lands? You take them from us who have always been true, always true to the government! You give them to our all-time enemies! That is not right!"

Howard patiently explained to his audience that their "possessory titles" to the land were not "absolute" or "legal." At his insistence, a committee was formed consisting of three freedmen, three white planters, and three Freedmen's Bureau representatives. It had authority to decide on the island's land ownership. (This practice was also adopted elsewhere on the Sea Islands.)

Howard still hoped to delay restoration of the property until Congress convened late in 1865. But the process of removing blacks from their assigned lands gathered momentum after he left the area to return North.

Saxton was still refusing to dispossess black landholders from the territories under his supervision, so Johnson removed him in January 1866. He was replaced by Davis Tillson, a Freedmen's Bureau official more sympathetic to presidential policy. Tillson issued an order allowing white owners to return to their former Sea Island farms and plantations. Tillson went so far as to charter a boat and accompany the first group, explaining personally to the blacks in residence that they would have to surrender their lands.

Blacks who were willing to sign contracts to work for white owners were allowed to remain. Others were driven from the islands either by Union troops or by white vigilante groups that began to terrorize black landholders throughout the Deep South during this period. One sympathetic New England schoolteacher later wrote of seeing all the freedmen on one Sea Island plantation leaving their newly acquired land with their hoes over their shoulders. "They told us that the guard had ordered them to leave the plantation if they would not work for the owners. We could only tell them to obey orders. After this many of the Sherman Negroes left the island."

For the moment, Howard's policy of delaying restoration had clearly failed. Yet shortly after Congress met in December 1865, the legislators debated the provisions of a new, postwar Freedmen's Bureau Bill designed to protect the rights of ex-slaves in peacetime. The final version of that bill was enacted by Congress over the president's veto in July 1866. It allowed freedmen deprived of their land by Johnson's restoration policy to lease twenty acres of government-owned land on the Sea Islands with an option to buy cheaply within six years. By then, however, almost all of the "Sherman Negroes" had lost their lands.

Also, by this time, Congress and Johnson were struggling bitterly for control of postwar policy toward the South. The outcome of that struggle would determine the nation's response to its millions of newly liberated blacks. Many of them probably shared the anguish of one Sea Island freedman who grieved shortly after his eviction: "They will make freedom a curse to us, for we have no home, no land, no oath, no vote, and consequently no country."

24 Civil War and Reconstruction

On February 23, 1861 (at a time when Sherman had just left his post at the Louisiana military academy), Abraham Lincoln slipped secretly into Washington after an all-night train ride. His aides had planned the night trip, fearing an assassination attempt at a previously scheduled stop in pro-Confederate Baltimore. On his special train the president-elect tried to sleep. But a drunken passenger kept singing the bouncy Southern melody "Dixie" over and over. Lincoln finally muttered to a companion, "No doubt there will be a great time in Dixie by and by." His concern over the impending showdown with the secessionist South was shared by most Northerners.

A thousand miles to the south, the Confederacy's president-elect took a different type of journey to his own inaugural. Lincoln had arrived in the nation's capital, according to one diplomat, "like a thief in the night." Jefferson Davis had traveled from his Mississippi plantation to Montgomery, Alabama—first capital of the rebellious states—like a conquering hero.

Davis was a moderate Southerner who had opposed secession until after Lincoln's election. Now this group had taken charge of the South's new government, replacing many of the zealous fire-eaters who had spread the gospel of disunion during the 1850s. Southern moderates had selected Davis as their president largely because he had declared himself in favor of a peaceful settlement with the North. A West Point graduate, Davis had fought ably in the Mexican War, represented Mississippi in both the House and the Senate, and served as President Pierce's secretary of war.

FIRST STEPS

While Davis pondered his cabinet, the Montgomery convention that had chosen him president wrote a Confederate constitution. For the most part the document copied the provisions of the federal Constitution. It included a bill of rights, and it even prohibited the slave trade. Slavery, of course, was pronounced legal throughout the Confederacy. In a significant speech at Savannah, the vice-president-elect, Alexander Stephens of Georgia, spoke candidly of the new government: "Its foundations are laid, its cornerstone rests, upon the great truth that the Negro is not equal to the white man; that slavery, subordination to the superior race, is his natural and normal condition."

The new Confederate congress began its work by legalizing for the South all Union laws that did not conflict with its new constitution. For two months after Davis's selection as president, the Confederate government waited for some sign of how Lincoln intended to deal with the secession crisis. Then came Sumter—and war.

A "Brothers' War"

When the Civil War began on April 12, 1861, Americans gave it various names. For secessionists it was a "War for Southern Independence" or "the War Between the States." Northerners, on the other hand, considered it "the War of the Rebellion" or simply "the War for the Union." Both sides agreed that, whatever else, it was a "brothers' war," severing links among families, personal friends, and public figures according to their sectional loyalties.

450

Mississippi politician and Confederate President Jefferson Davis did not provide the kind of flexible leadership the South needed badly during the Civil War. (Brady Collection, U.S. Signal Corps, National Archives)

Lee was a vigorous fifty-five when the Civil War began. Like Washington, he fought against difficult odds and was much admired by his troops. (Valentine Museum, Richmond, Va.)

This deeply painful division reached even into Abraham Lincoln's family. A Kentucky officer named Ben Hardin Helm was the husband of Mary Todd Lincoln's sister. He spent several days at the White House talking to old West Point friends. Some of them were already preparing to head south and join the Confederate army. As Helm—still uncertain—concluded his visit, Lincoln gave him an envelope containing a major's commission in the Union army. The two men grasped hands warmly and exchanged good-byes. A few days later came the news that Helm had chosen the Confederacy.

But another Kentuckian, Fort Sumter's Robert Anderson, accepted Lincoln's promotion to brigadier general that same month. He then left for the front to help keep his native state in the Union.

A third officer, a fervent Unionist, turned down Lincoln's offer to be commander of all Northern troops. Instead, he accepted command of the Confederacy's eastern force, the Army of Northern Virginia. "If Virginia stands by the old Union, so will I," Robert E. Lee declared. "But if she secedes (though I do not believe in secession as a constitutional right, nor that there is sufficient cause for revolution) then I will follow my native state with my sword and, if need be, with my life."

When Virginia finally broke with the Union, Lee followed.

In many ways the Confederate struggle for independence resembled the American revolt against British rule two generations earlier. Some revolutions are a struggle for colonial independence from a ruling country. Such a revolution occurred in North America in the 1770s. Other revolutions result when one section of a country tries to break away from the whole, leading to an internal war between the nation and the breakaway section. This type of separatist revolt may occur when the people of a particular region feel that their interests and values are directly threatened by those who control the national government. Such was the case in the South after Lincoln's election.[1]

National uprisings, such as the American Revolution, and separatist revolts, such as the Civil War, usually take place only after great soulsearching among those rebelling. The American people do not shift their loyalties easily. Washington, Franklin, and other Revolutionary leaders had served the British Empire faithfully for decades in war and peace. Lee, Davis, and other key Confederate leaders had served the American government

---

[1] More recently, separatist revolts have taken place in Nigeria (where the Ibo province of Biafra revolted unsuccessfully) and in Pakistan (where the Bengali area formerly known as East Pakistan won its independence and became the new country of Bangladesh).

before the South seceded. They finally revolted because they believed the Southern way of life—a culture based upon slavery—was directly threatened by Republican control of the central government.

Mobilization

In the early months of the Civil War most Americans seemed to expect the conflict to be bloody but brief. Few realized what lay ahead. "No casualties yet, no real mourning, nobody hurt," wrote Mary Boykin Chesnut, the wife of a high Confederate officer, in June 1861. "It is all parade, fuss, and fine feathers."

A few leaders believed the situation was more serious. Among them were Lincoln and his generals and their counterparts behind the Southern lines. Mrs. Chesnut noted what Jefferson Davis had told her one evening: "Either way, he thinks it will be a long war, that before the end came we would have many a bitter experience. He said only fools doubted the courage of the Yankees, or their willingness to fight when they saw fit."

Nor did most Southerners underestimate the extent of Northern resources. In almost every respect—population, capital, and raw materials— the Union had the advantage over the Confederacy. Most important, the North could produce endless

RESOURCES OF THE UNION AND THE CONFEDERACY, 1861

	UNION	CONFEDERACY
Population	23,000,000	8,700,000*
Real and personal property	$11,000,000,000	$5,370,000,000
Banking capital	$330,000,000	$27,000,000
Capital investment	$850,000,000	$95,000,000
Manufacturing establishments	110,000	18,000
Value of production (annual)	$1,500,000,000	$155,000,000
Industrial workers	1,300,000	110,000
Railroad milage	22,000	9,000
		*Including 3,500,000 slaves

supplies of guns, ammunition, ships, and other war equipment. The South, on the other hand, had increasing difficulty in keeping its soldiers supplied.

Neither side began with much of an army. There were only eighteen thousand men in the regular army in 1860, with about eleven hundred officers. Only a small number of these had significant combat experience, and most of them resigned to join the Confederate army, so that the South's officer corps was initially better trained than the North's. These officers, Northern and Southern, prepared to fight a conflict far different, in strategy and tactics, from those for which they had been trained.

Both North and South started the war using a system of volunteer enlistments. At first they recruited men for only a few months, since most leaders on both sides believed that the war would be short.

On April 15, the day after the surrender of Sumter, Lincoln issued a proclamation calling up "the militia of the several States of the Union, to the . . . number of seventy-five thousand, in order to suppress [the rebellion] and to cause the laws to be duly executed." The initial news of Sumter's capture outraged Northerners of almost every political persuasion—Douglas Democrats, Constitutional Unionists, Whigs, and Republicans alike. Such unity would prove short-lived. But while it lasted, people as dissimilar as abolitionist ex-pacifists and formerly pro-Southern businessmen all hailed the president's call for troops. Patriotic meetings were held in towns and cities throughout the Union, demanding swift action against the rebellious states. Eager volunteers rushed to join military units in almost every Northern community.

"Before God it is the duty of every American citizen to rally around the flag of the country," shouted an ailing Stephen A. Douglas at a Chicago mass meeting. Douglas, still Lincoln's most influential Northern Democratic opponent, had gone to the White House immediately after Sumter's fall to pledge to Lincoln his complete support in restoring the Union.

As the fighting dragged on, however, it became apparent to both sides that volunteers would not provide enough manpower. Even the cash bounties offered to those who enlisted would not bring in enough volunteers. Casualties mounted in 1862. First the undermanned Confederacy and then the Union turned to drafting soldiers by lottery. Wealthy or influential young men, North and South, could, and often did, avoid going to war. They could provide a paid substitute, who might cost as much as $600. Or they could claim exemption on grounds that their civilian work was essential. (Slaveholders who grew cotton, for example, could avoid service this way.) By the end of the war, the South's troop shortage had become extreme. By then, the Confederacy had begun drafting and training thousands of slaves.

FIGHTING THE CIVIL WAR

Late in May 1861 the Confederate government moved its capital to Richmond. This was done partly because the large Virginia city could accommodate the growing Confederate bureaucracy more easily than Montgomery could. The move also dramatized the Confederacy's promise to defend the Upper South. Besides, Richmond was an important rail and road center. With Northern and Southern capitals and armies now only a hundred miles apart, the area of Virginia and Maryland became, for obvious reasons, the war's pivotal theater of operations.

A thick layer of gloom spread over Washington as Lincoln and his generals prepared for a Southern attack. There was talk that, for the second time in half a century, an American president might be forced to flee the White House, pursued by an invading army.

Southern Strategy

Although a number of important battles were fought during the war, the Confederates resorted to an overall guerrilla strategy that resembled Washington's in the American Revolution. A friend wrote Jefferson Davis complaining of the Confederacy's "purely defensive" strategy and of its reluctance to launch a full-scale attack on the North. Davis replied: "Without military stores, without the workshops to create them, without the power to import them, necessity, not choice, has compelled us to occupy strong positions and everywhere—selecting the time and place of attack—to confront the enemy without reserves." In other words, the South chose to conduct an "offensive defense." It tried to select the time and place for major battles carefully. At other times Southerners harassed Northern armies with cavalry raids led by such intrepid commanders as "Stonewall" Jackson, J. E. B. Stuart, Nathan B. Forrest, and John S. Mosby.

Confederate army commanders realized that it was impossible to prevent Union invasions of the South. They knew too that they had neither the manpower nor the resources to mount a full-scale invasion of the North. So the Confederates worked instead to maintain their armies in the field while fighting back the Union troops thrown against them. They hoped that a war-weary Northern public would finally force Lincoln's government to negotiate a peaceful settlement. Lee and Davis recognized, as Washington did during the 1770s, that a revolutionary army wins by not losing—that is, by displaying the capacity to endure.

Northern Strategy

Recognizing the Southern strategy, Lincoln and his generals committed Northern armies from the beginning to a policy of total war against the

THE CIVIL WAR IN THE EAST, 1861-1863

Union moves · Confederate moves · ★ Battle · 0 10 20 30 40 50 MILES

Fighting broke out on April 12, **1861,** when Confederate batteries opened fire on Fort Sumter in Charleston harbor. The Union quickly began a naval blockade of Confederate shipping. The first major engagement occurred on July 21 at Manassas Junction, Virginia. There an advancing Union army under Irvin McDowell was defeated in the first Battle of Bull Run and driven back to Washington, D.C.

The year **1862** witnessed the first naval battle between ironclads—the Union ship *Monitor* and the Confederate ship *Virginia* (formerly the *Merrimack*)—on March 9 near Norfolk, Virginia. The Union offensives of that year began in March with McClellan's Peninsula Campaign, an attempt to take Richmond from the southeast. He advanced slowly to within a few miles of the city. Confederate forces inflicted heavy casualties on his troops at the end of May. During the subsequent Seven

Days' Battle (June 26–July 2) Lee and Jackson forced McClellan to retreat and abandon the campaign. The Confederate army moved northward to win the second Battle of Bull Run (August 29–30). From there Lee and Jackson advanced into Maryland. Near Sharpsburg, McClellan engaged the Confederates in the Battle of Antietam (September 17). Although militarily the battle was a draw, Lee withdrew to Virginia. McClellan was replaced as Union commander by Burnside, whose overwhelming force was shattered at Fredericksburg (December 13).

In **1863** Hooker took command of the Union army, only to be defeated at Chancellorsville (May 2–4). However, Confederate losses there included "Stonewall" Jackson. Lee marched into Pennsylvania and was defeated at Gettysburg by a Union army under Meade (July 1–3). Lee retreated to Virginia, his second offensive a failure.

South. They were dedicated to the complete destruction of Confederate military power and civil authority by every necessary means. George Templeton Strong wrote in his diary in November 1861:

> Were I dictator at this time, my military policy would be (1) to defend and hold Washington, Western Virginia, Kentucky, Missouri; (2) to support Unionists in North Carolina and in eastern Tennessee; (3) to recover and hold (or destroy with sunken ships) every port and inlet from Hatteras to Galveston.

Strong's proposals resembled the North's actual strategy during the war, which was threefold: (1) to encircle the South in an ever-tightening military net by blockading its ports; (2) to divide the Confederacy in half by seizing control of the Mississippi and Tennessee rivers; (3) to capture Richmond and destroy the main Confederate armies in Virginia, where most Southern troops were concentrated. Strong believed, as did Lincoln and his

Many a Civil War battle exacted enormous tolls in men. Confederate dead lie in a shallow trench at Chancellorsville. Watching a dramatic panorama earlier in the war, Lee had remarked: "It is well that war is so terrible—we would grow too fond of it." (Library of Congress)

officers, that if "the rebels of the South can be locked up and left to suffer and starve," victory would follow.

Superior to the South in its navy, the North was able to impose a blockade of Southern harbors. The Confederates counteracted with fast blockade runners, joined by a number of private merchantmen. In the early years of the war they managed to slip past Union vessels in five out of every six attempts. But the Union blockade became increasingly effective. By 1865 it had choked off Southern cotton exports to Europe, as well as imports of arms and supplies.

In September 1862, President Lincoln visited with General McClellan and his officers at Antietam. (Brown Brothers)

War in the East

The outcome of the Civil War was decided not by naval encounters but by land battles. Northern armies began poorly but improved their performance every year. Confederate forces scored impressive victories at the first and second battles of Bull Run in July 1861 and August 1862. At Fredericksburg, Virginia, in December 1862, the North suffered a crushing defeat, with over twelve thousand casualties.

In May 1863, at Chancellorsville, Maryland, outnumbered Southerners won another victory, though it cost them one of their best generals, "Stonewall" Jackson. They imposed a stalemate on the Virginia front and, several times, threatened to capture Washington itself.

Lincoln searched desperately for Union commanders capable of breaking the stalemate and executing major offensive operations. In the process he appointed a succession of commanding generals—George McClellan, John Pope, McClellan again, Ambrose Burnside, Joseph Hooker, and George Meade. One time, after McClellan had failed to pursue a retreating Confederate force, he reportedly received this letter: "My dear McClellan: If you don't want to use the Army of the Potomac, I should like to borrow it for a while. Yours respectfully, A. Lincoln."

The turning point of the Civil War in the East came in July 1863. Confederate troops under Lee marched into southern Pennsylvania, where they encountered a Union force near Gettysburg. After three days of costly fighting, Lee's invasion was repulsed decisively on July 3.

Each side had over seventy-five thousand troops involved, and the South suffered almost twenty-five thousand casualties. "The results of

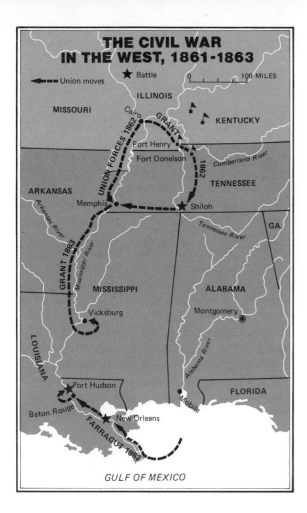

THE CIVIL WAR IN THE WEST, 1861-1863

← → Union moves   ★ Battle   0 ___ 100 MILES

ILLINOIS
MISSOURI
Cairo
GRANT
KENTUCKY
Fort Henry
Fort Donelson
Cumberland River
UNION FORCES 1862
1862
TENNESSEE
ARKANSAS
Arkansas River
Memphis
Shiloh
Tennessee River
GA.
GRANT 1863
Mississippi River
MISSISSIPPI
ALABAMA
Vicksburg
Montgomery
LOUISIANA
Alabama River
Port Hudson
FLORIDA
Baton Rouge
Mobile
FARRAGUT 1862
New Orleans
GULF OF MEXICO

Meanwhile, in the west, the Union won a series of important victories in **1862.** In February Grant captured Fort Henry on the Tennessee River and Fort Donelson on the Cumberland. Moving southward in Tennessee, he was attacked at Shiloh (April 6–7), but Union reinforcements forced the Confederates to withdraw into Mississippi. Union forces also made progress in their drive to gain control of the Mississippi River. Farragut bombarded and captured New Orleans in late April and proceeded up the river to Baton Rouge. To the north, a combined naval and land expedition defeated the Confederate fleet at Memphis on June 6 and captured the city.

In **1863** the Union continued its campaign to secure mastery of the Mississippi. Grant began attacking the Confederate stronghold of Vicksburg in May, and the city surrendered on July 4. With the fall of Port Hudson on July 9, the entire Mississippi was in Union hands and the Confederacy split in two.

this victory are priceless," rejoiced the normally pessimistic Strong. "Philadelphia, Baltimore, and Washington are safe. The rebels are hunted out of the North, their best army is routed, and the charm of Robert Lee's invincibility broken."

War in the West

The South's strategy of tying down and wearing out Union forces worked reasonably well in the East. Elsewhere, however, better-equipped and better-led Union troops won a series of important victories.

In February 1862 federal troops and a gunboat flotilla led by Ulysses S. Grant captured Fort Henry, on the Tennessee River, and Fort Donelson, on the Cumberland River. These moves forced Southern General Albert S. Johnston to abandon Kentucky and parts of Tennessee to the Union.

Admiral Farragut's capture of New Orleans in April 1862 and a series of Northern victories farther up the Mississippi—capped by defeat of the Confederate fleet at Memphis in June—brought most of the river under Union control. Arkansas, Louisiana, and Texas were thus isolated from the rest of the Confederacy.

In the West the decisive point was reached the day after Lee's defeat at Gettysburg. On July 4, 1863, Vicksburg fell. This key Confederate port surrendered after a six-week siege by Union troops. A final Confederate stronghold on the Mississippi—Port Hudson, Louisiana—fell later that same month.

Grant's remarkable success in this western campaign led to his appointment as Lincoln's seventh and last commanding general. Grant appealed to Lincoln for many of the same reasons he did to most Northerners. Wrote one admirer of Grant: "He talks like an earnest businessman, prompt, clearheaded, and decisive, and utters no bosh."

Final Campaigns

Grant took command of the Union forces in the spring of 1864. In May, he and Meade led a Northern force of 100,000 men against Lee's army, which had regrouped in Virginia after its Gettysburg defeat the previous year. It was in the same

This painting by William H. Overend depicts "An August Morning with Farragut: The Battle of Mobile Bay." (Courtesy, Wadsworth Atheneum, Hartford)

A wood engraving from the Illustrated London News *showing the enlistment of Irish and German immigrants on the Battery in New York City. (Museum of the City of New York)*

U. S. Grant cared less about the cut or condition of his uniform than he did about success in the field. Lincoln said of him: "I can't spare this man—he fights." (Brady Collection, U.S. Signal Corps, National Archives)

month that Union troops led by Sherman began their push to Atlanta.

For the remainder of the war Grant and Sherman pursued the same strategy of wearing down the enemy that Davis and Lee had hoped earlier would win for the Confederacy. No longer did Union forces concentrate on capturing Richmond or other Southern territory for its own sake. Instead, they struck directly at the remaining Confederate armies and resources—as Sherman did in Georgia. They aimed to inflict so heavy a price in casualties and physical devastation, that a war-weary South would be forced to surrender.

Beginning in June 1864, Grant's army tied down most of Lee's forces near Petersburg, Virginia. That fall Sherman led his famous march to the sea from Atlanta to Savannah. From Savannah, Sherman's forces turned north and extended their scorched-earth tactics into South Carolina and North Carolina.

Grant's troops, meanwhile, left their Petersburg trenches for frequent assaults on Lee's thinly manned lines. By early April 1865, Grant had blocked Lee's effort to retreat southward. Lee's army had by then been reduced by death and desertions from fifty-four thousand to thirty thousand men. Lee believed that further fighting was useless and that Confederate defeat was inevitable. He surrendered to Grant at Appomattox, Virginia, on April 9, 1865.

Despite pleas from Jefferson Davis for continued resistance, even if only by guerrilla bands in the Southern hills and forests, the rest of the Confederate armies still in the field surrendered by the end of May. Union troops finally occupied Richmond after Davis and other Confederate officials had fled. For all practical purposes Southern resistance had ended by the time Jefferson Davis was captured on May 10.

A Summing Up

The Civil War has been described as the "first modern war." A number of weapons and tactics associated with later military struggles were first used in its major campaigns. The basic weapon for the infantry, both Union and Confederate, was the single-shot, rifled musket, which had a range and accuracy two or three times greater than earlier, smoothbore guns. Troops could now engage in deadly fire from distances of a quarter to a half mile. Trench warfare, which later dominated much of World War I, came into being, and close-range or hand-to-hand combat was no longer inevitable.

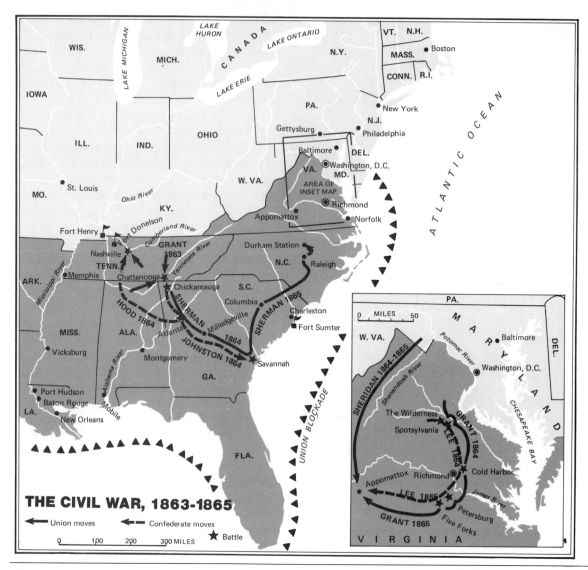

THE CIVIL WAR, 1863-1865

← Union moves   ←--- Confederate moves   ★ Battle

0   100   200   300 MILES

The major military actions of the fall of **1863** occurred in the west. On September 9 Union forces maneuvered the Confederates out of Chattanooga, Tennessee, without a battle. Moving south into Georgia, the Union army was stopped at Chickamauga (September 19–20) and driven back into Chattanooga. In October Grant was given command of all the Union's western armies. At the Battle of Chattanooga (November 23–25) he defeated the Confederates in engagements on Lookout Mountain and Missionary Ridge.

In **1864** Grant, now in supreme command of the Union armies, took charge of the Virginia front. He began a campaign to destroy Lee's army and take Richmond. Grant struck again and again; at the Battle of the Wilderness (May 5–6), at Spot-

sylvania (May 8–12), and at Cold Harbor (June 1–3). Lee parried Grant's blows, inflicting heavy casualties on his opponent. In this one-month period the Union army lost approximately sixty thousand men, a number equal to Lee's total strength at the beginning of the campaign. But the North could provide reinforcements of men and supplies; the South lacked reserves of both. Grant pressed on, moving south to Petersburg. He failed to capture it in a bloody four-day battle (June 15–18). However, his subsequent nine-month siege of the town cut Richmond off from the Deep South.

In the west, Union forces under Sherman moved out of Chattanooga in May 1864 to begin their invasion of Georgia. The opposing Confederate general, Joseph E. Johnston, fought a series of

This increased firepower of the infantry threatened both artillery and cavalry. A bank of cannon could no longer offer a solid defense; and the dash of a cavalry charge became mere vainglory when riders could easily be picked off, one by one, from a distance.

The American genius for creating new technology, shown earlier with such peaceful innovations as the cotton gin, was amply demonstrated during the Civil War, when Gatling guns (machine guns), repeating rifles, ironclad ships, and even submarines made their appearance (the latter were, for the most part, failures).

Railroads and telegraph lines revolutionized military communications, particularly for the Northern armies, who sent an estimated 6 million telegrams over fifteen thousand miles of wire set up by the Signal Corps. The most spectacular railroad supply system was that maintained for Sherman during the siege of Atlanta: sixteen hundred tons of supplies arrived daily in sixteen trains from Union depots northwest of the city. European military observers flocked to the United States to study the lessons the New World's "internal war" had to offer the Old World's future struggles.

The Civil War was a modern war in the important sense that it required a break with traditional military thinking in order to achieve victory. Initially most Civil War generals on both sides regarded cities and territories—not enemy armies—as their objectives. They hoped to win by

CIVIL WAR MANPOWER

	UNION	CONFEDERACY
Total serving in armed forces	1,556,678	1,082,119
Killed in battle or died from wounds	110,070	94,000
Died from illness	249,458	164,000
Wounded	275,175	100,000

maneuvering rather than by fighting. By contrast, Lincoln's overall strategy was to move on all fronts simultaneously in order to crush the enemy's forces and gain control of his resources. This warfare of annihilation was a plan that tradition-bound generals scorned. Only in Grant and Sherman did Lincoln find generals who would employ his strategy successfully. They were willing to break the rules to play, and win, a new and deadly game.

Casualties on both sides in the four years of "internal war" totaled almost 40 percent of the armies; several hundred thousand soldiers gave their lives to battle. The South lost its separatist revolt for lack of manpower and equipment. "They are too many for us," Mary Boykin Chesnut despaired two days before Lee's surrender. "Nine tenths of our army are under ground!" she anguished in her diary. "Where is another to come from? Will they wait until we grow one?" Time had run out for the Confederacy, and its will to endure had been crushed.

defensive actions but continued falling back toward Atlanta. John B. Hood, who replaced Johnston in July, suffered heavy losses in two pitched battles near Atlanta. It was occupied by Union forces on September 2. After the fall of Atlanta, Hood moved northwest to threaten Tennessee and the Union army's long lines of communication. Sherman sent part of his army to counter Hood's forces. He led the rest of his troops in a virtually unopposed march to the sea from Atlanta to Savannah, which fell on December 22. Meanwhile, Union forces shattered Hood's army at Nashville, Tennessee (December 15–16).

In **1865** Sherman continued his scorched-earth policy as he moved north from Savannah into North Carolina, where Johnston, restored to com-

mand, slowed his advance somewhat. In Virginia the Confederates, outnumbered more than two to one by Grant's reinforced army, were unable to lift the siege of Petersburg. On April 1, Lee's last attack (at Five Forks) was repulsed, and on April 2 he evacuated Petersburg and Richmond, moving westward. A Union army under Philip H. Sheridan, which had marched south through the Shenandoah Valley, blocked his path. Virtually surrounded by an overwhelming force, Lee surrendered to Grant at Appomattox on April 9. On April 18, Johnston surrendered to Sherman at Durham Station, North Carolina. Final Confederate capitulations occurred in Alabama (May 4) and Louisiana (May 26).

LIFE ON THE HOME FRONTS

In the long run it would have been far cheaper to purchase the abolition of slavery, although such a course was unthinkable to both sides in 1861. Estimates of the war's total cost ran as high as $3 billion for the South and $5 billion for the North. This was three to four times the total estimated value of every slave in the Confederacy. Both the Union and the Confederacy had great difficulty in paying their enormous bills for war equipment, soldiers' salaries, and operating expenses. Both sides resorted to such financial measures as raising taxes, issuing various types of bonds, and printing vast quantities of paper money unsupported by gold or silver reserves.

Crisis in the South

The overriding desire for victory led to sweeping changes in the South. Some affected the master–slave relationship. Southern slaveholders had defended their right to absolute control over their bondsmen in antebellum days. When war came, they watched helplessly as the Confederate government and Southern state governments transferred hundreds of thousands of slaves from private plantations to more urgent labor in the war effort. Slaves even became Confederate soldiers shortly before Appomattox. And throughout the war Southerners relaxed their close supervision of slave movements and activities.

Normal political life also came to a halt in the South during the war. There was no two-party system (as in the North). There was only one all-inclusive ruling, but unruly, "government party." Within the Confederacy there were people who opposed Davis's conduct of the war. They spoke their minds freely. Yet the demands of fighting a separatist revolt prevented any change in government.

The war not only changed master–slave relations and Southern politics, it also altered the Southern economy. The cherished doctrine of states' rights received rough treatment at the hands of Confederate leaders. These men were determined to assume every power they needed to wage war. Davis centralized and nationalized the economy to a remarkable degree. If occasion de-

manded, he interfered freely with the rights of capitalists. The Confederacy did more than seize slaves for war work. It closely regulated foreign commerce. It confiscated food and equipment for the army from private farms. It created government-run industries to produce military equipment. And it tightly controlled what was left of private enterprise.

The Confederacy even created a Cotton Bureau, which took over planters' cotton supplies. The Cotton Bureau paid a set price for the entire crop. By running the Northern blockade, the government acted as the sole Southern salesman in Europe. Government supplies of cotton were used as security for the Confederacy's foreign loans. But the blockade grew daily more effective, and Confederate revenues from European cotton sales – its one important source of revenue – dwindled correspondingly during the war's final years.

In spite of truly heroic effort and sacrifice, the South was destitute by the end of the war. "We have no money, even for taxes, or for their confiscation," wrote Mrs. Chesnut in April 1865. "Our poverty is made a matter of laughing." Millions came close to starving. Confederate officials recommended the nutritional values of such fare as squirrels and rats to make up for the dire shortage of food. At the time of its surrender, Lee's army had enough ammunition to provide each man seventy-five rounds – but no food.

Southern economic devastation by 1865 could be measured in many ways. Compared to 1860, there were 32 percent fewer horses, 30 percent fewer mules, 35 percent fewer cattle, and 42 percent fewer pigs. Cotton crops were destroyed or rotted unpicked in the fields. Few factories remained in operation. There was almost no trade. Only a handful of banks were left, and they were nearly empty.

Prosperity in the North

"We hear they have all grown rich," Mrs. Chesnut complained about Northerners in 1865. "Genuine Yankees can make a fortune trading jackknives!" Industrial growth in the North began before the Civil War, of course. But it was vastly accelerated by wartime demands to equip and sup-

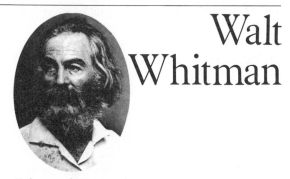

Walt Whitman

(Library of Congress)

The poet who was best able to bring together the vitality and idealism of his generation was Walt Whitman. He was born in 1819 in Huntington, Long Island, the son of a carpenter-farmer father with leanings toward Quaker thought, and a sympathetic and understanding mother with very little education. He grew up in a family of nine children of whom both the oldest and the youngest were mentally retarded. Walter, as he was known in the family, left school early in his eleventh year and started a process of self-education that included moving from job to job—as printer's devil, compositor, carpenter, schoolteacher, newspaper writer, and editor.

Whitman's ideas were generated by his childhood in the farming and fishing community on Long Island—his associations with the haymakers and eel fishers, the baymen and pilots —and by the stimulating life of New York, the city in which he worked. He roamed the streets, rode the ferries, and went regularly to the theater and the opera. Early in his life, books had become important to him. He read the Bible, Shakespeare, Ossian, the Greek tragic poets, the ancient Hindu poets, the Nibelungenlied, and the poems of Dante as well as Scott.

Politics were soon a consuming interest. The adult Whitman became an ardent Jacksonian and supporter of the Democratic party. Most of his newspaper jobs were with Democratic journals. The *Democratic Review* was one of the fine literary journals of the time and, through Whitman's work there, he met such literary figures as Hawthorne, Poe, Bryant, Longfellow, Thoreau, and others.

Whitman was especially imbued with the fire of Emerson's transcendentalist ideas. When *Leaves of Grass* appeared, Emerson wrote: "I am not blind to the worth of the wonderful gift of *Leaves of Grass.* I find it the most extraordinary piece of wit and wisdom that America has yet contributed. . . . I greet you at the beginning of a great career." But *Leaves of Grass*, in its first two printings in 1855 and 1856, was not a success. Some readers found it incomprehensible while others found the sexual implications shocking. With the mellowing of the author's language, finally in 1860–61, the volume began to sell.

The Civil War became a critical influence in Whitman's life. Several of his articles at this time dealt with Broadway Hospital where he spent time helping the wounded. Then, in December 1862, he visited his wounded brother, George, a Union soldier, and suddenly realized that he had himself become a part of the war effort. With a part-time job for support, he spent the next three years serving the wounded in hospitals around the city of Washington and sometimes on the battlefields.

In 1865 Whitman published *Drum Taps,* the poems he had written during the war. Some poems are martial outbursts, describing the mobilization of the army. Others are quieter, describing a field hospital or his own lonely vigils with the dying and the dead.

Drum Taps was being printed when the news of Lincoln's assassination reached Whitman. He was inspired to write the dirge that many critics consider his masterpiece. The poem stressed the triumph that peace and beauty achieve in death, for death brings a joining of man and nature. It begins:

When lilacs last in the door-yard bloom'd
And the great star early droop'd
  in the western sky in the night,
I mourn'd—and yet shall mourn
  with ever-returning spring.
O ever-returning spring!
  trinity sure to me you bring;
Lilac blooming perennial
  and drooping star in the west,
And thought of him I love.

ply the army. The number of Northern factories increased from fewer than 140,000 in 1860 to over 250,000 by 1870. Railroad mileage doubled during this decade. Growth in the North was aided not only by government contracts for arms and military supplies. It was helped also by wartime currency inflation, huge federal subsidies to railroads, and protective tariffs for industry.

The result was enormous inflation—high prices but also tremendous profits. There was rapid expansion in industries ranging from wool production to mining, from petroleum to iron manufacturing. Farmers prospered, too, because of the increased demand for every staple crop. Most merchants and shippers shared in the boom. Banking facilities were enlarged greatly after Congress passed several new banking acts. Senator John Sherman wrote his brother General William Sherman about the impact of the war on Northern capitalists: "They talk as confidently of millions as they formerly did of thousands." George Templeton Strong complained that the sedate prewar culture of New York City was being "diluted and swamped by a great flood-tide of material wealth."

A shortage of manpower on Northern farms and in factories stimulated immigration from Europe. In 1865 alone, 180,000 new immigrants arrived on Union soil. In 1866 and 1867 the number spurted to 300,000 yearly.

Perhaps most important in the North, as in the Confederacy, was the role played by the government in stimulating economic growth. Southern Democrats had dominated Congress and the executive branch until the 1850s. They had blocked such measures as the protective tariff, a national banking system, and railroad subsidies. Now the Republicans were in control. They favored industrialization and economic growth. To further their aims, they adopted the Morrill Tariff of 1861, which raised duties. They passed the National Banking Acts of 1863 and 1864, which aided national banks at the expense of state banks. In addition, Congress awarded land-grant subsidies to transcontinental railroads and stimulated Western settlement with the 1862 Homestead Act, which offered land to settlers for nominal sums.

The Republicans changed not only the economic habits of the North but its political life as

well. Lincoln found it no easier than Davis did to govern a country at war. Throughout the conflict the president was attacked from all sides of his wartime government coalition, which was known as the Union party. Abolitionist Republicans (known as Radical Republicans) denounced him for moving too slowly on the question of emancipation, while War Democrats denounced him for moving at all on the problem. Moderate Republicans criticized the lack of military progress by the Northern armies.

Compared to the Confederacy, the North had a poor wartime record in the field of civil rights. In spite of Union victories, many Northerners opposed the war. Lincoln authorized a number of arbitrary military arrests of such civilians, especially Peace Democrats—called "Copperheads" by their enemies. He suspended the privilege of habeas corpus[2] to keep pro-Confederate Northerners in jail once arrested.

In both sections, North and South, the war interfered with civil liberties, but in different ways. Northerners were more likely to be thrown in jail for opposing the war. Southerners were more likely to be punished for resisting government confiscation of their property. These interferences involved of course the civil rights of *white* people. Neither government troubled itself much about the rights of blacks, free or slave.

FREEDOM FOR BLACK PEOPLE

As soon as war broke out, Northern black men tried to enlist in the Union army. They were not allowed to do so, however, until the fall of 1862. Eventually, over 186,000 blacks served as Union soldiers—almost 15 percent of all Northern troops. They were usually led by white officers and they were paid less than white troops. Union commanders were divided in their attitudes toward

---

[2] This privilege, guaranteed by the Constitution, provides that an arrested person can demand that legal authorities show why he or she has been imprisoned. A writ of habeas corpus (Latin words meaning "you have the body") thus protects a person against being held in jail without cause.

using black soldiers. Some welcomed them. Others, like Sherman, did not.

The Emancipation Proclamation

Northern policy toward slavery changed during the war. Many Republicans in the government believed sincerely in emancipation. Lincoln, though, had always regarded it as secondary compared to the overriding importance of winning the war and reuniting the nation.

Like most Americans at the time, Lincoln believed that blacks were inferior. He never felt certain that 4 million ex-slaves could reach full equality with whites in the United States. Throughout the Civil War he tried unsuccessfully to link his moves toward emancipation with efforts to colonize freed blacks. None of these efforts worked out.

Lincoln had been elected on a platform that pledged to restrict slavery but not abolish it. He moved cautiously toward emancipation, mainly because of his military and political problems in conducting the war. Radical Republicans in Congress kept pressuring him for swift abolition. Even many moderate Northerners became fervent converts to emancipation as war casualties mounted, if only to punish the Confederacy. Such Unionists did not change their attitudes toward *black people* (and their supposed inferiority). They only changed their minds about *slavery.*

The situation was complicated by the fact that thousands of runaway slaves took refuge with the Union army. There, they were often treated — as with Sherman's army — as both a help and a hindrance. Thousands of blacks, however, did join Union army ranks. Lincoln, along with most Northerners, grew more sympathetic to emancipation.

Congress took the first step by abolishing slavery in the federal territories in June 1862. Then, in September 1862, Lincoln issued a preliminary proclamation. In it he stated that he would issue a final document on January 1, 1863, freeing the slaves in all states then in rebellion. This final document was the Emancipation Proclamation.

The Emancipation Proclamation actually freed very few people when it was issued. It did not apply to slaves in the border states fighting on the Union side. Nor did it affect slaves in Southern areas already under Union control. Naturally, the states in rebellion did not act on Lincoln's order. But the proclamation did show Americans, and the rest of the world, that the Civil War was now being fought to end slavery.

For all practical purposes the 3½ million black slaves in the South found themselves free within days after Lee's surrender. It was only with final ratification of the Thirteenth Amendment, however, in December 1865, that slavery was ended completely and legally throughout the United States.

Treatment in the North

Though the Union eventually fought to free black people, those who lived in the region faced many difficulties. In 1860 free Northern blacks numbered 225,000. Most of them were restricted to menial jobs. A rigid pattern of segregation in schools, hospitals, transportation, and other public facilities kept blacks and whites separated. Roughly 93 percent of Northern black people lived in states where they could not vote. (Only five New England states allowed blacks to cast ballots in 1865.)

Blacks were the victims of race riots throughout the North during the war. The most destructive took place in New York City in the summer of 1863. There, anger among the city's Irish working class at a new federal draft law exploded into violence during four days and nights of rioting. The new law allowed wealthy citizens to avoid the draft by buying the services of substitute soldiers — something poor laborers clearly could not afford.

Mobs of Irish workers rampaged over Manhattan Island from July 13 to July 16. They burned, looted, and killed. The rioters' main targets were free blacks and, to a lesser extent, white abolitionists and wealthy citizens. The city's outnumbered police force, also composed largely of Irishmen, fought the rioters with great bravery and discipline, finally putting down the rioting with the help of federal troops. By that time, some twelve hundred persons, mostly black, had been killed.

Confederate soldiers, after surrendering and disbanding, begin the journey home. (Culver Pictures)

Many thousands were injured. Property worth millions was damaged or destroyed. Other Northern cities, especially in the Middle West, experienced similar draft riots. Antagonism toward black people ran high throughout the North during the war years.

After the War

The Thirteenth Amendment did not settle the basic questions about the future status of black Americans, especially in the postwar South. Former slaves were now free. But free to *do* what? Free to *be* what? What did freedom mean to someone raised in slavery?

Many ex-slaves simply stayed on their plantations, working for the same masters. Their old habits altered little at first, although now the whites were often as poor as their former bondsmen. "The Negroes seem unchanged," Mrs. Chesnut wrote, referring to her one-time slaves. Other former slaves left their old homes, usually for an uncertain future.

Whatever the fate of individual freed slaves, one characteristic of Southern emancipation was its peaceful nature. Despite the fears of antebellum white Southerners, there were no bloodbaths or vengeful attacks by ex-slaves on their former masters. Black people responded to their new freedom with dignity and grace.

Early in the twentieth century Benjamin Botkin and other folklorists traveled through the United States, recording the recollections of aged ex-slaves. One elderly man recalled:

> The end of the war, it come just like that—like you snap your fingers. Soldiers, all of a sudden, was everywhere—coming in bunches. Everyone was a-singing. We was all walking on golden clouds. Hallelujah! Everybody went wild! we was free. Just like that, we was free. It didn't seem to make the whites mad, either. They went right on giving us food just the same. Nobody took our homes away, but right off colored folks started on the move. They seemed to want to get closer to freedom, so they'd know what it was—like it was a place or a city.

The experience was exciting yet frightening for blacks, people like those who had joined Sherman's army on its march to Savannah. Many of them had never gone beyond the borders of their own farms. One ex-slave commented to Botkin:

> We knowed freedom was on us, but we didn't know what was to come with it. We thought we was going to be richer than the white folks, 'cause we was stronger and knowed how to work, and the whites didn't, and they didn't have us to work for them any more. But it didn't turn out that way. We soon found out that freedom could make folks proud, but it didn't make 'em rich.

As soon as the war was over, blacks began to organize and work for their own advancement. Historians sometimes overlook the fact that, even in 1860, there were 261,000 free blacks in the South. Tens of thousands of them were literate. These men and women—like the leaders who met with Stanton and Sherman—formed an important black leadership base at the end of the war. Many took part in black conventions held in a number of Southern cities in 1865 and 1866. They petitioned the federal government to assist freedom by granting them the franchise, protecting their civil rights, and providing land and economic aid.

THE FIRST YEAR OF RECONSTRUCTION

The basic dilemma of Reconstruction for all those who lived through it, black and white, Southerner and Northerner alike, was its revolutionary nature. Like the Civil War itself, the postwar period had no examples on which to model itself, no constitutional provisions by which policy makers might be guided.

Compared with reconstruction periods that have followed more recent civil wars in Russia, Spain, and China, the American experience was notably mild. Confederate leaders were neither shot nor driven into exile. Indeed, many resumed their careers in American politics. Only a few, such as Jefferson Davis, were imprisoned, and these mainly for a brief period. No Confederate property was confiscated. Nor was any redistribution of wealth forced on the defeated South by the victorious North.

Lincoln's Approach

In Lincoln's second inaugural address, delivered a month before his death, he called for a generous settlement with the defeated South: "With malice toward none, with charity for all . . . let us strive on to finish the work we are in, to bind up the nation's wounds."

As early as 1862 Lincoln had indicated his desire to restore a defeated Confederacy quickly and without revenge against either its leaders or its people. Lincoln suggested a basis for Reconstruction in December 1863. He called for amnesty[3] (except in the case of key leaders) for Southerners who pledged loyalty to the Union. Southern states in which 10 percent of the 1860 electorate took such a loyalty oath and accepted emancipation would be restored immediately to the Union.

Governments in Arkansas, Louisiana, and Tennessee met Lincoln's provisions in 1864. But Congress refused to seat their representatives. The problem was complicated by the fact that Lincoln believed that the executive branch should control

---

[3] Amnesty is a form of pardon for offenses against the government—especially to a group of persons.

Reconstruction, whereas Congress wanted this power for itself. Congressional attitudes were partly a reaction to the vast expansion of presidential authority under Lincoln during the Civil War.

Republicans in Congress were led by Radicals Thaddeus Stevens of Pennsylvania in the House and Charles Sumner of Massachusetts in the Senate. They were afraid that the Democratic party, led by Southern ex-Confederates, would quickly return to national power. So they offered a much tougher Reconstruction plan in a measure known as the Wade-Davis Bill. It provided that a majority of voters in each Southern state take an "ironclad oath" swearing to their *past* as well as to their *future* loyalty. Obviously, if the electorate were composed only of whites, no ex-Confederate state could honestly meet this provision. The bill also required that the Southern states abolish slavery in their constitutions, repudiate the Confederate war debt, and disfranchise Confederate leaders. Congress passed the Wade-Davis Bill on July 4, 1864. Lincoln killed the measure with a pocket veto. Then Congress passed the nonbinding Wade-Davis Manifesto, reasserting the provisions of the earlier bill.

Therefore, by mid-1864, the stage was set for a postwar confrontation between the president and Congress on Reconstruction policy. Was the South to be restored quickly, its new state governments falling into the hands of ex-Confederate whites with a minimum of federal interference? (This is what Lincoln wanted, though he did urge Southern whites to allow at least educated blacks to vote.) Or should the Southern states undergo fundamental political changes before they could rejoin the Union? Should they allow blacks to vote and hold office, while disbarring ex-Confederate leaders and perhaps confiscating their land?

Assassination

With the war almost over, Lincoln's thoughts had turned increasingly to the problem of reconstructing the South. After a trip to Richmond early in April 1865, he spent several days working out various programs.

On the night of April 14, Good Friday evening, President and Mrs. Lincoln went to Ford's Theater in Washington to see a popular play, *Our American Cousin.* Shortly after 10 P.M. a half-crazed Southern sympathizer named John Wilkes Booth shot Lincoln as he watched the play. Booth then stabbed another member of the president's party, leaped onto the stage, rushed from the theater, and rode away. (He was shot down on April 26 by Union troops that had pursued him into Virginia.)

The wounded Lincoln was taken from Ford's Theater to a nearby house. There, family, friends, and government officials kept an all-night vigil. The president remained unconscious until his death at 7:22 the following morning. "Now he belongs to the ages," said Secretary of War Stanton, one of those at his bedside.

Word of Lincoln's assassination spread quickly via the telegraph. The first reaction to the event, shared by most Northerners and even many Southerners, was one of profound shock: "I am stunned," wrote George Templeton Strong, "as by a fearful personal calamity."

For Lincoln was highly popular in the North at the time of his death, a result of Union military victories beginning in 1863 and culminating in Lee's surrender. During the war itself, Southerners—as one might expect—had little affection for "Uncle Abraham." Many Northerners felt the same way, especially in the early years. One such person was Strong, an aristocrat and avowed snob. He never liked Lincoln's often-crude manner of speech and fondness for telling jokes. Yet these very qualities endeared the president to most other Americans. And even Strong, like other Unionists, responded to Lincoln's firm leadership and genuine anguish at the war's increasing toll in human suffering: "It must be referred to the Attorney General," Lincoln once told Strong about a request to pardon a criminal. "But I guess it will be all right, for me, and the Attorney General's very chicken-hearted."

By the war's end, most Northerners probably agreed with Strong's high estimate of Lincoln's wartime achievement. The president's "weaknesses are on the surface," Strong wrote on April 11, 1865. "His name will be of high account fifty years hence, and for many generations thereafter."

Johnson was an honest but tactless man forced to cope with uniquely difficult circumstances. He had to follow Abraham Lincoln in the presidency, and he had to confront the problems of postwar reconstruction. He failed. Jefferson Davis said he had "the pride of having no pride." (Library of Congress)

Johnson's Plan

Lincoln's death placed the burden of reconstructing the South on the shoulders of his former vice-president, Andrew Johnson. Johnson was a War Democrat from Tennessee and a one-time Radical on the Reconstruction issue. Once in the White House, however, he soon adopted Lincoln's basic proposals. Unfortunately, Johnson completely lacked Lincoln's basic sympathy for the problems of freed blacks. Also, he was a dogmatic man. He showed almost none of Lincoln's tact in dealing with political opponents.

Johnson, like Lincoln, believed that Reconstruction was a matter to be handled by the pres-

ident. His position was strengthened by the fact that Congress was not in session for several months after he took office. Johnson readmitted the states of Arkansas, Louisiana, and Tennessee. In May 1865 he issued his own Reconstruction plan. It provided that whites in each Southern state who pledged their future loyalty to the Union could elect delegates to a state convention. This convention had to revoke the ordinance of secession, abolish slavery, and repudiate the Confederate war debt. Then the state would be restored to the Union. Johnson granted amnesty to almost all Confederates who took the oath of allegiance. The exceptions were wealthy people and high officials. Even they could apply for a presidential pardon. By late 1865 all the Southern states except Texas had complied with these provisions. (Texas did so early in 1866.)

Southern Regulation of Blacks

Congress believed that the government had a duty to assist freedmen after the war. So in March 1865 it created the Freedmen's Bureau, a temporary federal assistance agency headed by Oliver O. Howard. The bureau distributed food and medicine to poor blacks (and whites), opened schools, supervised land distribution to freedmen, and tried to defend the civil rights of Southern blacks. (It exercised these functions in helping "Sherman's Negroes" in the resettlement program.)

The Freedmen's Bureau, however, could not protect the physical security of black Southerners without the help of Union troops. This problem was urgent. Brutal riots against blacks occurred in Memphis and New Orleans in 1866, and scattered acts of anti-Negro violence occurred throughout the South.

Yet after Appomattox, Union troops were mustered out of the army at a rapid rate. By the end of 1865 only 150,000 soldiers remained of the million serving six months earlier. Many of these were stationed on isolated Western posts fighting Indians.

Under these conditions it was impossible for Union troops to offer the 4 million Southern blacks, most of them recently freed, any real protection. Most white Southerners had been raised to

Stern, intense, and militant, Thaddeus Stevens called for strict measures to punish the Southern rebels. (Library of Congress)

Charles Sumner, once admonished during an argument, "But you forget the other side," thundered in reply: "There is no other side!" (Library of Congress)

believe that blacks had no civil rights that whites were bound to respect. Killings, beatings, burnings, and other forms of physical terror directed against blacks—mostly to keep them out of politics—began soon after the war's end. Violence against blacks was often carried out by white secret societies. Several were formed after the war, primarily to keep blacks from voting. The most famous, the Ku Klux Klan, was founded in 1866. The turmoil increased during the 1870s.

Many whites in the South adopted other means to reduce black people to a state of virtual enslavement. In every Southern state new govern-

ments were elected by voters according to the provisions of Johnson's Reconstruction plan. But the Johnson state governments, as they were called, allowed no blacks to vote. They adopted so-called Black Codes to regulate the actions and behavior of freedmen. Southern whites claimed that such codes were necessary because of the threat of social disorder as a result of emancipation. There had been no major instance, however, of blacks rioting against whites anywhere in the region.

The Black Codes had some provisions to protect blacks. They legalized marriages between blacks, for instance. They also gave blacks the right to sue and testify in court. But the codes consisted mainly of restrictions. They supervised the movements of blacks, prevented them from carrying weapons, and forbade intermarriage between blacks and whites. Contracts, sometimes for life, forced black people to remain at their jobs. In some states, blacks could not own land or work at any job other than farming without a special license. Black children were forced into certain job apprenticeships.

Reaction in the North

Northern Republicans, both Radicals and moderates, attacked the Johnson state governments. They denounced the Black Codes and called for their immediate repeal. Most Radicals believed that the defeated Southern states should be treated, in Thaddeus Stevens's phrase, like "conquered provinces," until more repentant leaders emerged.

When Congress reconvened in December 1865, representatives and senators elected under the Johnson state governments applied for admission. Republicans in Congress refused to admit them. These Southerners who now claimed loyalty to the Union included fifty-eight former Confederate congressmen, six of Jefferson Davis's cabinet members, and four Southern generals. Most amazing of all was the presence of Alexander Stephens of Georgia, who eight months earlier had been vice-president of the Confederacy!

The 1866 riots in Memphis and New Orleans gave Northerners additional evidence that the white South remained unrepentant. Thus it seemed inevitable that there would be a power struggle between Johnson and congressional Republicans over who would control the Reconstruction process. Who was sovereign in the federal government, the president or Congress? Who could decide?

RADICAL RECONSTRUCTION

Congress answered these questions to its own satisfaction by taking the initiative completely out of Johnson's hands. By 1867 the legislature had won control. It dominated the government for the next ten years.

The Republicans who controlled Congress developed their strategy mainly through the Joint Committee on Reconstruction, which was dominated by the Radicals. This group asserted that Southern states could be readmitted only after meeting congressional requirements. The Joint Committee moved a series of measures through Congress between 1865 and 1867. Most of the bills were vetoed by the hapless Johnson, then repassed by a two-thirds majority.

First, in February 1866, came the new Freedmen's Bureau bill. It expanded the bureau's authority to protect Southern blacks, giving it the right to try in military courts persons accused of violating the civil rights of freedmen.

A Civil Rights Act of April 1866 granted to blacks the same civil rights as those enjoyed by whites. The measure also asserted the right of the federal government to interfere in state affairs to protect a citizen's civil rights.

In order to fortify their position, congressional Republicans in June 1866 adopted and sent to the states the Fourteenth Amendment. In effect, it gave blacks full citizenship. If a state denied the vote to blacks, its representation in the House would be reduced. The amendment also forbade ex-Confederate officials from holding federal or state office again without receiving congressional pardon. The Joint Committee declared that any Southern state wishing readmission would have to ratify the Fourteenth Amendment. The Johnson state governments in the South voted against ratification. (The amendment was eventually ratified in 1868.)

President Johnson hoped his Republican opponents would be defeated in the 1866 congressional election, and he campaigned personally against them. After a wild and bitterly fought campaign, however, anti-Johnson Republicans swept the election. They carried every Union state but three.

A Strong Program

When Congress met after the election, Republicans enacted their program into law. They

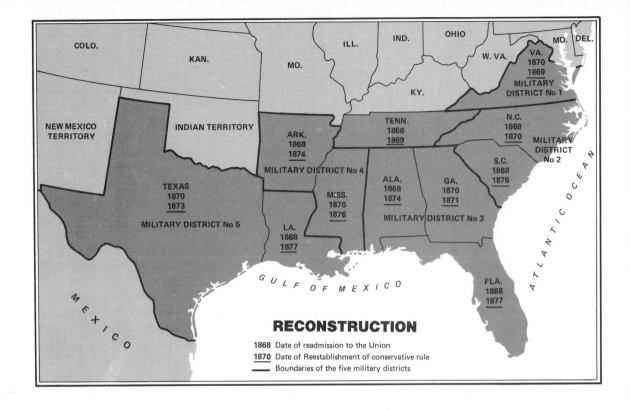

RECONSTRUCTION

1868   Date of readmission to the Union
1870   Date of Reestablishment of conservative rule
——   Boundaries of the five military districts

began with the First Reconstruction Act of March 1867. Significantly, the bill's final form came from a moderate, Republican John Sherman. By this time the moderates agreed with Radicals on most key issues of Reconstruction. This law abolished the existing Johnson state governments. It provided for universal male suffrage—that is, for black as well as white voting.

    The First Reconstruction Act also authorized temporary military rule of the South. Ten former Confederate states were still outside the Union. (Tennessee had ratified the Fourteenth Amendment and had been readmitted.) These states were divided into five military districts. To rejoin the Union, a state had to call a constitutional convention elected by universal male suffrage. This body, in turn, had to create a new state government that would ratify the Fourteenth Amendment and guarantee black suffrage. Three subsequent congressional acts strengthened the powers of federal army commanders in the South.

The final act in the congressional drama of Radical Reconstruction involved the effort in 1868 to remove the president through impeachment. Congress had good reason to believe that Johnson would do everything in his power to sabotage the Reconstruction acts. From 1865 to 1868, he had worked to impede every major step Congress had taken to assist Southern blacks or to enforce a harsh settlement upon the white South. In the process, Johnson had systematically interfered with congressional statutes, practically crippling effective operation (for one thing) of the Freedmen's Bureau throughout the South (as in his interference with Sherman's land program) by presidential directives.

    Johnson, moreover, had appointed as federal officials in the region (including even provisional governors) ex-Confederates who had not yet even taken the oath of allegiance to the Union. He used his presidential appointment powers ruthlessly to subvert congressional aims on Reconstruction, claiming for himself absolute direction of the process even after Congress had rejected his early effort to form state governments without first obtaining its approval. Johnson's view of presidential authority was a broad, almost modern one (as Lincoln's had been—but during the wartime emergency). But at all times, Johnson lacked his predecessor's tact in dealing with those who disagreed with him—especially in Congress—tact that might have made his view of presidential power more palatable to his political enemies.

Johnson's recurrent efforts to undermine the program of congressional Reconstruction through issuing conflicting orders to federal officials (both military and civil) in the South provoked Republican moderates and radicals to combine in self-defense. An unprecedented special session was called which passed two measures on March 2, 1867.

One of the measures virtually deprived Johnson of command of the American army by requiring him to issue all military orders through the general of the army, Ulysses S. Grant. The second was the Tenure of Office Act. It prohibited the president from removing those officials whose appointments had been made with Senate consent, without again securing Senate approval. This law meant that Johnson could not, for example, arbitrarily fire Secretary of War Stanton. This leading Radical was the man who—along with Saxton and Howard—had tried to block presidential interference with Sherman's land distribution policy. Johnson disregarded the measure and dismissed Stanton. Then the House passed a resolution impeaching Johnson on eleven charges, including alleged violations of the two March 2 bills.

After a Senate trial, the president was acquitted, although even some of his supporters acknowledged that they were less concerned with retaining Johnson—considering him an inept and insensitive chief executive—than they were with upholding the office of the presidency. If Johnson were successfully removed by impeachment, they felt, the process would rupture violently the normal relations between the three coordinate branches of national government. Both sides in the struggle argued from reasonable positions, and the entire impeachment process indicated the under-

lying strength of the constitutional mechanisms, even when tested in the midst of dire political crisis.

A two-thirds majority is needed to convict the president on an impeachment charge. Thirty-five senators voted for his conviction, while nineteen (including seven Republicans) voted for acquittal. Thus Johnson was saved by a one-vote margin.

After his acquittal, Johnson grudgingly complied with the tacit promises made by his supporters to obtain the votes of borderline senators. No longer did he interfere actively—for the brief remainder of his presidency—with enforcement of duly passed congressional statutes on Southern Reconstruction or with those officials charged with enforcing these laws. For the moment, Congress controlled the Reconstruction process.

The effort to unseat Johnson was the most daring episode in the Radicals' Reconstruction plans. A few Radicals such as Stevens tried to push through bills confiscating 394 million acres of land owned by the seventy thousand chief leaders of the Confederacy. (Charles Sumner called the antebellum plantations "nurseries of the Rebellion.") But such measures found little support among the party's moderate majority, and therefore they did not pass.

Most aims of the Radicals were fairly limited. They worked chiefly for Republican political control of the national government. They also hoped that coalitions of black voters and friendly whites would dominate Southern politics, thereby preventing national revival of the Democratic party.

But Republicans did not have any direct social or economic goals. Only a small number of Radicals were committed to complete equality for black Americans. There was no large-scale program to provide landless freedmen with an economic base. Many blacks had been promised "forty acres and a mule." But the thousands resettled on abandoned lands—such as "Sherman's Negroes" of the Deep South—were soon dispossessed.

After the attempt to impeach Johnson, Radicals left the problems of Reconstruction in the hands of federal commanders and new state governments in the South. The quarrel between legis-

Southern black men vote in large numbers for the first time. (The Bettmann Archive)

lative and executive branches over Southern policy ended in 1868, when Republican Ulysses S. Grant was elected president. By then the central drama of Reconstruction had shifted from Washington to the South itself.

The New Radical Governments

Beginning in 1867, so-called Radical state governments were set up according to congressional regulations. New black voters made up a majority of the Radical electorate in five states—Alabama, Florida, Louisiana, Mississippi, and South Carolina. Elsewhere in the South, white Radical majorities were supported by black voters. By 1870 more than 700,000 blacks and 627,000 whites were registered as voters under the Radical state constitutions.[4]

Congress readmitted Louisiana and six other states to the Union under Radical rule in June 1868. By the end of 1870 all ten ex-Confederate states had been readmitted to the Union.

Throughout the South blacks filled public offices for the first time. These were not, however, usually the highest offices. Nor did blacks hold office in proportion to their percentage of voters. Only one state legislature, that of South Carolina, ever had a black majority. No black ever became a Reconstruction Southern governor. (Some states, though, had black lieutenant governors.) There were two black United States senators and fifteen congressmen during the entire period of Radical rule.

Many black political leaders were educated men. Some were among the most distinguished figures in the entire South. Francis L. Cardozo, for example, South Carolina's state treasurer, held degrees from the universities of London and Glasgow, making him perhaps the best-educated politician in the South of either race.

Who were the Radicals in the South? They included many different groups. Some were South-

erners, most of whom had been prewar Whigs or secret Union sympathizers during the war. Many Southern businessmen and even a few planters joined the Radicals. They hoped that the new governments would have enough help from Northern capitalists and Republican politicians to rebuild the South's shattered economy. Radicals also included nonslaveholding farmers, who, while they disliked blacks, hated ex-Confederates even more for having led them into what they considered (at least after its loss) "a rich man's war and a poor man's fight." These Southern-born Radicals were called scalawags (an often undeserved term) by former Confederates.

Other Radicals were Northerners. Tens of thousands of them went south after the war for a variety of reasons. Hostile whites referred to them bitterly as carpetbaggers, whose only aim was to fill their luggage with ill-gotten Southern wealth. Yet many were teachers—their carpetbags stuffed only with McGuffey's Readers. Like the people who went to the Sea Islands, their aim was to set up schools for the freedmen. Northern soldiers returned to the South seeking good land; five thousand went to Louisiana alone. Businessmen sought opportunities to invest capital and to profit from the region's economic reconstruction. A number of politically ambitious people did arrive to take part in the Radical governments. But they were by no means all opportunists.

Charges of Corruption

It has often been said that Radical state governments were corrupt. There is some truth to this charge. Legislators in South Carolina, for example, paid $200,000 for $18,000 worth of furniture for the state capitol. Louisiana's Radical governor, H. C. Warmouth, left the state with a personal fortune of half a million dollars, most of it acquired illegally. Similar fortunes were made throughout the South.

Several points should be noted, however, about corruption in the Radical governments. At this time scandals tainted the Grant administration and many Northern state and local governments. The historian John Hope Franklin has termed public dishonesty after the Civil War "bi-

---

[4] The Fifteenth Amendment, adopted in 1870, forbade any state from preventing citizens from voting because of race, color, or "previous condition of servitude." This was a clear effort to eliminate the hypocrisy of some Northern states that demanded suffrage for blacks in the South while continuing to deny it at home.

Louisiana was one of five Southern states to have a majority of black voters. Between 1868 and 1896 the state had 133 black legislators—38 senators and 95 representatives. They were never numerous or strong enough to control political life in Louisiana, though Oscar Dunn (center) did lead a struggle against corruption and extravagance. (Louisiana State Museum)

A black family, most likely sharecroppers, stands in front of their cabin and storehouse. (Brown Brothers)

sectional, bipartisan, and biracial." (Actually, the *blacks* in Congress were not implicated in the Grant scandals, although many of their *white* colleagues were.) State governments everywhere ran up enormous debts. Postwar fortunes in the South were made by Radicals and ex-Confederates, Republicans and Democrats, alike. Given the level of immorality in American politics, North and South, during Reconstruction, it seems fair to say that the Radicals were no more corrupt than other politicians at the time.

In fact, most Radical state funds were spent rebuilding a ruined economy. Somehow, the Radicals managed to begin reconstructing Southern highways, railroads, hospitals, and orphanages.

They also began building schools; many Southern states had had no public school system before the war. The rebuilding had to be done for an additional 3½ million people. These were the ex-slaves, who were now citizens and entitled to the use of public facilities.

An Evaluation

Historians have long debated whether Radical state governments in the South ruled poorly or well. Opinions on this question depend in part on attitudes about whether (or when) blacks should have been allowed the franchise and a role in governing. We tend to forget how short a time Radical governments actually ruled. Tennessee never underwent this type of control. Virginia, North Carolina, and Georgia had returned to conservative hands by 1871. Arkansas, Alabama, and Texas had done so by 1874. And it was all over by 1877.

Some provisions of the Radical state constitutions found approval even among ex-Confederates. The documents ended imprisonment for debt, for example, and did away with property qualifications for voting. Basically, ex-Confederate whites objected less to the corruption of Radical state governments than to their very existence—especially to the presence of blacks on the political slate. Radical rule did not end because of its failure to meet the economic and social problems of the South. Radicals were driven from power because of their insistence on meeting these problems through biracial political cooperation.

THE END OF RADICAL RULE

Two trends put an end to Radical Reconstruction. One was the increasing hostility of white Southerners. The other was the growing indifference of its Northern Republican sponsors.

Southern hostility not only increased. It grew more violent. Thousands of blacks and white Radicals lost their lives to armed bands of whites such as the Ku Klux Klan and local "rifle clubs" that roamed the South during the 1870s. Federal troops and black state militia could suppress only a small number of these groups. Congress passed several Force Bills, making it a national offense to interfere with any citizen's civil rights (including his right to vote). But they had little effect, since only a few thousand federal troops remained in the South to enforce the laws against guerrilla groups like the Klan. To compound the Radicals' problem, Congress repealed its ironclad oath in 1871. No longer did Southerners have to swear that they had always been loyal to the Union. In 1872 a general amnesty restored civil rights (including the right to hold office) to all but about six hundred Confederate officials.

As white terrorists harassed the remaining Radical state governments, Northerners became indifferent. Republicans in Washington grew increasingly weary of the struggle to protect black civil rights. "The whole public," complained President Grant, "is tired of these outbreaks in the South."

The death or retirement of such Radical leaders as Stevens and Sumner helped restore control of Congress to more conservative, business-minded Republicans. A combination of Democrats and reform-minded "Liberal Republicans" nearly won the presidency in 1872 on a platform pledging an end to federal support for Radical regimes in the South. In 1874 the Democrats regained control of the House for the first time since before the war.

Public attention strayed even further away from the South after 1873, when a major depression swept the country. The business slump threw hundreds of thousands out of work and shifted political attention from postwar Reconstruction to the problem of economic recovery.

The Compromise of 1877

In 1876 both presidential candidates, Republican Rutherford B. Hayes and Democrat Samuel B. Tilden, promised even before the election to restore "home rule" to the South. Both pledged to remove federal support for the three remaining Radical state governments—those of Louisiana, South Carolina, and Florida. They implied that Southern whites could now handle all problems connected with blacks, including political rights.

The election ended in a unique stalemate. Two sets of returns arrived from the three states yet in Radical hands. The Radicals claimed that Hayes had won, while Democrats insisted on a Tilden majority. The nineteen doubtful electoral votes (including one disputed Oregon elector) meant the difference between a one-vote Hayes margin and a clear Tilden sweep. Congress finally accepted the recommendation of a specially appointed commission to award all the disputed votes to Hayes, thereby making him president. The South, in turn, received a pledge from Hayes that all remaining federal troops would be removed from the three Radical states, that federal subsidies would be provided for a Southern transcontinental railroad then under construction, and that a Southerner would be appointed to the cabinet.

After Hayes took office, Radical rule promptly collapsed in the three remaining states.

The violence of new vigilante groups, such as the Knights of the Ku Klux Klan, contributed to the overthrow of Republican rule and the demise of Reconstruction. A secret, terrorist society, the Klan formed in 1867 to restore white supremacy by harassing Reconstructionists, intimidating black voters, forcing black officials into resignation, and depriving freedmen of their rights. The tactics of the Klan ranged from pressure, ostracism, and bribery, to arson, beatings, and murder. (Culver Pictures)

This so-called Compromise of 1877 marked the final surrender of the North's promise to defend black political and civil rights against the former white Confederates.

During the decades that followed, Democratic state governments defeated black efforts to participate in Southern politics. In every subsequent election fewer blacks voted.

Violence toward black people increased for the rest of the century. The great majority of Southern blacks farmed other people's lands as tenants or sharecroppers. They were forced into a subordinate place in Southern life, being neither slaves nor completely free persons.

Suggested Readings
Chapters 23-24

Sherman's March

Burke Davis, *Sherman's March* (1980); Lloyd Lewis, *Sherman, Fighting Prophet* (1932); K. P. Williams, *Lincoln Finds a General: A Military History of the Civil War* (4 vols., 1949–56); T. H. Williams, *McClellan, Sherman, and Grant* (1962).

The Civil War

Mark M. Boatner, III, *The Civil War Dictionary* (1959); Bruce Catton, *Centennial History of the Civil War* (3 vols., 1961–63); David Donald, ed., *Why the North Won the Civil War* (1960); Clement Eaton, *A History of the Southern Confederacy* (1954); Shelby Foote, *The Civil War* (3 vols., 1958–74); George Frederickson, *The Inner Civil War* (1965); Paul W. Gates, *Agriculture and the Civil War* (1965); David T. Gilchrust and W. David Lewis, eds., *Economic Change in the Civil War Era* (1965); Harold M. Hyman, *A More Perfect Union: The Impact of the Civil War and Reconstruction on the Constitution* (1973); Mary E. Massey, *Bonnet Brigades: American Women and the Civil War* (1966); Allan Nevins, *The War for the Union* (4 vols., 1959–71); Peter J.

Parish, *The American Civil War* (1975); James M. McPherson, *The Negro's Civil War* (1965) and *The Struggle for Equality: Abolitionists and the Negro in the Civil War and Reconstruction* (1964); J. G. Randall and Richard Current, *Lincoln the President* (4 vols., 1945–55); J. G. Randall and David Donald, *The Civil War and Reconstruction* (2nd ed., 1961); Benjamin P. Thomas, *Abraham Lincoln* (1952); Emory Thomas, *The Confederacy as a Revolutionary Experience* (1971); Frank Vandiver, *Their Tattered Flags* (1970).

Reconstruction

W. R. Brock, *An American Crisis* (1963); Robert Cruden, *The Negro in Reconstruction* (1969); John Hope Franklin, *Reconstruction After the Civil War* (1962); Rembert W. Patrick, *The Reconstruction of the Nation* (1964); Kenneth M. Stampp, *The Era of Reconstruction, 1865–1877* (1965); Hans L. Trefousse, *Impeachment of a President* (1975); C. Vann Woodward, *Reunion and Reaction: The Compromise of 1877 and the End of Reconstruction* (1951).

Americans thought about their Civil War in many different ways. But most of them agreed, North and South, that it was somehow a conservative war. Each side thought of itself as the conserving protector of an inherited social and political order. It was difficult for Americans to understand that what lay ahead was not a restoration of stability but a surprising burst of activity and change. The United States was transformed into a modern industrial nation in the last third of the nineteenth century. That transformation is the subject of Unit Five.

In an odd way, the people who could best have understood the revolutionary transformations of American society were those who had been most completely defeated by it: the American Indians. From the time of Jamestown, they had watched white society grow in size and power. Now, the forces of expansion increased dramatically. Railroads, miners, cattle ranchers, and farmers spilled out over the Great Plains to the Pacific Coast with fresh speed and energy.

The westward expansion of white settlement often encountered resistance from Indian tribes already living in the region. Many of these Indians had been removed forcibly during the 1830s and 1840s from the Old Northwest and the Southeastern states. Now, in the Far Western territories, they again found themselves highly vulnerable. The expansion of settlers in the West during the mid-nineteenth century put an end to the relative isolation that had guaranteed security and survival to Indian culture.

No group of Indians resisted more fiercely the destruction of their identity and experienced more vividly the intrusions of white soldiers and settlers than did the Sioux. Chapter 25 describes their persistent but ultimately unsuccessful struggle to maintain autonomy, a struggle that culminated briefly in the dramatic Sioux victory over George Armstrong Custer and his 7th Cavalry at the Battle of the Little Bighorn. Chapter 26 then examines the factors that contributed to settlement of the American West: the influence of the frontier on American life, the Indian wars capped a generation later by the "ghost dance" agitation of 1890, and the major "frontiers" of white expansion west of the Mississippi—mining, cattle, and agricultural.

The examination, in Chapter 27, of the career of President James A. Garfield and of his assassination in 1881 by a crazed, disappointed office-seeker introduces the climate of political tensions. Chapter 28 then traces the conditions that made political careers such as Garfield's possible and describes party politics in late-nineteenth-century America.

During the same decades in which postwar America was expanding westward, a new economic landscape took shape in the East and Middle West. New inventions and manufacturing processes changed the manner in which Americans earned their livings and produced their goods. Giant factories developed and enormous cities quickly evolved with great immigrant and working-class populations. Along with industrial and urban growth came a complex series of conflicts between employers and workers, immigrants and native Americans, the newly prosperous and the desperately poor.

INDUSTRIAL
AMERICA

UNIT FIVE

One of the most significant industrial conflicts of this era occurred in Chicago in 1894 during the economic depression of that decade, the worst known by Americans up to that point. The clash involved the workers in Eugene V. Debs's American Railway Union and the country's railroad companies, after Debs's union called a strike against George Pullman's railway car company. The Pullman strike brought transcontinental rail traffic to a virtual halt (ended only after intervention by federal troops), led to the jailing of Debs, and caused the destruction of his union. Chapter 29 tells the story of this troubling episode, possibly the most important labor-management conflict in the United States during the violence-ridden 1890s. Chapter 30 then examines the background of urban and industrial development leading to the Pullman strike.

Social and economic change created strains on political parties and governmental institutions, which intensified during the depression of the 1890s. Agrarian protest led to the creation of a new, farmer-led party, the Populists. Populism is discussed in Chapters 31 and 32.

What comes through, then, from the late nineteenth century is a mixed picture of incredible industrial growth and geographical expansion alongside moments of crisis and bloodshed—with political leaders looking on as almost helpless and often confused spectators.

25 Battle at the Little Bighorn

The Sioux called the land Paha Sapa, a hunting and burial ground holy to their people. White railroad surveyors, prospectors, and soldiers called the land the Black Hills. For the whites, the territory promised to provide either new railroad lines, undiscovered gold, or fresh paths of glory. The struggle for control of the Dakota hill country and surrounding areas, territory sacred to the Sioux and attractive to the Americans, opened in 1874, the eighth year of peace between the two.

It began with a military "invasion" of the Black Hills that violated an earlier treaty between the United States and the Sioux, an agreement guaranteeing that whites would never enter Paha Sapa. Twelve hundred men of the 7th Cavalry set out from Fort Abraham Lincoln, North Dakota (near Bismarck), to explore the Black Hills during the summer of 1874 and to collect information useful for constructing a new fort there. The soldiers also intended to help prepare the way for safe transit through the region by Northern Pacific Railroad work crews. General Philip H. Sheridan, the Civil War hero who now commanded the Army's Division of the Missouri (which included all cavalry in the area), had ordered the Black Hills survey. Later, settlers would undoubtedly follow in the wake of railroad construction.

The 7th Cavalry brought with it two companies of infantry, five dozen Indian scouts, artillery, Gatling guns, and a staff of scientists. A party of prospectors also accompanied the 1874 expedition, fanning across the Black Hills in search of gold. The troops also brought with them into Paha Sapa a contingent of newspapermen. This was no surprise to anyone familiar with the 7th Cavalry's publicity-hungry commander, the flamboyant Lieutenant Colonel George Armstrong Custer.

Custer was a powerfully built figure, tall and slim, who wore his blond hair long and who normally dressed in buckskins on his campaigns into Indian country—in every respect a personally distinctive figure.[1] The Sioux called him Pahuska, "the Long Hair," according to some accounts,

---

[1] The Indians assigned a variety of nicknames to the flamboyant Custer.

The massive column of cavalry, artillery, and wagons which George Armstrong Custer commanded on his 1874 expedition into the Black Hills is shown in this photograph by W. H. Illingworth. (National Archives)

and "Yellow Hair" according to others. His obsession with gaining public attention first brought him notoriety during the Civil War. Born in Ohio in 1839, the son of a farmer and blacksmith, Custer had always yearned for a soldier's life. He graduated at the bottom of his West Point class in 1861 but, almost immediately afterward, went into combat at the Battle of Bull Run. He fought bravely through many campaigns on the eastern front during the Civil War, rising to the rank of major general of volunteers by the time the war ended. Custer gained a reputation as an impetuous, daring commander and as a "dandy" in both dress and manner. His most notable success came in April 1865, at the war's close, when he and his men relentlessly pursued Lee's exhausted Confederates across Virginia during that final campaign. The Confederate flag of truce just prior to Lee's surrender came to Custer's cavalry division.

Transferred to the Southwest after the war's end, Custer dropped in rank to captain once the massive volunteer Union army was officially disbanded in 1866. When the 7th Cavalry was organized that same year, Custer joined it as a lieutenant colonel and served during an unsuccessful campaign in 1867 against various Indian tribes, including the Sioux. He was court-martialed on charges arising from the failed campaign and suspended for a year but rejoined the 7th Cavalry in 1868. Custer defeated Black Kettle's Cheyenne that fall in a skillfully fought battle at the

Custer joins his staff officers and their wives on a hunting and camping expedition. He appears in a white hat in the center of the photograph. (National Archives)

Washita River, one that created his reputation as an effective Indian fighter. For the next two years, Custer fought a variety of tribes on the Southern plains and in Kansas, experiences he described in a self-promoting 1874 memoir published first in *Galaxy* magazine and then as a book called *My Life on the Plains.*

After several relatively inactive years, Custer again came to public notice in 1873, when he led units of the 7th Cavalry against Crazy Horse and his Sioux warriors in battles across the Yellowstone Valley. Custer was guarding a surveying group then working in the valley, an assignment that served as prelude to his even more provocative expedition into the Black Hills the following year.

Custer's force trekked through the Black Hills for two months before returning safely to Fort Abraham Lincoln. Its journey had been interrupted regularly as Custer sent messengers who announced the exciting, if premature, news that gold could be found in the Black Hills "from the grass roots down." Upon returning, newsmen who accompanied the cavalry alerted the country to the potential bonanza awaiting energetic American prospectors in the Black Hills.

The rush was on. Thousands of gold hunters, intent upon new finds, penetrated the area despite half-hearted efforts by the military to keep them out. The cavalry would occasionally take intruding miners into custody but usually freed them within a short time and allowed them to resume prospecting. By 1875, gold *was* discovered in the hills and in large quantities, a fact that reinforced the unwillingness of military authorities to protect Indian treaty rights to Paha Sapa against the incursions of whites staking claims there. The various Sioux bands and other tribes in the Dakotas, most notably the Cheyenne, stirred uneasily. Several Indian raiding parties even chased away groups of prospectors. For the moment, however, neither the cavalry nor the Sioux forced matters to the point of war.

The Sioux had first come to Paha Sapa a century earlier. During the period before European settlement, they had lived in the Northeast, apparently settling by the sixteenth century around the Mississippi River. At that time, the Sioux were hunters, lived in forests, ate wild rice and corn, and fought constantly with other tribes, including the Algonquins and Chippewas who eventually drove them farther westward. Among the three major Sioux "families"—each of which was fragmented into a number of smaller bands—was one called the Tetons, which figured most prominently in the confrontation with American soldiers over the Black Hills during the 1870s.[2] The Tetons had crossed the Mississippi by the early eighteenth century. They began roaming the plains, hunting buffalo, and waging war, greatly increasing their mobility through the use of horses.

Although the first Sioux warriors probably entered the Black Hills during the 1770s, most Tetons stayed along the Missouri River (near present-day South Dakota) at that time. When Lewis and Clark moved upriver past the Teton villages in 1804, they nearly came to blows with the fierce tribesmen.[3] In the end, the Sioux became friendlier toward the explorers, and normally Americans could travel up the Missouri without interference from the Tetons. During the decades after Lewis and Clark's expedition, the Tetons gained control of most of the Dakotas—including the Black Hills—and became fur-trading partners of American mountain men and trappers who moved into the region. By the 1840s, Sioux factions spread out over the entire central plains. They fought for dominance against new tribal enemies in the region and against one another.

Throughout the 1840s, growing numbers of settlers traveled through the Dakotas and Wyoming in wagon train caravans along the Oregon Trail until the government finally purchased Fort Laramie on the Platte River from a fur-trading company to use as a military outpost. After the arrival of federal troops, unrest spread among the Sioux and other Western tribes until U.S. Indian agents summoned a council of all the tribes in the area near Fort Laramie, at Horse Creek, in 1851. More than ten thousand plains Indians showed up, along with government agents, fur traders, and an assortment of other whites, to confer with the

---

[2] Tribal names often proved as confusing to whites as the descriptive and extended personal names taken by Indians. The three branches of the Sioux family—Tetons, Santees, and Yanktons—considered themselves (and thus named themselves) "allies," a word that became "Lakota" to the Tetons, "Dakota" to the Santees, and "Nakota" to the Yanktons. The Tetons themselves were divided into *Southern* and *Northern* Lakota bands. Among the Southern Lakotas were the Brulés and Oglalas; the Northerners included Hunkpapas, Miniconjous, and other branches in the tribal family. Among the Sioux leaders prominent in the events that followed, Red Cloud was an Oglala, Crazy Horse an Oglala, and Sitting Bull a Hunkpapa.

[3] See Chapter 11, p. 221.

Red Cloud (1822–1909) was the leading Oglala Sioux Chief through the Sioux War and the decade which followed. He twice traveled to Washington in the 1870s to present Indian views of their treaty rights to government officials. (The Bettmann Archive)

superintendent of Indian affairs and his associates. The latter group came from Washington to seek assurances that the Oregon Trail caravans could move safely without fearing Indian attack and that tribal warfare on the plains did not threaten whites already living there.

Most of the Sioux gathered there eventually agreed to a treaty that guaranteed safe passage along the Oregon Trail and granted permission to the American government to construct forts along the trail. In return, the United States pledged to pay the Indians a yearly amount in provisions and trade goods, and to use troops stationed in the region to guarantee fair dealings between whites and the Sioux. For several years, peace came to the Platte country. But a series of brutal encounters in 1854–55 between soldiers and Sioux, which involved casualties on both sides, led to the imposition in 1856 of a new treaty upon the Sioux in an attempt to prevent further hostilities.

Again relative peace came to the central plains as army units enforced Sioux rights against intruding settlers. This time the amity came to an abrupt end in 1864, when local militiamen, led by Colonel J. M. Chivington, massacred several hundred Cheyenne in Sand Creek, Colorado, triggering unrest in the neighboring Dakotas and Wyoming.[4] Oglalas and Brulés joined forces, with six thousand Sioux coming together the following year in raiding parties against both wagon trains and soldiers. The armistice over raids against the Oregon Trail had ended. American troops countered with a punitive expedition against the Sioux in 1865, their ranks bolstered by new recruits from the Union armies in the East, now freed by the end of the Civil War for battle against the Indians.

At this point, there intruded into the life of the Sioux a Montana prospector and road builder. John Bozeman developed a trail leading directly from the mining camps of western Montana to the major wagon road eastward through the Platte country. The Bozeman trail cut right through Sioux hunting grounds supposedly guaranteed against white in-

---

[4] See Chapter 26, p. 512.

cursions by the 1851 treaty. When both army officers and government negotiators tried to persuade the Sioux to agree to allow whites to use the
Bozeman trail, and also to let the railroads build lines and the army forts
within their territory, the entire region exploded into warfare. In northern
Wyoming, warriors led by Red Cloud, the younger (and fiercer) Crazy
Horse, and other Sioux chiefs successfully ambushed a party of soldiers
led by Captain William J. Fetterman, killing and mutilating eighty-one
soldiers, Fetterman's entire command. The massacre infuriated American troops in the area, and a series of bloody skirmishes between Indians
and soldiers, which came to be known as the Sioux War, dragged on for
the next two years.

Pressure on the Grant administration from Easterners sympathetic
toward the Indians, along with the obvious inability of the army to defeat
Red Cloud (the chief Sioux war leader), forced the government finally to
yield. Not only the Bozeman trail but three forts along the trail were
abandoned, at least temporarily, thereby removing the chief causes of Indian anger. Red Cloud's warriors set the torch to the abandoned Fort C. F.
Smith, while his Cheyenne allies burned Fort Phil Kearny. Yet another
treaty with the Sioux was signed in 1868. By its terms, they received a
number of gifts as an inducement to accept the pact. But the Indians
believed they had won the right to remain free of white interference and
settlement throughout the central plains, both north and south of the
Platte River. The actual terms of the document, however, about which
the Sioux appear to have been deliberately misled by the government
negotiators, conceded as Sioux and Cheyenne hunting lands *only* the
northernmost portions of the area in question, including the Black Hills,
while stipulating that the tribes must live at government-created agencies—receiving their treaty provisions there—on an area west of the Missouri River in South Dakota.

For the next two years, in an effort to persuade the roaming bands
of Indians to settle on their allotted reservations under the supervision of
government agents, army units pursued the Sioux, rounding up a number
of bands while slaughtering buffalo herds to deprive the Indians of any
major alternative to food provided by the agencies. Finally, in 1870, in a
last effort to persuade the Sioux to accept the treaty's terms through additional negotiation, government officials invited Red Cloud, the Oglala
war chief, and Spotted Tail, his counterpart among the Brulés, to travel
to Washington and meet President Grant.

Accompanied by several old friends from among the area's white
traders, Red Cloud and twenty other Oglalas set out on a journey which
took them not only thousands of miles but, in the process, centuries in
cultural time. After being escorted from Fort Laramie to the railroad station at Pine Bluff rather than to the closer rail depot at Cheyenne—where
white settlers' hostility toward the Sioux led to fears that Red Cloud and
his party might be lynched—the group boarded an east-bound train. (Up
to that point, few Oglalas had ever seen a train much less ridden on one.)
After traveling through towns along the Platte Valley, the train reached
Omaha, the first city the Indians had ever encountered. From there, they

proceeded to Chicago, whose tall buildings and unfamiliar industrial sprawl appeared to amaze and awe the Sioux delegation.

When the party reached Washington, Red Cloud confronted Spotted Tail's delegation of Brulés, who had traveled east separately. After quarreling, the two chiefs negotiated privately to settle their differences before meeting with government officials: Spotted Tail agreed to defer to Red Cloud as spokesman for the Indians, although no Sioux council had made any such distinction in rank between the two. Their hosts tried to impress the Sioux with displays of American military power, setting up demonstrations of giant cannon fired down the Potomac River and trying in a variety of ways to instill in the Indians a recognition of the extraordinary military force available to the United States. They did not succeed. Red Cloud proved intransigent in his discussions with Interior Department and army officials concerning their demands that he lead his people to their assigned reservation. The Oglala chief responded angrily to a reading of the 1868 treaty, insisting that he had never agreed to the provisions cited when the treaty was read at Fort Laramie. An impasse was reached when it became clear that the administration insisted on the Sioux conforming to the treaty's provisions without any revisions.

Before returning west, Red Cloud and his party traveled to New York, where he spoke to a crowded assemblage—well-covered by Eastern journalists—at the Cooper Union Institute. The meeting was arranged by sympathizers who hoped to rouse public opinion on behalf of the Indians' concerns. The scene itself was an unlikely and unprecedented one. Red Cloud and the other Oglalas stood or sat on the platform dressed in their ceremonial Sioux outfits and observed by an audience of well-tailored white New Yorkers. "You have children, and so have we," Red Cloud told them through his interpreter. "We want to rear our children well, and ask you to help us in doing so." He recited a long catalog of alleged wrongs committed against his people by white soldiers and settlers, complaining about the betrayal he felt at learning the terms of the 1868 treaty. Chief Red Dog, who spoke next, put the matter more succinctly:

> When the Great Father first sent out [white] men to our people I was poor and thin; now I am large and fat. This is because so many liars have been sent out there and I have been stuffed full with their lies.

When Red Cloud returned to Fort Laramie, he found thousands of Sioux and Cheyenne gathered nearby to await his report. Red Cloud remained angry at being forced onto a reservation supervised by government agents, but at the same time, much of his fury had cooled on the return trip. He even seemed flattered by the lengths to which government officials and private citizens in the East had gone in urging him to keep the peace between Indians and whites on the plains. After gaining approval from American military leaders for the Sioux to continue trading in the area (a right denied by the 1868 treaty to the Indians though without their knowledge at the time), Red Cloud agreed to take his Oglalas onto a reservation north of Fort Laramie.

The Indians celebrated what they considered a great victory over the Americans, having forced the government to back down on a few onerous treaty provisions, after which Red Cloud traveled among the different Sioux encampments in the area throughout the summer. He described to the tribal councils his trip to the East and recommended peaceful acceptance of the reservation agencies. In most instances, the Sioux followed his lead. Late that same summer of 1870, the Indians began arriving at the various military forts to be escorted to their reservations and receive provisions.

Red Cloud himself waited until early October before taking his people to Fort Laramie. Again the haggling over terms began: Would the Indian agent he dealt with be someone Red Cloud chose or a government appointee? Where would the site of the agency be? The arguments became heated until another Oglala chief, Man Afraid of His Horse, turned the dispute toward solution: "There is too much talk," he exclaimed. "Give us our presents and let this other matter lie where it is." The U.S. commissioners sent to negotiate with the Sioux traveled to the Oglala camp on October 7 bringing wagons filled with the gifts promised by "The Great Father" (President Grant) in exchange for peace: blankets, bolts of cloth, clothing, knives—but no guns or ammunition. The policy of placating Red Cloud and the other Sioux leaders had ensured a period of peace for the Platte country.

During the four years that followed, the peace held. Nevertheless, there were frequent quarrels between Red Cloud and government-appointed agents, constant arguments between various Indian notables and agents over the type and extent of supplies to be provided, and a number of minor shootouts between the Sioux and the whites. But the troubles began in earnest only after Custer led his expedition into the Black Hills during the summer of 1874. Several times during the previous year, there had been engagements between Custer's troops and Crazy Horse's band in the Yellowstone Valley. Only in 1874, however, did the prospect of a full renewal of warfare emerge.

Again Red Cloud took the lead in trying to maintain the peace. This time, however, his authority among the Sioux was undermined by younger, more militant chiefs including Crazy Horse, Sitting Bull, and Gall. Once more Red Cloud journeyed to Washington with a delegation, not only to protest Custer's violation of the Black Hills sanctuary but also to lay before the Great Father his bitter disputes with the Indian agent on his reservation. Red Cloud's 1870 trip had begun uncertainly but ended in triumph. During the spring of 1875, however, his hopes for a friendly reception in Washington were quickly shattered.

The Oglala chief and his party reached Washington only to find there delegations from other Sioux agencies on the Missouri River. The Indians learned from President Grant himself that the American government now wished to purchase the Black Hills, and for days officials pressured the chiefs to agree to the sale. The Sioux leaders gained time, finally, by insisting that they could not conclude arrangements without first consulting the tribal councils. The government, in turn, agreed to dispatch a special commission to the area that autumn to join with the entire Sioux Nation in council and negotiate the purchase.

Adding personal embarrassment to tribal frustration for Red Cloud was an episode that dimmed his reputation among white supporters in the East. By the time the Sioux chiefs reached Washington in 1875, the novelty of such Indian delegations to the city had worn off. Unscrupulous local businessmen sensed the prospect of easy profit. In Red Cloud's case, a hotel keeper collected the Oglalas at Union Station and brought them to his establishment. Red Cloud's friend and adviser, a white trader named Leon Palladay, remained drunk and unhelpful for the entire stay, while the hotel keeper escorted his Oglala guests out for nightly visits to what official reports would later refer to simply as "bad houses." Red Cloud, meanwhile, innocent of basic attitudes toward such matters among his sternly moralistic white supporters, proceeded to submit his hotel bill to the commissioner of Indian affairs. He, in turn, denounced Red Cloud for his improprieties in front of his fellow chiefs and declined to reimburse the hotel keeper for arranging the itinerary. Other well-meaning Eastern sympathizers accused Red Cloud of such vagaries as "obtuse and unsub-duable [sic] Indianism," a charge that only could have pleased the chief had he understood it.

Upon returning to their Missouri River agencies, Red Cloud and the other Sioux found their different bands in an agitated state as a result of prospectors' continuing penetration into the Black Hills. A number of Sioux led by Crazy Horse had already left the reservations and begun raiding miners' settlements. By September, when the government commission arrived at the Red Cloud Agency to begin negotiating for the Black Hills, more than twenty thousand Indians had gathered there. The setting became wildly inappropriate as a place for calm and reasoned discussion of the proposed sale, although the commission met several times in full council with all of the chiefs who had come.

None of the Sioux leaders could claim to serve as a spokesman for the entire nation, as Red Cloud had sometimes done (without authority) while in Washington in 1870. Any such attempt would probably have led to an Indian civil war on the spot. Under the circumstances, a number of Sioux chiefs spoke, mainly to express their opposition to sale of the Black Hills. (Some, like Crazy Horse, simply boycotted the meeting.) Several sessions produced no agreement and a rising state of tension. Commissioners and soldiers alike became anxious as hundreds of Indians would suddenly ride in a charge toward the council site during a negotiating session before turning aside at the last moment. At the final council session on September 23, the commissioners sat under an open tent awaiting the chiefs while thousands of Indians rode or walked through the nearby hills.

Two hundred Sioux dressed for battle suddenly bore down on the tent, circled it, and began firing their rifles in the air while chanting war songs. "The Black Hills is my land and I love it," ran one Sioux chant, "And whoever interferes will hear this gun." After that band had spread out in front of the commission, another band rode down at a signal from the hills and repeated the performance, then another, until seven thousand Sioux warriors circled the negotiating tent. At that point, the major chiefs—Red Cloud, Spotted Tail, and the others—proceeded to dismount and to sit in their own circle some distance from the tent, discussing among themselves what points should be raised with the commissioners and who should speak first as the primary chief. Their conclave dragged on for over an hour.

The warriors grew restless as they waited. Finally, one young Sioux named Little Big Man, a follower of Crazy Horse's, rode toward the tent holding a rifle and shouting that he intended to kill all the whites who had come to steal the Black Hills. Although other nearby Indians quickly grabbed Little Big Man's gun and shunted him aside, the vastly outnumbered soldiers and commissioners remained unnerved, fearing the outbreak of a major battle. Meanwhile the other Sioux continued to shout insults at the whites, aimed their guns at the soldiers, and rode up and down past the cavalry troops, who gripped their pommels and guns tightly. At last, a single Oglala chief, Young Man Afraid of His Horse, shouted to the others to disband and return to their camps until tempers had cooled. Reluctantly the Sioux warriors heeded this instruction, and the soldiers found it possible to escort the commissioners back to the Red Cloud Agency without incident. But they did not summon another general council of all the Sioux bands and, instead, began calling various leading chiefs to the agency for separate negotiations.

Those few Sioux willing to talk about selling the Black Hills demanded a price that no American negotiator at the time could accept. Red Cloud, for example, asked that the Sioux be fed and provisioned for seven generations and, in addition, that the United States pay $600 million. Other Sioux leaders named their own figures and demands. Red Dog was possibly most vocal of all when he denounced the trail Custer's men had made through the hills as the "Thieves' Road" and Custer himself as "chief of all the thieves." The Indians knew what spurred such sudden interest on the part of the American government in the Black Hills: "Paha Sapa," Little Bear exclaimed during one meeting with the Washington representatives, "is the House of Gold for our Indians. We watch it to get rich." The commissioners countered Red Cloud's exuberant demand for $600 million with an offer of $6 million for the Hills plus payment to the Sioux of $400,000 a year for the mining rights. In typical fashion, though, the negotiators reserved for the government the right to cancel the deal after giving two year's notice! The meeting ended without agreement.

After returning East, commission members recommended that the Grant administration adopt a tougher policy toward the Sioux and begin pressuring the tribe to comply with the terms of the 1868 treaty or face the loss of food and supplies. Implicit in the commission's report was an assumption that once the Sioux had been forced to submit to American authority and return to their agency reservations, they would prove more amenable to the earlier proposal to purchase not only the Black Hills but also the adjacent Bighorn and Powder river territories.

A get-tough policy soon took effect. Indian Office officials responded to the commission's report, to recommendations from military commanders in the area, and to direct instructions from President Grant. They directed that all bands of Sioux then roaming the central plains return to their assigned agencies by January 31, 1876, or face military action to force them back. Like so many other actions taken during the previous decades to "deal with" American Indians, however, this stern new approach appeared far easier to enforce when initiated on the Potomac than when implemented on the Platte.

Even those Sioux who wanted to comply with the order to return to the agencies by January 31 faced serious difficulties. The directive first reached the agencies around Christmas time during an extremely severe winter. Spreading the message to the different Sioux bands scattered among campsites in the hills over hundreds of miles proved arduous in itself. One runner sent out by an Indian agent to alert Sitting Bull's band and other insurgent Sioux finally returned to the agency on February 11, long after the deadline had past. Also, the snow and bitter cold allowed the Sioux to attempt delaying tactics. Crazy Horse told the runners that he could not move his people in such poor weather. Although most of the Sioux living outside the reservations apparently had no intention of fighting the American troops at this point, neither did they seriously consider complying with the humiliating directive from Washington.

An estimated three thousand Sioux, among them several hundred warriors, remained outside the agencies in mid-February, when local agents requested help from General George Crook's military units. Crook and his officers soon turned their attention to the task of subduing the major leader of Indian resistance on the plains, Crazy Horse, who—upon receiving the order to return—led his people away from the direction of the nearby Red Cloud Agency to the more isolated Powder River country. There Crazy Horse could link up more easily with other Sioux militants in the area—including the famous medicine man Sitting Bull—and with his Cheyenne allies.

Although Crazy Horse had received warnings from friendly Sioux in the south that General Crook's troops had begun marching toward him, he and his followers were apparently taken by surprise on March 17, 1876, when six companies of cavalry (about 450 men) led by Colonel J. J. Reynolds attacked his village, captured his pony herd, and destroyed the encampment. Crazy Horse regrouped and led an assault on Reynolds's force, managing to recapture most of the horses. Reynolds than retreated, pursued by Crazy Horse's band for twenty miles. Because of the large number of wounded troopers, and because he lacked a base camp within the area, Crook was forced to return to the Platte until spring.

Crazy Horse became a hero to the Sioux because of his standoff with Crook at Powder River, and at a council of the Oglalas, the warriors named him their primary chief. Crazy Horse then ordered messengers sent to those Oglalas who had remained on the agency reservations, seeking recruits for a spring battle against the soldiers. Hundreds of Sioux

General Crook's headquarters in the Dakota Territory during his 1876 campaign against the Sioux includes tents improvised from wagon frames. (National Archives)

abandoned the agencies to join the insurgents. By June, the Indians that gathered near the upper Rosebud River under Crazy Horse's leadership numbered several thousand, including not only Oglalas but also Sitting Bull's Hunkpapas, Cheyennes led by Two Moons, and fragments of Teton Sioux bands from the different agencies and from as far away as Minnesota. Although Red Cloud and other chiefs on the reservations who had negotiated with the whites for years chose to remain at the agencies, many of their younger warriors—including Red Cloud's son—brought guns and ammunition northward to Crazy Horse's camp for the climactic struggle to prevent the whites from taking over their remaining lands.

Nor was the first battle long in coming. During the second week in June, Sitting Bull and his Hunkpapa followers held their ceremonial Sun Dance. Sitting Bull himself served as the main dancer, proclaiming at the end of the rite that he had experienced a vision: A horde of dead white soldiers had fallen upside down into his camp. Only days later, on June 17, the vision became a reality.

The previous day, some Cheyenne scouts came upon Crook's forces camped on the west side of the Rosebud River near its head. Crazy Horse's major encampment at the time lay near a tributary of the Bighorn River known as the Little Bighorn, and the scouts rode back quickly to spread the news. After a council of the chiefs was held, more than a thousand warriors rode out in darkness toward the Rosebud. After settling in behind a hill near Crook's camp, the Sioux waited while scouts went out to determine the strength and formations of the soldiers. Crook had planned a surprise assault on Crazy Horse's camp, but now, his own men had been caught without warning. The Sioux scouts ran into some of Crook's Crow Indian scouts on a hilltop separating the two camps, and after both sides fired some shots, the Crows raced back shouting "Lakota! Lakota!" The cries alerted Crook's men, who hastily prepared for battle as the first wave of Sioux, both on horses and on foot, chased the Crow scouts into the American perimeter.

The Indians directly attacked Crook's cavalry, sometimes in bitter hand-to-hand struggle, and the battle proceeded wildly on both sides. Crook still directed troop movements intent upon attacking the Sioux camp, his original plan, but a series of furious Indian assaults kept him pinned down. One of Crook's officers, Colonel Anson Mills, later described the Sioux as "charging boldly and rapidly through the soldiers, knocking them from their horses with lances and knives, dismounting and killing them, cutting off the arms of some at the elbows in the middle of the fight and carrying them away." The Sioux and their Cheyenne allies repelled all of Crook's efforts to force his troops onto the offensive toward their village. But the Indians could not decisively destroy Crook's forces either. Both sides had planned an ambush; both sides failed.

In the end, Crook withdrew from the Battle at the Rosebud to a camp farther south, which delayed his offensive against the rebellious Sioux for a month. The army lost nine troopers, a larger number of Indian scouts, and suffered twenty-one wounded. Only eleven died in Crazy Horse's ranks, with another five wounded. Although Crook and his officers later described the engagement in official reports as a victory, it amounted to another standoff and—in some ways—to a triumph for the Sioux who had temporarily gone on the offensive. For the first time, Indians had amassed a large contingent of troops to fight in an organized manner similar to the campaign tactics used by the U.S. Army itself.

After his indecisive encounter with Crazy Horse at the Rosebud, Crook decided not to proceed against the Indians again until reinforcements had arrived. His general plan of operations remained the same and involved trapping the Sioux and Cheyenne between several advancing columns of soldiers: one commanded by Crook himself; another led by Colonel John Gibbon, which was coming from western Montana; and a third under General Alfred Terry, which had proceeded from the Missouri River westward toward the battle area.

George Armstrong Custer had been assigned originally to command the column now led by Terry, but in mid-March, Custer was ordered to report to Washington to testify concerning allegations of fraud among Indian agents. His testimony reinforced the existing criticism of administration Indian policies and angered President Grant, who stripped the popular Custer of his command. Grant ordered Terry placed in charge and even directed that Custer not be permitted to join the campaign. Only after protests from journalists and politicians sympathetic to Custer—and after requests from Terry and other military officers—did the president back down and restore Custer's rank and regimental command, but Grant left Terry in charge of the column.

Four days after Crazy Horse and Crook had clashed at the Battle of the Rosebud, on June 21, Terry's troops and those of Gibbon met on the Yellowstone at the mouth of the Rosebud. There Terry conferred with Gibbon and Custer about a plan of attack, Crook having left matters in their hands. They received Major Marcus Reno's report that the bulk of Sioux forces had moved to the Little Bighorn River country. Terry planned to trap the Indians in a pincer between two columns. His force, combined with Gibbon's, would return to the Bighorn River and march up alongside it until reaching the mouth of the Little Bighorn. Custer, meanwhile, would take the 7th Cavalry on a slow march (to allow time for Terry and Gibbon to reach their destination) up the Rosebud parallel to the larger Terry-Gibbon route. According to Terry's plan, Custer should arrive at the Little Bighorn late on June 25, and the attack from both columns would come the following day. If all went well, the Sioux would be trapped between the two forces and crushed.

At noon on the following day, June 22, the 7th Cavalry under Custer marched out followed by pack animals carrying supplies for its more than six hundred soldiers and forty-four Indian scouts. A single newspaper reporter, inevitable in any campaign fought by Custer, accompanied the column. Apparently disregarding Terry's instructions to proceed up the Rosebud at a leisurely pace, Custer marched his men relentlessly. They reached the Indian trail that connected the Rosebud and the Little Bighorn on the evening of June 24, a full day ahead of schedule. Custer rested only a few hours before pushing ahead through the night, marching along the trail with his men and reaching the Little Bighorn Valley early on the 25th.

Did Custer hope to "steal a march" on his fellow commanders and attack the main Sioux forces himself, thereby winning whatever share of glory might accompany the feat! Or did he genuinely fear, as he told his officers at dawn on the 25th, that Indian scouts had discovered their presence and that therefore they had to prepare an attack without waiting until the following day! Or, as a third possibility, was Custer's haste a complex mixture of *both* ambition and anxiety! The question would soon become the subject of intense national debate, military inquiries, journalistic probing, and historical analysis. It has remained so to this day.

Whatever his motives, Custer decided to attack what turned out to be the main Indian village alone, on June 25, rather than on the following day in combination with Terry's and Gibbon's forces. The Sioux and Cheyennes who were camped along the Little Bighorn River's west bank over a three-mile stretch—though Custer could not have known any of this—were clustered in sub-tribal groupings with their lodges in five giant circles: four of them Sioux—Crazy Horse's Oglalas, Sitting Bull's Hunkpapas, the Miniconjous, and the San Arcs—and one Cheyenne. Although the precise number of Indians that Custer's 650 men marched against remains undetermined, there were probably between ten and fifteen thousand (a third of them warriors) awaiting the soldiers at the Little Bighorn encampment.

Several groups of Crazy Horse's scouts had spotted Custer's column as it advanced toward the river, but the Sioux and Cheyenne bands seemed unconcerened until just before the cavalry reached their village. Nor could Custer have imagined how extensive that village had become or how populated. Nothing demonstrates this fact more clearly than Custer's decision, early on the morning of the 25th as he approached the Little Bighorn River, to divide *his* column into three groups. He planned to surround the Indians who lay ahead, attack from two sides, and prevent them from escaping his trap — Terry's plan in miniature!

Shortly before reaching the river, Custer directed Major Reno to take three companies of soldiers and scouts and cross the Little Bighorn, attacking from the north. Custer ordered Captain Frederick Benteen, meanwhile, to take another three companies to scout the bluffs to the south, holding his men in reserve as reinforcements. Custer himself led five companies in a march along the river, intent upon crossing further downstream. (Another company would remain with the pack animals and supplies.) His apparent hope was to trap the Indians between Reno's forces, now moving north of him, and his own soldiers.

Reno and his troops rode directly across the river, unsuspectingly, seeing only a thin line of Indians amassed against him. According to later Indian accounts, the arrival of Reno's troops took at least some of the braves by surprise: "Like that the soldiers were upon us. Through the tepee poles their bullets rattled." Reno's "attack" on the upper end of the large encampment ended suddenly, when he fell under assault himself by hundreds of warriors led by Crazy Horse, Gall, and other Sioux chiefs. "Come on Lakotas," Crazy Horse supposedly shouted while rallying his

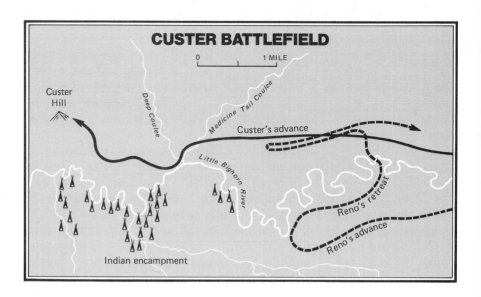

CUSTER BATTLEFIELD

men for the battle. "It's a good day to die!" The Indians attacked in such numbers that Reno frantically withdrew his men to a thicket of trees near the river, eventually ordering them to retreat to bluffs which overlooked the Little Bighorn from the west and north. By the time Reno's men (or what remained of them) — he would lose a third of his troopers that day — reached the bluffs, Benteen and his three companies had also begun riding in to join them. Together, after hurriedly digging in as best they could, the remnants of Reno's and Benteen's outnumbered companies fought off their attackers.

Neither officer knew what had become of Custer and his five companies. Whatever thoughts may have preoccupied George Armstrong Custer on the eve of battle remain lost to us. We do know that the exuberant officer, before leading his troops down a ridge to cross the river farther south, according to plan, displayed at least one evident sign that he had begun calculating the dimensions of the battle more realistically. A hastily scribbled message went off just prior to his attack: "BENTEEN. Come on. Big village. Be quick. Bring packs. P.S. Bring packs."

With that note dispatched, and possibly under the impression that Reno's men had routed the Sioux at the village's northern end, Custer led his men down a slope alongside the river to begin his charge. Within a matter of minutes, he and his troops found themselves fighting back a horde of attackers: Crazy Horse's Oglalas, the Cheyenne, Gall's Hunkpapas, and still other Sioux bands pressed toward the cavalry units to cut down any soldier they could reach.[5] Somehow, in the melee, Custer

---

[5] Although Sitting Bull was the better-known leader and the Hunkpapas' chief medicine man, Gall remained their most prominent leader in this and other battles.

managed to lead those of his men who remained alive and fighting up a high slope to mount a final defense. The troopers apparently tried to organize a defensive ring on the hill, but the Indians quickly surrounded them. Hundreds, possibly several thousand, warriors either shot arrows and fired at the soldiers from nearby shelters or rode relentlessly around the besieged enclave shouting taunts and firing at will.

Exactly when Custer died, or who killed him, remains unknown. Several leading Indian warriors later claimed to have killed Custer, but their accounts conflict. Most of the Sioux and Cheyenne in the battle did not even know Custer was present until the battle had ended. "He did not wear his long hair as he used to wear it," Sitting Bull said the following year, "but it was the color of the grass when the frost comes. . . . Where the last stand was made, the Long Hair stood like a sheaf of corn with all the ears fallen around him." It probably took the waves of Sioux and Cheyenne warriors less than an hour to ride through the small bloody ring of cavalrymen for the last time. To be certain that not a soldier remained alive, the Indians shot countless arrows and fired numerous rounds of ammunition into the fallen bodies.

Reno and Benteen had waited on the bluffs until mid-afternoon, unaware of Custer's fate, despite the fact that their Sioux and Cheyenne attackers had left to pursue Custer's units hours earlier. (Whether Reno should have ordered his men earlier to try and relieve Custer's embattled companies has remained a vigorously debated subject both in contemporary investigations of the episode and in later historical accounts.) Finally, one advance company led by Captain Thomas B. Weir moved downstream about a mile. Weir's men scaled a hill facing the direction from which shooting had been heard hours earlier. By then the shooting had stopped, and the smoke- and dust-filled battleground which lay in front of them prevented any clear recognition of the carnage. After being joined by Reno and the rest of his troops on the hill, the soldiers again came under attack by a number of Indians. Once more the Reno–Benteen forces were surrounded.

Retreating again to defensible positions on the bluffs overlooking the Little Bighorn, the 7th Cavalry survivors beat back continuing waves of attackers until dark. The Indians continued shooting arrows and bullets throughout the night. A smaller number of warriors resumed the assault on the following morning, but even these soon broke away after receiving word from scouts that a large column of soldiers (Terry's and Gibbon's troops) had been sighted marching up the Little Bighorn. By the time the main body of cavalry reached Reno and Benteen on the bluffs, Crazy Horse's entire force—several thousand Sioux and Cheyenne—had already left and were heading south toward the Bighorn Mountains.

A tour through the battleground showed that all of Custer's 212 men had died, along with another 47 from Reno's and Benteen's companies.[6] An additional 52 were wounded. Most of the dead bodies had

---

[6] One recent scholar has argued that available evidence indicates at least some of Custer's men committed suicide at the end—presumably fearing torture if captured—rather than fighting to the death, although all such hypotheses can never be adequately verified.

been scalped and completely stripped of clothing and equipment. Custer's corpse had one bullet in the head and another in the body but, although stripped, remained otherwise unmutilated.

The Indians retreated into the mountains for a long period of celebration. Their exact losses are unknown. After burying the dead, Crook and Terry led their commands into separate base camps away from the Bighorn to wait for reinforcements. Although the army already had two thousand soldiers available for battle to oppose possibly three thousand Sioux and Cheyenne warriors, and despite the army's preponderance in military equipment and firepower, neither Crook nor Terry thought it safe to pursue the Sioux and Cheyenne bands again before obtaining substantial additions to their units from the East. The Indians, meanwhile, gave no evidence after the battle at the Little Bighorn of preparing for a general assault on American soldiers elsewhere but returned to their normal lives now that the cavalry had withdrawn. For Crazy Horse, Sitting Bull, Gall, and the other chiefs, as for their followers, the summer of 1876 was a season of triumph. But how brief the season would prove to be.

In the East, Americans reacted to what quickly became known as the "massacre" of Custer and his men with an immediate sense of horror and outrage. The ambitious Custer achieved, in death, the measure of fame and public admiration—despite the persistence of detractors—that he had been denied during the years following the Civil War. Unfortunately for the Sioux, their defeat of Custer—and before that of Crook—had come in 1876, not merely in the midst of a presidential election year but in the middle of the nation's centennial celebration (capped by the great international exposition at Philadelphia). The Battle at the Little Bighorn shocked Easterners into recognizing that a major Indian war was in progress comparable to the ones that had been fought and won a decade earlier. For a time, public outcry led to a search for scapegoats. Military officers blamed Indian agents for misleading them about the number of warriors involved and for allowing hundreds of Indians to leave the reservations during the spring and join the hostile bands. In Washington, many officials in turn blamed the military officers for not crushing the Sioux outbreak in its earliest days. Custer's critics, meanwhile, accused him of disobeying orders and of recklessly risking the lives of his men in order to regain lost popularity and political influence. Custer's defenders pointed to the threat of an imminent Sioux attack on his unit, had he not attacked himself, and denied that Terry's instructions precluded a command decision on the spot such as the one made by Custer. Also they tried to shift some of the blame to Major Reno for failing to ride quickly enough to Custer's rescue. Most army officers appeared, however, to share General William Tecumseh Sherman's assessment that the *entire* campaign, including Custer's role in it, "had been planned on wrong premises," especially on the assumption that the Terry-Gibbon-Custer units would confront less than a thousand Indians. None of the army officers in the area anticipated confronting a Sioux-Cheyenne force of three to five thousand warriors.

This 1877 photograph of bones scattered on the Little Bighorn battlefield near the scene of Custer's final defense displays graphically the results of the Indian victory. (National Archives)

After Custer's defeat, the hardships of winter and the persistence of military campaigning against the Indians combined to destroy the ability of Sioux or Cheyenne to resist. The bands that had gathered at the Little Bighorn before battling Custer had all gone their separate ways in the months that followed. By the fall of 1876, both Crook and Terry felt sufficiently strong (and reinforced) to resume campaigning, this time in punitive expeditions, against those Indian groups that remained outside the reservations. In one of the most bizarre turnabouts of the entire struggle, hundreds of Sioux who had left their agencies to join Crazy Horse the previous spring now blithely returned for the winter, expecting to be fed and cared for without retribution until the following spring. The returnees discovered that army troops had taken over all of the Sioux agencies, however, and were confiscating guns, ammunition, and horses from all those who might have participated in the earlier battles against Crook and Custer.

Crazy Horse remained the major target for army military operations in the area, and on September 9, 1876, in northwestern South Dakota (north of the Black Hills), at Slim Buttes, the major military battle during the months following Custer's defeat occurred. A contingent of cavalry under Captain Anson Mills ran across the village of a Sioux chief named American Horse. Mills captured and destroyed the village, killing a number of Indians including American Horse, but not before American Horse managed to send word to Crazy Horse asking for help. Crook's main force reached the village shortly before Crazy Horse arrived with six hundred warriors. After firing at the soldiers from a distance, the Oglala chief and his band withdrew, clearly uninterested in further direct combat that year.

Instead Crazy Horse led his people into winter quarters near the Rosebud River in the Wolf Mountains. There, on January 8, 1877, an army unit under Colonel Nelson A. Miles, although smaller in number than the warriors encamped, attacked the village and routed the Indians. Throughout the winter months, army units pursued the remaining followers of Crazy Horse, a dwindling number each month, and many of these—although not the chief himself—surrendered as the snows came and the cold grew ever more bitter. A similar fate overtook Sitting Bull, Gall, and their Hunkpapas. Although the chiefs continued to hold out, a number of their followers drifted into the agencies during the winter to give themselves up. Finally, in February 1877, the two major Hunkpapa chiefs led several hundred Sioux diehards over the Canadian border into frigid sanctuary beyond the reach of American vengeance. Sitting Bull, and his followers, remained in Canada until July 1881, when he returned to surrender, bringing with him fewer than two hundred people. Even the Cheyennes, allies of the Sioux at the Little Bighorn, had been defeated by a unit of Crook's cavalry in December 1876 at Powder River, and their remnants joined Crazy Horse's remaining band.

With Sitting Bull safely established in Canada by the spring of 1877, Crazy Horse remained the only major holdout among all the rebellious chiefs of the previous year. He had watched in anguish as his people endured the winter freezing from lack of warm clothing, near starvation because of a shortage of food, and often desperately ill and dying. On May 6, 1877, responding apparently to messengers from Crook who falsely promised that Crazy Horse and his followers could have their own agency in the Powder River country, the great war chief led eleven hundred men, women, and children into the Red Cloud Agency to submit.[7] They marched in singing their own war songs, obviously anything but penitent. Crazy Horse surrendered personally to General Crook.

After he entered the agency, Crazy Horse was watched closely by the Indian scouts employed by the army. Crook and his officers suspected that their adversary was defeated but not subdued, and that he planned some further act of resistance. On September 4, Crook ordered out a huge combined force of cavalry and Indians to arrest Crazy Horse, who fled at first but was persuaded later that day to surrender. The following day, September 5, while waiting in a guard room at Fort Robinson, Crazy Horse recognized that he was being put into prison and drew a knife from under his blanket to resist. In the scuffle that followed, an Indian guard stabbed the Oglala chief. He dropped to the ground mortally wounded, supposedly crying out to those around him: "Let me go, my friends. You have hurt me enough."

But long before Crazy Horse met his end, the Sioux had lost their difficult struggle to retain Paha Sapa and the other lands that had been guaranteed them by treaty. So angry had Congress become at news of Cus-

---

[7] By that time, Red Cloud no longer ruled the Indians at the agency that bore his name. Under military orders, he had been deposed in favor of his rival, Spotted Tail, because he was suspected of complicity in the previous year's uprising.

ter's massacre that it delayed acting on appropriations for feeding and supplying the Sioux that winter. The bill that finally passed provided funds for the Sioux but contained a provision that no money would be granted until the Indians surrendered the Black Hills, Powder River, and Bighorn territories—the areas that the previous year's commissioners had unsuccessfully sought to purchase. In addition, the Sioux now had to agree to leave those areas for new reservations either on the Missouri River or within Indian Territory (later Oklahoma). The measure authorized another commission to proceed directly to the Sioux agencies to obtain agreement from the chiefs.

This time, the commission members found no rebellious Sioux threatening their negotiations with war dances and daring displays of horsemanship. They began their work at the Red Cloud Agency, if only because in the East most whites still considered Red Cloud the primary Sioux chief. After threatening the Indians there with possible starvation should they refuse to surrender the lands and agree to their own removal, the commissioners needed only two days to obtain the chiefs' signatures. (Nor did the negotiators even bother trying to observe the provision in the 1868 treaty with the Sioux stating that three-quarters of all adult males in the tribe had to approve new agreements with the United States.[8]) The commission members repeated this menacing approach at the other Sioux agencies, determining correctly that submission by Red Cloud's Oglalas would make the other Sioux bands even more reluctant to resist.

The Sioux tragedy now came round to its ironic final act. Although the chiefs present at the agencies reminded the commissioners that they had remained peaceful throughout the recent violence and had taken no part in the battles against the army, they were still being dealt with like conquered adversaries: forced to sign a treaty ending a war in which they had not fought, confiscating their lands and removing them from their homes. The threat of starvation finally compelled the chiefs to agree to the harsh terms. "Your words are like a man knocking me in the head with a stick," commented Standing Elk, one of the Sioux chiefs. "What you have spoken has put great fear upon us. Whatever we do, wherever we go, we are expected to say yes! yes! yes! yes!—and when we don't agree at once to what you ask of us in council, you always say, You won't get anything to eat! You won't get anything to eat!"

Agreement on the new treaty thus came quickly, and along with pursuit of the few remaining bands of "hostile" Sioux by General Crook's soldiers during the fall of 1876, it marked the end of the last major Sioux uprising. The struggle for control of the Black Hills and the central plains had ended.

---

[8] The Supreme Court, in a 1980 decision, ordered the U.S. government to pay the Sioux Indians 105 million dollars for its having illegally seized the Black Hills through this 1877 treaty. Sioux leaders rejected the payment, however, demanding the return of the Black Hills and 11 *billion* dollars in damages.

The West: Frontiers in Transition 26

T he West" may have been hard to fix precisely on a map during the nineteenth century, but the region (whatever its boundaries) remained critical to national development. It influenced America politically, economically, culturally, and in the realm of the imagination. In this sense, the destruction of Custer and his troops at the Little Bighorn during the American centennial year represented, for many in the country, an intolerable attempt to block the inevitable movement of white settlement into one of the remaining Western frontier areas. Along such frontier lines, the Sioux and other Indian groups had been engaged since the colonial period in last-ditch struggles to maintain their independence and to avoid subordination to white intruders. Crazy Horse's temporary triumph over the outnumbered cavalry in the Black Hills recapitulated earlier and equally short-lived Indian assaults on white soldiers and settlers invading their lands. The pattern could be traced as far back as the Pequot War along the New England Puritan frontier and to Powhatan's earliest attacks on the Jamestown settlement. Indian resistance could delay, but it could not halt, the onslaught of Americans hungry for Western land.

THE WESTERN FRONTIER: THEORY AND PRACTICE

During the second half of the nineteenth century, the American frontier "disappeared." The last remaining areas *beyond* the frontier line, which had been reserved by treaty for the various Indian nations, all fell prey to the dominant national passion for continued westward expansion.

The United States became a continental nation in this half century, as an outline of state admissions vividly demonstrates: California (1850), Minnesota (1858), Oregon (1859), Kansas (1861), Nevada (1864), Nebraska (1867), Colorado (1876), Montana (1889), Washington (1889), North and South Dakota (1889), Wyoming (1890), Idaho (1890), and Utah (1896).[1] The four decades separating the admission of California and the census of 1890 saw the constant movement of immigrants into the plains and Rocky Mountain areas, until cities, towns, and other settlements lined almost the entire previously unsettled interior of the country. "Up to and including 1880," the head of the U.S. census noted in his 1890 report, "the country had a frontier settlement, but at present the unsettled area has been so broken into by isolated bodies of settlement that there can hardly be said to be a frontier line."

Only three years after that official pronouncement, a historian named Frederick Jackson Turner pondered this monumental change. Turner, in an essay on "The Significance of the Frontier in American History," argued that the frontier had nurtured the characteristic political and cultural values of American democracy. "To the frontier," wrote Turner,

> the American intellect owes its striking characteristics: That coarseness and strength combined with acuteness and inquisitiveness; that practical, inventive turn of mind, quick to find expedients; that masterful grasp of material things . . . ; that restless, nervous energy; that dominant individualism . . . and withal that bouyancy and exu-

[1] Only the admission of Oklahoma (1907), New Mexico (1912), and Arizona (1912) remained in order to complete creation of states which Alaskans describe as "the lower forty-eight."

Homesteaders who have spread out their various possessions under makeshift shelters appear determined and confident in this 1889 photograph. "Holding Down a Lot in Guthrie," by C. P. Rich. (National Archives)

berance which comes with freedom—these are traits of the frontier, or traits called out elsewhere because of the existence of the frontier.

To the frontier, according to Turner, had come in every period first the traders and fur trappers exchanging goods with the Indians (and, in the process, altering and "destabilizing" traditional tribal patterns), then the farmers who pioneered in the wilderness and brought white communal settlement. Along with the farmers came miners (such as those who flooded into the Black Hills in the mid-1870s), artisans, lawyers, doctors, and businessmen until the frontier region in question became thoroughly "civilized." Many of its earliest white inhabitants—traders, trappers, farmers, and possibly miners—had moved on by then to new frontiers farther westward. Turner's formulation contained within it elements of hard truth and more than a bit of the romantic mythology Americans have always associated with Western frontier regions. Thus on the frontier, Turner found a "perennial rebirth" of society and of those "forces dominating American character."

What had made all this possible, of course, was the existence of a vast area of "free," or at least cheap, land—"the Western wilds, from the Alleghe-

nies to the Pacific"—which, scarcely a generation before Turner, Americans had thought virtually inexhaustible only to learn differently. One historian, commenting on Turner's work, described the American frontier aptly as that portion of settlement "at the edge of the unused."

Subsequent historians have criticized harshly a number of Turner's specific theories concerning the significance of the frontier for American national development and national character. Among other things, Turner deeply underestimated the role played by inherited values brought into the wilderness or frontier areas from either foreign countries or Eastern settled areas. And he had only a crude understanding of how so-called "frontier" values actually reflected complex patterns of belief which had emerged in a variety of American environments. Turner also never fully considered the degree to which *urban* growth and not westward movement along the frontier served as the primary "safety valve" (a favorite Turner term) for rural discontent, with the cities receiving the bulk of surplus agrarian population by the mid-nineteenth century.

Whatever the validity of his critics' judgments, Turner's writings expressed profoundly the old Jeffersonian dream of a small-holder agrarian republic, extending itself across the entire continent in an age of rapid and massive technological change. "American democracy," wrote Turner, "was born of no theorist's dream; it was not carried in the *Susan Constant* to Virginia, nor in the *Mayflower* to Plymouth. It came out of the American forest, and it gained new strength each time it touched a new frontier. Not the Constitution, but free land and an abundance of natural resources open to a fit people, made the democratic type of society in America for three centuries." Individualism and American nationalism, along with democracy, seemed largely frontier products to Turner. His observations applied, of course, *only* to white settlers along the frontier. The Indian tribes, and blacks forced to follow the Southern frontier trail, participated in the process of moving the frontier farther westward largely in the role of either impediments to American development or perennial victims of its success.

**THE LAST FRONTIER,
c.1860-1890**

┼┼┼┼ Railroads
••••••• Cattle trails
⚒ Mining sites
🐂 Cattle raising areas after 1880

0   100   200   300 MILES

GOVERNMENT LAND POLICIES AND WESTERN SETTLEMENT

Earlier in the nineteenth century, despite the expansionist energies evident among Americans from the time of the Louisiana Purchase (1803) to the annexation of Texas (1845), it seemed possible that the Indians might be left undisturbed in a "Permanent Indian Frontier" (the government's term) within the Rockies, the Great Plains,

and what some referred to as the Great American Desert. Explorers, traders, and fur trappers continued to intrude into these areas. They included Lewis and Clark on their path-breaking journey, Zebulon Pike's Southwest travels (1806–7), and William Ashley's trip up the Missouri to the Rocky Mountains which began in 1822. Yet the American government still pursued a policy of creating Indian "reservations" in the plains for tribes, such as the Cherokees, displaced from Eastern lands.

These reservations were supervised by agents from the Bureau of Indian Affairs, created in 1824 under the War Department. Then the relentless pressures of Western settlement—which exploded in 1848 with the discovery of gold in California and later with the prospects of wealth through mining gold and silver in the Rockies—brought hundreds of thousands of new settlers into what would become Colorado, Nevada, Montana, the Dakotas, and elsewhere. The rush into the Black Hills beginning in 1874 was only a late phase in this process.

When tribal lands became attractive or valuable to white settlers, as in the case of the Sioux and Paha Sapa, the government invariably declined to enforce its treaty obligations and began dislodging the Indian population by force if necessary. Just as a number of Southern tribes were driven westward during the 1830s on the deadly "Trail of Tears" and on other occasions (see Chapter 14), so the bulk of Indians in the Old Northwest were forced from that area during the 1840s. Andrew Jackson probably spoke for most white Americans of his day when he stated the issue in his usual blunt manner: "What good man would prefer a country covered with forests and ranged by a few thousands to our extensive Republic, studded with cities, towns, and prosperous farms, embellished with all the improvements which art can devise or industry execute, occupied by more than 12 million happy people?" The policy of Indian removal accelerated in both North and South during the Jackson era, creating the conditions for conflict in subsequent decades farther west once pressures for more "removals" resumed during the 1860s. The sweep of American settlement westward made the Indian wars on the plains and elsewhere in the Far West virtually inevitable.

Although settlement of the West had proceeded without strong assistance from the national government until the Civil War, the process accelerated with passage of the Homestead Act (1862). Any citizen or immigrant seeking citizenship, who was twenty-one or—if younger—the head of a family, could obtain 160 acres of land free, after payment of a small registration fee. The land became the settler's property after living on it for five years. Alternatively, homesteaders could *buy* land from the government for $1.25 per acre after living

on it for only six months. The Homestead Act helped, to some extent, to create a class of small land-holding farmers in the West. Between 400,000 and 500,000 homesteaders settled on over 80 million acres of public domain land under the act.

Unfortunately, these land claims represented less than one-sixth of the total public domain lands disposed of by the government (or held back from disposal) under the Homestead Act. Most Western settlers continued to purchase non-Homestead land, either buying publicly owned lands directly from local, state, or federal governments or buying land from the railroads, which, themselves, received vast amounts of acreage from the national government and the states. The Central Pacific and Union Pacific alone obtained through congressional authorization a bonanza in public land: ten square miles for every mile of track it completed (twenty square miles in federal territories). During the last half of the nineteenth century, railroad companies obtained from the states and the U.S. government over 180 million acres, more than double the total amount dispensed to individuals under the Homestead Act. In some Western states, the railroads and land speculators owned up to a quarter or more of the total available land.

Railroad entrepreneurship in the West began during the 1860s at a time when transportation from the East came either through a difficult overland route by stage coach or through travel by ship, either around the coast of South America or with a land connection across the Isthmus of Panama. In all cases, the routes were long and often dangerous. Wagon train caravans moving along the Oregon Trail during the 1840s or 1850s, for example, confronted the threat of Indian attacks throughout the journey despite the treaties (described in Chapter 29) which tried to minimize the danger. Only a small number of widely scattered army garrisons along the trail protected settlers and migrants. Nor, for the most part, were routes westward such as the Oregon Trail genuine "roads"; they merely traversed the existing land without improving it. Travel to the Pacific Coast from St. Louis, the last major link to the settled East, generally took three to four weeks before the Civil War, and a journey by ship could take much longer.

Despite the development of transcontinental railroads, stagecoaches such as this typical Concord type, continued to crisscross the Western states and territories, well-guarded against bandits and Indian attacks (as seen in this 1867 photograph). (National Archives)

The mail traveled faster, especially after imaginative businessmen established a "pony express" service between St. Joseph, Missouri, and Sacramento, California, in 1860. Riders carrying mail pouches in relays, alternating at stations along the route, cut the westbound travel time to a week and a half. The telegraph line reached the West Coast in 1861, allowing news from the East to circulate nationwide in a matter of moments. The coming of the railroads westward then com-

A railroad line spanning the continent would not have been possible without the help of thousands of Chinese laborers, who did much of the work on the Central Pacific. (Southern Pacific Railroad)

pleted the process of creating an efficient system of transcontinental travel and communication. Railroad investors profited enormously in construction of the Western tracks from government land policies during the post–Civil War era.[2]

Corporations, speculators, lumbermen, and mining interests also profited from several other laws passed during these decades. Their intent—like that of the Homestead Act—had been more admirable than their results. Three statutes passed during the 1870s resulted in benefiting large land purchasers more than small homesteaders. The Timber Culture Act of 1873, which granted an additional 160 acres to those homesteaders who planted trees on a quarter of their acreage, worked to the benefit of ranchers and speculators, not small farmers. So, too, did the Desert Land Act of 1877, which extended to homesteaders the right to claim 640 acres of land in return for a promise to irrigate the dry acres within three years. The measure often helped large ranchers to acquire free grazing lands and miners to stake additional claims—in both cases *without* irrigating more than nominal amounts of the public domain. The Timber and Stone Act of 1878, another "bonanza" measure, allowed purchases of a maximum of 160 acres of forest land in the West for $2.50 an acre. It proved invaluable to lumber companies, ranchers, and land speculators, all of whom used "dummy" purchasers—individuals who signed over acreage just purchased to the *real* buyers—in order to gain millions of acres at nominal cost.

In the South alone, much of the 47 million acres of public domain that Congress set aside in 1866 to provide small homesteads (eight acres each) ended, within a decade, in the hands of speculators. Congress finally had to repeal the legislation and open the land for general purchase. Although several attempts were made by legislators during the 1889–91 period to reduce speculation in public lands, it was too late. The bulk of America's public lands in the West had already fallen under the control of wealthy investors, railroad companies, mining and lumbering interests, large ranchers, and business corporations.

---

[2] For a discussion of railroad growth in the decades following the Civil War, see Chapter 30, pp. 574–576.

THE INDIAN FRONTIER

Even Indian removal and forced resettlement on isolated reservations did not insulate the tribes completely from contact with whites. In California alone, the hundred thousand new Gold Rush migrants of 1848–52 often confronted local Indians, sometimes with disastrous results. An estimated fifty thousand Indians died from diseases brought by the whites after the discovery of gold in 1848.

Throughout the Western territories, such epidemics decimated the Indians during the 1840s and 1850s. The diseases were carried originally by whites passing through Indian lands on their way to farm or prospect, but many Indians (understandably) came to believe that whites *deliberately* spread the infections in order to weaken Indian resistance. Smallpox and cholera, especially, plagued a number of tribes—including the Mandans, Comanches, and Kiowas—making white penetration of territories previously held by the Indians far easier.

The U.S. Army, though small, played an important role. As hundreds of thousands of miners and farmers spread out through the prairie and mountain regions during the 1850s, military units scattered through the area attempted to negotiate safe passages across Indian lands for the caravans of "prairie schooners" and mining expeditions. (Such discussions concerning the Oregon Trail, for example, brought the army and Sioux into continuous contact while negotiating treaties in 1851 and 1856.) Passage of the Kansas–Nebraska Act in 1854 (see Chapter 22, p. 424) and renewed interest in westward migration during the 1850s led to increased pressures upon Indian nations to renegotiate earlier treaties and to surrender to the United States lands previously granted the tribes (as the Sioux did in 1856). Such "negotiations" led to the United States obtaining almost 18 million acres from Indian tribes as a result of twelve treaties signed in 1854 alone, with the Indians retaining less than 10 percent of the lands supposedly guaranteed by earlier agreements. Rarely did federal troops or authorities try to protect Indian treaty rights against the intrusions of new settlers, whether in Kansas during the 1850s or anywhere

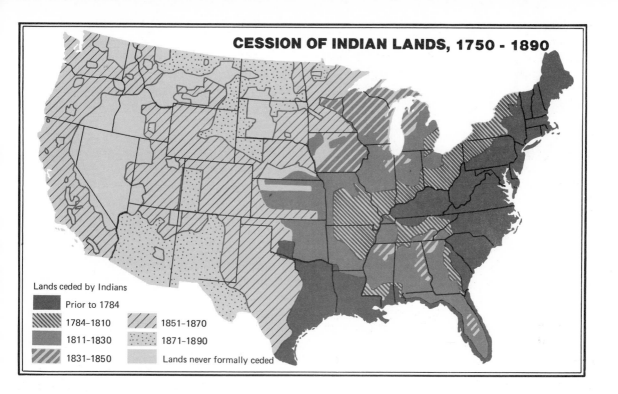

CESSION OF INDIAN LANDS, 1750 - 1890

Lands ceded by Indians
- Prior to 1784
- 1784–1810
- 1811–1830
- 1831–1850
- 1851–1870
- 1871–1890
- Lands never formally ceded

else in the West. White officials generally adopted a cynical attitude toward the validity and permanence of these pacts.

When the Indians finally began resisting white expansion during the early 1860s, the Western tribes often found themselves better prepared to fight back than they had been earlier. The plains Indian warriors had a measure of mobility through fighting on horesback, and they enjoyed a dependable source of food and provisions from the buffalo herds. White hunters began destroying the herds partly to sell food to railroad workers and skins to fur traders but also, in part, to deprive the Indians of this resource. The vast areas over which the Western tribes now roamed, moreover, afforded numerous retreats where they could regroup and plan surprise attacks on settlers and soldiers alike.

During the Civil War, neither North nor South managed to recruit reliable support to any significant degree among the Western tribes. The Indians remained divided on whether they had much to gain from backing either the Union or the Confederacy. But the war years did bring renewal of the earlier struggles between Indians and American military forces, this time along the Western frontier.

The Indian Wars

The conflicts reached as far east as Minnesota, where large bands of Santee Sioux raided settlements in less sparsely populated areas, killing over five hundred until defeated. Many of the Santee Sioux involved in the "Great Uprising" fled to the plains, where they joined other branches of the Sioux people in continuing resistance. As federal troops began returning East from Western garrisons after the outbreak of the Civil War, Apaches, Navahos, and other Southwestern tribes stepped up their raids on virtually unprotected mining towns and camps. Both Confederate and Union officials responded angrily to the assaults, and after a punitive expedition led by the former frontiersman and current Union officer Kit Carson, both the Navahos and Apaches were forced onto reservations.

Contemporaries viewing this photograph would have been surprised to find, in these unlikely formal and Eastern clothes, Kit Carson—the most famous explorer and "mountain man" of his era. Carson's exploits were popularized throughout the country in the mid-nineteenth century through biographies, novels, and Western travel books. (Brown Brothers)

Farther north, the influx of miners into Colorado after 1858, when gold was discovered, led to conflicts with the Cheyenne and Arapahos. (Discoveries of silver in Nevada's Comstock Lode in 1859, followed by new gold and silver finds in Idaho and Montana during the next half-decade led to comparable mining booms in those territories.) Three years of sporadic warfare in Colorado followed, pitting Union soldiers against both Cheyennes and Arapahos, when the Indians refused to be herded onto a small reservation near the upper Arkansas River at Sand Creek.

Both tribes raided and killed widely, stirring widespread anger throughout the territory among white settlers before they negotiated what the Indians believed was a peace treaty with Colorado officials. Led by Black Kettle and Little Antelope, the Cheyenne and Arapaho then moved to nearby Sand Creek. There, in late November 1864, a thousand Colorado militiamen, led by a Protestant minister, Colonel J. M. Chivington, surprised the Indians and massacred at least half of the five hundred persons in the camp. Chivington's militia killed everyone, women and children included. They behaved so barbarically that Colonel (later General) Nelson A. Miles denounced the Sand Creek Massacre as the "foulest and most unjustifiable crime in the annals of America."

In the East, a number of Americans protested the massacre bitterly. Denunciations filled the press and sparked congressional debate. But Chivington resigned from the militia in order to escape court-martial. He remained a hero to local settlers and returned to Denver, where he displayed before theater audiences more than a hundred Indian scalps taken by whites at Sand Creek. Within a year, a number of tribes in Colorado and surrounding areas—including the Arapaho, Cheyenne, Comanche, and Kiowa—had been forced to accept smaller reservations in isolated areas far from white settlements and to give up their treaty claims to more attractive land now occupied or coveted by Americans.

Hardly had the Indians in Colorado been "pacified" when military action began against the Sioux in Montana and Wyoming. Again the immediate cause of hostilities was the intrusion of white miners into territory previously guaranteed by treaty to the Indians. The struggle over constructing the Bozeman Trail from Montana's mining camps and the new forts along the trail led, as we have seen, to the ambush of Captain Fetterman's command in 1866, followed by two years of skirmishing between Indian and white man. In the end, the army abandoned the Bozeman Trail and the forts, at least temporarily, and the Sioux agreed to a new treaty in 1868 which brought six years of peace to the region until Custer led his expedition into the Black Hills in 1874. Much of the conflict which followed over the next three years involved differing views of the 1868 treaty, which stated that the Sioux would settle under supervision of government agents on smaller and more isolated reservations than they were willing to accept.

The reservation settlement policy extended to other Indian tribes elsewhere in the West. In the decade which followed the signing of the 1868 treaty with the Sioux, the Colorado tribes as well as the Blackfeet, Crow, Mandan, Pawnee, Osage, and Shoshoni Indians all encamped in newer, more compact reservations outside the main areas of white settlement. The Indians did not accept calmly the humiliations of forced resettlement. Between 1871 and 1886, federal troops fought a continuing war against the Apache in the Southwest, for example, which ended only with the capture in 1886 of Geronimo, the tribe's last prominent war leader. The Modocs rose up in 1872–73, and from 1875 to 1877, as Chapter 25 described in detail, the Teton Sioux and Cheyenne fought effectively for a time against General Crook's better-equipped and better-supplied forces in South Dakota and Montana. Even earlier, between 1868 and 1874, General Sherman's officers and men in the West engaged in over two hundred battles with Indian tribes to subjugate those that remained unwilling to accept the new, smaller, and usually more isolated reservation agencies as their homes.

Possibly the most gallant and imaginative of the Indian insurgents at this time was the leader of the Nez Percés, whom whites called Chief Joseph but whose people knew him as Heinmot Tooyalakekt—"thunder traveling to loftier mountain heights." The name proved prophetic. Bands of Nez Percés traditionally had roamed the states of Oregon, Montana, Washington, and Idaho. The favored home of many in the tribe, equivalent in importance to the Nez Percés as Paha Sapa (the Black Hills) was to the Teton Sioux, was the Wallowa Valley in the Oregon Territory. This area had been granted to the Nez Percés by an 1855 treaty with the Americans but was soon taken back under the provisions of another treaty in 1863 reducing tribal lands. The tribe was assigned in 1863 to a small reservation in Montana near the Washington border, miles from its beloved Wallowa Valley. "Old Joseph," then chief of the Nez Percés, and two-thirds of the other chiefs would not sign the 1863 treaty, and for the next decade, conflicts arose over land claims.

Old Joseph died in 1873, the same year that President Grant reversed the 1863 treaty and designated the Wallowa Valley "as a reservation for the roaming Nez Percé Indians." Grant, responding to

In this dramatic photograph, Chief Joseph of the Nez Percés, who led the most extraordinary defensive campaign of the Indian Wars of the 1870s, displays the self-possession and dignity that won him many white as well as Indian admirers. (Brown Brothers)

support for the tribe's claims among Eastern politicians and reformers, ordered white settlers to leave the Wallowa. But older white residents refused to budge and additional wagon trains of homesteaders continued to arrive. The Nez Percés were threatened with having to fight to regain the Wallowa, despite Grant's decision, and in 1875, still another presidential order reversed the 1873 statement and reopened the Wallowa to American settlement. Grant's reversal showed how frail even the most reasonable Indian land claim could seem to government officials when confronted with pressures for expanded white settlement. Conferences in 1876 between Old Joseph's son, Chief Joseph, new leader of the tribe, and American military officers and Indian agents proved futile. The Nez Percés were ordered to return to their designated reservation by April 1877 (just as the Sioux had been instructed to return to *their* agencies by January 31, 1877, during the events which led to the confrontation between Crazy Horse and Custer).

Chief Joseph had opposed war with the American settlers and soldiers. But in his absence, small bands of Nez Percé warriors had attacked and killed parties of whites. Although the fatalities numbered less than twenty, alarmed whites in the Far West feared a general uprising of Nez Percés. The reluctant Joseph found himself forced to lead his aroused tribe into battle. The Indians won an initial victory against a combined force of U.S. cavalry and volunteer militia, leaving thirty-four whites dead while incurring almost no losses themselves. In the months that followed, additional companies of soldiers were dispatched to defeat Joseph's warriors, who numbered less than two hundred.

Finally the Nez Percés retreated eastward greatly outnumbered by the pursuing army units. Never has a retreating force in American history performed more gallantly. The amazing march of the Nez Percés (who included five hundred women and children) covered almost a thousand miles. On several occasions, when Joseph and his men stopped to fight back, they inflicted heavy losses on the cavalry. The Indians continued to beat back the American soldiers pursuing them while moving across Idaho, Wyoming, and Montana. Units of cavalry finally closed in on the Nez Percés on September 30, 1877, less than thirty miles from safe refuge at the Canadian border on the northern tier of the Bear Paw Mountains. The fighting became fierce for several days, after which the soldiers settled in for a siege. Bitter cold and snow flurries made life agonizing for survivors in the Indian camp.

Chief Joseph decided to surrender on October 4. The following day, he rode into the army lines to capitulate personally to Colonel Nelson Miles. (Only Crazy Horse's surrender to General Crook the previous May matched this moment of drama during the Indian wars of that era.) It was here that Chief Joseph made the remarks which brought this extraordinary Indian leader and his people the admiration and sympathy of many white Americans:

I am tired of fighting. Our chiefs are killed. . . . It is cold and we have no blankets. The little children are freezing to death. My people, some of them, have run away to the hills, and have no blankets, no food . . . . Hear me, my chiefs, I am tired; my heart is sick and sad. From where the sun now stands, I will fight no more forever.

Joseph and the other Nez Percés were taken by railroad car and flatboats to the Indian Territory, before being allowed to return to a reservation in Washington—though not to the Wallowa Valley—in 1885.

More Indians starved or perished from diseases brought by white settlers than died through battle wounds. Unless the Indians accepted supplies from the agencies run by government officials on reservations and at forts, they found food becoming scarcer. Professional buffalo hunters, collecting hides for tanning, slaughtered an estimated 13 million of the animals in the two decades after the Civil War. The great herds upon which plains Indian tribes had previously depended for a reliable food supply and other needs were exterminated. By 1883, an expedition found only two hundred buffalo left in the entire West. Thus was created the Indians' dependence upon food and other supplies obtained at reservation agencies.

Far fewer died in battle on either side than from other causes. An estimated five thousand Indians perished in military combat with armed whites during the Indian wars of the nineteenth century, while seven to eight thousand whites died in the conflicts. The figures suggest that, for all the extended brutality of the wars and the bitterness engendered on both sides, Indian tribal autonomy was destroyed as much through the combined toll of diseases brought by whites and the destruction of traditional hunting grounds as through military defeats. Once the railroads had ensured a steady supply of military resources where needed throughout the West, as well as an ever-growing community of white settlers who could not be forced out, the final traces of tribal independence in the region were doomed. Indians were left with the difficult choice of retreating onto the impoverished reservations and remaining dependent upon food and supplies provided by government officials, trying to assimilate into the hostile white settler communities, or making an armed last-stand fight against overwhelming odds. After the 1870s, even that third choice was largely foreclosed.

From the Dawes Act to the Ghost Dance

An Indian chief once suggested sardonically that American whites should place the Indians on wheels to make it easier to transport them from old reservations to new ones. So often had the tribes been forced from land "guaranteed" by treaty during the nineteenth century that many of them were not surprised when the American government, in the name of a "reformed" Indian policy, decided in the 1880s to try to break up the reservations themselves. The new policy had been brewing in the American imagination for some years. Eastern philanthropists and other self-professed friends of the Indians, horrified at the mistreatment of the Western tribes by Indian agents and settlers, began during the 1870s to believe that the best method of "humanizing" their condition was to transform the Indians into "civilized" yeoman farmers akin to the white settlers. The essential elements in the new policy involved destroying tribal influence over individual Indians, converting to Christianity all Indians alienated from their tribes, educating them, and teaching them to farm. Once this process had been completed, the "problem" of the American Indian would approach solution. So the reformers believed.

Anthropologists would later call such policies an effort to encourage "behavioral assimilation" by the Indians, "acculturation" to the larger American society. Writers such as Helen Hunt Jackson, in her indictment of government policy toward the Indians in *A Century of Dishonor* (1881) and her novel *Ramona* (1884), accepted this policy, as did virtually all those in the Eastern states—and in the American government—who considered themselves sympathetic to the problem. Unless Indians learned to adjust to white culture, the reformers argued, either they would be destroyed in a renewal of futile skirmishing with *un*friendly whites seeking reservation lands or their old tribal culture would gradually die out as they failed to adapt.

The new policy came into effect with the passage of the Dawes Severalty Act of 1887. Under that act, which formed the basis of U.S. government policy toward the Indian tribes until the 1930s, individual Indians and their families would receive 160 acres of land each in exchange for leaving the tribal reservations and trying to function like a comparable white farmer in the same area. Indians were being tempted away from their defeated *collective* identities within the tribes, in effect, and urged to assume new (and totally unfamiliar) lives as self-sufficient farmers, for which few of them had the training or values at the time. To guard against the type of cynical speculation that had affected other land distribution statutes, the government retained title to the 160 acres for a quarter century, although Indians could lease the lands (and often did at minimal cost to whites who took advantage of the Dawes Act to add to their own holdings).

The Dawes Act obviously accelerated the destruction of American Indian culture. Reservations were broken up, and much of the acreage formerly "owned" by Indian tribes became the property of white ranchers, farmers, and speculators. Indians, who had enjoyed at least nominal possession of 135 million acres in the 1880s, had lost almost two-thirds of this by the 1930s, when the policy came to an end. A well-intentioned, but patronizing, effort to help Indians assimilate into white American society reinforced, over time, the American Indian's isolation and subordination.

During the late 1880s, the plains Indians made one brief and belated attempt to revive tribal identity and dignity. It began in a religious mode comparable to what anthropoligists would call a "revitalization movement." It ended in stark tragedy.

There emerged among the Paiute Indians of Nevada during these years a self-proclaimed "prophet" and preacher named Wovoka, also known as Jack Wilson, who insisted that—while in an unconscious state due to illness in 1888—he had received messages from the Indian Great Spirit. Wovoka began preaching a message of redemption and insurgency: The buffalo herds would reappear on the plains; whites would leave the area and their society be destroyed; Indian tribal cultures would once again reign over the entire West.

The new prophet cautioned against attempting any violent rebellion to drive out the whites, preaching instead the crucial importance of renewing ancient Indian spiritual beliefs through practicing a series of songs and dances—especially a ceremony that became known as the "Ghost Dance." The news of Wovoka's messianic teachings spread quickly throughout the tribal reservations on the Great Plains and inspired thousands of Indians. Many took up the Ghost Dance, especially younger ones who—in an earlier age—would have been earning their place in the tribe as warriors but were now confined instead to an inactive and humiliating existence.

As the Ghost Dance spread among the tribes, Wovoka's nonviolent message of eventual redemption (obviously influenced by Christian missionary preaching) became translated into angrier and more militant preachments. Many would-be tribal warriors prepared for some form of armed conflict with the whites, apparently in the belief that special shirts sanctified in the Ghost Dance ceremonies could repel soldiers' bullets. Older tribal leaders, many of whom had fought in the earlier wars, knew better but were hard-pressed to keep the new movement in check. Federal troops were placed on alert throughout the region, and Indian agents on several reservations warned of possible armed outbreaks. Fearful white farmers again kept their guns close at hand and waited.

The confrontation between followers of the Ghost Dance and federal authorities came in 1890 and, as a generation earlier, it again pitted the Sioux (including, among others, the venerable Sitting Bull) against the 7th Cavalry. Many of those troopers who had either fought at the Little Bighorn fourteen years earlier or had lived with its memories now awaited a final moment of retribution. The troopers, prepared for combat, occupied portions of one Sioux reservation and, after a series of inconclusive encounters between insurgent Indians and the cavalry, the focus of unrest shifted to Sitting Bull's Standing Rock Reservation. There, the Indian agent, a long-time enemy of the old In-

dian chief, believing that the chief intended to join Ghost Dance warriors on the neighboring Pine Ridge Reservation, sent a unit of Indian police to arrest Sitting Bull in mid-December 1890. After some scuffling between Sitting Bull's followers and the Indian police, the chief and several of his warriors were killed.

Settlers and soldiers in the region feared that Sitting Bull's death foreshadowed a major uprising of the entire remaining Sioux Nation, a revolt led by the Ghost Dance movement's leaders, Kicking Bear and Short Bull. In fact, no such rebellion took place. Instead, a Sioux chief named Big Foot, who sought to negotiate an end to the troubles, traveled to Pine Ridge. Big Foot's band was overtaken by the 7th Cavalry and escorted to a site near Pine Ridge called Wounded Knee.

The accumulated tensions of the entire region finally exploded into violence at Wounded Knee. There, on December 29, 1890, while the cavalry was in the process of disarming the Indians, the troops watched as a medicine man intoning Ghost Dance songs stirred a young Indian into shouting while waving his rifle in a threatening manner. A scuffle between cavalrymen and the Indian ensued, a shot was fired, a few other Indians began shooting at the troops, and the cavalry opened fire. By the time the gunfire subsided, several hundred Indians had been killed or wounded, a third of them women and children. Smaller skirmishes between Ghost Dance warriors and soldiers occurred elsewhere in the region, but the movement was soon completely suppressed. With the collapse of the Ghost Dance movement, the plains Indians concluded their last tragic episode in a long and losing nineteenth-century battle for survival.

THE MINING FRONTIER

The gold rush that sent thousands of miners into the Black Hills of South Dakota during the mid-1870s and precipitated the conflict between the Teton Sioux and the American army was the last of several major mining discoveries in the trans-Mississippi West which brought in their wake rapid influxes of white settlers. In each case, territories which had previously been sparsely

populated and relatively tolerant of Indian tribes living contiguously to white enclaves suddenly became inhospitable to the Indians. The pressures of mining communities for military protection, access roads, and freedom to explore lands previously guaranteed by treaty to the Indians led inexorably throughout the West to the armed conflicts that triggered Indian uprisings during the 1860s and 1870s. Another consequence of the mining frontier's spread throughout the western third of the United States was imposition of a tough "reservation" policy designed to ensure maximum isolation and supervision of the Indians.

Over a hundred thousand new settlers from the Eastern states and a number of foreign countries entered California within a year after gold was discovered there in 1848. Ambitious miners spread out not only across California's hills but, beginning in the 1850s, moved into Nevada, Idaho, and other territories in search of precious metals. During the 1850s, mining camps became firmly established not only in these areas but also in Montana, Oregon, Arizona, Wyoming, and Colorado. Although the two greatest "booms" occurred in Colorado and Nevada, often overlooked in discus-

sions of the mining frontier was the remarkable degree of mobility exhibited by prospectors throughout this period. Individuals generally brought only a small amount of gear and equipment with them, making it possible to move quickly from place to place following the trail of rumors announcing major gold or silver "strikes." The overwhelming majority of miners, moreover, were either single men or, if married, their families were elsewhere so that they were free to pursue their fortune. Towns sprang up quickly at the site of each new mining boom, as thousands of prospectors and those who profited from them—restaurant and saloon operators, storekeepers, assayers, gamblers, prostitutes, and hotel keepers—clustered in the mining communities of the Far West. Virginia City (Nevada), Silver City and Boise (Idaho), Bozeman and Helena (Montana), Denver and Central City (Colorado), and similar towns grew and declined with equal rapidity, depending upon the nearby mining prospects.

When gold deposits were found near Pike's Peak in Colorado in 1858, almost as many prospectors headed for that territory as had descended upon California a decade earlier. Along the dif-

Mark Twain

Born Samuel Langhorne Clemens in the "western" frontier village of Florida, Missouri, on November 30, 1835, the writer who later called himself "Mark Twain" embodied in his career, his personal style, and his imaginative themes the region of his boyhood. As with many other Americans during this period, Samuel's father had often resettled, speculating on higher land values. From Virginia, the elder Clemens traveled to Kentucky, Tennessee, and Missouri, settling finally in Hannibal, Missouri, when Samuel was four.

Although he later exploited portions of his boyhood life in books such as *The Adventures of Tom Sawyer* (1876), *Huckleberry Finn* (1885), and *Life on the Mississippi* (1883), only long after

Samuel Clemens left Hannibal did the town and the area preoccupy his literary concerns. At first, the restless boy began to wander in search of adventure and not wealth, as in his father's case, though in his mature years Mark Twain pursued riches passionately in life while demeaning it in literature. But for young Samuel, as later for Huckleberry Finn, the Mississippi River town of Hannibal seemed to have settled down too quickly to a staid and mundane pattern of daily life. To watch the steamboats plying up and downriver, as Samuel often did, became an inexorable goad to travel after the elder Clemens's death.

At the age of seventeen, Samuel left Hannibal and spent the next few years as an apprentice to a newspaper publisher and then as a journeyman printer under his older brother Orion. During the mid-1850s, he traveled to St. Louis, New York, and Philadelphia, taking various printing jobs along the way. At one point, the adventurous youth entertained a scheme to harvest cocoa in South America's Amazon country, only to discover in New Orleans in 1856: "When . . . I inquired about ships leaving for [Brazil] . . . that there weren't any and . . . that there probably wouldn't be any during that century." So much for the *South* American frontier. Apparently undaunted, Samuel gained a position on a Mississippi River boat, first as an apprentice and then as a pilot. From this experience came his literary pseudonym, Mark Twain, a river term meaning two fathoms deep.

After the outbreak of the Civil War, Twain's opportunity for adventure (though not fighting) had arrived. Through the influence of a friend in Lincoln's cabinet, his brother received an appointment as a secretary to the governor of the Nevada

ferent trails into Colorado, thousands of wagons emblazoned with emblems announcing the miners' destination (the most famous of which was the oft-repeated "Pike's Peak or Bust!") brought an onslaught of new residents. Most of them reached either that location or some other likely spot in the Colorado gold fields, but few of them prospered. Those who found no precious metals in Colorado then often headed farther west in 1859 to the

newly discovered gold and silver fields of Nevada's "Comstock Lode," where prospectors tapped the largest deposits of silver ever located in the continental United States. Others traveled to Idaho and Montana where gold and silver were found.

Certain developments proved to be common to most of these frontier mining territories in addition to their unfriendly treatment of local Indians. To maintain law and order within the new mining

Territory. Twain became his brother's personal secretary, a post virtually without duties, which allowed him time (among other things) to begin a new vocation in Nevada—then the site of a mining boom—as a frontier journalist. From these adventures in the West would come *Roughing It* (1872), a lively descriptive account of the miners, lumberjacks, and other frontier characters encountered by Twain intertwined with the exaggerated tales that characterized Western humor.

Twain himself had tried his hand at mining before becoming a reporter in 1862. His account of Virginia City, Nevada, during the silver boom especially delighted Eastern readers (and reads almost like one of the Aztec descriptions of Cortez's men's pursuit of precious metals):

> Joy sat on every countenance, and there was a glad, almost fierce intensity in every eye, that told of the money-getting schemes that were seething in every brain and the high hope that held sway in every heart. Money was a plenty as dust; every individual considered himself wealthy, and a melancholy countenance was nowhere to be seen. There were military companies, brass bands, banks, hotels, theatres, "hurdy-gurdy houses," wide-open gambling palaces, political pow-wows, civic processions, street fights, murders, inquests, riots, a whiskey mill every fifteen steps . . . .

In California Twain produced the story that brought him almost immediate national fame. He had fled to San Francisco from a Nevada felony indictment after challenging the editor of a rival paper to a duel. There, in 1864, Twain heard a tale about an unusual jumping frog which he later used in "The Celebrated Jumping Frog of Calaveras County." The master of a frog named Daniel wagered that his pet could outjump all others, but a stranger outwitted him by slipping Daniel a dose of quail shot:

> "Then he says, 'One-two-three-git!' and him and the feller touched up the frogs from behind, and the new frog hopped off lively, but Dan'l give a heave, and hysted up his shoulders—so—like a Frenchman, but it warn't no use—he couldn't budge. . . ."

Twain's use of authentic Western dialect caught the imaginations of Americans, and the story—which first appeared in *The New York Saturday Press*—was quickly reprinted in newspapers throughout the country. Twain's first "travel" book, *The Innocents Abroad* (1869), brought him national popularity as a humorist, in great demand both as a writer and as a lecturer. In the decades ahead, he moved East, settling in Hartford, Connecticut, into a varied career as writer, publisher, and businessman. The public valued his genius as a novelist, essayist, and travel narrator. Although his themes ranged both into history and "Old World" fantasy—as in *The Prince and the Pauper* (1882) and *A Connecticut Yankee in King Arthur's Court* (1889)—Twain held the interest of readers more steadily in the tales built on his lost Hannibal boyhood which immortalized Huck Finn, Tom Sawyer, the slave Jim, and their generation. The demand for more *Western* stories from Twain never flagged, especially in an era when industrial growth dominated the Eastern states. Many Americans at the time viewed Twain's Hannibal world with a mixture of nostalgia and fascination as a society characterized by the opportunity for individual adventure and unrestrained freedom. Twain became increasingly dyspeptic and misanthropic in his later years. He died in 1910.

towns, which attracted a high percentage of outlaws and others preying upon the honest prospectors and tradesmen, townsmen formed "vigilance committees." Often these groups took the first steps toward establishing legal governments within the communities and in the larger territory. After the first individual fortunes had been made in an area, generally with claims staked upon land where gold or silver could be found easily as on hill surfaces or through "panning" and "placer mining" (methods that involved washing the metal out from other rocks using pans or easily constructed water troughs), most ordinary miners found the difficulties of extracting metals from below the ground too burdensome. Quartz mining—extracting the precious ore with expensive equipment that would dig out rock deposits far below the ground—required large investments in capital.

Miners involved in the Black Hills gold rush of the mid-1870s helped to develop the South Dakota town of Deadwood, seen here in 1876, the year of the Custer massacre. (Culver Pictures)

Soon wealthy bankers and businessmen from cities such as San Francisco began investing heavily in mining properties throughout the Far West, and such giants as the "Bonanza Kings," who controlled Comstock Lode mining throughout the 1860s and 1870s, had their companies based in San Franciso more often than in Nevada itself. Absentee financiers and entrepreneurs who could afford the huge initial investment in the equipment, mining engineers, and the labor force required for subsurface mining soon overshadowed smaller prospectors throughout the Western territories. The mining companies purchased and took over individual claims in much the same manner as consolidations began to occur within Eastern manufacturing industries during the same period. Often, the incorrigible thousands of independent panning and placer miners would sell out to a company and simply move on to less developed territories and pursue new claims, a phenomenon that brought the intruding prospectors into the Black Hills during the 1870s and provoked the Sioux War of 1875–77.

Although resident Indian tribes invariably suffered from the incursions of white prospectors, the mining frontier during these decades stimu-

lated the American economy significantly through the shipment of hundreds of millions of dollars worth of newly discovered precious metals either to the East or to other countries. The boom also encouraged the technological development of the mining industry in the West and elsewhere, brought hundreds of thousands of new settlers into the region (many of whom remained to farm or pursue other business careers once the boom had ended), and helped to expedite the development of transcontinental road and rail systems throughout the Western United States.

THE CATTLE FRONTIER

Several related factors during the 1860s combined to turn the grasslands of the Great Plains into open range and to stimulate the creation of a major cattle industry there. The Indian tribes that had previously roamed the ranges had either been driven onto reservations or into a last-ditch fight for survival; the buffalo herds, which had devoured grazing lands, were being systematically slaughtered; and the transcontinental railroads being built provided reliable means to transport Western beef to Eastern markets.

Cattle raising had been a major New World industry since colonial days, and centuries before the United States came into existence, Spaniards had raised cattle and horses for sale. During the eighteenth century, Spaniards brought cattle into Texas where Mexican ranchers watched over thousands of head grazing on the open range, even collecting them in yearly roundups for cattle and horse drives to markets in Spanish Louisiana. During the early nineteenth century, farmers in the Old Northwest drove cattle from the Ohio Territory to markets in Philadelphia, and by the 1840s, a clear market link from Texas to St. Louis existed by way of New Orleans.

The Mexicans were the first cowboys. They were called *vaqueros*. From them came the distinctive equipment of the American cowboy, including chaps, saddles with horns and *la reata*, the lariat. Under the Mexicans, cattle ranching flourished in the land between the Nueces River and the Rio Grande. Americans settling in Texas, even while still owned by Mexico, quickly learned the techniques of ranching.

Millions of cattle roamed freely throughout western and southern Texas by the 1850s; these descendants of the earlier Spanish herds had gradually evolved into Texas longhorns. An estimated 5 million longhorns and other cattle grazed on the Texas plains during the Civil War years, although given the state's isolation both from the major markets of the Northeast and from many Confederate markets, there was only minimal economic gain made by local ranchers between 1861 and the war's end.

When it became apparent to Texans in 1865, after Appomattox, that they could sell their cattle to Eastern purchasers for thirty to forty dollars a head at the railroad, instead of the three to five dollars they received locally, ranchers began banding together and organizing roundups for the trek northward. The first such "long drive" occurred in the spring of 1866, when, after drives often lasting for a month and a half (frequently through dangerous Indian territory), hundreds of thousands of cattle reached the nearest railhead east at Sedalia, Missouri. At Sedalia and other railheads, cattle buyers and railroad companies built large stockyards and opened land to allow the herds to graze before shipment.

By the following year, 1867, the long drive had shifted direction to Abilene, Kansas, along the newly developed Chisolm Trail. Texas roundups for the "beef trail" northward began to occur during the summer, and within a few years, such Kansas towns as Ellsworth, Dodge City, and Wichita competed with Abilene for the profits to be gained from receiving the great herds. Chicago and Kansas City became centers of the meat-packing industry, and they constructed huge stockyards in which to receive the incoming cattle. An estimated 5 to 7 million head of cattle reached Kansas railheads from Texas during the two decades which followed the first long drive. Refrigerator cars had been developed and placed in operation on the railroads by 1875, making it possible to prepare American beef easily for markets throughout the world. Between 1875 and 1885 alone, over 5.5 million steers were driven to market in this process.

A new class of wealthy cattle barons emerged, making the small rancher's role in the long drive — which had been important in the early years — a subordinate one, much as the mining companies displaced individual prospectors during these same years. Land speculators and investors, both American and European, began purchasing huge tracts of land throughout the West upon which to raise cattle for market. New railroad lines, determined to wrest the shipping advantages in the cattle industry from Kansas, opened from Texas to Montana. Because of the Desert Land Act, the Homestead Act, and other government measures, a small number of ranchers acquired enormous tracts of land upon which to stock their cattle. By the early 1880s, the price of beef in the East reached more than sixty dollars a head. Giant herds from Montana to Texas, a "cattle kingdom" which extended from the borders of Canada to those of Mexico, were raised and slaughtered to feed an apparently insatiable appetite for beef on the part of Easterners. Throughout the West during this era, periodic "range wars" broke out between homesteaders and sheepherders who fenced in land for crop raising and sheep grazing purposes, and cattlemen determined to graze and water their vast herds on an "open range."

Several factors ended the "bonanza" in beef by the mid-1880s. Foremost among these was the overproduction of cattle throughout the country, which soon forced market prices down from highs reached in 1882. Also contributing to the decline were a combination of circumstances: The violent struggles between cattlemen protecting their open range and both sheepherders and wheat farmers intent upon fencing in the range to protect their own investments; the consequent fencing in of available waterholes along the cattle trails, which added to the difficulties of any long drive; and the crippling accidents of weather during the 1885–87 period. A series of horrendously cold and blizzard-filled winters beginning in 1885 left hundreds of thousands of cattle dead, and the disastrously dry summers during that same period limited the amount of grass and water available for grazing purposes among the surviving herds. Ranchers began disposing of their cattle at prices almost as low as the pre-1866 market levels. The Eastern markets became glutted with beef at bargain prices, and a number of companies—and small ranchers—lost everything.

During the decades that followed, serious cattlemen stopped speculating in land and stock, turning instead to the scientific development of improved breeds and the careful scrutiny of herd levels. The result was a massive reduction in the numbers of available animals—a decline in millions—throughout the "cattle kingdom" and consequent stabilization of the American cattle industry. Railroad expansion into most areas which held large ranches made further treks to distant railheads unnecessary. Even ranchers began fencing in their scarce available grazing lands. By the end of the century, the age of the adventurous long drives along the cattle frontier remained only a romantic memory.

THE FARMING FRONTIER

Of all the waves of frontier settlement in the trans-Mississippi West—fur trapping, trading, mining, cattle raising, and farming—the farmers re-

mained both the most numerous and the most economically important throughout the late nineteenth century. Two million farms in the United States in 1860 increased to 5.7 million by 1900, much of the growth occurring in the West. With the herding of Western Indian tribes onto reservations came an opportunity to transform the barren, low-rainfall areas of the Great Plains and the prairies. The railroads also played a major role in bringing grain farming to the newly opened areas. The United States became Europe's chief supplier of wheat, and corn was also exported in ever-expanding amounts during the post-Civil War decades.

The lack of plentiful water supplies in the plains areas that were under cultivation forced farmers to innovate, and they used a variety of techniques to preserve a sufficient supply of water. Windmills, though costly, were one ancient method of collecting water; deep wells were dug with new and expensive well-digging equipment; farms were surrounded carefully with barbed wire to prevent stray or passing cattle and other animals from trampling crops and—most importantly—from using up available water supplies. And plains farmers also developed an appropriate technique for the climate known as "dry farming"; in order to absorb and retain available snow, rainwater, and subsurface water, they dug furrows that were a foot deep (far deeper than normal for such crops). New farm equipment, such as harvesters, improved plows, grain drills, and special mowing machines, also improved the plains farmer's ability to harvest high-yield crops, despite the inadequate rainfall. (See Chapter 30, p. 573.)

The mechanization of prairie agriculture led to dramatic gains in production, increasing twenty-fold in the post-Civil War decades the number of acres of wheat an individual farmer could grow and reducing from sixty to three the number of hours of personal labor needed to grow each acre. The acreage of wheat in production in the United States went from 20 million before 1875 to 35 million in the following decade. Millions of immigrants from Europe and migrants from more settled areas of the country, meanwhile, flooded into the Great Plains region, resulting in its rapid settlement during these decades.

Despite depressingly arduous living conditions — extremes of weather in which bitterly freezing winters alternated with dry summer heat spells, initial reliance upon crude sod houses often dependent upon buffalo or cow chips for fuel because of lack of wood, sporadic threats of renewed Indian attacks, crop failures, the high cost of manufactured goods, and a profound sense of isolation due to the large acreage of most farms and distance between neighbors — the plains farmers survived and prevailed. Despite all the problems, the Homestead Act and railroad company land sales accelerated the growth of the entire region. Exports of wheat, corn, beef, pork, and other foodstuffs, in large measure from the plains and prairie states, became a more important source of American foreign exchange for most of the late nineteenth century than even manufactured goods. At the same time, the plains farmers found themselves increasingly dependent upon a variety of circumstances beyond their control for economic survival: the price of manufactured farm equipment, railroad rates, the fluctuations in prices offered for products by foreign and domestic grain markets,

Homesteaders like this Montana farmer took advantage of the government offer of cheap land in the West. Those who mastered the harsh climate turned the Great Plains into the breadbasket of America. (Bureau of Reclamation/National Archives)

and competition for a large share of the world market with growers from other countries.[3]

All of these problems led to political insurgency in the plains and prairie states during the 1890s, the decade of the "Populist revolt." But in the early decades of settlement along the agricultural frontier in the trans-Mississippi West, the attractions of owning larger farms and growing increased yields of wheat and other grains brought millions of farmers to a desolate region. Within a single generation, their labors had overcome both natural disasters and man-made obstacles to tame and transform the entire area.

---

[3] See Chapter 32 for an extended discussion of agricultural problems and the farmer's response during the 1890s.

Suggested Readings
Chapters 25–26

Battle at The Little Bighorn and the Sioux

Dee Brown, *Bury My Heart at Wounded Knee* (1971); George E. Hyde, *Red Cloud's Folk* (1957); Alvin M. Josephy, Jr., *The Patriot Chiefs* (1961); James C. Olson, *Red Cloud and the Sioux Problem* (1965); E. I. Stewart, *Custer's Luck* (1955); Robert Utley, *The Last Days of the Sioux Nation* (1963) and *Frontier Regulars: The U.S. Army and the Indian, 1866-1890* (1973); Stanley Vestal, *Sitting Bull* (1932).

The Frontier and the West

Ray Allen Billington, *Westward Expansion: A History of the American Frontier* (1967) and *America's Frontier Heritage* (1967); Thomas D. Clark, *Frontier America: The Story of the Westward Movement* (2nd ed., 1969); Howard R. Lamar, *The Far Southwest, 1846–1912* (1966); Henry Nash Smith, *Virgin Land: The American West as Symbol and Myth* (1950); Frederick Jackson Turner, *The Frontier in American History* (1929); Walter P. Webb, *The Great Plains* (1931) and *The Great Frontier* (1932, rev. ed., 1964).

The Plains Indians and American Indian Policy

R. K. Andrist, *The Long Death: The Last Days of the Plains Indians* (1964); R. G. Atherton, *William Tecumseh Sherman and the Settlement of the West* (1956); Henry L. Fritz, *The Movement for Indian Assimilation, 1860–1890* (1963); Wayne Gard, *The Great Buffalo Hunt* (1959); W. T. Hagan, *American Indians* (1961); Helen Hunt Jackson, *A Century of Dishonor* (1881); R. W. Mardock, *Reformers and the American Indian* (1970); James C. Mooney, *The Ghost Dance Religion and the Sioux Uprising of 1890* (reprinted, 1965).

The Cattle Frontier

Lewis Atherton, *The Cattle Kings* (1929, reprinted 1957); E. E. Dale, *The Range Cattle Industry* (1920, reprinted 1969); Robert R. Dykstra, *The Cattle Towns* (1970); J. B. Frantz and J. E. Choate, *The American Cowboy: The Myth and the Reality* (1955); Gene M. Gressley, *Bankers and Cattlemen* (1966); E. S. Osgood, *The Day of the Cattleman* (1929, reprinted 1957); Walter P. Webb, *The Great Plains* (1931).

The Mining Frontier

Dan De Quille, *History of the Big Bonanza* (1876, reprinted 1947); W. S. Greever, *The Bonanza West . . . 1848–1900* (1963); Rodman W. Paul, *Mining Frontiers of the Far West, 1848–1880* (1963); D. A. Smith, *Rocky Mountain Mining Camps* (1967); Mark Twain, *Roughing It* (1872).

The Farming Frontier and Government Land Policies

Everett Dick, *The Sod House Frontier, 1854–1890* (1954); Gilbert C. Fite, *The Farmer's Frontier, 1865–1900* (1966); Paul W. Gates, *History of Public Land Development* (1968); James C. Malin, *The Grassland of North America* (1948); R. M. Robbins, *Our Landed Heritage: The Public Domain, 1776–1936* (1942); Fred A. Shannon, *The Farmer's Last Frontier: Agriculture, 1860–1897* (1945); R. M. Wik, *Steam Power on the American Farm* (1953).

The Assassination 27 of Garfield

On the morning of July 2, 1881, the president of the United States, James Abram Garfield, was strolling toward a waiting train in a railroad depot in Washington. The train, scheduled to depart at 9:30 A.M., was to take him on the first leg of a trip to Williams College, his alma mater. There he was to address a class reunion and enroll his two sons. Walking alongside the president and chatting with him was the secretary of state, James G. Blaine, a close political associate and friend. Already inside the train were Garfield's two sons and other members of his cabinet.

The president and the secretary of state walked toward the train platform. Neither noticed a thin, bearded figure dressed in shabby and unpressed clothing, staring at them from a few feet away. The two men broke off their conversation for a moment and prepared to step aboard the train.

Suddenly the man who had been watching them drew a pistol from his pocket. He pointed it at the president and fired twice. Garfield fell to the ground, crying out only "My God!" before he fainted. Blood spurted onto his gray traveling suit.

At the sound of the shots, Blaine lunged toward the assassin. But when he saw the president lying on the ground, he quickly returned to his side. Along with others who had reached the scene, Blaine raised the wounded man's head. Garfield regained consciousness almost immediately.

Garfield's two sons and the cabinet members rushed from the train to join the crowd of onlookers. Some railroad workers gently lifted the heavy-set man and placed him on a ragged mattress, brought hastily from a nearby room. The first physician to arrive was Dr. Smith Townsend, the District of Columbia health officer. The doctor assumed from Garfield's appearance that the chief executive was dying. Townsend gave the injured man aromatic spirits of ammonia and some brandy to ease his pain. Then he inspected the more serious of the two wounds Garfield had received—the one on the lower right side of his back. Garfield winced. The doctor's touch had reopened the wound. Townsend's face and man-

SHOT DOWN.

President Garfield Dangerously Wounded.

AN ASSASSIN'S WORK.

Fired at Entering the Railroad Depot at Washington.

THE SERIOUS HIP WOUND.

Carried in an Ambulance to the White House.

CHEERFUL IN THE FACE OF DEATH.

Grave Symptoms Succeeded by a More Hopeful Condition.

A STRONG MAN'S STRUGGLE

Arrest and Imprisonment of the Criminal.

CHARLES JULES GUITEAU.

An Erratic Creature of Low Antecedents—His Strange History.

MRS. GARFIELD'S SORROW

She Reaches Washington and Meets Her Husband.

INTENSE EXCITEMENT—WORLDWIDE SYMPATHY

SCENE OF THE ASSASSINATION.

Map of Washington Showing Location of the Baltimore and Potomac Railroad Depot.

After less than six months in office President Garfield was shot by a disgruntled office seeker. Charles Guiteau, as Secretary of State James G. Blaine looked on. Though the president was in a public place, he had no Secret Service protection. (Library of Congress)

ner remained grim but, somewhat mechanically, he assured Garfield that his back wound was not serious. "I thank you, doctor," replied Garfield in evident pain, "but I am a dead man."

After firing the shots, the assassin calmly returned the pistol to his pocket. Then, as anxious and curious spectators surrounded the bleeding president, he rushed toward a railway station exit. Just as he reached it, the exit's massive door burst open. The man who had shot the president found himself face to face with Patrick Kearney, a District of Columbia patrolman. Kearney had been running toward the sound of the shots. In an attempt to flee past the policeman, the slender, dark-complexioned figure mumbled in an excited voice, "I have a letter to send to General Sherman."[1]

Kearney, sensing that the agitated man was somehow connected with the earlier pistol cracks and the crowd now gathering on the platform, held onto him. Several railroad employees raced to the exit and reported that the president had been shot. The policeman then rushed his prisoner away from the scene. As they left the station, the man finally spoke, saying: "I did it. I will go to jail for it; [Vice-president] Arthur is President."

When Kearney reached the police station, his fellow officers would not believe that Garfield had been shot. It took a few minutes before they accepted the patrolman's story. Kearney himself, still excited over having captured the man who had tried to kill the president, did not even take possession of the prisoner's gun until they had reached the stationhouse. For that matter, only then did the patrolman think to ask the assassin his name. The prisoner reached into his pocket, withdrew a small printed calling card, and handed it to Kearney, who stared at the name and address: Charles Guiteau, Chicago, Ill.

The president, meanwhile, had been carried to a police ambulance, which rushed him back to the White House. There he was placed in a second-floor bedroom. Dozens of physicians, family members, government officials, and well-wishers scurried about the sickroom for the remainder of the day. A hoard of newspapermen also managed to reach the sickroom door. They pestered each visitor to the president's bedside for fresh news of his condition.

The physicians all agreed that Garfield's back wound was too serious to allow immediate removal of the bullet. They felt they could do nothing but give the president large doses of morphine to dull his pain. Their frequent bulletins to the waiting reporters seldom varied in content: "The President's wounds are grave. He remains pale, weak, and cold. Although he is not bleeding profusely *externally,* there is every chance of massive *internal* hemorrhaging."

To doctors and reporters alike, this meant only one thing: the president was dying. Several members of Garfield's cabinet joined his family

---

[1] William Tecumseh Sherman was then commanding general of the American army.

and physicians in the sickroom. Together they waited for further developments throughout the long night. At one point the secretary of war walked out into the corridor for a breath of air. He turned to a reporter and said: "How many hours of sorrow I have passed in this town." With this remark, Robert Todd Lincoln, Abraham Lincoln's son, reentered the sickroom.

Garfield's spirits, and his condition, improved greatly once his wife reached his bedside. She had been recuperating in New Jersey, following a malarial infection, but hurried to rejoin her husband on receiving word of the shooting. A special train brought her to Washington. Arriving at the White House in the early evening, she spent a few minutes alone with Garfield. Then she stationed herself outside his sickroom, praying and waiting for news. The president, after being told that she had gone to bed, fell asleep himself.

An hour later Garfield awoke. He turned to the attending physician, D. W. Bliss, who had taken charge of his treatment, and asked about his chances for recovery. He told the physician, as Dr. Bliss later remembered, "that he desired a frank and full statement, that he was prepared to die and feared not to learn the worst." Dr. Bliss, somewhat less than frank, replied: "Mr. President, your injury is formidable [but] in my judgment you have a chance for recovery." Garfield smiled and, placing his hand upon the doctor's arm, answered simply: "Well, doctor, we will take that chance." The warmth, good humor, and optimism that had characterized James Abram Garfield throughout his rise to the presidency did not desert him during this final struggle for life.

Garfield's rise to the presidency paralleled the success story of several other nineteenth-century American presidents. He was a man of humble origins and, like President Lincoln before him, had the good sense to be born in a log cabin. The log cabin had become the American symbol of homespun integrity and was therefore very useful to budding politicians.

Garfield, who was born in Ohio in 1831, was a seventh-generation American. His ancestors came to Massachusetts Bay with John Winthrop. His father was a pioneer Ohio farmer who died when Garfield was two. His mother, Eliza, raised the future president and three other children in bitter rural poverty.

As a boy, Garfield worked at a variety of jobs, helping to support his mother while striving to earn an education. After graduating from a neighboring school called Western Reserve Eclectic Institute (later changed to Hiram Institute), Garfield worked his way through Williams College in Massachusetts. He graduated from there in 1856. Returning to Ohio, Garfield served first as a teacher and then—though still in his twenties—as principal of Hiram Institute. In 1858 he married Lucretia Rudolph, his childhood sweetheart.

Throughout the 1850s Garfield exhibited the talents that were later to win him high political office. In 1859 he ran for, and won, the Republican seat in the Ohio Senate. He made friends easily, worked

furiously, displayed great tact and an ability to compromise, took few extreme positions, and—above all—sought to please. When the Civil War began, the young state legislator organized a volunteer infantry regiment composed largely of his former students. Although he had no previous military experience, he mastered the appropriate army training manuals quickly and well.

Colonel Garfield's regiment was assigned to the Union army command in Kentucky. There it defeated a much larger force of Confederate soldiers at the Battle of Middle Creek in January 1862. This victory earned Garfield the rank of brigadier general. After fighting at the Battle of Shiloh, he had to leave the field because of poor health. When he returned to active duty in 1863, he served with distinction during the important Battle of Chickamauga. Garfield left the army in December of 1863 with the rank of major general. He had been elected to the House of Representatives that fall.

Garfield was then thirty-two and extremely popular in Ohio's Western Reserve district. This area returned him to Congress seven more times. His skill as a legislative leader and orator quickly made him a leading Republican in the House. So great was his personal popularity that Ohio voters reelected him despite the fact that they did not agree with him on many issues.

Garfield, like all successful officeholders, quickly learned the skill of political survival: when to speak out on an important question, when

The public's view of Garfield as a home-spun, simple man was reinforced by the fact that he was "the last of the log cabin presidents." This painting of his birthplace in Orange, Ohio, gives us a nostalgic view of the pure and pastoral life of Garfield's youth. (Library of Congress)

The warmth and good humor which impressed his fellow politicians emerge in this photographic portrait of James Abram Garfield. (Brown Brothers)

to blur an issue, and when to remain silent. During Hayes's administration Garfield's talent for bringing together different viewpoints within the Republican party led to his selection as House minority leader. Early in 1880 he was elected by the Ohio legislature to a six-year Senate term. But he never filled this seat.

It was in that year that the Republicans held their convention to nominate a presidential candidate. They were bitterly divided among three leading contenders—former President Ulysses S. Grant, Senator John Sherman of Ohio, and Senator James G. Blaine of Maine. There was a three-way deadlock on thirty-four ballots. On the thirty-fifth a break occurred. Garfield's name was put forward as a compromise candidate. On the thirty-sixth, Garfield, who had gone to the convention as Sherman's campaign manager, emerged with his party's nomination for president.

Blaine quickly became a close political ally. Sherman remained cordial, if untrusting. Grant's managers (particularly the influential New York Senator Roscoe Conkling) never forgave Garfield, despite the fact that Chester A. Arthur, Conkling's colleague from New York, was chosen to be Garfield's running mate. Garfield and Conkling did eventually smooth over their differences, and the Republicans carried a close election with a popular plurality of only ten thousand votes. James Garfield, a mild-mannered and unforceful politician, became president of the United States.

During his years in Congress, Garfield and his family had lived modestly. When Congress was in session, they stayed in Washington. At other times they made their home in Mentor, Ohio, a small agricultural town on Lake Erie, twenty-five miles from Cleveland. They had a farm there, which they called Lawnfield. Garfield enjoyed the farm work and rural way of life. He left Mentor for the last time in 1881, for Washington and his inauguration. The letters he wrote during his few months as chief executive show that he often yearned to return to peaceful isolation.

Although Garfield had been a professional politician for more than twenty years, by the time he entered the White House, he retained an avid interest in cultural matters. This interest, no doubt, was a carry-over from his days as a student, teacher, and college principal. Throughout his adult life he corresponded with some of the country's leading men of letters and reformers.

But Garfield himself was not a reformer. Throughout his legislative career he allied himself with railroad, industrial, and other established interests. He expressed skepticism about reforms dealing with woman suffrage, contempt for proposals to assist the Indians, and indifference toward efforts to aid blacks. Above all, Garfield was a party "regular"—a politician whose primary concern was advancing his own fortunes and those of his party.

Garfield did not know that one of the proposals he ignored would eventually mark him for an assassin's bullet. The issue was civil-service reform, which advocated filling government posts by qualifying tests rather than by political appointment. Some minor steps toward such reform were taken by Garfield's predecessor in the White House, Rutherford B. Hayes. But Garfield let the matter drop when he became president.

Instead, he put up with the hundreds who came weekly to the Executive Mansion in search of government jobs. True, they annoyed him. Daily he was besieged by a "band of disciplined office hunters who drew papers on me as highwaymen draw pistols."[2] One of the constant job-seeking visitors to the White House who "drew papers" on the president was a forty-year-old Chicago lawyer, bill collector, and itinerant preacher named Charles Julius Guiteau.

Charles Julius Guiteau's life contrasted starkly with that of James Abram Garfield. Garfield had married happily and raised a family. His efforts as student, educator, soldier, and politician were all rewarded. The president remained secure in his early religious beliefs. He numbered among his friends and admirers not only the most powerful people in America but also many of its intellectuals. The road from log cabin to

---

[2] White House security measures were not as strict then as they are now. Visitors were free to come and go, so that they might well run into the president as he was walking in the Executive Mansion.

Charles Guiteau claimed to believe that Garfield's death was a necessity that would unite the Republican party and save the Republic. He claimed that the idea had come to him under "divine pressure." (Library of Congress)

White House had been, by and large, a smooth one that he traveled with outer serenity and inner contentment. Garfield represented, for many of his generation, living proof of the continued American formula for achievement: personal integrity plus hard work plus trained intelligence yield success and happiness.

Both the personal life and public career of Charles Guiteau had been marked by frustration and failure. He was born the fourth of six children on September 8, 1841, in Freeport, Illinois. Jane Howe Guiteau, his mother, died when he was seven. The boy was raised by his father, Luther Wilson Guiteau, a Freeport bank official and religious disciple of John Humphrey Noyes.[3] Charles was usually cared for by his older sister, Frances, who maintained an interest in the boy's welfare even after her marriage to George Scoville, a Chicago lawyer.

Guiteau, like Garfield, worked extremely hard as a young man, helping his father at the bank and tending to family chores. Both young men were enthusiastic Republicans; both were physical- and mental-fitness buffs; and both dreamed of eventual success. But the quarrels between the young Guiteau and his domineering father were frequent and stormy. In 1859, the same year that Garfield became principal of Hiram Institute, Guiteau decided to leave Freeport to seek his fortune.

The first goal he set for himself was that of obtaining a college education. Guiteau went to the university college at Ann Arbor, Michigan, where he attempted to register. The teachers there asked that he first train for university work by enrolling at a Michigan preparatory school. Lonely, needing funds, and keenly feeling his lack of academic preparation, Guiteau turned to religion for solace. Not surprisingly, be became interested in his zealous father's faith, the teachings of John Humphrey Noyes. In June of 1860, Guiteau left Ann Arbor to join the Oneida Community.

The Oneida Community, like other utopian settlements in mid-nineteenth-century America, was based upon religious fellowship and the principle that both work and worldly goods would be shared. Guiteau was no happier at Oneida than he had been at Ann Arbor. He was unpopular among other members of the community. Neither then, nor at any other point in Charles Guiteau's life, did he manage to keep a single close friend. A bad-tempered, solitary, and nervous figure, he often came under attack for selfishness and conceit at the community's important mutual-criticism sessions. In 1865 Guiteau left the community.

For the next fifteen years Guiteau's life consisted mainly of a series of career failures. He borrowed constantly from family members, was always in debt, and often ran away to escape arrest. He flitted back and forth between New York City and Chicago (where his sister lived). Hoping and expecting some great new career—which would be achieved instantly—Guiteau generally found himself teetering on the edge of despair.

---

[3] John Humphrey Noyes was the founder of the Oneida Community, an experimental communal colony in upstate New York.

Guiteau attempted a succession of enterprises. After leaving the Oneida Community, he tried to found a religious newspaper. But he failed. He spent a short time in 1867 as a subscription and ad salesman for the Reverend Henry Ward Beecher's influential weekly paper, the *Independent*. He soon gave up the post. Then he spent a year threatening a lawsuit against Noyes and his other former brethren at the Oneida Community. He tried to blackmail them into paying him $9,000. Otherwise, he threatened to publicize the colony's controversial sexual practices.[4] Guiteau's own father denounced his son publicly for this betrayal of Oneida. Guiteau finally stopped his abusive letters to Noyes after the latter threatened to prosecute him.

Guiteau next moved to Chicago, where he apprenticed in a law office. He was admitted to the Illinois bar in 1868. He made only one appearance as a trial lawyer. Inevitably, he lost the case. After this, his legal practice consisted almost entirely of bill collecting, a trade he followed with little success until 1875

In 1869 Guiteau had married an eighteen-year-old girl, Anne Bunn. The union lasted five turbulent years, during which he often beat his wife severely and sometimes even locked her in a closet overnight. In 1874 his wife divorced him.

By then, Guiteau had acquired a reputation as a sleazy and dishonest bill collector. He served a brief jail sentence in 1875 for petty fraud and abruptly, that same year, shifted his career plans once more. The penniless lawyer now announced plans to raise $200,000 in order to purchase a Chicago newspaper. Attempts to borrow the money failed miserably. Guiteau retreated to his family again. During a visit to his sister Frances, he threatened her with an ax. A physician who examined Guiteau after this incident recommended that he be placed in an insane asylum. Guiteau fled.

Now Guiteau adopted yet another vocation. He became an itinerant preacher and wandered across the country, selling religious pamphlets and preaching a version of John Humphrey Noyes's theology. Apparently Guiteau earned almost no money between 1875 and 1881. Yet somehow he managed to survive on the misplaced trust of creditors.

In 1880 a new vision of success appeared to Guiteau, this time a political one. He wrote an incoherent pro-Garfield essay and had it privately printed. Then he attached himself to the Republicans' New York City campaign headquarters. There he became one of the many unwanted and unused hangers-on. Though he did nothing to bring it about, Guiteau viewed Garfield's election as a personal triumph. He immediately began making plans to apply for a high post in the diplomatic corps.

Guiteau wrote several letters to Garfield and other important Republican leaders, in pursuance of his plan. In them he asserted his im-

---

[4] The community held that traditional marriage and family patterns bred selfishness and, thereby, many evils in society. Therefore, monogamy was banned, and children were cared for by the entire community.

Roscoe Conkling, head of the Stalwarts, was a political boss who believed that "parties were not built by deportment or gush." He ruined his political career in an attempt to thwart Garfield's policies. (Library of Congress)

Senator Thomas C. Platt, a faithful political crony of Roscoe Conkling, followed his lead in resigning from the Senate. Promptly dubbed "Me Too" Platt, his loyalty cost him his Senate seat. (Library of Congress)

portance in the party's New York victory and requested assignment to various foreign ministries. Eventually, he decided on the Paris consulship. He moved to Washington—one jump ahead of his creditors—to press this claim.

During the early months of Garfield's presidency, from March to June 1881, Guiteau became a familiar face at the White House and in the State Department corridors. He pestered Garfield and Blaine about the Paris post at every chance, by letter and even in person (when he managed to push his way through). "Never bother me again about the Paris consulship so long as you live," Blaine shouted at the pesky figure after one such May encounter. By then, Guiteau had decided that Blaine was a "wicked man." He demanded Blaine's dismissal in notes to Garfield that became increasingly intimate in tone. A new scheme for glory now began to hatch in Guiteau's crazed mind: a plan to murder the president.

Guiteau was not familiar with firearms. As his obsession grew more vivid, he purchased a revolver and practiced shooting on the banks of the Potomac. He took to following the president and observing his daily routine. On several occasions prior to the fateful day he came close to executing his scheme, only to back down at the last minute. By his shooting Garfield, his disturbed mind reasoned, not only would his political friends be raised to power but he, too, would share in it.

Finally, on July 2, 1881, Charles Julius Guiteau, a man whose life had epitomized failure, managed to carry out the last of his innumerable schemes. He shot the president. Guiteau later acknowledged:

> I have had an idea [since my youth] that I should be President, and it has never left me. When I left Boston for New York, in June 1880 [to campaign for Garfield], I felt that I was on my way to the White House. My idea is that I shall be nominated and elected as Lincoln and Garfield were—that is, by the act of God.

Many blamed Garfield's factional opponents in the Republican party's Stalwart wing[5] (somewhat unfairly) for having allowed the assassin even a minor place within their ranks in New York during the 1880 campaign. Some even blamed Vice-President Arthur. Until Garfield selected him as a running mate, Arthur had been a loyal associate of the country's leading Stalwart, Senator Roscoe Conkling of New York. Arthur remained loyal to Conkling despite his new responsibilities as vice-president.

In May 1881, Garfield insisted on appointing an anti-Conkling Republican to an important patronage post—Customs Collector for the Port of New York. Conkling and his New York Stalwart colleague, Thomas C. Platt, both resigned from the Senate. Arthur supported their decision. Conkling and Platt hoped, by resigning, to put pressure on their Senate colleagues to reject the president's nominee on the grounds of "senatorial courtesy." They planned to win Senate reelection from the

---

[5] The Stalwart wing was centered in New York. It actively opposed civil-service reform. Guiteau claimed to be a Stalwart, acting for the good of that faction in shooting Garfield.

New York state legislature and then to return to Washington with added power. This was the dispute between Garfield and the Stalwarts that Guiteau claimed had triggered his decision to kill the president.

In the end, Conkling and Platt lost the struggle—and their power. The two were brought down in July 1881 by Conkling's personal arrogance and an ill-timed peek over an Albany hotel transom by a political opponent, who found Platt in the company of a prostitute. Platt withdrew from the contest the same day that Garfield was shot, in order not to hurt Conkling's chances. It was no use. Neither man gained reelection. Thus, ironically, Garfield had begun to win his struggle against Conkling for control of the Republican party at the very moment he was cut down by the maddened Guiteau claiming to be a Stalwart.

Garfield himself never blamed his political opponents for the shooting. Garfield also forgave his vice-president for supporting Conkling's reelection bid. During Garfield's struggle to recover from the shooting, Arthur remained at his New York City home, grief stricken and withdrawn from public notice. Garfield turned the daily management of government over to his cabinet. The rumors of a Stalwart conspiracy guiding Guiteau's hand quickly died away.

The wounded president lingered between life and death for seventy-nine days. He remained in his second-floor sickroom, only rarely writing official dispatches or dealing with government business. Doctors, medical consultants, and free advice poured into the White House to assist in the president's treatment. But the bullet remained lodged in his back while physicians continued their painful probing. Nothing seemed to help.

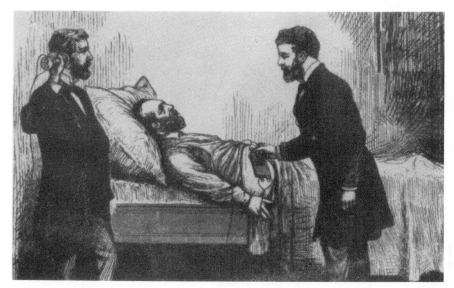

A reproduction of a contemporary sketch shows two doctors attempting to discover the location of the bullet in Garfield's body through the use of a strange telegraph-like apparatus. They never succeeded in removing the bullet. (Culver Pictures)

At first the president's condition improved. But a mid-July rally turned into a late-July decline. In Washington's sweltering summer heat, Garfield ran a fever that only occasionally broke. His normally robust 200-pound frame had shrunk to 120 pounds by late August. When early September brought a record heat wave, the doctors decided to move Garfield to the cooler temperatures of his oceanside summer house at Elberon, New Jersey. He was carried there by special train on September 6, but his condition continued to deteriorate. Still, almost at the end, his spirits remained good. He even tried to cheer those around him.

On the night of September 19, with only an old friend, Captain D. G. Swain, and one servant attending him, Garfield's final agony began. He awoke suddenly, clutched his heart, and cried out, "How it hurts here!" Swain handed the president a glass of water, but it failed to help. The president cried: "Swain, can't you stop this?" Then Garfield fell into a coma. Within moments Dr. Bliss and Mrs. Garfield entered the room. Mrs. Garfield sat down calmly and held her husband's hand. But the strain was too much, and she had to leave the room. Dr. Bliss remained with his patient for a few minutes, then walked quietly to a nearby study and wrote in his medical log: "Applying my ear over the heart, I detected an indistinct fluttering that continued until 10:35 when he expired. The brave and heroic sufferer, the nation's patient, has passed away."

The waiting had ended; the grieving began. Garfield's seventy-nine days of suffering before death, borne with stoic dignity, made the slain president a hero in the eyes of his countrymen. His body was brought back to Washington on September 21 to lie in state in the Capitol rotunda. Thousands—Southerners and Northerners, Democrats and Republicans alike—filed past to pay their last respects. The world's rulers also mourned. The president's widow received condolence messages from Queen Victoria of England; the emperors of China, Russia, and Japan; the kings of Belgium, Italy, and Spain; the Pope; and the sultan of Turkey.

American advocates of civil-service reform found an obvious moral in Garfield's assassination by a disappointed office seeker. Throughout his long death agony, reformers organized countless meetings protesting the spoils system and demanding government appointments based on merit alone. "Garfield dead," one historian later wrote, "proved more valuable to reformers than Garfield alive."

The great majority of Americans, however, mourned Garfield's passing less cynically. On September 23 a special train carried the president's casket from Washington to Cleveland for burial. Crowds lined the entire route to honor the dead president, just as sixteen years earlier throngs had wept as Lincoln's funeral train followed a similar route from the East back to Illinois. Some 250,000 people from throughout the Midwest jammed Cleveland's streets for Garfield's funeral ceremony. Thousands of tributes—sermons, memorial leaflets, and letters—reached his widow at their Mentor home. The nation's grief seemed remarkably intense, considering the fact that Garfield, unlike Lincoln, had not been a war leader. Moreover he had held the highest office in the nation for only a few months.

In New York, Walt Whitman heard of the president's death. In his journal he wrote some lines that expressed the genuine sorrow felt by less eloquent Americans:

> The sobbing of the bells, the sudden death-news everywhere,
> The slumberers rouse, the rapport of the People,
> (Full well they know that message in the darkness,
> Full well return, respond within their breasts, their brains, the sad reverberations,)
> The passionate toll and clang—city to city, joining, sounding, passing,
> Those heart-beats of a Nation in the night.

Another New Yorker also recoiled at the awful news that evening. At Chester Alan Arthur's house the bell rang at midnight. A reporter informed the servant who answered the door that Garfield had died. "Oh, no, it cannot be true," cried Arthur, who overheard the news. "It cannot be. I have heard nothing." His face was pale, and he was crying. When the reporter persisted, Arthur could say only "I hope—My God, I do hope it is a mistake."

The man who had just become president turned and walked back to his study, where a small group of silent friends now waited. The bell rang again, and a messenger handed Arthur a telegram sent by a number of Garfield's cabinet members. It confirmed the president's death and advised Arthur to take the oath of office immediately. Arthur's friends rushed out to find a judge who could administer the oath. Someone checked it for the exact wording. Within minutes a state supreme court justice, roused from his bed, administered the oath of office to the vice-president. The next morning President Chester A. Arthur left for Washington.

On September 20, two days after Garfield's death, his assassin sent a letter to Chester Arthur. He wrote, "My inspiration is a godsend to you, and I presume you appreciate it. It raises you from $8,000 to $50,000 a year. It raises you from a political cipher to President of the United States with all its power and honors. For the Cabinet I would suggest as follows. . . ." President Arthur never answered the letter. Instead, he ordered Guiteau tried promptly. He personally helped select the prosecuting attorneys.

Guiteau, however, still seemed convinced that the Stalwarts would somehow rescue and reward him. His confidence waned, though, as the trial date neared. He continued to deny responsibility for the killing. He insisted that divine inspiration made him pull the trigger. "I am here as God's man, and don't you forget it." No independent lawyer would touch the case, despite a newspaper appeal for such assistance. When the trial began on November 14, 1881, Guiteau's brother-in-law, George Scoville, served as defense counsel.

Lines between the defense and prosecution arguments were drawn clearly from the start. Scoville argued that his client was an insane religious fanatic and therefore could not be held legally responsible for his actions. Furthermore, the defense insisted that Garfield's wounds were not necessarily mortal. The president had died, Scoville claimed, only because of incompetent medical treatment after the shooting.

Both defense arguments had merit, although the prosecution, of course, denied them. It insisted that Guiteau, although morally evil, had killed the president while in complete possession of his faculties. He had done so for calculated political motives—namely, as a malicious and disappointed job seeker.

The case against Guiteau, then, centered on the question of his sanity. Both prosecution and defense attorneys presented "expert" medical testimony to prove their respective contentions. A majority of the doctors who had examined Guiteau found the prisoner sane within the prevailing legal definitions of sanity, which were far broader than those of today. But Guiteau demonstrated his unbalanced mental state by frequently interrupting the trial to shout abusive statements at everyone, including his own lawyer. He continued to claim divine inspiration.

The prosecution argued that such outbursts were merely a cynical act by Guiteau, who was trying to portray himself as mad. Apparently the jury believed this. It took only a half-hour on January 25, 1882, to find Guiteau guilty of murder. The prisoner vented his anger by shrieking: "My blood will be upon the heads of [this] jury. God will avenge this outrage." One doctor who had observed the trial daily, George M. Beard, a noted psychologist, disagreed strongly with the jury's decision. Beard later wrote:

> The physicians called in to make a diagnosis mistook the symptoms of insanity for the symptoms of wickedness. [This] error is quite as natural for nonexperts in insanity in our time as that of the village physician of Salem, Dr. Griggs, in witchcraft times, in attributing insanity to possession by the devil.

Nevertheless, on February 3, Judge Walter Cox sentenced Guiteau to hang.

Before sentencing, Guiteau addressed the court a final time. He insisted again that Garfield's killing had been "God's act, not mine." He compared his fate to Christ's and threatened bloody divine vengeance on the United States if he was hanged. In the months before his execution the condemned man continued to believe that President Arthur would issue a last-minute reprieve or pardon.

Finally, Guiteau recognized the reality ahead of him. Four days before his death, while in his cell, he scrawled a "Scene between the Almighty and my murderers." In this imaginary scene God confronts Guiteau's persecutors, including President Arthur, and condemns them along with the entire American nation. A few days later, on June 30, 1882, Charles Guiteau was hanged. He went to the scaffold, fighting back tears and singing a childlike hymn he had written especially for the occasion. Then he gave a final shout: "Glory hallelujah! I am with the Lord. Glory, ready, go!"

Politics in Transition 28

The economic and social landscape of the United States in the nineteenth century underwent dramatic change. The period might best be termed a transitional one, characterized by the emergence of a new, industrial society. In the decades after the Civil War the preindustrial issues that dominated the antebellum era were overridden in importance by the realities of a rapidly maturing industrial society. New economic and social factors, some of them grim, were changing life. They included transcontinental railroads, a truly national market for goods, a growing monopoly in oil, the factory system, and new technology in steel and other industries. In addition, there were deplorable urban living conditions, millions of new, non-English-speaking immigrants, rising labor violence, growing discontent among farmers, and brutal poverty among workers and farmers.

These factors were clearly visible. But both Republican and Democratic politicians managed to avoid confronting them. Not until a paralyzing business depression in the 1890s and the rise of a new third party, committed to reform, did politicians finally start to deal with the problems brought about by industrial development. Before then, in the 1870s and 1880s, political leaders were more concerned with traditional issues, particularly the currency and tariffs. They argued, for example, over whether the amount of currency in circulation should be expanded or reduced. And they debated whether the United States would benefit more from raised or from lowered tariffs.

Why did politicians avoid considering the problems of the new industrial society? Basically, they (and voters too) were incapable of redirecting their attention from the intense issues arising out of the Civil War and Reconstruction. With the end-ing of war and the termination of Radical rule in the South, the old issues had disappeared. But this transitional generation of politicians, raised in the antislavery battles of the 1850s, was simply unprepared to face the new problems of an industrial nation.

Some steps were taken during this period to deal with elements in the changed economy, but these proved to be less than effective. Politicians of the era were themselves too deeply involved in the development of American industries to take an active role in helping to regulate them. Only in the face of the new political forces and new conditions of the 1890s did politicians begin to bring the unregulated corporate system under some measure of public supervision. It took more than two decades for them to realize that they could no longer ignore the urgent economic and social problems created by post-Civil War industrial growth.

THE POLITICAL GENERATION

Through the 1870s and 1880s, politics continued along at an unhurried pace. Leaders tried to avoid difficult issues. In large part the people who entered politics during this period were average men, like Garfield, who displayed little achievement beyond their ability to win votes.

In *The American Commonwealth* (1888) James Bryce, an English historian, noted that in a country where all careers are open to those having talent and where "political life is unusually keen and political ambition widely diffused," the highest positions in the land are seldom "won by men of brilliant gifts."

Why did eminent figures usually not choose to run for political office in this period? First, for talented people American politics did not seem interesting or important. In European countries, officeholders in national governments generally held much more power over people's lives. First-rate men were attracted to vocations in which they felt they could make a significant impact. Politics in America was not one such vocation.

A second reason for the lack of brilliant people in politics was that success generally required a slow rise through the party ranks. The long apprenticeship in party loyalty necessary to achieve office discouraged ambitious people who wished to move quickly into positions of prominence. Also American voters, then as today, were distrustful of anyone who seemed overly eager for political power, however capable.

Finally, persons of outstanding ability may not have entered politics simply because the era seemed a quiet one, at least compared with the age preceding it. Profound ideological questions no longer separated the parties. The problems of slavery, sectional divisions, and civil war were settled. Few issues were significant enough to attract talented people into politics.

President Garfield's home in Mentor, Ohio, was the kind of country setting most national politicians of this era preferred. Their living patterns represented a nostalgia for an older, simpler way of life in an increasingly complex industrial society. (Library of Congress)

Small-Town Background

Given the lure of other fields, the slowness of the process of reaching the top, and the relative quietness of the times, the ordinary quality of those who held high public office is hardly surprising. Nor is it surprising to find that those who did make politics their career shared very similar patterns of life. In fact, most successful figures in late nineteenth-century national politics, including the great majority of congressmen and senators, had backgrounds similar to that of Garfield. They came from small towns and cities like Garfield's Mentor, Ohio, rather than from large cities or predominantly rural areas. Furthermore, most began their careers in such professions as law, business, the ministry, or teaching.

During the 1860s and 1870s the number of politicians having business interests increased. But most politicians remained provincial in their values and outlook on life. They were aloof and sheltered from the habits and problems of urban-industrial society. They brought to national affairs a viewpoint similar to that of their pre-Civil War counterparts. Most national elected officials, in fact, had little direct personal contact with the major new realities of a changed America—cities, industries, and immigrants.

As with most of the national politicians of this period, the Republican presidential candidates were men with roots in small cities and towns. And in 1884 all the Republican candidates but James G. Blaine came from the Midwest. Thus, even if Charles Guiteau had managed to build a successful career for himself in a city like New York, his urban and Eastern ties would probably have blocked his road to the White House.

An urban man might have been more successful, however, as a Democrat. The Democrats generally nominated presidential candidates from big cities during these years: Horatio Seymour (1868), Horace Greeley (1872), Samuel Tilden (1876), and Grover Cleveland (1884, 1888, 1892). But of this group only Cleveland succeeded in becoming president. Thus, while they controlled many of the cities and even had respectable showings in congressional elections, the Democrats largely failed to take the presidency.

Civil War Experience

As important as a small-town background seemed to be in achieving political success, there was another factor at least as important in advancing a politician's career—his Civil War record. This was true at all levels in American politics but particularly in regard to seeking the presidency. Indeed, another reason why Guiteau could never have become president was that he had not served in the Union Army.

For many Northern voters, Republicanism was practically a family religion, sanctified by wartime sacrifices. (Most Northerners had lost at least one family member in the fighting.)

The Republican presidential candidates were usually Civil War generals. General Hayes succeeded General Grant in the presidency. He, in turn, was succeeded by General Garfield. As death and old age thinned out the number of high-ranking officers, Colonel Benjamin Harrison, and, finally, Major William McKinley entered the White House.

The Democrats, for their part, failed to choose nominees having a military background, at least on the national level. The single Democratic candidate who was a Union military man was General Winfield Scott Hancock. He lost to Garfield in 1880. It is understandable that Union officers were not nominated. The Democrats depended, for the most part, on Southern support for victory. In local and regional elections, of course, where Southern support was irrelevant, Democrats could play on old Civil War loyalties to win elections. But the presidential prize eluded them.

Codes of Personal Conduct

The victorious politicians of this period, besides sharing a small-town background and Civil War experience, were also strong believers in the strictest of moral codes. They usually presented themselves to the public as family men who lived their private lives according to the rigid ethical precepts of American middle-class culture. We do not know, of course, whether this was fact or sheer image building. The author of Garfield's semiofficial campaign biography wrote, for example: "No profane word, no unseemly jest is ever heard at Lawnfield [his home]. No wines sparkle on its table. The moral atmosphere is sweet, pure, and healthgiving to heart and soul. It is a Christian family—a Christian home."

Prior to the Civil War a politician's personal habits and morality had rarely influenced the success of his political career. Neither Andrew Jackson's background of frequent duels nor Henry Clay's inveterate gambling prevented these men from seeking the highest prize in American politics. During the middle of the nineteenth century, however, the American family adopted a stern moral code on such questions as sexual behavior, drinking, and gambling. Voters began to apply these standards to vote seekers as well.

Perhaps the only national politician of the era successfully to overcome hostility toward "loose" morality was Grover Cleveland. He won the presidency in 1884 despite the fact—brought out in the campaign—that in his youth he had fathered an illegitimate child. Ironically, voters that year were offered a choice between repudiating either Cleveland's single offense against private morality or James G. Blaine's questionable public morality. While a senator during the 1870s, Blaine had allegedly accepted money and stocks from railroad companies in return for political favors. When the returns were in, the electorate had registered its preference for a candidate with a single confessed private lapse to one probably tainted with several instances of political corruption.

ELECTING A PRESIDENT

National politics during the 1870s and 1880s was not oriented toward issues, although some of the older issues did play a part in the elections. Basically, politicans were concerned with party affiliation and moral, ethnic, and religious differences among the electorate. Three basic factors shaped presidential elections of the late nine-

Democrat Grover Cleveland, who had won the presidency in 1884 and lost it four years later, returned to challenge the Republican incumbent, Benjamin Harrison, in 1892. Cleveland also served as reform governor of New York before becoming president. (Culver Pictures)

teenth century: a close balance in voting strength between the two major parties, high voter turnout, and a stress on party loyalty.

The Closeness of Contests

The statistics for every presidential election of the era show clearly that the parties were evenly matched. In the disputed 1876 election, Republican Rutherford B. Hayes was elected by one electoral vote, although he had received almost 250,000 fewer votes than his Democratic opponent, Samuel J. Tilden. In 1880 Garfield defeated the Democratic candidate, Winfield Scott Hancock, by a comfortable electoral majority. But his nationwide popular margin was a mere 7,368 votes. Actually, Garfield received only a plurality of the votes—48 percent; a third-party candidate,

James B. Weaver of the Greenback-Labor party, cut into the major parties' totals.

Democrat Grover Cleveland's presidential election history is an interesting one, for he crossed and recrossed the narrow line between victory and defeat. In 1884 Cleveland won with less than 49 percent of the popular vote. His margin in the popular vote was only 63,000. When he was defeated by Republican Benjamin Harrison in the 1888 election, Harrison received the majority of electoral votes despite receiving 96,000 fewer popular votes. Cleveland again became president in 1892 when he received 360,000 more votes than Harrison. In this race a new third party, the Populists, received over one million votes. Thus a presidential candidate once more won with only a plurality, not a majority, of the popular vote.

The closeness of these presidential contests helps to explain the efforts usually made by both Republicans and Democrats to blur their basic differences over issues at the national level. Although the Republicans supported high protective tariffs, for example, there were many in the party, including Garfield, who favored much lower rates. Similarly, the Democrats were a low-tariff party. But Cleveland's decision to press the tariff-reduction issue during his first term cost the party support from many high-tariff Democrats and independents who might otherwise have voted for him when he ran again. In order to make its position seem close to that of the other party, and hoping thereby to gain votes, each party had to muffle its internal conflicts and contradictions.

Because of the narrow margins of victory in each presidential election, both Republicans and Democrats were essentially in competition for the support of a small group of swing voters in a few doubtful states. These voters shifted back and forth between the major parties throughout this period. Business help was often invaluable in swinging the key votes and deciding the outcome of the election. Garfield's election in 1880 owed much to the fact that John D. Rockefeller instructed his thousands of salesmen in various states in the Midwest to work actively for the Republican ticket. Similarly, in 1888, Harrison's victory was due in part to corporate money that helped finance intensive drives for votes in a few key states.

Turnout of Voters

Another basic factor in presidential elections in the late nineteenth century was a surprisingly high voter turnout. This phenomenon is somewhat more difficult to explain. There were no dramatic public issues bitterly dividing the two parties as there had been earlier—and would be in the near future. Part of the explanation, however, can be found in the popular view of elections as spectacles.

Both parties waged furious campaigns. Republicans "waved the bloody shirt"—that is, they reminded the voters of Southern Democratic disloyalty during the Civil War. Democrats, in turn, pointed to the corrupting influence of business on the Republican party.

Political campaigns were often the greatest show in town. Huge numbers of voters marched in torchlight parades. They listened for hours to familiar but rousing partisan oratory. As participants in and spectators of such grand displays, voters reaffirmed their strong allegiance to and identification with their party.

Importance of Party Loyalty

Political loyalties among politicians and voters were clear and strong during this period. However blurred the political issues might be, this kind of loyalty strengthened the party as an institution in American life.

Among politicians, party loyalty, or regularity, was extremely important at the national level. Presidential power, which had reached a high point with Lincoln's wartime authority, declined after the crisis of civil war ended. Presidents were

Election night, 1892, in New York City is typical of voter enthusiasm in this era. Despite political corruption and the lack of great issues, excitement over politics ran high. (Culver Pictures)

largely at the mercy of Congress to achieve their programs. The president's political task was two-fold: (1) to "carry" enough congressmen of his own party into office when he was elected and (2) to hold their loyalty once he was president.

Concerning the former, presidents were not too successful. No president during this entire era governed for his entire term with a majority of his own party in control of Congress. The Democrats, for example, won control of the House in 1874, lost it in 1880, regained it in 1882, lost it in 1888, and won it back in 1890. Although Republicans controlled the Senate throughout this period, except for the 1879–81 session, for all but two years they held no more than a slim three-vote Senate majority. There was considerable turnover in congressional membership during the 1870s and 1880s, particularly in the House.

It was even more difficult for a president to hold the party loyalty of congressmen after election. There were numerous factions in both parties. Various means of keeping the party together seemed to work, however. By the end of the era, congressional caucuses were a device used in both parties. They generally decided the legislative policies that all members were expected to, and usually did, abide by. A congressman who did not support the party could be disciplined in a number of ways. Leaders might deny him important committee assignments. They might refuse to help him in the passage of the numerous private bills that every congressman introduces yearly on behalf of his constituents. If necessary they would oppose his renomination. In these circumstances, most congressmen, of course, obeyed the dictates of their party's leaders.

Party loyalty among American voters was more easily assured. American voters adhered as firmly to their party allegiance as they did to their religious faith. If one was raised as a Democrat (or Republican), one usually remained a Democrat (or Republican) for life.

Recent studies point to the importance of ethnic backgrounds and religion as factors in the political behavior of most Americans in the period following the Civil War. A voter's ethnic, cultural, and religious ties shaped his party loyalty as much as it did his attitudes on specific economic or political issues. For example, in order to help capture the votes of the immigrants, who badly needed employment, civil-service reformers in each party complained about the use of the spoils system by urban political machines in the other party. Although jobs were dispensed through political patronage under the spoils system, and recent immigrants were thus unlikely to get them, few of these immigrants favored introducing a merit system. This, they felt, might result in jobs being awarded mainly to native-born Americans who had had greater opportunity to receive education and training.

Religious beliefs were also a factor in determining political affiliation. Recent voting studies have shown that during this period the more an individual's religion stressed correct behavior rather than strict adherence to doctrine alone, the more likely he was to vote Republican. Some Protestant religious denominations viewed politics as a moral battleground, in which state power should be used to regulate ethical behavior. For example, they supported laws prohibiting the sale of alcohol. Members of these denominations tended to support Republicans for office, whether in the 1850s or the 1890s. Certainly, Republican opposition at the state level to using public funds for parochial schools (schools particularly important for many new immigrant families) and the party's support for prohibition (viewed as an assault on Democratic-voting Catholic immigrant "drinkers") attracted large numbers of native-born Episcopalian, Congregationalist, Presbyterian, and other similar voters.

This does not mean that immigrant groups and church members voted in blocs for a single party. Nonetheless, ethnic and cultural ties did indeed influence political loyalties in the period of the 1870s and 1880s.

THE REPUBLICANS IN POWER

For three decades, from 1861 to 1892, the Republicans (except for Democrat Cleveland's 1885–89 term) governed nationally, despite the close political balance between the parties. During this period, as already stated, the president was extremely dependent on Congress. In fact, more often than not, Congress—not the president—determined party policies and the legislation that emerged from Washington.

Americans did not seem to want strong presidents during this period. Certainly they did not appear to need them, because of the relative stability of the times. None of the Republican presidents—Grant, Hayes, Garfield, Arthur, or Harrison—managed to wrest control of Republican policies from the Senate and House leaders.

Men like Blaine and Conkling remained the party's most influential national spokesmen throughout the period. They largely shaped national legislation during the era. Since they were Republicans, they believed in an effective and energetic national economic policy. In general, the purpose of this policy was to encourage industrial expansion. For this they were often criticized by Democratic politicians who retained their party's traditional faith—that government should not meddle actively in the economic lives of Americans.

But the Republican party, founded in an era when the national government had to expand its powers to preserve the Union, saw nothing wrong with continuing this trend at the war's end. To encourage economic development, party leaders aided business in every possible way. In accomplishing this purpose, they forged an informal alliance between the national government and the great majority of businessmen—bankers, industrialists, and merchants in foreign trade. While this alliance furthered economic growth, it had other less fortunate consequences as well. It gave the era a reputation for corruption unparalleled in American history until then.

Corruption under Grant

It is ironic that people who lived by strict small-town moral codes in their private lives found it difficult to maintain the same kind of integrity in public affairs. Political corruption was widespread in this period. The Grant years in particular saw some of the worst offenses against honest government in the nation's history.

A series of cabinet scandals during Grant's administration involved many people close to the president himself. His secretary of the navy sold work to contractors rather than taking honest bids. His secretary of war sold extremely profitable traderships on Indian reservations. Department of the Interior officials worked hand in hand with dishonest land speculators.

Some of the worst scandals involved the Department of the Treasury. Grant's secretary of the treasury farmed out the collection of unpaid taxes to a private contractor who kept half of the money collected. The president's own private secretary protected a Whiskey Ring of corrupt Treasury inspectors. These officials received millions of dollars in bribes from liquor distillers to avoid payment of federal taxes. Through Grant's personal bungling, the Department of the Treasury cooperated with two New York stock speculators, James Fisk and Jay Gould, to manipulate the government selling of bullion. The two men cornered the gold market briefly in September 1869, forcing anyone else who needed gold to pay an exorbitant price for it. Although they caused a panic in the money market, Fisk and Gould made a fortune on the deal. Once they were exposed, Grant did little to punish the guilty parties in his administration.

The opportunities for politicians to profit through corrupt practices increased vastly as a result of the economic boom of the 1860s and 1870s. Many national leaders like Garfield had carefully watched their money while young, to further their education and careers. Suddenly they were responsible for handling millions of dollars in government funds. Politicians found themselves able to reap tidy sums (and benefit the country) simply by helping businessmen with government funds or favorable legislation.

The railroads were notorious seekers after these government favors. Railroad owners paid millions in bribes to public officials each year to secure cash subsidies, gifts of government land, and favorable legislation. Both Garfield and Blaine were linked to such transactions, although no specific criminal charges were ever made against either of them.

During Grant's administration, Garfield apparently profited, along with numerous other public officials, from a shady company known as the Crédit Mobilier. This was a purchasing and construction corporation organized by a few stockholders of the Union Pacific Railroad in the late 1860s. The Union Pacific stockholders retained control of the Crédit Mobilier, to which they awarded huge and fraudulent contracts connected with building the railroad. Congressmen of both parties, including Garfield, were bribed with money and stocks in the Crédit Mobilier to avoid congressional inquiry into these transactions. Before the affair was exposed in 1873, the Crédit Mobilier (despite the Union Pacific's virtual bankruptcy) had paid yearly dividends to stockholders that often exceeded 300 percent of the original investment. Moreover, sometimes these excessive profits went to congressmen who had paid nothing for the stock in the first place!

Although the Grant administration provides the most famous instances of scandal, governmental corruption was not limited to the national level or to Republicans alone. In fact, some of the worst instances of corruption took place at the city level, where Democrats were more likely to be in control. New York City, for instance, was run by a Democratic political organization, or "machine," known as the Tweed Ring (see page 547). Its political leader, "Boss" William Marcy Tweed, and members of his machine stole over $100 million in public revenues ($14 million in one profitable day).

Civil-Service Reform

An important source of Tweed's money was from kickbacks forced from people who wanted city jobs. Once in office, the machine politicians had the power to distribute jobs. Many reformers of the era thought that this spoils system for filling political posts should be eliminated and replaced with a merit system. This, they thought, would do away with much of the corruption that had plagued the country at all levels.

Grant's successor, Rutherford B. Hayes, ordered that officeholders not be asked to make political contributions or be required to do political campaigning. But these orders were largely ignored. Garfield, as noted in the previous chapter, backed away from Hayes's civil-service commit-

ment. With Garfield's death, public attention focused on Guiteau, not merely as his assassin but as a symbol of the various evils that Americans identified with the spoils system of selecting officeholders.

Although the most blatant instances of national corruption had taken place a decade or more earlier, in 1883 Congress responded to the public outcry by passing the Pendleton Act. President Arthur, himself a one-time spoilsman, had lobbied hard for the bill. The act established a bipartisan Civil Service Commission, appointed by the president. Its purpose was to conduct competitive examinations to choose officeholders on the basis of merit. Arthur appointed three solid reformers as civil-service commissioners.

The original measure did not solve the entire problem, however, since the merit system affected only about one of every ten federal jobs. The others were to be filled as political appointments. Nonetheless, the Pendleton Act gave the president the authority to expand the number of positions classified as merit jobs. By 1900 over 40 percent of federal posts had been brought under the civil-service heading. This percentage has expanded in every decade since.

CONTINUING BUSINESS INFLUENCE

The assault on the spoils system did not have much effect on business influence within the national government. Businessmen tried less often to buy favors from individual politicians. Instead, increasing numbers of them began either running for office themselves or supporting politicians committed to business policies, through legal campaign contributions. Industrialists and bankers poured millions into Republican campaign treasuries.

Even more important than business involvement in presidential contests, however, was the growing importance of senators who represented large corporate interests. By 1900 such businessmen, most of them Republicans, comprised a third of the Senate. Fifteen senators were involved in railroads; fifteen in extractive industries—

William Marcy Tweed

From one perspective, William Marcy Tweed was three hundred pounds of grand larceny. From another, he was a major figure in the development of American city government. He was appropriately named after the New York Democratic politician William Marcy, who had openly boasted that victors were entitled to spoils. As the boss of post-Civil War New York City, Tweed devised a method of dealing with an altered city. Most "respectable" New Yorkers wanted no part of it. If Tweed made himself a substantial profit, he could say, as a later Tammany official did, "I seen my opportunities and I took 'em."

By 1870, nearly a million people were crowded into the southern half of Manhattan Island, almost half of them immigrants. The city's startling growth had put enormous strains on its housing, public transportation, sanitation, and health facilities. The financial and social leaders of the city regarded the new residents with a mixture of disdain, foreboding, and bewilderment.

Tammany Hall, New York City's Democratic organization, had been working with immigrants, especially the Irish Catholics, for nearly seven decades before Tweed took over in the mid-1860s. Tweed and other leaders now increased their efforts to meet (and profit from) the incoming flood. Tammany Hall members greeted newcomers from Europe at the docks, helped them get settled, and assisted them in becoming voting American citizens.

With such support, the Tweed Ring controlled city politics. Close associates of Tweed held office as mayor and controller. The boss himself served the public as chairman of the General Committee of Tammany Hall, president of the Board of Supervisors, deputy street commissioner, and state senator. He was grooming his close ally, Governor John T. Hoffman, for the Democratic nomination for the presidency of the United States.

The Ring, however, was interested in public office less for its own sake than as a lever on the door to the public treasury. During five years of almost uncontested power, the Tweed Ring stole between $30 and $200 million. By one estimate, only 15 cents of every tax dollar went for legitimate purposes. The Ring's classic achievement was a court-

(United Press International)

house that cost $12 million to build, when $3 million would have been enough. Its costs included $179,729.60 for three tables and forty chairs.

Graft on such a scale could not and did not go unnoticed. Yet Tweed, sure of his power, responded to all charges with a sneering, "Well, what are you going to do about it?" Tammany's immigrant voters remained loyal, and Tweed even survived an investigation. But when, in 1871, two high level Ring members began turning over evidence to the New York *Times*, the end came with startling swiftness. Tweed, in a desperate move, offered the *Times* $500,000 to abandon its probe, and a similar sum to *Harper's Weekly* cartoonist Thomas Nast, suggesting that he might like to study art in Europe. Neither accepted the bribes, and soon the Tweed Ring was shattered both at the polls and in the courts. Tweed was in and out of prison for the next five years; he died in jail at age fifty-five.

TWO GREAT QUESTIONS.

'TWAS HIM.

Thomas Nast's cartoons exposed the unsavory Tweed Ring. *(Culver Pictures)*

minerals, oil, and lumber; nine in banking and finance; six in commerce; and three in manufacturing. Wealthy members of the House or Senate were not captives or "puppets" of the business interests with which they held close ties. But, on issues affecting the national economic life, their policies tended to favor businessmen and monied interests rather than farmers, laborers, and the poor. And they made only token efforts to regulate American industry or finance.

Currency Expansion

Favoritism toward business interests is shown clearly in the monetary programs enacted by Congress in the era. The debate involved the amount of currency in circulation. Farmers and most other debtors favored an increase in the amount of money issued by the government. Businesses, on the other hand, especially banking interests, wanted the opposite.

To understand the farmers' demands, it is important to keep in mind that this group was experiencing especially hard times during this period. The mechanization of agriculture was a mixed blessing to farmers. It greatly added to their ef-ficiency, but it helped create vast surpluses and consequent falling prices. Wheat, for example, which had sold for $2.50 a bushel in 1868 dropped to an average of 78 cents a bushel in the late 1880s.

While prices continued dropping, the cost of running farms remained high. Many farmers, for instance, were at the mercy of railroads that held a monopoly on transportation in their areas. These railroads often charged excessively high rates for carrying agricultural products to markets. Besides the cost of transportation, the cost of land, machinery, and tools was also quite high.

Faced with high costs and declining prices for their own products, farmers usually went into debt by mortgaging their land and goods. In the 1880s the number of mortgages soared. Of the total number of farms in the country, over 40 percent were mortgaged. In some areas, like Kansas, the figure was closer to 60 percent. Interest rates on these mortgages were high—6 to 15 percent on land and 10 to 18 percent on goods.

This pro-greenback cartoon portrays a gold-nosed government octopus linking itself to big business with its tentacles while strangling labor, farmers, and small business. (Culver Pictures)

Farmers felt that government could relieve their distress by pumping more money into the economy. The government had increased the amount of paper money—greenbacks—in circulation during the Civil War in order to finance the war effort. After the war the government began to withdraw these greenbacks from circulation. This cutback in currency was hitting the indebted farmer particularly hard because he had borrowed when money was "cheap" or plentiful. Now he had to pay his debts in currency worth much more than its original value.

From the bankers' point of view, of course, the situation was ideal. They had a stake in seeing that money became scarcer. They would profit more on the repayment of loans, since the value of a dollar increases as its supply decreases. The government agreed with this viewpoint.

During the Hayes administration, the Specie Resumption Act of 1875 was passed, committing the United States to returning to a gold standard by 1879. The Treasury Department, to help ensure the successful "resumption of specie payments" (as it was called) in 1879, began to reduce the number of greenbacks in circulation. This policy (and the Treasury's refusal to print additional issues of greenbacks) combined with an increase in overall productive output during the 1875–79 period to cause a total decline in the money stock. This was a direct slap at debtor interests, particularly farmers, coming as it did during the worst depression in American history up to that point.

The financial community benefited greatly, not only from the 1875 Resumption Act but from an earlier statute, in 1869, which provided that bonds issued during the Civil War should be paid off in gold. The banking community, of course, held most of these bonds. The provision meant that war bonds that had been bought with greenbacks worth less than 40 cents to the dollar could now be turned in for currency worth 100 cents to the dollar.

The resumption of specie payments (payment in gold alone) so enraged some farmers that they banded together to form a third party. They were joined by many recruits from labor and became the Greenback-Labor party in 1878. In the short run the movement was unsuccessful, since it failed to win many votes or to change the government's policy on currency. In the long run, however, it was significant in laying the basis for a far more powerful agrarian movement during the 1890s.

Agitation for expanding the currency did not stop after the initial failure of the Greenback movement. In fact, a new strategy was tried—a demand that silver be coined into dollars. In 1873 the government had stopped coining silver and put the country onto the gold standard—that is, backed money with gold alone. But in the 1870s the supply of silver increased tremendously because of the discovery of new silver deposits in the West. Many charged that silver had been demonetized illegally. By the 1880s farmers and other debtor groups saw in the "remonetizing" of silver a way of getting cheaper money. This in turn would raise crop prices and obtain for them relief from their debts.

Those who agitated for silver were partially successful during the 1870s. The Bland-Allison Act of 1878 required the Department of the Treasury to buy not less than $2 million and not more than $4 million worth of silver each month to back the dollar. Unfortunately, the government continuously bought the lesser amount. Though the silver interests were placated, farmers did not get much relief.

The Tariff Issue

Another government policy that tended to favor business interests at the expense of other segments of society involved the tariff. The tariff debate, as old as the country itself, took on new importance with the coming of the industrial age. The original justification for a tax on imports was to protect infant industries from the competition of foreign manufacturers. But long after competition from abroad ceased to be a threat, the tariff still remained high on most goods. And it was going higher.

Again those particularly hurt by the tariff were the farmers. They complained that they had to sell their goods competitively on an open world market. But they had to purchase tariff-protected manufactured and processed goods such as farm

An anti-tariff cartoon of the 1880s shows the spiraling bad effects of a high tariff. The tariff wall results in a glut of products on the home market, consequent cuts in production, and then widespread unemployment, at least in this hostile cartoon. (Culver Pictures)

machinery and oil. In fact, consumers in general suffered from the imposition of high tariffs. Without the competition of cheaper imported goods, they paid whatever prices domestic manufacturers set—prices that were often determined by monopolistic practices.

Republicans were by no means the only supporters of high protective tariffs. Factions in both parties backed business interests (or farmer interests) on this matter. But it was not until a Democrat, Grover Cleveland, took office that there was a serious challenge to high tariffs. Cleveland's advocacy of a lowered tariff provided the leading issue in his reelection bid in 1888. He was defeated, as noted earlier, partly because he had alienated the pro-tariff faction in his own party. But his downfall came mostly because businessmen poured millions of dollars into the campaign of the Republican candidate, Benjamin Harrison.

Harrison repaid his business backers by supporting the highest tariff in the nation's history. The McKinley Tariff of 1890—named after its sponsor, William McKinley—aimed not just at discouraging competition but at eliminating it altogether. It raised rates from an average of 38 percent to an average of almost 50 percent. It clearly marked a triumph for American industrialists.

Token Reform

Although business influence was at its height, the government could not afford to ignore the public altogether. Some steps were taken in this period to deal with elements in the changed economy. But these proved to be less than effective. Congressmen from both parties joined in passing two basically mild bills to regulate the new giant industries.

The Interstate Commerce Act in 1887 set up a federal commission (the ICC) to oversee "reasonable and just" rates on the nation's railroads. Congress did not provide the commission with any strong enforcement powers, however. Its only avenue was the courts, and these generally consisted of pro-business conservatives. Moreover, the persons who were appointed as commissioners during the 1890s were sympathetic to the railroads. This, of course, further prevented the ICC from making any serious efforts to regulate the lines in order to ensure fair and equal treatment for all shippers.

A second law, the Sherman Antitrust Act of 1890, was also supposed to curb big business. Anticipating public reaction to the high McKinley Tariff, congressmen hoped that the Sherman Act would quiet agitation. Unfortunately, the act provided only mild and ineffective penalties against companies that formed combinations in restraint of trade. Furthermore, it was rarely applied during the 1890s. Only five years after the law was passed, the Supreme Court handed down a decision in *U.S. v. Knight* that exempted most industries from its provision. A monopoly, according to the court, was not itself illegal. It became so only when it served to restrain interstate trade.

The immediate effect of such token efforts was to prevent a massive public outcry. In the long run, though, they only added further grievances to the growing list of problems confronting the country. The nation had lived through more than two decades of conservative rule resulting from the informal alliance of business and government. Pressure mounted in various parts of society to bring about meaningful reforms.

Suggested Readings
Chapters 27–28

Garfield

Robert G. Caldwell, *James A. Garfield: Party Chieftain* (1931); David M. Jordan, *Roscoe Conkling* (1971); Allan Peskin, *Garfield* (1978); Thomas C. Reeves, *Gentleman Boss: Chester A. Arthur* (1975); Charles E. Rosenberg, *The Trial of the Assassin Guiteau* (1968); Theodore C. Smith, *Life and Letters of James Abram Garfield* (2 vols, 1925).

Politics in Transition

Daniel J. Elazar, *The American Partnership* (1962); John A. Garraty, *The New Commonwealth, 1877–1890* (1968); Ari A. Hoogenboom. *Outlawing the Spoils* (1961); Robert D. Marcus, *Grand Old Party: Political Structure in the Gilded Age* (1971); H. Wayne Morgan, *From Hayes to McKinley* (1969); David J. Rothman, *Politics and Power: The U.S. Senate, 1869–1901* (1966); John G. Sproat, *"The Best Men": Liberal Reformers in the Gilded Age* (1968); Irwin Unger, *The Greenback Era* (1964); Allen Weinstein, *Prelude to Populism* (1970).

Republican Politics

Vincent P. DeSantis, *Republicans Face the Southern Question* (1959); Stanley P. Hirshon, *Farewell to the Bloody Shirt: Northern Republicans and the Southern Negro, 1877–1893* (1962); Leonard D. White, *The Republican Era, 1869–1901* (1958); Robert H. Wiebe, *The Search for Order: 1877–1920* (1968); C. Vann Woodward, *Origins of the New South* (1951).

Cleveland and the Democrats

Horace Samuel Merrill, *Bourbon Democracy of the Middle West, 1865–1896* (1969) and *Bourbon Leader: Grover Cleveland and the Democratic Party* (1957).

The Tweed Ring

Alexander B. Callow, Jr., *The Tweed Ring* (1966); Seymour Mandelbaum, *Boss Tweed's New York* (1965).

The Pullman Strike: Workers in Revolt 29

Rarlely had the McHenry County Jail held such a popular and notorious inmate. The year was 1895, and the place—Woodstock, Illinois. When the man walked out of jail into the chill November day, he went directly to the Woodstock train station. There he found awaiting him representatives of more than fifty unions, all of whom accompanied him on the short railroad trip to Chicago.

Over a hundred thousand people jammed the Chicago train station to greet the train from Woodstock. They cheered lustily as the train arrived and their man moved his way happily through the admiring crowd. Arrangements had been made for him to ride in a carriage drawn by six white horses during the following celebration in honor of his release from jail. Instead he chose to walk in a massive parade, and the festivities included his receiving a wild ovation from a large convention hall audience. Many in Illinois regarded the released prisoner, whose name was Eugene Victor Debs, as a conquering hero.

Yet Debs had conquered nothing. As president of the American Railway Union (A.R.U.), he had complied with the decision of its members to strike against the powerful Pullman Company, a firm that held a virtual monopoly on the construction of railway cars. The conflict, which centered in Chicago, had eventually spread, paralyzing railroad lines from coast to coast, with more than 150,000 men on strike. The battle escalated in political and economic importance, pitting organized labor against a giant corporation backed by a sympathetic national government. Debs went to jail during the course of the strike and, in the process, became a symbol, to working people throughout the country, of resistance to business dominance of labor–management relations. The Pullman strike was the third major conflict between American capital and labor during a decade of strife in which there were thousands of other strikes.

With the rise of large-scale industrial corporations, the struggle between American workers and capitalists replaced slavery as the nation's chief social dilemma after the Civil War. Corporations used millions of unskilled or semiskilled laborers, and these workers, often from recent

This cartoon portrays the activity of Eugene V. Debs's American Railway Union in an unfavorable light. Debs appears as a gimlet-eyed, crowned figure tyrannically halting all railroad activity on the national "Highway of Trade." An appeal to agrarian opinion can be deduced from the various indications, for example, "Grain Elevator Closed," of slowdowns in farm shipments wrought by the strike. (Library of Congress)

immigrant backgrounds, clustered in the teeming cities and factory towns. As had happened with slavery, the two major political parties avoided the subject as much as possible, and the conflict was dramatized by violent direct action—largely public protests and strikes. The drama was especially heightened during three strikes of the 1886–95 period, the last of which involved Pullman—and Debs.

The first of these three labor tragedies, the Haymarket bombing, also occurred in Chicago. During an 1886 city-wide campaign for an eight-hour day and other demands, workers called a meeting to support strikers at the McCormick Reaper works. Police tried to break up the assembly, and someone in the crowd threw a bomb, killing several policemen. Public outrage over this "Haymarket Massacre" led to the conviction of seven anarchists for conspiracy and murder, though without any evidence of any of them being directly linked to the bombing or of their plotting violence on the occasion. Four of the defendants were hanged, three received long prison sentences, and one committed suicide in jail.

Six years later, during the Homestead Strike of 1892, the Carnegie Steel Company hired a private army of three hundred Pinkerton Detective Agency operatives to protect the company's hired substitute workers (strikebreakers) from union workers attempting to keep the plant shut down. Members of the iron- and steelworkers unions fought a battle with the Pinkertons, killing three while losing ten of their own men. Carnegie Steel succeeded in smashing the union with the aid of Pennsylvania state militia. The company then reopened, using nonunion or "scab" labor (as unionists referred to the strikebreakers). But of the three great strikes in late nineteenth-century America, the trouble at Pullman reverberated most noticeably throughout the American scene. It involved a pro-business president of the United States, a strikebreaking attorney general, a pro-union governor, a paternalistic corporate tycoon, thousands of troops, and hundreds of thousands of workers in some capacity. Above all, it involved Eugene Victor Debs, who emerged from the strike—and from prison—as the hero of America's industrial poor.

For Debs, the journey to Pullman began at Terre Haute, Indiana, in 1855. The oldest son of French parents, Eugene was taught by his father, a grocer, to appreciate fine books and the dignity of human labor. After graduating from grammar school, Debs found his first job at a local factory, scraping paint from railroad cars. Later he worked as a car painter and then as a locomotive fireman at a lordly wage of one dollar a day. The frequent railroad accidents of his day made Debs's last job hazardous, and finally, he heeded his mother's anxious pleas and agreed to quit. Meanwhile, he had been studying bookkeeping at night, and he soon gained a clerkship in a grocery firm, where he remained for five years. Up to then, Debs's career had followed classic Horatio Alger lines, not unlike the early years of another Midwesterner soon to become president, James Abram Garfield.

Yet Debs's ambition and thirst for knowledge drove him to greater activity. After he was elected president of a local literary society in 1875, his talent at public speaking emerged. Although he was no longer working for the railroad, he became a charter member and secretary of the local lodge of the Brotherhood of Locomotive Firemen that same year. Helping to organize the brakemen and switchmen, Debs warned against strikes and violence. "We are not engaged," he avowed, "in any quarrel between capital and labor." Debs gave up his job as a grocery clerk after being elected Terre Haute City Clerk in 1879. Then, with election to the Indiana legislature at the age of twenty-nine, Debs appeared to be well launched on a promising political career. But he lacked obsessive ambition and acquired an idealistic disgust with the corruption of state politics which led him to quit the legislature after a single term.

By this time, Debs had become totally involved in activities that would lead to formation of the American Railway Union. He was chosen secretary treasurer of the Brotherhood of Locomotive Firemen in 1880 and promptly set about rebuilding the union. It had suffered along with other unions during the depression of the 1870s, but Debs helped put it back on its feet, even donating an entire year's salary to the union fund. In the thirteen years that followed, Debs increased the circulation of the Brotherhood's journal from fifteen hundred to thirty-seven thousand copies per month, reflecting an extraordinary growth in overall union membership.

But Debs dreamed of uniting *all* unions within the railroad industry under a single union banner. He recognized that, instead of fostering unity and strength, the existence of a variety of unions among railroad employees fostered suspicion and rivalry. Under these conditions, railroad corporations found it easier to deal with each "brotherhood" separately, confident that other railway unions would not support joint negotiations. Many of the skilled firemen, engineers, and conductors remained nonunion, for that matter, and there had been virtually no effort to organize the vast number of unskilled or semiskilled workers on America's railroads.

Debs introduced his idea of one large union embracing all skilled and nonskilled workers before the Brotherhood of Locomotive Firemen's convention at Cincinnati in 1892, and after an intense organizing process, the American Railway Union (A.R.U.) emerged in Chicago on June 29, 1893, with Eugene Victor Debs as its first president.

The A.R.U. had a democratic constitution: Ten or more workers could establish a local union; district conventions would be held annually; and a national convention would be held every four years in Chicago to elect the executive board. This board, in turn, would choose the president and other chief officers. The union stated its intention also to avoid strikes and settle grievances peacefully, presumably in order to assuage the fears of railroad officials that the unification of railway workers' organizations would bring in its wake disruption and violence. Each local union was charged with electing a board of mediation, which would attempt to negotiate settlements between aggrieved workers and local management. If the problem continued, it could be referred to the general board of mediation. Failure here would bring the matter to the attention of the president and the directors of the A.R.U., who would make a final effort to resolve the issue peacefully. The union board had no power itself to call a strike, but at this stage, it would call for votes from union locals on unresolved negotiations and, then, abide by their decision. Dues in the A.R.U. were only a dollar per year.

The organization did not concern itself only with the higher wage philosophy (or "bread-and-butter" unionism) of other craft unions. The A.R.U.'s political wing, its department of legislation and cooperation, campaigned and lobbied for the eight-hour day, safety laws, and restriction of Sunday work. The union also offered low-cost life and disability insurance, helped its unemployed members find work, and gave lectures for its workers on economics and related subjects.

But the test of the union's high principles would come not through the wording of its constitution or its subsidiary practices but when the American Railway Union confronted management. A victory in the Great Northern Strike some ten months after its founding soon swelled the ranks of the A.R.U. The Great Northern line stretched twenty-five hundred miles and employed about nine thousand workers, less than half of whom were organized. The depression that began in 1893 caused the company to slash wages three times in seven months, until they averaged less than forty dollars a month, lower than those paid by any other Pacific transcontinental line. When workers demanded higher wages, and the A.R.U. sent a letter calling for a meeting with union representatives to railroad magnate James Hill, he ignored the letter.

The A.R.U.-imposed strike, which began in Montana, soon paralyzed the entire Great Northern line. Unorganized workers and those usually loyal to management, such as station agents and yard masters, this time supported the workers' demands. Some mail trains and a few locals were allowed to run, but no transcontinental train operated by the company completed its trip. The company, in turn, imported strikebreakers, but the united front of railroad workers—supported by some farmers and businessmen in the towns along the Great Northern route—convinced the railroad owners to settle. (Western farmers and small businessmen had opposed the actions of powerful railroads in past decades and often sympathized keenly with the grievances of workers who lived in their localities.)

After only eighteen days of the strike, Hill and Debs agreed to arbitration. Fourteen representative businessmen in St. Paul and Minneapolis, acting as arbiters, found that the demands of labor were just and awarded the workers substantial wage increases. In the weeks following the strike, the A.R.U. gained two thousand members a day. One year after its founding, it had become the largest trade union in the United States, with 425 locals and 150,000 members. Returning to his Terre Haute home after settling the strike, Debs expressed personal satisfaction:

> As our train pulled out of the yards the tokens of esteem, which I prize far more highly than all others, was in seeing the old truckmen, men whose frames were bent with years of grinding toil, who received the pittance of from eighty cents to one dollar a day, leaning on their shovels and lifting their hats to me in appreciation of my humble assistance in a cause which they believed had resulted in a betterment of their miserable existence.

The man who was shortly to become Debs's chief adversary, George Mortimer Pullman, was born on March 3, 1831, in the town of Brocton in western New York. Pullman, like Debs, came from a poor family. His father, a dissatisfied farmer, became a carpenter, and Pullman was raised in the traditional American environment of a solid work ethic and a devotion to family and religion. Like Debs, Pullman left school at fourteen to become a clerk, in his case in a small general store. When his father died in 1853, young George, the eldest son, took over his father's work on state contracts, moving homes that were too near the banks of the Erie Canal, which was then undergoing extension. In 1855, Pullman left for Chicago to work on a similar project.

He set himself to the task of raising the streets along Lake Michigan and the Chicago River to guard against flooding and unhealthy conditions. Pullman was both practical and ambitious, and he set about ingratiating himself with highly placed Chicagoans in the business community: dressing conservatively, speaking only after carefully selecting his words, affecting a reserved and sophisticated manner. Eventually Pullman began thinking about constructing railroad sleeping cars.

The notion was hardly novel. By 1855 several railroads were advertising "sleepers," and a few companies had already opened shops to build them. Between 1850 and 1860 railroad mileage in the United States tripled, and it had become apparent that a transcontinental line would soon make coast-to-coast travel possible. Pullman described the three-and-a-half-day trip between Chicago and New York, which he had taken himself, as a "nightmare," and he determined to make that journey more bearable, perhaps almost comfortable. Narrow, hard-backed seats and rattling windows made long excursions in ordinary coaches a hardship, and the first sleepers contained no more than wooden shelves, perhaps with a hard mattress, on which the traveler might find some rest.

After an initial partnership on the idea, Pullman bought out his partners by 1867. The Illinois State Legislature issued a charter (which some states still required for all corporations), creating "Pullman's Palace Car Company." Pullman quietly sold the first million dollars of stock to Chicago businessmen and railroad tycoons. After building a model sleeping car, the "Pioneer," the company began contractual agreements with railroads for the production of these distinctive cars. Demanding from railroad companies that they promise to keep the outside of their cars in good appearance, Pullman built all the sleeping cars they needed, maintained their interiors, and received all profits above the regular fare from ticket sales for the cars.

Pullman introduced the dining car "Delmonico" in 1868, the name taken from a famous New York restaurant. Chefs in the car could make 250 meals a day, thereby eliminating the need to stop at local towns for meals.

The elegance and comfort of a Pullman dining car emerge from this photograph of one such "palace car" in actual service. (Brown Brothers)

Transcontinental rail travel became a reality after work on the country's first coast-to-coast line was completed with the driving of the Golden Spike on May 10, 1869, at Promontory Point, Utah. The following year, Pullman's company introduced a luxury "excursion" car, which wealthy travelers could hire; the car came complete with a steward, cook, and two waiters. "Parlor" cars, another Pullman innovation, provided swivel easy chairs. The manufacture of separate cars that could be used as offices, a wine room, smoking room and barber shop prompted one editor to label such trains a "rolling village."

Pullman's interest and concern with working-class conditions, reflecting the man's persistent paternalism toward his own employees, led to a social experiment conducted within his own business. In 1872, Pullman read a Victorian romance, Charles Rade's *Put Yourself in His Place,* which dramatized the dreadful living conditions of English workers. He also viewed with dismay the results of the depression of 1873 and the labor unrest in 1877. Beginning in the early 1870s, after the tragic Chicago Fire of 1871, the cost of urban property forced some companies to relocate in the suburbs. Many businessmen began wondering if the morale and morals of the work force would improve once employees were moved away from large cities. Pullman himself had served as vice-president of the Citizens' Law and Order League to enforce the prohibition of liquor sales to minors during the 1877 railroad strikes. He was won over, also, to supporting a model town movement among his own employees. But Pullman described the move as a "strictly business proposition," expecting that his new model town would attract city working-men of the highest character: prompt, hardworking, sober, and indifferent to labor "agitators" such as the organizers of railway unions.

Pullman put his idea of launching a great experiment in town—and character—development into action when he purchased four thousand acres on the western shore of Lake Calumet, twelve miles south of central Chicago (now a part of Chicago's South Side). Surrounded on one side by the lake and on the other by Pullman's private property, the town-site was suited to be free of any "disruptive elements." Nearly all railroads entering Chicago from the South or East passed through the Calumet region. A young New York architect who had designed Pullman's mansion in New Jersey, Solon Spencer Beman, was called in to supervise town planning. The first Pullman Car shops and workers' homes, made partly of brick from the deposits of clay at the bottom of the lake, were completed in 1881. A farm on the outskirts of the model town soon produced vegetables for the towns of both Pullman and Chicago. Streets were named after famous inventors, and trees were planted. The Arcade Building contained over thirty shops, stood ninety feet high, and stretched a full city block. Pullman himself donated over five thousand volumes to launch the town's library.

George Pullman put his personal stamp, in fact, on almost every aspect of life in the new community. He insisted on choosing plays for the Arcade Theater. The bar of the Florence Hotel, named after Pullman's favorite daughter, was the only place in town that sold liquor. The large nondenominational Greenstone Church was created to bring a spiritual center to the community, but various denominations—Catholic, Methodist, Episcopalian, and Presbyterian—soon held their own separate services. "As all the world knows," boasted one Chicago newspaper, the town of Pullman "is an industrial hive of many thousand busy workers, all placed in an environment unique and unmatched the world over for solid comfort and luxuriousness."

From the beginning, however, Pullman's village "utopia" displayed signs of erosion and difficulty. For one thing, males outnumbered females greatly (and in 1885 the men in the town were clearly of marrying age and disposition, their average age being twenty-nine). Average salaries in Pullman were higher than elsewhere, not because of better productivity or beneficent employers, but because three-quarters of those who labored in the Pullman Palace Car Company's repair and manufacturing shops were skilled workers. Also, by 1885, the majority of Pullman's population was foreign-born and not the native Americans previously expected to swell the community. Furthermore, the population proved to be unstable. The town had grown in size by 1893 to 12,600, with the average stay only a little over four years.

One reason for the instability was Pullman's refusal to sell any of his property, thereby preventing his workers from owning their own homes. Many resented this lack of freedom and began moving to the new surrounding communities, purchasing homes or land on which to build. The issue of rent became a sore point with Pullman residents. Rents in the town, it later became known, were 25 percent higher than elsewhere in Chicago; the company insisted its accommodations were superior.

In paternalistic fashion, George Pullman exercised enormous personal control over his town. He had little difficulty in obtaining the election of politicians favorable to his interests. In the town itself, the Pullman Company appointed all officials. Labor union officials and speakers judged "radical" or otherwise unacceptable were not allowed to rent public halls or speak in them. Many of the town's residents lived in fear of constant observation. Tenants considered undesirable could be evicted within ten days.

Workers charged, in 1887 and again in 1889, that the foreman in the Pullman shops had been instructed to influence the workers to vote for Pullman's favorite candidates, and several were cited as having pressured voters to cast ballots for the Republican party, standing close enough to the polls to check on how particular men voted. When the issue of annexing the town of Pullman to Chicago went on the ballot during the 1889 elections, Pullman used every resource to fight the measure. Company coercion, critics charged, led to discharges of workers who circulated pro-annexation petitions or refused to sign anti-annexation ones. In the end, the area was incorporated into the city of Chicago, but Pullman lost none of his power. He succeeded in electing compliant candidates to the City Council. The lack of any role in decision making destroyed what little civic pride workers might have felt in the model town, eventually undermining George Pullman's social experiment.

Much of the underlying discontent surfaced with the Panic of 1893 (a stock market and general financial collapse) followed by a depression that seemed to worsen with each month. After a period of record profits, Pullman Company business declined dramatically during the late summer of 1893. Many orders for cars were canceled, and the company laid off most workers in its construction division. Pullman believed, however, that by reducing the prices on his cars by 25 percent, he could continue to employ many workers who would otherwise be fired. The railway unionists interpreted Pullman's move, however, as purely a business measure designed to keep competitors from infringing on the company's share of the market.

Whatever his motives, Pullman determined that he could keep large sections of his labor force employed only by slashing wages in all divisions of the company, regardless of which units might still be showing profits. Employment was staggered, with some men working only ten or twenty hours a week at earnings too low for decent survival. Wages were cut by one-fourth to one-third, but the company continued to pay 8 percent dividends to its stockholders. The high rent workers paid for company-owned housing was simply withheld from their paychecks. Matters seemed to be heading for inevitable collision between union and management.

The struggle between railway workers, led by Debs, with his passionate belief in economic equality, and a company headed by Pullman, who believed with equal intensity in free enterprise capitalism, now came to a head in the latter's model town. In early April 1894, town workers gathered in the surrounding communities of Grand Crossing and Kensington to organize nineteen locals of the American Railway Union with a combined membership of four thousand men. Organizing a union, itself, violated Pullman's most deeply held paternalistic belief in his own ability to deal correctly—and without outside interference—with his workers, a belief that had led him to construct the town of Pullman in the first place. Now large numbers of his workmen seemed determined to betray his trust, or so Pullman reasoned.

The union organizers recognized the weakness of labor protest during a period of dire depression and cautioned the new recruits against a strike. The Pullman workers then selected a grievance committee, which presented demands to a company vice-president, insisting either that wages be restored to earlier levels or rents on their homes be lowered. Pullman himself claimed that raising wages would prevent the company from competing effectively with other manufacturers of railroad cars, and he refused to compromise with the union committee. When a superintendent fired three men who had served on the grievance committee, possibly in retaliation for committee criticisms aimed at him, workers immediately seized upon the firings as evidence of the company's bad faith.

That same night, May 10, 1894, after a long meeting in nearby Kensington, the A.R.U. grievance committee voted unanimously to strike, although without fixing a date for the walkout. The next morning, a rumor spread (which proved to be false) that the company had decided to close down the shops at noon in retaliation. The strike committee immediately called for men to leave their workplace to avoid layoffs before their planned strike. Three thousand employees walked off their jobs before noon, and by evening, company officials posted a notice that announced: "The works are closed until further notice." When the committee stationed three hundred strikers as guards for the express purpose of protecting Pullman property against vandals, the company accused them of picketing, the legal right to which was not then protected. After Debs came to inspect conditions in the town, he urged citizens of the area to donate generously to the relief committee.

When the first national convention of the American Railway Union met in Chicago in June, a special committee proposed that unless the Pullman Company agreed to negotiate within the next four days, union members would refuse to service or deal with Pullman cars. Pullman's works in St. Louis and Ludlow, Kentucky, would also be struck. When company officials refused to talk to union representatives, the boycott began on June 26. Debs ordered all sleeping cars cut from the trains and sidetracked. Within days, more than 125,000 railroad workers in the Central and Western states were on strike against their employers, who tried to force them to link Pullman cars onto various trains.

Workers were not the only group that had organized as a result of the trouble at Pullman. Responding to the formation of the American Railway Union in 1893, railroad managers met later that year to form an employers' group eventually known as the General Managers' Association. That August the organization worked out uniform low wage rates, which each railroad would pay certain categories of workers, explaining "that a reduction of wages of employees, however much to be regretted, is imperative." Three days after the A.R.U. boycott went into effect, the association announced that any worker fired by a railroad for refusing to perform certain work prohibited by the A.R.U. would be blacklisted and forbidden to work on *any* railroad within the General Managers' jurisdiction. Strikebreakers would be given special protection and permanent positions.

Despite the importation of strikebreakers from all parts of the country, the railroad strike spread from Chicago, extending to California in the West and to northern New York in the East, involving over 150,000 workers. Many trade unions and other labor organizations throughout the country supported the boycott, and unions actively campaigned to persuade middle-class or wealthy Americans not to ride in Pullman cars. Unity, public support, and high morale all seemed to signal a possible victory for Pullman workers and the A.R.U.

Sensing defeat, the railroads now sought to bring the federal government into the dispute. John Egan, coordinator of anti-strike activities for the General Managers' Association, admitted on July 2 that the railroads have been "fought to a standstill." Since there was no "other recourse left," federal troops should be called out. If so, he argued, "the strike would collapse like a punctured balloon. It is the government's duty to take this business in hand, restore law, suppress the riots, and restore to the public the service which it is now deprived of by conspirators and lawless men."

Fortunately for Pullman and the railroad executives, Egan had an ally in Attorney General Richard Olney, a man who had worked as a corporate lawyer for several railroads, including the Chicago, Burlington, and Quincy, before joining Grover Cleveland's cabinet. Olney remained a director of the Burlington and was also a codirector with George Pullman of the Boston and Maine line. When a large band of unemployed workers traveled to Washington as part of "Coxey's Army" that year, Olney saw to it that General Jacob Coxey and the other leaders — who demanded government action to alleviate the industrial distress caused by the depression — were arrested. Olney exercised direct control over United States marshals and district attorneys, enabling him to create situations that would involve the government deeply in the Pullman labor dispute.

The issue of the movement of mail finally brought the federal government into the conflict. Although the American Railway Union had no intention of interfering with the mail and even offered to furnish men to help operate mail trains as long as Pullman cars were not attached, railroad officials — and, soon, the General Managers' Association — adopted the policy of refusing to allow any operation of trains carrying mail unless the full number of cars, including Pullman sleepers and diners, were included. No law required that sleepers or other Pullman cars be attached to trains carrying the mail, and President Cleveland's administration could easily have avoided any complications by ordering that mail trains omit Pullman cars until after the strike settlement. As head of the Justice Department, however, Richard Olney defined a mail train as one including all cars that are normally hauled when mail is delivered. Anyone detaching any car from this train would be considered guilty, according to Olney, of obstructing the mail.

With railroad officials busily linking Pullman cars to mail trains throughout the stricken areas, the Post Office Department in Washington soon began receiving reports of delays in the mail in such places as Hammond, Indiana; Hope, Idaho; and San Francisco. When the division superintendent of the railway mail service at Chicago protested the matter to the A.R.U., Debs explained that all union strikers had withdrawn from work and could not be held responsible for the consequences of this passive disobedience.

After receiving a telegram from Attorney General Olney ordering him into action, Thomas Milchrist, U.S. attorney at Chicago, spoke before a meeting of the General Managers. He wanted the names of persons who disconnected Pullman cars from mail trains so that arrest warrants could be issued. Olney now authorized the federal marshal at Chicago to appoint fifty deputies and appointed Edwin Walker as special attorney for the federal government's case against the strikers. Walker, a corporate lawyer who remained on the payroll of railroads throughout the strike, served both as the Illinois counsel of the Chicago, Milwaukee, and St. Paul line and as general counsel for the General Managers' Association.

Events in the Chicago suburbs of Blue Island and Riverdale provided further justification for the government's increased legal effort against the A.R.U. Near riot conditions prevailed in both places, with men obstructing the tracks. On July 1, the United States marshal telegraphed Olney: "The situation here tonight is desperate. I have sworn in over 400 deputies, and many more will be needed to protect the mail trains. I expect great trouble. Shall I purchase 100 riot guns? . . ."

Such news convinced Olney that the Justice Department should apply for a broad injunction, a court order prohibiting the American Railway Union from striking against the railroads. The injunction would be based on the Sherman Antitrust Act of 1890, passed as a result of pressure by labor, small business, and farmers to prosecute *business* monopolies acting in restraint of trade. As corporate lawyer for the railroads, Attorney General Olney repeatedly refused to apply this law to illegal business combinations but immediately recognized its potential for fighting labor unions. Olney's decision was fortified as early as April 1894, when a federal judge named Jenkins ruled that the Sherman law could be interpreted to forbid combinations of employees from quitting work as a group. "Whatever other doctrine may be asserted by reckless agitators," Jenkins wrote, "it must ever remain the duty of the courts, in the protection of society, and in the execution of the laws of the land, to condemn, prevent, and punish all such unlawful conspiracies and combinations."

The federal district court in Chicago responded to the government's request by issuing the most sweeping injunction in American history up to that date. When U.S. Attorney Milchrist submitted his petition for injunction to the judges on July 2, Edwin Walker suggested that it be broadened and strengthened to include not merely the damages to interstate commerce presumably caused by the union's strike but interference with the United States mail as well. This would increase a less significant penalty for violating the injunction to a term in the penitentiary for criminal conspiracy. Walker got the injunction he requested.

The court order claimed that Pullman cars and similar ones were indispensable to the successful operation of trains. Strikers were charged with conspiracy, using force to discourage strikebreakers, and destroying railroad property. They were ordered to stay away from all railroads and forbidden even to persuade any other employee to walk off the job. Any form of communication designed to encourage workers to quit in support of the strike was declared illegal—even the sending of telegrams! The decision of the court was so favorable to the cause of railroad corporations that the New York *Times* approvingly called it a "Gatling gun on paper." The Chicago *Times,* more critical, described the power of injunction over labor unions as "a menace to liberty . . . a weapon ever ready for the capitalist."

As a result of the disturbances and the need to enforce the injunction, five thousand deputy marshals were recruited for Chicago alone. Two-thirds of these were armed and paid by the railroad companies to which they bore direct responsibility. After the men had been recom-

mended by the railroads, they were sworn in as deputy federal marshals without any examination of their qualifications or background. The consequence was that a number of drunkards, thieves, and questionable characters became law enforcement officers, and they often provoked unnecessary disturbances and made dubious arrests. The huge force of deputy marshals proved extremely costly, moreover, and one Chicago marshal argued that since most of the deputies had been employed by the railroads to protect their property, companies should help bear the costs of paying salaries and room-and-board costs. The General Managers replied with a straight face that all expenses had been for the "maintenance of Federal law and the authority of Federal Courts, and therefore ought no more to be paid by the railroads that by any individual citizen."

At first, shortly after the strike began, Attorney General Olney had considered the possibility of sending federal troops to Chicago. Eventually, he convinced President Cleveland and his closest advisers of the need for drastic action. When the United States marshal reported to Washington that a mob at Blue Island had overturned a mail train and several baggage cars, which now stood in the way of other trains, and requested federal troops, government intervention was assured. On July 3, federal troops were ordered from Fort Sheridan into Chicago to protect federal property and to prevent interference with interstate commerce and the U.S. mails.

This move by the national government triggered a far-reaching controversy between two very different Democratic officeholders, the conservative president, Grover Cleveland, and the reformist Illinois governor, John Peter Altgeld. Upon learning about Cleveland's intention to send in troops, Altgeld denied that federal assistance was needed:

> At present some of our railroads are paralyzed, not by reason of obstruction, but because they cannot get men to operate their trains. For some reason they are anxious to keep this fact from the public, and for this purpose they are making an outcry about obstructions in order to divert attention. . . It is true that in several instances a road made efforts to work a few green men and a crowd standing around insulted them and tried to drive them away, and in a few other cases they cut off Pullman sleepers from

trains. But all these troubles were local in character and could easily be handled by the state authorities.

Normally presidents did not use their constitutional authority to send the army into a state to protect it against internal violence unless requested to do so by the state's legislature or governor. But Cleveland could base his action on a Civil War statute intended to give President Lincoln the power to send troops into the rebellious states of the South, and a Reconstruction statute that allowed President Grant to send troops to protect black citizens in Southern states. Armed with these legal precedents, the president wired Governor Altgeld insisting that he was acting under constitutional authority and that he had no intention of interfering with local authorities. Unconvinced, the Illinois governor countered with a final telegram:

> If this is the law, then the principle of self-government either never did exist in this country or else has been destroyed, for no community can be said to possess local self-government, if the executive can, at his pleasure, send military forces to patrol its streets under pretense of enforcing some law.... The troops you have ordered to Chicago are not under the civil authorities, and are in no way responsible to them for their conduct. They are not even acting under the United States Marshal or any Federal officer of the State, but are acting directly under military orders issued from military headquarters at Washington, and in so far as these troops act at all, it is military government.

The Chicago *Evening Journal* promptly labeled Altgeld an "anarchist."

The arrival of federal troops in Chicago, combined with the high tension of the nationwide Pullman strike and the general frustration of the working force brought on by hard times, soon led to violence. On the Fourth of July, rioters and vandals moved from the stockyards to the property of the Rock Island Railroad, throwing switches and setting fire to trains. Two days later, mobs destroyed $340,000 worth of railroad property, burning over seven hundred cars at the Panhandle yards in South Chicago. While protecting a train on the afternoon of July 7, a militia company was attacked by a mob armed with both stones and guns. After

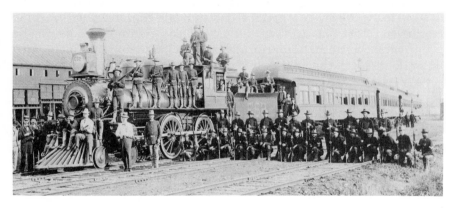

U.S. Army troops guarding a train during the Pullman strike. President Cleveland—personally sympathetic to the railway companies and anti-union—had ordered the troops into duty despite no clear-cut threat to the U.S. mails or public order. (Library of Congress)

demanding that the crowd disperse, the commander ordered a bayonet charge. Several in the crowd continued to shoot at the militiamen, who were now ordered to fire at will. This fight at Loomis Street left four rioters killed and twenty wounded. On the same day deputy marshals and federal troops were sent to seven Chicago depots to move the mail trains. Equipped with one hundred rounds of ammunition each and orders to disperse all interfering strikers, they began the process of clearing the roads for interstate commerce.

It was evident by this time that the American Railway Union's strike was in trouble. Some A.R.U. members and Chicago radicals believed that only a *general* strike by all workers in that city of 1 million people could save the cause that had begun with the dissatisfied workers of Pullman. At a mass meeting on July 8, representatives of over a hundred unions agreed to a city-wide strike beginning on July 10 if George Pullman did not agree to accept a settlement by arbitration. When company officials again refused to negotiate with a committee representing the workers, the Trades and Labor Congress called on all Chicago unionists to walk off the job. The plan failed totally. Fewer than twenty-five thousand workers responded to the plea. Few felt that such a show of support would have much effect in any case, with the city under what amounted to martial law. Many waited to see what action, if any, the executive conference of the American Federation of Labor (A.F. of L.) the nationwide bread-and-butter unionists' organization, would take when it met in Chicago on July 12.

Meanwhile other developments had convinced workers they should be wary of hasty action. Since the federal courts had issued the injunction against the A.R.U. strikers, any encouragement of the strike by others had become illegal. Strike leaders in Chicago could not help coordinate resistance in the Western states without subjecting themselves to arrest, and hundreds of union officials throughout the country were now arrested. Finally, on July 10, a federal grand jury in Chicago returned indictments against the officers of the A.R.U. Debs and his colleagues were arrested for conspiring to obstruct the mails and interfering with interstate commerce. They were released on bail the same day, but not before deputy marshals and deputy post office inspectors raided the union's headquarters. No one was left to deal with telegrams or to coordinate strike activities in any organized fashion.

Trade unions affiliated with the A.F. of L. had called on the federation's president, Samuel Gompers, to come to Chicago for a review of the situation. Gompers and two dozen top union officials met on July 12 in that city to discuss what action their organization should take in the great strike. Although some called for a nationwide walkout, the majority urged caution, doubting the wisdom of such a drastic step. That evening, Debs appeared at the meeting, suggesting that at this point the best action the A.F. of L. could take would be to offer the General Managers' Association an end to the boycott in return for a guarantee that all union members be allowed to return to their jobs.

With the strike already lost, however, the A.F. of L. refused even to act as a go-between in the dispute, offering only a suggestion that one of its members accompany Debs to the railway Managers' Association headquarters. Knowing that the railroad executives would not meet with him, Debs turned down the offer. Then, as a gesture of sympathy, the A.F. of L. leaders decided to contribute $1,000 to Debs's legal defense. While the Detroit *Free Press* and other conservative papers praised Gompers and his colleagues for "saving the people of this country from a most far-reaching and bloody revolution," more militant unionists viewed the A.F. of L. inaction as a betrayal of working people.

But the stand taken by Gompers and the A.F. of L. represented the growing conservative views generally held by influential craft unions in the labor movement. Spurning direct political involvement or attacks on capitalism, the A.F. of L., which had been founded the previous decade, had no interest in restoring the preindustrial conditions, which had supposedly existed prior to the Civil War and the advent of large-scale corporate development. Gompers and his associates accepted both the existence and the domination of corporate monopolies, seeking only to better working conditions and status within such a capitalist system. Rather than organizing workers industry-wide, as Debs had attempted in the American Railway Union, the A.F. of L. consisted of individual craft unions of skilled workers loosely affiliated in the national organization. Such a structure inevitably weakened the bargaining position of less-skilled or more poorly organized laborers. In the case of the Pullman strike, many A.F. of L. men had actually hoped for the defeat and destruction of the A.R.U., since the latter organization had depleted the ranks of railroad brotherhoods affiliated earlier with the A.F. of L.

Debs and other A.R.U. officials were again arrested on July 17 on contempt of court charges for violating the injunction. The defendants were charged with continuing to send telegrams urging railroad employees to leave their jobs and thus interfering with interstate commerce. When the contempt hearing began on July 23, the defendants denied that they had violated any restraining order, claiming that only the railroad workers themselves had the power to strike while top officials could only advise under the union's constitution. Debs also insisted that he and other A.R.U. officials had urged strikers repeatedly against lawlessness and violence. Counsel for the defense even argued that the railroads, not the unionists, were guilty of conspiracy, having formed an illegal combination (the General Managers' Association) to reduce wages. A young attorney named Clarence Darrow quit the Chicago and Northwestern Railroad to join the defense team for the A.R.U. Prosecuting attorney Edwin Walker granted that the defendants had warned strikers against violent resistance. Still, the accused, Walker argued, had continued to urge others to join the strike in violation of the injunction.

Judge William Woods found the defendants guilty, citing the applicability of the Sherman Antitrust Act. Although Woods acknowledged that the relevance of this law to a labor union had not been present in the "original measure," he believed that it had since undergone a modification widening its scope to include the conspiracy of boycotting Pullman cars as an interference with transportation across state lines. The union officials, he held, had gone beyond a simple boycott of Pullman sleepers to taking action to stop the movement of trains. High A.R.U. leaders may not have moved trains with their own hands, but they were responsible for union members who did. Debs was sentenced to six months in jail, other officials to three months. The defense counsel appealed the case on a writ of habeas corpus (technically, requesting an explanation of the reason for the prisoner's detention).

The case of *In re Debs* (1895) became one of the most celebrated in American legal history. Darrow and the defense argued that the Sherman Antitrust Act was not applicable and that the A.R.U. officials had never engaged in a conspiracy: "Refusing to work for a railroad is no crime, and, though such action may incidentally delay the mails or interfere with interstate commerce, it being a lawful act, and not done for the purpose, it is no offense." The prosecution, represented by Attorney General Olney, Assistant Attorney General Whitney, and Edwin Walker, contended that the executive branch, armed with the power to protect interstate commerce, had the obligation to enforce the law by seeking an injunction. Union leaders must be held responsible for the actions of their members, unless "it be true that a man can wantonly touch the match to powder and yet be blameless because not rightly realizing the ensuing devastation."

In denying the writ of habeas corpus to Debs, Justice David J. Brewer spoke for the U.S. Supreme Court in upholding the power of the national government over interstate commerce. He cited John Marshall's decision in *McCulloch* v. *Maryland,* and then proclaimed:

> The strong arm of the national government may be put forth to brush away all obstruction to the freedom of interstate commerce or the transportation of the mails. If the emergency arises, the army of the Nation, and all its militia, are at the service of the nation to compel obedience to its laws.

Convinced that the union had helped obstruct commerce, the Supreme Court held that the federal circuit court had possessed the authority to issue the injunction.

Richard Olney received the hearty congratulations of the business community for winning the government's case. American labor unions, on the other hand, responded anxiously, fearing future injunctions. Governor Altgeld believed that the federal government had still not proved that Debs and the other defendants had violated the law. Altgeld felt the union leaders had not received a fair trial in the overheated Chicago atmosphere of the day.

One thing was certain: The strike had failed. The day after the arrest of the A.R.U. leaders, on July 18, 1894, a notice appeared outside of Pullman: "These gates will be opened as soon as the number of operatives is sufficient to make a working force in all departments." Two weeks later those leaders of the A.R.U. still free held a special convention belatedly calling off the strike.

For Eugene Victor Debs, the experience of the Pullman strike proved bitter but enlightening. He emerged from the Woodstock jail a committed socialist and would suffer imprisonment on several other occasions in his career as the leader of the American Socialist party. For the Pullman workers, the strike proved disastrous. The collapse of the protest — and of the A.R.U. — left thousands of them unemployed or blacklisted. Workers who had opposed having their wages cut by the Pullman Company following the Panic of 1893 now found themselves destitute, some of them joining the wandering poor of the depression-wracked supposedly Gay Nineties.

But many people, from wealthy businessmen to large numbers of the middle class down to the skilled workers of the A.F. of L., applauded the failure of the Pullman strike as the defeat of a radical threat to American institutions. The destruction of the American Railway Union, for such people, seemed a victory for George Pullman's convictions (shared by millions of his fellow countrymen) in favor of hard work, duty, and the freedom to accumulate property. The evolving beliefs of Eugene Victor Debs, though nonviolent and egalitarian, still appeared as something vaguely anarchic and foreign to more traditional Americans and would await a more responsive hearing from future generations.

Urban-Industrial America: A New Society 30

Both Eugene V. Debs and George Pullman had witnessed profound changes in the America of their youth during the decades preceding the Pullman strike. When Pullman was born in 1831, for example, the *village* of Chicago stretched sparsely along the western shore of Lake Michigan, and even Pullman's birth area in western New York was hardly past the frontier stage at that time. Debs, although born twenty-four years later, was still in his early twenties when Reconstruction ended. Both men had been raised in a preindustrial, largely rural or small-town, predominantly Protestant United States, where a majority of Americans were either farmers or those whose livelihoods depended upon agriculture in some manner. By the time Debs and Pullman confronted one another in the struggle between the American Railway Union and the General Managers' Association, virtually all of the fundamentals of that earlier world had been transformed. The United States had changed dramatically during the late-nineteenth century as a result of rapid and widespread industrialization, urbanization, and immigration.

Modern America's formative period, from 1860 to 1900, began in civil war and terminated in imperial expansion. The population increased from 31 million to 76 million in these forty years. During these decades, after fighting a bloody war of national unity and liberating its slave population (only to abandon the freedmen to sectional serfdom), the United States expanded its industrial system and developed a network of urban slums (and factory towns) in which millions of immigrants and native-born migrants to the cities were absorbed. Returning to the United States from England in 1868 after a seven-year absence, Henry Adams observed that he felt as strange as if he had been a returning merchant from the year 1000 B.C., "so changed [was America] from what [it] had been ten years before." Adams noted that it took the remainder of the century and the "energies of a generation" to fill out the economic and social structure of modern America—its "capital, banks, mines, furnaces, shops, powerhouses, technical knowledge, mechanical population, together with a steady remodeling of social and political habits, ideas, and institutions to fit the new scale and suit the new conditions."

These developments all played some role in strikes such as the one which occurred at Pullman. The enormous growth of the railroad network after the Civil War allowed George Pullman to turn his attention from his previous, unpromising job of raising Chicago's lake-side streets to pursuing his vision of manufacturing sleeping, dining, and other "palace" cars that would better accommodate more affluent passengers traveling along transcontinental track. At the same time, the process of urbanization in Chicago, with the concurrent growth of normal social problems in the poorer quarters of cities—unhealthy tenements, high crime rates, prostitution, and alcoholism among them—led Pullman to establish the model town in which, he hoped, his workers would free themselves from such influences. (Pullman counted "labor agitators" and unions among the unhealthy influences to be countered in his new community.)

Pullman found, however, that the problems of labor–management conflict themselves could not be brushed aside simply because of his self-professed paternalism. The very existence of the factory system and underpaid laborers engendered the industrial strife which George Pullman tried so earnestly to eliminate. Moreover, despite his best efforts, the working force itself became more unruly and heterogeneous in background, as native-born laborers were replaced by an increasing number of immigrants in the Pullman works. The need to expand the factory labor force under the industrialism of late-nineteenth-century America helped spur massive immigration to the United States from all parts of Europe. Among other reasons for the often systematic recruitment of foreign laborers, many employers considered the newcomers potentially more controllable than native-born workers. Most residents of Pullman were foreign-born, and Debs himself was the son of French immigrants.

Together, these developments contributed to a major transformation of preindustrial American society. Immigrant factory workers in the late-nineteenth century, many of them Catholics or Jews fresh from peasant background in eastern and southern Europe, brought their distinctive religious and cultural experiences, which often included values and assumptions that were far different from those of the earlier northern European, Protestant norms of pre-Civil War America. The new immigrants found themselves forced to cluster in separate ethnic enclaves, unwelcome because of bigotry in neighborhoods dominated by native-born (or older immigrant) Americans, and often enmeshed in ethnic conflicts with new immigrants from different countries or ethnic backgrounds. When workers attempted to organize in order to protest wages, hours, and factory conditions, they often found their employers were far more effectively organized (as at Pullman) and were prepared to attack peaceful unionism as the alleged product of immigrant radicalism and domestic "labor agitators." Episodes such as the Pullman strike illustrate, in addition, the extent to which the national government was willing to

IMMIGRATION BY REGION, 1860-1920

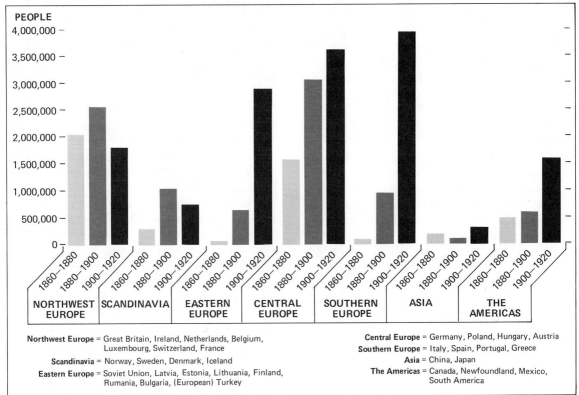

Northwest Europe = Great Britain, Ireland, Netherlands, Belgium, Luxembourg, Switzerland, France
Scandinavia = Norway, Sweden, Denmark, Iceland
Eastern Europe = Soviet Union, Latvia, Estonia, Lithuania, Finland, Rumania, Bulgaria, (European) Turkey
Central Europe = Germany, Poland, Hungary, Austria
Southern Europe = Italy, Spain, Portugal, Greece
Asia = China, Japan
The Americas = Canada, Newfoundland, Mexico, South America

commit itself to an overt defense of business interests against those of the working class at this time.

Whatever the complexities of class conflict, however, life had undergone fundamental change for all Americans during these decades. Only one out of ten citizens had lived in urban areas in 1800, but that number approached 50 percent by 1900. Before, the lights of city streets had been illuminated by gaslighters, but by late century, one man could throw a switch and brighten many city blocks using Thomas Edison's incandescent electric light. In every area of existence, such major changes were identified with industrialization and urban growth. By the 1880s, it was almost impossible for people of all classes to overlook the startling changes and often-grim realities of an industrial society that had grown to rapid maturity during the single decade and a half following the Civil War.

TECHNOLOGICAL INNOVATION

The Mechanization of Agriculture

A combination of factors helped to incorporate American farming into the larger industrial system beginning in the 1860s. Campaigns against the Indians had opened up enormous areas of land west of the Mississippi, and railroad lines expanded to link farmers with rail depots in the Midwest for transshipment to Eastern and world markets. Scientific methods and improvements in farm machinery brought greater yields on land already under cultivation. From 1860 to 1910, farm acreage more than doubled, from just under 400 million to almost 900 million acres, while the number of farms tripled from 2 million to well over 6 million.

The development of better farm machinery not only brought the rapid cultivation of the prairies and plains; it provided labor-saving innovations, enabling fewer people to produce a given yield. Teams of horses or oxen pulled heavy steel plows, digging through the prairie sod as wooden or even cast-iron plows had never done. The subsequent development of the efficient steel plow made these large teams unnecessary, lowering still more the cost of clearing virgin land. Farm equipment manufacturers turned out seed plant-

ers, cultivators, mowers, threshers, and binders, all of which brought enormous increases in productivity. By 1900, output per man-hour in the cultivation of wheat and oats, for example, was four times as great as that of 1840. It took one farmer sixty-one hours to harvest twenty bushels of grain in 1830; by 1900, he could accomplish the same task in under three hours.

Mechanization also added to the factors encouraging the historical tendency of many American farmers toward speculation. They purchased land, developed farms, and then sold out to newcomers, moving farther west to buy more land at cheaper prices. More important, with machinery available for a variety of agricultural tasks, many farmers and their children—as well as farm laborers—found less demand for their labor than in the pre-Civil War decades. Not only did the agricultural revolution provide the crops needed to supply the populations of developing American cities; it also helped create a large displaced agricultural class which sought new opportunities for employment through migration to urban areas, where its members found themselves in competition for jobs with the new immigrants. The revolution in farm technology thus helped accelerate the major migration from rural to urban America in the late-nineteenth century that continued into the mid-twentieth century.

Communication

With the rise of great railroad networks and mass markets for industry, improved means of transcontinental (and transoceanic) communication became essential. For one thing, the large corporations, which began to increase in importance in the last quarter of the century, required methods for keeping in touch with their various offices across the country and abroad. Through the efforts of individual investors, major breakthroughs in applied research helped fill the void. In 1866 Cyrus W. Field repaired and improved the transatlantic cable which had been completed by his company (and used briefly before it stopped working) in 1858. When E. A. Callahan of Boston developed a better stock ticker, businessmen on both sides of the Atlantic had economic developments literally at their fingertips. Thomas Alva Edison became a veritable one-man invention factory. From laboratories at Menlo Park, New Jersey, the hard-driving Edison and his associates developed practical and usable new electric light bulbs, storage batteries, phonographs, and hundreds of other devices which quickly found their way into widespread business and consumer use.

By far the most important invention, revolutionizing communication, was the telephone. Alexander Graham Bell, its inventor, emigrated from Scotland, first to Canada and later to Boston. There he taught speech to the deaf before becoming fascinated with experiments to transmit speech electrically. On March 10, 1876, Bell succeeded in transmitting a sentence over the telephone, and his new invention became a highlight of the Centennial Exposition that year in Philadelphia. (Bell's fame spread after the Exposition's most famous foreign guest, Emperor Dom Pedro of Brazil, paid a widely reported visit to the telephone exhibit on June 25 — the day that Custer and his men were wiped out at the Little Bighorn!) Citywide telephone exchanges began in 1878, and use of the instrument both accelerated the pace of industrialization and changed the nation's sociocultural patterns. (Sixteen million telephones were installed in the half century following Bell's first halting transmission.) Farsighted individuals who were prosperous enough to afford the invention during its earliest decades sought — and gained — an immediate communications advantage over their competitors, and those deprived of the invention (for example, Eugene V. Debs and the other A.R.U. leaders following their arrest and removal from strike headquarters) often suffered unfavorable consequences. Within just a few years after its invention, the telephone had ceased to be a luxury and had become a necessity for the successful conduct of affairs in American economic and political life.

Growth of the Railroads

For a generation, the railroad locomotive, as it sped across the American continent, was the prime symbol of industrial development. As late as 1865, at the end of the Civil War, only about thirty-five thousand miles of railway track existed. By

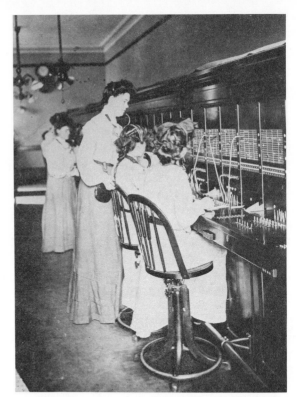

Women operating a turn-of-the-century telephone switchboard. (Culver Pictures)

1910, the United States had almost a quarter of a million miles of track, with capital investment in railroads surpassing the total investment for manufacturing. European capitalists and investors, a majority of them British, owned over one-third of all American railroad securities. The United States had one of every three miles of railroad track in the world by 1890. At the peak of railway construction in the 1880s, the industry employed over 200,000 workers. Huge government loans and land grants — beginning in the 1860s — helped to speed the rate of construction and to make the railroad magnates among the wealthiest of Americans.

Gangs of Chinese laborers moved the construction of the Central Pacific lines east from California, while Irish immigrants worked westward on the Union Pacific lines from Nebraska. The two railway construction programs met at

The financial speculator and railroad tycoon Jay Gould was one of the most unscrupulous (and successful) of the post-Civil War entrepreneurs. (Brown Brothers)

Promontory, Utah, and in ceremonies held on May 10, 1869, a silver sledge drove in the golden spike that connected the Atlantic and Pacific coasts by rail. The line reduced long-distance travel time significantly. A transcontinental journey now took only seven days, much less than previously and a short enough time to attract many new passengers to the railroads. Yet the trip remained long enough to give George Pullman a likely market for his new sleeping and dining cars.

Aided by government funds and land grants as well as by enormous investments from private capital sources, American railroad builders indulged in destructive competition and reckless speculation. Juggling rates to lure traffic away from competing lines only served to disrupt the flow of traffic. To compensate for the lower rates necessary to compete with rival lines, railroad en-

trepreneurs often charged inflated rates in non-competitive territory. These practices discriminated against the towns and cities along those routes, a condition that provoked an enormous resentment of virtually every railroad company among local businessmen and farmers during the late nineteenth century. When, in addition, railroads attempted to divide traffic through prior agreement by entering into "pooling" arrangements, the arbitrary power of the great rail companies seemed further magnified in the American heartland.

Possibly the most unscrupulous of the breed was railroad magnate Jay Gould, whose practices typified the worst of corporate behavior on the lines. Having already gained control of the Erie Railroad through stock manipulation, Gould and his associates next seized the Union Pacific line, adding to his personal wealth by forcing its directors to buy up some of his own smaller railroads. Gould used comparably underhanded tactics to gain control of the Texas and Pacific and the Southern Pacific. Through a combination of stock manipulations, threats to competing railroad owners, and well-timed alliances, by 1890 Gould held nearly complete control of transportation in the Southwest.

The passage of the Interstate Commerce Act in 1887 made pooling agreements between railroad magnates illegal, but the outright mergers continued. Through the maneuvers of Wall Street's powerful J. P. Morgan and the bankruptcies that struck several lines during the depression of the 1890s, railroad lines were increasingly consolidated. After 1900, the transcontinental railroad industry began a slow and steady decline in economic and political power. This change was wrought by many factors, among them the growth of intracity and "interurban" transportation lines, development of the internal combustion engine and the automobile, and the draining elsewhere of vital investment resources for railroad modernization by financiers who increasingly dominated the great railroad companies.

During the last four decades of the nineteenth century, the railroads—for all their corruption and unfair practices—had a significant impact on Western settlement. They remained crucial in opening up large areas of the United States for agriculture, mining, and cattle development by new settlers. Western territories along transcontinental railroad right-of-ways, none of which could have been developed as quickly without the trains, became states between 1876 and 1896. The great railroads made large towns out of small ones, helped transform villages into cities, transported immigrant settlers, and moved products nationwide, into and from factories engaged in mass production, thereby creating the basis for a national economic market.

THE RISE OF THE CORPORATION

The Factory System

The Industrial Revolution, in both Europe and the United States, had the effect of turning innumerable independent craftsmen into laborers while, in the process, changing the basic relationship between employer and employee. Prior to the Civil War, although large-scale business enterprise existed in such fields as iron production and textiles, most Americans who worked in industry did so in small shops. In this small-scaled environment, skilled shoemakers or blacksmiths, for example, acquainted with every part of their trade, labored for the most part under conditions and time constraints that they set for themselves. Thus men such as George Pullman's father (or Pullman as a young man) did personalized work for

Factories such as this badly ventilated textile room, jammed with machines, employed large numbers of women and children who often worked sixty- to eighty-hour weeks. (Brown Brothers)

An Influx of Newcomers

The United States has always been a "nation of nations." All Americans, even the original Indian inhabitants, are either immigrants or the decendants of immigrants to American lands. Over the centuries, every year has brought its share of foreigners seeking political refuge, economic opportunity, and additional freedom. Their numbers reached a high point during the late nineteenth and early twentieth centuries, when millions of immigrants reached the United States, mainly from Europe. The point of entry for many of these New Americans was New York harbor. At Ellis Island, portrayed imaginatively in Ben Shahn's mural "Arrivals," immigrants were received and their applications for admission processed before they were allowed to proceed on to their eventual destinations. No other country in the history of the world has voluntarily absorbed as many newcomers, ambitious but normally impoverished, as did the United States during the boom decades of immigration.

[For further information on the foreign observers quoted in this essay, see "Notes on Sources."]

PICTORIAL ESSAY   FIVE

My uncle Olaf, a seaman, used to come to us between voyages, and he was all the time talking about America; what a fine place it was to make money in. The schoolmaster told us one day about the great things that poor Swedes had done in America. A man who had lived in America once came to visit near our cottage. He said that food was cheap in America and that a man could earn nearly ten times there as in Sweden. So at last it was decided that my brother was to go to America.

[AXEL JARLSON, 1903]

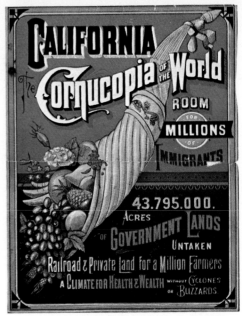

Railroad poster soliciting immigrants

The emigrants flocked into the mess-room from the four doors to twenty immense tables spread with knives and forks and toppling platters of bread. Nearly all the men came in their hats — in black glistening ringlety sheepskin hats, in fur caps, in bowlers, in sombreros, in felt hats with high crowns, in Austrian cloth hats, in caps so green that the wearer could only be Irish. A strange gathering of seekers, despairers, wanderers, pioneers, criminals, scapegoats.

[STEPHEN GRAHAM, 1913]

Between Decks in an Emigrant Ship

We carried our luggage out at eight, and in a pushing crowd prepared to disembark. At 8:30 we were quick-marched out of the ship to the Customs Wharf and there ranged in six or seven long lines. All the officials were running and hustling, shouting out "Come on!" "Hurry!" "Move along!" and clapping their hands. Our trunks were examined and chalk-marked on the run—no delving for diamonds—and then we were quick-marched further to a waiting ferry-boat [for Ellis Island].

[STEPHEN GRAHAM, 1913]

Immigrants disembarking in New York City

I visited Ellis Island yesterday. The central hall is the key. All day long, through an intricate series of metal pens, the long procession files, step by step, bearing bundles and trunks and boxes, past this examiner and that, past the quick, alert medical officers, the tallymen and the clerks. On they go, from this pen to that, pen by pen, toward a desk at a little metal wicket—the gate of America. Ellis Island is quietly immense. It gives one a visible image of one aspect at least of this world-large process of filling and growing and synthesis which is America.

[H. G. WELLS, 1906]

We were carefully examined, and when my turn came the examining officials shook their heads and seemed to find me wanting. I confessed that I had only five cents in my pocket and had no relatives here, and that I knew of nobody in this country except Franklin, Lincoln, and Harriet Beecher Stowe, whose Uncle Tom's Cabin I had read in a translation. One of the officials, who had one leg only and walked with a crutch, with a merry twinkle in his eye said in German: "You showed good taste when you picked your American acquaintances." I learned later that he was a Swiss who had served in the Union army during the Civil War.

[MICHAEL PUPIN, 1874]

A doctor examining boys at Ellis Island

Waiting for processing at Ellis Island

There was a bootblack named Michael on the corner. When I had time I helped him and learned the business. Francisco, too, worked for the bootblack, and we were soon able to make the best polishes. Then we thought we would go into business.

We had said that when we saved $1000 each we would go back to Italy and buy a farm, but now that the time is coming we are so busy and making so much money that we think we will stay. We meet many people and are learning new things all the time. We were very ignorant when we came here, but now we have learned much.

[ROCCO CORRESCA, 1902]

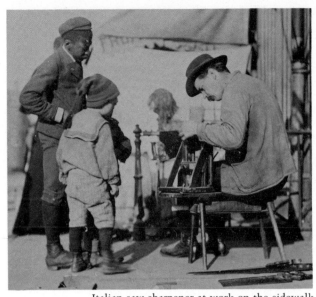

Italian saw sharpener at work on the sidewalk

George Bellows, *Cliff Dwellers*

The inhabitants seem to have come from all quarters of the globe and to represent every known type. The streets, wide as they are, are yet too narrow to hold the masses of people who surge to and fro in them. Everyone is busy; everyone carries a parcel containing articles of clothing or food. Bargaining goes on in all the languages imaginable, and one hears an Italian praising his oranges as in the piazza of St. Lucia; a German discussing sausages of doubtful origin with a French urchin, who plays the part of a chef at the corner of the street; and Russian emigrants share their vodka, as a token of friendship, with Polish Jews.

[COUNT VAY DE VAYA UND LUSKOD, 1908]

The work given to the new arrivals is generally of a rudimentary nature, but it teaches them to work, and the wages, although low, at least enable them to live, besides giving them the chance of joining the great labor unions of the country and taking if ever so small a part in the industrial pursuits of the people among whom they have come to live.

[COUNT VAY DE VAYA UND LUSKOD, 1908]

Immigrant iron workers in Pennsylvania

Jewish hot potato vendor, New York City

In the evening my sister and I took a walk; she went shopping and asked me to go with her. I saw a Jewish sign (in Hebrew letters) in a window reading "Kosher Butcher." I stopped and admired it very much and said to my sister, "This is the first time I see Hebrew letters in a window." In Rumania it is not allowed. Then I started to realize what anti-Semitism really meant and what an anti-Semitic country Rumania was.

[ROBERT MYERS, 1913]

The German in America is badly off. Where in the world can he find a wife? He has little opportunity for family life. So the young people get acquainted only in public places, in restaurants, concerts, the theater, balls. But what can they learn of each other there? Everything, except that which relates to a wife and her duties.

[KARL GRIESINGER, 1858]

German band, Cincinnati

Those who are Americanized are American, and very patriotically American. Those who are not thus nationalized are not in the least internationalized. They simply continue to be themselves; the Irish are Irish; the Jews are Jewish; and all sorts of other tribes carry on the traditions of remote European valleys almost untouched. Very often these exiles bring with them not only rooted traditions, but rooted truths.

[G. K. CHESTERTON, 1921]

Program for festivities at a Milwaukee *Turnverein* (German social and athletic club)

Polish store, Chicago

I made the acquaintance of two local
celebrities (Irish), namely Paddy Ryan
and Michael McDonald. Paddy is a fighting man lately defeated in the twenty-
four-foot ring by a compatriot, Sullivan.
Michael McDonald runs a granite quarry.
But his principal importance arises from
his political position. He is supposed to
direct and control what is called the
rowdy element in Chicago—largely made
up of our countrymen—and this gives
him very great local influence. He is a
rough diamond, with a decisive masterful
way about him, which clearly marks him
out as a leader of men. His friends claim
for him that he returned the present
mayor of Chicago—the first Democratic
mayor returned for Chicago for thirty
years.

[LORD RUSSELL OF KILLOWEN, 1883]

Irish politicians, Chicago

Returning to the log
house, we spent the
evening—twenty-one
Swedes altogether—in
games, songs, and
dancing, exactly as if
in Sweden. I felt my-
self happy in being
with my countrymen,
happy to find them so
agreeable and so
Swedish still in the
midst of a foreign land.

[FREDRIKA BREMER,
1850]

Harvesting, by the Swedish American painter Olaf Krans

The Chinese have built a great part of the Northern Pacific from the Continental Divide to the Pacific. As we sped along, we came upon their encampments again and again in forest glades, by the shores of the rivers and lakes, on the outskirts of the cities — always a community apart. It is said to their credit that they insist, when they can, on being located near water for purposes of personal cleanliness.

[LORD RUSSELL OF KILLOWEN, 1883]

Chinese workmen on a Western railroad

In a place so exclusively Mexican as Monterey, you saw not only Mexican saddles but true vaquero riding — men always at the gallop up hill and down dale, and round the sharpest corner, urging their horses with cries and gesticulations and cruel spurs, checking them dead with a touch, or wheeling them right-about-face in a square yard. In dress they ran to color and bright sashes. Not even the most Americanized could always resist the temptation to stick a red rose into his hatband.

Mexican horseman in California

[ROBERT LOUIS STEVENSON, 1879]

Child labor was common in late-nineteenth-century American industry and was on the increase at the century's end. Children often worked grueling schedules on extremely dangerous machines. (Brown Brothers)

customers whom they knew by name as members of the community; apprentice employees often worked for an employer they knew well and with whom they might socialize or even share lodgings. As the process of mass production undercut such traditional arrangements, however, skilled craftsmen often had no alternative but to surrender their status and independence by selling their only remaining commodity of value: their labor.

Unlike the preindustrial shop, factory work centered around the machine and not the worker. In a large industrial factory, workers often never saw the actual owner of the enterprise or encountered the thousands, possibly millions, of customers who used the finished product. Few Pullman workers ever met the occupants of a sleeper or dining car, much less a specially constructed one, and throughout American industry, the factory laborers functioned in an increasingly impersonal working environment. No longer did they have the control enjoyed by preindustrial craftsmen over the pace or design of the article they were helping to construct.

The division of labor within factories brought about by production-line techniques and interchangeable parts, moreover, often created specialized, monotonous work routines, and workers frequently did not even understand the complete process involved in construction of a finished product. Such routine often led to a loss of pride in workmanship and alienated laborers from any interest in their work except for the compensation involved. In his novel *The Jungle,* Upton Sinclair described such a dreary work routine in a Chicago meat-packing plant:

> Near by him sat men bending over whirling grindstones, putting the finishing touches to the steel knives of the reaper; picking them out of a basket with the right hand, pressing first one side and then the other against the stone, and finally drop-

Samuel Gompers

(Culver Pictures)

Samuel Gompers was an unlikely figure to emerge as the first great leader of the modern American labor movement and its chief spokesman for almost forty years. English-born in 1850 to Jewish parents in a London tenement, a socialist in his youth, Gompers later repudiated his early radicalism and—as head of the American Federation of Labor—devoted his life to fighting for practical improvements in the wages, hours, and working conditions of union laborers. His role as the most successful immigrant leader of the American working class seems, in retrospect, a personal odyssey comparable to the immigrant-industrialist Andrew Carnegie's rapid rise among American capitalists. More than any other union leader, Gompers set the direction, policy, and philosophy of the mainstream American labor movement throughout the formative decades of modern industrial growth.

Gompers's parents brought him to New York at the age of thirteen. The elder Gompers was a skilled worker, a cigar maker, who emigrated with his family to the United States in 1863. Samuel had been removed from school in London at the age of ten to apprentice, first to a shoemaker and then to his father in the craft of cigar making. The family settled on New York's East Side, where Gompers began his career as a labor activist in 1864, when he joined the Cigarmakers' Union. He married three years later.

Although formal schooling ended for Gompers in England, he read widely and—like other knowledge-hungry East Side immigrants—took advantage of the many free lectures available at nearby Cooper Union and elsewhere in the city. A fellow worker and radical exile from Europe, Ferdinand Laurrell, helped to steer Gompers toward cautious acceptance of socialism. Gompers studied Marx and other socialist theorists, but eventually he heeded Laurrell's warning never to allow *concepts* of working-class behavior to blur his own experienced perception of working-class realities in the United States. "Learn all [the Socialists] have to give," Laurrell advised, "read all they publish, but don't join." Gompers did not formally associate with the socialists and, even while still under the influence of their writings, he concentrated in a non-doctrinaire manner upon daily union activities. He served as president of the Cigarmakers' Union from 1874 to 1881, steering it in 1877 through a disastrous strike conducted during the worst year of that decade's depression.

Gompers and associates who shared his practical views of union functioning (including some socialist "moderates") took the lead in 1881 in creating the Federation of Organized Trades and Labor Unions of the United States of America and Canada. This was primarily a federation of unions

ping them with the left hand into another basket. One of these men told Jurgis he had sharpened three thousand pieces of steel a day for thirteen years.

By 1900, there existed more than 10 million such workers; millions were women, and almost a fifth were children between the ages of ten and fif-

teen. The number of children in the industrial work force tripled between 1890 and 1900 alone. Although real wages actually increased overall during the last four decades of the nineteenth century, owners paid scant attention to the number of hours their laborers put in or to working conditions that threatened their employees' safety and health.

of skilled crafts workers. For the next half decade, Gompers attempted to devise a "federated" structure capable of providing adequate central direction to the movement without abusing the self-governing quality of each individual union. When the federation was reorganized as the American Federation of Labor in 1886, Gompers was elected president. He remained in that post until his death in 1924, except for a single year, 1895, when militants within the A.F. of L. managed to unseat him briefly. But Gompers swept back into office the following year and remained in charge for the next three decades until his death.

By the time he helped found the American Federation of Labor Gompers was deeply suspicious of radicals and "theorizers" within the union movement. He opposed national unions such as the Knights of Labor that promoted and pursued either a program of overt political goals or the creation of "substitute economies" run by workers—such as cooperative stores and cooperative businesses—designed to displace capitalist enterprise. Gompers believed such efforts were futile and distracted unions from their primary task: uniting the working class to improve its economic and human conditions. Rather than attempting to overthrow or supplant capitalism, the American working class should—Gompers believed—accept the inevitability of the country's economic system and struggle always for an ever-increasing share of its rewards. "He held," one historian wrote, "that labor was always right."

Gompers opposed efforts by the American labor movement to take independent political action through the creation of a separate labor or farmer-labor party (such as the Populists). He believed such efforts were doomed to defeat because of the exceptional conditions of American society.

Although every national union within the A.F. of L. remained autonomous, Gompers devoted himself to encouraging unity within the American working class, bitterly opposing creation of more than a single union for each craft or industry. He urged labor to use collective bargaining at every opportunity to maximize its gains—and its power—over the owners of industry. Firmly opposed to violent or revolutionary action by labor organizations, Gompers was a devoted "gradualist" who—whenever possible—threw the support of the national A.F.of L. behind the resolution of local labor disputes. (Gompers's role in the Pullman strike is discussed in Chapter 29, p. 568.)

Although an anti-imperialist after the Spanish-American War, Gompers was no pacifist. He supported President Wilson's decision to intervene in World War I in 1917 and organized a War Committee on Labor, composed of both union and employer representatives, to aid the war effort. At the Versailles Peace Conference, Gompers served on the Commission on International Labor Legislation. Toward the end of his life, he wrote several books on the conditions of workers in the United States and Europe, the most famous of which (his memoirs), *Seventy Years of Life and Labor*, appeared posthumously in 1925.

To the end of his life, Samuel Gompers's intellectual benchmark remained the same simple test which he had applied since his days as a cigar maker: Judge actions by the way in which they affect the practical conditions under which the American working class lives and labors. Support those steps that improve its conditions; oppose the rest. "Study your union card, Sam," Gompers approvingly quoted his friend Ferdinand Laurrell at one point in *Seventy Years*, "and if the idea doesn't square with that, it ain't true."

Industrial workers found many factors hindered attempts to improve their conditions. No federal laws sought to correct these abuses, and few states or municipalities helped in protecting laborers. Owners used detectives and armed guards, where necessary, to impede or halt entirely any form of labor organizing, and most workers labored ten hours a day, six days a week. In some cases, owners built company towns which not only sought to impose a strict measure of social and political control on its work force, but also paid workers in "scrip" rather than cash, forcing them to buy needed food and clothing at inflated prices in company-owned stores.

GILLAM.

Attempts to foster a spirit of common interest among factory laborers also ran afoul of the tangle of ethnic and racial antagonisms that existed within the working force. Shrewd industrialists tried to capitalize on such antagonisms by mixing workers from distinctly hostile nationalities or races within the same factory and thereby minimizing the possibility of united activity in unionizing. Black workers, rarely able to gain factory jobs under ordinary circumstances, were often brought in as strikebreakers, as were recently arrived immigrants from non-English-speaking European countries, encouraging hostility toward both groups from native-born working-class whites. Poor immigrant laborers from Europe accounted for a large percentage of the factory working class. Unaccustomed to decent wages or treatment in their home countries, most had come to the United States for a chance to better their economic conditions and eagerly accepted the lowest paid jobs as a first step up the American ladder, while older (often better-organized) native laborers ac-

cused them of driving down the general wage level. Hostility toward immigrant laborers was most pronounced in the industrial cities and towns of the Northeast and Midwest. Farther west, such economic conflict within the working class combined with overt racism in stirring bitter anti-Oriental feeling. The leading anti-Oriental figure in California during this period was, ironically, an Irish immigrant. Denis Kearney, head of the Workingman's party in that state, used racist invective and the support of white workers to have a clause inserted in the new 1879 California state constitution prohibiting corporations from hiring Chinese workers. Throughout the United States, then, the new laboring classes faced not merely the obstacles thrown up by their industrial employers but, also, older traditions and attitudes which made working-class unity and concerted action extremely difficult to achieve.

The Struggle to Unionize

Despite employer resistance and working-class disunity, those who led or took part in the Pullman strike inherited a tradition of industrial union activity already a half-century old. In Jacksonian America, factory workers and craftsmen attempted to form their own unions. Few of these trade organizations lasted beyond the Civil War. In the half-century afterwards a number of major unions were formed. Almost all these unions employed the strike weapon, though rarely with complete success. During the 1880s, for example, over 24,000 strikes occurred in the United States, involving over 6½ million workers.

During the turbulent depression years of the 1890s, 3 million people were thrown out of work, perhaps 15 to 20 percent of the country's work force. Over 7,000 strikes were called during this period. Between 1894 and 1896 numerous small armies of the unemployed marched on Washington demanding federal relief assistance.

At the national level the union movement faced a number of difficulties in the half-century after the Civil War. Several national unions rose and fell because of unsuccessful strikes, the opposition of the middle class, and the inability of unions to hold the loyalty of most workers. The National Labor Union played a prominent role briefly during the depression of the 1870s. The Knights of Labor, under the leadership of Terence V. Powderly, became a major force in the labor movement in the following decade. These unions favored improvement of the American worker's economic state and a broad program of reform within American society.

The Knights had many self-employed or salaried middle-class Americans in its membership. During the 1880s it tried unsuccessfully to organize a series of strikes and to set up cooperative factories and stores—owned by the workers themselves—as an alternative to the privately run corporations. Leaders of the Knights were blamed for the Haymarket Affair of 1886 and were attacked as "anarchists." Actually, they had played no part in the bombing. Membership in the Knights of Labor nevertheless declined from 700,000 in 1886 to 74,000 by 1893. The union played an insignificant role in the labor movement during the 1890s, joining finally with the agrarian-led Populist party. By 1900 it had lapsed into obscurity.

American socialists were also influential in the union movement during these decades. Socialists were important in the Knights of Labor, the Western Federation of Miners, and other groups. After the failure of the Pullman strike, Eugene V. Debs joined the movement.

The leading force within American unionization during this period, however, was the American Federation of Labor (A.F. of L.). It was a loose confederation of independent craft unions and semi-industrial affiliates such as the ILGWU. The A.F. of L. was formed in 1881 under the leadership of Samuel Gompers. A one-time socialist, Gompers criticized earlier union organizations such as the Knights for stressing general reforms in American society.

The labor movement, Gompers believed, should concentrate exclusively on winning economic gains for the working class. It should leave the tasks of reform to others. Union leaders should devote all their time and energy to raising workers' wages, reducing hours, and improving working conditions. Gompers also believed that unions should avoid independent political action, such as the affiliation of the Knights with the Populist party in the 1890s. Instead, labor should support its political friends and oppose its enemies, regardless of party. When asked at a congressional hearing what the unions wanted, Gompers replied simply: "More!"

By the time of the Pullman strike, the A.F. of L., under Gompers's cautious leadership, had become the country's dominant national labor organization. It was also the most powerful union politically and economically up to that time.

The Corporate Form of Business

The United States went from being fourth among the world's manufacturing nations in 1860 to first by 1900, producing greater quantities than the combined productions of Britain, France, and

Germany (the world's other leading industrial powers). By the century's end, most manufacturing occurred within giant corporations, and the corporation replaced the family firm or partnership as the major business vehicle of American enterprise in the post-Civil War era. The earliest corporations, of course, had been chartered prior to the Civil War, and the idea, in embryo, goes back to the joint stock companies that had sponsored the settlements of various colonies such as Massachusetts Bay and Virginia.

Before the Civil War, however, the existence of a corporation in some field of business enterprise did not necessarily suggest an organization of private capital engaged in the *unrestricted* pursuit of profit and growth. The earliest corporations in the Jacksonian period, and before then, were chartered by state legislatures and supported by public funds. They were hedged with numerous obligations to the communities and state that they served, and they constituted quasi-public bodies. As individual sources of capital searching for investment grew in the antebellum period, "mixed corporations" of private *and* public monies became common. The Second Bank of the United States was the best known of such institutions. During the 1840s and 1850s, a growing number of entrepreneurs helped lobby state legislatures to pass *general* laws of incorporation, allowing new businesses to incorporate freely simply by registering and paying uniform fees, but without consent — or restriction — from state lawmaking bodies. By the end of the Civil War, these laws of incorporation and the considerable accumulation of capital in private hands had begun fostering rapid industrialization unrestrained by any sense of public purposes, however nominal.

The corporation's advantages over other forms of business organization were many. Under the legal title of incorporation, many individuals could invest money by buying stock in the company, but if the project failed, none of the investors could be held personally liable for the corporation's debts (unlike the personal liability involved in partnerships and family firms). The corporation also made it possible to concentrate industry into larger and larger units than had been conceivable under previous forms of organization. In producing for a mass market, corporations could control all stages of production, from obtaining raw materials and the tools that made machines in their factories, to turning out the product itself, to supervising and directing sales divisions responsible for transporting, advertising, and marketing particular products. This kind of expansion connecting related areas in the business process became known as "vertical integration." It was increasingly important as the economy became dominated by the national market. This domination had been facilitated by the construction of the transcontinental railroads, which allowed single corporations to rapidly deploy and transfer goods and services back and forth across the country. Businesses in virtually every major area of American life — from steel to tobacco, oil to farm equipment, Pullman cars to pork canning — now found themselves producing for a continental and even global market, which had been inconceivable, given the level of transportation, communication, and business organization, prior to the Civil War. American business, because of the corporations, spawned a "new class" of entrepreneurs — Pullmans, Rockefellers, Carnegies, Swifts, and Dukes — who would dominate the nation's economy in the late-nineteenth century. Individual businessmen might now fall, retire, or die, but the life of their corporation would outlast them.

Just as the formation of corporations helped to concentrate various industries into larger and more powerful units, agreements among corporations within an industry served to weaken competition and further consolidate control. The strategy of "pooling" between railroad directors or manufacturers aimed at dividing a given market and fixing agreed-upon prices within an industry. Although such "pools" were nominally outlawed, at least on the railroads, under the Interstate Commerce Act of 1887, they persisted within manufacturing industries. Another form of business consolidation and monopolistic centralization within a given industry came with the development of the "trust," first exploited within the oil industry by John D. Rockefeller in creating the Standard Oil Company in 1879. Under this form, several companies sold or assigned their stock to a single group of "trustees," which allowed corporations to appear legally independent while the same group of men, the "trustees," made decisions governing all of them for the common good of the trust. This method allowed a significant measure of centralized management within an industry, although not "officially" under a single monopolistic corporation. Beginning in the 1880s, the term "trust" came to be used to describe all huge corporations, even some that were centrally owned as well as managed and not technically trusts.

Case Studies in Consolidation: Morgan, Carnegie, and Rockefeller

By the turn of the century, giant corporations had come to dominate most major American industries. One or at most several firms held commanding positions within an industry, generally, and played a preemptive role in pricing policies, setting wage rates, purchasing practices, and all other areas of corporate life in their separate realms. These firms represented the victors in an economy-wide process of consolidation, whereby leading businesses drove out, purchased, or otherwise subordinated their less-successful competitors. Often the process was characterized by lengthy warfare between major competitors within an industry in which the victors would absorb the managerial talents, plants, and markets of the firms that did not survive the struggle. Most of the major new capitalists who emerged in the late nineteenth century reveled in the battles for preeminence within their respective industries, endorsed maximum consolidation, and dismissed as "impractical," within the conditions of modern industrial society, a return to a marketplace of smaller, more competitive, and widely scattered firms. Among the major firms to emerge by the first years of the twentieth century as leaders within their fields were such giant consolidations as the Standard Oil Company, International Harvester, American Tobacco, and the United States Steel Corporation. The leaders of business in late-nineteenth-century America constituted a new class of entrepreneurial millionaires, virtually all of whom made their fortunes in post Civil War America; the careers of Pullman in railway cars, Rockefeller in oil, Carnegie and Frick in steel, Swift and Armour in meat packing, Duke in to-bacco, and others testified to the extraordinary wealth to be gained by the economic oligarchy which emerged as one consequence of American industrialization.

Three of the most familiar and important figures in this process were the banker J. Pierpont Morgan, the steelmaker Andrew Carnegie, and the oil magnate John D. Rockefeller.

The role of American banking underwent a major change when business corporations began selling stocks and bonds to finance projected expansion rather than relying upon the individual investment of elite merchants and local private bankers. After the Civil War, bankers on Wall Street and elsewhere in the financial markets increasingly served as intermediaries between industrialists and a wide variety of investors because of the bankers' connections with foreign capitalists as well as their links to banking houses, insurance companies, and other revenue sources. Impressed by the apparent ease with which savings could be profitably invested into the fast-developing American industrial economy, foreign businessmen quadrupled their investments in the United States between 1860 and 1900.

The most spectacular success of this new generation of bankers was J. P. Morgan. A tall and commanding figure, Morgan was the son of a rich Hartford, Connecticut, merchant who had established a bank in London. He enjoyed a privileged youth: European travel and education, his father's private collections of rare books and art masterworks, and frequent excursions on one of his father's three huge yachts.

Since it was Morgan's business to finance corporations, he became increasingly involved in their internal affairs. Chaotic competition and instability threatened to drive capitalists from many investment markets, especially during economic downturns. During the depression of the 1870s, for example, 40 percent of all railroad bonds were in default. Many roads went bankrupt, as did many others during the even more stringent business depression of the 1890s. (See Chapter 32, p. 620.) In 1885, Morgan intervened to end ruinous competition between the New York Central and the Pennsylvania lines which threatened investors in both companies. After this intervention, Morgan

The best-known American businessmen of their era in typical poses: financier J. P. Morgan and his wife ride in his horse-drawn carriage; steelmaker Andrew Carnegie relaxes at his Scottish estate with walking stick and collie; John

D. Rockefeller, who dominated the oil industry, takes his "constitutional" in top hat and cutaway. (From left to right—Brown Brothers, Brown Brothers, and Culver Pictures)

and his associates reorganized railroads steadily, reducing their indebtedness and consolidating smaller lines into larger systems. By 1900, Morgan had brought order to the railroads while helping to reorganize other industries, such as steel, where he put together the country's first billion dollar capitalization in 1900—the United States Steel Corporation. He and other major investment bankers became increasingly influential in the financing and management of major industries.

Unlike Morgan, who was a well-born native son from a business background similar to that of most of the corporate elite of his day, Andrew Carnegie typified the "rags to riches" mythology so popular among Americans of all classes. In this,

Carnegie was *a*typical of the American business elite. Born to working-class parents in Scotland, Carnegie emigrated with them to the United States at age thirteen. At eighteen, he became a telegraph clerk in the office of a Pennsylvania Railroad official. During the Civil War, Carnegie impressed his employers and other business contacts with his hard work and entrepreneurial acumen. Investment information received from business associates had already made Carnegie a wealthy man by the age of twenty-eight. In 1872, he entered a project to build an enormous steel plant, near river and railroad transportation, twelve miles from Pittsburgh.

Technological advances and expanding vertical integration in the industry brought wealth

ping facilities—all to ensure the continuity of raw materials in the production process and the expeditious distribution of finished steel once produced.

As Carnegie grew more powerful and wealthy, he also became more distant and alienated from the problems of ordinary working people. While delivering personal instructions to his associates from a castle in Scotland, which he purchased and often repaired to, Carnegie observed from across the ocean the progress of efforts to defeat the Homestead strikers in 1892. The steel magnate, an immigrant himself, manipulated throughout his career the ethnic prejudices of his laborers to the company's advantage. In some cases he deliberately assigned men of different nationalities to a single workroom in order to encourage ethnic conflict and thus impede union organizing.

In the end, Carnegie's personal domination of the company gave way to the financial power of the investment houses which had begun to dominate manufacturing corporations by the turn of the century. After price wars broke out between competing firms in the steel industry, J. P. Morgan stepped in to negotiate for the purchase and amalgamation of the industry's leading firms. Carnegie sold his company for nearly half a billion dollars in 1901, and the new super-corporation that emerged that year, United States Steel, boasted control of three-fifths of the entire American steel industry. In his later years, the childless Carnegie used much of his fortune for philanthropic enterprises.

One industrialist of that turbulent era who did not lose control of his company was John D. Rockefeller, possibly the most famous (or notorious) of the entrepreneurs who dominated the new national firms: "Captains of Industry" to their admirers, "Robber Barons" to their enemies. Rockefeller developed the first and still most famous of all corporate trusts, Standard Oil Company (founded in 1870). He loathed competition and was dismayed by the beehive of competing enterprises that existed among producers and refiners of oil when he entered the industry. Rockefeller, a successful Cleveland produce commission merchant, invested in Pennsylvania oil refining in the 1860s. He soon gained an advantage over his competitors by acquiring special rates and secret rebates from

and fame to the young immigrant. Carnegie and his associates increased production rapidly, first by adopting the Bessemer process of developing steel, which involved blowing air through the molten iron to drive out the impurities, and later by accepting the open-hearth method of smelting. Steel production in the Pittsburgh area, where Carnegie centered his efforts, also benefited because it was in the midst of Appalachian coal fields and had access, via barges sent from the Great Lakes, to iron ore from the huge fields, such as the Mesabi Range, in upper Michigan and Minnesota. Anxious to guarantee a market for his steel company (one in which he continued to own the majority of stock), Carnegie made rails and built railroad bridges, bought coal and iron mines, and purchased ship-

railroads. Since transportation costs amounted to about a fifth of the total costs for refiners, Rockefeller's methods allowed him to undersell, and gradually to eliminate, most of his competitors. Rockefeller set up the Standard Oil Trust in 1879, reorganizing it three years later. He bought out seventy-four refining companies and, by the 1880s, controlled about 90 percent of the country's oil-refining capacity. (At this time, among other uses, oil was a favored illuminant in the nation's cities.) When rival companies built the first oil pipelines, thus threatening the transportation advantage of Standard Oil's agreements with the railroads, Standard soon gained a controlling interest in the United Pipe Lines Company. This represented another step in the direction of vertical integration. By 1900, the corporation was producing everything from kerosene to tank wagons, and engaged in production, refining, and distribution, while marketing both nationally and worldwide.

The Standard Oil Trust, organized in 1879, centralized company operations. Stockholders from twenty-seven supposedly competing companies turned over their shares to a board of nine trustees, receiving trust certificates in return. In practice, Rockefeller and his closest associates controlled all major decisions. With competition removed, profits soared. Again small producers and consumers protested at the aggregation of power that Rockefeller and other corporate giants had gained. Such discontent brought the passage of the Sherman Antitrust Act, which, in practice, had little immediate impact upon Standard Oil operations, though it did declare illegal trusts in restraint of trade. The Ohio Supreme Court broke the Standard Oil Trust in 1892, but Rockefeller managed in 1899 to establish another Standard Oil Company, this time in New Jersey and this time as a "holding company." In this variant of earlier methods, the "holding company"—a corporation itself—took control of the stock of other corporations which it managed, building up a cluster of supposedly semi-independent companies actually dominated by the single holding company. After Standard Oil's new incarnation came United States Steel, another holding company, this time under the auspices of the Morgan firm. Rockefeller remained proud of the entire process, trumpeting his support for industrial concentrations: "The day of combination is here to stay. Individualism is gone, never to return."

STRANGERS IN THE LAND

The Shift in Immigration

Except for the considerable numbers of African slaves (see Chapter 18), American society in the early national period remained extremely homogeneous. The vast majority of white Americans at the time came from English and Scottish ancestry, with possibly 10 percent of the population deriving from various parts of Germany. Three massive waves of immigration transformed the ethnic composition of American society with growing complexity during the nineteenth and early twentieth centuries.

Although the bulk of the first wave of immigration came during the 1840s and 1850s, the process actually got under way after the War of 1812. During the period from 1815 to 1860, 5 million immigrants came to the United States from abroad. Overwhelmingly northern European, these newcomers comprised a variety of nationalities departing from their home countries for both economic and political reasons: 1.7 million Irish fleeing from the horrible potato famine and desperate poverty; 1.3 million Germans escaping from the political turmoil during the revolutions of 1848 and hard times during the 1850s; Scandinavian peasants leaving land that was often unproductive; and an assortment of Englishmen, Swiss, Belgians, and others. Except for the Irish Catholics, most of these northern Europeans were Protestants from Anglo-Saxon or Nordic cultures; they scattered among the farms, small towns, and (especially the Irish) cities, where the non-Irish majority found relatively rapid acceptance.

A second wave of immigration from 1860 to 1890 sent another 10 million to the United States, again substantially from northern and western Europe. Of the 788,000 immigrants who came during 1882, the peak year in this wave, 87 percent were from those sections of Europe, and only 13 percent came from southern and eastern European countries.

Then the ethnic pattern changed starkly. Beginning in the 1880s, and accelerating during the 1890s, a third wave of immigration continued until World War I choked off the flood of new migrants from Europe. Thirteen million new immigrants came to the United States during the 1890–1914 period, the overwhelming majority from southern and eastern Europe: Italians, Austro-Hungarians, Poles, Russians, Greeks, Turks, Rumanians, and others whose appearance, clothes, customs, and languages appeared strange to older Americans. During the peak year of the new immigration, 1907, when 1,285,000 immigrants arrived, 19 percent came from northern and western Europe, and 80.7 percent came from southern and eastern European backgrounds. Most of the newcomers were Catholics and Jews, rather than Protestants like a majority of the earlier migrants, and they generally proved less likely to adopt quickly, or less interested in adopting, native-American Protestant cultural patterns.

The arrival of these great numbers of new immigrants coincided with the rapid industrialization and urbanization of American society in the late-nineteenth century. Unlike older immigrants, who had often sought farms in the countryside or jobs as artisans and small businessmen

Immigrants arriving at Ellis Island are examined for disease by a uniformed health inspector while they wait to enter the United States. (Culver Pictures)

U.S. GROWTH OF POPULATION, 1870-1910

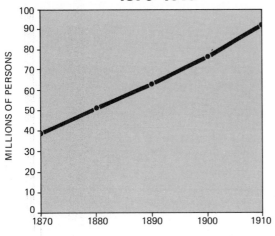

in the towns, the newer immigrants (after 1880 particularly) settled in the larger cities and factory towns, often gaining employment in the industrial plants that now proliferated throughout the country. By 1900, two-thirds of the foreign-born in the United States lived in cities and the larger towns. (Even the company town of Pullman had a foreign-born majority by 1890.) Four-fifths of the population of greater New York by the 1890s consisted of foreign-born workers or those of foreign parentage, and in most other major cities, at least a third of the population (sometimes far more) came from these groups. For many newer immigrants, political oppression was again a factor in their decision to come to the United States: Greeks fleeing Turkish persecution, Russian Jews escaping czarist "pogroms," and Hungarians or Serbs escaping the domination of Hapsburg Austria. Economic ambition overshadowed all other reasons for post–Civil War immigration, however, as it had in the past. The overcrowding, poverty, and dire conditions of urban life which awaited the largely rural peasants who came to the United States must have made the dream of beginning a new life in America seem, initially, a hollow one. For most immigrants during this period, a slum tenement replaced the "old country's" thatched-roof cottage. Most often settling in distinct ethnic areas, their numbers crowded the urban landscape.

Sometimes older immigrants of the same nationality assisted newer arrivals in finding work and housing. Just as often, however, these old-timers sought to exploit the newcomers on behalf of employers seeking cheap labor, corrupt city political machines, or simply their own benefit. Still, these "padrones" or patrons (although the word is of Italian origin, such *padrones* were found in *all* ethnic communities) provided a beneficial connection between the world of the newly arrived immigrant (often non-English-speaking) and the life of the broader American community. Political machines also played a major role in trying to absorb the new immigrants—providing assistance, employment, advice, and services (in exchange for votes and political loyalty) upon which the first-generation Americans often depended until becoming better established.

Although few of the newer immigrants managed to assimilate completely into American society immediately after arriving in this country, many hurdled the chief barrier to assimilation—learning English—with amazing rapidity. Public school classes were free, an institution unheard of in the "old country," and immigrants utilized the public schools and other educational opportunities to break the language barrier. Often voluntary institutions such as political parties and labor unions also provided language training, among other things, for the immigrants. Many of the foreign-born members of Eugene V. Debs's American Railway Union, for example, found themselves becoming "Americanized" in the very process of struggling to win their strike against Pullman. Settlement houses such as Jane Addams's Hull House in Chicago and Lillian Wald's Henry Street Settlement in New York also proved invaluable in helping immigrants to learn America's language and customs. The roads to establishing an American identity remained as varied for late-nineteenth-century immigrants, in short, as they had been during earlier decades.

The Nativist Backlash

Strong ethnic prejudices arose against the newcomers, because of the coincidence of their arrival at a time when the brutalizing aspects of industrial development grew increasingly apparent, and because of their cultural contrast with older

The hope, determination, and anxiety that characterized the immigrants' earliest perceptions of the United States can all be discerned in this vivid photographic portrait of a family newly arrived from the "Old Country." (Brown Brothers)

Americans. Many native white workers blamed foreigners who accepted menial jobs at poor pay for causing an alleged decline in general wage rates (alleged but not real), while middle-class Americans, reacting to such events as the participation of German anarchists in the Haymarket Riot in Chicago, generalized their fears concerning immigrant *radicalism.*

That only a minuscule percentage of the new immigrants were politically active in radical groups made little impression on the fantasy-ridden imaginations of fearful native-born Americans. One typical nativist newspaper editorial categorized the new immigrants as "long-haired, wild-eyed, bad-smelling, atheistic, reckless foreign wretches, who never did an honest hour's work in their lives." American Protestants attacked the arrival of large numbers of Catholics as part of an alleged conspiracy to make the United States subservient to the Catholic Church, an updating of the anti-Catholicism of the 1830s and 1840s. (See Chapter 16, pp. 314–5.) Rutherford B. Hayes claimed that Catholics dominated the Democratic party, a profound oversimplification and untruth, while President Grant argued that unless public

schools were kept free of Catholic influence, the country might face a new civil war.

Nativists on the West Coast vented their hostility against Orientals even more than against immigrant workers from Europe. In California, racist attitudes toward newly arrived Chinese workers created tensions that sometimes broke into violence. By 1880, over 100,000 Chinese had immigrated to the Pacific Coast. Although most did not directly compete with white labor for jobs, disappointed native Americans and Irish immigrants who had expected to get rich quick vented their frustrations on the scapegoat Asians. When mobs in San Francisco rioted against the Chinese in 1877–78, even wealthy businessmen employing Oriental labor could no longer fight the prevailing sentiment. Shortly after the 1879 California Constitution prohibited the hiring of Chinese workers, Congress (in 1882) passed the Chinese Exclusion Act, suspending for a decade all immigration from China and forbidding those already in the country from becoming naturalized citizens.

Movements to restrict immigration drew varied but growing support elsewhere in the country, winning widespread acceptance from native white working-class organizations. The American Federation of Labor and a number of its constituent craft unions, for example, campaigned actively for exclusion. The virulently anti-Catholic American Protective Association, organized in 1887, blamed Catholic newcomers for everything from labor violence to the depression of the 1890s. Other nativists stressed ethnic rather than religious differences, claiming that the influx of foreigners would surely destroy the supposed racial purity of Anglo-Saxon America. Such intolerance led to the passage, not once but four times in these decades, of a bill that proposed a literacy test aimed at excluding peasants from southern and eastern Europe. Each time, however, a presidential veto quashed the legislation. It would take the even more hostile nativism of a later generation to close down large-scale immigration.

THE URBAN SCENE

Matching the influx of immigrants into the larger cities during the late nineteenth century was a domestic folk migration, from town and farm to city, within the United States. The country had been overwhelmingly rural at the beginning of the century, with less than 5 percent of Americans living in large towns or cities. The proportion of urban population began to grow remarkably after 1840, increasing from 11 percent that year to 28 percent by 1880 and to 46 percent by 1900. A country with only six cities boasting a population of more than 8,000 in 1800 had become one with 545 such cities in 1900; of these twenty-six had a population of more than 100,000. By the latter year, three American cities held more than a million people. (In the entire ancient world, only Alexandria and Rome had a population of more than *half* a million.) Much of the migration producing an urban society came from smaller towns within the United States, but the combination of new immigrant and old American "settlers" on America's "urban frontier" in the late nineteenth century proved extraordinary.

The greatest decade of post–Civil War urban expansion occurred during the 1880s, when 101 cities more than doubled their size. Some growth rates were little short of spectacular: Kansas City

increasing 1,000 percent in population, Minneapolis growing from 47,000 to 164,000, Omaha from 30,000 to 140,000.

The growth of cities and the process of industrialization fed upon each other. The agricultural revolution stimulated many in the countryside to seek a new life in the city and made it possible for fewer farmers to feed the large concentrations of people needed to provide a work force for growing numbers of factories. At the heart of urban growth was this interconnected process: agricultural technology creating a surplus in food supply and farm labor; industrial growth providing economic opportunities for millions of unskilled laborers in the factory systems. Cities also provided ready and convenient markets for the products of industry, and huge contracts in transportation and construction—as well as the expanded market in consumer goods—allowed continued growth of the urban sector of America's overall economy.

The face of cities was revolutionized by such innovations as electric trolley systems, elevated lines, and subways which replaced horse-drawn trolleys, thereby allowing considerable expansion of the city limits while helping to curb a significant urban problem—horse pollution. These new transportation systems allowed the beginnings of American suburban life, as travel to the inner city was reduced from hours to minutes.

Other technological developments stimulated the process of urbanization. The Bessemer converter provided steel girders for the construction of skyscrapers. Refining of crude oil into kerosene, and later the development of electric lighting as well as of the telephone, brought comforts to urban areas unavailable to rural Americans and helped attract many of them from the farms into the cities. In every era, the lure of the city included a major psychological element for country people; the bustle and gregariousness of urban life (with all its dangers) seemed particularly intriguing to those raised in rural isolation.

Between 1880 and 1900, townships in several Midwestern states (notably Iowa and Illinois) as well as New England actually declined in population as people left for the largest cities. Farms were often abandoned, and by 1890, the number of industrial workers nearly equaled those in agriculture—an economic and social milestone in United States history. Yet urbanization was not equally distributed. Although nationwide 46 percent of the population lived in cities by 1900, in New England that figure grew to 85 percent, and in the Middle Atlantic states to 70 percent. In addition, certain states were evidently more urban than others; more than half of all Americans living in cities resided in New York, Pennsylvania, Massachusetts, Illinois, and Ohio. A large proportion of these were immigrants, and two-thirds of all foreign-born Americans were also urbanites.

Industrialization had helped to modernize and populate the cities, but few rational efforts were made to plan this development. Cities grew in an unschematic and often-unexpected manner. City government officials often became involved in corrupt relations with those business interests that had special interests in road building, sewage construction, waterworks, and transportation systems. Sanitation facilities remained primitive in many cities—often human wastes were deposited into nearby rivers which were also used for urban water supplies (as in the case of Philadelphia)—and local governments struggled to keep pace with the massive growth in urban areas (and consequent demands for even rudimentary sewage and water

The growth of New York City depended upon improved transportation facilities like the Brooklyn Bridge. The bridge's completion in 1883 made it possible to live outside Manhattan and commute to work by a steam car, by carriage, or on foot. (Museum of the City of New York)

services). Paved roads remained uncommon in the outlying areas of even the largest cities. All cities were confronted with the problems of inadequate financing and massive problems of growth—especially in areas dominated by the industrial working-class poor.

Population density in some major cities seems incredible in retrospect. New York City, for example, was the most overcrowded city in the *world* in 1890, with eighteen being the average number of persons per house compared with five nationwide. With his assistants, the journalist and reformer Jacob Riis surveyed New York's tene-

The vibrant bustle of life on New York's Lower East Side, overcrowded with immigrants buying and selling as they stroll through the district, emerges powerfully in this turn-of-the-century photograph. (Culver Pictures)

ments in 1890 and found that more than half the city's population (1.2 million) lived in such squalid quarters. The worst tenements—and there were thirty-seven thousand of them in Manhattan alone—lacked proper toilet facilities or access to sunlight. Rats and other disease-carrying animals and insects roamed the city's slums, and the overall environment was hardly fit for human habitation. The American novelist William Dean Howells, after a tour of the tenement district, described "the well-worn look of mothers, the squalor of the babes, the haggish ugliness of the old women, the slovenly frowsiness of the young girls," in short the "poverty-smell which breathes from the open doorways."

Although the immigrants had known poverty and sickness all too well in the old country, these conditions and the cultural shock of urban sprawl caused great distress among the newcomers. Living conditions, poverty, and ethnic tensions

all contributed to a rising crime rate in which murder and robbery became frequent occurrences in the slum neighborhoods. The extremes of human misery and degradation were common sights in American cities during the 1880s and 1890s, with the gulf between economic and social classes both dramatic and widening. The challenge to reformers of improving these conditions without provoking social explosions seemed, at least until the 1890s, at variance with the prevailing complacency of middle-class America and the assertive materialism of the new industrial elite.

CULTURAL PERCEPTIONS OF AN INDUSTRIAL AGE

Social Darwinism

The new ideology of industrializing America understandably reflected the interests of the new economic elite, though the major capitalists were not alone in formulating arguments to rationalize the numerous changes in economic practices since the Civil War. Businessmen, economists, ministers, and conservative academics joined in asserting that the profit motive within a competitive free marketplace stimulated people to invest funds that would promote economic welfare and a better society. In this view, without government intervention to restrict competition, the workings of the marketplace under laissez-faire capitalism would force out inefficient producers, and the best managers — an economic elite — would be left to run the nation's successful businesses. Such ideas, which had solid roots in the eighteenth-century free market theories of Adam Smith, found encouragement in Darwinian evolutionary theory. The English biologist Charles Darwin argued that the process of natural selection enabled only the fittest biological strains to survive. Herbert Spencer, another English theorist, and the American philosopher William Graham Sumner, carried Darwinian biological analysis into a further realm of analysis, applying it to the "laws" supposedly governing the development of society. The version of Social Darwinism that emerged offered as scientific truth a rationalization for the stark business expansionism of the post–Civil War decades and the obvious extreme contrasts of wealth and poverty which industrialization had helped produce. Proponents argued that without governmental interference in the "natural" processes of business, the men best able to adapt to their economic environment would accumulate wealth. In this view, men such as Morgan, Carnegie, and Rockefeller represented the triumph of social evolution.

Although Darwinian evolutionary theory belied the Biblical belief in creation, many American religious leaders showed no hesitation to link godliness to material accumulation. In his famous "Acres of Diamonds" speech, for example, Baptist minister Russell Conwell insisted: "I say that you ought to get rich, and it is your duty to get rich." A one-time clergyman became the country's most popular "success myth" novelist. During a career that lasted three decades, Horatio Alger wrote tales of young men who overcame obstacles in their early lives to stand at the beginning of adulthood prepared to shed their "rags" for "riches" through continued hard work, enthralling young American readers, who purchased over 200 million copies of Alger's writings. Alger's books, though not directly concerned with the mature realities of men engaged in industry or finance, projected, through the ambitions and fantasies of his young heroes, an inescapable sense of the impending "romance of business" within their lives.

The few obvious and spectacular rags-to-riches stories within the American industrial elite, notably Carnegie's, persuaded large segments of the public that wealth lay within the grasp of any person who had sufficient abilities and worked hard enough to acquire it. Poverty, the Social Darwinists argued, was caused by personal weaknesses or shortcomings, since each man had control over his own economic fate. Some even disapproved of public schools or any other ameliorative actions by government which would enable those less fit to rise and destroy the delicate (if imaginary) mechanism of natural selection in which the Social Darwinists believed. The most that certain businessmen, notably Andrew Carnegie, would concede in modifying the chilly Darwinist argument was to assert that businessmen would serve as "stewards" for the new wealth (God's surrogates), dispensing private philanthropy to the needy and thereby rendering compassionate redress to the cruel workings of economic nature. Carnegie embodied this notion in his "gospel of wealth."

Ironically, the spread of Social Darwinist ideas came at a time when the giant corporations had eliminated much of the competition previously existing in the economy and, more than occasionally, sought government protection in a variety of ways: through favorable financial legislation, higher tariffs on manufactured goods, and even troops to use against union workers striking (as in the Pullman dispute). Most businessmen, it must be recognized, tempered any belief in a Darwinian economic world with moral and religious convictions drawn from their Protestant backgrounds, convictions that allowed them to rationalize their recent acquisition of great wealth and power as the apparent fulfillment of Divine Will according to which (in the eyes of many devout Christians) even the pattern taken by industrial development seemed to become a portion of God's larger plan for America.

Literary Responses

The illogical borrowing of biological research by some theorists to explain the development of American industrial society, as well as the glaring abuses arising from the practices of unregulated capitalism, soon drew criticism from a variety of writers intent upon exposing the evils — and questioning the values — of the new society. Economist Thorstein Veblen, the son of Norwegian immigrants, brilliantly portrayed the behavior of the new industrial rich in his *Theory of the Leisure Class* (1899). Veblen introduced the idea of "conspicuous consumption" to attack the monied elite, sardonically portraying the need displayed by wealthy Americans to exhibit their power by spending and consuming without regard to the necessity of any purchase or the value of any product:

> The utility of consumption as an evidence of wealth is to be classed as a derivative growth. . . . Unproductive consumption of goods is honorable, primarily as a mark of prowess and a perquisite of human dignity; secondarily, it becomes substan-

tially honorable in itself, especially the consumption of the more desirable things.

Some American authors began to focus on the problems of industrialization in their work. Stephen Crane, best-known for his Civil War novel *The Red Badge of Courage* (1895), also wrote a far more daring novel for that rigidly moralistic Victorian era, *Maggie: A Girl of the Streets* (1891). *Maggie* tells the tale of an impoverished girl in New York's Bowery district and her corruption, descent into a life of prostitution, and subsequent death. Crane evokes the life of the city itself as leading inexorably, as in Greek tragedy, to Maggie's personal disaster.

William Dean Howells's reaction to the 1886 Haymarket Strike, his fascination with the ideas of single-tax advocate Henry George (see Chapter 34), and his adoption of socialist views spurred him to write novels strongly critical of American social structure. In *Annie Kilburn* (1889) Howells rejected the inadequate and paternalistic forms of charity that emerged in a New England town, and in *A Hazard of New Fortunes* (1890) he described the social conflict inherent in a violent strike. Although the bulk of Mark Twain's fiction seemingly ignored the problems of industrialization (except as material for a technological fantasy in *A Connecticut Yankee in King Arthur's Court*), his 1873 novel *The Gilded Age,* coauthored with Charles Dudley Warner, was a satirical account of Washington political and social behavior under the stresses of economic development. The title of Twain's novel became, in a later period, the most popular catchphrase applied to the materialistic era in which it was written.

Although post–Civil War industrial development and materialistic ideology produced its share of critics at the time, it was not until the economic depression and social upheavals of the 1890s that most Americans began to confront seriously (for the first time) the social impact of industrialization, immigration, and urbanization. Meanwhile, the convergence of these developments had transformed virtually every aspect of national existence and created the contours of a new urban-industrial society in the post–Civil War decades.

Suggested Readings
Chapters 29–30

The Pullman Strike

Stanley Buder, *Pullman: An Experiment in Industrial Order and Community Planning, 1880–1930* (1967); Ray Ginger, *The Bending Cross: A Biography of Eugene Victor Debs* (1949) and *Altgeld's America* (1958); Almont Lindsay, *The Pullman Strike* (1964); Samuel Yellen, *American Labor Struggles* (1936).

General Studies

Thomas C. Cochran and William Miller, *The Age of Enterprise: A Social History of Industrial America* (1961); Rendigs Fels, *American Business Cycles, 1865–1897* (1959); John A. Garraty, *The New Commonwealth, 1877–1890* (1968); Samuel P. Hays, *The Response to Industrialism: 1885–1914* (1957); Robert Higgs, *The Transformation of the American Economy, 1865–1914* (1971); Edward C. Kirkland, *Industry Comes of Age: Business, Labor and Public Policy, 1860–1897* (1961); Glenn Porter, *The Rise of Big Business, 1860–1910* (1973); Robert H. Wiebe, *The Search for Order, 1877–1920* (1968).

Industrial Development and Business Leadership

E. G. Campbell, *The Reorganization of the American Railroad System, 1893–1900* (1938); Alfred D. Chandler, *Strategy and Structure* (1962); Robert W. Fogel, *Railroads and American Economic Growth* (1964); H. J. Habakkuk, *American and British Technology in the Nineteenth Century* (1962); Louis M. Hacker, *The Course of American Economic Growth and Development* (1970); R. W. and M. E. Hidy, *Pioneering in Big Business, 1882–1911: History of the Standard Oil Company* (1955); Jonathan Hughes, *The Vital Few* (1966); Matthew Josephson, *Edison* (1959) and *The Robber Barons* (1962); E. C. Kirkland, *Men, Cities and Transportation,* (2 vols., 1948); David Landes, *Unbound Prometheus* (1969); Ralph Nelson, *Merger Movements in American Industry* (1959); Allan Nevins, *A Study in Power: John D. Rockefeller* (1953); H. C. Passer, *The Electrical Manufacturers, 1875–1900* (1953); Robert E. Riegel, *The Story of the West-* *ern Railroads* (1926); Charles Singer et al., eds., *A History of Technology, vol. V: The Late Nineteenth Century, c.1850 to c.1900* (1958); W. P. Stassman, *Risk and Technological Innovation* (1974); John F. Stover, *American Railroads* (1961); G. R. Taylor and I. S. Neu, *The American Railroad Network, 1861–1890* (1956); Peter Temin, *Iron and Steel in the Nineteenth Century* (1970); Joseph F. Wall, *Andrew Carnegie* (1971); H. F. Williamson and A. R. Daum, *The American Petroleum Industry* (1959).

The Industrial Working Class and the Union Movement

David Brody, *Steelworkers in America* (1960); John R. Commons et al., *History of Labour in the United States* (4 vols., 1918–1935); Henry David, *History of the Haymarket Affair* (1936); Charlotte Erickson, *American Industry and European Immigration, 1860–1885* (1957); John A. Garraty, ed., *Labor and Capital in the Gilded Age* (1968); Samuel Gompers, *Seventy Years of Life and Labor* (2 vols., 1925); Gerald N. Grob, *Workers and Utopia* (1961); M. A. McLaurin, *Paternalism and Protest: Southern Cotton Mill Workers and Organized Labor, 1875–1905* (1971); Henry Pelling, *American Labor* (1960); Terence V. Powderly, *Thirty Years of Life and Labor* (2 vols., 1925); Robert Smuts, *Women and Work in America* (2nd ed., 1971); Philip Taft, *The AFL in the Time of Gompers* (1957); Lloyd Ulman, *The Rise of the National Trade Union* (1955); Norman J. Ware, *The Labor Movement in the United States, 1860–1895* (1929); Leon Wolff, *Lockout: The Story of the Homestead Strike of 1892* (1965).

Immigration and Urbanization

Robert Bremner, *From the Depths: The Discovery of Poverty in America* (1964); Leonard Dinnerstein and Fred C. Jaher, eds., *The Aliens: A History of Ethnic Minorities in America* (1970) C. N. Glaab and A. T. Brown, *A History of Urban America* (1967); Constance M. Green, *The Rise of Urban America* (1965); Oscar Handlin, *The Uprooted* (1951); John Higham, *Strangers in the*

Land: Patterns of American Nativism, 1860–1925 (1955); Maldwyn A. Jones, American Immigration (1960); Seymour Mandelbaum, Boss Tweed's New York (1965); Blake McKelvey, The Urbanization of America, 1860–1915 (1963); Lewis Mumford, The Culture of Cities (1938) and The City in History (1961); Jacob Riis, How the Other Half Lives (1890); Moses Rischin, The Promised City: New York Jews, 1890–1914 (1962); Arthur M. Schlesinger, The Rise of the City, 1878–1898 (1933); Barbara Solomon, Ancestors and Immigrants (1956); Philip Taylor, The Distant Magnet: European Immigration of the U.S.A. (1971); David Ward, Cities and Immigrants: A Geography of Change in Nineteenth Century America (1971); S. B. Warner, Streetcar Suburbs . . . 1870–1900 (1969) and The Urban Wilderness: A History of the American City (1973).

Business Ideology and Business–Government Relations

Lee Benson, Merchants, Farmers, and Railroads (1955); Thomas C. Cochran, Railroad Leaders, 1845–1890: The Business Mind in Action (1966); Sidney Fine, Laissez Faire and the General Welfare State, 1865–1901 (1956); Richard Hofstadter, Social Darwinism in American Thought (1959); Edward C. Kirkland, Dream and Thought in the Business Community, 1860–1900 (1956); Gabriel Kolko, American Railroads and Regulation, 1877–1916 (1965); William Letwin, Law and Economic Policy in America: The Evolution of the Sherman Antitrust Act (1965); Robert G. McCloskey, American Conservatism in the Age of Enterprise (1957); William Miller, ed., Men in Business (1962); G. H. Miller, Railroads and the Granger Laws (1971); Hans B. Thorelli, The Federal Antitrust Policy (1955); Irving G. Wyllie, The Self-Made Man in America (1954).

The Culture of Early American Industrial Society

A. I. Abell, The Urban Impact on American Protestantism, 1865–1900 (1942); Warner Berthoff, The Ferment of Realism, 1884–1919 (1965); Van Wyck Brooks, New England: Indian Summer, 1865–1915 (1940); L. A. Cremin, The Transformation of the School, 1876–1957 (1961); John Tracy Ellis, American Catholicism (1956); Howard Mumford Jones, The Age of Energy, 1865–1915 (1971); Alfred Kazin, On Native Grounds (1942); Henry F. May, Protestant Churches and Industrial America (1949); Lewis Mumford, The Brown Decades: A Study of the Arts in America, 1865–1895 (1931); Barbara Novak, American Painting of the Nineteenth Century (1969); Lawrence R. Veysey, The Emergence of the American University (1965); Larzer Ziff, The American 1890's: Life and Times of a Lost Generation (1966).

Farmers in Revolt: The Election of 1896

31

For a week, arguments had raged through the lobby and corridors of Chicago's Palmer House hotel. Bellboys no longer looked up when a long-haired Southerner or a flat-voiced Midwestern farmer loudly debated a well-dressed Eastern delegate, or when reinforcements for both sides rushed to join the verbal melee. Only when it seemed the discussion would turn into a fistfight did hotel employees quietly suggest that the gentlemen might like to continue their chat elsewhere.

Since delegates to the Democratic National Convention had begun arriving in Chicago, these employees had heard the same argument many times. At its most basic level, it seemed dull, a technical question of economics. The United States government, in this year of 1896, promised to pay to each holder of a dollar bill one dollar in gold. Overexcited Democrats from the South and the West now demanded that the government be empowered to redeem its paper money in silver as well as gold. Equally aroused politicians from New York, Pennsylvania, and Massachusetts angrily retorted that such a policy would destroy the credit of the government.

Chicagoans grown sick of the nonstop bellowing over the currency issue in most of their downtown hotels, restaurants, and bars, could find no relief outside. Marching, shouting, pro-silver convention delegates filled the sidewalks and streets, singing along with the marching bands imported by each presidential candidate to improve his chances.

If there was an eye to this emotional storm, it was probably an upstairs corridor at the Sherman House, the hotel where a small, "foreign-looking" politico held court. He would beckon to a waiting silverite, hold a short, animated conversation in which he did most of the talking, and dismiss his auditor and summon another in the same gesture. The next man would then scuttle forward to talk to John Peter Altgeld, governor of Illinois and the closest thing at the moment to a leader of the silver forces.

Altgeld had been through controversy two years earlier, when the Pullman strike had paralyzed Chicago, and he had refused to call in fed-

New York financier William C. Whitney, a lifelong Democrat despite his substantial wealth, had supported Grover Cleveland in 1884 and 1892, and served as Cleveland's secretary of the navy. (Culver Pictures)

eral troops, arguing that local forces were adequate to maintain order. When President Grover Cleveland sent in troops anyway, Altgeld berated his party's leader. He was in turn attacked by conservatives all over the country, the Chicago *Tribune* calling him "the lying, hypocritical, demagogical, sniveling Governor of Illinois."

Earlier, Altgeld, realizing that the move might make him a "dead man politically," had pardoned the three Haymarket anarchists still in prison. He had long been troubled by charges of prejudice on the part of the judge and jury and by the inadequacy of the evidence against the accused. This action caused the more conservative elements of the press to conclude that Altgeld was an anarchist himself.

Neither of these acts, however, bothered the silver forces who looked to him for leadership. Many of the Southern and Western farmers now thronging Chicago had but recently risen up. In Alabama schoolhouse meetings and Kansas county conventions, they had taken the Democratic party away from its astonished former owners.

The silver Democrats had swept state after state, and now they came to Chicago with a clear majority of the delegates. But the more perceptive among them would have traded any one of the marching bands for a strong presidential candidate. Altgeld, the most important figure in the movement, was disqualified because he was German-born, although he had come to America at the age of three months. With the silver forces divided among several weak candidates, silverites feared a compromise that would allow the outnumbered gold men to name the candidate.

They feared one gold man in particular. In ability and intellect, William Collins Whitney was the only man in Chicago comparable to Altgeld. Both were farm boys who had become city lawyers—Altgeld in Chicago, Whitney in New York. But whereas Altgeld had gone into labor law and politics, Whitney had worked for the Vanderbilts, the railroad magnates, and moved on rapidly to build his own future. With the same brilliance and ruthlessness with which he had amassed $40 million, Whitney had engineered Cleveland's nomination and election in 1892 and was viewed as the most effective organizer in American politics.

Whitney rolled into Chicago as the brains of the "gold train," carrying the elite of the Eastern Democrats to the convention. The train, stocked with choice food and wines, carried cabinet officers, United States senators, and state party bosses. In previous years, this group had controlled the Democratic party; six of the last seven Democratic candidates for president had come from New York, and the seventh from Pennsylvania. Now they journeyed nervously, hoping that Whitney could work his magic and save them from humiliation.

Whether Whitney could do it, or whether the silver forces could agree on a candidate, remained in doubt when the convention opened. Fifteen thousand people jammed Chicago's Coliseum, facing giant portraits of Jackson, Jefferson, and James Buchanan, with galleries rising in rows above the convention floor.

William Jennings Bryan, a thirty-six-year-old former congressman from Nebraska, owed loyalty to neither Whitney nor Altgeld. A strong

The thirty-six-year-old "boy orator," Nebraska Congressman William Jennings Bryan, was hoisted onto the shoulders of supporters, following his powerful "Cross of Gold" speech at the Democratic Convention in 1896. (Culver Pictures)

silverite, he had his own ideas about who should lead the movement. On the convention's second night, before returning to his modest, two-dollar-a-day hotel room, Bryan uttered the following words to his wife and a friend: "So that you both may sleep well tonight, I am going to tell you something. I am the only man who can be nominated. I am what they call the logic of the situation."

The next day, the delegates waited expectantly as Bryan, famous as an orator but hardly considered a serious candidate, approached the stage to close the debate over the platform. Bryan began by warning that farmers were through with meekly asking the East for assistance. He reviewed the previous year's steady growth of silverite protest and challenged those Eastern gold Democrats who argued that returning to a dual monetary

William Jennings Bryan's "Cross of Gold" metaphor had little appeal to his opponents in the business and industrial communities, no more than the candidate himself or his proposals for economic reform. The cartoon depicts Bryan as a trampler of scripture and vendor of sacrilegious souvenirs and accuses him of dragging Christian symbols into the dust. (Culver Pictures)

standard—gold *and* silver—would "disturb" the country's business interests.

The petitions of farmers had been scorned by Eastern men of wealth, Bryan shouted. Their entreaties had been disregarded, and—"when our calamity [the depression] came"—their begging had been mocked. "We beg no longer," he cried, "we entreat no more; we petition no more. We defy them!" From that moment, Bryan held most of his fifteen thousand listeners in his hands. Their cheers interrupted him constantly as he heaped scorn upon the Eastern gold Democrats and their arguments. The audience's enthusiasm reached its height as Bryan's speech drew to a close. Even the most hostile listener would be forced to acknowledge that Bryan had transformed the convention briefly into a sort of revival meeting.

"You shall not press upon the brow of labor this crown of thorns," cried Bryan, in one of the most famous perorations in American history. "You shall not crucify mankind upon a cross of gold!" For five seconds Bryan stood in dead silence, his arms outstretched in a Christlike pose.

Then the convention went mad. Dignified judges and legislators screamed and danced in the aisles. Silverites carried Bryan on their shoulders. State after state dipped its standard in front of Nebraska's, while silver politicians fought through the crowd to pledge Bryan their votes.

One gold delegate grabbed a nearby newsman, hauled him to his feet, and bellowed, "Yell, damn you, yell!"

"I have enjoyed a great many addresses, some of which I have delivered myself," remembered Clarence Darrow, who would one day debate the Creation with Bryan in a Tennessee court, "but I never listened to one that affected and moved an audience as did that. Men and women cheered and laughed and cried. They listened with desires and hopes and finally with absolute confidence and trust. When he had finished his speech, amidst the greatest ovation I have ever witnessed, there was no longer any doubt as to the name of the nominee."

Bryan's nomination on a silver platform delighted the South and the West. Two people less enthralled were the kingmakers of the convention, Whitney and Altgeld. Whitney, along with much of the stunned Eastern democracy, immediately announced that he would neither support nor vote for the ticket. Altgeld, despite the triumph of silver, was also disappointed. "It takes more than speeches to win victories," he told a friend the day after Bryan's triumph. "I have been thinking over Bryan's speech. What did he say, anyhow?"

Three weeks earlier, down the river in St. Louis, the Republicans had named Bryan's opponent. Their convention contrasted sharply with the hubbub and activity of the Democrats'. It was, one newspaper noted mournfully, the dullest convention anyone could remember.

Which was exactly how Marcus Alonzo Hanna wanted it. Hanna had worked for three years to lock the convention up for his friend William McKinley of Ohio, and he wanted no disturbance that might unlock it. Although Eastern Republicans demanded a flat statement in support of gold and Republicans from Rocky Mountain silver-mining states wanted *their* metal endorsed, Hanna determined that the issue would not get out of hand.

McKinley had followed the path of the ambitious small-town Ohioan to success in Republican politics, the same trail that had led James Garfield to the White House. A former congressman and governor, McKinley had written the party's last tariff bill in 1890, a high tariff measure to "protect" American industries. "McKinley was no intellectual giant," a friend admitted, but he understood politics, made friends easily, and came from the right state for a Republican candidate.

McKinley had every asset for political success except money. And while he did not possess much of that himself, he had the next best thing: an extremely wealthy friend and political backer. Mark Hanna, though he owned a shipping company, a bank, a street railway, an opera house, and much of the Cleveland area's Republican party, was more than just rich. He had been born to money. He married much more of it. He then made a great deal more for himself and had thoroughly mastered all his businesses. Hanna believed in the durability of the new industrial system. If the system could weather violent strikes, surely it could also withstand the threat of free silver. He had informed the panicky members of the Cleveland Union League Club, "There isn't going to be any revolution. You're all a lot of damned fools."

Mark Hanna, McKinley's campaign manager in the 1896 election, boss of the Ohio Republican machine and later of the national one, was a wealthy industrialist anxious for political power. (Culver Pictures)

Over the years, Hanna had mastered national politics with McKinley as he had mastered his own shipping empire. With negotiating skill and with a personal expenditure of $100,000, Hanna won most of the delegates west and south of Pennsylvania for his candidate and brought him to St. Louis in possession of a clear majority of convention delegates.

Only the money question provided any interest. McKinley himself, now under pressure from both sides, had during his congressional career supported both gold and silver at different times. "McKinley isn't a gold-bug, McKinley isn't a silver-bug," mocked Speaker of the House Thomas Reed, who was his only real rival. "McKinley is a straddle-bug." Throughout the preconvention campaign, the candidate simply refused to answer letters asking his views on currency. When Easterners complained, Mark Hanna roared, "I don't give a damn what Wall Street thinks of McKinley's silence; they can go to hell down there. We are not going to nominate McKinley on a Wall Street platform."

Hanna now skillfully allowed the Eastern Republican bosses to push him into a flat declaration for gold, thus easing their resentment over McKinley's nomination. A handful of silver Republicans walked out, eventually to support Bryan. Hanna, wearing a blue shirt with white polka dots and an enormous diamond in his tie, watched happily as the convention overwhelmingly nominated his friend.

The nominee, who had fought for thirty years for the protective tariff, did not believe that currency could really decide the election. "Thirty days from now," McKinley told a friend, "you won't hear anything about silver."

The friend disagreed. "Thirty days from now," he told McKinley, "you won't hear about anything else."

In this extraordinary election year, one more party met in convention. The wave of rural anger and desperation that had rolled over the Democrats had created an entirely new party, the Populists, also known as the People's party. Growing steadily in strength since its first appearance in 1890, the Populist party increasingly stressed silver as the answer to the farmer's problems. If the Populists had joined with the Democrats, who had declared for other reforms as well as silver, the combined ticket might have swept the country, but with two separate silver tickets, Hanna's Republicans might enjoy an easy victory.

The Populist delegates who now marched into St. Louis bore little resemblance to the Republicans who had preceded them. Populists were a ragtag collection of veterans from earlier third parties, like the Grangers and the Greenbackers, and bankrupt farmers hoping desperately for help from the movement, with a scattering of urban radicals, including some Socialists and a few labor people. It was not the usual free-spending convention crowd; many in it were poor, and some had walked to St. Louis or skipped meals to get there. To complete the bucolic atmosphere, the Populists presented awed Eastern reporters with a dazzling array of beards and whiskers, a sight rarely seen among urbane men of fashion.

On the key issue of endorsing Bryan, the Populists split along sectional lines. Midwestern and Western Populists, accustomed to cooperate

with Democrats and encouraged by Democratic National Chairman James K. Jones, favored fusion with the Chicago ticket. Gaily singing, "We'll shoot the gold-bugs, every one," they were willing to join every effort to help boost the chances of silver. "I care not for party names," declared "Sockless Jerry" Simpson of Kansas. "It is the substance we are after, and we have it in William J. Bryan."

For Southern Populists, fusion with the Democrats was more distasteful. Like all political questions below the Mason-Dixon line, the Populist movement had become entangled in the race issue. Southern party members had declared racism to be a tool of the wealthy in oppressing the farmers and had welcomed blacks into the party. Hundreds of thousands of black farmers had joined the Colored Farmers' Alliance, working closely with the Southern Farmers' Alliance. In Georgia, Populist leader Tom Watson had called out dozens of white party members to stand guard over the house of a black leader who had been threatened. In North Carolina, white Democrats were stunned when a Populist legislature with black members adjourned for a day after the death of Frederick Douglass.

Because of such policies, Southern Populists had been beaten, shot at, and defrauded by the ruling Democratic machines. They would not now support a Democratic candidate. "Avoid fusion as you would the devil," wired Watson from Georgia. "Texas is here to hold a Populist convention," cried one Southerner, "and we're going to do it before we go home."

Although the Populists lacked the organization of the older parties, making high-level wheeling and dealing difficult, a compromise did emerge. The party would nominate Watson for vice-president. To assure

The delegates to Populist conventions, such as this one (held in a huge tent), were an amalgam of alliance leaders, politicos, visionaries, and other enthusiasts. In 1896 their ranks were divided over the presidential nomination, since free silverites and fusionists favored the Democratic candidate, William Jennings Bryan, who was to win the Populist nomination as well. The third party rejected the Democrats' vice-president nominee in favor of Georgia Populist Tom Watson, a concession to those who wanted an independent Populist slate. (Culver Pictures)

the Southerners that the more numerous fusionists planned no betrayal, the vice-presidential ballot was held first. Only after Watson had been put on the ticket did the Populists name Bryan for president. The pro-fusion convention chairman did not bother to inform delegates of the telegram he had received saying that Bryan did not want the nomination without Sewall.

Now that he was the candidate of two major parties, not to mention the National Silver party, the Single-Taxers, the Christian Socialists, and a faction of the Prohibitionists, Bryan offered himself and his remedies to a stricken country. The unrest in American politics only reflected a greater instability in the American economy, as the United States entered the fourth year of the most severe depression in its history.

At its worst point, the depression of the nineties left two and a half million workers unemployed. Some Americans were reported to have starved to death. Many employers responded to depression (and the labor surplus) by cutting wages. In response, strikes exploded across the land. Half a million workers walked out, and the disputes prevented another two-thirds of a million persons from working. The Pullman strike centered in the Chicago railyards, and Altgeld had tried successfully to keep Cleveland from intervening. It was only one of a series of bitter struggles.

A single pathetic protest best reflects the desperation of the depression of the 1890s. A small businessman from Ohio, Jacob Coxey, vowed to send "a petition in boots" to Congress, asking for a $500 million public-works program to help the unemployed. "Coxey's Army," as it was derisively dubbed, never numbered more than six hundred, but it was

"Coxey's Army" of unemployed, shown on their way to Washington in 1894, wanted to petition Congress for work relief. While not driven out at bayonet point (as was to be the case with the "Bonus Army" of 1932), the five hundred or so of Coxey's troops who arrived at the Capitol were confronted by police and placed in custody for endangering the public health. General Coxey was arrested for walking on the grass and put in jail. (Culver Pictures)

reported by newspapers as if it were a vast horde come to sack the Capitol and lay waste the District of Columbia. Correspondents dogged the "army" on its slow journey through Pennsylvania, writing about the half-dozen comic-opera figures capering on elderly horses, ignoring the ragged unemployed marching with something like hope in their eyes. Only a few hundred reached Washington, where Congress ignored them and Coxey was arrested for walking on the Capitol lawn.

Despair ran even deeper on American farms throughout the Great Plains and down into the cotton fields of the South. There, the depression only intensified the crisis that began in the late 1880s. Overproduction was crushing the army of wheat, corn, and cotton growers. The more the farmer produced, the lower prices fell, forced downward by the law of supply and demand. Many gave up, and thousands of covered wagons rolled East across the Mississippi, bearing signs reading, "In God We Trusted, In Kansas We Busted."

Farmers reacted to this situation with stunned anger, believing that *they*, and not the railroad owners or the farm-machinery producers or the meat packers, formed the backbone of the country. Yet debts piled higher and higher, while middlemen profited handsomely. There was something wrong somewhere, probably a calculated conspiracy to defraud farmers of their rightful share of national wealth, they felt.

In a thousand sun-baked courthouse squares, farmers cheered orators who demanded action. "What you farmers have to do," declared Mary Lease, a fiery woman known affectionately as "Mary Yellin," "is raise less corn and more hell!" In 1890, several farm groups had organized the Populist party to do just that. The Populists had elected three senators and twenty-five congressmen that year, and in 1892 its presidential candidate had carried four states and polled over a million votes. The party also elected governors and state officials, sometimes allying with an older party on a combined ticket.

The Populist showing in 1892 startled most of the country—and shocked the East. Populists demanded government ownership of railroads and telegraphs. Their platform also demanded an end to gambling in stocks, the direct election of the president and United States senators, and the secret ballot. And in a clear attempt to aid the mortgaged farmers, the Populists asked for no limit on the coinage of silver.

Requiring money to be backed only by gold, reasoned the Populists, greatly limited the amount in circulation. If the government could print money based on silver as well, and bought all silver mined in the country for that purpose, the resulting inflation would make mortgages easier to pay off and would raise farm prices. They spurned the arguments of bankers and industrialists that Europe would not accept money based on silver and that such a program would produce financial chaos. The Populists saw the issue as a battle of Eastern greed against Southern and Western sweat. "It is a struggle," explained "Sockless Jerry" Simpson, "between the robbers and the robbed."

The story of most presidential elections begins with the congressional election two years earlier. In the fall of 1894, in the midst of a depression and a farm crisis, the voters emphatically rebuked Cleveland and the Democrats. "The Democratic losses will be so great," predicted Thomas Reed, "that their dead will have to be buried in trenches labeled 'Unknown.' " The morning after the election, the trenches contained 113 of the 218 Democrats in the House. Cleveland's policies had shattered his party. Under intense pressure from their constituents, and with no reason to remain loyal to the administration, Democrats from the South and the West rushed to embrace "free" silver.

Now the Democrats and the Populists had a candidate to go with the issue. Bryan, having captured the nomination with his stirring oration, now embarked upon a radically different kind of campaign. Presidential candidates, by tradition, remained at home, pleased and flattered by the efforts their friends were making on their behalf, but pretending to be far too modest to campaign for themselves. In the four months between convention and election, Bryan altered this pattern, traveling eighteen thousand miles, making six hundred speeches, and addressing approximately five million persons. Republicans mocked his nickname, "the Boy Orator of the Platte," pointing out that the Platte River was six inches deep and a mile wide at the mouth; but Bryan's entranced audiences had apparently not heard the quip.

Across the nation, even in the supposedly hostile East, they yelled as the Democratic convention had yelled. After Bryan's triumphant tour of New England, a friend told him that he had never seen such a response. "You ought to come with me to Ohio, Indiana, and Kansas," smiled the confident nominee. "These people have given us a great reception in the East, but the West is on fire."

A Bryan speech in the West resembled a revival meeting more than a political rally. The crowd listened not with the skepticism usually accorded politicians, but with total trust and belief, cheering and responding at all the right moments. Before crowds so thick he sometimes could not reach the speaker's platform, Bryan painted a picture of a new America—a country whose abundant wealth would not be controlled by a small group, a country in which farmers would have their rightful place, in which the land across the Mississippi would not be an exploited colony of the East. Young and good-looking, Bryan appeared "every inch an Apollo," and farm wives as well as farmers were swept along in the spell of the new champion of the West.

Conservatives and Republicans, on the other hand, feared for their ticket. Hanna, panicked at the reception Bryan received that summer, went to McKinley, who was observing political tradition in his hometown of Canton. Hanna insisted that McKinley must campaign. The GOP candidate shook his head. "I might just as well put up a trapeze on my front lawn and compete with some professional athlete as go out speaking against Bryan," he reasoned. Hanna, reconsidering, agreed, and went off to New York to start his own campaign.

Joined by James J. Hill, railroad magnate of the Northwest, Hanna began visiting corporation offices. "I wish that Hanna would not talk so freely about money," complained one insurance company president, but the Ohio industrialist refused to play the hypocrite. He never denied that he proposed to beat Bryan by getting and spending more money than had ever been seen in an American election. Hanna extracted a quarter of a million each from John D. Rockefeller and J. P. Morgan. Four Chicago meat packers gave $100,000 apiece, and Hanna assessed banks and insurance companies one-quarter of 1 percent of their assets. The books of the Republican National Committee showed collections of $3.5 million, twice those of any previous campaign, but other estimates ranged from $10 million to $16 million being spent to beat silver. Cartoons in Democratic newspapers depicted Hanna in a suit checked with dollar signs.

With the money, Hanna sent out hundreds of speakers, preceding and following Bryan, including many converted Democrats. (He caused a furor at one luncheon by growling that some of the turncoat Democrats were not worth what it had cost to convert them.) Hanna's funds also enabled Republican headquarters to send out 250 million pieces of mail, including 120 million pamphlets, many of them in German, Swedish, Polish, Italian, Yiddish, and other languages. "He has advertised McKinley," complained the young Theodore Roosevelt, "as if he were a patent medicine!"

Bryan meanwhile had enough problems with his own party. Most major Democratic newspapers in the East refused to support the ticket. Immediately after Bryan's nomination, while gold Democrats were still stunned, Henry Watterson, editor of the influential and conservative Louisville *Courier-Journal*, wired from Europe, "Another ticket our only hope. No Compromise with Dishonor."

Taking that for their slogan, gold Democrats met in Indianapolis and nominated Senator John M. Palmer of Illinois, former Union Army general, for president, and former Confederate general Simon Bolivar Buckner of Kentucky for vice-president. The two old campaigners stumped actively, less for themselves than just to shake Democrats loose from Bryan. "Fellow Democrats," invited Palmer toward the end of the campaign, "I will not consider it any great fault if you decide to cast your vote for William McKinley." The Cleveland administration supported Palmer; when the secretary of the interior endorsed Bryan in August, Cleveland promptly fired him.

Bryan had also been unable to deal with the Populists' gift of a second running mate. Watson had accepted under the impression that the Democratic nominee, Arthur Sewall, would retire, making Watson the candidate of both Democratic and Populist parties. Democratic chairman Jones, no longer the eager seeker of Populist support, replied coolly, "Mr. Sewall will, of course, remain on the ticket, and Mr. Watson can do what he likes." What Watson did was to campaign through the West, urging Populists to vote for Bryan-Watson instead of Bryan-Sewall. (In most states, the slates combined on a single ticket of electors, with the vote to be cast for the vice-presidential candidate who led in the state's popular vote.) This policy was suicidal, since in the event of a Bryan victory neither Watson nor Sewall would share his majority and the Republican Senate would elect a vice-president. In the Democrats' idea of fusion, charged Watson, "We play Jonah while they play whale." Bryan dealt with the problem after a fashion by never formally accepting the Populist nomination.

A few Populists would never have supported Bryan anyway. "The Free Silver movement is a fake," sneered Henry Demarest Lloyd, one of the movement's few intellectuals. "Free silver is the cow-bird of the reform movement. It waited until the nest had been built by the sacrifice and labor of others, and then it laid its eggs in it, pushing out the others which it smashed on the ground." So saying, Lloyd groused off to vote Socialist Labor.

Feeling that their entire way of life was threatened, however, Republicans and conservatives intensified their attacks on Bryan. "Anarchists, Socialists, and destructives in society" supported Bryan, according to a Republican senator; *Harper's Weekly* compared Bryan and Altgeld to leaders of the French Revolution. But despite such invective, or perhaps because of it, the Republican New York *Herald* predicted in October that Bryan would get 237 electoral votes, thirteen more than needed for victory.

Hanna, however, had spotted the Nebraskan's weakness. "He's talking silver all the time," noted the Republican national chairman, "and that's where we've got him." The Chicago platform, with many planks favorable to labor, had gained Bryan the endorsement of Socialist leader Eugene V. Debs and J. K. Sovereign of the Knights of Labor, as well as the indirect support of Samuel Gompers of the American Federation of Labor. But even when speaking to workers, Bryan never stressed those planks, preferring to concentrate on currency. However attractive inflation appeared to a farmer with a heavy mortgage, it looked far different to a steelworker working twelve hours for a dollar a day. Bryan apparently saw no reason to broaden his appeal; as one observer commented, Bryan led a political revolution without understanding it.

The Nebraskan would have had problems with urban workers, who were largely immigrants, anyway. He neither drank nor smoked nor gambled, and he always wore about him an aura of rural, prudish evangelism. This cultural difference could not but make segments of the urban labor force uneasy. Their apprehensions about the Boy Orator of the Platte increased when Monsignor John Ireland, a ranking Catholic leader, came out against free silver.

Both McKinley and Hanna had excellent reputations among labor groups. McKinley had signed several prolabor bills as governor of Ohio, and his refusal to send troops to break a strike had once led the Chicago *Herald* to compare him with Altgeld. Hanna had rarely suffered any labor trouble in his far-flung enterprises, and was known to have bellowed during one major strike: "Any [business] man who won't meet his men halfway is a goddamn fool!"

McKinley proved to be a formidable campaigner in his own way. Although he would not go to an audience, audiences came to him, to sit on his front lawn and listen to him speak from the porch. Seven hundred and fifty thousand people came to Canton that fall, encouraged by the

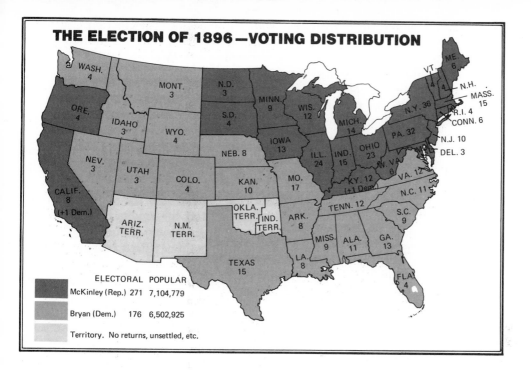

THE ELECTION OF 1896—VOTING DISTRIBUTION

ELECTORAL POPULAR
McKinley (Rep.) 271 7,104,779
Bryan (Dem.) 176 6,502,925
Territory. No returns, unsettled, etc.

special rates provided by friendly railroads. The reduced fares, a Democratic newspaper commented sourly, made it cheaper to visit McKinley than to stay home.

Many industrialists now decided to aid McKinley in their own way. "You may vote any way you wish," some factory owners were reputed to have informed their workers, "but if Bryan is elected on Tuesday the whistle will not blow on Wednesday." The idea spread rapidly, and a number of workers claimed to have received such warnings at factory gates or in their pay envelopes. "Boys," said a Bryan adviser, "I am afraid this beats us."

Possibly it did, although it was more likely that Hanna's efforts had decided the outcome. On November 3, Bryan came up half a million votes short. He carried no state north of the Mason-Dixon line or east of the Mississippi. He still might have won, but he lost four Democratic border states as well as California, Oregon, Iowa, Minnesota, and North Dakota in the West. In several of these states the vote was close, with the Palmer Democrats holding the balance. Bryan's rural stalwarts managed to win mainly the agrarian strongholds of the South and most of the prairie states for their eloquent standard-bearer.

Democrats charged that the Republicans had simply bought the election. The Democratic party, said Altgeld bitterly, was "confronted by all the banks, all the trusts, all the syndicates, all the corporations, all the great papers. It was confronted by everything that money could buy, that boodle could debauch, that fear of starvation could coerce."

The returns outlined the voters who decided the election. Bryan had failed to break through labor's fears, carefully fostered by Republican propaganda. He had failed to persuade dairy farmers that silver would help them, and he lost every dairy state, from Ohio to Wisconsin. Although he had repudiated the Democratic administration, the party could not escape the nation's bitterness over the depression. "I have borne the sins of Grover Cleveland," explained the candidate who most strongly opposed Cleveland's "Bourbon Democracy."

Republicans rejoiced at the election result. Hanna had saved the gold standard; the forces of "anarchism" (as conservatives fearfully viewed Bryan's Democratic and Populist supporters) had been beaten back. McKinley could be expected to offer the country a "safe" administration. He was confidently expected to retain the gold standard, raise tariff rates still higher, and avoid reforms.

Bryan cushioned his disappointment somewhat by writing a book on the campaign. In deference to both his beliefs and his own career, he called it *The First Battle.* He was certain that during his lifetime the forces favoring major reforms in America would regroup for future political campaigns. The 1896 election result, therefore, saddened him less than it did many of his agrarian supporters, about whose frustrations Vachel Lindsay wrote in an elegy to the campaign:

Election night at midnight:
Boy Bryan's defeat.
Defeat of western silver.
Defeat of the wheat.
Victory of letterfiles
And plutocrats in miles
With dollar signs upon their coats,
Diamond watchchains on their vests
And spats on their feet . . .
Victory of the neat.
Defeat of the aspen groves of Colorado valleys,
The blue bells of the Rockies,
And blue bonnets of old Texas,
By the Pittsburgh alleys.
Defeat of alfalfa and the Mariposa lily.
Defeat of the Pacific and the long Mississippi.
Defeat of the young by the old and silly.
Defeat of tornadoes by the poison vats supreme.
Defeat of my boyhood, defeat of my dream.

National Politics and the Crisis of the 1890s 32

The political turbulence of the 1896 election followed a long history of farm protest against the new industrial America. Great leaders had assured the small farmer, armed with the vote, that he was the backbone of America. The Populists were only the last of a series of farm organizations to reflect the farmer's growing belief that since the Civil War the balance of power and wealth had shifted to the corporations—and that the balance must be redressed.

Although the thrust of the farmer's complaints remained the same, issues varied over the last three decades of the nineteenth century. Originally, farmers had demanded stricter control of the railroads. Then, in two separate movements, currency reform seemed the root of the problem. Finally, the Populists focused on the process of government corruption and demanded a change in the selection of leaders; they wanted direct election of senators, primary elections, and secret ballots.

The Populist party achieved some significant gains in state government, but after 1896 it never posed a national threat. Some farmers would be swayed by the reformist rhetoric of Theodore Roosevelt; others, as we saw, remained with Bryan and the Democrats. A few would take a different path; when Oklahoma was admitted to the Union in 1907, it contained more Socialists than any other state in the nation. But with the rise of the cities, whatever the farmers did would matter less and less politically. The failure of the farmers' movement therefore was written not only in election returns but in census figures.

SETTLING THE WEST

Even after the passage of the Homestead Act during the Civil War, and despite subsequent government actions to make settlement of the plains attractive, Americans were reluctant to farm much past the Mississippi Valley. The notion of the Great American Desert, where nothing would grow and Indians abounded, died hard. Settlers heading west would rather go all the way to California or Oregon than stop in between in Kansas, Nebraska, or the Dakota territory.

After the war, heavy government subsidies helped to crisscross the plains with new railroad track. Roads like the Kansas Pacific, the Southern Pacific, and the Santa Fe appeared out of nowhere. Only heavy settlement of the area could make them profitable. The railroads, along with Western newspapers and local boosters, set out to recruit the needed settlers.

There was enough land for all of them. Not only did the government provide land virtually free to settlers under the Homestead Act, but the railroads had received millions of acres of public land in subsidies. They now used this land to lure farmers, selling it as cheaply as twenty-five cents an acre, and offering easy credit terms.

As a result of this effort, a tremendous boom in Western land took place. The population of the Dakota territory soared 853 percent between 1870 and 1880, and that of Kansas and Nebraska tripled. Some settlers mortgaged their homesteads to buy more land. Eastern and European money eagerly bought up Kansas mortgages, confident that prices would continue to rise. Not only settlers, but towns and cities went deeply into debt with the expectation that the boom would last forever. Well into the 1880s, bumper crops and financial boom flourished together. Farmers deeply in debt to banks and agricultural machinery companies still considered themselves rich because of the book value of their heavily mortgaged land holdings.

Due to gains in membership during the 1873 depression, the Grange could claim twenty thousand local lodges, mainly in the Midwest and South. On Independence Day, 1873, proclaimed as the "Farmers' Fourth of July," the Illinois lodge shown convened at an outdoor rally.
(Culver Pictures)

THE GRANGERS

Having come out to the West through the benevolence of the railroads, plains settlers slowly learned how completely they had fallen into the power of the railroad barons. Only by the railroad could they send their produce to Chicago and New York, and only by the railroad could they bring out the farm machinery and barbed wire necessary to tame the plains. Towns flourished or went bankrupt depending on the route of the road.

But even as new settlers rode the Rock Island Line out to the plains, agrarians farther east were learning how helpless they too were against the railroad. From Ohio to Minnesota, farmers had united into the Patrons of Husbandry, also known as the Grange. The Grange was partially a social institution, but also a cooperative alliance with some political interests. By the early 1870s, it had taken over several legislatures and had passed bills regulating railroad freight and storage rates. The railroads immediately attacked the new laws in the federal courts.

In the first decision, *Munn* v. *Illinois* (1877), the Supreme Court upheld an Illinois Granger law regulating Chicago grain storage companies. But over the next ten years, as Presidents Hayes, Arthur, Cleveland, and Harrison appointed a series of corporation lawyers as Supreme Court justices, the Court slowly whittled away at *Munn* v. *Illinois*. In 1890, in *Chicago, Milwaukee, and St. Paul Railway Company* v. *Minnesota,* it practically prohibited the states from regulating any railroad engaged in interstate commerce. The Grangers rapidly faded from political significance.

CRISIS ON THE PLAINS

Two blows—one a sudden act of nature, the other a steady process of technical advance and hard work—broke the speculative bubble on the plains. In 1886 and 1887, the weather turned on the homesteaders. Blistering summers with little rain were followed by miserable winters. Thousands of settlers were at once wiped out financially and began the slow, painful trek back east of the Mississippi. The inflated prices of land collapsed, and investors no longer clamored for plains mortgages.

The settlers who survived, when the rains returned and their corn again grew high, faced a worse problem. East of the Mississippi and in much of the West as well, advances in farming technology and efficient use of chemical fertilizers had tremendously increased American agricultural production. This increase sent the prices of wheat, corn, and hogs skidding downward. If, in a frantic attempt to catch up, farmers increased production, further price drops resulted. A bushel of wheat had plummeted from $1.19 in 1881 to 49 cents in 1894. The American farmer, whose productivity using indifferent soil had astounded the world, was being

The dry and dusty Great Plains had once been an unpleasant obstacle for westward-bound pioneers. After the Civil War, both the railroads and the federal government stimulated Western settlement. Although many families failed, those who remained transformed the unpromising flatland into a fertile source of grains and livestock. (Culver Pictures)

destroyed by his own success. Farmers now found it more profitable to burn corn for fuel than to sell it at current prices.

Farmers could blame themselves for creating part of the predicament. Many, out of greed, had dangerously overextended themselves. Before giving up entirely, farmers would mortgage virtually everything they owned. In Kansas and North Dakota, for example, the number of mortgages declared in 1890 amounted to one for every two citizens. Many, having mortgaged their horses and wagons, did not even have the option of fleeing to the East. A steady deflation since the Civil War, with less and less money in circulation, had crippled the mortgaged farmer. He had to pay back his loan in dollars that had doubled in value since he borrowed them.

Yet, farmers had also worked hard, and they now felt bitterly that the rules had been changed on them. They had no difficulty in coming up with people and institutions to blame. Somewhere, the farmers knew, someone was getting rich from their labor.

Railroads stood at the top of the list of indictments. There was little competition among the roads servicing the plains. Generally, only one ran into an area, and the farmer had no choice as to how to ship crops to market. Even when two railroads were within traveling distance, they had generally agreed upon rates beforehand, and the farmer again had little or no choice. Large growers received preferential rates, a practice justified by the railroads' claim that they must turn a profit on their investment. Farmers retorted that the railroads now had far more stock outstanding than the road was worth.

Even without considering the Granger cases, farmers expected little help from their state governments. The railroads exerted great power in the governments of many states.

Farmers also denounced other businesses that they felt were exploiting them. They charged that the farm machinery companies had formed a trust to keep the prices of their equipment high. Livestock raisers attacked the Chicago meat packers for making huge profits.

The plains farmers also stressed the need for remonetizing silver, a cause they had adopted from the Greenbackers. Since the time of the earlier reform movement, in the late 1870s, the situation had worsened for debtors. A dollar, worth twice its 1865 value in 1877, was worth three times its 1865 value by 1895. To heavily mortgaged farmers, this meant a financial war of attrition that they were bound to lose. Behind the country's virtual abandonment of silver money—"the Crime of '73"—they saw an alliance of their enemies: railroads, grain storage companies, money lenders, Wall Street, and foreign bankers.

This bitterness was fed by the intensity of the farmers' outrage, which had roots far deeper than economics. The center of American life was shifting rapidly to the city, and the farmer felt abandoned and despised. National magazines began carrying more and more stories and articles about city life, and the farmer saw his children deserting farm areas for the more exciting cities. Worst of all, a deep and justified suspicion existed that the new urbanites laughed at farm folk and looked down on them as "hicks." The conditions of farm life, especially in the West, were not such as to foster tolerance toward critics or opponents. Existence on a plains homestead was a constant round of hard physical labor and mind-numbing chores, allowing little contact with the outside world.

SOUTHERN AGRICULTURAL PROBLEMS

Although the problems of the Southern farmer differed from those of the plains homesteader, the two were partners in misery. When the plantation system collapsed at the end of the Civil War, millions of acres became available for land-hungry poor whites and freed slaves. Few of them, however, could afford to buy the land outright, and investors eager to buy up Nebraska mortgages showed no interest in Alabama cotton land.

Poor farmers in the South, therefore, were compelled to obligate themselves heavily to use the land. Most farmers, including the great majority of blacks, became sharecroppers, farming someone else's land and turning over a large portion of

THE INCREASE OF FARM TENANCY IN THE SOUTH—1890

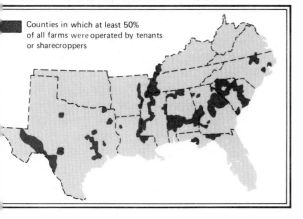

Counties in which at least 50% of all farms were operated by tenants or sharecroppers

the crop to the owner. Generally, the Southern farmer kept no more than half of the harvest. Many kept only one-third.

To support themselves while the crops were growing, farmers mortgaged themselves again, this time to local storekeepers. (Very often, moreover, the landowner and the storekeeper were the same person.) In exchange for supplies, the storekeeper received a lien on the farmer's crops. The crops, when they came in, rarely amounted to enough to wipe out the standing debt. Year by year, the debt increased, obligations to the storekeeper-land owner preventing the sharecropper from leaving the land. The result was a system of peonage. For black farmers, it was not much better than slavery, and, as the twentieth century approached, more and more white farmers also became "croppers."

Further, the landowners and storekeepers demanded that the farmer grow the crop that could be most easily turned into cash—namely, cotton. This prevented Southern farmers from growing enough food crops to maintain their families and took a heavy toll on Southern soil, which now required large doses of fertilizer. To make matters worse, the price of cotton was rapidly declining; from 1870 to 1890 it was cut almost in half.

Moreover, Southern farmers shared with the plains settlers the problems of currency appreciation and the railroads. In the South, railroads allied themselves with the Democratic rather than the Republican party, but they controlled state govern-

ments just as effectively. Southern farmers came to share their Western compatriots' interest in railroad regulation, and, being as deeply in debt, shared also a growing enthusiasm for free silver.

THE COMING OF THE FARMERS' ALLIANCE

Throughout American history, farm organizations had sprung up, scored some temporary successes, and then faded away. But in the late 1880s, a group appeared and began to spread with astounding speed. Helped along by the able leadership of several remarkable personalities, Farmers' Alliances enrolled millions of members in the South and the West. By the end of the decade, the Southern Farmers' Alliance had enrolled three million members, with another million and a quarter in the Colored Farmers' Alliance. The Northern Farmers' Alliance, composed overwhelmingly of farmers from states west of the Mississippi River, counted about another million. No previous farm organization had been able to come close to such numbers.

Like the Grange, the Alliance was partly social in its objectives, giving farmers a chance to get together occasionally. Also, like the Grange, it distributed pamphlets seeking to educate farmers about their condition and the reasons behind it. In many states, both in the West and the South, the Alliance took an active role in politics and managed to elect legislators favorable to its aims. In some states, it established railroad commissions, only to find, as the Grange had, that such controls turned out to be inadequate. The Alliance, however, had far greater numbers than the Grange had ever claimed, as well as a more impressive geographical distribution.

Political scientists and reformers in the 1870s and 1880s frequently complained that "Gilded Age" politics lacked meaning. They professed to find little difference between parties, and charged that elections reflected not popular choices on issues, but only a sordid struggle for government offices and power. True or not, soon after the farmers' massive entry into politics, the parties indeed began to represent different ideas.

This culminated in the bitter struggle of the 1896 campaign, when each side expected the destruction of the country should the other side win. It also culminated in the destruction of the balance between parties, leading to an unbroken, sixteen-year Republican rule in Washington.

While farmers gained strength, the tariff continued as the dominant issue on the surface of American politics. The farmers eventually came to oppose the tariff, seeing it as one more example of governmental aid to the rich and powerful, but they never felt as strongly about it as they did about silver and railroads. Republicans, however, saw the high tariff as one of the keys to American (and their own party's) prosperity.

As Congress gathered in 1889, Republicans for the first time in fourteen years had working control of the presidency, the Senate, and the House. In 1890 they seized the opportunity, under the leadership of William McKinley, to pass the highest tariff in history. The McKinley bill flatly intended to protect as many American industries as possible from foreign competition.

The bill roused widespread opposition. Most Democrats attacked it; some were even known to send peddlers through the Midwest with items to sell at wildly inflated prices (which would be blamed on the tariff). When the votes were counted that November, Democrats had won an overwhelming victory, capturing heavy control of the House. Many senior Republican congressmen, including McKinley himself, lost their seats.

THE FOUNDING OF THE POPULIST PARTY

Alliance members in both the South and the West entered politics on a large scale in 1890. In the South, Alliance members won impressive victories within the Democratic party, running against railroads and their alliances with conservative, or "Bourbon," Democratic leaders. The Alliance elected three governors and claimed control of eight state legislatures. More than forty Southern Democratic congressmen announced that they favored the Alliance platform. The election also produced dramatic leaders for the Southern farmers, such as one-eyed "Pitchfork Ben" Tillman of South Carolina and slight but fiery Tom Watson of Georgia.

The plains farmers, however, had resolved to strike out for themselves. Angered by their lack of power within the existing party system, many farmers decided to bolt to the new party. From Minnesota to Colorado, farmers sang, "Good-bye, My Party, Good-bye," and named independent tickets. All across the plains, orators for the new party described Democrats and Republicans as nothing more than different fronts for the same railroad machine. A large number of the new agitators were women: Mary Elizabeth Lease, a lawyer with four children, became one of the most popular speakers on the plains. Older reform protest figures joined in large numbers, and the Populists—although predominately agrarian in membership—also contained many Socialists, "Single Taxers" (followers of Henry George), "Nationalists" (disciples of the Utopian Socialist Edward Bellamy), and Knights of Labor within their ranks.

From the 1890 returns, the new party seemed to make a promising start. It elected great numbers of state legislators and two United States senators. Five Alliance congressmen were chosen from Kansas and two more, along with a sympathetic Democrat named William Jennings Bryan, from Nebraska. Where the Alliance could not muster enough strength to win, it got the votes of enough normally Republican farmers to elect a large number of Democrats.

Both sides in the debate over a third party gained from the election. Westerners were now confident that a new party could succeed, the Southerners that they could gain control of the Democratic party. In a series of conventions over the next year, from Florida to Nebraska, they fought the issue out. Slowly the Southerners, unhappy at the conservatism of the national Democratic leadership, began to come around. At the organization of Congress, twenty Southern Democrats joined the Western Alliance men in supporting Tom Watson for Speaker of the House. Finally, in July 1892, delegates from the Northern and Southern Alliances and other organizations met in Omaha to take the final step, to nominate an independent Populist candidate for president of the United States.

Their candidate, and their platform, reflected the party more closely than convention products usually do. General James Baird Weaver, the candidate, was a veteran of the Civil War and of two decades of activism for reform and Prohibition. He had run for president as the Greenback candidate in 1880 and served three terms in Congress as a Greenback Democrat. As a new Populist and an old soldier, Weaver campaigned over the entire country.

"We meet in the midst of a nation brought to the verge of moral, political, and material ruin," warned the 1892 Populist platform. The time had come, the Populists announced, when either the railroads would own the people or the people would own the railroads. They demanded the end of national banks and the issuance of all money by the government, based on free coinage of silver. The program reflected the party's largely rural and agrarian base. Therefore, although there were planks that defended the right of unions to organize and denounced the oppression of factory workers, these were not central Populist concerns. And, although the platform also demanded a graduated federal income tax, direct election of senators, and other constitutional or political reforms, these were not critical matters for Populists.

What the new party wished, above all, was a series of reforms designed to help American farmers overcome what they felt were the unfair handicaps imposed upon agriculture in the United States by industrial growth. The most important of these demands was strict regulation or government ownership of the nation's railroads, which farmers believed discriminated against them. They also wanted an increase in the supply of money through remonetizing silver, since the Bland-Allison Act had been largely ineffective. Finally, they proposed establishing a government subtreasury warehouse system in which farmers could deposit their crops and receive loans up to 80 percent of the current market value of these crops. They would redeem the crops and sell them when open market prices has risen to acceptable levels. With this radical platform and a radical candidate, the Populists prepared to go before the nation.

One reason for the willingness of some Southern Alliance members to leave the Democratic fold was the rapidly deteriorating condition of that party. Grover Cleveland, defeated for reelection in 1888, appeared to be the overwhelming favorite for his third nomination. Cleveland had never been much of an economic reformer. Since leaving the White House, he had practiced law in partnership with J. P. Morgan's attorney on Wall Street. He opposed free silver coinage even more strongly than the incumbent Republican president, Benjamin Harrison.

Despite Cleveland's nomination, the Southern Alliance split wide open over the question of leaving the Democrats. Regardless of any other issues, the Democrats were known in the South as "the white man's party." Joining the Populists meant public branding as a traitor to the white race. The South's best-known Alliance politicians were on opposite sides of the split. Tillman, governor of South Carolina and boss of the state Democratic party, refused to bolt, despite his well-known hatred for Cleveland; Watson led his Georgia followers into the Populist party and nominated a full state ticket to oppose the Democrats.

The Populists alarmed the white Southern establishment even more by openly appealing to the black vote. In many Southern states they allied closely with the Republicans, for whom blacks normally voted (when they were allowed to vote). In the campaign that followed, Southern Democrats used any weapon they could to smash the Populist–Republican–black alliance. Blacks were terrorized into staying away from the polls or marched there by force to vote Democratic. When General Weaver campaigned in the South, Democrats broke up his rallies; Mary Lease claimed that in Georgia they made "a walking omelette" of the Populist candidate. Opponents shot at Populists, pressured them with economic threats, and, if necessary, stuffed the ballot boxes.

Without the race issue, Populist campaigners faced little violence on the plains. There the Democrats, who were the minority party, established working arrangements with the Popu-

Songs, revelry, and flag waving characterized this election night crowd in 1892. Republican Benjamin Harrison and Democrat Grover Cleveland had few differences in policy, except on the tariff, but Populist ex-Union General James B. Weaver ran on a platform of economic reform that won him twenty-two electoral votes in the West. (Culver Pictures)

lists in most states. Democrats partially accepted the Populist platform, and Cleveland supporters, positive that they could not carry Kansas or Nebraska, planned to hurt Harrison by giving the states' votes to Weaver. The Democratic National Committee even supplied some under-the-table funds to the Populists for that purpose.

When the returns came in, Populists took a mixed view of the results. Cleveland won, but Weaver had polled a million votes (almost 10 percent) and carried five states, and the party claimed five senators and ten congressmen. Yet Populism had failed to make any serious inroads in the South, and had carried only Kansas on the plains.

The decline that had spurred the nation's farmers to take active steps for their own relief had no such effect on the rest of the country's workers. They failed to join the Populist movement. Several factors help to explain this. For one, the Populists never succeeded in breaking down the traditional political loyalties of most Americans, since party loyalty was extremely important to voters at this time. Even under the impact of economic depression, most people remained with their normal parties.

It was also true that the depression that began in 1893 occurred during a Democratic administration—Cleveland's second term. This resulted in political gains for the major opposition party even more impressive than those made by the Populists. In fact, Republicans almost doubled their number of House members in 1894—moving

An ex-slave whose achievements in a thirty-five-year career spanned several important realms of national experience, Booker T. Washington may have been the single most influential American of his era in the field of race relations. His claim to greatness rests on his accomplishments as a teacher, educational pioneer, social theorist, fund raiser for philanthropic causes, adviser to presidents, writer, politician and, most importantly, as the undeposed spokesman for black Americans.

Born on a Franklin County, Virginia, plantation in 1856, Booker T. Washington lived in a slave cabin with his mother, sister, and brother until emancipation, when the family moved to West Virginia. In later years Washington credited his mother's "high ambitions for her children" as a dominant influence on his early years. He taught himself the alphabet using a Webster spelling book and, soon afterwards, he attended night school where he learned to read and write. In 1872, he entered Hampton Institute. He earned his board as a janitor while studying at Hampton, and graduated in 1875 after training as a brick mason.

Most of Washington's adult life was spent in the South, first as a teacher in another Negro school before joining Hampton's staff in 1879 and then, two years later, becoming the head of a new Negro school being organized at Tuskegee, Alabama, which became world famous as the Tuskegee Institute.

During the 1880s, Washington addressed educational groups and public gatherings, in both the North and the South, covering such topics as race relations, the importance of education for black Americans, and the virtues of black–white harmony at almost any cost (including a temporary pause in Negro demands for political rights and legal equality until a strong educational and economic base had been created).

Undoubtedly Washington's most famous statement of his central themes came during an 1893 speech at the Cotton States and International Exposition at Atlanta. At the Exposition, Washington called for friendship between the races while bluntly accepting the pattern of caste segregation then prevalent in every section of the country: "In all things that are purely social we can be as sepa-

Booker T. Washington

(Culver Pictures)

rate as the fingers, yet one as the hand in all things essential to mutual progress." Washington was praised by white moderates throughout the country. At the same time, many other black political leaders viewed the speech with dismay as an invitation to continued white interference with expressions of Negro militance.

Washington established rural extension programs at Tuskegee Institute designed to assist Southern farmers, helped found the National Negro Business League, and participated in many other activities intended to maximize black economic action and educational opportunity. In addition to these accomplishments, Washington wrote ten books and numerous articles. His most famous book, *Up From Slavery* (1901), further enhanced his extraordinary public reputation. Washington died while still maintaining his rigorous work schedule at the age of fifty-nine in November 1915. Even critics of his "accommodationist" philosophy have recognized that, within the pantheon of American black leaders, Booker T. Washington served as the monumental personal bridge linking the tragic centuries of slavery with the twentieth-century struggle by Negro Americans for full equality.

from 127 to 244—while the Democrats lost 113 seats. This was the most rapid major reversal of national political strength in American history, marking the first step in ending the close balance between the parties that had existed during the 1870s and 1880s.

Besides the depression working against them, there were other factors that the Populists could not overcome. The South presented the Populists with a unique set of problems that impeded their growth. There the new party attempted, for the first time since Reconstruction days, to create a biracial political coalition of black and white farmers against the business interests that still dominated most Southern state governments. For a time they made striking gains. But the political opponents of Southern Populism played upon deeply felt racial fears and hostilities so effectively that, by the end of the decade, the new party had lost almost all its influence in the South. In that region, in fact, Populism had the ironic effect by 1900 of elevating the race issue to an intensity and importance that it maintained throughout most of the twentieth century until the 1970s.

Populist strength was sapped, especially in the industrial states, by internal tensions among its diverse sources of support. Such tensions between utopians and pragmatists often characterize reform movements. The Populists' agrarian leaders tended to be the movement's practical figures. Their overriding concern was for specific, immediate, and achievable goals such as free coinage of silver, the subtreasury plan, and other measures that would improve the economic bargaining position of most American farmers.

workers was unemployed. Four out of five Americans were living at subsistence level. As his first order of business, then, Cleveland would have to deal with a problem that had not figured in the campaign at all. And the price of farm products continued to decline disastrously on the world markets, while production costs skyrocketed.

Observers offered many explanations for the depression and suggested many ways to deal with it. The conservative Cleveland accepted the prescription offered by big business. Confidence, he contended, had been shaken by the Sherman Silver Purchase Act, passed three years earlier by Congress as a sop to silver feeling. Cleveland claimed that the country had lost faith in its currency and noted the rush to exchange Treasury Department silver certificates for gold, a rush that was rapidly depleting the nation's gold reserves. In the midst of the depression, with sentiment for unlimited silver coinage sweeping the South and West, Cleveland called Congress into special session to repeal the law and silver coinage altogether. Using all his powers of patronage, Cleveland jammed repeal through Congress.

Worst of all, Cleveland's policies seemed to have no effect on the depression. Banks still closed their doors, workers remained unemployed, and gold continued to pour out of the Treasury. By early 1895, the Treasury had only a three-week gold supply left. Cleveland and his secretary of the treasury now arranged to buy $60 million in gold from a syndicate headed by J. P. Morgan and the Rothschilds, paying an extraordinarily high rate of interest. Cleveland's action may have saved the treasury, but it did nothing for his popularity.

DEMOCRATS, DEPRESSION, DISASTER

Shortly after Cleveland took office for the second time, a business panic ushered in yet another of the series of depressions that had struck the nation at twenty-year intervals throughout the nineteenth century. Banks began to fail in 1893, and businesses laid off millions of workers in the cities and factory towns. By 1894, at the height of the depression, probably one out of every five

MCKINLEY AND PROSPERITY

The Republicans' comfortable though hard-fought victory over Bryan in 1896 appeared to put an end to the threats of radicalism and Populist agrarianism. Aided immensely by an economic upturn during the summer and fall of 1896, especially by a significant rise in farm prices, depression gave way to recession at an accelerating pace which soon produced recovery and defused agrarian protest. Mark Hanna had advertised McKinley as the

"Advance Agent of Prosperity." Hanna appeared to be right, and Bryanism appeared to be doomed.

Perhaps the most striking feature of the 1896 election, however, was the Republicans' ability to put together a national majority that cut across class lines. McKinley won the votes not only of industrialists and the middle class, but also of a majority of urban workers. Bryan failed to capture the cities and the votes of most industrial laborers, despite prolabor planks in the Democratic platform. Many urban workers evidently felt that their economic interests were better protected by a pro-business Republican president than by a Democratic candidate who spoke (in the rich twang of Midwestern rural America no less) mainly about the problems of farmers. Moreover, Bryan had failed to hold together many of the Democratic party's traditional supporters in business, the middle class, and various ethnic groups. This failure may have been the single most important factor in his defeat.

But if Bryan failed in 1896 to create that farmer–laborer–small-businessman coalition that he believed could win national power and make needed political and economic reforms, he did succeed in laying the groundwork for such reformers, not only within the Democratic party but among Republicans as well. In the process, Bryan set a precedent for active presidential campaigning that almost all subsequent major party candidates followed in the twentieth century. In the end, therefore, the struggle for change in American society gathered momentum during the late 1890s despite Bryan's defeat, despite the disappearance of Populism, and even despite the country's return to economic prosperity.

McKinley's cabinet, even more conservative than the bimetallist president, wanted no tinkering with the financial machine. For his part, McKinley, who was not a reactionary on most issues, insisted on raising the tariff even beyond the demands of most conservatives. The resulting Dingley Tariff of 1897 pushed rates upward to an average of 52 percent.

Prosperity, not political enthusiasm, provided the key to the McKinley administration's success. The economic upturn of 1896–97 continued full force. Thus the strongest argument of

the silverites—the contention that reliance on gold, a metal in short supply, strangled and would continue to strangle the nation's debtors—no longer applied. New discoveries of gold in Australia, Alaska, and South Africa dramatically increased supplies, and a strong inflationary trend accompanied the return to agricultural and industrial prosperity. In 1900, Congress and McKinley gave the country the Gold Standard Act, a law which committed the federal government to a single monetary standard: gold. Another section of the law aimed at increasing the amount of national bank notes in circulation. Within a year, the dollar total of such notes almost doubled.

Nineteen hundred was also a presidential election year. From the start, McKinley had little to worry about. Bryan, again the Democratic candidate, made little headway, and confusion over campaign strategies revealed his dilemma. Populism was dying during the late 1890s as rapidly as it had grown in the early years of the decade. Sensing this, Bryan tried to make anti-imperialism his central campaign theme. A bored or even hostile response caused him to switch in midstream, and he gave primacy to the monopoly issue. Bryan did not abandon the free-silver stand (he insisted on a silver plank in the Democratic platform), but obviously his "second battle" would be no rerun of the first, except in the election returns. McKinley again won handily, and to conservative Republicans all things seemed right.

Prosperity's "advance agent" did not live to enjoy the fruits of this happy political situation. Within six months of his second inaugural, William McKinley was dead, victim of an assassin's bullet. In September 1901, McKinley journeyed to Buffalo, New York, to open the Pan-American Exposition of that year. Waiting for him amidst an almost adoring public was a young man named Leon Czolgosz. The Detroit-born son of Polish immigrant parents, Czolgosz was twenty-eight in 1901. He had survived, barely, the economic troubles of the nineties. He espoused the ideas of radical anarchists, though he had never joined any group in the movement.

In 1901, he decided to kill the president. Without difficulty, Czolgosz joined the mass of people crowding around McKinley, who was "receiving" in one of the exposition buildings, shaking hands with all comers. Two shots rang out; one of them wounded McKinley mortally. A few days later the president died, and Theodore Roosevelt, a young New York Republican who had been chosen for the vice-presidency in order to slow down his political career, became the new president.

Roosevelt differed from McKinley greatly in style and slightly in principles. It would be Roosevelt's job, first, to restore domestic tranquillity, which had been jolted by the third presidential assassination in almost as many decades. Then, he would be charged with maintaining prosperity, so recently returned, while consolidating America's new and enlarged role in the world. To these tasks, Roosevelt would add one of his own: the advocacy of reform in American society, with growing boldness as his presidency progressed.

Suggested Readings
Chapters 31–32

Election of 1896

Robert F. Durden, *Climax of Populism: The Election of 1896* (1964); Paul W. Glad, *McKinley, Bryan and the People* (1964); Stanley Jones, *The Presidential Election of 1896* (1964).

The Gilded Age

Paolo E. Coletta, *William Jennings Bryan: Political Evangelist, 1860–1898* (1964); Harold U. Faulkner, *Politics, Reform and Expansion, 1890–1900* (1959); Ray Ginger, *The Bending Cross: A Biography of Eugene V. Debs* (1948); Paul W. Glad, *The Trumpet Soundeth: William Jennings Bryan* (1959); J. Rogers Hollingsworth, *The Whirligig of Politics* (1963); Richard J. Jensen, *The Winning of the Midwest* (1971); Edward C. Kirkland, *Industry Comes of Age* (1961); Paul Kleppner, *The Cross of Culture* (1970); Morgan Kousser, *The Shaping of Southern Politics* (1974); Margaret Leech, *In the Days of McKinley* (1959); H. Wayne Morgan, *William McKinley and His America* (1963); Arnold M. Paul, *Conservative Crisis and the Rule of Law, 1887–1895* (1960); Larzer Ziff, *The American 1890s: Life and Times of a Lost Generation* (1966).

Populism

Allan G. Bogue, *Money at Interest* (1955); Lawrence Goodwyn, *Democratic Promise: The Populist Movement in America* (1976); John D. Hicks, *The Populist Revolt* (1931); Walter T. K. Nugent, *The Tolerant Populists: Kansas Populism and Nativism* (1963); Norman Pollack, *The Populist Response to Industrial America* (1962); Martin Ridge, *Ignatius Donnelly* (1962); Fred A. Shannon, *The Farmers' Last Frontier: Agriculture, 1860–1897* (1945); Francis B. Simkins, *Pitchfork Ben Tillman* (1944); C. Vann Woodward, *Tom Watson: Agrarian Rebel* (1938).

The new century brought to Americans confidence in their own ability to control the nation's destiny. It also brought concern for the unresolved problems of industrial growth, urban squalor, and immigrant poverty. The business depression of the 1890s had ended by 1898, returning the country's middle and upper classes to full prosperity. A global empire had been won with little cost or exertion.

The chapters that follow describe the decades of confidence, concern, and change within American society from 1900 through the Depression. The first of these chapters, on the Triangle Fire, dramatizes the lives of Southern and Eastern European immigrant workers in New York City garment factories. Underpaid and impoverished, they struggled to unionize the clothing industry. Only when a flash fire killed scores of young female workers at the Triangle Company did their appeal for better working conditions receive a hearing.

Chapter 34 then opens with a discussion of the urban world within which most of these recent immigrants lived. The chapter explores the varieties of industrial reform efforts. Since the political life of progressive America (1900–17) often concerned the struggle for change, Chapter 34 examines connections between reform activities and partisan politics.

Popular confidence rose during these decades partly because of the ease with which the United States assumed a leading role in world affairs. Chapter 35 portrays one of the unhappier consequences of that new role — the unsuccessful revolt by Filipino nationalists against American takeover of their islands. The Philippine Revolt serves as the context for a general discussion in Chapter 36 of American foreign policy. The chapter traces developments from the country's brief involvement in the Spanish-American War to its costlier participation in World War I. The connections between domestic concerns in progressive America and the nation's actions as a major global power emerge clearly.

One of the great human dramas of the twentieth century was Charles Lindbergh's nonstop flight across the Atlantic in 1927, which captured the imagination of a world hungry for genuine heroes and fascinated with the new machine technology in fields such as aviation. The story of Lindbergh's pioneering flight unfolds in Chapter 37 at several levels: as an absorbing family drama, a saga of personal courage against enormous physical and technical odds, and an account of the way in which his flight reflected other major elements in American culture during the decade. Lindbergh's quiet heroism spans the entire narrative.

American society in the 1920s forms the subject of Chapter 38, accompanying the story of Lindbergh's flight. The self-proclaimed "New Era" of America's business civilization produced its own distinctive brand of politics, a broad measure of mechanical and economic progress, and a variety of bitterly fought cultural conflicts. The United States viewed itself and the world with confident detachment during the period which followed World War I, though the issues that separated urban and rural America during the 1920s never found satisfying resolution. The contradictions and conflicts of the "Roaring Twenties" emerge in the

PROGRESSIVE AMERICA

chapter: prohibition and the spread of a more tolerant social morality, religious fundamentalism, the political resurgence of extremist groups such as the Ku Klux Klan, complacent Republican government amidst the persistence of Progressive reform struggles at the congressional and state levels, business domination of American society and the decline of unionism as an economic force, ethno-cultural intolerance and the emergence of an alienated intelligentsia.

After the stock market crash of 1929, the middle- and upper-class prosperity which had characterized the "New Era" gave way to growing unemployment and business collapse. The Hoover administration operated in the lengthening shadow of a nationwide depression, unrelieved and ever-worsening, despite various inadequate government attempts to reverse or remedy the decline. The optimism which had characterized America's technologically advanced civilization had all but disappeared after four years of the worst economic depression the United States had ever experienced. What lay ahead during the 1930s seemed, to most Americans at the close of the Hoover administration, possibly the most critical test since the Civil War for the future of democratic society in this country.

33 The Triangle Fire

In September 1909, two hundred Jewish and Italian immigrant workers at New York City's Triangle Shirtwaist Company walked off their jobs. The previous year, Triangle's owners had organized an Employees Benevolent Association, a so-called company union, designed to head off unions organized by the workers themselves. But the tactic had not worked. Protesting miserable working conditions and poor pay, the workers at Triangle—most of them young women—sought to gain recognition of their own union by their employers. They were led by officials from the recently organized International Ladies' Garment Workers' Union (ILGWU). They had also received the support of the Women's Trade Union League (WTUL).

The Triangle strikers, as well as workers in other shirtwaist shops in the city, were forced to work in crowded, unclean factories. Fire hazards and unsanitary conditions presented a serious threat to their health. Windows and doors in the shops were often nailed shut. Rarely did the sun penetrate the factory lofts, which workers referred to as sweatshops.

Long hours and low wages added to the workers' discontent. Most employees in New York's garment factories worked a fifty-six-hour, six-day week. When a factory owner had a rush order, he could force employees to work overtime at night or on Sunday without pay. Wages in the shirtwaist industry were as low as six dollars a week. Employers often deducted penalties from workers' pay for mistakes made in sewing clothes. They charged the workers fees for "renting" the machines and using electricity. In addition, employees were subjected to a series of petty fines for talking, smoking, or singing on the job.

It was against such conditions and in the face of active opposition by the police, who were openly sympathetic to the factory owners, that the workers finally took a stand.

The strike dragged on into winter. Workers at nonstriking shirtwaist companies grew angrier as they watched police and hired thugs abuse the striking employees. On the evening of November 22 the city's shirtwaist workers held a mass meeting at Cooper Union to discuss the situation.

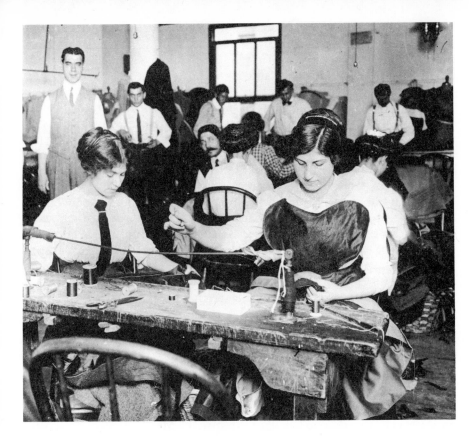

Sweatshops like the one shown here were common to the garment industry. Unskilled women laborers usually worked under skilled male machine operators in crowded, poorly ventilated, and unsafe shops. (Brown Brothers)

Within a few days, between ten thousand and twenty thousand workers, mainly young women, had walked off their jobs. The strike affected over five hundred shirtwaist and dressmaking companies, including all the smaller shops and most of the big companies in the city. "The Uprising of the Twenty Thousand," as the ILGWU called the walkout, was the first industry-wide strike of immigrant workers in New York City. It was also the largest strike by women ever staged in the United States up to that time.

The shirtwaist[1] industry was a relatively recent one. The 1900 federal census described it as a "branch of the garment industry that has developed during the last decade." Before 1900 many of the garments produced in New York City and elsewhere came from workshops in ghetto slum apartments. Families were paid according to the number of garments produced. This piecework system proved inefficient. Clothing production gradually shifted to new loft buildings constructed especially for the trade.

---

[1] The shirtwaist was a tailored blouse for women usually made of sheer cotton and styled somewhat like a man's shirt.

By 1910 New York had become the national center for the garment industry. The city's six hundred shirtwaist and dress factories employed over thirty thousand workers. They sold more than $50 million worth of clothing annually. In the new shops skilled machine operators, usually men, supervised crews of young women who performed simple, unskilled tasks. At large factories, such as Triangle, the machine operators, called contractors, were paid by the owners not only for their own work but for the labor of their crews as well. The contractors, in turn, paid weekly salaries to their female assistants. This system was often abused by dishonest contractors, who cheated young women workers out of their proper wages.

Four out of every five workers in the garment trades were women. In the Uprising of the Twenty Thousand, 75 percent of the strikers were young women between the ages of sixteen and twenty-five. Almost all had been born abroad or to recently arrived immigrant families. Most of the workers were either Jewish or Italian. Most of the factory owners were Jews.

The 1909 garment trade's strike marked the first time that many of these immigrant workers managed to set aside their mutual fears and suspicions to work for common economic interests. The strike brought Jewish and Italian women together on the picket line and in the union. Thus it set a pattern for future cooperation in the labor movement among the city's ethnic communities. Jewish union organizers learned a smattering of Italian, while Italian leaders acquired enough Yiddish to make themselves understood. Political and community leaders from each ethnic group worked together on behalf of the strikers. Meyer London, a socialist lawyer who later became one of the country's first Jewish congressmen, cooperated with Fiorello La Guardia, a young state legislator who later became the country's first Italian congressman. La Guardia, the son of a Jewish mother and an Italian father, symbolized the alliance then being forged by the two groups.

Black workers were frequently hired as strikebreakers, or scabs, in the garment factories. Several hundred of them joined the Uprising of the Twenty Thousand. One black shirtwaist striker—a "real born American," as she described herself—kept a diary of the events. In it she recorded her shop's reaction to the November 22 call for a general strike:

> It's a good thing, this strike is. It makes you feel like a real grown-up person. . . . I simply can't get over the way little Ray Goldousky jumped on a chair and suddenly, without a minute's notice, stopped the electricity [in the shop]. Why, we were simply stunned. Before you could say Jack Robinson, we all rose, slipped on our duds, and marched down the stairs, shouting, yelling, and giggling about our walkout, as they called it.

Similar incidents in New York's garment factories that week shocked the industry's manufacturers into taking action against the strikers. Anti-strike activities ranged from encouraging police brutality against strikers to organizing company unions among the minority of

workers who did not support the strike. Employers also tried "carrot-and-stick" tactics. They offered incentives to those who remained on the job but hired hoodlums to beat up workers on the picket line. The anonymous shirtwaist striker noted in her diary that the Triangle Company promised nonstrikers "from fifteen to twenty dollars weekly, free lunch, and dancing during the noon hour." These tactics, however, failed to break the morale and unity of the shirtwaist strikers. The Uprising of the Twenty Thousand continued throughout the bitterly cold winter of 1909–10.

Somehow the tens of thousands of strikers managed to maintain orderly picket lines at each shop. Every day the police dragged away dozens of frozen, poorly clad young women from the lines. By Christmas day, the arrests tallied 723. Yet those who were arrested and later bailed out of jail usually returned to the picket lines the next day.

The strike was an important event not only for women garment workers but also for woman suffrage reformers, ghetto community leaders, labor officials, and socialist politicians. All these groups donated time and money to make the strike a success. The "uptown" supporters were joined by several of the city's most active reform groups: the Women's Trade Union League, the National Women's Suffrage Association, the Political Equality Association, and the National Civic Federation.

A host of muckraking reporters,[2] academics, social workers, and other professionals also worked on behalf of the strikers. Many of these middle- and upper-class reformers were German Jews whose ancestors had come to the United States during the mid-nineteenth century. The

---

[2] Muckraking reporters were writers of the late nineteenth and early twentieth centuries who exposed corrupt conditions in business and government.

strike gave them an opportunity to display their solidarity with poorer Jews from the Lower East Side, most of whom had recently left Eastern Europe for the United States.

Everywhere on the Lower East Side community leaders worked in support of the strike. They included union officials from the United Hebrew Trades, Socialist party orators from both the Jewish and Italian communities, sympathetic rabbis and priests, and editors of Jewish newspapers. A number of other New York newspapers supported the striking workers, as did many of the city's residents. An open meeting held on December 5 drew over eight thousand pro-strike demonstrators. Pressure mounted on the garment trade employers to resolve the dispute.

A settlement was finally reached in February 1910. The agreement came in two stages. It represented a victory for the union, though not a total triumph. At first the shirtwaist workers rejected several compromise offers arranged by arbitrators who brought the two sides together. Then a number of smaller manufacturers began settling privately with the ILGWU. In these agreements, however, neither the union nor the union shop was recognized.

By February 15, 1910, only 1,100 workers, from thirteen shops, were still away from their jobs. The ILGWU officially declared the strike over. More than three hundred firms had accepted the union's terms completely, and nineteen shops (including Triangle and other large firms) had agreed to open-shop compromises, that is, to allow employers to continue hiring *non*union as well as union employees. The garment workers had made several important gains in the settlements: reduction of the workweek to fifty-two hours, a two-hour limit on night work, wage increases of 12 to 15 percent, and a promise by employers to end the contractor system of payment.

Later that year, prominent Jewish citizens of New York City helped to arrange a second agreement between employers and workers. Louis Brandeis, a Boston lawyer, served as chief arbitrator between union and management. Brandeis skillfully played on their common Jewish background. Many employers had begun as poor workers.

On Labor Day evening both sides agreed to a "Protocol of Peace," which became a milestone in American industrial relations. Its provisions included a privately run Joint Board of Sanitary Control—representing union, management, and the public—set up to oversee health and safety conditions in garment factories. Although the agreement eventually broke down, the Protocol represented a significant victory for the ILGWU. Its membership skyrocketed from four hundred to sixty thousand workers in the months following the "uprising."

At the Triangle Company, however, the union remained unrecognized. Many strikers were not rehired, and most of the strikebreakers who had worked during the walkout were kept on the payroll. Some workers complained that the major effect of the settlement was to end the phonograph music and dancing contests that had been provided for nonstriking employees. Work returned to normal at the country's largest shirtwaist shop, at least until the afternoon of March 25, 1911.

The Triangle Shirtwaist Company occupied the top three floors of a new loft structure, the Asch Building, in lower Manhattan. The ten-story building, constructed in 1901, was located on the northwest corner of Greene Street and Washington Place. It stood next to New York University and a block east of Washington Square. Since the turn of the century, over $150 million had been spent on the construction of loft factories in lower Manhattan. The new buildings, made of brick or stone, were supposed to be fireproof, but they had wooden frame interiors that could easily catch fire. Few of the buildings had adequate fire escapes or staircases.

Using such buildings, manufacturers took advantage of cheap insurance rates, low operating costs, and a concentrated labor supply. State law required employers to allow 250 cubic feet of air per worker. But the law did not specify where the air space should be. Loft buildings, with their ten-foot-high ceilings, enabled owners to crowd hundreds of employees onto a floor and still meet the space requirements. (The extra space was above the workers' heads; it was not distributed among employees.) At Triangle about five hundred people jammed the Asch Building's top three floors.

The Triangle employees never had a fire drill. Even though several small fires had occurred on the premises in 1909, no improved safety measures had been taken. There were only two narrow staircases leading down from the Triangle's top three floors. All but one of the doors leading to the stairways were kept closed (often bolted) to prevent employees from loitering or stealing fabric. The single fire escape in the building went down only to the second floor, so that it was difficult to reach the street in case of emergencies. The only other means of descent were two small freight elevators, each about five feet square. Huge piles of cloth, tissue, paper, rags, and cuttings covered the company's tables, shelves, and floors. The floors and machines were soaked with oil, and barrels of machine oil lined the walls.

As the day's work drew to a close on Saturday, March 25, five hundred Triangle workers finished their chores and prepared to leave the building by the one open door on the eighth floor. A company guard stationed at the exit checked the women's handbags for cloth fragments. The time was 4:30 P.M. Saturday's weather was brisk and sunny—a perfect early spring afternoon.

Hardly had the guard rung the closing bell when a young woman employee on the eighth floor ran up to Samuel Bernstein, the company's production manager, and cried: "There is a fire, Mr. Bernstein." The manager and several other men, who had battled a small fire on the floor two weeks earlier, tried to put out the blaze with pails of water. But the flames shot up even higher. One of the men later remembered: "It was like there was kerosene in the water; it just seemed to spread it." Bernstein quickly realized that it would be impossible to stop the fast-spreading flames. He shouted to an assistant: "You can't do anything here. Try to get the girls out!" Bernstein and a few others tried to lead the stunned workers out in orderly fashion. But screams of "Fire!" soon filled the eighth floor.

Panic and confusion spread with the inferno. The 225 eighth-floor workers scurried across the smoke-filled room toward the various exits. As they ran, many called out the names of relatives — sisters and brothers, fathers and mothers — who also worked for Triangle. A young bookkeeper on the floor, Diana Lipschitz, sent an urgent message by interoffice teletype to the tenth floor: "The place is on fire. Run for your lives." The bookkeeper who received the message at first thought that Diana was joking. But the flames soon spurted through the tenth-floor windows, igniting bundles of cloth. Employees on that floor spread the alarm and hurried toward the exits. Because the Asch Building was supposedly fireproof, the blaze could not damage the walls or floors. But the flames curved in a swirling mass through the eighth-floor windows and engulfed the ninth and tenth floors within minutes.

On every floor workers pressed against one another in a desperate effort to reach the exits. The intense heat from the surrounding flames seared their bodies. Those on the eighth floor who had pushed their way down the congested stairway collapsed on lower floors, where firemen later found them.

Employees on the ninth floor, meanwhile, had not received even a teletype warning of the blaze. They learned of the danger only when the fire darted through the windows, bursting into pockets of flame. Most of the women dashed frantically toward exits. Others froze in fear and remained at their machines. When they discovered that the door next to the freight elevators was locked, the women rushed toward the other stairway. Over 150 workers fought for access to the twenty-inch passageway that led to the open stairway.

On the tenth floor those who did not escape by the roof crowded into the two freight elevators. Jammed with fleeing workers, the cars began their descent to the ground floor. Then, some workers still trapped on the top floor started jumping into the elevator shafts to land on top of the descending elevators. One elevator operator, Joseph Zito, recalled that so many girls hit the top of his car that it would not work: "It was jammed by the bodies." Nineteen bodies were later found wedged into one of the elevator shafts. The other elevator broke down when its power circuit became waterlogged by the spray of the fire hoses.

By 4:45 P.M. the top three floors of the Asch Building were engulfed in flames. Escape was no longer possible.

By this time, the fire on the top floors of the Asch Building was visible in the street below. Within minutes a crowd gathered around the building to stare at the blaze. One policeman watching the scene observed: "It's mighty hard work burning one of those fireproof buildings, but I guess it's lucky it's Saturday afternoon. It looks as if everyone is out of the place." Suddenly, an object that looked like a bale of dress material dropped from an eighth-floor window. A reporter from the *New York World*, who had joined the bystanders, described what followed:

> "Somebody's in there all right," exclaimed the spectator. "She's trying to save the best cloth."

Another seeming bundle of cloth came hurtling through the same window, but this time a breeze tossed open the cloth and from the crowd of 500 persons there came a cry of horror.

The breeze had disclosed the form of a girl shooting down to instant death on the stone pavement beneath.

Before the crowd could realize the full meaning of the horror, another girl sprang upon the window ledge. It seemed that she had broken open the window with her fists. Her hair, streaming down her back, was all ablaze, and her clothing was on fire.

She stood poised for a moment, her arms extended, and then down she came. Three other girls at the same moment threw themselves from various windows, and other girls could be seen clinging to the window frames, struggling for breath and trying to decide between the death within the factory room and the death on the stone pavement and sidewalk below.

The firemen's nets caught only a few of those who jumped. More often, as Fire Captain Howard C. Ruch recalled, the bodies—which struck the ground with a force almost a thousand times their actual weight—"didn't break through the nets; they just carried them to the sidewalk. The force was so great it took the men off their feet; they turned somersaults over onto the bodies." Sometimes, a group of girls would join hands before jumping from the ledge, soothing their fears in a joint death fall.

Fifteen minutes after the firemen arrived, the fire was brought under control. In those few minutes, forty-six people jumped to their deaths. The charred remains of one hundred workers were later recovered from inside the building. Most of those who perished were Jewish. All but twenty-one of the victims were women, and a dozen were so badly burned or disfigured that they were almost unrecognizable. In fact, seven persons were never identified.

The sidewalk in front of the Triangle Company was strewn with the bodies of those who had jumped to their death at the height of the blaze. (Brown Brothers)

The Triangle Fire **633**

Thousands of mourning relatives and friends filed through the temporary morgue on the East 26th Street pier to identify the victims. Some were never identified. (Brown Brothers)

Hundreds of workers had managed to escape the flames. Those injured, stunned, and weeping survivors soon filled the hospitals and ghetto apartments of the Lower East Side. Police officials hurriedly tried to find coffins for the dead. On East Twenty-sixth Street a huge, enclosed pier was converted into a temporary morgue. The Triangle dead were piled up on sidewalks near the Asch Building while firemen watered down the smoldering building.

Police Department "death wagons" rode throughout the evening, bringing the dead to the temporary morgue. Policemen searched through personal belongings in an effort to identify victims. Fourteen engagement rings were later found on one floor alone of the Triangle factory. These and other rings collected at the morgue testified to a particularly bitter aspect of the tragedy, namely, the marital hopes and expectations of this young and largely female contingent of workers. Some of the victims had stuffed their skimpy pay envelopes inside their clothing. Others still had their wages clutched in their hands.

Many of the Jewish families on the Lower East Side had relatives or friends working at Triangle, and the community's grief was almost unbearable. Tens of thousands rushed to the East Twenty-sixth Street pier searching for missing friends or relatives. They were joined by numerous Italian and other immigrant families. The police finally let the frantic throng through the pier a few dozen at a time. Inside the temporary morgue the bodies of the Triangle victims had been laid out in coffins in neat rows.

Horrifying scenes of recognition filled the night. A mother, discovering her daughter's body, would break down into uncontrollable wailing and have to be escorted out. A young woman, finding her sister's charred body, would simply faint. Some women completely lost control and tried to kill themselves, either by swallowing poison or by jumping off the pier. Police and onlookers stopped at least a dozen such attempts.

In the days following the fire, the Triangle victims were buried quietly by their familes. Friends and relatives from the Lower East Side attended the funerals. They poured out their grief and sorrow. Reformers and community leaders arranged a series of memorial meetings to honor the victims. A fund-raising appeal conducted by the Red Cross, Jewish community groups, and the WTUL collected over $120,000 to assist needy families. Several of the victims had been the sole supports of their families, in either New York or "the old country." Half a dozen families had lost two sisters (one sister, a widow with five children); another had lost two brothers. In one Italian family a mother and two daughters were killed in the fire.

On April 5 a symbolic mass funeral was held in lower Manhattan. Over 100,000 people—mainly women who lived and worked on the Lower East Side—marched silently in the rain for five hours to honor the Triangle dead. As they approached the Asch Building, the women who marched gave way completely to their emotions. According to one paper's report, they uttered "One long-drawn-out, heart-piercing cry, the mingling of thousands of voices, a cry that was perhaps the most impressive expression of human grief ever heard in this city."

Who was to blame for the tragedy? This question haunted New Yorkers in the weeks that followed the Triangle disaster. "That a terrible mistake was made by somebody," The New York *Times* observed, "is easier to say now than to point out just where the blame for this destruction of human life may be placed."

The city's fire department bore a share of the responsibility, despite the bravery of those who fought the blaze. The department had failed to enforce even those few mild safety laws that were on the books. Moreover, its equipment was inadequate for fighting fires in the city's new loft buildings. The tallest fire ladders reached only to the sixth floor, although half the city's factory workers—more than 300,000—worked in lofts above this floor. Some of the department's safety nets were so weak that they broke under the force of falling bodies.

The City Buildings Department, too, had to accept a measure of the blame. The Asch Building, like most of New York City's garment shops, lacked adequate safety features. Several months earlier, a factory inspector had warned the owners of the Asch Building of such violations as insufficient exits and locked stairway doors. But the department made no effort to ensure that these conditions were corrected. There were only forty-seven inspectors in Manhattan to check over 50,000 buildings. Of these buildings 13,600 had been listed as dangerous by the fire department the previous month. Inspectors managed to visit 2,000 buildings in March, but the Asch Building was not among them.

Nor were the fire insurance companies innocent of blame. Insurance brokers in New York suffered heavy losses from the nu-

Not much remained of the "fireproof" Asch Building once the fire had run its course. The Triangle owners collected insurance money for losses in equipment and property damages though their building had inadequate safety features. (Brown Brothers)

merous fires that occurred in the city's loft buildings. Yet the insurance industry failed to insist on safety standards that might have reduced fire hazards. Rather, they preferred to pay off after a fire and then raise a company's premium costs. Higher policy rates also meant higher commissions for insurance brokers. During the 1890s a group of insurance companies attempted to offer cheaper rates to manufacturers who installed sprinkler systems in their factories. These companies were soon driven out of business by the city's powerful insurance industry. It was simply easier and more profitable to leave the "fireproof" firetraps alone and settle afterward.

At the time of the fire the Triangle Shirtwaist Company carried insurance policies totaling $199,750. The Triangle owners eventually collected full repayment for their losses in equipment and property damage. Under the terms of these insurance policies, they were also given an extra indemnity of $64,925 or $445 for each worker killed. The company's owners defended themselves against charges of responsibility for the fire by pointing out that building inspectors had never entered a complaint against the firm and that an employee carelessly dropping a cigarette might well have started the fire.

On April 11, a week after the public funeral for the Triangle victims, the company's owners, Isaac Harris and Max Blanck, were indicted by a grand jury and charged with manslaughter. Their trial began in New York eight months later, on December 4. Crowds of women gathered outside the courtroom each day screaming "Murderers! Murderers!" A heavy police guard was called in to protect the defendants. Harris and Blanck— "the shirtwaist kings"—engaged as their defense counsel a well-known Jewish lawyer, Max D. Steuer.

In order to simplify the case, the state decided to try the pair only for responsibility in the death of a single worker, Margaret Schwartz, who died in the fire because of the locked ninth-floor door. Most testimony centered on three questions: (1) Was the ninth-floor door kept locked regularly? (2) Was it locked at the time of the fire? (3) Most importantly, did Blanck and Harris know it was locked?

The jury took less than two hours to find the shirtwaist kings not guilty. As one jury member told a newsman: "I believed that the [door] was locked at the time of the fire. But I could not make myself feel certain that Harris and Blanck knew that it was locked."

One interesting sidelight to the tragedy emerged during the trial. The Triangle owners kept their exit doors locked for fear that employees would steal garments or pieces of fabric. At one point the prosecutor asked Isaac Harris: "How much in all the instances would you say was the value of all the goods that you found had been taken by these employees? You would say it was not over twenty-five dollars, wouldn't you?" Harris turned pale before responding: "No, it would not exceed that much."

If Harris and Blanck had been convicted, the Triangle fire might have been forgotten more easily. The public might have been satisfied that justice had been done. As it turned out, the acquittal of Blanck and Harris sparked a new effort to improve the conditions under which New York City's laborers worked. Responding to public pressure, the state legislature created the New York Factory Investigating Commission in June 1911 to study working conditions in the state.

Among the commission's most active members were two politically powerful New York City Democrats, State Assembly Majority Leader Alfred E. Smith and State Senate Majority Leader Robert F. Wagner, Sr. They helped throw the Tammany machine's full support behind the commission's many proposals for reform. Other members included Samuel Gompers of the A.F. of L. and Mary Dreier of the WTUL. Many experts on factory safety and working conditions assisted the commission. Among them were progressive reformers such as Belle and Henry Moskowitz, and young social workers such as Frances Perkins, who later became the nation's first woman cabinet member as secretary of labor.

The Triangle Commission, as it was popularly called, went far beyond an investigation of fire hazards alone. It studied almost every type of labor problem in New York. In 1911 the group held public hearings in the state's major manufacturing cities and heard 222 witnesses. Staff field inspectors visited 1,836 factories in twenty industries. Smith, Wagner, and their associates talked with factory workers who had lost limbs because of unsafe machinery. They examined the "doctored" records kept by many companies on employees' wages and hours. Commission investigators watched hundreds of women leaving factories at 5 A.M., after working ten-hour shifts. They studied the horrible conditions in the disease-ridden tenements where workers lived.

On farms in upstate New York, commission members observed migrant women working alongside their children for eighteen hours and more a day. In canneries across the state they saw children of five working full time. The conditions wore no party label; the worst offenders among New York's manufacturers included both Republicans and Democrats. In a factory belonging to a leading upstate Democratic progressive, for example, Smith and Wagner found "the vilest and most uncivilized conditions of labor in the state."

Between 1911 and 1915, Smith and Wagner introduced over sixty bills based on their investigations. Despite much conservative opposition in the legislature, the two Tammany Democrats managed to pass fifty-six of their proposals by fusing the votes of Democratic regulars and anti-machine reformers. The bills they passed called for the creation of a Bureau of Fire Prevention and the enforcement of strict fire safety codes (including compulsory fire drills and the installation of sprinklers in factories). Two other major bills provided for an increase in the number of factory inspectors and a strengthening of the supervisory authority of the state's Department of Labor.

One of the most hard-fought proposals in the legislature was a bill calling for a fifty-four-hour workweek for women and minors. When cannery owners objected to the measure, Smith replied sarcastically that they wished to revise the Bible to read "Remember the Sabbath to keep it holy—except in canneries." The bill passed. Other laws forbade night factory work for women, prohibited smoking in factories, and called for better ventilation and sanitary facilities. Child labor was outlawed in tenement manufacturing and canneries. Sunday work was forbidden ("one day's rest in seven"), and insurance (worker's compensation) was provided for employees injured in accidents. Other laws forbade employment of children under fourteen (anywhere) and required improved working facilities, rest periods, and minimum wages for women and children.

In the Triangle Commission's four years of existence, Smith and Wagner helped to pass the most enlightened code of industrial reform in the country. Their work served as a model for legislators in other states and foreshadowed many of the federal laws enacted under the New Deal. In the following decades, both men were to become leading progressive Democrats, and their concern for the improvement of working conditions in the state stemmed in large measure from their experiences on the Triangle Commission.

This sense of what Frances Perkins called "stricken conscience" was felt by Smith, Wagner, and Perkins—as well as by many of their colleagues in the legislature. Among them was a young, unknown Democratic senator from upstate who rose before the state senate one day to speak on behalf of a bill for a reduced workweek. The measure previously had been defeated by only one vote. Wagner had since rounded up an additional vote for the bill, and still another supporter—Manhattan's colorful

East Side Democrat, "Big Tim" Sullivan—was now racing across Albany to cast the tie-breaking ballot.

The youthful Democratic senator began "filibustering" (speaking on irrelevant subjects—mainly, in this case, on birds) to stall for time until Sullivan could reach the senate floor. When Republican leaders opposing the bill complained that the subject of birds had nothing to do with the bill, the speaker responded that he was "trying to prove that nature demands shorter hours." His filibuster continued until Sullivan arrived. Only then, confident that the bill would now pass, did Senator Franklin Delano Roosevelt return to his seat.

34 New Waves of Reform

The miserable working conditions that provoked the great shirtwaist industry strike of 1909 were typical of American manufacturing in the half century of industrial growth that followed the Civil War. Workers in manufacturing plants toiled an average of fifty-nine hours each week. They earned less than $10 per week for their backbreaking labor.

By contrast, most of their employers—the manufacturers, bankers, and merchants who directed the course of economic development in the United States—profited handsomely from the workers' long hours and low wage rates. Between 1860 and 1900 the country rose from fourth to first place among the world's industrial nations, producing more in 1900 than Britain, France, and Germany combined.

The rewards for business success during this period were high indeed. In 1890 an estimated 200,000 people owned 70 percent of the country's wealth. A survey taken in 1892 showed that close to 4000 people had become millionaires since the Civil War. Almost all of these individuals made their fortunes in manufacturing, railroads, trade, or finance. This great concentration of wealth among America's upper classes only added to the discontent of the nation's industrial laborers.

PROBLEMS OF UNIONIZING

Union organization seemed to hold the only promise of changing the working conditions of American workers. But despite the efforts of union leaders and rank-and-file organizers throughout the period, no strong, united workingman's association emerged among the industrial labor force of the United States. Instead, in this era of economic growth, industry-wide unions came and went. The ILGWU, for example, was only the latest in a line of unions attempting to organize the garment industry, the earlier ones having failed at the task.

At the turn of the century, 10 million men and women, over a third of the entire labor force, worked in factories. Yet the union movement had succeeded in organizing less than 4 percent of America's industrial workers.

Those who led or took part in the Uprising of the Twenty Thousand inherited a tradition of industrial union activity that went back to Jacksonian America. (See Chapter 30, p. 581.) By the early twentieth century the infant ILGWU, which was to lead the great shirtwaist strike of 1909, had counterparts in every other industry in the country. Like the garment union, most of these organizations were small and had to struggle for existence. The experience of the 1909 garment workers' strike demonstrates many of the difficulties encountered in organizing.

Rarely were unions at this time as successful as the ILGWU in persuading workers from different ethnic backgrounds to put aside their fierce hatreds and work for common goals. Indeed, the 1909–10 strike was the first time that most of New York City's Jewish and Italian workers actually banded together in one union. More often, tensions among nationality groups, differences in language, and racial hostilities within the working class hampered union organization.

Employers skillfully exploited these ethnic and national hostilities to divide workers. When Jews went on strike, Italians would work, and vice versa. When both groups went on strike, blacks were called in to scab. Furthermore, the influx of Southern and Eastern European immigrants in the

late nineteenth and early twentieth centuries kept wage rates down in most industries. More often than not, the labor supply greatly exceeded demand. Employers had little difficulty filling the unskilled and semiskilled positions at their plants.

Employers resorted to a variety of tactics to defeat the efforts of union organizers. These included the use of violence (for example, by the hoodlums who attacked ILGWU picketers), and the hiring of scabs (another tactic employed by Harris and Blanck). Employers also used blacklisting—the denial of work to union officials by all the firms in an industry—and lockouts of striking workers. Firms like the Triangle Company sometimes enlisted the aid of sympathetic policemen and judges who harassed strikers with arrests and court action. Another important weapon of management was the yellow-dog contract, in which new workers agreed not to join a union as a condition of their employment.

The leading force within American unionization during this period was the American Federation of Labor (A. F. of L.). It was a loose confederation of independent craft unions and semi-industrial affiliates such as the ILGWU. By the time of the New York garment-industry strike, the A. F. of L., under Gompers's leadership, had become the country's dominant national labor organization. It was also the most powerful union politically and

Samuel Gompers, shown here at a meeting to organize the 1909 garment workers' strike, founded the American Federation of Labor around such craft unions. Using both the strike and collective bargaining, he forged a powerful national labor organization. (Brown Brothers)

economically up to that time. Because of the powerful constraints that impeded union organizing, however, the influence of the A.F. of L. on industrial working conditions remained minimal.

REFORMERS IN THE LATE NINETEENTH CENTURY

Union leaders were not the only people concerned about the conditions of American workers. Socialists, middle- and upper-class reformers, and city politicians all worked to improve conditions for American laborers. Their solutions to the problems posed by industrial society, though, were as different as the backgrounds from which these reformers emerged.

The Socialist Vision

In the late nineteenth century a group of socialist writers became the first generation of critics to tackle the dilemmas of urban-industrial America. They were grouped as socialists because they held in common the belief that ownership and control of industry, land, and resources should be shared by the community as a whole. These writers put forth a series of proposals for a complete overhaul of American institutions. In *Progress and Poverty* (1877–79) Henry George attacked the inequities of private land ownership and the evils of urban-industrial life. Edward Bellamy's *Looking Backward* (1888) presents a vision of a socialist utopia. His book became a best seller in the 1880s and 1890s. Henry Demarest Lloyd's *Wealth Against Commonwealth* (1894) attacked the corrupt business practices of the Standard Oil Company. Other influential critics of American industrial life included economist Richard Ely, "social gospel" minister Washington Gladden, and utopian writers Ignatius Donnelly and William Dean Howells.

Uppermost in the minds of these late-nineteenth-century reformers was the notion that, if conditions in the nation's slums, factories, and farms were not improved quickly and drastically, the United States would explode into class warfare. Surely, they reasoned, abused workers would not tolerate such conditions indefinitely. They believed that a social catastrophe was close at hand. It could be prevented only by an immediate and total alteration in the nation's social and economic structure.

They offered no single remedy. Some, like Lloyd, Bellamy, and Howells, believed in a socialist commonwealth. They argued, though, over the details of utopia and how to achieve it. Others, like George, felt that a single tax on unearned income from land would somehow provide enough money to solve the nation's problems. All these reformers were united in believing that a single problem underlay all the social ills of the United States. Find and correct the overriding problem—"the root of our social difficulty," as George put it—and Americans could begin moving toward an era of moral and social perfection.

In this utopian vision of the United States these late-nineteenth-century reformers resembled their pre–Civil War, preindustrial counterparts. Garrison, Emerson, and Fuller had also walked a thin line between social criticism and religious prophecy. However "practical" their remedies, therefore, people like George and Bellamy were basically seers. They preached a gospel of total reform, without which total catastrophe would result.

The Settlement House Movement

The struggle to improve the lives of the immigrant poor, both in the factories and in the ghettos, was aided by a number of middle-class reformers and socially conscious members of the American upper classes. Women like Mrs. Belmont and other affluent leaders of the Women's Trade Union League who were active in the shirt-waist strike are representative of this trend.

During the 1880s and 1890s many college-educated women became concerned with the slum conditions under which immigrant workers lived. They helped to organize settlement houses in the ghettos of East Coast and Midwestern cities. There, foreign-born workers received food and shelter and learned how to speak English. They were given help in understanding and exercising their rights as Americans. In 1889 Lillian Wald founded the Henry Street Settlement in New York City. Jane Addams and Ellen Gates Starr founded Chicago's Hull House that same year. Others followed.

By 1910 over four hundred settlement houses had been established in the country's slum districts. On New York's Lower East Side, settlement workers assisted the victims of the Triangle fire and their families. In the previous year they had provided money and support for the striking garment workers. As valuable instruments for Americanizing immigrant communities, the settlement houses helped immigrants to improve their working and living conditions at a time when most middle-class Americans remained indifferent or even hostile toward the foreign-born poor.

Municipal Reorganization

For some reformers, however, the settlement-house movement seemed an inadequate response to the many problems of America's en-

Jane Addams

(The Bettmann Archive)

E ven as a little child, she seemed inclined toward special work of some sort. In fact, she was anxious for a career." This is how, with some dismay, Mrs. John H. Addams described her stepdaughter Jane. After all, a girl born to a prosperous family in Cedarville, Illinois, in 1860 was not supposed to have such ambitions.

Jane's heart had been set on the newly opened Smith College for Women, but her father's wish was that she follow the path of her older sisters and enter the Rockford (Illinois) Seminary. She did as he asked and entered the seminary in 1877. Here, the foundations of her feminism were laid down, and, resisting pressure from Anna Sill, Rockford's indomitable head, to become a missionary, Jane decided to become a doctor. Accordingly, she enrolled in the Woman's Medical College of Pennsylvania. Unfortunately, she was never physically strong, and her health broke, forcing her to withdraw.

For eight troubled years she traveled, read, and attended the social functions that suited Mrs. Addams's plans for her. It was a period of frustration, nervousness, and unhappiness. At long last, during a European tour with her friend Ellen Gates Starr, an idea began to take shape in Jane's mind. In London she witnessed a match-girls' strike and later she visited Toynbee Hall in London's East End, the University settlement that sought to alleviate the bitter human consequences of industrialization.

The two young women discussed their ideas and decided to return home to implement them. They searched for a suitable base of operations and found the decaying Hull mansion in the heart of one of the poorest districts in the city, a crowded area bursting with Greek, Italian, Russian, German, Sicilian, and other immigrants. In September of 1889, they moved in, and invited the neighbors to stop by.

Before long two things happened. First, neighbors, most of them immigrants, started coming—to attend lectures and to form clubs. Second, a number of talented men and women moved into Hull House. By 1893, Hull House was the center of some forty clubs, a day nursery, gymnasium, dispensary, and playground, cooking and sewing classes, courses in art, music, and language, a cooperative boardinghouse for working girls, and a little theater. Each week two thousand people entered its doors.

Under Jane Addams's leadership, Hull House took on another, more far-reaching task. It became a clearing house for various reform movements. The residents pressured legislators to act on such matters as child labor, factory inspection, recognition of labor unions, protection of immigrants, and industrial safety.

Jane Addams did not permit her energies to be siphoned off into the special enterprises sponsored by Hull House, but she remained the focus and center of the undertaking. She became sought after as a lecturer. Honors were bestowed upon her. She became the first woman president of the National Conference of Charities and Correction and in 1910 became the first woman to receive an honorary degree from Yale University. In 1931, sharing the award with Nicholas Murray Butler, she was given the Nobel Peace Prize.

A heart attack laid her low in 1933, and in 1935 she was stricken with cancer. She died at the age of seventy-four. She had been at Hull House for forty-six years and it stood as her most enduring monument.

larged industrial cities. It was somewhat like putting bandages over a festering infection without treating the infection itself first. For such reformers the roots of the infection seemed clear: the inefficiency and corruption of urban political machines in alliance with equally corrupt business interests. Democratic politicians such as Al Smith and Robert Wagner, Sr., viewed New York's Tammany machine as the logical friend of the immigrants. But reformers such as Henry George and, later, Fiorello La Guardia believed that the political machines merely exploited the innocent immigrants, using their trust and votes to line the pockets of ward heelers, city officials, and local businessmen.

Reform groups such as the National Civic Federation (which later helped to organize the Triangle Fire Commission investigation) sparked a concern among voters for driving the political machines from office. These groups sought to run urban government more efficiently and less corruptly than the machines. They also tended to be dominated by wealthy citizens, leading businessmen, and other upper-middle-class or upper-class figures within their communities.

Municipal reformers, then as today, included businessmen, lawyers, ministers, and journalists—professionals concerned with the concentration of power in the hands of working-class-supported political machines and giant corporations. Many were native-born Protestants. Most had had little direct contact with foreign-born, largely Catholic and Jewish immigrants until they began a career of reform.

Quite often, these basic cultural differences between immigrants and reformers made it difficult, if not impossible, for the two groups to join successfully. Their interests were also often in direct conflict. New immigrants depended on the very political favors—jobs and other assistance from local political bosses—that the reformers wanted to eliminate. Moreover, immigrant culture was more tolerant of gambling and drinking than the reformer's tradition of stern Protestant moralism. These differences over values certainly diluted the effect of municipal reformers in curing urban ills.

A NEW GENERATION OF REFORMERS

Many of those who had opposed unions and other reform movements prior to the 1890s gradually became convinced of the need for basic reforms in American society. They had been deeply affected by the tumultuous events of the nineties: the depression, the social unrest on farms and in factories, the deepening class conflict.

By the turn of the century many middle-class Americans saw the dangers. Conservative journalists such as William Allen White, "big business" lawyers such as Clarence Darrow and George Norris, and middle-of-the-road Republicans such as Theodore Roosevelt had all concluded that the future political and social health of the American republic depended on a variety of reforms. They sought improvements in the conditions under which the urban poor lived. They also wanted to bring giant trusts under governmental supervision in the public interest. These various reform interests came together in a movement that historians have labeled "progressivism."

The Progressive Movement

However different progressive reformers were in their social and economic concerns, most shared certain fundamental beliefs. For one thing, unlike the Bellamys and Georges of the previous generation, they did not believe in imminent social catastrophe. Rather, they were highly nationalistic and optimistic about the future of the United States. Herbert Croly, one of their most influential writers, argued that this "promise of American life" consisted of "an improving popular economic condition, guaranteed by democratic political institutions, and resulting in moral and social [improvement]."

Nationalism and reform, then, went hand in hand. Both impulses were based on an idealistic faith in American potential. Most progressives believed that a decent society could be created through gradual reform rather than revolutionary changes. The reformers of the previous generation had not been so confident.

Ida M. Tarbell's stunning exposés revealed the way giant corporations gained advantage over competitors. Her landmark study of the oil industry in McClure's magazine established it as the leading muckraking periodical. (Library of Congress)

Lincoln Steffens, one of the leading reformer journalists, wrote numerous articles exposing political corruption in city government. His autobiography gives an accurate account of the development of the muckraking movement. (Library of Congress)

Upton Sinclair is best remembered for his novel, The Jungle, which told of brutal and unsanitary conditions in Chicago's stockyards. The public revulsion it aroused resulted in the passage of the Meat Inspection Act of 1906. (Culver Pictures)

Progressive reformers harnessed their optimism about domestic affairs to a firm belief in the value of Christian morality. It was within this "ethical climate" that much reform legislation of the era took shape. To Frances Perkins the new climate was dominated by "the idea that poverty is preventable, that poverty is destructive, wasteful, demoralizing, and that poverty in the midst of potential plenty is morally unacceptable in a Christian and democratic society." An end to poverty, injustice, and unregulated economic power, the preservation of the nation's natural resources, a return to honest government—all this, the progressives believed, would follow from applying Christian ethics to reshaping the social environment.

Another belief shared by progressive thinkers was a confidence in the use of "experts" to manage public affairs. Professional advisers such as those who had assisted the Triangle Commis-

sion would provide rational, scientific measurement of the country's problems; they would also suggest efficient means for tackling social ills. Often this argument for "efficient" and "scientific" government cloaked the efforts of business groups and wealthier Americans to retain control of government—especially at the city and state level—and to deny power to the immigrant-supported urban political machines. In short, there was an important elitist, "anti-democratic" dimension to *certain* aspects of progressivism.

Progressive reformers called for the establishment of investigating bodies at all levels of government, and the use of expert advisers—brain trusts—to help city and state governments develop programs of reform. They urged the creation of regulatory agencies to supervise business practices. Progressives also favored the establishment of nonpartisan commissions or councils to eliminate machine corruption in city government. The independent commission form of city government originated in Galveston, Texas, in 1900. By 1914 it had spread to over four hundred American cities, although not to most larger ones.

Finally, most reformers of the era believed strongly in the value of publicizing social problems as a first step toward solving them. As early as 1898 Congress had established a commission to study the giant business trusts. The commission eventually published nineteen volumes on American social and economic problems. In addition, many states set up investigatory groups to study business corruption. This technique of exposure was carried out most systematically under the reform governorship of Robert M. LaFollette in Wisconsin from 1901 to 1906. LaFollette's efforts to uncover business abuses and press for needed social legislation set a pattern for reform administrations in other states.

Newspapers and magazines provided a forum for investigations of social problems by muckraking journalists. Ida Tarbell wrote an explosive exposé of the Standard Oil Company. Lincoln Steffens studied corrupt city political machines. David Graham Phillips examined Senate corruption. Magazines such as *McClure's* and *Harper's Weekly* increased their circulation to the hundreds of thousands by championing reform.

New Politics for the Cities

Nowhere was the belief in the need for "rational" government stronger than at the local level. Progressives were as appalled by corrupt city politics as they were by dirty tenements and unsafe factories. Beginning in the 1890s, municipal reform groups won control of a number of cities and began dealing with slum and factory conditions. In New York City, for example, after driving Tammany Hall from power in 1901, Mayor Seth Low worked closely with reformers to improve parks and playgrounds, tighten housing laws, and strengthen the city's health services to the poor. But, despite Mayor Low's efforts, much remained to be done, as conditions in the city at the time of the Triangle fire demonstrated.

In other cities, too, the concern for social reform proved strong. During the 1890s and 1900s three remarkable Midwestern businessmen—all self-made millionaires—became pioneers in urban reform. Their cities served as models for social reformers throughout the country.

Hazen Pingree, mayor of Detroit, Michigan, from 1889 to 1896, and then governor of the state, fought corruption by politicians and local industrial groups, especially street railways and gas companies. Pingree authorized the construction of a city-owned electric lighting plant and urged public ownership of other such utilities. In Toledo, Ohio, Samuel M. "Golden Rule" Jones, mayor of the city from 1897 to 1904, established free kindergarten day-care facilities for working mothers, pressed for a minimum hourly wage and other social legislation, and supported public ownership of utilities.

Thomas Johnson, Cleveland's mayor from 1901 to 1909, became a social reformer after reading Henry George's *Progress and Poverty*. He, too, fought the private utility interests and urged public ownership. Johnson sponsored a number of social welfare projects, including the construction of municipal bathhouses (a crucial urban health measure, since many tenement houses did not have adequate bathroom facilities) and careful inspection of consumer meat and dairy products.

All three Midwestern mayors ran nonpartisan governments, dominated by professional administrators and reformers who took over the jobs that had formerly been filled by political appointees. Unfortunately, driving political machines from office did not always produce improvements in ghetto or factory conditions. Unlike Mayors Pingree, Jones, and Johnson, many municipal reformers were anti-democratic elitists, less interested in improving slum conditions than in eliminating the power and corruption of immigrant-supported political machines. In Pittsburgh, for example, two-thirds of those involved in trying to revise the city's charter came from upper-class backgrounds and were closely tied to the city's leading banks and industries.

Changes at the State Level

Many of the major reforms of this period were achieved at the state level. In a number of states progressive reformers were elected governors. Among them were Robert LaFollette in Wisconsin, Charles Evans Hughes in New York, Hoke Smith in Georgia, Hiram Johnson in California, and the Southern-born president of Princeton University, Woodrow Wilson, in New Jersey. Each state had its special problems, each its particular group of "entrenched interests." In Massachusetts, the railroads and insurance companies dominated; in California, it was the powerful and corrupt labor unions.

Almost all reform governors fought for stricter regulations of railroads, public utilities, and industries within their states. They tried to force corporations to pay a fair share of taxes and to conserve natural resources like forests and mines, which provided raw materials for industry. Finally, they fought to make state government more democratic through such reforms as the initiative, the referendum, and the recall.[1]

During the first two decades of the century, many states enacted broad programs of social legislation dealing with the wages and hours of factory workers, the employment of women and children, and safety conditions in tenements and factories. Maryland adopted the first statewide workmen's compensation law in 1902. A year later Oregon passed a law restricting women's industrial work to ten hours per day. Illinois adopted the first measure providing public assistance to mothers with dependent children in 1911. And Massachusetts passed the first minimum wage law (applying to women and children) in 1912. All these measures were landmarks in the struggle of progressive reformers to achieve economic and social justice for all Americans.

Amending the Constitution

Suffrage—the right to vote—had been a central concern of the woman's rights movement for

---

[1] The initiative is a device by which a small number of citizens, sometimes as few as 5 percent, can bypass the legislature and force a vote upon measures at general elections. The referendum forces legislatures to return proposed laws to the electorate, who then approve or reject the proposals. The recall, perhaps the most controversial device, allows the electorate to remove an elected official from office. It requires a special election, called after a certain number of voters have signed a petition asking for the official's removal.

several decades. In 1910 the American labor force included over 8 million women, many of them college-educated. During this period 36 percent of all professional jobs were held by women. Yet, prior to World War I only eleven states had granted women the right to vote.

Between 1914 and 1919 woman's rights advocates gave the suffrage issue national importance by conducting a massive campaign of petitions, lobbying, picketing, and nonviolent demonstrations. The campaign was sponsored by two national associations of woman suffrage advocates, led by Carrie Chapman Catt and Anna Howard Shaw. The picketing and demonstrations that had brought public sympathy for the demands of shirtwaist employees during the Triangle strike worked with similar effect for the suffragettes. The involvement of women in war work during World War I brought the movement increased public support. In June 1919 Congress responded by passing the Nineteenth Amendment, giving women the right to vote. The amendment received final state ratification in August 1920. Later that year, for the first time, American women in every state voted in a presidential election.

Another progressive interest, the temperance movement, had been a concern of reformers since before the Civil War. Municipal reformers joined the anti-alcohol drive for two major reasons. First, there was much political corruption associated with urban liquor interests. Second, reformers felt that alcoholism was destroying the moral fiber and social well-being of many Americans.

The prohibitionists made their first gains at the local and state levels. A number of Southern and Western states voted themselves "dry." During World War I many of the same groups that later pushed the woman suffrage amendment through Congress secured passage of the Eighteenth Amendment, which forbade the sale and distribution of alcoholic beverages. Ratified by the states in January 1919, the amendment took effect the next year. It was considered the most impressive (yet the most debatable) triumph of progressive moralism.

In 1913 progressive reformers won two other important victories. The Sixteenth Amendment instituted a federal income tax. And the Seven-

Women concentrated on making political gains in the early twentieth century. An intense campaign, and their increasing importance in the labor market, finally gained them full suffrage on a nationwide basis by constitutional amendment—the Nineteenth. (Library of Congress)

teenth Amendment provided for direct election of senators instead of their election by state legislatures. An amendment prohibiting child labor passed Congress under intense reform pressure. It met strong opposition from the business community, however, and failed to win ratification by the states.

PROGRESSIVISM IN THE WHITE HOUSE

With the death of William McKinley on September 14, 1901, Theodore Roosevelt became the third man in less than forty years to succeed to the presidency because of an assassin's bullet. At forty-

three, he was the nation's youngest president. Roosevelt came to the White House with a distinguished career in public service. He had served as state legislator, federal official, city police chief, army colonel, governor of New York, and vice-president. An energetic and impulsive man, Roosevelt responded candidly to McKinley's death: "It is a dreadful thing to come into the presidency this way; but it would be a far worse thing to be morbid about it."

Roosevelt's Square Deal for America

Roosevelt moved cautiously during the next few years to take control of the Republican national machinery from McKinley's close friend Senator Mark Hanna of Ohio. In his first term he made few reform proposals. He did, however, publicize reform more and more, especially as his second term drew to a close. During this period no other American did as much as Theodore Roosevelt to educate his fellow citizens to the need for political and social change. He called the presidency "a bully pulpit." He often mounted its steps to criticize "malefactors of great wealth" and others—trusts, political bosses, destroyers of natural resources—who endangered his vision of a "square deal" for all Americans.

But Roosevelt did far more than simply publicize reform. Despite his strong party loyalties and keen appreciation of political patronage, he brought into government service a remarkable number of reformers. Roosevelt appointed William Howard Taft as secretary of war, conservationist Gifford Pinchot as chief of the Forest Service, James R. Garfield (the son of the former president and a dedicated conservationist) as secretary of the interior, and the great jurist Oliver Wendell Holmes, Jr., as Supreme Court justice.

Unlike his Republican predecessors in the White House, Roosevelt worked for the support of the black community. He solicited Booker T. Washington, president of the Tuskegee Institute in Alabama, as his chief adviser on Southern Republican appointments. Washington's relationship to Roosevelt was perhaps the high point of the black leader's national influence during a long and distinguished public career.

Washington was born into slavery in 1856 and, after a difficult struggle for his own education, founded Tuskegee in 1881 with assistance from Northern white philanthropists. Tuskegee, under Washington's leadership, stressed vocational training, reflecting his beliefs that blacks in the South could advance only by concentrating on economic training and self-improvement. Washington's basic message seemed eminently reasonable to many blacks and whites in the region, especially considering the rise in violence directed toward blacks, the spread of caste segregation, and the overall white hostility toward black aspirations during the late nineteenth and early twentieth centuries in America.

Washington's views drew support from Roosevelt and many other white progressives, who did not (for the most part) believe in a politically equal role for blacks. Washington came under increasing attack during his final years, however, from younger black leaders such as W. E. B. DuBois. The new breed—often Northern-born and well-educated professionals—demanded *immediate* ac-

tion to achieve full political and civic equality for black Americans, and they condemned the Tuskegee educator for advocating patience and (or so they believed) accepting a subordinate role for blacks. Many of Washington's critics knew little, however, about his quiet, covert efforts to raise money needed to launch legal battles against segregation statutes, or of his efforts to ensure that (at least in the North) blacks were organized as an effective political voting block. It was in this context that Washington interpreted his connection with Theodore Roosevelt as still another opportunity to secure influence and exercise patronage on behalf of his Southern black constituency and their white allies.

Underlying Roosevelt's actions and policies during his administration were certain firm beliefs shared by other progressives as well. Among them was the belief that government must begin to intervene in the economy to bring unregulated businesses under control. It was argued that such a move would reduce class tensions in American society as well. Toward this end Roosevelt lobbied actively to push several important reform measures through Congress. The Elkins Act of 1903 forbade railroads to give rebates[2] to large industrial companies. The Hepburn Act of 1906 strengthened the powers of the Interstate Commerce Commission (ICC) to regulate the nation's railroads.

Nevertheless, Roosevelt sometimes needed prodding from the public—for example, on the question of food and drug regulation. Americans were alerted to the vile conditions under which Chicago slaughterhouses and processed-meat plants operated by Upton Sinclair's 1906 novel *The Jungle*. (Ironically, socialist Sinclair's portrayal in that same book of the horrendous living and working conditions among Chicago's immigrant community was ignored by many of its readers.) Pressure from muckrakers and from reformers such as Dr. Harvey W. Wiley of the Department of Agriculture forced passage in 1906 of both a Pure Food and Drug Act *and* a meat-inspection bill. The former

---

[2] Rebates were special rates, lower than the published ones, granted secretly to users who accounted for a large share of freight traffic. Farmers felt especially cheated by these special rates, usually granted to industries.

Theodore Roosevelt surrounded himself with conservationists like John Muir who believed that the natural environment must be protected. Through Roosevelt's influence, 148 million acres of forests were set aside for national parks like Yosemite, seen in the background. (Library of Congress)

banned the production or sale of fraudulently labeled or adulterated goods. Meat packers and other manufacturers managed to adulterate the measures themselves, however, so that the final versions provided, among other things, that the government and not business pay the costs of inspection. Still, the laws were milestones in their day.

In these and other regulatory measures, Roosevelt received much support from the business community. For many business leaders, federal action seemed the most rational response to the country's growing industrial problems. Thus the railroads favored tighter federal regulation to eliminate the rebate system, which had become bothersome, and avoid even more rigid state regulation. Similarly, giant lumber corporations endorsed federal intervention to enforce a rational set of guidelines for the industry.

An energetic outdoorsman, Roosevelt did much to educate the American public to the need for environmental protection. The Newlands Act, passed in 1902, authorized federal funds for the construction of dams and reclamation projects in the West. In 1907 Roosevelt signed an executive order converting over 17 million acres of forest land in Western states to national reserves. He also withdrew from private sale many valuable natural resources, including coal and mineral lands, oil reserves, and water-power sites. In 1908 he summoned the nation's conservation experts to a

White House National Conservation Congress. Its purpose was to plan future policies for the protection of natural resources.

Busting the Trusts

In 1902 Roosevelt began a policy of "trust busting." He moved to break up many of the giant corporations that had been organized by industry mergers during the previous decade. At first Roosevelt sought only to regulate the trusts through appropriate legislative channels. He asked Congress to pass legislation authorizing the federal licensing of corporations, full disclosure of company earnings and profits, and other supervisory measures. But the conservative majority in Congress rejected these proposals. So Roosevelt took on the trusts himself, using the powers given to the president by the 1890 Sherman Antitrust Act.

The president's first target was the National Securities Company. This was a consolidation of three major railroad systems: the Northern Pacific, the Great Northern, and the Chicago, Burlington, and Quincy. New York banking houses, led by Rockefeller and J. P. Morgan, had organized the merger to put an end to damaging competition among the three lines. Roosevelt ordered his attorney general, Philander C. Knox, to file suit against the Northern Securities Company for violating the Sherman Act. In 1903 the Supreme Court declared the merger illegal and ordered the Northern Securities Company dissolved.

Roosevelt brought similar antitrust actions against several other giant corporations. These included Standard Oil, the American Tobacco Company, and DuPont. In this policy, which proved highly popular politically, Roosevelt asserted the supremacy of federal authority over private economic interests.

In his antitrust campaign Roosevelt insisted that he opposed not large corporations as such, but corporate action against the public interest. The exact nature of that interest, Roosevelt felt, was something the president must judge. He wrote: "Our objection to a given corporation must be not that it is big, but that it behaves badly." In 1902 Roosevelt used his authority to force the settlement of a coal strike that threatened to deprive residents of the East Coast of fuel during the winter months. With the aid of Wall Street banker J. P. Morgan he forced coal company executives to accept a settlement favorable to the United Mine Workers. It was the first time that an American president had intervened in a labor dispute on behalf of the striking workers.

Roosevelt's actions toward big business, however, were not always consistent. He came to private arrangements with U.S. Steel and other giant corporations to avoid invoking antitrust action. In some labor disputes he called in federal troops as strikebreakers. At heart, he believed that the federal government had to play the role of a neutral third party in resolving major disputes on industrial relations.

Roosevelt had been elected to the presidency in his own right in 1904, winning by the greatest landslide of any presidential contest since the pre–Civil War period. When he left the White House at the end of his second term in 1909, he bequeathed to his hand-picked successor, William Howard Taft, a well-formulated set of reform proposals for congressional action. These proposals included thorough governmental regulation of business, federal supervision of the stock market, a federal workmen's compensation law, and compulsory arbitration of labor disputes.

Taft and the Old Guard

The new president showed little interest in carrying out Roosevelt's proposals. Not that Taft opposed reform completely. During his four years as president he supported the constitutional amendments providing for an income tax and for direct election of senators. In addition, Taft initiated twice as many antitrust actions as Roosevelt, although, unlike his predecessor, he never acquired an image as a trust buster. Under Taft's administration Congress established the eight-hour day for government workers, widened the ICC's authority to include interstate communications systems, and extended a tax on corporate profits. Taft also gave genuine and vigorous support to the conservation movement.

In other areas, however, Taft remained a conservative, politically allied to the Republican

Old Guard. In 1910 Taft's interior secretary, Richard Ballinger, made an agreement with private firms allowing them to develop valuable coal and water-power sites in Alaska. Chief Forester Gifford Pinchot objected to this decision, but Taft supported Ballinger and fired Pinchot. This move infuriated Roosevelt and marked the beginning of a political break between the two men.

Taft also supported Republican conservatives in their battle for control of Congress against a coalition of reform Democrats and Republicans. He worked actively for the defeat of leading Republican insurgents in the 1910 congressional election. Again Taft's actions angered Republican reformers, among them Senator Robert LaFollette, the party's most prominent progressive. Later that year Taft cooperated with the Republican Old Guard in helping to pass the Payne-Aldrich Tariff, a high-tariff measure beneficial to big business. The battle over the Payne bill split congressional Republicans into conservative and progressive wings. Roosevelt, as usual more politically astute than Taft, had dodged the issue. GOP reformers wished to lower the tariff, while most conservatives favored upward revision. Long before the close of his term in office, Taft had lost the support of most Republican reformers. They turned again to Teddy Roosevelt for leadership.

The Election of 1912

Roosevelt did not disappoint them. Beginning in 1910, he toured the country, supporting party insurgents against Taft and denouncing the Ballinger-Pinchot affair. He made it evident that he wished the Republican party's nomination for an unprecedented third term in the White House. Roosevelt's active campaigning helped him to capture the presidential primaries in six states. But in most states presidential nominations were made by party conventions rather than by primary elections. Taft had gained control of the party machinery during his four years in office. Thus in June 1912 the Republican national convention nominated Taft for a second term.

Republican progressives led by Roosevelt and LaFollette then split from party ranks. In August 1912 they organized the Progressive party,

Many cartoons, such as this one, appeared during the 1912 presidential nominating conventions. Cartoonists had a field day depicting Roosevelt and the "Bull Moose" party. (Library of Congress)

which nominated Roosevelt for the presidency. The new party attracted the attention of the country's leading reformers. Its 1912 convention, held in Chicago, was attended by such figures as Jane Addams, William Allen White, and George W. Perkins—all activists in the era's various reform movements.

"We stand at Armageddon, and we battle for the Lord!"—Roosevelt shouted this rallying cry to Progressives at the Republican convention in June 1912. He was a man with a mission. He wanted to regain the presidency because he had a Progressive program, his "New Nationalism," that he wanted to see enacted into law. In his characteristic way he was ready to do battle. "I feel as fit as a bull moose," he told reporters.

When he lost the nomination, the Progressives would not accept the end of their dream. On August 5, 1912, they met as the newly formed Progressive, or "Bull Moose," party. Here in Chicago they would nominate Roosevelt as their presidential candidate.

The religious note that Roosevelt had sounded at the Republican convention seemed to find its real audience here. One historian has described the delegates as "a group of well-dressed, serious citizens with the respectability of Sunday School superintendents." The gathering seemed more like a religious revival meeting than a political convention. Speaker after speaker took the podium to deliver rousing, emotion-packed sermons on social justice. An already converted audience listened intently and often tearfully. Occasionally they would be moved to respond with hymns, feet stomping, and quotes from the Bible.

These were the men and women who, for years, had sought reforms in their own communities. They were frequently isolated from the rest of society because of their beliefs. One writer described them as "men of character who had fought against local grafting politicians. College professors, social workers, businessmen of vision and independence, farmers tired of seeing agriculture on the cross—[all] were enlisting in a cause they loved for unselfish service."

On the second day of the convention Roosevelt rose to present his "Confession of Faith" in political and economic reform. Before he could speak, fifteen thousand people came to their feet to welcome him. They poured out all of the emotions that had been building in them since he was denied the Republican nomination.

Roosevelt did not disappoint them. His mood matched theirs. When it came time for him to accept their nomination, he launched the crusade in fervent, enthusiastic terms:

> Six weeks ago here in Chicago, I spoke to the honest representatives of a convention which was not dominated by honest men; a convention wherein sat, alas! a majority of men who, with sneering indifference to every principle of right, acted so as to bring to a shameful end a party which had been founded over half a century ago by men in whose souls burned the fire of lofty endeavor. Now to you men who, in your turn, have come together to spend and be spent in the endless crusade against wrong, to you who face the future resolute and confident, to you who strive in a spirit of brotherhood for the betterment of our nation, to you who gird yourselves for this great new fight in the never-ending warfare for the good of mankind, I say in closing what I said in that speech in closing: We stand at Armageddon and we battle for the Lord.

The Progressive party platform reflected a broad concern for major reforms in American life. It called for tighter governmental regulation of giant industries and financial companies, national presidential primaries, women's suffrage, and the initiative, referendum, and recall. Progressives also favored the prohibition of child labor, minimum wage standards for women, workmen's compensation, and a variety of banking and currency reforms.

On July 2, the Democrats nominated for the presidency a moderate reform candidate, Governor Woodrow Wilson of New Jersey. The Democratic platform favored collective bargaining for unions and revisions in the country's banking system. Unlike the Progressives, the Democrats sought the abolition of giant corporations rather than their regulation. Wilson called his program the New Freedom.

The Republicans, too, ran on a platform of moderate reform. They favored, among other legislation, tighter regulation of trusts and banking and currency changes. Thus, although Taft was more conservative than either Roosevelt or Wilson, he could hardly be considered an opponent of reform. A fourth candidate, Socialist Eugene V. Debs, ran on the most radical platform of all. Debs had led the American Railway Union during the Pullman Company strike of 1894. He served a jail term for his efforts, emerged from prison a confirmed socialist (largely the result of having read the works of other American socialists such as Edward Bellamy and Henry Demarest Lloyd). Debs ran for the presidency as the socialist candidate five times. He again served a jail sentence during Wilson's second term as president because of his opposition to American involvement in World War I. In this curious election of 1912, therefore, all four candidates were committed in varying degrees to reform.

In the end the Republican split sent Wilson to the White House. Roosevelt received 4,126,000 votes and Taft 3,483,000. Had these votes been combined, the Republicans could have retained control of the presidency. Wilson received 6,286,000 popular votes, less than 45 percent of the total. But he won enough state pluralities to capture a majority of electoral votes. For the first time since the depression of the 1890s, the presidency returned to Democratic hands. In the election the Democrats gained control of both houses of Congress. Thus the new president had a working majority to pass his legislative program.

Wilson and the New Freedom

During his first term in office Wilson proceeded to enact his programs. Though he applied stern moral standards to the conduct of foreign relations, Wilson was a skillful realist about domestic affairs. He quickly tossed the notion of breaking up the trusts into the political ashcan. Instead, adopting Roosevelt's more moderate idea of regulating giant corporations, he helped push several bills through Congress to achieve this purpose.

The Federal Trade Commission Act of 1914 established a bipartisan body to supervise industry and prevent unfair methods of competition in interstate commerce. The Clayton Antitrust Act, passed that same year, strengthened the 1890 Sherman Act by spelling out specific business practices that violated the antitrust laws. The Clayton Act also restrained the government from using court injunctions against striking unions.[3] Though on paper the new law seemed a powerful weapon, it actually did little to regulate the behavior of giant corporations or aid organized labor.

One reason for this was that Wilson began permitting corporate leaders and their lobbyists to meet informally with administration officials and regulatory commission members in efforts to settle possible violations without penalty to industry. Businessmen quickly became adept at "co-opting" those nominally charged with overseeing them. In 1913 Wilson helped to steer through Congress the Underwood Tariff, the first downward revision in tariff rates since before the Civil War.

In December 1913 Congress passed the Federal Reserve Act, which created the present American banking system. The new law established twelve regional Federal Reserve banks, which were to serve member banks in their various geographic districts across the country. The Federal Reserve banks issued paper currency, supervised bank credit, and controlled other banking practices. The act also required existing national banks to become members of the Federal Reserve.

The financial "Panic of 1907," which severely disrupted the business community, had persuaded even many conservative bankers and businessmen of the need for greater national coordination of the banking system. The Federal Reserve System's regulatory mechanisms, it was hoped, would prevent the recurrence of such massive runs on banks by depositors demanding immediate currency payments. The 1913 Act also marked the acceptance of this new quasi-governmental institution as a means of both regulating the national banks and setting overall monetary policy for the United States.

Wilson was supported in all these measures by his close associations with Southern Democrats. Some historians have called his election "the revolution of 1912" because, for the first time since the Civil War, Southerners regained a large measure of national influence. Born and raised in the South, Wilson felt most comfortable with those from his native region, many of whom became his closest advisers. He appointed a number of Southerners ambassadors and awarded others with high-level government jobs. Several of his cabinet members came from the South; others, like Wilson himself, were of Southern background ("the South in exile," as some called it).

The Senate majority leader, Thomas Martin of Virginia, and the House majority leader, Oscar Underwood of Alabama, worked closely with the new president. During Wilson's administration fifteen out of seventeen Senate committees were led by Southern chairmen. These senators helped to formulate Wilson's domestic program and steer it through Congress. The Federal Reserve Act was largely the work of three Southerners, including Wilson's secretary of the treasury, Carter Glass of Virginia. The Clayton Antitrust Act was sponsored by Henry Clayton of Alabama, and House Majority Leader Underwood led the fight for the tariff-revision bill.

---

[3] An injunction is a court order requiring or forbidding certain activities. Business and government have sometimes used the injunction as an anti-union weapon to prevent strikes.

Protest and Progress

But Wilson's Southern background also had less fortunate consequences. Segregation officially came to Washington under Wilson's regime. Governmental offices and other public facilities in the city were ordered segregated by race. In doing this, Wilson was only following a practice that had become common after Reconstruction. In the late nineteenth century, "Jim Crow" laws[4] — that is, laws keeping blacks and whites apart in all public places — were enacted throughout the South (with little protest from the North). In 1896, in the case of *Plessy* v. *Ferguson*, the Supreme Court ruled that "separate but equal" facilities were constitutional. The decision was based to some extent on pseudoscientific assumptions of the day shared by many middle-class progressives in both the North and South. They believed that blacks (as well as Southern and Eastern Europeans) were essentially inferior. With the approval of the court, white supremacy asserted itself, in segregated railroad cars, restaurants, schools, and other public facilities and institutions.

In the early twentieth century the problems of black Americans were brought to the nation's attention by a group of young black businessmen and professionals under the leadership of the great scholar W. E. B. DuBois. In 1905 they founded the militant Niagara Movement to press for an end to Booker T. Washington's policy of "accommodation" with whites. The leaders of the Niagara group sought a return to active agitation for complete political and civil equality of blacks with whites — the earlier goals of Radical Reconstruction.

Four years later, members of the Niagara Movement and white supporters of black civil rights formed the National Association for the Advancement of Colored People (NAACP) DuBois was appointed editor of the NAACP's journal *The Crisis*. Active in the new organization were several reformers who would support the garment workers' strike that same year: Lillian Wald, Jane Addams, and publisher Oswald Garrison Villard (William Lloyd Garrison's grandson). The NAACP grew rapidly in the next decade. It quickly took the lead in opposing the segregationist policies of the Wilson administration.

Wilson found himself under growing pressure from other groups of reformers as his first term drew to a close. There seemed little chance that he could again slip into the White House through a split in Republican ranks. Roosevelt had rejoined his party, and most Progressives were unhappy with Wilson's refusal to support social welfare legislation. Concerned over the political situation, Wilson began a determined campaign to win over reform-minded voters by pushing several progressive measures through Congress.

The Federal Farm Loan Act, passed in May 1916, aided domestic agriculture by expanding the credit resources of American farmers. The Adamson Act, passed the same year, provided an eight-hour day for railroad workers. The Kern-McGillicudy Act created a model workmen's compensation program for federal employees. In August of 1916 Congress attempted to deal with the problems of child labor by passing the Keating-Owen Act, which outlawed the interstate shipment of products manufactured by children under fourteen. (Two years later the law was declared unconstitutional.) Wilson nominated progressive lawyer Louis Brandeis to the Supreme Court and fought for his confirmation in Congress against conservative opposition. Brandeis became the first Jewish Supreme Court justice.

During the election of 1916 Democrats stressed Wilson's skill at maintaining American neutrality during the growing war in Europe (see Chapter 36). But it was the president's energetic sponsorship of reform measures that won him the support of the labor movement and most middle-class reformers. In a hard-fought campaign against Republican Charles Evans Hughes, Wilson won reelection by narrow popular and electoral margins. In his second term he devoted most of his attention to the problems of fighting a war and winning the peace. Domestic reform took a back seat to world affairs during Woodrow Wilson's last four years in office.

---

[4] The laws got their name from a song sung by Thomas Rice in a Negro minstrel show.

Suggested Readings
Chapters 33–34

Triangle Fire

Daniel Aaron, *Men of Good Hope: A Story of American Progressives* (1951); Irving Howe, *World of Our Fathers: The Journey of the East European Jews to America* (1976); Moses Rischin, *The Promised City: New York's Jews, 1870–1914* (1960); Leon Stein, *The Triangle Fire* (1962); Charles E. Zaretz, *The Amalgamated Clothing Workers* (1934).

Synthesis and Interpretations

Samuel P. Hays, *Response to Industrialism, 1885–1914* (1957); Richard Hofstadter, *The Age of Reform* (1955); Gabriel Kolko, *The Triumph of Conservatism* (1963); Christopher Lasch, *The New Radicalism in America* (1965); Henry F. May, *Protestant Churches and Industrial America* (1949) and *The End of American Innocence* (1959); Robert H. Wiebe, *The Search for Order, 1877–1920* (1968) and *Businessmen and Reform* (1962).

States and Cities

Robert H. Bremner, *From the Depths: The Discovery of Poverty in the United States* (1956); Roy Lubove, *The Progressives and the Slums: Tenement House Reform in New York City, 1890–1917* (1962); Zane L. Miller, *Boss Cox's Cincinnati* (1968); Irwin Yellowitz, *Labor and the Progressive Movement in New York* (1965).

Roosevelt, Taft, and Wilson

Donald F. Anderson, *William Howard Taft* (1973); John Blum, *The Republican Roosevelt* (1954); William H. Harbough, *The Life and Times of Theodore Roosevelt* (1961); Arthur S. Link, *Woodrow Wilson and the Progressive Era* (1954) and *Wilson* (5 vols., 1947–1965); George E. Mowry, *The Era of Theodore Roosevelt, 1900–1912* (1958).

The Progressive Movement

Samuel P. Hays, *Conservation and the Gospel of Efficiency* (1959); Gabriel Kolko, *Railroads and Regulation, 1877–1916* (1965); Richard Lowitt and George W. Norris, *Making of a Progressive* (1963); Blake McKelvey, *The Urbanization of America, 1860–1915* (1963); William O'Neill, *The Progressive Years* (1975); Philip Taft, *The A. F. of L. in the Time of Gompers* (1957); David Thelen, *Robert La Follette and the Insurgent Spirit* (1976).

Progressive Journalism

David M. Chalmers, *Social and Political Ideas of the Muckrakers* (1964); Charles Forcey, *Crossroads of Liberalism* (1961); Richard Hofstadter, *The Progressive Historians* (1968); Justin Kaplan, *Lincoln Steffens* (1974); David W. Noble, *The Paradox of Progressive Thought* (1958).

Reform Movements

Lawrence Cremin, *The Transformation of the School: Progressivism in American Education* (1961); Jeremy P. Felt, *Hostages of Fortune: Child Labor Reform* (1965); Eleanor Flexner, *Century of Struggle: The Women's Rights Movement in the United States* (1974); David Kennedy, *Birth Control in America: The Career of Margaret Sanger* (1970); Roy Lubove, *The Professional Altruist: The Emergence of Social Work as a Career, 1880–1930* (1965); James H. Timberlake, *Prohibition and the Progressive Movement* (1963).

The 35
Philippines Revolt

At age thirty, Emiliano Aguinaldo was a seasoned revolutionary. The son of a prosperous farmer from the island of Luzon, he was a member of the Katipunan, the Filipino movement for independence. In August 1896, Aguinaldo joined a revolt against Spain, which had held the Philippines as a colony since the sixteenth century. Two months later the rebels proclaimed the existence of the Tagal Republic. When the first president of the republic died, Aguinaldo became president and commander in chief of the insurgent forces.

But revolutionary organization and high-sounding titles alone could not defeat the Spanish in the field. Nor could Spain's colonial power crush the rebels. In December 1897, after more than a year of see-saw guerrilla warfare, both sides recognized the stalemate and signed a treaty.

Spain, apprehensive over the threats posed to its Caribbean empire by rebellion in Cuba and political unrest in Puerto Rico, agreed to consider reforms in the Philippines. In turn, Aguinaldo and other leaders of the rebellion agreed to leave their country for three years. They went to Hong Kong, a British colony on the southern coast of China. Meanwhile, the Spanish deposited 400,000 pesetas in a Hong Kong bank in the rebels' name. If Spain enacted the promised reforms, this trust fund would be used to educate Filipinos abroad. If Spain failed, the insurgents could use the money to buy arms and resume the war.

The Filipinos soon became convinced that they had been tricked. Spanish Governor-General Miguel Primo de Rivera did not declare a general amnesty, as expected. Reforms acceptable to the rebels did not come to pass. The trust fund that rested in Hong Kong now seemed to the rebels to be no more than hush money, a bribe to silence Filipino leaders. From their headquarters in the British colony, the insurgents began planning for future campaigns.

During this period, rebellion in Cuba brought on a crisis in Spanish–American relations. (Americans and their government were sympathetic to freedom movements in Latin America.) As Spain and the United

States moved closer to war, the Filipino rebels thought about an alliance with the United States. Then, in April 1898, Aguinaldo learned that the American consul in Singapore, W. Spencer Pratt, wanted to discuss important matters of interest to both countries. The Filipino agreed to meet with Pratt in Singapore.

The Aguinaldo–Pratt talks took place in the Raffles Hotel, legendary center of "East Asian intrigue" and British colonial power at the turn of the century. Pratt claimed that Spain had broken the terms of the truce. He urged Aguinaldo to resume the rebellion. The consul added some important news: "As of the other day, Spain and America have been at war. Now is the time for you to strike. Ally yourselves with America, and you will surely defeat the Spaniards!"

Aguinaldo was clearly interested in this proposal, but he remained cautious: "What can we expect to gain from helping America?" Pratt assured him: "America will give you much greater liberty and many more material benefits than the Spanish ever promised you." When Aguinaldo asked whether such an arrangement could be put in writing, Pratt sidestepped. He obviously had no authority to speak for Washington. Yet he continued to offer verbal assurances.

Consul Pratt also told Aguinaldo that he would try to arrange for the rebels to be transported to Manila on American ships. Pratt contacted Commodore George Dewey, commander of the United States Pacific fleet in Hong Kong. The cable to Dewey read: "Aguinaldo, insurgent leader, here. Will come Hong Kong. Arrange with Commodore for general cooperation insurgents Manila if desired." The Yankee sailor answered quickly and tersely: "Tell Aguinaldo come as soon as possible." When informed of Dewey's okay, Aguinaldo promised that if his forces obtained sufficient arms the Filipino people would rise against the Spanish. Pratt, seldom at a loss for reassuring words, told him that Dewey felt that "the United States would at least recognize the independence of the Philippines under the protection of the United States Navy."

Commodore Dewey never met with Aguinaldo before the United States Pacific squadron sailed for Manila. A few years later he denied all knowledge of a political deal. Dewey dismissed Consul Pratt as a "busybody," a man whose letters he simply filed and ignored. Toward the Filipinos, Dewey adopted a paternal and disapproving stance. "They seemed to be all very young, earnest boys," he recalled. "I did not attach much importance to what they said or to themselves."

Certainly Dewey did not believe the rebels' boasts that they already had thirty thousand armed men in the Philippines, with many more available. Why then did Dewey agree to take Aguinaldo and other Filipino leaders to Manila? By his own account, to get rid of them. "They were bothering me. I was very busy getting my squadron ready for battle, and these little men were coming aboard my ship at Hong Kong and taking a good deal of my time." So he consented to transport the rebels, though in the end only one Filipino went along.

Despite his denials, Dewey did want something from the Filipinos. He needed troops to occupy Manila and other parts of the Philippines if

The Spanish fleet is depicted in this robust sketch of an encounter during the Battle of Manila Bay against Dewey's American squadron. (The Bettmann Archive)

and when he defeated the Spanish navy. Aguinaldo and his followers might help Dewey accomplish the job.

On May 1, 1898, American forces defeated the Spanish navy in Manila Bay. The spectacular victory reaffirmed the rise of American military power on the world scene. The United States squadron blew the remnants of the decaying Spanish navy out of the water. (Some of Spain's ships were hulks, rotting at dockside, with guns that would not function.) Within a few hours it was over. Spain no longer ruled the Philippines. Yet Manila remained to be captured and occupied. The Spanish army had not been routed, nor had its commander indicated a willingness to surrender.

The victory at Manila Bay reopened the question of Dewey's need for Filipino support. From his ships Dewey could do nothing. Spanish artillerymen had allowed Dewey to anchor close to Manila's shore, but the commodore was reluctant to subject the city to a prolonged bombardment. Moreover, his small Marine battalion was an insufficient landing force. The commodore felt that with five thousand troops he could end the war in one day. But he did not have five thousand troops. Insurgent Filipinos were the only immediately available source of military manpower.

Early in May, Dewey sent for the rebel leader. Aguinaldo and a dozen of his associates arrived from Hong Kong in Manila on a United States Navy auxiliary vessel. Within a few days Dewey and Aguinaldo

Commodore George Dewey created the conditions for United States involvement in protracted guerrilla warfare in the Philippines. He needed Filipino help to defeat Spain but did not reckon with Filipino nationalist feelings after the conflict. (Naval Photographic Center)

met for the first time. Their versions of the encounter are as different as the men themselves.

According to Aguinaldo, the American commander repeated the familiar assurances about American disdain for acquiring colonies and its support of Filipino independence. Dewey also requested that the insurgents resume fighting. He supplied them with sixty-two rifles and some abandoned Spanish naval guns. The United States commander stressed that all promises were guaranteed "by the word of honor of Americans." Finally, Aguinaldo claimed that Dewey instructed him to have a Filipino national flag prepared. It would be hoisted as soon as Spain surrendered.

Dewey presented an equally questionable account of the events. Shortly after meeting with Aguinaldo, Dewey claimed, the secretary of the navy instructed him to avoid entangling the United States in alliances with the Filipino insurgents. Dewey complied because he was bound by obedience and because he did not like the insurgents. He had little faith in their cause. He considered the soft-spoken Aguinaldo an "unimpressive little man," though he recognized the Filipino's enormous prestige among his people.

Dewey admitted that the insurgents might be of service in clearing the shoreline from the naval base of Cavite, which the Americans had now occupied, to Manila City. Thus he allowed the rebels to enter the Cavite arsenal. But he warned that Filipinos and Americans should keep at a distance from each other. The United States commander continued to maintain that Aguinaldo had been forced on him by the barrage of pleas from the American consuls in Hong Kong and Singapore. Dewey also insisted that he never believed the Filipinos wanted independence. How could they? Aguinaldo "considered me as his liberator, as his friend."

Friend would soon become foe, and Aguinaldo himself bore some of the blame for his later disillusionment with the United States. During his months of exile in Hong Kong and his first few weeks back in the Philippines, Aguinaldo seemed to accept everything the Americans promised. His proclamations and public letters of the time praised the United States in lavish terms.

The distance that Dewey sought to create between himself and Aguinaldo was quickly established. American officers had begun complaining about the many Filipinos inside the Cavite naval base. These "natives," they argued, might be friends or foes. So Dewey told Aguinaldo that he and his men must leave the arsenal but could remain in the town of Cavite. From its headquarters in the town, the Aguinaldo movement grew. Enlistees poured in, many of them armed with captured Spanish rifles.

On May 21 Aguinaldo felt militarily strong enough to issue a proclamation outlining his ultimate aims: "Everything appears favorable for attaining independence. The hour has arrived for the Philippines to belong to her sons." Aguinaldo advised his men to fight a "civilized" war, warning that "if we do not conduct ourselves thus, the Americans will decide to sell us or else divide up our territory, as they will hold us incapable of governing our land." Like it or not, Aguinaldo knew, the Filipinos would have to deal with the United States.

Throughout May, Manila remained in Spanish hands. The Americans had made no commitments to the rebels, but United States troops were on the way. In June the Filipino insurgents announced the establishment of a provisional government and issued a declaration of independence.

On June 23, Aguinaldo declared himself president of the revolutionary government. In an effort to win support from the United States and other nations, the Filipinos promised to work for two primary goals: independence and the establishment of a representative, republican country.

By the time Aguinaldo formally declared independence, he and his forces controlled most of Cavite province and almost surrounded Manila. From the panic-stricken city, Dewey received requests from Spanish officials to help evacuate foreign and Spanish civilians, as well as wounded soldiers. Some were placed aboard foreign ships in the harbor. Aguinaldo, mindful of the need to wage war in a manner approved by Europeans, allowed civilians and wounded soldiers to pass through his lines. His cooperative spirit reached its height in mid-July when he helped pick the spot for a landing of United States soldiers. Thanks to the insurgents' advice, admitted Dewey, "we were able to land our troops within easy striking distance of their objective," a position more than halfway between Cavite and Manila.

Emilio Aguinaldo was evaluated differently by his enemies and his own people. To Dewey he was at first a nuisance and later an "Oriental despot." To the Filipinos, however, he symbolized their hope for independence. (U.S. Signal Corps/National Archives)

But American gratitude did not mean acceptance of the Filipino forces as a political entity. According to Dewey, in fighting their way up the coast and surrounding Manila, the insurgents had merely prepared "a foothold for our troops when they should arrive." American army units, under General Wesley Merritt, entered Manila on June 30. From then on, the war against Spain became an exclusively American affair.

American soldiers quickly moved to replace the Filipinos in the trenches dug near the Manila fortifications. One of General Merritt's officers tried to convince the insurgents to pull out of the line and turn their trenches over to the Americans. In return he offered to supply the rebels with cannon and other artillery. The local Filipino commander consulted Aguinaldo. Aguinaldo would comply, but only if the request and the offer were put in writing. This concession demonstrated the Filipino leader's desperate desire for legal recognition of his government's standing. Pull out first—then we will furnish the paper, answered the Americans. Aguinaldo ordered his troops out of the trenches. But they never saw the cannon, nor did their commander receive written confirmation. Once again, as in Cavite, Aguinaldo had yielded to an American request under American pressure. This decision proved extremely costly to the rebel cause.

With insurgent forces neutralized and Aguinaldo's political status in doubt, the American capture of Manila proceeded swiftly and with little bloodshed. On August 13 the city capitulated. The United States now ruled the Philippines. On August 17 a War Department dispatch said that Filipino insurgents would not form part of the occupation forces:

> The United States, in possession of Manila City, Manila Bay and harbor, must preserve the peace and protect persons and property within the territory occupied by the military and naval forces. The insurgents and all others must recognize the military occupation and authority of the United States.

What was in store for the Philippines beyond the period of military occupation? In Washington, President McKinley began the process of reconciling the facts of conquest with the arguments of territorial expansionists. At first McKinley opposed taking all of the Philippines, though he held open the possibility that the situation might change. The president favored keeping Luzon, the large island in the northern part of the archipelago, and establishing a United States naval base at Manila. McKinley wished to show Europe that "a lofty spirit" guided American actions. But he also supported the "general principle of holding on to what we get."

These statements reflect McKinley's personality and his tactical approach to political decision making. The president worked hard to create the impression that he was forced to act. He wanted to make it appear that public opinion and the pressure of events directed the outcome of the Philippine conflict. In reality, as McKinley surely realized, the decision to take Manila made full-scale American involvement in the Philippines unavoidable.

The Treaty of Paris, which ended the Spanish–American War, was signed on December 10, 1898. Spain agreed to grant Cuba independence and to cede Puerto Rico and the tiny Pacific island of Guam to the United States. The United States also received the Philippine Islands, for which it paid Spain $20 million. "A goodly estate indeed!" crowed the head of the American delegation. He wrote President McKinley: "Perhaps the treaty may be an acceptable Christmas offering to you from the American commission."

During the negotiations between the United States and Spain, Aguinaldo tried desperately to gain legal standing for his revolutionary government. On August 6, shortly before Manila capitulated, he issued a memorandum to all foreign powers. It asked recognition of the belligerent status of the insurgents, a first step toward full diplomatic recognition. It also sought support for their ultimate aim of independence. He claimed to control fifteen provinces—an assertion not far from the truth at the time—and that the nine thousand Spanish prisoners in his hands were being treated with the "same consideration observed by cultured nations." Aguinaldo declared that the Philippines had "arrived at that state in which it can and ought to govern itself." But other countries refused to recognize the rebels. Nor did the United States indicate a willingness to consider Philippine independence seriously. Filipino insurgents were not America's allies, stated a directive from Washington. They had merely cooperated with Americans "against a common enemy."

Under these circumstances, tension between Americans and Filipinos mounted. In December 1898, President McKinley sent a message to the new military commander in the Philippines, General Elwell S. Otis. The president assured Otis that the United States wished to pursue a policy of "benevolent assimilation" in the islands and bestow the "blessings of good and stable government." But he warned Otis that all obstacles to achieving these ends were to be removed. Before publishing McKinley's message, General Otis cut out several sections critical of the Filipino rebels. When a junior United States officer in the city of Iloilo mistakenly printed the entire text, Filipino resentment grew.

The insurgents' reactions in January 1899 were firm but still friendly. Aguinaldo rejected the American claim to rule his country and accused the United States of betraying a loyal ally. In the United States another Filipino leader, Felipe Agconcillo, tried to reason with the new colonial power in terms of its own declared ideals: "I cannot believe that in any possible action on the part of the American republic toward my country there is an intention to ignore, as to the ten millions of human beings I represent, the right of free government." He concluded his memo with the warning that the accidental or impetuous act of one Filipino or American soldier might trigger a full-scale war.

On Feburary 4, 1899, just such an act occurred. An American soldier on guard duty near Manila challenged a Filipino to halt. When the Filipino disobeyed, the sentry shot and killed him. Fighting between Americans and Filipinos, confined during the previous six months to isolated incidents, broke out all along the outskirts of Manila. The war was on. And as even Dewey had to admit: "Perhaps the insurrection was bound to break out."

Inevitably, each side circulated conflicting reports about the incident. The Filipinos accused the Americans of deliberate provocation. They denied that they had initiated the attack, adding that they were unprepared and that several of their leaders were on leave. They also asserted that Aguinaldo had believed the initial exchange of shots to be accidental. The day after the incident, the rebels claimed, one of their generals proposed an immediate cease-fire to General Otis. But Otis rejected the offer, and ordered the fighting to continue "to the grim end."

McKinley responded with an equally one-sided account. First, he brushed off the cease-fire claim: "There appears to have been no such application." Second, McKinley claimed, no American officer had promised the rebels independence.

Throughout the war, American military leaders tried to demean the enemy. American officials viewed Aguinaldo as a bandit, who robbed his own people and lived in luxury on the proceeds of his looting. Whatever Aguinaldo's shortcomings, he remained the leading Filipino insurgent for two years, the chief symbol of resistance to colonial power and of hope for independence.

General Otis, who predicted a quick and easy suppression of the rebellion, failed at the job. Otis boasted that his twenty-one thousand

THE PHILIPPINES REVOLT, 1896–1902

AGUINALDO CAPTURED MARCH 1901 •Palanan

✈ Battle

0   MILES   200

LUZON

AGUINALDO PUT ASHORE ✗
APRIL 30, 1898

•San Isidro
•Malolos

SPANISH FLEET DESTROYED ✈• MANILA TAKEN AUGUST 13, 1898
MAY 1, 1898   *MANILA BAY* CAVITE
BATANGAS

*PHILIPPINE
ISLANDS*

*SOUTH CHINA
SEA*

SAMAR

PANAY   •Balangiga
Iloilo•   *LEYTE* *LEYTE GULF*
CEBU

NEGROS   *BOHOL*

PARAGUA

*MORO
TRIBE*

SULU SEA   *MINDANAO*

PACIFIC OCEAN

*SULU
ISLANDS* *CELEBES SEA*

troops would crush the insurgents in a few weeks. He repeated this promise with depressing regularity for the next twelve months. The gap between his fantasies and the realities of the Philippine war can be measured by the increased number of troops the general soon demanded. Shortly after the outbreak he had asked for thirty-five thousand. A year later he had seventy thousand men and wanted thirty thousand more.

In the spring of 1899, the United States Army drove northward from Manila to occupy — or pacify, as the government called it — the island of Luzon, center of Tagal resistance. In April, American forces captured the insurgent capital of Malolos. Aguinaldo and his followers fled farther north. But in mid-May they had to give up their provisional capital at San Isidro. Then, instead of mounting an all-out American attack, General Otis halted the advance. The rainy season had just begun, and many of the troops were scheduled for immediate return home. So Otis, a cautious field commander, suspended military operations.

Back in the White House McKinley remained optimistic. He assured Theodore Roosevelt that "Otis had things entirely in hand and that the insurrection would be speedily put down certainly after the opening of the dry season."

In the meantime, a mixed civilian-military commission headed by the president of Cornell University, Jacob Schurman, was formed to investigate conditions in the Philippine Islands. The Schurman Commission issued a preliminary report in the fall of 1899 which found much to praise in the Filipinos. It expressed great interest in the islands' natural resources and potential for economic growth. But the report stressed that immediate self-government was out of the question and that the American presence must continue to ensure peace and order. The commissioners concluded: "Whatever the future of the Philippines may be, there is no course open to us now except the prosecution of the war until the insurgents are reduced to submission." The report delighted McKinley.

Most Americans agreed that Filipinos were unprepared for self-government. Some, like Republican Senator George H. Hoar of Massachusetts, protested that Filipinos should be left to govern themselves, whatever the results. But the majority felt otherwise. They predicted that an American pullout would quickly produce internal wars and anarchy. This they were sure would be followed just as quickly by the intervention of other foreign powers. Theodore Roosevelt hoped that Filipinos might be able to govern themselves at some future, undetermined date. But he warned that the "consent-of-the-governed doctrine must not be pushed to an extent that would restore savagery."

William Howard Taft, at the time a federal judge, later went to the Philippines as the first American governor. He accepted the mistaken notion of Filipino inferiority. In 1902 the Senate committee investigating the war asked Taft whether Filipinos were in fact so ignorant that a few leaders could easily misguide them. Taft replied: "That is quite possible, and that is one of the chief reasons why the Filipino people are utterly unfit for self-government." Americans had to lead the way, Taft asserted, because the Filipinos lacked any knowledge of how to carry on a government. The United States could not remain "blind to their serious defects, many of which are due to the environment, social and political, which has been presented by their history of three hundred years."

General Robert P. Hughes spoke more bluntly. In referring to one of the Filipino ethnic groups, he testified: "These people do not know what independence means. They probably think it is something to eat. They have no more idea what it means than a shepherd dog."

The suspension of American offensive operations in the spring of 1899 gave Aguinaldo and his followers time to regroup—and make a key decision. The insurgents knew they could not defeat the rapidly growing United States forces in conventional warfare. From then on, Aguinaldo and his staff decided, Filipino rebels would engage in guerrilla tactics. In order to succeed, they would have to depend on their own countrymen's support, voluntary or forced, and on their ability to blend in with the civilian population.

Aguinaldo's tactical switch posed new and serious problems for the United States Army. When a later American general, Arthur MacArthur, resumed his northward advance in Luzon in October 1899, his

Combat in the Philippines was particularly grueling. Fought in jungle terrain against twin unseen enemies — the guerrilla insurgents and disease — the war produced over 7,000 American casualties. (Library of Congress)

men had trouble distinguishing friend from foe among the Filipinos. The guerrillas tried to wear down the enemy by ambushing American patrols and firing at night into towns occupied by United States troops. Along the trails between villages, Filipino rebels set booby traps — pits lined with sharpened bamboo spears and covered with foliage. General Hughes complained: "As to actual engagements, they were very few. It was very hard to get an engagement of any kind. You could get what we would call a little skirmish, and probably there would be ten or twelve killed."

Though Americans denied that the Filipino army had any legal standing, guerrilla prisoners were not automatically executed as rebels. Instead, a generous American amnesty policy for the insurgents allowed for a decent gap between the official United States position and the actual treatment of those Filipinos who wished to surrender.

Many insurgents did surrender and swear allegiance to the United States. Some even joined American troops to crush the rebels. Combat reports often mentioned the Macabebe soldiers. They were Filipinos who fought with and supported the United States throughout the war. But American officials in the Philippines rejected the idea of forming an all-Filipino regiment, "To put in command of a Filipino a thousand men with a thousand rifles would not be wise," warned Taft. Still, many Filipinos cooperated with the Americans, and, as in most wars, the majority of the population remained uninvolved. These facts bolstered the American argument that Aguinaldo and his forces actually hurt the Filipinos more than anyone else.

Filipinos who continued to resist and rejected the American offer of amnesty received rough treatment. Captured insurgent leaders were shipped to Guam, and "enlisted men" were imprisoned. For a short while, Americans even set up "security" camps for Filipino civilians. (This same tactic, when employed by Spain in Cuba, had enraged the American public.) In the insurrectionary province of Batangas, American officials ordered a ban on all trade, hoping that wealthy Filipinos who supported the insurgents would yield to the pressure.

In the field, United States soldiers routinely burned Filipino villages. Sergeant Leroy Hallock testified that he had participated in the burning of a village of over three thousand people. He claimed that he had heard of other burnings, including a town of ten thousand inhabitants. Another enlisted man recalled: "If a column was marching along and was fired upon, it was the practice to burn the buildings in that neighborhood. That impressed the natives with the fact that they could not fire upon us with impunity, although they did not often do very great damage." No specific orders had been issued authorizing such indiscriminate reprisals, but they continued.

The issue that stirred the most controversy during the Philippine war, both in the islands and in the United States, was the "water cure." This was a method of torturing prisoners by forcing them to swallow enormous quantities of water. The water cure apparently became the standard means of obtaining information from rebel prisoners and civilians suspected of aiding the enemy. Charles S. Riley, an enlisted man from Massachusetts, described repeated attempts to question the *presidente*, or mayor, of a Filipino village:

> One of the men of the Eighteenth Infantry went to his saddle and took a syringe from the saddlebag, and another man was sent for a can of water . . .

Filipino guerrillas were not highly regarded as soldiers by the American military. General Arthur MacArthur claimed that they "could not hit a stack of barns" with their guns. But it took 70,000 American troops three years to defeat them. (U.S. Signal Corps/National Archives)

holding about five gallons. Then a syringe was inserted, one end in the water and the other end in his mouth. The water was forced into his mouth from the can, through the syringe. The syringe did not seem to have the desired effect, and the [army] doctor ordered a second one, and a handful of salt was thrown into the water. The interpreter stood over him in the meantime asking for information. Finally he gave in and gave the information.

When reports of such atrocities began to leak out in the American press, officials disavowed them. But William Howard Taft added the final irony in this unsuccessful attempt by American civil and military officials to deny the facts, unpleasant but true, of widespread torture: "There never was a war conducted," insisted Taft, "whether against inferior races or not, in which there was more compassion and more restraint and more generosity than there have been in the Philippine Islands."

Early in 1900 the superior military strength of the United States forces began to make itself felt. In May, General Otis resigned rather than work under the all-civilian Taft Commission, which had been sent to Manila to set up a civil government. Otis's replacement, General Arthur MacArthur, already on the scene, harried the Filipino guerrillas whenever and wherever he could find them.

But the biggest setback for the insurgents' cause came with the capture of Aguinaldo himself. During late 1900 and early 1901, Aguinaldo's whereabouts remained a mystery. Some American military men and journalists began circulating rumors of his death. MacArthur knew better. In February 1901, United States troops captured an insurgent soldier carrying dispatches from Aguinaldo to rebel officers in the field. The messages did not pinpoint the location of rebel headquarters, but they indicated that the captive knew where to find Aguinaldo. Interrogation began, and before long the courier talked: Aguinaldo could be found in the village of Palanan, in the mountains of Luzon near the northeast coast.

But how could the Americans get to Aguinaldo? Thirty-six-year-old Brigadier General Frederick Funston, head of a volunteer regiment from Kansas, had a plan. The intercepted messages called for the movement of small groups of rebel reinforcements toward Aguinaldo's headquarters. Funston decided to use eighty Macabebe scouts pretending to be rebel reinforcements. He and four other American officers would go along, supposedly as prisoners. One additional and crucial element remained: several Tagals loyal to the United States would be needed to pose as leaders of the expedition. Funston found three such men; the messenger who had been captured was to be their guide. General MacArthur gave his approval to the plan, but with misgivings. Instead of wishing Funston well, he remarked: "I fear I shall never see you again."

The march to Palanan proved more difficult than the capture itself. The expeditionary force landed by gunboat on the east coast of Luzon, about a hundred miles from its objective. In heavy rain, the men had to struggle for several days across rough terrain near the shoreline and then through dense jungle. It had been decided, for reasons Funston never made clear, that the Tagal officers and the Macabebes would enter the village about an hour before the Americans.

On March 23, 1901, the Macabebes arrived in the rebel camp. They were relieved to find only a handful of insurgent soldiers to greet them. The Tagal officers entered rebel headquarters to confer with Aguinaldo and his staff. As the conversation wore on, all but two of the insurgent officers drifted out of the room. An expedition officer leaned out of the window to give the Macabebes the signal to open fire. Aguinaldo, thinking that his own men were firing in the air to welcome the fresh troops, rushed to the window to tell them to stop wasting ammunition. At that point one of the Tagal officers seized Aguinaldo. The others opened fire on the insurgent guards. It was all over before Funston and his American companions arrived.

At the sound of the firing, Funston had rushed to the rebel headquarters. Aguinaldo now asked if the "capture" was some kind of joke. When Funston identified himself, Aguinaldo's shoulders drooped in resignation and defeat. On March 28 the group returned to Manila. Aguinaldo was imprisoned in the governor's mansion. When General MacArthur arrived, ever skeptical, he asked Funston: "Where is Aguinaldo?" Funston was able to reply triumphantly: "Right in this house."

Aguinaldo had sworn many times that he would never be taken alive. For several weeks American officers pressured him to swear an oath of allegiance to the United States. On April 19 he agreed to take the oath. He promised to issue a proclamation calling on Filipinos to lay down their arms in order to avoid further bloodshed. Aguinaldo's declaration suddenly made him a hero in American eyes. The New York *Times,* which had once described Aguinaldo as an "enslaver" and a "criminal aggressor," now found him to be "honest and sincere," a "natural leader of men with considerable shrewdness and ability."

On July 4, 1901, Taft took over as civil governor of the Philippines. He left a revealing account of his reception in Manila: "The populace that we expected to welcome us was not there, and I cannot describe the coldness of the army officers and the army men who received us any better than by saying that it somewhat exceeded the coldness of the populace."

Still, the rebellion—the ill-fated and barely understood war of national liberation—continued. Its center shifted southward to the island of Mindanao. The inhabitants of the island were Moros. They were Moslems who opposed the American presence but had never accepted the authority of the Tagals in Manila. Fire fights and armed conflict broke out. One fire fight in northern Mindanao left ten Americans dead and forty wounded. Fighting between American troops and Moro rebels continued off and on for another twelve years.

In the meantime, the "unfriendly" island of Samar exploded. Company C of the regular Ninth United States Infantry was stationed on the island in the fishing village of Balangiga. Hundreds of Filipino workmen, supposedly loyal to the United States, fell on the Americans with knives, bolos (machetes), and bare hands. A few soldiers escaped in a boat to another island. They were the only survivors. The massacre at Balangiga would not be forgotten. For the next six months American troops called for revenge, in the same way that a previous generation of American soldiers had sought to avenge Custer's defeat at the Little Bighorn.

Major Littleton Waller of the Marines received the punitive assignment. The area commander, General Jacob ("Hell-Roaring Jake") Smith, told Waller that he wanted the Samar rebellion ended quickly. Smith ordered Waller to remove all Filipino civilians from the island's interior and place them in stockades. Those who resisted, especially those capable of bearing arms, were to be considered enemies and shot. Waller asked what the cutoff point was. Anyone more than ten years old, replied Smith. Waller and his men did as they were told.

The pacification of Batangas province followed the same script. Miguel Malvar, head of the revolutionary government there, had five thousand men and was better organized than the rebels on Samar. The American general, J. Franklin Bell, an ambitious young man who only three years before had been a lieutenant, waged an intense campaign, herding thousands of civilians into security camps. In April 1902, after several months of dodging and fighting on the run, Malvar surrendered. The last sustained pocket of armed Filipino resistance had been eliminated.

The war between American troops and Filipino rebels had lasted more than three years. Countless Filipinos had lost their homes in the burning of towns and villages. Thousands of rebel soldiers had been killed or wounded in the fighting. The United States had not gained an easy victory. Almost as many Americans died in the Philippine conflict as in the war with Spain. And the rebellion had cost the United States $160 million, or eight times the "indemnity" paid to Spain for the islands.

On July 4, 1902, the United States government declared the Philippine insurrection officially over. President Roosevelt then sent a special message to the Army.

The president praised American soldiers for the rapid accomplishment of this mission, despite great hardships in more than two thousand skirmishes and battles. Teddy Roosevelt was still mentally fighting Indians, for he went on to say: "Utilizing the lessons of the Indian wars [the army] relentlessly followed the guerilla bands to their footholds in mountains and jungle and crushed them." With surprisingly few exceptions, the president maintained, American troops had been humane and kind to both prisoners and civilians. They had fought bravely against "a general system of guerilla warfare conducted among a people speaking unknown tongues, from whom it was almost impossible to obtain the information necessary for successful pursuit or to guard against surprise and ambush." The army, declared Roosevelt, had added honor to the flag.

Becoming a World Power 36

By 1900 many Americans questioned the presence of American soldiers in the Philippines. Wasn't the war with Spain fought to liberate Cuba, an island ninety miles off the coast of Florida? Why, then, was the United States involved in places halfway around the globe? Whose interests were served by such overseas commitments? Answers to these questions lay tangled in the history of late-nineteenth-century America and in the international power struggles of an imperialist age.

For most of the nineteenth century, Americans had been more than content to search for and use the wealth of their own country. America was their Garden of Eden. And although many of its products were sold overseas (much cotton went to Britain, for example), the United States had avoided foreign political involvements. America had allied itself with a European power only once in its history—during the Revolutionary War, when it signed an alliance with France. Concerned with domestic problems and opportunities, Americans had concentrated on developing their own continent.

GAINING AN OVERSEAS EMPIRE

Two major factors helped to change this attitude and promote American interests overseas. First, domestic industry grew at an astounding rate during the second half of the nineteenth century. A massive and efficient transportation network was constructed across the American continent. Much of the country's agriculture was mechanized, and heavy industries were established. By 1900 the United States was the world's leading economic power, one that could play an influential role beyond its own territorial borders.

Second, the major nations of Europe had been scrambling for empire in Asia and Africa. They were carving up these two continents into colonial dependencies, much as Spain had done three centuries earlier in the New World. As the nineteenth century ended, Americans entered into the same race. American power was to expand not only into the Caribbean and the rest of Latin America but into the Far East as well.

Arguments for Empire

Basically, the United States shunned overseas *political* involvement. But many Americans argued for *commercial* expansion during the late nineteenth century. Why shouldn't the United States seek additional markets for its agricultural products and manufactured goods? The periodic recessions and depressions in the decades following the Civil War reinforced the argument for commercial expansion. Many business leaders had begun to feel that domestic markets were saturated. The new industrial (and agricultural) complex seemed to be producing more goods than Americans could buy. Substantial cuts in production were out of the question. They would only put large numbers of American workers and farmers out of work. In turn, unemployment might cause political unrest and social instability. Perhaps the surplus from American factories and farms could be channeled into enlarged and more profitable markets overseas.

Other expansionists argued for American imperialism on strategic grounds. The chief spokesman for this point of view was Alfred T.

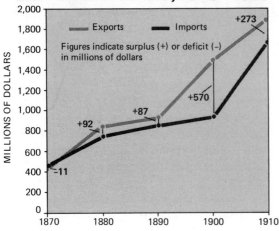

U.S. FOREIGN TRADE, 1870-1910

Figures indicate surplus (+) or deficit (−) in millions of dollars

- Exports
- Imports

+273
+570
+87
+92
−11

MILLIONS OF DOLLARS

2,000
1,800
1,600
1,400
1,200
1,000
800
600
400
200
0

1870 1880 1890 1900 1910

Mahan, a naval officer and instructor at the Naval War College. In 1890 Mahan advanced his theory in a series of lectures, which he later published as *The Influence of Sea Power on World History.* Mahan asserted that through the ages naval power had been primarily responsible for national or imperial power. He also held that no country could maintain commercial expansion without a strong navy and overseas ports (bases, for example, in the Philippines and other Pacific islands).

Mahan's ideas quickly gained favor with imperialists in every major European country. More important, they also influenced several American foreign policy makers at the turn of the century. Chief among the American advocates of a strong navy were Roosevelt, McKinley's assistant secretary of the navy, and John Hay, who served as secretary of state under McKinley and later under Roosevelt himself.

Expansionism also had its defenders outside the business and military communities. Many Americans prided themselves on the myth of Anglo-Saxon racial superiority and the dominance of Western culture. For both selfish and humanitarian reasons, they argued that the United States had a moral duty to uplift and enlighten its less civilized neighbors. The culture and religion of the Anglo-Saxons should be exported to "heathen" lands for everyone's good. This spirit was captured in 1899 by the British poet of imperialism Rudyard

Kipling. His "White Man's Burden" was written and first published in the United States. It reflected the mood of many Americans who were then debating the virtues of keeping the Philippines.

Current theories of evolution seemed to support the claims of Anglo-Saxonists. In his book *Origin of Species* (1859) Charles Darwin argued that through the process of natural selection only the "fittest" would survive. Individual animal species might adapt and prosper while others declined and perhaps disappeared. So-called Social Darwinists extended these generalizations to the domains of the social scientist, businessman, and politician. That is, individual nations and empires might attain greatness at the expense of their less fit neighbors. These ideas were powerful "scientific" supports for the missionary zeal of the expansionists.

Extending the Monroe Doctrine

Although the United States moved cautiously and with uncertainty at first, it soon began to behave like a world power. Its debut on the world scene as a leading economic power provoked a great deal of controversy. But as the nineteenth century drew to a close, the prospect of increasing commercial activity abroad became highly attractive to American businessmen and politicians alike.

Even Grover Cleveland, who opposed acquiring new territories, supported commercial expansion. The severe depression that began during his second administration (1893–97) gave the president added reason to seek foreign markets. Commercial expansion might cure some of America's economic ills. It might help the nation start its slow climb back to prosperity. But a drastic change would be needed in the pattern of America's overseas trading. Historically, farm products—not manufactured goods—had been the country's main export and source of foreign exchange. American business leaders began arguing for expanding the sale of industrial goods to nonindustrialized countries such as China, the Philippines, and Latin American nations.

As early as 1889, Benjamin Harrison's secretary of state, James G. Blaine, had organized the first Pan American Congress, to promote American commerce in the Western Hemisphere and increase United States influence in Latin American affairs. During the 1890s a significant number of American businessmen responded to this opportunity by investing in Latin America. The United States thus began the process of replacing Britain as Latin America's major foreign investor. Both Harrison and Cleveland supported these efforts.

Cleveland's Latin American policy received a major test in 1895 when a crisis arose between Britain and Venezuela. The two nations disagreed over the boundary line between Venezuela and British Guiana. When the British threatened to use force against Venezuela, some Americans demanded that President Cleveland step in and apply the Monroe Doctrine to curb the European power. Stung by accusations of cowardice and beset by domestic problems. Cleveland decided to force a confrontation. He insisted that Britain submit to arbitration of the boundary dispute. Sensing that Cleveland was not bluffing, the British agreed.

The president's actions led to an important extension of the Monroe Doctrine: European powers could no longer resolve conflicts in the Western Hemisphere by military means. In a note to the British government, Secretary of State Richard Olney declared that the United States considered itself "practically sovereign" in this hemisphere. The will of the United States, Olney boasted, "is law." American industrial power and growing military and naval power made these phrases more than empty words.

The Problem of Cuba

Another incidence of American expansionism concerned Cuba, the island ninety miles south of Florida. Americans have always been interested in Cuba. From the early decades of the republic, American politicians eyed the island with interest and greed. By the beginning of the nineteenth century, Spain had lost most of its overseas empire. The remnants of that empire—Cuba, Puerto Rico, and the Philippines—became all the more valuable to the Spanish as their power waned. During the second half of the nineteenth century, substantial American trade developed with the Spanish islands of the Caribbean. The sit-

uation appeared stable. But periodically groups of Americans called for absorbing Cuba, either by purchase or by force.

Cubans resented Spanish rule, which was repressive and corrupt. They had revolted unsuccessfully in the 1860s. By the 1890s they had had enough. At that time, the economic crisis in the United States had reduced the American sugar trade with Cuba. The Spanish island colony suffered sharply from the effects of the American depression. In 1895 a Cuban revolutionary movement called Cuba Libre ("Free Cuba") moved for independence. The Cuban rebels embarked on a new war of national liberation, a war similar to the revolution then under way against Spanish rule in the Philippines.

Neither Cuba Libre nor the Katipunan in the Philippines had sufficient strength to push out the Spanish without outside help. But Cuban rebels engaged in guerrilla warfare to wear down the Spanish soldiers. The Cubans also burned sugar plantations and anything else of value, hoping to drive out Spanish landowners. In response, Spanish officials set up *reconcentrados*, or "detention camps," for civilians suspected of helping the rebels. Thousands of Cubans died in the camps because of poor food, inadequate sanitation, and lack of medical attention.

The United States had been sympathetic but strictly neutral during the earlier Cuban revolution. But in the 1890s Americans gave increasing support to the Cuban rebels. A variety of factors led Americans toward direct intervention in Cuba. First, Americans had little sympathy for Spain and its culture. Many still believed in the "black legend."[1] Second, Spanish troops were committing atrocities. (Little did most Americans think that their own soldiers would shortly be acting in a similar manner to suppress the Filipino revolt.) Third, many American businessmen had investments in Cuba, though these investments were small. Finally, an increasing determination among Americans to become the dominant Caribbean power

---

[1] This was the English notion—dating back to the days of Queen Elizabeth and the defeat of the Spanish Armada—that the Spanish were a particularly cruel and treacherous people.

made events in Cuba of vital concern to Washington.

The Cuban question soon became a leading issue in United States politics. During the 1896 presidential election year, Congress passed a resolution calling for recognition of the belligerent status of the Cuban rebels. President Cleveland, a Democrat who opposed territorial expansion, rejected the resolution. Cleveland's successor in the White House, Republican William McKinley, also opposed intervention in Cuba. McKinley was apparently less eager for expansion than most other members of his party. The Republican platform of 1896 was avidly pro-expansionist and favored involvement in the Caribbean. McKinley remained firm at first.

But events in Cuba and America's desire to impose its will in the Caribbean won over McKinley's promises. "Jingoism"—boastful patriotism—soon took hold of the nation. Two sensationalist New York City papers, William Randolph Hearst's *Journal* and Joseph Pulitzer's *World,* helped to stir up the interventionist frenzy. Both Hearst and Pulitzer ran stories, some of them deliberate lies, attacking Spanish cruelty in Cuba and praising the rebels. The stories spread to other newspapers across the country. By early 1898 it had become clear that Spain could not put down the Cuban rebellion. Nor would the United States allow the stalemate to continue much longer.

On the night of February 15, 1898, an explosion aboard the U.S.S. *Maine* in Havana harbor settled the issue of United States intervention. The battleship had been sent to Cuba to demonstrate American concern for the Cuban situation. The explosion killed 260 American sailors. Spain, which had the most to lose from American intervention in Cuba, hastily sent notes of regret to Washington. The cause of the explosion was never determined. But public opinion in the United States placed the blame squarely on the Spanish. "Remember the *Maine*" became the slogan of American interventionists. The United States government began to pressure Spain to grant Cuba independence. But Madrid would not accept the loss of its Cuban colony.

On April 11, 1898, McKinley sent a message to Congress, asking for authority to use American troops in Cuba. The president described Americans as "a Christian, peace-loving people" who still hoped to achieve a just solution through diplomacy rather than war. But Spain would not modify its position, even with the certainty of American armed intervention. By late April the two nations were at war.

War with Spain

The Spanish-American War of 1898 was over within a few months. American forces dominated Spanish military and naval power. Spanish soldiers and sailors fought bravely, but they were hopelessly ill-equipped for war. Spain won no battles and suffered heavy losses. American casualties were light. Many more soldiers died from disease than from enemy fire.

When the fighting ended in the summer of 1898, United States forces had won Cuba and Puerto Rico. In the Philippines, Dewey's squadron held Manila Bay while awaiting the arrival of American troops. Spanish officials reluctantly agreed to meet with American negotiators to hammer out a treaty that would end Spain's status as an imperial power.

During the short struggle, American expansionists achieved their longstanding wish to annex Hawaii. In 1893 a revolutionary movement backed by American businessmen successfully overthrew the Hawaiian monarchy and sought annexation to the United States. But, like Texas between 1836 and 1845, Hawaii had to sit out a period of uneasy independence—five years—until United States politics entered into an expansionist phase. By mid-1898 annexationist forces had gained a majority in the House and the Senate. Congress passed a joint resolution declaring Hawaii a territory of the United States.

When Spanish and American negotiators met in Paris to work out the terms of a peace, the fate of the Philippines had not yet been established. But all signs pointed to a continued American presence on the islands. President McKinley's indecisive stance fooled few people—least of all Emilio Aguinaldo and other Filipino leaders. The president had clearly been drawn into the expansionist camp. For several months McKinley played a waiting game while expansionist forces in

The year 1900 had been called the year of yellow fever in Cuba. The Spanish-American War had brought thousands of American troops there. Now, with the war over, hundreds of men lay near death from the disease in Columbia Barracks in Havana. Doctors and nurses worked untiringly to try to save the victims, frustrated by lack of knowledge as to what caused the disease and how it was transmitted. Among them was a dedicated army doctor, Major Walter Reed.

On his return from Cuba, Reed strode into the office of the surgeon general of the United States Army in Washington, D.C., and requested that he be sent back to Cuba with the equipment and personnel needed to conduct a full study of the dangerous, often fatal, disease—yellow fever.

Walter Reed, a practicing doctor and a research scientist, was suited to the task he sought. Born in 1851 in Farmville, Virginia, he showed as a boy the love of knowledge, force of character, self-control, and sense of honor that marked his whole life. At sixteen he entered the University of Virginia by special permission. In nine months he graduated, third in his class. He then went to Bellevue Hospital Medical College in New York and received the degree of M.D. a year later.

After hospital experience and work as an inspector of the Board of Health in Brooklyn, Reed decided to enter the army as a surgeon in 1874. He wanted a future that would be secure so that he could carry on scientific research. The examinations for a commission in the Army Medical Corps were notoriously difficult, but he passed them brilliantly in 1875.

He was commissioned in February 1875, married on April 25, 1876, and left immediately for his station in Arizona. Thus began several years of garrison duty at army posts in the West. In 1890 he was assigned to duty in Baltimore and this gave him the opportunity for special studies in bacteriology at Johns Hopkins University. Up to the time he began his investigations into yellow fever, his most important work had been the study of typhoid fever in army camps during the Spanish-American War. One of the conclusions of this study was that the common house fly is a typhoid carrier.

Walter Reed

(Culver Pictures)

Now he urgently wanted to discover how yellow fever was transmitted. The theory then accepted was that a person caught the disease upon coming into contact with the clothing or bedding of an infected person. Dr. Reed did not agree. Several clues had been uncovered leading to the possibility that a certain kind of mosquito carried the disease and infected people with its bite.

Soon his orders came through. He was to return to Cuba to organize and direct the work of three doctors. Reed and his group set up the experimental situation. In one building, volunteers slept on bedding that had been in contact with yellow fever victims. In another, volunteers lived in uncontaminated surroundings but were exposed to the suspected mosquitoes. Those bitten by the mosquitoes did contract yellow fever. The culprit was proved to be a mosquito of the species *Aedes aegypti*.

Armed with the knowledge that the mosquito was the culprit, United States sanitary engineers launched on the Herculean task of cleaning up the filth in and around Havana in which the mosquitoes bred. They were so successful that by 1902 there was not one case of yellow fever in Cuba. It was also eradicated from the United States, where epidemics had struck periodically on the Eastern seaboard. And when work began on the Panama Canal, the mosquito-control measures taken there removed workers from the peril of yellow fever.

THE SPANISH-AMERICAN WAR, 1898

★ Battle ← U.S. moves ◄■■■ Spanish moves

THE PACIFIC CAMPAIGN

Military action in the Spanish-American War of 1898 occurred largely on two fronts, the Philippines and Cuba, although a brief and almost bloodless American invasion of Puerto Rico led to rapid surrender of the island's Spanish garrison. Hostilities commenced in the Pacific. The United States Asiatic Squadron under Commodore George Dewey sailed from Hong Kong in late April to attack the Spanish Philippines. On May 1 Dewey destroyed the Spanish naval force in Manila Bay with no loss of American lives.

In the Caribbean theater, the Spanish fleet under Admiral Pascual Cervera arrived in Santiago Harbor in May and was blockaded there by an American naval squadron. The blockade was reinforced June 1 under the command of Rear Admiral William T. Sampson. In late June, United States troops under General William R. Shafter landed in Cuba at Daiquiri and Siboney and marched on San-

tiago. This force included the Rough Riders, a volunteer cavalry regiment under Colonel Leonard Wood and Lieutenant Colonel Theodore Roosevelt. On July 1, the troops captured the heights north and east of Santiago in the battles of El Caney and San Juan Hill. They then began an artillery bombardment of Santiago.

On July 3, Admiral Cervera attempted to run the United States blockade and escape from Santiago harbor. But Sampson's force destroyed the entire Spanish fleet in a four-hour battle along the coast. The Spanish garrison of Santiago soon surrendered (July 17). Hostilities were ended in the Caribbean by July 25.

In the Pacific Dewey's naval squadron was reinforced in July by the arrival of American troops under General Wesley Merritt. On August 13, United States troops and Filipino guerrillas occupied the city of Manila.

the Senate gathered support for a Spanish-American treaty.

In the end, McKinley demanded what he had perhaps had in mind all along. Determined to "educate the Filipinos, and uplift and civilize and

Christianize them," McKinley asked Spain to give up all of the Philippines. The Spanish had to agree. The Treaty of Paris was signed in December 1898. The United States gained control of Cuba, the Philippine Islands, Guam, and Puerto Rico.

Most Americans had supported the war with Spain. But the Treaty of Paris, which proposed immediate acquisition of an American overseas empire, ran into stiff opposition. Many Americans feared that imperialism would tarnish American democracy at home by imposing arbitrary rule abroad upon alien peoples who were, in addition, nonwhite. (Racism played an important role in the anti-imperialist movement at the time.) Others objected to imperialism on moral grounds. Nations or cultures, they argued, should not be taken over by larger nations merely because they were too weak to resist. An anti-imperialist movement organized to fight the peace treaty. In the Senate many Democrats and a minority of Republicans opposed imperialism. William Jennings Bryan, the Democratic presidential candidate of 1896, led the antitreaty forces.

But at the last minute Bryan changed his course. The day before the vote on the treaty, fighting broke out between American troops and Filipino rebels. Americans regarded the uprising as a show of ingratitude on the part of the Filipinos. Bryan announced that the challenge had to be met firmly. He threw his support to the treaty, though he declared that he would continue to oppose imperialism. The Senate ratified the Treaty of Paris in Feburary 1899. Bryan, who again opposed McKinley in the election of 1900, attempted to make imperialism the central issue of the campaign, but he and the Democrats were defeated overwhelmingly. The American people had voted for empire.

The Search for Asian Markets

Early in the nineteenth century a few American businessmen had entered into a prosperous trade with China. Even with the "opening" of Japan in the 1850s, however, the volume of United States trade in Asia never reached the proportions anticipated by American business leaders. By the end of the century, overproduction in America's

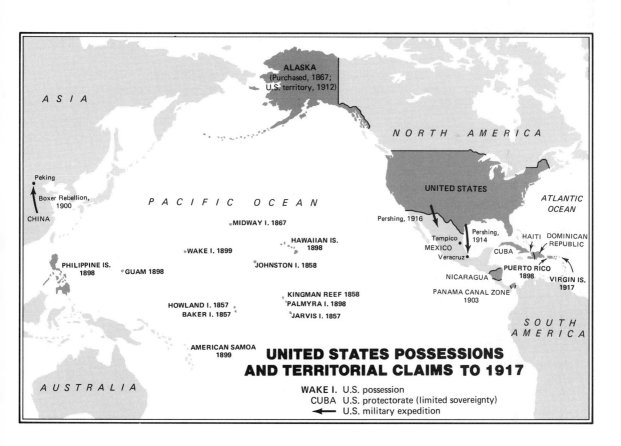

UNITED STATES POSSESSIONS AND TERRITORIAL CLAIMS TO 1917

WAKE I. U.S. possession
CUBA U.S. protectorate (limited sovereignty)
⟵ U.S. military expedition

This Chinese Boxer, a member of the society whose official title was the Fist of Righteous Harmony, believed that his country's survival depended upon expulsion of foreign powers threatening to divide China for economic profit. The Boxer Rebellion nearly led to the extinction of China as a national entity. (U.S. Signal Corps/ National Archives)

factories generated new and powerful pressures for foreign trade. The lure of the China market made itself felt again.

But participation in the China market could not be accomplished without political involvement in Asia. The European powers had already carved up China into "economic spheres of influence."[2] American businessmen believed they could compete successfully in China if they were given a fair opportunity. In September 1899, Secre-

tary of State John Hay sent a series of diplomatic notes to Japan and the major European powers. In the notes he asked them to support a new trade policy in China. This policy became known as the Open Door. Hay recognized the existence of foreign spheres of influence in China, but he asked the European nations to grant other countries free-trade privileges within these spheres—thus keeping the Chinese door open to all who wanted to trade there. Hay also called on the European powers to guarantee Chinese "territorial integrity" —that is, to avoid outright political partition of the country. The European nations did not formally reject Hay's proposals, though some grumbled about American interference. Hay announced boldly that the Open Door was accepted by all, although he was too sanguine in this judgment.

While America was seeking support for its Open Door policies, a group of Chinese nationalists, called Boxers, organized to drive foreigners from their country. In 1900 they began killing foreign missionaries and diplomats. Survivors fled to Peking and the temporary safety of the British legation. There, they withstood a two-month siege until troops from their own countries relieved them. The United States participated by rushing in troops from bases in the Philippine Islands. The Boxer Rebellion was ended. Within a few months peace—and imperialism—were reestablished. In July, Hay issued a second series of diplomatic notes. In them he asked the victorious European powers to preserve Chinese territorial integrity. Hay reaffirmed America's desire to "safeguard for the world the principle of equal and impartial trade with all parts of the Chinese Empire." Not wishing to risk a major war, the imperialist powers agreed not to divide up China. They accepted instead a sum of money from the Chinese in payment for their losses.

In comparison with other powers, the United States had acted as a friend and protector of China. But did the Open Door represent an American willingness to guarantee Chinese territorial integrity? The United States had not signed a formal agreement with China, or with any other foreign nation, to enact its Open Door policy. Hay quickly admitted that his country would not go to war to enforce the Open Door—not in 1900 at any rate.

---

[2] A nation often established with other nations a world area where it would hold a dominant economic position. Once other countries agreed to accept this arrangement, the area in question would be free from the competition of other nations.

European imperialistic powers had battled to a draw in China with the creation of economic spheres of influence. Hay's Open Door declarations filled the partial vacuum created by this stalemate. The Open Door would work to America's advantage only so long as no other major power embarked on an all-out push to dominate China.

INTERVENTION IN LATIN AMERICA

The growth of United States industrial and military power, combined with America's interest in the Caribbean, meant that Britain's position as the leading Caribbean power would not last long. In 1895, during the first Venezuelan crisis, the Cleveland administration had asserted America's new role in the Western Hemisphere. The events of the next decade confirmed this role.

Building a Canal to the Pacific

A fifty-year-old treaty between Britain and the United States became an early casualty of America's new attitude of expansion. The 1850 treaty called for participation by both nations in the construction of any canal across Central America. In February 1900, Secretary Hay negotiated another accord with the British ambassador, Lord Pauncefote. Under the Hay-Pauncefote Treaty, Britain granted the United States exclusive rights to build a canal. But the American government was prohibited from fortifying it. This compromise did not satisfy the United States Senate. The treaty was quickly rejected. Hay returned to the negotiating table, pulled a few teeth from the reluctant British lion, and produced a second agreement. The revised treaty placed no limitations on military fortification of the canal. The United States had only to promise that during peacetime all nations could use the canal on equal terms.

Americans next turned their attention to the question of where the Central American canal should be built. The shortest route was across the Isthmus of Panama, a province owned by Colombia. The Colombian government had sold the rights to the Panama site to a French company,

Roosevelt's famous boast that "I took the canal zone and let Congress debate" is caricatured here. Roosevelt is seen heaving his shovelful of Panamanian soil on Bogota, capital of Colombia, the country from which Panama was detached. (Library of Congress)

headed by Ferdinand DeLesseps (builder of Egypt's Suez Canal). After several unsuccessful attempts to build a canal, the French offered to sell their rights for $109 million. Another proposed site, in Nicaragua, was a much longer route. But it was less expensive and free of foreign entanglements.

President Roosevelt and Congress argued the relative merits of both routes and initially favored the Nicaraguan site. Then, early in 1902, the French company lowered the price for sale of its rights to $40 million. Roosevelt quickly changed his mind in favor of the Panama site. Permission also had to be obtained from Colombia. In January 1903, Secretary Hay signed a treaty with Colombia agreeing to pay $10 million and an annual rent of $250,000 for a one-hundred-year lease on a canal zone in Panama.

But the Colombian senate, in a burst of patriotic pride and financial self-interest, rejected the canal treaty. President Roosevelt complained about the "bandits" of Colombia and their insistence on national honor. Roosevelt considered intervening in Panama under the terms of an 1846 treaty with Colombia. This granted the United States the right to maintain "free transit" across the isthmus. But United States troops were then busy fighting in the Philippines. Besides, the 1846 treaty required the agreement of Colombian authorities for the use of force in Panama.

In November 1903 a revolt in Panama settled the canal question. The revolt was organized by Philippe Bunau-Varilla, an agent of the French canal company. The Panamanian rebels received immediate United States aid. American ships were sent in to prevent Colombian forces from landing on the isthmus. Within a few days the new Panamanian government declared independence. Bunau-Varilla was appointed its chief representative to the United States. Bunau-Varilla and Secretary Hay quickly came to an agreement on an American-operated canal. Under the treaty the United States granted diplomatic recognition to Panama and obtained a perpetual lease on a canal zone.

Roosevelt's "big stick" diplomacy in Panama received sharp criticism from some Democrats in Congress. But the majority of Americans approved of the deeds and the bluster of their president. Some years later Roosevelt acknowledged with few apologies: "I took the canal zone and let Congress debate, and while the debate goes on, the canal does also."

In 1914 the Panama Canal opened to merchant shipping. The canal was acclaimed as a marvel of American engineering. It also put the finishing touch on a program for United States domination of the Caribbean and economic penetration of Latin America.

Policing the Caribbean

While negotiations were being carried on in Panama, a second international crisis erupted in Venezuela. The dispute involved an attempt by European powers to collect debts owed their citizens by Venezuela. In December 1902, Britain, Germany, and Italy sent warships to blockade the Venezuelan port of La Guaira. An international court decided that the three nations that had blockaded Venezuela should be given priority in collecting their debts.

Roosevelt contested this decision. America could not permit European powers to use force to settle disputes in the Western Hemisphere. When a similar financial crisis arose in 1905 in the Dominican Republic, another Caribbean country, Roosevelt moved quickly to avoid European intervention. American officials took over the government and the financial affairs of the Dominicans.

In 1904 Roosevelt announced to Congress that the United States would not tolerate "chronic wrongdoing" by any Latin American country. If political or economic developments in Latin America invited the danger of European intervention, the United States would intervene first. The president's message, which became known as the Roosevelt Corollary to the Monroe Doctrine, asserted the role of the United States as an "international police power" in the Caribbean. The statement was actually a broad departure from the earlier doctrine.

Elsewhere in the world, Roosevelt also tried to project an American presence in global affairs in a variety of ways: by mediating (at Portsmouth, New Hampshire) an end to the Russo-Japanese War, by participating along with European heads of state in the Algeciras Conference of 1906 called to negotiate conflicting Great Power claims in Morocco, by sending the American fleet ("the Great White Fleet") on a "goodwill" tour of the world that had the effect of demonstrating America's growing naval might, and by pressing Congress for modernization of the armed forces.

Dollar Diplomacy

Theodore Roosevelt's successor, William Howard Taft, pursued Roosevelt's policies in Latin America. He favored economic penetration of foreign nations, a policy that became known as dollar diplomacy. Taft urged American capitalists to invest millions of dollars in overseas ventures, especially in the Caribbean. Such investments, he said, would bring Wall Street handsome profits. More important, they would serve the interests of American security. Also, American guardianship of the Western Hemisphere would benefit the people of Latin America. It would ensure them political stability and economic growth.

Nicaragua mounted the most serious challenge to the new American policy. Nicaraguan President José Zelaya, a strong opponent of the United States, tried to avoid the snares of dollar diplomacy. In 1909 he canceled special economic privileges granted to an American mining company. Zelaya's downfall came quickly. A revolutionary movement, supported by American businessmen, overthrew the Nicaraguan president. The United States granted diplomatic recognition to the new regime, took over the government's finances, and sent in the Marines to protect American interests. The pattern for implementing dollar diplomacy had been clearly established.

Idealism Versus Intervention in Mexico

In 1913 Woodrow Wilson, a Democrat, moved into the White House. In his campaign Wilson had promised a more liberal internationalism. He wanted a new foreign policy to curb the growing imperialist impulse. Wilson's choice for secretary of state, the anti-imperialist William Jennings Bryan, gave some indication that Republican policies would be modified or abandoned. Wilson stated that his aim in Latin America was to support "the orderly processes of just government based upon law, and not upon arbitrary or irregular force, and to cultivate the friendship of our sister republics of Central and South America."

But idealistic aims proved no match for great power realities. As president, Wilson used military force in Latin America even more than his Republican predecessors. Seeking to bring peace and "constitutional liberty" to the unstable governments of Latin America, he sent troops into the Caribbean to put down a rebellion in Haiti. A year later, in 1916, the president ordered United States Marines into the Dominican Republic. There a military government was established under the Department of the Navy. Troops remained in both countries throughout Wilson's administration.

Wilson played his strongest and most controversial role as a moralist when he intervened in the Mexican revolution that had begun in 1910. The president at first refused to recognize the government of General Victoriano Huerta, who had

risen to power in 1913. An unsavory politician, Huerta had ordered the murder of his predecessor, Francisco Madero, Mexico's first freely elected president in decades. Wilson wanted Huerta to resign and permit free elections in Mexico. Though such goals might have been welcomed by the Mexican people, they could hardly be imposed from outside by persuasion alone.

Huerta refused to budge from the presidential palace in Mexico City. But Wilson remained determined to "teach the South American republics to elect good men." Early in 1914 the president allowed ships to supply arms to Huerta's foes. In April, Huerta's forces arrested a group of American sailors who had landed at the port of Tampico. Washington demanded formal apologies. Huerta agreed but only on the condition that the United States support his government. Wilson and Bryan refused. When the president learned that an arms shipment from Germany—intended for Huerta's forces—was nearing the Mexican port of Veracruz, he decided to act.

In the meantime, Congress had granted Wilson permission to use armed force against Huerta. A message went out to the United States naval commander in the Caribbean: "Take Veracruz at once." American forces quickly seized Veracruz. Mexican opposition rose within a few days. Fighting broke out, and both sides suffered heavy casualties. Wilson, who had not anticipated bloodshed, found himself in an embarrassing position. Americans protested the involvement—and the death of United States soldiers. Withdrawal of troops had to be arranged by a mediating commission of three South American countries.

Wilson's problems regarding Mexico were not over, however. Huerta was overthrown in July 1914 by the Constitutionalist forces of Venustiano Carranza. As the new president tried to consolidate power, civil war again broke out in Mexico. In November 1915 Wilson gave unofficial support to Carranza's government. This move angered other pretenders to the Mexican presidency, particularly "Pancho" Villa. Operating in northern Mexico, Villa decided to teach the "gringos" a lesson. Early in 1916, Villa's forces stopped a train and killed sixteen American engineering students. Villa then crossed the border to raid the New Mexico town of

General John J. Pershing and his hastily mobilized American troops invaded Mexico in 1916 in pursuit of "Pancho" Villa. The mission was a failure and may even have convinced Germany of America's military unpreparedness. (U.S. War Dept. General Staff / National Archives)

Columbus, an act of revenge that cost seventeen American lives. The calculating and cold-blooded Villa hoped to lead America into military intervention in Mexico. Then, as the leading opponent of the United States, he would gain support from those people who supported Carranza.

Villa guessed correctly about United States intervention. But he misjudged its political consequences. Americans were enraged by Villa's actions. General John J. Pershing—soon to gain fame and glory as commander of the United States Army in France—led a "punitive" expedition deep into Mexico. Villa could not be found. Instead, American troops fought a bloody skirmish with Carranza forces. The battle was unwanted by both sides. The incident threatened another Veracruz. But anti-interventionists in Congress won out over those who wanted war. Early in 1917 Pershing's forces were withdrawn from Mexico. For most Americans it had become clear that Wilson's Mexican policy meant continuous trouble. By this time, too, the

American people had become far more concerned with developments in Europe, where a devastating war had been raging since 1914.

THE UNITED STATES AND WORLD WAR I

Europe had enjoyed a period of relative peace during the century after Napoleon's defeat in 1815. International rivalries did not die down, and many short but limited wars broke out. Yet Europeans managed to avoid a general war. European leaders relied on the balance of power to maintain peace and political stability. But in 1914 the assassination of Archduke Franz Ferdinand, heir to the Austro-Hungarian throne, set off a chain reaction that resulted in World War I. Two powerful blocs emerged quickly once the war began: the Central powers (Germany, Austria-Hungary, and Turkey) and the Allies (Britain, France, Italy, and Russia).

The United States tried to stay out of the war. Whatever their personal opinions or sympathies, most Americans preferred neutrality. In 1914 Wilson issued a proclamation calling on all Americans to remain impartial "in thought as well as in action." But over the next three years a combination of factors edged the United States closer and closer to the side of the Allies and involvement in the European war.

The Road to War

European powers violated America's rights as a neutral nation. American shippers tried to continue, and even expand, commerce with both sides. As in the case of the Napoleonic Wars a century before, American interests quickly clashed with those of Britain, the world's leading sea power. The British declared the North Sea a military zone. Before a neutral ship could pass through British waters, it had to enter a British port. There the ship's cargo was examined for war materials. British escorts would then lead the neutral ship through minefields to safety. Many Americans protested, and Wilson publicly condemned the British practice. But the United States clearly was not

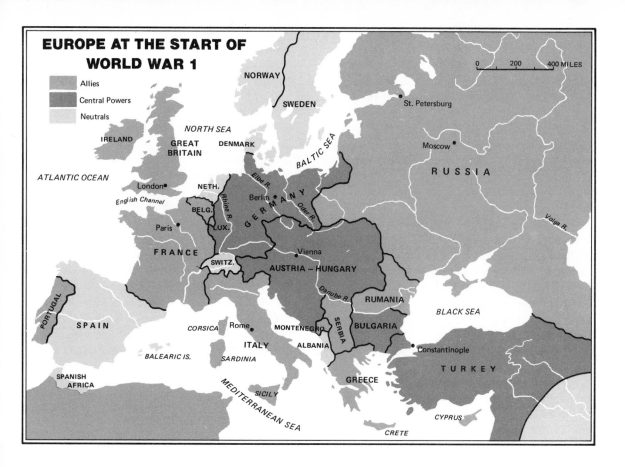

EUROPE AT THE START OF WORLD WAR 1

Allies
Central Powers
Neutrals

NORWAY
SWEDEN
St. Petersburg
NORTH SEA
IRELAND
GREAT BRITAIN
DENMARK
BALTIC SEA
Moscow
RUSSIA
ATLANTIC OCEAN
London
NETH.
Elbe R.
Berlin
GERMANY
Oder R.
Volga R.
English Channel
BELG.
Rhine R.
Paris
LUX.
FRANCE
SWITZ.
Vienna
AUSTRIA – HUNGARY
Danube R.
RUMANIA
BLACK SEA
PORTUGAL
SPAIN
CORSICA
Rome
MONTENEGRO
SERBIA
BULGARIA
ITALY
ALBANIA
Constantinople
TURKEY
BALEARIC IS.
SARDINIA
GREECE
SPANISH AFRICA
MEDITERRANEAN SEA
SICILY
CYPRUS
CRETE

going to make the issue a cause for war. No American lives were lost as a result of the British regulations. No American seamen were impressed into the British navy, as in the War of 1812.

The Germans knew that their navy was no match for British sea power. For the most part, German battleships and cruisers remained at anchor in home ports. Instead, the Germans turned to the submarine as a means of crippling their enemies. The British blockade of Continental Europe, launched soon after the war, threatened the German people with starvation. Germany fought back by declaring all-out submarine warfare. The Germans announced that any belligerent ships found in the waters surrounding the British Isles would be torpedoed without warning. Loss of life in such cases usually ran high.

Wilson denounced the German declaration as a violation of American neutral rights. Many Americans condemned submarine warfare as immoral. In the spring of 1915 the British passenger liner *Lusitania* was torpedoed by a German submarine off the Irish coast. Over 1000 people died, including 128 Americans. Germany refused to accept responsibility for the incident or pay indemnities for American losses. The Germans pointed out that Americans had been publicly warned not to sail on British ships. Besides, the *Lusitania* carried arms as well as passengers. But Wilson drafted a strongly worded note to the Germans insisting that they end their surprise attacks. Secretary of State Bryan resigned rather than sign the message, which he believed was an ultimatum to Germany. When another British ship was torpedoed a few months later, Wilson threatened to cut off diplomatic relations with Germany. The Germans, fearful of drawing the United States into the war, gave in to Wilson's demands: German submarine commanders would no longer fire on British passenger liners without warning.

Economic factors also contributed to American intervention on the side of the Allies. The United States had always traded more with Britain than with Continental Europe. The onset of world war, combined with British domination of the seas, ensured an expanded trade with Britain and its allies. Americans might have to endure annoying British regulations, but at least most American ships could get through to Britain. Between 1914 and 1916 Allied purchases in America quadrupled. It soon became apparent that Britain and France would need loans in order to continue trading. Wall Street stood ready. Anti-interventionists, led by Secretary of State Bryan, argued that such loans were contraband and would inevitably drag the United States into the war. Again Wilson proclaimed strict neutrality. But he did not move to prohibit credit to the Allies. The loans were big business, after all, and the United States economy was booming.

Moreover, America was closely tied to Britain, both culturally and politically. Since the end of the nineteenth century, relations between Britain and the United States had improved dramatically, though the two nations had not entered into a formal alliance. Most Americans sympathized with Britain and its allies. German Americans, as well as Irish Americans who opposed Britain's policies in Ireland, were notable exceptions. One of the strongest supporters of Britain was Wilson himself. The president admired British culture and the parliamentary form of government. In contrast, Germany's image in America had suffered a complete change during recent decades. Americans had once viewed Germany as a country of poets and philosophers. They came to view it now as a stark and frightening nation of militarists.

Within the context of these three factors—neutral rights, economic interdependence, and cultural ties—Wilson tried to maintain a course of neutrality. By 1916 the war had reached a stalemate. Neither side seemed capable of gathering enough strength to defeat the other. Hundreds of thousands of soldiers died in a series of brutal, inconclusive battles. Wilson attempted to use American prestige and the threat of use of American power to negotiate a European peace. His trusted adviser, Colonel Edward M. House, crossed the Atlantic several times to confer with foreign ministers and heads of state. European statesmen listened to House—America was too powerful to ignore—but they did not heed his message. They had fought too long and suffered too many losses to accept Wilson's "peace without victory." The British and French skillfully encouraged Wilson and House, counting ultimately on American intervention to bring an Allied victory.

The war dragged on indecisively for three years. Early in 1917 Germany renewed unrestricted submarine warfare, cutting off food and supplies to the French and British. Germany knew that this action would bring the United States into the war. But Berlin hoped to smash the Allies before a large American force could be mobilized and sent to Europe.

Wilson acted. Early in 1917 Washington received news of a revolution in Russia and the establishment there of a constitutional government. The overthrow of the Russian czar removed many of the moral problems that Wilson faced in seeking support for American involvement on the side of the Allies. In April the president asked Congress to declare war on Germany. Wilson called upon Americans to embark on a great crusade, a "war to end all wars" and make the world safe for democracy. In his message to Congress Wilson noted: "It is a fearful thing to lead this great peaceful people into war. But the right is more precious than peace."

The Great Crusade

When the United States entered World War I, the major European powers were nearly exhausted. On both sides men previously considered too old or too young for combat were pressed into military service. But after April 1917 the Allies suddenly had a great new reservoir of manpower to draw upon—the young manhood of the United States. The regular American army was small. Close to a million soldiers had to be recruited initially (over 4 million were eventually sent). But America prepared willingly to meet the demands of Wilson's crusade. Military conscription was ac-

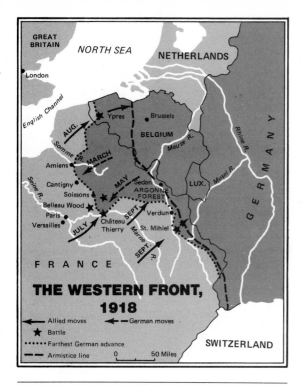

THE WESTERN FRONT, 1918

← Allied moves   ← ← German moves
★ Battle
••••• Farthest German advance
— — Armistice line

0   50 Miles

War broke out in Europe in July **1914,** one month after Serbian nationalists had assassinated Archduke Franz Ferdinand of Austria. In early **1917,** after the Germans renewed unrestricted submarine warfare against all shipping, the United States broke off diplomatic relations with Germany. Provoked by continued German submarine attacks, the United States declared war on Germany in April **1917.** The United States entered the war on the side of the Allies as an associated power. In June an American Expeditionary Force under General John J. Pershing arrived in France.

In March **1918,** after years of trench warfare, the Germans began an offensive with the Second Battle of the Somme, intending to reach the English Channel. The Allies (including the U.S.) set up a unified command for the Western Front under French General Ferdinand Foch. In May, the German armies approached to within fifty miles of Paris. The turning point of the war came in July, when the German advance was stopped at the Second Battle of the Marne. Allied advances in the second half of 1918 were marked by major offensives at Belleau Wood in June–July, Ypres in August, St. Mihiel in September, and the Meuse-Argonne Forest drive of September–November.

The military position of the central Powers deteriorated rapidly during the summer of 1918. On November 11, an armistice was signed.

cepted by most Americans with fewer objections than during the Civil War or during the war in Vietnam. Still, hundreds of thousands of young men—pacifists, socialists, and German Americans prominent among them—refused to serve.

The German submarine campaign achieved startling success during the first six months of 1917. But the Allied navies soon devised an effective countermeasure: the convoy system. A single ship crossing the Atlantic had little chance against the German submarine fleet. But a large group of troop ships and freighters traveling together could reach Europe in relative security. The rate of sinkings by German submarines fell rapidly. Most important, nearly all American soldiers completed the passage to France safely.

The large but still untested American army —General John J. Pershing's American Expeditionary Force—went into action late in 1917. French generals, hungry for more manpower, had originally called for small-sized American units, which they wished to integrate into their own commands. Pershing worked cooperatively with the French commanders and with the Allied commander in chief, Marshal Ferdinand Foch. But he and other senior American officers insisted that the Americans operate as an independent army.

American soldiers soon were allotted their own sector of the Western Front to defend. American troops also helped the Allies hold their positions. Then they joined the Allied counteroffensive in the summer and fall of 1918. By November Germany was beaten. The Kaiser fled into exile in Holland. Worn out by four years of brutal warfare and beset by unrest at home, Germany asked for peace.

At home, America had organized its wartime economy as quickly and effectively as it had mobilized its soldiers. The United States had begun to prepare for war as early as 1916. In that year Congress created the Council of National Defense, a mixed governmental and business commission. During the war the council supervised a network of agencies that controlled every aspect of the American economy. Under Bernard Baruch the War Industries Board supervised the allocation of raw materials and set production goals. The Food Administration controlled prices, and a War Trade

The Meuse–Argonne offensive in World War I was noted for its vastness—1,200,000 American troops—and its human costliness—over 120,000 casualties. Sergeant Alvin York, the prewar conscientious objector, became famous here for his single-handed capture of 132 Germans. (U.S. Signal Corps/National Archives)

Board regulated imports and exports. Congress established at least half a dozen other agencies, all of which reported to the president.

Wilson used his presidential war powers to the limit in waging a battle against dissent. Most Americans supported the war. But sizable minorities did not. German Americans opposed United States support of the Allies for ethnic reasons. Socialists and radicals condemned the war as a "capitalist" venture for profit. During the first months of American participation, German Americans suffered the abuse (and sometimes the assaults) of their fellow citizens. But when it became certain that Germany would have to yield to the Allies, radicalism came to be regarded as the prime threat to Wilsonian peace. In November 1917 Communist forces in Russia overthrew the new constitutional government and withdrew their nation from the war. With the new "Red scare," radical dissenters replaced German Americans as the nation's principal outcasts. (See Chapter 38, pp. 729–32.)

A government propaganda machine, the Committee on Public Information, was set up to publicize war efforts and to censor information or newspaper opinions unfavorable to the Allied cause. Congress enlarged the offensive against dissent by passing strict laws against sedition. By the time the war ended, almost all Americans had been enlisted in the crusade.

Wilson the Peacemaker

At the war's end Wilson turned his energies and ideals to the formidable task of obtaining a fair and lasting peace. The president had outlined his proposals for peace—the Fourteen Points—even before the armistice. The Germans surrendered in November 1918, hoping that Wilson's peace program would guide Allied policy.

The American president called for a new world order. It would help to eliminate worldwide political and economic rivalries. He sought to substitute international cooperation for the unstable and dangerous balance-of-power politics that had led the world to war. Wilson also proposed national self-determination for ethnic groups in the decaying European empires. Finally, Wilson called for a "general association of nations," a league of all the countries in the world. The league's members would cooperate actively to avoid future international conflicts.

In January 1919 Allied negotiators met at the palace of Versailles a few miles from Paris. The peace conference was attended by Wilson and other Allied heads of state: Premier Georges Clemenceau of France, Prime Minister David Lloyd George of Britain, and Premier Vittorio Orlando of Italy. Clemenceau's obsession with French security, though understandable, gave Wilson the most trouble. Lloyd George sought a middle ground, though he always kept the interests of the British Empire in mind. Orlando, junior partner of the Allies, did not participate in most of the "summit" deliberations.

The treaty that emerged from Versailles was a compromise. But it still remained compatible with Wilsonian goals. The president was defeated overwhelmingly on several issues. Despite Wilson's call for "open convenants of peace, openly arrived at," most of the treaty negotiations took shape in secret conferences among the Allied "Big Three"—Wilson, Lloyd George, and Clemenceau. Wilson compromised on national self-determination, allowing European leaders to redraw the political map of Europe. He agreed that Germany and its allies should pay staggering amounts in war damages. The Allied powers greedily divided up Germany's colonies, ignoring the wishes of the inhabitants of those areas. Nonetheless, some of the Fourteen Points were incorporated into the treaty. Perhaps most important for Wilson, the Treaty of Versailles called for the establishment of an international peacekeeping body, the League of Nations.

But dedication to ideals does not ensure success in politics, as Wilson quickly found out. Wilson brought the treaty and the League home to debate and disaster. A small group of isolationists in the Senate were opposed to any American participation in an international league. They feared that a headlong rush into internationalism would curb essential American rights and hurt American interests. Other American senators wanted to be convinced. If Wilson had confided in these senators and attempted to work out a compromise with them, the treaty and the League of Nations might have been saved.

The Fight Over the League

On July 19, 1919, Woodrow Wilson submitted the Treaty of Versailles with its League of Nations covenant to the United States Senate. A poll taken earlier in the year showed that sixty-four senators—the necessary two-thirds majority—favored ratification. Surveys also showed a majority of Americans favoring the League. But time and events had reduced that figure. Everyone knew that trouble lay ahead.

One source of the trouble was Wilson himself. He had created hostility by neglecting to ask any leading Republican to accompany him on the peacemaking mission. Then, too, he was a stub-

Despite President Wilson's desire for "Open Diplomacy," the Treaty of Versailles, signed on June 28, 1919, was largely the work of the "Big Three." Shown here as they left the Palace of Versailles: French Premier Georges Clemenceau, to the left, hat in hand, followed by President Wilson, with British Prime Minister David Lloyd George on the right. (Culver Pictures)

born man. Once he made a decision, he was certain that it was right. He refused to compromise.

Another source of trouble lay in the diverse reactions of the senators to the treaty and the League. Some thought the treaty dealt unfairly with various nations. Others had no trouble with the treaty itself but feared that the League would take away American independence and possibly lead the United States into war again. And there were those who thought the treaty provisions were unjust and that the League would only uphold these injustices. Several Republicans objected to the League simply because they thought that members of both parties should have been involved in its creation.

Battle lines were being drawn. There were forty-seven Democrats and forty-nine Republicans in the Senate, divided into three discernible groups. First there were those who were willing to ratify the treaty immediately — forty-three Democrats. Then there were the "reservationists" — about thirty-five Republicans and one Democrat — who wanted some of the provisions changed before they would agree to vote for ratification. Finally there were the "irreconcilables" — the remaining Republicans and three Democrats. This last group vowed never to sign the treaty under any circumstance.

At the center of this controversy was Senator Henry Cabot Lodge of Massachusetts, the new chairman of the Foreign Relations Committee. Lodge disliked Wilson and objected to the treaty, which he thought was too easy on Germany. He was therefore, at heart, an irreconcilable. But he thought he knew a better way of defeating the treaty. As he said to one senatorial colleague, "I do not propose to beat it by direct frontal attack, but by the indirect method of reservations."

Before the treaty went to the Senate for a vote, it was stalled for two months in the unfriendly Foreign Relations Committee. When it emerged forty-nine revisions and amendments were attached to it. The disheartened Wilson was adamant. Democratic senators were not to vote for it with these "Lodge reservations." "Never! Never!" said Wilson. "I'll never consent to accept any policy with which that impossible name is so prominently identified."

He kept his word, and enough Senate Democrats stayed loyal to him to defeat the treaty with reservations. On November 19 it was all over. The Senate adjourned and the treaty that Wilson thought would be his crowning achievement would not be considered again. The United States would never join the League of Nations.

Wilson saw all Senate opposition to the treaty as betrayal of the highest trust, the cause of world peace. During the long debate, he had cracked the whip of party discipline over Democratic senators and had gone on the campaign trail seeking public support for his treaty. The trip ended tragically when Wilson suffered a stroke, which left him partially paralyzed. It was in this enfeebled state that Wilson watched the Senate reject the treaty and, with it, his dream of American leadership for world peace as a member of the League.

Wilson began looking ahead to the presidential election of 1920, which he hoped to turn into a "solemn referendum" on the League. The election became instead a referendum on Wilsonian politics. Republican Warren G. Harding, who promised Americans a retreat from internationalism and a return to "normalcy," won a landslide victory. All hope for American participation in the League of Nations vanished.

Suggested Readings
Chapters 35–36

Philippines Revolt

John M. Gates, *Schoolbooks and Krags: The U.S. Army in the Philippines, 1898–1902* (1972); Teodoro M. Kalaw, *The Philippine Revolution* (1969); Joseph L. Schott, *The Ordeal of Samar* (1964); Leon Wolff, *Little Brown Brother: America's Forgotten Bid for Empire* (1961).

Becoming a World Power

Howard K. Beale, *Theodore Roosevelt and the Rise of America to World Power* (1956); Walter LaFeber, *The New Empire: An Interpretation of American Expansion, 1860–1898* (1963); Christopher Lasch, *American Liberals and the Russian Revolution* (1962); H. Wayne Morgan, *America's Road to Empire* (1965); Robert E. Osgood, *Ideals and Self-Interest in America's Foreign Relations* (1962); Betty M. Unterberger, *America's Siberian Expedition* (1956); William A. Williams, *The Roots of the Modern American Empire* (1969).

Imperialist Stirrings

Robert L. Beisner, *Twelve Against Empire: The Anti-Imperialists* (1968); Edward F. Berbusse, *The United States in Puerto Rico, 1898–1900* (1966); Clarence C. Clendenen, *The United States and Pancho Villa* (1961); Foster R. Dulles, *The Imperial Years* (1956); Raymond A. Esthus, *Theodore Roosevelt and Japan* (1966); P. Edward Haley, *Revolution and Intervention: The Diplomacy of Taft and Wilson with Mexico, 1910–1917* (1970); David F. Healy, *The United States in Cuba, 1898–1902* (1963); Thomas J. McCormick, *China Market: America's Quest for Informal Empire* (1967); Paul A. Varg, *Missionaries, Chinese, and Diplomats* (1958); Rubin F. Weston, *Racism in U.S. Imperialism* (1972).

War with Spain

Frank Freidel, *The Splendid Little War* (1958); Julius W. Pratt, *Expansionists of 1898* (1936); William A. Swanberg, *Citizen Hearst* (1961).

Wilson and Diplomacy

Edward H. Beuhrig, *Woodrow Wilson and the Balance of Power* (1955); N. Gordon Levin, *Woodrow Wilson and World Politics* (1968); Arthur S. Link, *Wilson the Diplomatist* (1957); Ernest R. May, *Imperial Democracy* (1961); Dana G. Munro, *Intervention and Dollar Diplomacy in the Caribbean, 1900–1921* (1964).

Wilson and War

Thomas A. Bailey, *Woodrow Wilson and the Lost Peace* (1944) and *Woodrow Wilson and the Great Betrayal* (1945); John M. Cooper, Jr., *The Vanity of Power: American Isolationism and the First World War* (1970); John A. Garraty, *Henry Cabot Lodge* (1953); Seward W. Livermore, *Politics Is Adjourned: Woodrow Wilson and the War Congress* (1966); Robert K. Murray, *Red Scare* (1955); Horace C. Peterson and Gilbert C. Fite, *Opponents of War, 1917–1918* (1957).

37

An American Hero: Lindbergh's Flight

Rough weather over the Atlantic kept the tall, slim pilot grounded in New York for a week. Six had already died in less than a year trying to be first to fly nonstop from New York to Paris, and now he awaited his chance. Other aviators were also preparing, but the obscure twenty-five-year-old who intended to make the trip without either copilot or crew had captured the imagination of both press and public. Newspapermen had nicknamed him "The Flying Fool."

Promoters and members of the press pursued the flier around New York. The promoters offered contracts contingent upon the success of his flight—$250,000 for a movie, $50,000 for guest appearances on the stage, and lucrative book proposals. The young man quickly turned down all but one. He had agreed to allow *The New York Times* exclusive rights to the story of his flight, but despite this "exclusive," he continued to meet with reporters from other papers while waiting for the weather to change.

The break finally came on May 19, 1927. The young man was in Manhattan planning to attend a Broadway musical. On an impulse, he asked an aide to phone the Weather Bureau for its latest forecast. "Weather over the ocean is clearing," came the report. "It's a sudden change." The two men headed immediately for Long Island's Curtiss Field, stopping on the way to eat a quick dinner and to buy food for the flight at a nearby drugstore—five sandwiches.

At the field, the flier noted with a mixture of surprise and apprehension that none of the other plane crews also planning a Paris flight seemed to be readying themselves for early takeoff. Apparently he would be the first to test the revised weather forecast over the ocean. He returned to Manhattan, brushed aside newsmen's questions, and reached his hotel room about midnight, hoping for a few hours sleep before starting out. Instead he found his mind alert and racing ahead without pause, reviewing the flight preparations and the excitement of the previous week:

> The days in New York have been tiring . . . but tiring in an unhealthy sort of way. If I had been working on the plane, pouring fuel in the tanks, and

walking over the field to watch its surface, I'd now be asleep. That's what I would have been doing except for the newspapers, and the crowds they've brought. But I wanted publicity on this flight. That was part of my program. Newspapers are important. I wanted their help. I wanted headlines. And I knew that headlines bring crowds. Then why should I complain? . . . Well, I'll be away from it all in the morning—this same morning, if the weather breaks. It will all be gone once I'm in the air, left behind.

He got no sleep that night. Instead, he rose about 2 A.M., and reached the field an hour later, where he remained undecided as to whether or not to take off that day. Mechanics lashed the tail skid of his plane to a truck for the trip to nearby Roosevelt Field, where conditions for takeoff were more favorable, while he considered his prospects. Rain continued to fall as a small band of newsmen, pilots, and other onlookers accompanied the police motorcyclists who escorted the towed aircraft on its slow transit between the two fields. It seemed "more like a funeral procession," the flier later wrote, "than the beginning of a flight to Paris."

After they reached Roosevelt Field, mechanics gassed the plane to capacity while tension built regarding the pilot's decision. Would he start out? The rain had stopped by the time "The Flying Fool" climbed into the plane's cockpit at about 7:40 A.M. Moments later, he signaled those nearby to kick away the blocks in front of the plane's wheels and started down the runway: "Wind, weather, power, load—how many times have I balanced these elements in my mind," the pilot later wrote, while I was "barnstorming from some farmer's cow pasture in the Middle West. . . . But here, it's different. . . . No plane ever took off so heavily-loaded [with gasoline]; and my propeller [was] set for cruising, not for take-off."

The runway remained soft because of the rain, and as the aircraft slowly gathered speed, spectators watched nervously. Finally the plane lifted off at 7:54 A.M., missing a tractor by about fifteen feet and clearing a telephone pole with about twenty to spare. Newspapermen raced off to file their story: Charles A. Lindbergh and his plane, *The Spirit of St. Louis,* were off to Paris.

Lindbergh's flight retraced, at airspeeds, the trans-Atlantic journey his father and paternal grandparents had made by ship as Swedish immigrants in 1860. The grandfather, a banker and politician named Ole Manson, left for the United States after decades of fighting for social reforms as a member of Sweden's Parliament. Although the facts remain obscure, Manson was convicted of embezzlement from a Bank of Sweden loan office in 1860 (he had served as a director of the bank). Manson blamed the conviction on his political enemies. Whatever the truth, the fifty-year-old Manson felt his reputation sufficiently stained to embark on a new life in America. He took with him his young second wife, Louisa, and their year-old son, Charles Augustus.

Physical courage, stubbornness, and coolness under pressure came to Charles Lindbergh as a family inheritance from grandparents and parents. In the United States, Ole Manson settled near Sauk Center, Minnesota, built a log cabin, and began a modest life as a homesteader under a new name, Lindbergh. The family later claimed that the change in name simply reflected Ole's desire to distinguish himself from the region's numerous Mansons, but it seems more probable that the ex-banker hoped the new name would help him forget his disgrace in the Old Country.

Ole and Louisa Lindbergh were at home on the American frontier. Once, while building a new house, Ole fell on a saw and tore a huge wound in his back, while also cutting through his left arm near the shoulder. It took three days for a doctor to reach the badly injured man. Ole survived, though his left arm was amputated. According to family tradition, Ole even held a burial ceremony for his left arm — bidding it a formal farewell — before resuming work on the farm.

Louisa's courage matched that of her husband. On one occasion, during the bloody Sioux uprising of 1862 in Minnesota, Louisa found herself alone and confronting a group of Indians. Although the Indians were Chippewas, not Sioux, they had been drinking and were decidedly unfriendly. Louisa refused to let them into the house or give them food, and when one Indian grabbed the family's only ax before leaving, she chased the intruders down the road, demanding its return. The Indian brave threatened to kill her, but one of the Chippewa women forced the ax away and returned it to Louisa. Louisa's grandson Charles considered that story one of his favorites and asked to have it told again and again.

The infant boy whom Ole Manson Lindbergh had brought to America, Charles Augustus, became a widely respected lawyer, known to everyone simply by his initials, "C. A." He represented banks and businesses, and invested in farmland. The death of his wife in 1895 left C. A. with two young girls to raise, and in 1901 he married Evangeline Lodge Land, the college-educated daughter of a Detroit dentist and inventor. She gave birth in that city on February 4, 1902, to the couple's only child, Charles Augustus Lindbergh, Jr. Charles Senior was then forty-three and Evangeline twenty-six.

The elder Lindbergh had become restless by then in his dual careers as lawyer and farmer. In 1906, he ran for Congress — and won — as an insurgent (or Progressive) Republican. Five-year-old Charles Jr. found himself living in Washington, D.C., where he remained for most of a decade. "I seldom spent more than a few months in the same place," Charles Jr. later wrote. "Our winters were passed in Washington, and our summers in Minnesota, with intermediate visits to Detroit." Young Charles never managed to attend the same school for a full year because of his parents' movements, and his family life was fragmented further by his parents' informal and never announced separation. Though Charles Jr. lived mainly with his mother, he also continued to spend much time with C. A. The arrangement provided a reasonable amount of stability in the boy's formative years.

While still in his teens, young Lindbergh watched his father's political career shattered because of C. A.'s opposition to American involvement in World War I. Congressman Lindbergh, like many Midwestern reformers of Northern European background, blamed the war entirely on profiteers, bankers, and munitions makers in Europe and the United States. In 1916, C. A. gave up his House seat to run for the Senate and lost to a more conservative opponent, partially because of his antiwar convictions. Lindbergh ran again — this time for the House — in 1918. By that time, the United States had entered the war, and hysteria against pacifists ran high in Minnesota (as elsewhere in the country). Charles Jr., then a teenager, often drove his father around the district to political meetings, as the elder Lindbergh was harassed by opponents for lack of patriotism.

Charles Lindbergh is shown here as a boy with his father, a complex and imaginative man who combined careers as a banker and a congressman. (Brown Brothers)

Young Charles was *not* present on one occasion, although he later heard about it in detail. His father found himself confronting a mob that had already beaten his driver while C. A. spoke. The former congressman walked coolly back toward his car, forcing the mob to give way, and he assisted his bruised driver into the automobile. Although shots rang out as the car drove off, Lindbergh insisted that his driver not speed away: "They will think we are afraid of them if we do." In the end, the courageous C. A. lost again and (this time) decided to retire from politics. President Wilson offered him a wartime post in Washington, but the offer fell through because of vitriolic attacks from Minnesota conservatives. A bitter man, he resumed his private law practice for several years before dying of cancer in 1924. His wife Evangeline, meanwhile, returned to a career as a Detroit schoolteacher, once their only son, Charles Jr., had begun to make his own life as a pilot.

Lindbergh did not rush into a career as an aviator. Instead, after graduating from high school in 1918, he spent two years farming on his father's land in Minnesota. Charles enjoyed the life but became restless. In 1920, he enrolled at the University of Wisconsin to study mechanical engineering. Even then, young Charles had his mind set on flying, even though the university did not offer a degree in aeronautical engineering. He remained at the university for three terms before announcing to his parents in the spring of 1922 that he wanted to become an aviator.

The United States then had fewer than 1200 civilian airplanes, many of which were World War I or prewar models, barely fit to fly. The idea of watching their son work at such a dangerous profession with only questionable chances for success disturbed both C. A. and Evangeline Lindbergh. But in March 1922 Charles Lindbergh became a flying student at the Nebraska Aircraft Corporation in the city of Lincoln. For a "tuition" fee of $500, payable in advance, Lindbergh found himself learning to fly, using converted Army training planes with open cockpits. Later that spring, he worked as a mechanic and helper assisting in "barnstorming" through the towns of southeastern Nebraska.

Barnstorming was the aviator's term for flying from one town to another, putting on air shows while taking anyone sufficiently air-minded who had the fee for a short flight over the country. In that part of Nebraska in 1922 they charged five dollars for a five-to-ten-minute flight.

Lindbergh helped, but also began performing stunts himself, such as "wing walking" and, in order to attract crowds, parachuting from the plane to the pastures or fields where the barnstormers performed. Wing walking involved "flying low over town while I was standing on one of the wing tips," a practice that, happily for them, his parents never witnessed. Lindbergh slowly gained acceptance in the small tightly knit fraternity of professional fliers in the area. They performed at county fairs, livestock exhibitions, and any place where they could collect an audience willing to pay for the privilege of watching them—many as young as Lindbergh—risk their lives in worn-out, patched-up planes.

Billboards along the barnstorming circuit referred to the newcomer as "Daredevil Lindbergh," but his fellow fliers usually called him "Slim." He seemed fearless even among a group accustomed to taking enormous risks daily. Lindbergh, in off hours, kept to himself and avoided the drinking bouts and womanizing that occupied his colleagues' spare time. What Slim wanted, one of them later recalled, was to perform the "daring stuff": wing walks, double parachute jumps (opening up one chute after the other), walks from one plane to another while in the air (conducted only by a ladder), and (when he found a chance) fancy aerial loops in planes belonging to those with whom he apprenticed. With his evident passion for the riskiest stunts possible, Lindbergh often came close to death, and he parachuted for his life at least four times from planes experiencing problems.

Within a year after he first began taking flying lessons, Lindbergh sought his own plane. Using savings and a bank note cosigned by his father, Lindbergh paid $500 in April 1923 for a war-surplus Curtis JN-4D army trainer known because of its initials as a "Jenny." He had flown a similar airplane only *once*, for half an hour, at flying school, but Lindbergh managed to get his newly purchased plane into the air and put it through a rough solo flight. After he landed, another young aviator more familiar with the craft explained to Slim that he had been flying with the Jenny's dual training controls still attached! Additional days of practice flying followed, before Lindbergh started barnstorming. During this period C. A. took his first airplane ride, and Evangeline soon went up in her son's Jenny. Unlike her estranged husband, Evangeline shared her son's excitement over flying. During the next few years, she often accompanied Charles Jr., seated precariously atop sacks of U.S. mail which he had contracted to deliver.

Lindbergh, soon after buying the Jenny, became eager to fly more up-to-date and powerful planes, most of which belonged to the Army Air Corps. In March 1924, he began a year's service as an air cadet, emerging the following March as a second lieutenant in the Army Air Service Reserve. By then, Lindbergh had become one of the most experienced and sought-after pilots in the region. While awaiting a response to his application for commission into the regular Air Force (then called the Air Service), Lindbergh went on barnstorming, taking assignments in "flying circuses" at fairs and exhibitions. He later described the performance in the air at such events in his usual laconic and perceptive manner:

> We started with wing-walking. The performer would climb out of the cockpit and walk along the entering edge of the wing to the outer bay strut, where he climbed up onto the top wing, and stood on his head as we passed the grandstand. After finishing his stunts on the wing he would go to the landing gear and from there to the center section, where he sat while the plane looped. . . . From the center section he went to the tail. . . .
>
> After wingwalking came the breakaway. This was accomplished by fastening a cable to the landing gear. The performer went out to the wingtip, fastened his harness to the loose end of the cable and to all appearances

fell off the wing. No one on the ground could see the cable and a breakaway always produced quite a sensation.

One of our feature attractions was the plane change. A rope ladder was attached to the wing of a plane and as one ship flew past the grandstand with the performer standing near the tip of the top wing, a second plane with the ladder attached, passed over the first, so that the ladder was in easy reach of the performer. We usually made two fake attempts to effect the change and actually counted on the third for success. In this way the feat looked more difficult.

The show usually ended with the performer parachuting from the plane or, if at night, with a fireworks display from the planes.

Lindbergh gave up barnstorming in 1925 when he began working for the Robertson Aircraft Corporation, testing planes and training student fliers. When Robertson finally gained a St. Louis to Chicago airmail contract early in 1926, Lindbergh became chief pilot on the route.

The first mail flight came in April 1926, after Lindbergh had chosen nine landing fields (mainly cow pastures with gasoline supplies and a telephone nearby) along the 285-mile route. Proving the feasibility of delivering mail by air became a passion for Lindbergh and the other fliers who worked for Robertson. While flying the mail late one night in September 1926 Lindbergh first considered tackling a far more extraordinary challenge to air travel: "Possibly—my mind is startled at its thought—I could fly nonstop between New York and Paris." Much later in his life, Lindbergh tried to reconstruct his thoughts:

> Why shouldn't I fly from New York? I'm almost twenty-five. I have more than four years of aviation behind me, and close to two thousand hours in the air. I've barnstormed over half of the forty-eight states. I've flown my mail through the worst of nights. . . . Why am I not qualified for such a flight?

Why New York to Paris, and not some other trans-Atlantic route such as Boston to London or Miami to Moscow? A $25,000 prize held the answer. It had been offered, first in 1919 but renewed in 1926, by a New York hotel manager of French background named Raymond Orteig for the first flight "from Paris or the shores of France, to New York, or from New York to Paris or the shores of France, without stop." Two Britons had already flown a much shorter nonstop route across the Atlantic in 1919, from Newfoundland to Ireland, a 1936-mile journey or less than two-thirds the distance (3600 miles) Orteig's prize demanded of a single flight.

For any plane to be capable of flying from New York to Paris, it would need special construction or modification. No existing aircraft had precisely the gasoline capacity and other structural specifications needed at the time. One disastrous attempt in September 1926, the same month Lindbergh first dreamed of making the flight, proved that even a specially designed plane faced grave odds. A Frenchman named Réne Fonck, his country's youngest World War I air "ace," took off, along with three crew members, in a huge three-engine biplane from Roosevelt Field. Fonck's biplane, specially built for the trip, proved too heavy to build up the power needed to take off. The overloaded plane dropped into an embankment at the end of the runway and exploded. Fonck and his navigator managed to escape, but the copilot and radio operator died in the blaze.

Lindbergh spent hours pondering the lessons of Fonck's disaster during the fall of 1926. First, he determined that New York to Paris by air, far from being a daydream, was feasible and realistic: "with the modern . . . air-cooled motor . . . and lightened construction, it would not only be possible to reach Paris but, under normal conditions, to land with a large reserve of fuel and have a high factor of safety throughout the entire trip as well."

Where, then, had Fonck gone wrong? Lindbergh concluded that the success or failure of the New York-to-Paris flight would depend on the ability of a plane to maximize its efficient use of gasoline. Fonck's plane had been too heavy and had carried far too much equipment (including a fully-cooked dinner). He would strip the interior of his own plane of every piece of gear not vital to the actual flight. Fonck had used a Sikorsky trimotored plane; he would seek a single-engine craft of minimal weight. Fonck had taken a three-man crew; he would fly alone.

Lindbergh had no qualms about his ability to manage the flight, but the immediate problem of finding the money and backing needed to purchase or build the right plane remained. Since he had only $2000 in savings Lindbergh devised a plan to interest a group of St. Louis businessmen (some of whom he already knew, as they were themselves aviators) in sponsoring the venture. He reasoned that should he succeed, he would publicize St. Louis as an aviation center, appealing to hometown boosterism of the sort that characterized prosperous cities such as St. Louis. Lindbergh prepared a memo, outlining the economic potential, for potential backers:

> St. Louis is ideally situated to become an aviation city. — We have one ⸢
> the finest commercial airports in the United States, and we will undou⸢
> edly become a hub of the national airways of the future. Some day airliners
> on their way from New Orleans to Chicago, and from Los Angeles to New
> York, will be landing on our airport.

Slim Lindbergh had come to know several of the businessmen "angels" while flying the mail in and out of St. Louis. Before contacting them, he set down a meticulous "plan of action" that linked his own fortunes on the flight with those of his adopted Midwestern home and even with the future of American aviation itself. The memo also indicated Lindbergh's recognition of the importance favorable media coverage could play in his plans:

ST. LOUIS — NEW YORK — PARIS FLIGHT

Action
1. Plan / 2. Propaganda / 3. Backers / 4. Equipment / 5. Co-operation of manufacturers / 6. Accessory information / 7. Point of departure / 8. Advertising

Advantages
1. Revive St. Louis' interest in aviation
2. Advertise St. Louis as an aviation city
3. Aid in making America first in the air
4. Promote nation-wide interest in aeronautics
5. Demonstrate perfection of modern equipment

Lindbergh went on to detail the need for cooperation from newspapers as well as from plane and motor manufacturers and government agencies such as the State Department and Weather Bureau. A realist, the young pilot listed only two possible results: "successful completion, winning $25,000 prize to cover expenses" or "complete failure."

Slim spent the fall, when not busy flying, approaching potential supporters. Several agreed to contribute, and Lindbergh began inquiring about planes for the flight. He met with a German aircraft representative from the prominent Fokker company, who offered to build a special trimotor for $90,000—at least six times what his St. Louis backers had committed themselves to spend. The German ridiculed the notion of any single-engine plane making the Atlantic flight. Lindbergh also wasted many weeks negotiating with the Wright Aircraft Corporation, trying to buy their excellent single-engine Bellanca plane. He pursued other companies with similar results. His frustration mounted as he read newspaper accounts of other aviators, far better financed, who had already begun preparing for the flight.

Time seemed to be conspiring against him until Lindbergh decided in desperation to contact a small, little-known San Diego company named Ryan Airlines. He sent a wire, signing the company name of his airmail route employer (with permission) in order to "get more consideration": "CAN YOU CONSTRUCT WHIRLWIND ENGINE PLANE CAPABLE FLYING NONSTOP BETWEEN NEW YORK AND PARIS. IF SO PLEASE STATE COST AND DELIVERY DATE. ROBERTSON AIRCRAFT CORP." Next day, Ryan replied "Yes," quoting an acceptable price that—with engine and instrument costs added—came to about $10,000.

But construction time worried Lindbergh. Ryan promised to deliver in *three* months and not sooner. "COMPETITION MAKES TIME ESSENTIAL," he wired back. "CAN YOU CONSTRUCT PLANE IN LESS THAN THREE MONTHS. PLEASE WIRE GENERAL SPECIFICATIONS." This time, Ryan promised to deliver in two months a plane with a 380-gallon gasoline capacity (enough for the 3600-mile flight). It would cruise at 100 miles per hour and use a relatively small (light-weight) 200-horsepower engine. It was during this period, in February 1927, that one of Lindbergh's St. Louis backers, banker-aviator Harold Bixby, suggested calling whatever plane Lindbergh used *The Spirit of St. Louis.* After several weeks in a new round of fruitless negotiations with Wright-Bellanca, Lindbergh went to San Diego to check out Ryan Airlines.

What he found on February 23 did not, at first, delight him: "The Ryan Airlines factory is an old, dilapidated building near the waterfront

... There's no flying field, no hangar, no sound of engines warming up; and the unmistakable smell of dead fish from a near-by cannery mixes with the banana odor of dope from drying wings." But Ryan quickly showed the St. Louis flier that it made up in its energy what it lacked in facilities. Ryan's youthful officials and engineers talked the enthusiastic lingo of experimental aviators so familiar to Lindbergh. He plunged into talks with the staff about new specifications vital for an effective single-engine plane designed to allow *one* flyer to make the New York-to-Paris run. The following day, Lindbergh wired Harry Knight, another St. Louis backer:

> BELIEVE RYAN CAPABLE OF BUILDING PLANE WITH SUFFICIENT PERFORMANCE. COST COMPLETE WITH WHIRLWIND ENGINE AND STANDARD INSTRUMENTS IS TEN THOUSAND FIVE HUNDRED EIGHTY DOLLARS. DELIVERY WITHIN SIXTY DAYS. RECOMMEND CLOSING DEAL. LINDBERGH.

Knight wired back his approval within twenty-four hours and Lindbergh turned his attention to practical problems of design and construction, working closely with the Ryan engineers. He recognized the advantages to be gained from having a new plane developed specifically for him and for the New York-to-Paris flight: "Every part of it can be designed for a single purpose.... I can inspect each detail before it's covered with fabric and fairings. And by knowing intimately both the strengths and weaknesses of my plane, I'll be able to tax the one and relieve the other according to conditions which arise." Five months had passed, however, since Lindbergh first decided to try for the Orteig prize. Several competitors seemed destined to attempt their flights long before *The Spirit of St. Louis* had touched off on any flight.

The entry application in late February 1927 from "C.A. Lindbergh," a "St. Louis mail pilot," was actually the *second* formal declaration for the Orteig prize received by the Washington-based National Aeronautic Association. The first had come from Lieutenant Commander Noel Davis who, along with a copilot, would fly a $100,000 trimotored Keystone Pathfinder biplane called *American Legion* after the sponsoring group. On March 2, Commander Richard E. Byrd also entered the race with another large $100,000 plane, this one designed by Germany's Fokker Aircraft and funded by New York businessman Rodman Wanamaker. Two experienced army pilots, Clarence Chamberlain and Bert Acosta, prepared to fly the Wright-Bellanca, now christened the *Columbia.* As if these were not enough, news came from France in late March that a pair of World War I fighter pilots, Charles Nungesser and François Coli, would fly from Paris to New York.

Not only did many competitors appear to be on the verge of making the flight months before Ryan Aircraft could complete his plane, but Lindbergh appeared hopelessly outclassed by this remarkable group of aviators. Byrd already had a world reputation for having been the first to fly over the North Pole, and Chamberlain's *Columbia* would soon set a world endurance record for remaining in the air more than fifty-one hours. Nungesser and Coli had been extraordinarily skilled and fearless pilots during World War I and were at the peak of their ability as aviators. The same could be said for every contestant in the race for Orteig's prize except for the unknown, relatively untried Charles Lindbergh.

All of the pilots waited impatiently for early spring and acceptable flying conditions over the Atlantic. But the onset of better weather brought a series of accidents that narrowed the field of entries and delayed other planes from embarking. Lindbergh, meanwhile, who had been hopelessly behind in his preparations, edged closer to departure date.

Byrd's first test flight in mid-April went smoothly, until the massive Fokker trimotor touched down for a landing. Suddenly the plane flipped over as its wooden and metal structure began tearing apart. By the time it stopped, the propeller and one engine were ruined, and the cockpit badly damaged. Although all four crew members survived, two were badly injured and Byrd was lucky to escape with a broken wrist. It would take weeks, possibly months, before *America* and its crew could resume test flights.

Two other planes crashed within a month. On the morning of April 26, ten days after Byrd's mishap, Davis and his copilot took off from Langley Field, Virginia, in the *American Legion* for a final test run before flying to New York for the takeoff to Paris. The plane carried several thousand more pounds of weight than planned in its original design, and after taxiing down the runway, it failed to clear a line of trees at the end. As the pilot dipped the plane to the right in an effort to avoid the trees, the *American Legion* lost altitude, drifted downward and crashed into a marsh, flipping over into a nearby mudbank. Both men died.

Twelve days later, on May 8, Nungesser and Coli took off from Le Bourget airfield near Paris in yet another massive aircraft, the *White Bird*. They soon disappeared from sight over the English Channel. The *White Bird* carried enough fuel to remain in the air for forty hours, and although the plane was seen over Ireland on its way out across the Atlantic, that was the last of it. (A reported sighting over Newfoundland—which provoked premature celebrations throughout France—proved a mistake.) Thus by the time Ryan Aircraft completed work on *The Spirit of St. Louis*, six men had already lost their lives, and another half dozen had been injured trying to make the nonstop trans-Atlantic flight.

Lindbergh and the Ryan staff had been working furiously from the moment contracts were signed on February 28. "During this time," Lindbergh recalled, "it was not unusual for the men to work twenty-four hours without rest, and on one occasion Donald Hall, the Chief Engineer, was over his drafting table for thirty-six hours." Lindbergh spent much of the time reviewing navigational details, checking out maps and weather charts, and attending to the most minute construction details on the plane. Everything structural on *The Spirit of St. Louis* related to the one task for which the plane had been designed. The pilot's seat was cramped, for example, but it suited Lindbergh, since it conserved space and enabled

The cockpit of **The Spirit of St. Louis** *was a model of stripped-down efficiency. The wicker seat was probably uncomfortable but lightweight. Only side windows were thought necessary since there was not much to see in flight. Legroom was limited by the controls. (National Air and Space Museum, Smithsonian Institution)*

him to supervise more directly the rest of the cabin equipment. Saving weight became the underlying principle of design and construction. Less weight meant more gasoline and a greater safety margin.

Lindbergh kept the plane stripped of excess equipment. He took neither radio nor heater; no parachute, nor much of the special navigational gear available on the larger planes. He even declined a request from a stamp collector to transport a pound of mail to Paris in exchange for $1000, both because it might lead to similar requests and because it would compromise his obsession with reserving extra weight for fuel.

He seemed indifferent to comfort and aesthetic considerations. The plane had no front windows, only an overhead glass skylight and two side windows. Although this meant that Lindbergh would have to peer out one of them for takeoffs and landings, the safety factor involved in keeping the strongest possible front profile on the plane as it crossed the storm-swept ocean seemed more important. Lindbergh also declined to carry hot meals or heating equipment, taking along only one day's worth of tinned army rations, two canteens of water (a gallon and a quart), and—at the last minute—a bag of sandwiches. "If I get to Paris," he reasoned, "I won't need any more, and if I don't get to Paris, I won't need any more either."

The rest of the safety equipment aboard *The Spirit of St. Louis* proved equally simple and sensible: "2 Flashlights / 1 Ball of string/ 1 Ball of cord/ 1 Hunting Knife/ 4 Red flares sealed in rubber tubes/ 1 Match safe with matches/ 1 larger needle . . . (1) Cup/ 1 Air Raft with pump and repair kit . . . 2 Air cushions/ 1 Hack saw blade." Two months to the day after the company had signed contracts, on April 28, the day the *American Legion* crashed, Ryan Aircraft completed work on *The Spirit of St. Louis* and prepared it for testing. By that time the press had begun covering Lindbergh's movements at the Ryan factory closely, and although he recognized the importance of friendly press coverage, the young flier bridled at the persistence and the sensationalism of the journalists. When, for example, Lindbergh took *The Spirit of St. Louis* up for its first test on April 28, he began a playful "dog fight" with a nearby navy fighter which had flown over for a look at the new plane. The next day, Lindbergh was horrified to read press headlines about his "near collision" with a navy fighter, stories that suggested he was an irresponsible pilot.

In the days ahead, Lindbergh continued to run tests on the plane, checking details involved in takeoffs and the way it handled under different weight loads while cruising in difficult wind conditions. By May 6, satisfied that the plane met his expectations, he prepared to leave. A storm prevented departure for another four days. Finally, late on May 10, after thanking his friends at Ryan, Lindbergh headed for St. Louis.

The trip proved anything but uneventful. The plane experienced engine difficulties while crossing the Rockies, problems Lindbergh managed to correct through adjustments in the air (and which he chose not to mention to backers when he saw them the next day). Fourteen and a half hours later (a new speed record for trips from the West Coast to St. Louis), *The Spirit of St. Louis* touched down. Reporters, pilots, and Lindbergh's friends and supporters were on hand to greet him. He learned, most importantly, that no other plane had yet completed the New York-to-Paris journey, and he delayed for only a day before flying on to New York.

There, for the first time in his life, Charles Lindbergh became a celebrity. One of the first people to greet Lindbergh at Curtiss Field, where he landed, along with the now ever present band of reporters and cameramen, was a public relations man named Richard Blythe. His firm represented the Wright Company, which had manufactured the engine placed in *The Spirit of St. Louis*. Blythe and his partner, both fliers, accompanied Lindbergh and acted as a buffer between the press and the aviator throughout his stay in New York. At the beginning, when raising funds had been a problem, attracting press interest to his flight had been one thing. Lindbergh now learned, however, how difficult it is to limit or divert public attention once it has been built up.

Flying did not equip the young man for what awaited him in New York. With newsmen and spectators jostling for a better view of Lindbergh and *The Spirit of St. Louis* when he arrived from St. Louis, shouting questions at him without pause and pressing atop the new plane, Lindbergh grew concerned for the safety of his airplane and for his own privacy. That apprehension increased as Blythe and others who represented his St. Louis and corporate backers began to encourage still greater public interest in the handsome aviator and his impending flight.

Not that much encouragement was needed. Newspaper reporters throughout the country had become fascinated with the story because of its extraordinary human interest and technical daring. The New York-to-Paris flight, at once attractive and deadly, provoked an outburst of celebrity worship for Lindbergh whom some papers now called "Lindy" while others gave him the hopeful nickname "Lucky." He became, in the eyes of the press and millions of ordinary Americans, a hero even before having performed his heroic deed: a hero for the moment manufactured by the interests of the papers and the public relations firms—the boy from the heartland who built at minimal cost a single-engine aircraft to fly alone to Paris, while competing against more heavily funded and prestigious aviators from both America and Europe. The comparisons were obvious, trite, and often made in the daily press: Horatio Alger with a pilot's license, David against the oceanic Goliath, Icarus, and many others.

Lindbergh presented the image of a supposedly small-town American youth who had mastered modern technology while retaining the older personal virtues—modesty, courage, self-restraint, a boyish manner, shyness, and dignity. The story proved matchless and intriguing for the New York press corps and, through them, for the rest of the country's newspapers in the days preceding Lindbergh's departure. This overnight change in his fortunes from an unknown airmail pilot to a national celebrity distressed Lindbergh, or so he claimed, because it distracted him:

> Depending on which paper I pick up, I find that I was born in Minnesota, that I was born in Michigan, that I was born in Nebraska; that I learned to fly at Omaha, that I learned to fly at Lincoln, that I learned to fly at San Antonio, in Texas. I'm told that my nickname is "Lucky," that I land and take off by looking through periscopes, that without them I can see only downward from my cockpit, that I carry "devices" on my plane which will enable me to "snatch a snooze" while steering a "beeline" for Paris.
>
> . . . . Every day I stay here will draw more of my attention from my plane and preparations. My problems are already shifting from aviation to reporters, photographers, business propositions, and requests for autographs.
>
> It wouldn't be so bad if I could go off quietly for an hour by myself. . . . But the moment I step outside the hangar I'm surrounded by people and protected by police. Somebody shouts my name, and immediately I'm surrounded by a crowd. Even at the hotel, newspapermen fill the lobby and watch the entrance so carefully that I can't walk around the block without being followed. There's never a free moment except when I'm in my room. It detracts from the health of one's body and prevents real clarity of thought.

In the midst of the initial chaos following his arrival in New York, on May 13, came a telegram from Detroit: "CAPT. CHARLES A. LINDBERGH/CURTISS FIELD, LONG ISLAND, N.Y./ARRIVE NEW YORK TOMORROW MORNING/MOTHER." Evangeline Lindbergh had read many press accounts about her son and, worried about the flight to Paris and Charles's state of mind, she decided to visit. Reporters in Detroit had already been pestering her regularly, and although an extremely shy woman, she found herself involuntarily swept into the drama and the unceasing publicity that surrounded Charles's impending try for the Orteig prize.

Evangeline stayed only one day in New York, and the diversion brought by her visit probably helped calm Lindbergh's nerves. He showed his mother *The Spirit of St. Louis* and dined alone with her throughout the visit. She, in turn, reassured herself that despite the misfortunes experienced by other aviators attempting the flight, Charles remained intent upon the journey and was capable of achieving it. At last, shortly before her departure for Detroit at the Garden City railroad station, mother and son met the press. This time, the questions were all directed to Evangeline, and she proved more than a match for the reporters:

"Was your son a good boy?"

"Just look at him."

"You had no trouble raising him?"

"He raised himself. I never had to worry about him."

"Kiss him, so we can get a good-by picture."

"No. I wouldn't mind if we were used to that, but we come from an undemonstrative Nordic race."

Lindbergh received only a motherly pat on the back before a smiling Evangeline boarded the train and waved good-bye.

Six days later, Charles displayed similar composure in his own last moments before takeoff at Roosevelt Field. As mechanics completed their final checks on *The Spirit of St. Louis*, its tanks carrying 25 gallons of gasoline more than the 425 gallons for which the plane had originally been designed, Lindbergh leaned out of one of the side cockpit windows, possibly calculating the risks that lay ahead. His plane carried its heaviest weight ever, the winds around the field were far from ideal for takeoff, the runway remained rain-soaked, and the plane's motor appeared to be turning at something less than full engine power. A decade earlier, during World War I, the Irish poet W. B. Yeats had written of another airman meditating on this private moment before takeoff:

I know that I shall meet my fate
Somewhere among the clouds above . . .
Nor law, nor duty bade me fight,
Nor public men, nor cheering crowds,
A lonely impulse of delight
Drove to this tumult in the clouds;
I balanced all, brought all to mind,
The years to come seemed waste of breath,
A waste of breath the years behind
In balance with this life, this death.

In this distinctive way, in the self-controlled and crisp manner so appropriate to a grandson of Ole and Louisa Manson and to C. A.'s and

Evangeline's only son, Lindbergh also "balanced all, brought all to mind." He turned his head from the cockpit to face a mechanic named Edward J. Mulligan, who had been working on the plane. "What do you think?" he asked Mulligan, who, after a moment, responded cautiously: "Rev her up again. We'll listen once more."

Other mechanics gathered around to hear *The Spirit of St. Louis*'s motor vibrate while Lindbergh opened its throttle. Finally, they moved away from the plane, nodding to one another. "She sound okay?" Lindbergh asked:

MULLIGAN: "The engine's doing as well as you can expect in this weather."

LINDBERGH (after peering down the wet runway for a moment): "Well, then, I might as well go. So long."

With that laconic farewell, the man who three months earlier in San Diego had not even known the exact mileage between New York and Paris started his plane down the field.

"What freedom lies in flying!" Lindbergh later wrote. "What godlike power it gives to man! I'm independent of the seaman's coast lines, of the landsman's roads. . . . I'm like a magician concocting magic formulas. The symbols I pluck from paper, applied to the card of a compass held straight by rudder and stick, will take me to any acre on the earth where I choose to go."

First, however, came his flight up the coast of Long Island and Connecticut. It proved anything but "free" from observers, even in the skies. Lindbergh realized soon after taking off that several newspapers had hired pilots to fly escort planes carrying cameramen close to *The Spirit of St. Louis* during its initial moments in the air: "as they drew in closer, cameras sticking out of cockpits and cabin windows, I was startled to find that I was not alone in the air." Finally, over Long Island Sound, he felt "alone at last, over the first short stretch of sea on the route to France":

> What advantages there are in flying alone! I know now what my father meant when he warned me, years ago, of depending too heavily on others. He used to quote a saying of old settlers in Minnesota: "One boy's a boy. Two boys are half a boy. Three boys are no boy at all." That had to do with hunting, trapping, and scouting in days when Indians were hostile. But how well it applies to modern life, and to this flight I'm making. By flying alone I've gained in range, in time, in flexibility; and above all, I've gained in freedom. . . . According to that saying of my father's, I'm a full boy—independent—alone.

For the next day, the world heard nothing about Charles Lindbergh and his plane. Throughout the United States and Europe, millions debated his probable fate and prayed for his safety.

He headed north over the three hundred miles of water from Cape Cod to Nova Scotia, "flying very low," he later wrote, "sometimes as close as ten feet from the trees and water," passing over a number of fishing boats as he proceeded northeastward. From the Nova Scotia coastline onward, Lindbergh confronted a variety of dangers any one of which could have ended his flight: the slow onset of sleeplessness for a pilot flying mainly on nervous energy with virtually no rest for almost two days; periodic storms and cloudbursts; possible engine troubles like the one that plagued his flight from San Diego to St. Louis; and the danger of ice collecting on the wings, which could send *The Spirit of St. Louis* spinning out of control in a moment. Only by extraordinary and continuous concentration, forcing himself at all moments to keep totally awake and his mind alert, did Lindbergh manage to proceed on course.

He had designed a route from Nova Scotia to St. Johns on the southern coast of Newfoundland, where he could be seen from shore, so that people would spot him there "in case I was forced down in the north Atlantic." After he flew over St. Johns at 7:15 P.M. New York time, almost twelve hours after takeoff, only the Atlantic's waters lay below with Europe an ocean to the east. No further word of Lindbergh's whereabouts would reach his anxious countrymen for almost an entire day. "No attempt at jokes today," humorist Will Rogers began his column the next morning. "A slim, tall, bashful, smiling American boy is somewhere over the middle of the Atlantic ocean, where no lone human being has ever ventured before. . . ."

Lindbergh (two months later) set down this account of what followed:

Darkness set in about 8 15 New York time and a thin, low fog formed through which the white (ice) bergs showed up with surprising clearness. This fog became thicker and increased in height until within two hours I was just skimming the top of storm clouds at about ten thousand feet. Even at this altitude there was a thick haze through which only the stars directly overhead could be seen.

There was no moon and it was very dark. The tops of some of the storm clouds were several thousand feet above me and at one time, when I attempted to fly through one of the larger clouds, sleet started to collect on the plane and I was forced to turn around and get back into clear air immediately and then fly around any clouds which I could not get over.

The moon appeared on the horizon after about two hours of darkness; then the flying was much less complicated.

Dawn came at about 1 A.M. New York time and the temperature had risen until there was practically no remaining danger of sleet.

Shortly after sunrise the clouds became more broken although some of them were far above me and it was often necessary to fly through them, navigating by instruments only.

As the sun became higher, holes appeared in the fog. Through one the open water was visible, and I dropped down until less than a hundred feet above the waves. . . .

After a few miles of fairly clear weather the ceiling lowered to zero and for nearly two hours I flew entirely blind through the fog at an altitude of about 1500 feet. Then the fog raised and the water was visible again.

On several more occasions it was necessary to fly by instrument for short periods; then the fog broke up into patches. These patches took on forms of every description. Numerous shorelines appeared, with trees perfectly outlined against the horizon. In fact, the mirages were so natural that, had I not been in mid-Atlantic and known that no land existed along my route, I would have taken them to be actual islands.

As the fog cleared I dropped down closer to the water, sometimes flying within ten feet of the waves and seldom higher than two hundred. . . .

The first indication of my approach to the European Coast was a small fishing boat which I first noticed a few miles ahead . . . a man's face appeared, looking out of the cabin window. . . . When I saw this fisherman I decided to try to get him to point toward land. I had no sooner made the decision than the futility of the effort became apparent. . . . In all likelihood he could not speak English, and even if he could he would undoubtedly be far too astounded to answer. However, I circled again and closing the throttle as the plane passed within a few feet of the boat I shouted, "Which way to Ireland?" Of course the attempt was useless, and I continued on my course.

Within an hour, at 6:30 P.M. local time, Saturday the 22nd, Lindbergh sighted before him the "rugged and semi-mountainous coastline" of southwestern Ireland near Cape Valentia and Dingle Bay. Twenty-eight hours in the air, two hours ahead of his own projected schedule, Lindbergh could hardly believe his own eyes: "I'm almost exactly on my route, closer than I hoped to come in my wildest dreams in San Diego. What happened to all those detours of the night around the thunderheads?. . . In edging northward, intuition must have been more accurate than reasoned navigation."

Lindbergh circled the Irish coastline several times with his charts spread before him, checking and double-checking. To his amazement, he had reached Europe within three miles of the point originally projected. Finally, he resumed course toward Paris:

> After leaving Ireland I passed a number of steamers and was seldom out of sight of a ship.
>
> In a little over two hours the coast of England appeared. My course passed over Southern England and a little south of Plymouth; then across the English Channel, striking France over Cherbourg. . . . The sun went down shortly after passing Cherbourg and soon the beacons along the Paris-London airway became visible.

By then Lindbergh had not eaten for thirty-two hours. Although he had no appetite, he forced himself after reaching the French coast to swallow down one of his five sandwiches as *The Spirit of St. Louis* continued on course.

Thirty-three and a half hours after leaving New York, Lindbergh prepared for the final moments of his 3600-mile flight:

> I first saw the lights of Paris a little before ten P.M., or 5 P.M. New York time, and a few minutes later I was circling the Eiffel Tower at an altitude of about four thousand feet.
>
> The lights of Le Bourget were plainly visible, but appeared to be very close to Paris. I had understood that the field was farther from the city, so continued out to the northeast into the country for four or five miles to make sure that there was not another field farther out which might be Le Bourget. Then I returned and spiralled down closer to the lights. Presently I could make out long lines of hangars, and the roads appeared to be jammed with cars.
>
> I flew low over the field once, then circled around into the wind and landed.
>
> After the plane stopped rolling I turned it around and started to taxi back to the lights. The entire field ahead, however, was covered with thousands of people all running toward my ship.

The surging crowd of onlookers surrounded *The Spirit of St. Louis*, excitedly shouting Lindbergh's name over and over while waiting for him to climb out of the cockpit. More than a hundred thousand people had come to Le Bourget, and units of the French police and army struggled helplessly with the crowd as it broke through every barricade. A human tide flooded the field, a spontaneous welcoming reception that prevented those who came more "formally" to greet the flier from reaching him. Neither French officials nor the American ambassador to France, Myron T. Herrick, nor even the two reporters from *The New York Times* who had come to claim their "exclusive," could break through the mob and reach the beleaguered plane or its pilot.

As the clock struck 10 P.M., The Spirit of St. Louis *came to rest on the runway at Le Bourget airport. To the French, who had gathered by the thousands to celebrate the "Flyin' Fool's" success, Lindbergh was the epitome of "a real American." (Brown Brothers)*

The frenzied reception unnerved Lindbergh after his many hours of solitude in the air. At first, he tried to get the people immediately surrounding the plane to hold back the rest of the crowd. This proved impossible, either because of language problems or—more likely—the simple difficulty of controlling the mob even if those closest to him had understood the gesticulating American:

> I cut the switch to keep the propeller from killing some one, and attempted to organize an impromptu guard for the plane. The impossibility of any immediate organization became apparent, and when parts of the ship began to crack from the pressure of the multitude I decided to climb out of the cockpit in order to draw the crowd away.
>
> Speaking was impossible; no words could be heard in the uproar and nobody apparently cared to hear any. I started to climb out of the cockpit, but as soon as one foot appeared through the door I was dragged the rest of the way without assistance on my part.
>
> For nearly half an hour I was unable to touch the ground, during which time I was ardently carried around in what seemed to be a very small area, and in every position it was possible to be in.

A pair of French aviators who had been watching the frenzied scene finally rescued Lindbergh. Fortunately the exhausted flier emerged unscathed from the friendly but furious mauling. The French fliers diverted the crowd by tossing Lindbergh's helmet toward another nearby American, a reporter named Harry Wheeler, who unthinkingly caught the object. Then, the French fliers pointed to Wheeler and shouted: "Here is Lindbergh!" which sent the mob descending upon poor Wheeler. The unfortunate reporter found himself lifted on innumerable shoulders despite angry protests until he finally reached Ambassador Herrick at the edge of the field. "I am not Lindbergh," Wheeler insisted, as the ambassador tried to present him with a bouquet of red roses. "Of course you are," Herrick responded. Finally, the Lindbergh decoy managed to explain the situation.

Lindbergh, meanwhile, was shoved into a car by the French fliers and driven to a nearby hangar. There he managed to catch his breath and regain his composure. Almost immediately Lindbergh expressed concern for the fate of his plane, fearing that the mob might tear it apart in search of souvenirs. His French rescuers assured him that the plane would be carefully guarded. Lindbergh asked about the fate of Nungesser and Coli: Had they been heard from since his departure from America? The answer was negative.

After Lindbergh had hidden in the hangar for about an hour, another French aviator, Major Pierre Weiss, appeared and escorted him to the reception area, where Ambassador Herrick and other officials had been waiting impatiently.

Until word came that *The Spirit of St. Louis* had been sighted over Ireland, Herrick had not given Lindbergh much chance for survival. Then, he engaged in a flurry of last-minute preparations for the arrival, and finally meeting Lindbergh, Herrick said simply: "Young man, I am going to take you home with me and look after you." Lindbergh seemed pleased at the simple, warm greeting and, as if momentarily forgetting its irrelevance, handed the ambassador a letter of introduction written to Herrick on Lindbergh's behalf by Theodore Roosevelt, Jr., son of the president. Both men smiled at the unnecessary introduction, and Lindbergh renewed his earlier question about the fate of his plane. Although assured that it had been removed from the field without serious damage, Lindbergh insisted on seeing for himself. Moving through the crowds once again, Lindbergh and the French aviators reached *The Spirit of St. Louis,* which they found reasonably intact and minimally damaged, although Lindbergh's logbook had been stolen and portions of the plane's fuselage ripped away.

Major Weiss and his two French colleagues then drove Lindbergh into Paris, where he and Herrick planned to meet at the American embassy. They parked the car near the Arc de Triomphe, under which they walked and paused for a moment of silence, honoring the war dead. It was almost 2 A.M. before Lindbergh reached the embassy. While waiting for Herrick to arrive (the ambassador's car creaked along in one of the massive traffic jams between Le Bourget and Paris), the hungry flier tore into a sandwich and a glass of milk.

When Herrick arrived, he asked if Lindbergh would be willing to meet briefly with the many American newsmen waiting elsewhere in the embassy. After gaining approval from *The New York Times* reporter still awaiting his "exclusive" story (which Lindbergh would provide in the days ahead), he held an impromptu press conference in the ambassador's bedroom.

By then, the tall, gangly flier had changed into pajamas normally worn by the corpulent Herrick. Seated on the bed, Lindbergh answered a flood of questions from the journalists gathered around, displaying his usual poise and candor.

Could he have flown any farther? "A thousand, or at least five hundred miles" with the remaining gasoline, he replied. "What about you? Could you have flown on? Weren't you too tired?" "I could have flown half the distance again. You know, flying a good airplane doesn't require nearly as much attention as a motor car."

The conference lasted less than ten minutes before Herrick stepped in. At last, sixty-three hours after he had risen sleeplessly from his New York hotel room, at 4:15 A.M., Charles A. Lindbergh went to bed in Paris.

Throughout the United States, celebrations had already begun. (Herrick, himself, would allude to the delight taken in Lindbergh's achievement even by cynics and sophisticates when he said in a widely quoted speech several days later: "I am not a religious man, but I believe there are certain things that happen in life which can only be described as the interpretation of a Divine Act. Lindbergh brought [France] the spirit of America in a manner in which it could never be brought in a diplomatic sack.") Before going to bed himself that morning, Herrick summoned an aide to dictate a cable to Evangeline Lindbergh in Detroit:

> Warmest congratulations. Your incomparable son has honored me by becoming my guest. He is in fine condition and sleeping sweetly under Uncle Sam's roof. Myron T. Herrick.

38 The 1920s: From "New Era" to Economic Collapse

B y the time Charles Lindbergh awoke in Ambassador Herrick's bedroom next morning, the entire world was aglow with acclaim. He had overnight become a celebrity-hero without peer in Europe or the United States. In the next days he toured France, Belgium, and England, feted by royal and political notables. Reinforcing the public's perception of his simplicity and self-possession, Lindbergh spoke little and stuck to very few themes: high hopes for the future of aviation, the pleasure at having successfully flown the New York-to-Paris hop (often referring in the plural "we," thus including his plane), and wishes for international friendship. Everywhere he appeared the crowds collected, and the press recorded his every word and gesture.

He had hoped to fly *The Spirit of St. Louis* back himself, but when President Coolidge sent a U.S. warship to bring pilot and plane back home, Lindbergh (now a captain in the Army Air Service Reserve) returned to Washington on June 11, 1927, triggering celebrations throughout the country. In the weeks ahead, Lindbergh flew *The Spirit of St. Louis* to every state in the Union.

By the year's end, Lindbergh settled into a new and exhausting life as a national hero. He continued to turn down financial propositions totaling in the millions (including offers to do movies, vaudeville tours, and other public performances exploiting his flight). He took three weeks off to seclude himself at the Long Island mansion owned by a new friend, millionaire and aviation patron Harry Guggenheim, to write thirty thousand terse words about his life and the flight experience. The book, aptly and modestly titled *We,* sold well and brought Lindbergh financial security. By the year's end, Lindbergh managed even to turn his thoughts to his personal life. After a December 1927 goodwill flight nonstop from Washington to Mexico City, where banker Dwight Morrow was the U.S. ambassador, Charles began courting Morrow's twenty-one-year-old daughter, Anne Spencer Morrow. Lindbergh then shifted his attention to the one field that interested him above all else; encouragement of commercial aviation in the United States. He began working with several groups of entrepreneurs, including two which would later evolve into the two great American transcontinental airlines, Pan American and T.W.A. Although he tried valiantly to avoid publicity, Lindbergh remained constantly in the public eye, still the heroic figure long after others had duplicated his flight across the Atlantic and long after the press had given its front pages to newer excitements.

More than the aviator's personal charm and attractiveness entered into the "Lindbergh myth." The young flier and his achievement attracted the unrelenting attention of his contemporaries and captured the imagination of his generation precisely because he seemed to personify many of the contradictory themes that characterized American society and culture during the 1920s. Lindbergh seemed to exemplify the union of the *old* Horatio Alger hero and the *new* mass culture celebrity. To an America surfeited with technological achievements, Lindbergh brought a momentary recognition that individuals could still master the new technology. In an affluent culture where the middle and wealthy classes were increasingly dominated by self-absorbed pleasure seekers, Lindbergh brought an unmistakable commitment to traditional American values: devotion to family, loyalty to friends, modesty, self-discipline, and a willingness to sacrifice comfort for duty.

Lindbergh, though no country bumpkin, retained the reputation of a self-possessed maverick while enjoying the support of the country's political and economic establishment. His ability to exploit the public's interest in his activities in the mass media—his ability to cultivate print and radio journalists without surrendering his independence—showed Lindbergh to be a master of advertising and public relations, both of which came into their own as American phenomena during the 1920s. In that cynical and disillusioned era of lawless Prohibition and relaxed Jazz Age morality, *the cult of innocence* itself found its quintessential expression in the adulation shown Charles Lindbergh by the American public and its publicists. "Romance, chivalry, self-dedication," wrote Frederick Lewis Allen, the decade's most effective chronicler, in *Only Yesterday*, "—here they were, embodied in a modern Galahad for a generation which had forsworn Galahads." In a decade characterized by massive changes within every major area of American life, Lindbergh came thus to exemplify both the most attractive qualities of the New Era and the ability of older American values to absorb and manage rapid change.

TECHNOLOGY AND ECONOMIC CHANGE

Many Americans described their society during the decade following World War I as a "New Era," a period of economic development linked to massive changes in machine technology. When the decade of the Twenties began, just over a third of American industry was electrified, but by the time of Lindbergh's flight, almost two-thirds of the power used in American industry came from electricity, a figure that reached 70 percent by 1929. The automobile led the growth sectors of the economy in the 1920s, stimulating development in related mass-production industries (among them steel, rubber, chemicals, and glass). A construction boom was accompanied by significant changes in mass communications (including both radio and telephone service nationwide). By 1927, 550 out of every 1000 households in the United States owned automobiles, 600 out of each 1000 had telephones, half of America's population enjoyed the use of

phonographs, and a quarter of the households had radios. By then, almost six out of ten Americans lived in cities, two-thirds of them in the nation's twenty-five largest metropolitan areas.

The United States had become a mechanized country dependent upon the systematic application of electrical power and machine technology. Lindbergh's designing of *The Spirit of St. Louis* for its assigned task, the New York-to-Paris flight, his developing each part and instrument within the plane for the plane's specific function, stood as a prime illustration for Americans in that era of their society's ability to mobilize human ingenuity and technological skill toward achievements that extended the range of individual performance.

To an extraordinary extent, the economy itself duplicated Lindbergh's solitary performance during the 1920s. American manufacturing industries grew three times faster than population during the decade, a growth in productivity due not to a larger labor force but to technological innovations and the rapid spread of mass production. In fact, despite the high industrial productivity of the 1920s, the white-collar segments of the working class grew significantly during the decade while blue-collar workers did not. Although the industrial working class remained relatively stable, over eight thousand separate firms disappeared between 1919 and 1930 because of mergers within American industry. The movement toward business consolidation, which had flourished in the first half decade of the century, resumed and accelerated under the sympathetic eyes of a government that encouraged giant combinations within the American economy.

Almost four thousand public utilities companies also merged out of existence between 1919 and 1927, and the number of banks was reduced significantly through mergers or because of failures. The top twenty banking institutions doubled their percentage of total loans and investments from 14 to 27 during the 1920s. Mercantile chains also expanded significantly at the expense of the small storekeepers. No single field of American enterprise escaped the merger movement during the decade.

Business values permeated American society and culture, and the federal government under

Henry Ford, the founding genius of the American automobile industry, as a young man. Ford's development of mass-produced, assembly line Model T's during the century's earliest decades transformed the automobile into an affordable conveyance for the millions. By the 1920s, Ford had become one of the most influential commentators in American society on a variety of social and political—as well as economic—subjects. (Culver Pictures)

three Republican presidents adopted the friendliest of attitudes toward private enterprise. "The man who builds a factory builds a temple," observed Calvin Coolidge; "the man who works there worships there." The chief "temples" of the era proved to be those in the automobile industry and other consumer durables, such as household appliances and goods (refrigerators, electric dishwashers, radios, toasters, and a hundred other products), which, along with the construction industry and electrical power, sparked investment in the 1920s.

The Age of the Automobile

At the time of World War I, when young Charles Lindbergh drove his father, "C. A.,"

around their Minnesota district in search of votes, the automobile had only begun to change from a luxury to a necessity for most Americans. There were only eight thousand autos in the United States in 1900, playthings for the rich until Henry Ford opened his first factory and, in 1908, began producing the Model T at the amazingly low price of $850. Ford vowed to "build a motor car for the multitudes," promising an automobile "so low in price that no man making a good salary will be unable to own one."

Ford simplified the design and eliminated decorative features in his Model T—much as Lindbergh, in developing his airplane, stressed simplification of design. Using a moving assembly line, and thus dividing his labor according to function, Ford reduced manufacturing costs significantly. His initial investment of $28,000 in the business soon brought him millions. Thousands of workers labored on Ford assembly lines in and around the city of Detroit, which became the country's automobile capital.

Paying constant attention to quality control and cost cutting on his assembly lines, Ford succeeded in creating a mass market for the automobile. His $850 basic price fell to about $500 in 1914 and to $300 by the 1920s. As people were encouraged to purchase cars on a monthly or weekly installment basis, and easy credit terms replaced the need to save the full price of an auto prior to delivery, the industry became big business. Success spawned collateral industries, dependent for much of their production upon automobile sales, not only older giants such as steel but also rubber, glass, petroleum, and a host of services—road construction, gas stations, restaurants, and motor inns. By 1929, there were 26.5 million autos in the United States, with the industry turning out additional millions yearly.

Ford's success also bred competition, and during the 1920s two other firms fought for a major share of the auto market. General Motors and Chrysler enjoyed the advantages of assembly-line manufacturing and also utilized Wall Street financing (which Ford distrusted) and aggressive marketing methods (which Ford resisted). General Motors was organized in 1908 as an umbrella corporation that absorbed earlier companies such as Chevrolet,

The automobile soon became a symbol of "the good life." Here a family enjoys a picnic on the grass with their Model T Ford parked behind them. (Brown Brothers)

Oldsmobile, and Buick. During the 1920s, GM overtook Ford in influence, trend setting, and total sales. GM had an efficient managerial structure far more integrated than Ford's and, because of its size, it could produce a wide range of automobiles attracting both the luxury-minded and the budget-conscious. Ford still vowed to produce an auto "that will last forever"; General Motors encouraged—even *planned*—for yearly obsolescence. Changes in color, body styles, and equipment were planned to induce customers to change their models frequently.

With over 26.5 million autos on the road by the end of the 1920s, American social life changed profoundly in less than a generation. New roads, part of the building boom of the Twenties, criss-crossed the United States, allowing for mobility undreamt of before. Railroads declined in importance, both for passenger transport and for freight, as automobiles and trucks proliferated. One new transportation technology displaced another, and

by the 1920s a new transcontinental trucking industry cut into the previous railroad monopoly on long-distance freight hauling.

As automobile use became common even among American families with modest income levels, the car became a primary "vehicle" in reinforcing a psychological belief in *personal* freedom. The freedom which Charles Lindbergh acclaimed as a prime benefit of *airplane* travel lay beyond the reach of ordinary Americans during the 1920s. Not so the "freedom" of choosing distance and destination when traveling in an "Olds" or a Model T. The American romance with the automobile filtered down from the upper and middle classes to workers and farmers. Few cultures have been as psychologically prepared to experiment in as many ways with a new mode of transportation as American society was with the automobile during the 1920s. Henry Ford's dream of an ordinary worker using a reasonably priced vehicle to "enjoy with his family the blessings of hours of pleasure in God's great open spaces," appeared close to realization.

Ironically, Ford the innovator regressed into an obsessive personal traditionalism during the 1920s. He waxed nostalgic for a lost, preindustrial, and simpler American world which his Model T had helped destroy. The prophet of technological change and mass production spent millions of dollars reconstructing his hometown, Greenfield Village. Thus, though a major force behind the emergence of a more frenetic and deracinated American culture, Ford (like Lindbergh) became a folk hero of the Twenties, partially as an arch defender of Old Small-Town America. "It was an evil day when the village flour mill disappeared," the designer of the Model T observed matter-of-factly, with no apparent recognition of the contradiction of his own life and values. He stood, as did Charles Lindbergh, both as a mover of new and modernizing forces and as a nostalgic survivor of a disappearing small-town world.

The Business World

New technologies affected production throughout American industry during the 1920s. Developments in the automobile and other major industries affected patterns throughout the economy. Most major corporations began investing heavily in research and development programs. Thus Charles Lindbergh spent much of his time in 1928 mapping out a nationwide "Lindbergh route" for a group of investors in the aviation field who wanted to combine transcontinental rail and air travel. The scheme proved to have less of a future, however, than Lindbergh's subsequent involvements with companies such as Juan Trippe's Pan American Airlines and T.W.A., which projected new transcontinental and worldwide commercial airlines. By the end of the 1920s, the industry which had its symbolic birth in 1903, when Orville and Wilbur Wright made their first short successful flight at Kitty Hawk, North Carolina, had be-

come an industry crowded with more than three dozen airline companies flying regular routes crisscrossing the United States. Lindbergh saw no contradiction between his own business-financed flying tours on behalf of commercial aviation, and his passion for breaking ground in adventurous worldwide flights that took him and Anne Morrow Lindbergh all over the world.

During the 1920s, American entrepreneurs sought new sources of profits through similar experimental innovations and diversification. The Du Pont Company, which started by manufacturing explosives, became a major producer of paints and dyes. General Electric moved from producing heavy equipment for industries into the manufacture of plastics and home appliances.

Most industries hired publicists or public relations firms to create a new "image" of business "partnership" with consumers and with their employees. In an effort to dampen worker enthusiasm for joining unions, which made almost no headway in the mass production industries of the 1920s such as automobiles and steel, corporate publicists developed a form of welfare capitalism popularly known as the "American Plan." As a part of this plan, major corporations encouraged employee purchase of company stocks, provided hospital and pension plans, and fostered a belief in the necessity of "cooperative" action by management and labor to maximize productivity and keep unions out. Although wages remained relatively constant throughout the 1920s, rising at less than a third of the rate of corporate profits, there was improvement. Real income for the average worker rose from $1308 in 1921 to $1716 by 1929. But the prosperity of the decade touched the majority of Americans far less than the affluent minority. The distribution of wealth in the United States remained profoundly uneven, dangerously so (though disguised by installment purchases). More than 87 percent of Americans—25 million families—had incomes of less than $2500 annually, while fewer than 3 percent—a million families—had incomes of over $5000. American Plan advocates succeeded in defusing most worker unrest by encouraging a commitment to industrial harmony. Through the activities of corporate publicists, the "image" of the businessman acquired a new popularity and re-

DEVELOPMENTS IN TECHNOLOGY, 1865–1930

(DATES REFER TO PATENT OR FIRST SUCCESSFUL USE)

YEAR	INVENTOR	CONTRIBUTION	IMPORTANCE/DESCRIPTION
1869	George Westinghouse	AIR BRAKE	Provided smoother and quicker braking action for railroad cars.
1874	Joseph Glidden	BARBED WIRE MANUFACTURE	Speeded the end of open grazing of cattle.
1876	Alexander Graham Bell	TELEPHONE	Made out of a cigar box, wire, and two toy magnets; revolutionized communication.
1877	Thomas Alva Edison	PHONOGRAPH	Extended availability of music to millions.
1879	Thomas Alva Edison	INCANDESCENT BULB	Made possible electric lighting.
1880	W. E. Sawyer	PRINCIPLE OF SCANNING	Established the possibility of using only a single wire or channel for transmission of a picture, thereby making television possible.
1888	George Eastman	HAND CAMERA	Revolutionized newspaper journalism.
1888	Nikola Tesla	FIRST MOTOR TO BE RUN BY ALTERNATING CURRENT	Made the transmission of electrical power over long distances possible.
1892	John Froelich	MOTORIZED TRACTOR	Powered by a 20-hp., single-cylinder gasoline engine; greatly increased agricultural efficiency.
1895	George B. Selden	INTERNAL COMBUSTION AUTOMOBILE ENGINE	Initiated a new mode of transportation.
1896	Guglielmo Marconi	WIRELESS TELEGRAPH	Formed the basis for radio transmissions.
1903	Orville & Wilbur Wright	FIRST FLIGHT OF A HEAVIER-THAN-AIR CRAFT	Marked the beginning of the air age.
1904	Thomas Alva Edison	SOUND MOTION PICTURE	Inaugurated a new entertainment/information medium.
1913	William M. Burton	CRACKING OIL-REFINING PROCESS	Made possible production of gasoline from kerosene.
1917	Ernst F.W. Alexanderson	HIGH-FREQUENCY ALTERNATOR	Made worldwide wireless transmission possible.
1918	Peter C. Hewitt F. B. Crocker	HELICOPTER	First helicopter to rise successfully from the ground.
1922	Herbert T. Kalmus	TECHNICOLOR PROCESS	Made possible color film.
1926	Robert Hutchings Goddard	ROCKET	First liquid-propellant rocket.

Posters such as this stylized appeal by a stellar Boy Scout to purchase government war bonds were part of a massive drive by the Wilson Administration to appeal to patriotic sentiments once the United States had entered World War I. (The Bettmann Archive)

buy nonessential products. Advertisers specialized in *creating* demand for radios, perfumes, sewing machines, electric washing machines and dishwashers, cosmetics, mobile homes, phonographs, and, of course, automobiles. Although an occasional celebrity such as Lindbergh turned down the quick profit advertisers offered for an endorsement of their products, many other celebrities, from baseball players to movie stars, proved less fastidious about celebrating the virtues of America's consumerism.

Advertisers prided themselves on keeping consumer demand at its highest pitch. A bestselling text for advertisers (published the year of Lindbergh's flight) observed with trenchant cynicism:

> Your average audience—which means *any* American audience as soon as you reach into the hundred thousands—is like that: $8-, $10-, $12-a-day workers; thirteen- or fourteen-year-old minds scarcely equal to second-year high school. Each gets a book every four months where public libraries reach them; four out of five haven't even this service. And one out of three families have no books in their home. . . . They all go to the movies every other week; and about one in four listens to the radio perhaps an hour a day. They like dark blue as a color and lilac as a scent. Writing themselves, they use a vocabulary generally fewer than a thousand words although each can understand, in reading, maybe six times that many. In their aggregate action the element of intellect is practically negligible.

The advertising industry's view of ordinary Americans both mirrored and reinforced the dominant belief of leading businessmen in their own superiority as an economic elite entitled to shape not only mass consumption patterns but the very directions of American society. The New Era represented the apex of American entrepreneurial confidence up to that point. The economic prosperity of the age encouraged consensus among Americans of all classes that American capitalism was moving in directions beneficial to all of society. Leading business voices stressed the preeminence of economic interests and of a material standard of values, a fear of popular interference, and an insistence upon "stability" (meaning noninterference in business decision making through government regulation or oversight). Republican political leaders appeared to share these views: "Brains are

spectability quite different from the widespread anti-business images of the Progressive era.

Advertising played a crucial role in the transformation of the businessman's image. The advertising industry tripled expenditures during the Twenties, and the modern Madison Avenue ad agencies came into their own. The techniques that had been used so successfully to market Liberty Bonds during the war now succeeded in the selling of consumer goods. Advertising, abandoning the ethic of thrift and savings, encouraged *efficient consumption*—spending earnings and, where necessary, using installment and credit purchases to

wealth," Calvin Coolidge observed, "and wealth is the chief end of man."

The complacent materialism of the era spread beyond the fields of business and politics. Many religious spokesmen stepped forth to preach the pro-business gospel. Appropriately, though, the classic statement of the New Conservatism came not from a minister but an advertising man, Bruce Barton, whose 1925 best seller, *The Man Nobody Knows*, turned Jesus himself into a proto-corporate executive who had "picked up twelve men from the bottom ranks of business and forged them into an organization that conquered the world." In Barton's view, then, the Christian church was nothing less than the General Motors of the Roman world. Barton urged all advertising men "to study the parables of Jesus," which are "the most powerful advertisements of all time." As for business, it was at the center of Jesus's ministry. Had He not Himself said, "Wist ye not that I must be about my father's business?"

Barton's vulgarization of Christianity differed little from Coolidge's *political* defense of business power. Politicians, ministers, and businessmen believed that the mass society and consumer culture that had brought prosperity to the United States would continue only under the unimpeded direction of those individuals who controlled American industry and finance.

NEW PATTERNS IN AMERICAN CULTURE

Just as the dramatic national impact of John Brown's raid in 1859 — and the rapid, cross-country preparations for that raid (along a Kansas–Canada– New England–Virginia axis) — had been made possible by the new improvements in transportation and communications of that day, notably the railroad and the telegraph, so too did Charles Lindbergh's 1927 flight reflect the technological advances that had spread through American society. Technological and cultural change, then as now, bore close and continuing links to one another in ways that were often taken for granted. Lindbergh's achievement dramatized a number of the newer patterns in both American technology and American culture, either by exemplifying them or by contrast.

Mass Communications

Charles Lindbergh was the first twentieth-century hero spawned with the total assistance of mass communications. He himself always appreciated the power of "the media." From his earliest plans for the New York-to-Paris flight, he calculated the ways in which newspapers could prove helpful to him. He played adeptly upon journalists' fascination with his relaxed and self-confident style, projecting himself eloquently not only with the press but — even more importantly — on radio and in motion pictures as his celebrity increased. With every major form of modern mass communication (except television) at his disposal his progress on the flight itself was relayed quickly via telegraph and radio. News of his whereabouts, except when he was over the ocean, was never far from the average American or European. In the Lindbergh phenomenon as elsewhere, the 1920s witnessed the evolution of mass communications — to a degree unimaginable a decade earlier — as a major fact of American life.

First came telephones, then radios, into average homes. Telephones had become standard equipment in middle-class households by the mid-1920s, and (countrywide) six out of every ten Americans enjoyed their use. Radio ownership spread even more rapidly. The first commercial broadcasting began in 1920 at Pittsburgh's station KDKA, which reported on the presidential election that year. Radio grew phenomenally. A quarter of the country's households had radios by the time of Lindbergh's flight, and that same year Congress passed an act creating a Federal Radio Commission to regulate stations and distribute wavelengths. This legislation confirmed that radio, like the railroads and telegraph lines before it, would develop as a privately owned enterprise under government supervision rather than as a government operation as in Europe. In 1926 the NBC radio network was founded, and CBS was created in 1927, thereby allowing hundreds of local stations to link up in unified networks. This allowed nationwide programming and helped spawn mass audiences for both programs and commercials.

Motion pictures also developed rapidly during the 1920s, their stars becoming far better known and more popular than most vaudeville or legitimate theater personalities. The medium invented by Thomas Alva Edison and others early in the century progressed quickly from the peep-hole, short feature "nickleodeon" films to serious, lengthy movies. The motion picture industry's center had shifted from the East Coast to Hollywood by the 1920s, as $1 million companies encouraged Wall Street investment in their operations much as their competitors in more sedate enterprises.

The next great innovation in the movies came the same year as Lindbergh's flight, 1927, when Warner Brothers produced the first sound feature film (a development that eliminated silent pictures within a matter of years). By then, Americans had developed a cadre of favorite film stars, celebrities whose movements they tracked not only on the screen but—between pictures—through sensationalist newspaper stories. Comedians such as Charlie Chaplin, cowboy stars such as Bill Hart, heroines such as Pearl White (whose adventures in the "perils of Pauline" series kept Americans gasping), seductresses such as Theda Bara, seducers such as Rudolph Valentino, and swashbucklers such as Douglas Fairbanks became the idols of millions because of their on-screen performances. The producers, including newspaper tycoon William Randolph Hearst, who offered Lindbergh phenomenal sums to make a movie (Hearst bid a reported $.5 million) all hoped to transform the young aviator into such a movie personality, a fate Lindbergh sensibly resisted. By the time he flew from New York to Paris, there were already more than seventeen thousand motion picture theaters around the United States. Movie going had become an ingrained habit for Americans of all classes. The cinematic dreams and stories provided by Hollywood often seemed the most important elements in the fantasy lives of millions.

The large circulation newspapers and magazines, often with readerships in the millions, supplemented the radio and motion pictures in creating daily perceptions of mass society. By the 1920s popular entertainment had become at least as important a function of newspapers and magazines as informing readers of news events. Special women's pages, comic strips, voluminous numbers of ads for consumer products, home features, and a general emphasis on sensationalism in news stories had come to characterize most newspapers. Thus Lindbergh's flight created a usable hero even more attractive than such sports celebrities as Babe Ruth, the movie stars, or the wife murderers, whose antics filled so many column inches of the nation's press. Lindbergh came to represent the "older" standards of American manners and morals in a decade of dizzying change in these areas: an apparent non-drinker in a prohibition era drowning in bootleg gin and speakeasy scotch; a mama's boy in a country whose family structure wobbled badly with almost one out of five marriages ending in divorce by 1929 (Charles's parents, C.A. and Evangeline, had chosen a more traditional method for disguising a broken marriage through their quiet separation); a romantic whose secretive courtship and marriage of sedate Anne Morrow had captured the imagination of young Americans rapidly tiring of the "flaming youth" image which advertisers and writers alike had assigned to the so-called Roaring Twenties.

The "New" Woman

Many of the elements that screen writers, novelists, and publicists celebrated in the supposed emancipation of American women during the 1920s had their roots in earlier decades. If we drew a composite portrait of the "flapper" (as the jargon of the era described this liberated woman because of her loose, knee-length dresses and freer body movements), we would emerge with a picture of a restless figure perpetually partying—drinking, smoking cigarettes in elegant holders, and engaging in casual sex. Although the flapper may have held down a job and even voted, the center of her life remained private and hedonistic, not public and professional. She *lived*, or so her celebrants portrayed her, for nights in speakeasies, dancing the Black Bottom and Charleston, drinking bootleg gin, and making love in hideaway apartments, or (when even this frenetic life became boring) traveling abroad to France and Spain to continue the party with different playmates.

How common were such life-styles among American women? Many women, primarily

younger ones of urban middle- or upper-class back-grounds, took advantage of the loosened restrictions to cut loose from many personal and family constraints. But the "new morality" did not emerge as a necessary by-product of Warren G. Harding's election in 1920. Rather, it had begun evolving in many ways long before the so-called Jazz Age. In 1890, six out of every one hundred American marriages ended in divorce. The rate had tripled by 1929. Decades of gradual increases in the total number of divorces and separations made marital ruptures more "respectable" or at least customary among middle-class Americans. Freedom from family constraints on personal behavior, which had long characterized women of the small American upper class, also spread widely among

The flapper symbolized the new woman's daring—her flouting of traditional social and moral restraints. Short, bobbed hairdos, knee-length skirts, and sheer silk stockings identify these four women as flappers, as do their night club surroundings. (The Bettmann Archive)

middle-class women during the 1920s, though the process had roots in the Progressive era when women active in a variety of reform movements—suffrage, settlement house, child labor, and peace protests among them—began to shape more independent lives for themselves.

Long before the suffrage amendment became law in 1920, many of these middle-class women sought jobs and liberation from the suffocating constraints imposed upon them by the Victorian family image of Ideal Motherhood. They demanded, either in addition to or in place of a homemaker's life, the pleasures of a leisure-oriented society.

Working-class women continued to work. As early as 1880, women accounted for 15 percent of the work force, a figure that had risen to only 20 percent by the 1920s. Only 10 percent or less of the 10 million women employed by 1930 enjoyed professional lives in teaching, social work, or other relatively high-status careers. Achieving the vote in 1920 did not give women significant political influence; only a minority of women, most of them middle- and upper-class, exercised the right, and women held few political positions of importance before the 1930s.

Even the great flapper heroines of American literature, women like Daisy Buchanan in F. Scott Fitzgerald's *The Great Gatsby* and Lady Brett Ashley in Ernest Hemingway's *The Sun Also Rises,* often appeared not fully liberated but, rather, trapped between competing sets of standards. The typical new woman of the 1920s may have reflected these competing tugs even more directly than the fictional flappers: holding down a monotonous and probably menial job by day while enjoying the clubs and speakeasies at night; working in organizations such as The League of Women Voters or Alice Paul's Women's Party but also delighting in the ridicule heaped upon reformers and their pretentions by H. L. Mencken; living independent of her family yet deeply concerned over eventual marriage; college-educated but dealing in her professional and social lives with men fearful of extended contact with educated women; partially alienated from older cultural values but also realistically conceding their persistence and dominance.

The Literary Life: Alienation and Detachment

Had Charles Lindbergh managed to evade the pursuing crowds once he landed at Le Bourget and visited a Paris far removed from the diplomatic world of Myron Herrick or the small circle of fellow aviators, he would have encountered in the city a flourishing colony of expatriate American writers and artists at work creating novels, poems, plays, essays, and paintings, a world removed from the detested business civilization of their own country. Gertrude Stein, supreme patroness of the American writers and artists colony in Paris (herself an earlier expatriate), dubbed the younger group a "lost generation," but in truth, they seemed not "lost" but purposeful and obsessively dedicated to their respective talents.

For many of the younger writers—people such as E. E. Cummings, John Dos Passos, and Ernest Hemingway—Paris provided the type of refuge from bourgeois society that many experimental American artists and authors had sought in New York's Greenwich Village during the prewar years.

World War I had been the great moral dividing line for these and other writers—Maxwell Anderson and William Faulkner among them—destroying whatever sentiments they had of reform and idealism as they witnessed the conflict that killed tens of millions and toppled empires. "I was always embarrassed by the words 'sacred,' 'glorious,' and 'sacrifice,' and the expression 'in vain,'" wrote Ernest Hemingway, a volunteer ambulance driver in the Italian army during the war. "We had heard them . . . and read them, on proclamations . . . and I had seen nothing sacred, and the things that were glorious had no glory and the sacrifices were like the stockyards at Chicago if nothing was done with the meat except to bury it." The war had been fought, complained the poet Ezra Pound, for a "botched civilization." Expatriate Americans transformed their bitterness—toward war, toward the ruling classes, toward their own country, and toward themselves—into a series of literary masterworks: T. S. Eliot's *The Wasteland* and other poems, Ezra Pound's *Cantos,* Ernest Hemingway's novels *A Farewell to Arms* and *The Sun Also Rises* (along with dozens of terse and sardonic pieces of fiction, which transformed the art of the short story), John Dos Passos's *Three Soldiers* and *U.S.A.,* E. E. Cumming's *The Enormous Room,* and many others. They were a generation of talented writers who had fled abroad only to find there, as within the United States, societies marked mainly by "chaos and shifting values."

The talented writer F. Scott Fitzgerald, shown here in the 1920s, became an extraordinarily popular novelist during the decade with his novels of bittersweet romance and youthful pleasure-seeking. (Culver Pictures)

But one did not have to retreat across the ocean to experience alienation and disillusionment. Within the United States itself, the optimistic and exuberantly hopeful undertones of so much of pre-1914 American literature had few echoes in the writing of the 1920s. F. Scott Fitzgerald found fame and a large reading audience as early as 1920 with his novel *This Side of Paradise*, about the wealthy and flamboyant youth of a generation "grown up to find all Gods dead, all wars fought, all faiths in man shaken." Fitzgerald's pleasure-seeking, passion-ridden characters seemed much like their exile counterparts: morally ambivalent and torn between old duties and new desires: "a new

generation shouting the old cries, learning the old creeds, through a revery of long days and nights; . . . a new generation dedicated more than the last to the fear of poverty and the worship of success. . . . "

Middle American boosterism found its satirist in Sinclair Lewis, himself a Midwestern product (from the same Sauk Center, Minnesota, which had given refuge to Ole Manson, Lindbergh's grandfather). Lewis created memorable characters, like George F. Babbitt in the novel of that name, preoccupied with economic success yet still as restless and unhappy personally—ultimately as disaffected from the values of the New Era—as any expatriate. The dreary and provincial life of entrepreneurial small towns became Lewis's most popular theme in novels like *Main Street* and *Babbitt*, though his ridicule always had its wistful and melancholic edge. Sherwood Anderson denounced the hypocrisies of small-town life in more mordant terms in *Winesburg, Ohio*. William Faulkner, whose disillusionment stemmed initially from war experiences, took the decay of traditional Southern society as his theme and setting in a series of novels beginning in 1929 with *The Sound and the Fury*. The contrast between traditional, ineffectual Southern gentility and the aggressively boorish new entrepreneurs such as the Snopes family became a major organizing element in Faulkner's worldview. The "discordant, broken, faithless rhythms" that so many writers of the 1920s found in American society were elevated into dramatic tragedy during the decade by playwright Eugene O'Neill, the first American dramatist to enjoy world recognition and respect. Although O'Neill began his career during the more hopeful prewar period, powerful treatments of personal and familial disintegration such as *Emperor Jones, Desire Under the Elms, The Great God Brown*, and *Mourning Becomes Electra* would win him three Pulitzer Prizes for drama in the 1920s.

Easily the most boisterous critic of the business civilization of the 1920s, however, was the newspaperman, H. L. Mencken, whose columns and essays fired endless salvos against the vulgar, self-deluding qualities of the New Era. Sending reformers into political life was equivalent to sending virgins into brothels, he scoffed; democracy was a fraud and middle-class Americans merely the "booboisie"; the rich were no better than the poor; all politicians were frauds and mountebanks, and the United States was largely a country of dolts. Mencken attacked all institutions and beliefs that came to his attention, but his popularity during the 1920s suggested the moral uncertainty just below the surface of New Era confidence.

Not all the writers of this decade, of course, held the realities and the promise of American society in such contempt. Thomas Wolfe's *Look Homeward Angel* (1929) introduced a hopeful and ambitious novelist whose social disillusionment would come later. The poet Robert Frost continued producing books throughout the decade that incorporated a variety of personal moods, while the black writers of the Harlem Renaissance—poets Countee Cullen and Langston Hughes and novelists James Weldon Johnson and Jean Toomer among them—portrayed a sorrow-filled but still vigorous world of urban Negro experience. Ellen Glasgow's novels rediscovered the virtues of Southern traditions, and poets such as Hart Crane (in *The Bridge* particularly), Robinson Jeffers, and William Carlos Williams pursued separate personal visions of experience which, though bleak, often remained detached from the major thematic concerns of literary disillusionment. Novelist Theodore Dreiser, the great naturalist writer, published in 1925 his masterwork, *An American Tragedy*, which combined an indictment of American materialism and a relentlessly tragic view of experience that owed less to events of the decade than to Dreiser's earlier vision of American society.

But American literature, despite differences in style and theme, produced few cheerleaders and enthusiasts for the business civilization of the 1920s. The image of the entrepreneur emerged most starkly in Fitzgerald's portrayal of the elusive and unscrupulous hero of *The Great Gatsby*, a man from the Midwest who had gathered his wealth illegally only to construct a new life and identity for himself in a Long Island mansion. There, Jay Gatsby placed himself at "the service of a vast, vulgar, and meretricious beauty." Despite all his efforts, Gatsby proved unable to recapture the dreams of his youth any more than Henry Ford's Greenfield Village reconstruction could re-create the lost world of village America.

Some critics have compared Jay Gatsby and Charles Lindbergh: simple and adventurous men struggling for their dreams in a commercialized country, Gatsby failing to achieve his while Lindbergh attained all he sought—fame, fortune, and the woman he idolized. But the more important comparison is often neglected: Gatsby tried to break all links to his origins and moral inheritance (as did so many Americans of the time); Lindbergh did not. He forged an accommodation between older values and the new economic and social patterns of American society which allowed him to retain an extraordinary and very serviceable balance. To that extent, he understood (probably without ever having read the words) Fitzgerald's admonition about the tragedy of the Gatsbys and their moral confusion during the Twenties: "so we beat on," Fitzgerald wrote, "boats against the current, borne back ceaselessly into the past."

NATIONAL POLITICS

During the 1920s, both major parties traded in their pre-war Progressivism for an openly pro-business policy. Republicans controlled the White House from 1920 to 1932 and dominated Congress for most of those years. But such twentieth-century "Hamiltonianism"—providing help where necessary and averting regulation where possible so that American business interests could pursue their ends unimpeded by government—characterized the behavior of government from Woodrow Wilson's second term through FDR's inaugural in 1933. As a result of American preparedness for possible involvement in World War I, followed by involvement in the 1917–19 period, Wilson virtually abandoned his earlier concern for antitrust regulation and had curbed his antibusiness rhetoric. A number of leading businessmen returned to leading roles within wartime government agencies. Progressive concerns about giant corporations melted away during the war years. Maximizing productivity and minimizing labor unrest seemed far more important than reform to Wilson's closest advisers.

The sense of national emergency did lead to a significantly expanded economic role for the fed-

eral government and a good deal of centralized economic planning. The railroads were placed under federal management and remained so until after the war. There was government-ordered rationing of food supplies and raw materials, and federal subsidies or price guarantees to producers stimulated large-scale increases in commodity production. Although the Wilson administration encouraged unionization within war-related industries (mainly as a vehicle of more effective labor control) and increased taxes upon the wealthy, the war brought enormous prosperity to American business along with restored respectability.

With the return of peace and the resumption of normal agricultural and industrial production by European competitors came economic problems, especially for American farmers, who (encouraged by government subsidies and patriotic pleadings) had increased production beyond all market demand. As millions of soldiers returned to their civilian occupations after 1919, readjustment pressures also hit the industrial sector. Unemployment climbed, inflation soared, strikes proliferated, and social tensions increased in the postwar 1919–20 period. Politically the Democrats—the party in

power—suffered at the hands of an angry electorate. They lost many seats in the 1918 congressional elections, and as Wilson endured his final years in office an invalid in the White House, Republicans mobilized for the 1920 campaign.

Harding and the Return to Normalcy

The Republicans nominated a conservative Ohio senator and newspaper publisher named Warren Gamaliel Harding. He proclaimed as his campaign theme the end of domestic reform and foreign involvement. The United States, said Harding, needed "not heroism but healing, not nostrums but normalcy . . . not experiment but equipoise, not submergence in internationality but sustainment in triumphant nationality." Such gaseous utterances by the Republican nominee caused Mencken to describe Harding's words as a string of wet sponges and led Wilson's son-in-law William G. McAdoo, himself a leading candidate for the Democratic nomination, to call a Harding speech "an army of pompous phrases roving over the landscape in search of an idea; sometimes these meandering words would actually capture a straggling thought and bear it triumphantly, a prisoner in their midst, until it died of servitude and overwork." Strikingly handsome and muscular, the gray-haired Harding "looked" presidential. His running mate, Governor Calvin Coolidge of Massachusetts, was best known to the delegates as an opponent of a controversial 1919 police strike in Boston. Both Harding and Coolidge were party regulars and conservatives, far from sympathetic to the insurgent Republicanism of a Theodore Roosevelt or a Bob LaFollette.

The Democrats gave their nomination to a pair of Wilsonians, burdened with the defense of an unpopular administration in a time of economic distress. Former Governor James M. Cox of Ohio and former Assistant Secretary of the Navy Franklin Delano Roosevelt of New York took on the onerous task of beating back the Republican surge.

The measure of their failure can be seen in the electoral results. Harding won 60 percent of the vote, 16 million to Cox's 9 million, and he collected 404 electoral votes to Cox's 127, winning everywhere outside the South. (The Socialist candidate, Eugene V. Debs, once the leader of the American Railway Union during the Pullman strike, gained almost a million votes, though he was then serving a term in a federal penitentiary for opposing the war. Wilson, vindictively, had refused to free Debs, but Harding released the old Socialist soon after taking office.)

Harding's administration was thoroughly conservative in its policy perspectives, though his presidency was not as totally inactive as portrayed by his many critics. His appointments to high office included cronies, later shown to be both corrupt and incompetent, but also several thoughtful selections: the aluminum tycoon Andrew Mellon as secretary of the treasury, former New York governor and 1916 Republican presidential candidate Charles Evan Hughes as secretary of state, and the head of American food relief efforts in Europe during and after World War I, Herbert Hoover, as secretary of commerce.

All three shaped new directions in American foreign and domestic policy. Mellon set out to cut government spending and to reduce taxes on the wealthy. In 1921, he succeeded in getting Congress to repeal the wartime excess profits tax,

and he later shaped tax policies favorable to the business community and to persons with high incomes. Congress quickly reversed the downward trend of tariff legislation, passing the Fordney-McCumber tariff bill of 1922 which led to massive increases in tariffs on both industrial and agricultural products. Hoover began a policy of "alliance with the great trade associations," encouraging consolidations within American industry and rarely invoking the antitrust statutes. "So long as I am Attorney General," declared Harding's close adviser Harry Daugherty, "I am not going unnecessarily to harass [business]men who have unwittingly run counter to the statutes." The Bureau of the Budget began its operations in the Harding years, and generally, government agencies went out of their way to seek methods to assist the business community.

In foreign affairs, although Harding had campaigned on a nationalist and isolationist platform, Secretary Hughes organized the Washington Disarmament Conference of 1921, at which the United States took the lead in successfully negotiating significant reductions in naval strength among the world's leading maritime powers.

In the end, however, Harding's presidency will be remembered less for its scattering of achievements than for the extraordinary spread of corruption at high levels of government. The moral tone of the Executive Mansion under Harding could not have been a greater contrast to the one exemplified by the president who preceded him and the one who followed. Theodore Roosevelt's daughter, Alice Roosevelt Longworth (wife of the speaker of the House, Nicholas Longworth), described one visit to the White House, where she found the president and various of his cronies at their ease: "the air heavy with tobacco smoke, trays with bottles containing every imaginable brand of whiskey [despite Prohibition] . . . cards and poker chips at hand, — a general atmosphere of waistcoat unbuttoned, feet on desk, and spitoons alongside." Harding, Mrs. Longworth concluded, "was not a bad man. He was just a slob."

In fact, Harding played poker only a few evenings a week, served liquor in violation of the law (along with millions of his countrymen) but rarely drank excessively, and still managed to work extremely hard at the job of president, far harder than his puritanical successor, Calvin Coolidge, who slept many an afternoon away. ("Four-fifths of all our troubles in this life would disappear," Coolidge once observed, "if we would only sit down and keep still.")

But Harding's life still displayed the moral laxness of a George F. Babbitt rather than the stern self-discipline of a Charles Lindbergh. After his death, it emerged that Harding had engaged (at different times) in at least two extramarital affairs, one with the wife of a hometown friend. Though weak and self-indulgent, Harding was no fool and no crook. But his small-town geniality, intellectual confusion, and casual attitude toward government appointments made him the victim of unscrupulous friends and associates, known collectively and informally to contemporaries as "the Ohio gang," who pillaged the federal treasury, solicited bribes, and made corruption an administration byword before Harding caught on. "My God, this is a hell of a job," he complained to journalist William Allen White in the spring of 1923, shortly before his death. "I have no trouble with my enemies. . . . But my damned friends, my God-damned friends, ... they're the ones that keep me walking the floor nights!"

The scandals that robbed Harding of sleep were of various kinds. The head of the Veterans Bureau, a friend of the president's named Charles Forbes, sold government property illegally. He went to jail. Another Harding friend, Jesse Smith, peddled influence at the Justice Department. He committed suicide. The custodian of alien property, Colonel Thomas W. Miller, was convicted of criminal conspiracy to defraud the U.S. government for the illegal disposition of profitable German chemical company patents being supervised by the government. (Miller worked in collaboration with Attorney General Daugherty and other leading Republicans in the fraud, but at two trials after Harding's death, Daugherty managed to escape conviction because of split juries.)

Harding's most unfortunate appointment, aside from Daugherty's, proved to be that of New Mexico Senator Albert B. Fall as secretary of the interior. In 1921, Fall and Navy Secretary Denby secretly leased valuable government oil reserves to private interests. Edward L. Doheny's company obtained the lease to California's Elk Hills reserve, while Harry F. Sinclair received one to Wyoming's Teapot Dome reserve. Investigation later revealed that the two oil men had given Fall more than $400,000 in gifts of cash and bonds, "loans," and cattle in exchange for the transfer of the leases. Denby and Fall both resigned, and Fall and Sinclair were each convicted. Fall became the first member of the cabinet to go to prison.

Harding never lived to see the outcome of the scandals. Nervous and depressed, he left on a speaking tour of the West and, while in Seattle in late July, suffered an attack first diagnosed as food poisoning. Physicians later discovered that he may have suffered a heart attack, and in any event, he died of natural causes in San Francisco on August 2, 1923. (Unfounded rumors circulated that he may have been poisoned by Mrs. Harding.) Tired, despondent because of the accumulation of evidence of betrayal by his closest Ohio friends, prone to high blood pressure, Warren Harding died before most of his fellow Americans had recognized the dreary failures of his administration.

Coolidge and the Triumph of New Era Politics

Calvin Coolidge, the president who (four years after taking office) would greet Charles Lindbergh upon his return from Paris, may have recognized in the young aviator qualities that he prized in himself: among them a self-discipline, a stern sense of duty, a taciturn disposition, and a wry ability to handle public attention without noticeably altering one's personal style.

Coolidge, whom William Allen White called a "Puritan in Babylon," took immediate steps to erase the stains of corruption. He quickly prosecuted "Ohio Gang" lawbreakers and chose, as Daugherty's replacement as attorney general, the former dean of Columbia Law School, Harlan Fiske Stone. Stone, in turn, placed in charge of a revamped Bureau of Investigation within the Justice Department (later the F.B.I.) a young and ambitious bureaucrat—untainted by Harding administration machinations—named J. Edgar Hoover, who established merit procedures for appointment and other reforms. Coolidge left the better Harding cabinet appointees in their positions.

The New Englander Coolidge quickly became a popular figure among Americans, an ascetic and crisp executive whose every appearance reinforced the public perception of honesty and sobriety. The contrast with the slack, gregarious Harding could not have been starker. Coolidge seldom smiled (Mrs. Longworth observed acidly that the new president had been "weaned on a dill pickle"), and he presented himself to his countrymen as an antidote to the Roaring Twenties aspect of the Harding years—the old virtues replacing the new vices.

Coolidge believed passionately, if that word could be applied to so limp a figure, in the benevolence of American capitalism and free enterprise. He admired men of wealth and accepted absolutely the notion that continued economic prosperity rested upon the abilities of business leaders. Under Coolidge, even more than under Harding, the federal government did virtually nothing to impede mergers and the development of trade associations, or to stop price fixing. By the mid-1920s, the federal regulatory agencies bulged with Republican appointees dedicated to noninterference with business. Coolidge's appointee as chairman of the Federal Trade Commission, a businessman named William T. Humphrey, went to the extent of denouncing the work of his own agency as oppressive and socialistic.

Although Wall Street speculation disturbed Coolidge, he did nothing to restrain the stock market. Such speculation increased with the triumph of Secretary of the Treasury Mellon's program of tax reduction. In 1924, Mellon (who served throughout the 1920s) persuaded Congress to cut maximum taxes on high incomes. At the same time, however, pressure from progressive legislators (who remained influential in Congress throughout the decade, despite the decline of reform at the presidential level) levied new gift taxes and higher estate taxes, and Coolidge signed the tax measure reluctantly. Two years later, Mellon succeeded in wiping out the progressive tax legacy of the Wilson years. Coolidge had won reelection by then, and progressives in Congress had become demoralized, failing to prevent passage of the Revenue Act of 1926, which wiped out the gift tax, cut estate taxes in half, and cut the maximum tax on incomes from 40 to 20 percent. In 1928, further reductions in corporate taxes passed in Congress.

The business community of the New Era received the advantages of *both* laissez-faire *and* Hamiltonian government policy: a free hand *and* special privileges. Supreme Court decisions during the 1920s confirmed corporate supremacy. Thus, in *Bailey* v. *Drexel Furniture Company* (1922), the Court declared void a federal law that taxed profits of companies using child labor, thereby reinforcing an earlier decision in *Hammer* v. *Dagenhart* (1918) that struck down a 1916 federal statute barring shipment of goods made by child labor in interstate commerce. The Court also declared unconstitutional a minimum wage law for the District of Columbia (*Adkins* v. *Childrens' Hospital*, 1923.) In a series of decisions during the decade, courts subjected unions to provisions of the Clayton Antitrust Act so that employers could once again use antitrust injunctions (as they had with the earlier Sherman Act) to break strikes. At every level of the federal and state court system, the 1920s saw the triumph of corporate power and the subordination of trade unions.

With the country prospering and the Democratic opposition divided, the Republicans faced happily the 1924 election and the prospects of a race with Coolidge at the head of the ticket. Coolidge's nomination came effortlessly, whereas the Democrats took a record 103 ballots at their New York convention before deciding on a nominee. The party could not choose between Governor Alfred E. Smith of New York—candidate of the big-city Democratic machines, urban ethnics, and opponents of Prohibition—and his opponent, William G. McAdoo, whose chief support came from the rural and small-town Southern and Western delegations. Finally, an exhausted convention nominated Wall Street lawyer John W. Davis, whose close connection with J. P. Morgan and Company and with large corporate interests guaranteed there would be no basic disagreement between the two major nominees on economic support for business.

Reformers in both parties broke away to organize a new Progressive party. Composed of insurgents from the major parties, labor and agrarian

Anarchist leader Alexander Berkman speaks to an I.W.W. rally in New York's Union Square. Both Berkman and his close associate in anarchist organizing, Emma Goldman, were deported during the "Red Scare" which followed World War I. (The Bettmann Archive)

reform leaders, socialists, and others dissatisfied with New Era politics, they nominated Wisconsin's Robert LaFollette for the presidency. Progressives stressed their old antitrust, anti-monopolistic planks, and their strength seemed confined largely to a regional power base in the Midwest, although they also ran well in the Northeastern cities.

Coolidge won easily in November, however, taking 54 percent of the popular vote to Davis's 29 percent (in electoral votes Coolidge had 382 to Davis's 136). Davis could win only twelve states, all in the South, while the Progressives out-tallied the Democrats in another dozen states and took 16 percent of the total vote. But the Progressives beat *both* parties in only one state, LaFollette's Wiscon-

sin, and with the death of LaFollette in 1925, America's independent reformers were left leaderless. Conservatives, however, interpreted Coolidge's victory as a mandate for continuing and extending the pro-business policies of New Era government.

Cultural Tensions and Rural–Urban Conflict

The Democrats' disaster in 1924 had its roots in the divisions between urban and rural wings of the party. These tensions had exploded during World War I, continued in the postwar period, and reached new heights of intensity during the 1920s. Periodically in American society, waves of hysteria over alleged threats to the safety of American democracy—as defined by the hysterical—have swept through the culture and eroded normal standards of political decorum. One such wave of intolerance led to the persecution of millions of Americans who opposed (or were thought to oppose) involvement in World War I: pacifists, Socialists, radical labor unions such as the Industrial Workers of the World (the "Wobblies"), members of such ethnic groups as German-Americans and Irish-Americans, and antiwar progressives all felt the brunt of officially sanctioned repression during the 1917–19 period. A conservative superpatriotic assault on radical, pro-German, or pacifist groups or individuals during the war itself spilled over in the 1919–20 period into a Red Scare, focusing on the supposed threat posed by Bolshevik supporters of the Russian Revolution.

Although the Red Scare's effects had begun to subside toward the closing months of the Wilson administration, the climate of cultural suspicion which provoked it continued. The 1920s saw the growth in numbers and political influence of a new Ku Klux Klan, widespread agitation for immigration restriction, an assault upon unionism, a general attack upon radicalism, a strident reassertion of fundamentalist religious beliefs, and an assiduous effort to enforce the Prohibition Amendment. These trends and movements contributed to the unrelenting stresses of conflict between older and newer groups in America. Rural and urban cultures fought for control of the country's destiny.

Wartime Coercion and Postwar Red Scare

American involvement in World War I did not create the intense suspicions toward dissenters and immigrants that characterized the 1917–19 period, yet the war encouraged government action to sustain and strengthen those attitudes. Millions of Americans objected to the country's participation in the war and, although over 24 million Americans registered for the draft in 1917–18, more than 163,000 men were arrested for refusing to register.

To encourage zealous public support for the United States's role in the conflict, Congress created the Committee on Public Information (COPI), a massive propaganda agency, which mobilized thousands of publicists from all walks of American life to create pamphlets explaining the Wilson administration's idealistic war aims and denouncing the Germans — normally referred to as the "Huns" — for alleged atrocities against civilian populations during battle. Directed by a Colorado progressive named George Creel, the COPI sent seventy-five thousand speakers around the country, who gave short talks designed to stir pro-war emotions ("four-minute men," as they were called), and encouraged production of motion pictures dramatizing the horrors of German brutalities in the field. Within a matter of months, involvement in the war became highly popular with most Americans, but the cost was the unleashing of often irrational hatreds and suspicions, directed not only toward the foreign enemy but especially toward those in the country thought to be "subversive" of the war effort. "Americanization" movements pressured immigrants into abandoning foreign-sounding names and bilingual family households. German words were Anglicized (sauerkraut, for example, became "Liberty cabbage"); a number of schools stopped teaching German; and German-Americans lived under the shadow of suspected disloyalty.

To quell internal dissent, Congress passed several statutes with the endorsement of the Wilson administration. The Espionage Act of 1917 provided tough jail sentences and fines for persons found guilty of aiding the enemy, obstructing recruitment for the army, or encouraging disloyalty. The statute also gave the attorney general power to ban the mailing of material — newspapers, pamphlets, and letters, for example — alleged to be seditious. The following year, the Sedition Act amended the Espionage Act to provide harsh penalties for a variety of vaguely worded "crimes": using "disloyal, profane, scurrilous, or abusive language" about the U.S. government, flag, military, or Constitution; making false statements that interfered with prosecution of the war; or advocating, teaching, or defending such acts. Other statutes also encouraged strict censorship of the foreign-language press and international mail or wires. Over fifteen hundred Americans went to jail for violating these wartime statutes, including Eugene V. Debs, the Socialist leader, and a number of other major figures in pacifist and Socialist ranks. Debs received a twenty-year sentence for a single speech advocating draft resistance. At the same time, the government moved to suppress the leaders of the Wobblies (I.W.W.) in a series of cases throughout the West, where the union was strongest, and thousands of informal civilian marshals worked in cooperation with the Department of Justice's Bureau of Investigation to harass suspected pro-Germans within their communities. Rarely did the offense involved meet the "clear and present danger" standard enunciated by the Supreme Court in 1919 when upholding the Espionage Act in *Schenck* v. *U.S.* The question, Justice Oliver Wendell Holmes wrote for the majority, was whether the words used were of such nature and in such circumstances "as to create a clear and present danger that they will bring about the substantive evils that Congress has a right to prevent." For the most part, those convicted posed no significant threat to the war effort and were neither traitors nor seditious; they simply opposed American involvement in the war.

The Red Scare which followed the armistice ending World War I continued to feed the anxiety among native-born Americans about alien dangers within the United States. The focus shifted from Germany to Russia, where the Revolution of 1917 had brought Lenin's Bolsheviks to power. Wilson had opposed the Bolshevik government's participation in the Versailles Peace Conference, and during 1918–20, American troops participated in several interventions in Russia. Fear of revolutionary unrest within the United States became widespread, however, for reasons that had little to do with Bolshevism and much to do with postwar social conflicts.

Labor unrest was a major component in the new climate of fear. In 1919 alone, unions called thirty-six hundred strikes involving over 4 million workers. The labor unions' wartime gains seemed threatened by the postwar decline in production and rise in unemployment. A general strike paralyzed Seattle for five days in January 1919. Officials who crushed the strike denounced the strikers as "Bolshevik-inspired." That same year, a massive but unsuccessful strike of steelworkers, many of whose leaders had backgrounds in the I.W.W. and Socialist movements, also raised the specter of labor radicalism, although the steelworkers' demands were hardly radical.

Conflicts between black and white workers led to race riots in cities such as Chicago, Washington, D.C., and St. Louis. Militant Negroes, many of whom had just returned from military service abroad, demanded decent economic and social treatment in the Northern cities to which hundreds of thousands of blacks had migrated from the rural South during the previous half decade. The white response often came in a return to violence, and along with the race riots, lynchings increased in number from thirty-six in 1917 to seventy-six in 1919. That same year, the revived Ku Klux Klan made its most significant membership gain since Reconstruction, taking on at least 100,000 members in the South alone and (more ominous still) spreading to the North.

With Wilson paralyzed by his earlier stroke, leadership in the pursuit of "subversives" fell to Attorney General A. Mitchell Palmer. Old-stock Americans like Palmer found little difference between the "Bolshevik" ideas of socialists (disregarding the fact that most socialists favored peaceful political change), the demands of union workers (especially immigrant workers whom Palmer believed susceptible to "foreign" influences), the protests by Negro veterans, and the continued agitation of feminists who wanted more than the vote. Palmer wrote in 1920:

Like a prairie-fire, the blaze of revolution was sweeping over every American institution of law and order a year ago. It was eating its way into the homes of the American workmen, its sharp tongues of revolutionary heat were licking the altars of the churches, leaping into the belfry of the school bell, crawling into the sacred corners of American homes, seeking to replace marriage vows with libertine laws, burning up the foundations of society.

Against such "enemies," what restraint could be shown? Palmer used a horde of government agents (foremost among them J. Edgar Hoover) along with private detectives to raid the headquarters of labor unions and radical organizations. In the process, he rounded up thousands of aliens (most of whom had committed no crime) and illegally deported hundreds. Playing on the popular identification of radicalism and terrorism, Palmer tried to exploit the Red Scare to win himself the Democratic presidential nomination in 1920. In April, he warned that Bolsheviks and others would revolt on May Day (May 1). Public buildings and officials' homes were specially guarded and state militias called out—but nothing happened on May Day. Palmer had overreached himself.

Congress soon turned to investigating *not* "radicalism" but Palmer's own behavior. In mid-September, when a wagonload of bombs exploded during the lunch hour on Wall Street, killing thirty-three people, injuring two hundred, Palmer again denounced a "Bolshevik plot" to overthrow the government. This time, the public took the Wall Street tragedy in stride as the evident work of demented anarchists or nonpolitical lunatics. By the end of 1920, with Harding elected president and promising an end to reform and foreign adventures, Americans discarded the hysteria that had sustained Palmer and his supporters for two years. "Too much has been said about Bolshevism in America," President-elect Harding opined, and his countrymen, turning to material pursuits and private pleasures, agreed.

Yet the intolerant attitudes of 1917–20 lived on into the Twenties. The labor movement had been tainted by the charge of alleged "radicalism" and remained on the defensive throughout the 1920s. Legislation to restrict immigration received

When a wagon filled with dynamite and scrap iron exploded in New York City's crowded Wall Street section on September 16, 1920, thirty-eight people were killed and hundreds injured. The perpetrators of the bombing were never tracked down. (Brown Brothers)

a decisive boost, and ultra-nativist sentiment combined with racist attitudes to swell the membership of the Ku Klux Klan. Despite the best efforts of the American Civil Liberties Union (ACLU), the rights of dissenting Americans were less protected in the 1920s than they had been prior to the ACLU's creation. The legacy of intolerance and hatred proved difficult to overcome in a country fiercely divided between rural and urban cultural perspectives.

"Two Nations": Rural–Urban Conflict

Conflicts between old-stock, native-born Protestant Americans—most populous in the country's small cities, towns, and rural areas—and newer immigrant arrivals, mainly Catholics and, to a lesser extent, Jews—centered in the industrial cities of the Northeast and Midwest—recurred in the years following World War I. Politically, the Democrats internalized the struggle, while the Republicans proved more successful in deflecting cultural arguments by focusing on a common pro-business set of New Era economic policies. The ur-

ban–rural struggle took a number of forms, and although the 1920 census showed that for the first time a majority of Americans lived in urban areas, new Americans generally remained on the defensive.

Immigration Restriction Hostility toward foreigners, especially those from Southern and Eastern Europe, continued after the easing of the Red Scare. In 1921 and again in 1924, Congress passed laws that discriminated blatantly against immigrants from Southern and Eastern Europe. The 1924 statute allocated immigration quotas to European countries in proportion to their "national origin" within the United States in 1890. Also, in the 1921 Act, Congress restricted the total number of immigrants to be admitted yearly. "America must be kept American," concurred Calvin Coolidge while signing the 1924 "National Origins Act."

The anti-immigrant passions of many old-stock Americans emerged blatantly during the long national debate over the Sacco-Vanzetti case, an issue that the novelist John Dos Passos noted would polarize the "two nations" of American culture: rural native-born and immigrant urban. Nicola Sacco and Bartolomeo Vanzetti, Italian-born anarchists, were accused in 1920 of murder during a robbery at South Braintree, Massachusetts. After their conviction and imposition of the death sentence, appeals began. Supporters argued that the two men had been convicted because of their radical views rather than on the basis of the evidence. Distinguished lawyers, writers, journalists, artists, and thousands of ordinary Americans took up their cause and demanded, at the least, clemency and a new trial. Despite protests throughout the world, both men were executed on August 23, 1927. The debate over their guilt or innocence continues to this day, but the trial record showed that their status as immigrants and foreign-born anarchist radicals undoubtedly prejudiced the fairness of the trial.

Racism Most native-born white Americans during the 1920s considered themselves "racially" superior not only to the country's subordinated Negro and Indian populations but also to the Catholic and Jewish immigrants against whom the restrictive legislation had been designed. The term "race" was often used in the broadest sense by white Americans of Anglo-Saxon, Nordic, and Teutonic backgrounds to justify discrimination against groups that threatened to transform America into a pluralistic, urban society.

Blacks, especially, bore the brunt of the racial segregation, in the North (where migrations of the previous decade had brought hundreds of thousands of Negroes) as well as in the South. Twenty percent of the black population lived outside the South by 1920, a 100 percent increase since 1910. After the race riots of 1917–19, white leaders reaffirmed their support for "white supremacy" in all areas of American life: Segregated public facilities and schools were common throughout the country, though legalized only in the South and border states. Violence continued throughout the 1920s, and 416 blacks were lynched between 1918 and 1927. The savage threat of lynching under which Negroes lived, especially in the South, led to House passage of an anti-lynching statute which Senate filibusters by Southern

members always managed to sidetrack. The National Association for the Advancement of Colored People (NAACP), organized during the Progressive era (see Chapter 34, pp. 655), continued its always difficult and sometimes dangerous work.

In New York and other cities that had experienced large influxes of Negroes, many thousands of blacks joined a new movement that abandoned racial integration as a goal and, instead, preached black nationalism: self-help, racial pride, and an eventual return to African homelands. Led by an eloquent West Indian orator named Marcus Garvey, and centered in New York's Harlem, the Universal Negro Improvement Association developed black-controlled businesses, including a Black Star Steamship Line, in which numerous blacks invested their hard-earned savings. But Garvey proved an inept businessman and both his entrepreneurial schemes and his "back to Africa" plans collapsed by mid-decade. After Garvey's 1925 conviction for mail fraud, his following turned to other saviors, or within themselves.

Rebirth of the Ku Klux Klan Although the resurgent Ku Klux Klan remained viciously anti-Negro during the 1920s, its anger was also directed toward Catholics and Jews—urban, immigrant newcomers. Klan propaganda played upon the fear of massive changes in cultural values, which deeply troubled native-born Americans: "The Klan. . . . has now come to speak for the great mass of Americans of the old pioneer stock," wrote Imperial Wizard Hiram W. Evans in 1926. "We believe that it does fairly and faithfully represent them, and one proof lies in their support." Evans was not exaggerating. Although the Klan engaged in acts of violence—lynchings, whippings, and other brutalities—it campaigned openly and enjoyed widespread support among "respectable" old-stock Americans in communities throughout the country. National Klan membership peaked at 2 million persons in 1924, and during the entire decade the Klan recruited an estimated 4 to 6 million Americans, primarily native-born. Unlike the rural Klan of Reconstruction days, its counterpart during the 1920s wielded great power in the cities where it appealed particularly to "country people," migrants to cities from small towns.

The 1920s: From "New Era" to Economic Collapse **733**

The Klan had its greatest influence and largest membership *not* in the South but in the Midwest. The "Invisible Empire," as some called it, used its secret rituals, cross burnings, white-hooded and -robed assemblages, and threats of violence to gain significant influence within both major political parties, especially among the Democrats. At the 1924 convention, Klan supporters succeeded in keeping the delegates from denouncing the Klan by name, and Klan-supported candidates included sixteen senators and eleven governors, along with a host of lesser officeholders. So confident and public had the Klan become that in August 1925 more than fifty thousand Klansmen strutted for hours down Washington, D.C.'s Pennsylvania Avenue in a parade of strength.

The Klan's influence declined rapidly after 1925, however, when its key national organizer, an Indianan named David Stephenson, was convicted of murder and sentenced to life in prison. Stephenson began revealing Klan secrets—the violence, the public officials corrupted, the internal strife—and a tarnished KKK lost its remaining shreds of respectability. Membership plunged downward, and the Klan's political power faded drastically for the remainder of the decade.

Resurgence of Religious Fundamentalism In the 1920s, fundamentalist churches experienced a surge of new membership and popularity. Looking around them, country people saw the frightening evidences of massive social and cultural changes: "new" immigrant masses, Catholic and Jewish; "liberated" Negroes no longer willing to accept subordination; wholesale violation of Prohibition; casual sexual mores; and other elements of life in urban America that seemed to them to pose direct threats to the old ways and the old faith. (When one of the new evangelists, a colorful preacher named Aimee Semple McPherson, walked on stage in her Los Angeles temple carting a pail filled with milk and proceeded to ask her audience which of those present had lived on farms, the entire audience stood up!)

Nor did the spread of more secular and rationalist approaches to religion please the theologically conservative fundamentalist preachers and their constituents. The crux of political con-

For more than half of his life, which lasted almost a century from Reconstruction to the 1960s, William Edward Burghardt Du Bois exerted an enormous influence as America's leading black intellectual. In a varied career that led him from the Republican to the Communist party, Du Bois made his mark as historian, sociologist, poet, teacher, editor, civil-rights leader, and pan-Africanist.

Born on February 23, 1868, W. E. B. Du Bois encountered racial prejudice as a boy even in the Berkshire mountain town of Great Barrington, Massachusetts. Unable to attend Harvard because he lacked sufficient money, Du Bois became the beneficiary of a scholarship fund, collected by neighboring whites, which allowed him to attend Fisk University, a Negro college in Nashville, Tennessee. After earning a bachelor's degree at Fisk in 1888, Du Bois finally entered Harvard University. He gained his B.A. in 1890, his M.A. in 1891, and after a period of study in Germany, his Ph.D. from Harvard in 1895. A dissertation on the African slave trade earned him the first Harvard doctorate ever awarded to a black student.

Du Bois taught for a short time at Ohio's Wilberforce College before accepting a fellowship from the University of Pennsylvania to study conditions in Philadelphia's black slums. The book that resulted from this study, *The Philadelphia Negro*, presented the most careful examination of urban black problems done up to that point. The young scholar moved to Atlanta in 1896 to teach at Atlanta University, where he remained until 1910, growing more deeply involved in the practical issues of Southern black life.

With the publication of his *Souls of Black Folks* in 1903, Du Bois declared his rebellion against the accommodationist arguments of Booker T. Washington (see Chapter 34, p. 649). In

troversy between religious fundamentalists and "modernists" in the 1920s came over the teaching of Darwinian evolutionary doctrine. A half-dozen Southern states passed laws forbidding such teaching, but it was in Tennessee in July 1925 that the controversy came to a head and reached national

this eloquent and anguished book, Du Bois celebrated Negro persistence in adversity, examined the dilemma of living as a subordinated black within dominant white America, and declared prophetically: "The problem of the twentieth century is the problem of the color line."

Rejecting the Washington philosophy of accepting segregation while fostering economic skills within the black community, Du Bois urged instead that black Americans carry their struggle into the political arena, protesting second-class treatment, demanding voting and other civil rights, and all the while developing an educated black leadership (a "Talented Tenth," as it became known). These ideas were advanced at a meeting of black activists—under Du Bois's leadership—at Fort Erie, Ontario, in July 1905, where they founded the "Niagara Movement." There Du Bois coauthored a "Declaration" calling for (among other things) voting rights for all blacks and an end to caste discrimination based upon color. Although the Niagara Movement dissolved after five national conferences, it helped to lay the groundwork for the founding of the National Association for the Advancement of Colored People (NAACP) in 1909.

From that moment, for the next several decades, Du Bois's career and the NAACP's growth were intertwined. He left Atlanta for New York in 1910 to become the organization's director of publicity and research and to edit its magazine, *The Crisis*, remaining in this capacity for the next twenty-two years before returning to Atlanta. In 1919, Du Bois organized the Pan-African Congress and served in the forefront of movements calling for independence for Europe's African colonies from that time until his death. A prolific writer, Du Bois published novels, poems, histories, and autobiographies as well as a stream of articles.

W. E. B. Du Bois

(Courtesy, The Moorland-Spingarn Research Center, Howard University)

Although Du Bois continued until the post-World War II period to hold important leadership posts at intervals in the NAACP, his relations with the group remained tempestuous and he frequently resigned because of policy disagreements. He began to turn increasingly toward a Marxist, pro-Soviet position during the 1940s, and in 1961 he formally joined the Communist party. He emigrated to Ghana in 1962 and died there the following year at the age of ninety-five. Throughout his long struggle for racial justice, W. E. B. Du Bois had reflected in his work and writings the anguish first revealed in *Souls of Black Folks* sixty years before his death: "I saw the race-hatred of the whites as I had never dreamed of it before—naked and unashamed!—I emerged into full manhood, with the ruins of some ideals about me, but with others planted above the stars . . . determined, even unto stubbornness, to fight the good fight."

proportions. Earlier that year, Tennessee had passed an "anti-evolution" statute, and a Dayton, Tennessee, high school biology teacher named John Scopes decided to challenge the law. After Scopes's arrest, two of the country's most important public figures journeyed to Dayton to take part in the trial. William Jennings Bryan, Democratic politician and fundamentalist, defended the statute (and the Bible), while Clarence Darrow, the agnostic criminal lawyer and iconoclast, defended Scopes (and Darwin). The champion of religion and the advocate of science struggled in a courtroom drama that captured the country's attention. Darrow subjected Bryan to a withering cross-examination, ridiculing his belief in a literal interpretation of the Bible, but in the end Scopes was convicted, fined, and fired. The law stood firm. Fundamentalism remained a powerful force within the society, if only because it reflected the anguished response of many devout old-stock Americans to their own economic deprivation and to the complex confusions of modern society. Bryan, who died shortly after the Scopes trial, remained a hero to his cultural compatriots, and the problem of controlling the ideas and curriculum which public school and public university students should be taught has remained a recurrent dilemma up to our own time.

Prohibition Most Protestants, not only fundamentalists, rallied to support the Eighteenth Amendment, ratified in 1919, which prohibited "the manufacture, sale, or transportation of intoxicating liquors" anywhere in the United States. Enforcement of Prohibition sharply divided rural and urban America, creating a vast market for illegal alcohol among the millions who refused to go "dry." The "noble experiment" of prohibition became big business, as crime syndicates in the larger cities made several billion dollars or more yearly from manufacturing and distributing "bootleg" liquor. The criminals often smuggled the liquor in from abroad, sold it either to wholesalers or to the thousands of "speakeasies"—establishments often providing entertainment as well as booze—which sprang up throughout the country. New York City alone had thirty-two thousand speakeasies in the 1920s.

Despite many arrests and convictions annually for violating the Volstead Act, which Congress passed to enforce the Eighteenth Amendment, those Americans interested in drinking had little trouble finding supplies wherever they lived. Gang wars among underworld syndicates engaged in bootlegging occasioned numerous murders, with the blood toll apparently greatest in the Chicago area, where Al Capone emerged as the leader of the city's underworld and the key figure in liquor traffic. Supporters of Prohibition viewed the amendment as a necessary check upon the "wets"

Chicago gangland boss Al Capone murdered and connived his way into control of the lucrative illegal liquor traffic in the Midwest. (Bettmann/Springer Film Archive)

—those who either drank hard liquor themselves or, though dry, favored repeal of Prohibition. The wets dominated the nation's cities and seemed most numerous among the Catholics and Jews of urban America.[1] For that reason alone, Prohibition became an issue that split the Democratic party down the middle by 1924. When Alfred E. Smith won the Democratic nomination in 1928, the issue of Prohibition—and the *other* cultural issues dividing rural and urban Americans—finally came to a head.

---

[1] In 1933 the Twenty-First Amendment was ratified, repealing the Eighteenth Amendment and again legalizing the sale of hard liquor except where it violated state or local statutes.

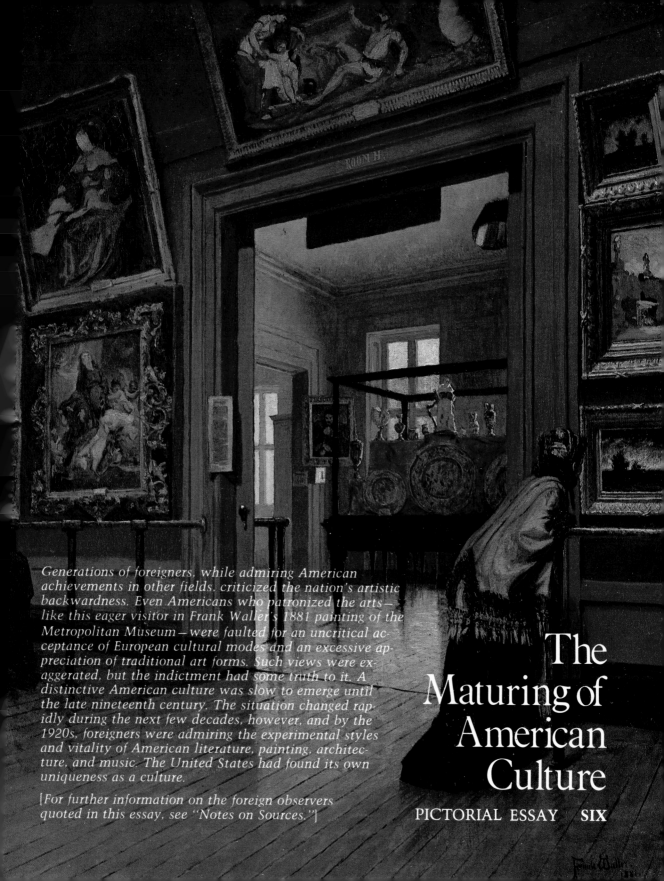

Generations of foreigners, while admiring American
achievements in other fields, criticized the nation's artistic
backwardness. Even Americans who patronized the arts—
like this eager visitor in Frank Waller's 1881 painting of the
Metropolitan Museum—were faulted for an uncritical acceptance of European cultural modes and an excessive appreciation of traditional art forms. Such views were exaggerated, but the indictment had some truth to it. A
distinctive American culture was slow to emerge until
the late nineteenth century. The situation changed rapidly during the next few decades, however, and by the
1920s, foreigners were admiring the experimental styles
and vitality of American literature, painting, architecture, and music. The United States had found its own
uniqueness as a culture.

[For further information on the foreign observers
quoted in this essay, see "Notes on Sources."]

The
Maturing of
American
Culture

PICTORIAL ESSAY   SIX

American art is still in a stage of evolution; the painters of today are the precursors of those who shall adorn the Golden Age which is to come. Though there have been, and are, individual artists of distinguished merit and ability, art itself is not yet fully developed nor understood. The nation has had hitherto neither time, opportunity, nor inclination to interest itself intelligently in the fine arts.

[COUNT VAY DE VAYA UND LUSKOD, 1908]

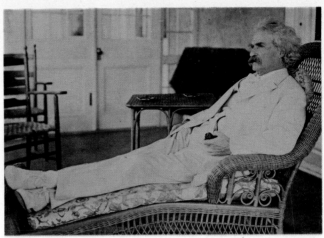

Mark Twain in 1907. By this time the writer had gained worldwide acclaim for such books as *The Adventures of Tom Sawyer* (1876), *Life on the Mississippi* (1883), and *The Adventures of Huckleberry Finn* (1885).

Behold! Mark Twain had curled himself up in the big armchair, and I was smoking reverently, as befits one in the presence of his superior. The thing that struck me first was that he was an elderly man; yet, after a minute's thought, I perceived that it was otherwise, and in five minutes, the eyes looking at me, I saw that the gray hair was an accident of the most trivial. He was quite young. I was shaking his hand, I was smoking his cigar, and I was hearing him talk — this man I had learned to love and admire fourteen thousand miles away.

[RUDYARD KIPLING, 1889]

The Last of Old Westminster, painted by James Abbott McNeill Whistler in 1862. The scene is London, where Whistler lived for much of his life. This work was followed by a number of outstanding portraits, including the famous one of his mother (which be actually titled *An Arrangement in Grey and Black*).

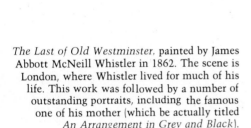

American paintings are no longer strange to Europe. In the art division of the last Paris Exposition, Americans took their share of the honors, and they are highly appreciated at most of the Berlin and Munich picture shows. Sargent and Whistler are the best known. Sargent, as the painter of elegant ladies, prosperous men, and interesting children, has undoubtedly the surest and most refined gift with his brush of any son of the New World. Whistler is doubtless the greater, the real sovereign. He fathoms each human riddle, and expresses it intangibly, mysteriously. Everything is mood and suggestion, the dull and heavy is lightened, the whole is rendered in rich twilight zones.

[HUGO MÜNSTERBERG, 1904]

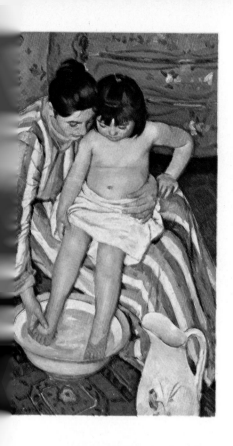

Miss Cassatt is a true phenomenon. In more than one of her canvases she is on the verge of becoming a notable artist with unparalleled natural feeling, penetrating observation, and a welcome subjection before the model which is the accomplishment of peerless artists.

[ALBERT WOLFF, 1881]

The Bath, by Mary Cassatt, dates from about 1891. The artist—who lived most of her adult life in Paris—liked to paint mothers and children. She communicated feelings of warmth and tenderness without sentimentality.

The taste for plastic art [in the United States] has slowly worked upward. Recent movements have left many beautiful examples of sculpture. Cities are jealously watchful now that only real works of art shall be erected, and that monuments which are to be seen by millions of people shall be really characteristic examples of good art. More than anything else, sculpture has at length come into a closer sympathy with architecture than perhaps it has in any other country. Such a work as Saint-Gaudens' Shaw Memorial in Boston is among the most beautiful examples of modern sculpture. Vigorous and mature is the American, in plastic art as well as in poetry.

[HUGO MÜNSTERBERG, 1904]

Mr. and Mrs. Isaac Newton Phelps Stokes, portrayed by John Singer Sargent in 1897. These prominent New Yorkers, though pictured in informal dress, epitomize the wealth and refinement typical of Sargent's subjects.

This work, showing Augustus Saint-Gaudens in his studio, was painted by Kenyon Cox in 1908. The sculptor was known for his public statuary, including Lincoln, in Lincoln Park, Chicago; General Sherman, near Central Park in New York City; and the Shaw Memorial on Boston Common.

People are inclined to smile at me when I suggest that you in America are at the commencement of a period of fine and vigorous art. The signs, they say, are all the other way. Of course you ought to know best. All the same, I stick to my opinion with British obstinacy, and believe I shall see it justified.

[JOHN GALSWORTHY, 1919]

Willa Cather builds her imagined world almost as solidly as our five senses build the universe around us. She has within herself a sensitivity that constantly presents her with a body of material which would overwhelm most of us. She has also a quality of mountain-pony sturdiness that makes her push on unfatigued under her load and give an accurate account of every part of it.

[REBECCA WEST, 1927]

On the threshold of her career, in 1902, Willa Cather had yet to gain a name for herself. She became noted for such novels as *O Pioneers!* (1913) and *My Antonia* (1918).

Six O'Clock was painted by John Sloan in 1912. He was one of a group called The Eight. They were known more familiarly as the Ashcan School because they depicted scenes of everyday city life rather than the more formal and traditional subjects favored by academic artists.

Sloan's canvas of girls under the elevated has more of New York in it than anything else I know.

[DIEGO RIVERA, 1942]

Robert Frost, as seen by artist James Chapin in 1929. The New England writer had by this time published some of his best-known poems, among them "Mending Wall," "Birches," and "Stopping by Woods on a Snowy Evening."

Characteristic of Frank Lloyd Wright's so-called prairie houses is this home in River Forest, Illinois. It was built in 1908. Wright's later works, noted for their daring innovation, included the Imperial Hotel in Tokyo, the Johnson administration building in Racine, Wisconsin, and the Guggenheim Museum in New York City.

The mission which this land has, like all others, is to discover its own being, to fulfill its task of representing itself. And if one puts his ear to the ground, then one hears millions of forces at work to forge and shape this individual being.

[ANTON ERKELENZ, 1927]

Eugene O'Neill is one of the really great figures in modern drama. O'Neill is an example of what I mean when I say America is producing, and will produce in ever greater quantities, an art I feel is indigenous; it belongs to the American soil. No European dramatist could possibly have written those plays. The drama, under him, has found a new type of artistic expression.

[GERHART HAUPTMANN, 1932]

Eugene O'Neill in 1921, at the start of his career. His greatest plays came later: *Desire Under the Elms* (1924), *Mourning Becomes Electra* (1931), and *The Iceman Cometh* (1946). In 1936 he became the first American playwright to win the Nobel Prize.

A scene from *Beyond the Horizon,* by O'Neill. Produced in 1920, it was the first full-length play by the dramatist to be acted.

What she gives us is a kind of sculpture in transition. Imagine a dozen statues expressive, say, of the cardinal phases of despair — the poses and gestures and facial expressions of the moment in which each of these phases reaches its maximum of intensity. Then imagine some hundreds of statues that represent, in faultless beauty, every one of the moments of slow transition between these cardinal phases, and you get the art of Isadora Duncan.

[ERNEST NEWMAN, 1921]

The great American photographer Edward Steichen captured some of the magic of dancer Isadora Duncan in this 1921 photo, taken at the Parthenon. Her flowing Grecian costumes and striking interpretive power transformed modern dance.

Gershwin's Rhapsody [in Blue] is by far the most interesting thing of its kind I have yet met with. It really has ideas and they work themselves out in a way that interests the musical hearer. Perhaps it is better not to prophesy. What is at present certain is that Gershwin has written something for a jazz orchestra that is really music, not a mechanical box of tricks.

[ERNEST NEWMAN, 1924]

Mexican artist David Siqueiros painted this *Portrait in a Concert Hall* (George Gershwin) in 1936. The composer, who died the following year, had followed his *Rhapsody in Blue* (1923) with *An American in Paris* (1928) and *Porgy and Bess* (1935).

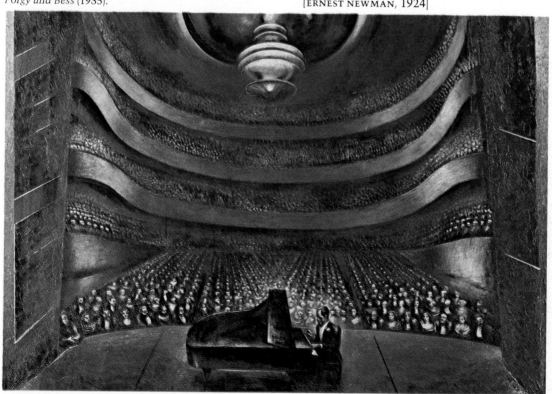

The outstanding achievement of American literature is the swiftness with which it strode from provincialism to half-acknowledged universality. Before 1800 there is nothing, save in the field of politics, which could command, or even deserve to command, a European audience; by 1900 it is true to say that there were few forms of creative effort in which Americans had not done work of the highest quality. America had moved to the very front of the cosmic stage. Henceforth it might be disliked; it could not be neglected.

[HAROLD LASKI, 1948]

It is hardly an exaggeration to say that Ernest Hemingway, more than any of his American colleagues, makes us feel we are confronted by a still young nation which seeks and finds its exact form of expression.

[NOBEL PRIZE CITATION, 1954]

Lunched with Sinclair Lewis. He is full of imagination. He tells me he wrote four or five novels before he wrote **Main Street**, but they were not successes. I asked him why that had not discouraged him. He laughed, he said it was no use being discouraged, that writing novels was all he could do, he might starve at it, but he was incapable of any other form of work. (Truly an artist!)

[CLARE SHERIDAN, 1921]

The young Ernest Hemingway was painted by Henry Strater in 1922. His best work, yet to come, included *The Sun Also Rises* (1926), *A Farewell to Arms* (1929), and *For Whom the Bell Tolls* (1940).

Sinclair Lewis, photographed with his wife in 1916. A year after his meeting with Clare Sheridan, he published one of his best-known novels, *Babbitt*. In 1930 he became the first American to win the Nobel Prize for literature.

The Election of 1928

After Calvin Coolidge announced that he did not "choose to run" in 1928, his party turned to Herbert C. Hoover, a shaper of the traditions and policies of the New Era. Known as "the Great Engineer," Hoover came from a small-town Western background and had risen to fame and fortune, Horatio Alger–style, first as a mining engineer and then through investments. He turned to public service, becoming food administrator during World War I and, later, as secretary of commerce under both Harding and Coolidge. Like Lindbergh, Hoover seemed a representative of old-stock, rural American values, despite his command of modern technology and new-found wealth.

Hoover's Democratic opponent, Alfred Smith, could not have contrasted more sharply in personality with the Great Engineer, though Smith too supported private enterprise and admired successful businessmen and bankers, many of whom had supported his presidential candidacy since 1924. Smith was a city product, a slum child who had risen to political prominence and some wealth while filling many political posts before becoming governor of New York. Although a reform governor, Smith shared Hoover's beliefs in the efficacy of New Era economic policies. His nomination in 1928 was an American milestone: the first new American to seek the country's highest office — Irish-American, Catholic, and anti-Prohibitionist, closely aligned with the Tammany Hall Democratic machine in New York, and identified strongly with immigrant Americans from backgrounds similar to his own.

Hoover, like Lindbergh, was a hero to small-town America. But Al Smith's New York ("Noo Yawk") accent gave away his ghetto origins and ignited emotional (often subconscious) reactions among those who listened to him. For better or worse, Smith epitomized ward politics, saloons, Catholic churches or synagogues, and the disturbing life of urban America.

Quite apart from the sincere opposition of the Prohibitionists, "the objection to Tammany, [and] the sectional objection to New York," Walter Lippmann had written in 1927,

> there is an opposition to Smith which is as authentic and, it seems to me, as poignant as his support. It is inspired by the feeling that the clamorous life of the city should not be acknowledged as the American ideal. . . . That, at bottom, is the opposition to Al Smith, and not the nonsense about setting up the Pope in the East Wing of the White House. . . . Here is no trivial conflict. Here are the new people, clamoring to be admitted to America, and there are the older people defending their household gods.

Lippmann was correct, and the election of 1928 became the most remarkable "symbolic" contest for the presidency since the McKinley–Bryan battle in 1896. Each candidate represented the best and most clear-cut definition of the values characterizing the culture that produced him. Small-town and urban America met head-on in 1928, and (for the last time) the cities lost. Hoover carried forty states, even cutting into Democratic territory in the solid South, and winning over 58 percent of the popular vote. Smith won the larger cities and received more popular votes than had the Democratic nominees in 1920 and 1924, but the issues lined up against him proved decisive. Not only did anti-Catholics, anti-Prohibitionists, and the opponents of urban immigrant culture eagerly champion Hoover, but just as important, Hoover's determination to continue a pro-business line appealed strongly to middle-class Americans. Even a large segment of the industrial working class voted for Hoover, who promised that the country neared "the final triumph over poverty."

But the election of 1928 also accelerated major shifts in voting behavior patterns. Working-class women voted in significant numbers for the first time in 1928, most of them favoring Smith. Throughout the country's cities, Democratic voting majorities were taking shape. If Hoover split the South, taking over 200 counties that had never voted Republican before, Smith swung 122 Northern counties out of their traditional GOP affiliations (a majority of these containing large Catholic majorities). The nomination of Al Smith and the election of 1928 helped define the forces — most of the South, urban immigrants, farmers, and workers — that would later create the New Deal coalition. None of this, of course, was certain at the time. Republican control of the country never seemed more secure than in the months following the 1928 election. The stock market responded to the voters' reaffirmation of New Era economics by spurting upward in dizzying fashion; the common stock average rose from 117 in December 1928 to 225 in September 1929, while brokers more than *doubled* money borrowed for additional stock speculations in the two years from 1927 to 1929. With that kind of Bull Market, what could go wrong?

UNPROSPEROUS AMERICA AND THE CAUSES OF ECONOMIC COLLAPSE

Despite the general prosperity of the Twenties, contrary signs were plentiful. Millions of ordinary Americans joined the great banking houses and financiers investing in the stock market, so that sales on the New York Stock Exchange quadrupled between 1923 and 1929. To keep pace with investor demand, stock prices rose well in excess of normal profit–production ratios. The Treasury Department, Federal Reserve Board, and other government agencies encouraged such speculation through easy credit policies. Wealthy investors, thanks to Mellon's tax policies, had plenty of money to play with. By the end of the decade, the total of American public and private debts amounted to no less than one-third of the national wealth. And business increasingly used its profits to increase corporate dividends rather than to reinvest in new plants or equipment.

The stock market led the easy money parade. Most investors borrowed from brokers. These "call loans" amounted to $1 billion or $1.5 billion during the early 1920s, then rose to $3 billion by 1926, $6 billion by 1928, and a staggering $8.5 billion by October 1929. Normal interest on such loans was about 5 percent, but interest rates rose to 12 percent by December 1928 and over 20 percent by March 1929 (the increase reflecting concern over the stability of many speculative investments). Only in early 1929 did most brokerage houses raise their margin requirements to as much as 50 percent (in short, speculators now had to put up half the money invested upon purchasing stocks). Throughout 1928–29, therefore, brokerage practices and the generally exuberant behavior of investors gave much cause for concern.

Other little-recognized weaknesses in the economy of the 1920s could have alerted Americans to the trouble ahead. First, income remained unevenly distributed to such an extent that, even with installment buying, the purchasing power of Americans had reached its limit. The unequal distribution of income grew more pronounced during the years of New Era economics, with one-third of national income in the hands of 5 percent of the population and one-half the income going to only 20 percent of the people, while the bottom 40 percent of the population received only a quarter of national income.

Income distribution aside, millions of Americans in both rural and urban areas lived out the "prosperous Twenties" in poverty, unaided by government funds when they became unemployed or when their crops failed. The overwhelming majority of Americans had no aggregate savings during this period. Industrial workers had lost many of the protections gained by unions during World War I, and union membership declined from 20 percent of the factory work force to about 10 percent.

Employers used both carrot and stick to subordinate their workers, and the tactics generally worked. Encouraging a limited measure of "welfare capitalism" and stock purchasing through the American Plan, businessmen also used company unions, court injunctions, labor spies, hired goons, and blacklists of union organizers to ensure "peaceful" and stable labor–management relations. The major unions, including the A. F. of L., themselves became increasingly conservative during this period. When major strikes broke out in industries such as textiles and mining, corporations —especially in the South—used local law enforcement authorities in strikebreaking.

For American farmers, the 1920s meant recession and low market prices. Despite the visibility of consumer affluence in the cities, farm purchasing power remained limited. Thus only a minority of the nation's farmers had running water or electricity in their homes, and such items as telephones and radios remained available to a far smaller percentage of rural Americans than elsewhere in the country. Under the American Farm Bureau's leadership, farmers turned increasingly to agricultural cooperatives—more than twelve thousand existed in 1921—to develop their own organized "trade associations" capable of negotiating successfully for crop-wide increases in wholesale prices. More often than not, such cooperatives could not mobilize a sufficiently large percentage of output to cause more than short-term gains in market price. Although more than 40 percent of the population still lived in rural areas, agriculture received a steadily declining share of national income, (less than 10 percent by 1929). Millions of farmers joined the procession of migrants to the cities seeking nonagricultural employment for which few had been trained.

Only the wealthiest farmers or those employed on corporate-owned farms could often afford the mechanized equipment and new technology needed to make a success of commercial agriculture in the New Era. For most farmers, the enterprise had become too difficult to manage as individual entrepreneurs, and their spokesmen turned increasingly to the prospect of government subsidy. These efforts centered around the McNary-Haugen bill, a measure that would have guaranteed farmers fixed high prices for their products based upon average market prices paid during the prosperous 1909–14 period. The bill provided for guaranteed government maintenance of such high prices, tariffs on imported farm goods, and the "dumping" or sale abroad of any surplus American farm commodities which could not be absorbed domestically at the subsidized or "parity" price. The bill contained no mechanism for enforcing limits on the amounts farmers could produce. All this made the legislation extremely popular among farmers and manufacturers dependent upon a prosperous rural sector. Congress passed the McNary-Haugen Act in 1927 only to have it vetoed by President Coolidge, who appeared more disturbed about "class legislation" favoring farmers than he did about the protective tariffs which buttressed business. The following year, Congress again passed the measure, but again Coolidge vetoed it. The Eastern-controlled, business-oriented Republican administration remained, to the end of the decade, indifferent to the small farmer.

Neither American farmers nor workers, then, enjoyed either the political clout or the economic resources needed to gain recognition from government at the height of the New Era. The fact that a large majority of Americans—immigrants, workers, farmers, blacks, most women, Hispanics, Indians, and others—lacked the purchasing power needed for full participation in the middle-class consumption prosperity of the 1920s did not seem to unduly trouble those in power.

Nor did the other warning signs of disaster attract much notice at the time. Although much of the decade's prosperity had been created by the automobile and construction booms, residential building declined from $5 billion in 1925 to $3 billion by 1929. The auto companies, while continuing to prosper, grew at a much slower rate after 1925. Thus decreases in auto production led directly to declines in allied industries, such as steel, rubber tires, and glass. The market for autos had become glutted, with most Americans who could afford cars—even on the most liberal credit terms—having already purchased them (26.5 million were on the road in 1929). The business cycle was headed toward an inevitable and major downturn unless some new source of investment in either the private or the public sector could be found to reverse upward the rate of production in basic industries. No such source emerged.

At the heart of the economy's warped and unbalanced character during the 1920s was the underlying assumption of the New Era that the interests of American business and the *public* interest were identical. When firms siphoned off productivity gains largely into higher profits and stock dividends, rather than raising wages or cutting prices in order to encourage consumer purchases, they ensured an eventual decline in buying power which threatened prosperity. The federal government chose to support almost any policy that the business community pursued, and with labor unions weak during the decade, no "countervailing" economic forces existed to challenge business actions.

The corporate sector, during the decade, increased its profits at more than twice the rate of growth in productivity, and in many cases profits became so large that corporations no longer needed to borrow funds in the money markets (thereby inhibiting the influence of Federal Reserve banks in controlling speculative growth). By the late

1920s corporations often invested their profits in the stock market for greater returns than more sober investments in plant expansion could provide. This process reinforced the ruinous stock market speculation of 1928–29 which raised stock prices to all-time highs.

The policies the federal government followed under the Harding and Coolidge administrations (policies inherited by Hoover, who helped shape many of them while secretary of commerce) reinforced the imbalances and encouraged the excesses within the U.S. economy. Tax cuts for the wealthy and for corporations reinforced the disastrous maldistribution of national income. The refusal of regulatory agencies to supervise and control the merger process left corporations insensitive to outside direction or to changes in market demand; abandonment of antitrust enforcement fostered rigidity within the private sector. Support for high tariffs made it more difficult for foreign countries to trade with the United States and hence either to purchase American goods or to pay the billions of dollars in war debts owed to the American government and private financial interests. European industry during the 1920s became increasingly dependent for investment upon massive infusions of American capital.

Because of government indifference and the overconfident perspective most Americans had toward corporate behavior during the 1920s, the major structural weaknesses in the economy were overlooked. Few analysts commented at the time on the perilous degree to which most major industries had overexpanded production past any valid profit ratio, or the basic weaknesses in overall purchasing power because of the maldistribution of income that allowed one-twentieth of the population to receive one-third of the country's personal income annually. Although the weaknesses in an almost unregulated banking system were also apparent during the decade, as over seven thousand banks failed and closed their doors even during the New Era years, little was done to make banking and finance more stable and responsible. The Austrian economist Joseph Schumpeter correctly complained about the emergence within U.S. banks, holding companies, and other financial institutions of a "new type of bank executive," a "banker-

promoter [who] financed speculation and loaded the banks with dubious assets, sometimes for personal profit, other times out of civic or corporate loyalties." For every Charles Lindbergh who emerged with a venturous scheme requiring speculative local financing—as his flight required from St. Louis bankers—a hundred more questionable self-promoters stepped forward to claim a piece of the action. If unregulated businesses and unrestrained banks were not enough unstabilizing forces within the economy, there was also an unreliable overdependence for prosperity upon the sale of consumer durable goods—automobiles, homes, electrical equipment, and other products. In hard times these unnecessary purchases were often the first to be deferred, as they were when the "Great Bull Market" of the 1920s finally crashed and collapsed in 1929.

THE NEW ERA COLLAPSES: CRASH AND DEPRESSION

Optimism about the economic future remained almost universal as late as the fall of 1929. "The economic condition of the world," opined financier-analyst Bernard Baruch in June, "seems on the verge of a great upward movement." The country's leading economist, Irving Fisher of Yale, agreed. "Stock prices have reached what looks like a permanently high plateau." Hoover, Mellon, and other administration figures shared this assessment. As if to confirm their confidence, the stock market kept climbing in the summer of 1929. American Telephone & Telegraph rose from 209 to 303 in those months, while General Motors went from 268 to 391. The high point was reached on September 3, and then the slide began, at first slowly, but continuously until the disastrous days of late October. Hoover and the country soon found themselves in a depression that seemed unresponsive to government moves. The downward economic spiral seemed irreversible.

Americans were unprepared for the sudden end of New Era prosperity, and the luckless Hoover plodded through his four agonizing years in office (1929–33) unable to halt the devastating depression that gathered momentum daily. A sense of desper-

President Herbert Hoover entered the White House in 1929 with the country still enjoying the last months of "New Era" prosperity, only to find himself wrestling with the unexpected and catastrophic problems of a stock market crash and national depression. (The Bettmann Archive)

ation gripped the nation, as all the old solutions and beliefs of the 1920s crumbled.

The Stock Market Crash

"The stock market crash," wrote literary critic Edmund Wilson, "was to count for us almost like a rending of the earth in preparation for the Day of Judgment." Despite overlooked danger signs of decline on the New York Stock Market beginning in September, the *plunge* began suddenly and unexpectedly on Thursday, October 24. Thirteen million shares were sold that day, and prices plummeted across the board: General Electric lost 47½ points, United States Steel 17½, and Westinghouse 34½. The news stunned the country, especially the 1.5 million Americans who had been "playing the market." Reassuring words

came from political and economic leaders. Hoover: "The fundamental business of the country . . . is on a sound and prosperous basis." J. P. Morgan, Jr.: "There has been a little distress selling on the Stock Exchange. I see nothing in the present situation that is either menacing or warrants pessimism."

Then came Black Tuesday, October 29. The market index for industrial stocks plunged 43 points and 16 million shares were sold. By the end of November the market index had declined to 224 from a September high of 452. As brokers called in billions in loans to clients, many of whom found themselves suddenly bankrupt and unable to repay debts incurred to finance market speculations, the downward slide continued. By mid-November about $30 billion in market value of listed stocks had been wiped out, losses that reached $75 billion by the summer of 1932.

The stock market hit bottom in July 1932, when the industrials index stood at 58 (from the 452 high in September 1929). Even the nation's blue-chip corporate stocks showed the dimensions of the catastrophe: A.T.&T. plunged from a high of 304 in 1929 to 72 in 1932; U.S. Steel went from 262 to 22; G.M. from 73 to 8; Montgomery Ward from 138 to 4. The speculative frenzy of the 1920s had ended in destitution and depression for millions as the collapse spread through the economy. By 1932, thousands of veterans who marched on Washington demanding immediate payment of a veterans' bonus would chant:

> Mellon pulled the whistle,
> Hoover rang the bell.
> Wall Street gave the signal,
> And the country went to hell.

Depression America

Not a corner of the American economy seemed capable of escaping the decline triggered by the stock market collapse. Five thousand banks failed during the Depression's first three years, wiping out billions in deposits and completely bankrupting millions of Americans (at the time the U.S. government had not yet begun insuring bank deposits). National income declined from $88 bil-

This graphic photograph of a "run" on a Vineland, New Jersey, bank during the early years of the depression shows a crowd of depositors crowding the bank's doors to try and retrieve their uninsured savings while the money lasted. (Collection of Ann Bloomenstein)

lion in 1929 to $40 billion by 1933, with a comparable drop in farm income (from $12 to $5 billion) and an even steeper slide in foreign trade from $10 billion to less than $3 billion. By 1932, industrial production had fallen to 54 percent of 1929 levels (or somewhat less than the 1913 levels, which wiped out the gains of the war years and the New Era).

Factories closed almost daily, and those still open cut their work forces and placed many remaining workers on part-time schedules. During the three years after the market crash, an average of more than 100,000 American workers were fired each week. Unemployment grew from 4 million in October 1930 to 7 million by the same period in 1931 and to more than 12 million (possibly as much as 14 or 15 million) by the fall of 1932. Whole cities appeared virtually out of work. In New York, there were a million jobless by 1932, another 600,000 in Chicago; 50 percent of the Cleveland work force was on the streets, 60 percent in Akron, and 80 percent in Toledo. In New England, 120,000 of the region's 280,000 textile

workers were unemployed by 1930 with more to follow. Probably a third of the country's 120 million residents in 1932 were either unemployed or belonged to a family of unemployed workers.

The Depression discredited the nation's politicians and economists, who offered little in the way of solutions beyond a continuing barrage of predictions that the worst had occurred and recovery was "just around the corner." Many ordinary Americans shared that opinion during the early years of collapse, basking in the "cheerful desperation" of a hope-suffused culture. "WASN'T THE DEPRESSION TERRIBLE?" ran a popular past-tense sign on billboards as unemployment continued to mount. One of 1931's most popular songs was the ditty "Life Is Just a Bowl of Cherries," and it would have been difficult to find many economic pundits in the 1929–33 period who predicted long-lasting distress. Will Rogers spoofed the reluctance of many Americans to sacrifice their luxuries in the midst of crisis: "We are the first nation in the history of the world," he wrote, "to go to the poor house in an automobile."

It was clear by 1931, however, that the Depression did not simply affect the United States but had become a worldwide calamity. The collapse of the European banking system in 1931 endangered repayment of billions owed to Americans and provoked more bank failures. The European panic also sealed the fate of American farmers, who faced overseas producers dumping products and driving down market prices still further. The world price of wheat went from $1.05 a bushel in 1929 to $.39 by 1932, corn from $.81 to $.33 a bushel, and cotton from $.17 a pound to only $.06.

"Cheerful desperation" gave way to despair and apathy as conditions worsened. At first, many unemployed Americans blamed themselves for the shame of poverty: "Melancholia and defeat were . . . the hallmarks" even of *protests* by the unemployed during the Hoover years, as millions began wandering the countryside and cities seeking work. Novelist Sherwood Anderson remembered "picking up hitchhikers on the highway who apologized for being down and out. They accepted the whole responsibility themselves." In July 1932 the *New Yorker* found Americans "in a sad, but not a rebellious mood." Studies of the jobless showed "that in broad terms, the unemployed who were active devoted their energy to looking for a job or surviving without one; the others were apathetic." Many observers noted a "sense of imminent catastrophe, not among those to whom it had already happened, but among those who might be next." The poet Carl Sandburg wrote:

Have you seen men handed refusals
 till they began to laugh
 at the notion of ever landing a job again—
Muttering with the laugh,
 "It's driving me nuts and the family too,
Mumbling of hoodoos and jinx,
 fear of defeat creeping in their vitals—
Have you never seen this?

The nation had entered into a period of profound psychological as well as economic depression. Millions had become alienated from traditional sources of authority—families, political parties, employers, government. None seemed able to offer effective help in coping with the catastrophe. In 1932 alone, more than 100,000 Americans, mainly Eastern European immigrants, applied for jobs in the Soviet Union. Each day's paper brought new tales of horror: the Pennsylvania man arrested in 1930 for stealing a loaf of bread from a neighbor to feed his starving children —who then hanged himself; the increasing number of suicides of unemployed workers; the street corner apple sellers; the malnutrition among the poor in every section of the country, unable to get adequate food (New York City alone had an average daily number of thirty-one breadlines in 1931); the makeshift communities ("Hoovervilles") that lined the empty lots and parks of major cities. Relief funds had run out by 1932 as many state and local governments went bankrupt. Many thousands roamed the country's roads seeking work, food, shelter—*something.*

Occasionally desperation turned into violence. The unemployed staged "hunger marches" on city halls demanding help. Membership in both the Socialist and the Communist parties increased significantly. Some cities witnessed food riots, and in the Midwest members of the insurgent Farm Holiday Movement withheld low-priced crops from market (often by the threat of violence against non-cooperating farmers) and forcibly prevented foreclosures on farms and homes.

Protests against the Hoover administration climaxed in the summer of 1932, when about seventeen thousand unemployed veterans descended upon Washington, D.C., as part of a "Bonus Expeditionary Force." They demanded the immediate payment of compensation certificates for veterans which Congress had authorized but which were not redeemable until 1945. The "invading" servicemen remained remarkably peaceful. Many in the Bonus Army camped on the Anacostia Flats across the Potomac from central Washington; others used abandoned government buildings and shacks near the Capitol itself. The house passed a $2.4 billion authorization bill to redeem the remaining certificates on June 15, but two days later the Senate defeated the measure. After the administration provided funds for travel expenses, a number of the veterans left Washington.

Thousands more refused to disband, however, and they clashed with D.C. police on July 28.

Amid the bright lights of Times Square hundreds of New York's hungry formed bread lines in 1932. Ironically, scarcity was not the problem. As Socialist Norman Thomas remarked: "It remained for us to invent bread lines knee-deep in wheat." (Wide World Photos)

President Hoover then ordered U.S. Army troops, led by Chief of Staff General Douglas MacArthur (among whose aides were two future World War II heroes, Dwight D. Eisenhower and George S. Patton), to drive the veterans out of Washington. In a bloody, day-long encounter, in which the largely unarmed and unresisting veterans faced four troops of cavalry, four infantry companies, and even some tanks, the remnants of the Bonus Army were routed from the city and their Anacostia shacks were burned. Although Hoover and MacArthur considered the ex-soldiers "a mob animated by the essence of revolution" (MacArthur's words), that judgment was as erroneous and morally obtuse as

many others made by the Hoover administration in its unsuccessful efforts to cope with the human realities of America's worst economic disaster.

Hoover and the Response to Depression

Herbert Hoover had come to the presidency a believer in far more active government involvement in the economy than his Republican predecessors, Harding and Coolidge. When the stock market crash turned into a depression, Hoover remained unfazed: "The cure for such storms is action." In the next four years, Hoover retained his faith in the fundamental soundness of the American economy. Throughout his presidency, he encouraged *voluntary* approaches to economic recovery where possible, with government acting as a catalyst in the process. Thus, a few days after the crash, Hoover began holding White House conferences of businessmen, bureaucrats, bankers, and labor leaders to discuss the crisis. Hoover believed that such cooperation between the private sector and government would restore New Era prosperity in a relatively short period of time. "He calls here," Senator Hiram Johnson observed caustically, "those who have much and have lost little." Yet none of the many conferences succeeded in delaying the downturns in the economy.

The President made his greatest mistake in underestimating the seriousness of the American economy's structural problems. A Hoover-supported tax cut passed by Congress in December 1929 had little economic impact, given the already low level of taxation at the time. (The federal budget of 1929–30, parenthetically, was the last balanced budget in American history.)

The Hawley-Smoot tariff bill, which passed Congress in June 1930, raised import duties to their highest levels (increasing duties on 75 farm products and 925 manufacturing items). It signaled a revival of economic nationalism in the United States at the expense of world trade at the very moment when the European economy was collapsing. Despite the bill's obvious negative impact upon our ability to sell American products abroad, if foreign countries retaliated by raising their tariffs, and despite its negative impact upon collecting the $12–15 billion in American investments abroad, Hoover rejected the almost unanimous advice of economists and signed the measure. The Hawley-Smoot tariff helped open an international tariff war between the United States and its European trading partners at the worst possible time.

Nor did the Hoover-sponsored agricultural program prove any more successful in halting the decline in farm income. The same emphasis on "voluntarism" characterized his approach in this area as well. The Agricultural Marketing Act of 1929 created a Federal Farm Board with a $500 million fund to buy farm surpluses (that were pushing down market prices) while encouraging the development of marketing cooperatives among crop producers. Although farmers organized many such cooperatives in the next two years, farm prices continued to decline, especially after the European crash in 1931. Since the Federal Farm Board could not enforce limits on production, its program failed to shore up American market prices. Dump-

ing of farm commodities at low prices became common throughout Europe. American crop production, meanwhile, continued to increase, further deflating world prices.

Hoover consistently opposed direct federal assistance to the needy. He urged instead two *indirect* approaches: federal assistance to states and localities, enabling them to borrow money for public works construction (thereby putting people into temporary government jobs while the private sector recovered), and federal coordination of voluntary and state–local relief efforts. Both methods proved grossly inadequate to combat the widespread hunger and distress. Political repercussions were predictable. In the 1930 elections, the Democrats gained control of the House and eight additional Senate seats, the first Republican setback since 1916.

By late 1931 Hoover agreed to revise some assumptions concerning voluntary approaches to economic recovery. A comprehensive recovery program requiring extensive federal participation evolved, and Congress agreed in 1932, despite bitter Democratic opposition. The main cog of Hoover's recovery machine was the Reconstruction Finance Corporation (RFC), passed by Congress in February 1932, capitalized at $500 million, and authorized to borrow an additional $1.5 billion. The RFC operated on the premise that a massive program of government loans to banks, railroads, life insurance companies, farm mortgage associations, and building and loan associations would stop the downward spiral, replacing private investment sources and helping to restore pre-1929 levels of purchasing power and employment. The RFC opened offices in fifty cities and within six months had loaned over $1.2 billion to five thousand borrowers. In the process, it restored some confidence in financial and credit institutions and saved the American financial structure from complete collapse. Also, Hoover pushed for a Federal Home Loan Bank Act, passed by Congress in July. This created a chain of banks authorized to loan money to institutions holding home mortgages and (hopefully) prevent foreclosures.

On the question of direct relief, however, Hoover stood firm and negative. He vetoed an election-year, Democratic-sponsored measure, the July

1932 Wagner-Garner Bill, which extended federal employment programs to states that had none and provided for more public works jobs and direct aid to individuals. Instead, Hoover supported an alternative measure, passed after the veto, in which Congress authorized the RFC to loan state and local agencies up to $1.5 billion to sponsor self-liquidating public works programs and provided an additional $300 million in temporary loans for bankrupt states unable to finance any relief efforts. Even those provisions could have helped only a small minority of Americans then enduring joblessness, poverty, and dire want as a result of the Depression.

In the end, although some of Hoover's bolder initiatives—the Federal Farm Board, the RFC, and the Federal Home Loan Bank—anticipated programs that would be developed under Democratic auspices in the 1930s, the administration remained far too cautious in its approach to America's most severe economic crisis. Hoover seemed, often, more concerned with saving the *business* of America than with helping individual Americans after four years of unrelieved depression. It was too much to take (for long), especially from a man who had blithely promised in 1928 to end poverty in the United States forever.

The Election of 1932

Not since the sectional crisis of 1860 had the United States begun an election year in so anguished and uncertain a state as in 1932. There seemed no end to the bad news and misery. While 25 percent of the work force looked for jobs that no longer existed, millions picked through garbage cans or roamed the highways in search of food. More ominous still, the unemployed and the ruined had finally begun to become restive. Farm Holiday Movement activists threatened "rebellion" in the heartland. Protests and marches of the unemployed increased in number and ferocity within the cities. In March 1932, five thousand jobless workers marched on Ford's River Rouge plant in Dearborn (near Detroit) demanding work. It took scores of company guards and local police to disperse the mob. Four men were killed. The head of Bethlehem Steel, Charles M. Schwab, spoke for

many bankers, industrialists, and politicians at the time when he said simply: "I'm afraid, every man is afraid."

Probably any Democrat could have defeated Herbert Hoover in 1932. The job went to the governor of New York, Franklin Delano Roosevelt, who broke with tradition and flew to Chicago to accept the Democratic nomination in person. "I pledge you, I pledge myself," Roosevelt told the convention, "to a new deal for the American people," and the term "New Deal" caught on. But the Democratic platform itself was filled (as was the Republican) with old shibboleths. At a time of economic desperation and social despair, both parties promised reductions in government spending, a balanced budget, and sound currencies. On Prohibition, the Democrats urged repeal and the Republicans only revision. Neither party's official statement seemed stocked with new ideas for tackling the emergency, and the campaign became mired in the usual rhetorical thrusts and counterthrusts. Not even Hoover's severest critics were convinced that Roosevelt offered an attractive alternative as president. Walter Lippmann, the country's most influential journalist, expressed the widespread reservations about Roosevelt's ability:

> Franklin D. Roosevelt is no crusader. He is no tribune of the people. He is no enemy of entrenched privilege. He is a pleasant man who, without any important qualifications for the office, would very much like to be President . . . [a man] who simply does not measure up to the tremendous demands of the office of President.

Hoover agreed; would the voters?

Roosevelt had been preparing himself for the presidency for many years. A relative of Theodore Roosevelt, Franklin came from the Democratic side of the family. First as assistant secretary of the navy and then, after recovering from a crippling attack of infantile paralysis, as governor of New York, FDR had followed TR's path to the White House (even down to a run for the vice-presidency, in his case unsuccessful, in 1920). As governor, replacing Al Smith, Roosevelt had been an active reformer, gathering around him an able group of academic and political assistants (known as the "Brain Trust") interested in major policy departures from New Era economics and social welfare programs. Whether he would retain the reform impulse if elected remained unknown in the 1932 campaign.

Election Day brought a Democratic sweep. Roosevelt's almost 23 million popular votes easily topped Hoover's almost 16 million. The new president won 471 to 59 in electoral votes, carrying 42 states. The Democrats took command of Congress by huge majorities (60 to 35 in the Senate and 310 to 117 in the House). Clearly, if Roosevelt intended new departures in policy, he had the political means to achieve them. A friend observed shortly after he took office that if Roosevelt's programs succeeded, he would be praised as the country's greatest president but, if they failed, he would be damned as its worst. Roosevelt replied: "If I fail [as President] I shall be the last one."

Suggested Readings
Chapters 37–38

Charles A. Lindbergh

Kenneth S. Davis, *The Hero: Charles A. Lindbergh and the American Dream* (1959); Nancy Eubank, *The Lindberghs—Three Generations* (1975); Charles A. Lindbergh, *"We"* (1927) and *The Spirit of St. Louis* (1953); Leonard Mosley, *Lindbergh: A Biography* (1976); Walter S. Ross, *The Last Hero: Charles A. Lindbergh* (1968). (Many of the quotations cited in Chapter 37 were drawn from Charles Lindbergh's two memoirs of his flight.)

The United States 1919–33: General Studies

John Braeman, R. H. Bremner, David Brody, eds., *Change and Continuity in America: The 1920s* (1968); John D. Hicks, *Republican Ascendancy, 1921–1933* (1960); William E. Leuchtenberg, *The Perils of Prosperity, 1914–1932* (1958); David A. Shannon, *Between the Wars, 1919–1941* (1965).

Technology and Economic Change

Erik Barnouw, *A Tower in Babel: A History of Broadcasting in the United States to 1933* (1966); Irving L. Bernstein, *The Lean Years: A History of the American Worker, 1920–1933* (1960); Alfred D. Chandler, *Strategy and Structure* (1962); Henry Ford, *My Life and Work* (1922); Ronald Gellatt, *The Fabulous Phonograph* (1965); Siegfried Giedion, *Mechanization Takes Command* (1948); Morrell Heald, *The Social Responsibilities of Business* (1970); F. C. Kelly, *The Wright Brothers: Fathers of Flight* (1943); F. L. Mott, *American Journalism* (1962); Allen Nevins and Frank E. Hill, *Ford* (3 vols., 1954–62); Beaumont Newhall, *The History of Photography* (1964); Otis Pease, *The Responsibilities of American Advertising* (1958); James W. Prothro, *Dollar Decade: Business Ideas in the 1920s* (1954); J. B. Rae, *The Road and the Car in American Life* (1971); Robert Sobel, *The Great Bull Market: Wall Street in the 1920s* (1968); George Soule, *Prosperity Decade: From War to Depression, 1917–1929* (1947); Keith T. Sward, *The Legend of Henry Ford* (1948); Philip Taft, *Organized Labor in the United States* (1964); Reynold M. Wik, *Henry Ford and Grass-Roots America* (1972); J. H. Wilson, *American Business and Foreign Policy, 1920–1933* (1971); Wilbur and Orville Wright, *Papers* (1953).

Cultural Patterns

Frederick Lewis Allen, *Only Yesterday* (1931); Loren Baritz, ed., *The Culture of the Twenties* (1969); Carl Bode, *Mencken* (1969); W. H. Chafe, *The American Woman: Her Changing Social, Economic and Political Roles* (1972); Malcolm Cowley, *Exile's Return* (1934); Paula S. Fass, *The Damned and the Beautiful: American Youth in the 1920's* (1977); Frederick Hoffmann, *The Twenties* (1955, rev. ed., 1966); Nathan I. Huggins, *Harlem Renaissance* (1971); Alfred Kazin, *On Native Grounds* (1942); Don S. Kirschner, *City and Country: Rural Response to Urbanization in the late 1920s* (1970); Arthur Knight, *The Liveliest Art* (1957); J. W. Krutch, *The Modern Temper* (1929); Oliver P. Larkin, *Art and Life in America* (rev. ed., 1960); Isabel Leighton, ed., *The Aspirin Age* (1949); J. Stanley Lemons, *The Woman Citizen: Social Feminism in the 1920s* (1973); R. S. and H. N. Lynd, *Middletown* (1929); Zane L. Miller, *The Urbanization of Modern America* (1973); Richard H. Pells, *Radical Visions and American Dreams: Culture and Social Thought in the Depression Years* (1973); Karl Schriftgiesser, *This Was Normalcy* (1948); Harold Seymour, *Baseball* (2 vols., 1960–71); Andrew Sinclair, *The Other Half: The Emancipation of the American Woman* (1962); Preston Slosson, *The Great Crusade and After* (1930); Marshall and Jean Sterns, *Jazz Dance* (1968); Edward Wagenknecht, *Movies in the Age of Innocence* (1962); Edmund Wilson, *Axel's Castle* (1931).

National Politics

S. H. Adams, *Incredible Era* (1939); LeRoy Ashby, *The Spearless Leader: Senator Borah and the Progressive Movement in the 1920s* (1972); David Burner, *The Politics of Provincialism: The Democratic Party in Transition, 1918–1932* (1968); Frank Freidel, *Franklin D. Roosevelt: The Ordeal* (1954); Oscar Handlin, *Al Smith and His America* (1958); John D. Hicks, *Republican As-*

cendancy, *1921–1933* (1960); B. C. and Fola La Follette, *Robert M. La Follette* (1953); K. C. McKay, *The Progressive Movement of 1924* (1947); Arthur Mann, *LaGuardia: A Fighter Against His Times, 1882–1933* (1959); Donald R. McCoy, *Calvin Coolidge, The Quiet President* (1967); E. A. Moore, *A Catholic Runs for President* (1956); Robert K. Murray, *The Harding Era* (1969); Burl Noggle, *Teapot Dome* (1962); Andrew Sinclair, *The Available Man: Warren Gamaliel Harding* (1965); W. A. White, *A Puritan in Babylon: The Story of Calvin Coolidge;* Robert Zieger, *Republicans and Labor, 1915–1929* (1969).

Cultural Tensions

Daniel Aaron, *Writers on the Left* (1961); Herbert Asbury, *The Great Illusion* (1950); Lois Banner, *Women in Modern America* (1974); Zechariah Chafee, *Free Speech in the United States* (1941); David M. Chalmers, *Hooded Americanism* (1965); Norman H. Clark, *Deliver Us From Evil: An Interpretation of American Prohibition* (1976); Felix Frankfurter, *The Case of Sacco and Vanzetti* (1927); Norman F. Furniss, *The Fundamentalist Controversy 1918–1931* (1954); W. B. Gatewood, Jr., ed., *Controversy in the Twenties* (1969); Ray Ginger, *Six Days or Forever* (1958); Joseph R. Gusfield, *Symbolic Crusade* (1963); John Higham, *Strangers in the Land* (1955); Kenneth T. Jackson, *The Ku Klux Klan in the City* (1967); J. W. Johnson, *Black Manhattan* (1930); M. A. Jones, *American Immigration* (1960); G. L. Joughin and E. M. Morgan, *The Legacy of Sacco-Vanzetti* (1948); Don Kirschner, *City and Country: Rural Responses to Urbanization in the 1920's* (1970); Alain Locke, *The New Negro: An Interpretation* (1925); Charles Merz, *Dry Decade* (1931); Paul L. Murphy, *World War I and the Origin of Civil Liberties in the United States* (1979); Robert K. Murray, *Red Scare* (1955); H. C. Peterson and G. C. Fite, *Opponents of War, 1917–1918* (1957); William Preston, Jr., *Aliens and Dissenters: Federal Suppression of Radicals, 1903–1933* (1963); A. S.

Rice, *The Ku Klux Klan in American Politics* (1961); Francis Russell, *Tragedy in Dedham* (1962); Andrew Sinclair, *Era of Excess: A Social History of the Prohibition Movement* (1962); R. G. Swing, *Forerunners of American Fascism* (1935).

The Market Crash and Early Depression Years

Frederick Lewis Allen, *The Lords of Creation* (1935) and *Since Yesterday* (1940); Robert Bendiner, *Just Around the Corner* (1968); Caroline Bird, *The Invisible Scar* (1965); John Brooks, *Once in Golconda: A True Drama of Wall Street* (1969); L. V. Chandler, *America's Greatest Depression* (1970); Roger Daniels, *The Bonus March: An Episode of the Great Depression* (1971); Milton Friedman and Anna J. Schwartz, *The Great Contraction, 1929–1933* (1965); John K. Galbraith, *The Great Crash, 1929* (1955); C. P. Kindelberger, *The World in Depression, 1929–1939* (1973); Donald J. Lisio, *The President and Protest: Hoover, Conspiracy, and the Bonus Riot* (1974); Grant McConnell, *The Decline of Agrarian Democracy* (1953); Broadus Mitchell, *Depression Decade* (1947); D. A. Shannon, ed., *The Great Depression* (1960); Bernard Sternsher, ed., *Hitting Home* (1970); Studs Terkel, *Hard Times: An Oral History of the Great Depression* (1970); Dixon Wecter, *The Age of the Great Depression* (1948).

The Hoover Administration

Robert H. Ferrell, *American Diplomacy in the Great Depression* (1957); Herbert Hoover, *Memoirs: The Great Depression* (1952); A. U. Romasco, *The Poverty of Abundance: Hoover, The Nation and the Depression* (1965); Arthur M. Schlesinger, Jr., *The Crisis of the Old Order* (1957); Jordan A. Schwarz, *The Interregnum of Despair* (1970); H. G. Warren, *Herbert Hoover and the Great Depression* (1959); Joan Hoff Wilson, *Herbert Hoover: Forgotten Progressive* (1975).

F ifteen million Americans were unemployed on March 4, 1933, when the new president, Franklin Delano Roosevelt, was inaugurated. Roosevelt stirred his audience when he told his stricken countrymen: "Let me assert my firm belief that the only thing we have to fear is fear itself." A despairing nation responded eagerly to Roosevelt's determination to act quickly and boldly in confronting the emergency.

Twenty-eight years later another new president, John Fitzgerald Kennedy, also used his inaugural speech to proclaim new energy in national affairs. "Let the word go out," Kennedy intoned, "that the torch has been passed to a new generation of Americans [willing] to pay any price, bear any burden, to assure the survival and the success of liberty."

Roosevelt's address rallied Americans to begin the process of economic recovery. Kennedy's speech summoned Americans to renew their leadership of the Western world. The three decades between these two orations saw the United States emerge from economic catastrophe to become the strongest and most prosperous country in world history. The following chapters trace the steps in this evolution.

The career of Eleanor Roosevelt, narrated in Chapter 39, portrays, through the experiences of America's most famous and influential twentieth-century woman, the country's transition from the relatively affluent twenties into the era of the Great Depression (and beyond). The accompanying chapter on the New Deal years discusses the social and the economic impact of the Depression on the American people as well as the political world of Franklin Roosevelt's pathbreaking administration. Together, the two chapters examine the formative decade of our modern national experience.

The attack on Pearl Harbor, dramatized in Chapter 41, highlights the beginning of a shift in national attention from domestic to foreign concerns. Roosevelt and his successors, determined to avoid future "Pearl Harbors," led the country in a search for collective security through treaty alliances. The wartime Grand Alliance of the United States, Great Britain, and the Soviet Union rapidly deteriorated after World War II. A new era of Cold War between the Western allies and the Soviet Communist camp began. Pearl Harbor thus vaulted the United States into a position of world leadership. Chapter 42 traces the development of that role from the 1930s to the Kennedy administration.

Running parallel to Cold War developments in foreign affairs were anti-Communist rumblings at home. The Alger Hiss case figured prominently in this. Hiss was a former high government official who was convicted in 1950 of having lied about involvement with a Russian agent. His case came to symbolize for many the threat of communism to American society. The Red Scare of which the incident formed a part was central to many political, social, and economic developments discussed in the next chapter. Among those developments are the nation's postwar return to affluence, the rise of a "military-industrial complex," and the evolution of social problems that would haunt the next decade.

MODERN AMERICA

UNIT SEVEN

39 Eleanor Roosevelt: An American Life

The coal miners were evidently a good distance beneath the surface. Only the lamps in their helmets illuminated the scene and revealed the surprise on their faces. "For Gosh Sakes!" one exclaimed to the other, "It's Mrs. Roosevelt!"

Eleanor Roosevelt may never have actually gone down a coal mine, but the most famous cartoon of the 1930s showed that people found the idea plausible. During the worst of the Great Depression, Mrs. Roosevelt went to many places no first lady had visited before, and she did things that the wife of no previous president had thought worth doing. She went to Appalachia, to the Gulf states' Black Belt, to Puerto Rico, and to just about everywhere else to see firsthand the worst poverty in a depression-stricken country. She explored the slums and alleys of the District of Columbia, which most politicians never saw during a lifetime in Washington. Driving with a friend, she visited one New Deal project after another, trying to see if they really helped the unemployed.

She also met people who had never before talked with a first lady. Through the Women's Trade Union League she maintained ties with working women and their leaders. She considered herself a personal friend of the activists in the American Youth Congress, even after Communists surfaced in the organization. Mrs. Roosevelt provided the New Deal's most open ear to the problems of blacks and worked ceaselessly to protect their rights in government programs. Walter White, head of the National Association for the Advancement of Colored People (NAACP), remarked once that only the thought of Mrs. Roosevelt kept him from hating all white people.

Mrs. Roosevelt tried to keep her husband available to new ideas and often drove the points home herself. "No one," recalled one New Dealer, "who ever saw Eleanor Roosevelt sit down facing her husband, and holding his eye firmly, say to him, 'Franklin, I think you should . . . .' will ever forget the experience." From her large correspondence she selected letters from people with ideas and from people needing help and laid them on his desk with the scrawled injunction, "F — read."

As first lady, Eleanor Roosevelt was an individual personality and not merely the wife of the president. She wrote a daily newspaper column, went on lecture tours, and spoke frequently on the radio. She held her own press conferences, the first president's wife to do so. She constantly tried to increase the role of women in the Democratic party and in government, telling a friend she considered that objective more important than any specific political issue.

Next to her husband, Mrs. Roosevelt was probably the best-known person in the country. Conservatives would amuse each other with "Eleanor stories," imitating her high-pitched voice and mocking her ungainly features. Friends remarked that her photographs did not do her justice. "My dear," she told one, "if you haven't any chin and your front teeth stick out, it's going to show on a camera plate."

People all over the United States knew Eleanor Roosevelt, and millions adored her. But her public life did not reflect her personal one. She agonized over a troubled marriage and suffered strained relationships with her children. Her private difficulties may have instilled in her the strength to sustain her public role, but they may also have caused her to seek among the poor and the disadvantaged the approval she could not find in her own family.

"My mother was one of the most beautiful women I have ever seen," runs the first sentence of Eleanor Roosevelt's autobiography. That beauty made a particular impression on her because she did not inherit it. Her mother and father were one of the most glamorous couples in New York society. In contrast, Eleanor remembered, "I was a solemn child, without beauty and painfully shy, and I seemed like a little old woman." Her exasperated mother called her "Granny."

Her early life did not tend to build either joy or self-confidence. The homely little Eleanor wore a back brace for two years to correct a curvature of the spine. She felt excluded from her mother's affections after the birth of her healthy, attractive, baby brother. Her father, Elliott (Theodore Roosevelt's younger brother), had begun the slow and painful process of drinking himself to death. He was away from home on one more effort to "dry out" when her mother died. Eleanor was eight years old when her mother's family decided that, because of her father's alcoholism, she and her brother should go to live with her maternal grandmother, a gloomy old lady in a gloomy old house in New York City, who hired governesses to deal with her unwelcome guests. The lonely Eleanor spent much time writing loving letters to her adored father. "He dominated my life for as long as he lived," she recalled, "and was the love of my life for many years after he died." Her father rarely answered her letters and more rarely saw her. He died two years after her mother. All her life Eleanor would be badly hurt when someone she loved disappointed her.

Eleanor was a good student, but—shy and awkward, dressed by her grandmother in children's clothes until she was fifteen—she made few friends when she was sent to school. And the few she made could not be

Eleanor, at age six, a shy, pensive child whom her mother addressed as "Granny." (UPI)

invited to her house because her maternal uncles were so often drunk. Her grandmother also severely limited Eleanor's visits to her uncle, Theodore Roosevelt, and his family. Theodore, then a rising young politician, had loved his brother and felt keenly for Eleanor. On her rare visits to his house, he embraced Eleanor warmly and tried hard to include her in the rough activities of his own brood. "Poor little soul, she is very plain," noted Theodore's wife Edith. "Her mouth and teeth seem to have no future. But perhaps the ugly duckling will turn out to be a swan."

This situation, Eleanor remembered, "began to develop in me an almost exaggerated idea of the necessity of keeping all of one's desires under complete subjugation." It also taught her something about people and their need to feel wanted. When she briefly visited a friend in the country, her hostess was surprised to find her writing to her young brother two days in a row. "I write him every day," Eleanor explained. "I want him to feel he belongs to somebody."

Her life improved dramatically when, at fifteen, she was sent to boarding school in England. The headmistress took an interest in the uneasy, gawky, but highly intelligent girl, and Eleanor, hungry for affection, responded happily to the attention. When she returned home, she had acquired enough self-confidence to enter New York society, although convinced that her appearance would keep her from achieving any great success. She soon limited her socializing and began teaching in a settlement house on the Lower East Side.

Yet Eleanor did not lack men who showed interest in her. She was soon seeing a good deal of her distant cousin, Franklin Delano Roosevelt. Their closest common ancestor had died in the seventeenth century. But the two Roosevelt families had always been friendly, although Theodore's Oyster Bay Roosevelts were Republicans and Franklin's Hyde Park Roosevelts were Democrats. Eleanor's father, Elliott Roosevelt, had been Franklin's godfather, and she had seen Franklin occasionally while she was growing up.

Franklin Roosevelt was then a popular and amiable Harvard student. He wrote editorials on school spirit for the *Harvard Crimson* and was good-looking enough to make people wonder what he saw in the ungainly, strait-laced Eleanor. His father, much older than Franklin's mother, had died when his son was at prep school, and Franklin's mother, Sara, now centered her life around her only child. For two winters she had taken a house in Boston to be near him at college. She bent every effort to break up his relationship with Eleanor, a romance she considered both premature and unsuitable. Nevertheless, they became engaged.

Uncle Theodore, now president of the United States, offered use of the White House for the marriage. But Eleanor chose her grandmother's house, selecting a day when the president would be in New York for the St. Patrick's Day parade. The outgoing Teddy Roosevelt—who, in the words of his acid-tongued daughter Alice, "wanted to be the bride at every wedding and the corpse at every funeral"—stole the show, although, in her wedding gown, Eleanor for once looked almost beautiful.

When the couple returned to New York from a European honey-

A tall, stately, and elegant bride, Eleanor was married to Franklin on March 17, 1905, in a society wedding at a New York town house. Wearing the long satin gown covered with Brussels lace in which her mother had been married, Eleanor, at twenty, appeared beautiful. She was given away by her uncle, Theodore Roosevelt, who had just been inaugurated as president, and whose daughter, cousin Alice, was one of the bridesmaids. (UPI)

moon, they found that Sara had rented them a house three blocks from her own. They spent weekends at Sara's country house at Hyde Park, a hundred miles up the Hudson River, and summers at Sara's house on Campobello Island off the coast of Maine. While Franklin began his law career, Eleanor settled down to bearing children, and Sara to telling her how. Sara had no qualms about being an interfering mother-in-law, and Eleanor lacked the self-confidence to decline her advice. "Franklin's children," she said later, "were much more my mother-in-law's than they were mine."

Sara used her money to control her son and daughter-in-law's lives, doling it out according to her own interests and whims. In 1908, she built a new house for Eleanor and Franklin, at 49 East 65th Street. She also built herself a new house—at 47 East 65th Street. Eleanor normally bore up well under the strain, but Franklin came home once to find her in tears. She had no feeling for her house, she sobbed; her mother-in-law had bought the land, selected the architect, and decorated the rooms. Franklin succeeded in calming her, but he did not really understand.

Soon, other interests provided some diversion for them. Legal business bored Franklin; in 1910 he received the Democratic nomination for state senator from the Hyde Park district. Aided by a national Democratic landslide and a good deal of Sara's money, he won the election. Eleanor had encouraged him to enter politics, but the prospect of meeting new people terrified her, and she found their two years in Albany painfully difficult.

Franklin's political career prospered swiftly. He became an early and active backer of the presidential hopes of Woodrow Wilson, then governor of neighboring New Jersey. When Wilson won in 1912, Franklin snared the job of assistant secretary of the Navy, the same position that had propelled Theodore Roosevelt to national prominence.

Washington seemed no warmer to Eleanor than Albany had, but she doggedly made the effort to fit in. To help with her social obligations, she hired a secretary who knew Washington, Lucy Mercer. Lucy, the twenty-two-year-old daughter of impoverished Maryland aristocracy, had all the social graces that Eleanor lacked. She also had a pretty face, a dazzling figure, and a velvety voice. When Eleanor and the children went to Campobello for summers, Lucy remained in Washington to look after the house and Franklin.

Franklin's association with Lucy soon turned into a love affair that was common knowledge among Washingtonians. The two often appeared together when Eleanor was away, and Lucy became a secretary in the Navy Department. Eleanor's cousin, Teddy Roosevelt's daughter Alice Roosevelt Longworth, assisted the lovers, inviting them both to her house. "Franklin deserved a good time," explained Mrs. Longworth. "He was married to Eleanor." Not surprisingly, Eleanor did not take this tolerant view when she came across revealing letters from Lucy. Furious, she offered her husband a choice: He must never see Lucy again, or Eleanor would sue for divorce.

The situation really offered Franklin no choice at all. He and Eleanor had five children whom he loved and enjoyed. And a divorce would destroy his political aspirations. For once his mother took Eleanor's side, threatening to cut him off financially. Franklin gave up his mistress. From that point on, however, his wife's bedroom door was closed to him. "I have the memory of an elephant," Eleanor quietly told a friend years later. "I can forgive but I cannot forget."

The episode had a profound effect on Eleanor's attitudes about life. "The bottom dropped out of my own particular world," she remembered later, "and I faced myself, my surroundings, my world honestly for the first time. I really grew up that year." Her attempt to build a life around husband and children had failed. As her children grew, she sought more and more to create a satisfying existence for herself outside her home.

In 1920 the Democratic party, seeking to capitalize on the Roosevelt name, nominated Franklin for vice-president. "I am sure that I was glad for my husband," Eleanor wrote later, "but it never occurred to me to be much excited." Nevertheless, she dutifully went on the campaign trail. At first she hated it, writing home: "I really don't see that I'm of the least use on this trip." But she soon became friendly with the reporters and drew close to Louis Howe, the wizened, coughing little man who managed her husband's political fortunes. Harding's landslide victory buried the Democratic ticket, but Eleanor emerged with an interest in politics. After the election, she joined the board of the New York State League of Women Voters.

The summer after Franklin's defeat the family went to Campobello as usual. Franklin felt particularly tired one afternoon and went for a swim in the icy bay. When that did nothing to revive him, he went to bed early. He awoke the next morning to find both his legs paralyzed. Weeks later, the Roosevelts received a definite diagnosis: At thirty-nine, Franklin had contracted polio.

For two weeks, Eleanor nursed Franklin constantly, sleeping on a couch in his room. "You will surely break down if you do not have immediate relief," the doctor warned. But she and Franklin managed to present to the world an image of cheerfulness, of confidence that he would recover and resume his political career. In the months of agony that followed, the world saw Franklin's courage; only Eleanor saw his desperation.

Eleanor's long career as a politician's wife exposed her to the demands of public life and to the public eye. During the campaign of 1920, when Franklin ran for vice-president, Eleanor joined Mrs. James Cox, wife of the Democratic presidential nominee, on a reviewing stand in Ohio to watch a parade in honor of the candidates. (UPI)

Eleanor now needed all of her own stamina in a struggle with her mother-in-law. Sara had never liked the strange people with whom her son had to associate in politics, and she felt that he should now retire to Hyde Park and become a gentleman farmer. Eleanor, equally determined, insisted that her husband should continue to lead an active life and not die slowly among his trees. She refused to allow people to treat him as an invalid, and she found a tireless ally in campaign manager Louis Howe, who now moved into the Sixty-fifth Street house.

With Franklin largely confined indoors, Howe trained Eleanor to keep her husband's name before the public. He attended meetings at which she spoke, and through pointed criticism, he managed to eliminate her nervous giggle. She chaired the Finance Committee of the Women's Division of the Democratic State Committee and joined the Women's Trade Union League. With growing confidence, she accepted invitations to speak on the radio and to write for magazines. She was becoming, to her own amazement, a prominent public figure.

Together, she and Louis Howe salvaged Franklin's career. But they did no less for Eleanor. Not only did she know that Franklin needed her; she was also creating a role for herself. When their youngest child went off to prep school, she broadened her activities to include full-time teaching at a New York private school. "I suppose," she once told an interviewer, "that if I were asked what is the best thing one can expect in life, I would say—the privilege of being useful."

But despite Eleanor's success and newly gained confidence, she could not withstand Sara's guerrilla warfare on the home front. With Franklin often away in the South, where the good weather and warm water assisted his therapy, Sara and Eleanor shared the responsibility of the children. With Sara's encouragement they soon learned to compare their busy mother, who had never been close to them and who now tried to teach them discipline and self-control, with their generous, available grandmother.

The political careers of the two Roosevelts meshed perfectly in 1928, when Governor Al Smith of New York won the Democratic presidential nomination. At the 1924 national convention, Franklin, in a stirring demonstration of his triumph over polio, had risen from his wheelchair and walked without assistance to the podium, where he gave the speech placing Smith's name in nomination. Four years later, Smith asked Franklin to nominate him again. The candidate also asked Eleanor, whose effectiveness in the New York party he had noted, to run national women's activities in his campaign.

Smith soon requested even more. A New York City Catholic himself, he wanted Franklin, as a well-known upstate Protestant, to run for governor. Roosevelt was reluctant—he had just invested most of his capital in a resort in Warm Springs, Georgia, where he thought the waters would help his legs. Eleanor refused to advise Franklin either way, and Smith wore him down. To critics who questioned Roosevelt's physical ability, Smith snapped, "The Governor of New York does not have to be an acrobat!"

Eleanor exerted herself more actively in Smith's presidential campaign than in her husband's. When the final returns buried Smith in defeat but gave Franklin a narrow win, she seemed more disappointed than elated. Nevertheless, she made preparations to assume new duties in Albany. "When I found I had something to do," she told a reporter once, "I just did it."

But things had changed in eight years. Eleanor would not—and indeed could not—again be merely a supportive wife. She spent only four days a week in the state capital; Monday through Wednesday she was in New York City to teach her classes. Her work for the Democratic State Committee also continued, although she removed her name from the organization's stationery. Even when present in the governor's mansion, Mrs. Roosevelt's approach to her role differed greatly from that of her predecessors.

Women's groups, which previously had met with hostility from the state government, now found an unaccustomed welcome in Albany, where Eleanor tried to advance their social programs with Franklin and the legislature. She also helped her husband by making unannounced

Governor Roosevelt's family, with Franklin's mother, the imposing Mrs. James Roosevelt, seated at the far right. Eleanor and her daughter Anna, then married to stockbroker Curtis Dall, held the grandchildren. During these Albany years, Eleanor was commuting by train to New York every week to teach at the Todhunter School, where she served as vice-principal. (Brown Brothers)

inspection tours of state institutions and reporting directly to him. During train rides between New York and Albany she handled an enormous load of letters from people who had problems with the state government. She also managed to keep the mansion going. Although the wall between Franklin and Eleanor had not come down, they functioned as a team. "We are really very dependent on each other," she once wrote him wistfully, "though we do see so little of each other."

Eleanor had adjusted to being the governor's wife, but she did not look forward to the next step. Franklin now led the field of Democratic candidates for president, and the Great Depression made his election a strong probability. But he had acquired a new group of advisers, who found Eleanor too idealistic for serious politics. Their first job, one of them told a new recruit, was "to get the pants off Eleanor and on to Frank." But Eleanor still tried to keep her influence with her husband; when, for political reasons, he came out against the United States joining the League of Nations, she refused to speak to him for three days.

When it became clear, by 23 million Democratic votes to 15 million Republican, that the Roosevelts were going to Washington, Eleanor made plans to keep herself busy. Just before the inauguration, she published a book entitled *It's Up to the Women* and accepted an offer to edit a magazine called *Babies—Just Babies.* She intended to continue her New York interests and remain active in women's causes. Riding to the inaugural ceremony with Mrs. Hoover, Eleanor asked her what she would miss most about the White House. Being taken care of, the outgoing first lady answered, not having to worry about anything. Eleanor silently promised herself that she would never adopt that attitude.

She was now confident enough to lend a little self-assurance to the wife of Roosevelt's vice-president. Despite her husband's long career in the House of Representatives, Mrs. John Nance Garner of Uvalde, Texas, feared the publicity of her new role and stood somewhat in awe of the famous personage who was now first lady. "If you see me making any mistakes, Mrs. Roosevelt," she asked uncertainly, "will you please tell me?" "Of course," Eleanor replied. "If you see *me* making any mistakes, will you please tell *me?*"

The country began to learn more about Eleanor when she became the first president's wife to hold her own press conferences—which were for women only. The male White House correspondents scorned the idea at first; as the conferences began to produce news, however, they too wanted to attend. But Eleanor refused, wanting to help the newspaperwomen, who were then barred from membership in the National Press Club. "So few women writers," she once complained, "many of whom are just as capable of handling the big stories as the men, get a chance to be front-page writers."

Eleanor followed this policy in other ways as well. The Gridiron Club of Washington correspondents traditionally gave an all-male dinner, inviting most of official Washington and visiting politicos. Eleanor began holding a Gridiron Widows Dinner the same night, inviting women reporters, cabinet wives, and women bureaucrats. She took a special interest in increasing the role of women in government and in the Democratic party, frequently inviting the handful of female officerholders to the White House. As a result of her efforts, she had the satisfaction of seeing, for the first time ever, women alternates chosen for the (all male) members of the Resolutions Committee at the 1936 Democratic convention.

Two months after Roosevelt's inauguration in March 1933, a new Bonus Army besieged Washington. Eleanor drove down to the campgrounds with Louis Howe. What should they do? "Well," answered Howe, "you're going out there and I'm going to take a nap." Eleanor walked alone into the tent city and talked to the men, telling them of her own volunteer work during World War I and promising to do what she could to help them. The unemployed veterans cheered as she left. Said one, in words that became famous, "Hoover sent the Army. Roosevelt sent his wife."

The president "sent his wife" to many other strange places. She continued the inspection tours she had started in New York, often arriving unannounced and virtually alone. (She flatly refused to have the Secret Service follow her around, although they finally forced her to carry a pistol in the glove compartment of her car.) She visited the poorest parts of the country and ate a five-cent meal with welfare mothers. She tried to get something done about the slums of Washington and once took two carloads of cabinet wives down into the tenements, trying to awaken their interest in the city. They thanked her but explained that their husbands took up most of their time.

As a first lady known to care about people, Mrs. Roosevelt received a flood of mail. The first year, 300,000 letters addressed to her poured into the White House. Eleanor, her secretary, and her staff read them all. If the problem lay with a federal agency, she got in touch with the agency head; if the problem was personal, she tried to counsel the writer or obtain assistance, using her friends in the Women's Trade Union League to check out the story.

Americans wanted to know more about this Mrs. Roosevelt, already known as the Conscience of the New Deal. She went on two lecture tours a year. Often, she surprised her audience: Speaking to the conservative Daughters of the American Revolution (DAR), she called on a new idea of patriotism, one "that will mean living for the interests of everyone in our country, and the world at large, rather than simply preparing to die for our country." She spoke often on the radio and in 1935 earned fees totaling $72,000. She gave the money directly to the American Friends Service Committee (AFSC), until a Republican congressman charged her with tax evasion. She then began accepting the money, paying the tax on it, and then giving the rest to the AFSC.

In 1936, Eleanor Roosevelt took the unprecedented step of agreeing to write a daily syndicated newspaper column. "My Day," largely a diary of happenings in her life and her thoughts on them, became widely read. Columns that might be controversial she cleared with her husband, who sometimes used them to test public reaction. Her topics were wide-ranging: In one colunn she might disagree with the idea that women could not be great playwrights, in another discuss her opposition to war toys, in yet a third express her sympathy for children of both sides in the Spanish Civil War. After speaking at an exclusive prep school, she wrote, "Several of the boys asked me about the unemployed as though the unemployed were some strange species of animal. . . . We should realize that the unemployed are individuals, human beings with all the tastes, likes, dislikes, and passions we have ourselves."

The columns gave Eleanor, a long-time supporter of organized labor, the chance to join a union herself. She became a loyal and working member of the Newspaper Guild, although she declined an offer to become its president. Eleanor had usually backed unions. Her interest in the Women's Trade Union League provided preparation for the White House years, during which she clearly stood on the side of workers against management. She tried to proceed as unabrasively as possible, but her bias in favor of such unions as the New York-based International Ladies' Garment Workers Union was clear. Sometimes, it must be said, she acted in a labor dispute, writing letters pleading the workers' case or expressing her views in print, without full knowledge of the facts. Eleanor would not cross a picket line, even for a polio benefit meeting; she once canceled an appointment with a dressmaker at a fashionable Fifth Avenue store whose employees were on strike. "I will have to wait before coming to see you again," she explained to the store owner, "until you have some agreement with your people which is satisfactory to both sides." Such New Deal measures as emergency relief, the prolabor section of the National Industrial Recovery Act, social security, and the Wagner labor relations law received Mrs. Roosevelt's enthusiastic support.

Nor did she neglect the even more thorny problem of farm labor. She fostered New Deal agencies to deal with displaced farm laborers and to help those trying to continue in their farm work. She also became involved in a crisis in Arkansas over sharecroppers' efforts to join the Southern Tenant Farmers Union. The federal government's attempts to have evicted sharecroppers resettled ran into stiff opposition from Arkansas growers and their political allies. Hoping to benefit from a personal acquaintance with Arkansas Senator Joseph Robinson, Eleanor told him the story as she understood it. Robinson remained unconvinced, blaming all the trouble on a "group of agitators." In the face of such stonewalling, Eleanor dropped the correspondence and worked behind the scenes to get immediate relief payments to the evicted sharecroppers.

The White House had brought Eleanor the feeling she most treasured—that of being useful. But although she clearly represented a major political asset to her husband, relations between them did not improve. Even apart from past hurts, their personalities differed too radically. Franklin found it essential to forget all his problems from time to time (exchanging banter with reporters or puttering with his stamp collection). But it seemed that Eleanor never could relax. Asked what she wanted for Christmas, she would answer, towels, sheets, pillowcases; at an election

In the early decades of the twentieth century, Eleanor strongly opposed woman suffrage, but once women had won the vote, she joined the Board of the League of Women Voters and began an intensive apprenticeship in public affairs. She became a staunch supporter of women's causes, a leader of women in the Democratic party, and the most prominent woman in American political life. Eleanor is shown here at the 1952 New-York Historical Society exhibit that traced the campaign for woman suffrage. (UPI)

night celebration, she "worried about whether anybody was being neglected and whether there was enough food." These very different traits, which enabled them to complement each other as a political team, kept them from taking any real joy in each other's company. Eleanor saw Franklin filling his need for feminine companionship with his daughter, his daughters-in-law, and his long-time secretary, Missy LeHand. "Missy was young and pretty and loved a good time," wrote Eleanor in her autobiography, and "occasionally her social contacts got mixed with her work and made it difficult for herself and others." (Eleanor did not know that Franklin also looked elsewhere for companionship, to an attractive woman in her forties who was now Lucy Mercer Rutherford. The presidential train frequently stopped for two or three days in South Carolina near the Rutherford plantation on its way to Warm Springs. Lucy also had a house in Washington, and during Eleanor's frequent trips out of town, Lucy often dined at the White House.)

Neither could Eleanor find much comfort in her children, whose marriages collapsed one after another. With the example of her mother-in-law always before her, Eleanor tried not to interfere: "I was almost obsessed with the idea that once the children were grown, they should not be subjected to the same kind of control that held such sway over me." But she could not create close relationships with them, although she tried. "We all turned out to have long memories," one of her sons wrote in 1973. "It was impossible to discount the coldness with which Mother treated us when we were young." Nor did her children inherit Eleanor's social conscience. "Mother!" cried her daughter once when she pressed Franklin on a reform issue at dinner, "Can't you see you are giving Father indigestion?"

The fact that she remained an outsider in her own family was perhaps what gave Eleanor such a strong interest in others who were outsiders — in the unemployed, in women, and, to a degree unique for an American national figure at the time, in blacks.

The latter interest created problems, since racial discrimination was everywhere around her, so ingrained as to seem beyond remedy. Still, Mrs. Roosevelt labored. It was no surprise that blacks were being short-changed in the distribution of New Deal aid, North and South. From the very start of the Roosevelt programs, Eleanor insited on reminding the administrators of the National Recovery Administration (NRA) and of emergency relief that wage and benefit payment scales that set lower rates for Negroes should not be permitted. Harry Hopkins, Roosevelt's "Minister of Relief," responded sympathetically, but, all too often, edicts from the top proved no match for low-level bureaucracy and deeply ingrained prejudices.

Eleanor could only hope that New Deal programs would "spill over" and that blacks would get some appreciable share of the benefits. Certainly her husband had no intention of mounting a presidential crusade specifically in favor of blacks and their rights. FDR counted too much on the votes of Southern Democrats in Congress for that. Even though Roosevelt all but monopolized the Negro vote by 1940, no amount of prodding from his wife could induce the president to support an anti-lynching bill in Congress.

Eleanor battled on against the prevailing currents. Why should the U.S. Navy, she asked Secretary Swanson, enlist Negroes only as kitchen help? Swanson, who probably found the inquiry distasteful in itself (but, after all, it did come from the first lady), responded firmly that during most of the 1920s blacks had not been allowed to enlist in the navy at all. Their relegation to service in ship galleys was necessary, he argued, because otherwise they might rise to be petty officers and be placed in authority over whites; that "would create dissatisfaction, and would seriously handicap ship efficiency." The notion of black naval *officers* was not even broached. All Eleanor could do was to counsel, if not console, a Negro correspondent: "These things come slowly and patience is required in all great changes."

Not only did Eleanor try to get government assistance for blacks; she publicly identified herself with their cause. She urged the appointment of blacks to many New Deal agencies, and for the first time since the days of Woodrow Wilson's "cleaning out of the Negroes" in the federal civil service, a small but noticeable number of blacks obtained middle-level government jobs. Eleanor refused to succumb to despair on the issue. She had frequent discussions with the head of the NAACP,

Walter White, and even forced a meeting between White and FDR over the anti-lynching bill. She spoke at commencements and other ceremonies at black colleges. She praised and aided Richard Wright, the young novelist, as well as other Negro intellectuals. She received black sharecroppers at the White House and visited them in the fields.

In November 1938 Mrs. Roosevelt attended the first Southern Conference for Human Welfare, an interracial meeting of educators and social workers. Birmingham, Alabama, the site of the conference, strictly enforced its segregation ordinance, forcing whites to sit on one side of the aisle, blacks on the other. Eleanor entered the room with Mrs. Mary McLeod Bethune, a prominent civil rights advocate, and, chatting animatedly, sat down with her in the black section of the front row. Immediately a policeman appeared next to Eleanor and loudly cleared his throat. Although he was not about to arrest the first lady, neither would he let her flout the law of the state of Alabama. Without looking up, Eleanor adjusted her chair slightly, so that she sat neither in the black nor in the white section. The policeman turned red, but left. "At a later meeting," Eleanor wrote, "word came to us that all the audience was to be arrested and taken to jail for breaking one of Birmingham's strongest laws against mixed audiences," but no police wagon appeared.

Early in 1939,, Mrs. Roosevelt again had the chance to put preaching into practice. The DAR had barred the use of Washington's Constitution Hall to Marian Anderson, a black singer of international repute. Eleanor, herself a member of the DAR, decided to break with precedent. She had never thought much of resignation as a means of protest, considering it preferable to work for change within an organization. But the DAR's refusal to budge on the issue caused her to resign and to express her reasons publicly. In April, Miss Anderson gave a triumphant open-air concert on federal property near the Lincoln Memorial, and a few months later, Mrs. Roosevelt presented her with the Springarn Medal, the NAACP's award for achievement. "It is the little things that the Roosevelts do," observed a Negro newspaper, "which make them great and increases in the mind of the thinking Negro respect for the New Deal and most of what it represents."

Eleanor also had a particular interest in another powerless group. She was instrumental in starting the National Youth Administration to aid the great numbers of young people made jobless by the Depression. She worked closely with leaders of the American Youth Congress (AYC), a left-wing organization demanding massive federal expenditures to provide employment for youth. In 1939, when the House Un-American Activities Committee subpoenaed the leaders of the AYC, Eleanor attended the hearings, sitting in the front row and knitting placidly like a benign Madame LaFarge. She had learned not to be frightened of names, perhaps because she had been called so many. (A friend once confessed to her of having voted in 1932 for the Socialist candidate for president. "So would I," Eleanor confided, "if I had not been married to Franklin.") After the student leaders had testified, she brought them back to the White House for dinner. In her column, she warned that if such witch hunting

During World War II, Mrs. Roosevelt toured army bases and military hospitals wherever Allied troops were stationed, from England to the South Pacific. Riding in jeeps, eating in mess halls, and visiting the wards, the president's wife displayed an energy and compassion that inspired the nation—and kept her in the news. "FIRST LADY DINES WITH DOUGHBOYS" cabled the United Press in 1943, as khaki-clad Eleanor appeared for lunch at an army camp in Australia. (UPI)

continued, "It is really going to take quite a strong-minded person with a great indifference to what may be said about him to join an organization, even one with whose principles he is in agreement."

Even after Communist control of the AYC became clear, Eleanor spoke at their national convention, asking amid angry heckling why they condemned Nazi aggression in Spain but not Soviet aggression against Finland. When her son commented that the AYC people obviously had bad manners, she turned on him angrily. "And who are you to talk about their bad manners?" she blazed. "You were brought up in plenty, trained to good manners. You never had to worry about getting a job. Who are you to talk about the manners of young people who had to fight for everything they got, and didn't get much?"

The outburst showed both Eleanor's great empathy for those in need and her difficulties with her own family. Possibly her problems at home strengthened her interest in, and her commitment to, the outside world. For whatever reason—out of an unhappy childhood, a shattering disappointment in marriage, and her husband's paralysis—Eleanor forged a career that affected the history of her country and permanently changed the role of the American woman in public life.

Eleanor Roosevelt, from her particularly privileged vantage point, had done much to become a significant figure on the New Deal scene. With the outbreak of World War II in 1939, she adjusted to new conditions as the United States edged toward involvement in that struggle. The success of fascist totalitarian regimes in Europe caused her to drop her former pacifism in favor of a more "realistic" attitude of moral and material aid to the Western democracies. On that point, she and Franklin saw eye to eye. Eleanor became a leader in the Office of Civil Defense

(OCD) during 1940 and 1941, working closely with a talented and flamboyant New Dealer, New York City's Mayor Fiorello La Guardia.

But when Japan attacked the United States in December 1941, Eleanor's course was set for wider horizons than those provided by OCD. She made a well-publicized trip to Britain in 1942 to visit Allied troops. The American buildup of armed forces overseas was proceeding at an astonishing pace, and even Eleanor's fabled stores of energy were hard pressed to keep up with all the war fronts. As a representative of the Red Cross and of the United Services Organization (USO), she became the First Gray Lady, earning the nickname the GI's Friend. When she made a wartime tour of the South Pacific, Admiral William "Bull" Halsey was decidedly impressed. During one twenty-hour stretch in New Caledonia, Mrs. Roosevelt inspected almost everything, including the many military hospitals. "When I say that she inspected those hospitals," Halsey reported, "I don't mean that she shook hands with the chief medical officer, glanced into a sun parlor, and left. I mean that she went into every ward, stopped at every bed, and spoke to every patient. . . . I marveled at her hardihood, both physical and mental. She walked for miles, and she saw patients who were grievously and gruesomely wounded. But I marveled most at their expressions as she leaned over them. It was a sight I will never forget."

The pace that both Roosevelts, Eleanor and Franklin, set for themselves during World War II was indeed killing. The president won his fourth presidential election in 1944 and prepared for a summit meeting of Allied leaders at Yalta in Russia. It was obvious by that time, however, that his physical condition had deteriorated badly. He no longer wished to drive his car, and he had even surrendered his beloved ritual of cocktail mixing to others. After Yalta, Franklin went down to Warm Springs for rest and recuperation. Eleanor, still in Washington, seemed to convince herself that her husband would regain strength. But on April 12, 1945, she learned that the president had died of a massive stroke. It was Eleanor who informed Harry Truman that he was the new president.

In Georgia, Eleanor had to bear the additional grief of learning that Lucy Mercer Rutherford had come to Warm Springs on April 9 and was with Franklin when he died three days later. Reflecting on Lucy's relationship with her husband as the funeral train moved toward Washington, Eleanor mused that Franklin "might have been happier with a wife who was completely uncritical. That I was never able to be, and he had to find it in some other people. Nevertheless, I think that I sometimes acted as a spur. . . ."

Franklin was gone, but Eleanor never abandoned the conviction that one had to be *useful.* Too many things remained undone; too many desperate people around the world needed help. After the war, Mrs. Roosevelt went on to represent and to voice the best of the American humanitarian impulse. She served as a U.S. delegate to the United Nations from 1945 to 1953, earning worldwide respect and love. For another nine years she fought her version of the good fight as a lecturer and "spur" in support of causes she considered just. Her optimism, if not infectious,

The founding of the United Nations in 1945, after FDR's death, provided an appropriate opportunity for Eleanor to utilize her political and diplomatic talents and to remain active in public life. During her challenging years as United States delegate to the General Assembly, Eleanor served as chairman of the Commission on Human Rights and was active in UNESCO. (Culver Pictures)

was certainly constant. She was, as her friend Adlai Stevenson expressed it following her death in 1962, a person who "would rather light a candle than curse the darkness."

Back in the early 1930s, when Soviet diplomat Maxim Litvinov made his first trip to the United States, President Roosevelt remarked that he regretted Madame Litvinov had not come with him. "Oh well, you know," answered the Russian, "very active woman, career of her own, constantly traveling, making speeches. Impossible to interrupt what she was doing. Came alone because she is individual in politics, just as I am."

· Said Franklin Roosevelt, "I think I understand."

The Great Depression and the New Deal: 40 America in the 1930s

E leanor Roosevelt assisted the New Deal in what was possibly its most important function—restoring the confidence of the American people in their government. Her husband, perhaps the country's master politician of the century, made the renewal of confidence a major objective, and in large measure he succeeded in achieving that goal. But Franklin Roosevelt also had to devise concrete policies, in legislation and in executive action, to deal with the crisis.

The administration's responses followed no set pattern and derived from no single philosophical base. The New Deal was, instead, an extended improvisation in public policy—trying first one program to deal with a problem, then another if the first one failed, and sometimes returning to the original idea. Over six years, in this zigzag pattern, Roosevelt and the New Dealers profoundly changed the face of American government and what the American people expected from it.

The New Deal did not end the Great Depression. It was World War II, with its massive government spending, that finally brought a full revival of production and an end to mass unemployment. By 1939, when foreign policy began to dominate his thinking, Roosevelt had shepherded the country from a crushing depression to a severe recession. Yet he could claim, for better or worse, to have preserved the American political and economic systems through a time when many expected that both would collapse.

ROOSEVELT

"The only thing we have to fear," declared the new president to a numbed nation, "is fear it-

self." Although the American people could search through the rest of his inaugural address without finding any reason not to be afraid and without learning what Roosevelt planned to do to ease their fears, they seemed to be comforted by his words as they had never been by Herbert Hoover's pronouncement of similar platitudes. Roosevelt's faculty for inspiring confidence by simple force of personality became one of his strongest weapons in the fight against chaos—as important as any bill he ever pushed through Congress.

Franklin Roosevelt was forty-seven when the stock market collapsed in 1929, fifty-one when he became president in 1933. His ideas about the world had already been formed. There is no evidence that the Depression changed those ideas significantly. He was in many ways a traditionalist. He was, as we have seen, a wealthy aristocrat: educated in exclusive private schools, a graduate of Harvard, and owner of a country estate where he liked to play at being a gentleman farmer. FDR was a suave, smiling, confident man, who seemed to take the institutions and beliefs of his country very much for granted. A more unlikely candidate for leadership in a revolution is hard to imagine. Roosevelt, wrote a bemused columnist during the 1932 campaign, was a pleasant man, with no particular qualifications, who would like very much to be president.

On the other hand, Roosevelt's confidence opened his mind to experimentation. Because he had no serious doubts about American values and institutions, he could accept almost any specific suggestion for reform. Above all, he often said, the country demanded action. As long as the action was limited in its scope and possible consequences, he was willing to try almost anything.

Roosevelt appreciated fully the seriousness

of the Depression. But he was nevertheless sure that, sooner or later, limited reforms would revive the economy. Then, all that would be needed would be adequate laws and regulations to prevent a repetition of the worst mistakes of the 1920s.

SAVING THE BANKS

Yet, as Roosevelt took the oath of office, it appeared doubtful that he would get the chance to try his reforms. Since the autumn of 1932, banks had been closing their doors, unable to pay depositors their money. In February, the governor of Michigan closed the state's banks for eight days to prevent collapse; state after state followed suit. By inauguration day on March 4, 1933, thirty-eight states had closed their banks; and before the sun rose on March 5, New York and Illinois had also closed theirs. The New York Stock Exchange and the Chicago Board of Trade shut down. "We are at the end of our rope," said Hoover in despair.

The day after inauguration, Roosevelt (with questionable legality) declared a national bank holiday. Four days later, he sent a mild banking reform and regulation bill to a special session of Congress. It went through both Houses in a day, although few congressmen knew what they were voting for. "The house is burning down," declared a Republican congressional leader, "and the President of the United States says this is the way to put out the fire." Roosevelt then spoke over the radio, in his first fireside chat, assuring the nation that banks were now safe. After they reopened, bankers were astounded to find that deposits exceeded withdrawals.

Roosevelt's response to the situation clearly demonstrated his attitudes—and disappointed many radicals. A frightened Congress would have passed almost anything Roosevelt had asked for, up to and possibly including a bill nationalizing the banks. But the president clearly intended to preserve capitalism as well as to stimulate recovery. It would, on the other hand, be a government-supervised capitalism. Two months later Roosevelt signed the Glass-Steagall Act, which strengthened federal controls over banks and set up the Federal Deposit Insurance Corporation (FDIC) to guarantee bank deposits up to $10,000 (now up to $100,000). Bank failures ceased immediately. Roosevelt had bought some time.

THE HUNDRED DAYS

Congress and the people now awaited, with both eagerness and anxiety, a legislative program that Roosevelt had not quite worked out. During the campaign, he and other Democrats had called for a cut in spending and a balanced budget, and the administration took a few halting steps in that direction. Awaiting the repeal of the prohibition amendment, it persuaded Congress to legalize beer, possibly to take people's minds off the Depression. Finally, the administration produced comprehensive farm and industrial recovery bills.

Both the National Industrial Recovery Act (NIRA) and the Agricultural Adjustment Act (AAA) sought to regulate the economy without changing its private enterprise character. The NIRA also reflected Roosevelt's desire to maintain the broad support he had enjoyed when he assumed office—to move against the Depression at the head of a coalition of government, business, and labor. (His approach in some ways resembled Wilson's approach to fighting World War I—the last period in which Democrats had controlled the federal government.)

The National Industrial Recovery Act was, in essence, a repeal of parts of the old Sherman Antitrust Act (see pp. 551–2). Under a federal agency known as the National Recovery Administration (NRA), corporations were encouraged to create associations to plan production and control prices. Such a step meant the end of effective competition, but the administration was prepared at this low point in economic activity to sacrifice competition to stability and recovery.

For workers, the act also proposed that employers agree on uniform standards for labor practices, wages, and hours. When some companies were slow to cooperate, the NRA created a blanket code of minimum wages and maximum hours. Companies that cooperated were awarded a flag with the NRA symbol—a blue eagle—to fly as evidence of their public spirit. Up to a point, it worked. Some workers—those who had jobs to begin with—began to work shorter days and take home fatter pay envelopes.

The Agricultural Adjustment Act was a similar but more radical attempt to alter prevailing economics. It recognized that the farmer had a peculiar problem. Manufacturers, when prices fell, could cut back production. The reduction in supply would, sooner or later, raise prices. But farmers had always met falling prices by trying to produce more, not less.

The law created an Agricultural Adjustment Administration (AAA) with the power to pay farmers cash subsidies *not* to plant or harvest crops. The agency could also buy up agricultural products, such as cotton or wheat, and store them. This scheme, it was hoped, would reduce supply and raise market prices. In other words, a government body, with the cooperation of farmers, would try to control agricultural production. The goal was to enable farmers to earn as much (in real dollars, or purchasing power) as they had earned during the prosperous years from 1909 to 1914—a standard known as parity.

The AAA worked better than the NRA. Using its new powers, the agency in 1933 paid out $160 million to farmers who plowed under about 10 million acres of crops. That same year, farmers also withheld about 6 million pigs in return for $30 million in government money—a controversial act, when millions of people did not have enough to eat. But these drastic measures worked—rein-

Dorothea Lange's 1940 photo of a Texas migrant laborer's family living in a trailer without sanitation or water in an open field indicates the depth of economic distress for millions even after seven years of New Deal relief and recovery programs. (National Archives)

MAJOR NEW DEAL DOMESTIC LEGISLATION

YEAR	ACT/ADMINISTRATION	PURPOSE
BANKING CURRENCY SECURITIES		
1933	EMERGENCY BANKING RELIEF ACT	To save failing banks by providing them with cash to pay their depositors.
	GLASS-STEAGALL ACT	To curb speculation by banks; set up the Federal Deposit Insurance Corporation to "insure" savings deposits up to $10,000.
	"TRUTH IN SECURITIES" ACT	To require corporations floating new securities to register them with the Federal Trade Commission.
1934	GOLD RESERVE ACT	To enable the president to fix the gold content of the dollar.
	SECURITIES EXCHANGE ACT	Set up the Securities and Exchange Commission to regulate the Stock Market.
1935	BANKING ACT	To reform and strengthen the Federal Reserve System by directing interest rates.
DIRECT RELIEF		
1933	FARM CREDIT ADMINISTRATION	To provide emergency relief to farmers in the form of mortgages.
	FEDERAL EMERGENCY RELIEF ACT	Set up the Federal Emergency Relief Administration to provide grants in aid to the states; also set up the Civil Works Administration to relieve unemployment by a temporary work relief program.
	FRAZIER-LEMKE FARM BANKRUPTCY ACT	To enable some farmers to regain their farms even after the foreclosure of mortgages.
	HOME OWNERS REFINANCING ACT	Set up the Home Owners' Loan Corporation to provide emergency relief to home owners in the form of government financed mortgage loans.
	NATIONAL INDUSTRIAL RECOVERY ACT	Set up the Public Works Administration to contract for heavy construction projects in order to increase employment.
	UNEMPLOYMENT RELIEF ACT	Set up the Civilian Conservation Corps to provide jobs for the unemployed on conservation projects.
1934	NATIONAL HOUSING ACT	Set up the Federal Housing Administration to insure mortgages for new construction and home repairs.
1935	WORK PROGRESS ADMINISTRATION	To relieve unemployment by light public works projects.
1937	FARM SECURITY ADMINISTRATION	To make short-term loans for rehabilitation of farms, and long-term loans for purchase of farms.

forced by drought in 1933 and 1934 that destroyed much of the wheat and corn crops. In 1933, farm prices were at 55 percent of parity; by 1936, at 90 percent. The act also had the indirect effect of forcing millions of tenant farmers and sharecroppers off the land, adding them to the unemployment rolls of the country's cities (and beginning a mass migration off the land that accelerated after World War II). Liberal New Dealers, including Mrs. Roosevelt, protested AAA contracts that allowed the

MAJOR NEW DEAL DOMESTIC LEGISLATION

YEAR	ACT/ADMINISTRATION	PURPOSE
REGULATION OF INDUSTRY AND AGRICULTURE		
1933	AGRICULTURAL ADJUSTMENT ACT	Set up the Agricultural Adjustment Administration to encourage stability in agriculture by attempting to control agricultural production.
	NATIONAL INDUSTRIAL RECOVERY ACT	Set up the National Recovery Administration to encourage corporations to create associations for planning production and controlling prices; created a blanket code of minimum wages and maximum hours.
1935	CONNALLY ACT	To prevent overproduction of oil.
	GUFFEY ACT	To control the coal industry.
	NATIONAL LABOR RELATIONS ACT (WAGNER ACT)	To give federal protection to the labor movement by making it illegal for an employer to refuse to recognize a labor union.
	PUBLIC UTILITIES HOLDING COMPANY ACT	To limit the development of holding companies and discourage financial concentration in public utilities.
1936	ROBINSON-PATMAN ACT	To prohibit wholesalers or manufacturers from giving preferential discounts or rebates to large buyers.
	WALSH-HEALY ACT	To set minimum wages and maximum hours for work done on federal contracts (enacted after NRA declared unconstitutional).
1938	AGRICULTURAL ADJUSTMENT ACT	To cut back farm production through marketing quotas, soil conservation payments, export subsidies, and crop loans. It began storage of surpluses.
	FAIR LABOR STANDARD ACT	To establish minimum wages and maximum hours; forbade child labor.
REFORM		
1933	TENNESSEE VALLEY AUTHORITY	Set up the Tennessee Valley Authority to develop the nation's water resources and, therefore, provide cheap electric power.
1935	SOCIAL SECURITY ACT	To create a system of old-age insurance for Americans.
	WEALTH TAX ACT	To make the federal income tax more equitable.
MISCELLANEOUS		
1934	RECIPROCAL TRADE AGREEMENTS ACT	To lower tariff barriers in order to improve foreign trade.
1939	HATCH ACT	To remedy corrupt campaign practices by prohibiting active political campaigning and soliciting by federal officials.
	REORGANIZATION ACT	To reorganize the executive branch for greater efficiency.

eviction of farm tenants. But the group of liberal and radical lawyers that had fought the policy was "purged" from the agency by Secretary of Agriculture Henry A. Wallace in 1935.

Wide ranging as they were, the NIRA and AAA were only a part of the legislative program achieved by FDR during the first months of his administration—the Hundred Days. He also demanded and received from Congress the Glass-Steagall Act, also known as the "Truth in Securities" Act, to regulate the stock market; and bills to provide emergency relief to farmers and home-owners in danger of losing their property. His advisers also persuaded Roosevelt to abandon his scruples over a balanced budget and set up the Federal Emergency Relief Agency to distribute half a billion welfare dollars to the states. Roosevelt, reversing the previous vetoes of two Republican presidents, signed a bill creating the Tennessee Valley Authority (TVA), a massive government hydroelectric power development in the Upper South.

Nowhere was the Depression more severe than in the forty thousand square miles of territory spanning seven states known as the Tennessee River Valley. Each year the river swelled to flood stage with an average fifty-two inches of rain that washed out the area's meager crops. There was little industry and no hope of more, income being not even half the national average. The Tennessee Valley Authority was easily the most creative and far-reaching experiment in regional planning undertaken in American history. The TVA built a series of dams for flood control, thus making successful farming possible in the region and providing an abundance of hydroelectric power. It also made the rivers navigable. Cheap power and easy water transport, in turn, made the area appealing to industry. Schools, improved health facilities, recreational opportunities, reforestation, and other social benefits also flowed from the TVA, which, as the decade wore on, became a successful—if controversial—model for subsequent regional planning efforts in the United States. It marked the first time that government had attempted to mobilize the natural, economic, and human resources of a region to effect a rapid change in the overall conditions of life for most citizens of the area.

RESPONSE

Long before the success of Roosevelt's program could be gauged, it became clear that he had captured the American imagination. The president's picture appeared in homes across the

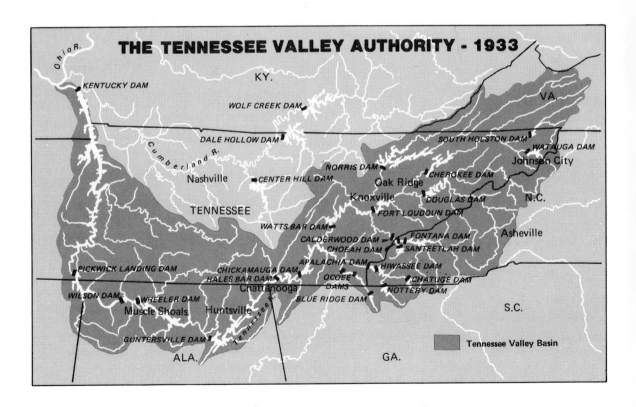

THE TENNESSEE VALLEY AUTHORITY - 1933

country; journalists estimated his popularity at up to 90 percent. "How do you account for him?" asked William Allen White, a progressive Republican. "Was I just fooled in him before the election, or has he developed?" People now felt the country had begun to move again. "President Roosevelt has done his part, now you do something," read a sign posted in a factory. "Buy something—buy anything, anywhere; paint your kitchen, send a telegram, give a party, get a car, pay a bill, rent a flat, fix your roof, get a haircut, see a show, build a house, take a trip, sing a song, get married."

Although Roosevelt's effect on music and marriage remains unclear, the economy did seem to respond to New Deal efforts. By spring 1934, the crisis had eased. Unemployment dropped, and business indicators picked up a bit. But that was as far as it went. The NRA's program of voluntary regulation of everything, from the steel industry to show business, apparently could do no more.

Despite Roosevelt's personal popularity, his programs were beginning to draw criticism from both the left and the right. At the low point of the Depression, during Hoover's last two years, Americans had been too demoralized even for radicalism. With millions of people living in shantytowns, the Socialist party ran a disappointing race in 1932, winning less than 900,000 votes, while the Communists polled only 100,000 votes. Now, as vitality seemed to return to the country, the left began to stir as well. Strikes erupted throughout the country in 1934, including a general strike in San Francisco. The greatest radical challenge, however, came not from Marxian philosophers but from uniquely American demagogues—notably Senator Huey Long of Louisiana (see page 777), who insisted that the New Deal had not been sufficiently reformist.

Wealthy businessmen argued, conversely, that Roosevelt had gone too far. In August 1934, the American Liberty League was organized. Originally financed by the Dupont family, the league soon gained enthusiastic support from leaders of such corporations as General Motors, Montgomery Ward, and General Foods. Calling itself nonpartisan, it could boast endorsement by the Democratic presidential candidates of 1924 and 1928— the conservative John W. Davis and the embittered progressive Al Smith. Smith felt that Roosevelt had cheated him out of the nomination and the presidency in 1932, and in his frustration he joined a group having little to do with his personal background or his political principles. "There can be only one capital," he warned appreciative Liberty Leaguers, "Washington or Moscow."

With such strident criticism apparently on the increase, New Dealers waited anxiously for the elections of 1934, hoping to hold their losses to under forty seats in Congress. The morning after election day, they were stunned and delighted to find Democratic gains in both houses, giving them the tightest control over Congress held by one party since Jefferson's day.

ENTER THE SUPREME COURT

With his massive electoral victories, Roosevelt controlled two of the three branches of government. Conservatives looked hopefully to the third, and the makeup of the Supreme Court seemed to justify their confidence. It would be almost two years before the legislation of the Hundred Days reached the Court, but when it did, it would find a Court roster that was unchanged, and probably unfriendly.

Of the nine men on the Court, seven had been named by conservative Republican presidents. Although Court decisions did not exactly follow a conservative pattern (two of the three liberal justices had been named by Republicans, while Justice McReynolds, possibly the most reactionary, had been nominated by Wilson, a Democrat), the Court did seem to bring the political and constitutional outlook of Calvin Coolidge to the judging of the New Deal. From early decisions, the administration learned to count four justices as against the New Deal, three as tending to sustain it, and two, including Chief Justice Charles Evans Hughes, as holding the balance of power. For Roosevelt, a bad situation was compounded by simple bad luck; throughout his first term, he did not have a single Court vacancy to fill.

The Court's first decisions only prolonged the suspense. It threw out a section of the NIRA, but it upheld Roosevelt's financial policies by a series of five-to-four votes. Then, in May 1935, the Court unanimously ruled the National Recovery Administration unconstitutional. "Extraordinary conditions do not create or enlarge constitutional power," admonished Chief Justice Hughes, as he read the judicial obituary for NRA.

In a way, the Court had done Roosevelt, a favor. The NRA, however useful it had been during the crisis of 1933–34, was collapsing, and many were charging, with some justice, that its industrial codes benefited big business at the expense of small producers. Clearly, the administration would need to try a new approach, and the Court had saved FDR from having to admit failure. Nevertheless, the president denounced the justices for adhering to a "horse-and-buggy" definition of interstate commerce. For the next two years, the administration would pass its bills looking uncomfortably over its shoulder at the Supreme Court.

THE SECOND NEW DEAL

Even before Black Monday, as the day of NRA's death came to be known for a while, Roosevelt had asked the new Congress to take bolder measures to deal with the Depression. The enactments of Roosevelt's second Congress differed greatly in philosophy from those of the first Hundred Days. Motivated by a combination of continuing economic hardship and the counsel of more liberal advisers (including Eleanor, who played a critical role at this time), and reacting to attacks from business and the Supreme Court, Roosevelt abandoned his earlier policy of stabilization and cooperation. He began to frame strategies for reforming the economic system that could bolster the poor and powerless and curb the power of business. The American Liberty League had not known when it was well off.

Faced by a stubborn persistence in the high rate of unemployment, Roosevelt shrugged off his hopes for a balanced budget and asked Congress for $5 billion for work relief. To administer the agency charged with spending this money, Roosevelt selected a controversial former social worker named Harry Hopkins, the man who would eventually become the second most powerful figure in the ad-

ministration. Thin and pale, apparently existing on cigarettes and black coffee, Hopkins seemed perpetually on the point of death from tuberculosis. But he possessed an incredible appetite for work and a keen social conscience. To those who suggested the economy would right itself in the long run without expensive government programs, he responded tartly, "People don't eat in the long run. They eat every day."

Hopkins' agency, the Works Progress Administration (WPA), soon employed three million people, paying a wage somewhere between relief and union wages. Careful not to take jobs away from workers already employed, WPA people worked on a wide range of projects, building or extending hospitals, schools, and playgrounds. The Federal Theater Project, Federal Writers' Project, and Federal Art Project subsidized unemployed hopefuls of varying talent while bringing subsidized drama and art to many isolated communities. The National Youth Administration tried to deal with the enormous number of needy young people, giving part-time employment to help many stay in school, providing training to many who had left school.

Between 1935 and 1941, more than eight million Americans were employed by the WPA. It spent over $11 billion on 250,000 projects. Another $4 billion was spent by a similar agency, the Public Works Administration (PWA), which built large-scale public projects and employed union labor. Critics charged that the programs were involved in useless "make-work" tasks, that WPA stood for "We piddle around," and that the whole organization was a taxpayer-supported boondoggle and patronage plum to get Roosevelt and other Democrats elected. Others pointed out that WPA took care of only about one-third of the unemployed, and that most of the others had to rely on the states or private charity for subsistence.

Shortly after Black Monday, the president demanded immediate passage of the five major administration bills, terming them "must" legislative items. Included in the crash program were the two bills that became the New Deal's most significant legislative accompishments. Despite the New Deal's reputation for innovation, however, neither of the two was really an administration idea.

Because of an assassin's bullet, Americans will never know just how serious a threat Huey P. Long posed to their political institutions. Unquestioned master of his own state of Louisiana, the most potent demagogue of the Depression, Long attracted national support with a hazy program of redistributing wealth, and the seductive slogan "Every man a king." He was preparing to run for president when he was murdered, but probably not even so gifted a politician as Long could have outmaneuvered Franklin Roosevelt. Still, Long did make Roosevelt—and a great many other people—extremely uncomfortable.

Long grew up in a middle-class but radical-populist family in northern Louisiana. After a brief spell as a traveling salesman, he used his savings and a small loan to put himself through a three-year law course in eight months. But he was interested in finding a way into politics. In 1918, at age twenty-five, he won election to the State Railroad Commission. After six years of denouncing corporations (especially the oil interests), he ran for governor, but lost. The day after his loss in 1924, he declared himself a candidate for 1928, and campaigned hard for four years. He won.

As governor, Long pushed through a reform program that included free textbooks, a large state university, an expanded road system, and a tax on oil production. He also worked unceasingly to extend his own power, firing people throughout the state government and replacing them with his own henchmen. When one of his bills came up in the legislature, Long would go down to the floor of each house and bellow orders at the legislators he controlled.

During his second year as governor, Long tried to pass a bill taxing the refining of oil as well. Aghast, the legislature killed the measure and impeached Long in a broad indictment covering virtually all impeachable offenses. Long barely managed to persuade, bribe, and threaten enough state senators to enable him to stay in office.

Tightening his control over the state, he began to develop a folksy image, calling himself "Kingfish" after a character in the radio program "Amos 'n Andy." The new nickname covered many activities; a U.S. Treasury agent reported to

Huey P. Long

(UPI)

his superiors that "Long and his gang are stealing everything in the state." In 1930 he defeated an incumbent U.S. senator and in 1932 played a large role in nominating Franklin D. Roosevelt for president. The Kingfish remained as governor for a year to ensure his control of the state before taking his seat in the Senate.

When he reached Washington, Long found the Democratic leadership too conservative for him, and within a year found he had problems working under President Roosevelt. Partly, the new president moved too slowly for Long; partly, Long was not born to follow.

From the second-best stage in the country (the U.S. Senate), the master showman began to assemble his own movement. He attacked the New Deal and offered his own program of Share Our Wealth. By 1935, he was receiving speaking invitations from all over the country and published a book modestly titled, *My First Years in the White House.* Roosevelt's advisers estimated he might poll several million votes as a third party candidate. Roosevelt showed his concern: he cut off federal patronage to the Long forces in Louisiana, and a small army of U.S. Treasury agents entered the state to examine Long's income tax returns.

In September 1935, the son-in-law of a Long opponent shot the Kingfish down in the lobby of the state capitol. According to legend, Long's last words were "God, don't let me die. I have so much to do."

Older people had suffered more in the Depression than any other group. Since 1933, an elderly physician from Long Beach, California, Dr. Francis Townsend, had been promoting a plan to give everybody over sixty years of age a federal pension of two hundred dollars a month, an admirable if difficult task given the lagging economy. The movement spread swiftly, and the impoverished elderly at last saw a chance for some dignity at the end of their lives. Several congressmen from both parties were elected with Townsendite backing in 1934, and although the House killed a Townsendite bill (avoiding a roll call, so that those against it would not be identified by name), both Houses saw the political necessity of doing something for the aged. By June, the Congress had passed Roosevelt's Social Security bill.

The bill provided that workers and their employers would contribute a small part of each year's earnings to a common fund. When a person reached retirement age (or could no longer work because of illness), he or she would receive a small pension from the fund. If a worker died, the survivors would receive benefits.

The Social Security Act of 1935 could in no way be considered radical. The pensions were much smaller than those suggested by Townsend, and payments would not start until 1942. Many

The Works Progress Administration employed millions of Americans on thousands of government-sponsored projects, such as the public park beautification efforts by this crew of tree planters. (The Bettmann Archive)

who needed coverage most, including farm workers and domestics, did not come under its provisions. Finally, while most industrialized countries had instituted old-age pension systems decades earlier, none had tried to pay for them out of workers' current earnings. (Roosevelt himself maintained that workers were assessed for policy reasons: "With those taxes in there, no damn politician can ever scrap my social security program.")

During the depths of the Depression, this 1934 street scene was repeated in every city in the nation. The efforts of voluntary agencies and local governments were not enough to help the vast numbers of destitute elderly and unemployed. The Social Security Act of 1935 not only provided immediate relief for the old and disabled, but also prospective annuities for those still at work—its most innovative feature. (UPI)

Social Security, however modestly begun, represented the longest step yet taken by the federal government toward becoming what Roosevelt's critics called a "welfare state," a government that involved itself directly in the financial security of its citizens.

Angered by the Court decision on NRA, convinced by business attacks on the administration that his dream of cooperation had died, Roosevelt now insisted on passage of the bill that would have the New Deal's greatest effect on the American power structure. He declared himself a strong supporter of the National Labor Relations Act (or Wagner Act), a bill he had previously ignored.

The Wagner Act, the most significant piece of prolabor legislation ever signed by an American president, became law at a time when organized labor had almost given up on Roosevelt. The act made it illegal for an employer to refuse to recog-

John L. Lewis led his union out of the A. F. of L. to help found the Congress of Industrial Organizations. Although a strong supporter of the New Deal, Lewis campaigned against Roosevelt's third-term effort in 1940 both because of his isolationist beliefs in foreign policy and a fierce personal feud with the president. (The Bettmann Archive)

nize a labor union favored by a majority of workers as their bargaining agent. The law also contained a list of "unfair labor practices"—an attempt to curb the power of employers in labor–management negotiations and strikes. And it set up the National Labor Relations Board (NLRB) to hear complaints and to supervise elections by workers who wished to unionize.

As a result of the act, labor unions tripled their membership, from a low of 3 million members in the early 1930s to about 9.5 million in 1941. Although this growth was marked by division between the craft unions of the American Federation of Labor (A. F. of L.) and a coalition of industrial unions formed in 1935 by the United Mine Workers' John L. Lewis, the Congress of Industrial Organizations (CIO), it raised organized labor to a

new position of power. Unions could now tell prospective members, with some exaggeration, "The President wants you to join," then call in the NLRB to hold elections by secret ballot among workers to choose a union. Possibly exceeding Roosevelt's own desires, the Wagner Act would eventually make Big Labor a political and economic force capable of challenging Big Business.

Of Roosevelt's other legislative demands, for which he kept a reluctant Congress in session through the hot Washington summer, the most dramatic was the "Wealth Tax." Throughout the 1920s, Secretary of the Treasury Andrew Mellon had steadily reduced taxes on the rich. Roosevelt now sought to reverse the trend, asking for higher tax rates on large personal incomes, a graduated corporate income tax, and federal inheritance taxes. Congress eliminated inheritance taxes but did institute the highest rates ever for the upper tax brackets: a 75 percent personal income tax, a 70 percent estate tax, and a 15 percent corporate income tax.

The Wealth Tax, a modest measure that Congress made even more modest, was as far as Roosevelt cared to go in the redistribution of America's wealth. Probably he only went that far under pressure from Senate liberals and a political need to ease criticism from the left. The bill had little real effect; by the end of the 1930s, the top one percent even held a slightly larger percentage of the diminished national wealth than it had before 1935.

But more than any other New Deal measure, except perhaps the Wagner Act, the Wealth Tax infuriated business. A Chamber of Commerce poll in September 1935 revealed that member organizations opposed the New Deal thirty-five to one. Many businessmen could not bring themselves to speak Roosevelt's name, referring to him bitterly as "that man in the White House." They looked forward with eagerness to the election of 1936, when the country could be redeemed from bureaucracy and Bolshevism.

TRIUMPH OF THE NEW DEAL

Having finally abandoned his hopes for a cooperative policy, Roosevelt welcomed the opportunity to confront political opponents of the New Deal. In his State of the Union message, he boasted of having "earned the hatred of entrenched greed." He drew a parallel between himself and Andrew Jackson, pointing out that in Jackson's fight with the Bank of the United States he had been opposed by the wealthy and most of the newspapers, and supported only by the people. "History," mused Roosevelt, "so often repeats itself."

Besides calling the New Deal socialistic and un-American, a few of Roosevelt's enemies even waged a whispering campaign against the president himself. His polio, they assured one another, had destroyed his mind; late at night, maniacal laughter was rumored to come from the Oval Office. The president was forcing on America a "Jew Deal"; his real name was Franklin Rosenfeld. A wealthy man, whose family money came from stocks, Roosevelt was "a traitor to his class."

To rid the country of this demon, Republicans selected as their candidate the mild-mannered governor of Kansas, Alfred M. Landon. Landon had a double claim to Republican admiration: He was the only Republican governor to win reelection in 1934, and he had balanced his state's budget. (Democrats pointed out that the state of Kansas had a budget roughly the size of New York City's Department of Sanitation.) Yet Landon was a weak choice to rally the fervid anti-New Dealers. He was a dull speaker, and he favored some portions of the New Deal. His most forceful claim was that Republicans could provide a cheaper and more efficient federal government.

Riding the crest of an improved economy, Roosevelt compared business to the elderly gentleman who, having been saved from drowning, turns angrily on his rescuer because he has not also saved his top hat. He ignored Landon and focused his attack on the plutocrats of the Liberty League. His campaign staff set up separate organizations, so that Republican progressives and prolaborites could support Roosevelt without having to align themselves with the Democratic party.

Just before the election, a newspaper wire service asked William Allen White for a story to run in case Landon won. "You have a quaint sense of humor," White wired back. James Farley, the professional politician who ran the Democratic

party and dispensed federal patronage for Roosevelt, predicted that the president would win every state but Maine and Vermont. Not even Roosevelt believed him.

But Farley was right. Carrying forty-six of the forty-eight states, Roosevelt beat Landon by 27 million to 16 million votes. He increased the already whopping Democratic majority in Congress, reducing the Republicans to sixteen votes in the Senate and less than a hundred in the House. The nation had overwhelmingly ratified the New Deal. "This," mourned the publisher of the Republican New York *Herald Tribune,* "is a great national disaster."

Roosevelt had done more than win an election and further depress the hearts of businessmen. He had redrawn the boundaries of American politics. From 1894 to 1930, Republicans had controlled every Congress except four during the Progressive Era. Roosevelt had changed the Democrats from the minority to the majority party in America.

Besides the Democratic South, the Roosevelt coalition found core support among the Catholic and immigrant voters in the large cities. Although many of these groups had previously voted Democratic, Roosevelt gave them, for the first time, heavy representation in top-level government positions. Of the 214 federal judges appointed by the three preceding presidents, for example, only eight were Catholics. Roosevelt, on the other hand, named 51 Catholics among the 196 federal judges appointed during the New Deal Era. The roll call of New Deal officials and advisers—including such names as Corcoran and Cohen, Frankfurter and Farley, Pecora and Bunche—symbolized this change for ethnic Americans. Big-city mayors, like La Guardia in New York and Curley in Boston, emphasized the point.

The third major factor in the coalition was organized labor, supporting Roosevelt in gratitude for the Wagner Act. Although labor had not yet gained the power and influence it was later to have in the Democratic party, it could supply a significant number of campaign workers. Furthermore, it could supply money, badly needed by a party that received few donations from business in 1936. The United Mine Workers became the

ELECTION OF 1936

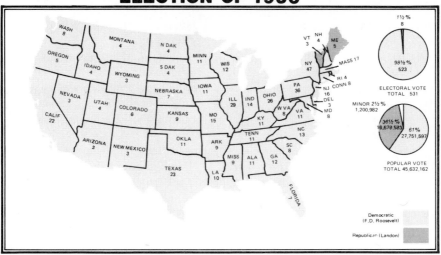

largest single contributor to the Democratic war chest, giving $469,000.

Finally, for the first time ever, Roosevelt had drawn large numbers of black voters into the Democratic party. In 1932, during the worst of a Depression that hurt blacks more than any other group, most black voters had clung to the GOP, the party of Lincoln. But in 1936 Roosevelt won most of the black vote. Remarkably, he effected this revolution while passing no civil rights legislation, while making no major black appointments, and while many New Deal programs existed in the South that were openly discriminatory. Yet relief, at least in the North and West, helped millions of blacks along with other poor people; Roosevelt did appoint black advisers to many departments and agencies; and blacks deeply appreciated Eleanor Roosevelt's frequently expressed concern for their plight. "My friends, go turn Lincoln's picture to the wall," advised one publisher. "That debt has been paid in full."

None of these groups had particularly strong feelings for the Democratic party. Their ties were to Roosevelt—and to Eleanor. Many of them idolized the couple. Yet they voted for Democratic governors, congressmen, and state legislators. Four times Roosevelt ran for president, and four times he was elected. By the time he died, the country had acquired the habit of voting Democratic.

THE COURT FIGHT

Roosevelt, with his massive congressional majorities, now contemplated a new round of reform. But all his plans might be frustrated by the Supreme Court. During 1936, the Court had killed the AAA, an administration act to regulate the coal industry, and a state minimum wage bill. Soon the Wagner Act and the Social Security Act would be coming up before the tribunal.

Roosevelt felt he had to act quickly. He dismissed the notion of a constitutional amendment; the negative vote of only thirteen state legislatures was needed to block passage. He also declined to consider a simple bill to expand the size of the Court, something Congress had done before. FDR finally came up with a tricky plan based on the false premise that the Court could not keep up with its work. It would allow him to make a new appointment for every justice over seventy who did not retire, and it would extend this principle throughout the federal court system.

The members of Congress, including many dedicated New Dealers, were stunned by Roosevelt's scheme. The Democratic chairman of the House Judiciary Committee announced, "Boys, here's where I cash in my chips." Republicans hung back, allowing the many irate Democrats to take the lead in fighting against the bill.

Worse for Roosevelt, the same electorate that had ringingly endorsed him was plainly disturbed over the bill. Many asked themselves if Republican charges that Roosevelt dreamed of becoming a dictator had some truth in them. With the rise to supreme power of Hitler and Mussolini in Europe, Americans clung closer to the institutions that they saw as the protectors of their own freedoms. The Supreme Court stood high on that list of respected institutions. Nevertheless, Roosevelt pushed hard for the plan.

The Court itself, in a variety of ways, actually killed the court-packing proposal. "If they want me to preside over a convention, I can do it," quipped Hughes publicly; but the chief justice, a skilled politician, led efforts by Court members to assure Congress that it could handle its work load. Louis Brandeis, at eighty the oldest and the most liberal man on the Court, lobbied personally against the bill.

Moreover, whether or not influenced by Roosevelt's attack, the Court seemed ready to take a friendlier view toward New Deal legislation. Within two months, it upheld both the Wagner Act and the Social Security Act by five-to-four decisions, and Roosevelt's supporters began to lose stomach for a fight. "Why run for a train after you've caught it?" asked one. Roosevelt's case seemed even less pressing when one of the conservative justices resigned.

But despite adverse public reaction and strong negative advice from congressional leaders, Roosevelt pressed for the bill even after it was obviously dead. One hundred sixty-eight days after the fight had begun, the bill was sent quietly back to committee. "Glory be to God!" proclaimed a senator who usually supported Roosevelt. The New Deal had sustained its first major legislative defeat.

When FDR proposed his controversial Court Reform Bill in 1937, contending that the justices were unable to cope with their work load, the **New Masses** *supported his views by depicting the "Nine Old Men" dozing off on the bench. Although the size of the Supreme Court had been altered before, constitutionally, many felt that the president's court-packing bill was political trickery rather than legitimate reform, and Congress rejected the bill. (Brown Brothers)*

A STRAIN ON THE NEW DEAL

Roosevelt's massive coalition of 1936, like any alliance of disparate groups, could not be maintained intact indefinitely. Its various elements had too many conflicting interests. The alliance began to break up shortly after the election. Industrial unionists of the CIO, newly armed with the Wagner Act, renounced the conservative leadership of the A. F. of L. and mounted a frontal attack on the most formidable anti-union forces—the steel and automobile industries. The nature of the campaign alarmed many people who had considered themselves liberals.

General Motors, as part of its campaign against the unions, paid out almost a million dollars to union-breaking private detectives between 1934 and 1936. Against such company spies and comparable tactics by management, normal union organization could hardly be expected to succeed. Early in 1937, workers occupied seventeen General Motors plants, refusing to come out until GM accepted the union. Thus began the "sit-downs." Strikers defied court orders; with wrenches and other makeshift weapons, they turned back company attempts to oust them. They received support and reinforcements from other unionists. In February, the country's largest corporation surrendered.

Despite an early and surprising capitulation by U.S. Steel, the battles in the rest of the steel industry were even worse. Police killed ten strikers on Memorial Day, 1937, at the Republic Steel plant in South Chicago. (A Senate committee later discovered that the company was the largest private purchaser of tear gas in the country.) The unions lost their battle with steel in 1937, yet within a few years the steel industry and other holdouts had to give in, worn down by a combination of skillful union organizers (many radicals among them) and New Deal support for the new unions through the NLRB.

The strikes terrified millions of middle-class Americans, who were alarmed by the violence and by what they considered a threat to private property. Neither were they pleased with Roosevelt's response to the situation: Although he publicly denounced the sit-down strikes, he did not send troops to break them, as most of his predecessors would have done. Millions of Roosevelt voters began drifting back to the Republican party.

They received an even stronger impetus to do so when the fragile economic recovery collapsed in the fall. Although there were still 8 million unemployed in 1937, other economic indicators had almost reached their pre-Depression level. Encouraged by those signs, Roosevelt, who had not accepted the idea of a permanent government role in the economy, tried to cut back and balance the budget. He sharply reduced expenditures in both the WPA and the PWA, bringing government "pump priming" of the economy to a virtual halt. With startling suddenness, the bottom dropped out of the recovery. The Dow-Jones averages fell from 190 to 117 in two months. An additional 4 million people were thrown out of work. Republicans— and others—began to speak sarcastically of the "Roosevelt recession."

THE LAST NEW DEAL CONGRESS

Hurriedly, Roosevelt recalled the Congress. But he was still reluctant to resume heavy spending. "Everything will work out all right if we just sit tight and keep quiet," he explained, sounding a lot like the man he had replaced five years earlier.

As on so many other issues, New Dealers warred for influence over the president. His secretary of the Treasury, Henry Morgenthau, argued that the government could not support the economy forever; having done all it could, the government must now pull back and let the economy right itself. But Harry Hopkins and the liberal wing called for a final acceptance of the policies of John Maynard Keynes, a British economist who argued that only the government, by pumping money into the economy through deficit spending, could cure a recession. In April 1938, as the recession worsened and congressional elections approached, Roosevelt regretfully abandoned for the last time his hope of a balanced budget. When Congress voted him $4 billion, he revitalized WPA and PWA, and slowly things began to improve.

Although the new Congress had the greatest Democratic majorities in history, Roosevelt could get little new legislation passed. He had weakened himself greatly in the Court fight. Conservative Southern Democrats, many of whom were alarmed by his popularity among blacks, now joined with Republicans to oppose his measures. Many anti-Roosevelt Southerners held positions of power in Congress, such as committee chairmanships won through seniority of congressional service. They could hurt the administration badly. This conservative coalition, formed to frustrate Roosevelt, would continue to dominate Congress for years after his departure.

Roosevelt, after a fight lasting more than a year, did manage to get one more reform bill out of Congress. The Fair Labor Standards Act, although seriously weakened by congressional conservatives, established a national minimum wage of twenty-five cents an hour (to rise over eight years to forty cents) and a workweek of forty-four hours (to drop to forty). It also prohibited child labor, something Wilson had tried to do twenty years earlier. Southerners, whose region paid the lowest wages in the country, fought hard against the bill. "Cotton Ed" Smith maintained that a man could live in South Carolina for fifty cents a day and called the bill a measure to destroy the South. The opposition succeeded in attaching many exemptions to the bill, but it was a beginning.

Roosevelt's other innovation required no congressional endorsement. In previous years he had winked at evidence of business collusion and combination, feeling that such activities stabilized the economy. Now, half convinced that business had conspired to prevent recovery in order to destroy him, he appointed a vigorous new assistant attorney general in charge of "trust busting," Thurman Arnold. Arnold more than quadrupled the size of the antitrust division of the Justice Department, raising its staff to 190 lawyers, and filed suits against such giant corporations as General Electric and Aluminum Company of America. Within five years, Arnold had filed almost half of the antitrust suits brought by the government since passage of the Sherman Act in 1890.

THE END OF THE NEW DEAL

In November 1938, Roosevelt reaped the fruits of middle-class alarm over sit-down strikes, the court-packing bill, and the Roosevelt recession. The Republicans gained eighty-one seats in the House of Representatives, nearly doubling their numbers there. Although Democrats still had a large majority in both Houses, the Republican–Southern Democratic alliance now virtually controlled Congress.

Roosevelt probably had little new legislation to suggest anyway, having gone about as far as he wanted to go. He seems to have entertained no further plans to strengthen government control over business or to deal with the problems of poverty and chronic high-level unemployment.

Moreover, foreign affairs were claiming an increasing part of his time. Roosevelt early saw the threat to the United States posed by European fascist dictators, and he wanted to strengthen the country and take a more active role in foreign policy. Southern congressional leaders were willing to support him on this—if he would soft-pedal domestic reform plans.

From 1933 to 1939, Roosevelt had tried to find cures for the Depression within the capitalist system. He never found a complete answer, and in the Roosevelt recession it became clear that he neither understood nor controlled the economy as much as he himself had once thought. Certainly, little change in the functioning or power distribution of the economy occurred during the 1930s. The New Deal had not been a coherent body of reform thinking that the nation could adopt; it depended for its dynamism mainly upon a strong personal belief in Roosevelt. People continued to cherish their old ideas about free enterprise.

But while Roosevelt may not have wrought deep changes in the American system, he had brought important changes to the American people. Workers saw their position in life anchored by strong unions. The elderly and the unemployed gained hope. Blacks received some recognition from the national government. Farmers saw their position greatly strengthened. Moreover, if Roosevelt's achievements sometimes appear small when compared to the magnitude of the crisis, they clearly loom large when compared to the efforts of previous administrations.

In the end, Roosevelt could at least claim that through his efforts the country had survived a difficult and dangerous period. Millions of Americans had been saved from starvation, and American institutions had come through largely intact. His greatest achievement may have been the appearance of stability and peacefulness in American government and society in 1939, when contrasted with the deprivations and uncertainties so painfully evident in the winter of 1932–33.

Suggested Readings Chapters 39–40

Eleanor Roosevelt

Tamara K. Hareven, *Eleanor Roosevelt: An American Conscience* (1968); James R. Kearney, *Anna Eleanor Roosevelt: The Evolution of a Reformer* (1968); Joseph P. Lash, *Eleanor and Franklin: The Story of Their Relationship Based on Eleanor Roosevelt's Private Papers* (1971) and *Eleanor: The Years Alone* (1972).

Franklin Delano Roosevelt

James M. Burns, *Roosevelt* (2 vols., 1956 and 1970); Frank Freidel, *Franklin D. Roosevelt* (5 vols. to date, 1952–1975); Alfred B. Rollins, *Roosevelt and Howe* (1962); Rexford G. Tugwell, *In Search of Roosevelt* (1972).

The New Deal

Leonard Baker, *Back to Back: The Duel Between FDR and the Supreme Court* (1967); John Braeman et al., *The New Deal*, I: *The National Level* (1975) and *The New Deal*, II: *The State and Local Levels* (1975); Paul K. Conkin, *The New Deal* (rev. ed., 1975); David E. Conrad, *Forgotten Farmers: Sharecroppers in the New Deal* (1965); Mario Eunaudi, *The Roosevelt Revolution* (1959); Sidney Fine, *Automobile Under the Blue Eagle: Labor Management and the Automobile Manufacturing Code* (1963); Daniel Fusfeld, *The Economic Thought of Franklin D. Roosevelt* (1955); Otis L. Graham, Jr., *Encore for Reform: The Old Progressives and the New Deal* (1967); Ellis Hawley, *The New Deal and the Problem of Monopoly* (1966); J. Joseph Huthmacher, *Senator Robert F. Wagner and the Rise of Urban Liberalism* (1968); Barry D. Karl, *Executive Reorganization and Reform in the New Deal* (1963); Richard S. Kirkendall, *Social Scientists and Farm Policies in the Age of Roosevelt* (1966); Paul A. Kurzman, *Harry Hopkins* (1974); Roy Lubove, *The Struggle for Social Security* (1968); William E. Leuchtenberg, *Franklin D. Roosevelt and the New Deal* (1963); Jane D. Matthews, *The Federal Theater* (1967); Thomas K. McCraw, *TVA and the Power Fight* (1971); Michael E. Parrish, *Securities Regulation and the New Deal* (1970); James T. Patterson, *Congressional Conservatism and the New Deal: The Growth of the Conservative Coalition in Congress, 1933–1939* (1967) and *New Deal and the States: Federalism in Transition* (1969); Richard Polenberg, *Reorganizing Roosevelt's Government: The Controversy Over Executive Reorganization, 1936–1939* (1966); C. Herman Pritchett, *The Roosevelt Court* (1948); Arthur M. Schlesinger, Jr., *The Age of Roosevelt* (3 vols. to date, 1957–1960); Charles F. Searle, *Minister of Relief: Harry Hopkins* (1963); Bruce M. Stave, *The New Deal and the Last Hurrah: Pittsburgh Machine Politics* (1970); Bernard Sternsher, *Rexford Tugwell and the New Deal* (1964).

America in the Great Depression

David H. Bennett, *Demagogues in the Depression* (1969); Irving Bernstein, *Turbulent Years: A History of the American Worker, 1933–1941* (1970); Lyle W. Dorsett, *The Pendergast Machine* (1968); Sidney Fine, *Sit-down: The General Motors Strike of 1936–1937* (1969); Walter Galenson, *The CIO Challenge to the AFL* (1960); Abraham Holtzman, *The Townsend Movement* (1963); Arthur Mann, *LaGuardia Comes to Power: 1933* (1965); Broadus Mitchell, *Depression Decade* (1947); Richard H. Pells, *Radical Visions and American Dreams: Culture and Social Thought in the Depression Years* (1973); Van L. Perkins, *Crisis in Agriculture* (1969); William Stott, *Documentary Expression and Thirties America* (1973); Studs Terkel, *Hard Times: An Oral History of the Great Depression* (1970); Charles Trout, *Boston, the Great Depression and the New Deal* (1977); Charles J. Tull, *Father Coughlin and the New Deal* (1965); T. Harry Williams, *Huey Long* (1969); George Wolfskill, *The Revolt of the Conservatives* (1974).

December 7, 1941: Attack on Pearl Harbor

41

On December 7, 1941, while negotiations to avoid war between the United States and Japan were proceeding in Washington, 353 Japanese planes attacked Pearl Harbor. This massive, audacious, and extremely successful attack on the Americans' principal—and supposedly impregnable—naval base in Hawaii came before Japan had even declared war. Grim-faced and resolved, President Roosevelt went before Congress to call it "unprovoked and dastardly" and "a day which will live in infamy."

Until this assault, Congress, like the country as a whole, had been sharply split between interventionists and isolationists. Now Congress and most Americans were furious at this shrewdly planned, superbly executed, and deadly raid. It dealt a staggering blow to American power in the Pacific. Congress swiftly and overwhelmingly voted to enter World War II. During the rest of the long, terrible conflict the single slogan that most readily aroused Americans to action was: "Remember Pearl Harbor!"

The attack on Pearl, referred to as Operation Z by the Japanese, had a history. A key figure in planning the attack was Admiral Isoroku Yamamoto, head of the Japanese Imperial Navy. If Japan's national interest called for war with the United States, the admiral reasoned, why not strike directly at the enemy fleet's Pacific home base? No mere "battleship admiral," the air-minded Yamamoto knew the possibilities of carrier-based warfare.

Yamamoto was neither a visionary nor overly optimistic. He was quite dubious about defeating the United States in war. He knew the country, having studied at Harvard and worked at the Japanese embassy in Washington during the 1920s. He had returned to Japan sobered by American industrial might. He harbored no illusions about *conquering* the United States. An invasion of the continental United States never figured seriously in Japanese war plans; Japan clearly lacked the resources for such a long-range, massive effort. "If I am told to fight regardless of the consequences," Yamamoto told the Japanese premier in 1940, "I shall run wild for the first six months, but I have utterly no confidence for the second or third years."

Isoroku Yamamoto, commander in chief of the Japanese Imperial Fleet, was a strong advocate of the navy's use of air power. Responsible for planning naval operations, he was the mastermind of the audacious attack on Pearl Harbor. (Naval Photographic Center)

Others in the Japanese military shared Yamamoto's fears over the probable consequences of war with the United States. Then why venture such a dangerous policy, such a desperate gamble? By 1940 Japan was an authoritarian society ruled by a civilian-military government. Its leaders agreed on the country's basic needs. Most important was access to the raw materials vital for a modern industrial nation. Without them, heavily populated Japan would become a third- or fourth-rate power. Without expansion the Japanese would be forced to tighten their belts even to stay alive.

So Japan decided to expand. In 1931 it took Manchuria from a helpless China. America and Western Europe objected strongly but ineffectively. In 1937 Japan launched a full-scale invasion of the rest of China. Despite Western protests the Japanese captured the coastal portions and overran much of the Chinese interior. By mid-1940 Japan's ally, Hitler, had conquered France, the Netherlands, and much of the rest of Europe, isolating Great Britain. Therefore, Tokyo reasoned that it could now expand Japanese control into Southeast Asia. It planned to establish a massive sphere of influence, "the Greater East Asia Co-Prosperity Sphere."

Thus, early in 1941, Admiral Yamamoto began planning his strategy. Success hinged on two factors: The attackers must achieve total surprise; and the bulk of the American fleet, especially the capital ships (battleships and carriers), would have to be at their moorings the day of attack.

While Japanese and American diplomats in Washington negotiated, naval aviators began months of intensive practice. When Yamamoto got wind of grumbling and possible footdragging, he threatened to resign if the plan was scrapped. Objections ceased. Yamamoto became for the moment the symbol of the Japanese navy. Under no condition would his fellow officers accept his resignation. Operation Z (named for the signal flag that Admiral Togo hoisted before trouncing the Russians) became a reality. If diplomacy failed, only the date of the attack on America remained to be fixed.

Meanwhile, political developments ominously paralleled the course of these military preparations. After France had fallen to Germany, Japan grabbed the northern half of French Indochina. It held back from the southern half—as well as from British Malaya and the Dutch East Indies (present-day Indonesia)—after the United States warned that action in these areas would have grave consequences. Roosevelt banned shipments of aviation gasoline and scrap metal to Japan, and increased American support to China. The American ambassador to Japan, Joseph C. Grew, noted: "We are getting ready, steadily, for the ultimate showdown."

By summer 1941 matters had become even more tense. Hitler had invaded Russia; Japan could now pursue its Asian policy without fear of Soviet armies. Japan advanced, occupying southern Indochina in late July. The Americans, British, and Dutch responded by seizing all Japanese financial assets in their areas of jurisdiction. They also ended Japan's access to their raw materials. The United States gave an official warning that, if Japan took any further steps "by force or threat of force," America would defend its "legitimate rights and interests."

In diplomacy's stilted language, these were strong words. The Japanese premier suggested that he and President Roosevelt hold a summit meeting, possibly in Hawaii. This could not be arranged. On October 16 a new premier, General Hideki Tojo, an all-out militarist, came to power.

Yet the national interests of both countries still favored more negotiations. Further talks would help hide Japanese war preparations—especially Operation Z, now in high gear. Washington would also benefit. It could use the extra time to reinforce its Pacific bases, particularly in the Philippines. In November 1941 Japan sent a veteran diplomat, Saburo Kurusu, to Washington to head a negotiating team. Diplomatic exchanges would obviously continue for at least a few more weeks.

At the same time, table-top maneuvers at the Japanese Naval War College demonstrated the most effective route for the Pearl Harbor attack force. The fleet would sail in a wide arc across the nearly deserted waters of the North Central Pacific. Then it would turn sharply south on reaching a point 500 miles north of Hawaii. Yamamoto thought that this route would give the best chance for surprise.

On November 5, while the Japanese and Americans negotiated in Washington, Yamamoto issued a secret order outlining the first phase of the Japanese offensive against Hawaii. The twenty-three attack ships included six carriers and two battleships under Admiral Chuichi Nagumo. He disliked the plan and still hoped the attack would somehow be canceled.

The Japanese strike force sailed on November 26. The attack date had been set for December 7 (Sunday morning) in Hawaii. The American navy—even though on military alert because of the dangerous diplomatic situation—had weekends off. So its ships usually anchored in the harbor on Friday and stayed there until Monday. Nagumo's orders did contain one escape clause. If the Washington negotiations succeeded, the attack was off. The fleet would then wait in the North Pacific for new orders.

Yet, any chance that diplomacy could ease the crisis was now vanishing. On November 20 the negotiator Kurusu made Tokyo's final offer: Japan would leave southern Indochina but remain in the northern part, as well as in China. The United States must not only lift its ban on oil to Japan but also cut off aid to China. Secretary of State Cordell Hull immediately rejected these terms. Fearful of being called appeasers, Roosevelt and Hull would make no concessions. The American note of November 26—the very day the strike force set sail—stated that America's embargo would continue until Japan withdrew from both Indochina and China.

Roosevelt and Hull, along with their top civilian and military colleagues, had good reason to distrust the sincerity of Japanese negotiations. Operation Magic of American naval intelligence had cracked Japan's diplomatic codes. On November 22—two days after Kurusu's

final offer and four days before the formal American reply to it—a cable intercepted from Tokyo read: "THIS TIME WE MEAN IT, THAT THE DEADLINE [November 29] CANNOT BE CHANGED! AFTER THAT THINGS ARE AUTOMATICALLY GOING TO HAPPEN."

What things? Most likely, reasoned the leaders in Washington, the Japanese planned to attack the Philippines and British and Dutch holdings in Asia. Hawaii seemed beyond the range of effective Japanese assault. So American short-sightedness was beginning to aid the future success of Operation Z. Knowledge of Magic was restricted to Washington's inner circle, to keep Tokyo from realizing its code had been broken. Thus American brass in Hawaii had no inkling of the intercepts.

All U.S. Pacific military commanders received some warning on November 27 to expect a hostile move by Japan. But Washington took no action during the next ten days. Only four Magic decoding machines existed then: two in Washington, one in the Philippines, and another in London. There were none in Hawaii. The commanders there, Admiral Husband E. Kimmel and General Walter C. Short, were not even told about the machine.

Admiral Kimmel had seriously considered, but then rejected, the idea of taking his fleet out of Pearl Harbor. In open water, he felt, the ships would be too vulnerable. His four carriers were not then available to provide air cover. (Three were bringing warplanes to American-held Pacific islands; the fourth was in San Diego for repairs.) Besides, moored safely in Pearl, his ships could be protected by the several hundred army planes stationed at Hawaiian bases. Still, Kimmel might well have sent most of the battleships out with the carriers to the other Pacific islands.

If Admiral Kimmel had initiated adequate air reconnaissance of the seas around Pearl Harbor, Operation Z might have been discovered and foiled. But neither he nor anyone else in authority expected Japanese hostilities to begin there. (UPI)

Premier Tojo is shown in a respectful posture before Emperor Hirohito at a ceremony celebrating the Japanese Empire's 2,600th anniversary. Tojo's rise to power helped determine Japan's course toward war. Hirohito's role was largely symbolic, but he supported Tojo's militarism and anti-Americanism. (U.S. Office of War Information/National Archives)

General Short reacted to the war warning by increasing the army's anti-sabotage defenses. Sabotage, he apparently thought, might come from Hawaii's large Japanese-American community. Instead of widely spacing his aircraft or protecting them in concrete shelters already constructed on the major fields, Short ordered the planes bunched together, wing tip to wing tip, so that fewer soldiers could then protect them against saboteurs. But Japanese Americans in Hawaii never aided Japan, although some Japanese diplomats were spies.

In short, the potential use of Magic had been botched. Hawaiian commanders never received copies of important decoded messages. These messages piled up at the few overworked decoding centers. As far back as September, and with increasing frequency thereafter, Tokyo asked the Japanese consulate in Honolulu for details on the location of American warships in the harbor. By November such naval maps were being transmitted to Tokyo twice a week. Some of these Magic intercepts were not deciphered and translated for many days after reception. Especially revealing Japanese messages of November 29, for example, waited until December 5 to be deciphered. Even then, they received little attention.

Even key Washington officials, including Roosevelt and Hull, apparently did not take the Magic decodings very seriously.[1] But in Tokyo the die had been cast. Hull's note of November 26 refusing to lift the American embargo infuriated Premier Tojo. He thought it proved beyond all doubt American insincerity in the negotiations. Tojo persuaded Emperor Hirohito to let Operation Z proceed. A palace meeting ratified the decision for war. Hirohito did not attempt to intervene. He believed, as he later told an aide, that the United States was looking for nothing less than Japan's humiliation.

Should Kurusu continue negotiating or at least pretend to? Of course he should, Tojo decided; it would facilitate operations. In Washington Kurusu asked a Japanese newspaperman rhetorically, "Am I being used as a smoke screen?" Indeed he was.

Kurusu's mission helped screen the task force then steaming across the North Pacific. After leaving port on November 26, the fleet enjoyed seven days of uneventful sailing. The weather cooperated. Light winds made refueling at sea relatively easy. Overcast conditions and generally poor visibility decreased chances of detection. Security precautions were rigidly enforced. No radio contact was made except within the fleet. At night a blackout was enforced. Most ships communicated by signal flags and blinkers. They did not even discard garbage to avoid leaving a trail.

---

[1] There were, however, several notable exceptions. On November 25 Roosevelt told Secretary of War Henry L. Stimson of his fears that Japan would strike on December 1 without declaring war, "for the Japanese are notorious for making an attack without warning." Stimson wanted to bomb Japanese convoys if they moved farther south. Roosevelt rejected the notion because "we are a democracy."

The fleet's passage north of the American base at Midway provided cause for some real concern. No American planes or ships spotted them, however. On December 6 there was the final fueling. Japanese intelligence from Hawaii reported the presence of many American warships there but no carriers or heavy cruisers. It was decided that the force would strike and destroy whatever was at hand.

A little past noon on December 6 all hands were summoned on deck. Their officers read them the emperor's war message. Yamamoto had also sent a statement: "The moment has arrived. The rise or fall of our empire is at stake." Then Admiral Togo's flag, the signal flag that gave its name to Operation Z, went up above the attack fleet's flagship. The crews shouted *"Banzai!"*—their battle cry—and turned the ships south toward Hawaii. All was ready for the great moment.

The launch itself was almost perfect. Pilots and flight crewmen were aroused at 3:30 A.M. The news that the Americans apparently had not adequately protected their ships encouraged the Japanese airmen. At zero hour (6 A.M.) the carriers were 200 miles from Oahu. As the ships rolled and pitched, the lead pilots waited eagerly for the order to take off. When it came, the first wave of 183 planes left the 6 carriers in 15 minutes, bettering their fastest practice runs. With Commander Mitsuo Fuchida in command, flying one of the high-level bombers, the air fleet headed for its target.

Overconfidence and negligence had made Americans complacent. Many viewed the Japanese as a society adept at imitating Western ways but with little creativity. Informed Americans knew that the Japanese had a history of attacking first and declaring war later, but most thought they would not dare attack the United States. In 1932 the American navy itself had successfully "attacked" the harbor during a mock raid. The event was quickly forgotten. The Navy Department filed the report in its archives as just another war-games exploit.

There were certainly some warnings during 1941. In January a Peruvian diplomat in Tokyo reported that a drunken Japanese official had boasted about Japan's plan to sink the American fleet and knock out Pearl Harbor. Ambassador Grew passed the "fantastic" rumor along to Washington. A few months later Grew noted that Japan was "capable of sudden and surprise action" with "a determination to risk all." In August, the chiefs of American naval and army aviation in Hawaii sent a gloomy memo noting Hawaii's vulnerability to air attack. They correctly predicted the use of six carriers in a dawn assault from the north.

The shortcomings of American defensive reactions were considerable, in view of what was known about Japanese intentions and how much more could have been learned if the data from Magic had been properly exploited. One man who worried a great deal was Admiral Kimmel. After November 27—the day Kimmel received the war warning from Washington—naval intelligence lost track of the Japanese fleet. Kimmel asked the head of his intelligence section at Pearl where the fleet was. The officer admitted he did not know. Not entirely in jest, Kimmel asked: "You mean to say that it could appear rounding Diamond Head [a famous high point close to Pearl Harbor] without our knowing it?" The intelligence officer answered: "I hope that it would be spotted before that."

Yamamoto had no intention of parading his ships past Diamond Head, impressive though the sight would have been. Instead, his planes crossed over Oahu's northern coast. At 7:49 A.M. Fuchida broke radio silence to signal Nagumo (and Yamamoto also, since Tokyo picked up the message). Attack by the first wave had begun, blessed with the key element of surprise. Fuchida's first signal was "To-To-To," repeating the opening syllable of the Japanese word for "charge." Soon he sent an even more welcome message: "Tora [Tiger], Tora, Tora," which meant that the Americans were almost completely unprepared.

They were indeed unprepared. Yet that same morning warnings had come. Five full hours before the attack began, Magic in Washington had decoded the final Japanese message breaking off negotiations. The officer in charge took the intercept straight to Admiral Harold R. Stark, chief of naval operations. Though impressed, Stark did not phone Admiral Kimmel.

Yet another chance to prepare for the attack was missed. This occurred on Oahu's north coast, precisely where Fuchida's squadrons would penetrate American air space. The Army Signal Corps had installed a movable radar station there. At 6:45 Private George Elliott, the enlisted man on duty at the station, noted the presence of a single plane on the radar screen.

But at 7:06 Elliott noted much larger blips on the screen, again moving toward Oahu from the north, and rapidly growing larger. He asked the advice of another soldier. They decided to call signal headquarters at Fort Shafter. But the only officer on duty there, a pilot, told them to forget about it. He knew that a dozen American planes were scheduled to arrive from California that morning. Again the Japanese had benefited from a stroke of luck. Fuchida's first wave was confused with reinforcements from the States.

After sending the signal "Tora, Tora, Tora," Fuchida fired a blue flare from his bomber. It informed pilots in planes without radios that surprise had been achieved. It would produce a prearranged pattern of attack, with the slow-flying but deadly torpedo bombers going in first. But apparently one group of pilots, their vision obscured by the cloud cover, had not seen the luminous signal. At least they did not wiggle their planes' wings in response. Fuchida then committed one of the few Japanese mistakes of the day. He fired a second flare.

This changed the flight plan. Two flares meant that dive bombers would attack first. Fighters and some dive bombers were to concentrate on American airfields and antiaircraft installations, rather than on the fleet. Happily for the Japanese, the commander of the torpedo bomber wing ignored the second flare. His forty heavy but superbly piloted aircraft peeled off and glided down to the prescribed low altitudes, heading straight for their principal targets, the battleships.

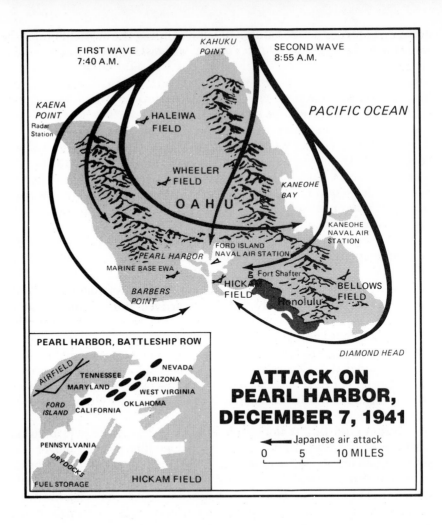

FIRST WAVE
7:40 A.M.

SECOND WAVE
8:55 A.M.

KAHUKU POINT

KAENA POINT
Radar Station

PACIFIC OCEAN

HALEIWA FIELD

WHEELER FIELD

KANEOHE BAY

O A H U

KANEOHE NAVAL AIR STATION

PEARL HARBOR
FORD ISLAND NAVAL AIR STATION

MARINE BASE EWA

Fort Shafter

HICKAM FIELD

BELLOWS FIELD

Honolulu

BARBERS POINT

DIAMOND HEAD

PEARL HARBOR, BATTLESHIP ROW

AIRFIELD

TENNESSEE
MARYLAND

NEVADA
ARIZONA
WEST VIRGINIA
OKLAHOMA

FORD ISLAND
CALIFORNIA

PENNSYLVANIA

DRYDOCKS

FUEL STORAGE

HICKAM FIELD

**ATTACK ON
PEARL HARBOR,
DECEMBER 7, 1941**

Japanese air attack

0   5   10 MILES

Meanwhile, in answer to the second signal, the faster planes went hunting for American aircraft at Wheeler, Hickam, Haleiwa, Bellows, and other fields. Wheeler housed most of the American fighter planes. These planes, already tested in combat, could hold their own against the more maneuverable Japanese fighters. But, owing to General Short's fear of ground sabotage, Wheeler's planes had been crowded together like sheep in a pen. The attackers quickly destroyed a third of the planes and damaged many more. Fires broke out in the hangars and storage buildings. One of them contained ammunition, which exploded, causing additional losses.

American military aviation tried to respond but it was useless. At Wheeler, for instance, most of the pilots were still sleeping. But Lieutenants George Welch and Ken Taylor, who were breakfasting at the officers' club, saw the dive bombers swoop. They rushed for a car and sped at a hundred miles an hour to an auxiliary airstrip unknown to the Japanese. There they took off, headed for a Japanese squadron, and shot down three planes before landing to refuel. During the dogfight one of the three machine guns in Welch's plane jammed. Taylor was wounded twice.

At Kaneohe Naval Air Station the commanding officer was drinking his morning coffee. When he heard planes, he glanced up. To his anger several V-formations of planes—all flying lower than regulations allowed—were turning toward the right into the bay where most of his thirty-three new flying boats were at anchor. He leaped to his feet shouting, "Those fools know there is a strict rule against making a right turn!" His young son, who was with him, exclaimed, "Look, red circles on the wings!" Realizing it was the Japanese rising-sun symbol, the commander rushed to his headquarters and set up a fierce antiaircraft fire against the invaders.

At the moment of attack only a fourth of the antiaircraft guns on the ships moored in the harbor were manned. Land-based antiaircraft guns could not respond immediately because ammunition had been stored to prevent deterioration. Their effectiveness increased as the morning wore on. Unluckily, the B-17s arrived from California about then. Weary after fourteen hours in the air, the American bomber pilots and crews thought they had flown into a nightmare. Columns of smoke rose from the ground. Airfields were ablaze, including the one the B-17s were supposed to use on Ford Island. Incredibly, not one Flying Fortress was shot out of the air. All landed at various fields, though some were shot at and destroyed after landing.

Admiral Kimmel and General Short had arranged to play golf together that morning. Kimmel rose early. At about 7:30 he received a phone call from a staff officer. The destroyer *Ward* had sighted a submerged submarine and dropped depth charges. Kimmel headed for his office. Just as he was leaving, he received a second call adding some details about the *Ward* incident. Suddenly, the officer at the other end shouted that Japanese planes were attacking. Kimmel ran out to his garden, which

The devastation on the ground after the attack was extensive. By 10 A.M. Hickam Naval Air Station was in chaos and a smoking ruin. (Navy Dept./ National Archives)

overlooked the harbor. What he saw froze him. The carnage was under way. The sky over the bay seemed alive with attack planes. Kimmel knew his ships were doomed.

Kimmel got to his headquarters at 8:10, during the height of the five-wave attack. There was nothing he could do but stand at the window and watch his fleet and men under attack. A spent Japanese bullet crashed through the window and bounced off Kimmel's chest. He felt that "it would have been merciful had it killed me."

Fuchida's pilots wanted to destroy the American fleet. Disappointed over not finding carriers in port, they concentrated on the battleships. Seven of the eight were lined up on Battleship Row in the harbor. Five were moored to the docks, and two were on an "outside" parallel column. Thus the two inside battleships could not be attacked by torpedoes. The dive bombers went after them. Soon every battleship had been hit.

On the *Nevada*, at one end of the row, Bandmaster Oden McMillan stood with his musicians, ready to play morning colors at 8 A.M. As they began "The Star-Spangled Banner," a Japanese plane dropped its deadly burden on the nearby *Arizona*, then peeled off just feet above the band. The *Nevada's* deck officer, Ensign Joe Taussig, shouted over the public-address system:: "All hands, general quarters. Air raid!" The *Nevada*, though damaged, tried to steam out to sea. The Japanese bore in, hoping to sink her at Pearl Harbor's mouth and thus close the port indefinitely. The *Nevada* took six bomb hits but made it to the other side of the bay, keeping the channel clear.

The *Oklahoma* took four torpedoes within one minute and began to capsize. The *California* sustained hits that caused her to settle slowly and finally sink. And so on down the row: *Tennessee, West Virginia, Maryland, Pennsylvania.* Fuchida, who was supervising the attack in his bomber overhead, frowned in disapproval as his pilots raced in. They were bunched up in their assault, instead of diving in stages as prearranged. But their formation no longer really mattered—every American ship was a sitting duck.

The worst disaster came when the *Arizona* blew apart and sank, trapping more than a thousand men inside. Later, it was claimed that a bomb had gone straight down her stack. But the probable cause of the disaster was the detonation of the ship's ammunition store. Whatever the cause, the gigantic pillar of fire and smoke rose 500 feet. The shock was so tremendous that, far above, Fuchida could feel his bomber tremble. Miraculously, many American seamen survived this searing blast. Some of these survivors tried to swim to shore and safety, but burning oil engulfed most of them.

The second wave, 170 additional planes, flew over at 8:55. Fuchida and his pilots had taken more time than planned because of additional bomb runs. The fresh attackers went to work shortly after the first wave pulled out. They encountered considerably more opposition from heavy antiaircraft fire and lost twenty-one planes. Towering columns of smoke cut visibility. Still, the second wave of bombers did considerable damage in its one-hour attack, knocking out some ships not previously hit. They withdrew at 9:45 to return to their carriers.

On Battleship Row the rescue effort began at once. Most of the giant ships were ablaze. One had overturned, while another had settled straight down into the mud. In the plotting room of the heavily damaged *West Virginia* Ensign Victor Delano watched smoke and oily water seep in. He and several others headed forward to another compartment. Just before closing a watertight door, they heard frantic calls from seamen blown from the deck above them by the explosions but had to go on. Delano then returned to the plotting room, risking his life to help a wounded sailor. Neither he nor his companion could get his footing on the oil-slick deck. The ship's angle compounded the problem.

Luckily, one compartment wall was a switchboard. By grabbing its knobs, they were at last able to reach the door. As the men moved forward, they could hear the shouts and pleas of others, sealed off by the watertight doors in compartments that were rapidly filling with water. The damage-control officer had ordered the doors closed. He knew that this order condemned many men to death. But opening the doors would merely cause the ship to sink quickly and doubtless drown even more men. Many of the men managed to make their way to the upper decks; others were able to swim to the surface by escaping through portholes. The harbor was filled with boats and launches rescuing the survivors.

The Japanese victory would have been more complete and would have had more serious consequences for the United States if American aircraft carriers had been in port. As it was, the Japanese had to be satisfied with destroying American battleships. (Navy Dept./ National Archives)

The overturned *Oklahoma* posed special problems. Dozens of men, perhaps hundreds, were still alive in a crazy house where floors had become ceilings. Partial flooding meant that air pockets existed in most compartments. There, survivors could exist for a time, if they treaded water or grasped whatever protruded from walls. About thirty men trapped in the dispensary waited an hour. Noting with alarm the decreasing amount of oxygen in the air, they decided to move. But where?

Diving into the water that covered most of the dispensary, they found a porthole. Though no one knew where it led, staying in the dispensary meant sure death. Those who were thin enough to squeeze through the porthole swam clear of the ship and were rescued. Others tried but could not squeeze through the porthole. They died in the dispensary.

Another group of sailors trapped near the *Oklahoma's* center seemed doomed beyond any hope. Amazingly, one of them dived downward through a funnel. He emerged directly under the capsized ship, reached topside, then swam clear of the wreckage and reached the surface. He led rescuers to his mates.

The rescue crews relied on this kind of information. Without it, they had no way of locating the living. Rescuers banged on ship hulls, and survivors lost no time in signaling back. Yet the sounds seemed to come from everywhere and nowhere. Several times crews laboriously cut holes in a hull, then found nobody.

Sometimes they unwittingly added to the tragedy. Acetylene torches consumed the oxygen in the air pockets once the hull had been punctured. Slower working pneumatic drills allowed precious air to escape as the water continued to rise in the compartments. Despite these dangers, inaction spelled sure doom for the trapped and so people worked through the night. They saved a surprising number of men.

The Japanese had fashioned a striking yet limited victory at Pearl Harbor. The casualty figures were all in their favor.[2] But, in the long run, Operation Z failed to cripple American power. First, no American carrier was in port; the war that followed showed conclusively that carriers were more vital than battleships. Second, American plane losses would soon be dwarfed by the huge air armadas that were already beginning to roll out of American factories. Third, the naval base itself had not suffered severe damage. Fourth, and possibly most significant, the Japanese—concentrating on ships and planes—had ignored the oil storage tanks. If Hawaii's fuel supply had been destroyed (as it easily could have been), Japan might have: (1) forced the carriers and other ships still functioning back to California for oil; (2) made Pearl useless as a base for several months and perhaps a year; and (3) thus given Japan freedom to expand in the Pacific without worrying about counterattacks. Instead, Pearl began

---

[2] All eight battleships in Pearl on December 7 were either sunk, capsized, or badly damaged. Ten other ships, including three cruisers and three destroyers, were also casualties. In military aviation 188 American planes were destroyed, and nearly all the others were damaged. About 100 civilians and 2,403 men in uniform died. Japan lost only twenty-nine planes, five two-man submarines, and a total of 54 lives.

to function right after December 7 as the staging area for a massive American buildup of military power.

By bombing the harbor, Japan gained some time—but little more. Even some of the sunken battleships came back to haunt their attackers. All but two were put back in service. But these consequences lay in the future. December 7 was Japan's day. The assault on Hawaii was only part of a mighty Japanese drive. Simultaneous attacks took place on the Philippines and on British and Dutch colonies.

Some diplomatic strings remained to be tied. The final Japanese note to Secretary Hull was supposed to be delivered at 1 P.M. But delay in decoding and typing the long document kept the Japanese diplomats from arriving at Hull's office until 2 P.M. In the meantime, Hull had read the Magic intercept of the note. Roosevelt got the news of the attack at 1:47 from Secretary of the Navy Knox.

Roosevelt called Hull at 2:05. The Japanese diplomats had just arrived and were in the waiting room. Roosevelt instructed Hull to receive them but say nothing about the attack. The Japanese ambassador, by way of apology, said he had been told by his government to hand over the note at 1 P.M. Hull pretended to read it (he knew its contents already) and handed it back saying it was "crowded with infamous falsehoods and distortions." With a disgusted shrug Hull dismissed the envoys.

In Tokyo, Ambassador Grew still hoped to achieve something positive. The day before the attack, Roosevelt had sent a personal appeal for peace to Emperor Hirohito. Grew asked for an audience with the emperor. At 7 A.M., Grew was awakened and told that the foreign minister wished to see him. Hoping to see Hirohito, Grew rushed to the ministry, only to be handed the note breaking off negotiations. Two hours later he heard that Japan had declared war on the United States and its European allies.

Japan greeted the news of war and victory at Pearl Harbor jubilantly. Newspaper extras appeared on the streets, and the radio alternated between martial music and patriotic slogans. At the end of December the fleet returned to Japan, and the government and people welcomed the heroes of Operation Z with celebrations and medals. Hirohito granted an audience to Nagumo, Fuchida, and several other task force leaders. The rising sun had reached its zenith. But Yamamoto, clearheaded as usual, warned that "this war will give us many headaches in the future."

Roosevelt and most Americans never doubted this. On December 8, when the president asked Congress to declare war on Japan, he assured his listeners that, whatever the cost, Japan would be vanquished.

42 The United States as a Superpower

After Pearl Harbor anything seemed possible for the Japanese. Their plan for domination of Asia (the Greater East Asia Co-Prosperity Sphere) became a reality, at least temporarily. Japan had signed a mutual security treaty with Nazi Germany, and Hitler hastily declared war on the United States shortly after Pearl Harbor.

Only twenty-three years had elapsed since the end of World War I. Now another generation of American youth would have to fight overseas. Ironically, America's entry into the war came after a decade of intense isolationist feeling.

A profound disillusionment with World War I had spread throughout the United States by the 1930s. It no longer seemed a clean-cut crusade to "make the world safe for democracy." Instead, some regarded it as a capitalist war that the United States had fought to protect loans made to European allies by American bankers. This in turn had benefited the arms manufacturers, the "merchants of death." Republican Senator Gerald P. Nye of North Dakota developed these themes in sensational congressional hearings during the mid-1930s. Nye's claims helped reinforce American support for isolationism as a foreign policy.

THE NEUTRALITY ACTS

The Neutrality Act of 1935 limited Roosevelt's ability to respond effectively to overseas aggression, even if American interests were endangered.

This law attempted to close the gap between a president's control of foreign relations and Congress's right to declare war. Henceforth, if war broke out anywhere, the president had to issue a proclamation of neutrality. More important, the law forbade shipping arms to any nation at war, whether victim or aggressor. Roosevelt sought power to ban or "embargo" shipments to unfriendly or aggressor nations while permitting arms to go to the victims of aggression. Congress refused this request.

Yet isolationist hopes proved no match for events in the later 1930s. Italy invaded Ethiopia in October 1935. Roosevelt invoked the Neutrality

Charles A. Lindbergh and Senator Gerald P. Nye stirred popular sentiment for isolationism. Americans had viewed World War I as a noble crusade. But Nye's munitions-industry investigations uncovered less noble reasons for this country's entrance into the war, which led Lindbergh to campaign for nonintervention in future world power struggles. (Acme Newspictures)

Act, this time willingly, since an arms embargo would hinder Italy more than Ethiopia. He also asked American oil producers for a "moral embargo" on shipments to Italy, limiting amounts to prewar levels. Ethiopia fell to the Italian invaders. Italy then quit the League of Nations, following the example of Japan and Germany. The foundations for the Axis alliance had been laid.

Further Triumphs for the Dictators

The menace to the Western democracies increased in 1936. Hitler armed the Rhineland, which had been demilitarized after World War I. General Francisco Franco, leader of Spain's fascists, led a revolt—which was ultimately successful—against the Spanish government. Congress reacted by passing a second Neutrality Act, tightening the isolationist provisions of the first law.

So the first series of fascist moves, instead of weakening isolationism, strengthened it. Believing the Atlantic and Pacific oceans afforded the United States ample security, isolationists argued that America should be a fortress prepared for any outside attack. But the United States should not meddle in foreign politics or wars. Yet most isolationists were not pacifists. They favored American rearmament, particularly a larger, two-ocean navy.

Rise of the Interventionists

In October 1937 Roosevelt sent up an anti-isolationist trial balloon, only to see it shot down quickly. In his "Quarantine Speech" he noted that an "epidemic of world lawlessness is spreading." Thus it was foolish to assume "that America will escape, that America may expect mercy, that this Western Hemisphere will not be attacked." To counter the threat, Roosevelt called for a quarantine of aggressor nations. Though some Americans agreed, the massive and negative outcry afterward caused Roosevelt to abandon his proposal.

A small but growing number of interventionists insisted, however, that the fascist Axis powers, if left unchecked, would eventually attack America. Like the isolationists, interventionists saw a world moving toward war. But, they also foresaw United States involvement—sooner or later. Better sooner, they thought, while Americans still had some overseas friends.

Events in 1938 and 1939 emphasized the failure of appeasement—the policy of buying off dictators with compromises. Compromises only brought new demands. France and Britain sold out part of Czechoslovakia to Germany at Munich in September 1938. Not satisfied yet, Hitler merely kept on expanding. Having already absorbed Austria as part of the German Third Reich, in March 1939 he occupied all of Czechoslovakia. Then he threatened Poland.

Hitler took advantage of Russian weakness (and Stalin, in turn, of the apparent German willingness to turn elsewhere for immediate conquest), and the two totalitarian dictatorships negotiated a nonaggression pact in August 1939. The Nazi–Soviet Pact allowed Hitler to turn his undivided attention to the conquest of Poland without fearing Russian retaliation. (As it turned out, Stalin's armies helped Hitler to dismember and then divide Poland the following month.)

Roosevelt had approved of appeasement at Munich, but by 1939 he realized his mistake. He began a long campaign to repeal, or at least soften, the neutrality laws. He spoke of "many methods short of war" that might discourage aggression. But Congress would have to allow some presidential flexibility. Congress did not budge. No one can say to what extent American inertia and isolationism helped Hitler decide on war. Nevertheless, the American attitude surely encouraged him. On September 1, 1939, Germany invaded Poland. Britain and France declared war on Germany two days later, and World War II was under way.

GLOBAL CONFLICT

The start of World War II put American views on neutrality to a real test. Hitler quickly conquered Poland and divided it with Russia. Roosevelt was legally bound to issue a proclamation of neutrality. He was far from neutral, however. Nor did he try to hide his pro-Allied sentiments.

For Roosevelt, defeat of the Axis was basic. If American isolation meant defeat for Britain and

France, American security would be disastrously, perhaps fatally, damaged. Thus, Roosevelt would go to war before letting the other Western democracies perish.

Since 1900 American foreign policy had increasingly involved British–American cooperation. Roosevelt would develop a close wartime friendship with Winston Churchill, Britain's prime minister.[1] Still, neither sentiment nor deep concern for the fate of democracy elsewhere in the world provided Roosevelt's chief motivation. He saw the savagery of dictators, especially Hitler. He concluded that, once Europe and Asia had been overrun by these "New Barbarians," America's turn would come.

Although Roosevelt accepted the risk of war, Congress would probably never have declared war prior to Pearl Harbor. Thus, Roosevelt's carefully worded pro-Allied efforts had to be made bit by bit. First, he asked Congress to repeal the arms embargo so that the United States might sell war goods to other Western powers. This passed with surprising ease. Now Britain and France might buy American arms but only on a "cash-and-carry" basis. Many Americans still hoped Hitler would be defeated without the necessity of making war loans to the Allies or placing American ships in Atlantic war zones.

These unreal hopes evaporated in the spring of 1940. Hitler launched a series of spectacular and successful campaigns that conquered much of Continental Europe. By May five countries had been overrun—Denmark, Norway, Luxembourg, the Netherlands, and Belgium. In June the "impossible" happened: France collapsed before the Nazi onslaught and agreed to German occupation of half its territory, including Paris. This left Britain the only effective Axis opponent.

Steps Toward Intervention

These events profoundly disturbed Americans and shifted the isolationist–interventionist

balance. Americans were shocked by the well-publicized picture of Hitler inspecting his new toy —the city of Paris—and dancing a little victory jig. What would come next? Americans might accept Allied defeats in limited wars, but this war seemed to have no limit.

Interventionists, who wanted massive aid for the battered Allies, grew bolder and better organized. Heroic British resistance to a German air assault on their homeland armed these interventionists with effective propaganda. The Committee to Defend America First, however, fought against any American involvement in the war. The America Firsters, like Charles Lindbergh, hero of the 1920s, argued that the war was simply none of our business. Many felt that a seemingly invincible Germany should not be stirred up unnecessarily.

Roosevelt moved shrewdly (1) to rearm America and (2) to aid Britain to the extent legally permissible and politically possible. Since 1940 was also a presidential election year, he had to be cautious. Meanwhile, Roosevelt broke the traditional ban on third-term presidents by running again. Significantly, Republican isolationists could not nominate their man, Senator Robert A. Taft of Ohio. An internationalist named Wendell Willkie, a utilities executive with little political experience, won the nomination.

In the midst of the campaign Roosevelt made a daringly unneutral move. He transferred fifty World War I destroyers to the British navy. In exchange the United States received a dozen British air and naval bases in the Western Hemisphere. Churchill said of this: "It marked the passage of the United States from being neutral to being non-belligerent [but involved]." Roosevelt won the election by a narrower margin than in 1936. Republican gains meant that Roosevelt had to take the views of the opposition party into greater account in facing the world crisis.

Every president who wins reelection regards it as a mandate for his policies. Now Roosevelt went even further than the destroyers-for-bases swap. He asked Congress for a Lend-Lease program. Under this law, passed in March 1941, the president would "lend" war material to countries whose security was deemed vital to American interests. The United States would become the "ar-

---

[1] The Roosevelt–Churchill correspondence consisted chiefly of long, candid cables between the two men. Roosevelt ended one such message: "It is fun to be in the same decade as you."

senal of democracy." By the end of World War II over $50 billion in Lend-Lease equipment and supplies had been distributed to America's allies.

Undeclared Naval Hostilities

Further support for Britain soon materialized. The American navy patrolled the western half of the North Atlantic, freeing British ships for duty nearer Europe. American ships and planes fed data on Nazi submarines to the Royal Navy. British ships used American ports freely, while this country kept sixty-five Axis ships tied up in its harbors. Some Americans joined the British or Canadian air forces, and British pilots trained at American airfields. The situation, as Germany knew, was not at all neutral. But Hitler was not yet ready to declare war on America; in the summer of 1941 he attacked Russia instead.

But American "nonbelligerence" soon provoked German countermeasures. When American warships began escorting Allied shipping halfway across the Atlantic, German submarines (or U-boats) responded. Several American destroyers were fired on; several merchant ships went down. In October a German submarine sank an American destroyer near Iceland. Congress then removed the last restriction of the neutrality laws: Armed American ships could now take war supplies directly to Britain. An undeclared naval war raged in the Atlantic.

Some members of the Roosevelt cabinet wanted an immediate declaration of war against Germany. But Roosevelt preferred to continue active nonbelligerence. He would arm those fighting the Axis (including Soviet Russia). He would cement relations with Britain, as in the meeting with Churchill that produced the Atlantic Charter.[2] And he would let the Axis powers decide when to declare war.

---

[2] The Atlantic Charter stated common British and American beliefs: The right of people to choose their own form of government and the need for worldwide economic cooperation and an international security system to prevent future wars.

Japan, not Germany, made the decisive move. The assault on Pearl Harbor and other bases in the Pacific on December 7, 1941, ended the isolationist–interventionist debate. It also united the nation. Roosevelt's critics, including Lindbergh of America First, now pledged their full support for the war. One major isolationist, Michigan's Republican Senator Arthur H. Vandenberg, conceded that Pearl Harbor had opened his eyes: "That day ended isolationism for any realist."

Could the war with Japan have been avoided? Not unless one of the two nations, Japan or the United States, had been willing to change its basic policy. Japan was determined to expand in China and Southeast Asia. The United States was determined never to recognize Japan's partial conquest of China; it was equally opposed to any Japanese moves against Allied colonies like British Malaya or the Dutch East Indies. Neither side would budge. Japan's decision to expand by force made conflict with America almost inevitable.

Americans had a long job ahead. It was made even longer when Germany and Italy honored their Axis commitments by declaring war on the United States just after Pearl Harbor. In one way, however, this step simplified matters. American leaders believed that Hitler, the greatest threat to democracy, should be defeated first. Japan could not be ignored—Americans would indeed "Remember Pearl Harbor"—but the war in Europe against Germany, Italy, and their Axis allies received top priority. Hitler, then at the height of his power, relished the idea of smashing Franklin "Rosenfeld." (Hitler had the strange notion that Roosevelt, an Episcopalian since birth, was Jewish.)

Whatever his motives, Hitler's actions caused the creation of the Grand Alliance, a coalition of all nations fighting the Axis. America, Britain, and Russia were senior partners. Starting with a declaration by "United Nations," signed in January 1942 by twenty-six countries, the alliance grew to forty-seven members by 1945. This provided the basis for the United Nations (UN). Technically, all were equal. But in reality the great powers ran the war largely to suit themselves.

Joining the Allies was a new step for the United States. Even in World War I, America was only an "associated power" rather than an "ally." The difference went beyond hairsplitting over the meaning of words. World War II was unique; Americans felt their own security threatened.

Big Three Relations

Within the Grand Alliance, or United Nations, the closest cooperation existed between Britain and the United States. Churchill and Roosevelt met almost a dozen times to develop the partnership and sometimes to prepare a united strategy against Russia, the other major ally. It was not that the Soviet Union was an uncooperative ally. After withstanding the first German offensive of 1941 (a surprise attack by a supposed ally), the Russians fought the Germans tenaciously. The Nazi army was spending itself in Russia, winning many battles but nothing decisive. Churchill and Roosevelt hastened to assure Stalin, the Soviet dictator, of their esteem. They promised military aid as soon as possible.

But Stalin wanted immediate action by his allies in the West. Specifically, he called for an Anglo-American invasion of Western Europe launched across the English Channel in 1942. But instead of a dangerous, and probably disastrous, cross-channel invasion of occupied France that year, Western leaders settled for landings in North Africa. This move took little pressure off Russia. Stalin angrily rejected suggestions that this weak move represented a so-called second front against Germany.

Further friction developed during preliminary discussions of the postwar political settlements. Stalin, like Roosevelt and Churchill, never doubted his side would win. He wanted a hand in carving national boundaries after the war. Roosevelt conceded this point, but Churchill usually tried to pacify but contain Stalin. Roosevelt often urged the postponement of political decisions until later in the war.

Events in Asia and the Pacific

The war was fought on many fronts. After the Japanese struck Pearl Harbor, they took over most of Southeast Asia. First they conquered the rest of French Indochina (Vietnam, Laos, and Cambodia). Then Malaya, Singapore, and Burma—all British colonies—fell. The Dutch East Indies were next. Australia was so sure its turn had come that it almost withdrew its troops from North Africa for a last-ditch homeland defense.

Meanwhile, the Japanese occupied most of America's colony, the Philippines. General Douglas MacArthur, the commander there when the Philippines were attacked (on the same day as Pearl Harbor), was ordered to Australia. What remained of the American army—including Filipino units—held out bravely for several months on the Bataan peninsula near Manila until overwhelmed by superior force. Most Filipinos opposed the Japanese invasion. The islands had been promised independence; the war upset this timetable, forcing a postponement until 1946.

The Japanese drive of 1941–42 was soon halted. Though a naval battle in the Coral Sea in May 1942 brought neither side victory, it removed the threat of a Japanese invasion of Australia. In June a key naval battle took place near Midway. Japanese strategy called for the capture of Midway, then a move against Hawaii. Japan probably should have made these two attacks right after Pearl Harbor. By mid-1942 things had changed. American aircraft carrier strength, though limited, was undamaged. Also, because Magic had broken the Japanese code, the American navy knew where to concentrate its forces.

Midway signaled the end of traditional naval warfare. Planes replaced guns and torpedoes as the most important offensive weapons. Enemy aircraft carriers were therefore the main target. Four Japanese carriers were sunk but only one American flat-top.[3] This gave the United States naval supremacy in the central Pacific, a factor of incalculable importance for the remainder of the Pa-

---

[3] All four of the carriers Japan lost at Midway had been used to attack Pearl Harbor. Likewise lost at Midway—or during the harsh fighting that followed in the Solomon Islands—were nearly all the daring Japanese pilots of December 7. Neither the flat-tops nor the aviators were ever properly replaced. Admiral Nagumo, who had led the victory at Pearl and the defeat at Midway, survived until 1944. Then he died, evidently by suicide, during the American capture of Saipan.

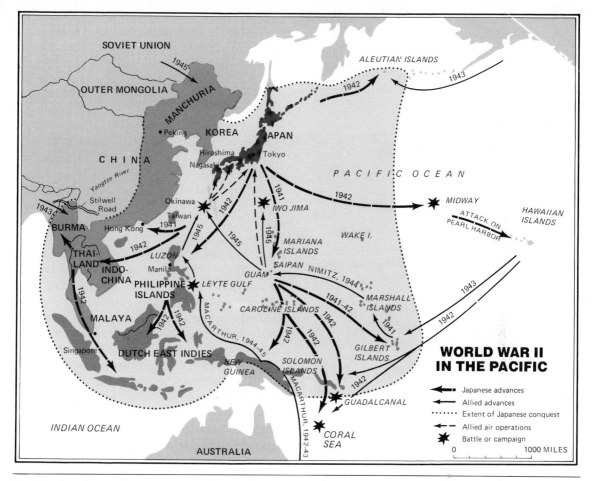

The day after the Japanese surprise attack on Pearl Harbor on December 7, **1941,** the United States declared war on Japan. On that same day, the Japanese invaded Thailand and Malaya. By late December they had captured Guam, Hong Kong, and Wake Island. The Japanese invasion of the Philippines began December 10; they took Manila on January 2, **1942.** General Douglas MacArthur retreated to Australia.

In February 1942 the Japanese took Singapore and, by early March, most of the Dutch East Indies. In June they seized two of the Aleutian Islands. The Battle of the Coral Sea was fought between Japanese and Allied forces on May 7–8, which stopped Japan's advance on Australia. The air and naval battle of Midway (June 3–6) was a turning point in the Pacific war, and within two months the United States was for the first time on the offensive.

The first major Allied offensive, beginning in August 1942, was fought at Guadalcanal. The Japanese were driven from it in February 1943. During March–August the Japanese were driven from the Aleutians. In the second half of **1943** the South Pacific offensive took place. It gave the Allies control of the waters adjacent to the Solomon Islands. A Central Pacific offensive was launched in November under Admiral Chester Nimitz,

during which the Allies took the Solomons, Gilberts, Marshalls, and Marianas. In December General Joseph W. Stilwell began a campaign in Burma; Burma was not completely retaken, however, until May 1945.

In June **1944** air attacks were opened against cities on the Japanese home islands. The Philippines campaign of June–December saw General MacArthur's return there. The naval Battle of Leyte Gulf (October 23–25), was a decisive defeat for Japan. It destroyed most of its remaining sea power. The Philippines campaign ended after the taking of Manila.

After heavy fighting, United States Marines took Iwo Jima in March **1945** and conquered Okinawa by late June. In May–August the greatest air offensive in the Pacific was launched against the Japanese home islands, culminating in the dropping of atomic bombs on Hiroshima (August 6) and Nagasaki (August 9). On August 8, the Soviet Union declared war on Japan and invaded Manchuria.

Japan surrendered and sued for peace on August 10. President Harry Truman announced August 14 as V-J Day. Japan's formal surrender took place September 2 in Tokyo Bay aboard the United States battleship *Missouri.*

The war in the Pacific was fought by island hopping—retaking island by island territory captured by the Japanese. This marine landing in the Solomons in 1943 helped push Japanese forces back to the home islands. (U.S. Information Agency/National Archives)

cific war. Moreover, the troop transports had turned back toward Japan after the Coral Sea action. The Japanese never again made a serious thrust in the mid-Pacific.

Coral Sea and Midway set the stage for Allied offensive operations. In August 1942 Americans landed on Guadalcanal in the Solomon Islands. The battle there was long and fierce—a warning of what lay ahead. This "island hopping" followed a long and bloody course from Guadalcanal in 1942 to Okinawa in 1945. In a series of landings on the various islands in between, United States troops fought for every bit of territory, notably the first few yards of each beachhead. Japanese resistance never let up. Even losing battle after battle did not diminish the enemy's will to fight.

After Midway, the Americans had sea and air superiority. The American fleet, especially the number of carriers, grew enormously. Even when the Japanese navy and air force came out in full strength (as when the United States recaptured the Philippines in 1944), Japan suffered staggering losses. On one day American pilots shot down nearly five hundred Japanese planes. At Leyte Gulf, much of Japan's navy was destroyed.

American submarines (though less publicized than German U-boats) sank hundreds of Japanese ships. Many of them were carrying raw materials from Southeast Asia to Japan's factories. By early 1945 Japan had no hope for victory. The war in China ground on inconclusively. The Pacific, which three years before had seemed to belong to Japan, was now an American lake. The only way left to preserve Japanese martial honor or punish the American invaders was suicide assaults by *Kamikaze* pilots.[4]

Events in Europe and the Mediterranean

The Allies mounted an equally relentless (and equally successful) effort in Europe and the Mediterranean. American and British forces overran North Africa and routed German General Erwin Rommel's *Afrika Korps*. In 1943 the Allies

---

[4] *Kamikaze* pilots crashed their planes, loaded with bombs, into American ships.

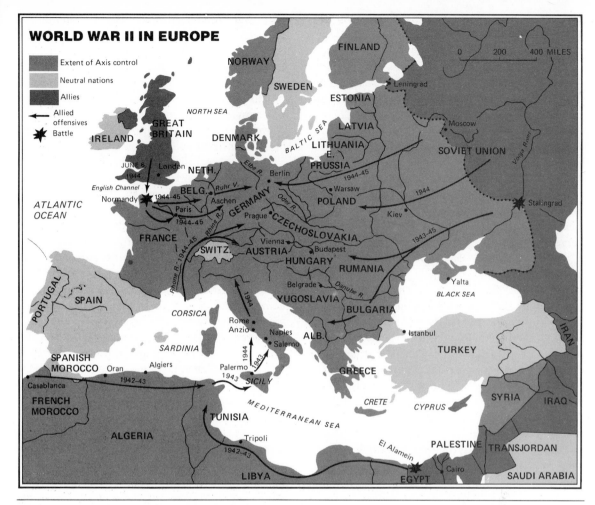

WORLD WAR II IN EUROPE

Extent of Axis control

Neutral nations

Allies

Allied offensives

Battle

When Germany was at the height of its power, its armies had overrun much of European Russia, defeated France, occupied Norway and Denmark, and held much of North Africa. In December **1941** England and the Soviet Union were the only allies in Europe still undefeated by Germany. The first United States troops for the European theater of the war arrived in northern Ireland in January **1942.** Six months later in North Africa, the British checked the Axis advance at El Alamein. In November General Eisenhower's Allied forces landed in North Africa. By May **1943** the Germans had been defeated there. In Europe the Russians defeated the German armies, attacking Stalingrad in December 1942 after a four-month siege—a major turning point. Thereafter the Russians began to take the offensive.

The Allied invasion of Italy began in July 1943. Italy's unconditional surrender to the Allies in September was followed by stiff German resistance in northern Italy. The Germans were not finally defeated there until 1945.

The air offensive against Germany began in January **1944** in preparation for an Allied invasion. On June 6, D Day, Allied armies invaded Normandy in northern France in a surprise attack. By August 10 this offensive was concluded and a second front in southern France was opened that began a drive up the Rhone Valley. All of France, Belgium, and Luxembourg was liberated by September. By this time the Russians had driven the Germans out of the Soviet Union and into Eastern Europe.

The battle for Germany began in September 1944. The first large German city to fall, Aachen, was taken in October. Within five months Belgrade, Budapest, and Warsaw had fallen.

A German counteroffensive in the west was launched in December 1944. The Germans almost succeeded in breaking through the American line in the Battle of the Bulge, but they were repulsed. Then a British offensive was launched in the Netherlands. By March United States troops had penetrated the Ruhr Valley and crossed the Rhine; a month later, they reached the Elbe. The Russians entered Berlin late in April. Berlin fell on May 2. The formal end of the war in Europe occurred on May 8. Germany surrendered unconditionally to the Allies.

invaded Sicily and then mainland Italy. Meanwhile, massive preparations for invading France went on, with Britain as the staging area.

On another front the Russians took terrible losses. Yet they stopped the farthest German penetration at the Volga River in the Battle of Stalingrad. For the next two years the "Eastern Front" saw many Russian advances and German retreats.

The invasion of France on June 6, 1944, put Hitler's neck in the noose. Despite strong resistance, Allied invaders stormed the Normandy beaches. Happily, Hitler insisted that the Normandy invasion was unimportant. He refused to concentrate his available forces there. After several nerve-racking weeks American tank columns led by General George S. Patton pushed beyond Normandy and raced across France.

But the Nazi army could not be crushed in 1944. It withdrew toward the Rhine. Germany, as helpless now as Japan, was the target of massive air attacks. (Over a thousand Allied planes participated in a single raid on Berlin.) Hitler still dreamed of victory, though he mistakenly believed his own people were betraying him. He forbade his generals to retreat. He hastened the murder of millions in concentration camps. Yet neither demonic raving nor barbarous cruelty could produce military victories. Early in 1945 the Allies pushed ahead on all fronts.

The Big Three leaders—Roosevelt, Stalin, and Churchill—had long been preparing for victory. Stalin and Churchill met in Moscow in October 1944. There they began carving out spheres of influence. Roosevelt wanted to end the war first and then make such decisions. The Axis must accept defeat and unconditional surrender; the Allies should not squabble until they had won. Thus the 1943 Big Three meeting at Teheran, Iran, had dealt mainly with wartime strategy.

By early 1945 territorial questions could not be further postponed. Germany would surely surrender that year; Japan was next in line. Russian participation in the invasion of Japan could mean a shorter campaign, with fewer Western casualties. What price would Stalin demand, though, to bring Russia into the Pacific war? The answer emerged at the Yalta Conference of February 1945, a Big Three meeting at a Russian resort in the Crimea.

Stalin set a high, though not outlandish, price. He wanted Russian power in the Far East to equal its extent in 1904, before his country lost the Russo-Japanese War. Russia was to receive the northernmost islands of the Japanese chain, plus territorial and commercial rights in Manchuria and northern China. In return, Stalin would declare war against Japan within three months of the end of the war in Europe.

The Yalta discussions produced agreement on another subject, which later became a matter of grave contention between the Soviet Union and the Western powers: the fate of Poland. At Yalta, Roosevelt and Churchill agreed to allow the Soviet Union to annex large areas of Eastern Poland, presumably as a buffer region against any future German attack. Stalin, in turn, agreed to allow "free elections" to be held after the war, although the commitment was a meaningless one given his views on the "necessity" for a "friendly" (that is, a Communist) regime in that country.

Polish-Americans and other opponents of the Yalta agreements would later denounce FDR for having "sold out" Poland and other Eastern European countries. Roosevelt, however, felt that he had exacted about as much as he could from Stalin on the question, given three elemental facts of international life: (1) the Russian armies would be controlling the country (as would American armies in Italy and a British one in Greece, countries where pro-Western governments were established); (2) Poland was clearly a security problem for the Soviet Union and not for the West; and (3) the issue was not of overriding importance to the United States compared to the future of Germany or securing Soviet entrance into the war with Japan.

Roosevelt's military advisers had warned that invading Japan without Russia might cost the United States a million casualties. The president had no wish for this. Nor could he count on the still untested atom bomb to end the war. Stalin's offer seemed the most reasonable choice.

The Yalta agreements included provisions for the division of Germany into zones of occupation. The Allied powers (the Big Three and France) would each occupy a section. Germany must also pay reparations for the wartime destruction it had

The strain of war was visible on FDR's face as he met with his allies, Churchill and Stalin, for the last time at Yalta. The concessions made to Stalin there to secure Russia's entrance into the Pacific war were denounced by some postwar critics as "appeasement." (Acme Newspictures)

caused. Stalin wanted to weaken Germany so that the Germans might never again attack Russia. Reparations would keep Germany feeble. Moreover, splitting Germany into occupation zones assured Stalin that the eastern zone would remain firmly under Soviet control.

Within a half year of Yalta, the Axis was subdued. In April 1945 Hitler committed suicide in Berlin as the Allies overran Germany. Four months later the Pacific war ended spectacularly and ominously. In the meantime, Roosevelt had died and been succeeded as president by Vice-President Harry S Truman.

The Atomic Bomb

Two American B-29s approached the southwestern tip of Japan on the morning of August 6, 1945. One of them was the *Enola Gay*. Its mission was to drop the first atomic bomb in the history of mankind. The target was the Japanese city of Hiroshima. At about 31,000 feet the doors of the bomb bay opened, and the bombardier released "Little Boy," a weapon that had twenty times the power of a ton of TNT. At 2000 feet the bomb detonated.

A young Hiroshima girl who was riding a trolley gave this account.

At that moment my eyes were suddenly blinded by a flash of piercing light and the neighborhood was enveloped in dense smoke of a yellow color like poison gas. Instantly everything became pitch dark and you couldn't see an inch ahead. Then a heavy and tremendously loud roar. The inside of my mouth was gritty as though I had eaten sand, and my throat hurt. I looked toward the east, and I saw an enormous black pillar of cloud billowing upward. "It's all over now," I thought.

As the plane made a sharp turn to avoid the blast, the tail gunner looked down at the falling bomb. Within seconds he was looking directly into the center of the atomic detonation. He watched the shock wave approach the plane like a shimmering heat wave. The mushroom cloud started forming immediately. He described it as "a bubbling mass of purple-gray smoke, and you could see it had a red core to it and everything was burning inside."

Within an instant 70,000 people died. Another 30,000 would later die of radiation burns and a strange new disease, radiation sickness. Approximately 75 percent of the buildings in Hiroshima were destroyed. As another eyewitness said of those first few seconds. "Everything had crumbled away in that one moment and changed into streets of rubble, street after street of ruins."

What caused the decision to use this devastating weapon? President Truman had been told that if the Japanese fought to the end in defense of their own islands, as they vowed, the war would last more than another year, and an additional half million American lives would be lost. He thought a quick one-two punch—one atomic bomb dropped, followed swiftly by a second on another target—would force Japan to surrender.

Historians have conjectured that there may also have been other reasons. Soviet–American relations were strained. Truman may have wanted to show the Russians that American strength was superior. Or he may have wanted to end the war before the Soviet Union could occupy Asia as it had eastern Europe. But Truman himself always insisted that his sole concern was ending the war in the Pacific quickly and with a minimum number of American casualties.

The atomic bomb did end the war. Three days after Hiroshima was bombed, Nagasaki suffered the same fate. The next day the Japanese asked for peace terms, though many Japanese still wished to fight to the death.

A HOT WAR TURNED COLD

History's greatest war ended with unconditional surrender by the Axis. Yet victory found the Grand Alliance anything but united. Differences over postwar policy produced visible strains, with the possibility of a new and dangerous confrontation. The United States and Russia were now superpowers. Their growing disagreements would soon be called a Cold War.

Soviet–American cooperation broke down completely after World War II. Eastern and central Europe came under Russian domination. The Baltic countries of Latvia, Lithuania, and Estonia ceased to be independent nations. Finland avoided the same fate by curbing its foreign policy in a treaty with Russia. The countries between Western-occupied Germany and the Soviet Union, plus the Balkan nations, became Soviet satellites. (Yugoslavia would later break away.) A Soviet empire emerged. Countries on its borders (Greece, Turkey, and Iran, for example) all felt the pressure of the new superpower.

The United States had hoped for cooperation, not conflict, among the major powers after the war. A return to the status quo and the isolationism of earlier periods was out of the question. Americans could not pull back as in 1919 and expect to maintain their interests in a vacuum. World War II had exhausted Britain and France. If North Atlantic leadership of the world was to continue, the United States had to step in. Thus Washington pushed for a new world organization, despite the League of Nations' failure and America's own sorry role in that failure.

Roosevelt had wanted a league. Unlike Wilson, though, he had made sure that Republicans participated in the sessions that preceded the founding of the United Nations in 1945 (soon after Roosevelt's death). The UN differed from the League in various ways. It was located in New York, not Geneva. More important, the great powers established a Security Council whose permanent members (the United States, Britain, France, Russia, and China) could defeat any proposal with a single negative vote. This big-power veto, a recognition of both national sovereignty and great-power interests, gravely limited UN effectiveness in crisis situations. Yet the veto was desired by all the large powers.

Containment in the Mediterranean

American hopes for postwar stability suffered as a result of Roosevelt's death. The late president had not mapped a precise blueprint for peacetime policy; he had become increasingly disillusioned with Russian behavior. But he did possess enormous prestige. This was not true of President Truman, a man without experience in either high-level administration or foreign policy. Truman's baptism of fire in summit diplomacy—direct meetings by heads of government—came in July 1945, when he, Stalin, and Britain's new prime minister, Clement Attlee, met at Potsdam, Germany. Full agreement proved impossible. With Japan still undefeated, Truman accepted postponement of various pending issues.

Russia's expansionism and the weakness of America's allies soon ruled out further delay. By 1947 Western Europe seemed profoundly unstable. Britain, France, Italy, and West Germany (not yet a separate country) were sliding economically downward, perhaps toward a chaos that could only benefit Russia. Britain had to give up its empire. The British move that most affected the United States was its decision to end aid to Greece and Turkey, Britain's anti-Communist Mediterranean allies. The Russians and Turks had been at odds for centuries. The post–World War II period proved no exception. The Soviets tried to gain parts of eastern Turkey and establish bases at the Dardanelles—Turkey's (and Russia's) gateway to the Mediterranean.

The Greeks (unfriendly toward the Turks but now allied with them as another target of Russian expansionism) also needed help. A Communist guerrilla movement was fighting the Greek government. Only active American intervention could keep Greece and Turkey out of the Soviet sphere. In March 1947 the president enunciated the Truman Doctrine "to help free peoples to maintain their free institutions" against the threat of "subjugation by armed minorities or by outside pressures." Congress appropriated $400 million to aid Greece and Turkey.

The congressional action and Truman's strong words were highly significant. They proved the Cold War had truly begun. The United States would, by threat of a third world war, contain Russia within the areas the Soviets had occupied or dominated in 1947. The support Truman received from Republicans in Congress signaled that the policy of containment had bipartisan support.

Containment in Western Europe

After containing the Russian advance in the eastern Mediterranean, the United States turned to Western Europe. Secretary of State George C. Marshall announced in mid-1947 American willingness to contribute huge sums toward European reconstruction. All Europe was included; even Russia sent envoys to a preliminary conference. But the Russians quickly withdrew and kept their satellites from joining the European Recovery Program (ERP), which is better known as the Marshall Plan.

Congress moved more cautiously than on Greece and Turkey. But a Communist takeover of Czechoslovakia in 1948 spurred it on. Billions of dollars flooded into Western Europe, stimulating the area's economic recovery. This also ended any early possibility that Communist parties there would reach power through elections.

The Western allies took an added step in containing Communist advances in Europe by creating a formal military alliance in 1949. The North Atlantic Treaty Organization (NATO) included a dozen North Atlantic nations. They pledged to take any action necessary "including the use of armed force, to restore and maintain the security of the North Atlantic area." To implement the promise to defend any NATO country attacked by an outside power, large numbers of United States troops were sent to Germany. The American navy took over from Britain in the Mediterranean.

Through NATO the United States in effect became the policeman for the Western world, a break with American tradition. Not since the French alliance of 1778 had the United States linked itself formally in a military alliance with another power. NATO made the containment policy a firm one. Though the Soviets exploded their first nuclear weapon in 1949, they knew that further expansion to the west was impossible without war. NATO was soon functioning, with General Dwight D. Eisenhower (Supreme Allied Commander in Europe during World War II) heading NATO's forces. Obviously Washington would not allow a Russian "iron curtain" to fall over Western Europe as it had over the Eastern portions.

COLD WAR EUROPE, 1945-55

NATO member 1949
(or by date of admission)

Warsaw Pact member 1955

U.S. Foreign Aid:
▲ Truman Doctrine 1946
● Marshall Plan 1948-52

0   250   500
Miles

ICELAND

Faeroe Is.

Shetland Is.

Hebrides

NORTH SEA

NO. IRELAND

IRELAND

GREAT BRITAIN

NORWAY

SWEDEN

FINLAND

DENMARK

BALTIC SEA

UNION OF SOVIET SOCIALIST REPUBLICS

ATLANTIC OCEAN

NETH.

BEL.

LUX.

FRANCE

SWITZ.

WEST GERMANY (1955)

EAST GERMANY

POLAND

CZECHOSLOVAKIA

AUSTRIA

HUNGARY

RUMANIA

CASPIAN SEA

PORTUGAL

SPAIN

Corsica

Balearic Is.

Sardinia

ITALY

YUGOSLAVIA

BULGARIA

ALBANIA

BLACK SEA

TURKEY (1951)

IRAN

GREECE (1951)

SYRIA

MEDITERRANEAN SEA

Sicily

Crete

Cyprus

LEBANON

IRAQ

MOROCCO

ALGERIA (France)

TUNISIA

The Struggle for Mainland China

Unsettling events in Asia contrasted sharply with the success of containment in Europe. Events in postwar China were particularly disappointing for Americans. Civil war broke out there between the Communists under Mao Tse-tung and the Nationalists under Chiang Kai-shek. Mao had fought for control of China long before the Japanese invasion. War with Japan temporarily united the two sides, but afterward, they returned to civil war.

By 1948 it became clear the Nationalists would lose. The next year Chiang fled to the island of Taiwan, while on the mainland Mao proclaimed his Communist government, the People's Republic of China (often referred to as Red China). Massive American military intervention might have pre-vented the Communist takeover, or at least so some American leaders thought, though few recommended it. And the history of later large-scale American involvement in Vietnam casts grave doubt on the wisdom of that course. In any case, two things were certain: By 1949 Red China possessed considerable power, and this power would increase.

The Korean Conflict

The United States refused diplomatic recognition to Red China. Yet soon after the Chinese civil war ended, Americans were forced to recognize the Red Chinese army in combat. The scene was Korea, which had regained independence from

George C. Marshall

One of George C. Marshall's biographers has described him as "the least typical of generals." He notes that what is remarkable in him is a "beautifully balanced mind thinking in terms of the dignity and integrity of the country which gave him birth."

Marshall was a soldier-statesman in the tradition of George Washington and Andrew Jackson. He was a military genius who turned diplomat, secretary of state, and secretary of defense after the close of his career as a professional soldier. His actions in war caused President Harry Truman to state in 1945: "In a war unparalleled in magnitude and horror, millions of Americans gave their country outstanding service. General of the Army George C. Marshall gave it victory." His actions in peace won him the Nobel Peace Prize in 1953. He was the first soldier ever to receive it.

Marshall was an absolute master of organization and military strategy. But he sometimes considered this talent a liability, for although his army career involved two world wars, he was never to lead troops in battle. He was considered too valuable a planner to be risked in field command.

In the 1930s Marshall had a tedious job as an instructor in the Illinois National Guard. But by 1936 his star began to rise. He was promoted to Chief of Staff of the Army on September 1, 1939, the opening day of World War II in Europe. Between that day and the end of the war Marshall built up the army and air corps from fewer than 200,000 men to over 8 million. It has been estimated that without his planning the invasion of Europe would have come a full year later than it did in 1944.

At war's end Marshall wished to retire. But President Truman asked him to undertake a diplomatic mission to China to try to bring the warring Nationalist and Communist forces together in a coalition government. The soldier hero's second career as a controversial statesman began.

After China Marshall was named secretary of state. He found himself in a new war—the Cold War with the Soviet Union. He helped to hammer out the Truman Doctrine and, of course, the Marshall Plan. Then he tried to retire again. This time, Truman wanted him to be secretary of defense.

(Wide World Photos)

In 1951 Senator Joseph McCarthy, whose crusade against communism became a witch hunt, lashed out at Marshall. He published a speech attacking Marshall's wartime strategy, his mission to China, and his actions as secretary of state. McCarthy accused this public servant of being "a man steeped in falsehood," who was guilty of "invariably serving the world policy of the Kremlin."

Marshall resigned soon after this vicious attack, because his effectiveness in office had been greatly reduced. It was a melancholy ending to a frequently brilliant and selfless career in the service of the nation. He was remembered by one of his colleagues in the State Department as "the image of the American gentleman at his best—honorable, courteous, devoid of arrogance, exacting of others, but even more of himself, intolerant only of cowardice, deviousness, and cynicism."

Japan in 1945. But now Korea had been divided into Communist-occupied North Korea and American-occupied South Korea. The Communist North invaded the South in June 1950, perhaps because Washington had declared Korea outside the zone of American vital interest. (U.S. troops had been pulled back to Japan.)

When South Korea asked for American help, Truman quickly provided it. Available combat forces (two American divisions stationed in Japan) were sent at once to Korea. Also, a Soviet mistake let Truman make the American response a United Nations venture. In June 1950 Russia was boycotting all UN meetings. The Security Council promptly branded North Korea an aggressor and authorized a UN military force to repel the attack. General Douglas MacArthur, leader of the occupation forces in Japan, also headed the UN army (mostly American soldiers) in Korea.

The Korean conflict was both a success and a failure for the United States. Two Koreas still exist. Thus the 1950–53 military effort there did prevent a Communist takeover. But this venture became a political liability for Democrats and a lasting frustration for all Americans. After a year of seesaw campaigns up and down the Korean peninsula, fighting ended close to the original dividing line.

Total victory was unattainable because the war had limited aims. And Washington permitted only limited means to achieve them. MacArthur, a great soldier and a great egotist, was especially frustrated. He had sent his troops to within sight of China's border in 1950, provoking full-scale Chinese intervention in Korea and an American retreat. Despite this—and the risk of bringing Russia into combat also—MacArthur wanted to bomb China and fight the war more vigorously. Truman refused. When MacArthur aired his contrary views in public, Truman fired him.

REPUBLICANS BACK IN POWER

Truman fought the war his way; he and his party then paid the political price. When the Republicans regained the presidency in 1952, after twenty years, they promised changes in foreign policy. Dwight Eisenhower and his party came into power in part due to charges that the Democrats had not resisted communism as strongly as they could and should have. Containment, declared the Republican campaign platform, was "negative, futile, and immoral." Once in power, the Republicans assured the country, not only would they stop losing countries to communism, but, they hinted, countries already Communist would be redeemed.

Eisenhower selected perhaps the ideal secretary of state to implement this policy. John Foster Dulles, a sixty-four-year-old Wall Street corporation lawyer, had long been one of the leading foreign policy spokesmen of the Republican party. Dulles's strong belief in the righteousness of the American system and the iniquity of communism appeared to have a great deal to do with the Christianity of the one and the atheism of the other.

Guided by this highly moralistic view of the world, Dulles managed American foreign policy for six years, from 1953 to 1959. While retaining the final power of decision, Eisenhower believed strongly in delegating authority to cabinet members, and he reposed special trust in Dulles. Dulles became the most influential secretary of state of the postwar era, at least until the coming of Henry Kissinger. The secretary made diplomacy a personal affair, visiting forty-seven countries and flying half a million miles during his tenure.

Liberation

The new Republican leaders proposed to differentiate themselves most dramatically from Truman with regard to the "captive nations" of Eastern Europe. The United States, said Dulles, should "make it publicly known that it wants and expects liberation to occur." During the election campaign, the policy had won the Republicans millions of votes from Americans of Polish, Hungarian, and other East European descent. Dulles quickly explained, once in office, that he meant that America should frequently restate its position that Eastern Europe should be free; he did *not* mean military action. Sustained moral pressure, maintained Dulles, would lead to liberation.

Secretary of State John Foster Dulles reporting on one of his many trips around the globe to President Eisenhower on May 17, 1955. Dulles had just returned from Europe where he signed a treaty restoring sovereignty to Austria and participated in the admission of West Germany to NATO. On several occasions, such as the one shown here, he briefed the president in informal public addresses that were broadcast to the nation from the White House. (UPI)

Brinkmanship and Massive Retaliation

Dulles labored hard and often to inform the world that the United States was not "scared to go to the brink," that it would not regard all-out war as unthinkable if its vital interests were threatened. As part of this strategy, Dulles purposely left unclear what situations would push the United States over the brink. Such a policy may have frightened America's enemies; it also discomfited America's allies.

Massive retaliation became a crucial corollary to brinkmanship. But it was partially forced on Dulles by the rest of the Eisenhower administration. As a result of the Korean War, defense spending had more than tripled, from $14 billion in 1950 to $49 billion in 1953. The cabinet's fiscal conservatives hoped to reduce expenditures and balance the budget. To curb military expenses, they imposed on the armed forces a policy called the New Look.

The New Look became more popularly known as the policy of "more bang for a buck." Atomic weapons, its proponents argued, could most economically defend the country, far more so

than large naval and land forces. By concentrating on American nuclear strength, especially the deterrent of the Strategic Air Command, the administration could prune the army and navy and cut the defense budget by 10 percent. Thus, when Dulles approached the brink, he threatened opponents with massive retaliation involving nuclear weapons. The logic of the administration's fiscal policies dictated the all-or-nothing approach.

Ending the Korean War

Eisenhower had pledged during his campaign, "I will go to Korea," to inspect battle lines and examine possibilities for peace. His visit, in December 1952, left him more than ever convinced of what he had believed from the start—Americans should not be fighting a land war in Asia.

The new president and his secretary of state rapidly began to test out their brinkmanship ideas. If the war did not end soon, Eisenhower proclaimed, the United States would take action "under circumstances of our own choosing." Chiang Kai-shek, driven by the Chinese Communists to the island of Formosa, began bombing raids against the Chinese coast. Finally, Dulles sent a message to the Chinese through the government of India: If a Korean agreement was not reached soon, the United States would seriously consider using nuclear weapons. Within two weeks, the Communists agreed to a settlement.

In its first innings, brinkmanship appeared to have scored a success. But some maintained that the war had ended largely because of stalemate on the battlefront and the death of Stalin two months earlier. In the next two years, Stalin's successors in Moscow appeared to be pursuing a more conciliatory role on several fronts, abandoning some territorial claims and improving relations with several countries. Eventually, the Soviets agreed to withdraw from their occupation zone in Austria, on condition that the reunited country follow a neutral foreign policy. The Soviets also indicated that they would be willing to solve the problem of German reunification the same way.

Dulles responded to all Soviet actions with deep suspicion. After the settlement of the Korean War, he explained, "This is the time to crowd the enemy—and maybe finish him, once and for all." Soviet overtures, he felt, reflected Soviet weakness, which the United States should exploit.

Problems in the Far East

If Dulles distrusted Soviet policies and aims, part of his attitude stemmed from Communist actions in the Far East, actions that the secretary interpreted as the direct work of the Kremlin. Since 1945, a dedicated Vietnamese nationalist and Communist named Ho Chi Minh had been at the head of a rebellion to drive the French out of Indochina. France appealed for American aid against communism, and this valued ally received millions of American dollars to finance its colonial war. But by April 1954 France was through in that area. French troops had entrenched and trapped themselves in a fortress near Hanoi called Dien Bien Phu. In May, the Dien Bien Phu garrison surrendered.

Meanwhile, the Communist insurgents and the French had begun negotiating in Geneva. After the fall of Dien Bien Phu, they agreed to divide Vietnam temporarily, with Ho Chi Minh taking over the north and the French remaining in the south. Internationally supervised elections, aimed at reuniting the country, were supposed to be held by 1956. The elections never took place. In South Vietnam, an American-backed regime, headed by a Vietnamese Catholic named Diem, established a separate government in Saigon. The United States poured in support, and elections, which everyone knew Ho Chi Minh would win, were postponed. Dulles, who attended the Geneva sessions as an unhappy "observer" (the United States did not sign the final accords), had salvaged something: a non-Communist South Vietnam. On the list of American Pyrrhic victories, the 1956 Geneva Conference ranks at the top.

Dulles had been frustrated in Indochina by a lack of support from America's allies. He now attempted to head off such embarrassments in the future by organizing the Southeast Asia Treaty Organization (SEATO) (ostensibly an Eastern NATO), comprising the United States, Britain, France, Australia, New Zealand, Thailand, Pakistan, and the Philippines. Many non-Communist but neutral states of Asia (India, Indonesia, Burma) refused to join or to align themselves with the United States. Nonetheless, Dulles believed he now had the means to repel future Communist advances in the region.

Toward a European Settlement

Neither Russians nor Americans expected substantive results from the Geneva conference of 1955. Neither side brought any new proposals to deal with the major East–West problem, the reunification of Germany. West Germany was being rearmed and had joined NATO, and the Soviet Union had organized its Iron Curtain satellites into the Warsaw Pact, which East Germany would join a few months later. Germany, like Europe, would remain divided for the forseeable future. The only positive result of the meeting was an intangible, rapidly dissolving "spirit of Geneva," which implied that the two countries would not seek to settle their differences by war.

This easing of tensions did not sit well with Dulles. It looked too much like American acceptance of the status quo, including permanent Soviet control of Eastern Europe. Accordingly, the United States continued to issue statements about "liberation" remaining a high-priority item in American foreign policy. Especially during the presidential election year of 1956, the administration would not forgo restating the crucial policy that differentiated it from the Truman administration.

Hungarian patriots hold an anti-Soviet demonstration on a torn-up Budapest street on October 24, 1956. In the week of bloody rebellion that followed, Soviet troops and tanks crushed the Hungarians' attempt to establish their own government. Although the United States joined in a UN resolution censuring the Soviets and was to admit thousands of Hungarian refugees in the wake of the revolution, it did not intervene in Hungary. (UPI)

But events soon demonstrated tragically the emptiness of these promises of liberation. In October 1956, discontent in Eastern Europe exploded in the streets of Hungary and forced changes in the government. Flushed with their success, Hungarians demanded the withdrawal of the Russian army, which began evacuating the country, or at least pulled out of Budapest. Eisenhower had been careful not to urge on the "rebels." But CIA-sponsored Radio Free Europe offered encouragement, and Dulles mentioned the possibility of American economic aid.

Hungary maintained its independence for several days. When the new premier announced that Hungary would withdraw from the Warsaw Pact, however, the Russians sent in their tanks. Hungarians resisted, pleading all the while for help from the West.

Given the realities of nuclear stalemate, Eisenhower never considered sending in American troops to Hungary. The Soviets would have construed such an action as an attack on them and would have responded, possibly with nuclear weapons. Despite the rhetoric of liberation, Eisenhower and Dulles had always known this. Now the East Europeans knew it too.

The Middle East

Dulles's problems were just beginning. At the time of the Hungarian revolution, the secretary's ability to influence world events suffered another dramatic blow, as a crisis erupted in the Middle East involving America's closest allies. Without consulting the United States, Britain and France took military action against Egypt. Their joint expedition produced only frustration for both European nations, and further frayed the bonds of the Atlantic alliance.

The crisis arose, in part, from Dulles's own bumbling. He had attempted to improve America's standing with the Arab nations by agreeing to aid in building the Aswan Dam on Egypt's Nile River. But by 1956 the young nationalist Egyptian leader, Gamal Abdel Nasser, had moved to establish ties with Communist countries as well. As a result, Dulles abruptly informed the Egyptians that the United States would not finance the dam (the Russians eventually did). Nasser, angered and humiliated, bolstered his prestige by nationalizing the Suez Canal.

This action infuriated the British and French, who considered control of the canal vital to their interests. When negotiations did not produce satisfaction, they allied with Israel in a combined attack on Egypt. (This development undoubtedly helped assure the Russians that they could move into Hungary without fear of Western reprisal.)

The United States reacted angrily, both at the invasion and at not having been consulted. Eisenhower immediately demanded that the British and French forces withdraw, before they had even reached the canal. Khrushchev, bidding for support among the Arabs, threatened Western Europe with nuclear weapons. Under pressure from both the Russians and the Americans, the British and French had no choice but to withdraw.

Dulles had ended the invasion, but he seemed to have accomplished little else. The affair injured NATO prestige and allowed the Russians to ingratiate themselves with Nasser, gaining a base on the Mediterranean. To maintain the American position, the United States, in early 1957, proclaimed the Eisenhower Doctrine, affirming its intent to support established Arab governments against subversion. By the end of that year, Eisenhower had strengthened American ties with Jordan and Saudi Arabia. A year later, he committed American troops for the only time in his presidency, ordering a landing by United States Marines in Lebanon as a show of American strength. As on previous occasions, Eisenhower moved in a far more limited fashion than his military advisers or his secretary of state had wanted.

Problems with the Third World

Eisenhower and Dulles presided over American foreign policy at a time when nationalism was rising throughout Asia, Africa, and Latin America. As shown by their difficulties in handling Egypt's Nasser, American policy makers had recurrent problems dealing with the new phenomenon. Although strongly opposed to old-style European colonialism, Americans did not know exactly what they wanted in its place.

Their major aim, to prevent the spread of communism, often lapsed into a policy of support for established regimes and opposition to virtually any insurgent movement, whether Communist-led or not. While this did not restructure American policy, the Eisenhower-Dulles world view often clashed with the plans of emerging Third World countries to quicken their own development. The United States sought to strengthen existing governments, assist development, and turn the new nations from communism with offers of military and economic aid. By 1961, Eisenhower was asking $4.2 billion from Congress for such aid.

The United States faced a particular problem in Latin America, where it tried to maintain traditional hemispheric influence and safeguard nearly $10 billion of American investment. Strains developed in an area that many Americans regarded as their backyard. In 1954, after the Central American republic of Guatemala took a turn toward the left, Dulles denounced the existing government. But more than words were involved. The CIA helped finance Guatemalan groups opposed to the left-leaning government in a successful seizure of power. Dulles had seemed to pay little attention to Latin America. But when rock-throwing crowds later attacked Vice-President Nixon in Venezuela, Washington began to worry. This concern came too late for Cuba. Fidel Castro's guerrillas overthrew a pro-American regime in 1958.

Sputnik and U-2

In August 1957 the Soviet Union startled the United States, and the world, by orbiting its first space vehicle, Sputnik. Whatever the implications for interplanetary travel, Sputnik symbolized rapid advances by the Soviets in rocketry and atomic warhead delivery systems. The United States had also advanced in these directions and had made great strides in developing nuclear submarines. More and more, international relations reflected a "balance of terror," with traditional considerations becoming less and less important.

Both sides now sought another summit conference to ease tensions and deal with international problems. But events seemed stalemated until Eisenhower decided to follow a more conciliatory policy. Dulles, terminally ill with cancer, had to retire in 1959. Ike invited Khrushchev to the United States, with an Eisenhower visit to Russia to follow. Khrushchev's visit passed pleasantly, including extensive conferences with the president at Camp David, the presidential retreat in Maryland. The two leaders agreed to hold a summit conference in Paris, in May 1960.

But before the conference could take place, the Russians shot down an American U-2 spy plane over Sverdlovsk, deep in Soviet territory. (This was the same type of spy plane later used over Cuba.) The United States denied that the plane had been on a spy mission until the Russians produced the pilot, who had survived and confessed. Eisenhower then took personal responsibility for the flights, which had started in 1956, stating that he was obligated to keep a close watch on Russia for the sake of American security.

Khrushchev, possibly because of pressure from Kremlin hard-liners and from the Chinese, used the U-2 incident to torpedo the summit conference. He delivered a long anti-American tirade at a news conference and demanded an apology from Eisenhower. The president refused; the proposed meeting evaporated; and Khrushchev canceled Eisenhower's invitation to visit Russia.

Eisenhower thus concluded his foreign policy stewardship on an embarrassing note, although his popularity at home soared after the summit debacle. During Ike's eight years in office, no one had been liberated from the Communist yoke—unless one can describe the creation of anti-Communist dictatorships in Iran, South Vietnam, and Guatemala as "liberation." Still, he had preserved peace and put some limits on defense spending. If he had not offered a daring or imaginative approach to the Third World, the Russians and later the Chinese would also learn the difficulty of maintaining relations between the "have" and the "have-not" nations.

Although Eisenhower was not active in the presidential campaign of 1960, his foreign policy came under attack. During his final presidential term, the United States had frequently seemed to be not acting but reacting, often too late, to Soviet initiatives. Democratic candidate John F. Kennedy made shrewd use of this issue in his campaign against Republican Vice-President Richard M. Nixon. Kennedy's promise to get the country "moving again" won him a narrow election victory. Americans looked forward to the 1960s, keenly anticipating his fulfillment of that pledge. But when the turbulent sixties had become history, many looked back with nostalgia to the eight relatively quiet years of the Eisenhower era.

Suggested Readings
Chapters 41–42

Pearl Harbor

Adolph A. Hoehling, *The Week Before Pearl Harbor* (1963); Walter Lord, *Day of Infamy* (1957); Roberta Wohlstetter, *Pearl Harbor: Warning and Decision* (1962).

Interventionists Versus Isolationists

Selig Adler, *The Isolationist Impulse* (1957); James M. Burns, *Roosevelt: The Soldier of Freedom* (1970); Mark Chadwin, *Hawks of World War II* (1968); Wayne S. Cole, *America First: The Battle Against Intervention, 1940–1941* (1953); Robert A. Divine, *The Reluctant Belligerent* (1965); Saul Friedlander, *Prelude to Downfall: Hitler and the United States, 1939–1941* (1967); Townsend Hoopes, *The Devil and John Foster Dulles* (1973); Manfred Jonas, *Isolationism in America, 1935–1941* (1966); Robert E. Osgood, *NATO, the Entangling Alliance* (1962); Martin J. Sherwin, *A World Destroyed: The Atomic Bomb and the Grand Alliance* (1975).

Depression Diplomacy

Dorothy Borg and Shupei Okamoto (eds.), *Pearl Harbor as History: Japanese-American Relations, 1931–1941* (1973); L. Ethan Ellis, *Republican Foreign Policy, 1921–1933* (1968); Lloyd C. Gardner, *Economic Aspects of New Deal Diplomacy* (1964) and *Architects of Illusion: Men and Ideas in American Foreign Policy, 1941–1949* (1970); David Green, *The Containment of Latin America* (1970); Allen Guttmann, *The Wound in the Heart: America and the Spanish Civil War* (1962); William L. Langer and S. Everett Gleason, *The World Crisis and American Foreign Policy* (2 vols., 1952–1953); John E. Wiltz, *From Isolation to War, 1931–1941* (1968); Bryce Wood, *The Making of the Good Neighbor Policy* (1967).

The Cold War

Selig Adler, *The Uncertain Giant: American Foreign Policy Between the Wars* (1965); Gar Alperovitz, *Atomic Diplomacy* (1965); Lynn E. Davis, *The Cold War Begins* (1973); John L. Gaddis, *The United States and the Origins of the Cold War* (1972); Akira Iriye, *The Cold War in Asia* (1974); Walter LaFeber, *America, Russia, and the Cold War* (1967); Joyce and Gabriel Kolko, *The Limits of Power: The World and United States Foreign Policy, 1945–1954* (1972); Gabriel Kolko, *The Politics of War* (1969); Robert J. Maddox, *The New Left and the Origins of the Cold War* (1974); Adam B. Ulam, *The Rivals: America and Russia Since World War II* (1972); Richard Walton, *Henry Wallace, Harry Truman and the Cold War* (1976); Daniel Yergin, *The Shattered Peace* (1977).

The Near East and the Far East

Dorothy Borg, *The United States and the Far Eastern Crisis of 1933–1938* (1964); Herman Finer, *Dulles Over Suez* (1964); Robert L. Neumann, *America Encounters Japan* (1963); John W. Spanier, *The Truman-MacArthur Controversy* (1965); Tang Tsou, *America's Failure in China, 1941–1950* (2 vols., 1963).

Wartime Diplomacy

A. Russell Buchanan, *The United States and World War II* (2 vols., 1964); Diane S. Clemens, *Yalta* (1971); Robert A. Divine, *Roosevelt and World War II* (1969); Herbert Feis, *Churchill, Roosevelt, Stalin* (2nd ed., 1967); Gaddis Smith, *American Diplomacy During the Second World War, 1941–1945* (1965).

The Hiss-Chambers Case: An American Mystery

43

Whittaker Chambers, star witness in the Hiss case, reflected on the importance of the case some years later and wrote to his children:

Beloved Children,

I am sitting in the kitchen of [our Maryland farm] writing a book. In it I am speaking to you. But I am also speaking to the world. To both I owe an accounting.

It is a terrible book—terrible in what it tells about men, more terrible in what it tells about the world in which you live. It is about what the world calls the Hiss-Chambers case, or even more simply, the Hiss case. It is about a spy case. All the props of an espionage case are there—foreign agents, household traitors, stolen documents, microfilm, furtive meetings, secret hideaways, phony names, an informer, investigations, trials, official justice.

But if the Hiss case were only this, it would not be worth my writing about or your reading about. It would not be what, at the very beginning, I was moved to call it: "a tragedy of history."

For it was more than human tragedy. Much more than Alger Hiss or Whittaker Chambers was on trial in the trials of Alger Hiss. Two faiths were on trial. Human societies, like human beings, live by faith and die when faith dies. At heart, the Great Case was this critical conflict of faiths; that is why it was a great case. On a scale personal enough to be felt by all, but big enough to be symbolic, the two irreconcilable faiths of our time—communism and freedom—came to grips in the persons of two conscious and resolute men. Both had been schooled in the same view of history (the Marxist view). Both were trained by the same party in the same selfless, semisoldierly discipline. Neither would nor could yield without betraying, not himself, but his faith [and] both knew, almost from the beginning, that the Great Case could end only in the destruction of one or both of the contending figures.

My children, as long as you live, the shadow of the Hiss case will brush you. In time you will ask yourselves the question: What was my father?

I will give you an answer: I was a witness. A witness, in the sense that I am using the word, is a man whose life and faith are so completely one that when the challenge comes to step out and testify for his faith, he does so, disregarding all risks, accepting all consequences.

Alger Hiss, chief among those high government officials accused of Communist connections, related the circumstances surrounding his involvement in the investigation:

In August 1948 I was living in New York City. For the preceding year and a half I had been president of the Carnegie Endowment for International Peace. To accept that position I had resigned from the State Department, where I was director of the office responsible for proposing and carrying out our policies in the United Nations.

My new work was closely related to what I had been doing in Washington, for the Endowment had decided to concentrate its activities on support of the United Nations as the appropriate means of furthering Andrew Carnegie's aim "to hasten the abolition of international war, the foulest blot upon our civilization."

On Monday, August 2, 1948 a reporter reached me by telephone at my apartment. He told me that, according to information coming from the Committee on Un-American Activities of the House of Representatives, a man named Chambers was going to appear before the committee the next morning and call me a Communist. The reporter asked whether I had any comment.

I did not. The untruthful charge of communism had been the lot of many who had been New Deal officials in the Washington of the 1930s and the early 1940s. I had not taken such charges seriously when made against others, and I saw no reason why I or anyone else should pay much attention to a similar fanciful charge that might now be made against me.

The next morning a witness named Whittaker Chambers appeared before the committee and said that years before he had been "attached" to "an underground organization of the United States Communist party" in Washington. He said that I had been a member of that group.

As I knew no one named Whittaker Chambers I chose to make my denials not only to the newspapers but in the same setting where the charges had been made. Therefore, I sent a telegram to the committee that same afternoon saying that I wanted to appear to deny Chambers's charges under oath.

Richard Nixon, then an obscure congressman from California, considered the case the first major crisis he would face while in public life:

My name, my reputation, and my career were ever to be linked with the decisions I made and the actions I took in that case, as a thirty-five-year-old freshman congressman in 1948. Yet, when I was telling my fifteen-year-old daughter, Tricia, one day about the [subject], she interrupted me to ask, "What was the Hiss case?"

I realized for the first time that a whole new generation of Americans was now growing up who had not even heard of the Hiss case. And now, in restrospect, I wonder how many of my own generation really knew the facts and implications of that emotional controversy that rocked the nation. I experienced [the case] not only as an acute personal crisis but as a vivid case study of the continuing crisis of our times, a crisis with which we shall be confronted as long as aggressive international communism is on the loose in the world.

The Hiss case began for me personally when David Whittaker Chambers appeared before the House Committee on Un-American Activities to testify on communist infiltration into the federal government. Never in the stormy history of the committee was a more sensational investigation started by a less impressive witness.

Chambers did not ask to come before the committee so that he could single out and attack Alger Hiss. The committee had subpoenaed him. Both in appearance and in what he had to say, he made very little impression on me or the other committee members. None of us thought his testimony was going to be especially important.

On his role as star witness in the case against Alger Hiss, Chambers said, "I have testified against him with remorse and pity, but in the moment of history in which this nation now stands, so help me God, I could not do otherwise." (Wide World Photos)

August 3, 1948. Six congressmen took their seats in a nearly empty House committee hearing room: Karl E. Mundt (South Dakota), John McDowell (New Jersey), John E. Rankin (Mississippi), J. Hardin Peterson (Florida), F. Edward Hébert (Louisiana), and Richard M. Nixon (California). Robert E. Stripling, chief investigator of the House Un-American Activities Committee (HUAC), called the sole witness waiting to testify—Whittaker Chambers. Chambers, not an impressive-looking witness, nevertheless had distinctive credentials. He had combined two public careers over the previous twenty years, as a gifted journalist and a translator. Educated at Columbia College, he was fluent in several languages and had translated from German into English such popular works as the children's book *Bambi.*

Chambers had been subpoenaed the previous day. In answer to Stripling's questions Chambers said that in the 1920s and 1930s he had been a Communist party member "and a paid functionary of the party." He added:

> In 1937 I repudiated Marx's doctrines and Lenin's tactics. For a number of years I had served in the underground, chiefly in Washington, D.C. The underground group [included] Alger Hiss. The purpose of this group at that time was not primarily espionage. Its original purpose was the communist infiltration of the American government. But espionage was one of its eventual objectives.

The committee members questioned Chambers at length about his charges. He pointed out that on several previous occasions in the past decade, he had given similar testimony to high State Department officials and to the FBI. No action, however, had ever been taken against any officials he had named as Communists. The witness went on to suggest that he and Hiss had been particularly close:

MR. STRIPLING: When you left the Communist party in 1937, did you approach any of these seven [alleged underground members] to break with you?

MR. CHAMBERS: No. The only one of those people whom I approached was Alger Hiss. I went to the Hiss home one evening at what I considered considerable risk to myself and found Mrs. Hiss at home. Mrs. Hiss is also a member of the Communist party. Mr. Hiss came in shortly afterward, and we talked and I tried to break him away from the party. As a matter of fact, he cried when we separated; but when I left him, he absolutely refused to break. I was very fond of Mr. Hiss.

Despite repeated questions by committee members, Chambers stood by his charges and pointedly denied that the alleged Communist underground group within the New Deal had ever committed espionage:

These people were specifically not wanted to act as sources of information. These people were an elite group, which it was believed would rise to positions—as, indeed, some of them did—notably Mr. Hiss—in the government. Their position in the government would be of much more service to the Communist party.

Newsmen present promptly reported the hottest news item in the morning's testimony: A senior editor of *Time* magazine had accused the president of the Carnegie Endowment of being a secret Soviet agent!

August 5, 1948. It was now Alger Hiss's turn to appear before the committee. He offered a striking contrast to his stout and untidy accuser. His handsome face seemed cool and relaxed. His tall, lean body was fitted with elegant, carefully pressed clothes. Furthermore, he displayed none of Chambers's evident nervousness under questioning. Hiss began his testimony with a prepared statement.

I am not and never have been a member of the Communist party. I do not and never have adhered to the tenets of the Communist party. I am not and never have been a member of any communist-front organization. I have never followed the Communist party line, directly or indirectly. To the best of my knowledge, none of my friends is a communist. To the best of my knowledge, I never heard of Whittaker Chambers until 1947, when two representatives of the Federal Bureau of Investigation asked me if I knew him and various other people. I said that I did not know Chambers. So far as I know, I have never laid eyes on him, and the statements made about me by Mr. Chambers are complete fabrications. I think my record in the government service speaks for itself.

Committee members questioned Hiss at length about his impressive government career. It included prior service as secretary to the great Supreme Court Justice Oliver Wendell Holmes and assistant counsel to the Senate's Nye Committee (see Chapter 42). He had also served with the solicitor general of the United States after which, for over a decade, he had held high posts in the State Department until he left in 1947 to head the Carnegie Endowment.

Then they questioned Hiss about Chambers's accusations:

MR. MUNDT: I wonder what possible motive a man who edits *Time* magazine would have for mentioning Alger Hiss in connection with [Communist involvement].

MR. HISS: So do I, Mr. Chairman. I have no possible understanding of what could have motivated him.

The committee members recognized by this time that, in Stripling's words, there was "very sharp contradiction" between Hiss and Chambers. One of the two men was a monumental liar. Yet according to Mundt, both men were "witnesses whom normally one would assume to be perfectly reliable. They have high positions in American business or organizational work. They both appear to be honest. They both testify under oath [yet their] stories fail to jibe."

At this point Congressman Nixon suggested that Hiss and Chambers "be allowed to confront each other so that any possibility of a mistake in identity may be cleared up." The other HUAC members ignored Nixon's suggestion, and the questioning continued. After Hiss had concluded his testimony, a large crowd of spectators and reporters rushed up to congratulate him. Nixon later expressed the feelings of most of them — and of most members of HUAC — when he said that a terrible mistake had been made. The committee, he thought, should not have allowed Chambers to testify without first checking into the possibility of such error.

A journalist confirmed this reaction when he asked Hiss: "How is the committee going to dig itself out of this hole?" HUAC was already being criticized widely for its careless handling of hearings. There was even a strong possibility that President Truman, if he won the upcoming 1948 election, would ask Congress to disband the committee. That same morning, while Hiss was denying Chambers's charges before the committee, Truman denounced HUAC's current spy investigation. He called it a red herring organized by the Republican-dominated committee to distract the public from the party's failure to pass an effective domestic economic program.

From the beginning, thus, the Hiss–Chambers case became an issue in national politics, threatening Republican chances in the fall elections. "This case is going to kill the committee," one reporter told Nixon after the morning session had ended, "unless you can prove Chambers's story." The reporter did not know that this was exactly what Nixon intended to do.

Richard Milhous Nixon was then a freshman representative from southern California. His family, like millions of others, had suffered during the Depression. He had worked hard from his earliest years. After largely supporting himself through college and law school, Nixon worked briefly in Washington and then served as a naval officer during World War II. Returning to California, he ran for Congress in 1946. In his campaign he charged his Democratic opponent with being a radical pro-Communist. The tactic was successful, and he won the election. During his first year and a half in Congress, he had not acquired any wide reputation beyond his home district. Soon this would change.

Nixon later wrote that when HUAC met privately after Hiss testified, "it was in a virtual state of shock." For his part Nixon argued:

> While it would be virtually impossible to prove that Hiss was or was not a communist — for that would simply be his word against Chambers' — we should be able to establish whether or not the two men knew each other. If

Alger and Priscilla Hiss at first denied any knowledge of Chambers, then conceded that they knew him under another name when he exposed numerous details of their personal lives to the committee. (UPI)

Hiss were lying about not knowing Chambers, then he might also be lying about whether or not he was a communist.

Nixon managed to persuade the acting committee chairman, Karl Mundt, to appoint him head of a subcommittee to question Chambers again. This time the session was to be private, with no spectators or press present.

August 7, 1948. The HUAC subcommittee headed by Nixon questioned Chambers secretly in New York City. Nixon asked in what period Chambers had known Hiss as a Communist. The witness answered "roughly, between the years 1935 and 1937." Chambers said Hiss knew him not by his real name but "by the party name of Carl." He also asserted that he collected Communist party membership dues from Mr. and Mrs. Hiss. According to Chambers, therefore, Hiss was a member of the Communist underground infiltrating the government. Moreover, he was also a dues-paying member of the party itself. At this point Nixon plunged into a detailed, rapid-fire series of questions testing whether Hiss had known Chambers. Specifically, Nixon noted, he wanted to know: "What should one man know about another if he knew him as well as Chambers claimed to know Hiss?"

Chambers apparently remembered a great deal about the Hisses, although as Nixon later admitted: "All of this information might have been obtained by studying Hiss's life without actually knowing him. But some of the answers had a personal ring of truth about them beyond the bare facts themselves." Chambers claimed he had seen the Hisses on numerous occasions. He had been a guest at their home several times. He also seemed to recall a great many details about the Hisses' private lives: nicknames for one another, eating and drinking habits, pets, personal mannerisms, relatives, the exteriors and furniture of their various homes.

Perhaps the most damaging details that Chambers provided about Hiss during the questioning concerned two episodes. One was the transfer of a car Hiss owned to another Communist with Chambers or an associate acting as intermediary. The other impressed Nixon because it had a "personal ring of truth." It concerned a hobby the Hisses and Chambers had in common. Both were amateur ornithologists, bird watchers. Chambers testified, "I recall once they saw, to their great excitement, a prothonotary warbler." At this point Congressman McDowell, also a bird lover, interrupted to ask, "A very rare specimen?" Chambers replied, "I never saw one. I am also fond of birds."

The mass of detail concerning the Hisses' lives restored a faith in Chambers's honesty among committee members.

August 16, 1948. At this closed session of HUAC Hiss seemed under severe strain. The cool composure of his earlier appearance before the committee had given way to a mixture of nervousness and anger. Nixon showed Hiss two pictures of Chambers and asked again whether he knew the man "either as Whittaker Chambers or as Carl or as any other individual." Hiss began to waver, admitting that "the face has a certain familiarity." Chief counsel Stripling and the committee members confronted Hiss with Chambers's detailed claims concerning their friendship. They probed for evidence confirming the *Time* editor's account.

Hiss repeatedly protested the committee's refusal to provide him with a transcript of Chambers's earlier testimony. He became increasingly hostile. He was angry that the committee found it difficult to decide whether truth was on the side of Chambers—"a confessed former Communist" and "self-confessed traitor"—or himself, a highly respected public servant. Stripling, in turn, snapped back sharply that Chambers had "sat there and testified for hours. He said he spent a week in your house, and he just rattled off details like that. He has either made a study of your life in great detail or he knows you."

Moments after this exchange Hiss announced: "I have written a name on this pad in front of me of a person whom I knew in 1933 and 1934 who not only spent some time in my house but sublet my apartment." Hiss was not sure this person—a free-lance writer named George Crosley—was Chambers. He insisted that he had not seen Crosley since 1934. Hiss gave a detailed account of this relationship, claiming to have met Crosley while he was legal counsel to the Nye Committee in 1933.

Crosley, he said, wished to write several magazine articles about the Nye Committee's munitions-industry investigation. Hiss added that he took a liking to the young journalist. When moving his family to a new apartment, Hiss briefly sublet his old apartment to Crosley and his family. At the same time he gave the journalist "an old Ford we had kept for sentimental reasons." Crosley never paid the rent money, according to Hiss. As for the car, "I threw it in along with the rent" because of a desire to "get rid of it." Deciding that he "had been a sucker and [Crosley] was a sort of deadbeat using me for a soft touch," Hiss said, he never saw the man again after 1935. (He later changed the date to mid-1936.)

Hiss also remembered taking several drives with Crosley and giving him "loans [he] never paid back." Once Crosley gave him "a rug he said some wealthy patron gave him. I have still got the damned thing." At one point Nixon asked Hiss about his hobbies. When the witness mentioned bird watching, Congressman McDowell asked: "Did you ever see a prothonotary warbler?" "I have right here on the Potomac," Hiss replied, unaware of Chambers's earlier testimony.

Several members of HUAC remarked during Hiss's testimony that either he or Chambers was obviously committing perjury. "Whichever one of you is lying is the greatest actor that America has ever produced," exclaimed Congressman Hébert. Before adjourning the bitterly tense executive session, the committee decided to have Chambers and Hiss testify publicly, together, nine days later on August 25. Actually, the pair confronted one another the following day at a hurriedly arranged HUAC meeting in New York City.

August 17, 1948. The session was moved up, according to Nixon, to prevent Hiss from gaining "nine more days to make his story fit the facts." In fact, there may have been another motive. The committee was uneasy over the death of Harry Dexter White, a former high Treasury Department official. He had died of a heart attack. White had appeared before a HUAC public hearing a few days earlier to deny charges leveled by Chambers that he had been either a party member or pro-Communist. He had asked for a postponement because of his bad heart but was refused. White had proved a good witness in his own defense despite the committee's attempt to browbeat him. Nixon and the other HUAC subcommittee members may have hoped to divert public outrage over White's untimely death following this grueling interrogation. They would shift attention to the still active Hiss–Chambers investigation.

Throughout the session, Hiss proved surprisingly irritable, angry, and defensive. He observed that Harry Dexter White's death had upset him greatly, so that testifying would be difficult. He also protested that the committee (despite promises to the contrary) had leaked portions of his previous day's testimony to the press. (Both Nixon and Stripling denied this charge.) Finally Chambers, who had been waiting in an adjoining room, was brought in.

> MR. NIXON: Sit over here, Mr. Chambers. Mr. Chambers, will you please stand? And will you please stand, Mr. Hiss? Mr. Hiss, the man standing here is Mr. Whittaker Chambers. I ask you now if you have ever known this man before.
>
> MR. HISS: May I ask him to speak? Will you ask him to say something?
>
> MR. NIXON: Yes. Mr. Chambers, will you tell us your name and your business?
>
> MR. CHAMBERS: My name is Whittaker Chambers. [At this point, Hiss walked toward Chambers.] I am senior editor of *Time* magazine.
>
> MR. HISS: Are you George Crosley?
>
> MR. CHAMBERS: Not to my knowledge. You are Alger Hiss, I believe.
>
> MR. HISS: I certainly am.
>
> MR. CHAMBERS: That was my recollection. [Chambers read from a magazine so that Hiss could test his voice pattern.]

Hiss then announced that Chambers was probably the man he knew as Crosley. Nixon and Stripling began a lengthy series of questions comparing Hiss's version of the relationship with Crosley—apartment rental, car transfer, gift of a rug, and other details—with the facts previously supplied by Chambers. Hiss, of course, denied that Crosley had been more than a casual acquaintance, saying, "He meant nothing to me." Chambers again stressed their common bond, stating, "I was a Communist, and you were a Communist." At last Hiss acknowledged, "I am perfectly prepared to identify this man as George Crosley." But he denied knowing whether "Crosley" had even been a Communist and pointed out that "it was a quite different atmosphere in Washington then than today." He insisted he had known Crosley only as a journalist.

Alger Hiss and Whittaker Chambers silently confront each other before the House Un-American Activities Committee on August 25, 1948. (Wide World Photos)

August 25, 1948. The hearing room was jammed with reporters and spectators. The hearing lasted nine hours. (Hiss testified for six, Chambers for three.) Not only Hiss but all seven other alleged members of the Communist cell whom Chambers had named had meanwhile testified before HUAC. Except for Hiss's brother, Donald, who joined Alger in specifically denying any Communist associations, the others refused to say whether they had been Communists. In their refusals all invoked the Fifth Amendment, which provides protection from possible self-incrimination.

From the start Hiss, accompanied by his lawyer, treated the occasion as a kind of trial. He was convinced that HUAC believed Chambers and wished mainly to prepare evidence for a perjury charge against him. Therefore, Hiss was extremely guarded in responding. He qualified his answers with phrases such as "to the best of my recollection" more than 200 times. On several occasions he accused HUAC of believing Chambers largely for political reasons. The Republican-controlled committee, he claimed, wanted to expose a top civil servant closely identified with Democratic administration programs—the New Deal, the Yalta agreements, and the United Nations.

The Hiss-Chambers Case: An American Mystery **829**

The day went badly for Alger Hiss. At the start both Hiss and Chambers were directed to stand. Hiss again identified the *Time* editor as Crosley. Chambers again claimed to have known Hiss in the Communist underground. Some of the most damaging passages for Hiss involved the Ford car. He had previously testified turning it over to Crosley along with his apartment.

Mr. Nixon: Did you give Crosley a car?

Mr. Hiss: I gave Crosley, according to my best recollection . . .

Mr. Nixon: You certainly can testify yes or no as to whether you gave Crosley a car. How many cars have you given away in your life, Mr. Hiss?

Mr. Hiss: I have had only one old car of a financial value of $25 in my life. That is the car I let Crosley use.

Mr. Nixon: My point now is, is your present testimony that you did or did not give Crosley a car?

Mr. Hiss: Whether I transferred title to him in a legal, formal sense; whether I gave him the car outright; whether the car came back—I don't know.

Unfortunately for Hiss, a title search by HUAC agents produced evidence that Hiss had transferred the car on July 23, 1936, to William Rosen, the alleged Communist about whom Chambers had testified earlier. The Hiss signature on the document had been notarized by W. Marvin Smith. He was a lawyer with the Justice Department. Smith told HUAC that he knew Hiss and that Hiss had personally signed the transfer in his presence. (Strangely, Smith fell or jumped to his death soon after he testified.)

Hiss now counterattacked. He denounced HUAC's investigation as a political attack on liberal Democrats. He reviewed his fifteen years of impressive public service and named as references for his achievements, personal character, and loyalty thirty-four prominent public figures. Nixon termed this an effort by Hiss to prove his "innocence by association," an ironic reference considering HUAC's past reputation for trying to show a witness's *guilt* by association.

During this day's testimony the two major witnesses reversed their previous roles completely. Chambers now became a cool, placid witness, calmly answering every question put to him. Hiss testified nervously and emotionally. But Hiss emphasized that some of Chambers's most obvious statements about him were incorrect. Thus the Hisses were not teetotalers and Hiss did attend church. Hiss's stepson was not a "puny little boy." Despite these and other errors about the Hisses, Chambers still displayed remarkable familarity with their private life.

Hiss offered some explanation for this apparent familiarity. He claimed that Chambers, with access to *Time's* excellent research records, could have discovered most of the personal material on Hiss in such publications as *Who's Who.* Congressman Hébert retorted: "Nobody could have read in *Who's Who* that you found a rare bird [the prothonotary warbler]." Hiss responded that he had "told many, many people." But this did not persuade the committee.

For his part, Chambers denied that he harbored any secret reason for wishing to ruin Hiss, as the latter charged. He went so far as to call Alger Hiss "the closest friend I ever had in the Communist party." Fighting back tears, he said softly:

> I am [not] working out some old grudge, or motives of revenge or hatred. I do not hate Mr. Hiss. We were close friends, but we are caught in a tragedy of history. Mr. Hiss represents the concealed enemy against which we are all fighting, and I am fighting.

By the time HUAC finally adjourned its August 25th session at 8 P.M., Alger Hiss had been placed on the defensive. Three days later HUAC issued an interim report. It called Hiss's testimony "vague and evasive," Chambers's "forthright and emphatic." In the committee's opinion "the verifiable portions of Chambers's testimony have stood up strongly; the verifiable portions of Hiss's testimony have been badly shaken."

The next act in this "tragedy of history" took place on a national radio show, *Meet the Press*. There, Chambers charged that "Alger Hiss was a Communist and may be now." Several weeks passed without Hiss responding. His supporters grew impatient. "Mr. Hiss has created a situation," complained the liberal Washington *Post*, "in which he is obliged to put up or shut up." Finally, on September 27, Hiss brought suit against Chambers for slander. By then the election campaign was in full swing. HUAC members (including Nixon) had returned to their various states. An exciting four-way battle for the presidency crowded "the Hiss–Chambers case" off the front pages.

Nixon himself faced no reelection problem. He had won his district's Democratic *and* Republican nominations, then possible under California's cross-filing system that allowed candidates to enter both primaries. He did campaign for other Republicans, however, regaling crowds with a dramatic account of the Hiss investigation.

In the presidential election Truman ran against Governor Thomas E. Dewey of New York, who avoided the anti-Communist issue because he believed no case could be made against Truman as "soft" on communism. After a hard-fought campaign Truman won a startling reelection victory. The Democrats, moreover, regained control of Congress.

Prospects for continuing the Hiss–Chambers inquiry looked bleak, since Truman still considered it a political red herring directed against his administration. After the election, many in Washington thought the president would try to abolish HUAC. The Hiss case itself dropped from public attention and went into its legal phase—a slander suit.

Deeply depressed by Truman's victory, Chambers even contemplated suicide (an action he considered at other critical points in the case). He also fretted at the possibility that a Justice Department controlled by Democrats might indict *him*, not Hiss, for perjury. Pressed by Hiss's attorney in pretrial dispositions for written proof of his charges and under severe emotional strain, Chambers (according to his own account) took a mid-November trip to Brooklyn. There he visited a nephew with whom, he claimed, he had left a package ten years earlier. The nephew drew from a disused dumbwaiter shaft the proof Chambers needed—a dusty envelope containing papers and microfilms that (Chambers later insisted) he had forgotten about until the libel suit jogged his memory.

The papers were dated from early 1937 through April 1938. If genuine, they indicated that Hiss had lied in claiming not to have seen "Crosley" or Chambers after mid-1936. Furthermore, the papers had apparently been typed on an old Woodstock typewriter that belonged to the Hisses until 1937 or 1938. (The exact date that the Hisses got rid of the machine would later become a major point at issue.) Chambers hurried back to his farm with this evidence and hid the microfilms. (He also hid several pages of notes on confidential government meetings in Harry Dexter White's handwriting.) On November 17, he submitted some of the material to Hiss's attorneys at a pretrial hearing—sixty-five pages of copied State Department documents, four memos in Alger Hiss's handwriting, and the envelope in which they had been hidden for a decade.

Chambers now claimed that he had tried until then to shield Alger and Priscilla Hiss from exposure as Soviet spies. But because of the pressures imposed by Hiss's libel suit, he had to reveal "that Alger Hiss had also committed espionage." Chambers then testified to Hiss's attorneys about a new claim. He alleged that he was a Communist spy for Russia from 1936 to 1938 and a courier for Hiss while the latter stole secret State Department documents. Some of these Mrs. Hiss had retyped. The *Time* editor now asserted that he had actually left the party in April 1938 rather than in 1937, since some of the stolen documents dated from the later period, although Chambers had referred to the April 1938 break date a number of times in his August 1948 HUAC testimony. Hiss vigorously denied this new charge. His lawyers grilled both Chambers and his wife about the contradictions between his previous and his new testimony.

The typed documents were explosive evidence. The Hiss and Chambers lawyers immediately turned them over to Alex Campbell, head of the Justice Department's Criminal Division. Campbell warned both parties to the slander suit not to discuss the envelope's contents (neither Campbell nor Hiss then knew of the microfilms) until the material had been investigated. But then a story in the pro-Hiss Washington *Post* indicating that the Justice Department might drop its investigation of Hiss spurred Nixon into action. Before leaving for a Caribbean vacation, Nixon—informed by an investigator for Chambers's lawyers about the stolen papers produced at the pretrial deposition—signed a subpoena ordering Chambers to provide HUAC with any further evidence he had relating to his charges against Hiss.

On December 2 HUAC staff members served the subpoena. A few days earlier, because of rumors that Hiss investigators were prowling around his farm, Chambers had taken the microfilms from his bedroom and hidden them in his pumpkin patch. Now he went to the hollowed-out pumpkin, removed the microfilms, and handed them to the HUAC

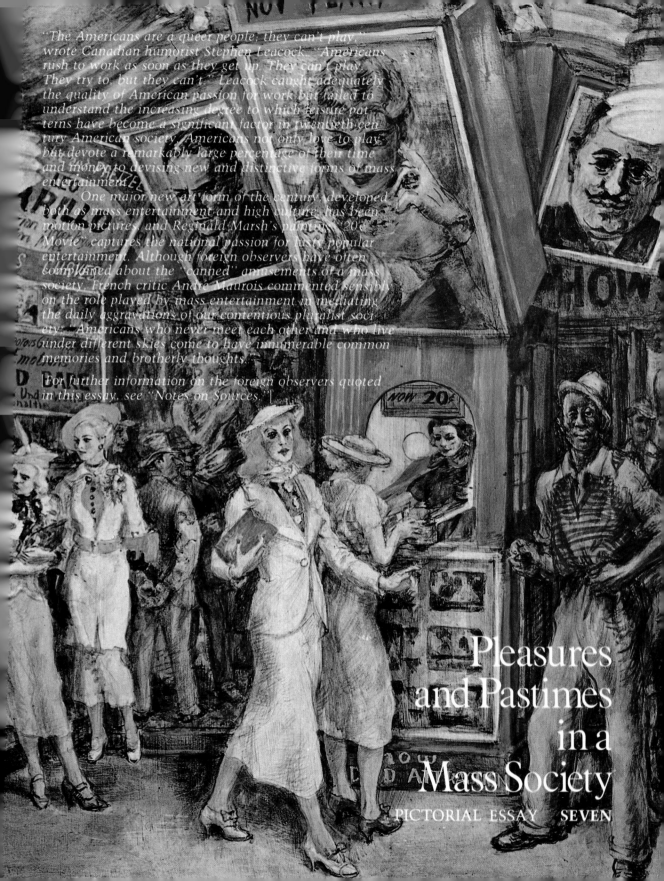

"The Americans are a queer people; they can't play,"
wrote Canadian humorist Stephen Leacock. "Americans
rush to work as soon as they get up. They can't play.
They try to, but they can't." Leacock caught adequately
the quality of American passion for work but failed to
understand the increasing degree to which leisure patterns have become a significant factor in twentieth-century American society. Americans not only love to play
but devote a remarkably large percentage of their time
and money to devising new and distinctive forms of mass
entertainment.

One major new art form of the century, developed
both as mass entertainment and high culture, has been
motion pictures, and Reginald Marsh's painting "20¢
Movie" captures the national passion for lusty popular
entertainment. Although foreign observers have often
complained about the "canned" amusements of a mass
society, French critic André Maurois commented sensibly
on the role played by mass entertainment in mediating
the daily aggravations of our contentious pluralist society: "Americans who never meet each other and who live
under different skies come to have innumerable common
memories and brotherly thoughts."

[For further information on the foreign observers quoted
in this essay, see "Notes on Sources."]

Pleasures and Pastimes in a Mass Society

PICTORIAL ESSAY   SEVEN

Stronger than in various other countries, and per-haps also than in Turkey, seems to be the predilec-tion in America for the lighter types of musical and theatrical entertainment — for jazz and operet-tas, or for comedies and thrillers rather than plays that have a pessimistic note or are centered around philosophical and social themes.

[ÖMER CELÂL SARC, 1959]

Broadcasting a radio drama, 1934

Scene from *Oklahoma!* (original production, 1943)

A scene from *Gold Diggers of 1933*

I could not agree that the creation of films is not an art at all, only an industry. It is actu-ally a curiously mixed activity, coming into a new category, needing all the resources and organization of a large industry, but by no means devoid of genu-ine artistic impulses.
The public looked to films for general enter-tainment, on a scale hitherto unknown, and accepted the moving pictures as a substitute for theaters, books, gossip, and dreams.

[J. B. PRIESTLEY, 1935–36]

Let's listen to Louis Armstrong on Broadway, the black Titan of the cry, of the apostrophe, of the burst of laughter, of thunder. An imperial figure, Armstrong makes his entrance. His voice is as deep as an abyss, it is a black cave. He bursts out laughing, he roars and puts the trumpet to his mouth. With it he is in turn demoniac, playful, and massive, from one second to another, in accordance with an astounding fantasy. The man is extravagantly skillful; he is a king.

[LE CORBUSIER, 1947]

Louis Armstrong

Elvis Presley and fans

Female teenagers are in the habit of greeting their heroes, the young crooners — the one best known being Elvis Presley, of the writhing hips and thighs — with a shrill yell that seems to issue from a single throat. The picture of young and well-dressed girls comporting themselves in this fashion is enough to send cold shivers down an adult's spine. Significantly, however, it has been observed that only the girls in the rows lit up by the stage lights break out in this yell; that is, only those who can be seen by the others. Moreover, they are looking not so much at the singer as at the other members of their own group.

[HERBERT VON BORCH, 1962]

I have studied hundreds of photos of Louis in his big fights, of Louis preparing for his big fights, of Louis just after his big fights. His face almost never changes. The man is dignified, in the toughest sport in the world, whether he's giving a licking or taking one. You canot get away from this impression of the man being so superbly equipped to fight that he didn't need the window-dressing of a big grin of confidence, or glib phrases by the publicity boys. Louis wasn't just a great fighter. He was an admirable man.

[HARRY CARPENTER, 1964]

The Brown Bomber, Louis and Schmeling Fight, by Robert Riggs

I do not pretend to understand even the coarser of the finer points of American college football, which must have been originally devised during an early revolutionary phase of American life, for like a revolution it is an odd mixture of secret plotting, with so many heads motionless and close together, and sudden violent action. When either side pressed towards goal, we all stood up. The danger over or the prize lost, we sat down again. The enormous clock ran off the seconds when the ball was actually in play. It stopped when the game stopped. And the game was always stopping.

[J. B. PRIESTLEY AND JACQUETTA HAWKES, 1954]

Miami defeats Holy Cross at the Orange Bowl, 1946

Willie Mays at second base, 1957

Bowling at a fifty-six lane alley, California

We went into a bowling alley. It is the old game of skittles which the dwarfs of Rip Van Winkle played, but it has been brought up to date. Instead of a wild gully, I found a bar with tables and chairs: the bowling alleys, set side by side, are of varnished wood, and when the bowling ball has knocked over the ninepins, it falls through a trap door and is returned by an automatic device to the player. The game is so popular that the alleys are booked for days in advance. It is monotonous to watch.

[SIMONE DE BEAUVOIR, 1947]

Robinson's character was the key. A fierce competitor, Jackie had in the early days to curb his angry pride. He ignored insults, and won recognition as a baseball player, on equal terms with others, whether white or black. Today ability is the key, not pigmentation. Some day Jackie's greatest honor will come when he is simply a name in a record book, when, because there was a Jackie Robinson and others like him, future generations have forgotten there was ever a need for a Jackie Robinson.

[CANADIAN SPORTSWRITER]

To observe the North American in a large crowd within the United States—at a World Series game or a popular football game—is one of the most cheering spectacles in the world. Here we have an enormous mass of people, well balanced, attractive, determined to enjoy to the utmost an afternoon of relaxation, applauding their favorite team but without ill will or malevolence toward the adversary, on the contrary always disposed to recognize and applaud the courage and skill of the opposition.

[DANIEL COSÍO VILLEGAS, 1959]

Cheerleaders at a high-school basketball game

Teenagers at a "sock hop," Carlsbad, New Mexico

Wisconsin Farm Auction. by Joan Arend Kickbush

Woman playing bingo in Muncie, Indiana

America is a modern land where technical ingenuity is apparent at every point, in the equipment of a kitchen as well as of a car, but at the same time a land of gardens, of flowers, of home activities, where a man, away from his office or his workplace, enjoys tinkering at his bench, making a piece of furniture, repainting his house, repairing a fence, or mowing his lawn. A land of luxury but also of simple pleasures. There is an America that strolls in the parks in its suburban Sunday clothes, or cavorts on the beaches, and plays baseball everywhere.

[JACQUES FREYMOND, 1959]

Father and son tossing a football, Newton, Iowa

Children playing at an
open water hydrant,
New York City

*The American smile, which has been so ridiculed by those who believe the in-
telligent thing is to know everything already—without, of course, knowing
much of anything at all—seems to me to be the expression of love for one's fellow
man, of the basic fact that in the United States it is firmly believed that living together is a blessing. This is derived, in my opinion, from the historical makeup of
the United States and from the American spirit, from its loneliness and the fact
that for so long the presence of other men was an occasion for joy.*

[JULIAN MARIAS, 1959]

Girls jumping rope,
Cleveland

representatives. "I think this is what you are looking for," he said. Within hours the press began headlining Chambers's mysterious "pumpkin papers" (actually not papers but microfilms). That same day Hiss confirmed that Chambers had turned over the typed stolen documents on November 17.

The Justice Department finally swung into action. Both Chambers and Hiss were called several times, beginning on December 6, to testify before a New York federal grand jury. After a hurried and well-publicized return from his Caribbean vacation, Nixon led HUAC in a new series of hearings. At one of these new sessions Assistant Secretary of State John Peurifoy (in charge of security matters) testified. He declared that the Soviet Union or any other foreign country possessing these microfilmed documents would have been able to break all the secret State Department codes then in use.

Clearly, the Republican-controlled HUAC, which had no legal authority to put Hiss on trial, was competing with the Democratic-controlled Justice Department for jurisdiction in what had now become a criminal case. Nixon frankly stated that his committee "did not trust the Justice Department to prosecute the case with the vigor it deserved." On December 9 Truman again labeled the case a red herring. On December 10 Chambers resigned from *Time*.

Under pressure to provide HUAC with all the evidence against Hiss in his possession, Chambers led two HUAC investigators to the pumpkin patch on his farm (an arrow identifies the patch) and retrieved the microfilms from a hollowed-out pumpkin where he had hidden them some time earlier. (Wide World Photos)

The Hiss-Chambers Case: An American Mystery **833**

On December 13 the FBI produced for the grand jury several old letters typed by Priscilla Hiss on the same machine that had typed the State Department documents. That day, Alger Hiss left the Carnegie Endowment on a three-month paid leave of absence. He never returned. The New York grand jury indicted Hiss on two counts of perjury on December 15. The first was for claiming he had not stolen State Department records and given them to Chambers. The second was for swearing he had not seen Chambers after January 1, 1937. Only the statute of limitations and the absence of witnesses who could back up the charge kept the grand jury from charging Hiss with espionage.

The former State Department official underwent two trials. The first ended on July 8, 1949, with a deadlocked jury that had voted eight to four to convict Hiss. The prosecutor at both trials, Thomas Murphy, presented several types of evidence to prove the government's perjury charges. These included evidence that the two men knew one another more intimately (after 1936) than Hiss admitted, that Hiss had been a Communist, and that Hiss had stolen the State Department documents. The weakest link in the government's case concerned Hiss's alleged communism. Only one witness, an ex-Communist named Hede Massing, confirmed Chambers's claim that Hiss had been a party member. Her testimony was challenged, however, by a defense witness who swore that Mrs. Massing had been confused about the question of Hiss's involvement when discussing it at a party.

At both trials Chambers repeated the story he first told to Hiss's attorneys in November 1948 during pretrial hearings involving the libel suit. According to this story, Hiss had been recruited for espionage by Chambers's Communist superior during the fall of 1936. Chambers said he served as Hiss's courier until April 1938. Then, according to Chambers, he broke from the party. (He previously testified to having left the party months earlier.) At this point Chambers turned the final batch of stolen documents over to his nephew in Brooklyn for safekeeping.

The microfilms and retyped State Department messages were at the heart of the case against Hiss. Prosecutor Murphy called them "immutable" witnesses, therefore presumably reliable ones. At neither trial did Hiss's attorneys challenge the testimony of an FBI expert who testified that a comparison of typing on the documents with letters written by Mrs. Hiss on the same machine established her as the typist. Nor did they challenge the argument that the documents had been typed on a Woodstock machine belonging to Hiss. Hiss did claim he had given the machine away sometime before the material was typed. But this claim was never proved conclusively in court, one way or the other. (Moreover, even three defense experts confirmed that the stolen documents had been typed on the Hiss Woodstock. Naturally, the defense did not put its own experts on the stand at either trial.)

The jury at the second trial convicted Hiss of perjury on both counts. After that, Hiss's lawyers began arguing that the typewriter itself was a false piece of evidence constructed by either Chambers or the FBI. They also argued that the typed documents had been prepared only to

implicate Hiss. (This argument, of course, did not affect the microfilmed documents or the handwritten Hiss memos.) Since the *defense* had actually located the typewriter in question prior to the first trial, Hiss's supporters began arguing that the FBI had somehow gained possession of the machine earlier, then "planted" it on the defense. This remains unproven even today, though those who argue that Alger Hiss was innocent tend to assume some degree of FBI involvement. The FBI files on the case, recently opened to researchers, failed to bear out this charge. They show that the FBI conducted a widespread, but unsuccessful, hunt for the Woodstock and that it was seriously embarrassed when the defense turned up the machine. Moreover, the key identification of the stolen typed documents is with *samples* of Mrs. Hiss's typing on *her* Woodstock.

At the Hiss trials themselves, the defense paraded a distinguished group of Americans before the jury to testify to Hiss's outstanding career and good character. At the same time, they tried to throw doubt on

Richard Nixon and chief HUAC investigator Robert Stripling are shown examining microfilms of secret State Department documents, the most damaging evidence against Hiss (Wide World Photos)

Chambers's reliability. They placed a psychiatrist on the stand who labeled Chambers "a psychopathic personality" with irrational hostilities.

Prosecutor Murphy ridiculed these defense efforts at both trials. He pointed repeatedly to the evidence that Hiss's lawyers could never adequately explain—the stolen government documents. The twelve jurors at the second trial, overlooking Chambers's minor inconsistencies, all believed Murphy. On January 21, 1950, they found Hiss guilty. Later appeals to overturn the verdict were rejected, and Hiss served forty-four months in prison. He emerged in November 1954, still proclaiming his innocence.

Hiss, now a convicted perjurer, did not return to the Carnegie Endowment, of course. He has had a series of obscure and ill-paying business jobs. He has written his version of the episode and worked continuously to renew public interest in the case. (The Watergate crisis revived attention in the episode because of its link to Richard Nixon. Hiss is presently seeking in federal court to overturn the 1950 conviction on grounds that he did not receive a fair trial.) Chambers returned to his Maryland farm, did special assignments as a journalist, and wrote his memoirs. In 1961 he died from a heart attack.

Nixon won a Senate seat in 1950, largely because of his efforts in the Hiss case. He went on to become vice-president in 1953. The House Committee on Un-American Activities temporarily regained its public prestige as a result of Hiss's conviction. Truman abandoned his effort to abolish it.

Less than three weeks after Hiss's conviction, a then obscure Wisconsin senator announced: "I have here in my hand a list of 205 people known to be members of the Communist party and who, nevertheless, are still working and shaping the policy of the State Department." With Joseph R. McCarthy's speech a new era of anti-Communist politics in the United States acquired its leader—and its name.

Affluence and Anti-Communism: 44 The Cold War at Home

The Depression ended—with a bang, not a whimper—when Japan attacked Pearl Harbor. The war years changed only marginally the lives of the two people who were later to become key figures in the Hiss case. Alger Hiss remained a top official of the State Department, while Whittaker Chambers rose in importance on *Time* magazine. But Richard Nixon saw his life altered dramatically. Although reared as a Quaker, Nixon yearned for some role in the war effort. He first joined a new government agency, the Office of Price Administration (OPA), created to regulate wartime price levels. Then the young lawyer joined the navy and served on various Pacific islands, handling duties as a supply officer.

Nixon spent a restless year in private practice in California before winning his first race for Congress in 1946. The war had clearly opened up significant career possibilities for Nixon, as it did for millions of his contemporaries. A nation still climbing uncertainly out of the Depression in 1941 had regained, by war's end, most of its pre-1930 affluence and self-confidence.

THE WORLD WAR II HOME FRONT

Almost 4 million Americans were still unemployed on the eve of Pearl Harbor. Other millions still labored at government-sponsored jobs for such agencies as the WPA. Some 40 percent of America's families lived below the $1500 annual minimum income needed for a family of four. (This amounted to only $30 a week to cover food, housing, clothing, and everything else!) Over 7.5 million workers earned salaries below the legal minimum wage of 40 cents an hour.

Still, there were many signs of change by 1941. The economy, thanks largely to $8 billion spent on defense production, was now strong, almost booming. Of the country's 134 million people, one-third held civilian jobs while one-tenth worked on defense contracts at top wages. Farm prices had reached a new high in 1940, as had average hourly wages in the two dozen major defense-oriented industries.

Moreover, on the eve of war, most Americans supported the pro-Allied policies of the Roosevelt administration. But polls showed that they did not expect a war to improve their condition much. Twelve years of depression had left the country somewhat doubtful of future prospects and skeptical of idealistic visions.

Bolstering Morale

The government went to great lengths to counteract pessimism and ensure the cooperative involvement of most Americans in the war effort. The Office of Civilian Defense (OCD) sponsored various programs to stimulate patriotism. These included "town meetings" throughout the country. Their basic objective was "that of awakening all the elements of the community to their responsibilities for total participation for victory." Patriotic sentiments were also aroused by stage, screen, and radio productions, all of which tried to bolster national morale, particularly in the first year, when news from the fronts was often grim.

Usually such entertainment aimed at stirring up hatred toward the enemy, Germans and Japanese. Seldom did it assert any positive American war goals. Movie heroes such as John Wayne and radio idols like Jack Armstrong ("the all-American boy") battled tirelessly against Nazi sab-

In 1943, women factory workers, "Rosie the Riveters" (the World War II slang for such indispensable workers) put the finishing touches on hundreds of control cabins for U.S. fighter planes at Douglas Aircraft's Long Beach, California, plant. (National Archives)

oteurs and Japan's "fanatical yellow hordes." American advertising encouraged sales of government war bonds or warned defense workers and soldiers to beware of possible spies in their midst. ("Loose lips sink ships!") Such efforts were remarkably successful in boosting home-front efforts.

Politically, the job of defending the country against attack had turned bipartisan even before the war began. A number of leading Republicans accepted Roosevelt's invitation in 1940 to help meet the impending emergency.

Mobilizing the Economy

Conversion to military preparedness had preceded Pearl Harbor. Total mobilization of both the American people and their economy, however, advanced swiftly after December 1941. An army of 1.6 million existed then. By war's end the number of troops who had served or were serving in the army, navy, marines, air corps (then still part of the army), and coast guard exceeded 15 million—including 200,000 women.

The home front resembled one vast factory. A few statistics tell much of the story. Many Americans felt that Roosevelt was being unrealistic when in 1942 he called for an output of 60,000 planes, 45,000 tanks, and 8 million tons of shipping. Yet in 1944 the nation's factory workers—keeping plants open 24 hours daily on continuous shifts—produced over 96,000 planes. By 1945 the country's naval yards had turned out over 55 million tons of merchant shipping and 71,000 warships. Federal purchases grew from $6 billion in 1940 to $89 billion by 1944. During the first six months of the war alone, the government placed over $100 billion worth of war contracts with private industry.

Total federal spending during the three and a half years of war amounted to over $320 billion, an amount twice as large as the total of all previous spending from 1789 to 1941! The government financed this vast increase partly through higher taxes on both corporations and individuals. Even after taxes, however, corporate profits doubled between 1939 and 1944 (reaching $10 billion that year). War production completed the job that the New Deal had begun of ending the country's economic depression. Much of the government's revenues came from taxes or public borrowing through war bonds. A still higher percentage came from running huge budget deficits throughout the war. The American national debt grew to $247 billion by 1945, nearly six times that of 1941.

Meanwhile, prosperity returned to the United States and unemployment vanished. Many women took full-time factory jobs to meet the shortage of labor created by the armed forces' need for men. Public confidence in the business community increased, replacing the widespread hostility apparent during the Depression decade.

Rationing and Inflation

Full employment during the war gave millions of Americans bigger bank accounts. It put more money in their pockets, though they had less to spend it on. "Disposable income" (income after taxes) increased from $67 billion in 1939 to $140 billion by 1945. Consumer spending alone rose from $62 billion in 1939 to $106 billion by 1945. Wartime rationing and shortages of consumer goods, as well as higher wages and profits, led to higher inflationary prices for those goods and services that were available.

The government tried to control inflation and regulate prices—which rose an average of 2 percent monthly during the war—by establishing official wage and price levels. It set ceilings on legal prices through OPA. Richard Nixon remembered his experiences in this agency as a time when he "became more conservative [and] greatly disillusioned about bureaucracy." Yet OPA did succeed in holding down runaway inflation throughout the war years, despite an enormous increase in the disposable income of most Americans.

Farm conditions improved. Farm income doubled during the war because of the demand for agricultural products by the armed forces and civilians alike. Despite a decline in the number of farm laborers, increased mechanization helped double farm output during the war years, 1941 to 1945. Legislation by powerful farm-bloc Democrats brought farmers' incomes to an all-time high.

Average weekly earnings among industrial workers also increased by 100 percent during the war years. Both the A. F. of L. and the CIO made "no-strike" pledges. But the number of strikes increased as prices and profits continued rising at a level greater than wage increases. Union membership increased from 10 to 15 million. The demand for factory workers led to a reduction of total unemployment from 5.6 percent of the work force in 1941 to 1 percent by war's end. More important, the war guaranteed the future of industrial unionism, which had grown with New Deal encouragement during the Depression.

The wartime domestic economy lay in the hands of a triple alliance of big government, big business, and big labor. The three differed on specific policies. But each accepted the need for negotiated settlements with the other two. Wartime cooperation among union leaders, government officials, and corporation heads—all eager to maximize production for the war effort—shaped a new industrial state in America.

The Atomic Bomb

The period's single most significant scientific and military achievement, which would notably affect postwar American policy, was the development of the atomic bomb. Wartime scientific research was placed in the hands of an Office of Scientific Research and Development (OSRD), headed by Vannevar Bush and James Conant. The United States benefited greatly from the work of refugee scientists, many of them Jews who had fled Nazi Germany or fascist Italy. Albert Einstein, Leo Szilard, and Enrico Fermi led this intellectual migration. It affected not only science but many other aspects of American life and culture.

At a cost of billions, a massively organized project was undertaken to develop an atomic bomb before the Germans, who were also working on the weapon. The secret program, known as the Manhattan Project, involved scientists, technicians, and industrial workers. It included design laboratories at Columbia University, the University of Chicago, the University of California at Berkeley, and —most important—at a central headquarters near Los Alamos, New Mexico. There, under the leadership of physicist J. Robert Oppenheimer, the first atomic device was assembled. It was detonated on July 16, 1945, at Alamogordo, New Mexico.

The bombs dropped subsequently at Hiroshima and Nagasaki led directly to Japan's defeat in August 1945. By then the United States had spent over $350 billion to achieve victory in World War II — apart from the tremendous cost in American casualties.

The Relocation Policy

The country paid not only a high cost in human life but also a certain moral cost for its victory. For the Japanese attack on Pearl Harbor led to what the American Civil Liberties Union called "the worst single invasion of citizens' liberties" during the war. This was the confining in relocation centers of 112,000 Japanese Americans (more than half of them born in the United States). After Pearl Harbor, white residents of West Coast states feared an internal threat from the Japanese Americans. They appealed to Roosevelt to remove the entire community from the West Coast.

Actually, there was no evidence whatsoever of sabotage. But officials such as California's attorney general, Earl Warren (later a great civil libertarian as chief justice of the United States Supreme Court), urged their evacuation to protect the region's civil defense. Bowing to these pressures, President Roosevelt signed an executive order in February 1942 authorizing the relocation of Japanese Americans to nine inland centers. Driven from their homes into what were virtually an American version of concentration camps, these loyal Japanese Americans needlessly suffered loss of their freedom, homes, land, and dignity. This unfair treatment did not deter over thirty-three thousand Japanese Americans from enlisting and fighting bravely for the United States. Although the Supreme Court upheld the relocation policy, the government later paid compensation to the displaced for their property losses.

THE TRUMAN YEARS

Franklin D. Roosevelt, reelected for an unprecedented fourth term in 1944, died in April 1945. He left to Vice-President Harry S Truman the

One young Japanese–American evacuee waits with her family's possessions in California before leaving by bus for a relocation center in the spring of 1942. (Clem Albers/National Archives)

responsibility for governing the world's most militarily powerful and economically prosperous nation. On learning of Roosevelt's death, Truman quite understandably felt "as though the moon and all the stars and all the planets have fallen on me."

Harry Truman was an accidental president. Roosevelt had chosen him for the vice-presidential nomination in 1944 almost as an afterthought. Truman had little formal preparation for holding the office. While vice-president, for example, he was not even told about the atomic bomb. Less than four months after taking office, he had to make the fateful decision whether to drop it on Japan.

A Missouri farm boy who served in World War I, Truman entered politics as a member of the notorious Pendergast machine that ran Kansas City politics. Although personally honest, he served this corrupt political machine loyally. Truman rose through its ranks and was first elected to the Senate in 1934.

Several factors helped Truman obtain the vice-presidency in 1944. Hardworking and extremely liberal (by Missouri's border-state standards), he had fought the Ku Klux Klan in his home state, battled loyally for New Deal programs, and served with distinction as chairman of a Senate committee that investigated irregularities in national defense spending.

Many of Truman's most pressing concerns during his first months in office were vitally important decisions on war policy and postwar settlements (see Chapter 42). Of immediate concern to the new president, once Japan surrendered, was the fact that the men overseas wanted to come home quickly. ("No Boats, No Votes," was the gist of GI mail.) Congress and President Truman responded by rapidly demobilizing (releasing from duty) the great bulk of American armed forces. By mid-1946 an army and air force that had numbered over 8 million troops the previous year was reduced to less than 2 million. A navy of almost 4 million was cut back to less than 1 million. Total military strength fell to 1.5 million by mid-1947, and Congress had ordered even this number reduced to under 1 million by January 1948.

Postwar Economic Policy

Congress allowed the 1940 draft to expire in mid-1947. Cold War military planning focused more and more on the defense shield provided by America's monopoly of nuclear weapons. Furthermore, the discharged servicemen found that Congress had provided generously for them. Under the Servicemen's Readjustment Act (which most people called the GI Bill of Rights), more than $13.5 billion was spent on veterans over the next decade. This money went not only for college educations and vocational training but also for special unemployment insurance (for a year) to smooth the return to civilian life. Funds were spent as well to provide medical services at veterans' hospitals and rehabilitation programs for the wounded. Finally, low-interest loans were made available to veterans to start businesses and to buy or build homes. This was particularly helpful because of the housing shortage at war's end.

There was widespread fear among the public, and many economists too, that without war spending the country would suffer a major postwar recession. A Council of Economic Advisers, created by Truman's Maximum Employment Act, committed Washington for the first time to using the nation's resources to ensure "maximum employment, production, and purchasing power." By mid-1946 Congress had also ended most wartime price and wage controls, cut taxes over $6 billion, and begun to tackle the massive problems of reconversion to a peacetime economy. These efforts were hindered by a wave of strikes and runaway inflation.

Auto workers struck for 113 days beginning in November 1945, and miners for a shorter period in mid-1946. Truman's decision to have the soft coal mines run by the government (control that continued until June 1947) lost him much support from businessmen. A railroad strike was settled the same month the mines were seized (May 1946) only when Truman threatened to take over the railroads, too. More strikes occurred in 1946 than in any other single year in American history. Over 4,750,000 workers were involved.

Truman faced a hostile congressional coalition of Republicans and anti-administration Southern Democrats in every area of his domestic program after Republicans won control of both Houses in the 1946 congressional election. This coalition responded to the strikes and general unrest among American unions with a tough law (passed over Truman's veto) regulating the labor movement. The Taft-Hartley Act of 1947 limited the president to seeking an eighty-day injunction to stop any strike that endangered "national health or safety" (rather than taking an extreme step like running an industry under government supervision). The new law also (1) required unions to accept a sixty-day "cooling-off" period before striking, (2) outlawed the closed shop, (3) restricted union involvement in political campaigns, and (4) required that union officials (but not company officers) take an oath that they were not Communists.

Congress also passed the Twenty-second Amendment to the Constitution limiting future presidents (although not Truman) to two full terms. This was a direct slap at FDR's four-term success. In various ways the Eightieth Congress prevented Truman from enacting his own legislative program.

The Fair Deal

The president called his program the Fair Deal. He viewed it essentially as an effort to continue the social welfare policies of Roosevelt's New Deal. Thus, soon after he took office, Truman had proposed to Congress legislation that would guarantee full employment, vastly expand public housing, and raise farm price supports. Other proposals aimed at continuing a permanent Fair Employment Practices Committee (FEPC) to block discrimination against blacks and other minorities, nationalizing atomic energy, and increasing the minimum wage. A few parts of the program passed quickly. Congress approved a civilian Atomic Energy Commission in mid-1946 that took control of peaceful uses of atomic energy. Most of the program, however, was blocked by the same

The culmination of Harry Truman's 1948 whistle-stop campaign was this triumphant pose before a crowd at St. Louis's Union Station. He called the headline "one for the books." (UPI)

Republican–Southern Democratic coalition that opposed Truman on so many issues.

Truman went on the offensive in 1948. He proposed not only the enactment of his entire Fair Deal program but also a set of civil rights proposals to guarantee first-class citizenship for black Americans. These included a permanent FEPC, measures against lynching and the poll tax, plus other laws that would ensure blacks full federal protection of their civil and political rights. After his renomination by a divided Democratic convention in 1948, Truman called Congress into special session to dramatize its opposition to his programs. He requested repeal of the Taft-Hartley Act and passage of civil rights, housing, health, and Social Security programs. Congress rejected it all.

This allowed Truman to conduct his successful "whistle-stop" campaign against what he called the "do-nothing Eightieth Congress." The public liked Truman's new stance as an aggressive, "give-em-hell" fighter. The Man from Independence scored the most smashing upset in American presidential history. The Democrats also recaptured both houses of Congress.

Still dominated in large measure by the Republican–Southern Democratic coalition, the

new Eighty-first Congress blocked Truman's farm program and his request for a permanent FEPC. But it did pass a major low-income housing and urban-renewal program, raised the minimum wage, abolished segregation in the armed forces, and enlarged existing conservation programs. All in all, it enacted more liberal legislation than any Congress since that of 1937–38.

The onset of the Korean War in June 1950, however, diverted the primary attention of Congress and the administration from home-front reforms to foreign policy. Little important domestic legislation passed in Truman's final two years in office. His energy between 1950 and 1952 was spent primarily fighting the Korean War and improving American security against communism abroad. Ironically, he also had to defend his administration against allegations of "softness" toward communism at home.

McCARTHYISM: "THE SECOND RED SCARE"

Truman reacted angrily whenever Republicans charged that his and Roosevelt's administration had "sold out" Eastern Europe and China to Communist control. To Republican cries of "Twenty Years of Treason," Truman replied that he had welded the free nations of Western Europe into military and political alliances against the Soviet Union's expansionism. The Truman Doctrine, the Marshall Plan, and NATO had largely restored European stability. China had been lost—not for lack of American help—but through Chiang Kai-shek's political and military weakness.

Elsewhere, American troops (along with UN forces) defended South Korea against Communist attack. Further, the Seventh Fleet prevented Communist invasion of the Chinese Nationalists' last stronghold, the island of Taiwan. To achieve this global strategy of containment, the Truman administration had increased defense expenditures from $13 billion in 1949 to $22.5 billion the next year and $44 billion by 1951. Military expenses absorbed two-thirds of the federal budget in 1952, up from only one-third in 1950. In the process of increasing defense spending so swiftly and enor-

mously, the country's gross national product rose from $264 billion in 1950 to $339 billion by 1952. A continued high level of economic prosperity was almost assured.

None of these facts, however, silenced Republican critics. They continued to attack Truman and Secretary of State Dean Acheson. Nor were Republican anti-Communist investigators like those on HUAC happy with Truman's efforts to rid the federal government of suspected subversives. The president, despite assurances from the FBI that the problem was under adequate control, had issued an executive order in May 1947 setting up a Loyalty Review Board. Its purpose was to check every federal employee and dismiss any found questionable "on reasonable grounds for belief in disloyalty." Over the next five years, such loyalty boards investigated over 6.5 million government employees and their families. Of this number only 490 were dismissed on loyalty grounds. The boards uncovered no cases of espionage, but the investigations wrecked the careers of many loyal government officials accused without adequate proof.

Prosecution of Leading Communists

Under mounting pressure from Congress after Alger Hiss's indictment, Truman prosecuted the eleven leaders of the American Communist party under the 1940 Smith Act. They were indicted for organizing a group advocating the overthrow of the American government by force. The Communist party leaders were convicted in 1949, and other prosecutions of Communists began, despite the fact that officials never claimed they had uncovered an *actual* conspiracy to overthrow the government. The Supreme Court upheld the convictions in 1951. Through such actions Truman contributed to a growing climate of American fear over communism.

No single episode did more to spread this Red scare than the indictment and eventual conviction of Alger Hiss. The fact that Dean Acheson and other high administration officials testified on behalf of Hiss lent a touch of credibility to charges that the Democrats, under Roosevelt and Truman, were soft on left-wingers.

At this point Senator Joseph McCarthy

began a series of speeches. It mattered little that McCarthy's figures for "known Communists" in the State Department varied from speech to speech. Britain had just arrested Communist Klaus Fuchs for atomic espionage; the new Communist government had full control of the Chinese mainland; and Americans were jittery over possible new Russian moves against Berlin. Accordingly, many people were prepared to believe that something dire was about to befall the United States. McCarthy himself never actually located a single "known Communist."

McCarthy's charges offended several Republicans in Congress, including Senators Margaret Chase Smith of Maine and Ralph Flanders of Vermont, who both denounced him publicly. Yet he was extremely useful to his party, despite his wild charges of disloyalty and Communist activity in government. A significant number of Americans approved of McCarthy's relentless attacks. McCarthy's method, like that of most successful demagogues, was simple. He used what Richard Rovere called "the multiple untruth," statements so complex and many-sided that they were extremely difficult to deny intelligently.

Flow of Political Melodrama

Among those McCarthy tried to smear were George Marshall (author of the Marshall Plan), Philip Jessup (later chief UN delegate under President Nixon), Secretary of State Dean Acheson, and even President Truman himself. In short, McCarthy turned this tactic of "red-baiting" against the Democrats. For a time, he had remarkable success. Little about his methods was new. He used the tactics of HUAC and even borrowed Nixon's files on the subject. From these he wrung a constant flow of political melodrama out of the noisy pursuit of "secret conspirators" and (occasionally) admitted Communists. There *were*, after all, thousands of American Communists, even a few who had reached middle-level posts in the Roosevelt years.

The onset of the Korean War in June 1950 gave McCarthy and other Republican opponents of Truman additional ammunition. If Communists were killing our soldiers in Korea, many Ameri-

cans reasoned, why give possible subversives the benefit of any doubt in this country? Loyalty oaths and security investigations soon involved millions of people in industries and labor unions, public schools and universities, as well as in government jobs at every level.

There is much irony in the fact that Truman spent his last two years in office using American and UN forces against Communist aggression in Korea while trying to prove that he was not a dupe or agent of communism at home. Truman's attorney general carried on a vigorous prosecution of alleged Communist agents. In April 1951 Julius and Ethel Rosenberg were convicted of having directed a spy ring that transmitted to the Russians diagrams and other data on the firing mechanism and internal structure of the atomic bomb. According to the Rosenbergs' accusers, this information had speeded up by years completion of the Soviet atomic bomb, which was first exploded in 1949. Ethel and Julius Rosenberg received the death sentence, while their accomplices were sentenced to long prison terms.

Such episodes persuaded Congress that tighter laws were needed to protect the country against domestic Communists. So it passed the McCarran Internal Security Act in 1950. This law established a Subversive Activities Control Board to keep track of Communist activities in America. The act ordered Communist organizations to register with the attorney general. Other provisions barred former members of totalitarian groups from the United States and forbade Communists to hold federal office or receive passports. Many of these provisions have since been declared unconstitutional by the Supreme Court. But the act passed by a two-thirds majority over Truman's veto, which showed how politically potent the anti-Communist issue had become.

"Korea, Communism, and Corruption"

The Democratic administration was very unpopular by 1952. Many voters accepted McCarthy's reckless charges against Truman and his associates, despite the Democrats' strong commitment to Cold War foreign policies. Truman's decision to seize the steel industry to prevent a nationwide strike in April 1952 (declared unconstitutional by the courts two months later) reminded Americans of his earlier troubles with labor and management. Several scandals involving big businessmen and some of Truman's associates had also come to light. Republicans raised the issue of widespread government corruption. The Korean War dragged on, with American casualties mounting in a war that was increasingly unpopular.

The issues of "Korea, communism, and corruption" that Republicans stressed in 1952 would probably have brought about the election of any candidate after twenty years of Democratic rule. Still, the out-of-power party took no chances. At their 1952 convention the Republicans rejected the candidacy of the able conservative Senator Robert A. Taft of Ohio because they were not sure he could win. They nominated General Dwight David Eisenhower—World War II hero, university president, commander of American NATO forces, and easily the most popular public figure in the country. The party then reaffirmed its concern for the anti-Communist issue by nominating Richard Nixon as vice-president.

The Democrats drafted Governor Adlai Stevenson of Illinois, a man who, though talented, was assailed by Republicans as an "egghead" because of his articulateness and elegant campaign style. Stevenson's efforts to defend Democratic achievements and promise a continuation of Fair Deal reforms fell flat. Many voters were tired after two decades of Depression, reform, world war, and Cold War. The public voted to make its grandfatherly first citizen, Dwight Eisenhower, president by an overwhelming 33 to 27 million popular vote margin and a 442 to 89 electoral majority. After two decades in the political wilderness the Republican party returned to full national power, winning not only the White House but also Congress.

THE EISENHOWER YEARS

With Eisenhower's inauguration in 1953, control of the federal government returned essentially—for the first time since Herbert Hoover—to businessmen. The new president's cabinet officers were either corporation executives or closely allied to the business community. Eisenhower was determined to run a less active presidency than either Truman or Roosevelt and was suspicious of the federal bureaucracy and New Deal—Fair Deal social welfare programs. He set himself the task of keeping the nation calm.

Eisenhower interfered less often than Roosevelt or Truman with his various department heads. Instead, he allowed each to make his own decisions with minimal overall supervision. Frequently, for example, Secretary of State John Foster Dulles and not Eisenhower made essential foreign policy decisions. Similarly Treasury Secretary George Humphrey slashed departmental budgets throughout the government—except for the military. The Joint Chiefs of Staff got many of the programs they wanted, especially those proposed by the air force and navy. The chain of command under Eisenhower thus often resembled that of a loosely organized corporation.

The Republican party's right-wingers became a real problem for Eisenhower. McCarthy, by his actions as head of the Senate's Government Operations Committee, posed a serious threat to Eisenhower's ability to rule. He publicly led the strong opposition to Eisenhower's nomination of career diplomat Charles E. Bohlen as ambassador to Russia because Bohlen had been Roosevelt's interpreter at Yalta! (However, Bohlen was eventually confirmed by the Senate.)

McCarthy's Fall

Until 1954 the administration tried to compromise with the senator. In that year, however, McCarthy opened an investigation of subversion in an army base at Fort Monmouth, New Jersey. This attack on the military and on Eisenhower's army secretary, Robert Stevens, for "coddling" Communists proved to be the last straw. It forced a reluctant Eisenhower to take a public stand against McCarthy and his tactics.

Senate hearings considered McCarthy's charges against the army. They reviewed the army's countercharges that the senator had sought special favors for an aide, David Schine, drafted into the army. The hearings were watched on tele-

Controversial Senator Joseph R. McCarthy of Wisconsin and his counsel, Roy M. Cohn, during the thirty-six-day-long Army–McCarthy hearings in 1954. The hearings went badly for him and began the rapid decline in his influence. (UPI)

vision by over 20 million Americans. McCarthy proved an adept television performer. But even more adept was the army's counsel, Joseph N. Welch. He baited McCarthy into losing his temper, thus widely exposing the browbeating tactics that McCarthy had used so effectively against unfriendly witnesses before his committee in the past. McCarthy's influence began to decline.

In December 1954 the Senate (supported by the Eisenhower administration) "condemned" Senator McCarthy for "conduct unbecoming a member." After this censure he lost his remaining political influence. He died in May 1957. But "McCarthyism" lingered on.

The reckless hunt for possible Communist subversives in American society, without proof of guilt or adequate safeguards for defense, continued to be a problem during the 1950s. Many thousands of Americans lost their jobs, suffered ruined careers because of blacklisting in their professions, and went to jail or even into exile because of it. The list of victims includes industrial workers and labor union officials, as well as prominent editors, broadcasters, and others in the arts.

"Peace, Progress, and Prosperity"

The Eisenhower years signified far more than simply the tail end of McCarthyism. Ei-

senhower avoided tampering with New Deal – Fair Deal programs, even presiding over some extensions for them. He created the Department of Health, Education, and Welfare, approved a measure that added 7 million people to the Social Security rolls, signed another that raised the minimum wage, and supported a housing act that greatly increased urban-renewal projects. The decline of such public facilities as schools, hospitals, and public transport systems also received little attention in the 1950s.

Eisenhower avoided the type of scandal that had rocked Truman's second administration. His relations with the Democratic leaders who ran Congress was generally amicable, unlike Truman's with congressional Republicans. Eisenhower regularly consulted House Majority Leader Sam Rayburn and Senate Majority Leader Lyndon Johnson, the two Texans who dominated Congress during the 1950s.

When the president decided to run for reelection in 1956, despite a serious heart attack in 1955, there were no major issues that the Democrats could exploit. Eisenhower had negotiated peace in Korea, run a basically budget-conscious and honest administration, and restrained McCarthyism. Also, he had flown to Geneva in 1955 for a summit meeting on peaceful coexistence with Russia's post-Stalin leaders (the first such meeting since Potsdam). He kept the country out of major foreign involvements in the Indochina crisis of 1954 and the Hungarian and Suez crises of 1956. Not surprisingly, Eisenhower again whipped Adlai Stevenson, winning a landslide 58 percent of the popular vote.

There seemed little public interest during the 1950s in rocking a very prosperous national boat. Eisenhower provided an image of safe, stable leadership that appealed even to many Democrats.

Farm income in the 1950s netted more for farmers than even the thriving war years. Moreover, the much larger pie had to be divided among a smaller farm population. Median family income rose from $4,293 in 1950 to $5,904 in 1960. By 1956 white-collar workers outnumbered those in blue-collar jobs. Even for those in the latter group (particularly those unionized) real spendable income increased by 60 percent between 1940 and

Polio is a disease of civilization. It strikes hardest where sanitation is highest. It is also a disease that most frequently strikes children. It can keep a victim bedridden for weeks in intense pain; but, much worse, it can cause severe, life-long paralysis, or even death. Since 1894, when the first cases of polio appeared in the Green Mountains of Vermont, epidemics of the disease had been a common and dreaded occurrence. And nothing could be done to prevent them until in 1953 a young researcher, Dr. Jonas Salk, announced the development of polio vaccine.

Dr. Salk's discovery was not one of medicine's happy accidents but rather the result of years of intensive research. Salk himself is said to have worked sixteen hours a day, six days a week over a long period of time before succeeding. His background had prepared him for such a test of endurance. Born in New York City on October 28, 1914, the son of an immigrant garment worker, he put himself through school largely by part-time jobs and scholarships. He entered New York University Medical School in 1934. There he met Thomas Francis, Jr., who was conducting a study on methods of killing influenza virus. In 1943, the two men field-tested a vaccine effective against both influenza A and influenza B.

In 1947, Salk joined the University of Pittsburgh School of Medicine as head of the Virus Research Laboratory. The polio vaccine that Salk finally developed was made by growing a representative strain of each of the three types of virus in a broth made with monkey kidney. The viruses were then killed with formaldehyde, which rendered them incapable of causing the disease. However, they did not lose the power to stimulate the human body to produce antibodies. These antibodies would give a person at least limited immunity to polio.

Salk, his wife, and their three sons were among the first to receive his vaccine. Then in the fall of 1954 a massive twelve-state test, sponsored by the National Foundation for Infantile Paralysis, was held. Almost one million schoolchildren in the primary grades participated. Half the children received the vaccine; the other half did not. The results were conclusive: In April 1955 the vaccine

Jonas Salk

(Wide World Photos)

was pronounced safe and effective in preventing polio.

By the summer of 1961, there was a reduction by approximately 96 percent in the amount of polio in the United States as a whole compared to the five-year period before the introduction of vaccination, even though only 50 percent of the population had been vaccinated. Contributing to the eradication of polio, an oral vaccine was being developed and tested by another American researcher, Albert Sabin. In 1959 Sabin's oral vaccine had been accepted for use by the Soviet Union and in August of 1961 it was approved for use in the United States. One year later, manufacture started, and the oral polio vaccine was licensed for general distribution.

Salk's discovery catapulted this shy, retiring man to instant and unwanted fame. He became a public figure deluged with offers to lecture and even to make his life into a movie. He was awarded a congressional gold medal for "great achievement in the field of medicine," and the people of San Diego voted to donate a tract of land on a bluff overlooking the Pacific on which to build an institute in his honor. The research center was dedicated in 1963. Under Dr. Salk's direction, it is now a leading center of research in immunology and cellular and molecular biology.

1960. Much of this prosperity came in new industries—dealing with military weapons systems and space technology. These greatly expanded after the Russians sent the world's first missile, Sputnik I, into space in 1957. Suddenly, Americans found they had a lot of catching up to do if they were to equal the Russians in scientific pursuits. Many people realized that American education had apparently gone slack, and government funds were quickly demanded to inject the schools and universities with new monies for the expansion and updating of their facilities.

UNSETTLED PROBLEMS

Yet various social and economic problems of enormous scope remained during the Eisenhower era. These would haunt Americans in the 1960s. For one thing, the affluent society remained a myth in 1960 for the 42 million people (almost a third of America's families) with annual family income levels of less than $4000. The "invisible poor," as Michael Harrington described them, were not "invisible" by choice. They were not so much unseen as ignored by those who had made dramatic economic gains.

"Making it" often involved drawing firm barriers between oneself and those left behind. Groups heavily represented among the poor were the elderly, unskilled or nonunion workers, migrant farm laborers, blacks, and Spanish Americans. The average black family income in 1960, for example, was $3,838 compared with $6,508 for white families.

The wartime FEPC had opened thousands of jobs in Northern industries to blacks. President Truman's 1950 executive order desegregated the armed forces and barred discrimination in federal employment. The next great civil rights advance for blacks came in 1954. The Supreme Court, in the famous case of *Brown* v. *Board of Education of Topeka, Kansas*, ruled unanimously that segregation in public school education was illegal.

The case, *Brown* v. *Topeka Board of Education*, came before the Court on December 9, 1952. It continued for over a year. The decision the Court handed down on May 17, 1954, presents the question the justices faced: "Does segregation of children in public schools solely on the basis of race, even though the physical facilities and other 'tangible' factors may be equal, deprive children of the minority group of equal educational opportunities?"

The Court answered this question with an affirmative: "We conclude that in the field of public education the doctrine of 'separate but equal' has no place. Separate educational facilities are inherently unequal." Later, the Supreme Court instructed schools to move "with all deliberate speed" to desegregate their facilities.

Although 792 of 2,985 biracial school districts had been integrated by 1959, none were in the Deep South or Virginia. There, massive resistance from leading politicians and local white citizens councils raised the level of racial tension to dangerous heights. In 1956 a hundred Southern congressmen promised to overturn the *Brown* decision by "all lawful means." Then in 1957 at Little Rock, Arkansas—with white parents threatening violence against court-ordered desegregation—Governor Orval Faubus called out the National Guard to bar nine black students from a high school. After a court order removed the guard, a riot broke out. Eisenhower, himself a moderate on the segregation issue, sent federal paratroopers to help escort the nine children into the school. Elsewhere, one Virginia county even closed its public schools to avoid integration. The University of Alabama, after a riot on the campus, expelled a black student admitted under Supreme Court order.

Meanwhile, blacks in Montgomery, Alabama, led by an eloquent young minister, the Reverend Martin Luther King, Jr., organized a boycott against segregation on local buses in December 1955. (See Chapter 47.) Segregation on interstate buses had been banned the previous month. King's "direct action" tactics spread to other Southern cities. Soon he and other Southern black ministers formed the Southern Christian Leadership Conference (SCLC) to fight discrimination and all forms of bigotry.

In February 1960 a student wing of the SCLC held the first sit-in at a Greensboro, North Carolina, lunch counter to protest segregation in public eating places. Two mild civil rights acts in 1957 and 1960 somewhat strengthened federal authority against efforts to keep blacks from voting or exercising other rights. But as the sixties began, Americans knew that the major battles to secure full equality for blacks lay ahead.

Other critical problems faced the nation as Eisenhower's second term ended. He himself emphasized a major one in a January 17, 1961, farewell speech.

> The conjunction of an immense military establishment and a permanent armaments industry of vast proportions is new in the American experience. The total influence — economic, political, even spiritual — is felt in every city, every state house, every office of the federal government. We must guard against the acquisition of unwarranted influence, whether sought or unsought, by the military-industrial complex. We must never let the weight of this combination endanger our liberties or democratic processes.

A fair warning, but Eisenhower himself had speeded the growth of the "military-industrial complex." The military and industrialists would become even more powerful during the twenty years following.

Return of the Democrats

America faced still other unsolved problems, but it entered the 1960s in a confident mood, sure of its purposes and powers. Though this confidence would not long remain, both 1960 presidential candidates reflected this basic assurance about the American future.

Richard Nixon, while defending the Eisenhower record, promised progressive and dynamic new policies. John Kennedy urged Democrats to rally behind him for vigorous leadership. Little separated the two candidates in terms of issues, domestic or foreign, except that Kennedy attacked a presumed decline of American prestige abroad under Eisenhower and an alleged missile gap that threatened to make the Soviet Union dominant.

Kennedy benefited from a united party. His Texas Protestant running mate, Lyndon Johnson, helped keep much of the South Democratic for the Catholic Kennedy. He also profited from television debates with Nixon, which helped undercut the Republican charge of inexperience and youth. (Kennedy was forty-three, the youngest man ever elected president.) Most of all, his election resulted from the strong support he received among Catholics and blacks — who gave him over 70 percent of their votes. Nixon received only mild backing from Eisenhower. Nixon's earlier career as a "red hunter" haunted him and hurt him severely among Democratic and independent voters in 1960. Still, Kennedy won by only a tiny popular margin — 113,000 votes out of 68,800,000 cast.

In his inaugural address Kennedy promised to lead the United States toward a New Frontier headed by young people: "The torch has been passed to a new generation of Americans, born in this century, tempered by war, [and] disciplined by a hard and bitter peace." The sense of promise and hope was strong among Americans that day, as the youthful new Chief Executive issued "a call to bear the burden of a long twilight struggle, year in and year out against the common enemies of man: tyranny, poverty, disease, and war itself." Few Americans doubted in 1961 that the country was adequate to these great tasks.

Suggested Readings
Chapters 43–44

Alger Hiss

Alistair Cooke, *A Generation on Trial: U.S.A. v. Alger Hiss* (1950); Allen Weinstein, *Perjury: The Hiss-Chambers Case* (1978); Meyer A. Zeligs, *Friendship and Fratricide: An Analysis of Whittaker Chambers and Alger Hiss* (1967).

The Truman Administration

William C. Berman, *The Politics of Civil Rights in the Truman Administration* (1970); Barton J. Bernstein (ed.), *Politics and Policies of the Truman Administration* (1970); Richard M. Freeland, *The Truman Doctrine and the Origins of McCarthyism* (1972); Alonzo L. Hamby, *Beyond the New Deal: Harry S Truman and American Liberalism* (1970); Earl Latham, *The Communist Controversy in Washington* (1966); Merle Miller, *Plain Speaking: An Oral Biography of Harry S Truman* (1974); Cabell Phillips, *The Truman Presidency* (1966); Allen Yarnell, *Democrats and Progressives* (1974).

The Eisenhower Administration

Charles C. Alexander, *Holding the Line: The Eisenhower Era, 1952–1961* (1974); Richard Dalfiume, *Desegregation of the United States Armed Forces* (1969); Peter Lyon, *Eisenhower: Portrait of a Hero* (1974); John B. Martin, *Adlai Stevenson of Illinois* (1976); Herbert S. Parmet, *Eisenhower and the American Crusades* (1975); James T. Patterson, *Mr. Republican* (1972).

Communism and Anti-Communism

William F. Buckley and L. Brent Bozell, *McCarthy and His Enemies* (1954); Richard Fried, *Men Against McCarthy* (1976); Walter Goodman, *The Committee* (1968); Robert Griffith, *The Politics of Fear* (1970); Robert Griffith and Athan Theoharis, *The Spectre* (1974); Alan D. Harper, *The Politics of Loyalty: The White House and the Communist Issue, 1946–1952* (1969); Louis Nizer, *The Implosion Conspiracy* (1975); Gary W. Reichard, *The Reaffirmation of Republicanism* (1975); Michael Paul Rogin, *McCarthy and the Intellectuals* (1967); Karl M. Schmidt, *Henry A. Wallace: Quixotic Crusader, 1948* (1960); Walter and Miriam Schneir, *Invitation to an Inquest* (1965); David A. Shannon, *The Decline of American Communism* (1959); Athan Theoharis, *Seeds of Repression* (1971).

Affluence

John K. Galbraith, *The Affluent Society* (1958); David M. Potter, *People of Plenty* (1954); Herbert Stein, *The Fiscal Revolution in America* (1969); Harold G. Vatter, *The United States Economy in the 1950's* (1963).

General Overview

John M. Blum, *V Was for Victory: Politics and American Culture During World War II* (1976); Jacobus Broek et al., *Prejudice, War and the Constitution* (1954); Robert A. Garson, *The Democratic Party and the Politics of Sectionalism, 1941–1948* (1974); Eric F. Goldman, *The Crucial Decade and After: America 1945–1960* (1960); Douglas Miller and Marion Nowak, *The Fifties: The Way We Really Were* (1977); Richard Polenberg, *War and Society: The United States 1941–1945* (1972).

A profound social and cultural gulf divides the two decades between the elections of 1960 and 1980. The burst of optimism about the American future that marked the early 1960s barely survived the assassination of John Fitzgerald Kennedy in 1963. By mid-decade, the United States had been shaken by a series of domestic upheavals ranging from the Black Power protests to campus demonstrations and the beginnings of anti-war agitation. As the United States became more deeply involved in the Vietnamese War under Presidents Johnson and Nixon, national self-confidence disappeared—a casualty of bitter social unrest at home and battlefield stalemate abroad.

Older allies and enemies began to challenge their earlier acceptance of American dominance in the world, while a confused and divided American people reassessed their national values, grievances, problems, weaknesses, and strengths. The three pairs of chapters in Unit Eight describe milestones in the United States's fateful encounter with the vicissitudes of historical tragedy and loss during the past generation.

Chapter 45 portrays the 1962 drama of the Cuban missile crisis—the Soviet-American confrontation that nearly unleashed World War III. The accompanying chapter, 46, charts the complex "decline of *Pax Americana*"—the erosion of the United States's domination of international affairs under the impact of the Vietnamese War and other problems. Martin Luther King's stirring leadership of the black struggle for equality in the U.S. and his violent death form the subject of Chapter 47, while Chapter 48 sketches out the contours of political stalemate and social crises in the 1960s. Finally, the Watergate ordeal—the gravest political and constitutional crisis in American life since the Civil War—emerges in Chapter 49, accompanied by an analysis of American politics and society in the 1970s in Chapter 50. This final chapter also contains a thorough analysis of foreign and domestic problems in the Ford and Carter presidencies through 1980, including an assessment of the 1980 presidential campaign.

All six chapters relate part of the overall story of the United States in what may prove to be the formative years of a new society: more sober and restrained in the exercise of its global influence, more committed than ever to correcting the inequities of its own socioeconomic order, and more faithful than in some earlier epochs to its noble, if imperfect, heritage of freedom and justice.

CONTEMPORARY
AMERICA

UNIT
EIGHT

45

Nuclear Brinksmanship: The Cuban Missile Crisis

For a week in October 1962 the United States and the Soviet Union, the two nuclear giants, stood facing each other in combat readiness. With the relatively "primitive" military weaponry of that time, probably no more than half a billion people were in actual danger. The year before, the Department of Defense had estimated a total of 120 million American casualties, should crisis deepen from confrontation into all-out war. A like number of Soviets would probably die, along with most of the populations of Europe and Canada. If the war spread to China, of course, the final toll would run incalculably higher.

The crisis of 1962 began with strange markings on photographs taken from a U-2 spy plane flying ten miles above the island of Cuba. No one disputed the CIA's interpretation of the pictures: On an island ninety miles from Florida, the Soviet Union was installing medium-range guided missiles, capable of carrying nuclear bombs to the United States.

The United States had had many problems with Cuba since 1959, when Fidel Castro led his rebels out of the mountains and toppled the existing American-supported Batista dictatorship. The U.S. government was wary of Castro; the CIA had noted the presence of many Cuban Communists in his government. When he began nationalizing extensive American holdings on Cuba, Washington refused his requests for loans. Just before leaving office in January 1961, Eisenhower decided to break diplomatic relations with Havana. Meanwhile, Castro steadily strengthened his ties with the Soviets.

On October 14, 1962, two United States Air Force pilots, flying specially equipped U-2 planes borrowed from the CIA, revealed how close those ties had become. When the U-2 photographs reached Washington, analysts from the Defense Intelligence Agency (DIA) agreed that the Cuban sites closely resembled missile bases in Russia. The head of the DIA sent two officers to show the pictures to his superior, Roswell Gilpatric, the second-ranking civilian at the Pentagon, who relayed the news on to the president's special assistant for national security affairs, McGeorge Bundy.

In his twenty-one months as president, John F. Kennedy had dealt often with "the Cuban question." Campaigning in 1960 as a dynamic alternative to the bland do-nothingism of the Eisenhower years, Kennedy charged that Republican policies had created a Communist state in Cuba. Once in office, Kennedy discovered that the Eisenhower administration had been fostering a CIA-sponsored invasion of Cuba by anti-Castro Cubans living in the United States. Kennedy agreed to back the plan, which suffered a humiliating defeat in April 1961, when Castro's troops routed the invaders at the Bay of Pigs on Cuba's south shore.

Early on the morning of Tuesday, October 16, 1962, Kennedy learned about the missile site photos. The president immediately called a

An American reconnaissance plane photographed Soviet freighters, loaded with intermediate-range ballistic missile parts, in a Cuban port. (UPI)

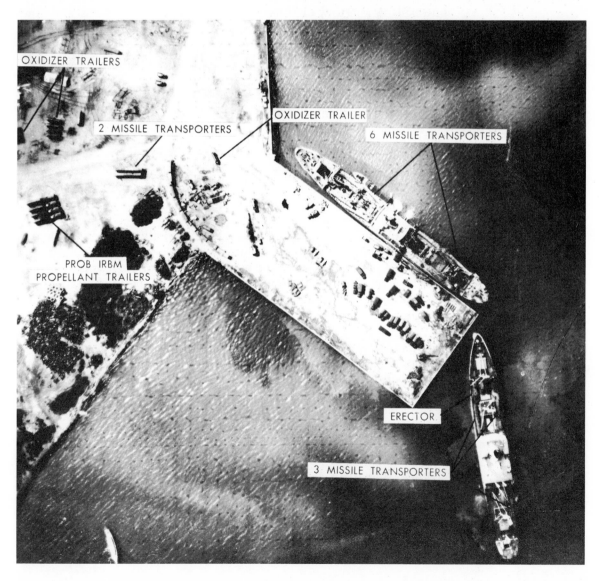

OXIDIZER TRAILERS

2 MISSILE TRANSPORTERS

OXIDIZER TRAILER

6 MISSILE TRANSPORTERS

PROB IRBM
PROPELLANT TRAILERS

ERECTOR

3 MISSILE TRANSPORTERS

Nuclear Brinksmanship: The Cuban Missile Crisis **855**

meeting for 11:45 that morning, summoning a group that would soon become known as ExComm, short for Executive Committee. Summoned were Vice-President Lyndon Johnson, Secretary of State Dean Rusk, Secretary of Defense Robert McNamara, Bundy, Gilpatric, Taylor, and a few other close advisers, notably the president's brother, Attorney General Robert Kennedy. "The President did not specify the problem over the telephone," recalled Robert Kennedy. "He said only that we were facing great trouble."

The news stunned the president's councillors. Despite evidence of great Soviet shipping activity to Cuba, they had never concluded that the Russians were putting missiles there. Unlike the United States, which had established missile bases in Turkey, Italy, and Britain, the Soviets had never before placed missiles outside their own borders. According to one explanation, they distrusted the Poles, the East Germans, and other satellite allies. Moreover, Khrushchev and his envoys had gone out of their way in recent months to assure the American government that no major moves would be taken by Moscow before the U.S. election in November. In light of the new evidence, it was clear they had been trying to stall until the missiles became operational.

Every one of the dozen men assembled in the Cabinet Room that morning agreed that the missiles must be returned to Russia with haste. A missile base in Cuba would greatly improve the Russians' nuclear capability and would subvert the U.S. warning system. It could threaten Latin America, vastly increasing the Soviets' prestige and diminishing U.S. power in the area. On the basis of his new strength, Khrushchev might demand American concessions in other parts of the world, such as the withdrawal of troops from West Berlin.

ExComm deliberated all day, moving briefly to the State Department in the afternoon and returning to the White House that evening. Rather than planning specific responses, they spent the first day discussing the overall situation, evaluating the effect of the missiles, and speculating on why Khrushchev had tried this awesome gamble. That night they had concluded only that something had to be done.

On Wednesday, October 17, ExComm met throughout the day in the State Department conference room to discuss policy options. No immediate consensus emerged. Although these twelve men, scuttling in and out of the meeting from their other official duties, all served the same administration, they regarded the problem from a dozen different perspectives.

The group considered diplomatic options first: either to make a private demand to the Russians that they get the missiles out or to take the case to the United Nations. But ExComm decided after brief discussion that diplomacy alone could not work. The Soviets would only stall for time while construction of the sites continued. Finally, the Soviets might demand a world conference on the missiles, further delaying any decision.

The military men on ExComm proposed a straightforward response: Send in B-52 bombers to blast the bases. According to evidence from stepped-up U-2 flights, between sixteen and thirty-two missiles would be ready for firing in a week. Bombing was the only strategy sure to eliminate the missiles before that point. This approach became known as "the fast track."

The most impassioned opposition to a military solution came from Robert Kennedy, the president's closest adviser, who rapidly emerged as a leading voice in the discussions. His intimate relationship with his brother added weight to his comments, and other cabinet officers tended to defer to RFK.

A surprise attack, argued Robert Kennedy, was not in the tradition of the United States. It would hurt the country in the eyes of the world and affront its conscience at home. The country that had been attacked without warning at Pearl Harbor would now seem to be following the Japanese example. "My brother," he warned the group, "is not going to be the Tojo of the 1960s." Furthermore, he doubted whether an air attack, even one referred to by the military as a "surgical strike," could be relied on to take out all the missiles. Very possibly, the United States would have to follow it up with an invasion and would have to accept a heavy toll in Cuban and American lives.

The "slow track," advocated by most nonmilitary advisers, included a naval blockade of Cuba. This would prevent the Russians from sending more missiles in and could be maintained until they removed the weapons already there. With the United States Navy's total control of the Caribbean and the eastern Atlantic, the blockade could be made to work. But, according to international law, a blockade is an act of war.

Although the slow and fast tracks emerged as the major alternatives, the lines in the room did not harden during the Wednesday session. Most participants changed sides at least once. ExComm argued the alternatives throughout Thursday and Friday. McGeorge Bundy, who had originally stood with Stevenson for a diplomatic approach, now led the "surgical" air-strike faction. Llewellen Thompson, former ambassador to the Soviet Union and the group's Kremlinologist, warned that bombing the missile bases was the worst course; Soviets would be killed, and Khrushchev's response to that could not be safely predicted. The Joint Chiefs unanimously argued for bombing; General Taylor suggested giving twenty-four hours' warning to minimize loss of life. McNamara argued that if the proposed blockade failed, the United States could then try bombing; but after bombing, the president could not go back to the blockade.

The discussions gave two new words to the American language — terms that would later be applied to hard-liners and soft-liners on Vietnam. Those favoring the air strike became known as "hawks," while supporters of the blockade were identified as "doves."

Slowly, a majority began to develop in favor of blockade. Treasury Secretary Douglas Dillon abandoned his support of the air strike, announcing himself convinced by the arguments of Robert Kennedy and McNamara. Former Secretary of State Dean Acheson, unable to support the blockade, left in a huff, "resigning" from the group.

On Saturday, ExComm made its report to the president. John Kennedy had campaigned in Chicago the day before but had canceled Saturday's appearances because he had "a cold." He now sat at the cabinet table in a chair designed to ease the pain in his back and listened to the final recommendations of each side. Neither faction could maintain that their policy would be safe or easy.

The president came down on the side of the blockade. He did not wish to back Khrushchev totally into a corner. Although he wanted to speak again with tactical bombing specialists, he doubted that bombing could guarantee destruction of all the missiles. Aware of the possible consequences, Kennedy nevertheless ordered the blockade, instructing McNamara to ready all U.S. forces for the confrontation. "I guess," he had told Acheson the day before, "this is the week I earn my salary."

Fifty-one hours later, Kennedy planned to announce the blockade on television. He directed his top speechwriter, Theodore Sorenson, to prepare the address, and Sorenson retired to his office with copies of the speeches made by Woodrow Wilson and Franklin Roosevelt in which they asked Congress to declare war.

The American military began moving well in advance of public announcements. Transport planes flew a thousand marines from Camp Pendleton, California, to reinforce the U.S. base at Guantánamo Bay, Cuba. The First Armored Division was loaded aboard special trains from Texas to Fort Stewart, Georgia, preparing its artillery for immediate use. One hundred eighty naval ships steamed toward blockade stations in the Atlantic, although their captains did not yet know their assignments.

The military was preparing for the possibility that the crisis would outgrow Cuba. Strategic Air Command planes began leaving their bases for civilian airports all over the country to guard against a sneak attack. B-52s loaded with atomic bombs were kept in the air at all times; as one landed, another would replace it in the sky. Crews tending ICBMs went on maximum alert. Warnings of an impending crisis went out to American military commanders all over the world.

Early Sunday morning, before going to church, President Kennedy reconfirmed his decision on the blockade after speaking to General Walter C. Sweeney, commander of the Tactical Air Force. Sweeney could pledge only 90 percent destruction of the missiles with an air strike. A few missiles would probably survive—and possibly be fired immediately at the United States. His mind now definitely made up, the president met with ExComm in the Oval Office at ten o'clock.

The Sunday morning session served to solidify the previous decisions and plans of operation. At the suggestion of Robert Kennedy, each participant brought his own ideas in writing. Assistant Secretary of Defense Paul Nitze's pocket contained a chilling but possible scenario: Construction work on the missiles would continue, forcing a U.S. air strike; the remaining missiles would be fired at the United States, which would have to invade Cuba and launch a "purely compensatory" attack on the Soviet Union. Nitze's scenario did not say what would happen next.

As Sunday afternoon passed into Monday evening, the government prepared itself. Sorenson's draft of the president's speech was edited, rewritten, and edited again. American women and children were evacuated from Guantánamo Bay. Spanish-language stations in Florida were checked to make sure that Monday night's speech could be heard in Cuba. General Thomas S. Power, commander of the Strategic Air Command, issued his final orders from underground headquarters near Omaha.

One substantive alteration was made in the speech. Abram Chayes, the State Department's legal adviser, and his assistant Leonard Meeker, persuaded the president not to use the word "blockade," widely considered to be an act of war. Instead, they suggested that Kennedy announce that he was placing a "quarantine" around Cuba. The semantic change in no way altered the plan.

Kennedy had one more task before he made his public announcement. The presidential jet had hopped around the country Monday, rounding up nineteen congressional leaders, most of whom were in their

Cuban refugees gather in a Manhattan hotel to watch President Kennedy's televised address to the nation on October 22, 1962. In the Monday night speech, the president outlined a seven-point program of American response to the missile crisis, including a limited "quarantine" of Cuba—in effect, a blockade.

home states campaigning. They came to the White House at five o'clock Monday afternoon, to be briefed by Rusk, McNamara, and John McCone of the CIA, and then to meet with the president.

Their reaction stunned and angered Kennedy. He had expected Republicans to question his approach and oppose his policies, but two Democratic leaders, Chairmen Richard Russell of the Senate Armed Services Committee and William Fulbright of the Senate Foreign Relations Committee, dismissed a blockade as ineffective and insisted on an immediate invasion. For an hour, Kennedy angrily repeated all the arguments from the meetings of ExComm. The congressmen were not convinced, so the president stormed out of the room to make final preparations for his speech.

Beginning with the traditional "My fellow citizens," Kennedy rapidly outlined the evidence of Soviet military activity on Cuba. The installation of missiles, he said flatly, "is a deliberately provocative and unjustified change in the status quo which cannot be accepted by this country."

To deal with the problem, Kennedy explained, a defensive quarantine would begin. "All ships of any kind bound for Cuba from whatever nation or port will, if found to contain cargoes of offensive weapons, be turned back." Later that evening, McNamara publicly confirmed what Kennedy had merely implied: Ships that did not turn back would be seized or sunk.

The United States, Kennedy continued, wanted immediate emergency sessions of the U.N. Security Council and the OAS. But although he talked of negotiations, the president issued a warning: Any missile launched from Cuba would be considered as coming from Russia "requiring a full retaliatory attack upon the Soviet Union."

A half hour after the president had begun speaking, the United States was in the middle of its most serious crisis since World War II.

"We have won a considerable victory," Dean Rusk told his undersecretary of state the next morning, waking him from his sleep on the couch in Rusk's office. "You and I are still alive." The absolute worst possibility—that Khrushchev would be so enraged he would immediately launch an attack on the United States, on Berlin, or on the Turkish missile bases—had not occurred. But the next move still belonged to the Soviets; it would come when an American ship tried to stop one of their vessels heading for Cuba.

That morning, Tuesday, October 23, the OAS met to vote on the blockade issue. The United States needed fourteen votes, a two-thirds majority, and the assistant secretary of state for Inter-American Affairs estimated one chance in four of getting that many. Latin American delegates listened to Rusk's speech and desperately called home for instructions. When a vote was taken, one by one the Latins rose and endorsed the position of the United States. The final vote was 19–0, with only Uruguay abstaining. The next day, when instructions came through from Uruguay, the vote became unanimous.

Opposing groups of pickets outside the White House at the end of October 1962 supported divergent strategies of retaliation against Soviet establishment of nuclear missile bases in Cuba, only ninety miles from the Florida coast. The hawks wanted the United States to bomb the missile sites in Cuba before they could be completed. The doves supported a naval blockade of Cuba that would continue until the missile bases were dismantled, a position endorsed by Attorney General Robert Kennedy and Secretary of Defense McNamara. (Dan Budnik/Woodfin Camp & Assoc.)

At the White House, the day passed in working out plans for the blockade to go into effect Wednesday morning at ten o'clock. If a vessel bound for Cuba refused to stop, the navy would attempt to cripple it by firing at the rudders and propellors—not to sink it. And rather than board the vessel by force, the navy would attempt to tow it into Jacksonville or Charleston.

ExComm worked out another contingency plan that day. To protect the missiles, the Russians had also installed SAMs (surface-to-air missiles) in Cuba. Since Tuesday, three U-2s a day had flown over Cuba. If a SAM destroyed a U-2, Kennedy and McNamara agreed that such an attack would require American bombers to destroy a SAM site, but that no action would be taken without the president's approval.

Still, the day brought no inkling of what the Russians might do. On the president's urging, his brother went to meet with Soviet Ambassador Anatoly Dobrynin, with whom he had developed a rapport. The meeting produced nothing, since Dobrynin denied that the missile bases even existed. Afterward, the ambassador attended a reception at his embassy for Lieutenant General Vladimir A. Dubovik. "We Russians are ready to defend ourselves against any acts of aggression, against ourselves or any of our allies," boasted the general. "Our ships will sail through."

The blockade would go into effect Wednesday morning, and Soviet ships were still steaming toward Cuba. Tuesday night, American intelligence picked up coded messages to the ships, but they were undecipherable.

Wednesday's regularly scheduled ten o'clock meeting of ExComm would coincide with the arrival of the first Russian ships at the blockade line. The president, sitting with his brother before the meeting, found apparent comfort in the thought that, had he not acted, he "would have been impeached." As the other members of ExComm gathered, the group quietly listened and waited. Some pored gloomily over the more recent U-2 photos, which showed that work on the missile sites was proceeding and that Soviet bombers were being uncrated and assembled. McNamara informed everyone that two merchant ships, the *Gagarin* and the *Komiles*, would reach the blockade line within minutes.

The next report ExComm received was not encouraging: A Russian submarine had joined the two ships. The group sat in frozen apprehension. The president held his hand over this mouth, but his eyes showed the strain. "We must expect that they will close down Berlin," he said, thinking ahead to the next step; "we must make the final preparations for that."

At 10:25, a CIA courier appeared at John McCone's elbow with a note. McCone read it rapidly and announced, "Mr. President, we have a preliminary report which seems to indicate that some of the Russian ships have stopped dead in the water."

Now information began to come in rapidly, confirming early reports. Twenty Russian ships near the line had indeed halted, and some had turned around and headed back across the Atlantic. "If the ships have orders to turn around," directed the president, eagerly grasping at the reprieve, "we want to give them every opportunity to do so."

A great burden seemed to have been lifted from the participants. Dean Rusk remarked bouncily, "We're eyeball to eyeball and I think the other fellow just blinked." In a more sober vein, Robert Kennedy reflected, "For a moment the world stood still, and now it was going around again."

The Soviets had not responded militarily, but the United States still did not know exactly what their next step would be. As ExComm had predicted, Khrushchev called for an international conference to discuss the problem. But his statement also struck a menacing note: "If the United States government carries out its program of piratical actions," he warned, "we shall have to resort to means of defense against the aggressor to protect our rights."

At 2:00 P.M. Wednesday, Acting U.N. Secretary General U Thant of Burma, pressured by alarmed Asian and African nations, asked for an end to both the American quarantine and the Soviet weapons shipments. He urged a two-week cessation of both, during which the parties could meet to resolve their differences. Khrushchev accepted the offer, but the United States did not. Time, ExComm felt, was essential. In two or three weeks, the missiles and bombers would be firmly established on Cuba. Before that happened, Khrushchev must be made to see the danger of keeping them there.

The navy was letting ships with nonmilitary cargoes through the blockade. Among Soviet ships, these were mostly tankers, which clearly did not carry missiles. Yet a faction on ExComm strongly urged stopping and searching one of the tankers to demonstrate American seriousness. After consideration, Kennedy rejected the idea as needlessly provocative.

Thursday, October 25, the United States presented its case to the U.N. Security Council. This day belonged to Adlai Stevenson, who had originally questioned the blockade and who was considered by some on ExComm to be too much of a dove. The Security Council meeting provided the most dramatic public moment of the crisis. Stevenson demanded of Soviet delegate Valerian Zorin whether the Russians had put missiles on Cuba.

> STEVENSON: Do you, Ambassador Zorin, deny that the USSR has placed and is placing medium- and intermediate-range missiles and sites in Cuba? Don't wait for the translation, answer yes or no.
>
> ZORIN: I am not in an American courtroom. . . . In due course, Sir, you will have your answer. . . .
>
> STEVENSON: I am prepared to wait for my answer until hell freezes over, if that's your decision. And I am also prepared to present the evidence in this room.

Stevenson then revealed blown-up photographs of the Cuban missile sites. Zorin refused to make any further statement, and the Security Council adjourned. The crisis was not resolved, but the exchange had focused worldwide attention on the photographic evidence.

Early Friday morning, October 26, the United States decided it was necessary to stop and search a ship. President Kennedy had personally selected the vessel, with great care. Although the *Marucla* was indeed sailing from Russia to Cuba, it was not a Soviet ship, but Panamanian-owned, registered in Lebanon, and chartered by the Soviets. Without incident, U.S. Navy men boarded the ship, inspected one of the holds, and then let it pass.

THE RANGE OF CUBAN–BASED SOVIET MISSILES

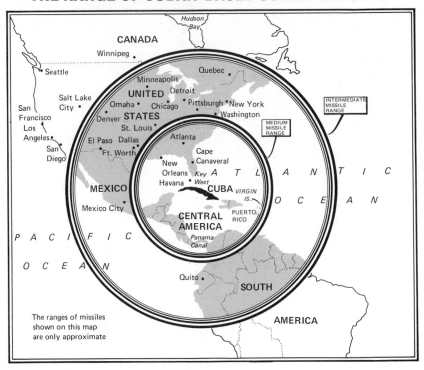

Still, depression and doubt reigned in ExComm on Friday as new evidence suggested that the Russians were speeding up construction. Even doves were coming to the conclusion that the United States would have to take more decisive action—an air strike against the missile sites, perhaps followed by an invasion.

McNamara warned that an invasion might entail forty to fifty thousand casualties. "They have a hell of a lot of equipment," CIA chief McCone warned. "And it will be damn tough to shoot them out of those hills." Nevertheless, the president ordered the State Department to prepare a program for civil government in Cuba after an invasion. That afternoon, ExComm developed plans for an air strike on the missiles.

The administration strove to make the urgency of the situation clear to the Soviets. Officials and congressmen now talked publicly of American readiness. Robert Kennedy warned Dobrynin that there were at most two days left. Now ExComm could only wait to hear from Khrushchev.

The first intimations of a response came in a roundabout, totally unexpected fashion. John Scali, diplomatic correspondent from ABC-TV, received an unusual phone call early Friday afternoon. It came from Alexander Fomin, an official at the Soviet embassy, who was rumored to be a colonel in the Soviet secret police. Could Scali meet him for lunch in ten minutes? To Scali's comment that he was busy, Fomin replied forcefully that it was urgent. Scali agreed to go.

Immediately after ordering his lunch, Fomin asked if the State Department would be interested in a three-part settlement: The missiles would return to the Soviet Union; the Russians would put no offensive weapons in Cuba in the future; and the United States would pledge not to invade Cuba. Scali said that he thought such a proposal showed promise. Upon the urging of Fomin, Scali went immediately to the State Department.

The department's intelligence chief took Scali to see Rusk. The secretary, after consulting with the White House, sent Scali back with positive words of interest and a warning against delay. Scali and Fomin met again at 7:35 that evening in a coffee shop around the corner from the Soviet embassy. After assuring himself that the statement came from the "highest circles," Fomin left to inform his superiors.

By that time, the White House teletype had already clacked out a strange letter from the American embassy in Moscow. It relayed a personal communication from Nikita Khrushchev to John Kennedy — a long, rambling letter, indicating a fear of war and a desperate search for a way out. Khrushchev wrote that he had seen war, and he detailed his experiences during two German invasions of his country. There were, he admitted, Soviet missiles in Cuba. But they were defensive, not offensive, weapons. (Khrushchev appeared to be playing the same semantic game with the word "defensive" that Kennedy had played in describing the "quarantine.") The missiles were there, Khrushchev said, because the United States had sponsored an invasion of Cuba, and Castro feared there might be another. The crisis must end before it spun out of control. If the United States would lift the quarantine and pledge not to invade Cuba, a solution might be possible. The Soviet Union would then have no further need to keep nuclear weapons in Cuba.

"Mr. President, you and we ought not now to pull on the ends of the rope in which you have tied the knot of war, because the more we pull, the tighter the knot will be tied," warned the Russian leader. "And a moment may come when the knot will be tied so tight that even he who tied it will not have the strength to untie it, and then it will be necessary to cut that knot. . . ."

ExComm went over the letter word-by-word, looking for traps and hoping not to find any. The group was not totally relieved: Khrushchev said nothing specific about withdrawing the missiles. But ExComm decided to treat Khrushchev's letter and Fomin's proposal as one single offer, an offer that the United States could accept.

Khrushchev's eagerness to extricate himself from the situation did not explain why the Soviets had put missiles in Cuba in the first place. Apparently, they wanted, first, to score a political victory and, second, to improve their country's military position. Khrushchev needed both in 1962. After four years of running his government's policy with a combination of probing, accommodation, and bluster, he had failed to gain ground. West Berlin remained in "enemy" hands, and the Soviets now faced opposition from the Chinese, who were beginning to chart a separate course from Moscow, one that threatened to flare into open hostility.

In the end, Khrushchev suffered greatly from the crisis. The Chinese denounced him for adventurism in putting the missiles in—and for cowardice in taking them out. Within two years, he, like Admiral Anderson, would be out of office.

Saturday, October 27, destroyed the fragile optimism of the night before. A new letter had arrived from the Kremlin, stripped of the rambling emotionalism of the first. The Soviet Union, Khrushchev wrote, would remove its missiles from Cuba when the United States removed *its* missiles from Turkey. Both major countries would pledge not to interfere in the affairs of their neighbors. Kennedy was not the only head of state who could issue an ultimatum.

ExComm studied the new note with perplexity. Had there been a *coup d'état* in the Soviet Union? Did Khrushchev no longer control the government? Thompson, the Kremlinologist, had his doubts. He speculated that Khrushchev's new communiqué was in response to the feeling of the Soviet military and his other advisers that he was losing face in the way he was dealing with the crisis. For the first time, awareness of a Soviet ExComm counterpart pervaded the group.

The new offer was ironic in one major respect. The Turkish missiles were hardly essential to American defense and were, in any case, obsolete. Months before, Kennedy had given orders that they be removed. But the Turks, eager to retain the economic benefits of the bases, opposed removal, and the president's order had not been implemented. Now the president faced an unpleasant choice: risking war over bases he no longer wanted, or giving European allies the impression that the United States would "sell them out" if its own security appeared in danger.

Other developments heightened the fragility of the situation. FBI Director J. Edgar Hoover notified Robert Kennedy that Soviet officials in New York were burning confidential documents, as though in preparation for war. McCone reported that construction of the bases on Cuba continued at a rapid pace. And the worst news was that Soviet missiles had downed an American U-2 in flight over Cuba. "There was the feeling," wrote Robert Kennedy, "that the noose was tightening on all of us, on Americans, on mankind, and that the bridges to escape were crumbling."

A decision to knock out the SAM bases could not be postponed much longer. Work continued on the bases, and they might be ready in a matter of hours. "It was generally agreed," remembered one member of ExComm, "that we couldn't go beyond Sunday without a further decision. At the very least . . . that would have been a decision to take out the missile sites by air attack." Invasion of Cuba would inevitably follow. Secretary of Defense McNamara stated that an air attack could be readied in forty-eight hours, but he would rather broaden the blockade to include petroleum.

Meanwhile, Khrushchev's letters remained unanswered. All Saturday afternoon, ExComm unsuccessfully tried to devise a way to remove the missiles from Turkey without giving the appearance of bowing to Soviet pressure. Rather, it drafted a series of responses refusing the terms offered by Khrushchev. Robert Kennedy found all of the drafts to be inade-

quate; they did not, in his opinion, sufficiently acknowledge the strong desire Khrushchev had shown for peace.

RFK then cut the knot brilliantly by suggesting that ExComm simply ignore Khrushchev's second letter and respond to the first—the one that offered withdrawal of Russian missiles but that did not mention the Turkish bases. He retired with Ted Sorenson to produce a draft. With some revisions, Robert Kennedy's letter went off to Khrushchev.

The same night, the attorney general met with Dobrynin and told him of the letter going to Moscow. Regarding the problem of the Turkish missiles, he told the ambassador that the United States could not remove them under threat. But Kennedy also told Dobrynin: "It was our judgment that, within a short time after this crisis was over, those missiles would be gone."

Dobrynin, however, was not optimistic, and neither were the Americans. ExComm met again at nine o'clock that evening to begin preparations for an attack not later than Tuesday. At 9:20 P.M., McNamara called twenty-four squadrons of the Air Force Reserve to active duty. Sixty thousand army and marine troops, the forces for the invasion, were ready in Florida and the Panama Canal Zone. "Now," said the president, utterly drained, "it can go either way."

Sunday morning, October 28, Kennedy was to meet at nine with McNamara and the generals to check details on the air strike. A few minutes before the meeting, Radio Moscow announced that at 9:00 A.M. (5:00 P.M. Moscow time) it would broadcast an important message. As the men in the White House listened, a Russian announcer read in English the Kremlin's response to the letter of the previous night. Khrushchev had agreed at last to dismantle and withdraw the missiles. The United States, in turn, would end the island's quarantine and pledge not to support any future invasion of Cuba. The crisis was over.

On October 31, 1962, President Kennedy met in his office with the U.S. Army Chief of Staff General Earle Wheeler, seated next to him, and two other key military officers to discuss American military preparedness. Fortunately for Kennedy, the Cuban missile crisis had ended three days earlier when Khrushchev agreed to remove the missiles if the United States would end its naval quarantine and promise not to invade Cuba. (UPI)

46 Pax Americana in Decline

The Cuban missile crisis provides a convenient dividing line for American foreign policy in the postwar era. It ended one period of U.S.–Soviet relations and inaugurated another. Since the start of the Cold War American diplomacy had consisted largely of responding to Soviet challenges, real or perceived. But in October 1962, the leaders of both superpowers peered into the abyss of thermonuclear war. What they saw frightened them as badly as some of their policies had frightened the world in the past.

The foreign policy pursued by Truman and Eisenhower in the 1950s, and continued by Kennedy in the early 1960s, assumed a bipolar world dominated mainly by the United States and the Soviet Union, in that order, and relied heavily on the threatened use of American atomic power to settle or deflect disputes between them. Although the two countries had never before come so close to an atomic exchange as during the Cuban missile crisis, public proclamations of their immediate readiness for mutual disaster, and the swollen size of nuclear stockpiles, was, for both, evidence enough of such intention.

The United States and the Soviet Union did not resolve their differences after the Cuban missile crisis; they still pursued widely differing objectives in the world. But both countries, as if sobered by the experience, began to take steps to guard against a repetition of the terrifying days of October by improving communication and deemphasizing "nuclear diplomacy." Not since 1962 have the populations of the two superpowers waited desperately to hear whether they would live out the week.

THE "NEW FRONTIER" IN FOREIGN AFFAIRS

As Democrats before him had done throughout the Eisenhower years, the campaigning Senator John F. Kennedy claimed in 1960 that the president had not used the country's full power to maintain its position and prestige. He charged that Ike's cuts in the military budget had limited America's power to act, had narrowed its options, and had caused the United States to lose its world leadership. Kennedy singled out Cuba as one example of the Republicans' misdirected foreign policy, and he accused Eisenhower of not doing enough to topple Castro.

As president, Kennedy did not allow any one adviser to exercise the amount of power wielded by John Foster Dulles under Eisenhower. But he made a strong effort to attract capable and perceptive individuals, such as McNamara from Ford Motor Company and Bundy from Harvard University. Less than two years after his inauguration, Kennedy's "team" was to become ExComm during the missile crisis.

Kennedy also tried to bring new ideas to international policy. Regarding the Third World, he expressed greater willingness to work with nationalist leaders. He initiated the Peace Corps, sending thousands of young Americans overseas to teach and work in underdeveloped countries. But, like Truman and Eisenhower, Kennedy intended to prevent the spread of communism, and to hold the line in Europe.

The sharpest break with Eisenhower's policies came in the area of defense. President Kennedy abandoned the concept of "massive retaliation" in favor of a new policy called "flexible response," which gave him more options in an emergency. One of Kennedy's favorite programs, the army's Green Berets (specially trained counterinsurgency fighters), reflected both his wish to bolster military capability and his desire for a more imaginative approach to the problems of Communist power and the Third World.

THE BAY OF PIGS

Regardless of Kennedy's new ideas and his new advisers, within months he sustained one of America's most humiliating foreign policy defeats. Cuba proved to be as painful a problem for him as it had been for President Eisenhower, and the new president sought a way to deal with Castro on American terms. "Communist domination in this hemisphere," declared Kennedy, "can never be negotiated."

Once in office, Kennedy learned that the CIA, under Eisenhower's orders, was training anti-Castro Cuban exiles for an invasion of Cuba. Kennedy seemed to have advocated just this kind of action while a candidate, and he ordered the program continued. American planners calculated that when the exiles landed in Cuba, one-third of Castro's army would join them, another third would desert, and the rest would not be able to withstand the invaders. Hoping to achieve this aim with as little direct U.S. commitment as possible, Kennedy canceled CIA air cover for the landing.

The invasion, in April 1961, failed miserably. Castro's forces remained loyal, fought well, and routed the invaders in two days. Moreover, the role of the United States in the fiasco could not be concealed. America had been caught intervening in the domestic affairs of another country—and, worse still, in a clumsy and ineffectual fashion. Kennedy regained some prestige in the United States by taking on himself all responsibility for the action, but the American position in the world had suffered a serious setback.

VIENNA AND BERLIN

Two months after the Bay of Pigs, Kennedy met for the first time with Khrushchev in Vienna.

Skeptical of the new president's strength, Khrushchev apparently tried to bully him, demanding "adjustment" of the situation in West Berlin and Taiwan; neither of the two areas, he warned, could stay as they were indefinitely. Kennedy replied with a defense of existing conditions and warned that the United States could not watch more territory go Communist without taking action. Khrushchev answered that revolution was sweeping the world; the Soviet Union, he said, would assist the process. Kennedy left the meeting angry and shaken.

Khrushchev seemed most perturbed over the status of Berlin. The four wartime allied powers still governed the city, deep in the center of Communist East Germany. West Berlin—consisting of the British, French, and American sectors of the divided city—stood as an island of prosperity and democracy in the midst of the then drab Russian satellite. The contrast itself galled Khrushchev enough, but West Berlin's position as an escape hatch for fleeing East Germans presented a more tangible problem. Three million East Germans, mostly the young and educated, had escaped to the West since the war, and by the early 1960s they were leaving the German Democratic Republic at a rate of 300,000 a year.

Khrushchev continued to demand changes in the situation; Kennedy continued to decline to make any concessions. Tension increased, and the United States began to build strength for a possible confrontation. Kennedy tripled the draft call, called up 150,000 reserves, and sent another 40,000 troops to Europe. The president of East Germany threatened to cut West Berlin off from the rest of West Germany—to reinstitute the Berlin Blockade. "I hear it said that West Berlin is militarily untenable," Kennedy told Americans in a TV address. "Any dangerous spot is tenable if men—brave men—will make it so."

On August 13, 1960, Khrushchev and the East Germans responded to the crisis by building a barrier around West Berlin (first barbed wire, later a brick wall), effectively cutting off further emigration. Although such an action violated the Four-Power treaty on Berlin, the United States took no action. The Russians had not touched West Berlin, and the United States would not go to war over a wall.

CONFLICTS WITH EUROPEAN ALLIES

From the start of Kennedy's term, American policy makers worried about a problem that the Cuban missile crisis—their greatest triumph—would only aggravate. The United States's relations with Western European nations, its closest world allies, seemed to be fraying. Although Kennedy felt the United States had convincingly demonstrated its commitment to defend Western Europe in the Berlin crisis, many Western Europeans continued to express dissatisfaction with their then subordinate role in the Atlantic Alliance and NATO.

Under Kennedy, the United States developed a two-part policy toward Europe. As an ultimate goal it urged a plan called the Grand Design, a united Western Europe (based on an expanded version of the European Common Market, the extremely successful economic alliance of France, West Germany, Italy, Belgium, Holland, and Luxemburg), which would share burdens and decisions with the United States. Until then, it urged Western Europeans to strengthen their conventional defenses while the United States controlled nuclear weapons.

Across both these plans fell the long shadow of France's President Charles de Gaulle. General de Gaulle wished to see France neither swallowed up in a greater Europe nor dependent upon the United States for its ultimate defense. He greatly distrusted both the Americans and the British, feeling that the Anglo-Saxons wished to control and divide the Western world between them. Despite American objections, he decided that France, like Britain, must have its own nuclear weapons.

The Cuban missile crisis, with its proof that the United States would engage in nuclear diplomacy without consulting its allies, intensified de Gaulle's determination. In January 1963, he vetoed British entry into the Common Market, thus frustrating a long-time American policy aim. He also loosened France's ties with NATO, formed a close relationship with West Germany, and began to make his own overtures to Eastern Europe.

The United States tried to discourage France, and other European nations, from building their own bombs with a plan called the Multi-Lateral Force. This project called for ships carrying nuclear weapons to be manned by mixed crews representing all the NATO powers, but it stirred no interest outside Washington. Although Britain ultimately joined the Common Market, France continued to pursue a course independent of the United States, and eventually pulled out of NATO.

THE BEGINNINGS OF DETENTE

But if the Cuban missile crisis damaged America's relationship with its allies, it greatly improved relations with "the other side." Following the confrontation, both the United States and the Soviet Union looked for ways to lessen the probability of nuclear holocaust—intentional or accidental. Soon after the days of October, they cooperatively set up a two-way "hot-line" linking the White House and the Kremlin with a separate teletype system. The ability to communicate quickly would, they hoped, greatly lessen chances of nuclear war arising from misunderstandings.

The thaw in the Cold War yielded even more specific results in August 1963, when the two superpowers signed a treaty banning nuclear tests in the earth's atmosphere. The agreement reflected in part the fears of both nations about their allies—fears that proved well-founded when France, Communist China, and Cuba refused to ratify the document.

Further, both powers seemed more inclined to recognize the problems of the other, and to see the necessity of accommodation. In June 1963, Kennedy expressed this growing tolerance in one of the best speeches of his career, declaring: "In the final analysis, our most basic common link is the fact that we all inherit this planet. We all breathe the same air. We all cherish our children's future. And we are all mortal."

ENTERING VIETNAM

Even with the nuclear pressures eased, major troubles loomed for the United States in a "fringe area." After the cancellation of the elections

Robert F. Kennedy

The life of Robert Kennedy, more so than most Americans of the 1960s, was profoundly shaken when his brother was shot on November 22, 1963. Before that day, he had operated as a satellite of his brother John, as his closest adviser, his campaign manager, and his attorney general. He had acquired a reputation for ruthlessness in pursuit of his brother's interests, often acting as "hatchet man" for JFK. After the day President Kennedy was shot down in Dallas, Robery Kennedy had almost to reassemble himself, to draw new strength from new people and projects.

In 1960, Robert Kennedy had told local Democratic leaders that he did not care what they thought of him, that he did not care what happened to him, that he wanted only to get his brother elected president. After John became the first president to name a brother to the cabinet, Robert still seemed to be characterized chiefly by a driving intensity. As attorney general, he devoted a large part of his own and the Justice Department's time to putting Jimmy Hoffa of the Teamsters, a labor leader he considered corrupt, in prison. Realizing, once assuming office, the desperate situation of Southern blacks, he assisted them to an extent no previous attorney general had considered. Kennedy's response to situations tended to be visceral rather than intellectual, but he could also be a poised and effective adviser as he was during the Cuban missile crisis.

After the death of his brother, a friend described Robert Kennedy as "a kind of bruised animal." He wanted to be Lyndon Johnson's running mate in 1964, but the two men had long hated each other, and their respective positions now infused a strong element of mutual resentment. Since his brother Edward was already senator from Massachusetts, Robert Kennedy (RFK) ran for the Senate from New York. He won, with the help of the growing legend of his martyred brother, family, wealth, and, ironically, a Lyndon Johnson landslide in the state.

Kennedy disliked both the routine of the Senate and the details of party leadership in New York. Although he made efforts to work in both directions, his real interest was developing and expanding his national constituency—Kennedy loyal-

(UPI)

ists, minorities, liberals—for an eventual attempt to reclaim his brother's office.

After publicly attacking Johnson's Vietnam War policy, he faced demands that he run for president in 1968. Certain that it was not politically wise, he refused, and Senator Eugene McCarthy of Minnesota first carried the antiwar standard. Only when McCarthy ran strong in the New Hampshire primary did Kennedy announce he would run. The first month of the campaign held one more surprise: Johnson withdrew from the race.

Old New Frontiersmen hurried to the support of the second (but not the last) Kennedy to run for president. McCarthy now refused to withdraw, and Vice-President Hubert Humphrey declined to challenge Kennedy in the primaries. Observers watched with awe—and foreboding—the intense emotion Kennedy evoked among widely differing groups. He won several primaries, but even after his June victory in the California primary, he faced a long and highly uncertain road to nomination at the convention. As he was leaving his victory party at a Los Angeles hotel, a young Palestinian-American named Sirhan Sirhan shot and killed Robert Kennedy.

intended to unite Vietnam, America had supported Ngo Dinh Diem's government in South Vietnam. Diem, a Catholic in a predominantly Buddhist country, had been having increasing problems with Communist Viet Cong guerrillas, and Kennedy chose to help him defeat the rebels. Much military and economic aid had already been sent to South Vietnam. And starting in 1961, Kennedy sent several thousand military personnel, including Green Berets, to aid Diem. Kennedy wanted to create a strong, pro-Western government in South Vietnam and to show that such a force, with American help, could defeat a Communist insurrection.

During 1961, Kennedy also dispatched both his vice-president, Lyndon Johnson, and General Maxwell Taylor of the Joint Chiefs of Staff to Vietnam to consult with Diem and examine the situation at first hand. Their reports to him, and his own reading of Mao Tse-tung and Che Guevara on guerrilla warfare, led Kennedy to increase the number of American soldiers and airmen in Vietnam. By November 1963, the U.S. presence had grown from a few hundred to sixteen thousand, some of them combat troops. The Diem government, however, did not seem to be doing its part.

Mounting discontent with Diem's government partly explained the ineffectiveness of the South Vietnamese effort. Buddhist leaders and others complained, justifiably, that the Saigon government was corrupt. Government officials gave favored treatment to their relatives, and they persecuted dissenters. Demonstrators demanded Diem's ouster, and several Buddhist monks gained international attention for their cause by publicly burning themselves to death. In Saigon crisis piled upon crisis as Diem retreated to the temporary security and isolation of his palace. Then, probably with the covert support, and certainly with the knowledge of the American government, the South Vietnamese military took over the country on November 1, 1963. Diem and his brother were executed. What Kennedy might have done next is speculation; he outlived Diem by three weeks.

LYNDON JOHNSON'S POLICY

In foreign affairs, as with domestic questions, Johnson was determined to continue Ken-

Senator Barry Goldwater of Arizona, presidential hopeful and popular conservative, waves to supporters as he arrives in San Francisco for the Republican National Convention in July 1964. In control of the convention throughout, Goldwater forces produced a conservative platform and jeered Nelson Rockefeller of New York when the liberal Republican governor proposed a strong civil rights plank. (UPI)

nedy's example. This determination, plus his own reading of international conditions, made victory in Vietnam a priority issue for him. Retaining Kennedy's foreign-policy advisers, including Rusk, McNamara, and Bundy, Johnson hoped to win the war without greatly increasing American involvement.

In the election of 1964, Barry Goldwater, the Republican candidate, severely criticized Johnson's policy, charging that the United States was taking a "no-win" approach. He even talked vaguely about bringing nuclear weapons into play. Against such an attack, Johnson campaigned as an opponent of a wider war. "We don't want our

President Johnson, amid supporters, arrives in Chicago in April 1964 to address a Democratic fundraising dinner. During the campaign for the presidency that fall, Republican nominee Goldwater criticized Johnson for not winning the war in Vietnam, while the incumbent president opposed enlarging the conflict or increasing American involvement. As the peace candidate, Johnson not only won the election handily but also received more votes, and a larger plurality, than any other presidential contender in American history. (UPI)

American boys to do the fighting for Asian boys," he declared frequently.

But Johnson also cultivated the image of toughness. In August 1964, American destroyers clashed with North Vietnamese torpedo boats in international waters. (Later, it was revealed that the American ships were convoying South Vietnamese raiders.) At the time, the North Vietnamese were steadily—but covertly—increasing both their military support for and control over the Viet Cong insurgents in the South. Denouncing the North Vietnamese action as piracy, Johnson ordered air strikes against their naval bases.

Shrewdly seizing the opportunity to enlarge the mandate for his Vietnam policy, he went to Congress for authority to "take all necessary measures to repel any armed attack against the forces of the United States and to repel any further aggression." Johnson had apparently been waiting for a chance to present to Congress such a resolution, similar to Eisenhower's Formosa resolution. In the years that followed, the Johnson administration would refer often to this resolution, known as the Tonkin Gulf Resolution, as the authority for all subsequent military actions. It passed unanimously in the House, and only two senators voted

against it, warning that it probably would lead the nation into a wider war. Johnson, the peace candidate in 1964, easily won the election.

ESCALATION

Shortly after Johnson's inauguration in 1965, the Viet Cong attacked an American base in Vietnam. The president then ordered sustained bombing of North Vietnam, allegedly to bring the Hanoi Communists to the peace table and force them to stop supplying the Viet Cong guerrillas in the South. But heavy American bombing produced the opposite result, steadily drawing the North Vietnamese even more deeply into the war and increasing the amount of supplies that came in from other Communist powers. During this period, the U.S. government apparently rebuffed various North Vietnamese "peace feelers," fearing that the South Vietnamese government was too weak even to negotiate, since the removal of Diem had not brought stability to Saigon.

The weaknesses of successive South Vietnamese governments further complicated the American effort. For four years after the fall of

When the Vietnam War escalated under President Johnson in 1965, the United States intensified bombing raids on North Vietnam and increased by eight times the number of American troops stationed in Vietnam. Here, soldiers from the U.S. 173rd Airborne brigade, having just received supplies by helicopter, continue a search-and-destroy patrol through the jungle in Phuoc Tuy Province, in June 1966. In the rear, this landing zone is guarded by an armored personnel carrier. (UPI)

Diem, governments came and went in Saigon. One of them lasted only eight days. No leader emerged strong enough to unite the non-Communist elements in the country, to control corruption in the South Vietnamese army, or to win the loyalty of the peasants. When a relatively stable government finally emerged, under two generals, it proved repressive and ineffectual, a creature spawned by U.S. aid and kept alive by the ever-increasing U.S. military commitment.

The worse the war went for Saigon, the deeper the United States became involved. Bombing raids intensified in the North and against Communist positions in the South until American planes ultimately dropped more bombs on Vietnam than had been used during all of World War II. In 1965 American troop strength in Vietnam increased from 23,000 to 180,000. By the end of 1967 there were nearly half a million American soldiers in the country.

The failure of the American expedition in Vietnam and Washington's determination to seek military victory worried and alienated many American allies. The United States tried desperately to attract support for the war, to make Viet-

nam appear a joint action similar to the UN Command in Korea. A few Asian countries—Korea, the Philippines, and Australia—made token commitments. But no NATO ally would join the United States in Vietnam, and France (the previous Western colonial power there) publicly derided American policy. The nature of the Vietnam War, the absence of a clearly defined front line, the inability to tell Vietnamese friend from foe—all these factors frustrated the U.S. effort. Indiscriminate use by American forces of napalm fire bombs and defoliant chemicals also weakened the moral position of the United States throughout the world.

Escalation of the war cost thousands of American lives and billions of dollars in equipment, divided public opinion at home, and strained foreign relations. Still, it did not lead to confrontation with the Soviets, who seemed content to let the United States sink deeper and deeper into the never-ending and costly Vietnam adventure. Soviet–American relations continued on fairly friendly terms during the period, although Russia supplied much of the arms used by the Communist Vietnamese. In 1968 the United States, the Soviet Union, and sixty-six other nations signed a nuclear

THE WAR IN SOUTHEAST ASIA

◄ ■ United States and South Vietnamese troop moves
◄ National Liberation Army moves
◉ Capital cities
● Major U.S. Bases
— Friendship Highway

0 _____ 100 MILES

With the defeat of the French at Dienbienphu in 1954, Vietnam was, in effect, divided into two countries: North Vietnam with its capital at Hanoi, and South Vietnam with its capital at Saigon. Soon Communists and nationalists began guerrilla and terrorist activity against the Saigon government, which received support and increasing amounts of military aid from the United States. These guerrilla forces, formally titled the National Liberation Army, came to be known as the Viet Cong.

In August **1964** North Vietnamese torpedo boats reportedly fired on United States ships in the Gulf of Tonkin. President Johnson ordered the bombing of North Vietnamese naval bases in retaliation. The United States was soon bombing North Vietnam regularly and also areas in South Vietnam held by the Viet Cong. In turn, United States naval bases, such as the one at Danang, were attacked. American bombers then attacked eastern Laos in an attempt to stop the flow of men and supplies from North Vietnam over the Ho Chi Minh trails. United States military involvement increased until nearly 540,000 American troops were in Vietnam.

In early **1968** the Viet Cong launched their Tet Offensive—simultaneous attacks on the major cities of South Vietnam. During an American counterattack, a massacre of Vietnamese civilians by American soldiers occurred ay My Lai. In the same year President Johnson called a limited halt to the bombing of North Vietnam on March 31 and a full bombing halt on November 1. In **1970** occasional air attacks were resumed.

United States and South Vietnamese forces drove deep into Cambodia in April 1970 in an effort to locate and destroy Viet Cong bases there. In February **1971** South Vietnamese troops, with United States air support, crossed the border into Laos in an unsuccessful attempt to cut the Ho Chi Minh trails.

In March **1972** the Viet Cong and North Vietnam launched a massive offensive, capturing the provincial capital of Quang Tri and scoring other successes; in May the United States began systematic bombing of all North Vietnam and mined North Vietnamese rivers, canals, and ports—including Haiphong Harbor.

Under President Nixon the number of American troops in Vietnam was drastically reduced—down to 65,000 in May 1972—and combat duties were transferred to South Vietnamese forces under a policy of "Vietnamization." In **1973** a cease-fire was concluded in Vietnam. In **1974** and **1975,** North Vietnamese units completely overran the South, and sent the South Vietnamese government fleeing. A unified Vietnamese regime was created, dominated by the North Vietnamese.

nonproliferation treaty, pledging not to assist additional countries in obtaining or developing nuclear weapons. President Johnson and Premier Kosygin met briefly, but amicably, during one trip by the Soviet leader to the United Nations headquarters in New York.

SANTO DOMINGO

Early in his administration, Johnson became engaged in a policy that, although as unpopular internationally as Vietnam, appeared more success-

ful. Since the violent death of its dictator, Rafael Trujillo, in 1961, the Dominican Republic had undergone several changes in government, and in 1965 a military dictatorship ruled the country. That year, a group of low-level officers and political radicals mounted what looked like a successful coup against the generals. The ruling junta appealed to the United States for help.

Johnson, acting on unconfirmed reports of Communist and Castroite participation in the revolution, sent in thirty thousand marines. He announced, however, that he was acting to safeguard the lives of Americans in the country. But when all American civilians had been evacuated, American troops remained, and Johnson then warned of Communist domination of the revolutionary forces.

Despite the resultant Latin American hostility, the Dominican intervention succeeded on one level. The left-wing revolution had been stopped, peace-keeping forces from the Organization of American States reinforced the Americans, and an election held in 1966 resulted in a pro-American president. But Johnson's action, like Kennedy's during the missile crisis, appeared to reconfirm in the minds of American leaders the effectiveness of armed intervention. Virtually all the members of ExComm were still holding top government posts during the Dominican intervention, and many remained to carry out further escalation in Vietnam.

JOHNSON STEPS DOWN

By early 1968, opposition to the Vietnam War echoed across the country. College students,

in danger of being drafted and sent to fight in a war whose casualties rapidly mounted, protested loudly. Some burned their draft cards or fled into exile. Johnson's Vietnam schemes had all gone awry. Even Robert McNamara, a key architect in formulating war plans, the "whiz kid" of the Pentagon, became doveish and began questioning the military effort. He dropped out as secretary of defense. An antiwar candidate, Senator Eugene McCarthy of Minnesota, began to challenge Johnson in the Democratic primaries. Virtually isolated in the White House, Johnson rebuffed all his critics, declaring, "I'm the only President you've got." He would try to tough it out.

In January, battle reports from Vietnam shattered the president's apparent composure. During Tet, the lunar new year, the Communists mounted their largest offensive of the war. They briefly captured Hué, South Vietnam's second-largest city, as well as parts of Saigon, besieging the American embassy for six hours. American forces counterattacked and recaptured the cities, but casualties were heavy on both sides. The Viet Cong and North Vietnamese seemed as strong as ever, despite a half million American troops and a steady barrage of optimistic public statements from the White House and the Pentagon. The Tet offensive revealed the obvious: The United States had failed

First Lieutenant William Calley, Jr., second from left, arriving at Fort McPherson, Georgia, to take the stand as the first defense witness in the court-martial of Army Captain Ernest Medina in September 1971. Medina was being tried by the army for his role in the My Lai massacre of March 16, 1968, when South Vietnamese civilians were shot to death by American soldiers who occupied their village. Calley himself was convicted of unpremeditated murder during the massacre and was imprisoned. (UPI)

to win the war in Vietnam, although in military terms, the offensive proved a major setback for the Communists.

Aided by the shock waves from the Tet offensive, McCarthy nearly defeated President Johnson in the New Hampshire primary. This strong antiwar showing led Robert Kennedy to enter the race as well. To add to Johnson's woes, his close friend Clark Clifford, the man who replaced McNamara, had also grown skeptical about the war. He began mobilizing sympathizers and amassing evidence in an effort to get the president and America off the Vietnam treadmill. Nightly television coverage of the war's daily brutality alienated additional millions of Americans, who saw no end in sight to the carnage—nor any victory.

On March 31, Johnson announced an unconditional stop to the bombing of North Vietnam. This met North Vietnam's first-step requirement for negotiations. Johnson then added that to keep his action from being interpreted as a political gesture, he would not run for reelection. The Vietnam War had added yet another American casualty to a very long list.

Suggested Readings Chapters 45–46

The Missile Crisis

Elie Abel, *The Missile Crisis* (1966); Graham T. Allison, *Essence of Decision: Explaining the Cuban Missile Crisis* (1971); Haynes B. Johnson, *The Bay of Pigs* (1964); Robert F. Kennedy, *Thirteen Days* (1969).

The Kennedy Years

Richard R. Fagen, *Cubans in Exile: Dissatisfaction and the Revolution* (1968); David Halberstam, *The Best and the Brightest* (1972); Maurice Halperin, *The Rise and Decline of Fidel Castro* (1972); John F. Heath, *John F. Kennedy and the Business Community* (1969); William Manchester, *The Death of a President* (1967); Bruce Miroff, *Pragmatic Illusions: The Presidential Politics of John F. Kennedy* (1976); Lewis J. Paper, *The Promise and the Performance: The Leadership of John F. Kennedy* (1975); Jack M. Schick, *The Berlin Crisis, 1951–1952* (1971); Arthur M. Schlesinger, Jr., *A Thousand Days* (1965) and *Robert F. Kennedy and His Times* (1980); Hugh Sidey, *John F. Kennedy, President* (1964); Theodore C. Sorenson, *Kennedy* (1965); Theodore H. White, *The Making of the President, 1960* (1961).

The Johnson Years

Edward J. Epstein, *Inquest: The Warren Commission* (1966); Philip L. Geyelin, *Lyndon B. Johnson and the World* (1966); Herbert Y. Schandler, *The Unmaking of a President: Lyndon Johnson and Vietnam* (1977); Doris Kearns, *Lyndon Johnson and the American Dream* (1976). (Additional biographies and studies of Johnson are cited in the "Suggested Readings to Chapters 47–48.)

The Cold War

Jerome Levinson and Juan de Onis, *The Alliance That Lost Its Way* (1970); James L. Sundquist, *Politics and Policy: The Eisenhower, Kennedy, and Johnson Years* (1968); Richard J. Walton, *Cold War and Counterrevolution* (1972).

Vietnam

Henry Brandon, *Anatomy of Error* (1969); Theodore Draper, *Abuse of Power* (1967); Bernard B. Fall, *Vietnam Witness, 1953–1966*; Seymour M. Hersh, *My Lai 4* (1970); George M. Kahin and John W. Lewis, *The United States in Vietnam* (1967); John B. Martin, *Overtaken by Events* (1966); Robert Shaplen, *The Lost Revolution: The U.S. in Vietnam* (1966).

47 Martin Luther King: The Man and the Dream

The day had been long and hot. The interracial crowd of 250,000 that started August 28, 1963, in a jubilant, festive mood at the base of the Washington Monument and marched triumphantly to the steps of the Lincoln Memorial had grown tired and restless in the heat of the late afternoon. They listened to freedom songs by Joan Baez, Bob Dylan, and Peter, Paul, and Mary. They heard demands for greater strides toward black equality from numerous civil rights leaders and celebrities. Exhausted marchers on the fringes of the crowd began to amble back toward the buses that had brought them. But Mahalia Jackson rose to the platform and sang most of the weary protestors back to life with her, "I Been 'Buked and I Been Scorned." Now came the last speaker of the day—Martin Luther King.

The band played "The Battle Hymn of the Republic" as King approached the microphone. Combining Baptist oratory with civil rights rhetoric, Martin Luther King preached to the marchers and to America about his vision:

I have a dream today.

I have a dream that one day [in] the state of Alabama . . . little black boys and black girls will be able to join hands with little white boys and white girls and walk together as sisters and brothers.

I have a dream today.

I have a dream that one day every valley shall be exalted, every hill and mountain shall be made low, the rough places will be made plain, and the crooked places will be made straight, and the glory of the Lord shall be revealed, and all flesh shall see it together.

This is our hope. This is the faith with which I return to the South. With this faith we will be able to hew out of the mountain of despair a stone of hope. With this faith we will be able to transform the jangling discords of our nation into a beautiful symphony of brotherhood. With this faith we will be able to work together, to pray together, to struggle together, to go to jail together, to stand up for freedom together, knowing that we will be free one day. . . .

And if America is to be a great nation, this must become true. So let freedom ring from the prodigious hilltops of New Hampshire! Let freedom

878

Two hundred thousand people, black and white, filled the Washington Memorial mall in August 1963 to give a visible form to Martin Luther King's dream of racial harmony. (Wide World Photos)

ring from the mountains of New York! Let freedom ring from the heightening Alleghenies of Pennsylvania!

But not only that; let freedom ring from Stone Mountain of Georgia!

Let freedom ring from every hill and mole hill of Mississippi. From every mountainside, let freedom ring.

When we let freedom ring, when we let it ring from every village and every hamlet, from every state and every city, we will be able to speed up that day when all of God's children, black men and white men, Jews and Gentiles, Protestants and Catholics, will be able to join hands and sing, in the words of that old Negro spiritual, "Free at last! Free at last! Thank God Almighty, we are free at last!"

Martin Luther King, Jr., was the most eloquent spokesman for racial justice in the 1960s. For many, his passionate plea for nonviolence was undercut by his own violent death at the hands of an assassin. (Wide World Photos)

The response was deafening. People wept and cheered. Martin Luther King had put into words the great emotional cry of American blacks who had been oppressed or ignored for three hundred years.

King triumphed that day. The minister himself probably believed that such dramatic changes were at hand, and there were reasons for his optimism. What had started eight years before in Montgomery, Alabama, as a campaign for desegregating a city bus line had grown into a national civil rights movement, and King, who had started his career as a minister in a small Southern Baptist church, had become the nationally recognized leader of American Negroes.

Martin Luther King, Jr., was born in Atlanta, Georgia, on January 15, 1929, the product of a complex inheritance. His maternal grandfather had founded the Ebenezer Baptist Church, and his father had nurtured it into one of the largest and most successful churches in the city. Martin inherited not only his father's name; it was also understood that he would be the next minister of the Ebenezer Church.

But King entered Morehouse College, an all-black male college in Atlanta, at the age of fifteen, still undecided about his future career. Despite his inheritance, he was then trying to choose between law and medicine. The ministry appeared to him as intellectually crude; he was too familiar with the image of the black pastor working his congregation into an evangelical fever. But by the end of his junior year, Martin announced his commitment to the church.

During his years at Morehouse, King began to develop the philosophical basis for his later belief in nonviolent protest against discrimination. Henry David Thoreau's justification for "Civil Disobedience" especially impressed the young man. "One has a moral responsibility to disobey unjust laws. . . . An unjust law is a code that is out of harmony with the moral law," wrote King later, much in the spirit of Thoreau.

King graduated from Morehouse at the age of nineteen. He could have moved directly into the ministry, as the assistant pastor of his father's church. He chose instead to continue his education by attending, first, Crozer Theological Seminary in Chester, Pennsylvania, and later, Boston University. It was at Crozer that King became acquainted with the writings of Mahatma Gandhi and became strongly attracted to the Indian leader's philosophy of pacifism.

While King pursued his graduate studies at Boston University, he was introduced to Coretta Scott, a graduate of Antioch College, whom he later married. The Kings stayed in Boston while Martin completed his dissertation and received his doctorate.

In May 1954, King accepted the pastorate of the Dexter Avenue Baptist Church in Montgomery, Alabama. That same month, the United States Supreme Court decided *Brown* v. *Board of Education of Topeka*. A unanimous Court declared racially separate school systems unconstitutional. Neither the Court nor the twenty-five-year-old minister realized it, but a new phase in the Negro struggle for equality was about to begin.

It started without fanfare, and, as it turned out, had nothing to do with the schools. On Thursday, December 1, 1955, Rosa Parks entered her usual crowded bus and took a seat behind the vehicle's white section. Farther down the line more whites boarded, and Mrs. Parks was ordered by the driver to give up her seat to a white man. She refused. The bus driver called the police, and she was arrested for violating the city's segregation code. Four similar episodes had occurred in Montgomery the previous year, but this time the black community responded.

The groundwork had been laid for concerted black action. Negro leaders had been active in NAACP (National Association for the Advancement of Colored People) programs, and many black women of the community had been working for equality of public facilities through their Women's Political Council. Jo Ann Robinson, head of the women's organization, had already formulated plans for a bus boycott by blacks; she had only been waiting for a defendant like Rosa Parks, a determined and respected member of the black community. When news of the arrest reached Mrs. Robinson, she approached various leaders to seek support for her plan. She first called Ed Nixon, an NAACP official who, in turn, telephoned the Reverend Ralph Abernathy and Martin Luther King, Jr. After King conferred with Abernathy, he decided to give the boycott his full support.

On Friday evening, December 2, black community leaders met at King's church and called a boycott for the following Monday, December 5. They spent the weekend getting news of the boycott to the rest of the black community. On Monday morning the bus boycott proved a total success. Blacks walked to work or used taxis driven by other blacks who had agreed to charge bus rates. Late that afternoon, the leaders met again. They decided, on the basis of this initial success, that the boycott would continue, and they founded the Montgomery Improvement Association (MIA) to superintend it. Martin Luther King, Jr., was elected president of the MIA, and blacks and whites alike recognized him as leader of the boycott. That evening, at a seven o'clock rally, King both challenged and inspired his audience with a call for community protest against the years of racial oppression. As the boycott continued throughout the next year, King would find not only Montgomery blacks ready for protest but the nation itself prepared to listen.

King and the MIA spent most of December attempting to negotiate with the city government. The city's lawyer warned that recognition of MIA's demands would destroy the social fabric of the South; the negotiations were doomed. By January 1956, the white Establishment, frightened by the overwhelming success of the black boycott, began to fight back, legally and extralegally. Police harassment of private car pools among blacks became commonplace. On January 30 King was arrested for speeding. His short imprisonment added impetus to the black movement, and a crowd gathered at the jail to demand his release.

While in jail, King learned that his home had been dynamited. King pleaded with his followers, for restraint. From the steps of his demolished porch, he spoke of love, not hate. "We want to love our enemies. We must love our white brothers no matter what they do to us." For the moment, violence was averted, and the crowd dispersed.

In February the city indicted the leaders of MIA for conspiring to interfere with normal business. By this time, the Montgomery bus boycott had become an issue of wider scope. King was fast becoming the national symbol of civil rights; his arrest and trial in March received extensive press coverage, and majority opinion seemed overwhelmingly sympathetic. The local judge found the MIA leaders guilty, but in a subsequent appeal, a higher court ruled the bus ordinance unconstitutional. The city appealed the ruling, and the case began a long journey through normal appellate channels that led eventually to the United States Supreme Court. King used the next three months to carry his message across the country, speaking at rallies from coast to coast.

Eleven months after the boycott began, MIA faced another crisis. In November the city issued an injunction against the carpool. Without the pool, the boycott would fail. On the morning of November 13, 1956, King and the other MIA leaders sat in a Montgomery courtroom fearing the worst as their trial wore on. Suddenly, during a recess, there was a

news bulletin that the Supreme Court had reached its decision: Segregated buses were indeed unconstitutional. Triumphantly, on the morning of December 21, 1956, King entered a bus and took a seat in one of the first ten rows. His success was marred, however, by the violence that followed. For a month, Montgomery experienced dynamitings and individual assaults, but eventually the city moved to establish peace. Seven white men were arrested and tried for participating in the violence. All were acquitted.

King and his supporters felt, however, that their legal campaign in Montgomery had succeeded. They had won their court battle and could now count the federal judiciary as an ally. More important, Montgomery had alerted the nation to the issue of civil rights for blacks in a specific, admirable, and dignified way.

In the years that followed, King devoted his energies to mobilizing his following and organizing his ideas. Meetings in early 1957 led to the formation of the Southern Christian Leadership Conference (SCLC), with King as its president. Originally, SCLC was intended to supplement the efforts of existing civil rights organizations such as the NAACP and the Urban League. But the leaders of these older, established groups opposed King's primary strategy of passive resistance. The NAACP felt that the best way to achieve racial equality was through the courts; Urban League leaders believed that black economic gains would provide the answer.

Not all of King's activities during these years were directed toward civil rights organizing. In February 1959, he and his family visited India, where he was received enthusiastically. King returned to America with an even deeper commitment to Gandhi's principles of nonviolence.

When King returned to America, his father offered him, for a second time, the co-pastorate of his Ebenezer Baptist Church in Atlanta. This time King accepted. By then the SCLC had grown into a full-fledged organization, with headquarters in Atlanta. King believed that to put Gandhian principles into action, he would have to devote more time to the civil rights crusade. In January 1960 he moved his family to Atlanta and prepared to escalate his campaign with an anti-segregation movement centered in that city.

Like the campaign in Montgomery, the Atlanta movement started quietly and simply. On February 1, 1960, in Greensboro, North Carolina, two black university students refused to leave a Woolworth's lunch counter when they were denied service. Within a week, their simple demonstration had sparked similar "sit-ins" in other major Southern cities. By March, the sit-in movement had reached Atlanta, where Atlanta University students issued a manifesto demanding an end to racial discrimination in education, housing, jobs, voting, law enforcement, hospitals, and entertainment facilities.

The lunch counter sit-ins, started in 1960 in Greensboro, North Carolina, proved an effective technique of protest against racial discrimination in public places. The proliferation of sit-ins in the early 1960s, and the attention they drew, contributed to the passage of the 1964 Civil Rights Act. (UPI)

The Atlanta campaign operated under the careful guidance of King and the SCLC. In April, King called a civil rights student conference, advocating the establishment of a permanent student organization (later to become known as SNCC—Student Nonviolent Coordinating Committee), a campaign of selective economic boycott, and creation of a volunteer army of student demonstrators. King was facing pressure from both sides of the black community. The student movement's potential for violence had to be controlled, while the older civil rights groups—the NAACP and the Urban League, which opposed the new civil disobedience techniques—had to be won over. King moved quickly both to maintain the momentum of protest and to retain control of the unfolding situation.

On October 19, he and thirty-six other demonstrators were arrested and charged with trespassing when they would not leave the lunch counter of Rich's department store after being denied service. King and the others refused to post bond. The judge proposed a two-month truce. Arrangements between the prisoners and the city government were being negotiated when an unexpected move by the DeKalb County authorities pushed King's case into headlines all over the nation. Six months earlier, the minister had been arrested in DeKalb County, Georgia, for driving with an invalid out-of-state license and had been placed on probation for twelve months. The DeKalb authorities maintained that King's October arrest violated his probation. The prisoner was transferred to DeKalb County and given a sentence of four months hard labor at Reidsville State Prison.

The imprisonment created national outrage, and demands poured into the White House for King's release. President Eisenhower declined to intervene in matters of local concern, however, and Vice-President Nixon, then embroiled in his presidential campaign against John F. Kennedy, refused to comment. But Kennedy showed no reluctance. After telephoning Mrs. King, the Democratic presidential nominee instructed his brother, Robert, to try and obtain King's release. King himself was not especially impressed by Kennedy's move, which he saw as one of political expedience, designed to win Kennedy black support at the polls in November.

In March 1961 the combined organizations of three civil rights groups—CORE (Congress of Racial Equality), SNCC, and King's SCLC—initiated a new program: the Freedom Rides. King was appointed chairman of the Freedom Rides Coordinating Committee. The rides were designed to "mobilize" the sit-in; the riders traveled from Washington, D.C., through the South to Montgomery, Alabama. Participants tested the segregation codes of each city en route by staging sit-ins in public facilities such as bus station waiting rooms and lunch counters.

The results were damaging to King personally and to his philosophy of nonviolence. The first riders met with disaster in Anniston, Alabama, where one of the buses was attacked and set on fire. The second bus made it safely as far as Birmingham. There, the riders were brutally beaten by a mob of whites while police looked on. The riders continued to Montgomery, but many demonstrators were left bruised and bloodied on the highway. King and seven hundred special marshals appointed by Attorney General Robert Kennedy rushed to Montgomery, but the damage was done.

King then decided to compromise: In May SCLC suggested a "temporary lull" in the Freedom Rides. This suggestion was totally ignored by SNCC, and during the summer of 1961 more rides and more violence occurred throughout the South. King had been labeled a moderate, and for a time lost much of his support among black youth. But there was more to come.

Albany, Georgia, typified many Southern black belt towns. The subordination of blacks was accepted and recognized. For the black community, Albany was not particularly better or worse than other Southern hamlets. But the events in Montgomery and other civil rights confrontation sites eventually had their impact on Albany.

SNCC decided to test the September 1961 Interstate Commerce Commission ruling that outlawed segregation in bus station waiting rooms. In October, nine students entered the white section of the Trailways bus depot in Albany and were arrested. When the ICC took no immediate action, black leaders decided to mobilize. The Albany Movement was born. Trial for the original "offenders" was set for December 11. That same day, five black and four white Freedom Riders arrived in Albany. They left their bus, entered the white waiting room of the station, and were arrested.

Their arrests touched off protest marches and more demonstrations. By December 15, many people were in jail. That day, King arrived in Albany to lead the campaign. The SNCC leaders reacted angrily to what they saw as a usurpation of their control. Their jealousy would seriously hamper the campaign's effectiveness.

Pitched battles between civil rights groups and city authorities continued. King and his followers staged sit-ins and marches. King was jailed twice, and the city refused to honor its December truce agreement, issuing injunctions against demonstrations of any kind. In July news of an assault on a pregnant black woman touched off a battle involving several thousand blacks and the police. This appalled King, and he called for a one-day moratorium on demonstrations, which served to alienate further the SNCC. Moreover, black leaders of the conservative NAACP and Urban League continued to hold King's methods ultimately responsible for the outbreaks of violence.

The struggle continued throughout August. King attacked the Kennedy administration for its failure to act. The Albany city officials refused to yield to any of the Albany Movement's demands, and the white community stiffened its determination to retain supremacy. September was a month of white retaliation. Within one week, the Ku Klux Klan bombed four black churches.

King, meanwhile, had returned to Atlanta, where he turned his energies toward another and larger-scale campaign—this time in Birmingham, Alabama. Albany had taught him that future campaigns must be better organized and must be directed toward an assault on specific issues rather than an attack on racial discrimination in general.

The industrial metropolis of Birmingham, Alabama, was especially tough on blacks. Its police commissioner, Eugene "Bull" Connor, was an outspoken racist, and King was anxious to challenge the city's overbearing white domination. King had no major worries about divided leadership here; Fred Shuttlesworth, leader of the black Birmingham community, was a long-time personal friend.

Neither did the Birmingham venture suffer from lack of organization. Many meetings and much paramilitary planning went into the formulation of "Project C" (C for confrontation). On April 3, 1963, the campaign opened with the declaration of "B Day" (B for Birmingham). For two days, blacks staged sit-ins and picketed in front of white businesses. On April 6 the second stage of Project C began. Shuttlesworth led forty-five people on a march to city hall. Connor had them arrested and jailed. The next day, Palm Sunday, another group of marchers set out for city hall to join those in jail. Three days later city officials obtained an injunction against the black leaders.

Again King had decided to defy the court order. On the morning of Good Friday, he and Abernathy led fifty hymn-singing marchers toward city hall as black spectators lined the streets shouting encouragement. Soon after they had begun, Connor ordered their arrest. King was placed in solitary confinement. Disturbed by her inability to find out what might have happened to her husband, Coretta King phoned President Kennedy for help. On Monday the president returned the call, giving Mrs. King personal assurances concerning her husband's safety.

While King and Abernathy remained in jail, matters worsened in the city. King's brother was imprisoned for demonstrating without a permit, and his arrest touched off further street disturbances. Governor George Wallace, who had personally defied court orders to desegregate the University of Alabama, was encouraging counterdemonstrations by whites. King and Abernathy were released on bail on April 20. The relatively mild sentences meted out to them six days later indicated that the white power structure feared the consequences of imprisoning King and thus creating a black martyr.

Early May saw more marches and more violence. On May 2, 6000 children marched, and 959 were arrested. For the next four days, the nation watched with horror as police swung their clubs and unleashed their dogs. By May 7, open rioting flared in the streets. Kennedy could no longer remain inactive. The next day King was rearrested and Kennedy made his move.[1]

Behind the scenes, the president had already put pressure on Birmingham businessmen to negotiate, and a truce was beginning to take

---

[1] Both President Kennedy and his successor, Lyndon Johnson, authorized FBI investigations into King's personal life. FBI Director Hoover, who was trying to find evidence that King's SCLC was "Communist-infiltrated," supervised an extensive probe of the black leader that included wiretaps and close surveillance of his activities. At one point, the FBI sent a note to King that threatened that if he did not commit suicide, compromising tape recordings of his personal life would be publicly released. The entire FBI probe continued right up to King's death; it never produced an iota of evidence that sustained the attacks on King's loyalty as an American. The entire episode—only recently revealed—was one of the most shameful abuses of governmental authority in recent American history.

shape. When King was returned to jail, Robert Kennedy immediately called Birmingham city officials to warn them of imminent federal intervention unless the city agreed to black demands that public facilities be desegregated. That evening King was released; the next morning, white officials agreed to meet with black leaders.

The outcome of those meetings in Birmingham was disappointing. The pact between the civil rights leaders and the city was informal, and in the following months the city reneged on much of it. Certainly the pact had not put an end to white violence. In the week after the compromise, King's brother's home was bombed, and more violence ensued. But on the national scale, Birmingham seemed a "success." King's personal prestige soared, and blacks in Birmingham took pride in what they considered a tactical victory. On May 20 the United States Supreme Court upheld the constitutionality of sit-ins. King had succeeded in arousing the country to the issue of civil rights. In June, after several years of directly confronting the issue, Kennedy called for a comprehensive civil rights bill.

After Birmingham, civil rights and Martin Luther King became truly national concerns. During 1963 and 1964, King received widespread personal recognition, but he also suffered severe moral defeats, as the country rocked with violence. On June 12, 1963, Medgar Evers, the NAACP field secretary, was murdered in Jackson, Mississippi. The militancy of black youth, which had surfaced briefly in the Albany and Birmingham campaigns, was on the rise. King found it increasingly difficult to keep the black movement identified with nonviolence.

Throughout June 1963, King toured the nation giving speeches and leading marches in the major cities. But the teachings of the Muslim separatist Malcolm X and other black leaders were also being heard. King's national fame was now drawing criticism from persons who equated his efforts with publicity seeking. He was seen as a creation of the media, as a peacefully protesting black man — an image more or less acceptable to the country's white majority. King had little control over his image, although he did try to reshape his program.

To gain more national support, King and the SCLC planned a March on Washington, to be held in August 1963. Though originally conceived in 1962, the plan took on special significance as the civil rights bill before Congress faced defeat by a Southern filibuster. In July leaders from five civil rights organizations and representatives of many national organizations sympathetic to the movement met in New York to plan the march. Black militants censured the meeting, charging that a white conspiracy was seeking to moderate black demands by limiting the demonstration's objectives. Despite this internal discord, the march went on, and King's emotional speech moved the world.

In the South, in Birmingham and Atlanta and elsewhere, violence continued. On September 22, 1963, yet another church was dynamited, this time in Birmingham. Four little black girls were killed and in the ensuing confusion Birmingham police shot and killed two black youths near the scene. In Atlanta, where past demonstrations had been generally peaceful, violent battles raged between blacks and policemen. But neither King nor the nation was prepared for the events of November 22, 1963. John Kennedy's assassination threatened not only King's dream—it threatened the American dream as well. To King, Kennedy's murder reaffirmed the malignant role of violence in the American way of life: "We mourned a man who had become the pride of the nation, but we grieved as well for ourselves, because we knew we were sick."

The events of 1964, in both the North and the South, further dramatized the extent of the illness. A drive to desegregate beaches and other public facilities in St. Augustine, Florida, proved both bloody and frustrating. Promises extracted from the city were quickly retracted, and racial polarization bred more violence. The Mississippi Freedom Summer is remembered more for the brutal slaying of three young civil rights workers—one black, two white—than for the significant gains in registering black voters. In the North, the cities of Rochester, Detroit, and Philadelphia were rocked by racial rioting. These disturbances foreshadowed the even greater violence in Los Angeles, Chicago, Detroit, and Newark in the summer of 1965. "Black Power," a slogan symbolizing violent retaliation to white oppression, became an increasingly popular rallying cry for militant black youth.

King feared that Johnson, Kennedy's successor, would oppose civil rights legislation. But his optimism was renewed in the early days of the new administration, as he and the president worked together amicably. On July 2, 1964, Johnson signed a new, tough civil rights bill into law. During this period, King's emphasis shifted from desegregation to an attack on poverty and economic discrimination. Johnson's antipoverty program, launched in August 1964, complemented King's moves, and prospects for continued support from the White House looked good.

The results of the 1964 voter registration drive in Alabama were impressive. The number of registered blacks rose from 6000 in 1947 to 110,000. But at the start of 1965, King returned to the South with plans for a new registration campaign. He singled out Selma, Alabama, as the campaign's focal point. On February 1, King, Abernathy, and 770 demonstrators marched on the courthouse and were promptly arrested. After being jailed for four days, and feeling the momentum dying, King organized a march from Selma to Montgomery to confront Governor Wallace. The marchers, however, threatened with violence, dispersed before reaching Montgomery. But in Selma, three white ministers sympathetic to the black movement were beaten, one of them fatally.

At this point, President Johnson made a historic move. Addressing Congress on March 15, he introduced a voting rights bill designed to guarantee black voting in the South. Johnson also called for a national drive to end racial discrimination. Thus he identified himself with the aspirations of blacks more strongly than had any other president: "Their cause is our cause, too. Because it is not just Negroes, but really all of us who must overcome the crippling legacy of bigotry and injustice. And we shall overcome." Two days later the Selma-to-Montgomery march received federal protection. On March 21 King and his supporters set out, triumphantly

CIVIL RIGHTS GROUPS

Year Founded	Group Name	Purpose
1909	National Association for the Advancement of Colored People (NAACP)	An association that aims to achieve equal citizenship rights for all American citizens, through peaceful and lawful means, by eliminating segregation and discrimination in housing, employment, voting, schools, the courts, transportation, and recreation.
1910	National Urban League	A community service agency that aims to eliminate racial segregation and discrimination in the United States and to help black citizens and other economically and socially disadvantaged groups to share equally in every aspect of American life.
1918	Southern Regional Council	A research and information center that seeks the improvement of economic, civic, and racial conditions in the South by providing community relations consultation and field services when requested by official and private agencies; distributing pamphlets that deal with desegregation of various public facilities, and fostering elimination of barriers to black voting registration.
1935	National Council of Negro Women	A coalition of twenty-five national organizations and concerned individuals that seeks to stimulate the development and utilization of the leadership of women in community, national, and international life.
1939	NAACP Legal Defense and Educational Fund	The legal arm of the civil rights movement that represents civil rights groups as well as individual citizens who have bona fide civil rights claims.
1942	Congress of Racial Equality (CORE)	A black nationalist organization that seeks the right of black people to govern themselves in those areas that are demographically and geographically defined as theirs.
1957	Southern Christian Leadership Conference	A coordinating and service agency for local organizations that aims to improve civic, religious, economic, and cultural conditions through non-violent resistance to all forms of racial injustice, including state and local laws and practices.

entering Montgomery four days later. Clearly, King had succeeded in rallying national support behind a voting rights bill.

Encouraged by his recent success, King decided the time had come to broaden his crusade: He began to express his opposition to the Vietnam War. In October 1964 he had won the Nobel Peace Prize. In keeping with his status as an international advocate of peace, he attacked the United States for waging war and for wasting federal funds sorely needed for domestic programs. This new stand cost him considerable support among many conservative black leaders. And it ended his chances of future support from President Johnson, whose administration had widened America's involvement in the war.

CIVIL RIGHTS GROUPS

Year Founded	Group Name	Purpose
1960	Student Nonviolent Coordinating Committee (SNCC)	A committee that sought to help poor people, eliminate slums, and reduce long working hours (now moribund).
1960	National Catholic Conference for Interracial Justice	A religious organization that initiates programs within and without the Catholic Church to end discrimination in community development, education, employment, health care, and housing.
1962	Scholarship, Education and Defense Fund for Racial Equality	An organization that creates programs to provide services in community development, including Eleanor Roosevelt scholarships for students who have demonstrated leadership in civil rights, leadership training programs, and technical assistance for newly elected black officials.
1962	Voter Education Project	A project created as part of the Southern Regional Council to investigate the causes and remedies of low political participation by southern blacks.
1963	Commission for Racial Justice	The commission's purpose is to make racial justice a reality in our national life.
1963	Law Students Civil Rights Research Council	An independent, civil rights legal organization that recruits, trains, and places law students in legal clerkship positions and aims to influence the attitudes of future lawyers about law and social change.
1964	A. Philip Randolph Institute	A nonmembership institution established to serve civil rights activists and promote cooperation between labor and the black community.
1964	Student Afro-American Society	A society that seeks to combat apathy toward the civil rights movement among black college students.
1970	Southern Poverty Law Center	An organization that seeks, through legal precedents it helps to establish via court decisions, to protect and guarantee the legal and civil rights of poor people of all races throughout the nation.

Adapted from *Gales Encyclopedia of Associations*

The King family moved North to Chicago in June 1966. There, King began a program of organizing black tenants to force their landlords to improve housing in the slums. The opposition to King's first assault on Northern abuses of the Negro was both sophisticated and well organized. Chicago's Mayor Richard Daley commanded one of the best-run municipal political machines in the history of American politics; also, the city's black leaders were disorganized and their political leader, Congressman William Dawson, owed his primary allegiance to Daley. Moreover, the problems of poverty and racism in an urban metropolis were unfamiliar to the Southern minister. In the end, they would prove to be more than he could control.

Reverend Martin Luther King, Sr., on June 12, 1977, at a press conference held before he spoke at a Baptist church in Knoxville, Tennessee. (Stephen Shames/Magnum)

King's announcement of a June march drew only criticism from black militants. Black Power advocates Stokely Carmichael and Adam Clayton Powell both called for excluding whites from the black movement. The June rioting in Chicago's black ghetto postponed the march until July 10, and the turnout was disappointingly small. The aftermath was even worse. Three more terrible days of rioting followed, and King found himself and the SCLC on the defensive.

Faced with the indifference of Mayor Daley and President Johnson, as well as an injunction that limited the size of any further demonstrations, King played his full hand—by this time a weak one. He called for a march on Cicero, a Chicago suburb and the center of white resistance to black demands. Two days before the march was scheduled, black leaders and city officials announced a compromise, but its terms brought no real victory for King and his program. He had obviously ended his Chicago campaign without making clear gains for the city's black poor.

Although King failed in Chicago, he did not desert his aim of economic racial equality. Rather, in the months following that drive, he devoted even more energy to economic issues. But the rumblings of discord that had started in Albany and had increased over the years now escalated into public attacks on King and the SCLC. Militant blacks characterized King's position as "tokenism," while conservative blacks condemned his anti-Vietnam pronouncements and held him personally responsible for black violence.

Although King continued to urge nonviolent resistance as the most effective way to minimize racial conflict, by 1967 he began to devote far more time and energy to the peace movement than to civil rights. In March and April he headed peace marches and spoke out against the war. Civil rights issues had become overshadowed by the growing national opposition to the war in Vietnam.

In April 1968 King began to plan a Poor People's March on Washington, D.C.—a two-barreled protest against domestic poverty and military involvement overseas. While details were being worked out by the SCLC staff, he received word that his help was needed by black organizers in Memphis, Tennessee. After conferring with his staff, King agreed to go.

A strike of Memphis garbage workers, mostly blacks, had become the focal point for organizing black protest. The effort appealed to King. He believed that a victory in Memphis would provide badly needed momentum for the supporters of nonviolent protest elsewhere in the country. Therefore, he announced plans for a peaceful march to support the garbage workers. But March 28, 1968, the day of the demonstration, was anything but peaceful.

Shortly after the march began, a group of young blacks began breaking windows. The confusion that followed quickly escalated into a riot. Fifty persons were injured, and more than twice that number were arrested. The march was a personal defeat for King. His inability to control his own followers triggered vicious attacks from all sides, and the city obtained an injunction against further demonstrations. Once again, King announced his decision to defy the court order and to lead another march. That evening, King delivered one of his most fiery sermons to a group of followers in a Memphis church, pleading with them to remain nonviolent toward their enemies. "I have been to the mountain," he intoned, reminding his supporters that he had witnessed the triumphs and tragedies of their movement for over a decade.

King did not march again. The next day, Thursday, April 4, 1968, King was shot in the head as he leaned over the balcony railing of his Memphis motel room. He died before reaching the hospital.[2]

World leaders and thousands of Americans gathered in Atlanta to attend his funeral. Although many speakers eloquently lauded his contributions to racial justice, a simple inscription carved on the slain minister's monument said it best: "Free at Last, Free at Last, Thank God Almighty, I'm Free at Last."

---

[2] Several months later, an escaped convict, James Earl Ray, was arrested, and confessed the crime. Ray later recanted his confession, but still serves a life sentence for the crime.

Dr. King's funeral, on April 9, 1968, was attended by 150,000 persons, who marched through the streets of Atlanta, after final ceremonies at the Ebenezer Baptist Church. King's murder, five days earlier, had been followed by riots in sixty-three cities across the nation. The riots, according to Dr. King's widow, were "an ironic tribute to the apostle of nonviolence." (Burk Uzzle/Magnum)

48 America in the 1960s: Crisis and Change

On January 20, 1961, John F. Kennedy became the thirty-fifth president of the United States. Though he won narrowly over Richard M. Nixon, for many Americans of all races Kennedy symbolized the same hope for a better future that Martin Luther King symbolized for blacks. But in the decade of the sixties, there were over 100,000 American casualties in the Vietnam War. At home, great masses of antiwar protestors spoke out. Black people vented their anger in civil rights protests and in violent riots in the ghettos. University students demonstrated their outrage at government defense research being conducted on their campuses. The voices of women loudly protested sexual inequality. The 1960s, in short, were characterized by an enormous release of energy both within the government and among groups seeking change within the society. What emerged was a mixture of achievement and anguish, confrontation and crisis, impressive social changes, and the most depressing of national tragedies.

THE KENNEDY ANSWER: THE NEW FRONTIER

In his acceptance speech at the Democratic Convention in 1960, Kennedy summarized what *he* hoped to do for his country—a formidable agenda—under the banner of the New Frontier. He promised to strengthen the economy by reducing inflation and unemployment. To improve the lot of the poor, he intended to provide medical care and increased social security benefits. Blacks were assured that their civil rights would be federally protected. Education was to receive additional federal funding. And all Americans would see the age of consumerism replaced by the virtues of commitment.

Kennedy's Cold War program involved "outgunning" the Russians. Using the "missile gap" argument in 1960 (the claim that Russia had a greater nuclear striking capacity than the United States), Kennedy supported increased defense spending designed to ensure that the existence of American arms superiority would deter Russia from initiating nuclear war. Concern over the nuclear arms race with Russia in the early sixties had ramifications at home. In 1961 and 1962, hundreds of Americans built nuclear fall-out shelters near or under their homes; millions of schoolchildren were drilled on where to go in case of an atomic war; a federal and civil defense bureaucracy plastered shelter signs and stored dehydrated emergency food rations in public buildings all over the country.

The shelters were not used, and the American people breathed sighs of proud relief after the Berlin and Cuban crises. But an important lesson had been learned. Although the Red Scare atmosphere of the fifties had not vanished completely, the outcome of the Cuban and Berlin crises definitely lessened perceived threats of Russian aggression.

Kennedy's domestic programs met with scant success. The civil rights issue exploded in 1961 and 1962, and all Kennedy could do was to ask for a cooling-off period. Kennedy's social reform plans faced stiff resistance from Congress. He failed to win approval for his education, tax revision, and Medicare programs. But he did win moderate increases in federal spending, expanded trade, and stabilized interest rates, which brought the economy out of the recession of the Eisenhower years. These gains, however, did not decrease the

Neil Armstrong took this photograph of Edward Aldrin preparing a scientific experiment on the surface of the moon. Their successful lunar landing fulfilled John Kennedy's promise of 1961 to put Americans on the moon before 1970. (UPI)

Gemini, involved two-man space trips. Apollo, the third phase, took men to the moon. This feat was first accomplished on July 20, 1969, when Neil Armstrong took his "giant step for mankind" on the moon.

Although few failed to be impressed by this major technological achievement, some wondered whether it was worth the cost. When three astronauts died on the launch pad in 1967, some scientists blamed their deaths on America's obsession to get to the moon first. Moreover, second to the defense budget, the moon shot proved to be the most expensive of Kennedy's programs. Many critics challenged this expenditure in light of other pressing domestic programs that were seeing their funding reduced or held to inadequate levels.

Despite the complaints and setbacks, Kennedy remained optimistic in 1963, and with some reason. The civil rights movement was gaining momentum. Kennedy's foreign policies won America prestige abroad and fostered American pride at home. In the summer of 1963, the Soviet Union and the United States agreed to ban aboveground nuclear testing. Although this agreement did not end the arms race, Kennedy reassured Americans that their air would no longer be polluted by radioactive materials. Kennedy's popularity began to soar. In the fall of 1963, the president planned a political tour to drum up support for his programs and for the Democratic party. The last stop planned was in Dallas. For Kennedy, it proved the final stop of his career. On November 22, 1963, Lee Harvey Oswald shot and killed the president. The assassin was himself gunned down the next day in the basement of the Dallas police headquarters. For the next week, the American people sat stunned while the events of Kennedy's life, death, and funeral filled the media. John Kennedy passed from the presidency into mythology. His actual achievements and failures became blurred and the promise he symbolized took hold of the public imagination. His life became an emblem of honesty and peace; his death, in turn, symbolized the violence in American life.

A presidential commission, headed by Chief Justice Earl Warren, investigated the assassination but did little to alleviate American suspicion. Warren and his colleagues concluded that Oswald had

5.5 percent unemployment rate. Kennedy's biggest domestic triumph was the space program, but even that achievement had its drawbacks.

The space program was partially, if not entirely, initiated as another race with the Russians. Distressed that Russia got into space first in the 1950s with Sputnik, Kennedy decided that Americans would be the first to land a man on the moon. On May 6, 1961, Alan Sheppard made the first American suborbital flight. Less than a year later, John Glenn circled the earth. Both flights were part of phase one, the Mercury project. Phase two,

President Kennedy's funeral procession, with its riderless horse, is shown here at the Capitol. At the time he was assassinated, November 22, 1963, Kennedy had been visiting Dallas in quest of Southern support for the 1964 presidential election. His successor, Lyndon Johnson, intended to memorialize Kennedy by enacting the legislative programs of the New Frontier. (UPI)

acted alone. But since many questions remained unanswered, the commission report only heightened public frustration and doubt. Conspiracy theories mushroomed. Most of them were implausible, but distrust of the offical explanation continues to disturb the American consciousness.

THE JOHNSON ANSWER: THE GREAT SOCIETY

If Kennedy symbolized a new breed of politicians, the man who inherited Kennedy's challenge stood for the old. Though Lyndon Johnson was only nine years older than Kennedy when he was sworn into office aboard Air Force 1, his style was quite different. Johnson's terms in Congress, including several years as Democratic leader of the Senate, had taught him the intricacies of power politics. Though this kind of political strength helped push his domestic programs through Congress, many Americans, especially younger ones, came to view excessive presidential power as a corrupting force.

In the first months after Kennedy's death, Johnson used his political might—and support from black leaders such as Martin Luther King—to ram through Congress a comprehensive Civil Rights Bill and to launch his antipoverty program. Other Kennedy bills that had bogged down also slid through Congress during Johnson's first year in office. Congress authorized federal funding for higher education, made appropriations for mass transit, and approved a tax cut. In May 1964, Johnson announced that this "drive" was part of his new program—the Great Society, "a place where men are more concerned with the quality of their goals than the quantity of their goods."

Johnson continued to press his domestic programs. In the fall of 1965, Congress passed an impressive number of domestic bills, many originating in or supported by the White House. Health care for the aged and indigent became law under Medicare and Medicaid. The Elementary and Secondary Education Act called for billions of dollars of assistance to low-income children, and private schools received federal assistance for the first time. A new cabinet post, the Department of Housing and Urban Development (HUD) came into existence. And numerous other bills to combat disease, clean up the environment, make highways safer, equalize immigration quotas, and provide more money for the war on poverty passed easily. Johnson's accomplishments in domestic areas drew applause and even astonishment. Apparently Lyndon Johnson could do no wrong—until his magical political fingers were burned to a crisp on Vietnam.

The "credibility gap" in foreign affairs grew out of the 1964 election. Like Wilson, who in 1916 campaigned as the man who kept the United States out of war, Johnson promised in 1964 that American boys would not do the job of Asian boys in Vietnam. Johnson fashioned his image as a dove,

In its third century the United States remains, in many ways, a difficult country to describe adequately. Today's travelers use buzz words, each valid up to a point, that capture only a portion of the whole: "diverse," "wealthy," "achievement minded," "troubled," "hopeful," "unhopeful," "ambitious," and many more. All the catch phrases of national character analysis seem abstract, however, without a firm sense of the people who have labored to build the America that exists. Their monuments may be as modest as a tiny New England village—this one is in Vermont—or as massive as Boulder Dam. But they have transformed in ways both impressive and sometimes destructive the land first explored by Europeans over 450 years ago and by Indians thousands of years before that.

Rarely have the foreign observers of American life been any less fascinated by its tribulations and triumphs than our own people. "It is not, then, merely to satisfy a curiosity, however legitimate, that I have examined America," wrote Alexis de Tocqueville 150 years ago; "my wish has been to find there instruction by which we may ourselves profit. . . . I confess that in America I saw more than America; I sought there the image of democracy itself, with its inclinations, its character, its prejudices, and its passions, in order to learn what we have to fear or to hope from its progress." That search continues in our own day.

[For further information on the foreign observers quoted in this essay, see "Notes on Sources."]

The Shaping of Contemporary America

PICTORIAL ESSAY   EIGHT

Already, three out of every five American families own homes. The horizontal trend which has replaced the vertical trend of the skyscrapers is covering the great green spaces around the cities with the individual houses of suburbia. Suburbia is a way of life. In the family-centered society which America has become in recent years, suburbia is regarded as the ideal place to rear children. In this world of carefully mowed lawns there already lives one-third of the nation.

[HERBERT VON BORCH, 1962]

Levittown. Pennsylvania

New York is a vertical city. It is a catastrophe with which a too hasty destiny has overwhelmed courageous and confident people, though a beautiful and worthy catastrophe. Nothing is lost. Faced with difficulties, New York falters. Still streaming with sweat from its exertions, wiping off its forehead, it sees what it has done and suddenly realizes: "Well, we didn't get it done properly. Let's start over again!" New York has such courage and enthusiasm that everything can be begun again, sent back to the building yard and made into something still greater, something mastered!

[LE CORBUSIER, 1947]

Skyscrapers, New York City

Joint session of Congress

The Capitol, Washington, D.C.

The Americans are proud of their Lincoln and Jefferson Memorials, and they enjoy showing visitors their National Art Gallery, a splendid white Tennessee marble building which looks pink after a rain. Next we visited the Library of Congress. As we walked around the city this evening in the warm moist air filled with swirling leaves, we saw the dome of the Capitol illuminated against the dark sky. Washington is not a provincial city but a melting pot for people from every state who come to do business, petition, or simply visit.

[NIKOLAI MIKHAILOV AND ZINAIDA KOSSENKO, 1960]

South Carolina plantation

On the banks of the Mississippi stands a stately home with pillared porch, dappled oak alley and a spacious lawn, on which magnolias shed their heavy-lidded blossoms. The home is open to visitors on Sundays, though a family is in residence. There is a guide in the shape of an overpowering lady who waits until the number of visitors meets her approval. The lady praises the past in a voice that echoes in the marble halls.

[JAN DE HARTOG, 1961]

Assembly line workers, Detroit

Steel works, Gary, Indiana

University of Chicago Law Library, designed by Eero Saarinen

I became aware of the pace of work in North America, a pace that was not the international one but that of Uncle Sam. During the eight-hour day people really attended to their job, and it was taken for granted that the chiefs would set an example of punctuality and dedication. Among us Chileans, and I believe also in all the Latin countries, the boss enjoys the privilege of arriving late at the office and staying away whenever he feels like it, and the employees, by the same token, can refrain from showing too much devotion to their work. Compared with us, the North Americans strike me as a much more powerful and better run machine.

[AMANDA LABARCA H., 1959]

American architecture has beauty, audacity, and a superb sense of scale, absorbing what is best in modern architecture in Western Europe, adapting itself to American needs, scenery, and wide horizons, and yet presenting what is exciting, new, and vital. The architect works in freedom and according to the needs he must satisfy and the function his building must perform.

[MORRIS BROUGHTON, 1959]

Parade at Taylor, Wisconsin

Then there are the cities, and especially those small towns that hold the secret of the United States—with their frame houses, their adjoining gardens always open to the view, their grass of a succulent and hospitable green, their tall, powerful trees, their modest and silent intimacy, softened in the whiteness of the snow or expressed passionately in the floral effusion of the springtime; their hospitable and secluded churches, their bustling schools, their solitary streets along which there shine at night, among the trees, the lights of so many open windows; and the business streets with the bank, the gasoline station, the tempting and ingeniously arranged shop windows.

[JULIAN MARIAS, 1959]

Wheat farm on the Great Plains

If you come from the Eastern states, or farther east still, from Europe, going west is a continuous journey of suspense, from the moment you are over the Appalachians and know that the Atlantic has gone for good. In the Midwest, the sky is a little wider, and the prairie is a kind of sea all its own; so much so that in the wheatlands of Kansas you get the illusion of great heaving yellow swells, and the silos float by like battleships on the horizon.

[ALISTAIR COOKE, 1968]

Boulder Dam is something more than a vast utilitarian device, a super-gadget. Enchanted by its clean functional lines and at the same time awed by its colossal size, you might be tempted to call it a work of art; as if something that began with utility and civil engineering ended somewhere in the neighborhood of Beethoven's Ninth Symphony.

[J. B. PRIESTLEY, 1935–36]

Taos is the most characteristic of all the reservations. We were struck at once by its beauty. On two sides of an open space, traversed by a stream, are enormous blocks of buildings, as high as they are long, in which adobe houses are encrusted and superimposed one above the other. The dominant color is a dull yellow, but red and violet cloths, hung to dry on the flat roofs and fluttering in the breeze, light up the sombre background.

[SIMONE DE BEAUVOIR, 1947]

Hoover Dam (Boulder Dam), on the Arizona–Nevada border

Taos Pueblo, New Mexico

Harbor Freeway, Los Angeles

Just leaving my hotel [in Los Angeles] I feel lost — the distance to the nearest drugstore is the same as between two villages in France. One's help- lessness in such vastness is paralyzing. In a car with a girl I said: "Let's go somewhere out of town. . . ." "But where?" she asked. "Oh, no mat- ter where . . . ," I smiled, ". . . where the city ends." "Los Angeles never ends," she said firmly.

[LEOPOLD TYRMAND, 1966]

San Francisco at night

Street signs, Las Vegas

A feature of Las Vegas hotels is that there are no windows or clocks. Gamblers must not be re- minded to go to bed. The less expensive gambling avenue caters for a poorer class of tourist and is known as Glitter Gulch. Its electric signs made it as bright as day. It is ridiculous to sneer at the lighted advertisements of the U.S. Romantic his- torians are always saying how wonderful Eliza- bethan London must have been "with all those painted inn signs swinging in the wind." Well, here you have it still alive. Why sneer? It is living, it is folk art, it is exquisite from an aircraft, and I personally like to be saluted by an electric cowboy a hundred feet high who waves his arm in a ges- ture of Hi!

[T. H. WHITE, 1964]

We sped toward the Mark Hopkins [and went to] the top floor. The walls were of glass, and we walked slowly around the room, looking at the myriad lights below; it was far more beautiful than Los Angeles at night, than even New York it- self, because of the bay traced out in shining lines against a background of dark water and also those fiery ladders rising from the sea. We looked for a long time. There are, in such travels, moments which are promises and others which are only memories: this one was complete in itself.

[SIMONE DE BEAUVOIR, 1947]

*There is enough wilderness in the world to increase very
greatly the number of national parks and to see to it that
some of them are preserved in their original condition
with access kept so strenuous that the solitary walker is
most unlikely to be crowded out.*

*And this perhaps is the ultimate meaning of the
wilderness and its preservation — to remind an increasingly urbanized humanity of the delicacy and vulnerability of all the living species — of tree and plant, of
animal and insect — with which man has to share his
shrinking planet. As he learns to observe their interdependence and their fragility, their variety and their
complexity, he may remember that he, too, is a part of
this single web and that if he breaks down too thoroughly the biological rhythms and needs of the natural
universe, he may find he has destroyed the ultimate
source of his own being. If somewhere in his community
he leaves a place for silence, he may find the wilderness
a great teacher of the kind of planetary modesty man
most needs if his human order is to survive.*

[BARBARA WARD AND RENÉ DUBOS, 1972]

Beach and cliffs, Kauai Island, Hawaii

Glacier Peak Wilderness, Washington

using overly optimistic cabinet and Pentagon reports on conditions in Vietnam. The South Vietnamese, Americans were told, had the war all but won; United States intervention would be discontinued. Voters believed the Democrats and returned Johnson to office in a landslide victory.

On February 7, 1965, Johnson approved air strikes on North Vietnam, and his image as a peacemaker was soon discarded. Explanations for the bombings did little to restore faith. Americans were told that in order for the war to be ended, it would have to be escalated. Debates on escalation raged across the country, but the Johnson administration wanted victory in Vietnam.

From then on, Johnson's main concern would be the war. Billions of dollars and thousands of lives were committed to the effort. Every night, Americans witnessed the atrocities of war on television screens and wondered which of their husbands, fathers, sons, or friends would die next. No other war in history was so graphically brought home to the nation. The impact of the media coverage of Vietnam, generally, was disastrous to Johnson. The administration's contention that the South Vietnamese supported the American-supported Saigon government was hard to reconcile with televised coverage of Buddhist riots and self-immolations.

But even harder to understand or believe was the notion that United States involvement truly aided the Vietnamese people. Night after night, Americans viewed the charred bodies of Vietnamese and their demolished villages — the aftermath of American air raids. And despite the confirmed reports of Vietcong and North Vietnamese atrocities, Americans were not ready to accept repeated napalm air strikes by U.S. planes or the slaughter of 347 Vietnamese men, women, and children by an American unit on a search-and-destroy mission at My Lai on March 19, 1968.

THE SUPREME COURT ANSWER: CIVIL LIBERTIES

The years of Vietnam involvement — and Vietnam disaster — were also years of major legislation broadening personal freedom. This expansion of civil liberties received support from the decisions of the Warren Court (named for Chief Justice Earl Warren, who presided over the court from 1953 to 1969). The majority of justices who served on the Supreme Court during these years believed strongly that individual freedoms must be preserved; they maintained that an active judiciary should protect these rights against local, state, and federal infringement. The impact of this judicial philosophy was felt in decisions on a wide range of cases, from the issue of civil rights to that of prayer in public schools.

The Warren Court dropped a major bombshell opinion in May 1954. In *Brown* v. *Board of Education of Topeka, Kansas*, Chief Justice Warren and all his colleagues maintained that separate education based on race, regardless of the "equality" of facilities offered to those separated, was inherently unequal. Segregation violated the equal protection clause of the Fourteenth Amendment.

The South, angered by the *Brown* decision, fought the ruling. In Arkansas, conflict over desegregation of a high school in Little Rock erupted into a confrontation between states' rights and federal power. The Arkansas governor attempted first to delay school integration and later to close the high school, but the federal courts were determined to fight school segregation. Ultimately, President Eisenhower had to send United States Army troops to Little Rock to enforce the court order. In subsequent cases involving school segregation, the Supreme Court has upheld the *Brown* ruling.

Still the evasions continued. One technique to evade the ruling was to close public schools and subsidize all-white private schools with county funds. In *Griffin* v. *County Board of Prince Edward County* (1964), the Supreme Court ruled that this practice "denied petitioners the equal protection of the laws." The next assault on the *Brown* decision came through "freedom of choice" plans adopted by many Southern states. Under these, parents could choose the student's school, and local custom ensured that black children attended black schools. The Supreme Court overturned this practice in subsequent rulings, which also held that the *Brown* decision required desegregation be accomplished as quickly as possible. These decisions did achieve immediate desegregation, but more than simply denying the constitutionality of segregation, they required that measures be taken to ensure desegregation.

In a number of other cases involving racial discrimination heard from 1955 through 1966, the Warren Court invalidated segregation of public facilities and laws prohibiting racial intermarriages. It also confronted the legality of convictions growing out of sit-ins. From 1961 through 1963, the Supreme Court concluded in several cases that demonstrators had lawfully exercised the right of free speech and that arrests had been based on illegal segregation codes. In cases involving housing, the Court ruled that discriminatory practices in sales and rentals were unconstitutional.

The judicial attack on discriminatory voter registration practices had ample precedent. As early as 1927, the Court invalidated Texas's "white primary" law. In 1949, an Alabama law requiring that voters understand and explain any articles of the state constitution was ruled "patently unconstitutional" under the Fifteenth Amendment. After passage of the Twenty-Fourth Amendment prohibiting poll taxes as a voting requirement, and the Voting Rights Act of 1965, the Supreme Court continued to rule against laws designed to deny blacks the right to vote. In a series of cases it upheld federal power to prohibit poll taxes, discrimination tests, and literacy tests as voting requirements.

While defending the rights of black people to equal protection of the law, the Warren Court also enunciated new procedures for guaranteeing the rights of political dissenters and accused criminals. With its attack on various acts designed to suppress political dissent, the Court undermined much of the legality of the McCarthy era assault on Communists, subversives, and political dissenters. In *Yates* v. *United States* (1957), the Warren Court held that, to be prosecuted under the Smith Act, it must be proven that an individual engaged in specific acts advocating revolution. Subsequent cases involving state prosecution of subversives resulted in Court declarations that states could not outlaw mere advocacy of the use of force, because to do so would deny freedom of speech. The requirements that government employees sign loyalty oaths was attacked by the Court in a number of cases from 1962 to 1967. In 1967, the Court held that the requirements of loyalty oaths "threatened the cherished freedom of association protected by the First Amendment." The right of persons to plead the Fifth Amendment to avoid self-incrimination was also reinforced by Warren Court rulings.

Perhaps the most revolutionary aspect of this civil liberties revolution came in cases involving the rights of suspected or accused criminals. In *Mapp* v. *Ohio* (1961), the Court applied an earlier ruling to invalidate the use in court of illegally obtained evidence. *Gideon* v. *Wainwright* (1963) obliged states to provide counsel for defendants who could not pay for their own attorneys. Confessions obtained under duress were declared a violation of due process. In *Escobedo* v. *Illinois* (1964) and *Miranda* v. *Arizona* (1966), the Court ruled out confessions obtained before defendants had been advised of the right to consult an attorney or the right to refuse to answer police questions. The right of the defendant to a jury trial was extended to include state criminal procedures in 1968.

Freedom of the press, protected under the First Amendment, posed difficulties for the Supreme Court in the 1960s. At issue was the constitutionality of censoring obscene or pornographic literature. As one writer expressed the problem, "obscenity, at bottom, is not crime; obscenity is sin." But the Warren Court tried to define obscenity constitutionally. The Court tended to vacillate between declaring some censorship invalid as a violation of the First Amendment and, at the same time, upholding censorship as the prerogative of the local community. As a result, the issue became more confused than before.

The Court also threatened many established patterns in American politics by a revolutionary decision, neatly summed up as "one man, one vote." This ruling (*Baker* v. *Carr*, 1962) declared that electoral districts for Congress and state legislatures had to be drawn so that they contained almost equal numbers of people. For generations, cities had been underrepresented in both state and national legislatures. In contrast, rural areas had enjoyed disproportionately higher political representation. The Court ruling threatened this prac-

Earl Warren

(UPI)

Of the three men generally considered great chief justices of the U.S. Supreme Court, Earl Warren served only about half as long as John Marshall or Roger Taney. He was over sixty when named to the Court and had never served as a judge before. Yet from 1953 to 1969, Chief Justice Earl Warren stirred up as much controversy—and helped write as much new law—as most men do in life-long judicial careers. While millions of Americans hailed the bold initiatives of the Warren Court, others bought billboard space and bumper stickers demanding "IMPEACH EARL WARREN."

The son of a Norwegian immigrant, Warren had slowly and painstakingly worked his way up in California politics, from Alameda County district attorney, to attorney general, to governor. Although a very private man, not given to backslapping, he rapidly became the most popular politician in the state, establishing a strong record as a liberal, effective administrator. Taking advantage of California's unique election laws of that era (laws that allowed "cross-filing"), he won both the Republican and Democratic nominations in 1946, and overwhelmingly won a third term in 1950.

Defeated as the Republican candidate for vice-president in 1948, Warren hoped for the presidential nomination in 1952. But instead, he helped Dwight Eisenhower win the prize. Shortly after the election, President Eisenhower, although himself a conservative, named his useful supporter chief justice. Ike—stung by Warren's liberal activism—later regretted the act, calling it the biggest mistake he had made during his presidency.

Less than a year after his appointment, on May 17, 1954, Warren spoke for a unanimous Court in *Brown* v. *Board of Education*, declaring racial segregation in public schools to be unconstitutional. At least one justice had been dubious about the ruling; the chief justice persuaded him that a decision of such importance had to be unanimous. *Brown* was the first of many decisions in which the Warren Court upheld the rights of minorities.

Not all of Warren's major decisions, however, received unanimous consent from Court members. In a long series of rulings on the rights of criminal suspects, the chief justice and four colleagues comprised the bare majority. In *Gideon*, they ruled that the state must provide a lawyer for any defendant unable to afford one; in *Escobedo*, that a suspect can have a lawyer present during questioning; in *Miranda*, that a suspect has the right to remain silent and refuse to answer questions.

In perhaps its most far-reaching decisions, the Warren Court ruled that legislative districts had to be drawn on the basis of population, rather than of county or township borders. These became known as the "one-man-one-vote" rulings, because they voided long-standing practices that gave rural voters greater political power than underrepresented city dwellers.

If such rulings caused right wingers to hang Warren in effigy, he also earned the distrust of the left while presiding over the Warren Commission, which investigated the assassination of President Kennedy. Warren issued a controversial report which asserted that Lee Harvey Oswald had been the lone gunman. By the time Warren retired in 1969, at age seventy-eight, some but not all of the bitterness directed against him and his Court by extremists had died down.

DISTRIBUTION OF FAMILY INCOME, 1936 AND 1962

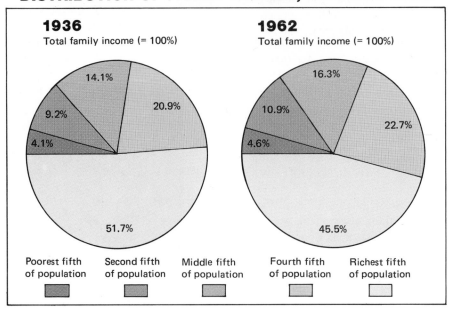

1936
Total family income (= 100%)

14.1%
9.2%
4.1%
20.9%
51.7%

1962
Total family income (= 100%)

16.3%
10.9%
4.6%
22.7%
45.5%

Poorest fifth of population   Second fifth of population   Middle fifth of population   Fourth fifth of population   Richest fifth of population

tice and shifted the balance of political power toward the cities.

But the Court provoked the most controversy in the 1960s by deciding against public school prayers. In 1962 the Court declared that the daily recitation of a nonsectarian prayer in New York schools violated the First Amendment injunction that "Congress shall make no law respecting an establishment of religion." One year later it declared unconstitutional a Pennsylvania statute requiring the daily reading of ten Bible verses. These decisions elicited vehement criticism from congressmen and the public. Some irate Court critics wanted to impeach Earl Warren. Attempts were made to pass a "prayer amendment" to the Constitution to overrule the Court's decision, but the measure stalled in the Senate.

By the end of the 1960s the Supreme Court had established an unprecedented record for defending civil liberties in a wide variety of areas. But in the final years of the decade, it became increasingly apparent that this trend toward judicial libertarianism would slow down. The Nixon appointees to the Supreme Court, like Warren Burger,

the man who replaced Earl Warren, began to shift the Court's balance toward a more conservative stand.

THE BLACK ANSWER: EQUALITY FOR ALL

The start of Martin Luther King's crusade in the late 1950s took most white Americans by surprise. Many still argued that blacks held inferior positions in society because they *were* inferior. They gave credence to the American work ethic—those who work hard get ahead, and those who fall behind have no one to blame but themselves—to rationalize the oppression of blacks. And Martin Luther King's new tactical program of civil disobedience, although the backbone of the Founding Fathers' opposition to George III, seemed decidedly alien. Still, King's actions forced thoughtful people to admit that perhaps racism *was* part of the American system. This proposition once accepted, King's nonviolent tactics could then be applauded. King merely asked for a fair share of the American dream; other militants who followed attacked the dream itself.

Although King's demonstrations (much to his dismay) were often accompanied by violence, it appeared that he was succeeding and improving American society's ability to cure its own ills. By 1965, several important federal measures put the seal of governmental approval on King's campaign. The Civil Rights Bill of 1964 outlawed racial discrimination in public facilities. The ratification of the Twenty-Fourth Amendment in 1964 ended poll taxes in federal elections. In August 1965, Johnson signed the Voting Rights Act, ending literacy tests and authorizing voter registration by federal examiners.

But some blacks remained angry over what remained undone. Since Birmingham, a feeling of frustration had been mounting. In 1965, the first of four successive summers of racial rioting erupted in the ghettos of Watts, Detroit, and Newark. Black militancy was superseding civil disobedience. During a march to Jackson, Mississippi, Stokely Carmichael of SNCC heralded the new black image—Black Power. Many black leaders tried to tone down the implications of Carmichael's approach, but the primary message came through. "Black and white together" (a stanza from "We Shall Overcome") was no longer viable. Black Power meant white exclusion from the movement. The new organization that promoted these ideals most truculently was the Black Panthers.

Even before this, another black, much more radical than King, Malcolm Little (or Malcolm X as he was known after he joined the militant, but separatist, Black Muslims), had already presented a serious challenge to King's moderate leadership in New York and other Northern cities. Malcolm X himself was killed at a New York rally in 1965. His

The nonviolent spirit of protest that characterized the early civil rights movement, as seen in the peaceful demonstration on the left, during the 1965 march from Selma to Montgomery, gave way to a mood of strident militance. The shift reflected increasing internal division within the movement, the growth in influence of separatist and nationalist leaders, and a mounting sense of frustration, most manifest in the ghetto riots of the later 1960s. (left, Dan Budnik/Woodfin Camp & Assoc.; right, UPI)

death—combined with King's and the killing of several Black Panther party leaders in Chicago in 1969—opened the way for an indecisive contest for public leadership of black Americans.

By the time Martin Luther King was assassinated in 1968, the crusade for black equality had been transformed for many militants into a campaign for black separatism. Even some followers of King's nonviolent philosophy began to question whether blacks would ever be integrated into American society on an equal basis; the Black Panthers and other tiny black nationalist groups had already decided that they would not—nor did they want to be. Although the Panthers were not the only black nationalists, they did receive the most publicity, thus providing Americans with a fractured picture of what black nationalism meant. In the end, some Panthers were killed in police raids. Others were arrested on a variety of charges. Still others shifted to electoral politics and community action to achieve their goals.

During 1968 and 1969, the years of "nonnegotiable" demands, black militants confronted college and university administrations. They called for more black admissions, black faculty, and black studies programs. At many schools, the administration moved quickly to satisfy the blacks. At others, black students took over buildings and conducted teach-ins to apply pressure on the administration. The long-range effects are hard to assess. Colleges and universities did admit more black students and hire more black faculty, but the gap in educational equality is not so easily closed.

The black response to the 1960s had more to it than black nationalist separatism. All black groups, from the NAACP to the Black Panthers, shared at least a common opposition to racial oppression. What they achieved through their varied approaches and policies still cannot be accurately measured, but by the end of the sixties, the slogan, "I'm Black and I'm Proud" had become a "nonnegotiable" reality.

THE STUDENT ANSWER: FREEDOM NOW

College life in the 1950s evokes images of football games, sorority and fraternity parties, and political apathy. But in the 1960s, a number of university students caught the public eye through political demonstrations, takeovers of school administration buildings, and antiwar protests. A variety of explanations have been offered for the new activism. Some maintain that it was the effect of keeping young people bottled up in institutions for the first two decades of their lives. Others contend that by the 1960s, universities had become so bureaucratic that students felt lost and alienated. Still others argue that the consumer culture of the 1950s provided no ideological goals for its youth. Whatever the explanation, students in the sixties demonstrated that they wanted their country to honor its commitments to free speech, equality of opportunity, world peace, and individual freedom. More often than not, the means they adopted to reach these goals defeated their purposes.

Many college and university students were introduced to the tactics of political activism in 1964, during the Freedom Summer and the Berkeley Free Speech Movement. Hundreds of students spent their summer vacation canvassing the back country of Alabama and Mississippi trying to get potential black voters registered. Others participated in the Freedom Rides. Many activist groups, such as the SDS (Students for a Democratic Society), became increasingly vocal in their opposition to the Vietnam War and to the anonymity of the university complex.

The first student movement to receive intensive national attention was the 1964 Free Speech Movement (FSM) at the University of California, Berkeley. Students and administrators disagreed over the use of a campus sidewalk for distributing student activist literature. When the university ordered the students' tables evacuated, they refused to leave. The confrontation escalated into an attack on the bureaucratic nature of the university itself. A student strike proved 50 percent effective. The next day, the faculty met and voted to remove all restrictions on speech. The FSM had won. Students learned that they had some power to change university policy.

The campus protests quickly spread. From 1965 through 1970, student disturbances rocked universities throughout the country. Many of these disturbances resulted in greater student participation in a university's management. But a backlash by conservatives, appalled at student militancy, was also taking hold. In California, these sentiments helped elect Ronald Reagan governor. Reagan appealed to the disaffected public with promises to discipline students and professors involved in the FSM.

This polarization increased when college campuses became the centers for antiwar demonstrations. Most of the participants and organizations in the antiwar movement had university or college connections. In 1965 numerous campus teach-ins took place; faculty and students discussed and debated American involvement in Vietnam, and most condemned the action. In September the SDS launched a campaign against the draft, declaring October 16–21 "Stop the Draft Week." Students responded with protest meetings and draft card burnings. Not all of the demonstrations were peaceful. A protest march from the University of Wisconsin on Dow Chemical Company (Dow had been selected because it manufactured napalm) ended in battles between the students and police. The week climaxed with a march on the Pentagon building itself. American TV viewers witnessed the spectacle of armed policemen beating off the protesters.

Organized student opposition grew, and so did violence. Another march on the Pentagon took place in October 1967. And again America witnessed bayoneted rifles confronting militant students.

Antiwar sentiment had been gathering momentum in other strata of society as well. Congress began expressing doubts about the war by the mid-1960s. In January 1966, Senators Mansfield and Fulbright began to hold committee hearings on the conduct of the war. In February, Mansfield announced that Americanization of the war had gained nothing. The Senate Foreign Relations Committee headed by Fulbright brought the congressional debate into American homes with televised hearings on American involvement. While these hearings did not appear to sway President Johnson, they gave some legitimacy to the antiwar movement among the moderate majority.

The student movements in the 1960s left their mark, especially in attacking the university's paternalistic tradition. Administrators and regents had to pay more attention to student needs, and students gained a larger voice in shaping policy. Still, the impact of student representation on policy formulation remained minimal.

The antiwar movement was more than somewhat successful in demonstrating the need to reevaluate American foreign policy, but much public hostility toward students surfaced in response to splinter extremist groups that preached revolution. Organizations like the Black Panthers and the Weathermen, although small in numbers, alienated a significant portion of the adult population. To many Americans, the student movement of the 1960s seemed but one part of a widespread and nihilistic counter-culture.

THE COUNTER-CULTURE

The term "counter-culture" is a handy label for describing the social upheavals of the 1960s. In simplest terms, the counter-culture represented an unorganized and varied attack by dissenters on established cultural norms. Student protest and antiwar activity were not the only elements of the movement. Nor were campuses the only settings for expressing counter-culture ideology or attitudes. The counter-culture "mind-set" defies succinct description. But in practice, the idea of a counter-culture implied a rejection of traditional cultural values.

American attitudes toward sexual experience underwent the greatest change. Sexual freedom became a national preoccupation – traditional sex roles were denounced. Young men rejected the time-honored outward manifestations of manhood by letting their hair grow long and adorning themselves with jewelry. Women rejected lace and frills, choosing blue jeans and workshirts instead. Young people of both sexes – in greater numbers than at any time in the past – openly rejected the taboos against premarital sex. College dorms went coed, and the practice of living together replaced or preceded marriage for many couples.

The entertainment world responded to the new sense of personal liberation by exploiting and promoting it. Rock musicians sang about sexual openness. Theater groups produced plays like "Hair" and "Oh! Calcutta," displaying nudity and simulated sex acts. Movies became progressively more sexually explicit. Certainly the easy availability of contraceptives (especially birth control pills) contributed to this revolution and its underlying philosophy—the belief that all existing middle-class inhibitions on sexual freedom must be repudiated.

In some cases, the general attack on sexual attitudes took organized forms. Many women began to denounce the repressiveness of sexual roles. A growing movement designed to eradicate male domination in American society, Women's Liberation, arose in the late 1960s. Schooled in the tactics of activism by earlier involvement in the black and antiwar movements, many women began to see their most pressing social problems in terms of gender, not class or race. "Male chauvinism" was added to "racism" and "imperialism" in describing so-called American repression of people's rights.

Like other movements in the decade, Women's Liberation adopted varied means for ending male dominance. Some organizations like NOW (National Organization of Women) advocated political techniques. Hiring policies in businesses and college and university campuses were attacked for practicing sexual discrimination. Women demanded stronger penalties for rape. A number of women supported legalized abortion. The women's groups lobbied for the passage of an Equal Rights Amendment, which they hoped would provide the same constitutional basis for woman's rights as the Fourteenth Amendment had for blacks, although a number of women fought the amendment as destructive of woman's special rights within American society. (See Profile of Betty Friedan, Chapter 50, pp. 934–35.)

Not all women involved in Women's Liberation saw politics as the correct or only path. Other women's organizations worked on issues closer to home. Female collectives and female consciousness-raising groups formed in most parts of the country. Other feminist groups rejected marriage, the traditional role of the mother as the primary parent, and the concept that the women's place was in the home. Some women extremists advocated an abandonment of heterosexuality. Many American women remained sympathetic to the movement's more immediate and practical demands for full equality in employment opportunities and pay scale, liberalized abortion laws, and expansion of day-care centers. Certainly the women's movement of the late 1960s and 1970s eroded the image that most women were content as homemakers alone.

Another institution that found itself under attack by the counter-culture was the family. The women's movement gave strength to this assault by questioning traditional sex roles within the family, but other counter-culture groups posed more serious threats. One such group was the Gay Liberation League. During the sixties, homosexuals denounced society's legal and moral sanctions against them. They demanded an end to job discrimination and to legal prosecution of their members.

Another challenge to established definitions of family came from the commune movement. Some young people in the sixties started living together in groups, reviving a tradition of utopian communal living with roots that went back to the 1840s. Some of the communes survived, although many—plagued by economic pressures and internal conflicts—quickly collapsed.

Other counter-culturists challenged basic American traditions and values, questioning the work ethic and the idea that American technological growth guaranteed progress. Some young Americans declared that technology degraded and corrupted life. They decided to return to the rural environment. Organic farming—agriculture without chemical fertilizers or pesticides—became a popular symbol of their philosophy. Others found the answer in Timothy Leary and the drug culture. Marijuana use skyrocketed in America. This, and other psychedelic drugs, became an integral part of the counter-culture.

The counter-culture thrived in the late 1960s and the early 1970s. Though American traditions had been attacked, they were not toppled. Yet a new level of tolerance for alternative life-styles was achieved. Nonconformity was tolerated to a far greater degree by the end of the 1960s than ever before.

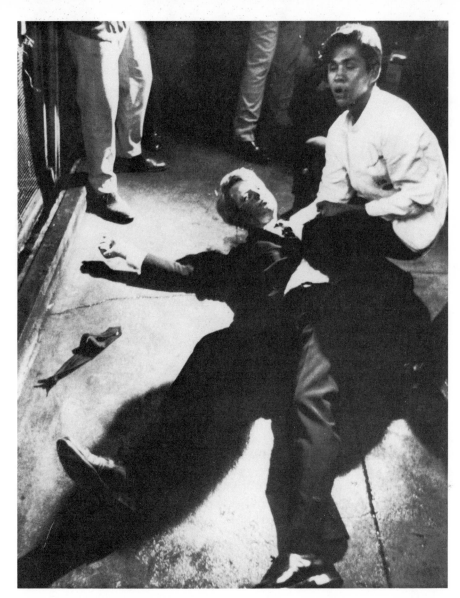

In a tragic reprise of his brother's assassination five years earlier, Senator Robert F. Kennedy lies mortally wounded at the Ambassador Hotel in Los Angeles on June 5, 1968. Kennedy, then campaigning for the Democratic presidential nomination in the California primary that had been held earlier that day (and which Kennedy had won), was shot and killed by a young Palestinian-American named Sirhan Sirhan, who was subsequently arrested and convicted of Kennedy's murder. (Wide World Photos)

THE MAJORITY ANSWER: A CONSERVATIVE PRESIDENT

Nineteen sixty-eight was a bad year for many Americans, and an especially bad one for Democrats. On January 31, the Viet Cong launched its Tet offensive in South Vietnam, illustrating a determination and ability to continue the war. The attack—though decisively repelled—spelled disas-

ter for President Johnson. After having assured the American people for more than four years that the United States was winning the war, he was forced to concede his overconfidence. In March, Johnson announced deescalation of the war and a drive for a negotiated peace. The second part of this televised message, however, stunned his audience. "I have concluded that I should not permit the presidency to become involved in the partisan divisions that

With the Democrats about to nominate Hubert Humphrey inside, the passions of demonstrators outside intensified—but so did the reaction of the police. Here police are shown dispersing demonstrators outside convention head-quarters. (Wide World Photos)

are developing in this political year. Accordingly, I shall not seek, and I will not accept the nomination of my party for another term as your president." Johnson, the shoo-in victor of 1964, had dropped out.

Johnson's dramatic withdrawal came in part because he could not hold the Democratic party together. Senator Eugene McCarthy had already effectively demonstrated that fact by nearly beating Johnson in the New Hampshire primary. Mc-Carthy's promise to end the war in Vietnam had won him the support of the student activists. His campaign in New Hampshire succeeded largely because of their volunteer efforts. After Johnson's withdrawal, Robert Kennedy, then holding a New York Senate seat, entered the presidential race. Vice-President Hubert Humphrey appeared on a few primary ballots as a pro-administration surrogate candidate. But McCarthy won some primaries and Kennedy others. Gradually, attention focused

on the last primary, California. There, Kennedy won by a narrow margin. There, too, leaving a victory celebration in a Los Angeles hotel, Robert Kennedy was murdered by a young Palestinian immigrant, Sirhan Sirhan.

This assassination—Kennedy's removal from the political scene—turned the Democratic convention into a struggle between an anti-administration wing, led but not controlled by Eugene McCarthy, and the party regulars, who rallied behind Hubert Humphrey. The regulars held a sufficient number of delegate votes to nominate Humphrey. But while the party regulars were winning inside the convention hall, the actions of demonstrators in the streets outside were losing them votes in the election. Thousands of people, most of them young, had come to Chicago not to attend the convention but to protest the Johnson administration's domestic and foreign policy.

U.S. GROWTH OF POPULATION, 1920–1970

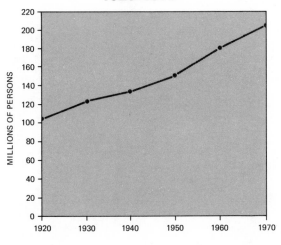

On millions of television sets around the country, Americans watched the two simultaneous events: The convention went on with the cumbersome and traditional speeches and roll calls, while outside, the police broke discipline and began to attack the demonstrators. Some protestors fought back with rocks, bottles, fists, and feet. But the main battle ended quickly. The police assumed control, and the crowd scattered to other parts of the city.

The federal government eventually indicted eight protest march leaders on conspiracy charges. But a spectacular trial produced no convictions. And little or no disciplinary action was taken against the Chicago police.

The convention itself was bitterly split between anti-Johnson forces and administration stalwarts. In that sense the battle almost assured the defeat of Hubert Humphrey, the presidential nominee and Johnson's vice-president, and the election of a Republican president that November. Richard Nixon easily won the Republican nomination at a much more peaceful convention in Miami, although the election itself proved close. Nixon won a marginal victory. He received fewer votes than in 1960 and won by only seven-tenths of one percent of the popular vote.

When Nixon took office, he promised to bring Americans into an era of retrenchment and tranquility. To accomplish this, he sought to placate the right while undercutting the left. But this center-of-the-road plan often ran into difficulties. The first three years of the Nixon administration ran a decidedly zigzag course. To appease moderate liberals, he advocated a sweeping reform of the welfare system that would set up a guaranteed minimum income for every family, but he ignored the issues of urban development and civil rights. In foreign policy, Nixon promised to end the Vietnam War, but to end it "with honor." His plan for accomplishing this surfaced slowly [see Chapter 50].

The economy presented even stickier problems. In 1969 Nixon promised no government interference and ridiculed the idea of economic controls. But rapid inflation and growing unemployment cut into his popularity. In August 1971 the president announced a three-month freeze on prices, wages, and rents, and after that he placed a ceiling on price and wage increases. Neither big business nor the unemployed were pleased, but Nixon had demonstrated a surprising flexibility.

If the silent majority was happy with Nixon, a vocal minority was not. The war in Vietnam continued, and despite United States troop withdrawals, the end did not seem near. In April 1970 Nixon announced that American troops had entered Cambodia. The promise of peace had been betrayed. Within days, protests erupted on campuses across the country. Four days after Nixon's announcement, students at Ohio's Kent State University were battling police and National Guardsmen. This now-familiar scene escalated to an unfamiliar and tragic climax. In the middle of a May 4 demonstration, National Guardsmen, without warning, opened fire on the students. Four students were killed, eleven wounded. Some of the dead were bystanders. During the rest of the month, buildings were burned and more battles took place on major college campuses. By the end of the month, hundreds of universities and colleges had been shut down, either by student strikes or by administrators fearful of violence. The President's Committee on Campus Unrest reported that, although the use of live ammunition was unwar-

*Days of anti-war dem-
onstrations broke out
at universities
throughout the
country after President
Nixon announced on
April 29, 1970 that
United States troops
had crossed the Cam-
bodian border. One of
the most violent of
these campus demon-
strations occurred at
Ohio's Kent State Uni-
versity, when students
hurled rocks at Na-
tional Guardsmen sent
to the scene by Ohio
Governor James
Rhodes. The guards-
men responded first by
firing tear gas but then
suddenly opened fire
on the students, four of
whom fell dead while
another eleven lay
wounded. The photo-
graph shows Jeffrey
Miller, one of the slain
students. (Black Star)*

ranted, the Kent State students shared the responsibility for the events of May 4, 1970. The Cambodia
spring of 1970 provoked the last of the large
campus demonstrations, but never before had student anger and frustration been displayed on such a
massive scale. The country itself, at the very beginning of the 1970s, remained bitterly divided and
troubled.

Suggested Readings
Chapters 47–48

Martin Luther King, Jr.

Lerone Bennett, *What Manner of Man* (1968);
Coretta Scott King, *My Life With Martin Luther
King, Jr.* (1969); Martin Luther King, Jr., *Why We
Can't Wait* (1964); David L. Lewis, *King: A Criti-
cal Biography* (1970).

Civil Rights and Civil Disorders

Richard Bardolph, *The Negro Vanguard* (1959);
Numan V. Bartley, *The Rise of Massive Resis-
tance* (1969); Robert Conot, *Rivers of Blood,
Years of Darkness* (1967); Harold Cruse, *The
Crisis of the Negro Intellectual* (1967); James

Forman, *The Making of Black Revolutionaries* (1972); David Garrow, *Protest at Selma* (1978); Charles V. Hamilton and Stokely Carmichael, *Black Power* (1968); John Hersey, *The Algiers Motel Incident* (1968); Steven F. Lawson, *Black Ballots* (1977); Anthony Lewis, *Portrait of a Decade* (1964); Louis E. Lomax, *The Negro Revolt* (1962); Marshall McLuhan, *Understanding Media* (1964); August Meier and Elliott Rudwick, *CORE* (1973); E. Frederick Morrow, *Black Man in the White House* (1963); Benjamin Muse, *The American Negro Revolution* (1968); Malcolm X, *The Autobiography of Malcolm X* (1965); Howard Zinn, *SNCC: The New Abolitionists* (1964).

The Supreme Court

Alexander M. Bickel, *The Supreme Court and the Idea of Progress* (1970); Albert P. Blaustein and Clarence P. Ferguson, Jr., *Desegregation and the Law* (rev. ed., 1962); Richard M. Dalfiume, *Desegregation of the U.S. Armed Forces 1939–1953* (1969); Richard Kluger, *Simple Justice* (1975); Samuel Krislow, *The Negro in Federal Employment* (1967); Philip B. Kurland, *Politics, the Constitution and the Warren Court* (1970); Clifford M. Lytle, *The Warren Court and Its Critics* (1968); Loren Miller, *The Petitioners . . . the Supreme Court . . . and the Negro* (1966).

J.F.K. and L.B.J.

Richard J. Barnet, *Intervention and Revolution* (1968); Carl M. Brauer, *John F. Kennedy and the Second Reconstruction* (1977); James MacGregor Burns, *John Kennedy* (1960); Rowland Evans and Robert Novak, *Lyndon B. Johnson* (1966); Frances Fitzgerald, *Fire in the Lake* (1972); J. William Fulbright, *The Arrogance of Power* (1967); Eric Goldman, *The Tragedy of Lyndon Johnson* (1969); David Halberstam, *The Best and the Brightest* (1972); Louis Heren, *No Hail, No Farewell* (1970); Roger Hilsman, *To Move a Nation* (1967); Townsend Hoopes, *The Limits of Intervention* (1969); Doris Kearns, *Lyndon Johnson and the American Dream* (1976); Harry McPherson, *A Political Education* (1972); Merle Miller, *Lyndon* (1980); Bruce Miroff, *The Presidential Politics of John F. Kennedy* (1976); George E. Reedy, *The Twilight of the Presidency* (1970); Herbert Y. Schandler, *The Unmaking of a President* (1977); Arthur Schlesinger, *A Thousand Days* (1965); Neil Sheehan, ed., *The Pentagon Papers* (1971); Theodore Sorenson, *Kennedy* (1965); Theodore H. White, *The Making of the President* (1961) and *The Making of the President, 1964* (1965); Tom Wicker, *JFK and LBJ* (1968).

Protests of the 1960s

Edward J. Baccioco, *The New Left in America* (1974); Lawrence M. Baskir and William A. Strauss, *The Draft, the War and the Vietnam Generation* (1978); William Henry Chafe, *The American Woman* (1968); Robert M. Fogelson, *Violence as Protest* (1971); Betty Friedan, *The Feminine Mystique* (1963); Christopher Lasch, *The Agony of the American Left* (1969); Norman Mailer, *Armies of the Night* (1968); Kate Millett, *Sexual Politics* (1970); Robin Morgan, ed., *Sisterhood is Powerful* (1970); Jack Newfield, *A Prophetic Minority* (1966); William L. O'Neill, *Coming Apart* (1971); Theodore Roszak, *The Making of a Counter-Culture* (1969); Kirkpatrick Sale, *SDS* (1973); Irwin Unger, *The Movement* (1974); Dan Wakefield, *Supernation at Peace and War* (1968).

Prosperity and Poverty

Edward C. Banfield, *The Unheavenly City* (1970); Erik Barnouw, *The Image Empire* (1970); Scott Donaldson, *The Suburban Myth* (1969); John C. Donovan, *The Politics of Poverty* (1973); Mark Gelfand, *A Nation of Cities* (1976); Otis Graham, *Toward a Planned Society* (1976); Jane Jacobs, *The Death and Life of Great American Cities* (1961); Charles E. Silberman, *Crisis in Black and White* (1964); Sam B. Warner, Jr., *The Urban Wilderness* (1972).

Watergate: The Nixon
49 Impeachment
Crisis

The young man on the witness stand was in serious trouble. Federal prosecutors had enough evidence to put him in jail for a long time. He had obstructed justice, failed to report a crime, and helped destroy evidence. Like many other people in similar situations, he was trying to soften the coming blows by testifying against his associates. But John Wesley Dean III, former White House counsel, differed from most informers. He was testifying during the last week of June 1973, not in court, but before a U.S. Senate committee probing illegal presidential campaign activities, as millions of Americans watched on television. Under penalty of perjury, John Dean was calling the president of the United States a criminal.

Tensely awaiting Dean's disclosures, the White House prepared to fight the accusations – the president's lawyer had already given the committee fifty questions designed to discredit Dean. Furthermore, the White House now claimed that Dean himself and former Attorney General John Mitchell had masterminded both the illegal activities and the attempt to cover them up.

Disowned by the White House and hopelessly ensnared by federal prosecutors, John Dean told his story for five suspense-filled days. Senators and committee lawyers questioned him closely, and journalists examined every word of his account for contradictions. All the while the White House offered opposing evidence. Everyone, especially the large television audience, searched Dean's face for clues as to his truthfulness. But at the end of his testimony, the committee and the public knew only what they had known before – either John Dean or Richard Nixon was lying. If Dean was lying, the country had just witnessed a dramatically effective performance. If President Nixon was lying, he might have to pay for it with his office – and with a criminal indictment.

On May 4, 1972, speaking at the funeral of J. Edgar Hoover, President Nixon had said, "The American people are tired of disorder, disruption, and disrespect for law. America wants to come back to the law as a way of life."

One month and thirteen days later, a night watchman at Washington's fashionable Watergate office/apartment complex noticed a door handle taped so that it would not lock. Frank Wills removed the tape, but on his next rounds he found the door taped again. At 2:30 A.M., convinced of the presence of intruders. Wills called the police. Within minutes of Wills's call police cars arrived. On the sixth floor, in the offices of the Democratic National Committee (DNC) the police found five men and a large amount of electronic equipment. They appeared to be attaching wiretaps to the DNC telephones. The police took them all downtown in handcuffs.

That afternoon the five appeared at a preliminary hearing to set bail. The government prosecutor stated that the burglars were carrying $2300, mostly in consecutively numbered $100 bills, plus elaborate and expensive electronic equipment. He asked the judge not to grant bail. When asked to state their occupations, one of the burglars (one of four Cuban Americans in the group) answered "anti-Communist." Their leader, James McCord, said that he was a security consultant recently retired from the Central Intelligence Agency.

The CIA connection and the presence of a reporter in the courtroom put the story on the front page of the next day's Washington *Post.* Then the Associated Press discovered for whom McCord worked as a security consultant—the Committee to Reelect the President (CRP), an independent group set up to run Richard Nixon's campaign and bypass the Republican National Committee. Contacted for a comment, John Mit-

The Watergate hearings reached a dramatic climax with the testimony of John Dean, here being sworn in before the Senate investigating committee by its chairman, Sam Ervin. To test the truthfulness of Dean's testimony, Senate investigators subpoenaed presidential tapes, and a confrontation with the executive branch resulted. (UPI)

Richard Nixon's former law partner, John Mitchell, became Attorney General in the Nixon administration. Mitchell and his wife Martha, whose running commentary on the Washington scene enlivened the gossip columns in the years before Watergate, are shown here in those happier days. (Fred Ward/ Black Star)

G. Gordon Liddy, former counsel to the Committee to Reelect the President, at court on January 30, 1973, for a session in the Watergate bugging trial. (UPI)

chell, former attorney general, close friend of the president, and current director of CRP (popularly pronounced "CREEP"), said, "There is no place in our campaign or in the electoral process for this type of activity, and we will not permit or condone it."

Bob Woodward, the Washington *Post* reporter who had happened to drop in on the hearing, found another lead. The *Post*'s police reporter had learned that one of the burglars carried an address book that included an entry: "E. Howard Hunt—W. H." Woodward called the White House and was given another number to call. When Woodward explained why he was calling, Hunt blurted, "Good God!" and then refused further comment. Although presidential press secretary Ron Ziegler dismissed the affair as "a third-rate burglary," the grand jury on September 15 brought in indictments against the five burglars as well as E. Howard Hunt and G. Gordon Liddy—McCord's boss at CRP. The prosecution indicated it would argue that these seven—and only these seven—had planned and executed the Watergate break-in.

Despite its scoop, the Washington *Post* seemed to lose interest shortly after the arrests. Woodward and the other Watergate reporter, Carl Bernstein, were reassigned. The paper regained interest only in late

Investigative reporters Carl Bernstein (left) and Bob Woodward (right) astounded the nation with their dogged inquiry into the Watergate burglary and their exposé of its ramifications in the Washington Post. Although their investigation drew intensive pressure from the White House, Woodward and Bernstein persisted with their diligent pursuit of all leads. (Mark Godfrey/Magnum)

July when the New York *Times*—the *Post*'s archrival—revealed that, before the break-in, fifteen phone calls had been made from the Miami home of one of the burglars to CRP. The *Post* now sent Bernstein to Miami. There, at the district attorney's office Bernstein found the bank records of the burglar, showing deposits of $114,000. Most of the checks came from Mexico.

Other evidence began to appear. The General Accounting Office found a large "slush fund of cash" kept at CRP. On a second trip to Miami, Bernstein learned of a practice called laundering—money was sent through a bank in Mexico so it could not be traced. The Mafia did it all the time, an aide to the Miami district attorney told him, and CRP had done it with $750,000 collected just before April 7 to beat the deadline established by a new law prohibiting secret political contributions. Bernstein also learned that Bernard Barker, one of the Watergate burglars, had told a friend, "I'm not worrying. They're paying for my attorney." Woodward and Bernstein now began digging in Washington, piecing bits of data together. The FBI was not pressing very hard on the case, they learned. Several people were known to have lied to investigators. Money was still going through the slush fund. Woodward also developed his own source—a high-ranking official whom he identified only as "Deep Throat." Another source was Hugh Sloan, a young Republican who had resigned as treasurer of CRP. Sloan would not talk for publication, on the advice of his attorneys. But he did confirm stories Woodward and Bernstein uncovered elsewhere.

Sloan's confirmation proved crucial for their next big story, the revelation that John Mitchell, while still attorney general in 1971, had approved payments from the secret fund. The two reporters, armed also with confirmation from sources in the Justice Department, told the story to Benjamin Bradlee, Washington *Post* editor. Bradlee examined the evidence and, after considering the interests of the paper and of Katherine Graham, its publisher, decided to let them go ahead with the story.

Bernstein called Mitchell, who had since resigned from CRP, asking him to comment on the story so far. "Jeeesus!" said Mitchell, stunned. Then: "All that crap, you're putting it in the paper? It's all been denied. Katie Graham's going to get her tit caught in a big fat wringer if that's published." The *Post* printed Mitchell's comments, and Mrs. Graham asked Bernstein if he had any further messages for her.

By October other newsmen—from *Time, Newsweek,* the Los Angeles *Times*—had picked up the story. On October 5 the Lost Angeles *Times* printed a long interview with Alfred Baldwin, who on the night of the Watergate break-in had been in a nearby motel, linked to the burglars by walkie-talkie. Baldwin said he had delivered logs of wiretapped DNC conversations to somebody at the Committee to Reelect the President. Each new discovery spurred Woodward and Bernstein to dig deeper. Encouraged by Bradlee, the two reporters now pushed to keep their advantage, but they could find only scattered fragments of evidence. Unwisely and illegally they tried to contact a member of the grand jury to find out what evidence the government was presenting. The grand juror reported it to a judge, who issued a warning—but without naming the culprits.

H. R. "Bob" Haldeman, former top White House aide, during a pause in his testimony at the Senate Watergate Committee Hearings, on July 30, 1973. Throughout his testimony, Haldeman denied John Dean's allegations that he had been involved in the Watergate cover-up. (UPI)

As November and December passed, the *Post* faced worse problems than judicial disapproval or professional rivalry. "Deep Throat" had warned that the White House was about to move against the *Post*. Under administration pressure to remain silent, the *Post*'s information sources dried up. Bradlee warned Woodward and Bernstein to do nothing they did not want known, to be careful on the telephone, and to have a lawyer handle all their personal tax matters. The White House began to exclude *Post* reporters from social occasions and, more significantly, to give news leads to its competitor, the Washington *Star*. People (known to be friends of the president) challenged the broadcasting licenses of the *Post*'s two Florida television stations. "As soon as the election is over," proclaimed Charles Colson, a White House aide with a reputation for ruthlessness, "we're going to really shove it to the *Post*."

The White House gave another sign of what Nixon's second term would be like. A few days after his easy reelection, the president gathered his cabinet, thanked them for their efforts, and announced that he planned major changes. He then turned the meeting over to H. R. Haldeman, his chief of staff, who liked to describe himself as "the president's son-of-a-bitch." "I'm not entirely sure you people understood what the president said," explained Haldeman to the secretaries of State, Defense, and the nine other departments. "When he said he wanted your resignations, *he meant he wanted your resignations.*"

Richard Nixon had often complained about lenient judges contributing to the breakdown of law and order in America. Even by Nixon's standards John J. Sirica was a tough judge. The son of an Italian immigrant, he had worked his way through law school as a boxing coach, and his stern philosophy on sentencing earned him the nickname "Maximum John." Even before the trial began, he had jailed one reporter for refusing to give tapes of an interview to the court. In the pretrial hearing, Sirica made his intentions clear. "The jury is going to want to know: What did these men go into that headquarters for? Who hired them? Who started this?"

All seven defendants had entered preliminary pleas of not guilty. But just before the trial opened in January, Hunt, who knew the four Cubans from his stint in the CIA, apparently persuaded them to plead guilty, as Hunt himself would. He promised that their families would be taken care of while they were in jail and that after a few months they would receive executive clemency. When the trial opened, all five pleaded guilty.

"Don't pull any punches—you give me straight answers," warned Sirica when the four burglars appeared before him to change their pleas. Who gave them their orders? Liddy, they answered, who was acting on his own. Had anyone mentioned executive clemency? No. Where had the $114,000 in the bank come from—the "hundred dollar bills floating around like coupons"? They didn't know—the money had arrived one day in the mail. "I'm sorry," said Sirica, "but I don't believe you."

The trial of Liddy and McCord lasted only two weeks. The prosecution argued that Liddy had received the money for legitimate security but had decided to use it for the break-in. Liddy refused to say anything; McCord insisted that he had bugged the Democrats to uncover plans for radical violence against the Republicans. Liddy was determined to keep his secret even in the face of repeated interrogation and a possibly long jail sentence. (He had earlier suggested to CRP a surefire way to guarantee his silence permanently—he would go to a specific place, and CRP could send somebody to shoot him.)

Day by day Judge Sirica grew angrier. As Theodore White wrote later, "Sirica's intelligence and dignity had been insulted by the testimony before him." Because he regarded the prosecution's questioning as inadequate, Sirica at one point dismissed the jury and asked one CRP witness forty-one questions of his own.

The jury took an hour and a half to find both Liddy and McCord guilty on all counts. After the verdict Sirica stated, "I have not been satisfied, and I am still not satisfied that all the pertinent facts have been produced before an American jury." And, he complained, "I don't think we should sit up here like nincompoops." He told all seven defendants that final sentencing would be based on their cooperation with investigators, including the Senate select committee that was then being formed to probe Watergate. Sirica put off sentencing until March 23. This would give the seven almost two months to ponder how much time they might spend in prison.

When John Sirica adjourned the trial on February 2, 1973, Watergate suspicions remained several steps away from the president. Little hard evidence implicated either the highest men at CRP or those closest to the president in the White House. In the next three months, one by one, the men who served as buffers between the scandal and the president went down.

On February 17, Nixon named L. Patrick Gray to head the FBI. As acting director, Gray had directed the bureau's investigation of Watergate, maintaining that the White House had not interfered. Although the president had so far refused to say whether administration officials would testify before the committee, Gray had no choice. Requiring confirmation by the Senate for his FBI appointment, he had to face the Judiciary Committee. On the first day of his confirmation hearings, Gray made a damaging admission without even being asked: While conducting the Watergate probe, he had met often with John Dean, counsel to the president, and shown all the evidence to him. But Gray denied that such action implied White House interference and offered to show the investigating files to the senators. Nevertheless, committee members were startled and disturbed by this admission.

Immediately the committee subpoenaed Dean. But the White House announced that Dean would not appear, citing "executive privilege" for the first though not the last time. Nixon also ordered Gray to keep his files confidential. That order came too late. On March 6 Gray released the FBI files, including one headed "Interview with Herbert Kalmbach" (the president's personal attorney). In the interview Kalmbach admitted that he had routed money for undercover political activities. The White House had been caught in an open lie, and now the scandal had reached a presidential aide. On the last day of Gray's doomed confirmation hearings, he revealed that Dean had "probably" lied to agents during the investigation.

Almost before the White House could absorb the impact of that assertion, John Sirica walked out of his chambers to find James McCord holding a letter for him. Three days later, on March 23, Sirica read the letter in open court. "Several members of my family have expressed fear for my life if I disclose knowledge of the facts in this matter," wrote the convicted burglar. But he wanted to talk. He said the defendants had been pressured to "plead guilty and remain silent"; also, that "others involved in the Watergate operation were not identified during the trial." Sirica postponed the sentencing of McCord. Hunt and the others who had pleaded guilty received "provisional" sentences of between thirty-five and forty years. Sirica told them that their final sentences would "depend primarily on whether or not you cooperate with the United States Senate."

Within days Washington knew that McCord, talking to Senate investigators, had blown the case wide open. McCord swore that Dean and Jeb Magruder, assistant director of CRP, had known beforehand of the break-in plan. He later added John Mitchell's name to the list. Hunt now testified before the grand jury. On April 2 Dean's lawyers told U.S. attorneys that he was willing to talk. Ten days later Magruder confessed to having committed perjury in the Watergate trial.

It seemed that many in the administration were racing to reach the federal prosecutors first, to plead guilty and perhaps lighten their sentences by implicating others more important. The prosecutors, of course, encouraged the panic atmosphere, telling Watergate figures that only early confession would count, that the government had virtually completed its cases. The confessional wave uncovered new issues. Why had the FBI not discovered the involvement of all these people earlier? Had there been, as McCord had indicated, a strong effort by the top government men to suppress the truth? Anyone involved in such efforts had committed a crime, obstruction of justice. Slowly interest shifted from the break-in to its aftermath — the cover-up.

Dean held the key, since he had met regularly with the president and his closest aides, Haldeman and John D. Ehrlichman. Haldeman warned Dean in early April, "Once the toothpaste is out of the tube, it's going to be very difficult to get it back in." But Dean had no intention of imitating Liddy by going stoically and silently to jail. He announced publicly on April 19 that he would not be made a "scapegoat." He had already turned over to the prosecutors documents implicating Haldeman, Ehrlichman, and Mitchell.

John D. Ehrlichman, formerly the key White House aide in charge of domestic affairs, appeared before the Senate Watergate Committee on July 30, 1973, for his fifth day of testimony. Ehrlichman attempted to discredit John Dean's testimony, as well as to defend his own role in the break-in of the office of Daniel Ellsberg's psychiatrist. (UPI)

Richard Nixon now saw only one choice. On April 30 he announced the resignation of Haldeman and Ehrlichman, "two of the finest public servants it has been my privilege to know." Speaking on television, flanked by a picture of his family and a bust of Abraham Lincoln, Nixon finished, "I must now turn my full attention to the large duties of this office. I owe it to this great office that I hold, and I owe it to you — to our country." Nixon also chose a new attorney general, Elliot Richardson, a man of unquestioned honesty, and Richardson in turn named a special Watergate prosecutor — Archibald Cox, a Harvard Law School professor and former U.S. solicitor general.

Less than three weeks later, the Senate hearings opened in Washington. Senator Sam Ervin of North Carolina, chairman of the Watergate committee, rejected the idea of calling in the higher-ups first. Instead the hearings started with the lesser fry, who confirmed what the committee already knew: Authority for the break-in had come from the top echelons of the CRP, and the defendants had been paid off during the trial. As the hearings gained momentum, the committee members rapidly became a focus of public attention. But Sam Ervin, the seventy-six-year-old chairman, stole the show. A constitutional conservative and anti-civil rights senator in the 1950s, by the late 1960s Ervin showed increasing concern for civil liberties and the boundaries of presidential power. He quickly captivated the nation with his drawling rebukes to witnesses — when his jowls would bounce and his eyebrows waggle with indignation. Responding to a complaint that he was badgering a witness, he responded, "I'm just a country lawyer from North Carolina. I just have to do it my way." Then, Samuel J. Ervin, scholar and Harvard Law School graduate, would lean back and smile not-so-innocently.

Important new revelations came out of the dramatic hearings. Magruder implicated a dozen White House and/or CRP people in the break-in and cover-up, including Haldeman, Ehrlichman, and Mitchell. Originally Liddy had suggested a program costing $1 million, involving electronic surveillance, kidnapping radical leaders and holding them in Mexico until after the Republican convention, and anchoring a yacht off the Miami coast during the Democratic convention that would be supplied with prostitutes and wired for sound and photographs. Magruder testified that when Liddy offered his plan in January 1972, Attorney General Mitchell balked—but mainly because of the cost. Mitchell, however, later approved a cheaper plan to bug the DNC.

Magruder had named everyone but the president. John Dean completed the list. He had met with Nixon four times to discuss the cover-up, Dean stated—once in September 1972 and three times in the spring of 1973. He had told the president details of the cover-up and had conveyed the demands of the Watergate burglars of up to $1 million in aid. The president had told Dean it could be raised. In their final meeting, which Dean suspected was being taped, Nixon had said his earlier statement had been a joke. Dean's account stood up under a full week of cross-examination.

So far no one had explained what had motivated the Watergate conspiracy. Dean said that the activities had arisen from an "insatiable appetite for all political intelligence, all coupled with a do-it-yourself White House staff, regardless of the law." Dean cited examples of White House paranoia, including the "enemies list"—a secret list of political opponents singled out to be harassed by the Internal Revenue Service (IRS) and other arms of the government. This list included Democratic politicians, reporters, and liberal show business people, such as Paul Newman, as well as various figures whose presence was difficult to explain, such as Joe Namath, quarterback of the New York Jets. Many of those listed proclaimed their delight at being considered a Nixon enemy.

Over the next four weeks the committee heard from all but one of the men accused. Mitchell continued to deny that he had ordered the break-in or conspired with anyone in the cover-up. He admitted only that he had kept information from the president in order to ensure Nixon's reelection. Mitchell proved himself a recalcitrant witness; at the end of his second day of testimony before the increasingly skeptical committee, he muttered sarcastically, "It's a great trial being conducted up here, isn't it?" Haldeman and Ehrlichman testified that John Dean had been the mastermind behind the cover-up and had misled them. The president's men were "stonewalling"—not without success from their point of view.

Soon another astounding development overshadowed their testimony. A committee investigator, talking to former White House aide Alexander Butterfield, discovered almost accidentally that the president had been taping conversations in the Oval Office since 1971. Three days later Butterfield told his story publicly, saying that only Nixon, Haldeman, and he had known of the White House tapes. It was no longer John Dean's word against Richard Nixon's.

On August 1 at a state dinner for Japanese Prime Minister Kakuei Tanaka, President Nixon said, "Let others spend their time dealing with the murky, small, unimportant, vicious little things. We will spend our time building a better world."

Outside, bumper stickers read: "Honk if you think he's guilty."

On October 10, NBC News interrupted a baseball game to broadcast a bulletin. Vice-President Spiro Agnew had resigned. While serving as vice-president, and earlier, as governor of Maryland, he had accepted illegal cash payments.

Over the summer of 1973, U.S. attorneys in Maryland had built a tight case against Agnew, but the evidence was not made public until August. Attorney General Elliot Richardson had watched the evidence accumulate since July and was now convinced that the Justice Department had a solid case against the vice-president. In September, before he was brought to trial, Agnew appealed to the House of Representatives, arguing that according to the Constitution a president or vice-president could not be indicted. However, the Democratic majority in the House showed little interest in helping Agnew out of his dilemma. Because Nixon too had maintained that the president was not subject to court action, he had a personal stake in the constitutional issues that would have to be decided if Agnew went to court. Richardson and the White House finally struck a compromise — over the protests of the Maryland prosecutors, who wanted to indict and convict Agnew.

The compromise was simple. Agnew resigned and pleaded no contest to one charge of income tax evasion. For this he received three years probation and a fine of $10,000. The judge announced that he would have sent Agnew to jail, given the evidence mounted against him. But Richardson in making the compromise had reasoned that it was of prime importance to have Agnew removed, since he was first in line as presidential successor. After all, Watergate might topple Nixon, or Nixon's health might break down. A long bribery trial would leave the problem of presidential succession dangerously in suspense.

Even after the Justice Department had released the evidence against him, Agnew was not contrite. Five days after resigning, the former vice-president addressed the nation on television, complaining that he was merely the victim of "the new post-Watergate political morality."

On October 6 the Providence *Journal* revealed that President Nixon on a salary of $200,000 had paid income tax of only $792.81 for 1970 and $873.03 for 1971.

Once the existence of the tapes became known, Archibald Cox wanted them. Two days after Butterfield's testimony, Cox requested nine crucial tapes. When the White House refused to deliver, claiming the tapes were covered by executive privilege, Cox went to court, asking Judge Sirica to order the president to give him the tapes. Earlier, Sirica had ruled that the tapes should be delivered to him personally, so that he could determine their relevance. The judge rejected the White House argument that the president had "absolute power" to withhold the tapes, and he denied that the constitutional doctrine of separation of powers protected the executive branch from court orders. Throughout September these issues were argued before the district court of appeals, with the White House, Cox, and Sirica himself submitting briefs.

On Friday, October 12, the court of appeals ruled 5 to 2 that Nixon had to deliver the tapes to the Senate. But it gave the president one week to work out an alternative arrangement with Cox. On the last day of the week Nixon announced a unilateral solution. He would make summaries of the tapes available to the court, and Senator John Stennis, a pro-Nixon Democrat from Mississippi, would verify the accuracy of the summaries. The president ordered Cox to cease court efforts to obtain the full tapes—or he would be fired.

The next day Cox held his own press conference. Almost apologetically, Cox said that the proposed arrangement ran counter to the pledges made when he became special prosecutor, and he would not stop seeking the tapes. He also stated that the president could not fire him—only the attorney general could.

At 8:31 that night the White House acted. Richardson had refused to fire Cox when ordered to do so and had resigned. William Ruckelshaus, deputy attorney general, had refused to fire Cox and had himself been fired. Solicitor General Robert Bork, convinced that someone had to carry out the president's orders, became acting attorney general and fired Cox. Reporters referred to the removals and resignations as the "Saturday Night Massacre."

Immediately after the announcement, callers jammed Western Union switchboards. In thirty-six hours 70,000 telegrams reached Washington, in four days 220,000, in ten days 450,000. Almost unanimously they denounced the president's action. Many newspapers called for Nixon's resignation. *Time* magazine, in its first editorial ever, asked that he quit. Nixon had badly misjudged the temper of the American people.

The White House held out for three days, then capitulated. On Wednesday Nixon's lawyer stood before Sirica to announce that the president would yield the tapes. "This president," he explained, "does not defy the law." Within two weeks the president named a new special prosecutor, Leon Jaworski of Texas, promising not to fire him without consulting congressional leaders.

But it all came too late. Congress had ample opportunity to gauge the widespread anger rising all across the country against Richard Nixon. Slowly the House leaders began moving toward impeachment. During the next eight months, while the House Judiciary Committee put its case together, the president's situation grew more and more desperate.

On November 17 Nixon spoke to a convention of newspaper editors at Disney World in Florida. He assured them, "I am not a crook."

On November 19 the president promised a group of Republican governors that there would be no more "bombshells" coming out of Watergate. The next day the White House told Sirica that one of the tapes—a conversation Nixon had with Haldeman three days after the break-in—had an eighteen-minute "gap" in it.

On December 20, Peter Rodino as chairman of the House Judiciary Committee named John Doar special counsel for the impeachment hearings. Doar was a Republican who had served in the civil rights division of the Justice Department. Congress rented space in a local hotel for Doar to carry out his work—he eventually filled it with a staff of 106 people. Soon the first partisan consequences of Watergate were felt outside of Washington. After Congressman Gerald Ford had been appointed to succeed Agnew as vice-president, a Democrat won the special election to fill Ford's seat in the House—the first Democrat to be elected by the district in sixty-four years.

But the scandal had not yet played itself out. On March 1, 1974, the Watergate grand jury indicted seven people in the Watergate cover-up, including Haldeman, Ehrlichman, and Mitchell. The Washington *Post* calculated that twenty-eight persons formerly associated with the White House or CRP had been indicted. On April 3 the Congressional Joint Committee on Internal Revenue Taxation, to whom the president had given all of his tax materials, ruled that he owed $432,787.13 in back taxes. The president said he would pay it.

Finally, on April 29, Nixon made a dramatic attempt to quiet the scandal. He released to the public twelve hundred pages of transcripts from the tapes. In a television address he argued that he had had little control of the 1972 campaign, since he had spent the year pursuing peace in Moscow and Peking. Incredibly, the president's transcripts were the most damning evidence yet. When Dean said that the defendants might want a million dollars, the President replied, "I know where it could be gotten. It is not easy, but it could be done." The tapes revealed an almost total concentration on political expediency, as well as appalling indecision. And they were studded with the phrase "expletive deleted"—meaning that a profanity had been edited out. Thus when Dean told the president that Hunt wanted $120,000 immediately, Nixon answered, "(Expletive deleted), get it." Instead of calming the storm, Nixon's release of the tapes touched off a new wave of demands for his resignation and seriously weakened his position as the Judiciary Committee hearings opened.

Unassuming Congressman Peter Rodino of Newark, New Jersey, would never be the folksy, Bible-quoting television star Sam Ervin had been. But in a methodical, cautious fashion, Rodino and Doar began organizing evidence, taking time to assemble every shred. In March, Rodino killed a move by committee liberals to subpoena Nixon. Instead Doar politely requested more tapes. In the spirit of fairness, Rodino's committee allowed the president's lawyer to participate in the hearings. Nevertheless, the White House attacked the committee's motivation and delayed supplying material.

When Doar began presenting evidence to the committee in May, many politicians complained about his and Rodino's slow, careful style. Some Democrats on the committee were ready to vote right away, and some Republicans charged that the Democrats were prolonging the agony. By the end of June, as Doar continued to present evidence with no vote in sight, Majority Leader O'Neill exerted pressure. But Rodino refused to be hurried. His committee included three conservative Southern Democrats, and Rodino wanted to hold all of them; it had seventeen Republicans, and Rodino wanted at least five of their votes. He did not want his committee to recommend impeachment on a narrow or party-line vote.

Finally in July the situation began to crystallize. Dean and other witnesses appeared before the committee. Doar made his final argument, summarizing the evidence for impeachment. Rejecting the administration argument—that impeachment required proof of a criminal act—he urged the committee to look at the pattern of all the president's acts, which added up to "the terrible deed of subverting the Constitution." He recommended four articles of impeachment: the Watergate cover-up; abuse of power, including using the CIA and IRS for political ends; failure to respond to committee subpoenas for the tapes; and the president's tax case.

At last the time had come for the committee members to make a decision. The thirty-eight members of Congress, barely known outside their own districts, had been readying themselves. The Southern Democrats had consulted with one another, as well as with Rodino and Doar. The half-dozen undecided Republicans had consulted with one another and with the Southern Democrats.

Meanwhile Leon Jaworski had been pressing for access to the tapes that had cost Cox his job—and the issue had reached the highest court in America. On the morning of July 24 the Supreme Court ruled that Richard Nixon must release the tapes. Speaking for a unanimous Court, Chief Justice Warren Burger, a Nixon appointee, declared that the courts, not the president, would decide what evidence was required by the courts: Nixon must hand over the tapes.

The president had run out of options. Defiance of the Supreme Court would precipitate impeachment by the committee and catapult the issue into the House and Senate. To avoid this, Nixon announced from San Clemente that he would surrender the tapes, although preparing them might take a little time. That same night the Judiciary Committee began its televised hearings. Each member opened with a fifteen-minute statement, which proved to be a fascinating review of the issues at stake. "This is no ordinary set of speeches," wrote one reporter. "It is the most extraordinary political debate I have ever heard—perhaps the most extraordinary since the Constitutional Convention."

On the third day the committee began considering the first impeachment article—charging that the president and his agents had acted "to delay, impede, and obstruct the investigation" and listing the means used. The last sentence stunned the room, although everyone had known it was coming: "Wherefore, Richard M. Nixon, by such conduct, warrants impeachment and trial, and removal from office."

Charles Sandman, Republican of New Jersey, opened the attack on the article, demanding "specificity"—hard facts. Proponents of the article, stung by the challenge, prepared to present justification for each clause. If Sandman and others wanted specificity, specificity they would get. For two days Democrats and Republicans rehashed the entire story: the payments to Hunt and the burglars, proven on the tapes; Dean's monitoring of the FBI investigation; the president's lack of interest in finding out the facts about the break-in; his discussing the case with Haldeman and Ehrlichman when he knew both were under suspicion; his knowledge of perjury all around him; his refusal to supply the tapes; his firing of Cox. The pro-Nixon Republicans listened to the exposition bitterly, noting only that no one had yet produced the "smoking gun" that would indisputably establish Nixon's guilt.

On the night of July 27, 1974, the Judiciary Committee passed the first article, recommending that the House impeach the president. The roll call ran down twenty Democrats, all voting aye in soft voices. The first four Republicans voted no; then one voted aye, and another, until six Republicans of the seventeen had voted to remove the president, head of their own party. Rodino, casting the last vote, made the total 27 to 11 for impeachment.

Many of the congressmen tried to compose themselves as they left the committee room to talk to reporters. Several, including Rodino, could not — they went into the antechamber and wept. The margin was big enough to counter the charge of partisanship. During the next week the committee passed two additional articles and defeated two more.

Although John Doar had not been able to present it, the "smoking gun" did exist. The president's lawyer, James St. Clair, had found it while listening to the tapes about to be turned over to Judge Sirica. He showed the transcript to Alexander Haig, a general serving as the president's chief of staff. Haig, who had assumed almost the duties of "acting president" while Nixon concentrated on his impeachment troubles, showed it to a Nixon loyalist in the Senate. The senator told Haig that the Senate would convict Nixon with this information. On the afternoon of August 2 Haig called Nixon defender Congressman Charles Wiggins, who was busy organizing the president's defense on the House floor, to the White House and showed him the key transcript. Wiggins went back to the Capitol and tore up his defense notes.

Haig and Republican leaders now sought a quick resignation. They tried to nudge the president toward that decision. On the afternoon of August 5 the president — at Haig's insistence — released three of the tapes, acknowledging that they "may further damage my case." The tapes, he stated, "are at variance with certain of my previous statements." But he did not believe the new evidence justified impeachment.

Later that night the incriminating transcript reached the press. It was taken from the tapes for June 23, 1972 — six days after the Watergate break-in. In it Haldeman informed Nixon that the FBI was pushing the investigation hard and would soon trace the burglars' cash back through Mexico to the CRP. The only way to avoid this, he told Nixon, was to direct the CIA to tell the FBI to back off for "national security" reasons. Nixon ordered Haldeman to do just that.

The next day, all ten Republicans who had supported the president on the Judiciary Committee announced that they would vote for impeachment. So did John Rhodes, the House minority leader. Senator Barry Goldwater, one of the Republican party's most respected politicians, told a group of senators, "You can only be lied to so often." Washington by now was discussing an Agnew-like deal: Nixon's resignation in exchange for immunity from prosecution. On Wednesday, August 7, Goldwater, Rhodes, and Senate Republican Leader Scott went to the White House. Impeachment by the House and conviction by the Senate would come, they told the president. Even they might have to vote to impeach on at least one article.

On Thursday evening Nixon became the first president of the United States to step down from office. His resignation took effect at noon of the next day, by which time Richard M. Nixon was already in an air force plane flying home to California. The Watergate crisis was over.

Surrounded by his family, President Nixon gave a resignation speech to his staff in the East room of the White House, before a tearful departure for San Clemente. After a year of trials and convictions, hearings and debates, subpoenas and revelations, impeachment by the House and conviction by the Senate now seemed inevitable. (Mark Godfrey/ Magnum)

Dreams Deferred: American Politics and Society in the 1970s

Many Americans considered Watergate as much a symptom as a cause of this country's troubles during the 1970s. During the early seventies, the nation endured the humiliation of a Communist take-over of all of Vietnam and an unceremonious departure of the remaining Americans and many Vietnamese supporters. Challenges to traditional post-World War II foreign policy assumptions in the post-Vietnam era eroded the country's anti-Communist consensus for half a decade, until public reaction to both the seizure of American hostages by Iranian revolutionaries and the Soviet invasion of Afghanistan restored broad public support for a strong national defense and firm diplomacy. As the United States entered the 1980s, Americans debated the uncomforting proposition that Russian military strength had come perilously close to surpassing our own, or had indeed done so, while the Soviet Union gave every indication of pursuing an aggressive global strategy that threatened the frail fabric of détente between the two superpowers.

Domestically, the 1970s brought an abeyance of the racial violence of the 1960s, though the economic, educational, and political gains that middle-class blacks had made did not noticeably improve life for the urban poor—black, Hispanic, and white—who experienced hard times throughout the decade. Nor did the economic condition of other Americans improve noticeably during the 1970s, as the country experienced two intense periods of recession, one of which continued as the decade closed. In essence, during the seventies the United States suffered its worst cumulative economic crisis since the Great Depression. Both in the earlier recession and, more pronounced, in the 1979–80 one, both unemployment and inflation rates rose to unprecedented modern heights. By the time of the Carter administration, the energy crisis, and its attendant oil shortages and price rises, had made an impact upon American consciousness and begun accustoming Americans to the realities of scarcity even amid consumer affluence. Environmental groups became more prominent and influential than ever before, and a diffuse but determined debate continued between advocates of unimpeded economic growth and those who favored accepting clear limits upon American consumption in the interests of global and national balance. Like the economy itself, the debate remained unsettled as the 1970s ended.

In the midst of continuing social and economic stresses, the forced resignations of the president and vice-president of the United States left the country stunned. Within ten years, the United States was governed by a president who was unseated by scandal, another who was unelected, and a third who became for a time the most unpopular one—according to the polls—in twentieth-century United States history. Polls showed that Americans had less confidence in politicians than in almost any other group or profession. Some comfort could be extracted from the performance of Congress, the courts, and the press during Watergate—all public institutions that displayed admirable strength and integrity.

By the time the country celebrated its bicentennial in 1976 with a range of patriotic observances and spectaculars, Americans seemed to have regained much of their optimism concerning future political prospects, an optimism that had been thrown into question by the Watergate scandals. The public paid far less attention to the scandals of the Carter administration, fewer in number and more personalized in nature than Watergate.

925

Americans seemed more concerned, as the decade closed, with assuring competent national leadership than with further reforming political institutions. By the late 1970s, there was widespread public concern that earlier reforms had seriously undermined the ability of the president, Congress, and the executive departments (including intelligence agencies) to perform. The issues that had seemed so overpowering at the time of the Vietnam and Watergate crises had faded from prominence. In their place had come growing concern over the prospects for rebuilding the American economy and reasserting U.S. power abroad.

THE NIXON ERA

Nixon Takes Over the War

When Richard Nixon entered the White House in 1969, his most urgent problem was the war in Vietnam. The issue had done much to destroy the previous administration and to get him elected. During the campaign he had announced—but refused to reveal details of—a plan to get the United States honorably out of Vietnam. As the futility of the Paris peace negotiations became apparent, Nixon's strategy assumed an even greater importance.

Gradually the president unveiled a policy of slow withdrawal of American troops with continued or increasing military and economic aid to the South Vietnamese government. This approach gained the name of "Vietnamization." Nixon broadened the idea to include *future* problems in Asia by proclaiming a "Nixon Doctrine"—that America would aid anti-Communist governments in Asia but would avoid further land wars on that continent.

Although Nixon would not accept outright defeat in Vietnam, neither would he let the war interfere with his broader aims in foreign policy. He had a particular interest in foreign affairs and often remarked that the country could almost run itself domestically. For advice and assistance, Nixon bypassed the State Department and relied on his special assistant for national security, a Harvard professor named Henry Kissinger.

The Nixon Administration and Dissent

The upheaval following the 1970 Cambodian invasion, while it did little to alter his foreign policy, deeply impressed Nixon. It appeared, as Jeb Magruder later told the Watergate Committee, that radicals and dissenters were tearing the country apart. The government launched strong public and covert efforts to stop them, by devising a broad plan calling for a council of all American intelligence organizations, including the CIA and the FBI. This group would be authorized to open mail, tap telephones, and conduct illegal break-ins. Files of the Internal Revenue Service were considered especially valuable for use against critics. In July 1970 President Nixon approved this plan. But steady opposition by FBI chief J. Edgar Hoover, who wanted no reorganization that affected his bureau, prevented the implementation of the scheme.

Nixon then carried his attack on dissenters into the political arena. During the congressional elections of 1970, Vice-President Spiro Agnew, whose attacks on the media had already gained him a wide following, proclaimed that the president would not be intimidated by "a disruptive, radical, and militant minority—the pampered prodigies of the radical liberals in the United States Senate." Nixon himself campaigned actively, claiming that "creeping permissiveness" allowed violent dissenters to "increasingly terrorize decent citizens." But the 1970 election results proved disappointing. Republicans gained only two seats in the Senate while losing nine seats in the House and seven governorships.

Nixon also had problems with the courts. Attorney General John Mitchell had obtained a lower court injunction to prevent the New York *Times* from publishing the "Pentagon Papers," but by a 6-to-3 vote the Supreme Court ruled that the newspaper had acted within its First Amendment rights. A year later, on June 19, 1972, a unanimous Court that included three Nixon appointees rejected Mitchell's contention that the president possessed inherent power to wiretap without a court order. The decision came two days after the Watergate burglars' arrest.

THE NATIONAL DEBT (1910-1980) AND THE GROSS NATIONAL PRODUCT (1931-1980)

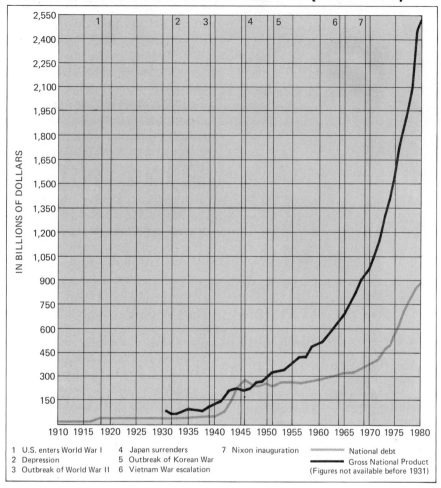

IN BILLIONS OF DOLLARS

1 U.S. enters World War I	4 Japan surrenders
2 Depression	5 Outbreak of Korean War
3 Outbreak of World War II	6 Vietnam War escalation

7 Nixon inauguration

〰〰 National debt
━━━ Gross National Product
(Figures not available before 1931)

Nixon and the Economy

Nixon had originally intended to reduce federal spending and work toward a balanced budget—an aim piously invoked by many presidents (including FDR) but seldom pursued. Nixon followed such a belt-tightening policy during his first year in power. By mid-1970 the country had entered a serious recession, and at the end of that year unemployment stood at 6.2 percent—almost twice the level under Johnson.

At the same time prices rose steadily. This unaccustomed combination of high unemployment, inflation, and limited economic growth soon acquired the name "stagflation," although Democrats preferred the political label "Nixonomics." Actually, the inflation was hardly Nixon's fault. It resulted largely from heavy spending for the Vietnam War and expanded social programs, combined with Johnson's refusal, for political reasons, to raise taxes. By 1971 the state of the economy posed a potent threat to Nixon's reelection, causing him to reverse himself on spending and taxes. By election time he had managed to force down the unemployment rate.

In August of 1971 Nixon made an even more startling turnaround. Throughout his career he had

During President Nixon's visit to China in 1972, he and Premier Chou En-lai reviewed the Chinese Red Guard. Scenes like this startled the American public, accustomed to thinking in Cold War terms. (UPI)

opposed government controls on wages and prices. But with little more than a year to go before the election, the president imposed a ninety-day freeze on wages and prices, which he labeled Phase I of a new economic plan. In the fall the economy entered Phase II, with limits on wage and price increases. Both phases worked fairly well, controlling inflation through 1972.

After the election Nixon began cutting back on government programs, especially social welfare programs. He inaugurated Phase III, a system of largely voluntary limits on increases. The removal of mandatory controls, combined with the additional money the administration had pumped into the economy, produced the sharpest burst of inflation since World War II.

Détente with Russia and China

Phase I was not the only shock Nixon produced in the summer of 1971. The president, who had been perhaps the country's leading anti-Communist for twenty years, announced that he would visit the People's Republic of China. Henry Kissinger had already secretly visited Peking and made arrangements for Nixon's trip.

Only a politician like Nixon, possessing impeccable credentials as an anti-Communist, could have altered American policy toward Communist China. The president's visit early in 1972 provided a startling experience for Americans still thinking in Cold War stereotypes. There was Dick Nixon, the man who had talked down Nikita Khrushchev, cozying up to Mao Tse-tung and Chou En-lai while admiring the Great Wall as if viewing Hoover Dam on a campaign tour. By the time of Nixon's visit the United States had acquiesced in the admission of mainland China to the United Nations. Shortly after the president's visit, China and the United States established offices in each other's capitals, although continued American support for the Nationalist Chinese on Formosa ruled out full diplomatic relations.

Three months later, Nixon was traveling again, this time to the Soviet Union. Nixon and Kissinger were determined to build on the easing of Soviet–American relations (détente) that had begun during the Kennedy and Johnson years. Since 1969 the two superpowers had been engaged in the SALT (Strategic Arms Limitation Talks) negotiations, and Nixon and Soviet leader Brezhnev now signed SALT I, a temporary and limited agreement to cut back on some new weapons. The leaders also agreed to expand trade, beginning with a large Russian purchase of American wheat. The total sale amounted to a quarter of the American crop for 1972, at a price well below that of the American market. For Americans the first concrete result of détente was a sharp increase in the price of bread.

Nixon did not intend, however, that more relaxed relations should include an American defeat in Vietnam. Indeed, his dealings with two Communist powers, Russia and China, who feared one another at least as much as each feared the United States, apparently enabled him to take bolder steps in Indochina. In March 1972, responding to expanded North Vietnamese activities in the south, Nixon first unleashed heavy American bombing on Hanoi and Haiphong (the largest cities of North Vietnam) and then mined the harbor of Haiphong, closing it to all ships. Despite rumblings from Moscow and Peking, as well as protests from many Americans, neither the Communist superpowers nor the American people reacted strongly to Nixon's new military offensive. The U.S. effort in Vietnam had become enormously expensive and costly in human as well as in dollar terms.

The Election of 1972

Nixon had greatly strengthened his political position with his trips to China and Russia as well as some easing of the recession. He also gained strength from political floundering on the Democratic side. Senator George McGovern of South Dakota led the forces of antiwar activists and students that had been led by Eugene McCarthy and Robert Kennedy in 1968. Benefiting from divided opposition and recent party reforms, McGovern won Democratic convention delegates faster than any other candidate. To most of the Democratic political pros and to labor leaders allied with the party, McGovern seemed too extreme. But he had enough delegates, barely enough, to win nomination, and he named Senator Thomas Eagleton of Missouri as his running mate.

McGovern's nomination did not heal the party division. Many Democratic politicians refused to rally behind him. He represented something novel on the American political scene. The "new politics" centered on youth, the rights of ethnic minorities, and the aspirations of women. McGovern proposed several controversial schemes — for example, that every family whose income fell below $10,000 should receive a yearly cash grant of $1,000. Ideas such as these, as well as the overly liberal impression he and his campaigners created, alienated many normally reliable sources of Democratic political power.

McGovern's slim chances faded when reports began to circulate that Eagleton had been treated for psychiatric disorders. That posed a problem which McGovern's maladroit response turned into a crisis. McGovern at first announced that he supported Eagleton "one thousand percent." But

soon he asked for the vice-presidential candidate's resignation, an act interpreted by many as both vacillating and ruthless. After four Democrats had publicly rejected McGovern's offer, Sargent Shriver, a brother-in-law of John and Robert Kennedy, became Eagleton's replacement.

Nixon, meanwhile, campaigned by seeming to be above politics. He stayed in the White House while presidential surrogates took on McGovern. To separate himself from the Republican party organization, he set up CRP (Committee to Reelect the President), and he put an emphasis on "Democrats for Nixon," a group of Democrats alienated by McGovern. Aiming for the largest victory possible, he refused to associate his campaign with those of Republican congressional candidates.

Nixon's personal victory, or at least McGovern's defeat, was enormous. The president carried forty-nine states, losing only Massachusetts and the District of Columbia. But while the president claimed a broad mandate, he had brought in only thirteen Republican congressmen, and his party had actually lost two seats in the Senate. The "deadlock of democracy" (GOP control of the White House and Democratic control of Congress) would continue.

PREPARING FOR THE SECOND TERM

Shortly after the election, Haldeman's demand for the resignation of cabinet members was echoed throughout the executive branch, and many high-level appointees were replaced by Nixon loyalists. The actions reflected a long-standing Nixon desire to centralize control of the executive branch by the White House.

The president also tightened control over the cabinet. Congress had earlier rejected a reorganization plan, but Nixon now named Kissinger, Secretary of the Treasury George Schultz, and Roy Ash, director of the Nixon-created Office of Management and Budget, as a "supercabinet," to whom other cabinet members would report. The supercabinet, in turn, would report to Haldeman and Ehrlichman. With such a structure, Nixon made himself the most isolated president of modern times.

The president also claimed ever-widening powers for his office. He issued a broad definition of "executive privilege," limiting the information Congress could require the executive branch to supply. He also announced that he would impound funds appropriated by Congress that he felt should not be spent, refusing to release $6 billion appropriated by Congress for environmental programs. In March, vetoing a number of spending bills, the president announced that even if Congress overrode his vetoes he would impound the money.

Nixon also celebrated his reelection with a treaty in Vietnam. Kissinger had announced a few days before the election that "peace is at hand." But snags developed, and Nixon responded with the heaviest bombing of the war in December—a saturation "carpet bombing" of parts of Hanoi. Shortly after Nixon's inauguration, the two sides signed a treaty calling for a permanent cease-fire and removal of American troops. But despite American troop withdrawal, the war continued among the Vietnamese, and U.S. B-52 bombers continued to pound Communist forces in Cambodia.

Government During Watergate

Despite Nixon's ambitious plans, Watergate quickly closed in on him. After McCord, Magruder, and Dean began talking, the president lost standing in the country, and what little influence he had retained over Congress evaporated. In August 1973 Congress forced Nixon to end the bombing in Cambodia. Shortly thereafter Congress passed the War Powers Act, stating that unless Congress approved an American military intervention within sixty days the president must withdraw troops. Nixon vetoed the bill, but both houses overrode his veto.

By then, Nixon's ability to govern was shaken. After the forced resignation of Agnew, Nixon hosted a White House extravaganza to announce his selection of House Minority Leader Gerald Ford as vice-president, the first exercise of a new presidential power under the Twenty-Fifth Amendment. A cabinet member remarked to House Majority Leader O'Neill that they might not see anything like it again for a long time. "No," answered O'Neill, "not for about eight months."

Within certain limits, however, Nixon could still act decisively. In October, Egypt, Syria, and Iraq, with heavy Soviet arms support, attacked Israel. Nixon, in the midst of the Agnew and Watergate crises, launched a huge American airlift to the Israelis, possibly preventing a disastrous defeat for the Jewish state. America's European allies, heavily dependent on Arab oil, refused to assist and publicly expressed their anger.

Despite the strain on the NATO alliance, Nixon and Kissinger could claim success in preventing Israel's extinction and, later, in negotiating a Middle East cease-fire. But when Nixon, warning of the danger of Russian intervention in the area, put all American forces on a worldwide military alert, the effects of Watergate-inspired skepticism became obvious. Americans openly speculated on how much Nixon's political difficulties had influenced him in calling the alert.

Even the president's success brought major problems. Four days after Nixon began airlifting supplies to the Israelis, on October 17, 1973, Arab oil-producing nations cut off petroleum shipments to the United States. At the time of the oil embargo, the United States was importing almost 2 million barrels of petroleum daily (more than a tenth of American consumption) from the Middle East and North Africa. Long before the embargo, however, the country had faced the prospect of shortages. Fuel consumption had been increasing far more rapidly than domestic fuel production. Moreover, the U.S. output of polluting fuels, such as coal, was being cut back for environmental reasons.

The Arab embargo intensified the country's problems, especially when the members of the Organization of Petroleum Exporting Countries (OPEC) exploited the situation to raise prices dramatically. Founded in 1960, OPEC had succeeded in doubling oil prices from their previous levels even in the years prior to the 1973 embargo, and both Arab and non-Arab members of the cartel agreed on a series of price hikes between October 1973 and January 1974 that quadrupled oil prices from their level prior to the latest Israeli–Arab war.

In the United States, the results were immediate and unpleasant. The price of heating oil tripled, and gas prices more than doubled – when gas was available. Long lines of cars formed outside and around gas stations, which remained open for only a few hours each day. Oil company profits also skyrocketed, further angering the public and arousing many politicians.

The president refused to enforce controls on either oil prices or profits, preferring instead to try to ease demand. A national speed limit of fifty-five miles an hour was adopted; Sunday gasoline sales were banned; and Nixon asked Americans to turn down their thermostats. With voluntary restrictions, and an unusually mild winter, the country came through the boycott.

During the winter, Kissinger, now secretary of state, made numerous trips to the Middle East, testing his hand at shuttle diplomacy. Since the Arabs refused to talk directly with the Israelis, he had to fly between the hostile capitals and succeeded in working out a disengagement of opposing troops. By March the Arabs ended the oil boycott, and the situation ended. But the U.S. government had failed to establish a long-term answer to the problem of diminishing energy resources.

Henry Kissinger's accomplishments in the Middle East provided the one and only consolation for Richard Nixon's administration in its last days. Through mid-1974, as Nixon approached his final reckoning, the White House became increasingly paralyzed. By the summer of that year, as the Judiciary Committee began its hearings, the president was almost entirely preoccupied with the unsuccessful efforts to clear his name and to remain in office.

THE FORD ADMINISTRATION

Gerald Ford's electorate had never been larger than the voters of Grand Rapids, Michigan. Still President Ford received strong support when he assumed the office. His openness seemed a welcome change after Nixon's secretiveness; Americans relaxed when he announced, "Our long national nightmare is over." The comic strip *Doonesbury* showed a brick wall around the White House being demolished. A television crew went into the White House to show the new president making his own breakfast.

Some of the beatific aura faded, however, a month after the inauguration – when Ford pardoned Nixon for any criminal actions committed during his presidency. Ford had said during his confirmation hearings that he did not expect to take such an action, and his new press secretary resigned in protest. At a time when most of Nixon's White House associates faced prosecution and possible jail terms, many Americans objected to Ford's action as charity misplaced and presidential power misused.

The pardon played a large role in the congressional campaign of November 1974. Republicans had originally thought that Ford, by replacing Nixon, would save the party from heavy congressional losses. Ford campaigned strenuously and tried to rally support for his policies with the slogan, soon to be ridiculed widely, "WIN – Whip inflation now." But Democrats increased their already large majorities in both houses of Congress.

Ford and the New Congress

In the new post-Watergate atmosphere, Democrats, with top-heavy majorities in Congress, now sought to take policy initiative away from the White House. Many journalists and political scientists had warned, after Vietnam and Watergate, that the presidency had become too powerful.

Congress and the president opposed each other on two major issues during the balance of Ford's term – the economy and the energy crisis. By early 1975 the economy appeared to be approaching disaster. Unemployment was running at levels near 10 percent, especially among auto workers and in the construction and aerospace industries. Although inflation had been brought under some control and the rate of price increases had slackened, economic growth had also declined.

Energy seemed to be at least as great a problem. Not only had OPEC quadrupled oil prices within a short period, but the United States's own supplies of oil could not last much longer. Intensive efforts to find and develop more, such as on the north slope of Alaska and off the Atlantic and Pacific coastlines, raised environmental questions and political controversy. The same problems applied to the development of America's huge supplies of coal, and widespread use of alternative fuel

The first man to reach the White House without ever winning a national election, Gerald R. Ford, shown here with his wife Betty, had entered the House of Representatives in 1948 as congressman from Grand Rapids, Michigan. After twenty-five years in the House, ten of them as minority leader, Ford was appointed to the vice-presidency when Spiro Agnew resigned in August 1973. He became president on August 9, 1974, upon Nixon's resignation. (Mark Godfrey/Magnum)

sources, such as solar and atomic energy, were decades and billions of dollars away.

Congressional militancy proved no match for problems of such magnitude. Democrats struggled in vain to produce an energy bill acceptable to one another, let alone strong enough to override a presidential veto. Congress did manage to produce a number of bills intended to boost the economy, but only one major measure—a compromise tax cut in the spring of 1975—became law. Most of the others were vetoed by Ford, and Democrats rarely managed to muster the two-thirds majority needed to override. Although the new Congress had restated some congressional prerogatives, it had again been shown that effective national government depended on strong presidential leadership.

Ford and Foreign Affairs

Congress had some success in deflecting Ford's foreign policy proposals. In March 1975 North Vietnamese troops launched a major offensive, and the South Vietnamese retreat quickly turned into a rout. With the Saigon government on the verge of collapse, Ford requested $700 million in emergency aid for South Vietnam and a smaller amount for Cambodia, also threatened by a Communist take-over.

At virtually the last moment in the fifteen-year Indochina War, Congress asserted itself and refused the request for aid, which would probably have come too late to change the outcome. By mid-April the Communist armies had captured the capital of Cambodia, and by the end of the month Saigon had fallen. The war was over.

But its final scene would remain to haunt Americans. Thousands of Vietnamese who had cooperated with the American forces tried desperately to get aboard departing American helicopters and ships. Many had been promised passage out of the country and had remained at their jobs on the strength of these assurances. Now American marines fought off the thousands of terrified Vietnamese swarming over the walls of the American embassy, begging to be taken along. One American devised a simple, hard rule for the last days: "Don't look in their eyes."

Post-Vietnam Foreign Policy

By mid-1975 it was becoming more and more difficult to see American foreign policy as an anti-Communist crusade. Ford had retained both Nixon's secretary of state, Henry Kissinger, and his policy of détente with the Russians. America and the Soviet Union reached a new level of agreement in the SALT talks and, along with the European powers, signed a major agreement at Helsinki calling for peace and recognizing territorial changes made at the end of World War II.

But some Americans, including many liberals, upset with Russian policy on the Middle East and treatment of Soviet Jews, began to question the value of détente. They pointed out that parts of the Helsinki Agreement, such as those calling for respect for human rights and free travel from country to country had been ignored by the Soviet Union. Those opposed to détente also cited the large Soviet involvement in Angola, where a withdrawal of Portuguese colonial authority had led to a civil war between Marxist and pro-Western factions. With hundreds of millions of dollars in Russian military aid, and several thousand Cuban soldiers, the Marxists won easily. But if Angola showed the unchanged nature of Soviet policy, it also illustrated the different attitude of Congress, which refused President Ford's request for aid to the pro-Western Angolans and directed an immediate end to all American involvement.

Aid to Angola and congressional attitudes were also involved in another controversy related to foreign affairs. Congressional committees dug out large amounts of evidence of illegal and disturbing activities by the CIA, including aborted assassination plots against foreign leaders. Ford announced new controls on the agency. But neither Congress nor the public seemed to consider the new directive the final answer, possibly because neither knew what actions would serve both the interests of American freedom *and* security.

Ford and the Economy

By early 1976 the economy seemed to be making some improvement. The president declared the recession over. Unemployment, although still high, had come down somewhat, and the stock market was running surprisingly high. The White House pointed to the improvement as an argument against further bills passed by Congress to stimulate the economy.

In the midst of the improvement at least one highly disturbing situation boiled over. New York City was rapidly going bankrupt and would soon be unable to cover its debt obligations. Nobody knew exactly how far the effects of a default by the nation's largest city would extend, but many people felt that it would have an appalling effect on the sluggishly improving economy. Others argued that New York had brought the problem on itself through fiscal mismanagement and overgenerous welfare and employee benefits. President Ford, bidding for conservative support, delivered a speech opposing federal aid to the city so strongly that the pro-Republican New York *Daily News* headlined the story, "FORD TO CITY: DROP DEAD."

In the end, Ford approved some federal aid. But while New York's problem remained to some extent unique, it gave a foretaste of what might happen to many American cities. Since World War II, the middle and upper-middle classes and many businesses had fled the inner city, while welfare costs and the cities' low-income population stayed behind. New York's plight reminded Americans that the urban crisis, while no longer receiving the attention it had during the 1960s, had not been solved or even eased.

THE BICENTENNIAL ELECTION

When the two major presidential candidates gained their parties' first-ballot nominations at the

Betty Friedan, theorist and organizer, emerged as a public figure during the 1960s as the first important leader of the contemporary women's rights movement. She achieved national recognition when her trailblazing book, *The Feminine Mystique,* was published in 1963, and she has remained a front-rank leader of American feminism since that time.

A true daughter of Middle America, Friedan was born in Peoria, Illinois, in 1921 and attended Smith College, graduating in 1942. After a period in graduate school studying psychology at the University of California at Berkeley, she married and devoted herself to raising three children. Friedan found herself profoundly dissatisfied with unrelieved domesticity and began speculating as to how widespread among other women her own feelings might be. A questionnaire sent to Smith College classmates showed that many others shared the bitterness at having been forced out of budding careers during the postwar period into lives as suburban matrons dedicated exclusively to their families.

The Feminine Mystique, which attacked the belief that personal fulfillment could be found in such unrelieved commitment to domesticity, became a best-seller and brought Friedan wide recognition. Its argument that most major institutions within American society (including the schools and colleges) had reinforced women's feelings that their sense of self-worth could only be derived satisfactorily from lives devoted exclusively to marriage and motherhood struck an especially responsive chord among women of Friedan's generation.

Turning from research to activism, Friedan helped found the National Organization of Women (NOW) in 1966 "to bring women into the mainstream . . . in truly equal partnership with men." She became NOW's first president and played a pivotal role in its earliest campaigns to achieve equal rights in employment, obtain passage of an Equal Rights Amendment (ERA), gain the creation of federally funded day-care centers for working mothers, and institute other reforms. As the women's movement grew, it found itself embroiled in factional struggles that left Friedan (among others) more often than not defending positions that more radical feminists felt were overly cautious. Friedan left the presidency of NOW in 1970 but continued her active career as both writer and organizer, becoming perhaps the most popular women's rights speaker on the campuses and before audiences of younger women.

She published a collection of essays and per-

party conventions, it appeared that the preconvention presidential battle had been cut-and-dried. However, although the 1976 campaign produced first-ballot nominations, things were anything but predetermined.

First, Gerald Ford had to fashion for himself a credible image as a presidential candidate, something more than the caretaker role assigned him by the Watergate mess and the Nixon resignation. Second, Ford had to fight off a strong challenger.

To avoid becoming an interim president, an appointed lame duck, Ford announced early that he would run for president. He became less apologetic about his status, acting more like a chief executive and less like a political accident. He even took to the skies, emulating Nixon's eye-opening visits to China and Russia, but not necessarily reaping the same results. Ford also stripped himself of another lame duck, the man he had appointed vice-president, New York's ex-governor Nelson Rockefeller—a person who carried an aura of liberal Republicanism about him. GOP conservatives still viewed Rockefeller with suspicion and wanted his head. They got it.

In the wings (the right wing, to be precise) stood Ronald Reagan, ex-movie star, former two-term governor of California, and still a dashing figure in his mid-sixties. He offered a fundamentalist Republican line, attacking the federal government, the welfare state, and détente. After a hard-fought battle in the primaries, the Republican convention nominated Ford on the first ballot. He chose Senator Robert Dole as his running mate.

In the enemy camp, the Democrats began the election year with more generals than buck privates. At least a dozen persons declared for the

sonal writings in 1976 called *It Changed My Life: Writings on the Women's Movement,* which combined memoir and history of the movement. In that book and in her speeches and writings elsewhere, Friedan has stressed a continuing theme in her perception of feminism: that it must avoid becoming identified with an aggressively anti-male or anti-societal set of beliefs and, instead, become a form of humanism—a "human liberation" movement, in her phrase. Throughout her career, therefore, Friedan has opposed within feminist ranks "an overfocus on sexual issues, on sexual politics, as opposed to the condition of women in society in general."

Although she has remained controversial, both within the women's movement and to its opponents, Betty Friedan's influence within feminism has normally been toward stressing pragmatic reforms to achieve an American society more equal in its daily treatment of men and women. More than one feminist has stressed, in words similar to those of Jean Sprain Wilson, Friedan's critical influence on the modern women's movement: "For sheer impact on the lives of American women, no book written in the sixties compares with Betty Friedan's *Feminine Mystique,* sometimes called the *Uncle Tom's Cabin* of the wom-

Betty Friedan

(Wide World Photos)

en's liberation movement." It will undoubtedly be as the author of that landmark book and later writings, even more than as a founder of NOW and persistent activist, that Betty Friedan will continue to leave her mark.

nomination. One of them, a Georgia politician with a permanent smile and an undistinguished record in his state's politics, seemed the least likely to succeed.

James Earl Carter, Jr. (he preferred to be called Jimmy) had announced in 1974 that he intended to become president. Those outside of his entourage thought Carter was as likely to walk on the moon. But Carter's persistence—and a brilliant strategic "game plan" by his close adviser, Hamilton Jordan—slowly changed his candidacy from something almost comic into something substantial. Though he was not taken too seriously before the primaries, Jimmy would not quit—soon enough his considerable political talents began to draw the public's attention.

In January 1976, Carter won Iowa delegates (and the attention of the media); a month later he

repeated with a win in New Hampshire. He was moving away from the pack, a process accelerated greatly in subsequent Southern primaries, which included his rout of Alabama's perennial maverick George Wallace. Democratic leaders such as Senators Henry Jackson and Birch Bayh pulled out of the contest. A few more entered. But it was over by early June, when Carter won the Ohio primary, and endorsements from most of the party's establishment poured in. So it was off to the Democratic convention in New York City in mid-July for this self-styled Georgia peanut farmer. (Actually the Carter family's wholesale peanut business and land holdings in Plains, Georgia, kept them moderately wealthy.)

Before the politicos got together, the country had an anniversary to face—July 4, 1976. President Ford spent the preceding days in Penn-

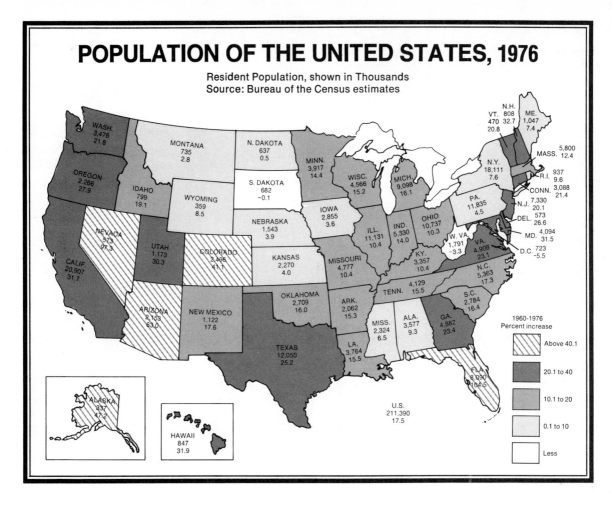

POPULATION OF THE UNITED STATES, 1976

Resident Population, shown in Thousands
Source: Bureau of the Census estimates

State	Population	%
WASH.	3,476	21.8
MONTANA	735	2.8
N. DAKOTA	637	0.5
MINN.	3,917	14.4
N.H.	808	20.8
VT.	470	
ME.	1,047	7.4
MASS.	5,800	12.4
OREGON	2,266	27.9
IDAHO	799	19.1
WYOMING	359	8.5
S. DAKOTA	682	-0.1
WISC.	4,566	15.2
MICH.	9,098	16.1
N.Y.	18,111	7.6
R.I.	937	9.6
CONN.	3,088	21.4
IOWA	2,855	3.6
NEBRASKA	1,543	3.9
PA.	11,835	4.5
N.J.	7,330	20.1
NEVADA	573	97.3
UTAH	1,173	30.3
COLORADO	2,496	41.1
KANSAS	2,270	4.0
ILL.	11,131	10.4
IND.	5,330	14.0
OHIO	10,737	10.3
W. VA.	1,791	-3.3
DEL.	573	26.6
MD.	4,094	31.5
CALIF.	20,907	31.7
MISSOURI	4,777	10.4
KY.	3,357	10.4
VA.	4,908	23.1
D.C.	723	-5.5
ARIZONA	2,153	63.0
NEW MEXICO	1,122	17.6
OKLAHOMA	2,709	16.0
ARK.	2,062	15.3
TENN.	4,129	15.5
N.C.	5,363	17.3
S.C.	2,784	16.4
TEXAS	12,050	25.2
LA.	3,764	15.5
MISS.	2,324	6.5
ALA.	3,577	9.3
GA.	4,882	23.4
FLA.	8,090	104.5
ALASKA	337	47.2
HAWAII	847	31.9
U.S.	211,390	17.5

1960-1976
Percent increase

- Above 40.1
- 20.1 to 40
- 10.1 to 20
- 0.1 to 10
- Less

sylvania—at Valley Forge and then at Independence Hall in Philadelphia, where one million persons celebrated America's two hundredth birthday. Then on to New York. The city and its neighbors spent a festive, frolicsome Sunday on the Glorious Fourth. The highlight of this spectacular was the procession of hundreds of ships and boats up the Hudson River, featuring sixteen "tall ships"— beautiful high-masted sailing ships from naval academies around the world. Not since the moon landing in 1969 had American morale received a greater boost.

New York's fourth of July euphoria lingered on a bit. Democrats in convention from July 12 through 15 took advantage of it. Carter knew he had the nomination, and to help re-cement the Democratic coalition, he put a Northern, prolabor liberal—Walter Mondale of Minnesota—on the ticket. At that point it looked as if Carter would trounce Ford.

But midyear polls and November election results seldom jibe. The campaign, not nearly so exciting as the primary fights, narrowed the margin established by the pollsters. Carter's religiosity (a "born again" Southern Baptist) was always an issue, but a lessening problem for him as he became better known.

Election year 1976 saw the return of direct presidential debates, a device used only once before, in 1960. This time the incumbent president, Ford, decided to gamble by debating with Carter three times. The debates were televised, and Carter later stated that it was his performances in the second and third debates that won him the election.

But rarely in close elections can a single factor be isolated as decisive. The 1976 election was close. Electoral vote counts usually show a good spread, but in 1976 the vote was Carter 297 to Ford 241. Carter got 50.4 percent of the popular vote (to Ford's 48.5 percent), so he could at least claim to be a majority president. But neither he nor Ford had excited the voters—only 53 percent of Americans eligible to vote did so, a drop of 2 percent since 1972, and a considerable drop from the 63 percent of eligibles who had voted in 1960. Many Americans simply did not care. And among the least involved in the electoral process were those in the eighteen to twenty-one age group granted voting rights in 1972. Despite the stay-at-homes, Carter had carried enough of the industrial Northeast, and his own near solid South to win election. It was

Former Georgia Governor Jimmy Carter, surrounded by his family, at the Democratic National Convention of 1976 in New York City. The front-runner in the primaries, Carter had stressed his role as a non-Washingtonian "outsider," at a time when the memory of Watergate put "insiders" under suspicion. (Elliott Erwitt/ Magnum)

virtually an East–West split, with Ford carrying most Western states.

Carter's inaugural day, January 20, 1977, was upbeat and informal. The address contained a characteristic biblical quotation and a plea that "we must again have faith in our country—and in one another." The president also issued an inaugural statement to the world, imprecise but reassuring, indicating that he appreciated both the extent and the limits of American power. Once installed, the president and Mrs. Carter walked from Capitol Hill to the White House, a distance normally traveled by a president in a glass-topped bullet-proof limousine. At night, inaugural parties replaced inaugural balls, and no one seemed to mind the informality.

THE CARTER ADMINISTRATION

All new presidents want to begin afresh. They want to bury old, divisive issues, those that can upset *their* administrations as much as the preceding ones. Jimmy Carter was no exception. On the day after he assumed office, Carter pardoned Vietnam era draft evaders, hoping thereby to begin healing the wounds inflicted upon the American body politic by Vietnam era domestic strife. Behind the gleaming smile and the insistence upon being inaugurated president (and addressed afterward) as Jimmy, not James, Carter lay a basically somber man, one who recognized that if Vietnam continued to haunt American politics, his own difficulties in the White House would be multiplied.

The Carter administration benefited also from a sharp decline in the bitter tensions of the Watergate crisis during the presidency of Gerald Ford. Although Ford often seemed unable to control personally the policy initiatives taken by strong-willed cabinet members such as Henry Kissinger, his own integrity and candor contrasted refreshingly with the secretive disingenuousness of the Nixon presidency in its final years. Ford played a vital role in restoring American confidence in and respect for the institution of the presidency. Jimmy Carter became the beneficiary of Gerald Ford's efforts to encourage a more "open presidency."

Carter reached Washington with less knowledge of the operations and personnel of national government than any president since Coolidge. He chose as his key advisers a number of officials who had served Presidents Kennedy and Johnson: among them Cyrus Vance as secretary of state, Michael Blumenthal at Treasury, Harold Brown at Defense, Joseph Califano at Health, Education, and Welfare, Zbigniew Brzezinski as national security adviser. Republican bureaucrat James Schlesinger became Carter's adviser on energy policy and later headed the Department of Energy, which he helped to create. The key post of budget director went to a Georgia banker and close Carter political associate named Bert Lance. Of this group, only Brown and Brzezinski lasted out the full 1977–80 period, resignations or firings leading to the others' departure. For domestic political and policy advice, Carter turned mainly to a trusted small circle of Georgians, including Lance and Griffin Bell, an Atlanta lawyer who became attorney general (and resigned in 1979). Others prominent in the Carter White House included Hamilton Jordan, the president's key political strategist, and Press Secretary Jody Powell.

The major domestic problems Carter confronted involved economic and energy policies. Unemployment had risen in 1977 to 7.5 percent of the American work force, and inflation continued at disturbingly high levels despite the continued recession. By 1978, inflation would return to double digit levels and continue spurting upward for the remainder of Carter's presidency. By late 1980 Carter had to contend with an annual inflation rate over three times the 4 percent he had confidently set as his 1980 goal in 1977.

Nor did Carter prove successful in implementing fully his energy proposals. In an April 1977 speech, Carter called for a separate Department of Energy and urged a variety of energy conservation measures—rather than measures to increase production—to handle the problem. The president proposed (among other things) an excise tax on cars with poor gas mileage, authority to levy a tax on gasoline which could reach a fifty-cent-per-gallon maximum, increased taxes on domestic crude oil to make it as costly as imported fuel (thereby lowering demand), tax incentives to encourage public utilities and other businesses to shift from oil to ("clean") coal production, and tax incentives to encourage homeowners to better insulate their houses. American dependence on foreign energy supplies had reached the point, Carter warned, where it amounted to a "moral equivalent of war."

But tough words do not necessarily resolve tougher problems. Over the next four years, Americans did conserve energy in unprecedented amounts—driving less, buying more fuel-efficient cars, carefully insulating their homes, heating their houses at lower temperatures in winter, and driving at slower speeds. However, although Americans proved less wasteful of energy, both because of its increased cost and for patriotic reasons, they did not rush to endorse the more extreme Carter proposals, such as a punitive gasoline tax. Just as Gerald Ford's Whip-Inflation-Now (WIN) campaign had petered out, Jimmy Carter's Moral Equivalent of War (or MEOW, as one unimpressed wit called it) evoked little popular or congressional enthusiasm.

Energy legislation moved glacially through Congress, and the compromise measure that finally emerged in mid-1978 bore little resemblance to Carter's original proposals. Legislators from the oil- and gas-producing states of the Southwest, aided by energy company lobbyists, succeeded in enacting provisions that "deregulated" natural gas over a seven-year period (allowing for gradual price rises) and quashed other special taxes that, they argued, would discourage efforts to find new domestic oil and gas supplies. On some aspects of the program, Carter proved successful: a Department of Energy was created; homeowners received tax credits for insulation and other energy conservation measures; and the worst gas-guzzling cars would be penalized. Although oil imports would surely be reduced as a result of new sources and conservation, American dependence on foreign petroleum supplies remained a major economic—and political—problem for the United States as the decade closed.

The Carter administration also proved far from adept in handling the country's proliferating economic woes. Upon taking office, Carter remained committed to a broad measure of economic voluntarism and, in this, reflected attitudes more commonly associated with previous Republican policy makers (always excepting Nixon's surprising turn toward price and wage controls in 1972). Despite his Democratic affiliation and despite Democratic sponsorship, since FDR's four terms, of broad government intervention in the economy, Carter consistently opposed government wage and price controls. Instead he tried to establish guidelines that business and labor would accept voluntarily, guidelines that had to be adjusted periodically from 1978 to 1980 as inflation became more severe (though they were seldom observed in the reasonably good economic times from 1977 to 1978). A special presidential adviser on inflation, Alfred Kahn, appeared on the scene to tilt with the inflation dragon, but though Kahn kept his good humor, the dragon clearly could not be easily slain.

Consumer prices continued a sharp rise throughout the Carter term. Inflation exceeded 20 percent monthly levels for a time, and public opinion polls confirmed that most Americans had come to view inflation as the country's worst domestic problem (even greater than unemployment, which also surged to the decade's highest levels in 1980). Nor was the United States doing any better within the international economy. The dollar continued its precipitous decline in world monetary markets, while the price of gold rose at a staggering pace throughout the Carter years, despite administration efforts (and efforts by American allies) to defuse the panic buying of gold. The U.S. trade deficit, caused in large part by the outflow of dollars for foreign oil purchases, also reached all-time multi-billion-dollar heights, made worse by the declining competitive situation of American products abroad. The increase in productivity among American workers was negligible for most of this period until (by 1980) there was no increase at all. Despite the administration's well-publicized efforts to hold the budget line on federal spending, the deficits continued unabated, and periodic announcements of an impending "balanced budget" became the butt of mordant jokes among economists and politicians alike.

These economic problems, and the manner in which Carter responded, had important political repercussions. Liberal Democrats complained that the president seemed more inclined to pursue traditional Republican economic policies, refusing to impose government controls on wages and prices while, at the same time, declining to support new and even more massive programs to assist the poor and disadvantaged. The rise in unemployment during the recession of 1979–80, induced in part by deliberate government measures designed to dampen spending and reduce the level of inflation, further angered many normally Democratic voting blocs. Significantly, America's skilled blue-collar workers, those employed in industries such as automobiles, steel, and construction—which in earlier decades had been the backbone of the economy—began to lose their jobs in alarming numbers. Many factors were responsible. The spectacularly successful efforts by Japanese and European industries to claim a large share of markets previously conceded to the United States, both in this country and abroad, played an obvious role. (Thus, in 1980 thirty of the fifty largest industrial companies in the world were based outside the United States.) Runaway inflation and astronomical interest rates also made investment in consumer durables, such as new homes and cars, far more difficult for consumers already overextended in credit purchases. Whoever was to "blame," the situation left Americans confused and angry, influencing political reactions. Hostility toward the Carter administration mounted as the decade drew to a close, and on the eve of the 1980 election, the president's popularity had fallen to the lowest figure ever recorded in a Gallup poll. Only 29 percent of those polled agreed that Jimmy Carter was doing a good job in the White House.

Nor could the president's handling of foreign affairs be called trouble-free or assured. Carter had come into office promising massive billion-dollar cuts in the defense budget. Soon after taking office, he seemed willing to fulfill those promises, even at the cost of stirring strong opposition among many military leaders and defense-oriented congressmen. He jettisoned production of the B-1 bomber, a proposed replacement for the vital but older B-52, and also scrapped plans for producing a neutron bomb (reversing himself under considerable pressure from Democratic liberals within and outside the administration). Instead Carter pinned much of his hopes for modernization of America's nuclear strike capability upon refurbished B-52s and submarines launching new cruise missiles, whose development he ordered accelerated, and upon a crash program to produce so-called Stealth bombers that could move undetected through Soviet radar patterns. The administration's calculated leaks of information on the super-secret Stealth program and the public announcement of the weapon became a 1980 campaign issue and drew strong criticism from the military, Congress, Republicans, and even the press.

During his early years in office, Jimmy Carter often attacked excessive military spending and so-called Cold Warriors who urged strengthening defenses and diplomatic firmness with the Soviet Union, chiding them for their "inordinate fear of communism." Carter reversed himself on all these positions by 1980.

From the moment he took office, the president appeared determined to pursue a policy of strongly (critics said "inordinately") championing human rights in both leftist and rightist dictatorships. He dispatched a public letter to Nobel Prize-winning Russian dissident leader Andrei Sakharov, expressing his identification with those in the Soviet Union striving to expand political freedoms. Carter told Sakharov that he intended to try to gain the release of imprisoned dissidents, not only in the Soviet Union but throughout the *unfree* world. This led to troubles with authoritarian governments in the Communist and Third World, that is with *most* of the world's non-democratic regimes, who resented American efforts to link good relations—even with many traditional friends of the United States—to improved treatment for "prisoners of conscience."

From all corners of the world came warnings that the United States should back down from its human rights meddling and mind its own business. The Soviet Union, in particular, stepped up arrests and harassments of dissidents in a direct response to the American challenge, holding several well-publicized trials of figures such as Anatoly Shcharansky as alleged Western agents. Meanwhile, right-wing dictatorships in Iran, the Philippines, Nicaragua, Brazil, and elsewhere, most of whom had long been U.S. allies, expressed bitter resentment at American opposition to their repression of political opponents. Within the United States itself, however, the Carter human rights policy received strong support from the public and within Congress, though critics pointed out that Washington seemed to be holding out false hopes to hundreds of millions of people living under tyrannical rule.

Relations with the Soviet Union remained delicate, not only because of the human rights issue but because the Russians understandably became even more wary of U.S. policy as the Americans drew closer to their Chinese Communist rivals. When the People's Republic of China and the United States established full diplomatic relations in January 1979, Moscow responded with denunciations of what was considered primarily an anti-Soviet development.

By that time, United States–Soviet negotiations on the limitation of strategic arms—the SALT II talks—neared successful conclusion after several years of extremely abrasive Russian diplomacy. President Ford and Premier Brezhnev had reached basic agreement at Vladivostok in 1974 on limiting various offensive weapons, but in March 1977 President Carter sent Secretary of State Vance to Moscow with proposals for deeper cuts in missiles and other weapons than ever previously agreed upon. The Russians attacked the Carter proposals but eventually resumed negotiations at Geneva which led, in June 1979, to the SALT II agreement. The Senate, after extended hearings and debate, postponed probable action on ratification of the treaty until at least 1981, and the entire arms control process remained virtually suspended as the Carter administration moved into the 1980 elections.

In the Western hemisphere, several crises arose late in the 1970s. In September 1977 the United States and Panama signed two treaties providing for complete return of the Panama Canal, in a series of stages, by the year 2000, while protecting the United States' rights to defend the canal in the event of military emergencies. Many American conservatives denounced this "giveaway" (the United States then held a perpetual lease on the Canal Zone) as further indication of America's loss of influence abroad; initially, a majority of the public polled agreed with this assessment. Senate debate on ratification raised virtually all the criticisms made of the treaty, but after lengthy discussion, the Senate in March and April 1978 approved the two treaties with Panama, both by sixty-eight to thirty-two margins. Sixteen Republican swing votes in favor of the treaties gave the administration the two-thirds margin needed for ratification.

The Carter policy on human rights and his more liberal views on noninterference with successful Third World revolutionary movements were tested in Latin America again in 1979, this time in the Central American nation of Nicaragua. There, the Sandinista Liberation Front, a left-wing revolutionary alliance that had fought to oust the dictator Anastasio Somoza, whose family had misruled Nicaragua since the 1930s, came to power in July 1979. Somoza fled to Miami, and Americans speculated as to whether Washington might try to intervene (covertly or openly) in the way the United States had encouraged the overthrow of the socialist Chilean government of Salvador Allende. This time, Washington acted with restraint, preferring to monitor the course of "Sandinista" rule closely to see if the new regime became openly anti-American and pro-Cuban (or pro-Soviet) rather than actively oppose the revolution.

In one major aspect of foreign policy, however, the United States did intervene diplomatically in a direct and forceful manner. Although Arabs and Israelis had been warring for decades, hopes soared in 1977 for at least a partial solution built upon earlier negotiations sponsored by Henry Kissinger under Presidents Nixon and Ford after the October 1973 War. At first, Carter tried clumsily to pressure the Israelis into attending a peace conference at Geneva, cosponsored by the United States and the Soviet Union, at which not only the Arab states but also the Palestinians (that is, supporters of the Palestinian Liberation Organization—P.L.O.—whose terrorist activities had made the group anathema to almost all Israelis) would be present. The Israelis refused to participate, although the new hard-line Prime Minister Menachem Begin visited Carter at the White House for talks in 1977, as did Egyptian President Anwar Sadat.

Suddenly, in November 1977 Sadat astonished the world by announcing dramatically that he wished to visit Israel to propose direct peace negotiations with the Begin government, easily the greatest shocker in summit diplomacy since Nixon's 1972 trip to Peking. After Begin extended an invitation to the Egyptian leader, Sadat flew to Israel and in a dramatic appearance before the Israeli Parliament (Knesset), pleaded the cause of peace between the two nations which had been at war for three decades.

Serious bilateral negotiations began and, as expected, bogged down until President Carter stepped in. He invited both Begin and Sadat, and their chief advisers, to a unique trilateral summit conference at Camp David, Maryland, in September 1978. After an extraordinary eleven days of negotiation, followed by a Carter trip to the Middle East to conclude the remaining unsettled issues, the two adversaries finally signed an Egyptian–Israeli peace treaty in March 1979. The treaty remained Jimmy Carter's supreme achievement in foreign policy between 1977 and 1980 — critics said perhaps his only one — and temporarily his popularity rose accordingly.

As for the Middle East, the treaty left the crucial question of Palestinian "autonomy," its definition and limits, unsettled for further Israeli–Egyptian talks. Eighteen Arab League countries angrily severed all diplomatic relations with Egypt for its "treachery" to the Palestinian (and Arab) cause. But the Camp David accords brought peace to Israel and Egypt at least, leading to Israel's phased return of the conquered Sinai territory to its former adversary and raising hopes for expansion of the negotiations to include Jordan, Syria, and other Arab states — and perhaps eventually some solution to the problems of Israeli security and a Palestinian homeland.

And then came Iran. The country's ruler, Shah Mohammed Reza Pahlevi, had been a close ally of the United States for more than a quarter century. By the 1970s, however, the Shah had become increasingly independent of American influence, thanks to the strengthening of Iran's economy because of the rising price of oil and the Shah's use of billions in oil revenues to make Iran the leading military power in the Persian Gulf region. At the same time that the Shah proceeded with an extensive modernization program designed to turn Iran into a mini-world power by the year 2000, his repression of political dissent and the rise of Islamic fundamentalism within Iran threatened the stability of his regime. Although not directly responsible for either political or religious opposition to the authoritarian, pro-Western Shah, the Carter administration did not help the ruler with its vocal attacks on human rights violations in Iran or with its confused signals from American diplomats and military advisers. Whatever the American role may have been, it added to governmental confusion in Iran, caused by prolonged strikes and riots in late 1978, which forced the Shah to step down and go into exile in January 1979.

In his place came the hero of the Iranian street crowds, an aging Muslim cleric, the Ayatollah Khomeini, who had been exiled by the Shah some years earlier and served from Paris as the leading symbol of resistance to the monarchy. Khomeini was an avowed and implacable foe of modernism, immorality, and the United States, all of which he identified with the hated Shah. Khomeini proclaimed the goal of establishing a Moslem theocratic Islamic republic in Iran dominated by religious leaders such as himself.

When the Shah left his Mexican exile for medical treatment in the United States, Khomeini and his advisers suspected (falsely) that his real purpose was to gather support for an attack on revolutionary Iran designed to place the Shah back on his throne (something the CIA had organized in 1953, when a nationalist government deposed the Shah). Militant revolutionaries in Iran used the Shah's entrance into the United States as an opportunity to escalate their confrontation with America, seizing the American embassy in Teheran in November 1979 and holding its occupants as hostages. Although some were later released, over fifty remained captives throughout 1980. An American commando-style rescue mission in April 1980 failed because of mechanical mishaps in the Iranian desert, leaving the hostages no closer to release than on their first day of captivity. Even the death of the Shah in July 1980 did not alter the situation.

At home Americans were furious. Shortly after the embassy seizure, Carter increased the strength of U.S. naval forces in the Persian Gulf. He also ordered the Immigration and Naturalization Service to search for illegals among the

many thousands of young Iranians studying in American colleges and universities. But the Iranian government — that is, the Ayatollah — refused to budge.

The administration renewed active U.S. military steps after years of cautious behavior for many reasons, not simply the continuing hostage crisis in Teheran. Foremost was the Russian invasion of Afghanistan in December 1979 to prop up a tottering Communist regime. Carter denounced the Russian move, fearing that in addition to Afghanistan (already a Moscow satellite even before the invasion), the Russians might strike toward Pakistan farther south, toward Iran, or toward the oil-rich pro-Western Arab kingdoms that line the Persian Gulf. Such a threat either to the West's access to vital oil supplies or to America's sometime ally, Pakistan, posed a direct and immediate challenge to U.S. strategic interests in the region.

The administration responded strongly to the Russian invasion, though critics charged that previous equivocations over the Iranian hostages and accommodations with Moscow may have en-

This extraordinary photo was taken on November 4, 1979, the day Iranian "student" terrorists seized the U.S. embassy in Tehran and took its personnel hostage. The picture shows the blindfolded diplomats being paraded in a humiliating manner by their captors hours after the seizure of the embassy. (UPI)

couraged the Soviets to invade in the first place. The president banned sales of American advanced technology and wheat to the Russians, controversial measures in view of the recession and hard times at home. Just as controversial, Carter called for the United States and other nations to boycott the July 1980 Summer Olympics in Moscow. The U.S. Olympic Committee agreed reluctantly to the boycott, and many (though not all) of America's allies — and Third World countries opposed to the invasion — also stayed home while the games were held.

More significant still, commentators of virtually all political persuasions agreed that the combination of Iran's seizure of American hostages and

Russian aggression in Afghanistan had dramatically altered the climate of public opinion in the United States on world issues and heated up the Cold War more strongly than at any time since the Cuban Missile Crisis of 1962. An overwhelming majority of Americans now supported significant increases in military spending to strengthen both national defense and our ability to respond effectively to perceived threats anywhere in the world. The "post-Vietnam psychosis," which had encouraged Americans in neo-isolationism and opposition to forceful actions abroad, proved remarkably short-lived. Television, which had played a significant role in fanning anti-Vietnam sentiment at the beginning of the 1970s, now stirred latent but powerful sentiments of patriotism in response to the protracted hostage crisis and the brutal Soviet military assault on a backward Asian society.

CAMPAIGN 1980

The Iranian crisis also provided President Carter with a winning strategy during the first phase of his campaign for reelection. Carter announced that he would remain at the presidential helm, in the White House and at Camp David, rather than campaign in person during the presidential primaries of January-June 1980. Critics sneered at this "Rose Garden strategy," a reference to a portion of the grounds surrounding the White House, but in view of Carter's abysmal standing in the polls in late 1979, the strategy of political silence might prove golden.

The president often seemed ineffectual (more critics raised the "competence" issue in connection with his administration than with any in recent memory) and had been grievously embarrassed a number of times. His close friend Budget Director Bert Lance, a former Georgia banker, had been forced to resign in 1977 when details of his complicated business arrangement came to light. (Lance was subsequently tried but acquitted of all criminal charges.) The U.S. ambassador to the United Nations, former civil rights leader Andrew Young, used pro-Third World hyperbole as a calculated method of international diplomacy for three years, often sounding off on issues in opposition to basic administration policy, until some unau-

thorized negotiations with representatives of the avowedly terrorist Palestinian Liberation Organization forced *his* resignation. Carter's brother Billy became the family embarrassment, taking $220,000 (a loan, claimed Billy) from the rabidly anti-United States government of Libya, chief national sponsor of international terrorist groups. A congressional committee in 1980 investigated not only Billy Carter's lobbying activities on Libya's behalf and his extraordinary "loan" but, also, possible efforts by Carter administration officials to intervene on his behalf despite an ongoing Justice Department criminal investigation. Carter himself appeared despondent in 1979 before his brother's "Libyan connection" became front-page news. He told a television audience about a "crisis of confidence," which made governing the country extremely difficult, a "malaise" gripping the American people and preventing them from rising to the expectations of their chief executive.

One Democrat who thought that the crisis of confidence could be localized in the White House was Senator Edward "Ted" Kennedy of Massachusetts, heir to the family political fortunes. Throughout 1979, Kennedy had been urged by a number of Democrats to challenge Carter for the presidency. Kennedy held back for good reasons. First, he did not match either of his assassinated brothers, John or Robert, in intellect or intensity of ambition. Also, in 1969, Kennedy had almost ended his political career at Chappaquidick, an island attached to Martha's Vineyard off the coast of Massachusetts. There, late one summer night, a young woman drowned when Kennedy drove his car off a bridge. The best that could be said for the senator was that he displayed poor judgment in the accident and in not reporting the episode until the following morning. (Kennedy avoided any possible presidential draft movement both in 1972 and 1976.) Ten years later, the idea of another Kennedy candidacy, one clothed in the tattered remnants of New Deal political alignments and New Frontier–Great Society programs, grew more attractive to liberal Democrats after three years of a Carter presidency.

Unfortunately for Kennedy, however, a *majority* of voting Democrats wanted no part of his reform prescriptions. "I'll whip his ass," Carter had volunteered at a White House reception when discussing the Kennedy challenge, and he proved true to his inelegant word. In primary after primary, the president—refusing to debate Kennedy and dramatizing his standing as national leader by remaining in the White House during the hostage crisis—easily bested Kennedy, who (until the last weeks) ran a ragged campaign. Although the challenger did sweep several large industrial state primaries in the spring, by convention time in August Carter had a clear majority of loyal delegates firmly in hand. Kennedy withdrew during the convention, handing the renomination to Carter without a fight.

The conservative swing visible among Democrats proved even more pronounced among Republicans. A number of challengers—Howard Baker, John Connally, Robert Dole, Phil Crane, and others—found themselves easily dispatched at an early stage by the front-runner, Ronald Reagan, the articulate former California governor. Reagan's chief opposition came from George Bush, a conservative in moderate's clothing, who accepted the consolation prize of vice-president at the Republican convention after last-minute negotiations by a Reagan aide failed to persuade former President Ford to accept the second slot.

Another Republican moderate whom Reagan had trounced decisively in the primaries, Congressman John Anderson of Illinois, bolted the GOP to organize a "National Unity Ticket" with former Democratic governor of Wisconsin Patrick Lucey as his vice-presidential running mate. (Lucey, a Kennedy leader, defected after the Democratic convention.) Anderson's campaign depended heavily for support on college students and the upper-middle-class political volunteers who had staffed the Eugene McCarthy and George McGovern campaigns in previous recent elections.

The debate between the President and his main challenger finally occurred on October 28. Both men took predictable positions on a whole range of foreign and domestic issues, but most press observers and pollsters agreed that Reagan emerged the clear winner in public perceptions of the two men. As a relaxed debater, far better informed on the issues than Democratic campaign oratory had led viewers to expect, Reagan emerged

(as had John Kennedy after the first 1960 debate with Richard Nixon) appearing decidedly "presidential."

Earlier in the fall, Carter's attempt to portray Reagan as a trigger-happy candidate likely to lead the United States into war, however inadvertently, appeared to have been effective in shifting the votes of numerous so-called moderates away from Anderson's "National Unity" campaign and into the Democratic column. Reagan, on the other hand, pursued successfully a steady attack on the Democratic incumbent for his unsuccessful economic policies. The continued high rate of inflation, high interest rates, and high unemployment worked to Reagan's advantage, when he demanded of voters (as he did in his closing comments during the debate): "Ask yourself, are you better off than you were four years ago?"

A flurry of diplomatic activity involving the possible return of the American hostages in Iran *might* have worked to Carter's advantage had any of the hostages actually been released. In the end, however, Reagan's surrogate Republican campaigners had alerted the press and public sufficiently to such a possible "October surprise" as to defuse any electoral gain to the Democrats. Nor did the Administration find it possible to respond with sufficient speed and enthusiasm to the conditions for release demanded by the Iranian government to obtain more than a negotiating channel prior to the election. As for the hostages, they remained in captivity. The Iranians reminded Americans of this fact vividly on November 4—Election Day—as thousands of demonstrators in Tehran paraded through the U.S. embassy grounds burning American flags and celebrating the first anniversary of the embassy's takeover.

In the United States, the American people chose a new president that day and by a margin which surprised virtually every pollster.. The Reagan–Bush ticket swept 44 states, winning 489 electoral votes with 51 percent of the popular vote. Jimmy Carter won only six states and the District of Columbia, taking 49 electoral votes with 41 percent of the popular votes. John Anderson won only 7 percent of the popular votes and no electoral votes; Anderson's double-digit support came mainly from the New England states. Carter con-

President-elect Ronald Reagan gestures toward Vice-President-elect George Bush during Reagan's first post-election press conference on November 6, 1980. Not only did Reagan triumph by margins far greater than virtually all pre-election predictions by pollsters, but the Republican Party gained control of the Senate for the first time since the mid-1950s. (Rich Lipski/UPI)

ceded defeat even before the polls had closed on the West Coast.

The victory went not only to Ronald Reagan personally but to the Republican Party, which swept to control of the Senate and also gained more than 30 seats in the House of Representatives. The Republicans also won four governorships and picked up more than 200 state legislative seats throughout the country. The 1980 election reflected a conservative sweep, although 48 percent of Americans still described themselves in 1980 as Democrats (with only 23 percent Republicans and 29 percent Independents). Polls also showed only 32 percent of the electorate calling itself conservative, with self-identified moderates a 43 percent

plurality and liberals down to 20 percent. Still, most observers viewed the 1980 election as a negative judgment on the excessive growth of the federal government during the 1960s and 1970s as well as a resounding rejection to the Carter administration's alleged ineptness in foreign and domestic affairs.

TOWARD A REAGAN ADMINISTRATION

The 227 million Americans of all backgrounds and creeds would begin the decade of the 1980s with new leaders, President Ronald Reagan and Vice-President George Bush. Reagan brought a varied background to the office. He spent more than a quarter-century as a Hollywood film star, serving in World War II and—after the war—being elected to six one-year terms as president of the Screen Actors Guild, where he led successful efforts to improve economic benefits and to prevent a takeover of the union by Communists and other radicals in the movie industry. Reagan drifted away from early Democratic New Deal beliefs toward a growing conservatism, crystallized from 1954 to 1962 in a new career as a spokesman for the General Electric corporation. Reagan remained nominally a Democrat until the early 1960s but campaigned for Richard Nixon in 1960 and for Barry Goldwater in 1964.

He won his first term as California's governor in 1966, running as a Republican, easily winning reelection in 1970. According to *Newsweek*, Reagan's two terms as governor "on balance (were) successful years running the nation's largest state—a passage in which he balanced a deep-red budget, held down employment by the state, pared the welfare rolls, and in other ways demonstrated his competence to govern." The two terms were marked by bitter disputes between Reagan and university faculty and students during the campus upheavals of the period (many of which occurred at the University of California at Berkeley). Most political observers consider Reagan's years as governor characterized by a moderate approach to the state's problems, generally, including his appointment to state government posts of more blacks, Hispanics, and other minorities than any previous governor. Reagan began running for the presidency seriously in the mid-1970s, unsuccessfully challenged President Ford in 1976, and continued his pursuit of the presidency in the years after Ford's defeat. Reagan and his second wife, the former Nancy Davis, were married in 1952, and Mrs. Reagan has played a prominent role in supporting her husband's political career over the past two decades.

Vice-President George Bush, like the new president, boasts an adopted Sun Belt constituency—in Bush's case, Texas. He served as U.S. Ambassador to the United Nations from 1971–73, Chairman of the Republican National Committee from 1973–74 during the Watergate climax, became President Ford's envoy to the People's Republic of China in 1974 and, in 1976, served as director of the Central Intelligence Agency. Bush's experience in foreign and national security affairs virtually assures him an active role as vice-president under Ronald Reagan comparable to Mondale's under Carter.

Often during the presidential campaign, Reagan quoted John Winthrop, the Puritan leader, who reminded his followers in 1630 when they arrived off the Massachusetts coast that their community would be "as a City set upon a hill, in the open view of all the earth; the eyes of the world are upon us. . . ." Reagan's acceptance speech at the Republican convention in August also reminded his listeners of the Pilgrim's Mayflower Compact, and he called upon other historical figures who dealt with the urgent crises of their own day—the Founding Fathers, Lincoln, Franklin Delano Roosevelt—to summon public attention to what he termed the "three grave threats to our very existence, any one of which could destroy us . . . a disintegrating economy, a weakened defense, and an energy policy based on the sharing of scarcity." Reagan called for "a rebirth of the American tradition of leadership at *every* level of government and in private life as well," and he offered a "pledge to restore, in our time, the American spirit of voluntary service, of cooperation, of private and community initiative" in place of what he attacked as the over-reliance upon federal government action under the previous administration.

Whether or not the Reagan administration can fulfill that pledge—and the many others made during the 1980 campaign—will be determined in the years to come. Most Americans—whether Republicans, Democrats, or Independents—would agree that the country's foreign and domestic future during the decade ahead will depend to a significant extent upon the success of the Reagan presidency in stimulating a new pattern of economic growth, controlling inflation, resolving the energy crisis, and restoring U.S. power and prestige. The new president entered office with a measure of public good will unprecedented in the past two decades. The promise of American life has emerged, in his comments, as a theme that overrides even the most serious problems, as in the spontaneous words with which he closed his acceptance speech:

> I've thought of something that is not part of my speech and I'm worried over whether I should do it.
>
> Can we doubt that only a Divine Providence placed this land, this land of freedom, here as a refuge for all those people in the world who yearn to breathe freely: Jews and Christians enduring persecution behind the Iron Curtain, the boat people of Southeast Asia, of Cuba and Haiti, the victims of the drought in Africa, the freedom fighters of Afghanistan, and our own countrymen held in savage captivity?
>
> I'll confess that I've been a little afraid to suggest what I'm going to suggest—I'm more afraid not to—that we begin our crusade joined together in a moment of silent prayer. God bless America.

Suggested Readings Chapters 49–50

Watergate

Carl Bernstein and Bob Woodward, *All the President's Men* (1974) and *The Final Days* (1976); John Dean, *Blind Ambition* (1976); William B. Dickinson, Jr., *Watergate: Chronology of a Crisis* (1974); Elizabeth Drew, *Washington Journal: The Events of 1973–1974* (1976); Leon Jaworski, *The Right and the Power: The Prosecution of Watergate* (1976); Richard Nixon, *RN* (1979); John Sirica, *To Set the Record Straight* (1979); Theodore H. White, *Breach of Faith* (1975); *The White House Transcripts* (1974).

The Nixon, Ford, and Carter Years: Politics

David S. Broder, *The Party's Over* (1971); Samuel Huntington, *The Crisis of Democracy* (1977); Leonard W. Levy, *Against the Law: The Nixon Court and Criminal Justice* (1974); Samuel Lubell, *The Hidden Crisis in American Politics* (1970) and *The Future While It Happened* (1973); Earl Mazo and Stephen Hess, *Nixon: A Political Portrait* (1968); Joe McGinnis, *The Selling of the President 1968* (1969); Clark Mollenhoff, *The Man Who Pardoned Nixon* (1976); Richard Reeves, *A Ford Not a Lincoln* (1974) and *Convention* (1977); Sumner Rosen, ed., *Economic Power Failure* (1975); Arthur M. Schlesinger, Jr., *The Imperial Presidency* (1973); James F. Simon, *In His Own Image: The Supreme Court in Richard Nixon's America* (1973); Jerald F. terHorst, *Gerald Ford and the Future of the Presidency* (1974); Theodore H. White, *The Making of the President, 1968* (1969); Gary Wills, *Nixon Agonistes* (1970); Jules Witcover, *Marathon* (1977).

The Nixon, Ford, and Carter Years: Foreign Policy

Coral Bell, *The Diplomacy of Détente* (1977); Henry Brandon, *The Retreat of American Power* (1973); Edward Friedland, Paul Seabury, and Aaron Wildavsky, *The Great Détente Disaster* (1975); Stanley Hoffman, *Primacy or World Order* (1978); Marvin and Bernard Kalb, *Kissinger* (1974); George Kennan, *A Cloud of Danger* (1977); Henry Kissinger, *White House Years* (1980); Walter LaFeber, *The Panama Canal* (1978); Anthony Lake, *The "Tar Baby" Option* (1976); Roger Morris, *Uncertain Greatness* (1977); John Newhouse, *Cold Dawn* (1973); Robert E. Osgood, et al., *Retreat From Empire?* (1973); Edward R. F. Sheehan, *The Arabs, Israelis, and Kissinger* (1976); Frank Snepp, *Decent Interval* (1977); John Stockwell, *In Search of Enemies* (1978).

The Nixon, Ford, and Carter Years: Society and Culture

Daniel Bell, *The Coming of Post-Industrial Society* (1976); Alexander M. Bickel, *The Supreme Court and the Idea of Progress* (1970); Otis L. Graham, Jr., *Toward a Planned Society: From Roosevelt to Nixon* (1976); Andrew Hacker, *The End of the American Era* (1971); Robert L. Heilbroner, *An Inquiry into the Human Prospect* (1974); J. Anthony Lukas, *Nightmare* (1976); Harland B. Moulton, *From Superiority to Parity: The United States and the Strategic Arms Race, 1966–1971* (1973); Jonathon Schell, *The Time of Illusion* (1975); the Staff of *The Washington Post, The Pursuit of the Presidency, 1980* (1980); Correspondents of *The New York Times, Reagan: The Man, the President* (1980).

In Congress, July 4, 1776. *The unanimous Declaration of the thirteen united States of America,*

When in the Course of human events, it becomes necessary for one people to dissolve the political bands which have connected them with another, and to assume among the powers of the earth, the separate and equal station to which the Laws of Nature and of Nature's God entitle them, a decent respect to the opinions of mankind requires that they should declare the causes which impel them to the separation.—

We hold these truths to be self-evident, that all men are created equal, that they are endowed by their Creator with certain unalienable Rights, that among these are Life, Liberty and the pursuit of Happiness.—

That to secure these rights, Governments are instituted among Men, deriving their just powers from the consent of the governed,—

That whenever any Form of Government becomes destructive of these ends, it is the Right of the People to alter or to abolish it, and to institute new Government, laying its foundation on such principles and organizing its powers in such form, as to them shall seem most likely to effect their Safety and Happiness. Prudence, indeed, will dictate that Governments long established should not be changed for light and transient causes; and accordingly all experience hath shown, that mankind are more disposed to suffer, while evils are sufferable, than to right themselves by abolishing the forms to which they are accustomed. But when a long train of abuses and usurpations, pursuing invariably the same Object evinces a design to reduce them under absolute Despotism, it is their right, it is their duty, to throw off such Government, and to provide new Guards for their future security.—

Such has been the patient sufferance of these Colonies; and such is now the necessity which constrains them to alter their former Systems of Government. The history of the present King of Great Britain is a history of repeated injuries and usurpations, all having in direct object the establishment of an absolute Tyranny over these States. To prove this, let Facts be submitted to a candid world.—

He has refused his Assent to Laws, the most wholesome and necessary for the public good.—

He has forbidden his Governors to pass Laws of immediate and pressing importance, unless suspended in their operation till his Assent should be obtained; and when so suspended, he has utterly neglected to attend to them.—

He has refused to pass other Laws for the accommodation of large districts of people, unless those people would relinquish the right of Representation in the Legislature, a right inestimable to them and formidable to tyrants only.—

He has called together legislative bodies at places unusual, uncomfortable, and distant from the depository of their public Records, for the sole purpose of fatiguing them into compliance with his measures.—

He has dissolved Representative Houses repeatedly, for opposing with manly firmness his invasions on the rights of the people.—

He has refused for a long time, after such dissolutions, to cause others to be elected; whereby the Legislative powers, incapable of Annihilation, have returned to the People at large for their exercise; the State remaining in the mean time exposed to all the dangers of invasion from without, and convulsions within.—

He has endeavoured to prevent the population of these States; for that purpose obstructing the Laws for Naturalization of Foreigners; refusing to pass others to encourage their migrations hither, and raising the conditions of new Appropriations of Lands. —

He has obstructed the Administration of Justice, by refusing his Assent to Laws for establishing Judiciary powers. —

He has made Judges dependent on his Will alone, for the tenure of their offices, and the amount and payment of their salaries. —

He has erected a multitude of New Offices, and sent hither swarms of Officers to harrass our people, and eat out their substance. —

He has kept among us in times of peace, Standing Armies without the Consent of our legislatures. —

He has affected to render the Military independent of and superior to the Civil power. —

He has combined with others to subject us to a jurisdiction foreign to our constitution, and unacknowledged by our laws; giving his Assent to their Acts of pretended Legislation: —

For quartering large bodies of armed troops among us: —

For protecting them, by a mock Trial, from punishment for any Murders which they should commit on the Inhabitants of these States: —

For cutting off our Trade with all parts of the world: —

For imposing Taxes on us without our Consent: —

For depriving us in many cases, of the benefits of Trial by Jury: —

For transporting us beyond Seas to be tried for pretended offences: —

For abolishing the free System of English Laws in a neighbouring Province, establishing therein an Arbitrary government, and enlarging its Boundaries so as to render it at once an example and fit instrument for introducing the same absolute rule in these Colonies: —

For taking away our Charters, abolishing our most valuable Laws, and altering fundamentally the Forms of our Governments: —

For suspending our own Legislatures, and declaring themselves invested with power to legislate for us in all cases whatsoever. —

He has abdicated Government here, by declaring us out of his Protection and waging War against us. —

He has plundered our seas, ravaged our Coasts, burnt our towns, and destroyed the lives of our people. —

He is at this time transporting large Armies of foreign Mercenaries to compleat the works of death, desolation and tyranny, already begun with circumstances of Cruelty & perfidy scarcely paralleled in the most barbarous ages, and totally unworthy the Head of a civilized nation. —

He has constrained our fellow Citizens taken Captive on the high Seas to bear Arms against their Country, to become the executioners of their friends and Brethren, or to fall themselves by their Hands. —

He has excited domestic insurrections amongst us, and has endeavoured to bring on the inhabitants of our frontiers, the merciless Indian Savages, whose known rule of warfare, is an undistinguished destruction of all ages, sexes and conditions.

In every stage of these Oppressions We have Petitioned for Redress in the most humble terms: Our repeated Petitions have been answered only by repeated injury. A Prince, whose character is thus marked by every act which may define a Tyrant, is unfit to be the ruler of a free people.

Nor have We been wanting in attentions to our British brethren. We have warned them from time to time of attempts by their legislature to extend an unwarrantable jurisdiction over us. We have reminded them of the circumstances of our emigration and settlement here. We have appealed to their native justice and magnanimity, and we have conjured them by the ties of our common kindred to disavow these usurpations, which would inevitably interrupt our connections and correspondence. They too have been deaf to the voice of justice and of consanguinity. We must, therefore, acquiesce in the necessity, which denounces our Separation, and hold them, as we hold the rest of mankind, Enemies in War, in Peace Friends. —

We, therefore, the Representatives of the united States of America, in General Congress, Assembled, appealing to the Supreme Judge of the world for the rectitude of our intentions, do, in the Name, and by Authority of the good People of these Colonies, solemnly publish and declare, That these United Colonies are, and of Right ought to be, Free and Independent States; that they are absolved from all Allegiance to the British Crown, and that all political connection between them and the State of Great Britain, is and ought to be totally dissolved; and that as Free and Independent States they have full Power to levy War, conclude Peace, contract Alliances, establish Commerce, and to do all other Acts and Things which Independent States may of right do. —

And for the support of this Declaration, with a firm reliance on the protection of divine Providence, we mutually pledge to each other our Lives, our Fortunes and our sacred Honor.

John Hancock
(MASSACHUSETTS)

NEW HAMPSHIRE
Josiah Bartlett
William Whipple
Matthew Thornton

MASSACHUSETTS
Samuel Adams
John Adams
Robert Treat Paine
Elbridge Gerry

DELAWARE
Caesar Rodney
George Read
Thomas McKean

NEW YORK
William Floyd
Philip Livingston
Francis Lewis
Lewis Morris

NEW JERSEY
Richard Stockton
John Witherspoon
Francis Hopkinson
John Hart
Abraham Clark

NORTH CAROLINA
William Hooper
Joseph Hewes
John Penn

MARYLAND
Samuel Chase
William Paca
Thomas Stone
Charles Carroll
  of Carrollton

SOUTH CAROLINA
Edward Rutledge
Thomas Heywood, Jr.
Thomas Lynch, Jr.
Arthur Middleton

RHODE ISLAND
Stephen Hopkins
William Ellery

CONNECTICUT
Roger Sherman
Samuel Huntington
William Williams
Oliver Wolcott

PENNSYLVANIA
Robert Morris
Benjamin Rush
Benjamin Franklin
John Morton
George Clymer
James Smith
George Taylor
James Wilson
George Ross

VIRGINIA
George Wythe
Richard Henry Lee
Thomas Jefferson
Benjamin Harrison
Thomas Nelson, Jr.
Francis Lightfoot Lee
Carter Braxton

GEORGIA
Button Gwinnett
Lyman Hall
George Walton

The Constitution of the United States of America

The preamble establishes the principle of government by the people, and lists the six basic purposes of the Constitution.

We the People of the United States, in Order to form a more perfect Union, establish Justice, insure domestic Tranquility, provide for the common defence, promote the general Welfare, and secure the Blessings of Liberty to ourselves and our Posterity, do ordain and establish this Constitution for the United States of America.

ARTICLE I • LEGISLATIVE DEPARTMENT

Section 1. All legislative Powers herein granted shall be vested in a Congress of the United States, which shall consist of a Senate and House of Representatives.

Representatives serve two-year terms. They are chosen in each state by those electors (that is, voters) who are qualified to vote for members of the lower house of their own state legislature.

Section 2. The House of Representatives shall be composed of Members chosen every second Year by the People of the several States, and the Electors in each State shall have the Qualifications requisite for Electors of the most numerous Branch of the State Legislature.

No Person shall be a Representative who shall not have attained to the Age of twenty-five Years, and been seven Years a Citizen of the United States, and who shall not, when elected, be an Inhabitant of that State in which he shall be chosen.

The number of representatives allotted to a state is determined by the size of its population. The 14th Amendment has made obsolete the reference to "all other persons"—that is, slaves.

A census must be taken every ten years to determine the number of representatives to which each state is entitled. There is now one representative for about every 470,000 persons.

Representatives and direct Taxes shall be apportioned among the several States which may be included within this Union, according to their respective Numbers, <u>which shall be determined by adding to the whole Number of free Persons, including those bound to Service for a Term of Years, and excluding Indians not taxed, three-fifths of all other Persons.</u> The actual Enumeration shall be made within three Years after the first Meeting of the Congress of the United States, and within every subsequent Term of ten Years, in such Manner as they shall by Law direct. The Number of Representatives shall not exceed one for every thirty Thousand, but each State shall have at Least one Representative; <u>and until such enumeration shall be made, the State of New Hampshire shall be entitled to chuse three, Massachusetts eight, Rhode Island and Providence Plantations one, Connecticut five, New York six, New Jersey four, Pennsylvania eight, Delaware one, Maryland six, Virginia ten, North Carolina five, South Carolina five, and Georgia three.</u>

Source: House Document #529. U.S. Government Printing Office, 1967. [NOTE: The Constitution and the amendments are reprinted here in their original form. Portions that have been amended or superseded are underlined.] The words printed in the margins explains some of the more difficult passages.

When vacancies happen in the Representation from any State, the Executive Authority thereof shall issue Writs of Election to fill such Vacancies.

"Executive authority" refers to the governor of a state.

The House of Representatives shall chuse their Speaker and other Officers; and shall have the sole Power of Impeachment.

The Speaker, chosen by and from the majority party, presides over the House. Impeachment is the act of bringing formal charges against an official. (See also Section 3.)

Section 3. The Senate of the United States shall be composed of two Senators from each State, <u>chosen by the Legislature thereof,</u> for six Years; and each Senator shall have one Vote.

The 17th Amendment changed this method to direct election.

Immediately after they shall be assembled in Consequence of the first Election, they shall be divided as equally as may be into three Classes. The Seats of the Senators of the first Class shall be vacated at the Expiration of the second Year, of the second Class at the Expiration of the fourth Year, and of the third Class at the Expiration of the sixth Year, so that one third may be chosen every second Year; and if Vacancies happen by Resignation, or otherwise, <u>during the Recess of the Legislature of any State, the Executive thereof may make temporary Appointments until the next Meeting of the Legislature, which shall then fill such Vacancies.</u>

The 17th Amendment also provides that a state governor shall appoint a successor to fill a vacant Senate seat until a direct election is held.

No Person shall be a Senator who shall not have attained to the Age of thirty Years, and been nine Years a Citizen of the United States, and who shall not, when elected, be an Inhabitant of that State for which he shall be chosen.

The Vice President of the United States shall be President of the Senate, but shall have no Vote, unless they be equally divided.

The Vice President may cast a vote in the Senate only in order to break a tie.

The Senate shall chuse their other Officers, and also a President pro tempore, in the absence of the Vice President, or when he shall exercise the Office of President of the United States.

The president pro tempore of the Senate is a temporary officer; the Latin words mean "for the time being."

The Senate shall have the sole Power to try all Impeachments. When sitting for that Purpose, they shall be on Oath or Affirmation. When the President of the United States is tried, the Chief Justice shall preside: And no Person shall be convicted without the Concurrence of two thirds of the Members present.

Judgment in Cases of Impeachment shall not extend further than to removal from Office, and disqualification to hold and enjoy any Office of Honor, Trust or Profit under the United States: but the Party convicted shall nevertheless be liable and subject to Indictment, Trial, Judgment and Punishment, according to Law.

No President has ever been successfully impeached. In 1868 the Senate fell one vote short of the two-thirds majority needed to convict Andrew Johnson. Twelve other officials—ten federal judges, one senator, and one Secretary of War—have been impeached; four of the judges were convicted.

Section 4. The Times, Places and Manner of holding Elections for Senators and Representatives, shall be prescribed in each State by the Legislature thereof; but the Congress may at any time by Law make or alter such Regulations, except as to the Place of chusing Senators.

Elections for Congress are held on the first Tuesday after the first Monday in November in even-numbered years.

The Congress shall assemble at least once in every Year, <u>and such Meeting shall be on the first Monday in December,</u> unless they shall by Law appoint a different Day.

The 20th Amendment designates January 3 as the opening of the congressional session.

Section 5. Each House shall be the Judge of the Elections, Returns and Qualifications of its own Members, and a Majority of each shall constitute a Quorum to do Business; but a smaller number may adjourn from day to day, and may be authorized to compel the Attendance of absent Members, in such Manner, and under such Penalties as each House may provide.

Each house of Congress decides whether a member has been elected properly and is qualified to be seated. (A quorum is the minimum number of persons required to be present in order to conduct business.) The House once refused admittance to an

Each House may determine the Rules of its Proceedings, punish its

Members for disorderly Behavior, and, with the Concurrence of two thirds, expel a Member.

Each House shall keep a Journal of its Proceedings, and from time to time publish the same, excepting such Parts as may in their Judgment require Secrecy; and the Yeas and Nays of the Members of either House on any question shall, at the Desire of one fifth of those Present, be entered on the Journal.

Neither House, during the Session of Congress, shall, without the Consent of the other, adjourn for more than three days, nor to any other Place than that in which the two Houses shall be sitting.

Section 6.   The Senators and Representatives shall receive a Compensation for their Services, to be ascertained by Law, and paid out of the Treasury of the United States. They shall in all Cases, except Treason, Felony and Breach of the Peace, be privileged from Arrest during their Attendance at the Session of their respective Houses, and in going to and returning from the same; and for any Speech or Debate in either House, they shall not be questioned in any other Place.

No Senator or Representative shall, during the Time for which he was elected, be appointed to any civil Office under the Authority of the United States, which shall have been created, or the Emoluments whereof shall have been encreased during such time; and no Person holding any Office under the United States, shall be a Member of either House during his Continuance in Office.

Section 7.   All Bills for raising Revenue shall originate in the House of Representatives; but the Senate may propose or concur with Amendments as on other Bills.

Every Bill which shall have passed the House of Representatives and the Senate, shall, before it become a Law, be presented to the President of the United States; If he approve he shall sign it, but if not he shall return it, with his Objections to that House in which it shall have originated, who shall enter the Objections at large on their Journal, and proceed to reconsider it. If after such Reconsideration two thirds of that House shall agree to pass the Bill, it shall be sent, together with the Objections, to the other House, by which it shall likewise be reconsidered, and if approved by two thirds of that House, it shall become a Law. But in all such Cases the Votes of both Houses shall be determined by Yeas and Nays, and the Names of the Persons voting for and against the Bill shall be entered on the Journal of each House respectively. If any Bill shall not be returned by the President within ten Days (Sundays excepted) after it shall have been presented to him, the Same shall be a Law, in like Manner as if he had signed it, unless the Congress by their Adjournment prevent its Return, in which Case it shall not be a Law.

Every Order, Resolution, or Vote to which the Concurrence of the Senate and House of Representatives may be necessary (except on a question of Adjournment) shall be presented to the President of the United States; and before the Same shall take Effect, shall be approved by him, or being disapproved by him, shall be repassed by two thirds of the Senate and House of Representatives, according to the Rules and Limitations prescribed in the Case of a Bill.

Section 8.   The Congress shall have Power to lay and collect Taxes, Duties, Imposts and Excises, to pay the Debts and provide for the common Defence and general Welfare of the United States; but all Duties, Imposts and Excises shall be uniform throughout the United States;

To borrow money on the credit of the United States;

To regulate Commerce with foreign Nations, and among the several States, and with the Indian Tribes;

To establish an uniform Rule of Naturalization, and uniform Laws on the subject of Bankruptcies throughout the United States;

To coin Money, regulate the Value thereof, and of foreign Coin, and fix the Standard of Weights and Measures;

To provide for the Punishment of counterfeiting the Securities and current Coin of the United States;

To establish Post Offices and post Roads;

To promote the Progress of Science and useful Arts, by securing for limited Times to Authors and Inventors the exclusive Right to their respective Writings and Discoveries;

To constitute Tribunals inferior to the supreme Court;

To define and punish Piracies and Felonies committed on the high Seas, and Offenses against the Law of Nations;

To declare War, grant Letters of Marque and Reprisal, and make Rules concerning Captures on Land and Water;

To raise and support Armies, but no Appropriation of Money to that Use shall be for a longer Term than two Years;

To provide and maintain a Navy;

To make Rules for the Government and Regulation of the land and naval Forces;

To provide for calling forth the Militia to execute the Laws of the Union, suppress Insurrections and repel Invasions;

To provide for organizing, arming, and disciplining the Militia, and for governing such Part of them as may be employed in the Service of the United States, reserving to the States respectively, the Appointment of the Officers, and the Authority of training the Militia according to the discipline prescribed by Congress;

To exercise exclusive Legislation in all Cases whatsoever, over such District (not exceeding ten Miles square) as may, by Cession of particular States, and the acceptance of Congress, become the Seat of the Government of the United States, and to exercise like Authority over all Places purchased by the Consent of the Legislature of the State in which the Same shall be, for the Erection of Forts, Magazines, Arsenals, dock-Yards, and other needful Buildings;—And

To make all Laws which shall be necessary and proper for carrying into Execution the foregoing Powers, and all other Powers vested by this Constitution in the Government of the United States, or in any Department or Officer thereof.

Section 9. The Migration or Importation of such Persons as any of the States now existing shall think proper to admit, shall not be prohibited by the Congress prior to the Year one thousand eight hundred and eight, but a tax or duty may be imposed on such Importation, not exceeding ten dollars for each Person.

The privilege of the Writ of Habeas Corpus shall not be suspended unless when in Cases of Rebellion or Invasion the public Safety may require it.

No bill of Attainder or ex post facto Law shall be passed.

No capitation, or other direct, Tax shall be laid, unless in Proportion to the Census or Enumeration herein before directed to be taken.

No Tax or Duty shall be laid on Articles exported from any State.

No Preference shall be given by any Regulation of Commerce or Revenue to the Ports of one State over those of another; nor shall Vessels bound to, or from, one State, be obliged to enter, clear, or pay Duties in another.

No Money shall be drawn from the Treasury, but in Consequence of Appropriations made by Law; and a regular Statement and Account of the Receipts and Expenditures of all public Money shall be published from time to time.

No Title of Nobility shall be granted by the United States: And no Person holding any Office of Profit or Trust under them, shall, without the Consent of the Congress, accept of any present, Emolument, Office, or Title, of any kind whatever, from any King, Prince, or foreign State.

Naturalization is the process by which an alien becomes a citizen.

Government securities include savings bonds and other notes.

Authors' and inventors' rights are protected by copyright and patent laws.

Congress may establish lower federal courts.

Only Congress may declare war. Letters of marque and reprisal grant merchant ships permission to attack enemy vessels.

Militia refers to national guard units, which may become part of the United States Army during an emergency. Congress aids the states in maintaining their national guard units.

This clause gives Congress the power to govern what became the District of Columbia, as well as other federal sites.

Known as the elastic clause, this provision enables Congress to exercise many powers not specifically granted to it by the Constitution.

This clause concerns the slave trade, which Congress did ban in 1808.

The writ of habeas corpus permits a prisoner to appear before a judge to inquire into the legality of his or her detention.

A bill of attainder is an act of legislation that declares a person guilty of a crime and punishes him or her without a trial. An ex post facto law punishes a person for an act that was legal when performed but later declared illegal.

The object of Clause 4 was to bar direct (per person) taxation of slaves for the purpose of abolishing slavery. The 16th Amendment modified this provision by giving Congress the power to tax personal income.

Section 10. No State shall enter into any Treaty, Alliance, or Confederation; grant Letters of Marque and Reprisal; coin Money; emit Bills of Credit; make any Thing but gold and silver Coin a Tender in Payment of Debts; pass any Bill of Attainder, ex post facto Law, or Law impairing the Obligation of Contracts, or grant any Title of Nobility.

No State shall, without the Consent of the Congress, lay any Imposts or Duties on Imports or Exports, except what may be absolutely necessary for executing its inspection Laws: and the net Produce of all Duties and Imposts, laid by any State on Imports or Exports, shall be for the Use of the Treasury of the United States; and all such Laws shall be subject to the Revision and Controul of the Congress.

No State shall, without the Consent of Congress, lay any duty of Tonnage, keep Troops, or Ships of War in time of Peace, enter into any Agreement or Compact with another State, or with a foreign Power, or engage in War, unless actually invaded, or in such imminent Danger as will not admit of delay.

ARTICLE II • EXECUTIVE DEPARTMENT

Section 1. The executive Power shall be vested in a President of the United States of America. He shall hold his Office during the Term of four Years, and, together with the Vice President, chosen for the same Term, be elected, as follows.

Each State shall appoint, in such Manner as the Legislature thereof may direct, a Number of Electors, equal to the whole Number of Senators and Representatives to which the State may be entitled in the Congress: but no Senator or Representative, or Person holding an Office of Trust or Profit under the United States, shall be appointed an Elector.

The Electors shall meet in their respective States, and vote by Ballot for two persons, of whom one at least shall not be an Inhabitant of the same State with themselves. And they shall make a List of all the Persons voted for, and of the Number of Votes for each; which List they shall sign and certify, and transmit sealed to the Seat of the Government of the United States, directed to the President of the Senate. The President of the Senate shall, in the Presence of the Senate and House of Representatives, open all the Certificates, and the Votes shall then be counted. The Person having the greatest Number of Votes shall be the President, if such Number be a Majority of the whole Number of Electors appointed; and if there be more than one who have such Majority, and have an equal Number of Votes, then the House of Representatives shall immediately chuse by Ballot one of them for President; and if no Person have a Majority, then from the five highest on the List the said House shall in like Manner chuse the President. But in chusing the President, the Votes shall be taken by States, the Representation from each State having one Vote; a quorum for this Purpose shall consist of a Member or Members from two thirds of the States, and a Majority of all the States shall be necessary to a Choice. In every Case, after the Choice of the President, the Person having the greatest Number of Votes of the Electors shall be the Vice President. But if there should remain two or more who have equal Votes, the Senate shall chuse from them by Ballot the Vice President.

The Congress may determine the Time of chusing the Electors, and the Day on which they shall give their Votes; which Day shall be the same throughout the United States.

No person except a natural born Citizen, or a Citizen of the United States, at the time of the Adoption of this Constitution, shall be eligible to the Office of President; neither shall any Person be eligible to that Office who shall not have attained to the Age of Thirty-five Years, and been fourteen Years a Resident within the United States.

In Case of the Removal of the President from Office, or of his Death, Resignation, or Inability to discharge the Powers and Duties of the said Office, the same shall devolve on the Vice-President, and the Congress may by Law provide for the Case of Removal, Death, Resignation or Inability, both of the President and the Vice President, declaring what Officer shall then act as President, and such Officer shall act accordingly, until the Disability be removed, or a President shall be elected.

The Vice President is next in line for the presidency. A federal law passed in 1947 determined the order of presidential succession as follows: (1) Speaker of the House; (2) president pro tempore of the Senate; and (3) Cabinet officers in order in which their departments were created. (So far, death and resignation have been the only circumstances under which a presidential term has been cut short.) This clause has been amplified by the 25th Amendment.

The President shall, at stated Times, receive for his Services, a Compensation, which shall neither be encreased nor diminished during the Period for which he shall have been elected, and he shall not receive within that Period any other Emolument from the United States, or any of them.

Before he enter on the Execution of his Office, he shall take the following Oath or Affirmation: — "I do solemnly swear (or affirm) that I will faithfully execute the Office of the President of the United States, and will to the best of my Ability, preserve, protect and defend the Constitution of the United States."

Section 2. The President shall be Commander in Chief of the Army and Navy of the United States, and of the Militia of the several States, when called into the actual Service of the United States; he may require the Opinion in writing, of the principal Officer in each of the executive Departments, upon any subject relating to the Duties of their respective Offices, and he shall have Power to Grant Reprieves and Pardons for Offenses against the United States, except in Cases of Impeachment.

This clause suggests written communication between the President and "the principal officer in each of the executive departments." As it developed, these officials comprise the Cabinet — whose members are chosen, and may be replaced, by the President.

He shall have Power, by and with the Advice and Consent of the Senate, to make Treaties, provided two thirds of the Senators present concur; and he shall nominate, and by and with the Advice and Consent of the Senate shall appoint Ambassadors, other public Ministers and Consuls, Judges of the supreme Court, and all other Officers of the United States, whose Appointments are not herein otherwise provided for, and which shall be established by Law; but the Congress may by Law vest the Appointment of such inferior Officers, as they think proper, in the President alone, in the Courts of Law, or in the Heads of Departments.

Senate approval is required for treaties and presidential appointments.

The President shall have Power to fill up all Vacancies that may happen during the Recess of the Senate, by granting Commissions which shall expire at the End of their next Session.

Without the consent of the Senate, the President may appoint officials only on a temporary basis.

Section 3. He shall from time to time give to the Congress Information of the State of the Union, and recommend to their Consideration such Measures as he shall judge necessary and expedient; he may, on extraordinary Occasions, convene both Houses, or either of them, and in Case of Disagreement between them, with Respect to the Time of Adjournment, he may adjourn them to such Time as he shall think proper; he shall receive Ambassadors and other public Ministers; he shall take Care that the Laws be faithfully executed, and shall Commission all the Officers of the United States.

The President delivers a "State of the Union" message at the opening of each session of Congress. Woodrow Wilson was the first President since John Adams to read his messages in person. Franklin D. Roosevelt and his successors followed Wilson's example.

Section 4. The President, Vice President and all civil Officers of the United States, shall be removed from Office on Impeachment for, and Conviction of, Treason, Bribery, or other high Crimes and Misdemeanors.

ARTICLE III • JUDICIAL DEPARTMENT

Federal judges hold office for life and may not have their salaries lowered while in office. These provisions are intended to keep the federal bench independent of political pressure.

Section 1. The judicial Power of the United States, shall be vested in one supreme Court, and in such inferior Courts as the Congress may from time to time ordain and establish. The Judges, both of the supreme and inferior Courts, shall hold their Offices during good Behaviour, and shall, at stated Times, receive for their Services, a Compensation, which shall not be diminished during their Continuance in Office.

This clause describes the types of cases that may be heard in federal courts.

The 11th Amendment prevents a citizen from suing a state in a federal court.

Section 2. The judicial Power shall extend to all Cases, in Law and Equity, arising under this Constitution, the Laws of the United States, and Treaties made, or which shall be made, under their Authority; — to all Cases affecting Ambassadors, other public Ministers and Consuls; — to all Cases of admiralty and maritime Jurisdiction; — to Controversies to which the United States shall be a Party; — to Controversies between two or more States; — between a State and Citizens of another State; — between Citizens of different States; — between Citizens of the same State claiming Lands under Grants of different States, and between a State, or the Citizens thereof, and foreign States, Citizens or Subjects.

The Supreme Court handles certain cases directly. It may also review cases handled by lower courts, but Congress in some cases may withhold the right to appeal to the highest court, or limit appeal by setting various conditions.

In all Cases affecting Ambassadors, other public Ministers and Consuls, and those in which a State shall be Party, the supreme Court shall have original Jurisdiction. In all the other Cases before mentioned, the supreme Court shall have appellate Jurisdiction, both as to Law and Fact, with such Exceptions, and under such Regulations as the Congress shall make.

The 6th Amendment strengthens this clause on trial procedure.

The trial of all Crimes, except in Cases of Impeachment, shall be by Jury; and such Trial shall be held in the State where the said Crimes shall have been committed; but when not committed within any State, the Trial shall be at such Place or Places as the Congress may by Law have directed.

Treason is rigorously defined. A person can be convicted only if two witnesses testify to the same obvious act, or if he confesses in court.

Section 3. Treason against the United States, shall consist only in levying War against them, or in adhering to their Enemies, giving them Aid and Comfort. No Person shall be convicted of Treason unless on the Testimony of two Witnesses to the same overt Act, or on Confession in open Court.

Punishment for treason extends only to the person convicted, not to his or her descendants. ("Corruption of blood" means that the heirs of a convicted person are deprived of certain rights.)

The Congress shall have Power to declare the Punishment of Treason, but no Attainder of Treason shall work Corruption of Blood, or Forfeiture except during the Life of the Person attainted.

ARTICLE IV • RELATIONS AMONG THE STATES

States must honor each other's laws, court decisions, and records (for example, birth, marriage, and death certificates).

Section 1. Full Faith and Credit shall be given in each State to the public Acts, Records, and judicial Proceedings of every other State. And the Congress may by general Laws prescribe the Manner in which such Acts, Records and Proceedings shall be proved, and the Effect thereof.

Each state must respect the rights of citizens of other states.

Section 2. The Citizens of each State shall be entitled to all Privileges and Immunities of Citizens in the several States.

The process of returning a person accused of a crime to the governmental authority (in this case a state) from which he or she has fled is called extradition.

A Person charged in any State with Treason, Felony, or other Crime, who shall flee from Justice, and be found in another State, shall on demand of the executive Authority of the State from which he fled, be delivered up, to be removed to the State having Jurisdiction of the Crime.

The 13th Amendment, which abolished slavery, makes this clause obsolete.

No Person held in Service or Labour in one State, under the Laws thereof, escaping into another, shall, in Consequence of any Law or Regulation therein, be discharged from such Service or Labour, but shall be delivered up on Claim of the Party to whom such Service or Labour may be due.

Section 3. New States may be admitted by the Congress into this Union; but no new State shall be formed or erected within the Jurisdiction of any other State; nor any State be formed by the Junction of two or more States, or parts of States, without the Consent of the Legislatures of the States concerned as well as of the Congress.

The Congress shall have Power to dispose of and make all needful Rules and Regulations respecting the Territory or other Property belonging to the United States; and nothing in this Constitution shall be so construed as to Prejudice any Claims of the United States, or of any particular State.

A new state may not be created by dividing or joining existing states unless approved by the legislatures of the states affected and by Congress. An exception to the provision forbidding the division of a state occurred during the Civil War. In 1863 West Virginia was formed out of the western region of Virginia.

Section 4. The United States shall guarantee to every State in this Union a Republican Form of Government, and shall protect each of them against Invasion; and on Application of the Legislature, or of the Executive (when the Legislature cannot be convened) against domestic Violence.

A republican form of government is one in which citizens choose representatives to govern them. The federal government must protect a state against invasion and, if state authorities request it, against violence within a state.

ARTICLE V • AMENDING THE CONSTITUTION

The Congress, whenever two thirds of both Houses shall deem it necessary, shall propose Amendments to this Constitution, or, on the Application of the Legislatures of two thirds of the several States, shall call a Convention for proposing Amendments, which, in either Case, shall be valid to all Intents and Purposes, as part of this Constitution, when ratified by the Legislatures of three fourths of the several States, or by Conventions in three fourths thereof, as the one or the other Mode of Ratification may be proposed by the Congress: Provided that no Amendment which may be made prior to the Year One thousand eight hundred and eight shall in any Manner affect the first and fourth Clauses in the Ninth Section of the first Article; and that no State, without its Consent, shall be deprived of its equal Suffrage in the Senate.

An amendment to the Constitution can be proposed (a) by Congress, with a two-thirds vote of both houses, or (b) by a convention called by Congress when two-thirds of the state legislatures request it. An amendment is ratified (a) by three-fourths of the state legislatures, or (b) by conventions in three-fourths of the states. The twofold procedure of proposal and ratification reflects the seriousness with which the framers of the Constitution regarded amendments. Over 6,900 amendments have been proposed; only 26 have been ratified.

ARTICLE VI • GENERAL PROVISIONS

All Debts contracted and Engagements entered into, before the Adoption of this Constitution, shall be as valid against the United States under this Constitution, as under the Confederation.

This Constitution, and the Laws of the United States which shall be made in Pursuance thereof; and all Treaties made, or which shall be made, under the Authority of the United States, shall be the supreme Law of the Land; and the Judges in every State shall be bound thereby, any Thing in the Constitution or Laws of any State to the Contrary notwithstanding.

The supremacy clause means that if a federal and a state law conflict, the federal law prevails.

The Senators and Representatives before mentioned, and the Members of the several State Legislatures, and all executive and judicial Officers, both of the United States and of the several States, shall be bound by Oath or Affirmation, to support this Constitution; but no religious Test shall ever be required as a Qualification to any Office or public Trust under the United States.

Religion may not be a condition for holding public office.

ARTICLE VII • RATIFICATION

The Constitution would become the law of the land upon the approval of nine states.

The Ratification of the Conventions of nine States shall be sufficient for the Establishment of this Constitution between the States so ratifying the Same.

DONE in Convention by the Unanimous Consent of the States present the Seventeenth Day of September in the Year of our Lord one thousand seven hundred and eighty-seven and of the Independence of the United States of America the Twelfth. In Witness whereof We have hereunto subscribed our Names.

G⁰ Washington
Presid' and deputy from
VIRGINIA

Attest: *William Jackson,* Secretary

DELAWARE
Geo: Read
Gunning Bedford, jun
John Dickinson
Richard Bassett
Jaco: Broom

MARYLAND
James McHenry
Dan: of St Thos Jenifer
Danl Carroll

VIRGINIA
John Blair
James Madison Jr.

NORTH CAROLINA
Wm Blount
Richd Dobbs Spaight
Hu Williamson

SOUTH CAROLINA
J. Rutledge
Charles Cotesworth
  Pinckney
Charles Pinckney
Pierce Butler

GEORGIA
William Few
Abr Baldwin

NEW HAMPSHIRE
John Langdon
Nicholas Gilman

MASSACHUSETTS
Nathaniel Gorham
Rufus King

CONNECTICUT
Wm Saml Johnson
Roger Sherman

NEW YORK
Alexander Hamilton

NEW JERSEY
Wil: Livingston
David Brearley
Wm Paterson
Jona: Dayton

PENNSYLVANIA
B Franklin
Thomas Mifflin
Robt. Morris
Geo. Clymer
Thos. FitzSimons
Jared Ingersoll
James Wilson
Gouv Morris

AMENDMENT I • (1791)

Congress shall make no law respecting an establishment of religion, or prohibiting the free exercise thereof: or abridging the freedom of speech, or of the press; or the right of the people peaceably to assemble, and to petition the Government for a redress of grievances.

Establishes freedom of religion, speech, and the press; gives citizens the rights of assembly and petition.

AMENDMENT II • (1791)

A well regulated Militia, being necessary to the security of a free State, the right of the people to keep and bear Arms, shall not be infringed.

States have the right to maintain a militia.

AMENDMENT III • (1791)

No Soldier shall, in time of peace, be quartered in any house, without the consent of the Owner, nor in time of war, but in a manner to be prescribed by law.

Limits the army's right to quarter soldiers in private homes.

AMENDMENT IV • (1791)

The right of the people to be secure in their persons, houses, papers, and effects, against unreasonable searches and seizures, shall not be violated, and no Warrants shall issue, but upon probable cause, supported by Oath or affirmation, and particularly describing the place to be searched, and the persons or things to be seized.

Search warrants are required as a guarantee of a citizen's right to privacy.

AMENDMENT V • (1791)

No person shall be held to answer for a capital, or otherwise infamous crime, unless on a presentment or indictment of a Grand Jury, except in cases arising in the land or naval forces, or in the Militia, when in actual service in time of War or public danger; nor shall any person be subject for the same offence to be twice put in jeopardy of life or limb; nor shall be compelled in any criminal case to be a witness against himself, nor be deprived of life, liberty, or property, without due process of law; nor shall private property be taken for public use, without just compensation.

To be prosecuted for a serious crime, a person must first be accused (indicted) by a grand jury. No one can be tried twice for the same crime (double jeopardy). Nor can a person be forced into self-incrimination by testifying against himself or herself.

[The date following each amendment number is the year of ratification.]

AMENDMENT VI • (1791)

In all criminal prosecutions, the accused shall enjoy the right to a speedy and public trial, by an impartial jury of the State and district wherein the crime shall have been committed, which district shall have been previously ascertained by law, and to be informed of the nature and cause of the accusation; to be confronted with the witnesses against him; to have compulsory process for obtaining witnesses in his favor, and to have the Assistance of Counsel for his defence.

AMENDMENT VII • (1791)

In suits at common law, where the value in controversy shall exceed twenty dollars, the right of trial by jury shall be preserved, and no fact tried by a jury, shall be otherwise reexamined in any Court of the United States, than according to the rules of the common law.

AMENDMENT VIII • (1791)

Excessive bail shall not be required, nor excessive fines imposed, nor cruel and unusual punishments inflicted.

AMENDMENT IX • (1791)

The enumeration in the Constitution, of certain rights, shall not be construed to deny or disparage others retained by the people.

AMENDMENT X • (1791)

The powers not delegated to the United States by the Constitution, nor prohibited by it to the States, are reserved to the States respectively, or to the people.

AMENDMENT XI • (1798)

The Judicial power of the United States shall not be construed to extend to any suit in law or equity, commenced or prosecuted against one of the United States by Citizens of another State, or by Citizens or Subjects of any Foreign State.

AMENDMENT XII • (1804)

The Electors shall meet in their respective states and vote by ballot for President and Vice-President, one of whom, at least, shall not be an inhabitant of the same state with themselves; they shall name in their ballots the person voted for as President, and in distinct ballots the person voted for as Vice-President, and they shall make distinct lists of all persons voted for as President, and of all persons voted for as Vice-President, and of the number of votes for each, which lists they shall sign and certify, and transmit sealed to the seat of the government of the United States, directed to the President of the Senate;—The President of the Senate shall, in presence of the Senate and House of Representatives, open all the certificates and the votes shall then be counted;—The person having the greatest number of votes for President, shall be the President, if such number be a majority of the whole number of Electors appointed; and if no person have such majority, then from the persons having the highest numbers not exceeding three on the list of those voted for as President, the House of Representatives shall choose immediately, by ballot, the President. But in choosing the President, the votes shall be taken by states, the representation from each state having one vote; a quorum for this purpose shall consist of a member or members from two-thirds of the states, and a majority of all the states shall be necessary to a choice. <u>And if the House of Representatives shall not choose a President whenever the right of choice shall devolve upon them, before the fourth day of March next following, then the Vice-President shall act as President, as in the case of the death or other constitutional disability of the President.</u> – The person having the greatest number of votes as Vice-President, shall be the Vice-President, if such number be a majority of the whole number of Electors appointed, and if no person have a majority, then from the two highest numbers on the list, the Senate shall choose the Vice-President; a quorum for the purpose shall consist of two-thirds of the whole number of Senators, and a majority of the whole number shall be necessary to a choice. But no person constitutionally ineligible to the office of President shall be eligible to that of Vice-President of the United States.

presidential candidate wins a majority, the Senate chooses from the two candidates having the highest number of votes. The portion underlined was superseded by Section 3 of the 20th Amendment.

AMENDMENT XIII ● (1865)

Section 1. Neither slavery nor involuntary servitude, except as a punishment for crime whereof the party shall have been duly convicted, shall exist within the United States, or any place subject to their jurisdiction.

Abolishes slavery.

Section 2. Congress shall have power to enforce this article by appropriate legislation.

AMENDMENT XIV ● (1868)

Section 1. All persons born or naturalized in the United States, and subject to the jurisdiction thereof, are citizens of the United States and of the State wherein they reside. No State shall make or enforce any law which shall abridge the privileges or immunities of citizens of the United States; nor shall any State deprive any person of life, liberty, or property, without due process of law; nor deny any person within its jurisdiction the equal protection of the laws.

This section confers full civil rights on former slaves. Supreme Court decisions have interpreted the language of Section 1 to mean that the states, as well as the federal government, are bound by the Bill of Rights.

Section 2. Representatives shall be apportioned among the several States according to their respective numbers, counting the whole number of persons in each State, excluding Indians not taxed. But when the right to vote at any election for the choice of electors for President and Vice-President of the United States, Representatives in Congress, the Executive and Judicial officers of a State, or the members of the Legislature thereof, is denied to any of the male inhabitants of such State, being <u>twenty-one</u> years of age, and citizens of the United States, or in any way abridged, except for participation in rebellion, or other crime, the basis of representation therein shall be reduced in the proportion which the number of such male citizens shall bear to the whole number of male citizens twenty-one years of age in such State.

A penalty of a reduction in congressional representation shall be applied to any state that refuses to give all adult male citizens the right to vote in federal elections. This section has never been applied. The portion underlined was superseded by Section 1 of the 26th Amendment. (This section has also been amplified by the 19th Amendment.)

Section 3. No person shall be a Senator or Representative in Congress, or elector of President and Vice-President, or hold any office, civil or military, under the United States, or under any State, who, having previously taken an oath, as a member of Congress, or as an officer of the United States, or as a member of any State legislature, or as an executive or judicial officer of any State, to support the Constitution of the United States, shall have engaged in insurrection or rebellion against the same, or given aid or comfort to the enemies thereof. But Congress may by a vote of two-thirds of each House, remove such disability.

Any former federal or state official who served the Confederacy during the Civil War could not become a federal official again unless Congress voted otherwise.

Section 4. The validity of the public debt of the United States, authorized by law, including debts incurred for payment of pensions and bounties for services in suppressing insurrection or rebellion, shall not be questioned. But neither the United States nor any State shall assume or pay any debt or obligation incurred in aid of insurrection or rebellion against the Unted States, or any claim for the loss or emancipation of any slave; but all such debts, obligations and claims shall be held illegal and void.

Section 5. The Congress shall have power to enforce, by appropriate legislation, the provisions of this article.

AMENDMENT XV • (1870)

Section 1. The right of citizens of the United States to vote shall not be denied or abridged by the United States or by any State on account of race, color, or previous condition of servitude.

Section 2. The Congress shall have power to enforce this article by appropriate legislation.

AMENDMENT XVI • (1913)

The Congress shall have power to lay and collect taxes on incomes, from whatever source derived, without apportionment among the several States, and without regard to any census or enumeration.

AMENDMENT XVII • (1913)

The Senate of the United States shall be composed of two Senators from each State, elected by the people thereof, for six years; and each Senator shall have one vote. The electors in each State shall have the qualifications requisite for electors of the most numerous branch of the State legislature.

When vacancies happen in the representation of any State in the Senate, the executive authority of such State shall issue writs of election to fill such vacancies: *Provided,* That the legislature of any State may empower the executive thereof to make temporary appointments until the people fill the vacancies by election as the legislature may direct.

This amendment shall not be so construed as to affect the election or term of any Senator chosen before it becomes valid as part of the Constitution.

AMENDMENT XVIII • (1919)

Section 1. After one year from the ratification of this article, the manufacture, sale, or transportation of intoxicating liquors within, the importation thereof into, or the exportation thereof from the United States and all territory subject to the jurisdiction thereof for beverage purposes is hereby prohibited.

Section 2. The Congress and the several States shall have concurrent power to enforce this article by appropriate legislation.

Section 3. This article shall be inoperative unless it shall have been ratified as an amendment to the Constitution by the legislatures of the several States, as provided in the Constitution, within seven years from the date of the submission hereof to the States by the Congress.

AMENDMENT XIX • (1920)

The right of citizens of the United States to vote shall not be denied or abridged by the United States or by any State on account of sex.

Congress shall have power to enforce this article by appropriate legislation.

Gives women the right to vote.

AMENDMENT XX • (1933)

Section 1. The terms of the President and Vice-President shall end at noon on the 20th day of January, and the terms of Senators and Representatives at noon on the 3d day of January, of the years in which such terms would have ended if this article had not been ratified; and the terms of their successors shall then begin.

The "lame duck" amendment allows the President to take office on January 20, and members of Congress on January 3. The purpose of the amendment is to reduce the term in office of defeated incumbents — known as "lame ducks."

Section 2. The Congress shall assemble at least once in every year, and such meeting shall begin at noon on the 3d day of January, unless they shall by law appoint a different day.

Section 3. If, at the time fixed for the beginning of the term of the President, the President elect shall have died, the Vice-President elect shall become President. If a President shall not have been chosen before the time fixed for the beginning of his term, or if the President elect shall have failed to qualify, then the Vice-President elect shall act as President until a President shall have qualified; and the Congress may by law provide for the case wherein neither a President elect nor a Vice-President elect shall have qualified, declaring who shall then act as President, or the manner in which one who is to act shall be selected, and such person shall act accordingly until a President or Vice-President shall have qualified.

Section 4. The Congress may by law provide for the case of the death of any of the persons from whom the House of Representatives may choose a President whenever the right of choice shall have devolved upon them, and for the case of the death of any of the persons from whom the Senate may choose a Vice-President whenever the right of choice shall have devolved upon them.

Section 5. Sections 1 and 2 shall take effect on the 15th day of October following the ratification of this article.

Section 6. This article shall be inoperative unless it shall have been ratified as an amendment to the Constitution by the legislatures of three-fourths of the several States within seven years from the date of its submission.

AMENDMENT XXI • (1933)

Section 1. The eighteenth article of amendment to the Constitution of the United States is hereby repealed.

Repeals the 18th Amendment.

Section 2. The transportation or importation into any State, Territory, or possession of the United States for delivery or use therein of intoxicating liquors, in violation of the laws thereof, is hereby prohibited.

States may pass prohibition laws.

Section 3. This article shall be inoperative unless it shall have been ratified as an amendment to the Constitution by conventions in the several States, as provided in the Constitution, within seven years from the date of the submission hereof to the States by the Congress.

AMENDMENT XXII • (1951)

Limits a President to only two full terms plus two years of a previous President's term.

Section 1. No person shall be elected to the office of the President more than twice, and no person who has held the office of President, or acted as President, for more than two years of a term to which some other person was elected President shall be elected to the office of the President more than once. But this Article shall not apply to any person holding the office of President when this Article was proposed by the Congress, and shall not prevent any person who may be holding the office of President, or acting as President, during the term within which this Article becomes operative from holding the office of President or acting as President during the remainder of such term.

Section 2. This article shall be inoperative unless it shall have been ratified as an amendment to the Constitution by the legislatures of three-fourths of the several States within seven years from the date of its submission to the States by the Congress.

AMENDMENT XXIII • (1961)

By giving the District of Columbia three electoral votes, Congress enabled its residents to vote for President and Vice President.

Section 1. The District constituting the seat of Government of the United States shall appoint in such manner as the Congress may direct:

A number of electors of President and Vice-President equal to the whole number of Senators and Representatives in Congress to which the District would be entitled if it were a State, but in no event more than the least populous State; they shall be in addition to those appointed by the States, but they shall be considered, for the purposes of the election of President and Vice-President, to be electors appointed by a State; and they shall meet in the District and perform such duties as provided by the twelfth article of amendment.

Section 2. The Congress shall have power to enforce this article by appropriate legislation.

AMENDMENT XXIV • (1964)

Forbids the use of a poll tax as a requirement for voting in federal elections.

Section 1. The right of citizens of the United States to vote in any primary or other election for President or Vice-President, for electors for President or Vice-President, or for Senator or Representative in Congress, shall not be denied or abridged by the United States or any State by reason of failure to pay any poll tax or other tax.

Section 2. The Congress shall have power to enforce this article by appropriate legislation.

AMENDMENT XXV • (1967)

Outlines the procedure to be followed in case of presidential disability.

Section 1. In case of the removal of the President from office or of his death or resignation, the Vice-President shall become President.

Section 2. Whenever there is a vacancy in the office of the Vice-President, the President shall nominate a Vice-President who shall take office upon confirmation by a majority vote of both Houses of Congress.

Section 3. Whenever the President transmits to the President pro tempore of the Senate and the Speaker of the House of Representatives his written declaration that he is unable to discharge the powers and duties of his office, and until he transmits to them a written declaration to the contrary, such powers and duties shall be discharged by the Vice-President as Acting President.

Section 4. Whenever the Vice-President and a majority of either the principal officers of the executive departments or of such other body as Congress may by law provide, transmit to the President pro tempore of the Senate and the Speaker of the House of Representatives their written declaration that the President is unable to discharge the powers and duties of his office, the Vice-President shall immediately assume the powers and duties of the office as Acting President.

Thereafter, when the President transmits to the President pro tempore of the Senate and the Speaker of the House of Representatives his written declaration that no inability exists, he shall resume the powers and duties of his office unless the Vice-President and a majority of either the principal officers of the executive department or of such other body as Congress may by law provide, transmit within four days to the President pro tempore of the Senate and the Speaker of the House of Representatives their written declaration that the President is unable to discharge the powers and duties of his office. Thereupon Congress shall decide the issue, assembling within forty-eight hours for that purpose if not in session. If the Congress, within twenty-one days after receipt of the latter written declaration, or, if Congress is not in session, within twenty-one days after Congress is required to assemble, determines by two-thirds vote of both Houses that the President is unable to discharge the powers and duties of his office, the Vice-President shall continue to discharge the same as Acting President; otherwise, the President shall resume the powers and duties of his office.

AMENDMENT XXVI ● (1971)

Section 1. The right of citizens of the United States, who are eighteen years of age or older, to vote shall not be denied or abridged by the United States or any state on account of age.

Lowers the voting age to eighteen.

Section 2. The Congress shall have the power to enforce this article by appropriate legislation.

1-1, Detail of "Raising the Liberty Bell," artist unknown —Courtesy, Kennedy Galleries, Inc.; 1-2 (top), Maryland Historical Society; (bottom), N.Y. State Historical Association—Courtesy, American Heritage Publishing Co.; 1-3 (left), (Thomas Anburey) *Travels Through the Interior Parts of America* (London, 1784)—Smithsonian Institution; (right), (Holm Campanius) *Kort Beskfrifnin om Provincien nya Swerige uti America* (Stockholm, 1702)— NYPL Rare Book Collection; 1-4, Trustees of the Dorset Natural History and Archaeological Society—Courtesy, American Heritage Publishing Co.; 1-5 (top), Massachusetts Historical Society; (bottom) Essex Institute, Salem, Mass.; 1-6 (top), The New-York Historical Society; (bottom), Painting by Ralph Earl from the Collection of Mrs. Cornelius Boardman—Courtesy, Metropolitan Museum of Art; 1-7 (top), The New-York Historical Society; (bottom), American Antiquarian Society; 1-8 (top), The New-York Historical Society; (center), Corning Museum of Glass, Corning, N.Y.; (bottom), Smithsonian Institution.

2-1, Detail of "Old State House, 1801"; 2-2 (top), Daughters of the American Revolution Museum, Washington, D.C.; (bottom), Moravian Historical Society, Nazareth, Pa.; 2-3 (top), Connecticut Historical Society; (bottom), Newport Historical Society; 2-4 (top left), (N. Heideloff) *Gallery of Fashion* (London, 1794)—NYPL; (top right), Detail of "The Shop and Warehouse of Duncan Phyfe, 168–172 Fulton Street, N.Y.C."—Metropolitan Museum of Art, Rogers Fund, 1922; (bottom), "The Dinner Party" by Henry Sargent, Museum of Fine Arts, Boston—Gift of Mrs. Horatio A. Lamb in Memory of Mr. and Mrs. Winthrop Sargent; 2-5 (top), NYPL Rare Book Collection; (bottom), The New-York Historical Society; 2-6 (top), Abby Aldrich Rockefeller Folk Art Collection; (bottom), Metropolitan Museum of Art, Rogers Fund, 1942; 2-7, National Gallery of Art–Gift of Edgar William and Bernice Chrysler Garbisch; 2-8 (top), Ann Parker; (bottom), Firestone Library, Princeton University.

3-1, Detail of "Buffalo Hunt"; 3-2 (top), Missouri Historical Society; (bottom), Museum of Fine Arts, Boston— Bequest of Henry L. Shattuck in Memory of the Late Ralph W. Gray; 3-3 (top), Northern Natural Gas Company Collection of the Joslyn Art Museum, Omaha, Neb.; (bottom left), Granger Collection; (bottom right), Culver Pictures; 3-4 (top), Northern Natural Gas Company Collection of the Joslyn Art Museum, Omaha, Neb.; (bottom left), (F. J. Meine) *The Crockett Almanacks* (Chicago, 1955)—NYPL Rare Book Collection; (botton right), Detail of "Spring Burning Up Fallen Leaves" by George Harvey—Brooklyn Museum; 3-5 (top), The New-York Historical Society; (bottom left), Collection of Mr. and Mrs. Leslie Cowan, Columbia, Mo.; (bottom right), Glenbow-Alberta Institute—Courtesy, American Heritage Publishing Co.; 3-6 (top), Detail of "Shooting for the Beef" by George Caleb Bingham; (bottom), "Flax Scutching Bee" by Linton Park—National Gallery of Art, Gift of Edgar William and Bernice Chrysler Garbisch (Courtesy, Time/Life Books, © Time, Inc.); 3-7, Boatmen's National Bank of St. Louis; 3-8 (top), (Mrs. Frances Trollope) *Domestic Manners of the Americans* (Kiel, Germany, 1835); (bottom), Minnesota Historical Society.

4-1, Detail of "The Nine-Forty-Five Accommodation," Stratford, Conn., by Edward Lamson Henry—Metropolitan Museum of Art, Bequest of Moses Tanenbaum, 1937; 4-2 (top), The New-York Historical Society; (bottom), Kennedy Galleries, Inc.; 4-3, "Travel by Stagecoach Near Trenton, New Jersey" by Paul Svinin—Metropolitan Museum of Art, Rogers Fund, 1942; 4-4 (top), Thomas Gilcrease Institute, Tulsa, Okla.; (bottom), Tulane University; 4-5 (top), Mariners Museum, Newport News, Va.; (bottom), Boatmen's National Bank of St. Louis; 4-6 (top), Thomas Gilcrease Institute, Tulsa, Okla.; (bottom), California Historical Society—San Francisco/San Marino; 4-7, Smithsonian Institution; 4-8 (top), Library of Congress —Courtesy, American Heritage Publishing Co.; (bottom), Granger Collection.

5-1, Detail of "Arrival" by Ben Shawn—E.P.A., Inc.; 5-2 (top), The New-York Historical Society; (bottom), Metropolitan Museum of Art; 5-3 (top), Bettmann Archive; (bottom left), NYPL Picture Collection; (bottom right), Bettmann Archive; 5-4 (top), Museum of the City of New York; (bottom), Los Angeles County Museum of Art; 5-5 (top), Bettmann Archive; (bottom), NYPL Picture Collection; 5-6 (top), Missouri Historical Society; (bottom left), Wisconsin State Historical Society; (bottom right), Chicago Historical Society; 5-7 (top), Chicago Historical Society; (bottom), Illinois Department of Conservation; 5-8 (top), Thomas Gilcrease Institute, Tulsa, Okla.; (bottom), Franklin D. Roosevelt Library, Hyde Park, N.Y.

6-1, Detail of "Interior View" by Frank Waller—Metropolitan Museum of Art, purchase; 6-2 (top), Culver Pictures; (bottom), Museum of Fine Arts, Boston; 6-3 (top), Art Institute of Chicago; (bottom left), Metropolitan Museum of Art; (bottom right), Museum of Modern Art—Gift of Friends of the Sculptor in 1908; 6-4 (top), NYPL Picture Collection; (bottom), Phillips Gallery; 6-5 (top), Amherst College Collection; (bottom), Hedrich-Blessing; 6-6 (top), Culver Pictures; (bottom), Museum of the City of New York; 6-7 (top), Edward Steichen; (bottom), Courtesy of Mr. Ira Gershwin and The Humanities Research Center, University of Texas at Austin; 6-8 (top), Museum of Art at Ogunquit; (bottom), Brown Brothers.

7-1, Detail of "Twenty-Cent Movie" by Reginald Marsh —Whitney Museum of American Art (Photograph by Bradley Smith); 7-2 (top left), Culver Pictures; (top right), Eileen Darby/Graphic House; (bottom), Brown Brothers; 7-3 (top), Globe Photos; (bottom), Time-Life Picture Agency; 7-4 (top), Capricorn Art Gallery; (bottom left), Acme News Pictures, Inc. (UPI); (bottom right), Hy Peskin/Time-Life Picture Agency; 7-5 (top), Ralph Crane/ Time-Life Picture Agency; (bottom), Francis Miller/ Time-Life Picture Agency; 7-6 (top), Nina Leen/Time-Life Picture Agency; (bottom), University of Wisconsin Dept. of Photocinema; 7-7 (top), Margaret Bourke-White/ Time-Life Picture Agency; (bottom), Leonard McCombe/ Time-Life Picture Agency; 7-8 (top), Peter Stackpole/Life Magazine, © Time, Inc.; (bottom), Frank Scherschel/ Time-Life Picture Agency.

8-1, "Vermont Vista"—Photograph by Esther Henderson/ Rapho/Photo Researchers; 8-2 (top), Van Bucher/Photo Researchers; (bottom), Charles Moore/Black Star; 8-3 (top left), Fred J. Maroon/Photo Researchers; (top right), Porterfield Chickering/Photo Researchers; (bottom), Bruce Roberts/Rapho/Photo Researchers; 8-4 (top left), Ford Motor Company; (top right), Charles E. Rotkin/Photography for Industry; (bottom), Hedrich-Blessing; 8-5 (top), Lucia Woods/Photo Researchers; (bottom), F. Hulnegle/Monkmeyer; 8-6 (top), Ray Manley/Shostal Photos; (bottom), Myron Wood/Photo Researchers; 8-7 (top left), Tom McHugh/Photo Researchers; (top right), Russ Kinne/Photo Researchers; (bottom), Joe Munroe/Photo Researchers; 8-8 (top), Jack Fields/Photo Researchers; (bottom), Ray Ateson.

Quotations by these foreign observers appear in the eight Pictorial Essays. Minor adaptations have been made in some quoted material, chiefly to modernize spelling and grammar. In the essays, the writer's name is followed by a date or dates. These represent the years in which the observations were made, if known. If the exact period is not known, the date represents the year in which the account was first published in the original language.

Anburey, Thomas *(Essay 1)* An officer in the British army during the Revolution, he journeyed through Canada and several of the colonies between 1776 and 1781. His *Travels Through the Interior Parts of America* was published in 1789.

Beaujour, Felix de *(Essay 1)* French consul-general in the United States from 1804 to 1816. His *Sketch of the United States at the Commencement of the Nineteenth Century* (1814) was highly critical of Americans as crude and money-grubbing.

Beauvoir, Simone de *(Essays 7, 8)* The noted French writer and philosopher made a nationwide tour of the United States between January and May 1947. *America Day by Day* (1953), based on her travels, shows her as an intelligent and sensitive reporter of the American scene.

Bernard, John *(Essays 2, 3)* This English actor made several professional tours in the United States between 1797 and 1811. Selections from his witty and gossipy *Retrospections of America* appeared at intervals later in the nineteenth century.

Birkbeck, Morris *(Essay 3)* An Englishman who relocated in southern Illinois in 1818. His writings greatly influenced other would-be settlers. The two quotations given here are from his *Letters From Illinois* (1818).

Blane, William *(Essay 3)* Little is known of this young Englishman other than that he lived from 1800 to 1825. His *Excursion Through the United States and Canada During the Years 1822-23* was published anonymously three years after his death.

Bremer, Fredrika *(Essays 3, 5)* A Swedish novelist well known in her day, who traveled in America from 1849 to 1851. Her impressions, in the form of letters to her sister, appeared in *Homes of the New World* (1853).

Broughton, Morris *(Essay 8)* A South African journalist and editor of *The Cape Argus*, he came to the United States in 1956 as a guest of the State Department. By his estimation, he traveled over 10,000 miles and visited over thirty states during his three-month stay here.

Burnaby, Andrew *(Essay 1)* A clergyman of the Church of England, Burnaby traveled in the colonies in 1759-60. His firm loyalty to the British crown is evident in his *Travels Through North America*, first published in 1775.

Capellini, Giovanni *(Essay 4)* An Italian professor of geology, Capellini toured the western United States in 1863. He recorded his scientific observations in a journal published in 1867.

Carpenter, Harry *(Essay 7)* An English sports expert, Carpenter was boxing and general sports columnist for *The London Daily Mail* from 1954 to 1962, as well as a full-time correspondent for the BBC. In his *Masters of Boxing* (1964) he spoke of Joe Louis as the "headmaster" of boxing.

Chastellux, Marquis de (Francois-Jean de Beauvoir) *(Essay 2)* A French army officer, he served as aide to Rochambeau during the American Revolution. His *Travels in North America in the Years 1780, 1781, and 1782* (1786) is a vivid and generally accurate account.

Chateaubriand, Francois-René de *(Essay 3)* This French novelist visited the United States for four months in 1791, but did not publish his *Travels in America* until 1827. It is a romantic work devoted mainly to the Indian as a "noble savage" rather than to the author's own experiences.

Chesterton, G. K. *(Essay 5)* The English poet and novelist visited the United States on a lecture tour in 1921. His book, *What I Saw in America,* was published in London in 1922.

Chevalier, Michel *(Essay 4)* As a young French engineer, he was sent by his government in 1834-35 to study transportation and public works in the United States. He praised the country in *Letters on North America* (1836).

Cobbett, William *(Essay 2)* Opinionated and outspoken, this English journalist was twice forced to flee to the United States, where he lived from 1792 to 1800 and again from 1817 to 1819. The selection quoted is from *A Year's Residence in the United States of America* (1818).

Colum, Padraic *(Essay 6)* This Irish man of letters made his home in the United States after 1914. He was a friend of many writers, including Robert Frost.

Cooke, Alistair *(Essay 8)* Of Anglo-Irish birth, this popular journalist and broadcaster has lived primarily in the United States since the 1930s, and became an American citizen in 1941. He is the author of many books on American culture. This selection comes from *Talk About America* (1968).

Corresca, Rocco *(Essay 5)* An Italian immigrant, he typified the penniless hopefuls who flocked to America to make their fortune. His "Biography of a Bootblack" appeared in a magazine, *The Independent,* in December 1902.

Dal Verme, Francesco *(Essay 1)* Member of a noble Milanese family. The journal and letters concerning his travels in 1783-84 were meant only for his relatives, but were published in 1969 as *Seeing America and Its Great Men.*

Danckaerts, Jaspar *(Essay 1)* A Dutchman, he belonged to a small Calvinist sect, the Labadists. He and Peter Sluyter spent thirteen months in America in 1679-80 looking for a place for the Labadists to settle (they chose Maryland). Danckaerts' journal was discovered in the nineteenth century by an American, and published in 1867.

Dickens, Charles *(Essay 3)* The famous English writer first toured the United States in 1842. His *American Notes,* published that same year, was highly critical of Americans. Out of this experience came his novel *Martin Chuzzlewit.*

Dubos, René—See Ward, Barbara

Erkelenz, Anton *(Essay 6)* A member of the German parliament, he wrote a book called *America Today* (1927), in which he expressed an optimistic belief that the United States would some day create a culture uniquely its own.

Freymond, Jacques *(Essay 7)* On his first trip to the United States (1949–1950), Freymond, a Swiss historian, studied at Yale University and made an ex-

tended auto tour of the country. He returned for a two-month trip in 1955.

Galsworthy, John *(Essay 6)* The noted English writer gave a series of speeches in the United States that were published in a volume called *Addresses in America* (1919).

Graham, Stephen *(Essay 5)* A British traveler and journalist who visited the United States in 1913. These quotations are from his work *With Poor Immigrants to America* (1914).

Grassi, Giovanni *(Essay 2)* This Italian Jesuit priest spent the years 1810-17 in the United States. His report, emphasizing general characteristics rather than specific people or places, appeared in 1819.

Griesinger, Karl Theodor *(Essay 5)* This German historian spent five years in the United States, although he did not find the American form of democracy to his liking. His *Living Pictures from America,* published in 1858, is characterized by a cutting and ironical humor.

Grund, Francis J. *(Essay 3)* A Bohemian journalist who spent several years in the United States during the 1830s. His book of observations—*The Americans in Their Moral, Social, and Political Relations*—was published in 1837.

Hall, Basil *(Essays 3, 4)* A retired English naval officer, he visited the United States in 1820 and in 1827-28. His *Travels in North America* (1829) is a valuable description.

Hamp, Sidford *(Essay 4)* This English youth was only seventeen when his uncle—who had helped found Colorado Springs—arranged for him to travel to the United States on a scientific expedition. His diary reflects his youthful enthusiasm.

Hartog, Jan de *(Essay 8)* A Dutch author and playwright who made a leisurely voyage in 1958–61 from Houston to Nantucket, largely by inland waterways. He gives a charming account of his adventures in *Waters of the Western World,* published in 1961.

Hauptmann, Gerhart *(Essay 6)* In 1932 this German playwright, a Nobel prize winner, visited the United States. He remarked on leaving that the high points of his trip had been meeting O'Neill and attending *Mourning Becomes Electra.* The critique quoted here is from an interview the same year with an American correspondent.

Hawkes, Jacquetta—See Priestley, J.B.

Hilbersheimer, Ludwig and Udo Rukser *(Essay 6)* These German architects praised the innovations of American architecture and especially the work of Frank Lloyd Wright. Their article appeared in a 1920 issue of the German journal, *Art and Artist.*

Jarlson, Axel *(Essay 5)* The story of this Swedish farmer's immigration to America illustrates how the members of a single family helped each other to settle in the United States. Jarlson's narrative was published in the January 8, 1903, issue of *The Independent.*

Josselyn, John *(Essay 1)* An English traveler who visited the American colonies in 1638-39 and again in 1663-71. This quotation is taken from the second of two books he wrote, *An Account of Two Voyages to New-England* (1674).

Kalm, Peter *(Essay 1)* A Swede who traveled in America from 1748 to 1751. As a botanist, he was interested mainly in plants and farming. (Mountain laurel is named after him—*Kalmia latifolia*.) His *Travels* appeared at intervals between 1753 and 1761.

Kemble, Fanny *(Essay 4)* A leading English actress, she first toured the United States in 1833-34, when she met and married a Philadelphian who owned cotton and rice plantations in Georgia. Her *Journal of a Residence on a Georgian Plantation in 1838-39* (1863) is an animated account.

Kipling, Rudyard *(Essay 6)* Between March and September 1889, the famous English writer (then only twenty-four) sent thirty-seven letters back to an Indian newspaper, as he traveled from India to England via the Far East and the United States. The last of his letters is titled "An Interview with Mark Twain." All this correspondence was published in *From Sea to Sea* (1890).

Klinkowström, Axel *(Essays 2, 3)* A member of an old Swedish family, Baron Klinkowström served as a naval officer, and visited the United States in 1818-20 primarily to investigate the practical workings of the steamboat. His *Letters on the United States* appeared in 1824.

Kossenko, Zinaida—See Mikhailov, Nikolai

Labarca H., Amanda *(Essay 8)* A distinguished Chilean educator, feminist, and public servant, she visited the United States ten times between 1911 and 1952. She represented Chile in the first General Assembly of the United Nations in 1946.

Lambert, John *(Essay 2)* Little is known of this Englishman's life except his trip to North America in 1806-09 to investigate the possibilities of hemp cultivation in Canada. The chief result was his *Travels Through Lower Canada and the United States of North America* (1810).

Laski, Harold *(Essay 6)* A noted British socialist, he taught history at Harvard University from 1916 to 1920. After returning to England, he devoted himself to teaching, writing, and journalism. His *American Democracy* was published in 1948.

Leacock, Stephen *(Essay 7)* The Canadian humorist and man of letters was also a distinguished political scientist and professor at McGill University. This quotation is from *Stephen Leacock's Laugh Parade*, published in 1940.

Le Corbusier (Charles Edouard Jeanneret) *(Essays 7, 8)* This Swiss-born French architect has been called "the voice and conscience of modern architecture." He visited the United States several times during his lifetime. His book *When the Cathedrals Were White* (1947) was devoted mostly to his impressions of America.

Lederer, John *(Essay 1)* This scholar and student of medicine explored the Piedmont and the Blue Ridge Mountains in 1669-70, the first European to do so. He then moved to New England, returning to his native Germany in 1675. His *Discoveries,* written in Latin, was translated and published in London in 1672.

Lyell, Sir Charles *(Essay 4)* The leading English geologist of the nineteenth century, he made four trips to the United States. His steamboat description is from *A Second Visit to the United States of North America* (1849).

Marias, Julian *(Essays 7, 8)* A Spanish philosopher, he helped found Madrid's Institute of Humanities. In 1951-52 Marias was a visiting professor at Wellesley College.

Martineau, Harriet *(Essay 3)* A writer, she spent the years 1834-36 in the United States, returning to her native England an ardent abolitionist. Her *Society in America* was published in 1837.

Maurois, André *(Essay 7)* The noted French critic and novelist was a frequent visitor to the United States, where he was a popular lecturer. In 1939 he published *Thirty-Nine States, Journal of a Voyage to America,* from which this quote is taken.

Mikhailov, Nikolai and Zinaida Kossenko *(Essay 8)* This Russian geographer and his wife, a psychiatrist, made a tour of America in 1960. Their account first appeared in a Moscow publication the same year and was later published in the United States as *Those Americans, a Travelogue* (1962).

Moreau de Saint-Méry, M. L. E. *(Essay 2)* A French judge, he fled to the United States in 1794 to escape the Revolution. He remained until 1798, an embittered critic of the American scene. His *Voyage to the United States* remained in manuscript form until it was published in 1913.

Münsterberg, Hugo *(Essay 6)* This German philosopher and professor at Harvard University wrote *The Americans* (1904) in order to dispel German prejudice against Americans.

Myers, Robert *(Essay 5)* A Jewish immigrant from Rumania, Myers came to the United States in 1913 and later became active in the labor movement. His recollections, *Stimmer* ["stutterer"]: *The Boy Who Couldn't Talk,* were published in 1959.

Newman, Ernest *(Essay 6)* From 1910 to 1940 he was the major British music critic. His review of Isadora Duncan quoted here was written in April 1921. Several years later, he moved to New York City, where he wrote music reviews for the *New York Evening Post.* The November 17, 1924, edition carried his appreciation of Gershwin's *Rhapsody in Blue.*

Priestley, J. B. and Jacquetta Hawkes *(Essays 7, 8)* The English novelist and critic lived in the United States in 1935-36; *Midnight on the Desert* (1937) grew out of this experience. In 1954 he and his wife Jacquetta Hawkes (an author and anthropologist) traveled in the American Southwest. Their wry and amusing collaboration, *Journey Down a Rainbow*, for which each wrote alternating chapters, was published in 1955.

Pupin, Michael Idvorsky *(Essay 5)* Born in Yugoslavia, the brilliant physicist sold all his belongings in order to come to America. In 1924, he won a Pulitzer Prize for *From Immigrant to Inventor* (1923), the story of his life.

Raeder, Ole *(Essay 4)* A leading Norwegian lawyer and judge, he was sent to the United States in 1847 to study the jury system. He regularly sent home newspaper dispatches, which were eventually published in 1929 as *America in the Forties*.

Rivera, Diego *(Essay 6)* In 1942 the celebrated Mexican artist spoke of his contemporary, John Sloan, to American art critic Walter Pach. Rivera himself had visited the United States in the 1930s, where he painted frescoes in Detroit, San Francisco, and New York. He was much impressed with American technology.

Ross, Alexander *(Essay 3)* A Scot, he worked for John Jacob Astor's Pacific Fur Company from 1810 to 1813, then for the Canadian North West Company until 1825. His *Fur-Hunters of the Far West* appeared in 1855.

Rukser, Udo — See Hilbersheimer, Ludwig.

Russell of Killowen, Lord *(Essays 4, 5)* Born in Ireland, this lawyer first visited America in 1883 and wrote a *Diary of a Visit to the United States of America* (published in 1910). He served as lord chief justice of England from 1894 until his death in 1900.

Sarc, Omer Celâl *(Essay 7)* This Turkish economist has spent much time in the United States. In 1950 he visited universities across the country as a guest of the State Department. He also taught at Columbia University and worked for the United Nations.

Schoepf, Johann David *(Essay 2)* A German scientist, he came to America as a physician for Hessian troops in 1777, and remained in this country until 1784. His *Travels in the Confederation* appeared in 1788.

Sheridan, Claire *(Essay 6)* A celebrated British sculptress, known for her busts of Lenin, Trotsky, and Gandhi. She met Sinclair Lewis in Washington, D.C., in April 1921. A vivid account of their meeting appeared in her book *My American Diary*, published the following year.

Stevenson, Robert Louis *(Essays 4, 5)* The Scottish writer crossed the United States in 1879 to visit an American woman he had met in Europe (and whom he eventually married). *Across the Plains* was published in 1892.

Tocqueville, Alexis de *(Essays 2, 3, 8)* This French statesman and writer was sent to the United States in 1831 by his government in order to study Ameri-

can penitentiaries. He is best known, however, for his two-volume *Democracy in America* (1835, 1840), widely regarded as one of the most insightful commentaries ever written on the United States.

Trollope, Frances *(Essays 3, 4)* An English novelist (and the mother of novelist Anthony Trollope), she visited the United States in 1827-30, trying unsuccessfully to set up a store in Cincinnati. Her *Domestic Manners of the Americans* (1832) is a humorous critique that much offended Americans of the time.

Tyrmand, Leopold *(Essay 8)* A journalist born in Warsaw, Poland, he moved to the United States in the 1960s. Portions of his writings, dealing with his experiences as a European in America, appeared in *The New Yorker*. They were collected in *Notebooks of a Dilettante* (1967).

Vay de Vaya und Luskod, Count *(Essay 4, 5, 6)* A Hungarian nobleman, he traveled widely as a diplomat for the Roman Catholic Church. Visiting the United States several times between 1903 and 1906, he described his travels in *The Inner Life of the United States* (1908).

Von Borch, Herbert *(Essays 7, 8)* This German writer's book *The Unfinished Society* (1960) was based on notes he made while working in the United States as a newspaper correspondent.

Wansey, Henry *(Essay 1)* An English clothier who retired to take up scholarship, he visited the United States in 1794. His observations were published in 1796 under the title of *An Excursion to the United States of North America*.

Ward, Barbara and René Dubos *(Essay 8)* Barbara Ward, an English social scientist, lectured frequently in the United States in the period after World War II. *Only One Earth* (1972) was written with the Pulitzer-prize winning microbiologist, René Dubos, who was born in France but moved to the United States in 1924.

Wells, H. G. *(Essay 5)* The famous English novelist visited Ellis Island during his first trip to the United States in 1905. He wrote of his impressions in *The Future of America* (1906).

West, Rebecca *(Essay 6)* Born in Ireland, she became known for her writings on history and politics. Her essay on Willa Cather was originally published by the *New York Herald Tribune* in September 1927, and was reprinted in *The Strange Necessity* (1928).

White, T. H. *(Essay 8)* Best known for his books on King Arthur, this English author kept a journal while on a lecture tour in the United States. It was later published as *America at Last, the American Journal of T. H. White* (1965).

Wolff, Albert *(Essay 6)* A French art critic, he wrote for the noted French newspaper, *Le Figaro*. This selection is quoted from his 1881 reivew of the Impressionists' sixth group exhibition.

Index

Allen Weinstein is a Professor of History at Smith College, where he directed American Studies for six years and teaches U.S. political and social history. In 1981, he served as the Commonwealth Fund Lecturer in U.S. History at University College, the University of London, and the previous year, he was a Fellow of the Smithsonian's Woodrow Wilson International Center for Scholars in Washington. His book, *Perjury: The Hiss–Chambers Case* (Knopf, 1978; Vintage paperback, 1979), received several awards, most recently a 1979 American Book Awards' finalist nomination in History Paperbacks. He directed The Twentieth Century Fund's study of the Freedom of Information Act's impact upon U.S. intelligence agencies and has lectured and published widely on government information policy. His previous books include *Prelude to Populism* and *American Negro Slavery: A Modern Reader* (with Frank Gatell, 3rd ed., rev., 1980). His articles have appeared in many scholarly periodicals and journals of opinion, both in this country and abroad. He has served on the Editorial Board of *The Journal of American Studies* and presently serves on *The Wilson Quarterly*'s Advisory Board. He has lectured throughout Europe and Israel, twice served as Senior Fulbright Lecturer in Australia, and has taught at Amherst College, Brown University, Hartford College for Women, Teacher's College (Columbia), and the University of Maryland.

Frank Otto Gatell, Professor of History at U.C.L.A., is the author of several books, including *John Gorham Palfrey and the New England Conscience*, and of a number of major articles on the historiography of the Jacksonian period and other subjects. He has taught at Stanford University, the University of Maryland, and the University of Puerto Rico. He has served several times as a Fulbright Professor in Latin America and lectured widely at universities throughout Latin America both in English and Spanish. His many published articles include several on the history of Puerto Rico and other aspects of Latin American history.